THE OXFORD HANDBOOK OF

THE INTERNATIONAL LAW OF GLOBAL SECURITY

THE OXFORD HANDBOOK OF

THE INTERNATIONAL LAW OF GLOBAL SECURITY

Edited by

ROBIN GEIß

and

NILS MELZER (EDS)

Assistant Editors:

JAMES DEVANEY

and

ELENI METHYMAKI

OXFORD
UNIVERSITY PRESS

OXFORD
UNIVERSITY PRESS

Great Clarendon Street, Oxford, OX2 6DP,
United Kingdom

Oxford University Press is a department of the University of Oxford. It furthers the University's objective of excellence in research, scholarship, and education by publishing worldwide. Oxford is a registered trade mark of Oxford University Press in the UK and in certain other countries

First Edition published in 2021
Impression: 1

Published in the United States of America by Oxford University Press
198 Madison Avenue, New York, NY 10016, United States of America

British Library Cataloguing in Publication Data
Data available

Library of Congress Control Number: 2020949074

ISBN 978–0–19–882727–6

Printed and bound by
CPI Group (UK) Ltd, Croydon, CR0 4YY

Contents

PART II PREDOMINANT SECURITY CHALLENGES AND INTERNATIONAL LAW

National and Transnational Security

International Security

Human Security

Economic and Resource Security

Environmental Security

PART IV POWER POLITICS, INTERNATIONAL LAW, AND GLOBAL SECURITY

PART V GLOBAL AND REGIONAL SECURITY MECHANISMS

Abbreviations

AC	Appeals Chamber
ACHPR	African Court of Human and Peoples' Rights
ACHR	American Convention on Human Rights
AFDI	Annuaire français de droit international
AFISMA	African-led International Support Mission in Mali
AFRC	Armed Forces Revolutionary Council
AGI	Artificial General Intelligence
AI	Artificial Intelligence
AICHR	ASEAN Intergovernmental Commission on Human Rights
AJIL	American Journal of International law
AMIB	African Mission in Burundi
AMIS	African Union Mission in Sudan
AMW Manual	Manual on International Law Applicable to Air and Missile Warfare, with Commentary (2010)
ANZJ Crim	Australian and New Zealand Journal of Criminology
APEC	Asia Pacific Economic Cooperation
APF	African Peace Fund
APSA	African Peace and Security Architecture
AP I	Additional Protocol I to the 1949 Geneva Conventions (1977)
AP II	Additional Protocol II to the 1949 Geneva Conventions (1977)
AP III	Additional Protocol III to the 1949 Geneva Conventions (2005)
ARSIWA	Articles on the Responsibility of States for Internationally Wrongful Acts
ASEAN	Association of Southeast Asian Nations
ASF	African Standby Force
AsianJIL	Asian Journal of International Law
ASIL Proc	Proceedings of the American Society of International
ATT	Arms Trade Treaty
AU	African Union
AUC	African Union Commission
AU PSC	African Union Peace and Security Council

BMJ	British Medical Journal
BPUFF	Basic Principles on the Use of Force and Firearms by Law Enforcement Officials
BRI	Belt and Road Initiative
BVR	Beyond Visual Range
BYIL	British Yearbook of International Law
CA 3	Common Article 3 to the 1949 Geneva Conventions
CanYIL	Canadian Yearbook of International Law
CAR	Central African Republic
CARICOM	Caribbean Community and Common Market
Case W Res JIL	Case Western Reserve Journal of International Law
CAT	Committee Against Torture
CBD	Convention on Biological Diversity
CCDCOE	Cooperative Cyber Defense Center of Excellence
CCLEO	Code of Conduct for Law Enforcement Officials
CCW	Convention on Conventional Weapons
CDC	Centre for Disease Control and Prevention
CEDAW	Convention on the Elimination of all Forms of Discrimination against Women
CESCR	Committee on Economic Social and Cultural Rights
CEWS	Continental Early Warning System
CFSP	Common Foreign and Security Policy
CFT	Combating (the) Financing of Terrorism
CIA	Central Intelligence Agency
CICC	Coalition for the International Criminal Court
CIL	customary international law
CIS	Commonwealth of Independent States
CITES	Convention on International Trade in Endangered Species of Wild Flora and Fauna
CJICL	Cambridge Journal of International and Comparative Law
CM	Committee of Ministers
CMLRev	Common Market Law Review
CoE	Council of Europe
Commentary AP I and II	Commentary on the Additional Protocols of 8 June 1977 to the Geneva Conventions of 12 August 1949 (Geneva/Dordrecht: International Committee of the Red Cross (ICRC)/Martinus Nijihoff Publishers, 1987)
Commentary GC I	Commentary on the Geneva Conventions of 12 August 1949 for the Amelioration of the Condition of the Wounded and Sick in Armed Forces in the Field.
Commentary GC II	Commentary on the Geneva Conventions of 12 August 1949 for the Amelioration of the Condition of Wounded, Sick and Shipwrecked Members of Armed Forces at Sea

Commentary GC III	Commentary on the Geneva Conventions of 12 August 1949 Relative to the Treatment of Prisoners of War
Commentary GC IV	Commentary on the Geneva Conventions of 12 August 1949 Relative to the Protection of Civilian in Time of War
CPA	Comprehensive Peace Agreement
CRC	Convention on the Rights of Child
CRPD	Convention on the Rights of Persons with Disabilities
CSBM	Confidence and Security Building Measures (OSCE)
CSCE	Conference for Security and Co-operation in Europe
CSDP	Common Security and Defence Policy
CTBT	Comprehensive Nuclear-Test-Ban Treaty
CTC	Counter-Terrorism Committee
CUP	Cambridge University Press
DC Cir.	US Circuit Court for the District of Columbia
DDC	US District Court for the District of Columbia
DDR	disarmament, demobilization, reintegration
DFS	United Nations Department of Field Support
DHA	Department of Humanitarian Affairs
DOJ	(US) Department of Justice
DPA	Department of Political Affairs
DPH	direct participation in hostilities
DPKO	United Nations Department of Peacekeeping Operations
DPRK	Democratic People's Republic of Korea
DRC	Democratic Republic of the Congo
EC	European Community
ECCC	Extraordinary Chambers in the Courts of Cambodia
ECB	European Central Bank
ECHR	European Convention on Human Rights
ECOMOG	Economic Community of West African States Monitoring Group
ECOSOC	Economic and Social Council
ECOWAS	Economic Community of West African States
ECtHR	European Court of Human Rights
EEZ	Exclusive Economic Zone
EHRR	European Human Rights Reports
EIA	Environmental Impact Assessment
EJIL	European Journal of International Law
EJIR	European Journal of International Relations
ELJ	European Law Journal
ETS	European Treaty Series
EU	European Union
EUFOR	European Union Force

EULEX	European Union Rule of Law Mission in Kosovo
EU NAVFOR ATALANTA	European Union Naval Force Somalia—Operation Atalanta
EWHC	High Court of Justice of England and Wales
FAFN	Forces Nouvelles de Côte d'Ivoire
FAO	Food and Agriculture Organization of the United Nations
FARC	Revolutionary Armed Forces of Colombia
FARDC	Forces Armées de la République Démocratique du Congo
FATF	Financial Action Task Force
FPC	Foreign Policy Concept (Russia)
FRY	Federal Republic of Yugoslavia
FSC	Forum for Security Cooperation
FTF	Foreign Terrorist Fighter
FYIL	Finnish Yearbook of International Law
FYROM	Former Yugoslav Republic of Macedonia
GAOR	General Assembly Official Records
GC I	Convention (I) for the Amelioration of the Condition of the Wounded and Sick in Armed Forces in the Field
GC II	Convention (II) for the Amelioration of the Condition of Wounded, Sick and Shipwrecked Members of Armed Forces at Sea
GC III	Convention (III) Relative to the Treatment of Prisoners of War
GC IV	Convention (IV) Relative to the Protection of Civilian Persons in Time of War
GCs	Geneva Conventions
GJIL	Göttingen Journal of International Law
GLJ	German Law Journal
GYIL	German Yearbook of International Law
HarvILJ	Harvard International Law Journal
HCJ	Israeli High Court of Justice
HIPPO	High-Level Independent Panel on United Nations Peace Operations
HPG	Hêzên Parastina Gel
UNHRC	United Nations Human Rights Committee
HRW	Human Rights Watch
HRLR	Human Rights Law Review
HRW	Human Rights Watch
HVO	Croat Defence Council
IAC	international armed conflict
IACHR	Inter-American Commission on Human Rights
IACtHR	Inter-American Court of Human Rights
IAEA	International Atomic Energy Agency

ICAO	International Civil Aviation Organization
ICBL	International Campaign to Ban Landmines
ICC	International Criminal Court
ICCPR	International Covenant on Civil and Political Rights
ICCWC	International Consortium on Combating Wildlife Crime
ICERD	International Convention on the Elimination of All Forms of Racial Discrimination
ICESCR	International Covenant on Economic Social and Cultural Rights
ICG	International Crisis Group
ICISS	International Commission on Intervention and State Sovereignty
ICJ	International Court of Justice
ICLQ	International and Comparative Law Quarterly
ICRC	International Committee of the Red Cross
ICSID	International Center for Settlement of Investment Disputes
ICTR	International Criminal Tribunal for Rwanda
ICTY	International Criminal Tribunal for the former Yugoslavia
IDI	Institut de Droit International
IDP	internally displaced people
IEDs	improvised explosive devices
IFOR/SFOR	Implementation Force/Stabilization Force in Bosnia and Herzegovina
IFRC	International Federation of Red Cross and Red Crescent Societies
IGA	Interpol General Assembly
IHL	international humanitarian law
IHRL	international human rights law
ILA	International Law Association
ILC	International Law Commission
ILM	International Legal Materials
ILO	International Labour Organization
ILR	International Law Reports
IMF	International Monetary Fund
IMO	International Maritime Organization
IMT	International Military Tribunal
IMTFE	International Military Tribunal for the Far East
INTERPOL	International Criminal Police Organization
INTERPOL CCC	INTERPOL Command and Coordination Centre
IOM	International Organization for Migration
IRRC	International Review of the Red Cross

ISAF	International Security Assistance Force
ITLOS	International Tribunal for the Law of the Sea
IUU	illegal, unreported and unregulated (fishing)
JAIL	Japanese Annual of International Law
JCPOA	Joint Comprehensive Plan of Action
JCSL	Journal of Conflict and Security Law
JDI	Journal du Droit International
JHIL	Journal of the History of International Law
JICJ	Journal of International Criminal Justice
JIEL	Journal of International Economic Law
JIM	Joint Investigative Mechanism (ECOWAS)
JWT	Journal of World Trade
KFOR	Kosovo Force
KLA	Kosovo Liberation Army
KRG	Kurdish Regional Government of Iraq
LAWS	lethal autonomous weapons systems
LJIL	Leiden Journal of International Law
LNTS	League of Nations Treaty Series
LOAC	law of armed conflict
MAPROBU	African Prevention and Protection Mission in Burundi
MARPOL	International Convention for the Prevention of Pollution by Ships
MD	Military Doctrine (Russia)
MDA	Maritime Domain Awareness
MDGs	Millennium Development Goals
MelbJIL	Melbourne Journal of International Law
MEZ	Maritime Exclusion Zone
MichJIL	Michigan Journal of International Law
MINUCI	United Nations Mission in Côte d'Ivoire
MINURCAT	United Nations Mission in the Central African Republic and Chad
MINUSCA	United Nations Multidimensional Stabilization Mission in the Central African Republic
MINUSMA	United Nations Multidimensional Integrated Stabilization Mission in Mali
MINUSTAH	UN Stabilization Mission in Haiti
MINURSO	United Nations Mission for the Referendum in Western Sahara
MISAB	Mission interafricaine de surveillance des Accords de Bangui
MJTF	Multinational Joint Task Force
MLC	Movement for the Liberation of Congo
MLR	Modern Law Review

MONUC	Mission de l'Organisation des Nations unies en République démocratique du Congo
MPEPIL	The Max Plank Encyclopedia of Public International Law
N.D. Ill.	US District Court for the Northern District of Illinois
NAM	Non-Aligned Movement
NATO	North Atlantic Treaty Organization
NDC	Nduma Defence of Congo
NFZ	no-fly zone
NGO	non-governmental organization
NIAC	non-international armed conflict
NILR	Netherlands International Law Review
NLA	National Liberation Army
NPM	National Preventive Mechanism
NQHR	Netherlands Quarterly of Human Rights
NSA	non-State actor
NSAG	non-State armed group
NSS	national security strategy
NUPI	Norwegian Institute of Foreign Affairs
NWP	Naval Warfare Publication
NYIL	Netherlands Yearbook of International Law
OAS	Organization of American States
OASTS	Organization of American States Treaty Series
OAU	Organization of African Unity
OCHA	United Nations Office for the Coordination of Humanitarian Affairs
ODI	Overseas Development Institute
ODIHR	Office of Democratic Institutions and Human Rights
OECD	Organisation for Economic Co-operation and Development
OECS	Organization of Eastern Caribbean States
OIC	Organization of Islamic Cooperation
OJ	Official Journal of the European Union
OJLS	Oxford Journal of Legal Studies
OMIK	OSCE Mission in Kosovo
ONUB	Opération des Nations unies au Burundi
ONUC	Opération des Nations unies au Congo
OPANAL	Agency for the Prohibition of Nuclear Weapons in Latin America and the Caribbean
OPCAT	Optional Protocol to the Convention Against Torture
OPCW	Organization for the Prohibition of Chemical Weapons
OSAPG	Office of the Special Adviser to the Secretary-General on the Prevention of Genocide
OSCE	Organization for Security and Co-operation in Europe

OTP	Office of the Prosecutor
OUP	Oxford University Press
P5	Five Permanent Member States of the United Nations Security Council
PAROS	Prevention of an Arms Race in Outer Space
PCA	Permanent Court of Arbitration
PCASP	privately contracted armed security personnel
PCIJ (series)	Permanent Court of International Justice
PKK	Partiya Karkerên Kurdistanê
PLO	Palestine Liberation Organization
PMC	private military company
PMSC	private military and security company
POC	protection of civilians
POW	Panel of the Wise (African Union)
PPP	perpetual peace projects
PSC	private security company
PSF	United Nations Rapid Deployment Police and Security Force
PSI	Proliferation Security Initiative
PSO	Peace Support Operation
PTA	Preferential Trade Agreement
PTBT	Partial Test Ban Treaty (Treaty Banning Nuclear Weapons Test in the Atmosphere, in Outer Space and Under Water)
PYD	Partiya Yekîtiya Demokrat
R2P	Responsibility to Protect
RBDI	Revue Belge de Droit International
RCEP	Regional Comprehensive Economic Partnership
RdC	Recueil de Cours de l'Académie de Droit International de la Haye
REC	Regional Economic Community
RFMO	Regional Fisheries Management Organization
RGDIP	Revue Générale de Droit International Public
RHDI	Revue Hellenique de Droit International
RIAA	Reports of International Arbitral Awards
RMC	Rules for Military Commissions
ROE	Rules of Engagement
RPA	remotely piloted aircraft
SCO	Shanghai Cooperation Organization
SCOR	Security Council Official Records
SCR	Supreme Court Reports
SCSL	Special Court for Sierra Leone
SDGs	Sustainable Development Goals
SEANWFZ	South-East Asia Nuclear Weapons Free Zone

SFOR	Stabilization Force
SIPRI	Stockholm International Peace Research Institute
SOFA/SOMA	Status of Forces/Mission Agreement
SOLAS	Safety of Life at Sea
SPT	Subcommittee on Prevention of Torture and other Cruel, Inhuman or Degrading Treatment or Punishment
SSR	security sector reform
SVP	Swiss People's Party
TAF	Turkish Armed Forces
TAM	Tribunal Arbitral Mixte
TC	Trial Chamber
TCC	troop contributing country
TCSL	transnational civil security law
TEZ	Total Exclusion Zone
TEU	Treaty on the European Union
TOC	transnational organized crime
TPNW	Treaty on the Prohibition of Nuclear Weapons
TPP	Trans-Pacific Partnership
TPSL	transnational public security law
TS	Treaty Series
TWC	Trials of War Criminals
TWQ	Third World Quarterly
UAV	Unmanned Aerial Vehicle
UCAS	Unmanned Combat Aerial Systems
UCK (KLA)	Ushtria Çlirimtare e Kosovës (Kosovo Liberation Army)
UDHR	Universal Declaration of Human Rights
UKAIT	United Kingdom Asylum and Immigration Tribunal
UKHL	United Kingdom House of Lords
UN	United Nations
UNAMID	United Nations-African Union Hybrid Mission in Darfur
UNAMIR	United Nations Assistance Mission in Rwanda
UNAMSIL	United Nations Mission in Sierra Leone
UNAVEM III	United Nations Angola Verification Mission
UNCIO	United Nations Conference on International Organization
UNCLOS	United Nations Convention on the Law of the Sea
UN COPUOS	United Nations Committee on the Peaceful Uses of Outer Space
UNDP	United Nations Development Programme
UNDSS	United Nations Department for Safety and Security
UNEF/UNEF II	United Nations Emergency Force/Second United Nations Emergency Force
UNEP	United Nations Environment Programme

UNFICYP	United Nations Peacekeeping Force in Cyprus
UNGA	United Nations General Assembly
UNHCHR	United Nations High Commissioner for Human Rights
UNHCR	United Nations High Commissioner for Refugees
UNICEF	United Nations International Children's Emergency Fund
UNIDIR	United Nations Institute for Disarmament Research
UNIFIL	United Nations Interim Force in Lebanon
UNIIIC	United Nations International Independent Investigative Commission
UNITA	National Union for the Total Independence of Angola
UNMIH	Multinational Interim Force in Haiti
UNMIK	United Nations Mission in Kosovo
UNMIL	United Nations Mission in Liberia
UNMIS	United Nations Mission in Sudan
UNOAU	United Nations Office to the African Union
UNOCI	United Nations Operation in Côte d'Ivoire
UNODA	United Nations Office for Disarmament Affairs
UNOMIL	United Nations Observer Mission in Liberia
UNOOSA	United Nations Office for Outer Space Affairs
UNOSOM II	United Nations Operation in Somalia II
UNPROFOR	United Nations Protection Force
UNSAS	United Nations Standby Arrangements System
UNSC	United Nations Security Council
UNSF	United Nations Security Force
UNSWLJ	University of New South Wales Law Journal
UNTAC	United Nations Transition Authority in Cambodia
UNTC	United Nations Treaty Collection
UNTEA	United Nations Temporary Executive Authority
UNTS	United Nations Treaty Series
UNWTO	United Nations World Tourism Organization
UP	University Press
USA	United States of America
USC	US Code
USV	Unmanned Seagoing Vessel
VaJIL	Virginia Journal of International Law
VCLT	Vienna Convention on the Law of Treaties
VUWLawRev	Victoria University of Wellington Law Review
WFP	World Food Programme
WHO	World Health Organization
WLR	Weekly Law Reports (UK)
WMD	weapons of mass destruction
WTO	World Trade Organization

YBILC	Yearbook of the International Law Commission
YIHL	Yearbook of International Humanitarian Law
YPG	Yekîneyên Parastina Gel
ZaöRV	Zeitschrift für ausländisches öffentliches Recht und Völkerrecht
ZOPFAN	Zone of Peace Freedom and Neutrality (ASEAN)

Table of Cases

International Courts and Tribunals

Economic Community of West African States (ECOWAS) Community Court of Justice

European Court of Human Rights (ECtHR)

European Court of Justice (ECJ)

Inter-American Court of Human Rights (IACtHR)

International Centre for the Settlement of Investment Disputes (ICSID)

International Court of Justice (ICJ)

International Criminal Court (ICC)

International Criminal Tribunal for the Former Yugoslavia (ICTY)

International Criminal Tribunal for Rwanda (ICTR)

International Tribunal for the Law of the Sea (ITLOS)

Permanent Court of Arbitration (PCA)

Permanent Court of International Justice (PCIJ)

World Trade Organization (WTO)

Ad Hoc International Arbitrations

Other International Bodies

African Commission on Human and Peoples' Rights

United Nations Committee Against Torture

United Nations Human Rights Committee

National Courts

Australia

Belgium

Canada

United States of America

Table of Instruments

Note: The present Table of Instruments does not constitute a comprehensive listing of all international documents referenced in the chapters of the *Handbook*, as this would be a fruitless task for a book of this size. Rather, we list here international treaties and the resolutions of the United Nations General Assembly, the Security Council, the Economic and Social Council, and the Human Rights Council, for which we have used abbreviated references in individual chapters. For all other international documents, a full citation is provided where they are referenced in the chapters themselves.

International Treaties

United Nations Resolutions

General Assembly

Security Council

Economic and Social Council

Human Rights Council

List of Contributors

Nayef Al-Rodhan is a Philosopher, Neuroscientist, and Geostrategist. He is Honorary Fellow at St Antony's College, University of Oxford, and Head of the Geopolitics and Global Futures Programme at the Geneva Centre for Security Policy.

Tilmann Altwicker is SNSF-Professor of Public Law, International Law, Legal Philosophy, and Empirical Legal Research at the University of Zurich.

Masahiko Asada is Professor of International Law at the Graduate School of Law, Kyoto University and President of the Japanese Society of International Law.

Christina Binder holds the Chair of International Law and International Human Rights Law at Bundeswehr University Munich and is a Board member and former Vice-President of the European Society of International Law.

Christopher J Borgen is Professor of Law and Co-Director of the Center for International and Comparative Law at St. John's University School of Law in New York.

Hilmer Bosch is a PhD candidate at the University of Amsterdam.

Katia Bouslimani is PhD Candidate in European Data Protection Law at the University Grenoble Alpes (CESICE) and Research Fellow for the Chair on the Legal and Regulatory Implications of Artificial Intelligence of the Multidisciplinary Institute in Artificial Intelligence, University Grenoble Alpes.

Congyan Cai is Professor of International Law at Fudan University School of Law, Shanghai, and an Honorary Professor at East China University of Political Science and Law (ECUPL) in China.

Simon Chesterman is Provost's Chair and Dean of the Faculty of Law, National University of Singapore.

BS Chimni is Distinguished Professor of International Law at O.P. Jindal Global University and an Associate Member of the Institut de Droit International.

Théodore Christakis is Professor of International and European Law, University Grenoble Alpes and Chair on the Legal and Regulatory Implications of Artificial Intelligence at the Multidisciplinary Institute in Artificial Intelligence. He is Co-Director of the Grenoble Alpes Data Institute and a member of the French National Digital Council.

Auden Davies-Bright is Lecturer at the Law School, Nottingham Trent University and a PhD candidate at the School of Law, University of Nottingham.

Adam Day is Director of Programmes at the Centre for Policy Research, United Nations University in New York.

Diane A Desierto is Associate Professor of Human Rights Law and Global Affairs at Keough School of Global Affairs, University of Notre Dame.

James Devaney is Lecturer in Law at the University of Glasgow.

Adama Dieng is former Under-Secretary-General and Special Adviser of the Secretary-General of the United Nations on the Prevention of Genocide. He was previously Registrar of the International Criminal Tribunal for Rwanda and Secretary-General of the Geneva-based International Commission of Jurists.

Cordula Droege is Head of the Legal Division of the International Committee of the Red Cross.

Helen Duffy is Professor of International Humanitarian Law and Human Rights at the Grotius Centre for International Legal Studies, Leiden Law School, Leiden University, and runs Human Rights *in* Practice, a strategic human rights litigation practice based in The Hague.

Helen Durham is Director of International Law and Policy at the International Committee of the Red Cross.

Hilal Elver is Global Distinguished Fellow at the Resnick Food Law and Policy Centre, UCLA Law School and a Research Professor at the University of California, Santa Barbara. She is also former United Nations Special Rapporteur on the Right to Food.

Jasper Finke is Legal Officer at the Federal Ministry of Justice and Consumer Protection, Berlin.

Steven Freeland is Professor of International Law at the School of Law, Western Sydney University, Adjunct Professor at the University of Hong Kong and a Director of the International Institute of Space Law.

Robin Geiß holds the Chair of International Law and Security at the University of Glasgow and is Director of the Glasgow Centre for International Law and Security. He also holds the Swiss Chair of International Humanitarian Law at the Geneva Academy for International Humanitarian Law and Human Rights.

Emanuela-Chiara Gillard is Senior Research Fellow at the Oxford Institute for Ethics, Law and Armed Conflict and a Research Fellow in the Individualisation of War project at the European University Institute. She is also an Associate Fellow in the International Law Programme of Chatham House.

Sabine Gless is Professor of Criminal Law and Criminal Procedure at the Faculty of Law, University of Basel.

Thomas Greminger is a Swiss diplomat and former Secretary General of the Organization for Security and Co-operation in Europe (OSCE).

Elise Gruttner is a Senior Research Officer for the Foreign Affairs, Defence and Trade Legislation and References Committees at the Department of the Senate, Parliament of Australia.

Douglas Guilfoyle is Associate Professor of International and Security Law at the School of Humanities and Social Sciences, University of New South Wales, Canberra.

Joyeeta Gupta is Professor of Environment and Development in the Global South at the Amsterdam Institute for Social Science Research, University of Amsterdam and the IHE-Delft Institute for Water Education. She was also Co-Chair of the United Nations Environment's Global Environmental Outlook-6 (2016–2019) and is presently Co-Chair of the Earth Commission.

Pierre Hauck is Professor of Criminal Law and Criminal Procedure at the University of Giessen.

J Benton Heath is Assistant Professor of Law, Temple University Beasley School of Law.

Gina Heathcote is Reader in Gender Studies and International Law at SOAS, University of London.

Christian Henderson holds the Chair of International Law at the School of Law, Politics and Sociology, University of Sussex.

Larissa van den Herik is Professor of Public International Law at the Grotius Centre for International Legal Studies, Leiden Law School, Leiden University.

Steven Hill is former Legal Adviser and Director of the Office of Legal Affairs at the North Atlantic Treaty Organization (NATO) Headquarters in Brussels.

Peter Hough is Associate Professor in International Politics at the School of Law, Middlesex University London.

Malcolm Jorgensen is Fellow of the Berlin Potsdam Research Group 'The International Rule of Law—Rise or Decline', jointly hosted by Humboldt University of Berlin, The Free University of Berlin and the University of Potsdam.

Markos Karavias is Director of the Asylum Service of Greece.

Jakob Kellenberger former President of the International Committee of the Red Cross, is President of the Board of the Swiss peace Foundation.

Claus Kreß holds the Chair for German and International Criminal Law, is Professor of International Law and Criminal Law and is the Director of the Institute of International Peace and Security Law at the University of Cologne.

Martina Kunz is Research Fellow on the AI Policy and Responsible Innovation Project at the Leverhulme Centre for the Future of Intelligence and a PhD candidate at the Cambridge Centre for Environment, Energy and Natural Resource Governance, University of Cambridge.

Benjamin F Kusi Brigadier General (Rtd) is the former deputy commandant of the Kofi Annan International Peacekeeping Training Centre. He also served as Deputy Force Commander of the United Nations Operation in Côte d'Ivoire (UNOCI) from April 2009 to August 2011.

David M Malone is Rector of the United Nations University and Under-Secretary-General of the United Nations.

Natasa Mavronicola is Reader in Law and Deputy Head of Research at Birmingham Law School, University of Birmingham.

Rob McLaughlin is Professor of International Law at the Australian National Centre for Ocean Resources and Security, University of Wollongong, Australia.

Nils Melzer is Professor of International Law at the School of Law, University of Glasgow, and the United Nations Special Rapporteur on Torture and Other Cruel, Inhuman or Degrading Treatment or Punishment. He also holds the Human Rights Chair at the Geneva Academy of International Humanitarian Law and Human Rights.

Eleni Methymaki is a DPhil candidate in Law at the Faculty of Law, University of Oxford.

Tibisay Morgandi is Lecturer in International Energy and Natural Resources Law at the School of Law, Queen Mary University of London.

Eva Nanopoulos is Lecturer in Law at the School of Law, Queen Mary University of London.

Hitoshi Nasu is Professor of International Law at the School of Law, University of Exeter and Senior Fellow at the Stockton Center for International Law, United States Naval War College.

Seán Ó hÉigeartaigh is the Director of the AI: Futures and Responsibility (AI:FAR) Programme at the Leverhulme Centre for the Future of Intelligence, and Co-Director of the Centre for the Study of Existential Risk (CSER), University of Cambridge.

Jerusha Asin Owino is a Visiting Scholar and PhD candidate at the Institute for International Peace and Security Law at the University of Cologne.

Asli Ozcelik is Postdoctoral Researcher in International Law at the School of Law, University of Glasgow and the Academic Coordinator of the Glasgow Centre for International Law and Security.

Sven Peterke is Professor of Public International Law at the Federal University of Paraiba.

Fausto Pocar is Professor Emeritus of International Law, Private International Law, and European Law at the University of Milan. He has served as a Judge of the International Criminal Tribunals for the former Yugoslavia (ICTY) and Rwanda (ICTR) and was President of the ICTY (2005–2008).

Arnold N Pronto is Principal Legal Officer in the Codification Division of the United Nations Office of Legal Affairs.

Ioana-Maria Puscas is Senior Research Officer for the Geopolitics and Global Futures Programme at the Geneva Centre for Security Policy.

James Revill is an Associate Fellow with the Harvard Sussex Program at SPRU, University of Sussex.

Alejandro Rodiles is Associate Professor of Public International Law and Law and Global Governance in the Law Department of ITAM University, Mexico City, and a faculty member of ITAM's Centre of Studies on Security, Intelligence, and Governance (CESIG).

Anna Roessing is a PhD candidate in Conflict, Security and International Order at the University of Bath.

Cecily Rose is Assistant Professor of Public International Law at the Grotius Centre for International Legal Studies, Leiden University.

Ben Saul is the Challis Chair of International Law at the University of Sydney and an Associate Fellow of Chatham House.

Michael N Schmitt is Professor of International Law at the University of Reading and the Francis Lieber Distinguished Scholar at the Lieber Institute of the United States Military Academy at West Point.

Ursula Schroeder is Professor of Political Science and Director of the Institute for Peace Research and Security Policy at the University of Hamburg.

Mirko Sossai is Associate Professor of International Law at the Department of Law, Roma Tre University.

Vladislava Stoyanova is Associate Professor at the Faculty of Law, Lund University.

Christian J Tams is Professor of International Law at the University of Glasgow and co-Director of the Glasgow Centre for International Law and Security. He is also an academic member of Matrix Chambers, London.

Pierre Thielbörger is Professor of German Public Law and International Law at Ruhr University Bochum and Executive Director of the Institute for the International Law of Peace and Armed Conflict (IFHV) in Bochum.

Kimberley N Trapp is Vice Dean (International) and Professor of Public International Law at the Faculty of Laws, University College London.

Bakhtiyar Tuzmukhamedov is Professor of International Law and Vice-President of the Russian Association of International Law. He served as Judge at the International Criminal Tribunals for the former Yugoslavia (ICTY) and Rwanda (ICTR) from 2009 to 2015.

Antonios Tzanakopoulos is Associate Professor of Public International Law at the Faculty of Law and Fellow in Law at St Anne's College, University of Oxford. He is a Door Tenant at Three Stones Chambers, and Secretary-General of the International Law Association.

Priya Urs is a PhD candidate and Teaching Fellow at the Faculty of Laws, University College London.

Jorge E Viñuales is the Harold Samuel Professor of Law and Environmental Policy at the University of Cambridge and the founder and former Director of the Cambridge Centre for Environment, Energy, and Natural Resource Governance (C-EENRG).

Gus Waschefort is a Senior Lecturer at the School of Law and Human Rights Centre, University of Essex. He is also associate researcher, South African Research Chair for International Law, University of Johannesburg.

Nathalie Weizmann is Senior Legal Officer with the United Nations Office for the Coordination of Humanitarian Affairs.

Nigel D White holds the Chair in Public International Law at the School of Law, University of Nottingham and is co-Director of the Nottingham International Law and Security Centre.

Elizabeth Wilmshurst CMG is Distinguished Fellow in the International Law Programme of the Royal Institute of International Affairs, Chatham House.

Helge Elisabeth Zeitler is a Counsellor (Environment, Climate) in the European Union Delegation at the United Nations.

INTRODUCTION

ROBIN GEIß AND NILS MELZER

A. The Big Picture

As UN Secretary-General António Guterres has poignantly stated: '[i]f I had to select one sentence to describe the state of the world, I would say we are in a world in which global challenges are more and more integrated, and the responses are more and more fragmented, and if this is not reversed, it's a recipe for disaster.'[1] Without doubt, the task of understanding the global security environment and delivering the necessary governance responses represents a central challenge of the twenty-first century.

Throughout the world, degraded security environments have produced massive population movements, deepening socio-economic fragility, and inequality. In addition, there are renewed risks of nuclear confrontation, prolonged wars have devastating humanitarian consequences, and terrorism and other forms of transnational crime have destabilized entire societies. This is not to mention increasingly common cybersecurity incidents, which gradually erode the edifice of international peace and security, or the enormous risks associated with pandemics, environmental degradation, and climate change, which are only now beginning to seep into public consciousness. It is no exaggeration to say that, today, humanity faces an existential crisis, and that the survival of humankind and the planet rests on our ability to identify and implement necessary governance responses. On a global scale, the central regulatory framework for such responses is public international law. Now more than ever, it is time to reinvigorate international solidarity, reinforce commitments to international law, and ensure its consistent implementation. It is the purpose of this *Handbook* to highlight the central role of public international law as part of an effective global security architecture and, in doing so, to make a modest contribution to addressing some of the most pressing legal and policy challenges of our time.

[1] UN Secretary-General António Guterres, 'Speech 2019' (WEF Annual Meeting, Davos, 24 January 2019) <https://www.weforum.org/agenda/2019/01/these-are-the-global-priorities-and-risks-for-the-future-according-to-antonio-guterres/> accessed 2 May 2020.

B. The Twenty-First-Century Global Security Environment

1. Globalization of the Security Agenda

Since the turn of the century the global security environment has become increasingly dynamic, complex, and volatile; and the causes, mechanisms, and consequences of national and international (in-)security have become increasingly transnational and global in nature.[2] Various powerful dynamics of a geopolitical, demographic, climatic, technological, social, and economic nature have been driving this trend,[3] which has now been taken to entirely new levels by the recent outbreak of the COVID-19 pandemic. The convergence of so-called 'old and new security challenges', such as the return to power politics, the rise of asymmetric and hybrid warfare, and the emergence of novel threats posed by potent non-State actors, technological innovation, as well as dramatically increased economic, pandemic, and environmental risks, have entailed a veritable globalization of the security agenda.

2. New Actors

The rise of non-State actors has been one of most significant dynamics shaping the global security environment since the end of the Cold War.[4] The diffusion of power and anticipated demise of the State associated with the growing influence of non-State actors may, at times, have been exaggerated. But the impact and relevance of a diverse range of non-State actors on global security has been a defining element of the twenty-first-century global security environment. Terrorist organizations, organized armed groups, and transnational organized crime have been a source and driver of insecurity. But States have also outsourced a growing range of security and governance functions to private actors, and transnational corporations and social media companies have accumulated unprecedented power, largely without adequate oversight and accountability as to their adverse impacts on human rights and environmental protection. At the same time, the role and influence of non-governmental organizations (NGOs) in global security

[2] Munich Security Conference, 'Munich Security Report 2019: The Great Puzzle: Who Will Pick Up the Pieces?' <https://securityconference.org/assets/02_Dokumente/01_Publikationen/MunichSecurityReport2019.pdf> accessed 2 May 2020.

[3] António Guterres, 'Vision Statement: Challenges and Opportunities for the United Nations' (4 April 2016) <https://www.un.org/pga/70/wp-content/uploads/sites/10/2016/01/4 April_Secretary-General-Election-Vision-Statement_Portugal-4-April-20161.pdf> accessed 30 October 2020.

[4] Gunnar Folke Schuppert (ed), *Global Governance and the Role of Non-State Actors* (Nomos 2006). See also Jean d'Aspremont, 'Do Non-State Actors Strengthen or Weaken International Law?—The Story of a Liberal Symbiosis' in Heike Krieger et al (eds), *The International Rule of Law—Rise or Decline?* (OUP 2019).

governance and politics has continuously grown. And there have been various important shifts towards the 'humanization' of international law and global security discourses, expressed in concepts like 'human security' and discernible in the evolving and consolidating legal status of individuals in international law.[5]

3. New Technologies, Interdependencies, and Vulnerabilities

New technologies, in particular, have added layers of uncertainty by triggering a new type of 'arms race' across economic, scientific and military fields, and by enabling disruptive power projections on an unprecedented level. An equally powerful driver of the globalized 'security agenda', has been the rapid growth of worldwide interdependencies (and corresponding vulnerabilities), not just for the global economy but also for global health and for interconnected, cyber-reliant societies more generally.[6] The COVID-19 pandemic, the Huawei 5G debate, and the proliferating 'trade and currency wars' are paradigmatic in this regard. In combination with the apparent preparedness of some States to 'weaponize' these interdependencies,[7] most notably in power struggles between the United States and China, these developments are testament to the pitfalls of globalization and evidence a multipolar and generalized securitization trend across a range of sectors.

4. Institutional and Normative Erosion

At the same time, international institutions, norms, and principles originally established to address global security challenges have themselves come under pressure in the face of dysfunctional power relations, the spread of zero-sum geopolitical strategies, and an ongoing backlash against globalization. Further, there is an increasingly widespread perception that State and Western-centric multilateralist structures have overpromised and underdelivered.[8] While power dynamics change and alternative visions of security, cooperation, and global governance emerge, most of them remain underexplored. As became evident at the 2020 Munich Security Conference, the world faces unprecedented global security challenges urgently requiring a coordinated response. Yet, factors

[5] Anne Peters, *Jenseits der Menschenrechte* (Nomos 2013).

[6] Anthea Roberts et al, 'Toward a Geoeconomic Order in International Trade and Investment' (2019) 22 Journal of International Economic Law 655.

[7] Henry Farrell/Abraham L Newman, 'Weaponized Interdependence: How Global Economic Networks Shape State Coercion' (2019) 44 International Security 42.

[8] Tanja A Börzel/Michael Zürn, 'Contestations of the Liberal Script: A Research Program' (January 2020) SCRIPTS Working Paper Series No 1 <https://www.scripts-berlin.eu/publications/Publications-PDF/SCRIPTS-WP1_final.pdf> accessed 2 May 2020. See also Munich Security Conference, 'Munich Security Report 2020: Westlessness' <https://securityconference.org/assets/user_upload/MunichSecurityReport2020.pdf> accessed 2 May 2020; Amitav Acharya 'After Liberal Hegemony: The Advent of a Multiplex World Order' (2017) 31 Ethics and International Affairs 271.

such as the decline of US global leadership, the rise of populist movements, and the emergence of an increasingly prominent ideological faultline between liberal democracy and nationalist authoritarianism, Brexit, and the UN Security Council's failure to end the wars in Syria, Yemen, Libya, and elsewhere, continue to obstruct multilateral and rule-based global governance responses.[9] Even amongst traditional allies, there is considerable dissonance, both as to what global security entails and whether it is to be achieved through protectionism or a renewed commitment to multilateralism.[10]

As a result of these dynamics, there is currently a pervasive sense that global security policies, norms, and institutions are failing to create sustainable security conditions and are increasingly inept in keeping pace with the complex and hyperdynamic environment of the twenty-first century. Ad hoc, palliative, and crisis-driven solutions that may stretch established rules and concepts (or sideline them entirely) too often appear to be the strategy of choice. This, in turn, serves to erode the explanatory power and operative purchase of long-standing legal paradigms and principles. Repeated high-level calls for holistic approaches to tackling today's threats to global peace and security have so far not sufficiently translated into actionable policies.[11]

Against the backdrop of these multi-level domain contestations, it is high time for deeper reflection about the role and relevance of public international law in today's global security environment. The notion of security is mentioned no less than thirty-four times in the Charter of the United Nations (UN Charter) and, therefore, clearly deserves consideration and analysis as a self-standing concept of public international law, not only in terms of a political aspiration but also in terms of individual and collective rights and duties. The challenges, trends, and dynamics sketched out here, have all been the subject of in-depth analysis and debate. Until recently, however, global security received only marginal attention as a self-standing theme in international law and the relationship between global security and international law has remained underexplored.[12] In part, this may be due to the fragmented nature of public international law, dealing as it does with security challenges through specifically tailored and partially insulated legal regimes. But it may also be ascribed to the fact that the relationship between global security and international law is as diverse, dynamic, and multifaceted as the concept of global security itself. The historic shift from the maintenance of inter-State peace in the early days of the United Nations towards the promotion of global security more broadly understood was followed, as globalization progressed, by increasingly complex global

[9] Eurasia Group, 'Top Risks 2020: Coronavirus Edition' (March 2020) <https://www.eurasiagroup.net/files/upload/top_risks_2020_coronavirus_edition_1.pdf> accessed 2 May 2020.

[10] The 'Alliance for Multilateralism', proposed by France and Germany in 2019, is exemplary in this regard, see Jean-Yves Le Drian/Heiko Maas, 'No, multilateralism is not outdated!' (*Le Figaro*, 12 November 2019) <https://www.diplomatie.gouv.fr/en/our-ministers/jean-yves-le-drian/press/article/joint-article-by-jean-yves-le-drian-and-heiko-maas-no-multilateralism-is-not> accessed 30 October 2020.

[11] See Guterres (n 3).

[12] But see Mary E Footer et al (eds), *Security and International Law* (Hart 2016); Avril McDonald/Hanna Brollowski, 'Security' MPEPIL (OUP, May 2011).

security governance models across a widening spectrum of sectors. This is reflected in concepts such as economic, environmental, and human security. Further, the relationship between these concepts has constantly evolved and grown in complexity. With the recent outbreak of the COVID-19 pandemic, a 'black swan event' of global proportions, we may well have entered yet another phase of accelerated and fundamental transformation, the far-reaching implications of which remain unpredictable at the time of writing. As with every major crisis, the recovery phase will present profound opportunities for visionary and extensive reform, for example for climate-positive recovery, greater inclusivity, and transformations in the global economy, but there is also a genuine risk that responses to the pandemic will consolidate and exacerbate existing inequalities and insecurities. At the present juncture, therefore, we hope that this *Handbook* may contribute to highlighting and reaffirming the important role of international law in defining, protecting, and transforming the global security architecture on all levels and in all dimensions, not only in the past and the present, but even more so in the future.

C. The Role of International Law in Global Security

There can be no doubt that to address the unprecedented scope, scale, and complexity of today's global security challenges, the world must act together. Any effective and sustainable global security governance system must therefore be built on the principles of solidarity, trust-building, and cooperation, as well as on certainty, predictability, and accountability. Both formally and substantively, therefore, the establishment and operation of any such system must be regulated by international law as the only universally accepted normative framework. The development and implementation of international law, however, is largely dominated, and often undermined, by some of the very same challenges that corrode the global security environment as a whole: dysfunctional power relations, zero-sum geopolitical strategies, and protectionism. Thus, deprived of their ability to adapt to the evolving security environment, multilateral legal and institutional security architectures still tend to operate based on outdated binary distinctions between peace and war, internal and external security, or public and private spheres. This is compounded by the fact that these architectures are often sectorally or spatially insular, failing to reflect contemporary realities of global transnationalism, interconnectivity, and interdependence.

Even in cases where genuine progress at the normative or institutional level can be found, such progress is not necessarily reflected at the implementation stage. A number of rather paradoxical constellations are testament to this reality. For example, the International Criminal Court's jurisdiction over the crime of aggression was finally activated in 2018 but at a time when instances of inter-State threats and unilateral uses of military force are rife, and when the fundamental prohibition on the use of force is showing alarming signs of erosion.[13] A visionary treaty on the prohibition of nuclear weapons will enter into force in January 2021, while at the same time the nuclear arms control architecture is rapidly falling apart in the face of renewed risks of nuclear confrontation.[14] Customary international law developments have closed significant regulatory gaps in the law applicable to non-international armed conflicts but the level of compliance with and enforcement of even the most basic tenets of international humanitarian law in the major armed conflicts of our time is appalling. Last but not least, there has been a notable increase in sophisticated and comprehensive national and international soft law instruments, legal manuals, governmental and non-governmental expert guidance, and norm clarification processes. Such soft law instruments increasingly claim legal precision to the 2nd decimal, whereas in reality even the meaning of legal concepts forming the very basis of the international legal order—such as sovereignty, armed conflict, and self-defence—have (re-)emerged as issues of contestation. As a result of all these trends, while formal international legal regulation has increased in scope and density, its capacity to translate normative aspiration into real-world governance, protection, and enforcement has in all likelihood decreased.

In this context, across the *Handbook*'s fifty-nine chapters, a number of overarching key dynamics, trends, and contestations have emerged that reflect the various intrinsic and extrinsic pressures and tensions international law is exposed to in the global security environment of the twenty-first century.

1. Exceptionalism, Emergency, and Crisis, and International Law

Narratives of exceptionalism, emergency, and crisis and how they inform the way States have tried to address global security challenges are a recurrent feature of many of the chapters included in this *Handbook*. In the past, States and other actors have often used politics of fear and securitization, narratives of insecurity, and images of real or perceived threats to broaden the scope of competence of the security apparatus and, in doing so, to solidify their positions and accumulate power. In the course of this process, established legal frameworks have often been stretched beyond recognition, severely undermining democratic processes and the rule of law both domestically and internationally. Well-known cases in point are the counter-terrorism legislation relating to pre-trial detention and bulk surveillance powers introduced in the aftermath of the attacks of 9/11, the proclamation of extended states of emergency in various countries, or the

[13] International Criminal Court, 'Assembly Activates Court's Jurisdiction over Crime of Aggression' (*ICC*, Press Release, 15 December 2017) <https://www.icc-cpi.int/Pages/item.aspx?name=pr1350> accessed 2 May 2020.

[14] Treaty on the Prohibition of Nuclear Weapons (7 July 2017) UN Doc A/CONF.229/2017/8.

recent decision to 'suspend' the right to asylum at the Turkish–Greek border.[15] In light of the recent outbreak of the COVID-19 pandemic and the ensuing 'full-spectrum crisis' caused by global lockdowns and other measures, but also in view of the even more existential climate crisis, these narratives will only gain in importance in coming years. In this context, and notwithstanding significant push-back reactions from domestic and international courts, the 'crisis theme' has widely been exploited to depict specific threats as emergencies temporarily requiring exceptional measures, which were subsequently perpetuated and, eventually, consolidated through legislation. Given the more ubiquitous, complex, and interdependent nature of contemporary security challenges, and the existential risks emerging from pandemic and environmental crises, prospects of major economic and political destabilization and a lasting global backslide on human rights and international peace and security may have become all but inevitable.[16]

2. Multipolar Securitization and International Law

Since the end of the Cold War, there has been a pronounced rise in the use of varying securitizing narratives in national and international politics. This has resulted in a rich body of scholarship and has prompted increasingly nuanced debate about the social construction of security issues.[17] In public international law discourse, the legal implications of the 'global war on terror' have for many years dominated debates. Depending on political preference, these debates typically focused on the enabling or constraining function of public international law, as well as the unintended side effects of counterterrorism for social, economic, and political structures. Whereas States were often quick to invoke international law's enabling functions, activating its constraining functions was, for the most part, a far more incremental process, driven by courts and civil society in particular. This is reflected in well-known debates and jurisprudence regarding, *inter alia*: the extraterritorial application of human rights law, due process and review standards applicable to targeted sanctions regimes, the justifiability of mass surveillance programmes, the concept and implications of civilian participation in hostilities, or the protective standards applicable to detainees captured in security operations.

The narrowing of the security agenda in the post-9/11 era has rightly been criticized and has in the meantime been superseded by a set of more diverse, multipolar securitization trends. In particular, the interconnectedness and interdependencies of the modern world and their impact on our natural environment have contributed to an increasing focus on areas such as health, science, resources, the environment, and the

[15] Greek Emergency Legislative Act, 2 March 2020 <https://docs.google.com/document/d/1yA782Vi56KnIhs2yVehXgkMYQeCieaPq5coWNHqh6xs/mobilebasic> accessed 30 October 2020.

[16] Michelle Bachelet, 'COVID-19 Pandemic—Informal Briefing to the Human Rights Council' (*UNHCHR*, 9 April 2020) <https://www.ohchr.org/EN/NewsEvents/Pages/DisplayNews.aspx?NewsID=25785&LangID=E> accessed 30 October 2020.

[17] Stéphane J Baele/Catarina P Thomson, 'An Experimental Agenda for Securitization Theory' (2017) 19 International Studies Review 646.

economy. The sheer complexity of many contemporary security challenges is, if anything, likely to amplify existing trends towards securitization that will likely be depicted as an 'inevitable' necessity. In this regard, contemporary debates about countermeasures taken in response to the COVID-19 pandemic should be seen as a harbinger of things to come.

The challenge for international law will be to engage with these multipolar securitization trends far more proactively and constructively than has been the case so far. In spite of the widely proclaimed objective to design 'more integrated responses', based on the complementarity of human rights, development, and security, such slogans have all too often amounted to nothing more than hollow rhetoric. There is a widely shared sentiment that, in reality, the human rights and development agendas were gradually subordinated to the security agenda.[18] In light of contemporary securitization trends, across the various sub-fields of public international law, the pressure is mounting to overcome these ideological and artificial divides and to recalibrate international law to the more holistic security governance demands of the twenty-first century.

With the Sustainable Development Goals, an overarching roadmap towards a more humane, sustainable, and just global security governance system already exists. But adjusting current institutional and normative structures with a view to effectively implementing these goals remains a key challenge. At the institutional level, ongoing reforms at the UN aim to break down silo mentalities and artificial barriers between development, peace, and global security.[19] At the normative level, prolonged armed conflicts, the so-called 'forever wars', increasingly raise questions about the interplay of developmental and humanitarian law regimes and, in particular, the role of economic, social, and cultural human rights in times of armed conflict. Multinational military operations, a model frequently used for specific global security governance tasks, are vested with a diverse range of executive powers raising complex questions about the interoperability of the various intersecting domestic, regional, and international legal regimes.[20] Similarly, the poverty–insecurity nexus needs to be better reflected in global security governance designs, and the continuous shrinking of the civic space attests to the urgency of taking the complementarity of human rights and security seriously.[21] Lastly, as the European Court of Human Rights rightly lamented in Medvedyev,[22] better

[18] Necla Tschirgi, 'International Security and Development' in Alexandra Gheciu/William C Wohlforth (eds), *The Oxford Handbook of International Security* (OUP 2018) 565.

[19] UN/World Bank, *Pathways for Peace: Inclusive Approaches to Preventing Violent Conflict* (World Bank 2018). Similarly, recognizing 'the nexus between sustainable development, humanitarian action, peace and security', the EU in 2017 committed to ensuring that its security objectives are fully aligned with objectives in the fields of development policy, peacebuilding, and conflict prevention. See EU, *The New European Consensus on Development: 'Our World, our Dignity, our Future'* (EU 2018).

[20] Robin Geiß/Heike Krieger (eds), *The Legal Pluriverse Surrounding Multinational Military Operations* (OUP 2020).

[21] UNGA 'Report of the Special Rapporteur on the Promotion and Protection of Human Rights and Fundamental Freedoms while Countering Terrorism: Impact of Measures to Address Terrorism and Violent Extremism on Civic Space and the Rights of Civil Society Actors and Human Rights Defenders' (1 March 2019) UN Doc A/HRC/40/52.

[22] *Medvedyev and Others v France*, App No 3394/03, 29 March 2010, para 101.

alignment, coordination, and harmonization is also desirable with regard to sectoral law enforcement regimes dealing with diverse transnational crime phenomena that have direct implications for human rights law.

3. Deformalization, Decentralization, and 'Decollectivization'

Predictability, transparency, and legal certainty are widely called for in today's volatile global security environment. Urgent calls from the UN Secretary-General or the G7 for States to clarify their legal positions regarding the application of international law in cyberspace are one such example.[23] In practice, however, there seems to be a preference for rapid, pragmatic, and informal responses as challenges arise and evolve case-by-case. It has become clear that the dynamic and integrated multi-actor responses required by increasingly interdependent and complex threat scenarios cannot be generated within traditional settings and formalized decision-making processes. Rather, what responses there have been so far have frequently taken the form of an opaque conglomerate of ad hoc measures, often characterized by self-help, power politics, and national discretion. While ad hoc solutions may usefully complement institutionalized responses, widespread deference to such approaches will circumvent and even corrode established institutional and normative frameworks. Resulting trends towards deformalization and decentralization have been widely analysed in international relations scholarship, typically with a focus on the post-American world order, which has been described as a 'multiplex world' or,[24] more pessimistically, 'no one's world'.[25] These trends towards decentralization, deformalization, and devolution are, if anything, likely to be further accelerated by emerging environmental and pandemic risks, which consequently increase the importance of regional and local governance arrangements.

These dynamics are affecting international law in various ways. At the meta-level, they put pressure on debates about the inner and outer limits of treaty interpretation,[26] including through subsequent agreements and subsequent State practice,[27] the

[23] UN Secretary-General António Guterres, 'Address at the Opening Ceremony of the Munich Security Conference' (Munich, 16 February 2018) <https://www.un.org/sg/en/content/sg/speeches/2018-02-16/address-opening-ceremony-munich-security-conference> accessed 2 May 2020; G7, 'Declaration On Responsible States Behaviour in Cyberspace' (Lucca, 11 April 2017) para 9 <https://www.mofa.go.jp/files/000246367.pdf> accessed 2 May 2020: 'To increase predictability and stability in cyberspace, we call on States to publicly explain their views on how existing international law applies to States' activities in cyberspace to the greatest extent possible in order to improve transparency and give rise to more settled expectations of State behavior.'

[24] Acharya (n 8).

[25] Charles A Kupchan, *No One's World: The West, the Rising Rest, and the Coming Global Turn* (OUP 2012).

[26] Ingo Venzke, *How Interpretation Makes International Law* (OUP 2012).

[27] Georg Nolte (ed), *Treaties and Subsequent Practice* (OUP 2013).

identification of customary international law,[28] and the systemic harmonization of interacting legal regimes.[29] As mentioned above, stagnating international codification processes have given rise to a proliferation of clarification manuals, soft law instruments, and expert processes within and outside traditional settings. The sheer amount of 'clarification' materials being produced could even trigger a second wave of fragmentation, thus increasing ambiguity rather than clarity and certainty. At the same time, on a more optimistic note, newly developed harmonization techniques might eventually enable courts and tribunals not only to contain centrifugal forces but even to better coordinate these developments across various sub-fields, enhancing the effectiveness and legitimacy of international law.[30]

Until relatively recently, deformalization, decentralization, and 'decollectivization' tendencies were perhaps most readily observable with respect to the international law on the use of force. In increasingly stark contrast to the original conception of the collective security regime, unilateral uses of force are becoming the rule rather than the exception.[31] The North Atlantic Treaty Organization's (NATO) intervention in Kosovo 1999, the US–British invasion and occupation of Iraq, Russia's invasion and annexation of Crimea, the banalization and institutionalization of targeted killings in the wake of the 'global war on terror', culminating in the killing of Iranian General Soleimani in Baghdad in 2020, or the controversial 2017 and 2018 missile strikes against Syria, are all pertinent examples of this alarming development. Many States appear to be willing to rely on increasingly expansive interpretations of the right to self-defence or humanitarian intervention and to remain passive in light of overt violations of the prohibition of the use of force, in gross underestimation of the long-term consequences. In our view, States' continued complacency in the face of repeated and increasingly bold transgressions against the most fundamental principles of the UN Charter severely undermines the stability and reliability of the current global security architecture and may well become part of the 'recipe for disaster' about which the UN Secretary-General has warned.

Furthermore, with COVID-19 and climate change, the world is now facing an unexpected full-spectrum crisis. Starting out as what was believed to be a local variation of a seasonal influenza, the COVID-19 pandemic quickly developed into an unprecedented health crisis of global proportions and, within weeks, brought the hyperdynamism of the entire world to a sudden halt, with still unpredictable, potentially devastating consequences for the global economy. Disrupting virtually all aspects of human life on the planet, the COVID-19 pandemic is likely to accelerate many of the trends and dynamics

[28] ILC 'Fifth Report on Identification of Customary International Law, by Michael Wood, Special Rapporteur' (14 March 2018) UN Doc A/CN.4/717.

[29] Anne Peters, 'The Refinement of International Law: From Fragmentation to Regime Interaction and Politicization' (2017) 15 International Journal of Constitutional Law (ICON) 671.

[30] ibid 672.

[31] During the Security Council debate on 'The maintenance of international peace and security: Upholding the United Nations Charter' on 9 January 2020, Austria stated that: 'We note with concern the increasing number of cases where armed force is applied unilaterally, invoking the inherent right of self-defense pursuant to Art 51 of the Charter.'

described in this *Handbook*. While radical uncertainty is likely to persist for as long as the pandemic continues, the initial reactions of many States are less than promising. A far cry from the solidarity and cooperation required to address the challenges of a rapidly spreading global pandemic, the G7 was incapable of agreeing on a text for a joint declaration;[32] world leaders chose to polarize and politicize the crisis, cut the funding of a critical multilateral organization such as the World Health Organization (WHO), and impose far-reaching derogations from human rights protections. Unfortunately, therefore, the world is likely to see an acceleration of these corrosive trends, further undermining the stability and integrity of the post-war world order based on a cooperative multilateral system of international peace and security, development, and human rights. Working to reverse these trends will be one of the central challenges in years to come.

4. Hidden Contestation, Ambiguity, and Creeping Indifference

Norm contestation in the widest sense, whether through actual breaches of the law or progressive reinterpretation, has always been an important driver of normative development.[33] High-profile contestations by powerful States always entailed a risk of undermining the normative power of international law.[34] As long as contestations were articulated openly and recognizable as norm challenges or norm development strategies as part of a diplomatic or judicial dialogue,[35] they allowed for, and indeed elicited, counter-contestations with the potential to confirm and consolidate the scope and substance of existing rules. Unfortunately, contemporary forms of norm contestation are often far more obscure and ambiguous and therefore lack the constructive potential inherent in transparent norm contestation. Increasingly, States appear to be pursuing strategies of ambiguity, relying on a hollow rhetoric of law. This entails the invocation of legal concepts in vague or hypothetical terms, on the basis of disputed facts and evidence and typically without any reliable clarification as to the precise legal reasoning on which the actions were based.[36] The ensuing ambiguity and the intended impossibility to decipher the exact transgressive scope of such actions tends to paralyse strong and clear counter-reactions and, therefore, fosters an attitude of passivity and creeping indifference, and undermines

[32] Associated Press, 'Pompeo, G-7 Foreign Ministers Spar over "Wuhan Virus"' (*Politico*, 25 March 2020) <https://www.politico.com/news/2020/03/25/mike-pompeo-g7-coronavirus-149425> accessed 30 October 2020.

[33] Jutta Brunnée/Stephen J Toope, 'Norm Robustness and Contestation in International Law: Self-Defence against Nonstate Actors' (2019) 4 Journal of Global Security Studies 73.

[34] Monika Hakimi, 'International Law in the Age of Trump' (*EJIL:Talk!*, 28 February 2017) <https://www.ejiltalk.org/international-law-in-the-age-of-trump/> accessed 2 May 2020.

[35] This was the case, for example, with regard to the concept of 'pre-emptive self-defense', the 'unable and unwilling justification', the 'global war against terrorism' or continuing attempts to shape and re-invent the interpretation of the notion of imminence in the context of Article 51 UN Charter.

[36] Christopher J Borgen, 'Kosovo, South Ossetia, and Crimea: the Legal Rhetoric of Intervention, Recognition, and Annexation' (*Opinio Juris*, 2 April 2014) <http://opiniojuris.org/2014/04/02/kosovo-south-ossetia-crimea-legal-rhetoric-intervention-recognition-annexation/> accessed 2 May 2020.

the credibility of lofty commitments to defend the rules-based international order. Countering such corrosive trends decisively and effectively is an absolute necessity, and no ensuing diplomatic, political, or economic disadvantage outweighs the risk of having to learn the lessons of two World Wars once more the hard way.

D. About this *Handbook*

1. Aims

The present book aims to provide a comprehensive map of the contemporary international security environment, and to explore the multifaceted relationship between public international law and global security governance. What is the state, role, and relevance of public international law in today's complex and highly dynamic global security environment? Which concepts of security are anchored in international law and what kind of security is it that international law ultimately helps to promote? Which dimensions of global security transpire from different sectors of public international law? How is the rapidly changing global security environment shaping international law, and how is international law in turn influencing other normative frameworks, as well as security governance models and policy responses to these challenges? Does international law ultimately foster or hinder the establishment and implementation of holistic and integrated responses to the security challenges of the twenty-first century?

2. Structure

To address these overarching questions and provide a bird's-eye view on how international law relates to global security, the *Handbook* casts a very wide net, both in terms of the topics and themes it addresses, but equally with regard to the diversity of views and approaches it includes. Thus, Part I of the *Handbook* explores general questions, trends, and dynamics regarding international law and global security, whereas Parts II and III consider a wide range of specific security challenges and security governance tools in light of the applicable international legal regimes. In the selection of relevant security challenges, Part II of the *Handbook* follows the Copenhagen School's classical conceptualization of security, focusing on key security themes and threats that are widely acknowledged as such at the national, regional, and international level. Part III in turn focuses on specific security governance tools in the widest sense, ranging from sanctions, peacekeeping missions, and the use of force to mediation and conflict prevention, as well as surveillance, criminal prosecution, and humanitarian intervention. Part IV provides a comparative perspective on relevant approaches, views, and practices of a select number of particularly influential States and regions—including China, Europe, the Global South, India, Russia, and the US. Finally, Part V considers principal global and regional security mechanisms including institutions such as NATO, the European Union (EU), the Organization for Security and Co-operation in Europe (OSCE), and Interpol, many of which have remained somewhat underscrutinized in their role as security governance actors in international legal scholarship.

3. Methodology and Style

The *Handbook* includes a plurality of approaches and orientations that reflect the spectrum and diversity of views and methodologies amongst mainstream positivists, critical scholars, and practitioners of international law. Some chapters take a classic, commentary-like and distinctly juridical approach, exploring legal frameworks that regulate a particular field or topic, analysing how these frameworks have evolved, and what their regulatory shortcomings or protective gaps are, or might be, in light of future challenges. Others take a more conceptual and theoretical approach, reflecting on whether a particular legal framework remains suitable to regulate a given topic, how law and politics interact with regard to a thematic field, what the drivers of security-related law-making are, and how global security could be conceptualized in a given field.

A related and recurrent feature throughout this *Handbook* is the fact that global security remains an extremely broad, relative, and mutable concept, highly influenced by political decisions and prioritization, and inherently elusive and contested. Given that virtually any aspect of international relations can give rise to security challenges, it is only natural that a reasonably comprehensive book on the international law of global security would have to address virtually any aspect of public international law. International law, in turn, is based on a range of similarly frayed, vague, and contested concepts such as sovereignty, people, or the international community. In his opening address to the 74th UN General Assembly in 2019, the Secretary-General of the United Nations affirmed that 'people have a right to security in all its dimensions'.[37] The *Handbook*'s wide-ranging and inclusive approach should therefore be understood as a way of embracing the 'fluidity' surrounding the multidimensional concept of global security and the various ways in which it interrelates with public international law in the twenty-first century.

Comprising fifty-nine chapters, this *Handbook* certainly aspires to be a comprehensive state-of-the-field compendium, but it does not—and could not—claim to be exhaustive. As the editors of this *Handbook*, we have aimed to capture key areas, central contestations, as well as broad patterns and transformative dynamics in public international law relevant to, and influenced by, contemporary global security challenges and discourses. Doing so has been an experience not only of professional privilege and academic passion, but also of profound humility. Most painfully, the sheer ubiquity and simultaneous

[37] UN Secretary-General António Guterres, 'Address to the 74th Session of the UN General Assembly' (*UN*, 24 September 2019) <https://www.un.org/sg/en/content/sg/speeches/2019-09-24/address-74th-general-assembly> accessed 20 May 2020.

ambiguity of the global security concept had to be balanced against practical and mundane confines of word counts and maximum page numbers. It is no exaggeration to say that, without the moderation patiently but relentlessly imposed by Oxford University Press, we may well have ended up producing an encyclopaedia rather than a handbook.

As a result, certain topics and themes had to be selected at the expense of others, sometimes based on criteria that may justly be deemed arbitrary. Thus, despite the *Handbook*'s diverse range of topics, and despite the extraordinary wealth of experience and expertise of no less than seventy-eight eminent contributors, all of whom count amongst the finest specialists in their field, we are keenly aware of the limitations inherent in this volume's purpose and design. It is, however, our hope that by providing the first comprehensive map of this emerging field of inquiry, the *Handbook* may come to be perceived as a useful starting point for further research in a subject area that is likely to define international relations and international law for generations to come.

E. Acknowledgements

The present *Handbook* is the result of three years of hard work and inspiration accomplished by countless individuals, only some of whom can be thanked individually here. First and foremost, we would like to thank the seventy-eight eminent scholars and practitioners who generously accepted our invitation to participate in this project. Each of them contributed an original chapter, which received its own precious place in the resulting, multifaceted mosaic of perspectives on an equally multifaceted topic. The *Handbook* is built on their invaluable expertise and long-standing experience, and we are immensely grateful for the enthusiasm and dedication each of them has shown throughout the entire process. We are truly delighted to have been able to count on such an illustrious group of authors with such a diversity and depth of professional and disciplinary backgrounds. It is clear that, without them, we could never have achieved our objective and brought this project to a successful conclusion.

A special debt of gratitude also goes to our two assistant editors James Devaney (University of Glasgow) and Eleni Methymaki (University of Oxford) for their invaluable support throughout the entire process. We are also immensely grateful to Jeanne Gillet (University of Glasgow), Daniel Westphal (Freie Universität Berlin), and Athene Richford (University of Glasgow) for their assistance throughout the entire editing process, and owe deep gratitude to the publication team at Oxford University Press for their unfailing support, especially Merel Alstein and Jack McNichol, as well as the project manager Dharuman Bheeman from SPi-Global, our copy-editor Jennifer Hinchliffe, and the various proofreaders. Last but not least, we wish to thank the anonymous peer-reviewers for their constructive feedback on the initial proposal for this *Handbook*.

It is our hope that our readers will find valuable insights into how public international law can contribute to the maintenance and promotion of global security and that the *Handbook* will make a modest contribution to the promotion of the transdisciplinary dialogues that are so urgently needed to address the global security challenges of the twenty-first century. If there is one conclusion we, as editors, can draw both from each individual chapter and the *Handbook* as a whole, it is that global security, despite all its ambiguities, is not an abstract concept, but that it is about averting individual human suffering and promoting the well-being of humankind and the planet. It is indeed high time to consider what 'a right to security in all its dimensions' should entail and how it can be implemented internationally for the benefit of all.

dialogues that are so urgently needed to address the global security challenges of the twenty-first century. If there is one conclusion we, as editors, can draw both from each individual chapter and the *Handbook* as a whole, it is that global security, despite all its ambiguities, is not an abstract concept, but that it is about averting individual human suffering and promoting the well-being of humankind and the planet. It is indeed high time to consider what a right to security in all its dimensions should entail and how it can be implemented internationally for the benefit of all.

PART I

INTERNATIONAL LAW AND GLOBAL SECURITY

CHAPTER 1

THE CONCEPT OF SECURITY IN INTERNATIONAL LAW

NIGEL D WHITE AND AUDEN DAVIES-BRIGHT

A. Introduction

SECURITY is not a fixed concept in international law. It is both maligned and central to the international legal order. Although normative and not just empirical, it is unclear whether the concept of security is a rule of international law, a legal principle, or an extra-legal value and, further, whether it can be truly separated from its companion star—'peace' as in 'peace and security'.

This chapter traces the development of 'security' in international legal discourse from State security, to collective security, to human security, to understand whether there has been a change of emphasis or, in fact, a deepening of security. National security focuses on the safety of the nation-State, which necessitates placing national interests over collective interests. According to Nasu, during the Cold War, 'national security from external military attacks and threats was recognised as the ultimate *raison d'être* of sovereign states'.[1] Collective security marks a transition in that the more national interests become diluted the more centralized a response becomes, and the concept of threats to peace and security is broadened to include events within States that have international repercussions. Furthermore, as noted by Rothwell, the 'traditional view of security defines it in military terms with the primary focus on state protection from threats to national interests', but with the end of the Cold War 'security discourse has expanded beyond the traditional military domain with the proliferation of security agendas, including economic

[1] Hitoshi Nasu, 'Law and Policy for Antarctic Security' in Allan D Hemmings et al (eds), *Antarctic Security in the Twenty-First Century: Legal and Policy Perspectives* (Routledge 2012) 19.

security, environmental security, food security, bio-security, health security and human security'.[2]

This chapter considers the debates about 'security' at a conceptual level, drawing on legal and political literature, and then sets them against developments in practice to see if a conclusion can be drawn on the precise nature and function of 'security' in international law. The chapter addresses the question of whether 'peace' and 'security' are, or should be seen as, norms of international law. This has the potential to bring greater systemic coherence to discussions about normative hierarchies found, for example, in the debates about the supremacy of 'security' obligations derived from the UN Charter. The lack of formal legal definition of security signifies that subjective views, particularly inter-subjective understandings of security, have facilitated the breakdown of the State–human security divide. The chapter concludes on the implications for this as security moves from being the primary purpose of international law and institutions to become a primary norm.

B. Current Status of the Debate

1. Peace and Security

'Peace' and 'security' are often found together in the sense of 'maintaining or restoring international peace and security'. Whereas 'peace' was traditionally conceived as the absence of 'war', in the post-Cold War era the UN General Assembly (UNGA) has defined it in a more positive sense so that 'inter-dependence and co-operation to foster human rights, social and economic development, disarmament, protection of the environment and ecosystems and the improvement of the quality of life for all are indispensable elements for the establishment of peaceful societies'.[3]

While this is a broad and open-ended definition of 'peace', 'security' is perhaps even more elusive, and it has not been the subject of formal definition or elaboration by the UN. According to Thakur, 'the concept of "security" is politically powerful, weakly conceptualised and intensely contested'.[4] In general terms 'security' is an absence of threats to States, groups, and individuals and implies methods to achieve a condition of security through measures designed to prevent threats from materializing. At the international level those measures include methods of peaceful settlement of disputes that might otherwise lead to threats or breaches of the peace, and more coercive measures such as non-forcible sanctions or the application of military force to combat threats and breaches of the peace.

[2] Allan D Hemmings et al, 'The Search for Antarctic Security' in Hemmings et al (n 1) 3.

[3] UNGA Res 46/14 (31 October 1991).

[4] Ramesh Thakur, *The United Nations, Peace and Security* (CUP 2006) 77.

The work of the Copenhagen School has been influential in shaping the concept of security understood as the absence of existential threats against States, other security actors, peoples, and individuals,[5] and reflects the way international law and security have developed in a fluid and inter-subjective way. Despite the continuing strength of national security, the concept of security has not only widened to include non-military threats, such as those arising from food or environmental insecurity, but has also deepened to encompass human security.[6] Clear evidence of the widening understanding of security is found in the pivotal post-Cold War UN Security Council (UNSC) summit held in January 1992. The UNSC had hitherto almost exclusively concerned itself with State and military security, but at that summit declared that the 'absence of war and military conflicts amongst States does not itself ensure international peace and security'. It further stated that 'non-military sources of instability in the economic, social, humanitarian and ecological fields have become threats to peace and security'.[7]

The Copenhagen School identifies those objects that are existentially threatened as 'referent objects'.[8] The referent object for security has 'traditionally been the state and, in a more hidden way, the nation'. This signifies that 'for a state, survival is about sovereignty, and for a nation, it is about identity'. However, following a constructivist approach 'securitizing actors can attempt to construct anything as a referent object'.[9] Thus, the 'referent object' is traditionally the State, although with new security agendas developing all the time, the referent object can be collective concepts such as the environment or regions such as the Antarctic; and this is reflected to some extent in the UNSC's expansion of the concept of 'threat to the peace'.[10] Although its 1992 Summit statement suggests a very wide conception of security, UNSC practice shows it has used its considerable discretion under Article 39 UN Charter to develop a core understanding of a 'threat to the peace' as 'impending or already initiated armed conflict between States'.[11] Krisch has identified an agreed expansion to cover 'classical security threats':[12] the proliferation of weapons of mass destruction;[13] terrorism;[14] internal armed conflicts;[15] and piracy.[16] Krisch then identifies more tentative developments towards threats to human security in the form of: protection of civilians in

[5] Barry Buzan et al, *Security: A New Framework for Analysis* (Lynne Rienner 1998) 5.

[6] ibid 8.

[7] UNSC 'Statement by the President on Behalf of the Members of the Council Concerning the Council's Responsibility in the Maintenance of International Peace and Security' (31 January 1992) UN Doc S/23500.

[8] Buzan et al (n 5) 36. [9] ibid. [10] Nasu (n 1) 25–6.

[11] Nico Krisch, 'Article 39' in Bruno Simma et al (eds), *The Charter of the United Nations: A Commentary* (3rd edn, OUP 2012) 1279.

[12] ibid 1280–3.

[13] UNSC Res 1718 (2006) (North Korea); UNSC Res 1737 (2006) (Iran); UNSC Res 1540 (2004) (non-State actors).

[14] UNSC Res 748 (1992) (Libya); UNSC Res 1267 (1999) (Taliban); UNSC Res 1333 (2000) (Al-Qaeda); UNSC Res 1373 (2001) (general legislation).

[15] UNSC Res 161 (1961). [16] UNSC Res 1816 (2008).

armed conflict;[17] violations of human rights;[18] and most controversially violation of democratic principles.[19]

Due to its inherent inter-subjectivity,[20] 'security' as a concept poses a considerable challenge in terms of detecting any definite normative or legal meaning, but there is no doubt as to the legal effects of 'security'. Security considerations often prevail in drafting and implementing laws. In terms of the international legal order, traditionally 'security' is not viewed as a legal principle but is seen, along with 'peace', as the primary 'purpose' of the UN Charter and the organization constituted by it.[21] The International Court of Justice (ICJ) declared that 'the primary place ascribed to international peace and security is natural, since the fulfilment of the other purposes will be dependent upon the attainment of that basic condition'.[22]

International legal analysis tends to focus on the principles of the UN Charter contained in Article 2, which include the principles applicable to the UN of sovereign equality and non-intervention, and duties upon States, primarily the obligation to settle disputes peacefully and the duty to refrain from the threat or use of force. However, Article 1 is important for international law more broadly because it sets the 'purposes', arguably the values that the UN system aims to achieve or uphold.[23] It is worth considering Article 1(1) UN Charter in greater detail because it only places security (partly) within the framework of international law by declaring that the maintenance of peace and security can be achieved through the taking of 'effective measures for the prevention and removal of threats to the peace', and by bringing 'about by peaceful means, and in conformity with the principles of justice and international law, adjustment or settlement of international disputes or situations'. Article 1(1) gives the UN the task of pursuing the peaceful settlement of disputes in accordance with international law but, read literally, does not subject UN coercive measures taken to tackle threats to the peace to the same legal framework.

The prospect of UN security action unbound by international law runs like a red thread through the Charter. First, there is the principle that the UN should not intervene in domestic affairs but this does not prejudice action taken by the UNSC under Chapter VII.[24] Secondly, the ban on the use of force allows for only two exceptions—self-defence and military action taken to combat threats to, and breaches of, the peace as authorized by the UNSC under Chapter VII.[25] The content of the Charter seems to favour 'security', especially the collective coercive type found in Chapter VII, over 'law'.

[17] UNSC Res 1296 (2000). [18] eg UNSC Res 688 (1991) (Kurdish region of Iraq).

[19] UNSC Res 841 (1993) (overthrow of elected government in Haiti); Krisch (n 11) 1284–8.

[20] Ian Johnston, 'Security Council Deliberations: The Power of Better Argument' (2003) 14 EJIL 437.

[21] UN Charter 1 UNTS XVI art 1(1).

[22] *Certain Expenses of the United Nations (Article 17, paragraph 2, of the Charter)* (Advisory Opinion) [1962] ICJ Rep 151, 168.

[23] Nigel D White, 'The Ties that Bind: The EU, the UN and International Law' (2006) 37 Netherlands Yearbook of International Law 57, 62–6.

[24] UN Charter art 2(7). [25] UN Charter arts 2(4), 51 and 42.

The achievement of peace and security is the *raison d'être* for the UN, and the enforcement of international law is secondary to that. However, paragraphs 2, 3, and 4 of Article 1 contain the basis for the development of a much more expansive and balanced legal architecture that could potentially provide a robust framework for security action by placing both the development of self-determination of peoples and the promotion of respect for individual human rights as purposes of the UN, alongside the achievement of peace and security. Within the human rights legal framework developed under the auspices of the Charter,[26] freedoms and rights are curtailed by considerations of security, both national and human. In turn, security has also been constrained by human rights. While security was only politically constrained in 1945, it has gradually been shackled by international law.[27]

2. State Security

Undoubtedly, States are a conceptual reality influencing all aspects of human life and interaction. Despite philosophical and political divergence in perspectives on the origins of the State,[28] they all converge on the articulation of the State as being essential and foundational to human existence. Human social and political interaction has given rise to the construct of 'the State' and national and international social, political, and legal systems rely on its existence for their foundation, structure, and legitimacy. Consequently, conceptualizations of State security are predicated on the foundational idea that States not only exist as independent entities but are also entities deserving of security—a State must be protected from threats to its existence. This security is of such paramount importance that individuals and communities will sacrifice themselves in its name. However, when discussing State security and the price people will pay for it, what it is that is being protected is a fundamental question rarely confronted, notwithstanding political rhetoric designed to inspire the requisite emotions and loyalties for the sacrifices to be made. This omission arguably exacerbates the lack of clarity around security as a concept and enables it to be utilized as a political tool,[29] which is exacerbated by structural inequalities within the international assembly of States.[30]

[26] Universal Declaration of Human Rights (UNGA Res 217A (III) (10 December 1948)) and the 1966 International Covenants on Civil and Political Rights (999 UNTS 171) (ICCPR) and on Economic, Social and Cultural Rights (993 UNTS 3) (ICESCR).

[27] Gabriël H Oosthuizen, 'Playing the Devil's Advocate: The United Nations Security Council is Unbound by Law' (1999) 12 Leiden Journal of International Law 549.

[28] eg Plato, *The Republic* (Christopher Rowe tr, Penguin Classics 2012); Aristotle, *Politics: Books I and II* (Trevor J Saunders tr, OUP 1995); John Locke, *Two Treatises of Government and a Letter Concerning Toleration* (Ian Shapiro ed, Yale UP 2003); Thomas Hobbes, *Leviathan* (Crawford B MacPherson ed, Penguin Classics 1981).

[29] eg as a referent object in a securitization agenda—Buzan et al (n 5).

[30] See eg Antony Anghie, *Imperialism, Sovereignty and the Making of International Law* (CUP 2005); Russell Buchan, *International Law and the Construction of the Liberal Peace* (Hart 2013).

The absence of a requirement for external validation in the legal criteria for statehood ostensibly demonstrates that the State is an artificial human construct produced by local human interaction, rather than a naturally occurring phenomenon.[31] The requirements of permanent population; defined territory; government; and capacity to enter into relations with other States,[32] focus on the internal character, structures, and effectiveness of the State and demonstrate that States have both a concrete and abstract form. The concrete form, the human population and physical landmass, are matters of fact independent of any sociopolitical constructs. The abstract form, the control exercised by a State over its territory through constructed power mechanisms, depends upon the physical aspect for its existence. The abstract form is what fulfils the second half of the Montevideo criteria and enables a State to interact with others. It is de facto dependent on external recognition in order to create and maintain inter-State relations and to assert its existence and sovereignty. It is this aspect of the State that requires security as it is not independent of the physical form and cannot autonomously assert itself—it is not a matter of fact, but rather a sociopolitically constructed reality. As such, maintenance and protection of the abstract form is the primary focus and purpose of State security, and protection of the physical form is a means to an end, rather than the end itself. This means that human lives can be sacrificed in the pursuit of State security.

The concept of sovereignty is essential to understanding State security as it is the assertion of legitimate impenetrability—the claim to independence from external forces. Although the Treaties of Münster and Osnabrück make no explicit reference to sovereignty and the rights it confers, the concept is traditionally seen as arising from the 1648 Peace of Westphalia which effectively recognized the independence of those human collectives existing within the Empire and the sovereign statehood of those committed to Christianity (whether Catholic or Protestant). Those States were not subject to external interference or control, such as that previously exercised by the Holy Roman Empire.[33] Modern-day divisions between the Liberal (predominantly Christian heritage) States and the non-Liberal (predominantly Islamic and other non-Christian heritage) demonstrate that perceived legitimacy and practical sovereignty follow adherence to particular values and political structures.[34] In the post-9/11 Age of Terrorism, State security is defined mainly, at least from Western perspectives, in terms of protection from Islamic terrorism and the destruction of democracy. What is being secured is the maintenance of the status quo and the measure is the absence of terrorist attacks and the resulting civilian casualties. However, as will be discussed in Section B.4, this measure of security is not sufficient, hence the development of the concept of human security.

[31] Convention on the Rights and Duties of States 165 LNTS 19 (Montevideo Convention) art 3: 'The political existence of the state is independent of recognition by other states.'

[32] ibid art 1.

[33] Ian Clark, *Legitimacy in International Society* (OUP 2005).

[34] See eg Anghie (n 30); Gerry Simpson, 'Two Liberalisms' (2001) 12 EJIL 537.

3. Collective Security

It has been stated that 'very generally we can delineate this area of international relations as any collective action designed to defuse situations that endanger the peace and combat threats to, and breaches of, (international) peace.'[35] In UN Charter terms, collective security mechanisms can both promote the peaceful settlement of disputes (under Chapter VI) and take coercive measures to combat threats to the peace, breaches of the peace, or acts of aggression (under Chapter VII). The UN was borne out of the alliance that defeated the Axis powers as an executive model with a great deal of centralized sanctioning power put into the hands of the primary organ, the UNSC. The UN Charter appeared so much more constitutionally and institutionally developed and 'action'-oriented than its predecessor. At the San Francisco Conference, the Soviet delegate stated that one of the characteristics of the UNSC 'was that actions should be fast and effective.'[36] Smaller States agreed on the basis that the Council should protect them from aggression and, moreover, 'that the interests of great and small powers in peace and security rested fundamentally upon the ability of the great powers to work together.'[37]

The Charter scheme for collective military action has not fully materialized. While the militarily limited, blue-helmeted peacekeepers have become a symbol of the UN and are under UN command and control, the idea of an army fighting for the UN, providing security by enforcing the peace, has not been realized. The early Cold War hardening of the positions of the superpowers meant that those parts of Chapter VII that envisaged agreements on the provision of forces to the UN, as well as means of controlling such forces through a Military Staff Committee,[38] never materialized.[39] As a result there is no reliable and deployable UN force capable of regularly confronting aggression and other threats to the peace.

Although peacekeeping realizes UN goals to a certain extent by maintaining an established peace between or within States, the UN collective security system was designed to confront, by coercive military means if necessary, threats to the peace, breaches of the peace and acts of aggression.[40] To do this it needs to be able to take military enforcement action against the will of the target State. It follows that there is no contradiction in the UN having or developing both a consensual 'police' function (in the form of peacekeeping) and a coercive 'military' function (in the shape of peace enforcement). As regards the latter, instead of the envisaged centralized military enforcement model found in Chapter VII, the UN and Member States have shaped a decentralized model of coercive enforcement action. In this model, a Member State or groups of States take coercive military action under UNSC authority to tackle a specified aggressor or a threat to the peace. Being dependent upon contributions from Member States, such a system does not, therefore, guarantee that the most serious ruptures of international peace are met

[35] Nigel D White, *Collective Security Law* (Ashgate 2003) xi.
[36] UNCIO XI (1945) 253. [37] UNCIO XI (1945) 276. [38] UN Charter (n 21) arts 43, 47.
[39] Leland M Goodrich et al, *Charter of the United Nations* (3rd edn, Columbia UP 1969) 323.
[40] UN Charter (n 21) art 39.

with collective military responses. Even if there are States willing to contribute to a UN authorized coalition, the UN's lack of effective continuing control over such operations means that the achievement of UN goals is by no means guaranteed. Command and control is delegated to Member States, who together may be part of a regional or defence organization such as the EU or NATO. The only real link between the military operation and the UNSC is the authorizing resolution, which is often open-ended.[41] Although States contributing to a coalition have reporting obligations to the UNSC, this does not normally lead to any exertion of continuing control over the operation by the UN. In effect, the coalition sets up its own command and control structure and conducts the military operations within the terms of the authorizing resolution, but at times stretching those terms beyond what appears to be the UNSC's collective will.[42]

4. Human Security

At the end of the Cold War, with the apparent victory of Western political and economic ideology,[43] the international security discourse moved away from the traditional State-centric approach and refocused on the individual human. With the major existential threat posed by inter-State conflict seemingly neutralized, attention could shift to the threats facing human groups caused by inequitable development and planetary exploitation. The term 'human security' was utilized by the UNDP's 1994 Human Development Report to promote the 'concern with human life and dignity'[44] and framed it in security terms in opposition to territorial security and the elimination of external threats to the State. The emphasis was on the ordinary human person and the insecurities faced by all persons across the globe: 'Human security means that people can exercise these choices safely and freely [—] and that they can be relatively confident that the opportunities they have today are not totally lost tomorrow.'[45]

After international failure to adequately address the various crises of the 1980s and 1990s, the concept of human security as a multi- or inter-sectional policy framework offered a fresh approach designed to combine different sectors and focus on the daily reality of people and of those who are actually affected when a State goes into crisis. Individual humans became the referent object within security discourse, reconceptualizing security on the micro level and securitizing the individual. This has arguably had a twofold effect. On the one hand, the individualizing of security harmonizes with human

[41] See criticism by Malaysia of UNSC Res 678 (1990), which authorized 'necessary measures' against Iraq in response to its invasion of Kuwait—UNSC Verbatim Record (29 November 1990) UN Doc S/PV.2963.

[42] See eg UNSC Res 1973 (2011) (the authorization to take 'necessary measures' to protect civilians in Libya).

[43] Francis Fukuyama, *The End of History and the Last Man* (Penguin 1992); Rick Fawn/Jeremy Larkins (eds), *International Society after the Cold War: Anarchy and Order Reconsidered* (Palgrave Macmillan 1996).

[44] UNDP, *Human Development Report 1994* (OUP 1994) 22.

[45] ibid 23.

rights discourse as it recognizes and prioritizes human dignity and integrity and the need for humans to be protected; on the other, it presents a threat to State security as it encourages the prioritization of human security, the needs of humans in countering existential threats, over the State. Thus, there is an inherent tension within the meta-security discourse as the security concerns of humans and States are arguably in opposition: the overarching threat to humans is the State (be it through armed conflict, economic development, social policies, environmental mismanagement, etc), and the primary threat to the State (in its abstract form) can only emanate from humans due to the State being a sociopolitical construct that relies on human interaction for its existence. Ultimately, international security discourse and policy may have utilized individual humans as the referent object, but the monopoly on power, the use of force and the subsequent ability to effect security has remained with the State. It is the State that sets the security agenda and allocates resources and it does so with self-preservation as its central purpose.[46] For example, human rights protecting the individual from the power of the State can be limited or derogated from in times of 'public emergency which threaten the life of the nation', demonstrating that the individual's 'right' to security is contingent upon it being in the State's security interests to afford security to certain citizens.[47]

Additionally, the securitization of the individual means that individuals can now be conceptualized as presenting a specific or even general threat to a State and its citizens. This in turn leads to the increased endangerment of individuals at risk from State abuse. Thus, although 'human security' was to create freedom from want and fear through the creation and maintenance of equitable global development and relevant normative frameworks addressing 'insecuritizing' factors,[48] the individualizing of security has arguably increased insecurity for certain persons in the Age of Terror. An example of this is the approach taken by States in addressing the current refugee crisis.[49]

Persons fleeing the insecurity of their homelands are viewed as a problem and a threat in themselves—State security is prioritized over the pressing human security issues. This is legitimized by State action in the form of UNSC resolutions, which reassert the State as the referent object through the continued securitization of terrorism by calling on States to ensure that refugee status is not 'abused by the perpetrators, organisers or facilitators of terrorist acts'.[50] This allows States to impose restrictions on movement and construct additional barriers for those humans in a position of insecurity and to reframe them as a possible security threat. The receiving States are engaging in fast-tracking,

[46] Robert Nozick, *Anarchy, State and Utopia* (Basil Blackwell 1974). [47] ICCPR (n 26) art 4.

[48] Commission on Human Security, *Human Security Now* (Commission on Human Security 2003).

[49] eg Arne Niemann/Natascha Zaun, 'EU Refugee Policies and Politics in Times of Crisis: Theoretical and Empirical Perspectives' (2018) 56 Journal of Common Market Studies 3; 'How is the migrant crisis dividing EU countries?' *BBC News* (London, 4 March 2016) <www.bbc.co.uk/news/world-europe-34278886> accessed 10 January 2020.

[50] UNSC Res 2178 (2014).

immediately returning refugees or sending them to transit countries.[51] Policies such as deportation, detention, and dispersal aim to discourage those seen as 'undeserving' or 'illegitimate' asylum seekers and refugees. In a reversal of the usual approach of not assuming guilt, the language of the relevant policies, directives, and legislation appear to assume a refugee is 'bogus' unless they are able to demonstrate otherwise. Those who are refused official refugee status face a destitute and uncertain future, similar to that of stateless persons.[52] After escaping the conflict at home, perceptions of individuals as a potential threat to the host State mean that their insecurity is increased. Humans fleeing conflict and persecution in their homelands are perceived as unwanted 'others' threatening the stability and social cohesion of European and other Western States, portrayed as 'a threat to national security, welfare security and national identity',[53] a threat to the human security of the existing populations as well as a threat to the State. In this way, the human security approach has been commandeered by the State to further its own security agenda.

C. Recent Developments and Contemporary Challenges

1. Counter-terrorism

A central difficulty in the effort to counter the threat of terrorism is that a universally accepted definition of terrorism remains elusive, resulting in an inevitably subjective and State or region-specific response. However, despite the lack of agreement on what exactly is 'terrorism', it is accepted that it is a negative concept,[54] and its successful securitization has changed the debates around, and conceptualizations of, security. Terrorism is the lens through which many aspects of national and international activities are now being viewed and it has had a unifying effect in the sense that all States are able to identify threats from groups that can be labelled as terrorist. There is thus general consensus that terrorism is a threat that must be countered. This has had an unparalleled impact on the sociopolitical sphere, not least in the development of understandings of State and human security. For example, justice is seen in overt security terms, which undermine

[51] Amnesty International, 'Dangerously Disproportionate: The Ever-Expanding National Security State in Europe' (2017) 21 <www.amnesty.org/download/Documents/EUR0153422017ENGLISH.PDF> accessed 28 February 2019.

[52] Emma Stewart/Gareth Mulvey, 'Seeking Safety beyond Refuge: The Impact of Immigration and Citizenship Policy upon Refugees in the UK' (2014) 40 Journal of Ethnic and Migration Studies 1023.

[53] ibid.

[54] Louise Richardson, *What Terrorists Want* (John Murray 2006) 19.

individual security factors such as human rights and access to justice.[55] This refocusing of State security concerns on the micro level through the concept of human security has led to increased dangers for individuals who are conceptualized as presenting a specific or even general threat to the State and its citizens.[56]

The individualizing of threats is exemplified in the current existential enemy threatening life and global values, particularly the West—international Islamic terrorism. This threat does not emanate from States, but from people. The enemy is not another State motivated by a conflicting ideology, rather it is other people who are conceptualized as seeking to destroy the everyday lives of ordinary, innocent citizens, breaking with the traditional inter-State security paradigm. Consequently, the appropriate and required response, responding in self-defence to this threat, is also people-centred. In an inversion of human rights, often the most vulnerable people, such as refugees, are seen as dangerous and States use the language of human rights to protect their own interests, often articulated as preserving the human rights of 'innocent civilians' (as opposed to potentially guilty ones).[57] The current international human rights legal framework, with no overarching legal authority and enforcement, does not adequately protect suspected individuals from abuses of State power when State security is considered to be at stake. The concessions made to States to encourage their buy-in to international human rights instruments allows (certain) States to ultimately wield their power with impunity—the only real deterrent being political fallout.

Interestingly, securitization of terrorism is articulated as a threat in itself, in the same way that disease is discussed as a general threat to human health, as opposed to a tactic used by people with a political agenda. This rhetorical sleight of hand enables governments to incorporate virtually any sociopolitical element that is inconvenient or threatens to disturb the status quo under the banner of terrorism, including ideological and political differences. It also allows a State to reinforce and protect its existence through the framing of certain beliefs and perspectives as being part of the national identity and of others as being wholly incompatible.[58] However, terrorism is not something that is capable of being defeated or eradicated in itself, as it is merely a tactic used by those without the coercive power of the State and will be used for as long as it remains

[55] See eg 'Abu Qatada wins Jordan Deportation Appeal' *BBC News* (London, 17 January 2012) <www.bbc.co.uk/news/uk-16590662> accessed 10 January 2020; James Slack, 'Hate Preacher to Go "Free in Months"' *Daily Mail Online* (London, 18 January 2012) <www.dailymail.co.uk/news/article-2087734/Abu-Qatada-deportation-Human-rights-mean-terror-cleric-CANNOT-sent-Jordan.html> accessed 10 January 2020; Graeme Wilson, 'Hate Preacher Abu Qatada Goes Free as Top Judge Sparks Outrage' *The Sun* (London, 13 November 2012) <www.thesun.co.uk/archives/politics/1039891/hate-preacher-abu-qatada-goes-free-as-top-judge-sparks-outrage/> accessed 10 January 2020.

[56] As discussed in Section C.2.

[57] Home Office, *CONTEST The United Kingdom's Strategy for Countering Terrorism* (Cm 9608, 2018); UNCHR, 'Human Rights, Terrorism and Counter-Terrorism' (Fact Sheet No 32, 2007) <www.ohchr.org/Documents/Publications/Factsheet32EN.pdf> accessed 10 January 2010.

[58] eg defining extremism as active opposition to fundamental 'British values', in the UK's counter-terrorism Prevent strategy. See Home Office, *Prevent Strategy* (Cm 8092, 2011).

effective.[59] Given that States have shown an increasing willingness to frame oppositional or alternative perspectives and ideologies as terrorist[60] in an effort to maintain the security of the State as it is, this significantly narrows the legitimate sphere in which citizens can operate. Consequently, the protections afforded to the individual from the coercive power of the State, such as human rights law, are subverted and compromised by the anti-terrorism narrative and viewed as a danger to the State and its legitimate citizens. This creates situations of injustice and insecurity for those suspected of terrorist activities or of having a religious or political ideology similar to those who have utilized terrorist tactics.[61]

In response to citizens travelling abroad to allegedly assist groups defined at home as terrorist, several Western States have enacted denationalization legislation in order to counter the perceived threat presented by these citizens returning home.[62] Thus, a person may be stripped of their citizenship on the basis of alleged involvement with groups utilizing the tactic of terrorism, creating a situation of extreme insecurity. In 2015, thirty-three people were deprived of their British citizenship by the Home Secretary after travelling abroad to countries such as Pakistan and Yemen, because it was considered 'conducive to the public good'.[63] This exercise of power was held to be lawful by the European Court of Human Rights.[64] The figure reportedly rose to 150 individuals in 2017.[65] Initially limited to those with dual citizenship, the power was extended in 2014 to include persons whom the Home Secretary considers to have reasonable eligibility to gain another nationality, although this power has yet to be used.[66] Thus, the UK is prepared to render a person stateless, removing the protections of the State from those

[59] Richardson (n 54) 22.

[60] eg Francesca Marshall, 'Student, 14, Referred to Terror Prevention Programme after he was "Groomed" by Anti-fracking Activists' *The Telegraph* (London, 30 July 2018) <www.telegraph.co.uk/news/2018/07/30/14-year-old-student-referred-anti-terror-programme-groomed-fracking/> accessed 10 January 2020.

[61] eg the killing of Jean Charles de Menezes by police in 2005, *Case of Armani da Silva v UK*, App No 5878/08, 30 March 2016; the freezing of assets on the suspicion of involvement with terrorist groups/activities, C-402/05 P and C-415/05 P *Kadi et al v Council of the European Union et al* [2008] ECLI:EU:C:2008:461 and C-584/10 P, C-593/10 P and C-595/10 P *Kadi et al v Council of the European Union et al* [2013] ECLI:EU:C:2013:518.

[62] Sangeetha Pillai/George Williams, 'The Utility of Citizenship Stripping Laws in the UK, Canada and Australia' (2017) 41 Melbourne University Law Review 845.

[63] Victoria Parsons, 'Theresa May Deprived 33 Individuals of British Citizenship in 2015' *The Bureau of Investigative Journalism* (London, 21 June 2016) <https://www.thebureauinvestigates.com/stories/2016-06-21/citizenship-stripping-new-figures-reveal-theresa-may-has-deprived-33-individuals-of-british-citizenship> accessed 13 November 2020.

[64] *K2 v UK*, App No 42387/13, 7 February 2017; Allan Travis, 'UK Can Strip Terror Suspects of Citizenship, European Judges Rule' *The Guardian* (London, 9 March 2017) <www.theguardian.com/uk-news/2017/mar/09/terror-suspects-british-citizenship-european-ruling> accessed 10 January 2020.

[65] Press Association, 'UK "has Stripped 150 Jihadists and Criminals of Citizenship"' *The Guardian* (London, 30 July 2017) <www.theguardian.com/uk-news/2017/jul/30/uk-has-stripped-150-jihadists-and-criminals-of-citizenship> accessed 10 January 2020.

[66] David Anderson QC, *Citizenship Removal Resulting in Statelessness: First Report of the Independent Reviewer on the Operation of the Power to Remove Citizenship Obtained by Naturalisation from Persons Who Have No Other Citizenship* (2016).

suspected of terrorism related activities,[67] thereby prioritizing State security over human security. Arguably this practice violates, or at least drastically alters, the social contract through the creation of overtly conditional citizenship and of an unequal status between naturalized citizens (with possible eligibility for alternative citizenship) and citizens born in the UK with no ties to another State (and so with no reasonable eligibility for alternative citizenship). A person subject to these powers may appeal the removal of citizenship through an inevitably lengthy and costly appeal process, while being prevented from returning home and having to communicate with lawyers from abroad,[68] thereby creating insecurity and raising serious access to justice concerns.

2. Drone Strikes

As discussed above, international law generally frames security as State security, either individually or collectively. Given the general prohibition on the use of force and the global imbalance in terms of military might in favour of the West (namely the USA), threats to State security do not emanate from other States as previously conceptualized, especially after the end of the Second World War. States powerful enough to threaten each other, such as Russia, China, and the USA, have largely adopted methods other than the use of force, such as allegedly influencing the outcome of elections,[69] malware or cyberattacks,[70] or cultural globalization.[71] Although these methods undoubtedly pose a threat to State security, they do not necessarily threaten its civilians or its existence and thus military responses are unlikely to be effective or easy to legitimize. Thus, following the Copenhagen School's logic, it is important for States to identify a threat that can be easily understood by the citizenry, the robber at the door seeking to take all that is held dear. Those utilizing terrorist tactics fit the bill and so are portrayed and targeted as presenting existential threats to States, despite there being no evidence that this is indeed the case. Terrorism poses a threat to individual humans, the safety and bodily integrity of the victims of shootings, bombings, and other violent acts, but arguably not the State itself.

It could also be argued that certain ideologies, such as those espousing an end to national borders and the establishment of alternative regional or even international modes of governance, pose a threat to statehood as currently understood. Hence

[67] The breadth of the discretion is not dependent on the successful prosecution of the suspected individual, but on the removal of citizenship being 'conducive to the public good'. See ibid 3.16.

[68] Parsons (n 63).

[69] See the various *New York Times* articles in 'Russian Hacking and Influence in the US Election: Complete Coverage of Russia's Campaign to Disrupt the 2016 Presidential Election' *New York Times* (New York, various dates) <www.nytimes.com/news-event/russian-election-hacking> accessed 10 January 2020.

[70] See eg Dorothy Denning, 'Cyberwar: How Chinese Hackers Became a Major Threat to the US' *Newsweek* (New York, 5 October 2017) <www.newsweek.com/chinese-hackers-cyberwar-us-cybersecurity-threat-678378> accessed 10 January 2020.

[71] See eg Edward W Said, *Culture and Imperialism* (Vintage Books 1994).

governments seek to delegitimize and eradicate certain ideological discourse, through counter-terrorism strategies,[72] which may encourage citizen-led movements to alter the status quo. However, an individual person cannot threaten a State's very existence. Nevertheless, the current articulation of security has had a direct impact on the methods used to protect States from external attack, namely, the targeting of individuals as though they present an existential threat to a State, treating individual humans as States in terms of threat, responsibility, and capacity. Concurrently, since 9/11, State counter-terrorism efforts have consistently shifted the focus to a Minority Report-style 'pre-crime' scenario, where State organs seek to anticipate and prevent terrorist incidents from occurring.[73] Although prevention is a central tenet of the majority of criminal law systems, the point at which security agents are intervening to counter the terrorist threat is pre-emptive, 'when the risk of harm is no more than an unspecified threat or propensity as yet uncertain and beyond view'.[74] A case in point is the drone strike against Reyaad Khan in Syria by the UK government in 2015.

Reyaad Khan was a UK citizen residing in Syria who was targeted and killed by a remote aircraft operated by UK armed forces on 21 August 2015. Then Prime Minister Cameron explained to the UK House of Commons that the strike had been taken as a self-defence measure and was in accordance with 'a comprehensive counter-terrorism strategy that seeks to prevent and disrupt plots against this country at every stage'.[75] The justification for the pre-emptive fatal strike against an individual outside the territory of the UK, and after the public events that were allegedly targeted had occurred without incident, was the unprecedented threat to State security presented by Islamic terrorism, requiring the UK to take such action in self-defence.[76] The legal arguments presented to justify the use of lethal force outside of an armed conflict situation and in violation of human rights law was the international principle of self-defence.[77] However, not only does anticipatory self-defence without an imminent threat present legal difficulty at an international level,[78] it also violates human rights law, such as the right to life, a fair trial, and individual liberty. The pre-emptive action does not require the establishment of the requisite *mens rea* or *actus reus* of the alleged criminal (terrorist) activity.[79] The targeting of individuals outside the usual safeguards of criminal or human rights law presents a serious threat to individual security and also to justice. Although this was a departure

[72] eg Eleni Courea, 'University Alerts Students to Danger of Leftwing Essay' *The Guardian* (London, 11 November 2018) <www.theguardian.com/education/2018/nov/11/reading-university-warns-danger-left-wing-essay> accessed 10 January 2020.

[73] Phillip K Dick, *Minority Report* (Gollancz 2002).

[74] Lucia Zedner, 'Seeking Security by Eroding Rights: The Side-Stepping of Due Process' in Benjamin J Goold/Liora Lazarus (eds), *Security and Human Rights* (Hart 2007) 259.

[75] Prime Minister David Cameron, HC Deb 7 September 2015, vol 599, col 25. [76] ibid.

[77] In contrast to the Prime Minister, a Joint Committee of Parliament found that Reyaad Khan was killed in an armed conflict involving the UK. See Joint Committee on Human Rights, *The Government's Policy on the Use of Drones for Targeted Killing (Second Report)* (2015–16, HL 141, HC 574) para 2.29.

[78] Nigel D White/Lydia Davies-Bright, 'Drone Strikes: A Remote Form of Self-Defence?' in Jens D Ohlin (ed), *Research Handbook on Remote Warfare* (Edward Elgar 2017).

[79] Zedner (n 74) 260.

from previous military action by the UK,[80] the precedent it sets is a dangerous one and further reinforces the securitization of terrorism and the expansion of State security.

3. Cybersecurity

Cybersecurity has proven a difficult area to achieve consensus. The issue has been discussed and resolutions have been adopted, primarily in the United Nations General Assembly (UNGA). In 1999, the UNGA adopted a resolution calling upon States to 'promote at multilateral levels the consideration of existing and potential threats in the field of information security' and went on to invite States to inform the Secretary-General on the advisability of 'developing international principles that would enhance the security of global information and telecommunications systems to help to combat information terrorism and criminality'.[81] The broad language of this resolution reflects a profound disagreement between the members of the UN, specifically within the permanent members of the UNSC. According to Mary Ellen O'Connell, Russia has promoted a treaty along the lines of the Chemical Weapons Convention to regulate cyberspace, which it viewed as a similar dual use issue: 'Russia's proposed treaty would ban a country from secretly embedding malicious codes or circuitry that could be later activated from afar in the event of war.' The US, however, differed in its approach following the success of the Stuxnet worm cyberattack, which infected computer software controlling centrifuges in an Iranian nuclear plant, thereby damaging or destroying them.[82]

It is difficult to construct a treaty or other legal regulatory mechanism that governs something as complex and multidimensional as the use of cyberspace. Achieving consensus on something that is both an important modern form of freedom of information and a threat to security is one of the greatest challenges facing the UN. In 2010, the UNGA identified a number of existing and potential threats in the field of information security. It urged States to develop 'strategies' to address 'threats emerging in the field, consistent with the need to preserve the free flow of information'. Intriguingly, the UNGA also considered that the 'purpose of such strategies could be served through further examination of relevant international concepts aimed at strengthening the security of global information and telecommunications systems'. It went on to invite States to look at the recommendations contained in the Report of the Group of Governmental Experts on Developments in the Field of Information and Telecommunications in the Context of International Security, in particular both the aforementioned 'concepts' as well as 'measures' that might be taken to strengthen information security.[83]

[80] Prime Minister David Cameron, HC Deb 7 September 2015, vol 599, cols 26–7.

[81] UNGA Res 53/70 (4 January 1999) (Developments in the field of information and telecommunications in the context of international security).

[82] Mary-Ellen O'Connell, 'Cyber Security without War' (2012) 17 JCSL 187, 205–6.

[83] UNGA Res 65/41 (8 December 2010).

Unfortunately, the Report did not develop the 'concepts' that might constitute a normative framework to shape the use of cyberspace.[84]

The responses to the UNGA's request to States contain some discussion of relevant 'concepts'. Australia, the US and the UK argued that existing international law was sufficient to provide a framework for protection from information security threats arising from a variety of actors (sovereign equality, the prohibition on the use of force, international humanitarian law, and the jus ad bellum).[85] The UN Institute for Disarmament Research has also taken this approach to existing legal frameworks for cyber war. A 2011 report by Melzer on 'Cyberwarfare and International Law' is a good example of the continuing restricted framework of the *jus ad bellum* and the *jus in bello*. Clearly, these are important areas of law which, as Melzer concludes, mean that 'the phenomenon of cyberwarfare does not exist in a legal vacuum, but is subject to well established rules and principles'.[86] However, such an approach narrowly confines cybersecurity threats to cyberwarfare in a literal sense, when many non-kinetic cyber operations and cybercrimes do not reach that level and yet may still constitute security threats.

One problem is to convert new understandings of security threats into legal concepts, principles, and rules that together will shape a legal regime, the purpose of which is to enable organizations and States, and other security actors, to address such threats. New technologies raise concerns as a cross-cutting issue of security in a number of areas. General principles and specific norms from various specialist areas of international law may be applicable: arms control law, human rights law, international humanitarian law, and international environmental law, to name the most obvious. *The Tallinn Manual on the International Law Applicable to Cyber Operations 2.0*, prepared by an international group of experts at the invitation of NATO in 2017, is an extensive analysis of all branches of international law relevant to cybersecurity.[87] However, when new technologies have been used to destabilize States, such as the 2007 cyberattacks on Estonia's internet capabilities, specialist legal regimes give way to discussions revolving around general principles of international law, such as non-intervention,[88] and sovereignty,[89] which can have limited traction in international affairs.

[84] See further the Reports of the Group of Governmental Experts (GGE): UNGA Res 68/243 (27 December 2013); (24 June 2013) UN Doc A/68/98, paras 16–25.

[85] UNODA, Disarmament Study Series 33: Developments in the Field of Information and Telecommunication in the Context of International Security (UN 2011) 22–3, 35–6, 56.

[86] Nils Melzer, 'Cyberwarfare and International Law' (UNIDIR 2011) 36 <http://unidir.org/files/publications/pdfs/cyberwarfare-and-international-law-382.pdf> accessed 10 January 2020. See also discussion of the first Tallinn Manual on International Law Applicable to Cyber Warfare in Dieter Fleck, 'Searching for International Rules Applicable to Cyber Warfare—A Critical First Assessment of the New Tallinn Manual' (2013) 18 JCSL 331.

[87] Michael N Schmitt (ed), *Tallin Manual 2.0 on the International Law Applicable to Cyber Operations* (2nd edn, CUP 2017).

[88] Russell Buchan, 'Cyber Attacks: Unlawful Uses of Force or Prohibited Interventions?' (2012) 17 JCSL 212.

[89] Phil Spector, 'In Defense of Sovereignty, in the Wake of Tallinn 2.0' (2017) 111 AJIL 219.

Furthermore, the problem of attribution of such attacks in terms of State responsibility adds to the problems of regulation. The strict rules on attribution of acts of private individuals to States as embodied in Article 8 of the ILC Articles on the Responsibility of States,[90] and the ICJ jurisprudence,[91] do not assist in inducing States to prevent acts of private individuals that interfere with the security of other States.[92] However, greater recognition should be given to the underdeveloped general principle of due diligence in international law, initially proclaimed by the ICJ in the *Corfu Channel* case when the Court pointed to 'every State's obligation not to allow knowingly its territory to be used for acts contrary to the rights of other States'.[93] This demonstrates that States have at least some positive obligations to prevent cyberattacks against other States launched from their territories, even if the territorial State is not the perpetrator.[94]

D. Outlook

It remains the case that security revolves around State security, and the protection of humans and other elements is in service to the protection of the State. It is an overarching norm that guides international relations and law and presents an existential threat to certain human groups and individuals. Thus, there is a tension between the duty of a State to its citizens (the social contract) and its commitment to its own survival, hence the framing of State security threats, such as different ideologies, as being threats to humans, thereby justifying the use of (potentially lethal) State power against its own citizens.

As a normative concept, security pervades the international legal order, and as the primary purpose of the UN it can be enforced through the coercive mechanisms contained therein. This makes security an exceptionally powerful concept and tool, and its subjective nature renders it potentially borderless and inherently dangerous. Intersubjective agreement is achievable on aspects of it, however the current tension between State security and human security, and the lack of certainty and clarity in the examples discussed above, illustrate that although security is an international legal norm, it falls foul of most if not all of the integral elements of what constitutes a 'good' law: clarity,

[90] ILC, 'Articles on Responsibility of States for Internationally Wrongful Acts' UNGA Res 56/83 (12 December 2001) Annex.

[91] *Military and Paramilitary Activities in and Against Nicaragua (Nicaragua v USA)* (Merits) [1986] ICJ Rep 14, 62–4; *Application of the Convention on the Prevention and Punishment of the Crime of Genocide (Bosnia and Herzegovina v Serbia and Montenegro)* (Merits) [2007] ICJ Rep 43 [406].

[92] Kubo Mačák, 'Decoding Article 8 of the International Law Commission's Articles on State Responsibility: Attribution of Cyber Operations by Non-State Actors' (2016) 21 JCSL 405.

[93] *Corfu Channel (UK v Albania)* (Merits) [1949] ICJ Rep 4, 22.

[94] Russell Buchan, 'Cyberspace, Non-State Actors and the Obligation to Prevent Transboundary Harm' (2016) 21 JCSL 429.

certainty, stability, compatibility with other norms and rules, and non-retroactivity.[95] Until some of these elements are remedied by achieving international consensus on the nature, purpose, and limits of security generally and within particular contexts, it will continue to operate as a primary norm that can eclipse or qualify all others, whether general norms such as non-intervention and sovereignty, or specific ones such as human rights laws and those designed to protect refugees.

[95] Lon L Fuller, *The Morality of Law* (Yale UP 1969) 39.

CHAPTER 2

THE GLOBAL SECURITY AGENDA

Securitization of Everything?

HITOSHI NASU

A. Introduction

THE geopolitical, socio-economic condition of the world that surrounds us today differs considerably from the one that our predecessors had to face. So does the global security agenda we are set to address. At the dawn of the United Nations (UN) era, the primary security concern that was universally shared amongst world leaders was, as enshrined in the preamble to its founding instrument, to 'save succeeding generations from the scourge of war, which twice in our lifetime has brought untold sorrow to mankind'.[1] Soon after its establishment, a new security concern hijacked the UN as the Cold War unfolded, which dominated world politics for over forty years, largely due to fears for the potentially catastrophic impact of a nuclear war.[2] The end of the Cold War, forty-five years later, was expected to be filled with a sense of euphoria towards world peace, but instead saw an expansion of the global security agenda, with the acknowledgement of a range of 'non-military sources of instability in the economic, social, humanitarian and ecological fields'.[3]

Since the end of the Cold War, the global security agenda has not only widened but also deepened, moving the focus of security concerns away from the sovereign State to include other objects such as the environment, social groups, and regional institutions. Critical to this development was the 1994 Human Development Report,[4] which introduced

[1] Charter of the United Nations 1 UNTS XVI (UN Charter) preamble.

[2] See, generally, Jane Boulden et al (eds), *The United Nations and Nuclear Orders* (UN UP 2009).

[3] UNSC Verbatim Record (31 January 1992) UN Doc S/PV.3046, 143.

[4] UNDP, *Human Development Report 1994* (OUP 1994) 22.

the concept of human security into policy discourse and provided a theoretical foundation for various human-centred policy initiatives including, most notably, the ban on anti-personnel landmines,[5] the protection of civilians in armed conflict,[6] and the 'responsibility to protect'.[7] The rise of terrorism and other transnational threats to the top of the agenda in the aftermath of the 9/11 terrorist attacks in New York added complexity to the global security environment.[8] A stream of non-traditional security issues has cascaded through to regional groupings such as the European Union (EU), the African Union (AU), and the Association of Southeast Asian Nations (ASEAN).[9]

The process of widening and deepening the global security agenda is premised upon the theory of securitization. Since its emergence, this theory has provided a critical perspective to security studies and contemporary debates about security governance. After briefly reviewing the trajectory of the theoretical debate, this chapter examines the institutional practice of securitization, with particular focus on the practices of the UN, EU, AU, and ASEAN as major international and regional security institutions. The understanding of how global and regional policy issues have been securitized in institutional practices is of particular significance to the development of international law because of the ways in which the process of securitization operates within, or interacts with, the existing structure of international law. The role of national security in the process of securitization of a global policy agenda also reveals normative constraint within the framework of international law.

B. Current Status of the Debate: Securitization in Theory

The Copenhagen School theorized the process of securitization as a more extreme version of politicization, by conceptualizing security as a self-referential practice to construct a shared understanding of an existential threat and the collective response to that

[5] Convention on the Prohibition of the Use, Stockpiling, Production and Transfer of Anti-Personnel Mines and on their Destruction 2056 UNTS 211. See, also, Richard A Matthew, 'Human Security and the Mine Ban Movement I: Introduction' in Richard A Matthew et al (eds), *Landmines and Human Security: International Politics and War's Hidden Legacy* (SUNY Press 2004) 3–19.

[6] Hitoshi Nasu, 'Peacekeeping, Civilian Protection Mandates and the Responsibility to Protect' in Angus Francis et al (eds), *Norms of Protection: Responsibility to Protect, Protection of Civilians and Their Interaction* (UN UP 2012) 119–21.

[7] ICISS, *The Responsibility to Protect: Report of the International Commission on Intervention and State Sovereignty* (International Development Research Centre 2001) 15; Gareth Evans, *The Responsibility to Protect: Ending Mass Atrocity Crimes Once and For All* (Brookings Institution 2008) 34–5.

[8] A case in point is the pathological use of human security as a justification for extraordinary counter-terrorism measures: Hitoshi Nasu, 'Human Security and International Law: The Potential Scope for Legal Development within the Analytical Framework of Security' in Mary E Footer et al (eds), *Security and International Law* (Hart Publishing 2016) 39–41.

[9] For more detail, see Eva Nanopoulos, Chapter 54, Jerusha Asin Owino, Chapter 53, and Diane A Desierto, Chapter 52 respectively, in this *Handbook*.

threat.[10] Drawing upon the 'speech act' in language theory, the process of securitization involves not only presentation of an issue as an existential threat by a securitizing actor (the securitization move) but also its acceptance by the relevant audience as such.[11] The emergence of this theory marked a significant departure from the traditional security studies, with a narrowly confined focus on the security of individual States and military issues, which were considered inadequate in the post-Cold War era.[12] The theory has provided an analytical framework for the concept of security, free from any specific object to be secured (such as the State) or a specific type of threat (such as military threats).[13]

The Copenhagen School defines successful securitization as comprising three components.[14] First, it must be argued (though not necessarily agreed upon by others) that a certain issue poses an 'existential threat' to a designated referent object such as a sovereign State, a non-State entity, or an institution.[15] Secondly, this designation enables legitimizing emergency measures or other steps that would not have been possible had it not taken the form of an 'existential threat'. Thirdly, such emergency action has effects on inter-unit relations (for example, inter-State relations) by breaking free of conventional rules. According to this view, securitization necessarily entails a violation of existing rules and is aimed to proffer collective justification for their breach,[16] inevitably causing tension with the normative foundations and values underlying existing rules. Ole Wæver also warns of political manipulation of securitization, observing that because 'something is a security problem when the elites declare it to be so', the elites 'can easily use it for specific, self-serving purposes [and this] is something that cannot easily be avoided'.[17]

The theory of securitization, simple as it is, has grown into a complex field of study in itself, particularly with further studies on how securitizing moves are accepted, rejected, or reversed (the process of de-securitization).[18] The field has expanded with a variety of theoretical and empirical studies, bringing with them plurality of different perspectives

[10] Barry Buzan et al, *Security: A New Framework for Analysis* (Lynne Rienner 1998).

[11] For details, ibid 23–45.

[12] Barry Buzan, *People, States and Fear* (Harvester Wheatsheaf 1991) 29. On its significance for broader areas of international relations theory, see Michael C Williams, 'Words, Images, Enemies: Securitization and International Politics' (2003) 47 International Studies Quarterly 511.

[13] Keith Krause/Michael C Williams, 'Security and "Security Studies": Conceptual Evolution and Historical Transformation' in Alexandra Gheciu/William C Wohlforth (eds), *The Oxford Handbook of International Security* (OUP 2018) 22.

[14] Buzan et al (n 10) 23–6.

[15] See Nigel D White/Auden Davies-Bright, Chapter 1 in this *Handbook*.

[16] Buzan et al (n 10) 24–5.

[17] Ole Wæver, 'Securitization and Desecuritization' in Ronnie D Lipschutz (ed), *On Security* (Columbia UP 1995) 54–5.

[18] See eg Lene Hansen, 'Reconstructing Desecuritization' (2012) 38 Review of International Studies 525; Megan MacKenzie, 'Securitization and Desecuritization' (2009) 18 Security Studies 242; Holger Stritzel, 'Towards a Theory of Securitization: Copenhagen and Beyond' (2007) 13 EJIR 357; Thierry Balzacq, 'The Three Faces of Securitization: Political Agency, Audience, and Context' (2005) 11 EJIR 171; Claudia Aradau, 'Security and the Domestic Scene: Desecuritization and Emancipation' (2004) 7 Journal of International Relations and Development 388.

to the theory of securitization.[19] The expansion of its scope has raised concerns that the tight conceptual core of the original theory has been trivialized such that everything can be securitized beyond the original narrow conceptual terms.[20] In fact, there is no normative limit to the theory of securitization.[21] The theory is limited only by its premise that places the survival of collective units and principles—the politics of existential threat—as the defining core of security studies in its original form.[22] This fundamental premise of the concept of security militates against any reductionism that human security is sometimes perceived to implicate with the focus on individuals as potential referent objects.[23]

As a theory to grasp the processes and dynamics of securitization, it is not designed to constitute a normative practice providing ethical and moral grounds for political agendas and actions.[24] Nevertheless, the theory is tainted with a normative bias against securitization. Buzan, Wæver, and de Wilde are unequivocal in stating that 'security should be seen as negative, as a failure to deal with issues as normal politics'.[25] The assumption that underpins this normative bias is that securitization necessarily calls for emergency action or special measures with less democratic control and legal constraint, as opposed to politicization that leaves political choice in making policy decisions. This normative aspect of the theory, misrepresented as that may often be,[26] poses a methodological problem that drives researchers to focus their study on de-securitization as the optimal long-term option,[27] rather than allowing them to explore a variety of different mechanisms and measures, particularly those legally justifiable, to address securitized issues. The distinction between normal and securitized politics has also increasingly become difficult to sustain, with the rise of risk management practices to address non-traditional sources of security threats.[28]

In addition to the expanded range of threats (from the traditional focus on military threats to non-traditional threats) and referent objects (from the traditional focus on

[19] Ralf Emmers, 'Securitization' in Alan Collins (ed), *Contemporary Security Studies* (5th edn, OUP 2018) 173; Thierry Balzacq/Stefano Guzzini, 'Introduction: "What Kind of Theory—If Any—Is Securitization?"' (2015) 29 International Relations 97; Thierry Balzacq, *Securitization Theory* (Routledge 2011); Bill McSweeny, 'Identity and Security: Buzan and the Copenhagen School' (1996) 22 Review of International Studies 81.

[20] Ole Wæver, 'Politics, Security, Theory' (2011) 42 Security Dialogue 465, 468–9.

[21] cf Rita Floyd, 'Can Securitization Theory Be Used in Normative Analysis? Towards a Just Securitization Theory' (2011) 42 Security Dialogue 427.

[22] Buzan et al (n 10) 27.

[23] Barry Buzan, 'A Reductionist, Idealistic Notion That Adds Little Analytical Value' (2004) 35 Security Dialogue 369.

[24] The Copenhagen School, however, appears to be hopeful that the theory could be used to 'maneuver the interaction among actors and thereby curb security dilemmas': Buzan et al (n 10) 31.

[25] ibid 29.

[26] Rita Taureck, 'Securitization Theory and Securitization Studies' (2006) 9 Journal of International Relations and Development 53.

[27] Jonathan Luke Austin/Philippe Beaulieu-Brossard, '(De)securitisation Dilemmas: Theorising the Simultaneous Enaction of Securitisation and Desecuritisation' (2018) 44 Review of International Studies 301, 309.

[28] Krause/Williams (n 13) 22.

the sovereign State to non-State objects), the process of securitization may also expand the range of options available to address security threats. Free from the normative bias implicated in the original theory, the emphasis of securitized measures may shift the focus away from extra-legal response, to risk regulation, authorization of new powers and mandates, and institutionalization of collective response. Indeed, the expansion of the global security agenda has led to a growing role for a variety of intergovernmental institutions, international expert bodies, domestic government institutions, and even private institutions to address a wider range of contemporary security challenges.[29] The practical impact of securitization through the practices of international institutions, as will be discussed below, provides a critical perspective to the normative value of securitization and its limit.

C. Recent Developments and Contemporary Challenges: Securitization in Practice

The process of securitization may take place in a variety of settings. In the practice of international law, this process has often entailed a parallel process of institutional evolution as a means to regularize the response to a newly identified security threat. This section reviews the institutional practice of securitization with the focus on the UN, EU, AU, and ASEAN to see how these international institutions have embraced securitization in their practices and what challenges have confronted them.

1. The United Nations

Born from the ashes of the Second World War, the UN has represented an institutionalized form of collective security for all nations as the means to regulate their behaviour and disputes amongst them,[30] with the primary responsibility for the maintenance of international peace and security vested in the UN Security Council (UNSC).[31] As such, it was designed, at least originally, to address traditional, military-oriented threats to the maintenance of international peace and security by providing an institutionalized mechanism to protect the territorial integrity and political independence of its Member States in a collective manner. While it remains, to date, the primary

[29] On different perspectives on the normative and legal challenges that institutional development has brought in dealing with various security threats, see Hitoshi Nasu/Kim Rubenstein (eds), *Legal Perspectives on Security Institutions* (CUP 2015).

[30] See, generally, Nicholas Tsagourias/Nigel D White, *Collective Security: Theory, Law and Practice* (CUP 2013); Alexander Orakhelashvili, *Collective Security* (OUP 2011).

[31] UN Charter (n 1) art 24.

security institution of a universal nature, the remit of its activities has expanded as the nature and range of contemporary security threats evolved.

The expansion of the global security agenda was recognized at the UN even during the Cold War, as illustrated by the adoption of UNGA Resolution 38/188 H in 1983, which called for 'a comprehensive study of concepts of security'.[32] The study, carried out by a group of governmental experts under this mandate, defined security broadly as 'a condition in which States consider that there is no danger of military attack, political pressure or economic coercion, so that they are able to pursue freely their own development and progress'.[33] Based on this broad definition of security, the study identified arms race and international diffusion of advanced military technologies as global security threats. It also referred to a wide range of other security threats, stating:

> In addition to these worsening military developments, there are serious new challenges to global political and economic problems. The emergence of new centres of political and economic power, resource scarcities, trade deficits, financial debts, over-population and threats posed by natural calamities and environmental degradation have combined to create hitherto unforeseen problems in the period following the Second World War. New actors, new issues, more complicated linkages between old issues all tug at the fabric of international relations. These circumstances challenge the capacity of the international community to adapt to the rapidity of global change and indeed create growing challenges in all aspects of human activities.[34]

At the end of the Cold War, the UNSC came to share the same view by acknowledging, as noted above, a range of 'non-military sources of instability'.[35]

It did not take long before the Council started applying such a broad notion of security to its mandate through practice. In 2000, it discussed the impact of HIV/AIDS on the maintenance of international peace and security,[36] setting a precedent for debating a broader security agenda.[37] It opened a floodgate to a variety of non-traditional security

[32] The agenda in full reads:

> [A] comprehensive study of concepts of security, in particular security policies which emphasize co-operative efforts and mutual understanding between States, with a view to developing proposals for policies aimed at preventing the arms race, building confidence in relations between States, enhancing the possibility of reaching agreements on arms limitation and disarmament and promoting political and economic security.

See UNGA Res 38/188 H (20 December 1983).

[33] UNGA 'General and Complete Disarmament: Study on Concepts of Security: Report of the Secretary-General' Annex (26 August 1985) UN Doc A/40/553, para 3.

[34] ibid para 5. [35] See n 3.

[36] UNSC Verbatim Record (10 January 2000) UN Doc S/PV/4087 and S/PV/4087 (Resumption 1); UNSC Verbatim Record (17 July 2000) UN Doc S/PV/4172.

[37] UNSC Verbatim Record (10 January 2000) UN Doc S/PV/4087, 2 (remarks of US Vice-President Gore). The same agenda was discussed subsequently in 2001, 2003, and 2005: UNSC Verbatim Record (19 January 2001) UN Doc S/PV/4259; UNSC Verbatim Record (17 November 2003) UN Doc S/PV/4859; UNSC Verbatim Record (18 July 2005) UN Doc S/PV/5228. For a critical perspective, see eg Stefan Elbe, 'Should HIV/AIDS Be Securitized? The Ethical Dilemmas of Linking HIV/AIDS and Security' (2006) 50 International Studies Quarterly 119.

issues, including terrorism,[38] proliferation of weapons of mass destruction,[39] food security,[40] energy and climate change,[41] and drug trafficking.[42] However, the expansion of the security agenda was not received without criticism or reluctance on the part of some Member States.

Securitization through Council practice has been subjected to jurisdictional and practical restrictions.[43] As an organ with the primary responsibility for the maintenance of international peace and security, the Council is empowered to address any international security threats within its competence. While there is room for different interpretations, Council Members have been vigilant in ensuring that the security agenda falls within the Council's competence by identifying a direct link to conflict and instability. For instance, UNSC Resolution 1308, adopted on 17 July 2000, emphasizes that 'the HIV/AIDS pandemic, if unchecked, may pose a risk to stability and security'.[44] Likewise, the issue of food security was largely considered in relation to its 'incontrovertible link' to conflict and instability.[45] On the other hand, the impact of climate change as a potential driver of conflict received a mixed response due to an over-stretch of the Council's mandate to essentially a development issue.[46]

The Council's role as regards a broader global security agenda is also constrained due to its institutional orientation focused on the exercise of collective enforcement powers as the means to address a security threat. The undefined term 'threat to the peace' has the

[38] UNSC Res 1373 (2001); UNSC Res 1624 (2005); UNSC Res 2353 (2017).

[39] UNSC Res 1540 (2004); UNSC Res 1887 (2009).

[40] UNSC Verbatim Record (3 December 2002) UN Doc S/PV/4652; UNSC Verbatim Record (7 April 2003) UN Doc S/PV/4736; UNSC Verbatim Record (30 June 2005) UN Doc S/PV/5220.

[41] UNSC Verbatim Record (17 April 2007) UN Doc S/PV/5663 and S/PV/5663 (Resumption 1); UNSC Verbatim Record (20 July 2011) UN Doc S/PV/6587 and S/PV/6587 (Resumption 1); UNSC Verbatim Record (11 July 2018) UN Doc S/PV/8307; UNSC Verbatim Record (25 January 2019) UN Doc S/PV/8451. For details, see Shirley V Scott, 'Securitising Climate Change: International Legal Implications and Obstacles' (2008) 21 Cambridge Review of International Affairs 603.

[42] UNSC Verbatim Record (December 2009) UN Doc S/PV/6233 and S/PV/6233 (Resumption 1); UNSC Verbatim Record (24 February 2010) UN Doc S/PV/6277; UNSC Verbatim Record (24 June 2011) UN Doc S/PV/6565; UNSC Verbatim Record (18 December 2013) UN Doc S/PV/7090; UNSC Verbatim Record (19 December 2018) UN Doc S/PV/8433.

[43] For the author's detailed analysis regarding these restrictions, see Hitoshi Nasu, 'The Place of Human Security in Collective Security' (2013) 18 JCSL 95.

[44] UNSC Res 1308 (2000) preamble.

[45] UNSC Verbatim Record (30 June 2005) UN Doc S/PV/5220, 11 (Philippines). See also, ibid 9 (Romania, UK), 12 (Japan), 13 (China, Greece), 14 (Benin).

[46] UNSC Verbatim Record (17 April 2007) UN Doc S/PV/5663, 10 (Qatar), 12–13 (China), 15–16 (South Africa), 17 (Russia), 24 (Pakistan), 31 (Namibia); UNSC Verbatim Record (17 April 2007) UN Doc S/PV/5663 (Resumption 1), 4 (Egypt), 10 (Venezuela), 11–12 (Sudan), 17 (Philippines), 21 (India), 27 (Cuba); UNSC Verbatim Record (20 July 2011) UN Doc S/PV/6587, 9 (China), 13 (Russia), 26 (Egypt), 27 (Argentina); UNSC Verbatim Record (20 July 2011) UN Doc S/PV/6587 (Resumption 1), 19 (Iran), 20–1 (Kuwait), 35 (Venezuela), 38 (Tanzania). UNSC Verbatim Record (11 July 2018) UN Doc S/PV/8307, 17 (Bolivia); UNSC Verbatim Record (25 January 2019) UN Doc S/PV/8451, 25 (Dominican Republic), 39 (Pakistan), 64 (Iran). See also, Aristotle Constantinides, '"Securitizing" Development: Advantages and Pitfalls of the Security Council's Involvement in Development Issues' in Christoffer C Eriksen/Marius Emberland (eds), *The New International Law—An Anthology* (Brill 2010).

potential to expand the range of threats against which the Council is authorized to take enforcement action.[47] However, many of the non-traditional security threats have called into question the extent to which the Council can play a useful role beyond raising public awareness or facilitating cooperation.[48] The legislative counter-terrorism and non-proliferation measures imposed by the Council are unique in that it employed its collective enforcement powers universally, rather than against any specific State, by requiring all Member States to implement them.[49] The adoption of such measures has inevitably been subject to political and practical limitations, as well as legal constraints.[50] Its institutional structure, based on the traditional notion of security, poses an inherent limit to the way in which the Council can employ its powers to address a broader global security agenda.

2. The European Union

With the adoption of the 1992 Maastricht Treaty, the EU started emerging as a regional security actor by creating the Common Foreign and Security Policy (CFSP) as one of three intergovernmental pillars of the Treaty on European Union (TEU).[51] Predicated upon systematic cooperation between EU Member States rather than on centralized Union competence,[52] the CFSP has provided an institutional platform for policy coordination on regional security issues.[53] The institutional reform under the 2007 Lisbon

[47] See, generally, Karel Wellens, 'The UN Security Council and New Threats to the Peace: Back to the Future' (2003) 8 JCSL 15; Inger Österdahl, *Threat to the Peace: The Interpretation by the Security Council of Article 39 of the UN Charter* (Iustus Forlag 1998) 85–8; Rob Cryer, 'The Security Council and Article 39: A Threat to Coherence?' (1996) 1 Journal of Armed Conflict Law 161; Peter H Kooijmans, 'The Enlargement of the Concept "Threat to the Peace"' in René-Jean Dupuy (ed), *The Development of the Role of the Security Council* (Martinus Nijhoff 1993) 111.

[48] Nasu (n 43) 115–20.

[49] Monika Heupel, 'Adapting to Transnational Terrorism: The UN Security Council's Evolving Approach to Terrorism' (2007) 38 Security Dialogue 477. For discussion on quasi-legislative resolutions, see eg Stefan Talmon, 'The Security Council as World Legislature' (2005) 99 AJIL 175; Matthew Happold, 'Security Council Resolution 1373 and the Constitution of the United Nations' (2003) 16 Leiden Journal of International Law 593.

[50] See Luis Miguel Hinojosa Martínez, 'The Legislative Role of the Security Council in Its Fight against Terrorism: Legal, Political and Practical Limits' (2008) 57 ICLQ 333, 344–54; Andrea Bianchi, 'Assessing the Effectiveness of the UN Security Council's Anti-Terrorism Measures: The Quest for Legitimacy and Cohesion' (2007) 17 EJIL 881, 893–910.

[51] Treaty on European Union [1992] OJ C191/1. [52] ibid art J.1(3).

[53] See, generally, Michael E Smith, *Europe's Foreign and Security Policy: The Institutionalization of Cooperation* (CUP 2004); Ole Wæver, 'The EU as a Security Actor: Reflections from a Pessimistic Constructivist on Post Sovereignty Security Orders' in Morten Kelstrup/Michael C Williams (eds), *International Relations Theory and the Politics of European Integration* (Routledge 2000).

Treaty did not change the fundamental characteristics of the CFSP,[54] of which the new Common Security and Defence Policy formed an integral part.[55]

Far from a supranational institution envisaged as the European Defence Community in the early 1950s,[56] the Common Security and Defence Policy is an extension of the rudimentary practice of joint action in peacekeeping and police operations.[57] The development of this policy and practice emerged from the conceptual framework set by the 2003 European Security Strategy, which for the first time defined the EU's security environment and challenges.[58] The 2003 Strategy identified, as new threats, terrorism, proliferation of weapons of mass destruction, regional conflicts, State failure, and organized crime.[59]

The exclusion of the CFSP from the centralized Union competences has signalled strong resistance on the part of EU Member States to transfer their decision-making authority on security matters. However, the EU Court has diluted this demarcation of competences in relation to a joint action measure that pursued a number of objectives across different policy areas.[60] Within the Liston Treaty framework, the European Commission and the EU Council have expanded their respective role on the security agenda by securitizing matters without prejudice to the demarcation of competences, for example, with the adoption of the 2010 Internal Security Strategy,[61] the 2013 Cyber Security Strategy,[62] the 2014 Maritime Security Strategy,[63] and the 2014 Energy Security

[54] Treaty on European Union, as amended by the Treaty of Lisbon amending the Treaty on European Union and the Treaty Establishing the European Community [2007] OJ C306/1 art 42(1).

[55] See eg Anne McNaughton, 'Institutional Competence and the Common Foreign and Security Policy of the European Union' in Nasu/Rubenstein (n 29) 78–81; Panos Koutrakos, *The EU Common Security and Defence Policy* (OUP 2013) 40–51.

[56] Martin Trybus, 'The Vision of the European Defence Community and a Common Defence for the European Union' in Martin Trybus/Nigel D White (eds), *European Security Law* (OUP 2007) 13; Edward Fursdon, *The European Defence Community: A History* (Palgrave Macmillan 1980).

[57] Frederik Naert, 'ESDP in Practice: Increasingly Varied and Ambitious EU Security and Defence Operations' in Trybus/White (n 56) 61.

[58] European Security Strategy: A Secure Europe in a Better World (Brussels, 12 December 2003) available at <https://europa.eu/globalstrategy/en/file/10/download?token=ubYn8qBQ> accessed 28 February 2019.

[59] ibid 3–5.

[60] See eg Case C-91/05 *Commission of the European Communities v Council of the European Union* [2008] ECR I-3651, paras 76–7 (finding that the contested decision should have been adopted under Community competence despite CFSP components). For commentary, see Joni Heliskoski, 'Small Arms and Light Weapons within the Union's Pillar Structure: An Analysis of Article 47 of the EU Treaty' (2008) 33 European Law Review 898, 906–8.

[61] Council of the EU, 'EU Internal Security Strategy' (25 February 2010) Doc 6870/10 (Presse 44).

[62] Commission/High Representative of the European Union for Foreign Affairs and Security Policy, 'Cybersecurity Strategy of the European Union: An Open, Safe and Secure Cyberspace' (Joint Communication to the European Parliament, the Council, the European Economic and Social Committee and the Committee of the Regions) JOIN (2013) 1 final. For detailed analysis, see Ramses A Wessel, 'Towards EU Cybersecurity Law: Regulating a New Policy Field' in Nicholas Tsagourias/Russell Buchan (eds), *Research Handbook on International Law and Cyberspace* (Edward Elgar 2014) 411–24.

[63] Council of the EU, 'EU Maritime Security Strategy' (24 June 2014) Doc 11205/14.

Strategy.[64] In April 2015, the European Commission issued the European Agenda on Security as a shared plan of action between the Union and Member States, identifying three areas where an effective and coordinated response at European level is required: terrorism, organized crime, and cybercrime.[65]

Securitization has played a particularly prominent role in the area of border control as the European integration process entailed a parallel development in restrictive migration policy against people from outside the EU.[66] In 2004, the Council established the European Agency for the Management of Operational Cooperation at the External Borders of the Member States of the European Union (Frontex) with a view to improving the integrated management of EU external borders.[67] Its mandate has subsequently been broadened, with the establishment of the Rapid Border Intervention Teams,[68] the European Border Guard Teams,[69] and the coordination of border surveillance operations.[70] In 2016, the European Border and Coast Guard was established to implement European integrated border management as a shared responsibility between the Union and national authorities.[71] Even though these arrangements are not to alter the respective competences of the Union and Member States, the lines of responsibility have been

[64] European Commission, 'European Energy Security Strategy' (Communication) (28 May 2014) COM (2014) 330 final.

[65] European Commission, 'The European Agenda on Security' (Communication) (28 April 2015) COM (2015) 185 final.

[66] See, generally, Violeta Moreno-Lax, 'The EU Humanitarian Border and the Securitization of Human Rights: The "Rescue-Through-Interdiction/Rescue-Without-Protection" Paradigm' (2018) 56 Journal of Common Market Studies 119; Sarah Léonard, 'EU Border Security and Migration into the European Union: FRONTEX and Securitisation through Practices' (2010) 19 European Security 231; Jef Huysmans, 'The European Union and the Securitization of Migration' (2000) 38 Journal of Common Market Studies 751.

[67] Council Regulation (EC) No 2007/2004 of 26 October 2004 establishing a European Agency for the Management of Operational Cooperation at the External Borders of the Member States of the European Union [2004] OJ L 349/1. The establishment of Frontex itself is not necessarily an outcome of securitization: see Andrew W Neal, 'Securitization and Risk at the EU Border: The Origins of FRONTEX' (2009) 47 Journal of Common Market Studies 333.

[68] Parliament and Council Regulation (EC) No 863/2007 of 11 July 2007 establishing a mechanism for the creation of Rapid Border Intervention Teams and amending Council Regulation (EC) No 2007/2004 as regards that mechanism and regulating the tasks and powers of guest officers [2007] OJ L 199/30.

[69] Parliament and Council Regulation (EU) No 1168/2011 of 25 October 2011 amending Council Regulation (EC) No 2007/2004 establishing a European Agency for the Management of Operational Cooperation at the External Borders of the Member States of the European Union [2011] OJ L 304/1.

[70] Parliament and Council Regulation (EU) No 656/2014 of 15 May 2014 establishing rules for the surveillance of the external sea borders in the context of operational cooperation coordinated by the European Agency for the Management of Operational Cooperation at the External Borders of the Member States of the European Union [2014] OJ L 189/93.

[71] Parliament and Council Regulation (EU) 2016/1624 of 14 September 2016 on the European Border and Coast Guard and amending Regulation (EU) 2016/399 of the European Parliament and of the Council and repealing Regulation (EC) No 863/2007 of the European Parliament and of the Council, Council Regulation (EC) No 2007/2004 and Council Decision 2005/267/EC [2016] OJ L 251/1.

blurred in practice, which has resulted in shifting operational priorities to maritime surveillance and patrols, rather than humanitarian action such as search and rescue at sea.[72]

3. The African Union

Largely dysfunctional in dealing with contemporary regional security issues and owing to the shift in focus in the 1990s towards regional management of security in Africa,[73] the Organisation of African Unity was transformed into the AU in 2000 with the adoption of the Constitutive Act.[74] As a regional organization aiming, amongst other things, to promote peace, security, and stability on the African continent,[75] the AU has a broad mandate that can accommodate a wide range of security agendas. This is reflected in the variety of common security threats identified in the 2004 Solemn Declaration on a Common African Defence and Security Policy.[76]

The 2004 Declaration adopts a broad, multidimensional notion of security, which 'encompasses both the traditional, state-centric, notion of the survival of the State and its protection by military means from external aggression, as well as the non-military notion which is informed by the new international environment and the high incidence of intra-state conflict'.[77] On that basis, the Union's Common Defence and Security Policy addresses, amongst other things: collective defence; small arms and light weapons; peacebuilding and peacekeeping; post-conflict rehabilitation and reconstruction; landmines; child soldiers; weapons of mass destruction; HIV/AIDS; infectious diseases; terrorism; humanitarian issues; and environmental matters.[78]

Notwithstanding such a broad notion of security adopted by the Union, the mandate of the Peace and Security Council—the primary organ responsible for peace and security in Africa—is confined to the prevention, management, and resolution of conflicts as 'a collective security and early-warning arrangement to facilitate timely and efficient response to conflict and crisis situations in Africa'.[79] Its activities have primarily focused upon conflict management due to capacity constraints and the intensity of conflict in

[72] See Daniel Ghezelbash et al, 'Securitization of Search and Rescue at Sea: The Response to Boat Migration in the Mediterranean and Offshore Australia' (2018) 67 ICLQ 315, 323–7.

[73] See, generally, Abou Jeng, *Peacebuilding in the African Union: Law, Philosophy and Practice* (CUP 2012) 123–5; Klaas van Walraven, 'Heritage and Transformation: From the Organization of African Unity to the African Union' in Ulf Engel/João Gomes Porto (eds), *Africa's New Peace and Security Architecture: Promoting Norms, Institutionalizing Solutions* (Ashgate 2010) 48–55; Robert I Rotberg, 'African Responses to African Crises: Creating a Military Response' in Robert I Rotberg et al (eds), *Peacekeeping and Peace Enforcement in Africa: Methods of Conflict Prevention* (Brookings Institution 2000) 98.

[74] Constitutive Act of the African Union 2158 UNTS 3. [75] ibid art 3(f).

[76] Solemn Declaration on a Common African Defence and Security Policy (adopted 28 February 2004) <http://www.peaceau.org/uploads/declaration-cadsp-en.pdf> accessed 28 February 2019.

[77] ibid para 6. [78] ibid para 10.

[79] Protocol relating to the Establishment of the Peace and Security Council of the African Union AU Doc 9/7/2002 art 2.

numerous African countries.[80] Even though the Peace and Security Council was tasked to harmonize and coordinate counter-terrorism efforts, its work in this area has been limited.[81]

Of the non-traditional security threats identified in the 2004 Declaration, the prevention and combating of terrorism is the only agenda that drew significant attention for regional cooperation. The AU facilitated regional cooperation, for example, with the adoption of the 2001 Dakar Declaration Against Terrorism,[82] the 2002 Plan of Action on the Prevention and Combating of Terrorism,[83] and the 2004 Protocol to the OAU Convention on the Prevention and Combating of Terrorism.[84] The level of cooperation achieved was not adequate,[85] however, as has been evident in the proliferation of terrorism threats on the continent.[86] The failure of the Union to engage in sustained regional efforts to address other non-traditional security issues, such as infectious diseases and the trafficking of small arms and light weapons,[87] also suggests that it lacks the institutional capacity and resources to address a wide range of regional security issues as envisaged in the 2004 Declaration.

4. The Association of Southeast Asian Nations

As a regional security institution in Southeast Asia, the ASEAN emerged to provide a political platform with a dual function:[88] the protection of political stability within each Member State; and the protection of regional stability from external interference at the

[80] See eg Isiaka A Badmus, *The African Union's Role in Peacekeeping: Building Lessons Learned from Security Operations* (Palgrave Macmillan 2015) chs 4–6; Kathryn Sturman/Aïssatou Hayatou, 'The Peace and Security Council of the African Union: From Design to Reality' in Engel/Gomes Porto (n 73) 74–9.

[81] Martin A Ewi/Anton du Plessis, 'Criminal Justice Responses to Terrorism in Africa: The Role of the African Union and Sub-Regional Organizations' in Ana María Salinas de Frías et al (eds), *Counter-Terrorism: International Law and Practice* (OUP 2012) 1009–10.

[82] Dakar Declaration Against Terrorism (17 October 2001) UN Doc A/56/513-S/2001/1021 Annex.

[83] AU, 'Plan of Action of the African Union High-Level Inter-Governmental Meeting on the Prevention and Combating of Terrorism in Africa' (11–14 September 2002) Doc Mtg/HLIG/Conv.Terror/Plan(I).

[84] Protocol to the OAU Convention on the Prevention and Combating of Terrorism UNTS A-39464.

[85] Martin Ewi/Kwesi Aning, 'Assessing the Role of the African Union in Preventing and Combating Terrorism in Africa' (2006) 15 African Security Review 32, 41–3.

[86] See, generally, Hussein Solomon, *Terrorism and Counter-Terrorism in Africa: Fighting Insurgency from Al Shabaab, Ansar Dine and Boko Haram* (Palgrave Macmillan 2015); John Davis (ed), *Terrorism in Africa: The Evolving Front in the War on Terror* (Lexington Books 2010).

[87] See Jürgen Haacke/Paul D Williams, 'Regional Arrangements, Securitization, and Transnational Security Challenges: The African Union and the Association of Southeast Asian Nations Compared' (2008) 17 Security Studies 775, 789–94.

[88] ASEAN was founded by the Declaration Constituting an Agreement Establishing the Association of South-East Asian Nations 1331 UNTS 235.

height of Cold War politics.[89] One of the foundational regional norms that underpin this security arrangement is the principle of non-interference in the internal affairs of one another.[90] While the precise scope of this principle remains unsettled,[91] it is generally understood as prohibiting a broad range of interference, such as criticizing another government's actions towards its own people,[92] which may not necessarily constitute an intervention prohibited under general international law.[93] A strict adherence to this principle was prominent in ASEAN's collective criticism against Vietnam's military advances in Cambodia to overthrow the Khmer Rouge regime,[94] despite the fact that the regime was responsible for mass atrocities during its reign from 1975 to 1979.

After the end of the Cold War, ASEAN's role on regional security has been gradually redefined to address various transnational security challenges. The 2003 Bali Concord II—a blueprint document for ASEAN's further regional integration into the ASEAN Community—provides that the ASEAN Security Community, as one of the three pillars of the ASEAN Community, subscribes to 'the principle of comprehensive security as having broad political, economic, social and cultural aspects'.[95] The ASEAN Charter, adopted in 2007 as the new constitutional instrument of the institution, formally incorporates comprehensive security as a regional norm, in accordance with which its Member States are to respond effectively to all forms of threats, transnational crimes and transboundary challenges.[96]

Under the principle of comprehensive security, ASEAN has been engaging in regional cooperation in select areas of non-traditional security.[97] For example, various regional initiatives for cooperation on counter-terrorism culminated in the adoption of the

[89] See eg Amitav Acharya, *Constructing a Security Community in Southeast Asia: ASEAN and the Problem of Regional Order* (3rd edn, Routledge 2014) 49–56; Alice D Ba, *(Re)Negotiating East and Southeast Asia: Region, Regionalism, and the Association of Southeast Asian Nations* (Stanford UP 2009) 42–100; Shaun Narine, 'ASEAN and the Management of Regional Security' (1998) 71 Pacific Affairs 195, 196–201; Pranee Saipiroon, *ASEAN Governments' Attitudes towards Regional Security 1975–1979* (Institute of Asian Studies 1982) 5–7.

[90] Treaty of Amity and Cooperation in Southeast Asia 1025 UNTS 319 art 2(c).

[91] See, generally, Lee Jones, *ASEAN, Sovereignty and Intervention in Southeast Asia* (Palgrave Macmillan 2012); John Funston, *ASEAN and the Principle of Non-Intervention—Practice and Prospects* (Institute of Southeast Asian Studies 2000).

[92] See Acharya (n 89) 56–9; Hitoshi Nasu, 'Revisiting the Principle of Non-Intervention: A Structural Principle of International Law or a Political Obstacle to Regional Security in Asia?' (2013) 3 Asian Journal of International Law 25, 36–7.

[93] *Military and Paramilitary Activities in and against Nicaragua (Nicaragua v USA)* (Merits) [1986] ICJ Rep 14 [205] (*Nicaragua*). See, also, Maziar Jamnejad/Michael Wood, 'The Principle of Non-Intervention' (2009) 22 Leiden Journal of International Law 345; Lori Fisler Damrosch, 'Politics Across Borders: Nonintervention and Nonforcible Influence over Domestic Affairs' (1989) 83 AJIL 1.

[94] See Acharya (n 89) 79–83.

[95] Declaration of ASEAN Concord II (2004) 43 ILM 18 section A, para 2.

[96] Charter of the Association of Southeast Asian Nations 2624 UNTS 223 art 1(8).

[97] See, generally, Mely Caballero-Anthony/Alistair D B Cook (eds), *Non-Traditional Security in Asia: Issues, Challenges and Framework for Action* (Institute of Southeast Asian Studies 2013).

ASEAN Convention on Counter-Terrorism in 2007,[98] with its follow-up in the 2009 ASEAN Comprehensive Plan of Action on Counter-Terrorism.[99] Cybersecurity is another area where ASEAN has been actively engaging in regional cooperation, as they started seeing comprehensive cybersecurity efforts increasingly vital to the region's pursuit of enhancing regional cyber capacity, interconnectivity, and infrastructure of information technology.[100]

These security challenges have not been handled in a uniform manner and ASEAN governments' domestic approach to each of these issues has varied and is driven by different national interests.[101] It is also difficult to make an accurate assessment as to how ASEAN initiatives for regional cooperation on non-traditional security issues have actually influenced domestic decision-making or practices due to the lack of relevant and sufficient information. Nevertheless, it is fair to observe that ASEAN has contributed, to a varying degree, to the securitization of a range of non-traditional security issues and has facilitated the implementation of the region's collective response, most notably through the adoption of regional plans of action.[102]

D. National Security and the International Rule of Law: Normative Constraint on Securitization

National security is not precluded from the process of securitization under international law. Indeed, national security can be considered as a reserved matter over which the sovereign State may exercise its exclusive competence, free from external interference under the principle of non-intervention.[103] It may also form a ground for an exception

[98] ASEAN Convention on Counter-Terrorism UNTS I-54629.

[99] ASEAN, 'Comprehensive Plan of Action on Counter-Terrorism' (11th ASEAN Ministerial Meeting on Transnational Crime, 30 June 2009) <https://asean.org/wp-content/uploads/2012/05/ACPoA-on-CT-Adopted-by-11th-AMMTC.pdf> accessed 14 May 2020.

[100] Hitoshi Nasu/Helen Trezise, 'Cyber Security in the Asia-Pacific' in Tsagourias/Buchan (n 62) 451–5.

[101] See eg, in the context of counter-terrorism operations, See Seng Tan/Hitoshi Nasu, 'ASEAN and the Development of Counter-Terrorism Law and Policy in Southeast Asia' (2016) 39 University of New South Wales Law Journal 1219, 1228–33.

[102] For a detailed study on the exercise of ASEAN's legal authority on regional security issues, see Hitoshi Nasu et al, *The Legal Authority of ASEAN as a Security Institution* (CUP 2019).

[103] cf *Nicaragua* (n 93) [205] (without specifically referring to national security); *Nationality Decrees Issued in Tunisia and Morocco* (Advisory Opinion) [1923] PCIJ (Ser B) No 4, 24 (noting that whether a certain matter is or is not in principle regulated by international law is 'a relative question; [which] depends upon the development of international relations').

to a treaty obligation when it is explicitly referred to as such in a treaty instrument.[104] In principle, the meaning of such exception clauses is determined through treaty interpretation and therefore they are not susceptible to securitization. However, the versatility of the national security ground as an exception to treaty obligations depends on how the respective provision is formulated. The use of open, subjective language in a national security exception clause is more likely to be susceptible to securitization,[105] compared to closed, enumerated exceptions.[106]

The process of securitization at the national level has only a limited impact on the global security agenda due to normative constraints under international law. National security, irrespective of its scope or definition, does not provide an independent legal justification under customary international law for violating any of the existing rules of international law.[107] A national security issue may form part of an existing legal justification such as the right of self-defence,[108] and other circumstances precluding wrongfulness, such as distress and necessity.[109] However, as the ICJ acknowledged in *Nicaragua*, 'the concept of essential security interests certainly extends beyond the concept of an armed attack',[110] which indicates that only a national security event that amounts to an armed attack could satisfy the requirement for the legitimate exercise of the right of self-defence. Similarly, a national security event that can be relied upon to invoke the plea of distress and necessity is restricted to cases where human life is at stake in the charge of a State official or where an essential interest of the State, its people, or of the international community as a whole is threatened by a grave and imminent peril.[111]

[104] See eg International Covenant on Civil and Political Rights 999 UNTS 171 arts 12(3) (freedom of movement), 13 (expulsion of foreigners without a fair hearing), 14(1) (public hearing of criminal trials), 19(3) (freedom of expression), 21 (peaceful assembly) and 22(2) (freedom of association); Convention relating to the Status of Refugees 189 UNTS 137 art 32; Geneva Convention relative to the Protection of Civilian Persons in Time of War 75 UNTS 287 arts 5 and 27(4).

[105] See eg Marrakesh Agreement Establishing the World Trade Organization, Annex 1A, 1867 UNTS 187 (GATT) art XXI; Annex 1B, 1869 UNTS 183 (GATS) art XIV *bis*; Annex 1C, 1869 UNTS 299 (TRIPS) art 73. Note, however, that the WTO Dispute Settlement Panel adopted the view that the existence of an emergency in international relations is an objective fact, capable of objective determination: *Russia—Measures Concerning Traffic in Transit*, Report of the WTO Panel (5 April 2019) WTO Doc WT/DS512/R, para 7.77. For analysis, see eg Dapo Akande/Sope Williams, 'International Adjudication on National Security Issues: What Role for the WTO?' (2003) 43 Virginia Journal of International Law 365; Hannes L Schloemann/Stefan Ohlhoff, '"Constitutionalization" and Dispute Settlement in the WTO: National Security as an Issue of Competence' (1999) 93 AJIL 424; Michael J Hahn, 'Vital Interests and the Law of GATT: An Analysis of GATT's Security Exception' (1991) 12 Michigan Journal of International Law 558.

[106] See eg UN Convention on the Law of the Sea 1833 UNTS 3 art 19.

[107] See ILC, 'Articles on the Responsibility of States for Internationally Wrongful Acts' UNGA Res 56/83 (12 December 2001) Annex (ARSIWA) art 3.

[108] UN Charter (n 1) art 51.

[109] ARSIWA (n 107) arts 21, 24 and 25. [110] *Nicaragua* (n 93) [224].

[111] ILC, 'Articles on the Responsibility of States for Internationally Wrongful Acts with commentaries' (2001) II(2) YBILC 26, 79 and 83. See also James Crawford, *State Responsibility: The General Part* (CUP 2013) 303, 308–1. Note, also, the dictum of the ICJ in the *Gabčikovo-Nagymaros Project (Hungary/Slovakia)* [1997] ICJ Rep 7 [51] on necessity that 'such ground for precluding wrongfulness [under customary international law] can only be accepted on an exceptional basis'.

This does not mean that the process of securitization at the national level cannot contribute to an expansion of the global security agenda. Indeed, as discussed earlier, counter-terrorism has been added to the global security agenda through securitization, as the issue became widely shared amongst the many States represented at the UN and other regional forums. The global public order, established under the UN collective security system, restricts the way in which international peace and security issues are to be addressed and, at the same time, facilitates the collective process of securitization where warranted.[112] This system imposes the normative constraint on securitization in that no State can unilaterally change the existing rules of international law by securitizing matters at the national level.

E. Conclusion

There is no doubt that the global security agenda has expanded beyond its narrow remit of 'sav[ing] succeeding generations from the scourge of war'.[113] While the prevention of armed conflicts remains fundamental to the maintenance of international peace and security, the nature and range of contemporary security threats has changed such that a broader range of transnational problems, including terrorism, human trafficking, infectious diseases, piracy and armed robbery at sea, and cyberattacks, have increasingly been characterized as a global security agenda. As has been reviewed in this chapter, the institutional practices of different international institutions (including regional ones) reflect this tendency, but more importantly, also demonstrate various limitations to the effects of securitization, which the theory tends to neglect due to normative bias against securitization.

First, securitization in institutional practices is not free from constraints imposed upon the institutional competence and capacity. The activities of international institutions (including regional institutions) are regulated by general rules of international law,[114] which necessarily limit the extent to which, and the way in which, a matter can be securitized on their agenda. The competence of an international institution to deal with any particular security issue is subject to an interpretation of its own constituent instrument. Thus, for example, the World Health Organization was deemed to lack competence to make a request for an International Court of Justice advisory opinion on the legality of the use or threat of nuclear weapons.[115] The demarcation of competence between the EU and its Member States has also been a contested ground as the regional

[112] See Tsagourias/White (n 30) 281–96.

[113] UN Charter preamble.

[114] *Interpretation of the Agreement of 25 March 1951 between the WHO and Egypt* (Advisory Opinion) [1980] ICJ Rep 73 [37]; *Conditions of Admission of a State to Membership in the United Nations (Article 4 of the Charter)* (Advisory Opinion) [1948] ICJ Rep 57, 64; *Jurisdiction of the European Commission of the Danube between Galatz and Braila* (Advisory Opinion) [1927] PCIJ (Ser B) No 14, para 179.

[115] *Legality of the Use by a State of Nuclear Weapons in Armed Conflict* (Advisory Opinion) [1996] ICJ Rep 66 [25].

security agenda expands into the European integration policy areas.[116] The institutional competence to securitize a certain issue may be questioned or rejected internally, as illustrated by the UNSC debate on the impact of climate change.[117]

Secondly, even in cases of successful securitization within the institutional competence of the international institution, the latter may lack necessary resources to carry it through to implementation. Resource constraint is a significant factor that inhibits the institution from actually taking up the securitized issue for collective action, as has been the case with the AU and, to a varying degree, ASEAN. The expansion of the security agenda adds burden to the international institution and national authorities, although the institution can play a useful role to facilitate cooperation and implementation, for example, with the adoption of a plan of action,[118] and to monitor the progress of implementation.

Thirdly, the implementation of any measure adopted to address a security threat must comply with relevant rules of international law that apply to the international institution or its Member States. The notion of national security does not provide an independent justification for violating any of the existing rules of international law, beyond the ones established under customary international law or specifically provided in treaty instruments, and this does not change as a result of securitization of any issue. This means that any expansion of powers to enforce a security measure or any security-based restriction upon the rights granted under the existing rules of international law requires careful consideration regarding its legal implications.

Notwithstanding these limitations, this chapter has also demonstrated that securitization may facilitate an expansion of institutional competence. It could also prompt negotiations for a new treaty or the development of State practice that adjusts or clarifies the substance of an existing rule of customary international law or the interpretation of a particular treaty obligation. Thus, as the global or regional security agenda expands through institutional practices, the interaction of securitization with the body of international law will continue to provide fertile ground for future research and critical analysis of international law.

[116] See Section C.2 (nn 60–72) and accompanying text.
[117] See Section C.1 (n 46) and accompanying text.
[118] As noted in relation to ASEAN in Nasu et al (n 102).

CHAPTER 3

THE TRANSFORMATION OF SECURITY CONCEPTS

Beyond the State

URSULA SCHROEDER

A. Introduction

The global security landscape has been transforming rapidly in the past two decades. While well-known inter-State patterns of conflict and cooperation remain relevant, the character of violent conflict has been changing, and transnational insecurity dynamics are on the rise. These developments increasingly challenge established concepts of global and international security. This chapter discusses to what extent the traditionally State-centric international norms and bodies of law concerning national and international security capture the current global security landscape.

At its core, this body of law governs the use of force between States, sets rules of conduct in violent conflicts, and seeks to maintain international security through collective security arrangements. Today's security environment, however, diverges considerably from conditions in the 'ideal-typical' Westphalian international system and legal order. Security is no longer seen exclusively as a matter of the State; violent conflicts are more often than not intra-State in nature; and collective security arrangements have proven to be mostly ineffective in crisis situations.

Three transformative trends characterize this 'new status quo' of the global security order.[1] First of all, the State is no longer the only recognized security actor of relevance. An expanding set of actors beyond and below the level of the State is invested in providing security or waging war, and creating other forms of insecurity. In many regions of the world, informal security providers such as civil defence forces, vigilantes, or customary authorities have long been crucial in providing security to citizens—in particular,

[1] See Nigel White/Auden Davies-Bright, Chapter 1 in this *Handbook*.

where State agencies have been either unwilling or unable to do so. Moreover, in many situations commercial security companies, not public institutions, provide security. Security has here become a commodity, bought and sold on the market.

Secondly, (in)security dynamics are no longer exclusively tied to State boundaries. Violent conflicts increasingly stay within or extend across State borders in complex, regional conflict constellations that do not adhere to border limitations, often impacting the civilian population to a disproportionate extent. Here, legal baselines regarding the conduct of hostilities often fail to apply. New forms of warfare increasingly challenge international humanitarian law originally designed to regulate armed conflict between States.[2] The increasing acknowledgement of security concerns that transcend the borders of individual States,[3] such as global health crises,[4] climate change,[5] transnational organized crime,[6] and terrorism,[7] has contributed to the erosion of States' abilities to provide security to their citizens on their own. The governance of these challenges increasingly requires scaling up to new spatial and territorial arenas beyond the State.[8] A third trend concerns not only the spatial scope, but also the speed of current (in) security dynamics. Rapid technological developments, in particular in the field of information and communication technologies, have enhanced the interconnectedness of people on a global scale. The emerging global digital information infrastructure brings with it its own threats and vulnerabilities, as the speed and the pathways of information diffusion have accelerated and broadened.[9]

This chapter outlines how this new status quo challenges orthodox assumptions in international law about the role of the State in providing security. Tracing the shift of security concepts away from the traditional focus on war and the State in a Westphalian international system, the chapter discusses the evolution of current security concepts in their historical and theoretical context. It then goes on to show how State-based security concepts have slowly made way for broader understandings of security over the past decades. At the same time, it argues that the successive broadening and deepening of security concepts has led to issues of coherence (and lack thereof) and concept stretching in the research field, while leaving crucial dynamics of contemporary security governance underexplored. In its second part, the chapter highlights several challenges posed by the ongoing and rapid transformation of global security dynamics and discusses their implications for international law.

[2] eg Nicolas Lamp, 'Conceptions of War and Paradigms of Compliance: The "New War" Challenge to International Humanitarian Law' (2011) 16 JCSL 225, 230.

[3] See Tilmann Altwicker, Chapter 4 in this *Handbook*.

[4] See J Benton Heath, Chapter 32 in this *Handbook*.

[5] See Joyeeta Gupta/Hilmer Bosch, Chapter 30 in this *Handbook*.

[6] See Pierre Hauck/Sven Peterke, Chapter 12 in this *Handbook*.

[7] See Helen Duffy/Larissa van den Herik, Chapter 11 in this *Handbook*.

[8] Shahar Hameiri/Lee Jones, *Governing Borderless Threats: Non-Traditional Security and the Politics of State Transformation* (CUP 2015).

[9] eg Joseph Camilleri, 'Insecurity and Governance in an Age of Transition' in Anthony Burke/Rita Parker (eds), *Global Insecurity. Futures of Global Chaos and Governance* (Palgrave Macmillan 2017) 23.

B. A Short History of Security Concepts

In contrast to other major concepts in political and social sciences, the concept of security has received comparatively little research attention, leading to its characterization as a 'neglected concept'.[10] Nevertheless, it is one of the defining concepts of modern life, as it has become the 'core value of our modern—or rather postmodern—society'.[11] A very short intellectual history of security concept formation is therefore crucial to understand changes in the protective practices of States and societies over time. Security, however, is not only a core concept to understand what societies value and how they are willing to protect such values, it is also a highly contested concept whose meanings have changed quite fundamentally over the past decades. In fact, the 'term "security" covers a range of goals so wide that highly divergent policies can be interpreted as policies of security'.[12] In a nutshell, Wolfers' early formulation conceptualizes security as the 'protection of values previously acquired'.[13] This is still a useful starting point in the current situation, where answers to the crucial questions of 'who is to be secured?' and 'by what means?' have transformed rapidly and have received increasingly diverse answers.

Conceptualizations of security, similarly to other concepts in social sciences, shift and change meaning in line with political and societal debates, and crucial historical developments. Security debates are, as Williams put it, products of historical, cultural and deeply political legacies.[14] These legacies, the following section argues, are quite visible in the different conceptualizations of security of the last decades. Consequently, this chapter will first introduce crucial baseline assumptions about the role of the State, military conflicts and the need for collective security, before proceeding to investigate the place of these assumptions with reference to the broadening and diversification of debates about security concepts in the field of international relations and security studies.

1. International Security, Military Power, and Collective Security

During much of the Cold War, questions of security policy were primarily discussed in terms of military power and Great Power politics. Partially in response to the failure of

[10] David A Baldwin, 'The Concept of Security' (1997) 23 Review of International Studies 5, 9.

[11] Christopher Daase, '"National, Societal", and "Human Security": On the Transformation of Political Language' (2010) 35 Historical Social Research 22.

[12] Arnold Wolfers, 'National Security as an Ambiguous Symbol' in Arnold Wolfers (ed), *Discord and Collaboration Essays on International Politics* (Johns Hopkins UP 1962) 484.

[13] ibid.

[14] Michael C Williams, *Culture and Security: Symbolic Power and the Politics of International Security* (Routledge 2007) 17.

the multilateral security institutions of the interwar period, in particular the League of Nations, security became narrowly understood as security of the State from external military threats.[15] With the State as core player in this perspective, 'national security' became an idea that bridged 'the interests of the state abroad and those of the state at home'.[16] During the height of the Cold War, strategic challenges related to the use of nuclear weapons dominated the agenda. Issues of national security were primarily discussed in terms of military power, and in particular nuclear power. Security studies, in this narrow Cold War perspective, were dedicated to 'the study of the threat, use, and control of military force'.[17] Previously, and as late as the mid-1950s, security had been 'viewed not as the primary goal of all states at all times but rather as one among several values', while 'national security was viewed as a goal to be pursued by both nonmilitary and military techniques of statecraft'.[18]

The international legal debate since the Second World War in some respects mirrors the focus of security studies on the State as the crucial actor and referent object of security, as outlined above. International security law is primarily found in the United Nations (UN) collective security system.[19] The collective security system under the UN Charter is designed as a 'sovereign-centred'[20] system that governs the use of force between States and outlines the rules governing the conduct of war (international humanitarian law). Collective security can be defined as 'a system, regional or global, in which each state in the system accepts that the security of one is the concern of all and agrees to join in a collective response to threats to, and breaches of, the peace'.[21] Collective security systems thus provide 'institutionalized procedures for legalizing collective response'[22] to threats to the maintenance of international peace and security. International law in the field of security deals with issues as diverse as the maintenance of international peace and security, the principle of the non-use of force by one State against another as well as with international humanitarian law during violent conflict. Intra-State conflicts are not explicitly encompassed by the UN's enforcement system under Chapter VII of the UN Charter.

This system of collective security has, however, increasingly come under stress, as it has failed repeatedly to fulfil its mandate and as States have opted more and more frequently to act outside the established collective security framework. In particular,

[15] See further Keith Krause/Michael C Williams, 'Security and "Security Studies": Conceptual Evolution and Historical Transformation' in Alexandra Gheciu/William C Wolforth (eds), *Oxford Handbook of International Security* (vol 14–28, OUP 2018) 19.

[16] Bill McSweeney, *Security, Identity and Interests. A Sociology of International Relations* (CUP 1999) 20.

[17] Stephen M Walt, 'The Renaissance of Security Studies' (1991) 35 Review of International Studies 211, 212.

[18] David A Baldwin, 'Security Studies and the End of the Cold War' (1995) 48 World Politics 117, 122.

[19] Hitoshi Nasu, 'The Expanded Conception of Security and International Law: Challenges to the UN Collective Security System' (2011) 3 The Amsterdam Law Forum 15.

[20] ibid.

[21] Vaughan Lowe et al (eds), *The United Nations Security Council and War. The Evolution of Thought and Practice since 1945* (OUP 2010) 13; also Alexander Orakhelashvili, *Collective Security* (OUP 2011).

[22] Nasu (n 19) 15.

the UN Security Council's (UNSC) role in maintaining international peace and security has been severely challenged, given the body's inability to overcome persistent deadlocks, for instance pertaining to the conflict in Syria.[23] Academic and policy debates about possible mechanisms to work around the UNSC's procedural challenges focus on, for instance, a renewed role for the UN General Assembly (UNGA) in authorizing the use of force in exceptional cases via UNGA Resolution 377 (V) ('Uniting for Peace' Resolution), as well as on the duty of States to exercise a 'responsibility to protect' (R2P) civilian populations in third countries in cases of gross and widespread human rights violations.[24] The introduction of a broader conception of collective security into the UNGA's 2005 'In Larger Freedom' report followed long-standing discussions about the challenges and failures of the collective security system in dealing with widespread human rights abuses and genocide in Rwanda, the Bosnian war, and elsewhere. According to this conceptualization, 'any event or process that leads to large-scale death or lessening of life chances undermines states as the basic unit of the international system and poses a threat to international security'.[25] The outlined developments and debates are part of a larger, global shift to significantly expanded security concepts in the post-Cold War era that will be discussed in the following section.

2. Broader and Deeper Security Concepts

Several undercurrents in the field of security studies have become increasingly dissatisfied with the outlined 'orthodox' perspective on security. Given the observable rapid and irreversible processes of transformation in world politics, purely State-centric and military-focused approaches to the study of threats and the provision of security were directly challenged by the actors who expanded understandings of security along several axes. Here, 'Broadening' the security agenda refers to the inclusion of a 'wider range of potential threats, ranging from economic and environmental issues to human rights and migration', while 'deepening' moved the agenda of security studies 'either down to the level of individual or human security or up to the level of international or global security, with regional and societal security as possible intermediate points'.[26]

An early focal point for these debates was environmental security. During the 1980s, as exemplified by the report of the Brundtland Commission[27] and early studies by

[23] eg Philippa Webb, 'Deadlock or Restraint? The Security Council Veto and the Use of Force in Syria' (2014) 19 JCSL 471.

[24] See, further, Erika de Wet/Michael Wood, 'Collective Security' in MPEPIL (OUP, July 2013).

[25] ibid.

[26] Keith Krause/Michael C Williams, 'Broadening the Agenda of Security Studies: Politics and Methods' (1996) 40 Mershon International Studies Review 229, 230; see also Barry Buzan, *People, States and Fear* (Harvester Wheatsheaf 1991); Ole Wæver et al, *Identity, Migration and the New Security Agenda in Europe* (Pinter 1993).

[27] World Commission on Environment and Development, *Report of the World Commission on Environment and Development: Our Common Future* (UN 1987).

Ullmann[28] and Tuchman Matthews,[29] environmental issues were first discussed as threats to security. The discussion of issues associated with climate change and environmental degradation more generally, such as large-scale droughts, floods or shortages in food supply, as security issues, heralded a starting point for the inclusion of a broader set of threats on security agendas worldwide. This early 'redefinition of threats'[30] moved the debate away from accepted thinking about 'national security in terms of military threats arising from beyond the borders of one's own country'.[31] Instead of focusing on the survival of the State in the face of possible external attacks, a broader understanding of the relevance of non-military threats emerged, in combination with the insight that security threats could also arise from within a State. Beyond the example of the possible 'drastic deterioration of environmental quality caused by sources from either within or outside a territorial state',[32] economic vulnerabilities and issues of resource security, global pandemics, and other health crises as well as food and energy issues became seen as possible sources of global insecurity. After the end of the Cold War, the development of these debates picked up pace and broader security concepts spilled over into the security strategies of States and international organizations.

Over time, the narrower security concepts of earlier generations of Cold War scholars gave way to broader security concepts with significantly changed assumptions about the origins of threats and the need for protection. In the latter case, not only the question of who or what can threaten security, but also the question of who or what is to be secured through security policies became pertinent. Moving away from the State as the exclusive 'referent object' of security, questions of societal and human security entered the debate, in which the State came to be seen as only one object to be secured amongst many. This expansion of security referent objects also stemmed from empirical discrepancies between the conceptual status of the State as the main provider of security and empirical realities in many regions of the world where the State has often played an ambiguous or outright negative role in the security of its citizens. The notion that State actors are often the source of security problems, rather than the solution to them, has become a commonly accepted proposition.[33] In fragile situations, State actors can be the main perpetrators of threats to the security of their own people.[34] In light of these findings, a concept of security that remains bound to the level of individual States and military issues became 'inherently inadequate'.[35] Several lines of thinking about how to extend the politics of protection to groups other than States emerged, chief amongst them the concepts of societal and human security.

[28] Richard H Ullman, 'Redefining Security' (1983) 8 International Security 129.

[29] Jessica Tuchman Mathews, 'Redefining Security' (1989) 68 Foreign Affairs 162.

[30] Ullman (n 28). [31] ibid 133. [32] ibid 134.

[33] eg Christian Davenport, 'State Repression and Political Order' (2007) 10 Annual Review of Political Science 1; Jean-Francois Bayart et al, *The Criminalization of the State in Africa* (Indiana UP 1999).

[34] Keith Krause, 'Is Human Security "More than Just a Good Idea"?' in Michael Brzoska/Peter Croll (eds), *Promoting Security: But How and for Whom?* Contributions to BICC's Ten-Year Anniversary Conference (Bonn International Center for Conversion, BICC Brief No 30 2004) 45.

[35] Buzan (n 26) 3.

The notion of societal security is primarily concerned with questions of identity.[36] This concept took shape during, and in the aftermath of, the proliferation of ethnonationalist conflicts during the 1990s. It reflects concerns with ideational issues overall and conceptions of society 'as an object of security in its own right'.[37] It can be defined as 'the defence of a community against a perceived threat to its identity'.[38] In ethnonationalist conflicts, as Krause and Williams further outline, 'competing claims to sovereignty, rather than the competition between existing sovereignties, often provide the source of conflict. What people are attempting to secure is an idea.'[39] Societal conceptions of security have become ever more relevant, as research has paid increasing attention to the phenomenon that, in particular but not only in the Global South, State boundaries do not normally coincide with societal boundaries. The primacy of State security has for the longest time led to security concepts that have forgotten to address not only the security concerns of Stateless people and minorities, but also the fact that societal integration functions on both smaller and larger scales than Statehood and sometimes even transcends the spatial dimension altogether.[40] As we will see in the remainder of this chapter, societal concepts of security point to community-focused, not State-centric, solutions to security challenges, while avoiding a singular focus on those threats and protective practices primarily concerning the security of individuals.

The latter aspects of security have become known, in the wake of the UN Development Programme's (UNDP) 1994 Development Report,[41] as 'human security'. A people-centred security concept par excellence, human security promised a necessary emphasis on the well-being of people anywhere on the planet, while shining a light on the many ways in which this security was being challenged. Based on two components, 'freedom from fear' and 'freedom from want',[42] human security brought traditional concerns with threats to survival, the staple of 'orthodox' security concepts, together with a broader engagement with sustainable human development. Human security can therefore aptly be defined as a concern 'with how people live and breathe in a society, how freely they exercise their many choices, how much access they have to market and social opportunities—and whether they live in conflict or in peace'.[43]

In the late 1990s, the rise of the human security concept led to the adoption of 'ethical' or 'normative' foreign policies based on humanitarian concerns, as the examples of the Norwegian and Canadian foreign policies showed.[44] A crucial departure from established lines of thinking that left the protection of its citizens to the State, human security shifted the emphasis from understanding the security of the State as a black box to the

[36] Wæver et al (n 26) 25.

[37] Bill McSweeney, 'Identity and Security: Buzan and the Copenhagen School' (1996) 22 Review of International Studies 81, 82.

[38] Ole Wæver, 'The Changing Agenda of Societal Security' in Hans G Brauch et al (eds), *Globalization and Environmental Challenges Hexagon Series on Human and Environmental Security and Peace* (Springer 2008).

[39] Krause/Williams (n 26) 244. [40] Wæver (n 38) 582.

[41] UNDP, *UNDP Development Report 1994: New Dimensions of Human Security* (OUP 1994).

[42] ibid 24. [43] ibid 23.

[44] Astri Suhrke, 'Human Security and the Interests of States' (1999) 30 Security Dialogue 265.

personal security of people 'in their homes, jobs and communities',[45] as then UN Secretary-General Boutros-Ghali argued. Security, in essence, became an individual good again. While societal security was concerned with the security of a collective, different from the State, human security in a certain sense reverted to earlier ideas of liberal thought and constitutes a 'rediscovery, of sorts, of…late eighteenth and early nineteenth-century politics'.[46]

3. New Security Concepts and Their Impact on Policymaking

Current security environments differ considerably from the relatively stable and heavily rules-based conflict patterns of the Cold War. Then, security was defined almost exclusively from the perspectives of the two adversaries in the East–West confrontation. It was military in nature and strongly based on the development of military capacities. Individual and societal concerns did not have a central place in security strategies. Today, security challenges are diverse, often transnational and not necessarily military or State-based in nature. Many old certainties of security policymaking no longer hold: violent conflicts between States have declined, with intra-State conflicts now making up the vast majority of active violent conflicts.[47] The increasingly internationalized character of war, namely those armed conflicts in which one or more States have contributed troops to one or both warring States, makes conflicts 'on average more violent, more difficult to solve, and last longer'.[48] Equally worrisome, 2017 was one of the most violent years since the end of the Cold War.[49] Dramatic increases in occurrences of non-State violence are also significant. Quite unlike the situation during the Cold War, violence and the use of force is now often non-State in nature and routinely transcends existing State boundaries.

Security responses, in line with these rapid transformations, also vary widely. Tracing the evolution of core security concepts over the past decades, we have seen that conceptualizations of security propagated in current research have changed almost beyond recognition. Security studies is a research field that has lost many of its certainties over the past years and has been in conceptual upheaval ever since.[50] At the same time, security policymaking has also become much more fragmented, with a vastly broadened set of issues to deal with and different military and non-military actor sets enlisted in the provision of security. More often than not, national security strategies are now 'comprehensive' in scope and integrate both military and a wide variety of non-military aspects into a State's security policies. In particular, in direct comparison to the narrow security

[45] Cited in: Emma Rothschild, 'What is Security?' (1995) 124 Daedalus 53, 56. [46] ibid.

[47] Kendra Dupuy/Siri Aas Rustad, *Trends in Armed Conflict, 1946–2017: Conflict Trends*, 5 (PRIO 2018).

[48] ibid. [49] ibid.

[50] eg Krause/Williams (n 15); J Peter Burgess (ed), *The Routledge Handbook of New Security Studies* (Routledge 2010).

strategies pursued during the height of the Cold War, broader security concepts have become part and parcel of national and international policies.

Within this 'broadening' move, the concept of human security has arguably become the most well-known and crucial extension of classical security concepts for the policy world. The policy implications of the human security concept are of particular relevance to the field of international law, as they challenge basic underpinnings of the international legal system in various ways. In itself, the idea of a human-centred approach is not alien to international law, as the latter has evolved to accommodate the principles of equality and non-discrimination, respect for human dignity, and the principle of humanity—all human-centred principles.[51] The Ottawa Convention banning landmines,[52] the Statute of the International Criminal Court,[53] and the Protocol to the Convention on the Rights of the Child,[54] are themselves 'human security treaties', as Oberleitner has pointed out when arguing that human security concerns are already shaping international legal documents.[55] At the same time, human security concepts fundamentally challenge traditional conceptions of security as the sovereign prerogative of States,[56] as well as the notion of States as the primary subject of international law. Human security, if taken seriously as a concept, could change the ways in which international law addresses issues of State sovereignty, humanitarian intervention, as well as the place of non-State actors in international law.[57] Currently, the UN's collective security system is still underpinned by a firmly 'state-centric, military-oriented conception of security'[58] and the question remains to what extent this can and will change in the coming years. In particular, the hotly debated issues of humanitarian intervention in the wake of the R2P norm emerging out of the 2001 Report of the International Commission on Intervention and State Sovereignty (ICISS)[59] resonate with the concept of human security. Both extend States' obligations beyond their territorial boundaries and both situate the ends of security policies firmly at the level of individuals made insecure by State or other actors. Human security, in short, is a wide-ranging concept that diverges considerably from orthodox assumptions about security provision. It has the potential to significantly alter debates about how to uphold international peace and security in international law.

[51] Hitoshi Nasu, 'Human Security and International Law: The Potential Scope for Legal Development within the Analytical Framework of Security' in Mary E Footer et al (eds), *Security and International Law* (Hart Publishing 2016) 32.

[52] Convention on the Prohibition of the Use, Stockpiling, Production and Transfer of Anti-Personnel Mines and on their Destruction 2056 UNTS 211.

[53] Rome Statute of the International Criminal Court 2187 UNTS 3.

[54] Optional Protocol to the Convention on the Rights of the Child on the Involvement of Children in Armed Conflicts 2173 UNTS 222.

[55] Gerd Oberleitner, 'Human Security: A Challenge to International Law?' (2005) 11 Global Governance 185, 195.

[56] Nasu (n 51) 32. [57] Oberleitner (n 55) 189. [58] Nasu (n 51) 36.

[59] ICISS, *The Responsibility to Protect. Report of the International Commission on Intervention and State Sovereignty* (International Development Research Centre 2001).

Since its arrival on the scene over two decades ago, human security has rapidly become a go-to concept for different policy communities, ranging from development and foreign policies to issues of global health and climate change. The interesting observation here is that the general premise of human security, namely that security provision should centre on human beings, has entered mainstream policy debates, even though the concept of human security itself remains relatively vague. Even more astonishingly, observers show that 'the language of human security has spread well beyond the policy communities, achieving a level of popular resonance that few would have predicted in the mid-1990s.'[60] Despite this intrinsic attractiveness, the concept of human security has attracted its fair share of criticism. In particular, its lack of conceptual coherence and its propensity towards stretching the concept of security to its breaking point have been debated at length. A core criticism reiterated in different ways is that it lacks a precise definition: 'everyone is for it, but few people have a clear idea of what it means.'[61] The existing inclusive or, depending on the observer, vague definitions of human security in fact allow for almost all harm to individuals to be framed as a question of human security. The breadth of the concept allows groups of different political persuasions to appropriate the concept for their own ends, but it also makes it difficult to clearly define what a human security policy would look like in practice.

C. Contemporary Challenges of Security Governance

The broadening and deepening of security concepts outlined above has fundamentally reconfigured more limited and narrow conceptualizations of security during the Cold War. However, these debates were waged and are still anchored primarily in the political and social contexts of the 1990s and early 2000s. Debates and current events have since moved on to reveal more complex patterns of local and global security governance. As will be shown in the following section, the rescaling of security politics, the often both local and global reach of security-related events, and the sometimes rather limited role of formal, State-based forms of security governance call into question core assumptions of international security law.

Security studies and studies of international law share a property that challenges their ability to fully take into account these complex security dynamics: both remain wedded to the State as the core security provider, and to categories of Statehood (control over a fixed territory, the existence of a centralized government, and a monopoly on the legitimate use of violence) that are based firmly on the European experience of State formation.

[60] Ryerson Christie, 'Critical Voices and Human Security: To Endure, To Engage or To Critique?' (2010) 41 Security Dialogue 169, 173.

[61] Roland Paris, 'Human Security: Paradigm Shift or Hot Air?' (2001) 26 International Security 87, 88.

As a research field that is, by birth, an Anglo-American discipline,[62] this focus on the Western model of the State and on Western security issues does not come as a surprise. However, the European model of State formation is of only limited relevance for major parts of the non-Western world, as its categories do not adequately capture security governance and insecurity dynamics in the non-West.[63] At the same time, faced with globalization-induced challenges, European States themselves are undergoing processes of fundamental transformation. Insights from studies of security provision in the Global South, as well as from research on globalization and from criminology, point us to alternative trajectories of security provision that need to be taken more fully into account.

1. Globalization and the Rescaling of Security Governance

Scholars interested in processes of globalization have developed several lines of thinking to better conceptualize complex patterns of security governance 'beyond the State'. The starting point is the observation that globalizing processes and the concomitant rise of 'borderless threats'[64] introduce new 'scalar constellations'[65] into traditional equations of security provision. The increasing range and depth of transnational connections, it is argued, needs to be accompanied by 'a new grammar and spatial imagination about risk and security which is not primarily based on geographical proximity'.[66] In a world of transnational organized crime, increasingly internationalized intra-State wars, and global pandemics, the methodological nationalism of earlier studies simply does not capture the range of boundary-transcending challenges and attempts to regulate them. In this context, recent studies have started to grapple with understanding the scope and scale of ongoing transformations of security governance at the global level. Hameiri and Jones focus on the transformation of State apparatuses into multilevel, regional, or global regulatory governance networks.[67] They argue that the prevalent focus on the role of 'new' security threats is misleading, as they are mostly not all that new. Instead, research should focus on the ways in which the regulation of non-traditional security threats leads to conflicts about the scale—national, regional, or global—at which these issues are governed. A second conceptual framework tackling similar issues is Abrahamsen and Williams' concept of 'global security assemblages',[68] which introduces

[62] Barry Buzan/Lene Hansen, *The Evolution of International Security Studies* (CUP 2009) 19.

[63] See further Pinar Bilgin, 'The "Western-Centrism" of Security Studies: "Blind Spot" or Constitutive Practice?' (2010) 41 Security Dialogue 615; Tarak Barkawi/Mark Laffey, 'The Postcolonial Moment in Security Studies' (2006) 32 Review of International Studies 329.

[64] Hameiri/Jones (n 8).

[65] Katja F Aas, '(In)Security-At-A-Distance: Rescaling Justice, Risk and Warfare in a Transnational Age' (2012) 13 Global Crime 235, 237.

[66] ibid 236. [67] Hameiri/Jones (n 8) 4.

[68] Rita Abrahamsen/Michael C Williams, *Security Beyond the State. Private Security in International Politics* (CUP 2011) 89.

the heuristic of a dual process of State disassembly and (global) reassembly to study processes of security privatization and its impact on global security. What these conceptualizations have in common is a shared concern with contemporary governance patterns that do not adhere to the 'neat order composed of territorially delineated units, commonly described as the Westphalian order'.[69] Instead, this research highlights the networked and cross-cutting character of sometimes fluid and shifting governance arrangements that can include both public and private actors in different constellations.

These findings, however, do not imply that the State is losing all relevance in security provision. Rather, on the contrary, although the State's functions are transforming, the State is not in full retreat. While privatization and globalization, as Abrahamsen and Williams outline, 'have empowered private actors, their growth cannot be seen as an automatic diminishment in the power of the state'.[70] The increased commercialization of security services has led to a situation where State regulators are joined in transnational security institutions by increasingly well-resourced private security companies that possess the 'material and ideational capacities to operate on increasingly global scales'.[71] Similar transformations in the governance of internal security provision have been characterized as shifts towards 'liquid security' from the 'solid-state technology of criminal justice to the fluid, endlessly mutable operations of the security industry'.[72] State structures are here not replaced by private security. Instead, the criminal justice system moves from being the dominant player to one amongst many.[73]

In short, current research on the governance of global security shows that interlinked processes transform the provision of security at the global level. On the one hand, the boundary-traversing nature of many security challenges has led to the rescaling of security governance to transnational sites beyond the borders of the State. Transnational associations of public and private actors do not replace the State in this analysis but add another layer of complexity to the governance of increasingly difficult to handle security challenges. On the other hand, commercial private security activities 'ranging from manned guarding and alarm installation, to risk analysis and surveillance, have expanded at a phenomenal rate'.[74] Their regulation, and the regulation of commercial security services during the conduct of hostilities, is a task that needs to be tackled at the global level. Here, questions of international law, in particular international humanitarian law, intersect with issues of commercial, non-State security provision. Concept development in the field of security needs to reconcile the expansion of specific forms of non-public, often transnational security provision that can be bought and sold on the market, with the role of State-based international security governance.

[69] Aas (n 65) 238.

[70] Rita Abrahamsen/Michael C Williams, 'Security Beyond the State: Global Security Assemblages in International Politics' (2009) 3 International Political Sociology 1, 4.

[71] ibid 5.

[72] Lucia Zedner, 'Liquid Security: Managing the Market for Crime Control' (2006) 6 Criminology and Criminal Justice 267.

[73] ibid 268. [74] Abrahamsen/Williams (n 70) 1.

2. Local (In)securities and Informal Security Provision

A second dimension of security provision that has not received the share of attention it deserves is the routine provision of security by a variety of informal actors in areas of limited Statehood.[75] Area-specific studies and studies of security provision in the Global South have shown time and again that the State is often not the primary provider of security in many areas of the world. The State in this sense is only one actor amongst many.[76] Limiting the rights and obligations of security provision to States, as is customary in the Westphalian system of States, therefore, does not sit comfortably with the histories and practices of security provision in many post-colonial States. Dispersed forms of security and justice provision that are tied to local, informal communities have a long history. According to some estimations, up to 80 or 90 per cent of primary security and justice provision in the Global South operates in this way.[77] Informal governance arrangements of this type are often highly localized. Security is guaranteed by a heterogeneous set of actors ranging from community protection mechanisms to for-profit commercial services.[78] Local protective practices are often most visible in extremely fragile situations. At the same time, security provision can be provided, for instance, by nationally operating non-State armed groups. Often characterized by fragmented, spatially heterogeneous and exclusive forms of protection, these ubiquitous forms of security provision by no means operate fully outside the sphere of the State, as they are bound up with the State in complex ways. A recent study of African States found that States and their security institutions operate alongside a large array of non-State bodies, 'some violently challenging state authority, others working alongside or co-operating with it'.[79] Beyond the Weberian paradigm of States monopolizing the means of violence over time, security arrangements here are characterized by complex interplays between formal and informal security actors and institutions.

To analytically capture this largely overlooked dimension of 'hybrid'[80] security governance, security concepts that focus on the Global South have paid closer attention to what security looks like 'from below' or 'in the vernacular'.[81] Based on Bubandt's

[75] The arguments in this section are further developed in Ursula C Schroeder, 'Security' in Thomas Risse et al (eds), *The Oxford Handbook of Governance and Limited Statehood* (OUP 2018). See also Christopher J Borgen, Chapter 15 in this *Handbook*.

[76] Joel S Migdal, *State in Society: Studying How States and Societies Transform and Constitute One Another* (CUP 2001). See also Markos Karavias, Chapter 24 in this *Handbook*.

[77] Peter Albrecht/Maria H Kyed, 'Introduction: Non-State and Customary Actors in Development Programs' in Peter Albrecht et al (eds), *Perspectives on Involving Non-State and Customary Actors in Justice and Security Reform* (International Development Law Organization 2011) 3.

[78] See further Bruce Baker, 'State and Substate Policing in Africa and the Boundaries between Them' (2012) 13 Global Crime 276, 278. Similarly, see Markos Karavias, 'Non-state Actors in Control of Territory as "Actors of Protection" in International Refugee Law' (2014) Revue Belge de Droit International 487.

[79] Niagale Bagayoko et al, 'Hybrid Security Governance in Africa: Rethinking the Foundations of Security, Justice and Legitimate Public Authority' (2016) 16 Conflict, Security and Development 1.

[80] ibid.

[81] Robin Luckham/Tom Kirk, 'The Two Faces of Security in Hybrid Political Orders: A Framework for Analysis and Research' (2013) 2 Stability: International Journal of Security and Development art 44.

conceptualization of 'vernacular security,'[82] these studies analyse the everyday experiences of ordinary citizens to understand how they perceive and cope with security challenges. This perspective adds a welcome layer of empirical analysis to concepts of 'human security' that have often remained outside everyday patterns of local insecurities and security provision. For the field of international law, grappling with non-State actors in security provision is not easy, as this phenomenon challenges the established hegemony of State-based security provision head on. However, the deeply rooted interactions between formal and informal security actors and institutions in many parts of the world, briefly described above, are no fringe phenomenon that only affects those States at the margin of the international system of States or those most at risk of high levels of fragility or State collapse. Instead, they make up continuing and vital parts of security provision in large areas of the world. Security concepts that cannot account for these dynamics run the risk of remaining divorced from the empirical realities they seek to capture.

D. Conclusion

This chapter has outlined how rapidly accelerating, complex, and increasingly transnational global security dynamics challenge established ways of understanding security in the fields of International Law and International Relations. In past decades, narrower security concepts based exclusively on the template of the State as a security provider and security referent object were adapted to incorporate a broader range of security issues ('broadening') and a larger set of security referent objects ('deepening'). This chapter has shown, however, that these moves sidestepped a crucial question, namely that of the primary role of the State in security concepts. Given the sometimes limited positive role of State security institutions in large parts of the world, and the rise of commercial security at both the local and global levels, security concepts should take into account these challenges to a State-based order. This chapter argued that paying closer attention to the role of non-State security actors and informal patterns of security provision, in particular (although not exclusively) in the Global South, will contribute to a better understanding of current security dynamics.

Such transformative dynamics are difficult to capture as the international law of global security continues to focus strongly on the role of States in providing security. At the same time, a trend towards the 'decollectivization' of security provision, that is, a departure from the collective security institutions of the post-Second World War world, has become visible. These parallel trends, the rise of non-State actors in global security and the increasing informalization of international cooperation outside established multilateral fora, call the carefully constructed intellectual edifice of collective security

[82] Nils Bubandt, 'Vernacular Security: The Politics of Feeling Safe in Global, National and Local Worlds' (2005) 36 Security Dialogue 275.

into question. Security governance at the global level today is a heterogeneous and fragmented field that increasingly depends on fluid actor constellations that include, but are not limited to, formal intergovernmental cooperation in multilateral institutions. Given recent political developments in the transatlantic and European arenas of security cooperation, the future of the current collective security system is uncertain.

CHAPTER 4

TRANSNATIONALIZATION OF SECURITY

TILMANN ALTWICKER

A. Introduction

'Security', in its many guises, is in a process of 'transnationalization', namely it is becoming a cross-border issue.[1] Thus, in the twenty-first century, the primary examples of sources of 'insecurity'—such as transnational terrorism, transnational crime, mass migration, cross-border environmental hazards, and problems of energy security—are no longer perceived as 'domestic affairs'. The ensuing processes of transnationalization are naturally also processes of transnationalization of and by international law.[2] The present contribution analyses the transnationalization of security insofar as this process makes use of, or is constrained by, international law.

From these preliminary remarks, it follows that the scope of this chapter is limited in three ways: First, it deals with problems of 'transnational security', namely with security problems that are constructed by the relevant actors as cross-border issues. Of course, not all security-relevant risks, threats, and vulnerabilities are transnational. For example, although security-relevant, local gang crime or small-scale environmental harm usually lacks a cross-border dimension. Further, it is important to note that there is no exhaustive list of transnational security problems. Transnational security problems

[1] 'Transnationalization', here, refers to processes of growing cross-border interaction, cooperation and transaction by State, economic, and civil society actors, see László Bruszt/Ronald Holzhacker, 'Three Converging Literatures of Transnationalization and the Varieties of Transnationalization' in László Bruszt/Ronald Holzhacker (eds), *The Transnationalization of Economies, States, and Civil Societies* (Springer 2009) 1, 3, 10–12.

[2] This contribution does not deal with the transformative effects the integration of transnational security has on domestic law.

neither reflect an ontological reality (they do not 'exist' out there) nor are they merely a subjective perception. Rather, transnational security problems are the product of effective securitization by the relevant actors (such as governments, international organizations, courts, and civil society actors).[3] In other words, transnational security problems are best viewed as an open-ended social construction by the relevant actors. Responding to transnational securitization in the twenty-first century, the transboundary nature of the effect of certain risks, threats and vulnerabilities has been made the object of intensified regulatory activity. This condition distinguishes 'transnational security' from security problems that are constructed either as predominantly domestic (eg, local handbag thefts) or as predominantly international (eg, international armed conflict) concerns. The present contribution distinguishes between 'transnational' and 'international' security as follows: While international security relates to inter-State security (traditionally affected by war or international armed conflict), transnational security relates to risks, threats, and vulnerabilities of a non-military nature, such as transnational terrorism (though this is contested), and, more clearly, transnational crime, cybersecurity, and even cross-border environmental hazards and energy security.[4] Second, the contribution addresses transnationalization only insofar as it relates to international law. It must be stressed that the phenomenon of transnationalization of security as such is far broader, affecting not only international law but also domestic law (criminal and public law) as well as European Union (EU) law. The domestic and the EU spheres of transnationalization of security, too, must be left aside due to the limited scope of this chapter.[5] Third, the contribution is naturally limited to transnationalization of security as a *legal* process, namely a process in which the relevant actors resort to legal norms. Consequently, the social or ethical dimensions of the transnationalization of security will not be addressed.

The present contribution makes two claims: The first claim concerns the potential of the transnationalization of security and its impact on international law. On the one hand, regulation of typical transnational security issues such as, for example, those concerning foreign terrorist fighters, cybersecurity, and transboundary hazards (including natural disasters and epidemics) has led to new forms of international lawmaking and implementation as well as to the inclusion of new security actors on the international level. The transnationalization of security has fuelled innovative forms of international cooperation and continues to have an impact on the development of international law. On the other hand, the transnationalization of security has sometimes challenged foundational international legal principles, in particular, the international rule of law and international human rights.

The second claim concerns international law as a constraint to the transnationalization of security. While international law seems to be the instrument of choice regarding

[3] Thierry Balzacq, 'The Policy Tools of Securitization: Information Exchange, EU Foreign and Interior Policies' (2008) 46 Journal of Common Market Studies 75.

[4] For further distinction between 'transnational public security' and 'transnational civil security' see Section B.

[5] For details, see Tilmann Altwicker, *Transnational Public Security Law* (manuscript on file with the author).

the regulation of transnational security issues (which naturally affect more than one State), international law is at the same time often ill equipped to function as an efficient problem-solver due to its conceptual and structural peculiarities. Broadly speaking, and in simple terms, it is the 'State-centredness' of the international legal order which often impedes efficient transnational problem-solving in the field of security (for example, by insufficiently acknowledging the actor status of transnationally operative private security companies, or by insufficiently capturing cross-border intrusions of the right to privacy of individuals as a violation of general international law). At the same time, it is precisely the 'State-centredness' of the international legal order that functions as a natural limit to the transnationalization of security by international law (for example, the principle of territorial integrity prohibiting acts of public authority on the territory of another State as well as any physical interference with the territorial space of other States). Other limitations for the transnationalization of security by international law often derive from foundational principles such as international human rights.

The chapter addresses the following research questions: what is the contribution of international law to the transnationalization of security? How has the transnationalization of security impacted international lawmaking (and implementation)? What international actors (institutions) are the main drivers of the transnationalization of security? Is there sufficient counterbalancing of international lawmaking by international human rights law (IHRL) (such as in UN Counter-terrorism Conventions)? And what are the limitations of transnationalization of security by international law in general?

The contribution is structured as follows. The second section dissects three major framings (perspectives about social reality) used for the transnationalization of security, namely, 'war', 'crime', and 'risk' and their conceptualization in international law.[6] The third section discusses the two major challenges faced in the transnationalization of security by international law: the problem of jurisdictional dysfunctionalities under international law and the problem of applying IHRL to transnational security cases. The fourth and final section evaluates the contribution of international law to the process of the transnationalization of security.

B. Current Status of the Debate

In the context of international law, transnationalization of security is, currently, operationalized by relying on three basic framings: 'war'-framing, 'crime'-framing, and 'risk'-framing.[7]

[6] As outlined above, 'international' security is distinguished from 'transnational' security by its military nature. However, this ideal-type distinction does not prevent the relevant actors from relying on 'war' as a perspective for securitization, even though the security problem may lack a military nature.

[7] The following is a shortened version of the discussion in Altwicker (n 5) 39–53.

In international law, 'war'-framing represents the conventional framing used for securitization. 'War'-framing was traditionally reserved for inter-State conflicts. However, in recent times, especially after the 9/11 attacks (and ever since), 'war'-framing has come to be used in other contexts as well.[8] For example, it has sometimes been used in respect of fighting transnational organized crime (especially in the fight against drug trafficking): In 1986, a US Commission dealing with cocaine distribution stated that the:

> testimony in this record portrays a state of war ... a situation in which large, sophisticated organizations, based abroad but with agents and collaborators within our borders, have launched a massive, well-armed and well-financed invasion of our country by sea and air, resulting in thousands of our citizens being killed or disabled.[9]

'War'-framing is also more frequently used with respect to cyberspace. There is visible transnational legal securitization regarding cyberwarfare, especially in the *Tallinn Manual 2.0* (outlining how the legal rules governing international peace and security apply to cyberspace).[10] The most prominent attempt at transnational legal securitization relying on 'war'-framing is the US-led 'war on terror'. It must be noted here that the 'war' approach to terrorism not only sought to legitimize the use of force against individual perpetrators but also, if not primarily, against other sovereign States believed to harbour terrorists. After having lost its political appeal for some time, this extended understanding of 'war' was recently revived in the context of fighting ISIL/Da'esh: Former French President François Hollande is quoted as saying that '[w]e are confronted with a group, Daesh, which has declared war on us'.[11] The existence of 'war' traditionally implies a law

[8] The terminology is commonly used in the debate concerning the correct legal framework for addressing transnational terrorism: See Jens David Ohlin/Larry May, *Necessity in International Law* (OUP 2016) 198 (distinguishing between a 'war model' and a 'law enforcement model'); David Kretzmer, 'Targeted Killing of Suspected Terrorists: Extra-Judicial Executions or Legitimate Means of Defence?' (2005) 16 EJIL 171, 176–204 (distinguishing between a 'law enforcement-model', an 'armed conflict-model', and defending a 'mixed-model' with respect to targeted killings of suspected terrorists).

[9] Quoted by Jay S Albanese, *Organized Crime: From the Mob to Transnational Organized Crime* (7th edn, Routledge 2015) 183. For the situation in Mexico see Carlos Vilalta, 'How Did Things Get So Bad So Quickly? An Assessment of the Initial Conditions of the War Against Organized Crime in Mexico' (2014) 20 European Journal on Criminal Policy and Research 137.

[10] The *Tallinn Manual 2.0* was drafted by international law experts, see <https://ccdcoe.org/research/tallinn-manual/> accessed 14 November 2020. The text is available in Michael N Schmitt (ed), *Tallinn Manual 2.0 on the International Law Applicable to Cyber Operations* (2nd edn, CUP 2017). Further, see John Stone, 'Cyber War Will Take Place!' (2013) 36 *Journal of Strategic Studies* 101; Gary McGraw, 'Cyber War is Inevitable (Unless We Build Security In)' (2013) 36 Journal of Strategic Studies 109. For criticism of this securitization effort see Thomas Rid, *Cyber War Will Not Take Place* (OUP 2013).

[11] Andrew Rettman, 'Hollande: French People "Under Threat"' (*EUobserver*, 26 July 2016) <https://euobserver.com/justice/134497> accessed 14 May 2020.

of exception and emergency powers.[12] In particular, 'war'-framing is used in the belief that tighter human rights obligations could be avoided.[13] In addition, 'war'-framing allows greater room for manoeuvre than 'crime'-framing, in particular, by legitimizing the application of the rules governing immunity of State armed forces.[14] This is of relevance, for example, in respect of extraterritorial targeted killings where a drone pilot may otherwise ultimately be charged with murder.

In general international law, 'war'-framing must be compatible with the understanding of international peace and security, the two key concepts of the security architecture established by the UN Charter.[15] Under the UN Charter, 'war' is the antonym to 'international peace'.[16] The meaning of the concept of 'international security' is more complex and multilayered, encompassing also the positive dimension of securing the circumstances conducive to peace.[17] In the text of the UN Charter, international peace and security are usually mentioned together and any interpretation must take their systemic connection into account.[18] Consequently, in an international legal context, the 'war'-framing of a threat not only denotes 'conflict' or 'hostilities', but also an attack on the order of living together, on the accepted principles necessary for maintaining international peace. Transnational terrorism is regularly condemned by the UN Security Council (UNSC) as a threat to 'peace and security'.[19] Unlike transnational terrorism, the other transnational security problems—cybersecurity, organized crime, environmental hazards—are usually not addressed as threats to 'international peace and security'. Other fields within international law dealing with 'war' are international humanitarian law (IHL) and international criminal law. International humanitarian law contains provisions, for example, protecting civilians against acts of terrorism in the context of

[12] Frédéric Mégret, '"War"? Legal Semantics and the Move to Violence' (2002) 13 EJIL 361, 365–70 (arguing that war-terminology paves the way for an 'ideal-typical state of exception'). See Joan Fitzpatrick, 'Speaking Law to Power: The War against Terrorism and Human Rights' (2003) 14 EJIL 241, 251 (who states—drawing on a point made by Oren Gross—that 'war on terror' is the 'quintessential "normless and exceptionless exception"').

[13] See the UNGA 'Report by the Special Rapporteur on Extrajudicial, Summary Or Arbitrary Executions, Philip Alston: Study on Targeted Killings' (28 May 2010) UN Doc A/HRC/14/24/Add.6, para 2, (criticizing that 'too many criminal acts have been re-characterized so as to justify addressing them within the framework of the law of armed conflict'). Furthermore, Alston wrote that '[t]o expand the notion of non-international armed conflict to groups that are essentially drug cartels, criminal gangs or other groups that should be dealt with under the law enforcement framework would be to do deep damage to the IHL and human rights frameworks', ibid para 56.

[14] ibid para 47.

[15] Charter of the United Nations 1 UNTS XVI art 1(1).

[16] On the concept of war in international law see Lothar Kotzsch, *The Concept of War in Contemporary History and International Law* (E Droz 1956). For a more recent treatment, Christopher Greenwood, 'The Concept of War in Modern International Law' (1987) 36 ICLQ 283; Marina Mancini, 'The Effects of a State of War or Armed Conflict' in Marc Weller (ed), *The Oxford Handbook of the Use of Force in International Law* (OUP 2015) 989–90.

[17] On the legal meaning of 'international security', Avril McDonald/Hanna Brollowski, 'Security' MPEPIL (OUP, May 2011) MN 2. On the positive dimension of the concept of 'international security', Rüdiger Wolfrum, 'Article 1' in Bruno Simma et al (eds), *The Charter of the United Nations: A Commentary* (3rd edn, OUP 2012) MN 8.

[18] McDonald/Brollowski (n 17) MN 3.

[19] eg UNSC Res 2083 (2012) preamble.

armed conflict.[20] However, IHL, in large part, does not apply to acts of transnational terrorism (or to other transnational security problems).[21] In sum, 'war'-framing is largely inappropriate for transnational security problems, and attempts to alter the international law understanding of 'war' in the wake of new transnational security threats have largely been unsuccessful.

Another framing used for transnational legal securitization in the context of international law is 'crime' or 'criminal behaviour'.[22] Just like 'war'-framing, 'crime'-framing is associated with certain background assumptions. Obviously, the major field responsible for generating background assumptions regarding the 'crime'-framing of threats is criminal law. First, at a basic level (but leading to intriguingly complex issues beyond the scope of this chapter), one can say that legal 'crime'-framing presupposes—depending on one's theory of criminalization—either some kind of public wrong(doing) or causation of harm to some protected legal interest.[23] This assumption clearly limits the range of transnational security problems to which 'crime'-framing may be applied. For example, 'crime'-framing is of limited use with respect to cross-border energy security or health concerns. Second, 'crime'-framing of threats assumes that the target of adverse measures, sanctions or punishment is not exchangeable. In other words, it is assumed that there is an identifiable individual who 'deserves' criminal sanctioning. As Jens Ohlin and Larry May write, the 'criminal law enforcement model assumes that the individual perpetrators will not necessarily be replaced by others, so that the key is to capture and prosecute the right individuals'.[24] This assumption is increasingly problematic with respect to the particularly pressing transnational threat of terrorism. In many cases, terrorists are replaceable and, therefore, the assumption is violated.[25] Third, 'crime'-framing presupposes that State authorities have the power and, generally, the political will to investigate and prosecute situations involving a transnational threat, or, at least, to cooperate with other States (for example, through mutual legal assistance in

[20] For international armed conflicts: Protocol Additional to the Geneva Conventions of 12 August 1949 and relating to the Protection of Victims of International Armed Conflicts (Protocol I) 1125 UNTS 3 art 51(2). For non-international armed conflicts (NIACs): Protocol Additional to the Geneva Conventions of 12 August 1949 and relating to the Protection of Victims of Non-International Armed Conflicts (Protocol II) 1125 UNTS 609 art 4(2)(d).

[21] Robert Kolb/Richard Hyde, *An Introduction to the International Law of Armed Conflicts* (Hart Publishing 2008) 203.

[22] From a legal perspective, this is discussed as a 'law enforcement'-model, Kretzmer (n 8) 176–86.

[23] The question of what conduct should be criminalized is notoriously contested, Antony Duff, 'Theories of Criminal Law' (2013) *Stanford Encyclopaedia of Philosophy* (discussing both the 'harm principle' and the theory of 'public wrongs' as candidates for a theory of criminalization). Examples are, for a theory relying on the 'harm principle', Joel Feinberg, *The Moral Limits of the Criminal Law: Harm to Others* (OUP 1987) 105 (stating that 'harm is a *wrongfully* set-back interest'), and, for a theory of legal moralism, Michael S Moore, *Placing Blame: A Theory of the Criminal Law* (OUP 2010) 69–70 (asserting that 'because an action is morally wrong [there] is always a legitimate reason to prohibit it with criminal legislation'). For a critical discussion, Larry Alexander, 'The Philosophy of Criminal Law' in Jules L Coleman et al (eds), *The Oxford Handbook of Jurisprudence and Philosophy of Law* (OUP 2004) 851–64.

[24] Ohlin/May (n 8) 198.

[25] This is the reason why Ohlin/May reject applying the 'law enforcement' model to transnational terrorists (ibid).

criminal matters). In other words, 'crime'-framing assumes that it is the obligation of the territorial State to take steps against transnational criminal offenders present in their territory. This assumption is seriously called into question in situations in which the transnational threat arises in places with fragile or limited Statehood (such as, for example, Yemen).[26] Fourth, with a few exceptions (such as inchoate crime), the crime-framing of transnational threats relates to past conduct. It is, thus, retrospective and repressive. Often, however, transnational security requires prospective cross-border action for which a criminal law-approach is insufficient. Fifth, 'crime'-framing presupposes that the conduct must in some way or another be 'harmful' to society or individuals, although not to such a degree that the survival of the State or parts of the population is threatened when 'war'-framing would be more appropriate. Again, with respect to some forms of large-scale terrorism (such as ISIL/Da'esh), this assumption has come under pressure.[27] Similarly, the assumption may also be violated in the case of States that are severely affected by transnational organized crime.

With respect to transnational terrorism, 'crime'-framing still seems to dominate present securitizing efforts. For example, the UN counter-terrorism conventions commonly address terrorism within 'crime'-framing, for instance when referring to terrorist offences[28] or criminal acts.[29] However, transnational legal securitization using the 'crime'-framing of terrorism has not been completely successful in the international legal context. For example, a motion to include terrorism amongst the international crimes recognized in the Rome Statute of 1998 was rejected.[30] To date, a 'crime of terrorism' is neither recognized in international treaty law nor in customary international law (though the latter point is contested).[31] While the 'crime'-framing of terrorism, internationally, seems to meet with opposition, it is the case that most States consider terrorism a serious crime in their domestic legal orders.[32]

[26] In recent years, some securitizers attempted to weaken this assumption connected with 'crime'-framing, and instead push for conditioned sovereignty under the 'unable and unwilling' standard, Jutta Brunnée/Stephen J Toope, 'Self-Defence against Non-State Actors: Are Powerful States Willing but Unable to Change International Law?' (2018) 67 ICLQ 263.

[27] Richard A Posner, *Not a Suicide Pact: The Constitution in a Time of National Emergency* (OUP 2006) 64–5.

[28] International Convention for the Suppression of Terrorist Bombings 2149 UNTS 256 art 3; International Convention for the Suppression of Acts of Nuclear Terrorism 2445 UNTS 89 art 2.

[29] Terrorist Bombings Convention (n 28) art 5.

[30] States, notably the US, voted against including terrorism in the Rome Statute mainly because terrorism was lacking a common definition, and because of fears of politicization of the ICC. See Antonio Cassese, 'Terrorism is Also Disrupting Some Crucial Legal Categories of International Law' (2001) 12 EJIL 993, 993–94, Richard J Goldstone/Janine Simpson, 'Evaluating the Role of the International Criminal Court as a Legal Response to Terrorism' (2003) 16 Harvard Human Rights Journal 13.

[31] Ben Saul, *Defining Terrorism in International Law* (OUP 2006) 190, 270; cf Antonio Cassese, 'The Multifaceted Criminal Notion of Terrorism in International Law' (2006) 4 JICJ 933 (arguing that there is a customary international definition of terrorism as an international crime in time of peace).

[32] UNSC Counter-Terrorism Committee, 'Global Survey of the Implementation of UN Security Council Resolution 1373 (2001) by Member States' (1 September 2011) UN Doc S/2011/463, para 12 ('Most states have now taken steps to criminalize terrorist acts in their domestic laws and regulations…').

Transnational securitization has given birth to a new field of law: transnational criminal law. The main function of transnational criminal law is to harmonize domestic criminal law. The transnationalization of criminal law has only been recognized in more recent times.[33] At the time when Neil Boister, in a path-breaking article published in 2003, established the term 'transnational criminal law', the underlying criminological concept of 'transnational crime' had already been in use for a while.[34] Indeed, the concept of transnational crime was used as early as the 1975 Fifth UN Congress on the Prevention of Crime and Treatment of Offenders, defining transnational crime—in contrast to international crime—as '"ordinary crimes" which are defined by national codes, but which involve (in terms of either the offender or the victim) nationals of different countries, or situations in which the crime takes place over several States'.[35] As Boister writes, this understanding of the concept of transnational crime later found its expression in the UN Convention against Transnational Organized Crime (UNTOC).[36] The debate on transnational criminal law currently focuses on questions of transnational standard-setting, predominantly concerning the role of human rights, such as the *ne bis in idem* principle.[37]

A final framing for transnational security problems is that of 'risk'.[38] In the past decade, the 'risk'-framing of security threats has received a lot of scholarly attention from

[33] See Neil Boister, 'Transnational Criminal Law?' (2003) 14 EJIL 953; Sadiq Reza, 'Transnational Criminal Law and Procedure: An Introduction' (2006) 56 Journal of Legal Education 430; David Luban et al, *International and Transnational Criminal Law* (2nd edn, Wolters Kluwer 2014); Valsamis Mitsilegas et al (eds), *Globalisation, Criminal Law and Criminal Justice: Theoretical, Comparative and Transnational Perspectives* (Hart Publishing 2015). For a useful overview on the problems see Sabine Gless/John A E Vervaele, 'Law Should Govern: Aspiring General Principles for Transnational Criminal Justice' (2013) 9 Utrecht Law Review 1.

[34] Boister (n 33) 953–4. Prior to Boister's article, a collection of essays had been published by Albin Eser/Otto Lagodny (eds), *Principles and Procedures for a New Transnational Criminal Law* (Max-Planck-Institut für Ausländisches und Internationales Strafrecht 1992).

[35] Fifth United Nations Congress on the Prevention of Crime and the Treatment of Offenders, 'Changes in Forms and Dimensions of Criminality—Transnational and National: Working Paper Prepared by the Secretariat' (1975) UN Doc A/Conf./56/3, para 118.

[36] Neil Boister, 'Further Reflections on the Concept of Transnational Criminal Law' (2015) 6 Transnational Legal Theory 9, 12. According to the United Nations Convention against Transnational Organized Crime 2225 UNTS 209 art 3, its provision on the scope of application, the Convention applies to a range of offences which are 'transnational in nature', including any offence that is 'committed in more than one State;...committed in one State but a substantial part of its preparation, planning, direction or control takes place in another State;...committed in one State but involves an organised criminal group that engages in criminal activities in more than one State; or...committed in one State but has substantial effects in another State'.

[37] See Gless/Vervaele (n 33) 8–9.

[38] For a useful overview of the concept of risk in a legal context, Jonathan R Nash, 'Law and Risk' in James Wright (ed), *International Encyclopedia of the Social & Behavioral Sciences* (2nd edn, Elsevier 2015). For other accessible conceptual studies, David Garland, 'The Rise of Risk' in Richard V Ericson/Aaron Doyle (eds), *Risk and Morality* (Toronto UP 2003) and Bruce Newsome, *A Practical Introduction to Security and Risk Management* (Sage 2014).

various disciplines.[39] Generally, risks result from situations, as Jonathan Nask writes, 'when there are multiple outcomes to which one might be subject. No single outcome will occur with certainty. Rather, each outcome... will arise with a certain probability.'[40] In a formal definition, 'risk', then, pertains to the 'probability of a particular event (or hazard) occurring and the consequent severity of the impact of that event'.[41] In other words, when there is a 'risk', we do not know for sure that the prospective event will materialize but we can state a probability of that event happening and we can assess the potential impact of that event. Thus, in contrast to 'crime'-framing, which is primarily retrospective and repressive in focus, the focus of 'risk'-framing lies on prospective and proactive action.

The legal contexts in which the 'risk'-framing of threats is adopted by securitizers have multiplied.[42] Other than in the case of 'war' or 'crime', given its ubiquitous presence, it seems impossible to name a specific legal field that is primarily responsible for generating background assumptions regarding the legal treatment of 'risks'.[43] For example, in domestic and EU law, framing threats as 'risks' has become common in areas as diverse as criminal law,[44] disaster law,[45] consumer protection law,[46] and even constitutional law.[47] Also in many fields of international law the turn to the 'risk'-framing is evident, such as in international environmental law, global health law, and in international investment law, to name a few.[48] In the international law context of disaster

[39] For a seminal overview see the articles assembled in Sabine Roeser et al (eds), *Handbook of Risk Theory: Epistemology, Decision Theory, Ethics, and Social Implications of Risk* (Springer 2012). Broadly speaking, the multi-dimensional phenomenon of 'risk' can be approached from several perspectives: a technical perspective, an economic perspective, a psychological perspective, a cultural perspective, and a legal or regulatory perspective; see Robert Baldwin et al, *Understanding Regulation: Theory, Strategy, and Practice* (2nd edn, OUP 2012) 88–93. For an early, seminal treatment of risks and the law see Stephen Breyer, *Breaking the Vicious Circle: Toward Effective Risk Regulation* (Harvard UP 1993).

[40] Nash (n 38) 504 (also on the difference between risk and uncertainty which lies in the quantifiability of the probability of outcomes).

[41] Baldwin et al (n 39) 83.

[42] The following survey of fields of reference is based on Tilmann Altwicker, 'Transnationale Gewährleistung Ziviler Sicherheit—Europäische und internationale Rahmenbedingungen' in Christoph Gusy et al (eds), *Rechtshandbuch Zivile Sicherheit* (Springer 2017) 150–6.

[43] For a collection of articles on legal securitization using a risk-framing approach in the context of EU law see Hans-Wolfgang Micklitz/Takis Tridimas (eds), *Risk and EU Law* (Edward Elgar 2015).

[44] Andrew Ashworth/Lucia Zedner, *Preventive Justice* (OUP 2014).

[45] Alexander Thiele, 'Zivile Sicherheit im Katastrophenrecht' in Gusy et al (n 42) 539–62.

[46] Tanja Ehnert, 'The Legitimacy of New Risk Governance—A Critical View in Light of the EU's Approach to Nanotechnologies in Food' (2015) 21 ELJ 44.

[47] For an early statement on the constitutional law discourse concerning risks, Dieter Grimm, *Die Zukunft der Verfassung* (Suhrkamp 1991) 197–220. Grimm already emphasized that the modern idea of prevention not only relates to 'technological security' (eg, nuclear power plants), but also to 'personal security'. In a far-sighted passage, Grimm states that the shift to risks is accompanied by the need to widen the instruments of public authority: Because 'personal security' does not deal with 'clear and present danger', means of coercion of individuals are not suitable any more, but must be complemented by information-gathering (ibid 207). For the constitutional law implications of 'risk'-framing see also Adrian Vermeule, *The Constitution of Risk* (CUP 2013).

[48] See the useful collection of articles in Monika Ambrus et al (eds), *Risk and the Regulation of Uncertainty in International Law* (OUP 2017).

prevention, the 1993 International Labour Organization (ILO) Prevention of Major Industrial Accidents Convention already speaks of 'risk management', 'emergency planning' and 'assessments of hazards' and thus applies 'risk'-framing.[49] Further, the 'Sendai Framework for Disaster Risk Reduction' utilizes 'risk'-framing.[50] Tellingly, the UN Secretary-General stated that this Framework shifts the focus from actual 'disaster management' to prospective 'risk management'.[51] It should be noted, however, that these instruments are international soft law and, thus, not formally binding.[52] Importantly, the 'risk'-framing also underlies a multiplicity of international counter-terrorism efforts, such as the Financial Action Task Force (FATF) Recommendations on Counter-Terrorist Financing and some provisions in the Terrorism Financing Convention.[53] 'Risk'-framing is also inherent in the system of individual targeted sanctions by the UNSC. The turn to individualized or 'targeted' sanctions commenced with the travel ban and financial restrictions taken against the National Union for the Total Independence of Angola (UNITA) in 1997 and 1998.[54] Presently, the sanctions regime on Al-Qaeda and ISIL/Da'esh is the singular example for the use of targeted sanctions in the fight against terrorism.[55]

The use of 'risk'-framing for cross-border security problems has given rise to two innovative legal fields: transnational public security law (TPSL) and, albeit still in its infancy, transnational civil security law (TCSL). International law plays a role in both of these fields, but, as already indicated, both are emerging as distinct legal fields. The first field, TPSL, refers to a distinct set of legal norms dealing with problems of cross-border

[49] Convention (No 174) Prevention of Major Industrial Accidents Convention 1967 UNTS 231.

[50] UNGA Res 69/283 (23 June 2015).

[51] UNGA 'Report of the Secretary-General: Implementation of the International Strategy for Disaster Reduction' (4 August 2015) UN Doc A/70/282, para 15.

[52] Altwicker (n 42) 151–3 (for more examples, also from EU law).

[53] FATF, 'Recommendations: International Standards on Combating Money Laundering and the Financing of Terrorism & Proliferation' (FATF 20112–2019); International Convention for the Suppression of the Financing of Terrorism 2178 UNTS 197 art 18 (requiring financial intermediaries to perform due diligence checks on their customers and transactions in order to minimize the risk of terrorism financing).

[54] UNSC Res 1127 (1997) para 4; UNSC Res 1173 (1998) para 11; UNSC Res 1176 (1998) para 2. Andrea Bianchi, 'Assessing the Effectiveness of the UN Security Council's Anti-Terrorism Measures: The Quest for Legitimacy and Cohesion' (2006) 17 EJIL 881.

[55] The sanctions regime was established in 1999 by UNSC Res 1267 (1999) (and has been amended since then). In December 2019, 261 individuals and eighty-four entities associated with ISIL/Da'esh and Al-Qaeda were listed on the sanctions list ('black list'), see UNSC 'Report of the Security Council Committee pursuant to resolutions 1267 (1999), 1989 (2011) and 2253 (2015) concerning Islamic State in Iraq and the Levant (Da'esh), Al-Qaida and associated individuals, groups, undertakings and entities' (20 December 2019) UN Doc S/2019/980. Individuals and non-State entities are added to the 'black list' by the sanctions committee, a subsidiary organ to the UNSC. Targeted sanctions typically comprise three measures: asset freeze, travel ban, and arms embargo, see Michael Bothe, 'Security Council's Targeted Sanctions against Presumed Terrorists: The Need to Comply with Human Rights Standards' (2008) 6 JICJ 541, 544–7, UNSC Res 1267 (1999); UNSC Res 1333 (2000) paras 5 and 6.

public security.[56] However, norms belonging to TPSL do not form a separate legal order or—much less—a system of legal norms. This is excluded because these norms originate from different legal sources. Norms in the domain of TPSL are created both on the State level (such as domestic criminal law norms prohibiting the provision of material support to a foreign terrorist organization) and on the supra-State level (for example international norms requiring the establishment of a system of customer due diligence as a tool to counter-terrorism financing).[57] What binds TPSL norms together is not their formal origin but commonalities in a more substantive sense: TPSL norms share the same subject matter (public security), the same scope of application (cross-border contexts), and their underlying regulatory mode (regulatory nature and authoritativeness).[58] Transnational Public Security Law norms are, furthermore, established by regional expert networks such as the FATF, which sets transnational standards for combating money laundering and terrorist financing.[59] Finally, non-State actors are increasingly involved in transnational standard-setting on issues of security. As early as 2003 there was, for instance, a self-regulation initiative by the Basel Committee on Banking Supervision, the International Association of Insurance Supervisors and the International Organization of Securities Commissions to combat money laundering and the financing of terrorism.[60] Furthermore, standard-setting by self-regulation or codes of conduct is emerging in the field of private military and security companies (PMSC) which are becoming increasingly engaged in the provision of transnational security.[61] For example, an initiative by Switzerland resulted in an International Code of Conduct (ICoC) for Private Security Service Providers to which, by 2013, 708 globally operating companies had committed themselves.[62]

The second emerging field, TCSL, presently, is only in its infancy. Transnational Civil Security Law is more comprehensive than TPSL. It encompasses all cross-border non-military risks, threats, and vulnerabilities, including environmental hazards, energy

[56] 'Public security'—in transnational contexts—refers to the management of man-made risks attributable to the conduct of non-State actors threatening the existence and functioning of public authority institutions, essential public services, survival of the population, risks of a serious disturbance to foreign relations or to peaceful coexistence of nations, risks to military interests, and the calm and physical security of the population as a whole or a large part of it, Altwicker (n 5) 26.

[57] Anne-Marie Slaughter/Jose E Alvarez, 'A Liberal Theory of International Law' (2000) 94 ASIL Proc 240, 245.

[58] TPSL norms are abstract-general norms shaping the obligations of individuals (regulatory nature). Further, TPSL norms are distinct by their authoritativeness, relating to the regulatory depth (the degree to which they constrain domestic policy choices), their potential to given direct effect in domestic legal orders, and the extent to which their implementation is subjected to international supervision. See, in detail, Tilmann Altwicker, 'Explaining the Emergence of Transnational Counter-Terrorism Legislation in International Law-Making' (2018) 24 Finnish Yearbook of International Law 3, 12–27.

[59] See <www.fatf-gafi.org/about/> accessed 14 May 2020.

[60] BIS, 'Initiatives by the BCBS, IAIS and IOSCO to combat money laundering and the financing of terrorism' (12 June 2003) <https://www.bis.org/publ/joint05.htm> accessed 14 May 2020.

[61] Erika Calazans, *Private Military and Security Companies: The Implications Under International Law of Doing Business in War* (Cambridge Scholars Publishing 2016) 112–19.

[62] See <https://icoca.ch/about/> accessed 14 November 2020 (I am grateful to Anne Peters for drawing my attention to these developments).

security, nutrition and food security, as well as health security.[63] While international and European legal documents still firmly assign the core responsibility to guarantee 'civil security' to nation States, there are attempts to create international best practice models, obligations to inform, consult or report on transnational civil security risks, and an increasing transnational harmonization of domestic regulation in the field of civil security.[64]

C. Recent Developments and Contemporary Challenges

The major cross-cutting and contemporary international law-related challenges in the field of transnational security are: jurisdiction under international law (and, consequently, unilateralization, internationalization, and privatization of transnational security), and the applicability of IHRL in contexts of transnational security.

The first, central challenge relates to jurisdiction. In general, a large number of legal problems surrounding transnational law are, at their core, problems of jurisdiction.[65] There is a tension between the territoriality of jurisdiction, entrenched in international law, and the de-territorialization of risks to public and civil security. In particular, the de-territorialization of security risks leads to conflicts with territorial jurisdiction when States are unwilling or unable to use their authority to identify and address cross-border security problems originating from, or located in, their territory. Other States, which consider themselves affected by a risk or threat originating abroad, are prohibited by international law from interfering with foreign territorial space in order to address the security problem. In particular, public authority actions outside a State's own territory are prohibited by the principle of territorial integrity, contained in Article 2(4) of the UN Charter and contained in various soft law documents.[66] The principle demands that all States must respect the territorial boundaries of other States and refrain from entering

[63] For more details, Altwicker (n 42) 137–60.

[64] Altwicker (n 42) 157–9. For the field of disaster relief see Sandesh Sivakumaran, 'Techniques in International Law-Making: Extrapolation, Analogy, Form and the Emergence of an International Law of Disaster Relief' (2017) 28 EJIL 1097 (arguing that a 'holistic body of international law relating to disaster relief' is emerging).

[65] eg in relation to cybersecurity—which is arguably the most 'transnational' of all cross-border security problems—some consider jurisdiction to be the greatest issue. See Stefanie Schmahl, 'Zwischenstaatliche Kompetenzabgrenzung im Cyberspace' (2009) 47 Archiv des Völkerrechts 284; Thomas Schultz, 'Carving up the Internet: Jurisdiction, Legal Orders, and the Private/Public International Law Interface' (2008) 19 EJIL 799.

[66] In particular, Declaration on Principles of International Law Concerning Friendly Relations and Co-operation among States in Accordance with the Charter of the United Nations, UNGA Res 2625 (XXV) (24 October 1970). On the principle of territorial integrity see Jost Delbrück/Rüdiger Wolfrum, *Völkerrecht* (vol 1/3, 2nd edn, De Gruyter 2002) 791. For details see Abdelhamid El Ouali, *Territorial Integrity in a Globalizing World: International Law and States' Quest for Survival* (Springer 2012).

the other's territory, airspace, or waters without the consent of the territorial State.[67] Traditionally, the jurisdictional challenge arising from the tension between the de-territorialization of public security risks and the territoriality of jurisdiction has been addressed in the form of inter-State problem-solving, namely by international law obligations requiring States to exercise (territorial) jurisdiction, mutual legal assistance, and extradition, as well as informal cooperation. These solutions are 'traditional' because they remain within the boundaries of inter-State cooperation.

The limitations of the traditional approach to jurisdiction have triggered three (partially complementary, partially contradictory) developments or shifts: unilateralization, internationalization, and privatization of transnational security. The solution of establishing an international legal framework requiring States to exercise their jurisdiction fails if States are unwilling or unable to exercise their (territorial) jurisdiction. This has propelled unilateral acts by certain States invoking the right to self-defence (such as in the case of extraterritorial targeted killings).[68] Other examples are enhanced (unilateral) transnational surveillance and cross-border data access.[69]

A further response to the problem of jurisdiction can broadly be described as 'internationalization of transnational security'. This means that cross-border security problems are increasingly brought within the purview of international (and regional) organizations, whose acts sometimes complement, sometimes supersede the unilateral efforts of States. Especially in the field of public security, there has been an increase in transnational security actors and interaction due to Europeanization (such as the EU Rule of Law Mission (EULEX) in Kosovo) and internationalization (including the UN Stabilisation Mission in the Congo (MONUSCO), targeted sanctions against individuals or groups engaged in terrorism, and quasi-legislative counter-terrorism resolutions by the UNSC). For example, the 2014 'Operation Onymous', the largest dark-web takedown so far, involved the cooperation of law enforcement personnel from seventeen countries and several regional and international organizations.[70] An important subphenomenon is increased bilateral police cooperation (such as cooperation on the basis of bilateral police treaties).[71] The problem of jurisdiction does not only concern the jurisdiction to enforce: UNSC quasi-legislation in the field of counter-terrorism has been justified by pointing to the fact that States had been reluctant or too slow in ratifying the necessary international legal instruments.[72]

[67] Delbrück/Wolfrum (n 66) 792. [68] Brunnée/Toope (n 26).

[69] Marko Milanovic, 'Human Rights Treaties and Foreign Surveillance: Privacy in the Digital Age' (2015) 56 Harvard International Law Journal 81. On cross-border data access see *United States v Microsoft Corp.*, 138 S.Ct. 1186 (controversy mooted by passage of the CLOUD Act).

[70] Tom Fox-Brewster, 'Silk Road 2.0 Targeted in "Operation Onymous" Dark-web Takedown' (*The Guardian*, 7 November 2014) <https://www.theguardian.com/technology/2014/nov/07/silk-road-20-operation-onymous-dark-web-drugs-takedown> accessed 14 May 2020.

[71] Hans-Joachim Cremer, 'Der grenzüberschreitende Einsatz von Polizeibeamten nach dem deutsch-schweizerischen Polizeivertrag: ein Vorbild für die Kooperation der Mitgliedstaaten der Europäischen Union auf dem Gebiet der Verbrechensbekämpfung' (2000) 60 ZaöRV 103.

[72] Altwicker (n 58) 43.

Finally, jurisdictional dysfunctionalities under international law have also inspired a recent move towards the privatization of transnational security. While the privatization of security tasks is predominantly taking place in the domestic sphere, it is not limited to it. Private security companies increasingly act transnationally (such as Academi in Iraq). Another example of the increased interaction between the different actors engaged in cross-border action relates to cases in which State law enforcement collaborates with foreign private Internet service providers to collect personal data from one of its users, adding a new layer of complexity to transnational security. The need to better cooperate with non-State actors is especially acute regarding cybersecurity. Significant problems arise regarding matters of cybersecurity due to the volatility of data.[73] While a recent UN Study on Cybercrime stated that the 'vast majority of cases fall within either the territorial or nationality principle', the greatest jurisdictional challenge arises from the problem of unknown, fragmented, or changing data locations.[74] In times of cloud computing and linked data, the Internet has become a global information space.[75] A significant problem with the traditional approach, which relies on inter-State cooperation (such as mutual assistance) is its formalized, time-consuming procedure. This is why some States are pushing hard for more efficient direct transnational access to data stored by non-State actors.[76]

A second major challenge concerns the application of international human rights in transnational security cases.[77] International human rights law, as it is traditionally conceived, is largely 'State-centred law'.[78] This 'State-centredness' is an obstacle in the context of transnational security. International human rights law paradigmatically concerns the bipolar normative relationship between a (non-State) rights-holder and the State as a duty-bearer. Private transnational actors are generally not considered as directly bound by IHRL (although there have been several attempts to extend the range of duty-bearers in the recent past).[79] Similarly, international organizations, although they can be bound by international human rights, are commonly not parties to international human rights treaties.[80] The lack of transnationalization of IHRL sometimes results in problematic

[73] For a good overview see Susan W Brenner/Bert-Jaap Koops, 'Approaches to Cybercrime Jurisdiction' (2004) 4 Journal of High Technology Law 3; Jonathan Clough, *Principles of Cybercrime* (2nd edn, CUP 2015) 475.

[74] UNODC, Draft Comprehensive Study on Cybercrime (UN, 2013) 196.

[75] Tom Heath/Christian Bizer, 'Linked Data: Evolving the Web into a Global Data Space' in James Hendler/Frank van Harmelen (eds), *Synthesis Lectures on the Semantic Web: Theory and Technology* (Morgan and Claypool Publishers 2011).

[76] On transnational direct access to personal data, see Tilmann Altwicker, 'Transnationale Direktanfragen im Kontext des Übereinkommens über Cyberkriminalität des Europarats' in Dieter Kugelmann (ed), *Migration, Datenübermittlung und Cybersicherheit* (Nomos 2016).

[77] Passage adopted from Tilmann Altwicker, 'Transnationalizing Rights: International Human Rights Law in Cross-Border Contexts' (2018) 29 EJIL 581, 583.

[78] Manfred Nowak/Karolina M Januszewski, 'Non-State Actors and Human Rights' in Math Noortmann et al (eds), *Non-State Actors in International Law* (Hart Publishing 2015) 124.

[79] Andrew Clapham, 'Non-State Actors' in Daniel Moeckli et al (eds), *International Human Rights Law* (OUP 2014) 535–8.

[80] Guglielmo Verdirame, *The UN and Human Rights: Who Guards the Guardians?* (CUP 2011).

protection gaps (including the inability of IHRL to address instances of transboundary pollution as an IHRL issue).[81] In recent times, the literature has pointed to a shift away from this 'State-centredness' in some areas of IHRL, especially with regard to the types of duty-bearers in order to address this gap (for instance by discussing the possibility of human rights obligations for transnational corporations and international organizations).[82]

D. Conclusion

What is the contribution of international law with regard to the transnationalization of security? The central argument defended above was that international law serves the role of both facilitator of, and constraint on, the processes of transnationalization of security. In some cases, an extensive interpretation of international law has enabled new approaches to transnational security. For example, the field of counter-terrorism has given rise to new forms of international lawmaking and inter-State cooperation. Other fields of transnational security, such as the international disaster relief law and the international environmental security law, have recently witnessed sustained international lawmaking efforts. However, international law has unilateral domestic law with transnational effect as its natural competitor in the regulation of transnational security. Thus, in some cases, international law has failed to serve as an effective legal framework to guide and constrain States' security ambitions. For example, in the context of cross-border surveillance, States have, until recently, been reluctant to submit their activities to an international legal regime.

International law also serves as a constraint to processes of transnationalization of security. Most importantly, the fundamental principles of the international legal order, such as the principles of territorial integrity and sovereignty, set a high argumentative threshold to transnationalization efforts in the field of security. Efforts by some States to dilute the constraining effect of these legal principles, most visibly by advocating a more permissive 'unwilling or unable' standard with respect to the right to self-defence against non-State actors, have so far proven to be unsuccessful. Problematically, however, IHRL has so far been unable to exercise its full potential as a constraint to transnationalization efforts in the field of security, mainly because IHRL is still largely State-centred. There are, however, cautious signals that some international actors are willing to give IHRL a transnational interpretation (for example by including direct

[81] For an argument that direct cross-border environmental harm should give rise to human rights claims see Alan Boyle, 'Human Rights and the Environment: Where Next?' (2012) 23 EJIL 613, 640.

[82] Wouter Vandenhole/Willem van Genugten, 'Introduction: An Emerging Multi-Duty-Bearer Human Rights Regime?' in Wouter Vandenhole (ed), *Challenging Territoriality in Human Rights Law: Building Blocks for a Plural and Diverse Duty-Bearer Regime* (Routledge 2015) 2 (for an overview on the literature). See also Lee McConnell, *Extracting Accountability from Non-State Actors in International Law: Assessing the Scope for Direct Regulation* (Routledge 2016).

references to European fundamental rights law in international agreements between the US and the EU).[83]

The continued relevance of international law in processes of transnationalization of security depends on its problem-solving capacity concerning transnational security issues. In some cases, international power-conferring norms can be given a 'transnational interpretation', such as the right to self-defence under Article 51 UN Charter (which can be interpreted as allowing the use of force against war-like acts of non-State actors). In other cases new cross-border competences of security actors can be contemplated (such as in bilateral police treaties). However, successful transnationalization of security does not only depend on the further transnationalization of competences in the field of security, rather it also requires continued counterbalancing by IHRL for legitimacy reasons. The relevance of international law in the field of transnational security thus ultimately depends on its capacity to provide an effective, legitimacy-ensuring framework for the transnationalization of security. In other words, international law must provide a framework within which a reasonable balance between transnational security interests of States and the interests of non-State actors can be found.

Acknowledgement

I am grateful to Alexandra Hansen for excellent research assistance. I thank the Swiss National Science Foundation (SNSF) for generous funding.

[83] Altwicker (n 77).

CHAPTER 5

GENDERED SECURITY

GINA HEATHCOTE

A. Introduction

SINCE the adoption of UN Security Council (UNSC) Resolution 1325 there has been recognition within international institutions that there is a link between women, peace, and security. This chapter examines the links between women, peace, and security in the activities of international institutions, such as the UNSC, and well beyond institutional settings. I draw on a range of feminist approaches to mark a shift towards gender (rather than women) and security and a need for further expansion of the field to acknowledge plural feminist approaches. The latter is demonstrated through an incorporation of indigenous feminisms, an analysis of gendered security at sea, and the impact of the politics of austerity within Western democracies.

I follow Duncanson's definition of gender as functioning as an individual identity and a symbolic system, that requires attention to the embodied realities of gendered lives and the nexus to larger power relations.[1] Approaches to women, peace, and security articulate gender as an individual identity in the sense of responding to women as a named group that experiences discrimination and who can be identified by virtue of a commitment to the gender binary. Within feminist writing such an approach has limited value as it tends to write out women's diversity or any mode of gender fluid and gender diverse lives, while legal outcomes tend towards liberal feminist framings focused on rights and the individual, the production of quotas for participation and limited means to address heteronormativity.[2] Addressing gender as a symbolic system opens gender analysis to deployment in the analysis of systems and structures of meaning as well as institutions.[3] Duncanson's further incorporation of both the embodied

[1] Claire Duncanson, *Gender and Peacebuilding* (Polity 2016) 7.

[2] Ratna Kapur, *Erotic Justice: Law and the New Politics of Postcolonialism* (Routledge 2005); Gina Heathcote, 'Participation, Gender, Security' in Gina Heathcote/Dianne Otto (eds), *Rethinking Peacekeeping, Gender Equality and Collective Security* (Palgrave Macmillan 2014).

[3] Carol Cohn (ed), *Women and Wars: Contested Histories, Uncertain Futures* (Polity 2013).

modes through which gender is experienced and the relation of gender to other sites of power relations draws from the work of postcolonial and intersectional feminist thinking to challenge the production of gender as monolithic, stagnant, or disconnected from other sites of discrimination and harm. I use Duncanson's understanding of gender as a symbolic system, invested in the embodied experiences of gendered individuals and intimately connected to adjunct power discourses, to examine the existing regime on women, peace, and security and to analyse potential future framings of gendered security in this chapter.

1. Women, Peace, and Security

Security Council Resolution 1325 (2000) is a thematic UNSC resolution described as a 'landmark' in the work of the institution due to its recognition of the potential impact of engaging women in peace and security and the impact of security on women.[4] Prior to Resolution 1325, the Council had only made the link between women and security in Resolution 1214 on the situation in Afghanistan and the gender apartheid under Taliban rule in the late 1990s.[5] Security Council Resolution 1325 emerged after a speech to the Council from the representative for Bangladesh in March 2000. The Bangladesh representative's provocation in the Council led to the drafting of Resolution 1325 by key civil society actors, including Women's International League for Peace and Freedom (WILPF).[6] The subsequent text, notably leaving out WILPF's anti-militarist approach, incorporated four pillars: participation, protection, prevention, and relief and recovery. The resolution has been widely recognized as encompassing a broad vision of the relationship between women, peace, and security and, although subject to persistent critique from various feminist spaces, is credited with changing institutional, local, State, and academic practice.[7]

In the subsequent two decades, the UNSC has produced nine additional resolutions on women, peace, and security and developed provisions on related gender issues within some situation-specific resolutions, as well as adjunct resolutions on the regulation of sexual exploitation and abuse within UN missions.[8] Of those additional nine resolutions, five resolutions—1820 (2008), 1888 (2009), 1960 (2010), 2103 (2013), and 2467 (2019)—focus on conflict-related sexual violence while the remaining four resolutions—1889 (2009), 2122 (2013), 2242 (2015), 2493 (2019)—are closer to the template

[4] UNSC Res 1325 (2000); Dianne Otto, 'A Sign of "Weakness"? Disrupting Gender Certainties in the Implementation of Security Council Resolution 1325' (2006–07) 13 Michigan Journal of Gender and the Law 113.

[5] UNSC Res 1214 (1998).

[6] Felicity Ruby, 'Security Council 1325: A Tool for Conflict Resolution?' in Heathcote/Otto (n 2).

[7] Sara E Davies/Jacqui True, *The Oxford Handbook on Women, Peace, and Security* (OUP 2019).

[8] eg UNSC Res 2272 (2016) (on sexual exploitation and abuse in peacekeeping operations). For an example of a situation-specific resolution invoking the language of the women, peace, and security agenda: UNSC Res 2040 (2012) on Libya.

of the original Resolution 1325 on women, peace, and security, and articulate a general approach.[9] Critiques of the resolutions extend from concerns with regard to the over-emphasis on conflict-related sexual violence,[10] the use of the word 'gender' without sufficient recognition of the gendered nature of men's lives,[11] an investment in a heteronormative gender binary across the resolutions,[12] and a disciplining role for gender in the resolutions that produce 'civilizing' regulations that are imposed on post-conflict States. Civil society actors have questioned the manner in which donor funds have used the language of women, peace, and security such that local feminist needs and agendas have been displaced, as well as the failure of the resolutions to develop an intersectional understanding of the operation of gender in diverse communities.[13] For Madhok, there is a need to 'supplement intersectionality with coloniality'; that is, to see intersectionality as an important feminist analytic tool that should not be severed from the geographic and temporal making and reconstituting of empire.[14]

2. Addressing Everyday (In)security

The ten resolutions on women, peace, and security have, in many ways, come to dominate international discourse on gendered security. However, despite the wide-ranging nature of the resolutions, the development of the field has been piecemeal and in no way comprehensive in the sense of building robust governance mechanisms for the implementation of change in relation to gendered security. For example, Resolution 2242 includes, in paragraph 5, the requirement that the UNSC itself:

> *Recognizes* the ongoing need for greater integration of resolution 1325 (2000) in its own work in alignment with resolution 2122 (2013), including the need to address challenges linked to the provision of specific information and recommendations on the gender dimensions of situations on the Council's agenda, to inform and help strengthen the Council's decisions ...[15]

[9] UNSC Res 1820 (2008); UNSC Res 1888 (2009); UNSC Res 1889 (2009); UNSC Res 1960 (2010); UNSC Res 2106 (2013); UNSC Res 2122 (2013); UNSC Res 2242 (2015); UNSC Res 2467 (2019); UNSC Res 2493 (2019).

[10] Karen Engle, *The Grip of Sexual Violence in Conflict: Feminist Interventions in International Law* (Stanford UP, 2020).

[11] Chloé Lewis, 'Systematic Silencing: Addressing Sexual Violence against Men and Boys in Armed Conflict and Its Aftermath' in Heathcote/Otto (eds) (n 2) 203.

[12] Jamie Hagan, 'Queering Women, Peace and Security' (2016) 92 International Affairs 313.

[13] Sophie Richter-Devroe, '"Here it's not about Conflict Resolution—We can only resist": Palestinian Women's Activism in Conflict Resolution and Non-Violent Resistance' in Nadje Al-Ali/Nicola Pratt (eds), *Women and War in the Middle East* (ZED Books 2009).

[14] Sumi Madhok, 'Coloniality, Political Subjectivation and the Gendered Politics of Protest in a "State of Exception"' (2018) 119 Feminist Review 56.

[15] UNSC Res 2467 (2019) para 5.

A quick survey of resolutions immediately after 2242, namely Resolutions 2243 through to 2250, shows limited incorporation of the substance of this provision.[16] A reference to conflict-related sexual violence appears in the preamble of Resolution 2243, on the situation in Haiti. In the next three resolutions, Resolution 2244, Resolution 2245, and Resolution 2246, all on the situation in Somalia, no provisions relate to either women or gender. In Resolution 2247, on Bosnia and Herzegovina, there is no reference to women, peace, and security issues, nor in Resolution 2248, on the situation in Burundi or in Resolution 2249, on threats to international peace and security caused by terrorist acts (a response to the terrorist attacks in Paris, France in November 2015). The latter absence is notable, given the additional links made between the Council's counter-terrorism work and the women, peace, and security agenda in Resolution 2242.

It is only in Resolution 2250, a general resolution on the maintenance of international peace and security and with a thematic focus on youth participation and youth initiatives relevant to security, that there is reference to CEDAW (paragraph 5), women (paragraph 16, amongst a list of groups to be empowered) and conflict-related sexual and gender-based violence (paragraph 7). The latter reference is interesting because it is phrased as follows:

> *Calls* on all parties to armed conflict to take the necessary measures to protect civilians, including those who are youth, from all forms of sexual and gender-based violence.

This is a wider framing of the responsibility of States parties to armed conflict than the women, peace, and security resolutions articulate.[17] The use of the phrase 'take the necessary measures' does invoke the language usually deployed by the UNSC to frame authorizations of military force under Chapter VII of the UN Charter,[18] while the adjunct framing in the context of protecting civilians links to the shift within peacekeeping mandates to broaden the scope of missions through the language of the protection of civilians.[19] Furthermore, paragraph 7 of Resolution 2250, although invoking the protection of youth, does address all civilians and articulates a need for protection 'from *all*' forms of sexual and gender-based violence (emphasis added). This is a potentially wide framing of the women, peace, and security focus, which has increasingly narrowed to conflict-related sexual violence, while in Resolution 2250 is inclusive of all forms of sexual and gender-based violence. As such, the failure to incorporate the Council's directive in Resolution 2242 in the subsequent seven resolutions is then, confusingly,

[16] UNSC Res 2244 (2015); UNSC Res 2245 (2015); UNSC Res 2246 (2015); UNSC Res 2247 (2015); UNSC Res 2248 (2015); UNSC Res 2249 (2015); UNSC Res 2250 (2015).

[17] Gina Heathcote 'Feminist Politics and the Use of Force: Theorising Feminist Action and Security Council Resolution 1325' (2011) 7 Socio-Legal Review 23.

[18] Gina Heathcote, *The Law on the Use of Force: A Feminist Analysis* (Routledge 2012); Gina Heathcote, 'Humanitarian Intervention and Gender Dynamics' in Fionnuala Ní Aoláin et al (eds), *Oxford Handbook on Gender and Conflict* (OUP 2018).

[19] Gina Heathcote, 'Women and Children and Elephants as Justification for Force' (2017) 4 Journal on the Use of Force and International Law 66.

picked up in Resolution 2250, but in a manner ultimately inconsistent with the existing women, peace, and security resolutions because of the link to enforcement action and the potential expansion of the women, peace, and security framework embedded in this resolution.

This short analysis opens up a range of issues that are yet to be tackled or addressed sufficiently within the wider women, peace, and security agenda that I take up in the remainder of this chapter. First, the framing of 'all forms of sexual and gender-based violence' in Resolution 2250 is extremely wide. Resolution 2250 seems to be both inclusive of wider feminist analysis of how gendered security norms produce complex forms of insecurity for women within communities and yet exclusive in the tying of gendered security to the production of direct forms of violence against specific gendered bodies. On the one hand, the very failure of the UNSC to address or include any aspects of women, peace, and security in the seven resolutions between Resolution 2242 and Resolution 2250 demonstrates a failure to abide by its own pronouncements in thematic resolutions, such as Resolution 2242. At the same time the framing of paragraph 7 in Resolution 2250 as directed at all parties to an armed conflict ignores the persistent feminist refrain that gendered security moves well beyond the need for militarized modes of security to articulate an understanding of everyday security to produce a transformation away from the status quo.[20]

3. Intersectional and Postcolonial Feminisms

To think differently about gender and about security in this chapter, I use the women, peace, and security resolutions to deploy Duncanson's model of gender as a symbolic system. Building on the analysis, above, of the schizophrenic outputs of the UNSC, which both attest to a series of commitments about its own development of gender initiatives in its thematic outputs and limited incorporation into situation-specific outputs, I use postcolonial feminisms to situate gendered security as constrained by the institutional frames it is produced within and through. This forms Section B of the chapter. In Section C, I return to the notion of everyday (in)security to look outside the expected frames of gender security. First, through an analysis of the nexus between sites of knowledge, environmental security, and legacies of colonialism, followed by a framing of security at sea as an additional site where security is imagined in extremely narrow terms to illustrate the necessity of developing intersectional feminist tools within security scholarship. I then examine how gendered insecurity occurs within peacetime States through the twin effects of the policies of neo-liberal States on austerity and the rise of populism. The chapter concludes by asserting that the UNSC has been a limited place

[20] Cheryl Hendricks, 'Women, Peace and Security in Africa' (2015) 24 African Security Review 364; Fumni Olonisakin et al, 'The Convergence and Divergence of Three Pillars of Influence in Gender and Security' (2015) 24 African Security Review 376; Catherine O'Rourke, *Gender Politics in Transitional Justice* (Routledge 2013).

for challenging gendered (in)security, not only for its selective action but also through the nexus to militarized security that does little to dislodge forms of everyday gendered insecurity. As such, I assert a postcolonial and intersectional feminism that moves and shifts in new ways to imagine human and environmental security for the future.

B. UNSC Resolution 2467 and Beyond

In this section, I provide a gender analysis of UNSC Resolution 2467 (2019). This resolution was drafted by Germany, who held the presidency of the UNSC in April 2019 and took the role of penholder. The draft proved controversial with Russia, China, and the United States all objecting to elements of the resolution. This was in contrast to previous women, peace, and security resolutions that have tended to pass with unanimous support from States and, via the arria formula,[21] receive unqualified endorsement from a wide range of States. Resolution 2467 focuses on conflict-related sexual violence and although it still continued an agenda for supporting punitive measures—sanctions and prosecutions—the draft introduced a reproductive health response to this form of gender-based violence. The draft underwent considerable re-writing before it was agreed to by Member States. In particular, the US objected to and challenged the health provisions in the draft, while China and Russia urged for caution in widening the UNSC's remit beyond a narrow focus on conflict-related sexual violence in armed conflict and the framing of gender-based violence as potentially incurring sanctions. The interventions of Russia and China are interestingly in tension with earlier language, already endorsed by the Council in Resolution 2250 on youth and security. However, rather than situating my analysis within the text of the resolution itself, in this section I look beyond the resolution to the role of UN institutions in shaping gender law reforms within international law.

Work on sexual and gender-based crimes within international institutions does not sit only within the outputs of the UNSC. As such, a study of gendered security benefits from an analysis of how institutional norms evolve and the different arenas where legal reform has been pursued. Chinkin and Rees describe Resolution 2467 as having enhanced legal value in part because of the cross-institutional parallels between UNSC, International Criminal Court (ICC), and the Committee on the Elimination of

[21] The 'Arria-formula meetings' are 'very informal, confidential gatherings which enable Security Council members to have a frank and private exchange of views, within a flexible procedural framework' and 'provide interested Council members an opportunity to engage in a direct dialogue with high representatives of Governments and international organizations—often at the latter's request—as well as non-State parties, on matters with which they are concerned and which fall within the purview of responsibility of the Security Council': UNSC, 'Working Methods Handbook' <https://www.un.org/securitycouncil/content/background-note> accessed 10 January 2020.

Discrimination against Women (CEDAW) outputs.[22] Similarly, O'Rourke argues that it is through the cross-institutional development of norms and practices that gender law reform has become an entrenched element of the international legal system with a robust structure for checks and balances across the various institutions.[23] In this section, I question what role this continually expansive area of work plays in the eradication of gendered (in)security. In particular, I am interested in the convergence of carceral and punitive feminist agendas that appear to be the constant across international institutions.[24] Importantly, a carceral and punitive set of gender law reforms, whether focused on sanctions against States or prosecution of individuals, remains within the format of the institutions it emerges from. As such, attempts to address the gender symbols and structures within those institutions remain unlikely as the punitive legal model dictates not only crisis thinking but a commitment to identifying perpetrators and rogue States rather than forging a model for working in concert.

The CEDAW General Recommendation No 35, on violence against women, provides an interesting example of this cross-institutional development. While wider in scope and drawing on a specific commitment to an intersectional understanding of gender-based harms, the recommendation flags armed conflict as a type of special circumstance that might compound violence against women, referencing General Recommendation No 30 on women in conflict prevention, conflict, and post-conflict situations. Paragraph 42 of Recommendation 35 identifies 'high rates of criminality and pervasive impunity, which may increase in situations of armed conflict or heightened insecurity'.[25] As such, although conflict-related sexual violence only appears in the footnote text of the recommendation, the reference here to crime and impunity implicitly invokes international criminal law where the focus of gender strategies has predominantly developed in relation to sexual violence. From a symbolic perspective, what is invoked and understood across these institutional outputs is gender-based violence and violence against women as channelled through the issue of sexual violence and regulated through a crime control model.

While paragraph 5 of Resolution 2242 calls for greater cross-resolution incorporation of the women, peace, and security framework, and the analysis, above, shows the limited ways in which this has been rolled out, the key space where convergence across institutional activities does emerge remains sexual violence. The commitment of the UNSC, the CEDAW Committee and the International Criminal Court to develop the law on sexual violence, in particular conflict-related sexual violence, therefore requires further

[22] Christine Chinkin/Madeleine Rees, 'Commentary on Security Council Resolution 2467: Continued State Obligation and Civil Society Action on Sexual Violence in Conflict' (July 2019) LSE WPS Working Paper Series <http://www.lse.ac.uk/women-peace-security/assets/documents/2019/reports/WPS-Commentary-Report-online.pdf> accessed 10 January 2020.

[23] Catherine O'Rourke, 'Feminist Strategy in International Law: Understanding its Legal, Normative and Political Dimensions' (2018) 28 EJIL 1019, 1021.

[24] Karen Engle, 'Feminist Governance and International Law: From Liberal to Carceral Feminisms' in Janet Halley et al (eds), *Governance Feminisms: Notes from the Field* (University of Minnesota Press 2019).

[25] CEDAW, 'General Recommendation No 35 on Gender-Based Violence Against Women, updating "General Recommendation No 19"' (14 July 2017) UN Doc CEDAW/C/GC/35, para 42.

scrutiny. A commitment to disrupting gendered (in)security would be specifically concerned with the symbolic elements of these agendas, the way power is configured and how different women's security is imagined via these legal developments.

Thinking through the way gender is deployed in UNSC Resolution 2467, in conjunction with larger gender law reform, articulates the ongoing imagining of a vulnerable, sexualized female victim and her specific insecurity in conflict and post-conflict situations. While the same institutions build spaces of agency through notions of gender expertise, for elite women in global forums and networks, a two-tiered representation of gender is built into security discourse. The *prompt* for action is continually configured as a vulnerable woman in economically weak States and those States suffering the impact of armed conflict on their territories. The *space* for action is imagined as occurring within the institution where the inclusion and expansion of gender advisers and gender experts becomes the solution. The two-tiered model ignores the insecurity of women in the global North and outside of conflict zones while exacerbating forms of victim feminism that are more often imposed and directed towards women in the global south. The CEDAW recommendations attempt, at some level, to disrupt such a thin account of feminist praxis, through the wider focus on violence against women and its larger remit outside of conflict zones, an element of which is the cross-referencing of human rights in the preamble of women, peace, and security resolutions since 2013. However, this post-2013 trend towards incorporating specific links between human rights and the women, peace, and security agenda does more to narrow the former than broaden the latter. Ultimately, a postcolonial feminist analysis of the carceral mode, the global inequalities, and the use of gender as a civilizing tool warrant a feminist agenda that looks beyond existing legal tools.

C. Contemporary Developments

> *'One way forward is to refocus international law on issues of structural justice that underpin everyday life.'*[26]

If the institutions of international law are replete with a narrow understanding of gender security, this section inquires as to the potential avenues for a transformative agenda. I introduce three mechanisms for reframing the international institutional approach to gendered (in)security that builds on 'footholds' already carved into existing law while attempting to actively think beyond the crisis politics of the UNSC.[27] I explore the possibility of feminist and security scholarly commitment to new frames of knowledge that embed and embrace postcolonial feminist accounts and an intersectionality methodology

[26] Hilary Charlesworth, 'International Law: A Discipline of Crisis' (2002) 65 Modern Law Review 377.

[27] Dianne Otto, 'The Exile of Inclusion: Reflections on Gender Issues in International Law over the Last Decade' (2009) 10 Melbourne Journal of International Law 11.

beyond that currently framed in the CEDAW recommendations.[28] The three mechanisms are short provocations into an existing system of gendered security that ignores indigenous voices, the complexity of security outside of traditional land-based armed conflict, and the impact of economic policy on the production of gendered insecurity in peacetime States. I have described the section as 'contemporary developments' as, although looking outside existing provisions on women, peace, and security, I draw on contemporary feminist writing from a whole host of settings that offer alternatives to the status quo—outside of the existing institutional apparatus.

1. Indigenous Security

'you stand for power, white people, but we stand for our land and the sea'[29]

There are many different indigenous knowledge traditions. As a preliminary provocation, I discuss the knowledge traditions of Aboriginal and Torres Strait Islanders in Australia in this section to sample and evidence the types of strategies that allow alternative praxis with regard to gendered security. My argument is not that Aboriginal and Torres Strait Islander peoples hold the (magic) key to a reimagined security, rather that analysis of tradition knowledge can help expose the poverty of existing institutional structures and thus provide a frame for addressing the complexity of insecurity in diverse places.

Aboriginal and Torres Strait Islander peoples understand law as implicated in their larger knowledge structures that incorporate a relation to land, kin, and ancestors.[30] As such, the security of individuals is connected to the security of the community, the land, and the continuation of traditions that connect to storytelling and remembering. Across the Australian continent, Aboriginal lore varies amongst the many different groups (nations) that lived on the territory prior to the arrival of the British colony. The creation of the Australian State after colonization and the designation of the land as *terra nullius* rely on a number of myths to ensure the perception of the territory and property that currently dominates Australian governance structures. Within the origin myths of women, peace, and security, gendered security is imagined as something that is ensured through law and thus largely constitutes part of an agenda for Australian peacekeeping and military missions abroad, in the sense of being a deliverable that accompanies Australian actors overseas rather than an issue of internal concern to the State. Settler colonies, like Australia, thus continue the project of imposing and delivering security elsewhere while denying the insecurity of first nations communities on their own lands

[28] Megan Campbell, 'CEDAW and Women's Intersecting Identities: A Pioneering Approach to Intersectional Identities' (2015) 11 Revista Direito GV 479; Lola Okolosie, 'Beyond "Talking" and "Owning" Intersectionality' (2014) 108 Feminist Review 90.

[29] Court transcript, *Gumana v Northern Territory of Australia and Others* [2005] FCA 50 cited in Frances Morphy, 'The Language of Governance in a Cross-Cultural Context: What Can and Can't Be Translated' (2007) 1 Ngiya: Talk the Law 93, 96.

[30] Irene Watson, *Aboriginal Peoples, Colonialism and International Law: Raw Law* (Routledge 2015).

and the role of the legal system in consolidating and entrenching insecurity.[31] For indigenous feminisms, this requires a linking of land, community, health, spiritual, and environmental (in)security to the existence of the nation State which denies Aboriginal and Torres Strait Islander knowledge as a form of governance.[32]

In addition, the women, peace, and security structure in the deployment of a narrow range of feminist approaches, largely liberal, radical, and cultural in their modes, limits the potential for an indigenous worldview, let alone multiple indigenous worldviews across first nations peoples, to be incorporated at the level of knowledge production and normative framings.[33] On the one hand, this is indicative of a larger challenge with regard to the assumptions about knowledge that construct international institutions, including the UNSC. Nevertheless, this should be of specific concern in the development of responses to gender and security because of the generally widespread feminist commitment to intersectionality.[34] This, by definition, asks for a response to gender and security that is plural in the modes of feminism offered as a solution to insecurity and thus inclusive of indigenous feminisms.

Key security concerns within Australian indigenous communities include the specific, deathly insecurity for Aboriginal and Torres Strait Islander women caused by high rates of domestic violence in remote Australian communities and high rates of incarceration for Aboriginal and Torres Strait Islander women across Australia.[35] Likewise, environmental insecurity across the continent is addressed by Aboriginal and Torres Strait Islander lore that both cultivates and cares for the environment in a responsible and sustainable manner. For example, while Aboriginal and Torres Strait Islander land management gained increased recognition during the horrific bushfires over the summer of 2019, indigenous practices of controlled (prescribed) burning have previously been identified as a means to reduce emissions while providing increased environmental and human security.[36] Aboriginal and Torres Strait Islander knowledge of country seems distant from the UNSC, and from the women, peace, and security agenda, in part because the knowledge sources this stems from are largely untranslatable in the context of an international institution that deploys military violence as the ultimate enforcement

[31] Chris Cuneen, 'Detention, Torture, Terror and The Australian State: Aboriginal People, Criminal Justice and Neocolonialism' in Greta Bird et al (eds), *Majah: Indigenous Peoples and the Law* (The Federation Press 1996).

[32] Aileen Moreton-Robinson (ed), *Sovereign Subjects: Indigenous Sovereignty Matters* (Allen & Unwin 2007).

[33] Catherine Powell, 'How Women Could Save the World if Only We Would Let Them: From Gender Essentialism to Inclusive Security' (2017) 28 Yale Journal of Law and Feminism 271.

[34] Nira Yuval-Davis, 'Human/Women's Rights and Feminist Transversal Politics' in Myra Marx Ferree/Aili Mari Tripp (eds), *Transnational Feminisms: Women's Global Activism and Human Rights* (NYUP 2006) 275.

[35] Mandy Wilson et al, 'Violence in the Lives of Incarcerated Mothers in Western Australia' (2017) 7 SAGE Open 1; Melissa Lucashenko, 'Violence Against Indigenous Women: Public and Private Dimensions' (1996) 2 Violence Against Women 378.

[36] Jeremy Russell-Smith et al, 'Managing Fire Regimes in North Australian Savanas: Applying Aboriginal Approaches to Contemporary Global Problems' (2013) 11(Online Issue 1) Frontiers in the Ecology and the Environment e55.

mechanism.[37] Similarly, contemporary feminist initiatives within global governance are not able to mobilize diverse sites of women's knowledge that might have a holistic understanding of gendered security: that is, integrated into a worldview that holds environmental security as a necessary element. Drawing on the transcript from the *Gumana* case, quoted above, this is a knowledge that stands 'for land and sea'.[38] However, even the conjoining of land and sea in security discourse has yet to occur, and certainly not land, sea, and gender as a way of thinking differently about when and where insecurity lies.[39]

2. Gendered Security at Sea

Picking up on the indigenous relation to both land and sea, a significant silence in women, peace, and security discourse is flagged—that is, analysis of security at sea through a gendered lens. Although naval forces are incorporated into standard security discourse and analysis, thus far there has been little, if any, analysis of how gendered security happens at sea. The oceans have always been an important component of inter-State defence and security, with the naval might of the Dutch and British embedded in the history of international law and colonialism.[40]

The obvious neglect of gendered insecurity at sea is apparent in contemporary women, peace, and security discourse. For example, human rights abuses at sea amongst fishing communities form a very specifically gendered mode of insecurity. These predominantly male communities have been identified as often operating under conditions of modern slavery, with the inaccessibility of vessels to enforcement bodies and the inaccessibility of land to victims, exacerbating the greed and violence that characterizes large numbers of seafaring communities. Poor mechanisms for the guarantee of labour rights further contribute to the conditions for the large numbers of victims of egregious human rights abuses at sea.[41] However, in the absence of direct State regulation of vessels, due to the inept model of registration, and any other form of effective regulation on the high seas, these are vast communities of predominantly men experiencing insecurity in a highly gendered exploitation of labour and via the desire for mobility through labour.

As a gendered security concern, modern slavery at sea raises important questions with respect to how security is understood (via States as victims) and responded to (via military means) and how distinctions between civilians and combatants is gendered, such that a large, global threat to male communities via gross violations of human rights is not perceived as a space of insecurity and not recognized as a specifically gendered form of insecurity. An intersectional feminist analysis might dislodge the fixation on

[37] Morphy (n 29). [38] *Gumana* case (n 29).

[39] Gina Heathcote, 'Feminism and the Law of the Sea: A Preliminary Inquiry' in Irini Papanicolopulu (ed), *Gender and the Law of the Sea* (Brill 2019).

[40] Norrie Macqueen, *Colonialism* (Routledge 2014) 9, 15.

[41] Ian Urbina, *The Outlaw Ocean: Journeys Across the Last Untamed Frontier* (Knopf Doubleday 2019).

women as the primary victims in the current women, peace, and security framework through a recognition of how intersectional privilege functions. Attention to the intersectional nature of privilege thus allows for recognition and response to how some men abuse and exploit other men and that the dominance of some men (and women) in international institutions is not indicative of a global male privilege but rather an intersectional male privilege.[42]

At a macro-level, in the post-millennium security environment, new spaces for collective security enforcement mechanisms, new threats, and provocations have emerged at sea. The violence and hostility of rogue actors off the Somali coast led to the authorization by the UNSC of the use of force in Somali territorial waters: a previously unprecedented form of collective security.[43] The coastal communities labelled as pirates include both male and female identifying actors, although the response to pirates as male actors remains prevalent.[44] Similarly, in other areas where security interests play out at sea, any gendered dimensions have remained suppressed by traditional approaches to security that ignore the existence of the women, peace, and security framework. This would include the UN Interim Force in Lebanon (UNIFIL) enforcement mission in Lebanon which requires a Maritime Task Force to police the territorial waters under a mandate that supports the Lebanese Navy in monitoring its territorial waters, securing the Lebanese coastline and preventing the unauthorized entry of arms or related materials by sea into Lebanon,[45] and the North Korean launching of missiles over Japan into the oceans, described as tests and with destinations in the high seas, which have been regarded by the US as hostile acts that subsequently escalated tensions between the two States. In the area of international law on collective security, the existing legal instruments for the most part only encompass the use of force on land and certainly no application of the women, peace, and security framework has been extended to the ocean. The gendered nature, and consequences, of the use of force on land have increasingly gained attention in the period subsequent to UNSC Resolution 1325 on women, peace, and security.[46] However, as yet no study of the application of the women, peace, and security resolutions to forces at sea has been undertaken, whether those forces be regular navies in peacetime, peacekeeping operations or enforcement missions, or actions against rogue actors at sea.

3. Gendered Security and Austerity Politics

In this third intervention, I look at an alternative perception of gendered security through a focus on austerity politics within peacetime States, in particular the UK.

[42] Heathcote (n 2). [43] UNSC 1846 (2008); UNSC 1851 (2008).

[44] Brittany Gilmer, 'Invisible Pirates: Women and the Gendered Roles of Somali Piracy' (2019) 4 Feminist Criminology 371.

[45] This was established under UNSC Res 1701 (2006). At the time of writing Brazil held the command role for the UNIFIL Maritime Task Force.

[46] Heathcote (n 18).

I argue that there is a need for responses to gender and security that look beyond the spaces of armed conflict to see how gendered insecurity emerges within repressive State agendas in a manner that frames and consolidates other forms of insecurity.

Since 2011, and arguably before, the UK conservative government has endorsed and constructed an economic agenda to implement a policy of austerity, in line with other Western liberal democracies in the early twenty-first century. A key concern of austerity agendas has been the retraction of baseline public services—including funding for health and education—as well as the imposition of increasingly restrictive policy to access State benefits, particularly for non-citizen residents within the State. The gendered consequences of this approach have been well documented and the impact on the delivery of key services to women, including responses to sexual and gender-based crimes, has meant the imposition of dangerous constraints on a previously robust civil society structure supplementing welfare, health, and education.[47] Scholars identify the nexus between the withdrawal of services and benefits to women as interlocking with the retraction of State support to disabled residents and to foreign nationals residing in Britain.[48] An intersectional feminist analysis not only asks how different types of harms are inflicted on different bodies but how those harms are magnified at the intersection of gender and race, gender and disability, or gender and sexuality.[49] Moreover, an intersectional feminist account interrogates how the construction of gendered harms via macro-level decisions intersects and is underpinned by racialized, homophobic and cis-phobic policies as well as the production of ableism as a normalizing force.[50]

The intersectional construction of power and privilege is as much about the maintenance of the status quo as it is about the embodiment of individual identities.[51] Consequently, when assessed and deployed in the international sphere, intersectionality engages a series of provocative questions about gendered security. First, it illustrates how attention to gender in isolation from other sites of insecurity is often used to underpin and maintain privilege, where gender becomes a disciplining tool that imagines and frames gender disadvantage as elsewhere: for example, in conflict and post-conflict spaces. Secondly, and following on from the latter, a gender analysis of security that lacks an intersectional framework in locating gendered insecurity as 'elsewhere' to the West ignores how in States, such as the UK, gendered insecurity is felt most severely by racialized communities, in genderqueer and LGBTI lives, and in the intersection with disabled experience of harm and vulnerability. Austerity in the UK is thus a reminder that notions of insecurity cannot be measured or studied away from the everydayness of privilege. Gendered insecurity is global in its manifestations, linked to macro power dynamics—both within and across national contexts.

[47] Elena Vacchelli et al, 'Is it Really Just the Cuts? Neo-Liberal Tales from the Women's Voluntary and Community Sector in London' (2015) 109 Feminist Review 180.

[48] Avtar Brah et al (eds), 'The Politics of Austerity' (2015) 109 Feminist Review.

[49] Hannah Jones et al, *Go Home: The Politics of Immigration Controversies* (Manchester UP 2017).

[50] Alyosxa Tudor, 'Dimensions of Transnationalism' (2017) 117 Feminist Review 20.

[51] Gina Heathcote, *Feminist Dialogues on International Law: Successes, Tensions, Futures* (OUP 2019) 56–7.

Not surprisingly, attempts to expand the women, peace, and security agenda beyond conflict and post-conflict settings has seen some pushback from States, as is noted, above, in the Russian and Chinese responses to Germany's original drafting of Resolution 2467. Despite the potential different agendas prompting China and Russia to act in this way to block this expansion of women, peace, and security, this is a good outcome if it is recalled that UNSC engagement is connected to its enforcement powers under Chapter VII of the UN Charter: military force and measures short of force, such as sanctions. As such, the broadening of UNSC engagement with gendered insecurities need not move outside of conflict or post-conflict spaces: rather, recognition of the intersectional and global power inequalities that play out via gender inequality might be the key to recognizing a need to move beyond militarized and carceral agendas towards challenging and arresting everyday violence. Nevertheless, feminist actors working to lobby States for new resolutions and new provisions within women, peace, and security would do well to question the convergence of Chinese and Russian agendas here. It is likely that the pushback on recognizing the gendered insecurity emerging from an approach to everyday insecurity would draw attention to a range of internal conflicts in which these States are engaged.

D. Conclusion

In 2019, when Germany held the pen for the drafting of UNSC Resolution 2467, thus attesting to a commitment to global reproductive justice, via the Council, national politics within Germany saw a rise in populism, nationalism and far-right political parties. Although by no means a development limited to Germany, the specific agenda of the German far-right group Alternative für Deutschland ('AfD'), outlined in the party manifesto, is a good example to question the external and internal dissonance on gender politics for States. While Germany juxtaposes itself against the US Trump administration via UNSC Resolution 2467, nationally the electoral gains of AfD demonstrate tolerance of a repressive, racist, homophobic party that directly opposes both women's rights and gender law reform, including an approach to reproductive justice that is anti-women.[52] The nexus between populism, austerity, and racialized violence in Europe becomes a space of increasing insecurity for many and, when understood through the lens of intersectionality, demonstrates how gendered insecurity must be understood as implicated in forms of violence that cannot be addressed by solely looking at women's lives. Furthermore, military solutions to gendered insecurity are unlikely to reduce patterns of insecurity produced by the rhetoric—and actions—of those committed to violent nationalisms.

[52] Alternative für Deutschland, 'Manifesto for Germany: The Political Programme for the Alternative for Germany' (2017) <https://www.afd.de/wp-content/uploads/sites/111/2017/04/2017-04-12_afd-grundsatzprogramm-englisch_web.pdf> accessed 10 January 2020.

The overview of gender and security in this chapter offers a space for rethinking how knowledge on gendered insecurity might be understood. It does not propose that the UNSC, as it currently exists with great power privilege knitted into its operations, be a space for articulating an indigenous feminist understanding of environment, community, and dispossession (although I sometimes wonder what that would look, sound, and seem like) or that the women, peace, and security agenda might be used to end the horrendous labour exploitations at sea, or that austerity practices in States in the global North, such as the UK, might be challenged through an expanded operation of international norms. I use each of these examples, instead, to configure and draw out the limited mechanisms available to feminists who wish to engage with the UNSC to challenge insecurity, as equally as the limitations of the UNSC as a forum to address such issues.

To conclude, this chapter is ultimately a plea for attention to plural feminisms. That is feminisms that operate both inside and outside of the UNSC: indigenous feminisms, environmental feminisms, masculinity studies, political economy feminisms, postcolonial feminisms, intersectional feminisms, and so on; and feminisms that attend to insecurity in peacetime States, conflict States, and post-conflict States but which do not build new sites of colonial interventions and which do not assume gender as a shorthand for women or that gender operates in a single mode. Feminisms that can respond to environmental insecurity, everyday insecurity, and the nexus between violent nationals and violent States need to be recognized and heard. Ultimately, from the perspective of plural feminisms, the UNSC remains a limited place for challenging gendered (in)security, through its select spaces of addressing women, peace, and security and through the persistence of militarized modes of security that are, by definition, unable to address everyday insecurities in peacetime or conflict States. As such, I advocate for postcolonial and intersectional feminisms that move and shift in new ways to imagine human and environmental security for the future. Plural feminisms are open to a diversity of voices and to an understanding of gender relations that could engage the complexity of a diversity of knowledge structures for future responses to gender and security.

CHAPTER 6

ACCIDENTLY INSECURE

PETER HOUGH

A. Introduction

INSECURITY surrounds us. Insecurity has always surrounded us. Nevertheless, the law and politics of security generally remain far removed from our everyday lives. States, and particularly their peoples, are threatened in myriad ways yet the political and legal practice of security invariably continues to focus on once grave threats now in decline. Armed conflicts continue to blight the world and render some of us insecure but the lives of the vast majority of people depend much more on being secured against less grand, abstract, and remote threats than a 'war against terror'. Most insecurities are more 'mundane' and close than war or terrorism. They reside in our workplaces, towns, roads, and homes. Insecurity is normal. The process of addressing insecurities needs also to be normalized. Large bodies of Public International Law have evolved in relation to insecurities faced in regards to war, human rights, or environmental change but the accidents that threaten most of us more are barely addressed in international affairs. 'Security' in law and politics has long been used as a synonym for military defence in both practice and analysis. Over recent decades some practitioners and analysts have come to embrace the notion that non-military threats like climate change, AIDS, or societal discrimination can also be treated as security matters and so given greater political priority. Accidents, though, are rarely construed as matters of security, even though they represent the biggest source of insecurity for most people across the world. This chapter explores why this is and considers the case for giving greater recognition to accidental insecurity in international law and politics.

B. Accidental Insecurity

Accidents are far removed from the conventional conceptualization of security politics and yet represent a much bigger threat to most people's lives than those most typical security concerns: war and terrorism. Most of the readers of this chapter are hundreds of times more likely to die in an accident than be killed by a soldier or terrorist, as illustrated in Table 6.1. 'War / political violence' is a category collating international war, civil war, terrorism, and human rights abuses and is still dwarfed by accidental deaths. It is also a figure generally in decline with 0.17 million deaths representing less than half the figure for 2001 and considerably less than almost any year in the twentieth century.[1] As Table 6.1 indicates, worldwide, only ill health represents a bigger killer than accidents in their various forms (and the bulk of these deaths are the result of old age or 'natural causes').

In spite of this, accidents are very infrequently thought of, and hence acted upon, as matters of security in international political and legal practice. However, structural or mechanical failings not instigated by natural phenomena (like earthquakes) or war represent a major risk to human life throughout the world and one that looks set to continue growing. The absence of direct, deliberate human causation with 'malice aforethought', has led to accidents being somewhat tolerated societally and not prioritized (or 'securitized') by governments in the same way as other causes of harm. Consequently they are very rarely considered the stuff of 'high politics' and generally held to be domestic rather than international legal matters.

However, accidents are not inevitable. They are rooted in contemporary societal practices and are, to a large degree, avoidable through political and legal actions. As such, accidents are actually no more unavoidable than other social systemic problems like war, terrorism, and crime. In addition, accidents are not purely domestic matters. They invariably have underlying socio-economic causes intrinsically linked to the global

Table 6.1 Top causes of death in the world (in millions) in 2015[2]

Disease / ill-health	51.07
Accidents	3.31
Suicide	0.83
Criminal violence	0.41
War / political violence	0.17
Natural disasters	0.02

[1] WHO, *The World Health Report: Reducing Risks, Promoting Healthy Life* (WHO 2002).

[2] 'The Global Burden of Diseases, Injuries, and Risk Factors Study 2015' (2016) 388 The Lancet 1447.

political and economic systems. With accidents, globalization blurs the traditional domestic–international dichotomy as it is now widely accepted to do for issues such as crime and health. In particular, as for all matters of life and death, with accidents the finger of fate points in familiar directions: towards the poor and the weak. For example, Africans are three times more likely to die in road accidents than Europeans even though they are far less likely to own a car.[3] In the US in 2001, the death toll on the roads every 26 days was the equivalent of the unprecedented 9/11 terrorist attacks.[4] It is an indication of how the politics of security has become skewed over time that the issue most associated with the discipline is a comparatively minor threat to most people in the world. The average citizen of the world is actually far less threatened by military action from another State or a foreign non-State actor than they are in ways rarely labelled as matters of security. Our insecurities are invariably close to home and familiar.

1. Transport Accidents

Just like the iceberg that sank the Titanic in the world's most well-known transport disaster, the chief risk to life posed by travelling lies submerged from full appreciation. As illustrated in Table 6.2, road traffic accidents claim well over a million lives per year worldwide, the biggest cause of all deaths apart from disease, and a figure that continues to rise. However, since such deaths occur so regularly and so universally they tend not to attract the sort of attention given to sporadic shipping, rail or air disasters and have for some time been almost uncontroversial. Indeed, Short argues that the scale and predictability of this death toll has served to distort the meaning of the word 'accident'. These are not accidents in the traditional sense of being unforeseen events since we do expect them and also know that it is the poor who bear the brunt of the carnage.[5] The vested interests of the oil industry, car manufacturers and motorists blind us to this hugely clumsy 'elephant in the room'.

This complacency has, to some extent, begun to change in the Global North as data, showing significant disparities in deaths between countries, has proved that car accidents can be reduced through governmental action. For example, in 2003 the French government initiated a campaign focused on the better enforcement of existing speeding restrictions, which produced an immediate 20 per cent drop in deaths annually.[6] Similarly, road deaths in New York in the 2000s were lower than when counting began in the 1920s and have halved in Sweden since 2000 as safety standards and a safety culture

[3] Global Health Observatory Data, 'Road Traffic Death Rate by WHO Region and Income Level' (*WHO*) <http://www.who.int/gho/road_safety/mortality/rate_text/en/> accessed 24 September 2017.

[4] Nick Wilson/George Thomson, 'Deaths from International Terrorism Compared with Road Crash Deaths in OECD Countries' (2005) 11 Injury Prevention 332.

[5] John Short, *Globalization, Modernity and the City* (Routledge 2012) 143–4.

[6] WHO, *World Report on Road Traffic Injury Prevention* (WHO 2004).

have evolved.[7] Invariably the most secure motorists drive on roads regulated by the most stringent legislation in the most developed and wealthy States.

Domestic political action on accidents has tended to be more stringent, however, for public rather than private transport. The greater bursts of killing in train, aeroplane, or ferry crashes are more newsworthy and heighten both public anxieties and a governmental sense of responsibility. Statistics show that people in the US are nearly twenty times more likely to die in a car accident than a train crash (and nearly 720 times more likely to die in a motorcycle crash!).[8] Americans (and most in the Global North), though, continue to prefer driving to travelling on public transport, even though the latter is markedly safer. However, when we do need to sail or fly, paying a premium to feel safe is largely accepted. Companies offering budget flights in the Global North cut costs in terms of catering and legroom but would never be likely to get away with cutting corners in terms of safety.

Again, however, insuring against public transport accidents is a cost much more likely to be absorbed in countries developed enough to sacrifice some profit for safety. The world's worst ever transport disaster, in the Philippines in 1987, saw over 4,000 passengers on the Don Paz ferry perish when it burned and sank after a collision. Cutting corners and packing more bodies on a ferry boat pushes up the profits but also, of course, the danger level. It is a similar story with air travel. Global deaths in the 2000s have halved from what they were in the 1970s but much of the remaining toll is attributable to flights with older, less safe aircraft in the Global South.[9]

The vast majority of maritime disasters today occur domestically in overcrowded ferries in the Global South. Since the sinking of the Don Paz all ferry disasters claiming over 500 lives have been in poor Global South States.[10] An annual average of 1,541 people died in ferry disasters between 2000 and 2014, with two-thirds of these deaths occurring in just five countries: Bangladesh, Tanzania, Indonesia, Senegal, and the Philippines.[11] Safety on international waters has greatly improved with over a century of regulations

[7] S N, 'Why Sweden has so Few Road Deaths' (*The Economist*, 26 February 2014) <https://www.economist.com/the-economist-explains/2014/02/26/why-sweden-has-so-few-road-deaths> accessed 22 January 2019.

[8] Deaths per billion miles in the USA 2000–14: motorcycle 237.57, car/truck 6.53, train 0.33, bus 0.2: American Public Transport Association, 'The Hidden Traffic Safety Solution, Public Transportation' (September 2016) iv <https://www.apta.com/wp-content/uploads/Resources/resources/reportsandpublications/Documents/APTA-Hidden-Traffic-Safety-Solution-Public-Transportation.pdf> accessed 14 November 2020.

[9] ICAO, 'Implementing the Global Aviation Safety Roadmap' (2011) <https://cfapp.icao.int/fsix/_Library/Global_Aviation_Safety_Roadmap_Part_2.pdf> accessed 8 April 2020; Aviation Safety Network, 'Statistics' (1 January 2018) <https://aviation-safety.net/statistics/> accessed 14 April 2020.

[10] Bart Jensen, '10 Worst Ferry Disasters Worldwide' (*USA Today*, 16 April 2014) <https://www.usatoday.com/story/news/world/2014/04/16/ferry-disasters-philippines-senegal-bangladesh-red-sea/7771799/> accessed 12 March 2018.

[11] Abigail Golden/Roberta Weisbrod, 'Trends, Causal Analysis and Recommendations from 14 Years of Ferry Accidents' (2016) 19 Journal of Public Transportation 17.

making safer the journeys of traders and tourists. Global deaths on cargo ships dropped below 100 in 2014, less than half the annual average in the first decade of the millennium.[12] International maritime safety standards centre on the Safety of Life at Sea (SOLAS) Conventions, initiated in 1914 in the wake of the Titanic disaster. Measures declared mandatory for all ships on the high seas included reduced speed limits after the sighting of ice, and lifeboat training for all crewmembers. In 1960, an updated version of SOLAS was then adopted by the UN's Intergovernmental Maritime Consultancy Organization, which later became the International Maritime Organization (IMO). The IMO, based in London, is today the focal point for a wide array of global maritime safety standards, such as the global Maritime Distress and Safety System, which from 1998 has ensured that any ship in distress can receive assistance even if it does not have a radio.[13]

Global flight safety standards are much more embryonic than those covering high sea travel. The International Civil Aviation Organization (ICAO), the relevant UN agency, has generally played a technical rather than regulatory role with safety standards left to governments. However, in 2006, in response to rising accident figures in the Global South, the ICAO worked with the airline industry to devise the Global Aviation Safety Roadmap, which seeks to harmonize national and regional safety standards up to Global North standards and share good practice. This roadmap metamorphosed into the Global Aviation Safety Plan, now reviewed every three years by the ICAO, which also produces annual reports detailing levels of State compliance with its standards. Global air standards, though, remain voluntary. Aeroplanes tend to be more 'national' than ships, where ownership and crews are frequently quite distinct from where a vessel is operating. As such, international standards, from the perspective of influential States, are deemed less necessary.

2. Structural Accidents

Like transport accidents, disasters due to structural building failures have occurred for as long as construction has been part of human life but have become far more common and dangerous in the industrialized age. Improved safety standards for public buildings in most countries have seen deaths reduced from a highpoint of the latter half of the nineteenth and early part of the twentieth centuries. However, accidents of this form cannot be eliminated altogether in a modern world characterized by crowded urban living and working. It is instructive to note that the Great Fire of London in 1666, which destroyed most of the city, claimed only an estimated five or six lives since escaping low

[12] 'Lives Lost at Sea' (*International Chamber of Shipping*) <http://www.ics-shipping.org/shipping-facts/safety-and-regulation/lives-lost-at-sea> accessed 20 March 2018.

[13] International Convention for the Safety of Life at Sea 1184 UNTS 2 ch IV; IMO, *GMDSS Manual* (IMO Publications 2019).

burning buildings was straightforward. Contrast this with the 2017 Grenfell Tower disaster in London in which seventy-one perished in a fire that destroyed one building.[14]

Building safety might be more obviously a domestic matter than transport safety but here also human insecurities are affected by globalization. Increased levels of migrant labour and tourism make building regulations, fire exits, and safety drills increasingly international matters. This is illustrated by considering the world's worst ever structural disaster. In 2015, during Hajj, over 2,000 chiefly foreign pilgrims died in a stampede at Mina near Mecca when a bottleneck was created by huge numbers of people arriving from different directions on to a particular street.[15] This was not the first major disaster to occur during Hajj. Over 1,400 perished in 1990 due to the collapse of a tunnel and there have been several other incidents before and since this. Over 400 of the pilgrims killed in 2015 were Iranian, which served to further sour relations between Riyadh and Tehran already strained by the Syrian and Yemen Civil Wars and a general Sunni–Shia 'Cold War'. Tehran considers the disaster to be illustrative of a Saudi neglect of foreign and particularly Shia pilgrims and has called for international management of the event.[16] That these disasters have occurred in an oil-rich State also further illustrates that, while it may be accompanied by improved safety standards, economic development is no panacea for security from accidents.

3. Workplace Accidents

Most clearly associated with modern living is industrialization, which is itself associated with far more hazardous forms of employment and production than pre-industrial economic activity. However, like structural disasters, major industrial accidents can be prevented, and the death toll has fallen in countries after undergoing industrialization. Most major disasters of this kind occur in countries in the early stages of industrial revolution and economic development. The world's worst ever accident, industrial or otherwise, occurred at Bhopal, India in 1984 on a pesticide plant run by the US-based MNC Union Carbide. A leak of 40 tonnes of the highly toxic chemical methyl-isocyanate (MIC), used in the production process, killed between 15,000 and 20,000 people living near the plant. Around 500,000 other people have since suffered from a range of long-term health problems and birth defects.[17] As an intermediate chemical (rather than the end product) MIC did not feature on the world's foremost safety inventory of the time, UNEP's

[14] 'Grenfell Tower: What Happened' (*BBC News*, 29 October 2019) <https://www.bbc.co.uk/news/uk-40301289> accessed 10 December 2019.

[15] Sarah Almukhtar/Derek Watkins, 'How One of the Deadliest Hajj Accidents Unfolded' (*The New York Times*, 6 October 2016) <https://www.nytimes.com/interactive/2016/09/06/world/middleeast/2015-hajj-stampede.html> accessed 8 December 2019.

[16] 'Hajj Stampede: Iran Leader says Saudis "Murdered" Pilgrims' (*BBC*, 5 September 2016) <http://www.bbc.co.uk/news/world-middle-east-37274243> accessed 30 March 2017.

[17] 'Bhopal Disaster' *Encyclopedia Britannica* (last updated 17 January 2019) <https://www.britannica.com/event/Bhopal-disaster> accessed 14 February 2017.

International Register of Potentially Toxic Chemicals.[18] Hence Indian authorities were unaware of its presence in the country and medics had no clear understanding of how to treat survivors. Investigations also proved that safety standards on the plant were weak and that previous fatal accidents had occurred. In particular, standards were far lower than at Union Carbide's home plant in West Virginia.

An industrial accident the scale of Bhopal has not occurred since 1984 and the notoriety of this disaster has seen the international trade in hazardous chemicals come to be better regulated. The 1998 Rotterdam Convention[19] is based on a system that ensures that the prior informed consent of State authorities is gained before importing chemicals like MIC. However, as with transport and structural disasters, the full picture of regular, small-scale accidents at work lies outside of international public and political attention. Twenty years on from Bhopal, the International Labour Organization (ILO) reported that the Indian government had claimed an annual total of 231 work-related fatal accidents, whereas the true figure was nearer 40,000.[20]

That major work-based disasters were not consigned to the past was confirmed in 2013 with history's second worst such event, which also doubled up as a structural failure. Over a thousand clothing workers, from several firms, perished in the Savar building collapse in Dhaka, Bangladesh. After the disaster it transpired that extra storeys had been illegally added to the building and workers told to continue operating there despite engineers expressing safety concerns at these extensions.[21] Additionally, like Bhopal, it became apparent that Savar was not just a Bangladeshi matter, since many major Western retailers had sourced clothing from this creaking death trap. The notion of a 'race to the bottom' by MNCs, highlighted by critics of economic globalization, is given credence by disasters such as at Bhopal and Dhaka.

An added transboundary and global dimension to many workplace accidents comes from the disproportionate number of victims who are migrant labourers. While confirmed figures are not available, reports have suggested a shocking death toll in Qatar, a country with one of the highest proportions of migrant workers and in the spotlight due to a massive construction drive towards hosting the football World Cup in 2022. Over 400 Indian and Nepalese construction workers in Qatar (who make up around half of the total migrant workforce) are believed to have died in both 2013 and 2014.[22]

[18] For a brief description: A Sundén/J W Huismans, 'The International Register of Potentially Toxic Chemicals (IRPTC) its Databank and Network Partners' (1990) 25 Toxicological and Environmental Chemistry 163.

[19] Rotterdam Convention on the Prior Informed Consent Procedure for Certain Hazardous Chemicals and Pesticides in International Trade 2244 UNTS 337.

[20] ILO, 'Introductory Report: Decent Work—Safe Work' (XVIIth World Congress on Safety and Health at Work, Orlando, 18–25 September 2005) 4.

[21] Ker Than, 'Bangladesh Building Collapse Due to Shoddy Construction' (*National Geographic*, 26 April 2013) <https://www.nationalgeographic.com/news/2013/4/130425-bangladesh-dhaka-building-collapse-world/> accessed 8 April 2020.

[22] International Trade Union Confederation, 'ITUC Special Report: The Case Against Qatar—Host of the FIFA 2022 World Cup' (March 2014) <https://www.ituc-csi.org/ituc-special-report-the-case> accessed 27 February 2019.

As with transport disasters and most forms of insecurity, however, large-scale or high-profile disasters like at Dhaka and Bhopal represent only a small, highly visible, fraction of the full picture. The vast majority of accidents in the workplace are individual or small scale. For example, official State figures acknowledge an annual average death toll of 2,623 between 2005 and 2016 in Chinese coalmines.[23] Overall the ILO have estimated that around a third of a million people a year in the world are killed in occupational accidents (including traffic accidents while working).[24] If deaths when commuting to or from work and by illness caused at work are included, this figure rises to over 2.3 million.[25] As Tapiola from the ILO has observed: 'If the daily global casualty rate at work would be concentrated in one place, it would be all over the first pages of the world's newspapers.'[26]

There is a long history of international law on accidents but the impact of this has been strikingly limited. As far back as 1929 the ILO's Prevention of Industrial Accidents Recommendation (R31) incorporated a resolution of the previous year's International Labour Conference that information be collated systematically on accidents and their causes. Numerous recommendations since then culminated in the 1993 Prevention of Major Industrial Accidents Convention.[27] Convention No 174 is hardly radical and its measures include calls for plants manufacturing hazardous substances to be located away from residential areas and the notification of residents in the event of a leak. Nevertheless, over twenty years after the Convention had entered into force in 1997, only eighteen States had ratified it.[28] Even allowing for the typical slowness of treaty ratification this shows that most governments do not pay much attention to international safety policy. The ratification rate for older ILO Safety Conventions is little better. The 1985 Occupational Health Services Convention, which requires that a State's occupational health services advise employers and workers on safety had, by 2018, been ratified by only thirty-three of the ILO's 187 Member States.[29] This is particularly telling since, while many developed States can cite the fact that they have more thorough domestic

[23] Danni Fu, 'Casualties of China's Coal Addiction' (*Sixth Tone*, 22 December 2016) <http://www.sixthtone.com/news/1727/casualties-of-chinas-coal-addiction> accessed 3 May 2018.

[24] ILO, 'Introductory Report: Global Trends and Challenges on Occupational Safety and Health at Work' (XIXth World Congress on Safety and Health at Work, Istanbul, 11–15 September 2011) 10.

[25] Tampere University of Technology/Workplace Safety & Health Institute/VTT Technical Research Centre of Finland, 'Global Estimates of Occupational Accidents and Work-Related Illnesses' (2014) <https://www.wsh-institute.sg/~/media/wshi/past%20publications/2014/global%20estimates%20of%20occupational%20accidents%20and%20work-related%20illness%202014.pdf?la=en> accessed 27 February 2019.

[26] Kari Tapiola, 'Human Security and the Role of the ILO' (Symposium commemorating the 50th anniversary of reopening the ILO Office in Japan, Tokyo, 27 December 2005) <https://www.ilo.org/public/english/region/asro/tokyo/conf/2005tbo/ed.htm> accessed 14 November 2020.

[27] 1967 UNTS 3.

[28] See UNTS <https://treaties.un.org/Pages/showDetails.aspx?objid=0800000280049ea&clang=_en> accessed 13 April 2020.

[29] 1498 UNTS 19. For the parties, see UNTS <https://treaties.un.org/Pages/showDetails.aspx?objid=08000002800ca75b&clang=_en>.

legislation as a basis for not ratifying the Industrial Accidents Convention, the ILO consider that few non-parties to Convention No 161 have equivalent existing laws.[30]

Global regulation with regards to the use and production of, rather than trade in, hazardous chemicals is less rigorous but has developed over time. A plethora of informal international standards in this area was brought together in 2002 under the Globally Harmonized System of Classification and Labelling of Chemicals (GHS), co-managed by three intergovernmental organizations: the Organization for Economic Cooperation and Development (OECD), the United Nations Committee of Experts on the Transportation of Dangerous Goods (UNCETDG) and the ILO. As well as setting labelling standards, this scheme includes requiring data sheets for workers involved in chemical transport to be provided and sets guidance information for governments on how to implement the scheme. The system began the process of ratification in 2003 and by 2017 had been implemented by seventy-two States. It should be noted, though, that harmonized global standards are becoming more popular due to the fact that they can facilitate trade by levelling the 'playing field' rather than because they enhance human security. The advent of the World Trade Organization (WTO) in 1995 has led to more focus on establishing global standards for traded goods in order to determine whether national standards in excess of this can be deemed to be barriers to free trade.

Safety standards for the production of nuclear energy and the transportation of its constituent elements and by-products tend not to be included in general international law on accident prevention. Instead, the responsibility for this lies with the International Atomic Energy Agency (IAEA), set up by the UN in 1957 to coordinate policy on both military and civilian uses of nuclear power. The IAEA has an International Nuclear Safety Advisory Group which has coordinated the establishment of a range of 'Safety Principles' and 'Codes of Practice on the International Transboundary Movement of Radioactive Waste'. Following the 1986 Chernobyl disaster and the end of the Cold War, the most extensive legal instrument on this area was concluded under the auspices of the IAEA: the Convention on Nuclear Safety.[31] Its ambit is quite broad, covering issues ranging from the siting and construction of power plants to emergency preparation. Despite its legally binding nature, however, being an 'international convention' and not IAEA 'principles' or 'codes of practice', the obligations contained therein are not particularly robust. According to the IAEA: 'The Convention is an incentive instrument. It is not designed to ensure fulfilment of obligations by Parties through control and sanction.'[32]

Hard international law protecting migrant workers exists but the significance of this legal regime is also highly limited. The 1990 International Convention on the Protection of the Rights of All Migrant Workers and Members of Their Families includes an obligation

[30] Jukka Takala, 'Introductory Report of the International Labour Office' (XV World Congress on Occupational Safety and Health, 12–16 April 1999) 4.

[31] 1963 UNTS 3.

[32] This paragraph draws from Peter Hough et al, *International Security Studies: Theory and Practice* (Routledge 2015) 282.

on States of immigration to ensure the 'security of person' (Article 16) but this is a notoriously poorly ratified human rights instrument.[33] As of 2018 the Convention had fifty-one Parties but none of these were Global North States, rendering it effectively meaningless.

4. Personal Accidents

In addition to those encountered while travelling, working, and congregating in public buildings, people also face a diversity of risks to their lives at home or at leisure. Electrical appliances and cooking facilities characteristic of modern living are further sources of 'everyday danger' confronting an ever-increasing proportion of the world's population. Table 6.2 lists the most prominent causes of accidental death across all of the categories and it is clear that many of these result from personal, domestic activities such as fires caused by deep fat fryers and children drowning in ponds. Again, domestic legislation has served to improve safety in the home in many countries but there is still an observable tendency to accept the possibility of such 'mundane' ways to die and the problem is most acute in the developing world.

Personal accidents of these forms are as far removed from the conventional image of security politics as is possible but, again, this is misleading. Securing people individually is well established in domestic law and politics and globalization serves to erode the national–international dichotomy. Tourism, business travel and migration make

Table 6.2 The top causes of accidental death (in 2015)[34]

Form of accident	Deaths (000s)
Road traffic injuries	1,362
Falls	528
Drowning	324
'Mechanical Forces' (eg guns, tools, suffocation)	201
Fires	176
'Foreign Body' (eg. choking)	152
Adverse effects of medical treatment	100
Animals	94
Poisoning	86
Environmental exposure to cold and heat	45
Other non-transport	134
Other transport	105
TOTAL	3,305

[33] 2220 UNTS 3.

[34] The Global Burden of Diseases (n 48).

everyday health and safety relevant for all. When abroad we expect that hotel room facilities have been safety-tested and that, outdoors, potentially dangerous stretches of water have been highlighted by warning signs. There is little precedent for personal accidents being addressed at the global level but the World Health Organization (WHO) have begun to do so with drowning, with a 2014 report making recommendations on national water safety plans, particularly with regards to children.[35] In recognition of the need to safeguard the security of tourists, the UN World Tourist Organization (UNWTO) in 1999 adopted a Global Code of Ethics for Tourism which includes ensuring a 'client's security' as an obligation of tour companies under Article 6.[36] This voluntary code was endorsed by the UN General Assembly (UNGA) in 2001[37] and the UNWTO have since campaigned for it to be transformed from soft law into an international treaty. This, though, has yet to happen and no hard law exists in regards to personal accidents.

C. Accidents and Risk

Deaths by accident are very much a feature of the modern world. There have, of course, always been accidental deaths but this form of threat to life is closely associated with technological development and has risen in accord with industrialization and the onset of modernity. While aspects of technological development can also be used to mitigate against them, accidental deaths can be viewed as unfortunate by-products of modernity. Health and safety legislation in developed countries has succeeded in reducing the potential hazards associated with transport, industrial production and the use of public buildings but, at the same time, people continue to travel more than ever and the industrial production and transportation of potentially hazardous substances continues to increase.

The inherent risks of modern living prompted sociologists in the 1990s to construct a new way of thinking about both societies and accidents, encapsulated in the term 'risk society'.[38] This paradigm posits that modern (or post-modern) societies have gone beyond thinking of accidents as avoidable and have come to accept them as an inevitability. Hence insecurity becomes normal: a part of life. Most of the conveniences and benefits of modern living come with some associated side effects. The huge toll of fatalities on the road is largely tolerated by societies because of the gains to be had from personal mobility. The most rigorous health and safety legislation could not make working

[35] WHO, *Global Report on Drowning: Preventing a Leading Killer* (WHO 2014).

[36] 'Global Code of Ethics for Tourism' (*UNWTO—World Tourist Organization*) <https://www.unwto.org/global-code-of-ethics-for-tourism> accessed 14 November 2020.

[37] UNGA Res 56/212 (21 December 2001).

[38] Ulrich Beck, *Risk Society: Towards a New Modernity* (Sage 1992).

in a modern petrochemical plant or offshore oil platform entirely safe. The workers on such plants are largely aware of this but accept the risk in exchange for monetary reward beyond what they might expect in a safer occupation.

The gamble for an individual in taking on some degree of risk in order to achieve greater rewards than attainable through safe behaviour is, of course, simple to understand and as old as history. What characterizes today's 'risk society' as different from previous generations, though, is the social dimension of risk-taking. Individuals can choose to play it safe by avoiding hazardous forms of transport or employment but may have little choice but to accept the possibility of, say, a radiation leak from their local nuclear power plant. Such an individual may well gain a pay-off from cheaper electricity but would be a largely involuntary participant in the deal and more vulnerable as well as wealthy, whether they like it or not.

From the perspective of society at large, avoiding all risk can be costly and may even increase insecurity. Scientific advances, such as the testing of new medicines, entail risks but also bring major societal benefits. The word 'security' derives from the Latin *sine cura*, meaning 'without care'. As such it is an elastic term since the 'cares' may be major fears or minor frustrations. Complete freedom from care is both impractical and undesirable. Human life that does not have any everyday concerns is unimaginable and a complete absence of risk-taking in society would eliminate much beneficial scientific progress and entertainment from life. However, the fact remains that lives are routinely put at risk in modern industrialized societies in the quest for overall State and societal progress.

The perception of the social dimension of risk, then, is crucial in determining the political demands people make of their authorities, beyond even the 'real' risk. Proponents of nuclear energy have long been irritated by the fact that the public in developed countries demand far greater restraints on this activity than other power stations with worse accident rates. An irony of the backlash against nuclear energy since the 2011 Fukushima disaster in Japan is that it has led to a revival of electricity powered by coal, an industry with a far worse track record of both accidents and pollution. In this case, of course, the calculation is complicated by a fear of the unknown, born not only of ignorance but also of a genuine lack of clarity as to the hazard presented by nuclear radiation. In fact, the true risk factor inherent in nuclear energy production can only be assessed by factoring in the implications for future generations in tackling nuclear waste, further exposing the limits of a conventional cost–benefit analysis in a risk society.

D. Accidents and Security

Since the 1990s, both academic and 'real world' political discourse has increasingly granted security status to non-military issues in 'widening' and 'deepening' the agenda of international political priorities. Many governments have 'widened' and become receptive to the notion of treating problems like pandemic diseases, environmental degradation, or transnational crime as matters of national security. Hence, we have seen the UN Security Council (UNSC) come to address HIV/AIDS (in 2000) and climate change (in 2007), and the 'Big 5' from that high table of realpolitik uniquely cooperate militarily to tackle piracy around the Horn of Africa. A few governments have gone further and 'deepened' in security politics by making individuals, rather than the State, the referent object of security. Amongst governments endorsing this concept of human security are those in Canada, Norway, and Japan who have been at the forefront of advocating the prioritization of human rights and safety over national interests in international affairs. This is a theme most prominently taken up in international affairs by the UN Development Programme (UNDP).

> The concept of security must change—from an exclusive stress on national security to a much greater stress on people's security, from security through armaments to security through human development, from territorial to food, employment and environmental security.[39]

However, security 'wideners' and even many human security advocates, while acknowledging that diseases, crime, environmental change, and natural disasters can sometimes be matters of security, are often still reluctant to grant this status to accidents. This reluctance seems to boil down to two objections: (i) There are no military or power politics dimensions inherent in accidents; (ii) Accidents are not deliberate attacks on countries or people.

Security wideners ignore accidents because there is rarely any scope for sending in troops to fight anyone or help clear up in the aftermath. Such thinkers, including some Realists, do accept that non-military issues can become 'securitized' and be privileged with 'national security' status but these issues are not defined according to the scale of human threat. The tendency has been, on the one hand, to select non-military issues which military forces can help deal with, such as fighting drugs barons abroad or assisting in civil emergency operations. On the other hand, 'securitization' has sometimes been granted to external non-military problems on the basis that they have domestic military repercussions. Issues such as AIDS or environmental degradation in distant countries may destabilize regional balances of power and trigger military conflict into which the onlooking government may be drawn or affected in some capacity. The aforementioned UNSC resolutions on AIDS and climate change were very much framed in this context. In most government policy and popular discourse security has become a noun rather than an adjective. Security is assumed to be the military defence of the State, regardless of whether this best enhances the security of its people or not.

A further barrier to the 'securitization' of accidents for some is the absence of direct and deliberate human causation. MacFarlane and Foong Khong, while advocating

[39] UNDP, *Human Development Report: People's Participation* (OUP 1993).

human security, opine that natural disasters and accidents 'fail the "organized harm" test—tsunami waves, traffic accidents, the spread of viruses and crop failure are usually not organized by individuals to do their victims in'.[40] What this reflects is that human security itself is a contested concept with more and less expansive versions having come to be employed in both academic and political discourse. A broader interpretation of human security is often characterized as combining 'freedom from want' and 'freedom from fear' (from the UNDP definition) in that it considers any issues with direct or indirect life-threatening consequences for individuals to be matters of security. Concerns amongst some advocates of an individual-focused approach to security that 'existing definitions of human security tend to be extraordinarily expansive and vague',[41] led them to favour a more restricted version based purely on 'freedom from fear'. This narrow version of human security concentrates on direct and deliberate violent threats, excluding less directly human-caused forms of insecurity like disasters. Recent Canadian governments have been supportive of such an approach in their advocacy of human security as a pragmatic determinant of when specific foreign policy actions—such as taking part in a humanitarian intervention or developing international human rights conventions—should be undertaken. In contrast, the Japanese government's endorsement of human security has tended to be more in line with the expansive version as favoured by the UNDP and has embraced human vulnerabilities due to poverty and related threats.

For advocates of more expansive human security there is a fatalism in assuming that only direct and deliberate threats to life can be deemed worthy of security status. The non-securitization of accidents makes sense only if you are to assume that the word 'security' actually amounts to a synonym for 'involves the military' rather than a description of how to make people less insecure. Must we deduce from this line of reasoning that anyone threatened or killed indirectly is not insecure? Are the 'collateral killings' of war or insurgency not military or terrorist victims? Accidents are actually no more unavoidable than other social systemic problems like war and crime, and people can be secured against them, at least to some degree.

The human agency argument is flawed on two levels. There is human agency in most accidents. Human failings, whether at the State, corporate or individual level, account for most accidents and, hence, can be addressed in political and legal actions. Indeed, it could be argued that the international community should feel a greater sense of responsibility when it comes to industrial accidents in particular since they have become more functionally connected to these events in enjoying the fruits of this hard labour. The contemporary deaths of Chinese miners or Indian construction workers in the Gulf States building skyscrapers for global banks and football stadia should trouble Western

[40] S Neil MacFarlane/Yuen Foong Khong, *Human Security and the UN: A Critical History* (Indiana UP 2006) 275.

[41] Roland Paris, 'Human Security: Paradigm Shift or Hot Air?' (2001) 26 International Security 87, 88.

consumers and governments as much as notorious domestic disasters did in the nineteenth and twentieth centuries.

Securing people against such things was a political task accepted by industrialized governments from as far back as the late nineteenth century when 'social security' laws began to evolve in response to changing economic and social conditions. The industrialization of Western European and North American States prompted the emergence of laws to protect those put at risk by these social changes based on a blend of compassion and pragmatism. An ideological consensus emerged in the late nineteenth century in support of the notion of State welfarism. The dangers associated with industrial employment and the economic uncertainties of trade prompted the emergence of interventionist liberalism (in place of its previous unfettered free-market version) and also paternal conservatism and the birth of socialism. The development of welfare systems in Western Europe, and to a lesser extent in North America, arose from a blend of altruistic human security concerns and internal State security interests. Germany, under the arch-conservative Bismarck, pioneered the idea of State protection for workers in the 1870s, prompted mainly by the pragmatic realism that reform from above was the best means of preventing revolution from below.[42] Bismarck's aim was not so much human security as State security: maintaining the unity of his newly formed country, which was witnessing some of the earliest manifestations of socialist thought.

There is compelling logic that globalization has now shifted some of this governmental responsibility to protect citizens to a wider level but this has yet to be fully recognized. The International Covenant on Economic and Social Rights,[43] setting out basic citizen entitlements, has come to be near-universally ratified but does not explicitly cite a government responsibility to protect people from accidents and has not had the impact of its sister International Covenant on Civil and Political Rights.[44] A 'responsibility to protect' those imperilled by political violence has been universally acknowledged in the UNGA since the 2005 World Summit Outcome Document,[45] so why should there not be such a responsibility for those imperilled by their government's or host government's political negligence?

With the inexorable rise of a coherent global economic system, global society is now awakening, albeit slowly, to this need for safety standards. Incidents of workers or residents near industrial plants in the Global South being killed are no longer unfortunate problems unconnected with the relatively safe lives of people in the Global North. Developed world consumers are functionally connected to these systemic failures as never before and are increasingly aware of this fact. The rise in the Global North of 'fair trade' products, in which the consumer pays a premium for goods imported from developing countries on the premise that the workers have not been exploited bears testimony to this.

[42] Peter Hough, *Understanding Global Security* (Routledge 2018) 223–4.
[43] 993 UNTS 3. [44] 999 UNTS 171.
[45] UNGA Res 60/1 (16 September 2005) paras 138–40.

However, global standards on the safety aspects of business and employment are limp when set against comparable standards for facilitating the trade in the produce of this process. The ILO have long-established guidelines on worker safety and the WHO have increased cooperation and good practice on safety standards in transport and social problems like drowning. However, these organizations do not have the same sort of authority in compelling States to protect workers and citizens that the WTO has in compelling them to allow goods they produce or consume into their countries. Hence, we see one reason why many political activists have come to view economic globalization as a dangerous exercise in unfettered liberalism, guided only by the profit motives of the Global North. It is indeed telling that, whereas the idea of freeing up the movement of products, services and money is well established as a global norm, the notion of a free movement of the workers producing such common goods is barely conceivable. The anti-migration turns in the US and UK, illustrated by the election of Trump and 'Brexit', make this ever more apparent.

What is needed, though, is not the abandonment of globalization but a more rounded notion of globalization which balances profits with responsibilities as is broadly the norm in the laws of most developed democracies. Such changes are slowly occurring. As with most areas of security, the gradual globalization of democracy and human rights offers some hope for improving personal safety from accidents since more and more people are able to demand action from their governments. In addition, recent evidence points towards the development of something of a 'union effect' on safety at the global level. The fact that the unionization of work forces increases human security was highlighted by contrasting safety records in the construction of sports stadia for the 2012 London Olympics (no deaths and a strong union role) with the 2014 Russian winter Olympics at Sochi (sixty deaths and no prominent union role).[46] If the Qatari World Cup construction industry (where workers' rights are effectively non-existent) is compared, the contrast is starker still.[47] Some progress in advancing this union effect globally has been made. Following up on pressuring the Bangladeshi government to legalize unions in the aftermath of the 2013 Savar disaster, a campaign by trades unions served to secure the release of Unionists imprisoned on trumped-up charges in 2017. That Unions, rights, and laws save lives has been apparent in Western Europe and North America for over a century and this is slowly coming to be recognized at the global level.

Securing people at work, at home, travelling, or at leisure is for governments and societies, though, more than charity or even duty. A more secure and healthy workforce and society is more productive and contented. Four per cent of global GDP is estimated to be

[46] Owen Tudor, 'Sochi Winter Olympics: Rights Suspended, 60 Workers Dead' (*Stronger Unions*, 8 February 2014) <http://strongerunions.org/2014/02/08/sochi-winter-olympics-rights-suspended-workers-dead/> accessed 23 January 2017.

[47] Trade Union Congress, 'Report of Congress 2014' (146th Annual Trades Union Congress, Liverpool, 7–10 September 2014) 17 <https://www.tuc.org.uk/sites/default/files/Report%20of%20Congress%202014%20-%20using%20new%20template%20rs.pdf> accessed 4 March 2019.

lost to accidents and around this amount was trimmed off the Japanese GDP by the single Fukushima nuclear disaster.[48] Exploiting workers and short-changing citizens is only profitable for so long when such people can be shown that there are alternatives. Disillusioned and angry workers have been a factor in nearly all revolutions and welfarism suits both sides of the social contract. Health and safety is the dull stuff of politics and business but it is, nonetheless, 'life and death' both for members of society and for governments and this has long been recognized as such in industrialized democracies. Globalization dictates that this can no longer be a purely domestic matter. With accidents, as with many other issues, enhancing human security is not just altruistic; it makes economic and national security sense as well.

E. Conclusion

Insecurity is increasingly multifaceted and 'normal'. However, the conceptualization of security remains highly specific and abnormal. Over time, security has come to be defined in International Relations solely as a noun rather than an adjective. The human part of a human condition had been lost and the term became synonymous with *realpolitik*, the interest of the State. The assumption that security is about the military defence of the State is a relic of the Cold War. In some ways this is understandable since the discipline of International Relations (IR), and its sub-discipline, Security Studies, only emerged in the 1930s and was thus very much forged in an era of unprecedented military threats. The total war of the Second World War and the 'total phoney war' of the Cold War, whereby whole populations were threatened by State quarrels in ways not previously seen, bound individuals to the fates of their governments like never before.

The scale of the threat posed by nuclear war in the second half of the twentieth century served to weld the security of individual people in many States to that of their governments. The State would assume the responsibility for protecting its citizens and demand their loyalty in return in a strengthened version of the social contract relationship articulated by political philosophers such as Hobbes and Locke from the seventeenth century. Hobbes' advocacy of the need for the *Leviathan* (meaning a strong State) to save individuals from the dangerous anarchy that would otherwise result from the pursuit of their own selfish interests was a major influence on thinkers like Morgenthau and the subsequent dominance of Realism in IR.[49] In the late twentieth century, anarchy was what characterized the international State system and the dangers came, to a greater extent than ever before, from other States. Hence the Realist approach to IR represented a revival of the Hobbesian understanding that the State was crucial to securing the lives of its citizens in a different guise.

[48] ILO, 'Introductory Report: Global Trends and Challenges on Occupational Safety and Health at Work' (XIXth World Congress on Safety and Health at Work, Istanbul, 11–15 September) 155, 187.

[49] Hans Morgenthau, *Politics Among Nations: The Struggle for Power and Peace* (5th edn, Knopf 1972).

Long before the Realist orthodoxy crystallized, though, political philosophy and State governance in Europe and North America acknowledged that security was also about the protection of individuals, as 'social security' came to be accepted as part of the State's obligations in the social contract by conservatives as well as liberals. Individual security is recognized in democratic States as overriding other values (at least most of the time) as is evidenced by health and safety laws restricting business activities and the whole notion of welfarism and economic and social rights. In global politics, though, issues of life and death frequently are not treated as priorities because they do not coincide with State gain or security. The blinkered pursuit of profit can enrich some but imperil others. If saving others from disaster is seen as an act of charity, rather than political duty, it will only happen infrequently and selectively. Actual threats to people are so far removed from the way in which issues are conventionally ordered on the political agenda by States that IR theory and international political practice needs to find ways of accommodating them or cease to be connected in any meaningful way with human behaviour and needs. Throughout the total war era of the twentieth century a case could be made that the security of individuals was inextricably tied up with that of their States but that era has now passed into history. Today the issues that threaten people's lives bear such little relation to those issues that dominate the international political agenda that State-centrism is impeding both the study and the practice of that most fundamental of political concerns: securing people. Sending in the building inspectors is less exciting than sending in the troops, but more likely to save our lives.

CHAPTER 7

GLOBAL SECURITY AND NEUROPHILOSOPHY

Understanding the Human Factor

NAYEF AL-RODHAN AND
IOANA-MARIA PUSCAS

A. Introduction

On 11 January 2007, China launched a ballistic missile from the Xichang Satellite Launch Centre situated in the Sichuan province. The missile was targeted at one of China's own ageing and non-operational weather satellites, at an altitude of 863 kilometres. This attack (known as 'direct ascent anti-satellite attack') completely destroyed the satellite and left around 3,000 pieces of space debris, which are expected to remain in orbit for many decades (at a speed faster than that of a bullet), effectively posing a threat of collision for other objects in Low Earth Orbit (LEO).[1] The Chinese anti-satellite (ASAT) test of 2007 is significant not just for the amount of debris it caused. It was an audacious technological achievement: the missile launched from the ground was able to hit a celestial target moving at 17,000 mph (over 27,000 kph).[2] Perhaps more critically, the test marked a turning point in the politics of outer space. For decades, the United States enjoyed unrivalled dominance in outer space, and US satellites could circle the Earth without any major challenges. In fact, the US had also carried out a test against a satellite during the Cold War, in 1985, when the ageing Solwind satellite was destroyed at an

[1] Brian Weeden, '2007 Chinese Anti-Satellite Test: Fact Sheet' (*Secure World Foundation*, 23 November 2010) <https://swfound.org/media/9550/chinese_asat_fact_sheet_updated_2012.pdf> accessed 12 September 2018.

[2] Garrett M Graff, 'The New Arms Race Threatening to Explode in Space' *WIRED* (San Francisco, July 2018) 47.

altitude of 555 kilometres, generating 250 pieces of persistent space debris and 800 to 900 smaller pieces.[3] Later, in the early 2000s, US interest in space-based weapons and ASAT capabilities increased again: notably, the US unilaterally withdrew from the Anti-Ballistic Missile Treaty in 2002 and in 2008 it destroyed a non-responsive satellite from its Aegis Sea-based missile defence system.[4] In parallel with these developments, in recent decades, the US and the entire mankind started to become profoundly reliant on the Global Positioning System (GPS), which is now indispensable for 14 out of the 16 infrastructure sectors considered critical by the Department of Homeland Security in the US.[5]

Following the 2007 Chinese test, all the satellites dotting the skies appeared starkly vulnerable. The US became immensely concerned about the potential of its adversaries acquiring advanced capabilities in space and the proposal for the creation of a Space Force in 2018 is largely a reflection of that concern.

In the summer of 2010, new stories emerged about a mysterious computer worm called Stuxnet. The virus had been active for about two years. Stuxnet was a 500-kylobite computer worm that had a particularly destructive capability: rather than simply infiltrating and stealing information from computers, it managed to create destruction in the physical world, more specifically on equipment and installations controlled by the infested computers. The news of the virus emerged first at nuclear facilities in Iran, which in January 2010 started to show unusual behaviour. During a visit by inspectors from the International Atomic Energy Agency at the Natanz uranium enrichment plant, the centrifuges that were used to enrich uranium gas were failing at a worryingly fast rate. The worm, physically inserted via an infected USB flash drive, found the controlling software of the centrifuges and installed itself into it, effectively taking control of the centrifuges, and attacking them in two rounds.[6] Stuxnet is amongst the world's first known digital weapons.

In 2014, Russia annexed Crimea, a process that started in February 2014 with Russian troops entering the peninsula, followed by a regional referendum on 16 March, under Russian coordination, to decide on its future. The vote, clearly in favour of absorption into Russia, was followed by international sanctions. The Crimean crisis was a stark reminder about the return of history and the persistence of geopolitics in the twenty-first century. Crimea enjoyed a large degree of autonomy in Ukraine but Russia's 300-year-long association with Crimea, which started when the peninsula was

[3] Laura Grego, 'A History of Anti-Satellite Programs' (*Union of Concerned Scientists*, January 2012) 5 <https://www.ucsusa.org/sites/default/files/2019-09/a-history-of-ASAT-programs_lo-res.pdf> accessed 14 November 2020.

[4] ibid 8–12. [5] Graff (n 2).

[6] Kim Zetter, 'An Unprecedented Look at Stuxnet, the World's First Digital Weapon' (*WIRED*, 3 November 2014) <https://www.wired.com/2014/11/countdown-to-zero-day-stuxnet/> accessed 12 September 2018.

incorporated into the Russian Empire under Catherine the Great in 1783, helped Russia legitimize the annexation ('Russia took back what it naturally belonged to it').[7]

These three examples, while in no way painting a full picture of the twenty-first-century security landscape, expose challenges in at least three domains: in outer space, in cyberspace and on land, in 'territorial politics'. In just a span of a little more than a decade, the world has traversed crises that amalgamate modern, postmodern elements, or both.

Many more types of emerging security threats can be added: climate change and bio-chemical warfare, from rogue States and individuals, spread of right-wing politics, violent xenophobia, and radicalization in new regions of the world. Additionally, the nature of intra-State and inter-State warfare is itself defined by immense complexity. In fact, the model of the troops of two nations in direct confrontation has been rarely seen in the past decades. A list compiled by researchers at University of California listing all the inter-State conflicts in the past two centuries, reveals that only very few such wars took place in recent years: one was the India–Pakistan war of 1999 (the Kargil War), another two examples are the invasions of Afghanistan (2001) and of Iraq (2003).[8]

Some of the 'long wars' today, such as Somalia (at war since 1991), Libya (since 2011), Mali (since 2012), South Sudan, Ukraine (in a frozen or 'invisible' conflict since 2014), or even the Democratic Republic of the Congo (at war between 1997 and 2003, but experiencing a resurgence of tensions recently), Syria, and Yemen—display varying complexities along geopolitical, ethnic, ideological, sectarian, economic (resource-related) lines. To make sense of these complexities, we often reach for easy binaries such as 'Islam vs the West', established super-powers vs emerging super-powers, or haves against have-nots, functional States vs failed States, or States that accept international norms vs rogue States.[9] In reality, none of these explanations can convincingly capture the complexities of the conflicts.

This chapter will attempt to return to the fundamental starting point in political theory: human nature, and in doing so, to go beyond conventional wisdom in International Relations. To understand conflict and to chart a way forward, we must re-examine our understanding of human nature. In doing so, the following section will draw on recent findings from neuroscience. No discipline has been able before to grasp human emotionality, rationality, or morality in neurochemical and neuroanatomical ways simply because the technological means were not available. Today, we are increasingly able to do so, with implications for the theory of human nature, understandings of good governance, and conflict prevention.

[7] Gwendolyn Sasse, 'Revisiting the 2014 Annexation of Crimea' (*Carnegie Europe*, 15 March 2017) <https://carnegieeurope.eu/2017/03/15/revisiting-2014-annexation-of-crimea-pub-68423> accessed 12 September 2018.

[8] Meredith Reid Sarkees, 'The List of Inter-State Wars' in Meredith Reid Sarkees/Frank Whelon Wayman, *Resort to War: A Data Guide to Inter-State, Extra-State, Intra-State, and Non-State Wars, 1816–2007* (CQ Press 2010).

[9] Jason Burke, 'Why is the World at War?' (*The Guardian*, 4 March 2018) <https://www.theguardian.com/world/2018/mar/04/why-is-world-at-war-syria-democratic-republic-congo-yemen-afghanistan-ukraine> accessed 12 September 2018.

B. Neurophilosophy and Global Security

In *Leviathan* (1651), written during the English Civil War, Thomas Hobbes laid out his political philosophy, which departed from a specific understanding of human nature. In chapter XIII, he writes:

> So that in the nature of man, we find three principal causes of quarrel. First, Competition; Secondly, Diffidence; Thirdly, Glory. The first, maketh men invade for Gain; the second, for Safety; and the third, for Reputation. (...) Hereby it is manifest that during the time men live without a common Power to keep them all in awe, they are in that condition which is called Warre; and such a warre as is of every man, against every man (...) And the life of man, *solitary, poore, nasty, brutish, and short.*[10]

Jean-Jacques Rousseau, publishing the *Social Contract* more than a century later, in 1762, believed in the innate goodness of man, and his perfectibility. He famously stated that 'man is born free and everywhere is in chains'.[11] Societies made humans more selfish, although at their core, in the state of nature, they were generous and living in harmony. Rousseau believed that man is naturally peaceful and timid, but becomes a soldier through the coercive pressure of the State.[12] Recognizing this inherent dynamic of competition between States (States started wars, not individuals, who normally would not resort to war), he proposed plans for perpetual peace, through federations acting as 'islands of peace' where a stable system could be created if the right balance of power existed.

Immanuel Kant developed his idea of perpetual peace in relation to a certain understanding of human nature. In *Perpetual Peace* (1795) or *The Doctrine of Virtue (Part II of the Metaphysics of Morals)* from 1797, Kant's theories on the State and International Relations emerged from his specific understanding of human nature. In Kant's view, humans had a dual character, 'negotiating' between an animal and rational side. The animal nature comes from the fundamental fact that humans are living beings, seeking their preservation, reproduction, personal pleasure and avoidance of pain. However, the rational nature is only specific to humans and it is the quality that allows humans to understand moral laws. Kant contended that, initially, all humans may choose to obey their impulsive sides simply because the temptation to seek pleasure is stronger.

[10] Thomas Hobbes, *Leviathan* (first published 1651, C B Macpherson ed, Penguin Books 1985) 185–6 (emphasis added).

[11] Jean-Jacques Rousseau, *The Social Contract* (first published 1762, Maurice Cranston tr, Penguin Books 1968) 49.

[12] Genevieve Blanchet, 'Jean-Jacques Rousseau's Contribution to International Relations Theory' (2002) 2 Glendon Journal of International Studies 15, 18.

Becoming moral is therefore, initially, very hard, but this difficulty can be overcome by developing human reason. In fact, reason would inevitably develop as all natural faculties developed throughout history, but it needed time and experience. Interestingly, Kant believed that a way for reason to emerge and develop was through the antagonism between people: hostility and conflict pushed people to find solutions and thus develop their reason. The ultimate purpose of human existence was to move towards a peaceful society, not to find happiness. Kant believed that if happiness was the higher purpose of humans, nature would not have bestowed them with reason because their natural instincts would have served them well enough in their pursuit of 'happiness'.[13]

States, for Kant, followed the same rules as humans: they were moral persons in the international society, just like individuals within States. Kant, like Hobbes, believed men formed States to escape fear because in a state of nature, they were fully able to pursue their wishes, but because *everyone* was able to do so, there was no guarantee of order and property. However, he recognized that the international society of States in his times was far from perfect and he proposed his vision of a league of States, bound together by their commitment to peace. This league would develop similarly to the way States are formed, through natural forces that will lead to the best possible balance. In this system, it was necessary to develop an international law and international constitution, which must acknowledge and respect all States, weak and strong.[14] Kant's conception of an international society of perpetual peace follows his philosophy of human nature, as ultimately dominated by reason. He wrote:

> This guarantee [of Perpetual Peace] is given by no less a power than the great artist nature (natura daedala rerum)[15] in whose mechanical course is clearly exhibited a predetermined design to make harmony spring from human discord, even against the will of man.[16]

The two dominant theories of International Relations (IR), Realism and Idealism/Internationalism, derived their intellectual origins from such contrasting and dichotomous views of human nature. One, exemplified by Thomas Hobbes, was pessimistic both about human nature (described as selfish and confrontational) and States. The other, exemplified by Kant and to some extent Rousseau, believed in an innate perfectibility of humans, of States and the international society, which would evolve towards peace.

Today, a growing body of evidence from neuroscience permits us to re-examine long-held claims about human nature and what it is that truly drives and motivates human behaviour.[17] Therefore, what defines 'man' now lends itself to more complicated

[13] Julie Barkley, 'Human Nature and Kant's Vision of International Society' (2000) 1 Glendon Journal of International Studies 36, 36–7.

[14] ibid 40–1. [15] 'the intricate nature of things'.

[16] Immanuel Kant, *Perpetual Peace: A Philosophical Essay* (first published 1795, M Campbell Smith tr, George Allen & Unwin Ltd, 1903) 143.

[17] It should be noted that neuroscience is both an evolving field, and that it is not a deterministic science.

conclusions, which debunk many assumptions about human nature, including the orthodox view about humans as predominantly 'rational' beings. In recent decades, these conclusions reached outside of the medical field and started to be explored by philosophers as well, who recognize that the premises of earlier schools of philosophy were speculative. Neurophilosophy, the interdisciplinary field connecting findings from neuroscience and philosophy, is relevant for global security and for understanding what can propel good governance, peace, and security.

1. A Reappraisal of Emotions

An important contribution of neuroscience to political philosophy has been its reappraisal of the centrality of emotions in decision-making, morality, or preferences for political ideologies.

While emotions have often been cast aside as hindrances to sound judgement, emotions have anything but a marginal role in decision-making and cognitive processes. For example, studies of the human amygdala—the most thoroughly studied brain structure involved in emotional processes in the brain—revealed some surprising facts. The amygdala is a subcortical almond-shaped structure in the anterior-temporal lobe and comprises a group of nuclei that are critical in fear-conditioned responses and, because of its connections with the cortex, it has a broader role in the detection of stimuli, including positive stimuli, and other cognitive functions, such as attention and memory.[18] Studies on the amygdala showed that it may have a role in modulating the neural circuitry for episodic memory through the amygdala's modulation of hippocampal consolidation and that psychological arousal results in activation of the beta-adrenergic receptors in the amygdala. The amygdala subsequently modulates hippocampal processing leading to enhanced memory consolidation. Simply put, emotional responses, which are crucial for future survival, are less likely to be forgotten.[19]

Emotions are also critical to decision-making. A dominant view, with strong roots in Western philosophical tradition, and thinkers such as Plato and Kant, held that emotions were stumbling blocks to rational thought, and as a consequence, to moral decision-making.[20] Emotions and reason were therefore seen as 'dual' systems. However, studies in recent years have verifiably refuted the claim that the two are separated or in conflict. Antonio Damasio had already hinted at the importance of emotions and feelings in building autobiographical memory and good decision-making, back in the 1990s, when his research led him to work with patients who had brain lesions.

[18] Jennifer Kubota et al, 'The Neuroscience of Race' (2012) 15 Nature Neuroscience 940.

[19] Elizabeth A Phelps, 'Emotion and Cognition: Insights from Studies of the Human Amygdala' (2006) 57 Annual Review of Psychology 34.

[20] Nayef Al-Rodhan, 'Neurophilosophy of International Relations: Implications for Sustainable Peace and Security' (*The Montreal Review*, June 2016) <http://www.themontrealreview.com/2009/Neurophilosophy-of-International-Relations.php> accessed 12 September 2018.

These patients were not able to make good decisions although the brain structures responsible for 'reason' were unaffected.[21]

In recent years, more evidence has emerged to support the claim that changing emotions alters decisions (and vice-versa). For example, stress affects decision-making in ways that can be now understood in neuroanatomical terms—with implications for governance.

Stress is a term commonly used nowadays, at times inaccurately. From a neuroscientific perspective, stress manifests through activation of the hypothalamic-pituitary-adrenal (HPA) axis (and sympathetic nervous system arousal, but that is more transient), which leads to a cascade of neuroendocrine changes, notably glucocorticoid release, which in turn affect regions of the brain involved in decision-making. Stress impacts the prefrontal cortex (PFC), which is considered to play a role in goal-direction decisions, and PFC-dependent tasks such as memory. Intense and prolonged stress impairs the hippocampus; however, mild stress can enhance hippocampal functions. Stress also enhances performance on striatal-dependent tasks—the striatum is usually linked to habit-based choices. Chronic stress was shown to impair several brain functions and prevent the good functioning of others: experiments showed that it resulted in neural atrophy of the medial PFC and dorsal medial striatum, a neurocircuit that is involved in goal-oriented actions, as well as hypertrophy of the dorsal lateral striatum, a region known to be responsible for learning new habits.[22]

Stress therefore incapacitates several regions of the brain and skews the mechanisms involved in making decisions, which, under normal circumstances, would follow different patterns. Other studies have also pointed to the detrimental impact of chronic stress. For example, studies about intertemporal choice revealed that stress is more likely to lead to the tendency to dismiss future rewards in favour of immediate rewards.[23] Other studies looked into moral decision-making and revealed that stress reduces the tendency to make utilitarian judgments in personal moral decisions and is thus consistent with the notion of egocentric moral choices.[24]

2. Neurophilosophy of Human Nature and Implications for Global Security

These studies carry important implications for political philosophy and theories of governance. Chronically stressful situations, such as conflict, deprivation, and any situation

[21] Jason Pontin, 'The Importance of Feelings' (*MIT Technology Review*, 17 June 2014) <https://www.technologyreview.com/s/528151/the-importance-of-feelings/> accessed 12 September 2018.

[22] Elizabeth Phelps et al, 'Emotion and Decision-Making: Multiple Modulatory Neural Circuits' (2014) 37 Annual Review of Neuroscience 263, 268.

[23] Kenta Kimura et al, 'The Biological Effects of Acute Psychosocial Stress on Delay Discounting' (2013) 38 Psychoneuroendocrinology 2300.

[24] Farid F Youssef et al, 'Stress Alters Personal Moral Decision Making' (2012) 37 Psychoneuroendocrinology 491.

that tests an individual's survival impulse will greatly shape their actions and the degree to which they can make 'moral' decisions. There is little evidence in neuroscience to point to innate morality or immorality. While there are species-specific commonalities in our nature, evident in our shared neurochemistry, we are otherwise left to circumstances.

A neurophilosophical understanding of human nature best describes humans as *emotional*, *amoral* and *egoistic*.[25] We are deeply *emotional* beings, and a vast neural circuitry mediates emotions' modulation of decision-making. Indeed, human experience is to a large extent mediated by emotions. Another defining trait is our *amorality*, which means that we are not intrinsically good or bad but we can be both at various times and in varying degrees, depending on circumstances. We are, however, not entirely blank slates. A more accurate description would be that of a *predisposed tabula rasa*, meaning we are born free of preconceptions of good or bad but we are endowed with a set of predispositions for survival encoded by genetics.[26] This is a powerful motivator throughout our existence, which is often not even expressed at a conscious level but more like an 'inbuilt microchip tuning us for survival'.[27] That is where our *egoism* manifests: as a drive for the survival of the self, which is a basic form of egoism.

This neurophilosophical account of human nature has immediate implications for IR theory and policymaking. Because our morality fluctuates depending on the environment, it is crucial to create and foster governance structures that allow the best, moral, sides of human nature to thrive. In other words, if the lowest threshold for survival is hard to attain, humans will do anything to survive, even commit acts seemingly 'immoral', or of pre-emptive violence.[28]

Key to countering this is to foster dignity-based models of governance. Integrating human dignity in governance is the single best predictor of sustainable governance, which in turn is the best predictor of human nature being at its best. The importance of dignity is often rendered starkly obvious in its absence. This can be seen even in the most advanced and prosperous Western democracies, where ample freedoms and liberties coexist with marginalization, discrimination, and alienation. The results are social tensions, the rise of hyper-populist political figures with destabilizing tendencies, and a climate of frustration or political apathy.

Contrary to what Francis Fukuyama professed three decades ago, liberal democracy has not become a universally adopted political system precisely because it did not focus

[25] Nayef Al-Rodhan, *'Emotional Amoral Egoism': A Neurophilosophical Theory of Human Nature and Its Universal Security Implications* (LIT 2008) 16–17.

[26] Nayef Al-Rodhan, 'Predisposed Tabula Rasa' (*OXPOL*, 15 May 2015) <https://blog.politics.ox.ac.uk/predisposed-tabula-rasa/> accessed 12 September 2018.

[27] Nayef Al-Rodhan, 'Who are we: Neurochemical man and emotional amoral egoism' (*The Montreal Review*, January 2015) <http://www.themontrealreview.com/2009/Who-are-we-Neurochemical-man-and-emotional-amoral-egoism.php> accessed 12 September 2018.

[28] Nayef Al-Rodhan, 'A Neuro-Philosophy of History: "Sustainable History"; with Dignity, and without Directionality' (*Blog of the American Philosophical Association*, 20 August 2018) <https://blog.apaonline.org/2018/08/20/a-neuro-philosophy-of-history-sustainable-history-with-dignity-and-without-directionality/> accessed 12 September 2018.

enough on weeding out the sources of disenfranchisement for all of the populace. Rather than the 'end of history', what is sorely needed today is a 'Sustainable History' model of governance, which places dignity at the centre. What is meant by dignity here is not merely the absence of humiliation but a more inclusive set of human needs, which carefully balance the *emotional*, *amoral* and *egoistic* attributes of human nature. These are: reason, security, human rights, accountability, transparency, justice, opportunity, innovation, inclusiveness.[29]

The consequences of this transcend domestic politics.[30]

3. Emotional Amoral Egoism of States

International Relations theorists such as Morgenthau significantly drew from accounts of human nature to make inferences about the character of States in the global arena. For Realists, to cite one example, States were like humans: driven by self-interest and *animus dominandi* (the desire to dominate), interested in maximizing their powers and resources. The international stage was highly competitive and anarchic as a result. While Realists imbued some ancient philosophical conclusions with a status of timeless truth (eg, Thucydides' famous line that 'the strong do as they will and the poor must endure'), which was overly fatalistic, the man–State analogy was methodologically sound and remains valid to date.[31] This means that States, too, are emotional, amoral, egoistic actors.

As extensive historical evidence demonstrates, States do not always behave 'rationally', and emotions and idiosyncratic factors very often come into play. Nationalism, in fact, is one expression of that subjective emotionality. Another one is strategic culture, which is a concept in strategic studies that matured during the Cold War especially in US policy circles. Jack Snyder had defined it in 1977 as 'the total sum of ideals, conditional emotional responses and patterns of habitual behaviour that members of the national strategic community have acquired through instruction of imitation and share with each other with regard to [...] strategy.'[32] The intellectual precursor of this paradigm was to be found in the so-called 'national character' studies, during the 1940s and 1950s, when US anthropologists and sociologists were employed to analyse the Axis powers.[33]

[29] Nayef Al-Rodhan, 'Proposal of a Dignity Scale for Sustainable Governance' (*CSS*, 2015) <https://isnblog.ethz.ch/politics/proposal-of-a-dignity-scale-for-sustainable-governance> accessed 12 September 2018.

[30] Al-Rodhan, 'Geopolitics of Dignity' (*OXPOL*, 17 June 2014) <https://blog.politics.ox.ac.uk/geopolitics-dignity/> accessed 14 November 2020.

[31] Al-Rodhan, 'A Neuro-Philosophy of History' (n 28).

[32] Jack L Snyder, The Soviet Strategic Culture: Implications for Limited Nuclear Operations (RAND 1977) <https://www.rand.org/content/dam/rand/pubs/reports/2005/R2154.pdf> accessed 12 September 2018.

[33] Nayef Al-Rodhan, 'Strategic Culture and Pragmatic National Interest' (*Global Policy Journal*, 22 July 2015) <https://www.globalpolicyjournal.com/blog/22/07/2015/strategic-culture-and-pragmatic-national-interest> accessed 12 September 2018.

Collective memory and highly emotional narratives about historical episodes continue feeding into visions of national security. China's 'century of humiliation' by Japan and the West created a powerful guide for the country in the following century and decades. To some extent, China's territorial disputes with Japan, such as over the Senkakus (or Diaoyu, as the islands are known in China) is ultimately of minimal strategic importance and is more a proof of the high emotional value each country attaches to the dispute.[34] Similarly, numerous conflicts within the Middle East, and also with outside powers, are strongly rooted in sensitive historical memories, such as the 1917 Balfour Declaration. The latter shaped the relations between the West and the Arab world and even a century later, it continues to be vividly remembered in the Arab world as a token of mistrust towards Western powers.[35] Pragmatic national interest, of course, does supersede emotional responses on many occasions, but the importance of accounting for the emotionality of States in global security should not be understated. Just like for humans, a baseline in international politics is survival, and territorial integrity and sovereignty are fundamental guiding posts of any foreign policy. Beyond that, any country's conduct will oscillate.

States are also amoral in the sense that their moral actions in foreign policy fluctuate depending on circumstances or on leadership. One recent example is how Italy responded to the ongoing humanitarian refugee crisis at its Southern borders—in different ways from other previous governments.

4. Just Power and Transcultural Understanding

The international domain is, however, different from domestic government as there is no centralized overarching power to keep abuses in check. While there are international legal mechanisms to prevent or retaliate for abuses, ranging from economic sanctions to military intervention, a state of anarchy formally remains in global politics because there is no global government. Therefore, while dignity-based governance can decisively stave off the worst of human nature in a domestic setting, the same logic cannot be equally transposed to international governance because the legal mechanisms for enforceability of laws are much weaker.

Nevertheless, once it is acknowledged that States embed 'emotional, amoral, and egoistic' features, it is easier to grasp how peace and security can be furthered in the global arena. One way to do so is to promote Just Power. In the century since the US left isolationism and become a hegemonic power in global politics, several conceptions of power have been theorized and entered official rhetoric. Hard, soft, and smart power captured

[34] DZ, 'Who really owns the Senkaku Islands?' (*The Economist*, 3 December 2013) <https://www.economist.com/the-economist-explains/2013/12/03/who-really-owns-the-senkaku-islands> accessed 12 September 2018.

[35] Nayef Al-Rodhan, 'The Arab-Islamic World and Global Geopolitics: Endogenous vs. Exogenous Factors' in BBVA Openmind (ed), *The Age of Perplexity: Rethinking the World We Knew* (Penguin Random House 2018) 206.

different aspects, eras and expectations in US foreign policy. The most recent of the three, 'smart power', was proposed as a concept by a 2006 bi-partisan Commission, which defined it as a skilful and intelligent use of both hard and soft power.[36]

In today's interdependent and deeply connected world, the 'smartness' of power is not sufficient. Indeed, a fundamental flaw in previous conceptions of power was that they insufficiently accounted for the agency of others, and for the dignity needs of others. Power in the twenty-first century can only be effective if it is smart, as well as just. Justice here is meant in a minimalist sense as fairness and respect for international law. 'Just Power' is critical for attracting support and encouraging compliance and legitimacy in international politics.[37] Power which manifests itself in dominating ways and is not committed to respecting the individual and collective dignity of others is inherently unsustainable. This new understanding of power goes hand-in-hand with a reform of global institutions, such as the UN. A reformed UN can go a long way in creating a greater sense of fairness in the system, especially if the structural asymmetry which is enshrined in the United Nations Security Council (UNSC) is abandoned, although that remains a distant prospect.[38]

5. From International to Transcultural Understanding

The notion of collective dignity here also has a security dimension. After 2001, the discourse of divisiveness between the West and Arab-Islamic world has fed fear, mistrust, and insecurity. The theory of a 'clash of civilizations', which had lost appeal in previous years, was quickly resurrected and added to State-centric and geopolitical explanations. Moreover, Samuel Huntington, who had proposed the theory, contended that geo-cultural differences are more enduring and more constant than the political ones, and therefore more difficult to resolve. Representations of human history as an account between multiple civilizations in conflict are extremely problematic politically, as well as historically incorrect. Instead, history can be best described according to the 'Ocean Model of Civilization', which regards human civilization as an ocean, into which many rivers flow. This is a more judicious account of human civilization because it rightly credits the role and contribution of other geo-cultural domains and thus sees civilization as a cumulative experience built in countless processes of exchanges and interactions.[39]

[36] Richard L Armitage/Joseph S Nye (eds), *CSIS Commission on Smart Power: A Smarter, More Secure America* (CSIS 2007) 7.

[37] Nayef Al-Rodhan, 'Sustainable Power is Just Power' (*e-International Relations*, 5 December 2013) <https://www.e-ir.info/2013/12/05/sustainable-power-is-just-power/> accessed 12 September 2018.

[38] Nayef Al-Rodhan, 'Just Power for a Reformed UN' (*OXPOL*, 7 June 2018) <https://blog.politics.ox.ac.uk/just-power-for-a-reformed-un/> accessed 12 September 2018.

[39] Nayef Al-Rodhan, 'The Islamic World and the West: Recovering Common History' (*YaleGlobal Online*, 15 July 2014) <https://yaleglobal.yale.edu/content/islamic-world-and-west-recovering-common-history> accessed 17 September 2018.

This could improve the relations between the West and the Arab-Islamic world. Contrary to the image now normalized in Western consciousness, Europe and the Arab world have a long history of mutual borrowings in areas as diverse as astronomy, medicine, mathematics, legal scholarship, architecture. The story of the rise of the West frequently omits telling this side of the story. According to the canon, this happened organically, autonomously, as Europe left the Dark Ages and moved towards Renaissance, the Scientific Revolution, and the Enlightenment. However, the West built significantly in those centuries on advances from the Arab-Islamic world, just like the latter had built, in its rise, from other cultures.[40] Reclaiming this forgotten chapter of commonality and mutual history could go a long way in advancing more transcultural understanding. This is especially needed in a time when the rift between 'civilizations' is rendered ever wider by populist leaders with an isolationist bent. This also has implications for global security. In extreme forms, discourses of incompatibility between cultures feed into violent rhetoric on both sides.[41]

6. Neuroscience of Divisive Politics

Studies in the neuroscience of social cognition and race provide further insight into divisive politics. Cultivating fear towards whoever is part of the 'out-group' is distinctly expressed in the brain and plays on ancestral predispositions of regarding the 'tribe' or close group as critical to survival. Research showed that the distinction between 'us' versus 'them' occurs in the prefrontal cortex and further studies revealed activation differences in the brain. When asked to make judgements about people considered 'similar', areas in the ventromedial PFC became active, whereas for people considered different, the activation happened in the dorsomedial PFC.[42] Different brain regions are therefore deployed in assessing similar or dissimilar people. The bias goes even deeper. fMRI experiments also showed how empathy is created differently: for those we will perceive as outsiders to the group, the 'mirror neurons' (usually involved in building empathy) will more likely switch off, thus blocking emotional connections.[43]

In the 1990s, new studies of race began in the US, using electrophysiological techniques and focusing in great detail on the role of the amygdala. The amygdala, as

[40] Nayef Al-Rodhan, 'Introduction: A Thousand Years of Amnesia' in Nayef Al-Rodhan (ed), *The Role of the Arab-Islamic World in the Rise of the West. Implications for Contemporary Trans-Cultural Relations* (Palgrave Macmillan 2012) 7.

[41] Nayef Al-Rodhan, 'The "Ocean Model of Civilisation", Sustainable History Theory and Global Cultural Understanding' (*OXPOL*, 1 June 2017) <https://blog.politics.ox.ac.uk/ocean-model-civilization-sustainable-history-theory-global-cultural-understanding/> accessed 14 November 2020.

[42] Bernard J Baars/Nicole M Cage, *Cognition, Brain and Consciousness: Introduction to Cognitive Neuroscience* (2nd edn, Academic Press 2010) 460.

[43] Mari Fitzduff, 'What Does Neuroscience Have to Offer Peacebuilders?' (*Oxford Research Group*, 12 September 2016) <https://www.oxfordresearchgroup.org.uk/Blog/what-does-neuroscience-have-to-offer-peacebuilders> accessed 17 September 2018.

described in the previous sections, is heavily involved in emotional learning, as well as in the unconscious assessment of threats. Two studies published in *Psychological Science* (2004)[44] and in *Nature* (2012)[45] showed, quite astoundingly, how brain activations shift from one brain region to another, as initial automatic response is met with egalitarian conscious beliefs. A 30-millisecond exposure of black faces led to an automatic activation in the amygdala, while extended exposure of up to 525 milliseconds led to an activation in the PFC and the anterior cingulate cortex, areas associated with inhibition and control, suggesting a tendency to impose upon oneself the societal goals to be unprejudiced and the aspiration now shared by many Americans that any behaviour that condones racial bias is unacceptable.

An optimistic conclusion emerged, however, from these studies, and which strengthened the premise that dignity-based governance is crucial in fostering social harmony. Because the brain is highly malleable, all prejudices can be unlearned, even those that are automatic. Changing the context for social interactions leads to a definitive change of responses in the brain—a conclusion that can be extended to any forms of divisive politics.[46] The same can be said about any and all excesses that our nature is inclined to fall into. One of them is power.

7. A Neurochemical Understanding of Power—Implications for Governance

Power is highly addictive and, circumstances allowing, it can devolve into extreme forms of totalitarian control. That is because, if power is addictive, absolute power is intoxicating. The main neurochemical (known today) which is involved in the neural circuitry of power is dopamine, the same neurotransmitter responsible for producing a sense of pleasure. Power creates an addictive high, compelling those in positions of power, at the very least, to maintain it at all costs.

The problem, again, is one of institutions. Leaders in positions of absolute power in systems with weak or no checks and balances will find it much harder to accept any loss of power or any change of status. Sudden withdrawal of power is like an abrupt withdrawal from drugs, which creates uncontrollable cravings. For dictators who enjoyed undisputed reigns in their countries, relinquishing power can never go smoothly and without violence.[47] These are some of the extreme neurobehavioural aspects of power

[44] William A Cunningham et al, 'Separable Neural Components in the Processing of Black and White Faces' (2004) 15 Psychological Science 806.

[45] Kubota et al (n 18) 941–4.

[46] Nayef Al-Rodhan, 'Us versus Them: How Neurophilosophy Explains our Divided Politics' (*World Economic Forum*, 3 October 2016) <https://www.weforum.org/agenda/2016/10/us-versus-them-how-neurophilosophy-explains-populism-racism-and-extremism> accessed 17 September 2018.

[47] Nayef Al-Rodhan, 'The Neurochemistry of Power: Implications for Political Change' (*OXPOL*, 27 February 2014) <https://blog.politics.ox.ac.uk/neurochemistry-power-implications-political-change/> accessed 17 September 2018.

addiction, which have been seen throughout history in leaders like Napoleon, Stalin, or Hitler and which manifest through manic behaviour, increased cognitive skills, lack of inhibition, narcissism, impulsiveness, and paranoia.

The same cannot be said, however, of leaders in functional democratic systems. While the temptation to accrue power and maintain it may also be high, the limitations imposed by consolidated institutions curtail ambitions of absolute rule. Moving forward into the twenty-first century, this is a crucial lesson in peacebuilding and regime change. For any political transition to happen effectively, especially in contexts of absolute rule, the change must be gradual. In such contexts, the withdrawal of power must be skilfully managed, so as not to unleash the destructive impulses that accompany unchecked power.

C. A Future Redefined by Technology: 'Game-Changers' and Existential Risks

As this chapter attempts to re-energize the debate on human nature in global security, it cannot leave out the inevitable question about the future of human nature in the twenty-first century. A range of technologies under development today already flag some of the existential risks besetting humanity going forward.

First, there are technologies external to us, which promise to change warfare and societies alike. Second, a range of internal technologies will alter our biology, enhancing certain functions or eliminating others.[48]

1. From Artificial Intelligence Agents to Enhanced Humans

The presence of artificial intelligence (AI) in society and increasingly on the battlefield is on the cusp of becoming the 'new normal'. Today, advances in robot intelligence are leading, for the first time, to discussions about robots' 'rights' and 'personhood', and under which conditions such a status could be considered—a discussion unthinkable just two decades ago. The question, however, is not only one of intelligence but also of morality. No matter how intelligent a machine is, it would need to possess a capacity for moral decision-making. That technology has yet to materialize; although developments with neuromorphic technology, which aims to mimic the human neural architecture of the brain, would mean effectively that a robot could 'think' like a human, thus displaying

[48] Nayef Al-Rodhan, 'Future Wars: Reshaping the Ethics and Norms of War' (*The Wilson Quarterly*, Summer 2015) <https://wilsonquarterly.com/quarterly/summer-2015-an-age-of-connectivity/future-wars-reshaping-the-ethics-and-norms-of-war/> accessed 17 September 2018.

human values.[49] Even so, the current pace of development of AI-based systems is enough of a matter of concern. For example, a 2016 study for the JURI Committee of the European Parliament on 'European Civil Law Rules in Robotics' stated that:

> People will work, cooperate, interact, have fun, live, and perhaps even fall in love, with highly sophisticated machines. Society will need to reconsider humanity's place in the face of these technologies. (…) The split between past and future societal models will be such that we cannot expect to take the emergence of information technology, the Internet or mobile phones as a starting point for reflection.[50]

In the domain of security, which is the main focus of this volume, AI is making its way on the battlefield, aiding human-led operations especially in maritime and air power, where human and social skills are less needed compared to domains such as urban warfare.[51]

But despite ground-breaking advances in weaponry and military technologies, the most unsettling and ultimate frontier of innovation is poised to be within our own bodies. In the military, the striking frailty of the human body is in sharp contrast with the fast development of sophisticated technologies. As Patrick Lin et al write, '[a]s impressive as our weapons systems may be…[a] soldier is still vulnerable to a fatal wound delivered by a single 25-cent bullet'.[52] In a 2003 Statement, the US Defense Advanced Research Projects Agency (DARPA) noted that fast advances in arms technology meant that humans remained the 'weakest link' in the US military. The solution would be found in enhancing soldiers' minds and bodies by technology.

Human enhancement refers to 'the use of innovative technologies to augment or enhance human functions and abilities beyond the replacement of dysfunctional cellular groups and organs'.[53] Enhancement is different from therapy and restorative medicine as it does not aim to heal or restore lost functions but to enhance healthy abilities above and beyond 'normal' levels. The thrust for DARPA's Bio-revolution, and the 'Enhanced Human Performance' project in particular, was motivated by an underlying goal 'to

[49] Nayef Al-Rodhan, 'Artificial Intelligent Agents: Prerequisites for Rights and Dignity' (*CSS*, 4 April 2018) <https://isnblog.ethz.ch/technology/artificial-intelligent-agents-prerequisites-for-rights-and-dignity> accessed 17 September 2018.

[50] European Parliament/Directorate-General for Internal Policies, 'European Civil Law Rules in Robotics: Study for the JURI Committee' (2016) PE 571.379, 6. <http://www.europarl.europa.eu/RegData/etudes/STUD/2016/571379/IPOL_ STU%282016%29571379_EN.pdf > accessed 17 September 2018.

[51] Kareem Ayoub/Kenneth Payne, 'Strategy in the Age of Artificial Intelligence' (2015) 39 Journal of Strategic Studies 793.

[52] Patrick Lin et al, 'Enhanced Warfighters: Risk, Ethics and Policy' (*The Greenwall Foundation*, 1 January 2013) 1 <http://ethics.calpoly.edu/greenwall_report.pdf> accessed 17 September 2018.

[53] Nayef Al-Rodhan, *The Politics of Emerging Strategic Technologies. Implications for Geopolitics, Human Enhancement and Human Destiny* (Palgrave Macmillan 2011) 178.

make the individual warfighter stronger, more alert, more endurant, and better able to heal'.[54]

The drive for enhancement in the military has a long history, and included anything from alcohol to drugs or psychostimulants. The use of amphetamines skyrocketed during the Second World War and the Vietnam War. Today, a drug more commonly used is Modafinil, which has been proven to sustain wakefulness for up to 40-h periods.[55] Another method includes brain stimulation with electricity. Neurostimulation harnesses the functions of certain nerves or brain areas and works by inhibiting or enhancing those functions. For example, stimulation of the PFC can enhance or diminish the tendency to lie (a potentially useful skill for soldiers who are captured and interrogated by the enemy), or encourage compliance with social norms.[56] A procedure known as transcranial direct current stimulation (tDCS) was demonstrated to help participants perform better at multitasking and overall vigilance.[57] It works by altering the sensitivity of certain brain cells, making them more or less active to something that will stimulate them later. Another method known as transcranial magnetic stimulation (TMS) uses instead the physics of electromagnetism to activate brain cells. Both have effects that can last up to days and cause changes in neurochemistry and neurophysiology.[58]

2. From Enhancement to Inevitable Transhumanism

The above-cited examples provide a glimpse into the extraordinary potential of technology to alter our physiology and brains, charting a new course for the future of humanity, one in which we will one day be able to take charge of evolution itself.[59] This is a very dangerous prospect because of the inevitable negative spillover effects.

In warfare, differences between enhanced and unenhanced soldiers will erode the cohesiveness of troops and put a strain on military values. In addition, they will raise numerous ethical questions and legal conundrums.[60] For example, if a soldier is

[54] Tony Tether, 'Statement' (Subcommittee on Terrorism, Unconventional Threats, and Capabilities, 27 March 2003) 12 <https://www.darpa.mil/attachments/TestimonyArchived(March%2027%202003).pdf> accessed 14 November 2020.

[55] Arthur Estrada et al, 'Modafinil as a Replacement for Dextroamphetamine for Sustaining Alertness in Military Helicopter Pilots' (June 2012) 83 Aviation, Space and Environmental Medicine 556.

[56] Chris Chambers, 'Neuro-enhancement in the Military: Far-fetched or an Inevitable Future?' (*The Guardian*, 7 October 2013) <https://www.theguardian.com/science/head-quarters/2013/oct/07/neuroscience-psychology> accessed 14 November 2020.

[57] Ian Sample, 'US Military Successfully Tests Electrical Brain Stimulation to Enhance Staff Skills' (*The Guardian*, 7 November 2016) <https://www.theguardian.com/science/2016/nov/07/us-military-successfully-tests-electrical-brain-stimulation-to-enhance-staff-skills> accessed 17 September 2018.

[58] Chambers (n 56).

[59] Nayef Al-Rodhan, 'Will Biology Change what it Means to be Human?' (*World Economic Forum*, 10 November 2014) <https://www.weforum.org/agenda/2014/11/synthetic-biology-designing-our-existence/> accessed 14 November 2020.

[60] Nayef Al-Rodhan, 'Transhumanism and War' (*Global Policy Journal*, 18 May 2015) <https://www.globalpolicyjournal.com/blog/18/05/2015/transhumanism-and-war> accessed 17 September 2018.

enhanced to withstand extreme levels of pain, how will the notion of torture evolve or be re-evaluated?

In society, enhancements with the help of technology and pharmaceuticals will have profound implications for social cooperation, prompting new forms of inequality between the enhanced and unenhanced, or aggravating existing divides between haves and have-nots, assuming that the wealthier could afford to have access to forms of enhancements to a greater extent than the less privileged. The consequences go deeper: enhancements could reinstate ways of ranking human beings into superior and inferior and it is hard to believe legal and normative efforts could effectively devise ways to counter that.[61]

The risks are greater down the line. As we gain more and more control over biological processes and are able to manipulate them, it is futile to hope that we will resist the temptation to pursue such interventions. Humans are neuro-chemically pre-programmed to 'feel good' and are strongly driven by a set of five motivators called the 'Neuro P5': power, profit, pleasure, permanency (understood as the drive to maximize one's chances of survival), and pride. When one or all of these motivators are boosted by technology, our nature will push us in that direction even if that may be counter-productive for us in the long term. Rather than exerting meaningful control over how we adopt enhancements into our lives, we will in fact continue pursuing them at a galloping pace. This will set us on the course of inevitable transhumanism.[62]

The existential risks cannot be understated. During millennia of evolution, our species successfully learnt reflexes and habits that have helped us survive and thrive. This also includes negative emotions, such as fear, remorse, guilt, which have been highly educational and have equipped us with tools for social cooperation. While technology may eradicate some of our 'weaknesses' and negative feelings, it may do so in the detriment of our 'humanity' and the essential aspects that define us as humans.

D. Conclusion

Writing on twenty-first-century security challenges is dauntingly complicated. As the opening lines suggested, threats and challenges come from multiple sources simultaneously: aggressive States and militarism, outer space politics, climate change, transnational crime, cyberwarfare, to name but a few. Finding a thread of commonality amongst these may seem difficult. This chapter delved into findings from neuroscience

[61] Nayef Al-Rodhan, 'The "Sustainable History" Thesis: A Guide for Regulating Trans- and Post-Humanism' (*e-International Relations*, 24 April 2018) <https://www.e-ir.info/2018/04/24/the-sustainable-history-thesis-a-guide-for-regulating-trans-and-post-humanism/> accessed 14 November 2020.

[62] Nayef Al-Rodhan, 'Inevitable Transhumanism? How Emerging Strategic Technologies will Affect the Future of Humanity' (*CSS*, 29 October 2013) <https://isnblog.ethz.ch/security/inevitable-transhumanism-how-emerging-strategic-technologies-will-affect-the-future-of-humanity> accessed 17 September 2018.

to reflect on conflict and governance in a more fundamental way: by looking into what drives human nature and what propels good governance at the domestic and international level.

The conventional wisdom that shaped the discourse on IR in the post-Second World War era can be revisited in light of new insights from neuroscience. This is a unique opportunity to reconsider how to improve our governance models, even the most 'successful' ones, by ensuring that human dignity is placed at the centre of all policies, as well as how to think about political transitions, regime change, and a sustainable future for all. In light of new advances in enhancement technologies, the kind of future we want to shape for humanity as a whole will be a primary responsibility and challenge for this century and beyond.

PART II

PREDOMINANT SECURITY CHALLENGES AND INTERNATIONAL LAW

NATIONAL AND TRANSNATIONAL SECURITY

CHAPTER 8

CORRUPTION AND GLOBAL SECURITY

CECILY ROSE

A. Introduction

As the news demonstrates on a nearly daily basis, corruption is a phenomenon, to varying extents, in all societies, from the highly stable, to the highly unstable.[1] Corruption, in other words, can hardly be seen as a feature of only insecure societies, emerging from or entering into armed conflict. Yet, some of the world's most spectacular contemporary corruption scandals have indeed been associated with various forms of global insecurity, whether in the form of impoverished and aggrieved local populations, extreme political instability, or violent uprisings. Moreover, social scientists have been able to show not only a correlation between corruption and insecurity, but also causal relationships, as corruption can contribute to insecurity, and insecurity can also give rise to corruption.

In concluding international and regional anti-corruption treaties, States have shown at least some awareness of these relationships, in particular the role that corruption can play in fostering political and economic instability. Anti-corruption treaties contain provisions on criminalization, enforcement, international cooperation, and prevention, which can be seen as a toolbox and a guide to combating corruption and perhaps, in turn, fostering global security. But these treaties also provide that in some instances,

[1] The Editorial Board, '"Lula" is in Prison and Brazil's Democracy is in Peril' (*The New York Times*, 12 April 2018) <https://www.nytimes.com/2018/04/12/opinion/lula-brazil-corruption-scandal.html> accessed 16 May 2020; Aodhan Beirne, 'Corruption in South Africa: A Guide to Our Recent Reporting' (*The New York Times*, 22 December 2018) <https://www.nytimes.com/2018/12/22/world/africa/corruption-south-africa-guide.html> accessed 14 May 2020; John Lloyd, 'The Roots of Putin's Power Machine' (*Financial Times*, 17 July 2019) <https://www.ft.com/content/4ebebedo-a163-11e9-a282-2df48f366f7d> accessed 16 May 2020; Valerie Hopkins 'Kosovo "Enslaved from Within" by Corruption, Says Incoming PM' (*Financial Times*, 15 December 2019) <https://www.ft.com/content/ddc2f794-060e-11ea-a984-fbbacad9e7dd> accessed 16 May 2020.

States are free to prioritize national security interests over anti-corruption interests. Fighting corruption and promoting global security may be viewed as competing or complementary initiatives under international law, depending on the circumstances.

This chapter begins in Section B by discussing the term 'corruption', which lacks a legal definition and can mean different things to lawyers and to social scientists. The chapter goes on to describe in Section C the various ways in which corruption and insecurity can relate to each other, before detailing the international legal framework concerning corruption in Section D. Finally, Section E touches on one of the challenges facing researchers who study the causes and consequences of corruption, namely the difficulties involved in measuring corruption and the impact of anti-corruption laws.

B. Defining the Term 'Corruption'

International lawyers and social scientists often do not use the term 'corruption' in the same manner, or to refer to the same set of conduct. The meaning of this term therefore merits a few remarks. Within the international legal field, the term 'corruption' itself has no legal definition. Numerous international legal instruments that are dedicated to combating corruption, and have 'corruption' in their titles, do not define the term.[2] In the case of the United Nations Convention against Corruption (UNCAC), the drafters omitted a definition of corruption because they could not agree upon a definition that would be compatible with a range of domestic legal systems and also they did not consider a definition to be necessary.[3] Instead, corruption in UNCAC and other anti-corruption treaties represents an umbrella concept, which refers to the various forms of criminal conduct that are defined in the treaty provisions. Because various types of corruption benefit from legal definitions, the absence of an overarching definition of corruption under international law poses no practical problems, and is therefore of relatively little significance. When international lawyers refer to 'corruption', they are referring to a set of crimes, including bribery, embezzlement, trading in influence, abuse of functions, and illicit enrichment. Although the term bribery is sometimes used (by lawyers and non-lawyers) as a synonym for corruption, bribery is, in fact, only one form of corruption, albeit the most common form. The term corruption does not, however,

[2] Inter-American Convention against Corruption (1996) 35 ILM 724; CoE Criminal Law Convention on Corruption ETS No 173 (CoE Criminal Law Convention); United Nations Convention against Corruption 2349 UNTS 41 (UNCAC); African Union Convention on Preventing and Combating Corruption (2004) 43 ILM 5 (AU Convention on Corruption); Arab Anti-Corruption Convention <https://star.worldbank.org/document/arab-convention-against-corruption> accessed 16 May 2020. But see CoE Civil Law Convention against Corruption ETS No 174 (CoE Civil Law Convention) art 2 (defining corruption as 'requesting, offering, giving or accepting, directly or indirectly, a bribe or any other undue advantage or prospect thereof, which distorts the proper performance of any duty or behavior required of the recipient of the bribe, the undue advantage or the prospect thereof').

[3] Cornelia Spörl, 'Article 2: Use of Terms' in Cecily Rose et al (eds), *The United Nations Convention against Corruption: A Commentary* (OUP 2019) 23.

encompass money laundering, a form of conduct which is related to, but separate from, corruption. Money laundering refers to the process of obscuring the illegal origins of the proceeds of crime, the source of which may be an act of corruption, or some other crime such as drug trafficking.

Social scientists and non-lawyers generally use the term corruption in ways that are both broader and narrower than the use of this term in the international legal field. These divergences are significant because when lawyers and non-lawyers (eg, social scientists) speak of 'corruption', they are often not referring to the same phenomena. According to a widely cited definition, corruption refers to 'the abuse of entrusted power for private gain'.[4] This definition is, however, under-inclusive (when compared with the acts of corruption set out in UNCAC, for example), because it focuses on the passive rather than the active side of corruption.[5] This definition easily captures the conduct of the public official who abuses his or her authority by accepting a bribe, for example, but it does not capture the conduct of the private sector official who bribes the public official. Far from abusing his or her authority, the private sector official may be carrying out a company policy concerning bribe payments. An expanded definition that captures both the active and passive sides of corruption would refer to 'the abuse of entrusted power for private gain or the exercise of improper influence over those entrusted with power'.[6]

Social scientists also sometimes conceive of corruption in ways that are significantly broader than the forms of corruption that are enumerated in international anti-corruption treaties, and are found in domestic criminal law. Social scientists have, for example, used the term corruption to encompass vote-buying in the context of rigged elections, illegal logging, the extortion of ransoms, and the extortion of rents through monopolistic practices.[7] While such conduct may be illegal and may also distort economies and political systems, these phenomena do not necessarily meet the definitions of any of the forms of corruption set out in international anti-corruption treaties. In other words, such conduct may be illegal, but not under domestic anti-corruption laws. Because this chapter approaches the subject of corruption and global security from the perspective of public international law, the term corruption will therefore refer to the

[4] Transparency International, 'What is Corruption?' <https://www.transparency.org/what-is-corruption#define> accessed 16 May 2020.

[5] 'Active' bribery, for example, refers to the promising, offering or giving of a bribe, whereas 'passive' bribery refers to the solicitation or acceptance of a bribe. UNCAC (n 2) art 15.

[6] Mlada Bukovansky, 'The Hollowness of Anti-Corruption Discourse' (2006) 13 Review of International Political Economy 181, 186; Cecily Rose, *International Anti-Corruption Norms: Their Creation and Influence on Domestic Legal Systems* (OUP 2015) 7. Another definition, posited by the political scientist Joseph Nye, also encompasses both the active and passive sides of corruption. Joseph S Nye, 'Corruption and Political Development: A Cost-Benefit Analysis' (1967) 61 The American Political Science Review 417 ('Corruption is behavior which deviates from the formal duties of a public role because of private-regarding (personal, close family, private clique) pecuniary or status gains; or violates rules against the exercise of certain types of private-regarding influence').

[7] Philippe Le Billon, 'Buying Peace or Fueling War: The Role of Corruption in Armed Conflicts' (2003) 15 Journal of International Development 413, 419; Fredrik Galtung/Martin Tisné, 'A New Approach to PostWar Reconstruction' (2009) 20 Journal of Democracy 93, 97–8.

various acts of corruption set out in international anti-corruption treaties, in particular UNCAC, which provides the most comprehensive enumeration of corrupt acts.

C. The Relationships between Corruption and Global Security

Corruption and global security relate to each other in a number of ways. Corruption is both a cause of global insecurity, and a consequence of it. In other words, corruption may lead to insecurity, and conversely, insecurity, as in post-conflict societies, may lead to corruption and to greater tolerance of it. In addition, corruption can also be a cause of security or stability, rather than insecurity. A body of social science literature, described in this section, supports all of these relationships. Finally, anti-corruption measures and campaigns may themselves inadvertently cause insecurity. This last possibility will be explored in Section D, concerning the international legal framework, as the relationship between anti-corruption measures and insecurity has not been addressed to a significant extent in the work of social scientists. Anti-corruption treaties, however, specifically address the possibility that anti-corruption measures could give rise to national security threats.

1. Corruption as a Cause of Insecurity

A limited body of social science literature considers how corruption may cause insecurity by creating economic or political grievances amongst a population, which may then express these grievances in a violent or destabilizing manner. Empirical studies published by economists in the mid-to-late 1990s demonstrated that a positive correlation exists between corruption and political instability.[8] Since then, social scientists have posited various reasons for the existence of a causal relationship between corruption and insecurity, in particular armed conflict. Corruption can fuel armed conflict by generating both economic and political grievances.[9] Economic grievances may stem, for example, from corruption's negative impact on investment, economic growth, and public spending on health and education.[10] By contributing to economic grievances amongst marginalized groups, corruption can reduce the

[8] Paolo Mauro, 'Corruption and Growth' (1995) 110 The Quarterly Journal of Economics 681.

[9] Le Billon (n 7); Carnegie Endowment for International Peace, 'Corruption: The Unrecognized Threat to International Security' (Working Group on Corruption and Security, June 2014) <https://carnegieendowment.org/2014/06/06/corruption-unrecognized-threat-to-international-security-pub-55791> accessed 14 November 2020.

[10] Paolo Mauro, 'Corruption and the Composition of Government Expenditure' (1998) 69 Journal of Public Economics 263.

opportunity cost of a violent uprising. In other words, marginalized groups have little to lose by engaging in violent, destabilizing conduct.[11]

Political grievances may result, for example, from major corruption scandals, which typically involve high-level public officials, such as a head of government, and large sums of money.[12] Such 'grand corruption' can undermine the legitimacy of the high-level official, his or her ruling party, and/or the government as a whole. Major corruption scandals may foment popular support for political change through peaceful and constitutional methods, but also through violent coups that create political and physical insecurity. Major corruption scandals in Brazil (2014–18), South Korea (2016), and Ukraine (2014) have, for example, contributed to political upheaval in these various corners of the globe. In the case of Ukraine, political upheaval escalated to the violent Euromaidan Revolution.[13]

The link between corruption and armed conflict can also be explained by reference to the concept of 'greed' rather than grievances.[14] Greed can motivate violent, destabilizing conduct by marginalized groups in countries where the ruling regime has control over 'economic rents'. The term 'economic rents', when used in the corruption context, refers to the extra amount (such as a bribe) that is paid for something due to an artificial limitation in supply (such as a government-imposed limitation on the number of available licences).[15] The risk of political violence may be heightened in States where the most lucrative 'rents' are controlled by the State itself, as is typically the case in resource-rich countries.[16]

A small body of empirical research both supports and challenges these greed- and grievance-based understandings of how corruption gives rise to insecurity. Empirical research supports, in particular, the existence of a causal relationship between corruption and the risk or likelihood of 'large scale ethnic violence'.[17] This line of research is premised on the conception of ethnic conflicts as grievance-based, and the idea that corruption forms an underlying motivation for ethnic violence, not a proximate cause of a particular violent action.[18] Corruption creates a way for ethnic groups to influence the political decision-making process, outside of formal political institutions, such as

[11] Hanne Fjelde, 'Buying Peace? Oil Wealth, Corruption and Civil War, 1986–99' (2009) 46 Journal of Peace Research 199, 202.

[12] Le Billon (n 7).

[13] CoE/GRECO, 'Fourth Evaluation Round: Corruption Prevention in Respect of Members of Parliament, Judges and Prosecutors—Evaluation Report Ukraine' (8 August 2017) Doc GrecoEval4Rep(2016)9 https://www.ecoi.net/en/file/local/1406684/1226_1503385695_grecoeval4rep-2016-9-ukraine-eng-docx.pdf accessed 16 May 2020; Anders Aslund, *Ukraine: What Went Wrong and How to Fix It* (Peterson Institute for International Economics 2015) 91–4.

[14] Le Billon (n 7) 418–19.

[15] Paolo Mauro, *Why Worry About Corruption?* (Economic Issue 6, IMF 1997); Francis Fukuyama, *Political Order and Political Decay: From the Industrial Revolution to the Globalisation of Democracy* (2014) 128–31.

[16] Le Billon (n 7) 418–19.

[17] Natascha Neudorfer/Ulrike Theuerkauf, 'Buying War Not Peace: The Influence of Corruption on the Risk of Ethnic War' (2014) 47 Comparative Political Studies 1856.

[18] ibid 1858.

electoral systems or State structures.[19] Networks of corruption have an exclusionary effect because they tend to form along ethnic lines, thereby benefiting some ethnic groups over others.[20] Members of one ethnic group may, for example, use bribes to influence political decision-making in favour of their ethnic group, to the detriment of other ethnic groups. Corruption can also distort political decision-making by creating an incentive for officials to prioritize expenditures that offer better opportunities for corrupt dealings, such as defence contracts, rather than education or health projects. When some ethnic groups have greater influence over decision-making processes than others, this can give rise to grievances amongst excluded ethnic groups, ultimately leading to ethnic violence.

Another empirical study, however, points in the opposite direction, meaning that social scientists have also shown that corruption can have a stabilizing effect in some circumstances, particularly in oil-rich States.[21] While both oil wealth and corruption are associated with a heightened risk of armed conflict, oil's harmful effect decreases with the level of corruption. Some oil-rich States, such as Saudi Arabia and Gabon, do not face violent opposition even though they engage in political corruption that damages the economy and society.[22] This can be explained by the fact that government actors can use income generated from oil wealth to bring about stability in the relationship between the State and society.[23] They may misuse oil revenue for the purpose of patronage or clientelism, meaning private payoffs that aim to preserve and expand political power.[24] By selectively distributing rents or 'sharing the spoils' of oil wealth with some groups, high-level government officials can create supporters who have a stake in the continuation of the existing political order.[25] Thus, in some oil-rich countries where State institutions are weak, political corruption may actually reduce the risk of violent uprising.[26]

2. Insecurity as a Cause of Corruption

Another strand of social science research on the relationship between corruption and global security focuses on how State-building in post-conflict societies creates unique incentives for corruption and breeds greater tolerance of corruption on the part of international actors.[27] Social science research based on case studies describes how post-conflict

[19] ibid 1859. [20] ibid 1858.

[21] Fjelde (n 11); see also Le Billon (n 7) 420–1. See, generally, Michael Johnston, 'The Political Consequences of Corruption: A Reassessment' (1986) 18 Comparative Politics 459.

[22] Fjelde defines political corruption as 'transactions between public and private actors through which collective goods are illegitimately converted in private payoffs. It involves high-level political officers and takes place at the formulation end of politics, where the decisions regarding public wealth are made.' Fjelde (n 11) 202. Fjelde can also be understood as referring to grand, rather than petty corruption (see fn 4).

[23] Fjelde (n 11) 201. [24] ibid. [25] ibid 202. [26] ibid 214.

[27] Susan Rose-Ackerman/Bonnie J Palifka, *Corruption and Government: Causes, Consequences and Reform* (2nd edn, CUP 2016) ch 10; Susan Rose-Ackerman, 'Corruption in the Wake of Domestic National Conflict' in Robert I Rotberg (ed), *Corruption, Global Security, and World Order* (Brookings Institution Press 2009). See also Galtung/Tisné (n 7); Jonas Lindberg/Camilla Orjuela, 'Corruption in

societies are especially susceptible to corruption due to the nature of post-conflict regimes. This susceptibility stems from the presence in post-conflict societies of many of the factors that are associated with corruption in any society, whether post-conflict or peaceful. These factors include 'poverty, weak institutions, lack of trust in law enforcement, a poorly functioning judiciary, and the marginalization of minority groups'.[28]

These factors can incentivize corruption in a number of distinct ways.[29] First, where infrastructure has been destroyed during a conflict, large infrastructure projects in the post-conflict period can represent prime opportunities for high-level officials to solicit bribes or embezzle funds. Moreover, in a post-conflict environment there may be pressure on governments to pursue reconstruction quickly, without strong financial controls. Secondly, large influxes of emergency or development aid in a post-conflict period represent funds that are separate from internal tax revenues and therefore increase the risk of misappropriation by public officials. Thirdly, organized crime groups may have emerged during the conflict, and may continue to grow in size and power after the conflict, as former combatants join the groups. Corruption is a key tool of organized crime groups, and may facilitate their capacity to undermine law enforcement and effectively merge with State entities.

Recent quantitative empirical research has gone beyond the existing qualitative empirical research, based on case studies and anecdotal evidence, by demonstrating that power-sharing arrangements in post-conflict States increase corruption levels.[30] One study focuses on power-sharing arrangements amongst a small circle of government and rebel elites, at the cabinet level of an executive branch. While power-sharing between the government and rebels might be necessary to achieve peace, such power-sharing is also a cause of increased levels of corruption, which can in turn threaten the prospects of maintaining peace in the long term.[31] These elites are conceptualized as individuals who will engage in rent-seeking behaviour by using public funds stemming from taxes, natural resources, and foreign aid to generate private income and to secure their power through patronage networks.[32] Because power-sharing arrangements tend to be temporary, elites may, in particular, have an incentive to capture as much of the State's resources as possible, before an elected government replaces the transitional, post-conflict government.[33] From a policy perspective, these findings suggest that power-sharing arrangements may bring short-term stability at the end of a conflict, at

the Aftermath of War: An Introduction' (2014) 35 Third World Quarterly 723; Carnegie Endowment for International Peace (n 9); Transparency International, *Corruption as a Threat to Stability and Peace* (Transparency International 2014); Philippe Le Billon, 'Natural Resources and Corruption in Post-War Transitions: Matters of Trust' (2014) 35 Third World Quarterly 770; Christine S Cheng/Domonik Zaum, 'Introduction—Key Themes in Peacebuilding and Corruption' (2008) 15 International Peacekeeping 301; Mark Philip, 'Peacebuilding and Corruption' (2008) 15 International Peacekeeping 310.

[28] Rose-Ackerman/Palifka (n 27) 316. [29] ibid.

[30] Felix Haass/Martin Ottman, 'Profits from Peace: The Political Economy of Power-Sharing and Corruption' (2017) 99 World Development 60.

[31] ibid 61. [32] ibid 62. [33] ibid 64.

the cost of heightened levels of corruption and delayed economic development, in the longer term.[34]

D. The International Legal Framework

Bearing in mind the various relationships between corruption and global security, this section begins by exploring the extent to which States concluded anti-corruption treaties on account of, or in response to, corruption's role as both a cause and a consequence of insecurity. The following also considers the extent to which anti-corruption treaty law can serve as tools or guides for States and also non-State actors seeking to combat corruption and promote global security. The 2003 UNCAC will be the focus of this analysis, although references will also be made to the Organisation for Economic Co-operation and Development's (OECD) 1997 Convention on Combating Bribery of Foreign Public Officials in International Business Transactions (OECD Anti-Bribery Convention)[35] and the regional treaties that States concluded both before and after UNCAC.[36] UNCAC will be the focus of this discussion in part because it is the most comprehensive anti-corruption treaty, as it not only includes provisions on criminalization, enforcement, and international cooperation, which are common features of transnational criminal law treaties, but it also includes more novel provisions concerning prevention of corruption and asset recovery. Moreover, UNCAC enjoys nearly universal participation, with 187 States Parties as of March 2020. UNCAC is therefore arguably the most significant anti-corruption treaty to date, even though many of its provisions impose vague or less than mandatory requirements on States Parties, and its actual impact in practice remains an open question that must be the subject of future research by lawyers and social scientists.

1. Insecurity as a Motivator of Anti-corruption Treaties

States have been motivated to conclude anti-corruption treaties in part because of corruption's role in creating insecurity. The preambular language in UNCAC and regional anti-corruption treaties shows that the drafters primarily conceived of corruption as a cause of insecurity, rather than the converse, namely, insecurity as a cause of corruption.[37] The preambles variously refer to corruption as a threat to the 'stability and

[34] ibid 71.

[35] Convention on Combating Bribery of Foreign Public Officials in International Business Transactions (1998) 37 ILM 1 (OECD Anti-Bribery Convention).

[36] See n 2.

[37] The treaties include no reference to insecurity as a cause of corruption, although the AU Convention does recognize 'the need to address the root causes of corruption on the continent', which would presumably include armed conflict. AU Convention on Corruption (n 2) preambular para 8.

security of societies',[38] to 'political, economic, social, and cultural stability',[39] and to the 'stability of democratic institutions'.[40] The drafters of the Inter-American Convention further considered that combating corruption is required for representative democracy, which is in turn an essential condition for 'stability, peace and development' in the region.[41] The references in these treaties to the link between corruption and stability or security are brief and vague, but they nonetheless suggest that the drafters were partly motivated by corruption's destabilizing consequences. Whether the drafters conceived of a causal link between corruption and insecurity in the form of armed conflict remains unclear. The only significant exception is the 1997 OECD Anti-Bribery Convention, which addresses the bribery of foreign public officials and makes no reference to the link between corruption and security or stability. The drafters of this treaty were instead motivated in good part by concerns about how foreign bribery distorts competition amongst businesses engaged in international business transactions.[42] The preamble also describes bribery as conduct that 'raises serious moral and political concerns' and 'undermines good governance and economic development'.[43]

UNCAC and the Inter-American Convention further acknowledge the link between corruption and other forms of criminal behaviour that are themselves causes of global insecurity. The preambular language of both of these treaties indicates that the drafters were concerned about the links between corruption and organized crime and money laundering, and the drafters of the Inter-American Convention also expressed deep concern about the link between corruption and the proceeds generated by drug trafficking, which undermine and threaten society.[44] In general, however, anti-corruption treaties make no reference to other forms of transnational crime that tend to involve corruption and that have destabilizing effects, such as migrant smuggling, human trafficking, and arms trafficking. Each of these three phenomena is addressed in protocols to the 2000 United Nations Convention against Transnational Organized Crime (UNTOC), the treaty that inspired the drafting of UNCAC. Although social science research supports linkages between corruption and other forms of transnational crime, it is perhaps unsurprising that States have addressed these phenomena through the conclusion of distinct instruments that deal with these issues in relative isolation (although UNTOC does contain a provision on bribery).[45] Treaties that deal with transnational

[38] UNCAC (n 2) preambular para 1.

[39] AU Convention on Corruption (n 2) preambular para 6; see also UNCAC (n 2) preambular para 3.

[40] CoE Criminal Law Convention (n 2) preambular para 4.

[41] Inter-American Convention against Corruption (n 2) preambular para 2.

[42] See, generally, Mark Pieth, 'Introduction' in Mark Pieth et al (eds), *The OECD Convention on Bribery: A Commentary* (CUP 2014).

[43] OECD Anti-Bribery Convention (n 35) preambular para 1.

[44] UNCAC (n 2) preambular para 2; Inter American Convention against Corruption (n 2) preambular paras 4, 8.

[45] United Nations Convention against Transnational Organized Crime 2225 UNTS 209 (UNTOC) art 8; Protocol to Prevent, Suppress and Punish Trafficking in Persons, Especially Women and Children, supplementing the United Nations Convention against Transnational Organized Crime 2237 UNTS 319; Protocol against the Smuggling by Land, Sea and Air, supplement the United Nations Convention against

crimes have been developed in a notably ad hoc manner, and tend to deal relatively separately with various crimes or methods of committing crimes, although newer treaties typically borrow from older treaties.[46]

2. Criminalization and Enforcement

The criminalization provisions of UNCAC and other anti-corruption treaties are meant to ensure that States Parties' domestic criminal laws allow them to prosecute a core set of corrupt acts. The enactment and subsequent enforcement of such domestic laws represent fundamental elements of anti-corruption measures and campaigns, alongside policy-based approaches to combating corruption. Yet, scholarship on corruption by social scientists often includes little or no discussion of legal approaches to corruption, and in particular domestic criminal laws.[47] The omission of any discussion of laws concerning corruption in most of the social science literature is especially noteworthy given that acts of corruption are criminal offences in virtually every State in the world, thanks in part to international anti-corruption treaties. The international legal approach to corruption is premised on domestic implementation of treaty obligations, and domestic enforcement. Like other transnational criminal law treaties, anti-corruption treaties do not make acts of corruption international crimes, but instead require States Parties to criminalize specific conduct in their domestic legal systems.[48]

Enforcement therefore takes place at the domestic level, under domestic criminal law, and not at the international level, before international criminal courts or tribunals. Some scholars and anti-corruption activists have advocated for the creation of an international court that could try individuals suspected of acts of corruption. Others have written about the need for an amendment to the Rome Statute of the International Criminal Court to include the crime of corruption, or the possibility of prosecuting corruption as a crime against humanity.[49] But at present these ideas are aspirational and present their own problems, as any international court tasked with prosecuting corruption would likely encounter serious challenges related to immunities and the collection

Transnational Organized Crime 2241 UNTS 507; Protocol against Illicit Manufacturing of and Trafficking in Firearms, Their parts and Components and Ammunition, supplementing the United Nations Convention against Transnational Organized Crime 2326 UNTS 208.

[46] Neil Boister, *An Introduction to Transnational Criminal Law* (OUP 2018) 32–3.

[47] But see Raymond Fisman/Edward Miguel, 'Corruption, Norms, and Legal Enforcement: Evidence from Diplomatic Parking Tickets' (2007) 115 Journal of Political Economy 1020.

[48] See eg UNCAC (n 2) art 15 (requiring each state party 'to adopt such legislation and other measures as may be necessary to establish as criminal offences' the active and passive bribery of national officials, when committed intentionally).

[49] See eg Sonja Starr, 'Extraordinary Crimes at Ordinary Times: International Justice Beyond Crisis Situations' (2007) 101 Northwestern University Law Review 1257; Ilias Bantekas, 'Corruption as an International Crime and Crime against Humanity' (2006) 4 JICJ 466. For a discussion of the international prosecution of transnational crimes generally, see Neil Boister, 'International Tribunals for Transnational Crimes: Towards a Transnational Criminal Court?' (2012) 23 Criminal Law Forum 295.

of evidence.[50] The focus of this chapter therefore remains on how anti-corruption treaties provide for domestic criminalization and enforcement for acts of corruption.

UNCAC requires States Parties to criminalize some, but not all of the forms of corruption set out in Chapter III of the Convention. UNCAC includes the most comprehensive enumeration of corrupt acts, but the treaty's comprehensiveness comes at the cost of uniformly mandatory obligations on States Parties. During the negotiations, when the delegations disagreed as to what should fall under the umbrella of 'corruption', they compromised by making the more controversial forms of corruption 'semi-mandatory', meaning that States Parties must only consider criminalizing certain types of corruption. UNCAC's mandatory criminalization provisions include various forms of bribery (active and passive bribery of national public officials, and active bribery of foreign officials and officials of public international organizations);[51] embezzlement, misappropriation or other diversion by a public official;[52] money laundering;[53] and obstruction of justice.[54] All of these forms of corruption had previously been included as mandatory criminalization provisions in other transnational criminal law treaties, including regional anti-corruption treaties, with the result that their inclusion in UNCAC was uncontroversial.[55] The drafters of UNCAC could simply lift language from existing treaty provisions.

All of UNCAC's other criminalization provisions, however, only require States Parties to consider adopting domestic implementing legislation or other measures. These semi-mandatory crimes include the passive bribery of foreign officials and officials of public international organizations;[56] trading in influence;[57] abuse of functions;[58] illicit enrichment;[59] and private sector bribery and embezzlement.[60] The obligation to consider is an obligation of conduct rather than an obligation of result, and could be satisfied, for example, by a debate in parliament about the adoption of legislation, even if the legislators ultimately decide against it.[61] These provisions are semi-mandatory for a range of reasons. The delegations could not reach a consensus regarding the mandatory criminalization of trading in influence, for example, because some States criminalize 'influence peddling' by intermediaries, while in other States such conduct would be characterized as lobbying, a legal form of behaviour.[62] Another controversial provision is illicit enrichment, which involves the criminalization of a 'significant increase in the assets of a public official that he or she cannot reasonably explain in relation to his or her

[50] For a discussion of the evidentiary problems likely to be associated with the prosecution of money laundering by the African Court of Justice and Human and Peoples' Rights, see Cecily Rose, 'Money Laundering and the African Court of Justice and Human and Peoples' Rights' in Charles C Jalloh et al (eds), *The African Court of Justice and Human and Peoples' Rights in Context* (CUP 2019).

[51] UNCAC (n 2) arts 15, 16(1). [52] ibid art 17. [53] ibid art 23.

[54] ibid art 25.

[55] See eg United Nations Convention against Illicit Traffic in Narcotic Drugs and Psychotropic Substances 1582 UNTS 95 art 3(1)(b); UNTOC (n 45) arts 6, 8.

[56] UNCAC (n 2) art 16(2). [57] ibid art 18. [58] ibid art 19. [59] ibid art 20.

[60] ibid arts 21, 22. [61] Cecily Rose et al, 'Introduction' in Rose et al (n 3) 12.

[62] Aloysius Llamzon, 'Article 18: Trading in Influence' in Rose et al (n 3) 194.

income'.[63] Many delegations had concerns about the inclusion of illicit enrichment in UNCAC, because they considered that it would conflict with the presumption of innocence, a fundamental principle in domestic legal systems.[64] As a result, most States Parties have decided not to criminalize illicit enrichment, especially developed States with advanced legal systems.[65] In light of the controversies surrounding some of the criminalization provisions in Chapter III of UNCAC, the crimes set out in in this treaty have to be understood as an exhaustive enumeration of possible forms of corruption, but not a reflection of the types of corruption outlawed in all domestic legal systems.[66]

UNCAC's provisions concerning the enforcement of anti-corruption laws address a range of issues concerning the capacity of States Parties to investigate and prosecute natural and legal persons for the acts of corruption that they have criminalized within their legal systems. The provisions on enforcement cover fundamental issues such as liability for legal persons; prosecution, adjudication and sanctions; jurisdiction; and statute of limitations—all issues that other anti-corruption treaties cover as well. The enforcement provisions also include more innovative articles that address cooperation with law enforcement authorities, cooperation between national authorities, and cooperation between national authorities and the private sector. Although UNCAC includes numerous provisions concerning enforcement, it does not address the possibility that anti-corruption prosecutions could themselves be destabilizing from a global security perspective.

This issue has, however, arisen within the context of the OECD Anti-Bribery Convention. Article 5 of the OECD Anti-Bribery Convention requires that domestic investigations and prosecutions of foreign bribery 'shall not be influenced by considerations of national economic interest, the potential effect upon relations with another State or the identity of the natural or legal persons involved'. Article 5 does not expressly indicate that national security is a factor that domestic enforcement authorities may not take into consideration, but the terms 'economic interest' and 'relations with another State' arguably encompass national security in some circumstances.[67] The term national security may be understood, for example, as referring not only to military and police security, but also to the general social and economic well-being of a State or its 'economic interests'. Furthermore, the overlap between national security and economic interests may be especially evident in the context of the defence industry, which is one of the most corrupt industries.[68] When defence companies based in a 'home State' conclude contracts for the sale of weapons systems to 'host States', the home State may have a strong economic interest in the success of the deal. Such weapons sales may also promote

[63] UNCAC (n 2) art 20.

[64] Oliver Landwehr, 'Article 20: Illicit Enrichment' in Rose et al (n 3) 220; see also Julio Bacio Terracino, *The International Legal Framework against Corruption: States' Obligations to Prevent and Repress Corruption* (Intersentia 2012) 114–24; Lindy Muzila et al, *On the Take: Criminalizing Illicit Enrichment to Fight Corruption* (World Bank 2012).

[65] Landwehr (n 64) 231. [66] Rose, (n 6) 106.

[67] Peter J Cullen/Mark Pieth, 'Article 5: Enforcement' in Pieth et al (n 42) 385–9.

[68] Transparency International, Out of the Shadows: Promoting Openness and Accountability in the Global Defence Industry (Transparency International 2018) 3–4.

relations between the home and host States. Allegations of bribery in this context typically involve accusations that a defence company has bribed a public official in the host State in order to obtain or retain a given defence contract. The investigation and prosecution of such a case could give rise to national security concerns if the investigation or prosecution would result in the disclosure of information about the host State's defence capacities or its national defence strategy.[69]

The United Kingdom's *Al Yamamah* case illustrates another way in which the prosecution of foreign bribery in relation to a defence contract may raise issues of national security.[70] In this case, the UK's criminal investigation threatened the national security interests of the United Kingdom itself, the 'home State' in this instance. In 2004, the UK's Serious Fraud Office (SFO) opened an investigation into bribes paid by the UK defence manufacturer, BAE Systems, to public officials in Saudi Arabia.[71] BAE allegedly bribed Saudi officials in the context of a valuable arms contract between the United Kingdom and Saudi Arabia, for which BAE was the main contractor.[72] After the Saudi government threatened to withdraw counter-terrorism cooperation with the United Kingdom should the SFO continue to pursue the investigation, the SFO dropped the case in 2006.[73] The SFO's decision to terminate the investigation led to litigation in UK courts, as two public interest groups, Corner House Research and the Campaign Against Arms Trade, brought an application for judicial review of the SFO's decision. The House of Lords, however, never reached the question of whether the SFO's decision conflicted with Article 5 of the OECD Anti-Bribery Convention, a provision which had not been incorporated into UK law at this time.[74] Instead, the House of Lords held that, as a matter of domestic law, the SFO Director had not exceeded his discretion by deciding that the public interest in pursuing the investigation was outweighed by the public interest in protecting the lives of British citizens.[75] This case nevertheless demonstrates the range of ways in which national security interests may arise in the context of anti-corruption proceedings and create dilemmas for prosecutors in their exercise of discretion. Article 5 of the OECD Anti-Bribery Convention arguably precludes prosecutors from terminating investigations or prosecutions on national security grounds, which may fall within the scope of 'economic interests' and 'relations with other States'. UNCAC, however, leaves this issue untouched, with the result that in the enforcement context, many States Parties are free to balance national security interests and anti-corruption interests as they see fit.

3. International Cooperation

In order to ensure that States Parties are able to investigate and prosecute acts of corruption, anti-corruption treaties include provisions on international cooperation,

[69] Cullen/Pieth (n 67) 385.

[70] *R (on the application of Corner House Research and others) v Director of the Serious Fraud Office* [2008] UKHL 60 (*Corner House Research*).

[71] ibid para 3. [72] ibid. [73] ibid para 11.

[74] ibid paras 43–8. [75] ibid paras 38–42.

in particular mutual legal assistance and extradition.[76] The acts of corruption set out in UNCAC and other anti-corruption treaties may or may not involve transnational conduct that could necessitate international cooperation in the gathering of evidence or the freezing of assets, for example. While the bribery of foreign public officials involves, by definition, conduct that crosses State borders, other forms of corruption are not necessarily transnational in character. But in cases where the alleged perpetrators have engaged in conduct in multiple jurisdictions, treaty provisions on mutual legal assistance may help to facilitate the taking of evidence and many other forms of assistance, including the searches and seizures of assets, the examination of objects and sites, the provision of financial and business records, the identification or tracing of proceeds of crime for evidentiary purposes, and the facilitation of the voluntary appearance of persons in the requesting State Party.[77] Corruption cases can also take on a transnational character where the accused or convicted person seeks to evade justice by fleeing to, or remaining in, a foreign jurisdiction, outside of the State conducting the criminal proceedings. In such cases, provisions on extradition facilitate the surrender of an accused or convicted person from the 'requesting State' that is conducting the proceedings, to the 'requested State' where the accused or convicted person is seeking safe haven.[78]

The intricacies of UNCAC's lengthy and detailed provisions on mutual legal assistance and extradition lie beyond the scope of this chapter. But one of the grounds on which States Parties may refuse a request for mutual legal assistance merits brief mention, as it concerns matters of security. If a State Party considers that the execution of a request for assistance 'is likely to prejudice the sovereignty, security, ordre public or other essential interests', then it may refuse the request.[79] This ground for refusal is not new to UNCAC, but in fact replicates an exception included in earlier treaties, including the European Convention on Mutual Assistance in Criminal Matters, and the 1999 Council of Europe Criminal Law Convention.[80] The word 'may', rather than 'shall' signifies the discretionary character of this provision, which allows but does not require States Parties to refuse mutual legal assistance requests on this ground. The term 'security' may be understood as having both external and internal dimensions, meaning that it encompasses both defence by the military against external threats, and police measures directed towards domestic security.[81] Requests for mutual legal assistance could conceivably raise security concerns where, for example, the public disclosure of information about the requested State's national security strategy might result. Like other

[76] UNCAC (n 2) also addresses other less common and/or more innovative forms of international cooperation, namely the transfer of sentenced persons (art 45); the transfer of criminal proceedings (art 47); cooperation between law enforcement, in particular the police (art 48); joint investigations (art 49); and special investigative techniques such as controlled delivery, surveillance, and undercover operations (art 50).

[77] ibid art 46. [78] ibid art 44. [79] ibid art 46(21)(b).

[80] European Convention on Mutual Assistance in Criminal Matters 472 UNTS 185 art 2(b); Coe Criminal Law Convention (n 2) art 26(2); UNTOC (n 45) art 18(21)(b).

[81] Dimosthenis Chrysikos, 'Article 46: Mutual Legal Assistance' in Rose et al (n 3) 462–3.

transnational criminal law treaties, UNCAC allows States Parties to prioritize national security concerns over international cooperation in relation to anti-corruption proceedings.

4. Prevention

The prevention of corruption is of particular relevance for this chapter on corruption and global security, in light of the causal relationship between corruption and insecurity, as discussed above. Given that corruption is an underlying cause of insecurity, legal and policy approaches to the prevention of corruption must be considered by policy-makers grappling with the subject of global security. For the most part, anti-corruption treaties do not address prevention.[82] This topic is typically omitted from transnational criminal law treaties, which tend to focus on criminalization, enforcement, and international cooperation. UNCAC, by contrast, includes an entire chapter on preventive measures. While these provisions in Chapter II of UNCAC are innovative and wide-ranging, they are also replete with qualifying language and semi-mandatory or non-mandatory language.[83] UNCAC's provisions on prevention address various aspects of the public sector and public administration, including human resources systems for civil servants, codes of conduct for public officials, rules for the conduct of the judiciary and prosecution service, public procurement and the management of public finances, and transparency in public administration. The private sector's involvement in corruption is the subject of provisions that concern auditing and accounting standards and the prevention of money laundering. Lastly, the chapter includes a provision on the participation of society, including non-governmental organizations and the media, in preventing corruption. Although these provisions on prevention are contained within an anti-corruption treaty, their scope is broader, as they concern many aspects of good governance in general.

The only mention of national security in the chapter on prevention may be found in Article 13, which concerns the prevention of corruption. Society's participation in the prevention of corruption depends in part on awareness of the existence, causes, and gravity of corruption, as acknowledged in the *chapeau* of the article. The publication of such information about corruption can, for example, take the form of reports by non-governmental organizations and media reports. Article 13(1)(d) accordingly provides that States Parties should respect, promote, and protect the freedom of society 'to seek, receive, publish and disseminate information concerning corruption'. This freedom may, however, be subject to certain restrictions, but these 'shall only be such as are provided for by law and are necessary ... for the protection of national security or ordre public or of public health or morals'. An interpretative note included in the *travaux préparatoires* for UNCAC indicates that Article 13(1)(d) is intended not to modify States

[82] But see Inter-American Convention against Corruption (n 2) art III.

[83] UNCAC (n 2) ch II.

Parties' existing human rights obligations, but to 'stress' the human rights obligations already undertaken by States Parties.[84] This qualifying language, in fact, replicates the language in the International Covenant on Civil and Political Rights, in the provision on freedom of expression (Article 19(3)).[85] The same concerns about the publication of sensitive information about defence capabilities and national security strategies may explain why States Parties included such a qualifier in Article 13, which already includes broad qualifying language in the *chapeau* (providing that each State Party shall take appropriate measures 'within its means and in accordance with fundamental principles of its domestic law'). The balance struck in Article 13 between freedom of expression and national security is therefore uncontroversial, when viewed from the perspective of international human rights law. In the anti-corruption context, however, this balance is a particularly sensitive one, in light of the fact that journalists who write about corruption are in practice uniquely vulnerable. According to the Committee to Protect Journalists, for example, nearly a third of all journalists whose murders have been linked to their work since 1992 were reporting on corruption (265 out of 857).[86] When viewed from this perspective, Article 13 as a whole does little to specifically address this well-known and very troubling phenomenon.

E. Contemporary Challenges and Outlook

Measuring the impact of international anti-corruption law represents one of the greatest contemporary challenges in the anti-corruption field. As discussed above, social scientists have been able to show that a causal relationship exists between corruption and insecurity. Furthermore, anti-corruption treaties address essential elements of any anti-corruption strategy that States could pursue for the purpose of achieving greater security or dealing with the aftermath of insecurity. Yet, the unanswered question is whether these anti-corruption laws can or have had any measurable impact on levels of corruption and security. Researchers have not demonstrated that these anti-corruption treaties are actually reducing corruption and thereby promoting security. Moreover, the reduction of levels of corruption is not even one of UNCAC's stated goals. Instead, UNCAC aims in part to promote anti-corruption measures and international cooperation. In other words, the goal is largely the implementation and enforcement of the treaty's provisions.[87]

[84] UNODC, Travaux Preparatoires *of the Negotiations for the Elaboration of the United Nations Convention against Corruption* (UN 2010) 146.

[85] International Covenant on Civil and Political Rights 999 UNTS 171.

[86] Committee to Protect Journalists, '1345 Journalists Killed' https://cpj.org/data/killed/?status=Killed&motiveConfirmed%5B%5D=Confirmed&type%5B%5D=Journalist&start_year=1992&end_year=2019&group_by=year accessed 16 May 2020.

[87] UNCAC (n 2) art 1.

Regardless of UNCAC's stated goals, measuring the treaty's impact is a very valid line of research, if very difficult to execute at present. The difficulties stem partly from the fact that data on levels of corruption are, in general, non-existent or unreliable. Perpetrators of corruption go to great lengths to conceal their transactions, and unlike other crimes, such as murder or arson, for example, the existence of corruption may go unreported or undetected, at least for some time. Commentators sometimes reference breathtaking estimates of the yearly cost of corruption or money laundering, but the methodological basis for these figures and the exact source of these estimates is typically unclear. Levels of corruption can, however, be measured indirectly, through proxies such as perceptions of corruption levels amongst the business community, which is the approach taken by Transparency International in its Corruption Perceptions Index.[88] Such measures of corruption are relative and indirect, but are currently among the only available data on levels of corruption. Thus, the relative impact of anti-corruption laws on perceptions may be measurable, but the absolute impact on corruption levels remains seemingly out of reach, at least for the time being.

In the meantime, treaty-monitoring bodies have produced a significant body of data about the domestic implementation of these anti-corruption treaties, and, to a lesser extent, the domestic enforcement of anti-corruption laws.[89] UNCAC, the OECD Anti-Bribery Convention, the Inter-American Convention against Corruption, and the CoE Criminal Convention all benefit from monitoring bodies which, to varying extents, gather information about compliance and issue recommendations to States Parties about how they should improve their domestic implementation and/or enforcement. These bodies have produced a wealth of information that allows researchers to assess whether States have undertaken necessary law reform, pursued enforcement actions, and engaged in international cooperation. These lines of inquiry do not necessarily allow for any conclusions to be reached about the impact of these treaties, but they do allow for conclusions about levels of compliance. Research on compliance is an essential first step; before researchers can measure whether enforcement actions deter corruption, for example, they must be able to establish whether States are in fact implementing and enforcing their treaty obligations in the first place.

Social scientists and lawyers still have much work to do in understanding the precise relationships between corruption and global security, and how international anti-corruption law operates in practice. Ideally, social scientists and lawyers would do some of this work together. Interdisciplinary collaboration has the potential to yield some insights, for example, into whether States are complying with their international legal obligations under anti-corruption treaties, and if so, to what end. More

[88] Transparency International, 'Corruption Perceptions Index 2019' https://www.transparency.org/cpi2019 accessed 16 May 2020.

[89] See eg UNODC, UNCAC Implementation Review Mechanism, 'Country Profiles' <https://www.unodc.org/unodc/en/treaties/CAC/country-profile/index.html> accessed 16 May 2020; OECD, 'Country Reports on the Implementation of the OECD Anti-Bribery Convention' <https://www.oecd.org/corruption/countryreportsontheimplementationoftheoecdanti-briberyconvention.htm> accessed 14 November 2020.

interdisciplinary work could also help to ensure that when social scientists and lawyers speak of 'corruption', they are referring more or less, to the same set of criminal acts. Only with more research about the links between corruption and security and the role of anti-corruption law, will policymakers and lawmakers have the necessary evidentiary basis for designing anti-corruption strategies in the future.

CHAPTER 9

INTERNAL STRIFE AND INSURGENCY

CHRISTIAN HENDERSON

A. Introduction

The terms 'internal strife' and 'insurgency' encompass a range of situations from peaceful and violent protests and demonstrations to rebellions against the government to full-blown armed conflicts. Such situations may either occur entirely between the governmental forces of a State and a non-State armed group (or between two such groups) or, as is more often the case, may be fuelled by third States or even involve them directly.[1] The uprisings of the Arab Spring since 2011, in particular the horrifying continuing crisis in Syria, provide a near textbook example of these different conditions of internal strife, and their actual and potential impact upon regional and global security.

Traditionally, international law neither expressly permitted nor prohibited individuals or groups within States to revolt against their government, or against each other,[2] nor provided much in the way of rules regulating their actions during the course of such internal strife, leading some to declare the 'neutrality' of international law regarding

[1] No universally accepted definitions of 'internal strife' or 'insurgency' exist. In Kelsen's view insurgency presupposes a civil war. Hans Kelsen, 'Recognition in International Law' (1941) 35 AJIL 605, 616. Another term used for 'insurgency' is 'insurrection' which has been described as 'a war of citizens against the State for the purposes of obtaining power in the whole or in part'. R P Dhokalia, 'Civil Wars and International Law' (1971) 65 Indian Journal of International Law 219, 225. According to Falk, insurgency requires 'a coordinated struggle with the objective of obtaining power in the state in whole or in part'. Richard A Falk, 'Janus Tormented: The International Law of Internal War' in James N Rosenau (ed), *International Aspects of Civil Strife* (Princeton UP 1964) 185–9.

[2] Christopher O Quaye, *Liberation Struggles in International Law* (Temple UP 1991) 212–13.

such issues.[3] Similarly, it was traditionally the case that '[g]overnments faced no limitations on their ability to quell internal uprisings'.[4] Today, while international law retains a certain neutrality regarding the right of individuals and groups to rise up against their government (or indeed each other), governments and State officials are no longer permitted to simply resort to forcible measures against individuals and groups within their territory; how they respond to the disruptive and possibly violent actions of these groups is more firmly regulated—and, with that, limited—by international law.

This contribution intends to provide a broad yet concise overview of the international legal frameworks that regulate internal strife and insurgency, with a particular focus on international human rights law (IHRL) and the applicability of the law of armed conflict (LOAC) and the ways that this framework interacts with IHRL. What is more, from a global security perspective, it is the possibility of outside intervention and the attendant frameworks and rules of international law that are arguably most pertinent and controversial. There have been several recent developments potentially impacting the international law governing internal strife and insurgency and the chapter will explore these and some of the recent situations that illustrate them, before concluding.

B. Legal Framework

1. Law Enforcement

Instead of starting with the imposition of obligations upon States, the law enforcement paradigm inversely begins with the rights of individuals under IHRL, with States' and State officials' obligations flowing from these.[5] In this respect, and with particular relevance to internal strife and insurgency, individuals have the right to life,[6] the right to be

[3] Oliver Corten, 'The Russian Intervention in the Ukrainian Crisis: Was *Jus Contra Bellum* "Confirmed Rather than Weakened"?' (2015) 2 Journal on the Use of Force and International Law 17, 22.

[4] Richard A Falk, 'Introduction' in Richard A Falk (ed), *The International Law of Civil War* (Johns Hopkins UP 1971) 11.

[5] States also have a general obligation to maintain law and order within their territory. See ICRC, *International Rules and Standards for Policing* (ICRC 2015) 18.

[6] International Covenant on Civil and Political Rights 999 UNTS 171 (ICCPR) art 6. Regionally, European Convention on Human Rights and Fundamental Freedoms ETS No 5 (ECHR) art 2; American Convention on Human Rights 1144 UNTS 123 art 4; African Charter on Human and Peoples' Rights 1520 UNTS 217 art 4. It is also protected under customary law. Generally, Bertrand G Ramcharan, 'The Right to Life' (1983) 30 NILR 297, 299. It has also been argued that the right to life is *jus cogens*. See Christof Heyns/Thomas Probert, 'Securing the Right to Life: A Cornerstone of the Human Rights System' (*EJIL Talk!*, 11 May 2016) <https://www.ejiltalk.org/securing-the-right-to-life-a-cornerstone-of-the-human-rights-system/> accessed 27 January 2020.

free from torture,[7] the right to liberty and security,[8] the freedom of thought and expression,[9] the freedom of association,[10] and the right to peaceful assembly and protest.[11] However, while several human rights are absolute, many others are not. Accordingly, while individuals have an absolute right to not be subjected to torture under any circumstances, there are situations in which either the interruption of a protest—including through forceful means—or even the taking of an individual's life may be lawful.

These rights are contained in various human rights treaties which state the rights and, if relevant, the strict conditions under which some may be limited or derogated from.[12] However, regulation of State actions concerning these rights is encased within the broader law enforcement paradigm, incorporating also 'softer' non-binding instruments, including the 1979 Code of Conduct for Law Enforcement Officials and the 1990 Basic Principles on the Use of Force and Firearms by Law Enforcement Officials.[13] Generally, this paradigm provides that State officials carrying out law enforcement duties, whether police or military personnel,[14] are exceptionally permitted to resort to the use of forcible measures when necessary, in particular where non-forcible measures 'remain ineffective or without any promise of achieving the intended result' or legitimate objective,[15] and only in a proportionate manner and to the extent strictly required.[16] In this context there is special attention given to the use of firearms.[17]

Even more restrictively, intentionally lethal force, whether or not through the use of firearms, is permitted solely when strictly necessary in order to protect life and less extreme measures are insufficient to restrain or apprehend the suspected offender.[18] In gauging whether such action meets this strict standard of necessity, it must be clear that a real and imminent threat to the life of either the law enforcement official concerned or others exists.[19] In addition, the use of intentionally lethal force must be strictly unavoidable, with other less-lethal means proving ineffective or without any promise of protecting life. Indeed, the right to life provides that 'no one shall be *arbitrarily* deprived of

[7] ICCPR (n 6) art 7. [8] ICCPR (n 6) art 9. [9] ICCPR (n 6) arts 18, 19.

[10] ICCPR (n 6) art 22. [11] ICCPR (n 6) art 21.

[12] See ICCPR (n 6) art 4(1). Certain rights, like the right to life, the freedom from torture, and the freedom of thought conscience and religion are expressly excluded, see ibid art 4(2).

[13] The Code of Conduct for Law Enforcement Officials was adopted by UNGA Res 34/169 (17 December 1979) Annex (Code of Conduct). The Basic Principles were adopted by the Eighth UN Congress on the Prevention of Crime and the Treatment of Offenders (27 August to 7 September 1990) and adopted without a vote by UNGA Res 45/166 (18 December 1990) (Basic Principles).

[14] Code of Conduct (n 13) art 1 (commentary). [15] Basic Principles (n 13) art 4.

[16] Code of Conduct (n 13) art 3 (commentary). See Stuart Casey-Maslen/Sean Connolly, *Police Use of Force under International Law* (CUP 2017).

[17] Basic Principles (n 13) art 9. Also, Code of Conduct (n 13) art 3 (commentary) (c).

[18] Basic Principles (n 13) art 9.

[19] *Nachova and Others v Bulgaria*, App Nos 43577/98 and 43579/98, 6 July 2005, para 95.

[their] life'.[20] And as the right to life is an individual right,[21] the necessity and proportionality of the use of lethal force must be assessed against the specific actions of individuals, not groups as a whole. Hence, it is not permissible to shoot with lethal force at a group of people merely because they are participating in a violent riot. Rather, a clear imminent threat posed by each individual targeted must exist.

2. The Conduct of Hostilities Paradigm

There may come a point during internal strife when a transition in the applicable legal frameworks occurs, from law enforcement operations to armed conflict. Given that the doctrine of belligerency and its associated ad hoc regulatory approach is mostly of historical significance today,[22] situations of violent and prolonged internal strife or insurgency that begin to challenge the authority of governmental authorities will normally be regulated under the law of non-international armed conflict,[23] as found in Common Article 3 (CA3) of the Geneva Conventions and the 1977 Additional Protocol II (AP II), as well as customary international law. There are, however, differences in the applicability of CA3 and AP II, in that while the 'elementary considerations of humanity' contained in CA3 apply to all States,[24] AP II, which develops and supplements CA3,[25] while having a higher threshold of applicability,[26] only applies to States that have signed and ratified the Protocol.

This framework specifically does 'not apply to situations of internal disturbances and tensions, such as riots, isolated and sporadic acts of violence and other acts of a similar

[20] ICCPR (n 6) art 6(1). See further UNCHR 'General Comment No. 36 on Article 6 of the International Covenant on Civil and Political Rights, on the Right to Life' (30 October 2018) UN Doc CCPR/C/GC/36. Contrariwise, ECHR (n 6) art 2 holds that no one shall be 'intentionally' deprived of their life. See *McCann and Others v UK*, App No 18984/91, 27 September 1995, para 148.

[21] Yuval Shany, 'Is Israel Justified in Shooting Protestors on Gaza Border?' (*Forward*, 7 April 2018) <https://forward.com/opinion/398307/is-israel-justified-in-shooting-protestors-on-gaza-border/> accessed 27 January 2020.

[22] But see Antonio Cassese, 'The Spanish Civil War and the Development of Customary Law Concerning Internal Armed Conflicts' in Antonio Cassese (ed), *The Human Dimension of International Law: Selected Papers* (OUP 2008) 128.

[23] Generally, Sandesh Sivakumaran, *The Law of Non-International Armed Conflict* (OUP 2012); Lindsay Moir, *The Law of Internal Armed Conflict* (CUP 2002); Jean-Marie Henckaerts/Louise Doswald-Beck, *Customary International Humanitarian Law, Vol I: Rules* (CUP 2005) rules 1–24, 3–76.

[24] *Case Concerning Military and Paramilitary Activities in and against Nicaragua (Nicaragua v USA)* (Merits) [1986] ICJ Rep 14 [114] (Nicaragua).

[25] It provides for a broader rage of fundamental guarantees in the protection of non-combatants, such as prohibiting collective punishment, hostage-taking, and pillage.

[26] In particular, armed groups must 'exercise such control over a part of [the State's] territory as to enable them to carry out sustained and concerted military operations'. See Protocol Additional to the Geneva Conventions of 12 August 1949, and Relating to the Protection of Victims of Non-International Armed Conflicts 1125 UNTS 609 (AP II) art 1(1).

nature'[27] but instead to protracted hostilities of a particular intensity.[28] So while internal strife might at first be governed solely by the law enforcement paradigm, if the severity and gravity of the situation on the ground reaches a certain point it then falls to be regulated by the LOAC. In addition, and connected to the intensity requirement, the armed group(s) involved must be sufficiently organized,[29] and any armed hostilities must have a nexus with the armed conflict.[30]

These vague criteria leave much room for disagreement as to whether they have been met, raising the question of how to assess whether LOAC has come into application. This evaluation is not always easy, as the International Tribunal for the former Yugoslavia has remarked, yet relevant factors include the number, intensity, and duration of individual confrontations, the type of weapons and other military equipment used, the number and calibre of munitions fired, the number of persons and type of forces partaking in the fighting, the number of casualties, the extent of material destruction, and the number of civilians fleeing combat zones.[31] In addition, if and when the UN Security Council (UNSC) begins to identify violations of LOAC (as well as to call upon the parties to refrain from violating LOAC), then it can be credibly claimed that the situation and applicable frameworks have shifted. The 2011 uprising in Syria is a pertinent example. While the internal strife began with demonstrations in Daraa, as the situation intensified the UNSC began to refer to violations of LOAC in its resolutions,[32] indicating that a shift in applicable legal frameworks had occurred.

However, it is not in fact a case of simply 'transitioning' from one framework (IHRL) to another (LOAC), given that IHRL continues to apply during armed conflicts.[33] Indeed, the law enforcement paradigm does not cease to apply during armed hostilities, although the way that it is interpreted and applied is altered and LOAC becomes the *lex specialis*.[34] For example, while all individuals have the right at all times to be free from arbitrary deprivation of their lives, during hostilities this must be read in light of the applicable LOAC rules.[35] In this respect, while in the context of law enforcement the taking of life is permitted only in exceptional circumstances,[36] the taking of life during

[27] ibid art 1(2).

[28] *Prosecutor v Tadić* (Decision on the Defence Motion for Interlocutory Appeal on Jurisdiction) ICTY-94-1-A (2 October 1995) para 70; *Prosecutor v Tadić* (Opinion and Judgment) ICTY-94-1-T (7 May 1997) para 562.

[29] ibid.

[30] Marko Milanovic/Vidam Hadzi-Vidanovic, 'A Taxonomy of Armed Conflict' in Nigel D White/Christian Henderson (eds), *Research Handbook on International Conflict and Security Law:* Jus ad Bellum, Jus in Bello *and* Jus post Bellum (Edward Elgar 2013) 291.

[31] *Prosecutor v Haradinaj et al* (Judgment) ICTY-04-84-T (3 April 2008) para 49.

[32] cf UNSC Presidential Statement 16 (2011) UN Doc S/PRST/2011/16, with UNSC Resolution 2139 (2014) para 1.

[33] Generally, Daragh Murray, *Practitioners' Guide to Human Rights Law in Armed Conflict* (OUP 2016). But see Israel's position in *Legal Consequences of the Construction of the Wall in the Occupied Palestinian Territory* (Advisory Opinion) [2004] ICJ Rep 136 [103]–[10]. See also *Legality of the Threat or Use of Nuclear Weapons* (Advisory Opinion) [1996] ICJ Rep 226 [24]–[25] (*Nuclear Weapons*).

[34] *Nuclear Weapons* (n 33) [25]. [35] See ECHR (n 6) art 15(2). [36] Section B.1.

hostilities depends on the *status* of the individual concerned either as a combatant (a member of a State's armed forces) or a member of an armed group to the armed conflict.[37] That said, the targeting of individuals may also be determined according to the *conduct* of the individuals concerned, in that civilians may be exceptionally targeted if and for such time they directly participate in hostilities.[38] As such, while no one shall be intentionally or arbitrarily deprived of their life, an intentional killing of a combatant, a member of an armed group, or a civilian directly participating in hostilities will not be deemed to be arbitrary as LOAC permits killing under these circumstances.[39]

Additionally, while killing under both frameworks is governed by a principle of necessity, in law enforcement the principle of 'absolute necessity' restricts force to a last resort and which pursues a legitimate aim, while under LOAC 'military necessity' to use force against legitimate targets is presumed. Furthermore, under the law enforcement framework, in gauging proportionality, a balance between the risks posed by an individual and the potential harm to this individual and to bystanders by a particular action is required,[40] whereas LOAC proportionality does not apply to legitimate targets of attack and also tolerates more incidental loss of life than the law enforcement paradigm.[41]

Both frameworks will be relevant when situations of civilian unrest—for example, demonstrations and riots—arise while combat operations against an armed group are taking place,[42] something which happened in early 2018 when Israel responded to protests by Gazan civilians while in an armed conflict with Hamas.[43] Indeed, 'the two situations of violence may even intermingle, for instance when fighters are hiding among rioting civilians or demonstrators'.[44] In such situations 'it may become difficult to distinguish fighters from rioting civilians and to identify the relevant applicable paradigm'.[45]

3. Outside Intervention in Internal Strife

While internal strife predominantly takes place within one State, and in that sense is internal, it may also have external elements, in particular in the form of third States

[37] Members of organized non-State armed groups which are a party to a non-international armed conflict are understood as 'individuals whose continuous function is to take a direct part in hostilities'. See Nils Melzer, Interpretive Guidance on the Notion of Direct Participation in Hostilities under International Humanitarian Law (ICRC 2009) 27 (ICRC Interpretive Guidance).

[38] AP II (n 26) art 13(3); ICRC Interpretive Guidance (n 37).

[39] But see ICRC Interpretive Guidance (n 37) 82.

[40] *Andronicou and Constantinou v Cyprus*, App No 86/1996/705/897, 9 October 1997, para 194; *Kerimova and Others v Russia*, App Nos 17170/04, 20792/04, 22448/04, 23360/04, 5681/05 and 5684/05, 3 May 2011, para 246.

[41] Gloria Gaggioli (ed), Expert Meeting Report: The Use of Force in Armed Conflicts (ICRC 2013) 2 (ICRC, Use of Force in Armed Conflicts).

[42] ibid 1. [43] See Section C. [44] ICRC, Use of Force in Armed Conflicts (n 41) 1.

[45] ibid.

directly or indirectly intervening. In this sense, the framework and rules governing intervention and inter-State use of force become applicable.

States are prohibited from intervening in the internal affairs of other States, that is, they are not permitted to employ coercion against other States so that political, economic, social or cultural choices are no longer made freely.[46] Coercion involving the use of force is, in particular, prohibited under Article 2(4) UN Charter and customary international law.[47] While self-defence and authorization by the UNSC represent exceptions to this prohibition,[48] if a State intervenes in another upon the invitation or consent of that State, for example to help the authorities maintain law and order or conduct hostilities against enemy fighters, then its actions do not engage the prohibition of forcible intervention in the first place.[49]

A State is an abstract entity and hence the question arises *who* may invite or give consent to the intervening State.[50] Under international law governments may invite outside intervention, while opposition forces or insurgents may not.[51] This is not to say that States do not intervene on behalf of opposition groups, but rather that they have not done so on the basis of a legal right to assist such groups.[52] Instead, States often deny that they are assisting opposition forces in another State, providing covert indirect support like weapons and training, which was the case for much of the Cold War.[53] Such support, while insufficient in itself to constitute an 'armed attack', thereby triggering the right to self-defence under Article 51 UN Charter, does nonetheless constitute a use of force under Article 2(4) UN Charter and customary international law.[54] Other forms of assistance, such as the provision of non-lethal equipment or the supply of funds, undoubtedly constitute acts of intervention in the internal affairs of the State concerned,

[46] *Nicaragua* (n 24) [202]; Declaration on Principles of International Law concerning Friendly Relations and Co-operation among States in accordance with the Charter of the United Nations, UNGA Res 2625 (XXV) (24 October 1970) para 1 (Friendly Relations Declaration).

[47] *Nicaragua* (n 24) [205].

[48] Charter of the United Nations 1 UNTS XVI (UN Charter) ch VII, art 51 specifically.

[49] See also ILA Committee on the Use of Force, 'Final Report on Aggression and the Use of Force' (Sydney 2018) s B.3 <http://www.ila-hq.org/images/ILA/DraftReports/DraftReport_UseOfForce.pdf> accessed 27 January 2020. See Louise Doswald-Beck, 'The Legal Validity of Military Intervention by Invitation of the Government' (1985) 56 BYIL 189.

[50] Consent may be ad hoc or contained within a treaty. See, controversially, Constitutive Act of the African Union 2158 UNTS 3 art 4(h).

[51] *Nicaragua* (n 24) [246]; *Armed Activities on the Territory of the Congo (DRC v Uganda)* [2005] ICJ Rep 168 [164]; Declaration on the Inadmissibility of Intervention in the Domestic Affairs of States and the Protection of Their Independence and Sovereignty, UNGA Res 2131 (XX) (21 December 1965) para 2 (Inadmissibility of Intervention Declaration).

[52] Christian Henderson, *The Use of Force and International Law* (OUP 2018) 353. More generally, States have not in general attempted to develop a legal right of humanitarian intervention in order to prevent, deter or end a humanitarian catastrophe within another State that takes place at the hands of the government or is something that the government is unable to do anything about. See ibid ch 10. While the UNSC possesses primary responsibility for the maintenance of *international* peace and security, it has also characterized internal strife and humanitarian situations as a 'threat to the peace' and subsequently authorized interventions under UN Charter (n 48) ch VII upon this basis.

[53] Henderson (n 52) 353.

[54] *Nicaragua* (n 24) [205].

but not a use of force.[55] In other cases, States have claimed that intervention in support of opposition groups is justified upon the basis of individual or collective self-defence.[56]

However, it may be that a State, in supporting an opposition group, claims to be intervening in support of the legitimate authorities of the State. This could be through a State installing a new regime, which subsequently extends an invitation to that State to intervene, as occurred with the Soviet Union's intervention in Afghanistan in 1979.[57] Alternatively, it may be claimed that an opposition group has assumed governmental authority through its de facto effective control of the State territory.[58] Indeed, effective control is the traditional method of identifying governmental legitimacy. Yet, it may also be claimed that an intervention has taken place upon the basis of an invitation from an opposition group with greater democratic legitimacy than the incumbent regime,[59] or upon the invitation of a democratically elected leader that has either been ousted from, or has yet to assume leadership of, a State. However, while the political goals underlying an intervention may include the (re)establishment of democratic government this has 'not led states to espouse a legal doctrine of "pro-democratic" invasion without UN authority'.[60]

Alternatively, a State may claim that an opposition group, and the 'people' they represent, possess the right of self-determination which justifies intervention in support. During the Cold War, national liberation movements were recognized as having the right to 'struggle' for self-determination,[61] although it was not clear whether 'armed struggle' was permitted. Nonetheless, while all States were urged 'to provide moral and material assistance to all peoples struggling for their freedom and independence',[62] in declaring that '[i]n their actions against, and resistance to, ... forcible action in pursuit of the exercise of their right to self-determination, such peoples are entitled to seek and to receive support in accordance with the purposes and principles of the Charter',[63] support involving the direct or indirect use of force would appear to have been excluded, as the Charter makes no provision for the use of force upon this basis. In addition, while no objective definition of a 'people' exists for the purposes of the right of self-determination, there also appears to be no 'support for the right to use force to attain self-determination outside of the context of decolonization or illegal occupation'.[64] While those in power—either through effective control or democratic credentials—possess the right to request

[55] ibid [228].

[56] See eg *Nicaragua* (n 24). The right of self-defence is located in UN Charter (n 48) art 51. It also exists under customary international law. See *Nicaragua* (n 24) [176].

[57] UNSC Verbatim Record (5 January 1980) UN Doc S/PV/2185.

[58] James Crawford, *Brownlie's Principles of Public International Law* (8th edn, OUP 2012) 152.

[59] Section C.

[60] Christine Gray, *International Law and the Use of Force* (4th edn, OUP 2018) 64. Such interventions more often take place under UNSC authorization (eg Côte d'Ivoire in 2011) or upon consent or invitation to intervene (eg The Gambia in 2017).

[61] Definition of Aggression, UNGA Res 3314 (XXIX) (14 December 1974) art 7.

[62] Implementation of the Declaration on the Granting of Independence to Colonial Countries and Peoples, UNGA Res 2908 (XXVII) (2 November 1972) para 8.

[63] Friendly Relations Declaration (n 46) para 1 (emphasis added).

[64] Gray (n 60) 73.

outside intervention, much will also turn on whether an intervention impedes the realization of self-determination.[65]

There is, in this respect, notable support for the 'negative equality' principle, meaning that if a civil war is in progress—and the outcome of the conflict is unclear—States should refrain from interfering and potentially influencing the outcome one way or the other, on the basis that to do so would negatively impact the right of self-determination.[66] During often messy civil wars adherence to this principle avoids the need to identify those with authority to consent or establish that an invitation has been validly given.[67] It also avoids escalating internal strife into an international armed conflict.[68] Yet, the principle also overlooks the absence of clarity as to what exactly constitutes a 'civil war' and whether one exists in the circumstances,[69] leaving much to subjective determination. In addition, if the principle only becomes applicable when the intensity of fighting has reached the level of civil war it 'appears to provide a greater right of self-determination to those with the capabilities to fight'.[70] In this respect, given that the negative equality principle is based upon not impeding the right of self-determination it should also arguably be applicable beyond full-blown civil wars to situations of domestic civil and political unrest.[71] It has, in any case, arguably not been followed in State practice,[72] while an absence of consensus amongst scholars remains.[73]

Scholars supportive of the negative equality principle also accept, however, that an intervention in support of one side in a civil war can justify a 'counter-intervention' in support of the other,[74] primarily on the basis that the initial intervention internationalizes the conflict with the negative equality principle thereby losing its relevance. Concerns might be raised regarding the potential abuse of such a principle. Indeed, this was arguably witnessed by the USSR's intervention in Czechoslovakia in 1968 and Afghanistan in 1979.[75] The required degree of prior intervention in order to permit counter-intervention is also unclear.[76] If adhered to, this principle could be seen as supporting the principle of self-determination, in that the purpose of a counter-intervention would be to

[65] Friendly Relations Declaration (n 46) para 5(5).

[66] Inadmissibility of Intervention Declaration (n 51) para 2. See also Friendly Relations Declaration (n 46) para 3(2); IDI, 'Resolution on the Principle of Non-Intervention in Civil Wars' (1975) 56 IDI Annuaire 545, 547; Independent International Fact-Finding Mission on the Conflict in Georgia, 'Report: Volume I' (September 2009) 277 <https://www.mpil.de/files/pdf4/IIFFMCG_Volume_I2.pdf> accessed 20 January 2020.

[67] Henderson (n 52) 363. [68] ibid. [69] ibid. [70] ibid 364.

[71] Quincy Wright, 'Subversive Intervention' (1960) 54 AJIL 521, 529.

[72] Dapo Akande, 'Would It Be Lawful for European (or other) States to Provide Arms to the Syrian Opposition?' (*EJIL Talk!*, 23 July 2011) <https://www.ejiltalk.org/would-it-be-lawful-for-european-or-other-states-to-provide-arms-to-the-syrian-opposition/> accessed 16 August 2019; Yoram Dinstein, *War, Aggression and Self-Defence* (6th edn, CUP 2017) 125–6.

[73] Gregory H Fox, 'Intervention by Invitation' in Marc Weller (ed), *The Oxford Handbook of the Use of Force in International Law* (OUP 2015) 828.

[74] Gray (n 60) 81; Geoffrey Marston (ed), 'United Kingdom Materials on International Law 1986' (1986) 57 BYIL 487, 616.

[75] Doswald-Beck (n 49) 224, 230–3.

[76] Tom Ruys/Luca Ferro, 'Weathering the Storm: Legality and Legal Implications of the Saudi-Led Military Intervention in Yemen' (2016) 65 ICLQ 61, 93.

reverse the negative impact of the original intervention. Yet, whether there is a need for proportionality between the prior intervention and the counter-intervention is another issue that remains unclear.[77]

Finally, it is possible that the purpose of an intervention may affect the way it is viewed legally.[78] For example, while an intervention which aims to aid government forces in the context of a civil war, and thus potentially interfere with the right of self-determination, may be unlawful, intervention with the government's invitation or consent for other purposes, such as fighting terrorism, may be seen as permissible.[79] While this can be observed to an extent in State practice,[80] identifying and confirming the legitimacy of the proclaimed purpose of intervention will often be problematic.

In the event of intervention, the applicable LOAC framework between opposition fighters and the government will still be that regulating non-international armed conflicts. If the intervening State intervenes on behalf of an opposition force indirectly—through the provision of weapons, funding, training etc—then while this might constitute a use of force against the territorial State the armed conflict will remain one between the governmental and non-governmental forces concerned.[81] If, however, the non-governmental forces operate under the effective control of the intervening State or the State intervenes directly with its own armed forces then the framework governing international armed conflicts becomes applicable.[82]

C. Recent Developments and Contemporary Challenges

There has been no shortage of incidents over recent years that fall within the purview of the topic of this chapter, producing challenges to the legal frameworks and having consequences for both regional and global security. The revolutionary spirit that has spread through Africa and the Middle East since 2011 (the 'Arab Spring') led to a wave of peaceful and violent demonstrations, protests and riots and in many cases insurgencies, civil wars, and foreign interventions. While the uprisings in Tunisia, Egypt, and Yemen resulted in the overthrow of the government, in Libya it led to a civil war with an intervention by NATO resulting in the killing of the leader, Muammar Gaddafi, and a regime

[77] ibid 94.

[78] Karine Bannelier-Christakis, 'Military Interventions against ISIL in Iraq, Syria and Libya, and the Legal Basis of Consent' (2016) 29 Leiden Journal of International Law 743.

[79] Henderson (n 52) 365–6.

[80] See eg the intervention of the Gulf Cooperation Council in Bahrain in 2011 and France's intervention in Mali in 2013.

[81] On this see *Nicaragua* (n 24) [195] and [228].

[82] On this see ibid [115] and [195].

change.[83] This intervention, while arguably conducted to protect civilians,[84] exemplifies the longer-term repercussions for internal and regional peace and stability of taking such action without any plans for the aftermath. On the other hand, the uprising in Bahrain was crushed by the government, supported by a direct intervention by several Gulf States,[85] while a catastrophic civil war continues to this day in Syria, fuelled by outside intervention by several States, most notably Russia, the US and Qatar. In the early days of the Syrian uprising there was condemnation of violations of IHRL by State agents,[86] followed by condemnation of violations of LOAC by both sides,[87] demonstrating the transition in applicable legal frameworks.

As further examples, demonstrations of both peaceful and violent nature in reaction to severe austerity measures took place in Greece in 2010–11,[88] while in April 2018 a nationwide revolt began against President Ortega in Nicaragua, initially in response to pension reforms. These later swelled into a broader rebellion to remove Ortega from power.[89] The violent response of Ortega's government led to the UN accusing it of 'a wide range of human rights violations…including extrajudicial killings, torture, arbitrary detentions, and denying the people the right to freedom of expression.'[90] Furthermore, the long-standing armed conflict between the Revolutionary Armed Forces of Columbia (FARC) and the government, which commenced in 1964, came to an end in June 2017, with FARC ceasing its activities and disarming under a peace agreement.[91] Civil uprisings also took place in Côte d'Ivoire in 2011,[92] The Gambia in 2016–17,[93] and Zimbabwe in 2018[94] in response to disputed election results, while

[83] James Meikle, 'Muammar Gaddafi is Dead, says Libyan PM', (*The Guardian*, 20 October 2011) <https://www.theguardian.com/world/2011/oct/20/gaddafi-dead-says-libyan-pm> accessed 27 January 2020.

[84] UNSC Res 1973 (2011) preambular para 5.

[85] BBC News, 'Gulf States Send Forces to Bahrain Following Protests' (*BBC News*, 14 March 2011) <https://www.bbc.co.uk/news/world-middle-east-12729786> accessed 27 January 2020.

[86] eg UNSC Resolution 2042 (2012) preambular para 4.

[87] eg UNSC Resolution 2139 (2014) para 1.

[88] BBC News, 'Three Dead as Greece Protest Turns Violent' (*BBC News*, 5 May 2010) <http://news.bbc.co.uk/1/hi/world/europe/8661385.stm> accessed 16 August 2019.

[89] Tom Phillips, 'Nicaragua: What's Driving the Uprising and What Comes Next?' (*The Guardian*, 20 July 2018) <https://www.theguardian.com/world/2018/jul/20/nicaragua-uprising-what-is-it-and-what-comes-next> accessed 16 August 2019.

[90] UNHCHR 'Press Briefing Notes on Nicaragua, Mali and Kashmir' (17 July 2018) <https://www.ohchr.org/EN/NewsEvents/Pages/DisplayNews.aspx?NewsID=23383&LangID=E> accessed 16 August 2019.

[91] Sibylla Brodzinsky, '"Welcome to Peace": Columbia's Farc Rebels Seal Historic Disarmament' (*The Guardian*, 27 June 2017) <https://www.theguardian.com/world/2017/jun/27/colombia-farc-weapons-war-government> accessed 16 August 2019.

[92] Christian Purefoy, 'What's Causing the Conflict in Ivory Coast?' (*CNN*, 5 April 2011) <http://edition.cnn.com/2011/WORLD/africa/04/03/ivory.coast.explainer/index.html> accessed 16 August 2019.

[93] Ruth Maclean, 'Troops Enter The Gambia after Adama Barrow is Inaugurated in Senegal' (*The Guardian*, 19 January 2017) <https://www.theguardian.com/world/2017/jan/19/new-gambian-leader-adama-barrow-sworn-in-at-ceremony-in-senegal> accessed 16 August 2019.

[94] *BBC News*, 'Zimbabwe Election: Troops Fire on MDC Alliance Supporters' (*BBC News*, 1 August 2018) <https://www.bbc.co.uk/news/world-africa-45035533> accessed 16 August 2019.

several States, for example Mali and Nigeria, have faced severe threats from insurgent Islamist groups.[95] While the consequences of these incidents have often remained internal, there are cases where civil unrest has had regional security consequences. In 2014, a series of protests and civil insurrection took place in Venezuela against the economic policies of the government.[96] This led to extensive migration to neighbouring States, including Brazil, Columbia, and Ecuador, which has resulted in the deployment of troops in light of security concerns arising from attacks by and against the migrants.[97]

In addition, and of particular note, Israel's response to the Great March of Return in Gaza in 2018,[98] during which Palestinians in the Gaza Strip demonstrated near the border fence with Israel, presented real challenges and raised questions regarding the appropriate application of the law, in particular the way in which the law enforcement and conduct of hostilities paradigms should interact and operate alongside each other. The rules of engagement of the Israeli Defence Force received particular attention, both in the blogosphere[99] and through a challenge brought by 11 NGOs to the Israeli Supreme Court in the *Yesh Din* case.[100]

In what was a notable development, Israel asserted that within the LOAC framework, which it claimed applied in this situation, there are two regimes regulating the resort to force: the 'conduct of hostilities' paradigm, and the 'law enforcement' paradigm. The law enforcement paradigm embedded within LOAC, according to Israel, is 'inspired by', but not similar to, the law enforcement regime under IHRL, and applies where demonstrations are organized by a belligerent party, take place in enemy territory, and are used by the belligerent party to further its hostile goals.[101] While under the law enforcement framework, as set out above, force is only permitted against individuals who pose an imminent threat to life,[102] Israel was of the view that under its LOAC-law enforcement paradigm the 'threat can be posed by a single individual, or by masses of individuals' and that force might be resorted to so as to 'address the threat before it materializes, even if

[95] *BBC News*, 'Mali Crisis: Key Players' (*BBC News*, 12 March 2013) <https://www.bbc.co.uk/news/world-africa-17582909> accessed 16 August 2019; *BBC News*, 'Who Are Nigeria's Boko Haram Islamist Group?' (*BBC News*, 24 November 2016) <https://www.bbc.co.uk/news/world-africa-13809501> accessed 16 August 2019.

[96] *BBC News*, 'Venezuela Student Protest Ends in Deadly Violence' (*BBC News*, 13 February 2014) <https://www.bbc.com/news/world-latin-america-26166094> accessed 16 August 2019.

[97] *BBC News*, 'Venezuela Crisis: Brazil Deploys Troops After Migrant Attacks' (*BBC News*, 20 August 2018) <https://www.bbc.com/news/world-latin-america-45242786> accessed 16 August 2019.

[98] Alia Chughtai, 'Palestinian's Great March of Return: The Human Cost' (*Al Jazeera*, 16 May 2018) <https://www.aljazeera.com/indepth/interactive/2018/05/palestinians-great-march-return-human-cost-180516110538165.html> accessed 16 August 2019.

[99] Elena Chachko/Yuval Shany, 'The Supreme Court of Israel Dismisses a Petition Against Gaza Rules of Engagement' (*Lawfare*, 26 May 2018) <https://www.lawfareblog.com/supreme-court-israel-dismisses-petition-against-gaza-rules-engagement> accessed 16 August 2019; Eliav Lieblich, 'Collectivizing Threat: An Analysis of Israel's Legal Claims for Resort to Force on the Gaza Border' (*Just Security*, 16 May 2018) <https://www.justsecurity.org/56346/collectivizing-threat-analysis-israels-legal-claims-resort-force-gaza-border/> accessed 16 August 2019.

[100] *Yesh Din v IDF Chief of General Staff*, HCJ 3003/18 and 3250/18, 24 May 2018.

[101] Lieblich (n 99). [102] Section B.1.

the danger itself is not immediate'.[103] In addition, the threat may be to the life of others but also 'when there is a clear threat to infrastructure'.[104] In essence, soldiers were permitted to fire live ammunition at anyone attempting to approach and damage the border fence, even if unarmed and posing no imminent danger.[105] Intentional lethal force was permitted against 'main inciters', regardless as to whether or not they were directly endangering any lives.[106] In this sense, Israel claimed that many of those killed were terrorists with a documented terror background.

On 24 May 2018, the Israeli Supreme Court unanimously rejected the NGOs' petition.[107] The position of the Court on several issues was not overly clear. Although it accepted Israel's argument that the relevant legal framework was LOAC, implicitly accepting its version of it with a law enforcement paradigm,[108] the Court did not clearly specify which paradigm within this framework—conduct of hostilities or law enforcement—covered targeting in the situation in Gaza.

Nonetheless, most controversy has actually arisen in the context of third State intervention. While such interventions have occasionally been justified as humanitarian intervention,[109] self-defence,[110] or as having received UNSC authorization,[111] most often they have been justified upon the basis of an invitation by, or consent of, the host State government. And it is in this context that several recent developments and challenges to the law can be seen.

While identifying the entity with legitimacy to invite or consent to outside intervention has never been clear,[112] the traditional criterion of effective control has been challenged in recent interventions. For example, there was widespread acceptance by the international community in 2013 of the legality of French military intervention in support of the Malian government, despite the fact that Islamist rebels controlled much of the north of the country and were gradually moving in on the capital.[113] It seems that the validity of

[103] Lieblich (n 99).

[104] *BBC News*, 'Did Israel Use Excessive Force at Gaza Protests?' (*BBC News*, 17 May 2018) <https://www.bbc.co.uk/news/world-middle-east-44124556> accessed 16 August 2019. In any case, Israel claimed that its actions would be lawful under the regular law enforcement paradigm found within IHRL, as potentially lethal force is permitted in order to quell a life-threatening riot under ECHR (n 6) art 2(c).

[105] ibid. [106] Chachko/Shany (n 99).

[107] See n 115.

[108] Justice Hayut, however, doubted whether it reflects international law.

[109] eg NATO intervened in Kosovo in 1999 to stop the severe repression by the Serbian authorities. Adam Roberts, 'NATO's "Humanitarian War" Over Kosovo' (1999) 41 Survival 102.

[110] eg a US-led coalition intervened in Syria in 2014 in collective self-defence of Iraq against so-called 'Islamic State' forces that had taken control of areas of both Iraq and Syria and had carried out heinous acts against civilians in both States. Christian Henderson, 'The Use of Force and Islamic State' (2015) 1 Journal on the Use of Force and International Law 209.

[111] eg in 2011 authorization was provided to NATO to intervene in Libya and to the UN Operation in Côte d'Ivoire (UNOCI) and French forces to intervene in Côte d'Ivoire. Christian Henderson, 'International Measures for the Protection of Civilians in Libya and Côte d'Ivoire' (2011) 60 ICLQ 767.

[112] Section B.3.

[113] Dapo Akande/Zachary Vermeer, 'The Airstrikes against Islamic State in Iraq and the Alleged Prohibition on Military Assistance to Governments in Civil Wars' (*EJIL Talk!*, 2 February 2015) <https://www.ejiltalk.org/the-airstrikes-against-islamic-state-in-iraq-and-the-alleged-prohibition-on-military-assistance-to-governments-in-civil-wars/> accessed 16 August 2019.

consent or invitation has, instead, more often been ascertained on the basis of recognition of the entity concerned having the authority or at least legitimacy to provide such consent. Traditionally, States have not tended to expressly recognize governments, but have rather left this to be implicitly determined in light of the interactions that take place with the entity concerned. More recently there have been examples of express recognition. This has sometimes been done collectively through the UNSC in an attempt to implement an election result. During the 2011 internal strife in Côte d'Ivoire, flowing from a disputed election between Alassane Ouattara and Laurent Gbagbo, the UNSC '[u]rge[d] all the Ivorian parties and other stakeholders to respect the will of the people and the election of Allasane Dramane Ouattara as President of the Côte d'Ivoire'.[114] Following this there was an intervention by the UN Operation in Côte d'Ivoire (UNOCI) and French armed forces to enforce the election result,[115] despite Alassane Ouattara not yet being in office, let alone in effective control of the territory.

Events in The Gambia in 2016–17 provide a further example. The sitting president, Yahya Jemmeh, refused to accept the results of the 2016 presidential elections and leave office, with the president-elect, Adama Barrow, immediately calling for assistance to enforce his electoral win after having been sworn into office.[116] His claim was supported by UNSC Resolution 2337.[117] Senegalese troops subsequently entered The Gambia as part of an Economic Community of West African States (ECOWAS) intervention.[118] On both occasions, while the UNSC did not expressly authorize the intervention, the support provided to the democratically elected leader was apparently sufficient to legitimize the ensuing intervention.

The UNSC has also been seen to support leaders who have been forced into exile, and are therefore no longer in effective control of the territory of the State. For example, President Abdrabbuh Mansour Hadi of Yemen issued an invitation to a Saudi Arabian-led coalition to intervene and oust the Houthi rebels that had forced him into exile in 2015. This invitation received general support and the UNSC 'took note' of the request,[119] the support arguably being offered upon the basis of Hadi representing the elected president of the country as opposed to being in effective control of it.

Upon the basis of these particular developments it is possible to conclude that 'broad international recognition of the person inviting outside intervention may effectively compensate to a large extent for the lack of effective control over territory',[120] with it also being inversely true that a general lack of recognition can negatively affect perceptions of the legality of invited interventions. For example, Russia intervened in Crimea in 2014 upon the invitation of President Yanukovych after he had been forced to flee the country and had been replaced by an interim government through an act of the Ukrainian

[114] UNSC Res 1975 (2011) para 1.

[115] *BBC News*, 'Ivory Coast: UN Forces Fire on Pro-Gbagbo Camp' (*BBC News*, 5 April 2011) <https://www.bbc.co.uk/news/world-africa-12960308> accessed 16 August 2019.

[116] Claus Kreß/Benjamin Nußberger, 'Pro-Democratic Intervention in Current International Law: The Case of The Gambia in January 2017' (2017) 4 Journal on the Use of Force and International Law 239.

[117] UNSC Res 2337 (2017) preamble.

[118] Maclean (n 93).

[119] UNSC Res 2216 (2015) preamble.

[120] Ruys/Ferro (n 76) 85.

parliament.[121] On this occasion, it was argued that 'any consent [Yanukovych] might have provided for the Russian action is unlikely to have been valid because he was no longer effectively acting as president of Ukraine',[122] and therefore he 'no longer had authority to represent Ukraine in relation to the use of force'.[123] Yet, while the legality of the interventions in Yemen and Crimea are viewed differently, in neither case was the individual concerned able to act effectively as President of their respective countries. As such, while democratic legitimacy has the power to 'validate an invitation to intervene by a government in exile that controls no territory',[124] the overriding factor appears to be the breadth and extent of the recognition that an individual and their government possesses.

The question arises whether recognition can also validate interventions on behalf of opposition groups or insurgents, if the latter pose a more democratic and stable future than the incumbent, perhaps democratically elected, regime. After the 2011 uprising in Libya, States began to recognize the National Transitional Council as the legitimate government, a recognition that was followed by the supply of arms and non-lethal military equipment and which permitted other measures such as the release of assets held in various States to the opposition forces.[125] This all took place while Colonel Gaddafi remained in power and retained effective control over most of the country, leading some to argue that such recognition and subsequent supply of arms was premature and therefore illegal.[126] By contrast, in the case of Syria States stopped short of providing full recognition to the Syrian National Council as the legitimate government, instead recognizing it as the 'legitimate representatives' of the people in 2012.[127] This lack of recognition arguably led to much greater resistance by States to the idea of supplying it with arms and non-lethal assistance. The potential for negative repercussions for regional and global security of such premature recognitions of an opposition group was arguably less in Libya than in Syria, given the collective involvement of the UNSC and the lack of a big power, such as Russia, in support of the Gaddafi regime. In none of these cases, however, did States attempt to develop a standalone right of pro-democratic intervention.

A lack of general adherence to the negative equality principle has also been witnessed. For example, as the internal strife in Syria morphed into a protracted civil war, and while

[121] *BBC News*, 'Ukrainian MPs vote to oust President Yanukovych' (*BBC News*, 22 February 2014) <https://www.bbc.co.uk/news/world-europe-26304842> accessed 16 August 2019.

[122] James A Green, 'Editorial Comment: The Annexation of Crimea: Russia, Passportisation and the Protection of Nationals Revisited' (2014) 1 Journal on the Use of Force and International Law 3, 7.

[123] Marc Weller, 'The Shadow of the Gun: Marc Weller Reports on the Legality of Events in Crimea' (2014) 164 (7599) New Law Journal.

[124] Fox (n 73) 833–4.

[125] Stefan Talmon, 'Recognition of the Libyan National Transitional Council' (2011) 15 American Society of International Law Insights, <https://www.asil.org/insights/volume/15/issue/16/recognition-libyan-national-transitional-council> accessed 27 January 2020.

[126] Akande (n 72).

[127] *BBC News*, 'Syria Conflict: UK Recognises Opposition, says William Hague' (*BBC* News, 20 November 2012) <https://www.bbc.co.uk/news/uk-politics-20406562> accessed 16 August 2019.

concerns were raised regarding the Russian supply of arms and subsequent deployment of its forces to assist the Assad regime, this was not on the basis that intervention in support of either party during a civil war was unlawful.[128] States that went on to support the opposition groups in Syria also did not justify their intervention on the basis of the principle of counter-intervention. Similarly, France's 2013 intervention in Mali at the request of the government came, and was accepted, after the Tuareg rebels of Le Mouvement national de liberation de l'Azawad (MLNA) had captured and controlled the entire northern part of the State and were less than 300 miles from the capital, although 'no state raised the "negative equality" principle or spoke in opposition to the French intervention.'[129]

In practice, when States have intervened they have attempted to convince others that they are not intervening in a civil war, but instead for an alternative purpose. For example, while it might be questioned whether the internal strife had reached the level of a civil war, the Gulf Cooperation Council (GCC) intervened in Bahrain in March 2011 principally on the grounds of 'contribut[ing] to the maintenance of order and stability' following an uprising in the State.[130] However, it later transpired that '[t]he GoB [Government of Bahrain] [had] expressed its concerns about a possible Iranian armed intervention in Bahrain' and 'that these concerns were among the principal reasons that it requested the deployment of GCC forces in Bahrain starting on 14 March 2011.'[131] Similarly, in intervening in Mali, France denied that it was intervening in the war between the government and the MLNA, but argued that it was instead acting against Islamist terrorist groups.[132]

The Saudi-led coalition intervention in Yemen—Operation Decisive Storm—that commenced on 26 March 2015 in response to armed activity by the Houthi movement could be seen as an intervention in a civil war on the basis of an invitation by Yemen's president. Indeed, it was launched to 'protect the people of Yemen and its legitimate government from a takeover by the Houthis.'[133] Yet, in its letter to the UNSC, Saudi Arabia placed clear focus not upon the consent or invitation but on the fact that the Houthi rebels were 'supported by regional forces' and 'had always been a tool of outside forces'

128 Christian Henderson, 'The Provision of Arms and "Non-Lethal" Assistance to Government and Opposition Forces' (2013) 36 University of New South Wales Law Journal 642, 669.

129 Fox (n 73) 828.

130 GCC, Secretary-General of the Cooperation Council, 'Notes and supports the positions of the GCC countries to contribute to the preservation of order and security in the Kingdom of Bahrain' (Riyadh, 15 March 2011) para 1.

131 M Cherif Bassiouni et al, 'Report of the Bahrain Independent Commission of Inquiry' (BICI, 10 December 2011) ch IV, para 1575 <http://www.bici.org.bh/BICIreportEN.pdf> accessed 16 August 2019.

132 UNSC 'Identical Letters dated 11 January 2013 from the Permanent Representative of France to the United Nations addressed to the Secretary-General and the President of the Security Council' (14 January 2013) UN Doc S/2013/17.

133 Press Release, 'Statement by Saudi Ambassador al-Jubeir on Military Operations in Yemen' (25 March 2015) <https://www.saudiembassy.net/press-release/statement-saudi-ambassador-al-jubeir-military-operations-yemen> accessed 27 January 2020.

and therefore there had been an act of 'aggression' against Yemen.[134] While it might, therefore, be argued that the forces intervened against the Houthi rebels, consent to intervene in a civil war was not considered a sufficient justification by itself with Saudi Arabia also claiming counter-intervention, although it is not clear whether, and to what extent, Iran was supporting the Houthi rebels.

A central problem with this 'purpose-based' approach to intervention during civil war, however, is identifying and confirming the legitimacy of the proclaimed purpose of the intervention. In Mali, for example, while all three groups that France intervened against had been determined to be of a 'terrorist' nature by the UNSC,[135] thus lending some legitimacy to the subsequent intervention, during the internal strife in Syria the Syrian government appeared to simply categorize all opposition forces as terrorist, meaning that winning the civil war and fighting terrorism had become indistinguishable.[136]

D. Outlook

While internal strife and insurgency traditionally remained outside the reach of international law and within States' *domaine réservé*, this chapter has attempted to demonstrate that this is no longer the case. Yet, while the law has not remained static and can no longer be said to be entirely neutral on this issue, in an attempt to shift the law further, particularly in the context of large-scale internal strife, proposals have been advanced for more 'internal' regulation so as to bring the actions of non-State actors and insurgents within the purview of international legal regulation of both the use of force and armed conflict.[137] Yet, the humanitarian imperative upon which proposals for a new framework governing 'internal *jus ad bellum*' and for a more developed internal *jus in bello* are based—in particular, providing the 'privilege of belligerency' to non-State armed groups with the aim of providing greater incentive for compliance with LOAC—has not been accepted without question.[138]

[134] UNSC 'Identical Letters dated 26 March 2015 from the Permanent Representative of Qatar to the United Nations addressed to the Secretary-General and the President of the Security Council' (27 March 2015) UN Doc S/2015/217, 5 (Saudi Arabia).

[135] UNSC Res 2100 (2013) para 4.

[136] UNSC, 'Identical Letters dated 26 January 2016 from the Chargé d'affaires a.i. of the Permanent Mission of the Syrian Arab Republic to the United Nations addressed to the Secretary-General and the President of the Security Council' (28 January 2016) UN Doc S/2016/80. Although, if there is no negative equality principle then there is no need to look for a purpose of the intervening force.

[137] eg Eliav Lieblich, 'Internal *Jus ad Bellum*' (2016) 67 Hastings Law Journal 687; Claus Kreß, 'Towards Further Developing the Law of Non-International Armed Conflict: A Proposal for a *jus in bello interno* and a New *jus contra bellum internum*' (2014) 96 International Committee of the Red Cross 30.

[138] eg Frédéric Mégret, 'Response to Claus Kreß: Leveraging the Privilege of Belligerency in Non-International Armed Conflict towards Respect for the *jus in bello*' (2014) 96 International Committee of the Red Cross 44.

Yet, what should become clear is that while the basic standards and expectations contained within the rules and principles of the existing frameworks remain strong, their implementation is not straightforward and remains hostage to the subjective whims of those relying on them. In addition, and as the ongoing catastrophe in Syria demonstrates all too vividly, what might begin as peaceful protest can morph swiftly into a civil war and then into what might be described as a regional or even global conflict, with interventions not simply by regional States but by those further afield. The consequences for both regional and global security are heightened from the risks of instability caused through, for example, migration, while outside intervention—as both Syria and Yemen have vividly demonstrated—has the tendency of prolonging civil conflict and, with that, drastically increasing the negative humanitarian consequences.

While commissions of inquiry have in some senses partially filled an accountability gap, enforcement of international law in the context of internal strife remains poor. Despite the emergence of the concepts such as the Responsibility to Protect, the bulwarks of sovereignty and territorial control continue to remain stumbling blocks in ensuring accountability in such crises.

CHAPTER 10

INTERNATIONAL LAW AND STATE FAILURE

ROB MCLAUGHLIN

A. Introduction

While each incidence of State failure 'is taken as a unique event',[1] State failure is not unusual or remarkable for its rarity in the international system, indeed it is for some 'a structural trait of the contemporary international system'.[2] Furthermore, State failure is a multivalent concept, approachable from political, historical, sociological, developmental, economic, and myriad other normative, functional, and thematic perspectives—one recent study of State failure in Africa, for example, prioritized the distorting economy and organization of violence as both an indicia and a consequence.[3] This chapter seeks to examine the concept of State failure from the perspective of international law as it concerns the facilitation, regulation, and occasionally the degradation of global security. The key point made is that international law, in this context, is primarily conceptualized as an enabler for security-informed responses to the phenomenon of State failure, and thus has been 'focused mainly on how to resurrect (…) [failed States], while limiting the number of people harmed'.[4] That is, international law approaches State failure from the perspective of restorative legal and institutional facilitation,[5] with a structural predilection for a State-centric security framework. This has resulted in the nexus between 'State failure' and international law being dominated by two interlinked purposes: (1) promoting

[1] Jeffrey Herbst, 'Responding to State Failure in Africa' (1996–97) 21 International Security 120, 126.

[2] The African Studies Centre et al, 'Report: Failed and Collapsed States in the International System' <https://www.ces.uc.pt/nucleos/nep/documentos/failed_collapsedStates-Report.pdf> accessed 18 August 2019.

[3] ibid 7. [4] Herbst (n 1) 120.

[5] Daniel Thürer, 'The "Failed State" and International Law' (1999) 81 International Review of the Red Cross 731, 760.

the normative continuity of 'Stateness'[6] for failed entities; and (2) managing the transition back to a minimum level of stable 'Stateness' with the least harm to the population and the international community.[7] That is, international law's approach to State failure is primarily one of remedy, not of acceptance. This is unsurprising given the empathy in international law and practice, as applied in State failure situations, for continuity in domestic legal arrangements—generally pending revision by the new government—in transitional and decolonization situations.[8] It is also evident in the predisposition of domestic courts to seek continuity with applicable pre-strife law when assessing litigation arising out of periods of civil war.[9] This chapter will consequently focus upon how international law defines, identifies, and facilitates initial responses to State failure. To this end, this chapter first seeks to evolve a working (and certainly imperfect) definition of 'State failure' from an international law perspective. The analysis then examines the adequacy of selected modes and indicators by which international law may recognize State failure. The chapter concludes with a brief comment on how international law generally structures initial responses to State failure.

B. 'Defining' State Failure

1. Definitional Approaches

There is no common or traditionally accepted definition of State failure; indeed, the 'conceptual vagueness' that surrounds it is 'reflected in the proliferation of terminologies concerning the phenomenon of state collapse—for example, collapsed state, failed state,

[6] I have adopted this term from Nicolas Lemay-Hebert, 'Statebuilding without Nation-building? Legitimacy, State Failure and the Limits of the Institutionalist Approach' (2009) 3 Journal of Intervention and Statebuilding 21, 23.

[7] Thus, proposals such as that by (*inter alia*) Herbst are normatively sound but functionally often limited to narrow purposes such as 'decertification' (for aid and assistance purposes) of States that fail to perform certain obligations—Herbst (n 1) 142–4.

[8] Regulation No. 1999/1 on the Authority of the Transitional Administration in East Timor (27November 1999) UNTAET/REG/1991/1. Generally, Michael Kelly et al, 'Legal Aspects of Australia's Involvement in the International Force for East Timor' (2003) 83 International Review of the Red Cross 101; Hansjörg Strohmeyer, 'Collapse and Reconstruction of a Judicial System: The United Nations Missions in Kosovo and East Timor' (2001) 95 AJIL 46. For a different, critical, perspective with respect to decolonization, see Reginald Austin, 'Namibia and Zimbabwe: Decolonisation and the Rule of International Law' (1982) 35 Current Legal Problems 203. On 'State failure reversal' or 'transformation', see, generally, Rosa Ehrenreich Brooks, 'Failed States, or the State as Failure?' (2005) 72 University of Chicago Law Review 1159, 1163; Jarat Chopra, 'Building State Failure in East Timor' (2002) 33 Development and Change 979; Stephen Krasner/Carlos Pascual, 'Addressing State Failure' (2005) 84 Foreign Affairs 153, 158–60.

[9] eg in the US Supreme Court, *Williams v Bruffy* 96 US 176 (1877).

fragile state, shadow state, lame Leviathan, weak state'.[10] Additionally, there is no clearly demarcated spectrum of State failure, and no attendant set of universal identifiers or milestones. There are certainly attempts to distinguish 'weak States' from 'failed States',[11] just as there are schematic approaches that coalesce around differentiating factors such as 'ability to broadcast power over (...) sovereign territory', or the imperfect degree to which a government maintains its 'monopoly on the legitimate use of violence'.[12] However there is no universally accepted categorization scheme that assimilates all such factors, coherently orders them, and then assigns legally meaningful and nuanced degrees of failure.

Arriving at a working definition of 'State failure' from an international law perspective thus requires three iterative steps. The first is to determine what 'State failure' is not; that is, which elements or concepts, often evident in State failure analysis—and thus potentially fundamental to any definition—are in fact contested or partial, and thus cannot provide a robust definitional foundation. The second step is to then ask what purpose would or could such an international law definition serve, for this will provide some guidance as to the nature of any definition. The final step is to then propose a working definition of 'State failure' in the context of international law.

2. The Contested Utility of Certain Concepts in an International Law Definition of State Failure

The first and most fundamental conceptual distinction to be drawn is that State failure is not the same as State extinction; it may be a waypoint on the road to that outcome, but it is not synonymous with State extinction, nor analogous to it. This is important because it means that the criteria in law for identifying a failed State need not necessarily be the same as for State extinction. This is evident in the prevalence of legally significant statements to the effect that a failed State's 'Statehood' has not disappeared.[13] Indeed, State extinction is rare—as some analysts have observed, '"State death" as a result of external

[10] Lemay-Hebert (n 6) 22; Jean-Germain Gros, 'Towards a Taxonomy of Failed States in the New World Order: Decaying Somalia, Liberia, Rwanda and Haiti' (1996) 17 Third World Quarterly 455, 456–8.

[11] Robert Jackson, *Quasi-States: Sovereignty, International Relations and the Third World* (CUP 1990) 26–31.

[12] Justin Hastings, 'Geographies of State Failure and Sophistication in Maritime Piracy Hijackings' (2009) 28 Political Geography 213, 213–14.

[13] eg the US (and many other States') policy position that the Transitional Federal Government (TFG) (now the Federal Government of Somalia) represented the unitary State of Somalia, regardless of (in the 2000s) both the TFG's limited geographic writ, and the existence of functioning sub-State entities claiming independence (such as Somaliland). On US policy with respect to the TFG, see Bronwyn E Bruton, 'Somalia: A New Approach' (Council on Foreign Relations Special Report No 52, 2010) 10, 19–20; on current US recognition of the FGS, see US Department of State, 'U.S. Relation With Somalia' (*US DoS*, 13 August 2018) <https://www.state.gov/r/pa/ei/bgn/2863.htm> accessed 18 August 2019.

invasion, common before World War II, has almost disappeared since 1945'[14]—whereas State failure is not. Crawford's survey of post-1945 State extinctions tallies to eight, of which only three were involuntary,[15] and his concept of 'State extinction' essentially focuses on the loss or preservation of the 'legal identity of the state over time'.[16] The CIA State Failure Task Force, on the other hand, identified 127 instances of post-1945 State failure.[17] The two concepts are thus related, but not identical. Indeed, it is arguable that the legal paraphernalia of State identity and recognition, and of identifying State failure, is in fact premised upon the *raison d'être* of preserving the particular State in existence as a legal entity, regardless of its current situation and the 'abeyance' of its ability to express its sovereignty. As Aust notes, it is the 'extinction of the international legal personality of a party' to a treaty that terminates treaty obligations;[18] degrees of inability to perform those obligations—from comprehensive incapacity through to sectoral inability—may well indicate State failure, but do not indicate State extinction.

Secondly, State failure is not necessarily synonymous with 'state collapse'.[19] Thürer argues, for example, that the 'failure' of 'Stateness' is also evident in 'aggressive, arbitrary, tyrannical or totalitarian' States—the 'opposite extreme' from anarchic or collapsed States,[20] albeit in such cases the failed State has ossified or frozen rather than disintegrated. In the 1990s, for example, Helman and Ratner identified at least three categories of 'failing' States, each evidencing different degrees and pathologies of failure, in which collapse was a subset but not a defining characteristic.[21]

This realization of the elastic and contextually determined limits of the concept of 'failure' also reveals that there is no causal correlation between a third definitional candidate—legitimacy—and State failure: 'the history of the modern state is in no small part a history of rulers who are illegitimate.'[22] This dismissal of a failure of legitimacy as the defining factor in State failure is not universally agreed, of course,[23] but it must be accepted that while the absence of legitimacy may often be connected with State failure, it is not fundamental to it. There are illegitimate governments whose States are not failing; there are failing States whose governments are—at the very least—formally legitimate, even if incapable or overwhelmed. Additionally, the indicia of legitimacy may well differ contextually and culturally, if not legally,[24] thus rendering it opaque as a readily and universally acceptable definitional foundation.

[14] Krasner/Pascual (n 8) 155; Robert Rotberg, 'The New Nature of Nation-State Failure' (2002) 25 The Washington Quarterly 85, 94–5.

[15] James Crawford, *The Creation of States in International Law* (2nd edn, OUP 2006) 700–17.

[16] ibid 700–1.

[17] Daniel Esty et al, 'State Failure Task Force Report: Phase II Findings' (1999) 5 Environmental Change and Security Project Report 49, 50.

[18] Anthony Aust, *Modern Treaty Law and Practice* (3rd edn, CUP 2013) 261–3, 270, 320–4.

[19] Lemay-Hebert (n 6) 21. [20] Thürer (n 5) 732–3.

[21] Gerald Helman/Steven Ratner, 'Saving Failed States' (1992–93) 89 Foreign Policy 3, 5.

[22] Jennifer Milliken/Keith Krause, 'State Failure, State Collapse, and State Reconstruction: Concepts, Lessons and Strategies' (2002) 33 Development and Change 753, 757.

[23] Rotberg (n 14) 85.

[24] eg Pierre Englebert/Denis Tull, 'Postconflict Reconstruction in Africa: Flawed Ideas about Failed States' (2008) 32 International Security 106, 110.

The fourth thing which State failure is not, is 'Etats sans gouvernement'. On one hand, this descriptor is inadequately narrow, argues Thürer, because State failure carries the implication that not only all functions of the State, but also many private functions, have collapsed.[25] Alternatively, as Brooks observes, it is too imprecise a description because it is necessary to 'distinguish between governance structures, which all societies require, and the particular governance structures that have characterized the modern state'.[26] That is, failed States often have non-State forms of governance (warlords, criminal gangs, commune, religious) actively expressing their mandates and competing for local priority. Consequently, it is not absence of government that is the issue—indeed, sometimes the challenge is actually a surfeit of competing governance options—but rather the absence of formal State governance. As Chopra noted, while correlating State anarchy or 'voids' with 'the absence of any recognizable state machinery' has a long and contested history, 'this polarized disagreement altogether miss[es] the fact that the population continues to exist, that market forces of whatever kind are always at work, and that the social structures of indigenous communities invariably generate sources of political legitimacy according to their own paradigm (…)'.[27] That is, absence of 'government' is clearly an imperfect indicator or definitional element of State failure. Furthermore, while there may often be 'governance' in fact,[28] whether international law is doctrinally capable of characterizing that governance as a legally acceptable or definable mode of governance is another matter.

Finally, State failure can be conceived of as the failure of conflict management mechanisms—particularly when manifested as an unacceptable absence of responsible jurisdiction, or the failure of capacity to deconflict jurisdictional rub points with other States.[29] This conception is itself open to multifarious taxonomies—an institutional-functional framework,[30] and distinguishing between anarchic and phantom States being but two.[31] It is not unknown to international law that physical space can be owned by none, however, this is generally accompanied by the caveat that such space is also usable by all. Thus, oceans and (albeit less universally accepted) space[32] are often

[25] Thürer (n 5) 733. [26] Brooks (n 8) 1184. [27] Chopra (n 8) 979–81.

[28] Herbst (n 1) 124–5.

[29] Cedric Ryngaert, *Jurisdiction in International Law* (2nd edn, OUP 2015) 5–10.

[30] Milliken/Krause (n 22) 757.

[31] Jean-Germain Gros, 'Towards a Taxonomy of Failed States in the New World Order: Decaying Somalia, Liberia, Rwanda and Haiti' (1996) 17 Third World Quarterly 455–9.

[32] United Nations Convention on the Law of the Sea 1833 UNTS 3 (UNCLOS) preamble, arts 125, 136. 150, 155, 311; impliedly in Treaty on Principles Governing the Activities of States in the Exploration and Use of Outer Space, including the Moon and Other Celestial Bodies 610 UNTS 205 arts 1–3; Agreement Governing the Activities of States on the Moon and Other Celestial Bodies 1363 UNTS 3 art 11. Generally, Christopher Joyner, 'Legal Implications of the Concept of the Common Heritage of Mankind' (1986) 35 ICLQ 190; John Noyes, 'The Common Heritage of Mankind: Past, Present, and Future' (2011–12) 40 Denver Journal of International Law and Policy 447; cf, Virgiliu Pop, 'Is Outer Space Proper the "Common Heritage of Mankind"?' (67th International Astronautical Congress, Guadalajara, Mexico, 26–30 September 2016); Edward Guntrip, 'The Common Heritage of Mankind: An Adequate Regime for Managing the Deep Seabed?' (2003) 4 Melbourne Journal of International Law 376.

described as components of the common heritage of mankind, but then overlaid with governance regimes to facilitate deconfliction. Similarly, vessels without nationality/ stateless vessels are not treated as physical sites in which no jurisdiction applies, but rather are immediately susceptible to the jurisdiction of any boarding State.[33] But failed States cannot be thought of, even temporarily, as the common heritage of mankind, for to do so would be to invite 'governance' interventions by any or all in the absence of a claims deconfliction architecture such as applies over those components of the oceans that are considered to be common heritage. That is, even the apparently comprehensive failure of a State to evidence any capacity to engage with other States in order to resolve disputes does not mean that it has become juridically unpinned from 'Statehood'. International law does not readily accommodate reversion to an undefined, porous, form of common heritage for which there is no alternative jurisdictional framework in place (as is the case for the oceans and, to a lesser extent, space).

3. What Purposes Might an International Law Concept of State Failure Serve within the Broader Context of Global Security?

Any attempt at defining State failure—in any disciplinary context—must be sensitive to the admonition that '[m]uch ink has been spilled on developing typologies of the forms of state failure, using either the degree of failure or its cause as a criterion'.[34] The purposes that an international law definition of State failure might therefore serve within this broader dialogue on State failure thus include to: (1) describe a process; (2) denote an endstate or outcome; (3) delineate a spectrum; or (4) identify constitutive factors. I shall briefly address each before proposing an initial international law-focused definition of State failure.

First, a definition of State failure may be designed to describe a process.[35] Thürer, for example, has described how '[f]ailing States are invariably the product of a collapse of the power structures providing political support for law and order, a process triggered and accompanied by "anarchic" forms of internal violence'.[36] Gordon has emphasized the process of disintegration and 'survivability': '[t]he common theme is overwhelmed governments that are almost, if not completely, unable to discharge basic governmental functions',[37] accompanied by failure to afford 'their populations even the most rudimentary

[33] UNCLOS (n 32) arts 92, 110; *Naim Molvan v Attorney General for Palestine (The 'Asya')* (1948) 81 Lloyds List Law Reports 277.

[34] Sebastian von Einsiedel, 'Policy Response to State Failure' in Simon Chesterman et al (eds), *Making States Work: State Failure and the Crisis of Governance* (UN UP 2005) 13.

[35] Esty et al (n 17) 68. [36] Thürer (n 5) 732.

[37] Ruth Gordon, 'Some Legal Problems with Trusteeship' (1995) 28 Cornell International Law Journal 301, 306.

standards of living'.[38] Consequently, an international law definition of State failure that focused upon describing a process would likely seek to prioritize the legal indicia of 'weakening'.

A second definitional approach is to denote State failure as an endstate or an outcome. Thürer, again, describes the political and legal consequence of State failure in terms of three interconnected outcome phenomena: geographical and territorial; political; and functional.[39] A similar approach is adopted by Milliken and Krause, who ultimately define State failure as 'a phenomenon that threatens to undermine the modern project of achieving political order'.[40] An international law definition of State failure that focuses upon the endstate will, consequently, likely privilege indicia of 'collapse'.

The third definitional approach is to conceive of State failure as a spectrum, a continuum of circumstances that afflict States with weak institutions.[41] Rotberg, for example, distinguishes between weak and failing States,[42] observing that a 'collapsed state is an extreme version of a failed state'.[43] This spectrum might range from failed States (such as Somalia), through failing States (such as Libya) through to weak States (such as Afghanistan), allowing for differentiations based upon the degree to which the State is 'plagued with corruption (…) unable to effectively police their territories (…) not able to prevent abuses by powerful private actors'.[44] At the other end of that spectrum is 'State decay',[45] which is not necessarily State collapse or State failure, although it may be a step towards that characterization.[46] The legal work required of this approach to State failure is the emphasis placed upon legal differentiations that nuance complexity and pathology. For example, a strong government may coexist with a weak State precisely because the government actively seeks to ensure institutional weakness to facilitate clientage, patronage, and corruption without fear of State organs interfering with or checking this power—as, for example, with Congo.[47] However, such a definition would also be required to accommodate the fact that while some State weakness can be a consequence of the 'ill will' of rulers, other incidences of State weakness may arise irrespective of the best intentions of rulers.[48]

Finally, an international law definition of State failure may seek to describe a linked amalgam of identifying factors, and indeed all three of the other definitional approaches briefly noted above, of necessity leverage such identifying factors or criteria to some degree. One approach, for example, is to privilege the institutional and functional dimensions of State failure.[49] The State Failure Task Force, employing a different 'factoral' approach, identified three 'clusters of variables' (all of which have legal dimensions)

[38] ibid 307–9. [39] Thürer (n 5) 733–44. [40] Milliken/Krause (n 22) 764.

[41] von Einsiedel (n 34) 13.

[42] Robert Rotberg, 'The Failure and Collapse of Nation-States: Breakdown, Prevention, and Repair' in Robert Rotberg (ed), *When States Fail: Causes and Consequences* (Princeton UP 2004) 1–50.

[43] Rotberg (n 14) 90.

[44] Neil Englehart, 'State Capacity, State Failure, and Human Rights' (2009) 46 Journal of Peace Resolution 163.

[45] Milliken/Krause (n 22) 754. [46] ibid.

[47] Englehart (n 44) 167. [48] ibid 177. [49] Milliken/Krause (n 22) 753.

that evidence 'a significant correlation with subsequent state failures: (1) quality of life; (2) openness to international trade; and (3) the level of democracy'.[50] Lemay-Hebert's taxonomy of approaches as either institutional or legitimacy-centric[51] certainly emphasizes the definitional predisposition to establish casual or networked linkages between a set of factors and variables.[52] Yet other scholars isolate the core State functions fulfilled by stable States, and define failure by their paucity or absence.[53] Thus any international law definition that centres upon identifying factors will tend to hinge around legally delineating factor hierarchies, and describe the relationship between these factors and their causal role in State failure. Although it is this tendency that my basic definition ultimately favours, this is but one approach. Other international law definitions will undoubtedly privilege different factors, or indeed prioritize different relationships or hierarchies from within the purposive spectrum.

4. State Failure as a 'Legal' Concept

Given the analysis thus far, it is arguable that one approach to constructing an international law definition of 'State failure' is to essentialize capacity/effectiveness, expressed as a legal principle,[54] as the key definitional attribute. That is, an international law definition ought not to fetishize legitimacy[55] for it has been argued that 'partial democracies, other things being equal, are on average three times more likely to fail' than either autocracies or full democracies.[56] My proposal, therefore, is that the 'international law essence' of State failure is defined by the *loss of capacity* of the State in question, to:

a. Represent, enforce, and apply the perquisites and obligations of *sovereignty*,[57] (including—most importantly—the capacity to mediate conflict and 'deal with' disaffection internally),[58]
b. In *compliance* with that State's international obligations.

However, while such an approach certainly emphasizes the failure of the 'civilising value of the State'[59], and prioritizes indicia that challenge the 'aspiration to viability'[60] implicit

[50] Esty et al (n 17) 60; descriptions of some of the more than 30 variables within these clusters, ibid 56–7.
[51] Lemay-Hebert (n 6) 22–3.
[52] Lemay-Hebert argues that State failure can never be solely attributed to institutional collapse ((n 6) 28).
[53] Stuart Eizenstat et al, 'Rebuilding Weak States' (2005) 84 Foreign Affairs 134.
[54] Crawford (n 15) 5. [55] eg Lemay-Hebert (n 6) 21–2, 24–5, 37–40.
[56] Esty et al (n 17) 53, 68.
[57] Sovereignty in this sense is 'an attribute of States, not a precondition', and is the '"totality of international law rights and duties recognized by international law" as residing in a particular territorial unit—the State': Crawford (n 15) 32.
[58] Krasner/Pascual (n 8) 155.
[59] Thürer (n 5) 760. [60] Milliken/Krause (n 22) 762.

in 'Stateness', it is important to avoid construing failure merely in terms of institutional loss of 'agency' and/or loss of control over 'agents'.[61] Such an approach would impose an unnecessarily narrow interpretation of State capacity as constituting 'willingness and capability of the state apparatus to carry out government policy',[62] because it may indeed be State policy to commit atrocity: Hence the necessary qualifier of State policy being *in compliance with international obligations*. Additionally, it is important to accept that while sovereignty in any given case of State failure may well be characterizable as a 'legal fiction', or subject to radically different historical or regional manifestations,[63] it is nevertheless normatively key to legally characterizing capacity and its absence.

C. Recognizing State Failure

The basic international law-focused definition of State failure outlined above leverages three general criteria: capacity; sovereignty; and compliance. These are not unproblematic but their utility as definitional components may be further buttressed by examining two associated matters. The first is to briefly review the most 'logical' alternative international law definition of State failure—a 'reverse Montevideo' approach. The second is to briefly outline the subsidiary adequacy or otherwise of some of the alternative international law-nuanced indicators or markers that speak to these three general components.

1. State Failure is not Montevideo in Reverse

The iconic modern legal expression of the attributes of 'Stateness' is undoubtedly Article 1 of the Montevideo Convention: 'The state as a person of international law should possess the following qualifications: a. permanent population; b. defined territory; c. government; and d. capacity to enter into relations with the other states.' Might State failure therefore be legally characterized as 'reverse Montevideo'? To some extent, the failed State can be conceptualized as the 'dark' mirror image of the 'successful' State,[64] and as Lemay-Hebert explains, '[e]very scholarly contribution on statebuilding adopts, whether consciously or unconsciously, a definition of what it intends to reconstruct: a definition of the state'.[65] The centrality of the Montevideo definition to 'Stateness' cannot be understated: Crawford describes the debate regarding recognition as generally bounded by constitutive or declaratory approaches, but he does so in order to adopt an appropriate interpretive methodology towards the Montevideo criteria.[66]

[61] Englehart (n 44) 164–6. [62] ibid 167.

[63] Among others, Herbst (n 1) 122, 127–30 on different conceptions of sovereignty in Africa.

[64] Brooks (n 8) 1160. [65] Lemay-Hebert (n 6) 23.

[66] Crawford (n 15) 19–28, 37–62.

While some successful entities do not unquestionably meet all Montevideo requirements and are still considered successful examples of 'Stateness' (Taiwan, Vatican City),[67] the Vienna Convention on the Law of Treaties (VCLT) Article 2(1) definition of a treaty as 'between states'[68] clearly excludes inchoate entities. This reinforces the idea that international law is focused upon continuity of 'Stateness' and does not have a well-developed, encapsulated regime for State failure—except to say it is not State extinction, nor is it recognition law in reverse. This indicates a significant hurdle for any attempt to use a reverse Montevideo approach to identifying a failed State: International law as it interacts with State failure is not equipped to determine the point of regression where a State slides back into a non-State, inchoate entity status, because international law takes as its underpinning normative fundamental that the maintenance of an entity's persisting 'Stateness' or 'Statehood' is the first priority, so that it can be recuperated (unless extinguished by incorporation or other affiliation into or with another State). Similarly, as the International Court of Justice has indicated,[69] international law is very permissive in terms of identifying individuals, offices, or institutions that might at any given time be said to represent or identify a State for treaty making purposes—this widely cast net is again indicative of the normative bias in international law to seek for and identify continuity of 'Stateness', rather than to readily accept or admit its absence or failure. Thus the emphasis in international law is clearly to stress 'Stateness' continuity—even if it is contested, or tenuous continuity. To that end, while international law may accept a temporary 'abeyance' of 'Stateness'—such as with transitional administration[70]—it does not readily contemplate regression to pre-Stateness status, nor does it willingly contemplate State extinction, except in the rarest and most limited circumstances. Thus, State failure in international law cannot be easily characterized as 'reverse Montevideo' because the whole enterprise of international law is normatively underpinned by continuities, and normatively opposed to State extinction or regression to a pre- or non-State entity status.

2. Specific Subsidiary Legal Indicia of State Failure?

Given that a 'reverse Montevideo' approach is an inadequate basis for identifying instances of State failure, if specific legal indicators are required to add colour and form to the three definitional elements identified above, it is necessary to look more broadly afield. One option is to list a series of structural and political shortfalls—to 'define the coexistence of civil war, political corruption, lawlessness, economic collapse, disease, ecological disaster, absence of basic infrastructure, and systematic human rights abuse

[67] Brooks (n 8) 1187. [68] See also Aust (n 18) 15–16.

[69] *Accordance with International Law of the Unilateral Declaration of Independence in Respect of Kosovo* (Advisory Opinion) [2010] ICJ Rep 403 [105]–[109].

[70] Among others, Rob McLaughlin, 'East Timor, Transitional Administration and the Status of the Territorial Sea' (2003) 4 Melbourne Journal of International Law 323.

as state failure'.[71] Rotberg's 'indicia' of State failure are similarly a mix of categorical and prudential, the ecumenical and the granular: weak or flawed institutions; inability to provide security; primacy of executive over legislative and judicial arms; deteriorating/destroyed infrastructure; slumped or failed privatization (formal or informal) of health and education; privileged economic opportunity; corruption; and so on.[72] However, distilling specifically international law-based indicators that may assist in identifying incidents of State failure—that is, factual indicators with a specific international law definition or consequences—is a narrower task. Some possible options include: Implications of the 'unwilling or unable' doctrine; evidence of wide-scale human rights law and law of armed conflict (LOAC) violations; withdrawal from international trade and economic regulatory fora, regimes, and norms; and external manifestations of governance failures (whether by design, or as a consequence).

The first possible international law-defined specific marker is the application of the (contested) 'unwilling or unable' doctrine[73]—that is, where a finding is made that a State is unwilling or unable to act against a threat emanating from within its borders, this constitutes an implicit indication of State failure. In many respects this candidate indicator is fundamentally a subset of a yet broader approach to identifying State failure, founded as it is in the assessed inability of a State to enforce the 'norm of territorial integrity'.[74] To this extent, it is arguably an inadequate international law-based indicia, for the inability of a State to take advantage of the territorial integrity norm, or to prevent others from trampling upon the norm with respect to the State in question, is not a good legal marker. This is because this particular norm can be trespassed upon in a wide range of circumstances—armed conflict, occupation, invasion—which do not necessarily indicate State failure as a precondition, rather than a consequence, of transgression of the norm. Employing the unable or unwilling doctrine as a marker thus lacks sufficient fidelity to distinguish—as Milliken and Krause do, for example—between State collapse as a failure of institutions (a formalist approach), and State failure as being fundamentally a consequence of 'functional failure' (a consequentialist approach).[75] And while it is certainly arguable that the most recent context in which the unwilling or unable doctrine has been applied—Syria[76]—also arguably evidences a high degree of State failure, the correlation is situational rather than definitive of either context. Taliban-controlled Afghanistan, for example, was a State considered unable (for political, ideological, and

[71] Tonya Langford, 'Things Fall Apart: State Failure and the Politics of Intervention' (1999) 1 International Studies Review 59, 78.

[72] Rotberg (n 14) 87–90.

[73] Daniel Bethlehem, 'Self-Defense Against an Imminent or Actual Armed Attack by Nonstate Actors' (2012) 106 AJIL 769.

[74] Lemay-Hebert (n 6) 33.

[75] Milliken/Krause (n 22) 765.

[76] eg Australia, UNSC 'Letter dated 9 September 2015 from the Permanent Representative of Australia to the United Nations addressed to the President of the Security Council' (9 September 2015) UN Doc S/2015/693; generally, Elena Chachko/Ashley Deeks, 'Who is on Board with "Unwilling or Unable"?' (*Lawfare*, 10 October 2016) <https://www.lawfareblog.com/who-board-unwilling-or-unable> accessed 18 August 2019.

other reasons) to act against a threat given succour within its borders,[77] but it could hardly be said that it was also on the failed State spectrum in the way that Syria (constituted by truncated and segmented areas of significant, or no, government control), or Libya (evidencing a more comprehensive loss of governmental control and its arrogation by a diverse network of competing non-State groups), were or are on that spectrum.

A second candidate for a clearly international law-informed marker of State failure is evidence of wide-scale human rights law and LOAC violations.[78] Again, however, the correlation of State failure with atrocity may be more coincidental than causative—Rotberg, for example, has argued that 'it is the enduring character of that violence (…) the direction of such violence against the existing government or regime, and the vigorous character of the political or geographical demands for shared power or autonomy that rationalize or justify that violence that identifies the failed state'.[79] Similarly, it must also be recognized that a tyrannical State can equally engage in wide-scale atrocity and violations against its own population—as for example has been reported in relation to the DPRK[80]—without that State being readily characterized as being on the State failure spectrum. This, of course, has implications for the responsibility to protect (R2P) doctrine[81] in that, while facilitating a legal path for territorially interventionist responses is often easier in State failure situations—for example, by finding an appropriate, acceptable, and accessible (and sometimes, manufactured) 'representative' to authorize what would otherwise be a territorial transgression[82]—it is much more difficult to overcome the absence of consent (or to manufacture it) in situations of atrocity inside a State that is not considered (yet) to be on the State failure spectrum.

A third candidate for an international law marker is withdrawal from international trade and economic regulatory fora, regimes, and norms. This is perhaps the most reliable international law-specific indicator. The State Failure Task Force, for example, found that

> [i]nvolvement in international trade, as measured by trade openness, is associated with a lower risk of state failure in virtually all states and all contexts (…) Interestingly, it appears that it is the involvement in international trade itself, and not the eventual prosperity that such trade provides, that is the key to this effect.[83]

77 UNSC Res 1333 (2000) paras 1–3. 78 eg Thürer (n 5) 740–6; Englehart (n 44) 163.

79 Rotberg (n 14) 85–6.

80 UNCHR 'Report of the Commission of Inquiry on Human Rights in the Democratic People's Republic of Korea' (2014) UN Doc A/HRC/25/63, eg paras 56–79.

81 ICISS, *The Responsibility to Protect* (International Development Research Centre 2011) Basic Principle 1B.

82 UN Transitional Authority in Cambodia (UNTAC) operation in Cambodia 1663 UNTS 27 (Paris Agreement). eg Paris Agreement art 3. See also Agreement concerning the Sovereignty, Independence, Territorial Integrity, and Inviolability, Neutrality and National Unity of Cambodia 1663 UNTS 27. Similarly, on Somalia, *inter alia* Herbst (n 1) 125.

83 Esty et al (n 17) 66; Brooks (n 8) 1162.

And while withdrawal from economic and trade processes may merely be a subset of Helman and Ratner's characterization of a failed State as one 'utterly incapable of sustaining itself as a member of the international community',[84] or Krasner and Pascual's observation that 'the traditional tools of diplomacy—demarches, treaties, dialogue—often have limited sway over actors unconcerned about their international image or legitimacy',[85] it may be that the first signs of incapacity and withdrawal may indeed manifest in the complicated trade and investment context. However, it does not necessarily follow that attempts to keep failing States tied into multilateral trade and investment fora and processes will arrest disintegration—the State Failure Task Force, for example, specifically noted that the record of 'bilateral and multilateral' policy and institutional engagement as a way to 'forestall' some State failures is at best inconsistent.[86]

A fourth candidate for an international law-defined indicator is the more amorphous category of governance failures, whether by design or as a consequence of other factors.[87] The externally observable deleterious effects of a lack of 'strong, capable institutions'[88] is often emblematized by loss of control of borders—'when its nominal borders become irrelevant and when one or more groups seek autonomous control within one or more parts of the national territory or, sometimes, even across its borders'.[89] Another international law-defined, but contextually under-analysed, potential governance failure indicator is a rise in piracy.[90] Hastings, for example, argues that discrete forms of piracy indicate different forms of State failure:

> Because they combine a passable transportation infrastructure and a market with a level of enforcement that is enough to discourage long-running hostage dramas, but are inefficient or corrupt enough to encourage pirates to seize ships and cargo, weak States actually are better breeding grounds for sophisticated pirates than failed States are. Conversely, failed States may be havens for criminals and terrorists, but the evidence here suggests that they are not havens for particularly sophisticated criminals and terrorists.[91]

Hastings thus concludes that different typologies of State failure can in fact create or foster different typologies of piracy:

> Proposition 1. The waters in or around failed States are disproportionately characterized by hijackings whose aim is exacting a ransom for the ship or crewmembers without disposing of the ship or its cargo.
>
> Proposition 2. The waters in or around weak States are disproportionately characterized by hijackings whose aim is to seize the ship and cargo themselves.[92]

[84] Helman/Ratner (n 21) 3. [85] Krasner/Pascual (n 8) 155.

[86] Esty et al (n 17) 68.

[87] Derick Brinkerhoff/Jennifer Brinkerhoff, 'Governance Reforms and Failed States: Challenges and Implications' (2002) 68 International Review of Administrative Sciences 511, 513.

[88] Krasner/Pascual (n 8) 154. [89] Rotberg (n 14) 90.

[90] Hastings (n 12) 213. [91] ibid 222. [92] ibid 215.

Another international law-nuanced governance failure indicator might be the loss of a State's monopoly on means of organized violence, given that failing States 'almost universally lack the requirements for successful stabilization.'[93] However, while such discrete variables can provide useful and legally nuanced or expressible markers, individually they are neither universal nor fundamental. Nor are they adequately refined in the manner of legal criteria, and collectively they do not constitute a coherent legal 'test' for State failure. Thus, given its normative focus on, and endorsement of, 'Stateness' continuity—even tenuous, contested, superficial, 'legal fiction' continuity—international law is relatively intolerant of State failure as a potential legal 'regime'. This is almost inevitable given that international law deals with State failure more as a context and a consequence, requiring the application of diverse and multiparty legal rights and obligations, than by offering a single, coherent set of criteria for identifying State failure situations.

D. Legal Responses to State Failure

One of the first definitive international security law responses that individual States may make to situations of State failure is to either buttress the legal fiction of State unity by reaffirming recognition of the 'government', or to switch recognition to a different group, declaring that this alternative group now represents the State in question. An example of the latter was the early French recognition of 'Libya's rebel leadership in the eastern city of Benghazi' as the new representative of Libyan sovereignty during that State's collapse.[94] However, a global security-informed response to State failure will often follow once sufficient, and sufficiently powerful, third States have formed a view that a State is on the State failure spectrum, and that a coordinated international response is required.[95] When this tipping point is reached, the UN is the first port of call.

1. The United Nations

Given that 'the collapse of a State anywhere in the world is seen as a matter for the international community, since the international system as a whole is felt to be endangered if

[93] Krasner/Pascual (n 8) 154–5; Englehart (n 44) 166, quoting Harvey Kline, *State Building and Conflict Resolution in Columbia, 1986–1994* (University of Alabama Press 1999) 66.

[94] Alan Cowell/Steven Erlanger, 'France Becomes First Country to Recognize Libyan Rebels' (*New York Times*, 10 March 2011), <https://www.nytimes.com/2011/03/11/world/europe/11france.html> accessed 18 August 2019; 'France Formally Recognises Libyan Rebels' Authority' (*France 24*, 10 March 2011) <http://www.france24.com/en/20110310-france-libya-first-country-recognize-libyan-national-council-envoy-exchange> accessed 18 August 2019.

[95] On Bosnia, eg Brendan Simms, *Unfinest Hour: Britain and the Destruction of Bosnia* (Penguin 2001) chs 1–3; William Shawcross, *Deliver us from Evil: Warlords and Peacekeepers in a World of Endless Conflict* (Bloomsbury 2000) chs 5–6; Paddy Ashdown, *Swords and Ploughshares: Bringing Peace to the 21st Century* (Weidenfeld and Nicholson 2007) chs 1, 6.

one of its members is seen to be no longer functioning',[96] the UN is well positioned as the primary clearing house for initial responses to State failure. To this end, the initial burden generally falls upon the UN Security Council (UNSC), given its primacy in the area of international peace and security.[97] In this respect, Thürer[98] and others have observed that there are four main pillars to UNSC responses to State failure: recourse to Chapter VII UN Charter; deployment of Peacekeeping Forces (noting, however, the critique that 'UN peacekeeping limps along, applying partial solutions to complex problems'[99]); broad mandate interpretation (again, however, noting the ambivalent record of the UN on this count[100]); and addressing 'all parties' to the conflict, including non-State actors.[101] These four factors then provide context for the specific type of security response, ranging from peace enforcement and transitional administration, through to less singular assertions of authority and control such as partnership with, and mentoring of, weak local institutions, negotiated and monitored factional power-sharing arrangements, and so on.[102]

Another option for UN action with respect to State failure could be a revival of the older concept of 'trusteeship', although this is an intensely problematic and deeply contested idea. UN Charter Articles 77 and 78, the normative weight afforded the principle of self-determination, and the practical fact that trust status is incompatible with sovereignty (the core attribute of 'Stateness'),[103] must thus moderate any enthusiasm for such revival. It should also be noted that the UN General Assembly (UNGA) holds a residual international peace and security mandate, and has established missions that deal with transition from one governance authority to another (such as with the UN Temporary Executive Authority (UNTEA), transitioning Irian Jaya from Dutch sovereign control to Indonesian sovereignty[104]) and with truce supervision (as with UN Emergency Force I in the Sinai[105]). It would thus be incorrect to argue that UNSC engagement points to an appropriately universal and robust State failure marker on the assumption that particular instances of State failure (if on the UN agenda) will always be dealt with by the UNSC. Indeed, the Uniting for Peace Resolution[106] remains extant and thus even within the UN system it is not the case that State failure (if it comes before the UN) will only ever be dealt with by the UNSC.

[96] Thürer (n 5) 736–7.

[97] Charter of the United Nations 1 UNTS XVI arts 24–5, chs VI, VII, and VIII.

[98] Thürer (n 5) 738–40. [99] Langford (n 71) 79.

[100] UNGA 'Report of the Secretary-General pursuant to General Assembly Resolution 53/35: The Fall of Srebrenica' (15 November 1999) UN Doc A/54/549, eg paras 503–4; UNGA/UNSC 'Report of the Panel on United Nations Peace Operations' (21 August 2000) UN Doc A/55/305-S/2000/809 paras 56–64.

[101] eg UNSC Res 2327 (2016) para 25.

[102] See eg Chopra (n 8) 980–2.

[103] eg Langford (n 71) 59–60, 66–73; Gordon (n 37) 315–35.

[104] Indonesia and Netherlands Agreement (with annex) concerning West New Guinea (West Irian) 6311 UNTS 274; UNGA Res 1752 (XVII) (21 September 1962).

[105] UNGA Res 997 ES-1 (2 November 1956); UNGA Res 998 ES-1 (4 November 1956); UNGA Res 999 ES-1 (4 November 1956); UNGA Res 1000 ES-1 (5 November 1956); UNGA Res 1001 ES-1 (7 November 1956); UNGA Res 1125 (XI) (2 February 1957).

[106] UNGA Res 377(V) (3 November 1950).

2. Other Legal Responses to State Failure?

Initial third State recognition responses, and initial restorative UN responses are not, however, the only forms of legal response to State failure. It is vital to recall that State failure also resonates in other legal arenas. For example, State failure can have practical consequences for the capacity of the failing entity to fulfil treaty obligations. However, the international community appears to adopt a predominantly 'business as usual' approach to such obligations, even to the extent of encouraging States on the State failure spectrum to adopt or enshrine further obligations—as with international encouragement (if not demands) in September 2013 that Syria accede to the 1993 Chemical Weapons Convention.[107] Another legal venue in which State failure has significant consequences is in commercial legal relationships—ranging from the consequences of State failure for international contracting and insurance practices (such as with shipping war and piracy insurance[108]), through to domestic courts dealing with contractual arrangements involving entities domiciled within a failing or failed State. In the British case of *Luther v James Sagor and Co* (1921),[109] for example, the court recognized and applied Bolshevik regulations that had been promulgated after recognition of the collapse of Tsarist authority in Russia, but prior to Britain's subsequent recognition of the Bolshevik government, regardless of the ambiguity as to the 'Stateness' of the Bolshevik entity at the relevant time.

E. Conclusion

There are two fundamental challenges confronting any attempt to formulate an adequate international law 'definition' of State failure. The first is the normative bias of international law towards the preservation of 'Stateness', reflected in the absence of a coherent approach to regressions in 'Stateness' that fall short of State extinction—that is, the exact situation that State failure is concerned with. The second challenge is that State failure can be defined and conceptualized in a multitude of ways: by discipline or theme (for example, in political or legal terms, or with a thematic emphasis on the incidence of violence); by conceptual purpose (scheme, process, endstate); or by indicators of conceptual content (atrocity, and so on). And while thematic and purposive approaches may provide useful—albeit inadequate—foundations for a global security-informed but legally expressed definition of State failure, approaches that focus on indicia such as legitimacy and governance are also problematic—primarily because of their contextual

[107] UNGA/UNSC 'Letter dated 19 September 2013 from the Permanent Representatives of the Russian Federation and the United States of America to the United Nations addressed to the Secretary-General' (24 September 2013) UN Doc A/68/398–S/2013/565 and UNSC Res 2118 (2013).

[108] eg Gotthard Gauci, 'Piracy and Its Legal Problems: With Specific Reference to the English Law of Marine Insurance' (2010) 41 Journal Maritime Law and Commerce 541, 544–50.

[109] *Luther v James Sagor and Co* [1921] 3 KB 532.

relativity. However, the concepts of sovereignty, capacity, and compliance are arguably fundamental to any security-informed but legally expressed definition of State failure, although they must be assimilated in a way that escapes the legalism implicit in formalist normativity. Consequently, it is my small contribution to the future direction of any debate that the legal indicators of State failure, and indeed any attempt at an international law definition of State failure, should of necessity coalesce around loss of capacity to act as sovereign, not loss of sovereignty per se; that is, State failure as an international law concept should focus upon the ability of the State in question 'to make sovereignty work,'[110] rather than on formal indicia drawn from differently focused doctrines and concepts that are underpinned by international law's normative predisposition towards emphasizing 'Stateness' continuity.

[110] Krasner/Pascual (n 8) 163.

CHAPTER 11

TERRORISM AND THE SECURITY COUNCIL

HELEN DUFFY AND LARISSA VAN DEN HERIK

A. Introduction

It is generally agreed that terrorism presents a security challenge, but consensus does not extend to how we should understand that challenge and still less to how best to address it. Traditionally terrorism was regulated in international law through specialized treaties.[1] However since 9/11, this conventional approach has given way to an unprecedented international response model in which the UN Security Council (UNSC) assumes a central role. Undoubtedly, during this time a vast global counter-terrorism architecture has developed, involving myriad regional and international dimensions, mechanisms, and processes.[2] But for two decades, the UNSC has become the dynamo of international counter-terrorism legislation and policy, using its unique role and powers to generate detailed regulation with wide-reaching effect.

This chapter discusses the UNSC's intense regulatory approach to counter-terrorism and its consequences, including the direct and indirect repercussions for affected individuals, and the broader global security landscape. The main argument is that the expansion of the UNSC's role has gradually opened up a space of indeterminacy and unaccountability. Two dimensions are explored here: (i) the creation of a quasi-permanent counter-terrorism sanctions regime under Chapter VII and (ii) the Council's ever-expanding 'legislative' activities, amongst others in relation to 'foreign terrorist fighters'

[1] UNGA 'Report of the Special Rapporteur on the Promotion and Protection of Human Rights and Fundamental Freedoms while Countering Terrorism' (3 September 2018) UN Doc A/73/45453 (unedited version), para 9 (SR 2018 UNGA Report).

[2] At the UN level, recent examples include the UN Office for Counter-Terrorism (2017) and the UN Global Counter-terrorism Coordination Compact (2018).

and incitement or provocation. It exposes underlying tendencies and ulterior effects of the UNSC's approach, including the expansive reach of undefined or ill-defined phenomena, a reflex of over-criminalization, and the increasing involvement of the private sector, including financial institutions, in the counter-terrorism sphere. The impact on human rights, participative democracy, the shrinking space for civil society, humanitarian assistance and peacebuilders, accountability, and rule of law is profound. The chapter tells a story of uncertain threats and unaccountable actors in counter-terrorism practice and the adverse effects on security in the long run.

B. Terrorism as a General Threat to Peace?

Terrorism has long featured on the international agenda. However, while previously considered a matter of general 'international concern', then in some contexts a 'threat to peace and security',[3] it has now been transformed into what the Council persistently describes as 'in all forms and manifestations [...] one of the most serious threats to peace and security'.[4] The number of resolutions repetitively condemning terrorism has increased following the rise of ISIL/Da'esh, also qualifying terrorism as a 'global and unprecedented threat to international peace and security'.[5]

However, while there is a certain universality in the perception of terrorism as a threat, and increasingly exorbitant descriptions of its nature,[6] consensus remains remarkably frail in relation to its definition and scope. The lack of an internationally accepted definition, and the existence of vastly divergent regional and national definitions, is well known.[7] Despite overwhelming expressions of support by States and institutions for defining terrorism and adopting a comprehensive counter-terrorism convention post 9/11, long-lasting controversies[8] have continued to impede consensus around the thorny definitional issue.

[3] eg the first UN General Assembly Resolution on measures to prevent terrorism: UNGA Res 3034 (XXVII) (18 December 1972); Declaration on Measures to Eliminate International Terrorism, UNGA Res 49/60 (9 December 1994) Annex, para 2: 'acts, methods and practices of terrorism constitute a grave violation of the purposes and principles of the United Nations, which may pose a threat to international peace and security', followed by UNGA Res 51/210 (17 December 1996); UNGA 'Report of the Secretary-General: Measures to Eliminate International Terrorism' (6 September 1996) UN Doc A/51/336.

[4] UNSC Res 2178 (2014) preambular para 1. Similarly, UNSC Res 2249 (2015); UNSC Res 2253 (2015); UNSC Res 2322 (2016); UNSC Res 2368 (2017); UNSC Res 2395 (2017); UNSC Res 2396 (2017).

[5] UNSC Res 2249 (2015) preambular para 5.

[6] Jane Boulden, 'The Security Council and Terrorism' in Vaughan Lowe et al (eds), *The United Nations Security Council and War: The Evolution of Thought and Practice since 1945* (OUP 2010) 608.

[7] Helen Duffy, *The 'War on Terror' and the Framework of International Law* (2nd edn, CUP 2015) ch 2. Neither terrorism nor the associated 'violent extremism' to which the Council repeatedly refers (eg, UNSC Res 2178 (2014), UNSC 2354 (2017)) are defined by the Council or in international law.

[8] Duffy (n 7) 34.

While there is also little consensus on how to respond to the undefined terrorist threat, UN counter-terrorism practice, including Council resolutions, has increasingly focused on strategies of prevention. This has evolved along several quite distinct, and at times contradictory, strands. One strand, led by the UN Secretary-General's Office and the UN General Assembly (UNGA), focuses on preventing the causes of, and contributors to, terrorism. Attention to the 'root causes' of terrorism peaked in the post-colonial period, but was marginalized during the 1980s, partly because of the perceived danger of justifying terrorism. In this context, the 1994 UNGA Declaration on Measures to Eliminate International Terrorism was seen as a milestone in condemning terrorism unreservedly,[9] and the immediate post-9/11 spirit followed this trend. However, aspects of this debate were revisited when the Secretary-General broached the need to consider the link between terrorism and its causes and contributors in his In Larger Freedom report in 2005.[10] In Uniting Against Terrorism of the following year, he then called for a comprehensive response to the underlying dynamics and 'conditions conducive to terrorism'; these included extremist ideologies, violent conflict, poor governance, human rights abuse, discrimination, exclusion, and socio-economic marginalization.[11] This comprehensive approach has since been widely endorsed at regional and international level—reflected, for example, in the World Summit Outcome Document,[12] and most critically as a pillar of the UN Global Counter-Terrorism Strategy.[13] In language that is now commonplace, the Secretary-General and the UNGA recognize 'that effective counter-terrorism measures and the protection of human rights... [are] complementary and mutually reinforcing'.[14] The UNSC has subsequently endorsed the need for 'measures, pursuant to international law, to address all drivers of violent extremism conducive to terrorism, both internal and external, in a balanced manner as set out in the United Nations Global Counter-Terrorism Strategy'.[15]

However, tension arises with the other strand of the Council's approach, which mandates increasingly coercive counter-terrorism measures. Human rights courts and bodies and civil society have frequently criticized the resulting rights violations and the use of counter-terrorism laws and policies to stifle and punish debate and dissent, the defence

[9] UNGA Res 49/60 (9 December 1994).

[10] UNGA 'Report of the UN Secretary General: In Larger Freedom: Towards Development, Security and Human Rights for All' (21 March 2005) UN Doc A/59/2005, para 16. Concept also visible in, eg, UNGA Res 72/284 (26 June 2018) preambular paras 36, 37.

[11] UNGA 'Report of the Secretary-General: Uniting against Terrorism: Recommendations for a Global Counter-Terrorism Strategy' (27 April 2006) UN Doc A/60/825, paras 20*i*, 21–38. (Uniting Against Terrorism Report).

[12] UNGA Res 60/1 (16 September 2005) para 82. For similar observations: G8, 'Statement on Strengthening the UN's Counter-Terrorism Program' (St Petersburg, 16 July 2006) <https://www.mofa.go.jp/policy/economy/summit/2006/un_terro.html> accessed 14 November 2020.

[13] UNGA Res 60/288 (8 September 2006) Annex (UN Global Counter-Terrorism Strategy), s I ('Measures to address the conditions conducive to the spread of terrorism'); UNGA Res 72/284 (26 June 2018) paras 10–12.

[14] Uniting Against Terrorism Report (n 11); leading to the UN Global Counter-Terrorism Strategy (n 13). See pillars 1 and 4.

[15] UNSC Res 2395 (2017); UNSC Res 2396 (2017).

of human rights, and peace-building initiatives.[16] Despite this, the UNSC's constant determination that terrorism poses a general threat to peace and security has provided the basis for unprecedented measures, including (i) the design of a quasi-permanent sanctions regime under Chapter VII and (ii) intense legislative activities obliging or calling on States to take myriad criminal, administrative, or other measures against a growing range of undefined phenomena. These are discussed in turn in the subsequent sections.

C. A Quasi-permanent Counter-terrorism Sanctions Regime

A central part of the Council's counter-terrorism arsenal has been the adoption of Chapter VII sanctions regimes, which over time have become quasi-permanent. This section discusses the evolution and transformation of the 1267 UN sanctions regime from its Taliban origins to its current focus on IS/Da'esh and beyond, questioning its status as a quasi-standing Chapter VII counter-terrorism sanctions regime, highlighting the role of private actors in its implementation and questioning its ulterior effects, for example, on development, humanitarian assistance, and peacebuilding.

1. The Evolution of the 1267 Sanctions Regime

The 1267 sanctions regime was established in 1999 as a regular sanctions regime,[17] created as a reaction to terrorist attacks in East Africa. Similar to other regimes, it imposed sanctions on elite decision makers exercising de facto control in Afghanistan, namely the Taliban.[18] After 9/11, Resolution 1390 reinvigorated the 1267 regime and extended it to address the threat posed by Al-Qaeda. Effectively, Resolution 1390 rendered the 1267 regime unique as it severed geographical ties and turned it into a sanctions regime with global reach.[19] This development was facilitated by the UNSC's generic determination of terrorism as a threat to international peace.

[16] 'Global Group of NGOs Deplore Lack of Attention to Human Rights in Latest Review of UN's Global Counter-terrorism Strategy by UN Member States' (*FIDH*, 11 July 2018) <https://www.fidh.org/en/global-group-of-ngos-deplore-lack-of-attention-to-human-rights-in> accessed 10 February 2019; SR 2018 UNGA Report (n 1) para 44; Fionnuala Ní Aoláin, 'The Complexity and Challenges of Addressing the Conditions Conducive to Terrorism' in Manfred Nowak/Anne Charbord (eds), *Using Human Rights to Counter-Terrorism* (Edward Elgar 2018).

[17] UNSC Res 1267 (1999).

[18] Lisa Ginsborg, 'UN Sanctions and Counter-Terrorism Strategies: Moving Towards Thematic Sanctions Against Individuals?' in Larissa van den Herik (ed), *Research Handbook on UN Sanctions and International Law* (Edward Elgar 2017).

[19] UNSC Res 1390 (2002).

Within a decade, the combined threat that the Taliban and Al-Qaeda posed in 2001 gradually morphed.[20] The distinction between the two groups became more predominant than their mutual connections, which made their grouping into one sanctions regime less obvious. Furthermore, with a view to promoting the comprehensive peace process in Afghanistan, the Afghan government requested a more flexible and expedient approach to delisting requests for Taliban members engaged in reconciliation efforts who had severed their ties with Al-Qaeda.[21] In light of these developments, the UNSC split the 1267 regime into two separate regimes, one targeting the Taliban as a national movement (the 1988 sanctions regime) and one targeting Al-Qaeda as a global actor (the 1989 sanctions regime).[22] Another major turning point came with Resolution 2253,[23] which expanded the regime further to cover ISIL/Da'esh.[24] The regime was renamed as the '1267/1989/2253 ISIL (Da'esh) and Al Qaeda' sanctions regime. The regime thus targeted quite different groups, including ones that actually opposed each other, and its targeting loop included those that were relatively loosely associated with them, such as the Organization of Al-Qaida in the Islamic Maghreb and others operating in Mali and the Sahel region.[25]

It has been observed that 'the current 1267 regime has evolved into the realm of the permanent exception'.[26] This permanence may be in tune with an enduring reality of an ongoing terrorist threat, with expanding scope and geographical reach. It is, however, more difficult to shoehorn it into Chapter VII's exceptional emergency status. For this reason, it has been suggested that a separate body (and not a UNSC sanctions committee) might be more opportune to address this threat.[27] Meanwhile, the UNSC has considered further expanding the regime to include targeted sanctions for individuals and entities involved in sexual violence and trafficking in persons in areas affected by armed conflict, thus expanding it beyond counter-terrorism.[28]

2. The 1267/1989/2253 Regime and its Broader Legacy for the Security Landscape

With the situation in Syria evolving, it remains to be seen what will ultimately happen to the 1267 regime. This notwithstanding, it is worth reflecting on 1267's legacy and its

[20] UNSC 'Eleventh Report of the Analytical Support and Sanctions Implementing Monitoring Team established pursuant to Resolution 1526 (2004) and extended by Resolution 1904 (2009) concerning Al Qaeda and the Taliban and associated individuals and entities' (13 April 2011) UN Doc S/2011/245, para 16.

[21] ibid para 17. [22] UNSC Res 1988 (2011); UNSC Res 1989 (2011).

[23] UNSC Res 2253 (2015). [24] UNSC Res 2170 (2014) paras 7, 18.

[25] UNSC Res 2295 (2016).

[26] Sue Eckert, 'The Evolution and Effectiveness of UN Targeted Sanctions' in van den Herik (n 18).

[27] ibid 68. [28] UNSC Res 2368 (2017) para 15.

broader impact on the security landscape through rule of law lenses. Its legacy can be situated in three domains: procedure, practice, and policy.

a. *Procedural Fairness: The Ombudsperson as a Legacy or a Memory?*

The litigation that the 1267 regime generated—with the *Kadi* case at the apex—is well known. The EU courts' judgments propelled institutional reform at UNSC level contributing to the creation of the Ombudsperson, and other procedural improvements concerning listing and review. While the latter improvements radiated to other UN sanctions regimes, extension of the mandate of the Ombudsperson to all UN sanctions regimes was repeatedly blocked. Indeed, when the 1267 regime was split into two separate regimes in 2011, the mandate of the Ombudsperson was restricted to the Al-Qaeda regime.

This political decision to limit the Ombudsperson mandate to Al-Qaeda was plainly at odds with the underlying principle established through litigation—that any listed individual should have a remedy, and a meaningful opportunity to challenge his or her listing. While scholars and litigators have challenged the sufficiency of the Ombudsperson's role, as a non-judicial process,[29] they have so far largely ignored the fact that the review it does provide is connected to one sanctions regime only. Yet the weak institutional embedding of the Ombudsperson within the greater UN bureaucracy and its very limited mandate for a single sanctions regime are fundamentally problematic. After all, once the 1267/1989/2253 sanctions regime ceases to exist, if ever, the institution of the Ombudsperson will fade with it. In its current set-up and through its exclusive linkage to the 1267/1989/2253 regime, the Ombudsperson thus risks eventually becoming a memory rather than an enduring legacy as an inseparable part of UN sanctions regimes.

b. *Practice on the Ground: Unintended Consequences and Other Implications of Terrorist Listings*

Financial institutions play a central role in counter-terrorism, and this was certainly the case for the 1267/1989/2253 regime where actual implementation depended on their cooperation.[30] The different dynamics that inform private implementation as opposed to State implementation, that is, de-risking and overcompliance, have produced serious unintended consequences, many of which remain to be addressed.[31] The intense chilling effect of international (terrorist) sanctions, and anti-money-laundering compliance requirements on humanitarian and development assistance and remittances, have been

[29] For counterarguments to judicial review as the best option: Devika Hovell, *The Power of Process; The Value of Due Process in Security Council Sanctions Decision-Making* (OUP 2016); Kimberly Prost, 'Security Council Sanctions and Fair Process' in van den Herik (n 18).

[30] Oldrich Bures, 'Private Actors in the Fight against Terrorism: Efficiency versus Effectiveness' (2012) 35 Studies in Conflict and Terrorism 712.

[31] Ginsborg (n 18) 99–103.

flagged by several actors.[32] In an effort to avoid this, it has been suggested that sanctions regimes should include exemptions for humanitarian actors similar to the Somali sanctions regime as standard.[33] Additionally, Article 50 of the UN Charter on the effects of Chapter VII measures on third parties could be reconceptualized as extending beyond States to the non-State entities that are adversely impacted by counter-terrorism measures such as charities, diaspora organizations, humanitarian agencies, and development actors.[34]

Many of the diverse, unintended consequences of terrorist designations have by now been brought to light. The International Peace Institute has indicated how these practices may effectively lead to criminalization of health care and humanitarian aid.[35] Referring to UNSC Resolution 2286 on the protection of civilians in armed conflict under international humanitarian law (IHL),[36] the paper highlights how, in fact, the counter-terrorism framework largely ignores or pays mere lip service to that body of law.[37]

A very similar effect has been observed in relation to international and local peace builders. The 'Building Peace in Permanent War; Terrorist Listing and Conflict Transformation' report flagged the shrinking space for peace facilitation, *inter alia* through the possible criminalization of third-party mediation.[38] It even argues that the consequences of sanctions and counter-terrorism measures more broadly on peace-building may not even be fully unintended, and that terrorist proscription has a

[32] Katie King et al, 'Understanding Humanitarian Exemptions: UN Security Council Sanctions and Principled Humanitarian Action' (April 2016) PILAC, Harvard Law School, Working Group Briefing Memorandum, 6 <http://blogs.harvard.edu/pilac/files/2016/04/Understanding_Humanitarian_Exemptions_April_2016.pdf> accessed 10 February 2019; see Emanuela-Chiara Gillard/Nathalie Weizmann, Chapter 28 in this *Handbook*; Human Security Collective/European Center for Not-for-Profit Law 'At the Intersection of Security and Regulation: Understanding the Drivers of "De-Risking" and the Impact on Civil Society Organizations' (March 2018) <https://www.hscollective.org/assets/Uploads/Reports/8f051ee3cb/Understanding-the-Drivers-of-De-Risking-and-the-Impact-on-Civil-Society-Organizations_1.pdf> accessed 14 November 2020.

[33] UNSC Res 1916 (2010) para 5; most recently reiterated in UNSC Res 2317 (2016) para 28. Also see UNSC 2397 (2017), para 25 on DPRK, and Gillard/Weizmann (n 32); UNGA/UNSC 'Compendium of the High Level Review of United Nations Sanctions' (June 2015) UN Doc A/69/941-S/2015/432, 55–6 and UNGA/UNSC 'Assessment Report: Achievements, Challenges and Opportunities Resulting from the Recommendations of the Compendium of the High-level Review of United Nations Sanctions' (23 June 2017) UN Doc A/71/943-S/2017/534, Recommendation 8.

[34] UN Charter 1 UNTS XVI art 50 focuses only on States: 'If preventive or enforcement measures against any state are taken by the Security Council, any other state, whether a Member of the United Nations or not, which finds itself confronted with special economic problems arising from the carrying out of those measures shall have the right to consult the Security Council with regard to a solution of those problems.'

[35] Alice Debarre, 'Safeguarding Medical Care and Humanitarian Action in the UN Counter-terrorism Framework' (International Peace Institute, September 2018) <https://www.ipinst.org/2018/09/safeguarding-humanitarian-action-in-un-counterterrorism-framework> accessed 20 April 2020; UNSC 'Report of the Secretary-General on the protection of civilians in armed conflict' (10 May 2017) UN Doc S/2017/414, para 43.

[36] UNSC Res 2286 (2016). [37] Debarre (n 35) 1, 10–12.

[38] Louise Boon-Kuo et al, *Building Peace in Permanent War; Terrorist Listing and Conflict Transformation* (ISCI/TNI 2015).

profound and transformative impact on conflict resolution resulting in the securitization of peacebuilding.[39]

c. *Policy Consequences of Intensified Use of Sanctions*

Beyond the unintended or unforeseen practical and legal consequences of the 1267/1989/2253 sanctions, the UNSC's intensified use of terrorist listings reflects a greater, notable trend in the international security landscape. As pointed out by de Goede and Sullivan, the 1267/1989/2253 lists are harbingers of the comeback of 'The List' as a governance device in security policies.[40] They have presented such lists as 'inscription devices',[41] allowing for the appreciation of specific material, political, and legal effects of the lists. A seemingly technical instrument that assembles and orders information, the list 'flattens complexity' and homogenizes what is not homogeneous, thereby blurring 'collateral realities'.[42] Intense political questions become reduced to technical exercises regarding the application of criteria, which are malleable and flexible, to information, which is risk rather than evidence-based.[43] The authors also expose the diffusion of agency involved in the formation and operation of lists, arguing that seeing how lists work as 'novel forms of transnational legal assemblage' allows for a fundamental rethink of the accountability problems that have arisen.[44]

The procedural fairness debate so far has also largely ignored the second life of the 1267/1989/2253 counter-terrorism lists, as they are copied and amended by other public and private actors which may continue to use the lists in their risk assessments or otherwise, even after delisting at UNSC level. These dispersed forms of global security governance, also conceptualized in terms of liquid postnational authority,[45] require new ideas on how to ensure proper remedies and protection for affected individuals.[46] In their absence, the intensified use of listings leaves designated individuals in the 'shadow site' of the current security system.[47] As such, the use of sanctions as surrogate accountability measures impacts on the international legal order in a truly fundamental manner.

3. Other International Legal Consequences of the 1267/1989/2253 Regime

Notwithstanding serious concerns and adverse impacts, the end of terrorist listings is not in sight. On the contrary, lists are proliferating. The US Magnitsky Act has extended

[39] ibid.

[40] Marieke de Goede/Gavin Sullivan, 'The Politics of Security Lists' (2015) 34 Environment and Planning D: Society and Space 67.

[41] ibid 70–3. [42] ibid 70. [43] ibid 73–6. [44] ibid 73.

[45] Nico Krisch, 'Authority, Solid and Liquid, in Postnational Governance' in Roger Cotterrell/ Maksymilian Del Mar (eds), *Authority in Transnational Legal Theory: Theorising Across Disciplines* (Edward Elgar 2016).

[46] De Goede/Sullivan (n 40) 73. [47] ibid 84.

the use of lists to other perceived security threats and foreign policy concerns, and other States are copying these initiatives.[48] Moreover, the 1267/1989/2253 listings are taken by some as hard-core facts that certain groups are terrorist without any further scrutiny or care. For instance, in the context of arguments regarding legality of the use of force upon invitation, some scholars maintain that consented use of force in civil war is legal if the purpose is to fight 'terrorist groups',[49] determined by reference to benchmark of UNSC listings.[50] This reliance on UNSC designations as indisputable facts neatly illustrates how the legal implications of terrorist designations extend far beyond the concrete context of a specific sanctions regime. Combined with the previous analysis of practical consequences, it is evident that the UNSC terrorist sanctions regimes have profoundly shaped and transformed the international security landscape, and will continue to do so for some time to come.

D. United Nations Security Council-mandated Anti-terror Measures: Indeterminacy and Implications

United Nationals Security Council Resolution 1373,[51] adopted in the aftermath of 9/11 under Chapter VII, mandated States to take a host of action against terrorism. This was described as the Council adopting an 'unprecedented', 'quasi legislative'[52] role. On the basis of the 'threat to international peace and security', which 'any act of international terrorism' was deemed to present,[53] States were obliged to, *inter alia*, limit movement, freeze assets, deny asylum, withhold any forms of services to persons engaged in or facilitating terrorism, criminalize, and punish with suitably severe penalties.[54]

The Council's failure to define the terrorism towards which this torrent of coercive measures was directed attracted stern criticism for 'opening the universal hunting

[48] Ewelina U Ochab, 'The Magnitsky Law is Taking Over the European Union' (*Forbes*, 10 December 2018) <https://www.forbes.com/sites/ewelinaochab/2018/12/10/the-magnitsky-law-is-taking-over-the-european-union/#333b8c441eca> accessed 20 April 2020.

[49] This view departs from the implications of the Nicaragua judgment that States have overall authority to request military assistance. Rather, it views military interference in civil strife, even on the side of the State, as prohibited with an exception based on legitimate purpose, such as the combating of terrorism. See eg Karine Bannelier/Theodore Christakis, 'Under the UN Security Council's Watchful Eyes: Military Intervention by Invitation in the Malian Conflict' (2013) 26 Leiden Journal of International Law 855.

[50] ibid 866. [51] UNSC Res 1373 (2001).

[52] Paul C Szasz, 'The Security Council Starts Legislating' (2002) 96 AJIL 901; José E Alvarez, 'Hegemonic International Law Revisited' (2003) 97 AJIL 873, 874; Stefan Talmon, 'The Security Council as World Legislator' (2005) 99 AJIL 175; UNSC Res 1373 (2001).

[53] UNSC Res 1373 (2001) preambular para 3.

[54] ibid paras 1(c), 2(a), 2(c), 2(g).

season on terrorism without defining it'.[55] The notorious lack of an agreed definition of 'terrorism' in international law provided a gap into which States' own definitions of terrorism and associated threats to the State have readily poured. A wave of legislative, policy, and practical change ensued, in which broad and diverse definitions of terrorism and associated activity were incorporated into domestic law. Exceptional laws, policies and practice were adopted, directed against this exceptional, but ill-defined, threat. The consequences for human rights were dire.[56]

Since Resolution 1373, the Council's detailed regulation of counter-terrorism has gathered pace.[57] Some things have changed positively in this UNSC practice, while others have got distinctly worse. Positive change can be seen in the language employed in resolutions. One feature of Resolution 1373, which was severely criticized, was the lack of reference to human rights, humanitarian, and refugee law.[58] This changed,[59] and it gradually became commonplace in Council resolutions,[60] like those of the UNGA and other organizations,[61] to cite the need for any measures taken to combat terrorism to comply with States' obligations under international law including international human rights, refugee, and humanitarian law.[62] This shift has, however, been criticized as insufficient, lacking in specificity (compared to detailed counter-terrorism measures) and meaningful oversight necessary to give laudable exhortations real effect.[63]

The key feature of Council resolutions that did *not* change after 1373 was the definitional deficit. In some ways this is particularly surprising as the UNSC in Resolution 1566 (2006) adopted 'guidance' on the core elements of a definition of terrorism, in part in response to evidence of how anti-terrorism resolutions were being used.[64] Resolution 1566's attempt to rein in far-reaching definitions was supported by the work of the former Special Rapporteur who delineated core elements of 'genuinely terrorist' conduct (involving serious acts of violence for particular purpose) to which counter-terrorism laws should be directed. However, in subsequent binding resolutions the Council continued to impose new obligations to act against terrorism and associated activity,

[55] Statement of Mr Jean-François Gayraud, Chief Commissioner of the French National Police, and of the French judge David Senat, in Duffy (n 7) 73.

[56] See Section C.1 on the Council's role and shifting approach to human rights standards. The Counter-Terrorism Committee (CTC) was established by UNSC Res 1373 (2001).

[57] There was a record number of resolutions in 2017; UNGA 'Report of the Special Rapporteur on the Promotion and Protection of Human Rights and Fundamental Freedoms while Countering Terrorism on the Human Rights Challenges of States of Emergency in the Context of Countering Terrorism' (1 March 2018) UN Doc A/HRC/37/52 (SR 2018 UNHRC Report).

[58] Human rights are mentioned only once in the specific context of asylum seekers.

[59] eg UNSC Res 1456 (2003).

[60] eg UNSC Res 1963 (2010) preambular para 4 and UNSC Res 1624 (2005); UNSC Res 2178 (2014); UNSC Res 2396 (2017); UNSC Res 2462 (2019).

[61] eg UN Global Counter-Terrorism Strategy (n 13), or the EU Directive discussed in this section.

[62] See n 13 and accompanying text.

[63] Fionnuala Ní Aoláin, Special Rapporteur on Terrorism and Human Rights, 'Statement' (73rd session UNGA, Third Committee, 17 October 2018) Item 74 (a–d), 7.

[64] UNSC Res 1566 (2004).

without even referring to its own 'guidance' defining terrorism, or limiting how the target should, and should not, be understood.

Far from curtailing the unruly reach and impact of what pass as 'counter-terrorism' measures, the Council's subsequent practice has compounded the problem. A series of resolutions governing incitement and provocation, 'foreign terrorist fighters', and financing of terrorism have vastly expanded the coercive measures mandated by the UNSC, including under Chapter VII, as well as the scope of behaviour covered by them. Directed towards various forms of activity associated with, or deemed supportive, sustaining, or facilitating of the undefined 'terrorist threat', these resolutions add multiple layers of indeterminacy to an already murky field.

The result is steadily increasing obligations on States to take an ever-wider range of coercive measures against an ever-broader and less well-defined phenomenon. Two illustrations of this trend and its insidious impact follow.

1. Incitement or Provocation

Promoted by the UK following the '7/7' London bombings, UNSC Resolution 1624 (2005) refers to 'all acts of terrorism irrespective of their motivation, whenever and by whomsoever committed, as one of the most serious threats to peace and security', and urges States to take 'all measures as may be necessary and appropriate and in accordance with their obligations under international law to counter incitement of terrorist acts'.[65] The Preamble goes further, expressing grave concern at the serious and growing danger posed by 'incitement of terrorist acts motivated by extremism and intolerance' and 'repudiating... attempts at the justification or glorification (*apologie*) of terrorist acts'.[66] However, neither 'terrorist acts', nor 'incitement', 'extremism', 'justification', 'glorification', or '*apologie*' are defined in the resolution, or elsewhere in international law.[67]

The UN Secretary-General, in his 2008 report on Human Rights and Terrorism sought to limit the scope of the 'incitement' in Resolution 1624, offering an approach compatible with human rights law.[68] The report draws a bright line between direct incitement to violence on the one hand, and glorification or *apologie* of past acts on the other, stating unequivocally that while 'the first may be legally prohibited, the second *may not*'.[69]

However, the Secretary-General's report appears to have done little to curb the much further-reaching effects of Resolution 1624 which has triggered a plethora of regional

[65] UNSC Res 1624 (2005) para 3 and para 1 on 'prohibiting by law' incitement to terrorism; Duffy (n 55).

[66] UNSC Res 1624 (2005) preamble.

[67] There was no reference to the UNSC's own definitional 'guidance' (UNSC Res 1566 (2006)).

[68] UNGA 'Report of the Secretary-General: The Protection of Human Rights and Fundamental Freedoms while Countering Terrorism' (28 August 2008) UN Doc A/63/337, para 61 (Secretary-General's Report).

[69] ibid.

standards, national laws, and prosecutorial practices directed against myriad forms of expression deemed to constitute direct or 'indirect' incitement.[70] These include EU responses which refer back to Resolution 1624,[71] in particular the EU Directive on Combating Terrorism (2017/541).[72] According to the Directive, States must criminalize listed terrorist offences, including public provocation, as well as threats to commit such offences, and preparatory acts, aiding and abetting, inciting or attempting to do so.[73] The recital notes explicitly that provocation covers '*inter alia, the glorification and justification of terrorism or the dissemination of messages or images ... including those related to the victims of terrorism, as a way to gather support for terrorist causes or to seriously intimidate the population*'.[74] While stricter than the UNSC resolution or its Council of Europe contemporary in some respects, this latest transnational iteration broadens out the Council's approach in other ways, covering anyone who 'makes available' in any way (re-posting, lending, distributing) a message or images which might prove 'dangerous'.[75] Ambiguous offences of advocating or making available 'dangerous messages' are a far cry from the direct incitement of violent acts of terrorism in the Secretary-General's report.

Most troubling is practice at the national level. Under the shadow of UNSC mandate, some States have incorporated new forms of 'indirect incitement' into hastily passed legislation, while others have subjected pre-existing laws to expansive interpretations.[76] The result is a broad spectrum of offences, and prosecutions, based on diverse forms of 'dangerous' expression, such as encouragement,[77] glorification,[78] justification,[79] apology,[80] possession,[81] dissemination or making available prohibited information or

[70] Duffy (n 55).

[71] EU Council Framework Decision on Combating Terrorism 2008/919/JHA of 28 November 2008 OJ L330/22, para 8.

[72] Directive 2017/541 of 15 March 2017 on Combating Terrorism OJ L88/6 ('EU Directive').

[73] ibid art 5 'public provocation to commit a terrorist offence'.

[74] Directive 2017/541 of 15 March 2017 on Combating Terrorism OJ L88/6 ('EU Directive') para 10 (emphasis added).

[75] ibid art 5.

[76] Duffy (n 55) 350–8, citing law and practice in UK, France, Spain, Egypt, Canada, and Turkey amongst others.

[77] eg UK Terrorism Act 2006, s 1 Encouragement of Terrorism.

[78] eg UK, Canada and Spain where the UN Human Rights Committee and/or UN Special Rapporteurs have expressed concern; Duffy (n 55) 350–1, and objections of the Dutch Council of State on grounds of vagueness.

[79] Russian Federal Law No 35-Fz (6 March 2006) on Counteracting Terrorism criminalizes 'justification of terrorism' and 'popularisation of terrorist ideas'.

[80] eg French Code pénal (Criminal Code) (FR) art 421-2-5 (Loi N°2014–1353, 13 November 2014), or reforms in the Honduran penal code (eg IACHR/UNHCHR 'Joint Press Release' (23 February 2017) <http://www.oas.org/en/iachr/expression/showarticle.asp?artID=1054&lID=1> accessed 21 April 2020).

[81] eg 'Possessing Things Connected with Terrorist Acts' and 'Collecting or Making Documents Likely to Facilitate Terrorist Acts'—Criminal Code Act 1995 (AU) Schedule, ss 101.4–101.5.

materials,[82] or professing to be a member of or associated with prohibited organizations.[83]

The human rights and rule of law implications are multidimensional. Through these measures the Council has mandated an expansive approach to criminal law—a body of law intended to be used exceptionally (ultimo ratio). Its force, and legitimacy, depends on respect for the basic principles of criminal law and human rights. Legality, and particularly stringent (and non-derogable) requirements of *nullum crimen sine lege*, are undermined by concepts such as encouragement and glorification which—as human rights courts and tribunals have frequently noted—are inherently vague, malleable, and susceptible to abuse. The principle of individual culpability is also at stake. The harm principle and principle of remoteness require a personal proximate link—through conduct and intent—between an individual and harm to a value protected by criminal law. Proportionality requirements ensure that individuals are punished commensurate with their own contribution to that harm. The requirement of restrictive interpretation of the law, where in doubt in favour of the accused, applies (*lex stricta*). Each of these are jeopardized in a context in which, in some cases, there is no need for the conduct to have created any harm at all, or even to have caused a risk of such harm, and the individual need not have intended to do so,[84] yet 'dissuasive' and often disproportionate sanctions apply.[85]

United Nations Security Council Resolution 1624 and its national offshoots have also heavily affected freedom of expression. In line with human rights law, criminalizing expression of opinion is permitted only exceptionally.[86] While expression cannot be prohibited on the basis that it is offensive, direct and public incitement to future violence can. However, in practice, broad offences such as aiding and assisting crimes of provocation have delinked the role of the individual from any act of violence or even from the creation of a real risk of such violence. As such, the bright line between legitimate limitations on speech that incites violence, and 'thought crimes' risks being gradually erased. As growing evidence of academics, artists, rappers, lawyers, journalists, bloggers, political dissenters, human rights organizers, protesters, environmental activists, indigenous women's groups, peace activists, and others being labelled 'propagandists' and terrorists continues to stream into light, the broader, longer-term implications for democracy become clear.[87]

[82] eg Dutch Wetboek van Strafrecht (Criminal Code) art 132 (as translated in *Prosecutor v Imane B et al*, Judgment of 10 December 2015, Case Nos 09/842489–14, 09/767038–14, 09/767313–14, 09/767174–13, 09/765004–15, 09/767146–14, 09/767256–14, 09/767238–14, 09/827053–15, 09/767237–14, 09/765002–15, and 09/767077–14, para 11.12). (Context Case) <http://uitspraken.rechtspraak.nl/inziendocument?id=ECLI:NL:RBDHA:2015:16102> accessed 17 April 2019.

[83] Strafgesetzbuch (Criminal Code) (DE) ss 129 and 129a.

[84] Examples in Duffy (n 55).

[85] eg UNSC Res 2462 (2019).

[86] As discussed more fully in Duffy (n 55).

[87] Turkey presents a striking example of eroding democracy through expansive use of such counter-terror laws. See eg Nils Muižnieks, Council of Europe Commissioner for Human Rights, 'Memorandum on Freedom of Expression and Media Freedom in Turkey' (15 February 2017) Doc CommDH(2017)5; Duffy (n 55) 358.

Resolution 1624 does not mandate or authorize States to enact broad-reaching crimes of expression or prosecute political dissent, and responsibility lies with implementing States. Cooperating States also have a responsibility to ensure they do not contribute to arbitrary prosecutions that fail to meet international standards.[88] It was not unforeseeable, however, in light of experience with prior resolutions such as 1373, that UNSC Resolution 1624 might contribute to the normative toolkit of repressive States. It would be followed by yet more powerful tools in response to the threats posed by 'foreign terrorist fighters'.

2. 'Foreign Terrorist Fighters'

In Resolution 2178 (2014), the Council obliged States to take extremely wide-reaching measures to prevent, disrupt, prosecute, and suppress the travel and return of 'foreign terrorist fighters' (FTFs). The resolution covers, *inter alia*, the recruitment, organization, transportation, training, financing, and various other forms of facilitation or support for the FTF phenomenon.

Alarm ensued that we were 'back to [the] post 9/11 chaos' of UNSC Res 1373, with grave rights implications.[89] But this did not apparently chasten the Council. United Nations Security Council Resolution 2396 (2017) went further, broadening States' obligations in relation to criminal justice, border security, and cooperation, calling for the creation of 'watch lists or databases' of suspect persons and information-sharing between States.[90] Resolution 2462 (2019) reached even further, underscoring the need for 'dissuasive criminal sanctions'.[91]

United Nations Security Council activity on FTFs since Resolution 2178 has catalysed global normative activity. States have changed legislation, developed policy and introduced a diverse array of measures aimed at preventing and punishing foreign travel and associated threats.[92] Key amongst them is burgeoning resort to 'administrative'

[88] eg the extradition dispute between Belgium and Spain concerning Valtonyc, a rapper being prosecuted for apology of terrorism, pending before Belgian courts and on referral to European Court of Justice.

[89] Martin Scheinin, 'Back to Post-9/11 Panic? Security Council Resolution on Foreign Terrorist Fighters' (*Just Security*, 23 September 2014) <www.justsecurity.org/15407/post-911-panic-security-council-resolution-foreign-terrorist-fighters-scheinin/> accessed 17 April 2019; OSCE, *Guidelines for Addressing the Threats and Challenges of 'Foreign Terrorist Fighters' within a Human Rights Framework* (OSCE/ODIHR 2018) 16–17.

[90] UNSC Res 2396 (2017). eg Fionnuala Ní Aoláin, 'The UN Security Council, Global Watch Lists, Biometrics and the Threat to the Rule of Law' (*Just Security*, 17 January 2018) <www.justsecurity.org/51075/security-council-global-watch-lists-biometrics/> accessed 17 April 2019.

[91] eg OSCE (n 89); Helen Duffy, '"Foreign Terrorist Fighters": A Human Rights Approach?' (2019) 29 Security and Human Rights 120.

[92] For an overview of measures applied in selected countries: IEP of Strasbourg/Council of Europe, 'Returning Foreign Terrorist Fighters in Europe: A Comparative Analysis' (October 2017) <http://mastereurope.eu/wp-content/uploads/2017/10/Returning-foreign-terrorist-fighters-in-Europe-.pdf> accessed 21 April 2020.

measures—by their nature adopted by the executive without normal political and often judicial oversight—such as citizenship stripping, blocking entry into, or transit through, States including one's own State, removal of travel documents, house arrest, control orders, and freezing of assets.[93] This is supported by increased use of surveillance, special investigative techniques, watch lists and databases, monitoring, and blocking of websites.[94]

Another striking feature of the FTF landscape is, once again, expansive criminal law. Criminal conduct may consist of travel or attempts to travel, 'facilitation', or 'justification' of such travel to prohibited areas with a 'terrorist purpose', irrespective of the individual's own intent. Broad approaches to what constitutes recruitment, training, or 'self-indoctrination',[95] raise questions as to the contribution of individuals to criminal harm. Punishing parental provision of small amounts of money to children abroad as 'FTF financing' raises doubts as to criminal culpability, and on the proper use of the criminal law *ultima ratio*.[96] The web of criminality has spun out of control, embracing activity that arguably goes far beyond—and has limited meaningful individual connection to—the violent activity at the heart of international terrorism. The explicit delinking of FTF from any 'specific terrorist act' in Resolution 2462 (2019) may further contribute to this trend.

While of course these resolutions follow the trend of explicitly acknowledging that States are obliged to adopt such measures consistently with other obligations,[97] a now familiar gap emerges between theory and practice. Long-standing problems associated with the lack of clarity surrounding 'terrorism'[98] are significantly compounded by the novel term 'foreign terrorist fighters', each element of which raises challenges in terms of legality, specificity, and foreseeability.[99] It is unclear how 'terrorist organizations' and entities should be identified, even those which are not apparently limited to those designated or listed on UN or regional terror lists with all the problems associated with those regimes.[100] What constitutes a 'foreigner', given ambiguity as regards dual nationals or persons with important personal, social, or family links to States beyond formal residence or nationality, is far from clear.[101] The reference to 'fighters' is also misleading, as

[93] OSCE (n 89) section 3.4. [94] ibid.

[95] eg viewing websites has been considered self-training in the Netherlands, or EU Directive (n 72) art 6 definition of recruitment.

[96] OSCE (n 89) 19, 35, 38.

[97] Note significant shift since the silence of UNSC Res 1373 (2001) in this respect.

[98] eg ECOSOC 'Promotion and Protection of Human Rights: Report of the Special Rapporteur on the Promotion and Protection of Human Rights and Fundamental Freedoms while Countering Terrorism, Martin Scheinin' (28 December 2005) UN Doc E/CN.4/2006/98, para 42.

[99] eg International Covenant on Civil and Political Rights 999 UNTS 171 art 15; European Convention for the Protection of Human Rights and Fundamental Freedoms ETS No 5 art 7.

[100] UNCTED, 'Implementation of Security Council Resolution 2178 (2014) by States Affected by Foreign Terrorist Fighters' (2015) para 158(b) <https://www.un.org/sc/ctc/wp-content/uploads/2016/09/FTF-Report-1-3_English.pdf> accessed 21 April 2020.

[101] UNSC Res 2178 (2001) para 6; Sandra Krähenmann, 'The Obligations under International Law of the Foreign Fighter's State of Nationality or Habitual Residence, State of Transit and State of Destination' in Andrea de Guttry et al (eds), *Foreign Fighters and International Law and Beyond* (Springer 2016) 235.

the scope of those covered by the provisions goes far beyond those in fighting roles or in any way 'participating in hostilities'.

The conflation of 'terrorism' and armed conflict also runs through Resolution 2178, with potentially insidious implications for IHL. Travel to participate in armed conflict is treated as terrorist fighting, irrespective of whether for example the individual is fighting against terrorist organizations, within the limits of IHL, or the opposite. The need to carefully distinguish terrorism and participation in conflict is increasingly recognized in international and domestic practice.[102] As a Belgian court found, 'if participants in an armed conflict fight in the knowledge that they will in any case be subject to prosecution under common criminal law or under terrorism legislation, there is no incentive to comply with (at least) international humanitarian law'.[103] There may also be less incentive to terminate conflicts if IHL's provisions for amnesties for participation (as opposed to war crimes) are effectively removed.[104] Unsurprisingly, FTF resolutions have also raised concerns as to the ability of humanitarian workers, including medical personnel, to provide care in conflict and access areas to provide relief to civilian populations. This compounds the problems highlighted above in relation to the impact of sanctions regimes.

Finally, UNSC resolutions have contributed to greater private actor engagement with the FTF threat in a range of contexts, with uncertain implications. The unwillingness of donors and financial institutions to provide essential funds and services, particularly in situations of armed conflict, has added to concerns that essential humanitarian work is rendered practically impossible.[105] The emphasis placed on criminalizing offences related to financing and support of FTFs,[106] including through the Internet and social media,[107] has led to stringent requirements of prompt removal of online content.[108] In September 2018, the President of the European Commission proposed new rules 'to get terrorist content off the web within one hour'.[109] As regards the identification of the amorphous scope and definition of the 'terrorist content' that must be removed from the Internet, the EU Commission cites back to the broad-reaching offences contained in Directive (EU) 2017/541 and domestic laws, and to information as to 'terrorist groups' identified as such by the EU or the UN.[110] Microsoft accordingly uses the UNSC sanctions list to guide an interpretation of 'terrorist content' that should be removed from its

[102] eg Ghent Court of Appeal, Decision of Case 939/2019 (8 March 2019) 26–7 (on file with authors). Belgian courts have ruled that individuals participating in an armed conflict cannot be prosecuted as terrorists but must be judged by the standards of IHL.

[103] ibid. [104] OSCE (n 89) 24–8. [105] ibid 27; Section C.2.

[106] EU Directive (n 72) para 5. [107] ibid para 6.

[108] EU Directive (n 72) art 21(1).

[109] European Commission, 'Press Release—State of the Union 2018: Commission Proposes New Rules to Get Terrorist content Off the Web' (12 September 2018) <http://europa.eu/rapid/press-release_IP-18-5561_en.htm> accessed 12 April 2019; European Commission, 'Proposal for a Regulation of the European Parliament and of the Council on Preventing the Dissemination of Terrorist Content Online' (12 September 2018) 2018/0331 (COD), 4.

[110] European Commission, 'Recommendation on Measures to Effectively Tackle Illegal Content Online' (1 March 2018) C(2018)1177final, 11.

online services,[111] while Google and Facebook both use national US sanctions lists for this purpose.[112] This has given rise to 'exceptional concern'[113] as to the chilling impact in practice on private actors, and broad-reaching implications for free speech in light of 'a growing trend [...] of self-regulation efforts among industry actors in response to online terrorist content and activity'.[114]

E. Conclusion

This chapter has explored a landscape of uncertain threats and unaccountable actors. Systematic acts of violence by terrorist groups have posed a range of threats—to the most basic rights of their victims, to the intensity of conflicts, to international peace and security. It is uncertain, however, whether all acts of terrorist violence constitute such a threat. More doubtful still is whether the vastly disparate array of conduct labelled as 'terrorism', 'extremism' or associated offences around the world, delinked from acts of violence, can conceivably be considered a threat to international peace and security. The loose and ever more expansive approach to security threats, absent definitions of relevant concepts, has brought a vast and growing range of conduct within the purview of counter-terrorism, much of which should not properly be considered 'terrorism' at all, still less be subject to onerous sanctions.

Perceptions of unprecedented threats have, however, given rise to exceptional measures of response. These have, in turn, spread out and been applied to less and less exceptional circumstances, and taken root, gradually becoming embedded as the new normal. A significant contributor has been the 'shift in counter-terrorism regulation and process'

[111] 'Microsoft's Approach to Terrorist Content' (*Microsoft Corporate Blogs*, 20 May 2016) <https://blogs.microsoft.com/on-the-issues/2016/05/20/microsofts-approach-terrorist-content-online/#sm.000o8cfog1gyufreset139jjonsg1> accessed 12 April 2019; UNCTED/ICT4 Peace Foundation, 'Summary Report: Private Sector Engagement in Responding to the Use of the Internet and ICT for Terrorist Purposes' (Zurich Workshop, 25 August 2016) 8 <https://ict4peace.org/wp-content/uploads/2016/10/Summary-Report-Zurich-Workshop-FINAL.pdf> accessed 12 April 2019.

[112] UNCTED/ICT4 Peace Foundation (n 111) 8.

[113] Special Rapporteur on the Promotion and Protection of the Right to Freedom of Opinion and Expression/Special Rapporteur on the Right to Privacy/Special Rapporteur on the Promotion and Protection of Human Rights and Fundamental Freedoms while Countering Terrorism, 'Communication' (7 December 2018) OL OTH 71/2018, 6 <https://spcommreports.ohchr.org/TMResultsBase/DownLoadPublicCommunicationFile?gId=24234> accessed 12 April 2019.

[114] UNCTED/ICT for Peace Foundation, 'Private Sector Engagement in Responding to the Use of the Internet and ICT for Terrorist Purposes: Strengthening Dialogue and Building Trust' 4 <www.un.org/sc/ctc/wp-content/uploads/2016/12/Private-Sector-Engagement-in-Responding-to-the-Use-of-the-Internet-and-ICT-for-Terrorist-Purposes.pdf> accessed 12 April 2019; European Council, 'Joint Statement of EU Ministers for Justice and Home Affairs and Representatives of EU Institutions on the Terrorist Attacks in Brussels on 22 March 2016' (24 March 2016) <www.consilium.europa.eu/en/press/press-releases/2016/03/24/statement-on-terrorist-attacks-in-brussels-on-22-march/> accessed 12 April 2019.

by the UNSC, the full implications of which deserve greater reflection than has been afforded to date.[115]

Sanctions regimes that are supposed to be temporary have now become quasi-permanent. Extensions of the criminal law reach further back into the pre-crime era, and further out to embrace an ever-broader range of 'neutral' activity that may have been deemed supportive of terrorism, gradually delinking criminal responsibility from terrorist acts of violence. The predominance of 'administrative measures' broaden the net, sometimes with comparably serious implications for the rights of those affected but with less due process of law. This chapter has illustrated how gradually, under the cover of UNSC mandate, counter-terrorism practice stretches to embrace a vast array of legitimate activity, from political dissent to artistic expression, journalism, and/or other human rights defenders.

Fundamental questions inevitably follow as to the threats posed by these responses. So far as they impede the work of journalists, lawyers, civil society organizers, educators, and environmental activists, amongst others, they pose a risk to human rights, democracy, and rule of law interlinked with peace and security. So far as sanctions and restrictions on travel and financing interfere with the work of humanitarian organizations, they run counter to the cause of peace and stability. So far as measures undermine IHL properly applicable in conflict, they have potential to disincentivize peace processes.

This complex reality of terrorism, threats, counter-terrorism, and counter-threats has been exposed and acknowledged increasingly. Its importance is reflected in now long-standing recognition at UN level of the centrality of addressing 'conditions conducive' to the spread of terrorism and violent extremism. But it does not necessarily correspond with the Council's practice, or appear to prompt the necessary evaluation of the effectiveness of the Council's role in addressing and contributing to 'threats and challenges'.

Problematic features of counterterrorist practice highlighted in this chapter—the lack of definition, exceptionalism and its spreading reach, and a lack of accountability—are hardly unique to the UNSC's role.[116] But they are seriously compounded by the exercise of the Council's unique powers. The contribution of the Council to multiple dimensions of unaccountability therefore deserves particular attention. This includes, within the Council, political accountability in the process of adoption of these far-reaching resolutions, which has at times been hasty, precluding debate, stakeholder consultation, and the opportunity for much-needed reflection. This has led to calls for 'a form of a priori human rights review for Security Council resolutions in the

[115] Ní Aoláin suggests the issue 'has gone largely unremarked by policymakers and scholars', Fionnuala Ní Aoláin, 'The UN Security Council's Outsized Role in Shaping Counter-Terrorism Regulation and its Impacts on Human Rights' (*Just Security*, 19 October 2018) https://www.justsecurity.org/61150/security-council-mainstream-human-rights-counter-terrorism-regulation accessed 20 May 2020.

[116] Duffy (n 7) ch 12 exploring characteristics of 'war on terror' practice, which have been exacerbated in recent years through the Council's role.

counter-terrorism domain that have a quasi-legislative character, and mandate criminal law regulation at the domestic level'.[117]

In turn, the limits of legal or judicial oversight of Council action are well rehearsed in academic commentary and prompted a flood of judicial practice in relation to sanctions. When this forced at least a measure of accountability, including the introduction of the Ombudsperson position, it is significant that this was not rolled out to other sanctions regimes and that institutional embedding remained weak. Likewise, the Council's inclusion of language on the need to implement resolutions consistently with human rights obligations, and its adoption of 'guidance' on a definition in UNSC Resolution 1566, were apparent responses to criticism. But its failure to put flesh on the bones of those obligations, to even refer to its own definition, and to engage in any meaningful review of the human rights and rule of law implications of implementation of resolutions, suggest a failure to take seriously and follow through on their own standards.[118]

The implications for the accountability of other actors also deserve reflection. States bear the obligations to implement consistently with human rights and humanitarian and refugee law, yet arguably they too have become less accountable for doing so under the shadow of Council mandate. Political oversight has been curtailed where expedited legislative processes have been employed in capitals around the globe. In substance, the Council has provided a veneer of legitimacy to measures adopted under Chapter VII powers, but where overwhelming evidence has emerged of abuse by States, the Council has not meaningfully engaged to ensure any form of accountability. Human rights courts and bodies have sometimes stepped into the breach, but are under-resourced, slow and poorly placed to act in a timely manner to prevent legislation and policies from acquiring effect. The problematic practice of many States in implementing Council resolutions inevitably mutes their authority and force to exercise pressure on the worst violators.

The various UNSC measures discussed in this chapter have also had implications for the role of private actors in counter-terrorism. Financial institutions, Internet providers and others have a role to play in the much-touted 'whole of society' approach to addressing security threats. But they have been required to take a host of measures linked to the implementation of resolutions that require careful balancing of the human rights issues that they are ill-suited to provide, with even less normative frameworks and accountability. This requires a fundamental rethink of how to organize and structure safeguards and accountability mechanisms in this space. Meanwhile other private actors, such as civil society groups, many of whom seek to address the 'conditions conducive to terrorism' at the centre of the global counter-terrorism strategy, are targeted and impeded in their work by anti-terrorism laws and practices.

Perhaps the most striking indicator of the accountability deficit, reflected across this chapter, is the resistance to learning lessons and correcting course in the counter-terrorism context. In light of the profound and wide-reaching implications of UNSC activism in this field, and criticism from a range of judicial and other authorities, it is pertinent to

[117] SR 2018 UNHRC Report (n 57). [118] ibid.

ask whether this will influence Council practice in the future. Will it grapple with the complexity of threats and challenges arising from terrorism and from its own responses to it? Or will it continue on the trajectory towards increasingly coercive approaches, towards an expanding range of uncertain threats, in the dubious pursuit of advancing peace and security?

CHAPTER 12

TRANSNATIONAL ORGANIZED CRIME

PIERRE HAUCK AND SVEN PETERKE

A. Introduction

Since the end of the Cold War, transnational organized crime (TOC) has become a major concern in the international arena. Two main events have fuelled the cross-border spread of organized delinquency in an increasingly interconnected world with old and new criminal opportunities: the collapse of the former Soviet Union and the process of globalization and economic liberalization. While the former played a crucial role in the expansion of criminal networks and activities, the latter has profoundly changed the dynamics and features of illegal markets. As criminal justice systems remain traditionally entrenched in the nation-State, they tend to struggle in facing these challenges.

With the growing recognition that combating TOC requires more effective international cooperation, an impressive international legal regime has been constructed around this subject matter. A good part of this framework consists of so-called 'suppression conventions' that oblige States Parties to criminalize certain 'evils', to enforce relevant domestic laws, and to cooperate with each other in the persecution of these illegal activities. An often-downplayed problem is that these instruments are 'rooted in the crime control policies of powerful Western states',[1] supposedly serving as models for other governments. They therefore tend to impose duties that are rather difficult to comply with for States with fragile institutions, often incapable of effectively delivering essential goods, such as safety and security.

Against this background, it is increasingly acknowledged amongst both scholars and practitioners that tackling TOC requires the use of a broader and far more differentiated approach that addresses not only the multiplicity of non-State actors who have links to organized criminal groups (such as rebels and terrorists), but also the promotion of

[1] Neil Boister, *An Introduction to Transnational Criminal Law* (2nd edn, OUP 2018) 20.

good governance, transparency and professional ethics. The sound implementation of this approach must be seen as pivotal for achieving both global justice and security.

The present chapter can only offer a concise introduction to this complex and highly controversial issue. To confine the analysis solely to the international legal regime relevant to TOC would, however, be of little help in understanding the various pitfalls being associated with it. Thus, this chapter begins by shedding some light on the basic notions of TOC (Section B), before pointing out some of the impacts attributed to this cross-border delinquency and its ties and linkages with other legal and illegal activities and actors (Section C). After a brief sketch of the international legal framework that is in place for countering TOC (Section D), attention is drawn to some of the challenges faced in further developing this regime and making it more effective (Section E).

B. The Notion of Transnational Organized Crime

The term TOC merges two controversial concepts, that is, 'organized crime' and 'transnational crimes'. Although policymakers, law enforcement agents, and many other State and non-State actors today use this term without major reluctance in their agendas, from a juridical perspective, it lacks a precise meaning. Serious doubts therefore exist with regard to considering TOC a concept of international law. Understanding where the two concepts originally come from and how far they have merged is of great help thus in inducing the necessary sense of scepticism on a debate revolving around phenomena whose empirical proof is often difficult, if not impossible.

1. Historical Background

From a historical perspective, organized cross-border deviance is nothing new. Piracy and privateering, slavery, and both the smuggling and trafficking in humans and weapons have been known for centuries.[2] These activities were profit-driven, required some degree of sophistication, and routinely involved a collectivity of persons. Yet, the first consistent use of the term 'organized crime' appears to have emerged only in 1919, when the Chicago Crime Commission, a civic organization that was created by businessmen,

[2] cf Frank Madsen, 'The Historical Evolution of the International Cooperation against Transnational Organised Crime: An Overview' in Pierre Hauck/Sven Peterke (eds), *International Law and Transnational Organized Crime* (OUP 2016) 6f; for details, Bruce Elleman, 'Historical Piracy and its Impact' in Gerben Bruinsma (ed), *Histories of Transnational Crime* (Springer 2015) 9ff; Marlou Schrover, 'History of Slavery, Human Smuggling and Trafficking 1860–2010' in Gerben Bruinsma (ed), *Histories of Transnational Crime* (Springer 2015) 41ff; Jonathan Grant, 'The Arms Traffic in World History' in Gerben Bruinsma (ed), *Histories of Transnational Crime* (Springer 2015) 71ff.

bankers, and lawyers to promote reforms of the criminal justice system perceived as rotten and corrupt, referred to 'the orderly fashion in which the so-called "criminal class" of an estimated "10,000 professional criminals" in Chicago allegedly could pursue "crime as business"'.[3]

During the Prohibition Era (1920–1933), the discourse on organized crime shifted towards 'gangsters and racketeers', such as Al Capone, accused of heading 'crime syndicates' and 'criminal organizations'.[4] After the Second World War, various presidential and congressional committees and working groups were established in the US to publicly deal with some of the underworld's presumed 'masterminds'. Many were descendants from Italian immigrants.[5] This politically inspired media event ended not only in the formulation of the xenophobic 'alien conspiracy thesis',[6] namely the notion that the US is controlled by a hierarchically structured criminal organization predominantly composed of 'Mafiosi', called the 'Cosa Nostra'; it also culminated in the creation of the world's first anti-organized crime legislation.[7]

These developments soon started to be discussed abroad, first of all in Western Europe. The result of this process was not a general rejection of the discourse on organized crime, although the 'ethnicity trap' and 'conspiracy thesis' were heavily criticized.[8] Rather, its meaning was gradually modified for conceptual purposes, increasingly centring on illegal markets and its supply through loosely connected criminal networks.

The term 'transnational crime' has its origins in the debate on transnationalism, transnational actors, and transnational organizations in the theory of international relations. Starting in the early 1970s,[9] this debate soon generated efforts with regard to its criminological conceptualization,[10] however, without properly distinguishing between transnational, global, or international dimensions. In 1975, the term was taken up by the Fifth UN Congress on Crime Prevention and Treatment of Offenders, where it was primarily used to refer to economic crimes committed by multinational corporations.[11]

[3] cf Klaus von Lampe, 'Not a Process of Enlightenment: The Conceptual History of Organized Crime in Germany and the United States of America' (2001) 1 Forum on Crime and Society 99, 104 with further references.

[4] Martin Neumann/Corinna Elsenbroich, 'Introduction: The Societal Dimensions of Organized Crime' (2017) 20 Trends in Organized Crime 1, 2.

[5] Von Lampe (n 3) 106.

[6] cf Jay S Albanese, *Organized Crime In Our Times* (6th edn, Anderson Publishing 2011) 138.

[7] Organized Crime Control Act, Public Law 91-452 (14 October 1970) 84 Stat 922, that contains the famous 'Racketeer Influenced and Corrupt Organizations Act' (RICO).

[8] cf Michael Woodiwiss, 'Enterprise not Ethnicity: An Interview with Dwight C. Smith Jr' (2015) 18 Trends in Organized Crime 41.

[9] Joseph S Nye Jr/Robert O Keohane, 'Transnational Relations and World Politics: An Introduction' (1971) 25 International Organization 329; Samuel Huntington, 'Transnational Organizations in World Politics' (1973) 25 World Politics 333.

[10] See eg William Clifford, 'New Dimensions in Criminality: National and Transnational' (1975) 8 Australian and New Zealand Journal of Crime 67.

[11] UN Secretariat, 'Report on the Fifth Congress Containing a Summary of the Proceedings, Conclusions and Recommendations as adopted by the Congress' Fifth UN Congress on the Prevention of Crime and the Treatment of Offenders (Geneva 1–12 September 1975) UN Doc A/Conf.56/10, paras 51–63.

With the end of the Cold War and the collapse of the former Soviet Union, this notion gradually shifted to the cross-border provision of all kinds of illegal products and services as a phenomenon of 'shadow globalization'.[12] It was then the internationalization of the 'war on drugs' during the Reagan administration with its focus on the eradication of 'cartels' as producers and transporters of narcotic substances, which created a significant overlap of the notions of organized and transnational crime.[13] A legal and political hallmark of this process was the adoption of the UN Convention against Illicit Traffic in Narcotic Drugs and Psychotropic Substances in 1988, as further explained below.

The Convention was soon followed by the first UN General Assembly (UNGA) Resolution on 'International Co-operation in Combating Organized Crime'[14] and other regional and universal events, such as the 1994 Naples Conference,[15] which consolidated the perception of cross-border delinquency as a 'new threat' to the international community, urgently requiring the internationalization of those criminal laws that had allegedly proven effective and useful for its suppression. Ultimately, it was the advent of the quickly negotiated 2000 UN Convention against Transnational Organized Crime (UNTOC)[16] that somehow internationally entrenched the use of the term 'transnational organized crime'.

2. Basic Criminological Notions of Organized Crime

Before looking into this treaty for clarifying the assertion that TOC is not a concept of international law, light needs to be shed on the academic debate on the concept(s) of organized crime. This explains to a significant degree the difficulties in achieving a consensus on how to define TOC, if, at all, desirable and possible.

Amongst criminologists it is today widely accepted that organized crime can be approached conceptually from essentially three angles.[17] The first is to centre on organized criminality, which necessarily implies a controversy on which forms of delinquency can and should be considered as sophisticated and serious enough to deserve this label. Obvious candidates are the trafficking in arms, art, drugs, humans, and wildlife species, frequently correlated with a set of enabling acts, such as (the threat of) violence, corruption, and money laundering.[18] A second option is to focus on organized criminals, namely to give preference to groups of offenders instead of activities. This is problematic in itself in the absence of individual criminal acts. Other problems with this approach

[12] David Felsen/Akis Kalaitzidis, 'A Historical Overview of Transnational Crime' in Philip Reichel (ed), *Handbook of Transnational Crime and Justice* (SAGE Publications 2005) 5.

[13] Margaret Beare/Michael Woodiwiss, 'U.S. Organized Crime Control Policies Exported Abroad' in Letizia Paoli (ed), *The Oxford Handbook of Organized Crime* (OUP 2014) 551.

[14] UNGA Res 44/71 (8 December 1989).

[15] UNGA Res 49/159 (23 December 1994).

[16] 2225 UNTS 209 (UNTOC).

[17] See, for a solid introduction, Klaus von Lampe, *Organized Crime. Analysing Illegal Activities, Criminal Structures and Extra-legal Governance* (SAGE Publications 2016) 15–35.

[18] Alan Wright, *Organised Crime* (Willan Publishing 2006) 49.

revolve around the question of to what extent it is legitimate and makes sense to include 'disorganized crime'[19] committed by highly informal and relatively short-living non-hierarchical networks[20] or by youth and street gangs.[21] Evidently, these two notions are not mutually exclusive and can be combined with notions of transnational crime. A third and much broader approach consists of conceptualizing these activities and actors as forms of extra-legal governance based upon the exercise of power and influence through criminal entrepreneurs.[22] Independent of the existence of the myriad diverging forms of deviance that can be labelled as TOC, it is this often-unqualified notion that causes considerable discomfort in societies and therefore provokes governments towards interventionist measures. Combined with the idea that organized crime no longer can be 'kept outside' and frequently comes from abroad, and that it inflicts serious harm to peoples and their institutions, TOC is seen by States as a threat to sovereignty, in particular, territorial integrity and political independence.

3. Transnational Organized Crime as a Concept of International Law

From the perspective of international law, in a way, the first two approaches have been incorporated into treaties. On the one hand, an internationalization and harmonization of criminal laws has been achieved through the so-called 'suppression conventions' which focus on specific transnational crimes. On the other hand, the UNTOC not only obliges its signatories to criminalize the participation in an 'organized criminal group' in their domestic legislation,[23] but even provides that the use of the term:

> shall mean a structured group of three or more persons, existing for a period of time and acting in concert with the aim of committing one or more serious crimes or offences established in accordance with this Convention, in order to obtain, directly or indirectly, a financial or other material benefit.[24]

Moreover, it proposes that '"structured group" shall mean a group that is not randomly formed for the immediate commission of an offence and that does not need to have formally defined roles for its members, continuity of its membership or a developed structure'.[25] While representing a minimum consensus that allows for some rudimentary delineations, as, for example, with regard to groups that strive for political change through violent means, the UNTOC neither contains a legal definition of 'organized

[19] Peter Reuter, *Disorganized Crime: The Economics of the Invisible Hand* (MIT Press 1983).

[20] Instructive: Jay S Albanese, *Transnational Crime and the 21st Century: Criminal Enterprise, Corruption, and Opportunity* (OUP 2011) 6–9.

[21] Pierre Hauck/Sven Peterke, 'Organized Crime and Gang Violence in National and International Law' (2010) 92 International Review of the Red Cross 407, 411.

[22] See, for an early proposal, Allan A Block, *East Side, West Side: Organizing Crime in New York 1930–1950* (Transaction Publishers 1983) vii.

[23] UNTOC (n 16) art 5. [24] UNTOC (n 16) art 2(a). [25] UNTOC (n 16) art 2(c).

crime' nor of TOC.[26] Yet, as detailed below, commonly rebels, insurgents, terrorists, and other parties to a political conflict finance their fight through involvement in benefit-orientated organized crime. Hence, the UNTOC might even apply in such circumstances. Conversely, other international criminal law, such as anti-terrorist conventions, may apply to acts that have been perpetrated by members of drug-trafficking organizations or other criminal networks.

C. Impacts and Linkages

Against this background, it is important to roughly understand the impacts that are attributed to TOC and the potential linkages between the groups involved.

1. Impacts

Due to the manifold legal, institutional, and socio-economic conditions for its flourishing, TOC has a series of direct and indirect impacts on countless actors in both the private and public sphere.[27] In most instances these impacts are negative, yet difficult to quantify and qualify. There is often no suitable data available on such secretive practices and structures.

Although it is true that TOC is a pervasive phenomenon, involving perpetrators and victims from all social classes, an important qualification has to be made with regard to those *modi operandi* that generate profits through the organized exploitation of human beings: the so-called 'modern forms of slavery' such as forced labour, debt bondage, domestic servitude, or sex slavery. They are often linked to human trafficking as another multibillion-dollar industry. The hundreds of thousands or even millions of victims of such commercial exploitation belong almost exclusively to marginalized groups. While these crimes must not always be transnational in nature, they can be observed all over the world. Yet it is in the countries of the global South, where the vulnerability for victimization tends to be considerably higher. There, extreme poverty, social inequality and exclusion often go hand in hand with dysfunctional State institutions, incapable or simply unwilling to offer these persons a reasonable degree of protection and resilience.

It is also in fragile and failed States of the global South where the criminal groups involved in TOC tend to be more predatory and violent. The general rule that they avoid the use of violence to not attract the attention of the authorities is often inapplicable, when some of the above-mentioned contributing factors accumulate, particularly if embedded in societies with parochial structures and traditionally low respect for formal

[26] See, however, UNTOC (n 16) art 3.

[27] See, for a more profound insight, Thomas Feltes/Robin Hofmann, 'Transnational Organised Crime and its Impacts on States and Societies' in Hauck/Peterke (n 2).

rules, or ridden by armed conflicts or the consequences thereof.[28] In that sense, the power 'of organized criminal groups to a large extent depends upon the strength and weakness of the states involved'.[29]

A case in point is illegal drug markets. The majority of them are relatively peaceful,[30] albeit harmful to societies. However, Mexico, Colombia, and many other Latin American countries are nowadays afflicted with outrageous drug-related violence. The worst atrocities are usually confined to those areas whose control is disputed between local gangs or other rivalling actors, the State's security forces included. Entrenched in the countries' prison systems or 'zones of impunity', yet connected to transnational drug-trafficking organizations, the ruling crime groups may even pay 'foot soldiers' for defending their turf against competitors or sporadically intervening law enforcement agencies, often kept away by corruption and threats.[31]

Interestingly, it is also in these extreme settings where certain positive impacts of TOC are easier to observe. It is less the fact that such illegal structures offer a considerable number of people a variety of jobs and incomes, but rather the often-neglected circumstance that their uncontested rule may have certain stabilizing effects. Through implementing 'social policies' in the form of financial assistance for the poorest, promotion of cultural events, etc, and avoiding unforeseeable, arbitrary actions against the obedient local population, they may even achieve greater social acceptance than the State. As in the case of the Italian mafias, territorial crime groups may therefore be viewed as phenomena of parallel governance or even quasi-governmental structures.[32] At the same time it must not be ignored that their existence and success are based on forced reciprocity, secured through corruption and other illicit activities which connect these 'underworld groups' with the 'upper world'.[33]

The long-term impacts of such situations however can be dramatic, destabilizing whole societies and endangering ongoing processes of democratization and development. While the potential of criminal associations to infiltrate the highest levels of politics, public authorities or justice systems may often be overrated, it is the general idea that they have such power and influence that causes fear and horror in the broader public. This 'moral panic' is frequently nourished by mass media, pressuring governments to demonstrate their capacity to act through sensationalist coverage of the most shocking

[28] Francisco E Thoumi, 'The Relationship between Illegal Drugs and Violence: Is There a Cause and Effect?' (2009–2010) 5 LLILAS Portal 38–9; Susanne Karstedt, 'Organised Crime, Democracy, and Democratisation: How Vulnerable Are Democracies?' in Caroline Y Robertson-von Trotha (ed), *Organised Crime. Dark Sides of Globalization* (Nomos 2012) 96.

[29] Cyrille Fijnaut, 'Organised Crime in Europe and Beyond: Some General Considerations' in Robertson-von Trotha (n 28) 16.

[30] Peter Reuter, 'Systemic Violence in Drug Markets' (2009) 52 Crime Law and Social Change 275.

[31] See eg Sven Peterke, 'Urban Insurgency, "Drug War" and International Humanitarian Law: The Case of Rio de Janeiro' (2010) 1 Journal of International Humanitarian Legal Studies 165.

[32] Diego Gambetta, *The Sicilian Mafia: The Business of Private Protection* (Harvard UP 1993) 71. See also von Lampe (n 17) 201–12.

[33] See eg Enrique D Arias, *Drugs and Democracy in Rio de Janeiro. Trafficking, Social Networks, & Public Security* (University of North Carolina Press 2006) 49.

crimes. These are fertile grounds for populist 'law-and-order' and discriminatory 'zero tolerance' politics that do not address the root causes but only 'militarize' public security.

Transnational organized crime also affects the efficiency of economic systems and therefore hampers both economic and sustainable development. Amongst others, it distorts free competition and reduces profits, be it directly, through racketeering activities or piracy, or indirectly, through the costs for prevention, repression or the reparation of damages that have been caused. Yet, caution is necessary with regard to general statements on this issue, too. The capacity of criminal enterprises to infiltrate the legal economy and to legitimize their proceeds through money laundering varies considerably from State to State. To that effect, criminal enterprises are, of course, opportunistic and practice 'forum shopping'.

Finally, the picture would be incomplete if one were to neglect the diverse impacts of TOC on nature. From illegal mining, the unauthorized dumping of toxic materials, to the illicit trafficking of wild flora and fauna,[34] these impacts may at times be truly devastating and far more harmful than counterfeit products or other forms of TOC.[35]

2. Linkages

The linkages between the groups that participate in TOC are as diverse as its impacts. Even before 9/11, States had turned their attention to the obscure interplay between TOC and other illegal non-State actors, especially terrorists and insurgents. There is little doubt that these groups may benefit from cooperative pacts for exchanging illegal goods and services. Indeed, such alliances exist, yet, due to the different objectives these actors pursue, they also pose distinct threats to States and societies. For this reason, the combined suppression of such 'dirty entanglements' has traditionally been viewed with great scepticism.[36] In the 1990s, this position slowly began to change. In academic writing, an important point of departure was the debate on so-called 'new wars', described as involving 'horizontal coalitions of local militia, break away units from disintegrating states, paramilitary and organized crime groups'.[37] The existence of 'war economies', in which the 'greed vs. grievance' dichotomy is essentially blurred, was increasingly perceived as a logical consequence of the end of the Cold War.[38] The chance that certain alliances between terrorist and organized crime groups may translate into processes of external (organizational) or even internal (motivational) convergences became theorized in the so-called 'crime–terror continuum'.[39]

[34] See Gus Waschefort, Chapter 33 in this *Handbook*.

[35] See eg Hennie Strydom, 'Transnational Organised Crime and the Illegal Trade in Endangered Species of Wild Fauna and Flora' in Hauck/Peterke (n 2).

[36] Bettina Weißer, 'Transnational Organised Crime and Terrorism' in Hauck/Peterke (n 2) 98.

[37] Mary Kaldor, *New and Old Wars: Organized Armed Violence in a Global Era* (Cambridge 1997) 16.

[38] Frank Madsen, *Transnational Organized Crime* (Routledge 2009) 65.

[39] Tamara Makarenko, 'The Crime–Terror Continuum: Tracing the Interplay between Transnational Organised Crime and Terrorism' (2004) 6 Global Crime 129.

After 9/11 the crime–terror nexus became a major issue on the international security agenda. To a great extent, this was due to the interest in countering the financing of terrorism and the conviction that the methods and tools for investigating the origins of these illegal funds would also prove useful for the suppression of drug-trafficking organizations, and vice versa. A merger of the 'wars' on terror and drugs into a 'war on organized crime' that would also include terrorists was therefore deemed promising.[40] In the meantime, research has shown that solid alliances between terrorist and organized crime groups are less common than often assumed.[41]

Yet it is quite safe to say that TOC 'can prolong and exacerbate conflict and stability or intensify its impacts on civil populations'.[42] It is therefore in the context of conflict or post-conflict situations where TOC is more and more perceived as a threat to international peace and security. Against this backdrop, the UNSC started entering into a series of 'experiments in international law enforcement',[43] that today go way beyond the targeting of the financial flows that fund terrorists and armed groups.[44] For example, it is now routine practice to equip peace operations with a mandate to counter TOC. Ironically, these missions have sometimes fuelled the local demand for certain illegal traffic, such as drugs and sex. Worse, peacekeepers have themselves been involved in organized crime and co-opted individuals with ties to criminal networks. This has not only undermined the already fragile confidence of the local populations in the efforts of the international community, it has also generated a debate on the so-called 'organized crime-peace operations nexus'.[45]

As TOC is essentially about money and power, politicians and State representatives are not immune from becoming involved in it. The traditional view is that such figures become corrupted and co-opted by the underworld for (not) taking certain decisions. The fear that drug-trafficking organizations may infiltrate such functional elites has stimulated a dubious debate on the potential emergence of 'narco-States'.[46] However, it has always been a fact, too, that governments not only clandestinely fund criminal groups, but also use them for all sorts of 'dirty jobs' abroad and at home. This includes the assassination of government members and opposition leaders, causing internal unrest for destabilizing countries, and making a case for direct and indirect interventions. There is rich evidence for the involvement of many Western governments in drugs and arms smuggling and the funding of insurgents and terrorists. A more

[40] Phil Williams, 'Terrorist Financing and Organized Crime: Nexus, Appropriation, or Transformation?' in Thomas J Biersteker/Sue E Eckert (eds), *Countering the Financing of Terrorism* (Routledge 2008) 133.

[41] Vanda Felbab-Brown, *Shooting up. Counterinsurgency and the War on Drugs* (Brookings Institution Press 2009).

[42] See eg UNSC Res 2388 (2017).

[43] James Cockayne, *The UN Security Council and Organized Criminal Activity: Experiments in International Law Enforcement* (Working Paper Series No 03, UN University 2014).

[44] eg UNSC Res 2312 (2016).

[45] Wibke Hansen, 'The Organized Crime–Peace Operations Nexus' (2015) 5 *PRISM* 63.

[46] Pierre-Arnaud Chouvy, 'The Myth of the Narco-State' (2016) 20 Space and Polity 26.

systematic debate on this issue was prompted in the late 1980s by famous US-criminologist William Chambliss, who coined the term 'State organized crime'.[47]

D. The International Legal Framework

With the growing recognition that the countering of TOC requires more intensive and effective international cooperation, an impressive international legal framework has been created. As it is composed of conventions and soft law documents of universal, regional, sub-regional, pluri- or simply bilateral reach, its systematic presentation[48] would exceed the purposes of the present contribution. Rather, the analysis will focus on the global level, where a series of 'core conventions' on TOC can be identified: namely the 1988 UN Convention against Illicit Traffic in Narcotic Drugs and Psychotropic Substances (1988 UN Convention),[49] the 2000 UNTOC and its three protocols, as well as the 2003 UN Convention against Corruption (UNCAC).[50]

1. United Nations Core Conventions on Transnational Organized Crime

While the 1988 UN Convention might be viewed as the starting point, this anti-drug-trafficking convention, instead of being the beginning, was rather the culmination of international legal responses to this delinquency, which stimulated the creation of a global drug control regime. Indeed, State practice concerning illicit drug trafficking can already be traced back to the 1912 Hague International Opium Convention[51] and most notably to the Geneva Convention of 1936 for the Suppression of the Illicit Traffic in Dangerous Drugs.[52] In Article 2 of this Convention, States Parties were required 'to make the necessary legislative provisions for severely punishing' acts like '(…) possession, offering (for sale), distribution, purchase, sale, delivery (…), brokerage, dispatch (in transit), transport, importation, and exportation of narcotic drugs'. Hence, trafficking in illicit drugs had to be established as a criminal offence at the domestic level, even though this was triggered by an international agreement. Subsequently, there seems to have been a political shift in that the 1961 Single Convention on Narcotic Drugs[53] mainly dealt with the legal control of narcotics in terms of administrative law rather than as criminal offences; it nevertheless contains provisions referring to criminal law: Article 4

[47] William J Chambliss, 'State-Organized Crime' (1989) 27 Criminology 183.

[48] See, for those details, Hauck/Peterke (n 2). [49] 1582 UNTS 95. [50] 2349 UNTS 41.

[51] 8 LNTS 187.

[52] 198 LNTS 299. cf Patrick Robinson, 'The Missing Crimes' in Antonio Cassese et al (eds), *The Rome Statute of the International Criminal Court: A Commentary* (Vol 1, OUP 2002) 498–9 and 523–4, listing the thirteen most important conventions.

[53] 520 UNTS 151.

creates 'general obligations' including domestic measures and international cooperation in the execution of the convention. Article 35(a) provides for 'arrangements at the national level for coordination of preventive and repressive action against the illicit traffic' and Article 36(1)(a) even stipulates a duty to ensure that all the aforementioned single acts of the 1936 Convention 'shall be punishable offences when committed intentionally'.[54] As such, this convention went beyond its predecessor by introducing provisions on money laundering and by exceeding the process of criminalization of drug trafficking by relating it to an international dimension.

At least since the 1961 Convention, which included explicit international cooperation provisions for the first time, international State practice has moved in a global direction. The main purpose of fulfilling the convention gradually became accompanied by the belief that the fight against drug trafficking could only be successful, when this crime was understood as an international phenomenon. The ratified measures included special provisions aiming at the transgressing character of international trafficking on a domestic scale. This comprehension is reflected in the provisions of the 1988 UN Convention establishing universal jurisdiction in a hitherto unknown understanding: Articles 4 (Jurisdiction), 6 (Extradition), 7 (Mutual Legal Assistance), and 8 (Transfer of Proceedings).[55]

Since then, developments have not stopped: The UN produced widely accepted resolutions covering illicit drug trafficking as a worldwide problem that need to be implemented through domestic and international strategies.[56] Action plans were drawn up and the year 2008 was set as a target date for all States with a view to eliminating illicit trafficking.[57]

The 2000 UNTOC is designed to be the premier global crime suppression convention in the fight against organized crime.[58] But instead of defining TOC, it relies on a double strategy of only criminalizing basic crimes (such as money laundering, corruption, and obstruction of justice[59]) and membership of an 'organized criminal group', whether acting transnationally or not. The importance of the latter condition primarily lies in triggering the convention's provisions on international cooperation (including joint investigations, extradition, and mutual legal assistance). However, as indicated above, due to its compromise nature and the challenge of grappling with a variety of legal traditions, it ultimately contains rather vague obligations so that the strength of the UNTOC (its flexibility due to its broad scope) is also its weakness because it cannot be used to prescribe to States Parties what to criminalize.[60] Another example is the obligation to establish the responsibility of legal persons, such as corporations or labour unions, involved in TOC. Their criminalization *stricto sensu* for involvement in such delinquency is '[s]ubject to the legal principles of the State Party[:] the liability of legal

[54] Convention on Psychotropic Substances 1019 UNTS 175 arts 21 and 22 share the same content.

[55] Similarly, Robinson (n 52) 499.

[56] UNGA Res 20/2 (10 June 1998).

[57] ibid paras 13–14.

[58] Neil Boister, 'The UN Convention against Transnational Organised Crime 2000' in Hauck/Peterke (n 2).

[59] UNTOC (n 16) arts 5, 8, and 23.

[60] Boister (n 58) 149.

persons may be criminal, civil or administrative'.[61] Furthermore, States Parties still have not agreed to a mechanism to review implementation.[62] Accordingly, the UNTOC faces the risk of being nothing more than a paper tiger.

Three supplementary protocols, the Protocol to Prevent, Suppress, and Punish Trafficking in Persons (2000),[63] the Protocol against the Smuggling of Migrants by Land, Sea, and Air (2000),[64] and the Protocol against the Illicit Manufacturing and Trafficking in Firearms, Their Parts and Components, and Ammunition (2001),[65] substantiate certain areas which the UNTOC left open. In these individual conventions, the specific misconduct of trafficking, smuggling and manufacturing is spelled out much more precisely. With regard to human trafficking and the smuggling of migrants, it is noteworthy that both documents are seemingly based on a holistic approach that recognizes the importance of preventing these crimes and respecting the rights of those exploited by criminal networks. The measures proposed to deal with the victims of human trafficking are, of course, far more detailed. Yet, they are not compulsory and the distinction introduced in treating smuggling and trafficking of human beings differently is often artificial in practice, because many migrants end up getting trafficked as a consequence of the vulnerability stemming from the fact that they entered another country illegally.[66]

The 2003 UNCAC contains both mandatory (such as the bribery of, or the embezzlement of, property by a public official) and non-mandatory (trading in influence or abuse of functions) criminal law provisions. These sections do not define the term corruption but circumscribe instead the phenomena by which corruption can appear. Though praised as a 'major step in the fight against corruption'[67] the political will to fully implement this convention is still missing, especially in those countries with a long history of political and grand corruption.[68]

2. Other Relevant International Regimes and Issues

In addition, TOC is addressed by other international regimes that deal with transnational crimes more generally. Here only a select few can be briefly mentioned.

[61] UNTOC (n 16) art 10(2). [62] Boister (n 58) 147.

[63] 2247 UNTS 319. Hans-Joachim Heintze/Charlotte Lülf, 'The UN Protocol to Prevent, Suppress, and Punish Trafficking in Persons (2000)' in Hauck/Peterke (n 2).

[64] 2241 UNTS 507. Andreas Schloenhardt, 'The UN Protocol against the Smuggling of Migrants by Land, Sea and Air (2000)' in Hauck/Peterke (n 2).

[65] 2326 UNTS 208. Aaron Fellmeth, 'The UN Protocol against the Illicit Manufacturing and Trafficking in Firearms, Their Parts and Components, and Ammunition (2001)' in Hauck/Peterke (n 2).

[66] Anne T Gallagher, *The International Law of Human Trafficking* (CUP 2010) 52; see also Vladislava Stoyanova, Chapter 21 in this *Handbook*.

[67] Michael Kubiciel/Anna C Rink, 'The United Nations Convention against Corruption and its Criminal Law Provisions' in Hauck/Peterke (n 2).

[68] ibid 237 with further references.

First, TOC often involves money-laundering activities and hence is subject to the pertinent international regime[69] that began evolving from 1989 onwards, when the G-7 commissioned a Financial Action Task Force (FATF) to look at the issue and make recommendations to fight this problem.[70] It was supposed to be a temporary task force with the mandate 'to assess the results of cooperation already undertaken in order to prevent the utilization of the banking system and financial institutions for the purpose of money laundering, and to consider additional preventive efforts in this field, including the adaptation of the legal and regulatory systems so as to enhance multilateral judicial assistance'.[71] The FATF's organizational framework today comprises the FATF, FATF-style Regional Bodies, and a range of international observer institutions that partner with the FATF to support the adoption and implementation of global anti-money laundering and combating terrorism financing (AML/CFT) standards.[72] In 2001, money-laundering control became fused with CFT.[73] In the wake of all these efforts, the relevant UN conventions set out the framework of the key money-laundering offences in general terms.[74] In this area, national and international cooperation is essential as well as the responsibility and engagement of the private (banking) sector.[75] Any assessment of whether these strategies have proven effective is difficult to undertake.[76]

Illegal trade in endangered species of wild fauna and flora also led to the conclusion of a convention, the 1973 Convention on the International Trade in Endangered Species of Wild Fauna and Flora (CITES).[77] In reality, there is a glaring gap between those commitments and compliance.[78] The 'pace, level of sophistication and globalized nature of wildlife and forest crime is beyond the capacity of many countries and individual organizations to address'.[79] Accordingly, these crimes still pose serious threats to the security, environment, and sustainable development of many countries.[80]

Transnational organized crime can also take the form of the sale of children, child prostitution, and pornography. The 1989 Convention on the Rights of the Child[81] has made a significant contribution to addressing this menace, particularly since the adoption of the 2000 Optional Protocol on the Sale of Children, Child Prostitution, and Child Pornography[82] on this subject matter.[83] Furthermore, globalized transnational

[69] Louis de Koker/Mark Turkington, 'Transnational Organisation and the Anti-Money Laundering Regime' in Hauck/Peterke (n 2).

[70] ibid 244.

[71] G7 Group of Nations, 'Economic Declaration, Paris Summit' (*G7 Research Group at the University of Toronto*, 16 July 1989) para 53 <http://www.g8.utoronto.ca/summit/1989paris/communique/index.html> accessed 28 August 2020.

[72] ibid 247. [73] ibid 241. [74] ibid 249. [75] ibid 252, 255. [76] ibid 259.

[77] 993 UNTS 243. Strydom (n 35) 264, 269. [78] ibid 275.

[79] Christian Nellemann et al (eds), *The Environmental Crime Crisis: Threats to Sustainable Development from Illegal Exploitation and Trade in Wildlife and Forest Resources* (2014 UNEP) 10.

[80] Strydom (n 35) 275. [81] 1577 UNTS 3. [82] 2171 UNTS 227.

[83] Thorsten Müller, 'Transnational Organised Crime and the Sale of Children, Child Prostitution, and Pornography' in Hauck/Peterke (n 2).

crime can be identified in the shape of crimes against cultural property[84] and, of course, in terms of cybercrime.[85]

Last but not least, attention must be drawn to the fact that TOC affects more established sub-areas of international law, including the international law on the use of force, international humanitarian law, and international human rights law. A case in point is the right to self-defence, the regulation of which by more or less clear-cut criteria, as stipulated in the UN Charter,[86] was a historic achievement. Until the terrorist attacks of 9/11 there was solid consensus between States and scholars that this right could not be invoked against such crimes, unless attributable to a State in accordance with the law of international responsibility. This consensus has begun to crumble.[87] It is now argued that an armed attack, as the core requirement to trigger the right to self-defence, may be committed by non-State actors, whether qualifying as terrorist or not.[88]

Moreover, an interface between TOC and international humanitarian law (IHL) is increasingly emerging due to the outlined crime–war nexus and the blurring of traditional paradigms with regard to the categorization of violent actors as belligerents. Even when applying internationally agreed criteria for the determination of a non-State party to an armed conflict, it can no longer be excluded that TOC groups may transform in such a way so as to achieve this legal status that implies both rights and duties.[89] In how far this is desirable is, of course, as controversial as the attempts to 'transnationalize' international human rights law for including the cross-border conduct of non-State actors by modifying some doctrinal concepts, such as jurisdiction or attribution of conduct, in order to avoid a direct horizontal effect of these obligations.[90]

E. Contemporary Challenges

The previous section has shown that there is no shortage of international instruments dealing with TOC. Many of them enjoy universal ratification. This is particularly true for the core conventions that have been in force for some time now. Yet it seems that TOC is on the rise. Is this impression correct and is the international community indeed

[84] Bernhard Kretschmer, 'Transnational Organised Crime and Cultural Property' in Hauck/Peterke (n 2).

[85] Dominik Brodowski, 'Transnational Organised Crime and Cybercrime' in Hauck/Peterke (n 2).

[86] Charter of the United Nations 1 UNTS XVI (UN Charter).

[87] Kimberly N Trapp, 'Can Non-State Actor Mount an Armed Attack?' in Marc Weller (ed), *The Oxford Handbook on the Use of Force in International Law* (OUP 2015).

[88] cf Karin Oellers-Frahm, 'What Matters Is the Armed Attack, not the Attacker' (2017) 77 Houston Journal of International Law 49.

[89] Sven Peterke/Joachim Wolf, 'International Humanitarian Law and Transnational Organised Crime' in Hauck/Peterke (n 2) 405.

[90] See eg Tilmann Altwicker, 'Transnationalizing Rights: International Human Rights in Cross-Border Contexts' (2018) 29 EJIL 581.

failing in the fight against these 'dark forces of globalization'? What needs to be improved and what are the latest developments in this respect on the international level?

Due to the lack of consensus of what exactly constitutes TOC and the above-mentioned difficulties to empirically qualify and quantify the myriad phenomena associated with it, it would be hypocritical to suggest that there is an academically satisfying answer to the question whether TOC is flourishing in such a way as to pose a serious threat to global security. Undoubtedly, the trafficking of drugs, human beings, and arms, as well as many other criminal activities, affect almost all States and societies today. Their control through international cooperation therefore is of common interest. This is a mammoth task requiring permanent and sustainable efforts on very different levels of responsibility and intervention.

With regard to the universal level, it is first of all important to appreciate that the international community has reacted to the challenges posed by TOC by setting up a regime of global security governance based on the international instruments described above.[91] This regime, which still might be regarded as emerging, has contributed not only to the harmonization of national legislation and the streamlining of cooperation procedures in criminal matters, but also to a more strategic and holistic approach to TOC. Institutionally, it is composed of a net of specialized international organs and organizations, including the UN Office on Drugs and Crime (UNODC). Created in 1997 as the Office for Drug Control and Crime Prevention, the UNODC today plays a key role in the coordination and supervision of the implementation processes of the UN conventions on TOC.[92] With its headquarters in Vienna, it closely collaborates with other UN bodies and intergovernmental organizations, such as the Commission on Crime Prevention and Criminal Justice[93] (which is its governing body[94]) or the Enforcement Committee of the World Customs Organization.[95] Amongst others, UNODC offers financial and technical assistance to governments and conducts relevant research. Today, it has country, liaison, project, and (sub)regional offices all over the world and operates in more than 150 countries.[96]

Nevertheless, no international 'police' exists with powers to investigate or arrest persons suspected to be involved in TOC, or to search and seize their assets. The main task of the International Criminal Police Organisation founded in 1923, today known as INTERPOL, essentially consists of enhancing international police cooperation through

[91] The term 'global security governance' still lacks precise definition. See eg Emilian Kavalski, 'The Complexity of Global Security Governance: An Analytical Overview' (2008) 22 Global Society 423.

[92] Boister (n 1) 397.

[93] ECOSOC 'Establishment of the Commission on Crime Prevention and Criminal Justice' Res 1992/1 (6 February 1992).

[94] UNGA Res 61/252 (4 December 2006) 8.

[95] See eg Carsten Weerth, 'The Structure and Function of the World Customs Organization' (2009) 4 Global Trade and Customs Journal 131, 142.

[96] Details available, UNODC 'Field Offices' (2019) <www.unodc.org/unodc/en/field-offices.html?ref=menutop> accessed 10 August 2019.

its hi-tech infrastructure of technical and operational support.[97] Due to the lack of a truly international law enforcement authority, it is absolutely crucial to continuously collaborate with the respective international organs and organizations for keeping up with the diverse challenges of countering TOC and making global security governance more effective.

It might be stated, however, that the so-called 'securitization'[98] of the discourse on TOC has become a challenge itself. In the last thirty years, the notion that it represents a very serious security threat has been successfully internationalized despite numerous concerns and criticisms.[99] As a consequence, almost all regional and universal security organizations have put this issue high on their agendas. It is today taken almost as self-evident that TOC must be treated as a 'non-traditional' or 'soft' threat to international security, traditionally understood as regarding questions of territory and sovereignty (national security). Although the broadening of the concept of international security is not wrong in essence, in practice it often goes hand in hand with sometimes inaccurate assessments of instances of collective delinquency and armed violence and the promotion of a 'politics of fear'[100] that frequently serve as an effective tool for claiming broader policing powers and more financial and human resources for the security sector.

Of course, many violent conflicts and security crises can only be understood by taking into account the malign actions and effects of TOC. They typically affect so-called 'failing' or 'failed' States of the Global South more dramatically.[101] A significant number is plagued by 'war economies' that commonly nourish the most serious forms of TOC. It is therefore coherent that the UNSC, which has the primary responsibility for the maintenance of international peace and security, focuses its attention on the detrimental role of TOC around zones of conflict. One must not forget, however, that there are a great number of States that are not affected by any internationally recognized armed conflict, but nonetheless show extremely high indices of (organized) crime and violence. There, the notion of a 'war among people',[102] in which armed gangs and criminal networks play the role of 'public enemies', is not only a popular but a crucial factor for the framing of questionable law-and-order policies. Pacifying these 'militarized' environments is certainly a challenge that requires responses from all relevant levels of authority, including the global level. Whatever their costs and design, such interventions must always be intelligence-driven and based upon a qualified and holistic assessment of the situation

[97] Roraima Andriani, 'Interpol: The Front Lines of Global Cooperation' (2007) 23 Crime and Justice International (98) 4.

[98] Barry Buzan, 'New Patterns of Global Security in the Twenty-First Century' (1991) 67 International Affairs 431.

[99] David Cape, 'Transnational Crime' in Mely Caballero-Anthony (ed), *An Introduction to Non-Traditional Security Studies: A Transnational Approach* (SAGE Publications 2016) 212.

[100] Helena Carapiço, 'Transnational Organized Crime as a Security Concept' in Felia Allum/Stan Gilmour (eds), *Routledge Handbook of Transnational Organized Crime* (Routledge 2012) 27.

[101] Paula Miraglia et al, 'Transnational Organised Crime and Fragile States' (OECD Development Co-operation Working Paper 3/2012, October 2012) 4 <https://www.oecd.org/dac/accountable-effective-institutions/WP3%20Transnational%20organised%20crime.pdf> accessed 20 May 2020.

[102] Peterke/Wolf (n 89) 403.

in loco, taking into consideration the specific cultural, legal and socio-economic conditions of a country or (sub)region.

From the international perspective, an essential point in this exercise is to respect State sovereignty and to promote the rule of law. This is usually achieved through strictly adhering to the procedures of international cooperation. An important condition for its smooth and relatively speedy functioning is the universal ratification of international conventions. In this respect, much progress has been achieved during the last two decades. Despite this success, there are still some international instruments that have not received universal acceptance, such as the 2001 Protocol against the Illicit Manufacturing and Trafficking of Firearms,[103] for example.[104] In other areas, such as cyber-criminality, there is no sufficient consensus amongst States to create such instruments so far.[105] And even those conventions that have attracted a vast number of States cannot necessarily be considered true success stories: they often lack effective implementation by many States Parties. A case in point is the 1988 UN Convention.[106] Now in force for roughly forty years, it has not measured up to the expectations that were placed on it by its framers.

Generally speaking, it is too easy to criticize certain States for being unwilling to comply with their international obligations. The same might be true for pointing to the traditional problems of international cooperation, such as lack of confidence in the other side, language barriers, and obscure national competencies, although these issues are often troublesome realities. Again, the problem is far more complex. For instance, some States with traditionally fragile institutions and problems in securing their national borders, have been pushed by the United States and other Western States into 'suppression conventions', without having the necessary resources and capacities to put them into practice.[107] They may have hoped to receive financial and technical assistance for slowly solving these deficiencies, but this has never really materialized or has been done without sustainable efforts. Whether this is the fault of a specific government is often difficult to answer. Yet, it seems safe to say that capacity-building is a challenge that must be taken more seriously on the enforcement level. If a country's law enforcement agencies are overtaxed with relatively simple forms of crime and violence, it cannot be expected that they will successfully confront more sophisticated forms of crime. Long-term

[103] 2326 UNTS 208.

[104] Ratification status: 118 (10 August 2019) <https://treaties.un.org/Pages/ViewDetails.aspx?src=IND&mtdsg_no=XVIII-12-c&chapter=18&lang=en> accessed 10 August 2019.

[105] There are, however, currently six regional agreements on this subject matter, amongst them, the Council of Europe 2001 Convention on Cybercrime ETS No 185, also open to ratification and accession by non-Member States (see arts 36–7 of the Convention). It has sixty-three Parties, including Japan and the USA. Its 2002 Additional Protocol, concerning the criminalization of acts of a racist and xenophobic nature committed through computer systems, ETS No 189, has thirty-two Parties.

[106] Christine Jojarth, *Crime, War, and Global Trafficking. Designing International Cooperation* (CUP 2009) 138.

[107] Jan van Dijk, *The World of Crime: Breaking the Silence on Problems of Security, Justice and Development Across the World* (SAGE Publications 2008) 318; David P Steward, 'Internationalizing the War on Drugs: The UN Convention against Illicit Traffic in Narcotic Drugs and Psychotropic Substances (1990) 18 Denver Journal of International Law and Policy 387.

solutions that adequately combine preventive and repressive approaches in the light of available resources must therefore be envisaged.

F. Outlook

This chapter has discussed the various forms of TOC as a phenomenon as well as the different ways by which international law is responding to such crimes. It has become clear that the international legal framework has contributed to the fight against TOC to a certain extent. But this analysis has also shown that these international legal measures are facing serious implementation problems. It has been admitted here that TOC may also pose, in extreme cases, a threat to global security, although one has to be very cautious with such a statement.

Transnational organized crime will probably exist as long as mankind lasts and there is no patent remedy for its suppression. However, solely relying on criminal law or international law or any other legal institution would clearly impose exaggerated expectations on the law. Neither global justice nor global security policy can solve this problem alone. The stabilization of weaker States, the consolidation of international cooperation, and real efforts towards achieving a global social policy could prove more effective in order to obviate the incentives and to avoid the reasons to commit TOC. Today, it remains as true as it ever was that, in Franz von Liszt's words, the best crime policy is good social policy.[108]

[108] Franz von Liszt, *Das Verbrechen als sozial-pathologische Erscheinung. Vortrag gehalten in der Gehe-Stiftung zu Dresden am 10. Dezember 1898* (Pöschel and Trepte 1899) 22, 168.

INTERNATIONAL SECURITY

CHAPTER 13

AGGRESSION

CLAUS KREß

A. Introduction

The concept of aggression has been gaining prominence since the end of the First World War. In its 1919 report to the Preliminary Peace Conference, the Commission on the Responsibility of the Authors of the War and on Enforcement of Penalties concluded as follows:

> The premeditation of a war of aggression, dissimulated under a peaceful pretence, then suddenly declared under false pretexts, is conduct which the public opinion reproves and which history will condemn, but by reason of the purely optional character of the institutions at The Hague for the maintenance of peace... a war of aggression may not be considered as an act directly contrary to positive law, or one which can be successfully brought before a tribunal such as the Commission is authorized to consider under its terms of reference.[1]

Simultaneously, the Commission placed aggression on the international legal policy agenda and stated: 'It is desirable that for the future penal sanctions should be provided for such grave outrages against the elementary principles of international law.'[2] While the League of Nations Covenant did not include provisions on international 'penal sanctions', the concept of aggression was taken up in its Article 10.[3]

The concept of (external) aggression had, however, not been defined in the Covenant. In the inter-war period, four different approaches to capture the essence of the concept can be discerned. Under the first model, as articulated in the Covenant itself and Article 1 of the 1923 Draft Treaty of Mutual Assistance,[4] aggression was linked to the infringement upon two distinct legal rights of States: political independence and territorial integrity. The second model consisted of the juxtaposition of aggression and defence,

[1] The text is reprinted in (1920) 14 AJIL 95, 118. [2] ibid 120. [3] 108 LNTS 188.

[4] Article 1 of the Draft Treaty of Mutual Assistance, in Stefan Barriga/Claus Kreß (eds), *The Travaux Préparatoires of the Crime of Aggression* (CUP 2012) 119.

as, for example, in Article 2 of the 1924 American Draft Treaty of Disarmament and Security.[5] Thirdly, aggression was defined as a violation of existing undertakings, including procedural restraints on the waging of war. This was the approach of Article 10 of the 1924 Geneva Protocol for the Pacific Settlement of Disputes.[6] Fourthly, the 1933 Soviet Draft Definition[7] relied on the priority principle. None of these models, however, proved capable of laying the ground for an international consensus definition. To the contrary, doubts regarding the very idea of defining aggression were raised. Perhaps best remembered is a statement made by the British Foreign Minister Chamberlain in 1927 that to define the aggressor would amount to 'a trap for the innocent and a signpost for the guilty'.[8]

This scepticism regarding the definition of aggression prevailed during the drafting of the UN Charter. As a result, apart from not defining it,[9] the Charter accords only limited significance to the concept of aggression within the legal regime governing the use of force by States:[10] Article 2(4), the prohibition of the threat or use of force, does not include the term 'aggression'.[11] Neither does Article 51 UN Charter.[12] This provision recognizes the right of self-defence, which, apart from the collective security system, constitutes the only exception to the Article 2(4) prohibition. In fact, the perception that, in view of the inter-war experience, it would have been difficult to produce a satisfactory consensus definition, was an important consideration in choosing the English term 'armed attack' instead of 'aggression' in Article 51.[13]

Article 39, the opening clause of the Charter's collective security system, contains the term 'act of aggression', the existence of which in a given case falls to be determined by the UN Security Council (UNSC).[14] Recalling Article 39, the UN General Assembly (UNGA), in 1974, adopted a definition of aggression (1974 Definition of Aggression).[15] As the term 'act of aggression' is used alongside the terms 'threat to peace' and 'breach of the peace' in Article 39, the UNSC is not bound to determine the existence of an act of aggression to activate the Charter's collective security system and authorize the use of force by one or more States in order to maintain or restore international peace and security (see Section B).

[5] Reprinted in Benjamin B Ferencz, *Defining International Aggression. The Search for World Peace. A Documentary History and Analysis*, vol I (Oceana Publications 1975) 124.

[6] Reprinted in Barriga/Kreß (n 4) 120.

[7] Maxim Litvinov (Union of Soviet Socialist Republics) 'Definition of Aggression', Doc. Conf. D/C.G.38, XIII:2 Monthly Summary of the League of Nations (1933), Annex. Reprinted in Barriga/Kreß (n 4) 126.

[8] HC Deb 24 November 1927, vol 210, col 2105.

[9] On the proposals to do so: Thomas Bruha, 'The General Assembly's Definition of the Act of Aggression' in Claus Kreß/Stefan Barriga (eds), *The Crime of Aggression: A Commentary* (vol I, CUP 2017) 146; Ferencz (n 5) 37–9, 285–361.

[10] On this regime, see Elizabeth Wilmshurst, Chapter 45 in this *Handbook*.

[11] cf League of Nations Covenant (n 3) art 10.

[12] 1 UNTS XVI. The French version of art 51 uses the concept 'agression armée'.

[13] Tadashi Mori, *Origins of the Right of Self-Defence in International Law. Form the Caroline Incident to the United Nations Charter* (Brill 2018) 225–8; Tom Ruys, *'Armed Attack' and Article 51 of the UN Charter. Evolutions in Customary Law and Practice* (CUP 2010) 60–8.

[14] UN Charter (n 12) art 53(1), containing a reference to the concept of 'aggressive policy', has, in that specific respect, become obsolete; Jürgen Bröhmer/Georg Ress, 'Article 53' in Bruno Simma et al (eds), *The Charter of the United Nations: A Commentary* (vol II, 3rd edn, OUP 2012) 1522–3.

[15] UNGA Res 3314(XXIX) (14 December 1974).

In the view of the International Court of Justice (ICJ)[16] and the International Law Commission (ILC),[17] the prohibition of aggression forms part of customary international law. Here again, though, the distinct legal significance of the concept compared to 'use of force' and 'armed attack' is of quite limited reach (see Section C). Contrariwise, the concept of aggression has been of considerable importance in the realm of international criminal law *stricto sensu*[18] since the latter's inception. In both the Nuremberg and Tokyo Tribunals' judgments, the concept of war of aggression constituted the State conduct element of a crime against peace on which the judges relied in reaching their convictions.[19] The UNGA in the Friendly Relations Declaration[20] confirmed that 'a war of aggression constitutes a crime against the peace', reconfirming this position in the 1974 Definition of Aggression.[21] Article 16 of the ILC Draft Code of Crimes against the Peace and Security of Mankind (1996 ILC Draft Code of Crimes),[22] substitutes the title 'crime of aggression' for 'crime against peace' and the concept of aggression for that of war of aggression in order to denote the State conduct element of that crime. The title 'crime of aggression' has been retained in the Rome Statute of the International Criminal Court (ICC Statute) and in particular in Article 8 *bis*, adopted in 2010 and containing the first explicitly articulated definition of the crime in a binding legal document.[23]

B. Act of Aggression under Article 39 UN Charter

1. The Legal Significance of the Concept of Act of Aggression within the UN Charter Collective Security System

A determination of an act of aggression by the UNSC paves the ground for the activation of the collective security system. If the relevant further conditions are fulfilled,

[16] *Barcelona Traction, Light and Power Co, Ltd (New Application: 1962) (Belgium v Spain)* (Judgment) [1970] ICJ Rep 3 [34].

[17] James Crawford, *The International Law Commission's Articles on State Responsibility. Introduction. Text and Commentaries* (CUP 2002) 246, 248.

[18] For international criminal law *stricto sensu*, see Claus Kreß, 'International Criminal Law' in Rüdiger Wolfrum (ed), *Max Planck Encyclopedia of Public International Law* (vol V, OUP 2012) 717–32.

[19] Carrie McDougall, 'The Crimes Against Peace Precedent' in Kreß/Barriga (n 9) 52–78.

[20] Declaration on Principles of International Law Concerning Friendly Relations and Co-operation among States in Accordance with the Charter of the United Nations, UNGA Res 2625 (XXV) (24 October 1970) principle 1(2) 2.

[21] UNGA Res 3314 (XXIX) (n 15) art 5(2), first sentence.

[22] Text and commentary are reprinted in Barriga/Kreß (n 4) 197–9; for the run-up to the adoption of that Draft Code, see James Crawford, 'The International Law Commission's Work on Aggression' in Kreß/Barriga (n 9) 234–8.

[23] For a comprehensive documentation of the negotiations, see Barriga/Kreß (n 4); for detailed scholarly analyses, see Kreß/Barriga (n 9) vols 1 and 2.

the Council may adopt enforcement measures including the authorization of the use of force by States.[24] Given that Article 39 is worded in the alternative though, the determination of an act of aggression by the UNSC is not a necessary condition for the activation of the Charter's collective security system: The Council may also adopt enforcement measures on the basis of the existence of a threat to the peace or a breach of the peace.

2. 'Act of Aggression' as a Legal Concept

Article 39 of the UN Charter grants the UNSC discretion. Even if the Council finds that the conditions for a determination of the commission of an act of aggression are present, it does not have to make such a determination. This is not to say, however, that the UNSC is free to give whatever meaning it wishes to the concept of an act of aggression.[25] Whatever the difficulties in construing it, 'act of aggression' in Article 39 constitutes an international legal concept[26] to which the recognized methods of treaty interpretation, including that due attention is given to the subsequent practice of States, apply.

3. Indications Regarding the Meaning in the UN Charter and the 1974 Definition of Aggression

a. *'Use of Force by a State'*

According to Article 1(1) of the UN Charter an act of aggression involves a breach of the peace. Assuming that the concept of 'peace' within the UN Charter means the absence of organized use of force, an act of aggression would necessarily presuppose a use of force. Yet, especially in view of State practice after the end of the Cold War, the definition of 'peace' is no longer unchallenged.[27] It is therefore not possible to conclude with certainty on the basis of the Charter's text alone that an act of aggression presupposes a use of force.

Any remaining doubts are dispelled, however, if Articles 1(1) and 39 of the UN Charter are read together with the 1974 Definition of Aggression.[28] It has been said that this

[24] On the UNSC 'authorization model', Niels Blokker, 'Outsourcing the Use of Force: Towards More Security Council Control of Authorized Operations' in Marc Weller (ed), *The Oxford Handbook of the Use of Force in International Law* (OUP 2015) 202–13.

[25] Nico Krisch, 'Article 39' in Simma et al (n 14) 1276.

[26] *Prosecutor v Dusco Tadic* (Decision) IT-94-1-AR72 (2 October 1995) para 29.

[27] Krisch (n 25) 1277–8.

[28] On UNGA Res 3314 (XXIX) generally, see Bengt Broms, 'The Definition of Aggression' (1977) 154 RdC 299; Bruha (n 9) 142–77; Thomas Bruha, *Die Definition der Aggression. Faktizität und Normativität des UN-Konsensbildungsprozesses der Jahre 1968 bis 1974 zugleich ein Beitrag zur Strukturanalyse des Völkerrechts* (Duncker/Humblot 1980); Constantin T Eustathiades, 'La Définition de l'Agression Adoptée aux Nations Unies et la Légitime Défense' (1975) 28 RHDI 5; Ahmed M Rifaat, *International Aggression. A Study of the Legal Concept: Its Development and Definition in International Law* (Almqvist/Wiksell International 1979) 222–80; Julius Stone, 'Hopes and Loopholes in the 1974 Definition of Aggression' (1977) 71 AJIL 224; Jaroslav Zourek, 'Enfin une Définition de l'Agression' (1974) 20 AFDI 9.

document 'does not bind the Security Council at all',[29] which is correct in the sense that the 1974 Definition of Aggression as a UNGA resolution is not binding upon the UNSC. Yet, the 1974 Definition of Aggression was adopted by consensus to provide the UNSC with guidance regarding its power under Article 39 to determine whether an act of aggression has been committed.[30] Therefore, it constitutes at the very least a supplementary means of interpretation within the meaning of Article 32 of the Vienna Convention on the Law of Treaties (VCLT)[31] regarding the interpretation of the concept of act of aggression in Article 39 of the UN Charter.

The generic definition contained in Article 1 of the 1974 Definition of Aggression closely follows the formulation of Article 2(4) UN Charter,[32] while the addition of the word 'armed' makes it unambiguous that non-physical coercion is not enough. Furthermore, and other than the non-exhaustive list of examples set out in Article 3, the definition under Article 1 of the 1974 Definition of Aggression is not subject to a different determination by the UNSC in a given case. The 1974 Definition of Aggression has therefore 'ended the discussion on "economic" and "ideological" aggression'.[33] By not reproducing the term 'threat', as used in Article 2(4) UN Charter, Article 1 of the 1974 Definition of Aggression makes clear that a threat of force does not amount to an act of aggression. Finally, this provision construes the term 'act of aggression' as conduct by a State.[34]

The international legal term of 'use of force' is not free from complexity.[35] It does not only imply the use of brute force but also includes the internationally unlawful presence of a State's military with a hostile intent in another State's territory. This is evident from the inclusion of invasions, (maritime) blockades, and the unlawful extension of the extra-territorial presence of armed forces originally sent with the agreement of the receiving State, in *litterae* (a), (c), and (d) in the list of examples of acts of aggression in Article 3 of the 1974 Definition of Aggression. As was already mentioned, (armed) force within the meaning of Article 1 of the 1974 Definition of Aggression refers to a physical effect and therefore excludes, for example, economic coercion. It is not necessary, however, that the physical effect be brought about by the release of kinetic force or the use of a weapon in any technical sense. All that is required is the use of an instrument capable of causing such an effect in a sufficiently direct manner. It is therefore possible for a State to convert a civil aircraft or a computer into an instrument for the use of force within the meaning of Article 1 of the 1974 Definition of Aggression.

b. *'Against the Sovereignty, Territorial Integrity or Political Independence of Another State, or in any other Manner Inconsistent with the Charter of the United Nations'*

As a rule, the prior valid consent of the State directly affected by the use of force negates the existence of a use of force 'against the sovereignty, territorial integrity or political

[29] Bruha (n 9) 166. [30] cf UNGA Res 3314 (XXIX) (n 15) preambular para 10.
[31] 1155 UNTS 331. [32] For the invariably minor deviations, see Bruha (n 9) 158–9.
[33] ibid 159. [34] The explanatory note on the term 'State' is reprinted in Barriga/Kreß (n 4) 181.
[35] For more detail, see Claus Kreß, 'The State Conduct Element' in Kreß/Barriga (n 9) 424–9.

independence of another State, or in any other manner inconsistent with the Charter of the United Nations', and by necessary implication the existence of an act of aggression. To the contrary, certain uses of force, which pursue a benign purpose, are not as such excluded from the concept of act of aggression.[36]

c. *'In the International Relations'*

The prohibition to use of force in Article 2(4) UN Charter only applies in the international relations of States. While not reproduced in Article 1 of the 1974 Definition of Aggression, this part of the provision remains implicit therein. Consequently, the use of force by a State against its own population on its own soil does not constitute an act of aggression.

The paradigmatic case of a use of force by a State in its international relations is one that occurs in the territory of another State. If the sovereign title to a certain piece of territory is disputed between two States, the prohibition in Article 2(4) UN Charter protects the State that exercises de facto control over the territory concerned. Therefore, a State that uses force to settle the dispute and to (re)gain control over the disputed territory violates Article 2(4) UN Charter, even if that State holds the sovereign title to the territory concerned. As a matter of systematic interpretation, this important point of law follows from the interplay of paragraph 4 with paragraph 3 of Article 2 of the UN Charter.[37] Subsequent State practice has confirmed this interpretation on several occasions. Paragraph 4 of Principle 1 of the 1970 Friendly Relations Declaration reads as follows:

> Every State has the duty to refrain from the threat or use of force to violate the existing international boundaries of another State *or as a means of solving international disputes, including territorial disputes and problems concerning frontiers of States* (emphasis added).

Both in the Falklands case (1982)[38] and the Eritrea–Ethiopia conflict (1998–2000),[39] this interpretation of the prohibition of the use of force prevailed.[40] Similarly, a State uses force in its international relations and thus within the meaning of Article 2(4) of the UN Charter if it hereby 'violate[s] international lines of demarcation, such as armistice lines,

[36] For more detail, see Kreß (n 35) 429–32.

[37] Olivier Corten, *The Law Against War. The Prohibition of the Use of Force in Contemporary International Law* (Hart 2012) 149.

[38] See UNSC Res 502 (1982) preambular para 3.

[39] Eritrea-Ethiopia Claims Commission, *Jus Ad Bellum—Ethiopia's Claims 1–8* (Partial Award) (2005) 26 RIAA 457, 465.

[40] This interpretation is without prejudice to the possibility, pursuant to UNGA Res 3314 (XXIX) (n 15) art 3(a), to qualify a military occupation, which has resulted from an unlawful (Kreß (n 35) 441) invasion or attack, as an act of aggression, and to the possibility to exercise, without undue delay (Kreß (n 35) 470–1) the right of individual and collective self-defence against such occupation.

established by or pursuant to an international agreement to which it is a party or which it is otherwise bound to respect',[41] provided that these lines run between two States.[42]

State, including the latter's armed forces or embassies, also concerns the international relations of those two States.[43] Such use of force may occur on the high seas as well as in the territory of the State that uses force.

Law enforcement action by a State on its own soil against foreigners does not, however, constitute a use of force in its international relations, irrespective of whether such action is lawful. At the same time, Article 3(d) of the 1974 Definition of Aggression covers the 'attack by the armed forces of a State on the… marine and air fleets of another State'. This demonstrates that a use of force within the meaning of Article 2(4) UN Charter may be directed against private targets belonging to another State. This raises the question whether a massive lethal attack by a State on its own soil directed against a group of nationals of another State without even the slightest appearance of a law enforcement character constitutes a use of force under Article 2(4) UN Charter so that it might amount to an act of aggression. While it is not inconceivable, as a matter of textual and teleological interpretation, such a broad reading of the prohibition of the use of force in the absence of an appreciable amount of supporting State practice remains controversial. This—in addition to the non-inclusion in Article 3(d) of the 1974 Definition of Aggression of that instance of a use of force—makes the qualification of such conduct as an act of aggression presently very doubtful.

d. *Two Forms of an 'Indirect' Use of Force*

Article 3(f) of the 1974 Definition of Aggression is sometimes referred to as circumscribing a case of 'indirect' aggression.[44] From the perspective of internal consistency of the list of examples in Article 3, *littera* f is problematic because it covers State conduct which would be more properly characterized as aid or assistance in the commission of an unlawful use of force by another State within the meaning of Article 16 of the ILC Articles on State Responsibility (ARSIWA) and customary international law.[45] The ILC has emphasized that 'the assisting State is responsible for its own act in deliberately assisting another State to breach an international obligation by which they are both bound' and that '[i]t is not responsible, as such, for the act of the assisted State'.[46] Against this backdrop, *littera* f has to be interpreted narrowly to preserve the highest possible degree of internal consistency within Article 3. The State conduct described in *littera* f

[41] Friendly Relations Declaration (n 20) principle 1(5), first sentence.

[42] Eritrea-Ethiopia Claims Commission (n 39) 467.

[43] Concurring Corten (n 37) 150–1; for a different view, Albrecht Randelzhofer/Oliver Dörr, 'Article 2(4)' in Bruno Simma et al (eds), *Charter of the United Nations: A Commentary* (vol I, 3rd edn, OUP 2012) 214–16.

[44] Rifaat (n 28) 273. The accuracy of the term 'indirect' is doubtful, hence it is placed in inverted commas.

[45] For detail on State practice, see Helmut Philipp Aust, *Complicity and the Law of State Responsibility* (CUP 2011) 91–7.

[46] Paragraph 10 in the commentary on Article 16 in Crawford (n 17) 151.

requires, first, that this State place a part of its territory at the disposal of another State. Secondly, this other State must use this territory for the perpetration of an act of aggression. Thirdly, the aggressor State within the meaning of *littera* f must have allowed the other State to make use of the territory placed at the latter's disposal for the perpetration of the act of aggression. Regarding the first requirement, it is not necessary that the State place the part of its territory at the disposal of the other State *with the intent* that this other State may use the territory for an act of aggression. As far as the second requirement is concerned, *littera* f does not specify the kind of act of aggression to be perpetrated by the other State; hence no restriction exists in that respect. Importantly, *littera* f describes the third requirement as 'the *action* of a State of *allowing* its territory... to be used...', instead of referring to the 'non-prevention of...' by that State. This choice of words in *littera* f is meant to indicate that the relevant State conduct comes at least close to some form of active collusion. It follows that the aggressor State within the meaning of *littera* f must foresee the perpetration of the act of aggression by the other State. Secondly, the non-prevention of the act of aggression of the other State, per se, though perhaps unlawful, does not amount to the State conduct described in *littera* f. The situation is different only if such non-prevention, under the prevailing circumstances, constitutes implicit permission vis-à-vis the other State to perpetrate the act of aggression. By the same token, a State which has declared its genuine opposition to the aggressive use of its territory but fails to enforce this position vis-à-vis the other State does not 'allow its territory... to be used...' and does not therefore commit an act of aggression within the meaning of *littera* f.

The inclusion of Article 3(g) of the 1974 Definition of Aggression (often referred to as 'indirect' aggression)[47] was particularly controversial during the negotiations, especially as far as the substantial involvement-limb was concerned. *Littera* g requires, first, that 'armed bands, groups, irregulars or mercenaries... carry out acts of armed force against another State of such gravity as to amount to the acts listed above'. Secondly, the aggressor State must have either 'sent' such persons or been 'substantially involved' in such sending. The categories of persons listed in *littera* g comprise all those who do not qualify as *de jure* or de facto organs of a State under Articles 4–6 ARSIWA.[48] The use of the term 'sending' suggests that those persons must move from the territory of the aggressor State across this State's border to carry out their acts of armed force. They will either move into the territory of the victim State or to a place where they can carry out acts of armed force against the land, sea, or air forces, or marine and air fleets of another State.[49] This also applies in case of the alternative State conduct of substantial involvement. While it is unclear in the English version of *littera* g whether this substantial involvement must be in the acts of armed force or in the sending, the French version

[47] eg Elena Sciso, 'L'aggressione indiretta nella definizione dell'Assemblea Generale delle Nazione Unite' (1983) 66 Rivista di diritto internazionale 253.

[48] For the delineation between the terms 'armed forces by a State' and 'armed bands, groups, irregulars, or mercenaries', see Kreß (n 35) 437–8.

[49] cf Maurice Kamto, *L'Aggression en Droit International* (Pedone 2010) 53–4, for whom attributability is all that matters.

unambiguously refers to the substantial involvement in the sending. The term 'armed force' in *littera* g should be given the same meaning as the term 'force' in Article 2(4) UN Charter. The qualification of 'gravity' is ambiguous, as the descriptions of the acts of aggression listed in 3(a)–(f) do not invariably imply the need for a certain gravity. Nevertheless, the emphasis on 'gravity' in *littera* (g) is not to be ignored and should be understood to exclude relatively minor incidents.

The 'sending' by a State of persons falling under *littera* g should be interpreted in conformity with the test of attribution under Article 8 ARSIWA. In that context, the ICJ requires effective control over specific acts: a very demanding threshold.[50] The unhappily worded[51] alternative of the 'substantial involvement' of a State 'in the sending' should, at the present stage of legal development at least, be confined to the exercise of overall control by the aggressor State over the persons concerned. Overall control was developed by the International Criminal Tribunal for the former Yugoslavia (ICTY) to mean control that goes 'beyond the mere financing or equipping... and involv[es] also participation in the planning and supervision of military operations'.[52] It is controversial whether the overall control test forms part of the customary international law on attribution. If this is answered in the negative,[53] the substantial involvement-limb of Article 3(g) of the 1974 Definition of Aggression should best be considered as *lex specialis* on attribution in the context of the prohibition of the use of force. It is true that the ICJ has so far refrained from elaborating upon the meaning of 'substantial involvement in the sending',[54] and its case law does not lend support to an interpretation that covers the exercise of overall control. However, to reject such a construction would be tantamount to rendering this alternative of *littera* g redundant.[55] Beyond that, the ordinary meaning of 'substantial involvement' is wide enough to cover even the (mere) toleration by a State of acts of armed force carried out by non-State actors from its territory against another State. The negotiations on the resolution lend some support to such a wide interpretation, since 'substantial involvement' replaced the proposal to require an 'open and *active* participation' (emphasis added). This interpretation could also be compatible with the State conduct described in *littera* f if the requirement is added that the State concerned placed part of its territory at the disposal of the violent non-State actors. Yet, for the following three reasons, 'substantial involvement' should, at the present stage, not be construed as extending to conduct beyond the exercise of overall control by a State over violent non-State actors. First, on closer inspection, there was no consensus

[50] *Application of the Convention on the Prevention and Punishment of the Crime of Genocide* (*Bosnia and Herzegovina v Serbia and Montenegro*) (Judgment) [2007] ICJ Rep 43 [400]–[407] (*Bosnian Genocide*).

[51] If a State does not send the group of persons concerned, there is no entity that sends those persons other than perhaps the leadership of the group itself. It is therefore difficult to make linguistic sense of the requirement of a substantial involvement in the sending of those persons.

[52] *Prosecutor v Tadic* (Judgment) ICTY-94-1-A (15 July 1999) para 145.

[53] *Bosnian Genocide* (n 50); contra, *Tadic* (n 52).

[54] Claus Kreß, 'The International Court of Justice and the "Principle of the Non-Use of Force"' in Weller (n 24) 584.

[55] eg Kamto (n 49) 55, who rejects the application of the overall control test under art 3(g), but fails to identify any independent scope of application for the alternative of 'substantial involvement in the sending'.

during the negotiations to give the term such a wide meaning.[56] Secondly, the ICJ has not so far demonstrated any inclination to adopt such a wide reading.[57] Thirdly, the USA's attempt following the 9/11 attacks to establish a new 'harbouring doctrine' of attribution has not met with a degree of approval within the international community sufficient to ascertain the existence of a new customary law rule on attribution—at least in the form of a *lex specialis* in the context of the prohibition of the use of force.[58]

e. *Instances of a Use of Force Beyond Article 3 of the 1974 Definition of Aggression*

According to Article 4 of the 1974 Definition of Aggression the list of acts in Article 3 is non-exhaustive. However, and because Article 4 only refers back to Article 3 ('the acts enumerated above'), any act of aggression qualified as such by the UNSC should still come within the general definition contained in Article 1 of the resolution.[59] It is impossible to come up with a comprehensive list of instances of use of force beyond Article 3, which may qualify as acts of aggression. By way of example, reference may be made to Article 3(d) to illustrate possible 'unlisted' instances of an act of aggression. *Littera* d covers some—but not all—sovereign extra-territorial emanations of the State. It omits, in particular, embassies and consulates. While the ICJ did not use the term 'aggression' in the *Tehran Hostages* case, it repeatedly used the term 'armed attack' to label the seizure of the US embassy in Tehran and the hostage-taking of its staff.[60]

f. *The Gravity Requirement*

Compared with Article 4, Article 2 'opens' the definition of the concept of 'act of aggression' in the opposite direction. This is true for the application of both Article 3, which contains a cross-reference to Article 2, and Article 1. Most importantly, Article 2 explicitly refers to the need for a use of force to be of 'sufficient gravity' in order to qualify as an act of aggression. This aligns with the preambular paragraph 5 of the Resolution, which states: 'aggression is the most serious and dangerous form of the illegal use of force'. The explicit stipulation of a gravity requirement in Article 2 in connection with the preamble is important because such a requirement is not implicit in all instances of

[56] For a meticulous analysis, see Bruha (note 28) 228–39. [57] Kreß (n 54).

[58] For detail, see Christian Henderson, *The Persistent Advocate and the Use of Force. The Impact of the United States upon the Jus ad Bellum in Post-Cold War Era* (Ashgate 2010) 153–70. In Claus Kreß, *Gewaltverbot und Selbstverteidigungsrecht nach der Satzung der Vereinten Nationen bei staatlicher Verwicklung in Gewaltakte Privater* (Duncker/Humblot 1995) 314–19, this author supported the existence of a *lex specialis* on attribution, extending slightly beyond the overall control test and based this position mainly on the 'substantial involvement-limb' in article 3(g) of the 1974 Definition of Aggression. In light of the analysis of subsequent State practice, as provided in Henderson, *The Persistent Advocate* 153–70, this author is no longer fully convinced that the case for such a *lex specialis* is strong enough. For a different view in light of the more recent practice, see Christian J Tams, 'The Use of Force against Terrorists' (2009) 20 EJIL 359, 385ff.

[59] Bruha (n 9) 166.

[60] *Case Concerning United States Diplomatic and Consular Staff in Tehran* (*United States of America v Iran*) (Judgment) [1980] ICJ Rep 3 [57], [64], [91].

possible acts of aggression listed in Article 3. The gravity threshold is not specified any further than by indicating that the sufficient gravity may result either from the act of aggression itself or from the consequences of the act. By making the lack of sufficient gravity only one of 'other relevant circumstances', Article 2 opens the definition even further. The lack of a reprehensible (collective) intent underlying the act could be one possible relevant circumstance other than gravity.

g. *The Unlawfulness of the Use of Force*

A use of force by a State must be internationally unlawful to qualify as an act of aggression under Article 39 UN Charter. While the Charter does not say so explicitly, the 1974 Definition of Aggression contains three compelling indications to that effect: Article 1 requires a use of force 'inconsistent with the Charter of the United Nations'; Article 2 speaks of a use of force 'in contravention of the Charter'; and Article 6 states that '(n)othing in this Definition shall be construed as in any way enlarging or diminishing the scope of the Charter, including its provisions concerning cases in which the use of force is lawful'. That the unlawfulness of the relevant State conduct is inherent in the concept of 'act of aggression' is buttressed by the fact that 'aggression' by a State has invariably been understood as implying unlawfulness since the early attempts to define the concept in the 1920s.[61]

Importantly, Article 6 of the resolution reveals that the attempt made by thirteen non-aligned countries to clarify the conditions under which a use of force is lawful under international law[62] remained unsuccessful. In fact, the 1974 Definition of Aggression remains silent regarding the 'cases in which the use of force is lawful'.[63]

4. The Practice of the Security Council

The UNSC is the organ with exclusive power to determine the existence of an act of aggression in order to activate the collective security system. The Council's practice and the reactions by Council Members and other States to this practice therefore constitutes at the very least a supplementary means of interpretation under Article 32 VCLT regarding the interpretation of 'act of aggression' in Article 39 UN Charter.

To date, the UNSC has not explicitly referred to the 1974 Definition of Aggression.[64] The Council has also been reluctant formally to determine the existence of an act of aggression under Article 39 UN Charter. The Council's preference to avoid such a determination became particularly clear in the case of Iraq's invasion of Kuwait, which the Council condemned 'only' as a 'breach of international peace and security'.[65] At the same time, the UNSC has repeatedly referred to 'acts of aggression' or 'aggressive acts' in its

[61] For those early attempts, see Section A.

[62] For the text of the draft proposal, see Ferencz (n 5) vol 2, 331–3.

[63] Article 7 adds constructively ambiguous language concerning, *inter alia*, the question of the lawfulness of a foreign State's use of force in support of a colonized people.

[64] Bruha (n 9) 168.

[65] UNSC Res 660 (1990) preambular para 2.

resolutions.[66] For example, while the Council abstained from determining that Iraq, by invading Kuwait, had committed an act of aggression, it nevertheless condemned Iraq for having perpetrated 'aggressive acts' in the form of 'acts of violence against diplomatic missions and their personnel' and 'violations of diplomatic premises and the abduction of personnel enjoying diplomatic immunity and foreign nationals'.[67] This latter example reveals that the UNSC will not use the term 'aggressive' only in the context of use of force of an extraordinary magnitude or duration. In fact, its practice so far has not shed much further light on the gravity threshold under the 1974 Definition of Aggression.

While the UNSC has predominantly used the terms 'act of aggression' and 'aggressive acts' in the context of conduct falling within at least one of the categories of Article 3 of the 1974 Definition of Aggression, it appears to have occasionally gone beyond that list.[68] Exceptionally, the UNSC has even used this terminology without clearly identifying a State as the author of the relevant use of force.[69] Such practice, however, is insufficient for establishing the Council's intention to deviate from the 1974 Definition of Aggression.

5. The Practice of the General Assembly

Overall, the UNGA has been less reluctant than the UNSC to use the term 'act of aggression', while it has also explicitly referred to its 1974 Definition of Aggression.[70] It has, for example, declared that 'Israel's decision ... to impose its laws, jurisdiction and administration on the occupied Syrian Golan Heights constitutes an act of aggression under the provisions of Article 39 of the Charter of the United Nations and General Assembly resolution 3314 (XXIX)'.[71] Nonetheless, the UNGA has also not been consistent in its practice. It has, for example, abstained from declaring that the Russian Federation's use of force in, and annexation of, Crimea in 2014 constituted an act of aggression under Article 39 UN Charter.[72] The same is true for Turkey's Military Operation 'Peace Spring' in Syria beginning in 2019.[73]

6. The International Court of Justice

The ICJ has yet to find a State responsible for committing (an act of) aggression. The Court has also not formulated a definition of '(an act of) aggression'. It has, however, repeatedly referred to the 1974 Definition of Aggression to interpret the concept of

[66] For a comprehensive analysis of the UNSC practice until April 2015, see Nicolaos Strapatsas, 'The Practice of the Security Council Regarding the Concept of Aggression' in Kreß/Barriga (n 9).

[67] UNSC Res 667 (1990) preambular paras 4–6, para 1. [68] Strapatsas (n 66) 186–91.

[69] ibid 183–5. [70] Bruha (n 9) 168. [71] UNGA Res ES-9/1 (5 February 1982) para 2.

[72] cf UNGA Res 68/262 (27 March 2014).

[73] Turkey's use of force has, however, been condemned as 'aggression' by the League of Arab States; see Resolution 8454, adopted by the Council of the League of Arab States (12 October 2019), and enclosed in (28 October 2019) UN Doc A/74/516–S/2019/818.

armed attack within the meaning of Article 51 UN Charter.[74] Most importantly, the ICJ, in the *Nicaragua* case, has devised a gravity threshold for the concept of armed attack, using language conspicuously similar to that of preambular paragraph 5 of the 1974 Definition of Aggression.[75] This could suggest that the ICJ, while it has so far—fortunately[76]—abstained from saying that 'armed attack' and 'act of aggression' are congruous concepts, believes that the same gravity requirement applies to both. In this context, it should be noted that the Court in the *Oil Platforms* case said that it did 'not rule out the possibility that the mining of a single military vessel might be sufficient to bring into play the 'inherent right of self-defence'.[77] This is significantly less stringent than the words 'most serious and dangerous form of the illegal use of force' in preambular paragraph 5 of the 1974 Definition of Aggression would *prima facie* appear to suggest. This would be relevant with respect to 'act of aggression', too, assuming that the ICJ wishes to maintain its jurisprudence to adopt the same gravity threshold for 'armed attack' and 'act of aggression'.

7. Conclusion

An act of aggression under Article 39 UN Charter presupposes an unlawful use of force by a State of a certain gravity. While it is difficult at the present stage to specify this gravity requirement, the practice of the UNSC and the ICJ case law would not appear to suggest that the use of force must be of an extraordinary magnitude or duration.

C. Aggression and Aggravated State Responsibility for a Serious Breach of a Peremptory Norm

According to the second sentence of Article 5(2) of the 1974 Definition of Aggression 'aggression gives rise to international responsibility', regulated by the customary law of State responsibility for internationally wrongful conduct. An unlawful use of force by a State need not, however, rise to the level of aggression to trigger State responsibility.

[74] For detail, see Dapo Akande/Antonios Tzanakopoulos, 'The International Court of Justice and the Concept of Aggression' in Kreß/Barriga (n 9) 218–24.

[75] *Military and Paramilitary Activities In and Against Nicaragua (Nicaragua v United States of America)* (Merits) [1986] ICJ Rep 14 [191].

[76] As is clear from Article 6 of the 1974 Definition of Aggression, there was no agreement amongst the drafters of that definition that by defining the concept of (act) of aggression they would by necessary implication define the concept of armed attack. For example, the important question as to whether the concept of armed attack necessarily involves the conduct by a State cannot be answered in the affirmative simply by reference to the fact that the concept of (act of) aggression implies State activity.

[77] *Case Concerning Oil Platforms (Iran v United States of America)* (Judgment) [2003] ICJ Rep 161 [72].

In fact, the ICJ recognized both in the *Nicaragua* and the *Armed Activities* cases that a violation of the prohibition to use force creates an obligation of the offending State to make reparation to the victim.[78] Yet, under Article 40 ARSIWA a 'serious breach by a State of an obligation arising under a peremptory norm of general international law'[79] triggers an aggravated regime of State responsibility,[80] within which aggression falls.[81] Article 41(2) ARSIWA states that '(n)o State shall recognize as lawful a situation created by a serious breach within the meaning of article 40, nor render aid or assistance in maintaining that situation'.[82] Even these special duties do not, however, articulate legal consequences distinctive of aggression if compared with a use of force not rising to that level. Whenever a territorial acquisition has resulted from a use of force third States have a customary duty not to recognize it. It is then difficult to see how the rendering of aid or assistance in maintaining such acquisition would not amount at least to implicit recognition.[83] Yet, under Article 41(1) ARSIWA, aggression also gives rise to a duty of all other States 'to cooperate to bring to an end through lawful means any serious breach within the meaning of article 40'.[84] To concretize this duty is no doubt difficult. Nevertheless, it is worth noting that it constitutes a distinct legal consequence of (an act) of aggression.

According to the ILC, aggression 'by (its) very nature require(s) an intentional violation on a large scale'.[85] However, neither has the Commission specified this gravity requirement any further, nor has it clarified whether it considers 'aggression' in the sense of a 'serious breach by a State of an obligation arising under a peremptory norm of general international law' and 'act of aggression' under Article 39 UN Charter identical. To date, the ICJ has not clarified those matters, either.[86] The Court referred to the concept of (act of) aggression in its groundbreaking *obiter dictum* on obligations *erga omnes* in the *Barcelona Traction* case, but without specifying its meaning.[87] The ICJ has not so far found that a State has committed (an act of) aggression. In the *Armed Activities* case, the Court instead found that Uganda's use of force in the Democratic Republic of the Congo

[78] *Nicaragua* (n 75) [292(13)]; *Armed Activities on the Territory of the Congo (DRC v Uganda)* (Judgment) [2005] ICJ Rep 168 [259]–[60], [345(5)].

[79] cf Article 40 ARSIWA in Crawford (n 17) 245.

[80] This regime has taken the place of the previous idea of a category of 'international crime of State', which met with firm opposition by several States. The special regime under ARSIWA arts 40 and 41 avoids any connotation of criminal law; see James Crawford, 'International Crimes of States' in James Crawford (ed), *The Law of International Responsibility* (OUP 2010) 405–14.

[81] Crawford (n 17) 246, 248. To date it remains an open question whether the prohibition of the use of force forms part of *jus cogens*. In *Nicaragua*, the ICJ has referred to a statement made by the ILC in 1966 that such is the case, but without endorsing it; *Nicaragua* (n 75) [190]. In the course of its subsequent work, the ILC has accorded the status of *jus cogens* only to the prohibition of aggression; see André de Hoogh, '*Jus Cogens* and the Use of Armed Force' in Weller (n 24) 1168–9.

[82] Crawford (n 17) 249.

[83] cf Friendly Relations Declaration (n 20) principle 1(10). The Assembly has recalled that duty, for example, in its resolution 'Territorial Integrity of Ukraine' UNGA Res 68/262 (n 72) preambular para 3.

[84] For an analysis of those duties, see Nina HB Jorgensen, 'The Obligation of Non-Assistance to the Responsible State' and 'The Obligation of Cooperation' in Crawford (n 80).

[85] Crawford (n 17). [86] Also, Akande/Tzanakopoulos (n 74) 225–6.

[87] *Barcelona Traction* (n 16) [34].

(DRC) constituted a 'grave violation of the prohibition on the use of force expressed in Article 2, paragraph 4, of the Charter' due to its 'magnitude and duration'.[88]

D. The Crime of Aggression

Since 17 July 2018, the International Criminal Court (ICC) can exercise its jurisdiction over the crime of aggression.[89] This date marks the end of a long and thorny journey, which began after the First World War. At the final stage of this journey, which commenced with the Rome Statute negotiations in 1995, two starting points were largely uncontroversial: The crime of aggression requires State conduct in contravention of the prohibition of the use of force and criminalization only extends to the leadership level. A number of other questions had given rise to long enduring controversies. The fundamental political tension underlying all those controversies was the desire of (typically) militarily weaker States for maximum protection from the use of force by foreign States vis-à-vis the fear of (typically) militarily more powerful States that their liberty of action in matters deemed of vital national importance might be curtailed. Hence, a first choice had to be made between various term(s) of reference: 'war of aggression', 'use of force', 'armed attack', 'act of aggression', 'aggression' or some combination thereof and/or addition thereto. A second and closely related issue concerned whether a generic definition or a list of the relevant forms of State conduct or a combination thereof was more appropriate. Finally, it had to be decided whether the UNSC should be authorized to determine the existence of the State conduct element of the crime.

1. 'An Act of Aggression which, by its Character, Gravity and Scale, Constitutes a Manifest Violation of the Charter of the United Nations'—The State Conduct Element

Article 8 *bis*(1) of the ICC Statute defines the crime of aggression as follows:

> For the purpose of this Statute, 'crime of aggression' means the planning, preparation, initiation or execution, by a person in a position effectively to exercise control over or to direct the political or military action of a State, of an act of aggression

[88] *Armed Activities* (n 78) [165]. For critical remarks on the non-characterization of Uganda's use of force as aggression, see Separate Opinion of Judge Elaraby ibid [9]–[20], and Separate Opinion of Judge Simma ibid [3].

[89] Claus Kreß, 'On the Activation of ICC Jurisdiction over the Crime of Aggression' (2018) 16 JICJ 1; also Darin Clearwater, 'When (and How) Will the Crime of Aggression Amendments Enter into Force?' (2018) 16 JICJ 31.

which, by its character, gravity and scale, constitutes a manifest violation of the Charter of the United Nations.

The first sentence of Article 8 *bis*(2) defines the concept of act of aggression for the purpose of paragraph 1 by adopting the language of Article 1 of the 1974 Definition of Aggression. The second sentence of Article 8 *bis*(2) stipulates that all the acts contained in Article 3 of the 1974 Definition of Aggression shall qualify as an act of aggression within the meaning of the generic definition. Article 8 *bis* thus chooses the term 'act of aggression' as the starting point for the definition of the State conduct element of the crime. The definition of the term 'act of aggression' for the purposes of Article 8 *bis* closely follows that in the 1974 Definition of Aggression. As in the case of the latter's Article 1, the existence of an act of aggression for the purposes of Article 8 *bis* requires an unlawful use of force by a State. As in the case of Article 3 of the 1974 Definition of Aggression, the list of instances of acts of aggression in Article 8 *bis*(2) is non-exhaustive.[90] This does not mean that a determination of the UNSC to qualify, in accordance with Article 4 of the 1974 Definition of Aggression, as an act of aggression a certain State conduct, not envisaged by the list, would also bind the ICC. To the contrary, Articles 15 *bis*(9) and 15 *ter*(4) of the ICC Statute state that '(a) determination of an act of aggression by an organ outside the Court shall be without prejudice to the Court's findings under this Statute'. The same must hold true with respect to a decision by the UNSC, in accordance with Article 2 of the 1974 Definition of Aggression, not to qualify an unlawful use of force by a State as an act of aggression, 'in light of other relevant circumstances'. At the same time, there are good reasons in support of the view that the ICC should construe the concept of act of aggression within the meaning of Article 8 *bis* of the ICC Statute in light of the gravity requirement set by the 1974 Definition of Aggression.[91] It is doubtful, however, whether the answer to the question if a certain gravity threshold is implicit already in the very concept of act of aggression is really significant in view of the specific and more demanding gravity requirement posed by Article 8 *bis*(1) of the ICC Statute. Article 8 *bis*(1) chooses the concept of act of aggression only as the starting point for the definition of the State conduct element of the crime of aggression. It also requires that the act of aggression must, 'by its character, gravity and scale, constitute(s) a manifest violation of the Charter of the United Nations'. This threshold clause, the insertion of which was central to reach the consensus, serves a double function.[92] In its qualitative dimension ('manifest by its character'), it aims to exclude from the definition those uses of force that fall in one of the grey areas surrounding the prohibition of the use of force. In its quantitative dimension ('manifest by its gravity and scale'), it requires a use of force of a certain intensity.[93]

[90] The point is controversial, for a full exposition see Kreß (n 35) 435–6.

[91] For an exposition of these reasons, see Kreß (n 35) 426–9.

[92] For more detail: Kreß (n 35) 507–12; also Andreas Zimmermann/Elisa Freiburg, 'Article 8*bis*' in Otto Triffterer/Kai Ambos (eds), *The Rome Statute of the International Criminal Court. A Commentary* (3rd edn, CH Beck 2016) MN 50–86; Carrie McDougall, *The Crime of Aggression under the Rome Statute of the International Criminal Court* (CUP 2013) 124–30.

[93] For more detail on how the words 'character', 'gravity', and 'scale' play together, also in light of the Understanding Seven, as adopted at the Kampala Conference, see Kreß (n 35) 510–12.

2. The Quantitative Dimension of the Threshold Requirement

This intensity threshold is higher than the intensity threshold for an armed attack under Article 51 UN Charter.[94] The most important consideration[95] in support of such a high intensity threshold is that only such a high threshold ensures an interpretation of Article 8 *bis* of the ICC Statute in conformity with customary international law. The Nuremberg and Tokyo *acquis* on the State component of crimes against peace chiefly results from Article 6(a) of the 1945 London Charter,[96] Article 5(a) of the 1946 Tokyo Charter,[97] and Article II(1)(a) of 1945 Control Council Law No. 10[98] as applied in the 1946 Nuremberg and 1948 Tokyo Judgments, as well as in the case law under Control Council Law No. 10 subsequent to the Nuremberg Judgment. In the relevant texts, the State conduct element was described by reference to the concept of war of aggression, with the one possible exception of Article II(1)(a) of 1945 Control Council Law No. 10, which, in addition to wars, speaks of 'invasions'. It is impossible to ascertain a subsequent development of customary international criminal law departing from that standard. A close analysis of the negotiations on the crime of aggression does not support a different conclusion. Clearly, a significant number of States supported a broad definition of the State conduct element of the crime of aggression, perhaps even without any intensity threshold.[99] But the USA consistently articulated the view and eventually went on record at the Review Conference in Kampala to state that 'it is only a war of aggression that is a crime against international peace'.[100] The UK did the same in an elaborate statement on 12 June 2000.[101]

While the overwhelming majority of delegations did not support a reference to the term 'war', this does not mean that all of those delegations favoured the absence of an intensity threshold for the unlawful use of force or the formulation of a fairly low intensity

[94] cf text Section C. [95] For a number of further considerations, see Kreß (n 35) 514.

[96] 82 UNTS 279. [97] TIAS No 1589.

[98] Control Council Law No 10 on Punishment of Persons Guilty of War Crimes, Crimes Against Peace and Against Humanity (1946) 3 Official Gazette of the Control Council for Germany 50.

[99] See, in particular, the 1999 Proposal by Greece and Portugal, reprinted in Barriga/Kreß (n 4) 343; and the 2000 Proposal by Greece and Portugal, ibid 375.

[100] For the US statement at the Review Conference in Kampala, see 'Untitled, undated text, distributed by the US delegation after the meeting of the Working Group on the Crime of Aggression on 7 June 2010', reprinted in Barriga/Kreß (n 4) 751. A further attempt made by the USA to emphasize the existence of a high intensity threshold led, after certain modifications, to the adoption, at the Kampala Conference, of Understanding Six, which begins by stating, and taking up the language contained in the fifth preambular consideration of the 1974 Definition of Aggression, that 'aggression is the most serious and dangerous form of the illegal use of force'.

[101] Elizabeth Wilmshurst (UK Delegation), 'Statement at the Preparatory Commission for the International Criminal Court, Working Group on the Crime of Aggression' UK Mission to the United Nations (New York, 12 June 2000) (on file with the author); Wilmshurst has expressed essentially the same view in her private capacity in 'Definition of the Crime of Aggression: State Responsibility or Individual Criminal Responsibility?' in Mauro Politi/Giuseppe Nesi (eds), *The International Criminal Court and the Crime of Aggression* (Ashgate 2004) 95.

threshold. For example, Germany did not attach decisive importance to maintaining the term 'war', but insisted on the need to cover only 'attacks of a particular magnitude and dimension and of a frightening gravity and intensity'.[102] This latter approach is in line with that of the ILC, which in Article 16 of its 1996 Draft Code of Crimes does not use the term 'war', but nevertheless states in the commentary that the 'action of a State entails individual responsibility for a crime of aggression only if the conduct of the State is a sufficiently serious violation of the prohibition contained in Article 2, paragraph 4, of the Charter'.[103]

To properly construe the intensity threshold posed in Article 8 *bis*(1), one must therefore ascertain what is meant in substance by the concept of war in the context of international criminal law. A first distinction to be observed is that between war in the technical and the material sense, the former requiring (only) a declaration of war and the latter being contingent (only) upon the eruption of comprehensive hostilities.[104] In the context of the crime of aggression, the point of reference must be 'war in the material sense'. There is accordingly no indication that the Nuremberg or Tokyo Tribunals built their case law on the concept of 'war of aggression' on the issuance of declarations of war.[105] The concept of war in the material sense is not to be confined to full-scale hostilities in accordance with Hersch Lauterpacht's often-cited definition of war in *Oppenheim's International Law*.[106] Rather, the concept of material war, as the Tokyo Judgment has confirmed,[107] encompasses that of limited war. This includes the use of force, the goal of which 'may be confined to the defeat of only some segments of the opposing military apparatus; the conquest of certain portions of the opponent's territory (and no others); or the coercion of the enemy Government to alter a given policy (eg, the Kosovo Air Campaign of 1999)'.[108]

3. The Qualitative Dimension of the Threshold Requirement

As discussed in Section B.3.g of this chapter, the openly worded reference in Article 6 of the 1974 Definition of Aggression to 'cases in which the use of force is lawful' can be read as an implicit acknowledgement of the existence of grey legal areas surrounding those cases. The 1974 Definition of Aggression has done nothing to clarify the law in that respect. Instead, the matter was left to be dealt with by the UNSC on a case-by-case basis. Such an essentially political solution would be inappropriate in the context of

[102] 'Proposal Submitted by Germany: The Crime of Aggression—a Further Informal Discussion Paper', reprinted in Barriga/Kreß (n 4) 369.

[103] cf Section A, text accompanying n 22.

[104] Yoram Dinstein, *War, Aggression and Self-Defence* (5th edn, CUP 2011) 9, paras 16–19.

[105] Article 5(a) of the 1946 Tokyo Charter (n 97) even explicitly embraces the concept of war in the material sense by including 'undeclared' wars of aggression.

[106] Hersch Lauterpacht (ed), *International Law: A Treatise by Lassa Oppenheim* (vol 2, 7th edn, David McKay Company 1952) 202, para 54.

[107] For references, see Kreß (n 35) 518–19.

[108] Dinstein (n 104) 12, para 30.

international criminal law. On the other hand, there was also no prospect of overcoming the deeply entrenched controversies in the course of the negotiations leading to the adoption of Article 8*bis* of the ICC Statute. This explains the latter's requirement that the act of aggression, 'by its character', constitutes a manifest violation of the UN Charter. This excludes those instances of use of force from the State conduct element of the definition, the legality of which forms the object of genuine disagreement between reasonable international lawyers. The relevant grey areas include,[109] most importantly, the use of force in anticipation of an imminent armed attack, the use of force in response to an armed attack by non-State actors emanating from the territory of another State that is either unwilling or unable to put this armed attack to an end, the use of force to save the life or limb of nationals abroad in a case of imminent danger and as a last resort, and the use of force to defend a civilian population against a widespread or systematic attack on life and limb carried out by that population's own government.

This last instance, most often referred to as 'humanitarian intervention',[110] was lurking in the background of the negotiations. As a matter of principle, international criminal law *stricto sensu* would be subjected to a most delicate tension, if this body of law criminalized the decision made by one or more State leaders at a moment of overwhelming need to use force to stop the commission of crimes under international law in their gravest forms—namely, genocide or a particularly grave form of crimes against humanity. The attempt made by the USA, and supported by other delegations, failed to reach agreement on an Understanding stating explicitly that such use of force is excluded from Article 8 *bis*(1) of the ICC Statute by virtue of its threshold clause.[111] But essentially, such use of force is nevertheless not one that, 'by its character', 'manifestly' violates the UN Charter. First, such use of force, as the result of the more recent practice of States,[112] has entered in a grey legal area. Secondly, the inclusion of such use of force within the definition contained in Article 8 *bis*(1) of the ICC Statute would create a divorce between this definition and customary international law. By cutting its customary roots, it would thereby oddly situate Article 8 *bis*(1) outside international criminal law *stricto sensu*. As was recalled at the outset,[113] no consensus on the international legal concept of aggression had emerged before the trials of Nuremberg and Tokyo. Neither of the two judgments articulates an explicit definition of the aggression component of the concept of war of aggression. If one looks at those judgments more closely, the hard core of the Tribunals' understanding of the aggression component is as follows:

> (i) war with the object of the occupation or conquest of the territory of another State or part thereof; (ii) war declared in support of a third party's war of aggression; and

[109] For an attempt comprehensively to set out these areas, see Kreß (n 35) 457–502.

[110] See Simon Chesterman, Chapter 44 in this *Handbook*.

[111] For detail on the negotiations, see Claus Kreß et al, 'Negotiating the Understandings on the Crime of Aggression' in Barriga/Kreß (n 4) 94–7; Kreß (n 35) 524–5.

[112] This practice is set out in detail in Kreß (n 35) 489–502.

[113] Section A.

(iii) war with the object of disabling another State's capacity to provide assistance to (a) third State(s) victim of a war of aggression initiated by the aggressor.[114]

But on further inspection, the Nuremberg and Tokyo *acquis*, especially if read against the background of the various attempts to define aggression made in the inter-war period, also provides for considerable and therefore noteworthy potential pointing towards an understanding of the aggression component which extends beyond this core. This may explain why the commentary on Article 16 of the ILC 1996 Draft Code of Crimes, while relying on the Nuremberg precedent, does not confine the latter's content to the hard core built on the judgments' description of the adjudicated cases, but more openly requires a 'sufficiently serious violation of the prohibition contained in Article 2, paragraph 4, of the Charter of the United Nations'.[115] This was essentially the starting point for the negotiations on Article 8 *bis* of the ICC Statute. For, as the foregoing analysis makes clear, the aggression component of the concept of war of aggression had not undergone any appreciable customary development subsequent to Nuremberg and Tokyo up to that point. In particular, the 1974 Definition of Aggression had not only left untouched, by virtue of its Article 6, the controversies surrounding the 'cases in which the use of force is lawful', but it had also, by virtue of its Article 2, left open the possibility for the UNSC not to qualify the unlawful use of force as an act of aggression because of 'other relevant circumstances', including the absence of a certain *animus aggressionis*. This means that only the negotiations on Article 8 *bis* of the ICC Statute and on its threshold requirement can have crystallized a customary law definition of crimes of aggression which includes the use of force to defend a civilian population against a genocidal campaign or other attacks of the most serious nature. These negotiations have indeed, through a year-long exchange of legal positions between States, crystallized customary law regarding the definition of the State conduct element of the crime of aggression, which goes beyond the hard core of the Nuremberg and Tokyo precedent. Most importantly, the State conduct element of the crime of aggression under customary international criminal law no longer requires a collective intent to annex or occupy or to pursue another objective, which is unacceptable to the international community as a whole. The State conduct element of the crime of aggression under customary international criminal law does also not exclude any use of force carried out with the purpose of enforcing an existing international legal obligation. This, however, comes with one important *caveat*: In view of the clearly recorded opposition by the USA, as supported by a number of other delegations, to the inclusion of the use of force in defence of a civilian population against a genocidal campaign or other attacks of the most serious nature, no customary international law to the contrary has crystallized through the negotiations process.

[114] Carrie McDougall, 'The Crimes against Peace Precedent' in Kreß/Barriga (n 9) 77.
[115] Section A, text accompanying n 22.

E. Aggression: An International Legal Concept on the Move Towards Clarification?

The international legal concept of aggression, be it under Article 39 UN Charter, in the context of the customary law regime of aggravated State responsibility, or as a crime of aggression, presupposes an unlawful use of force by a State qualified by a certain seriousness. For the purposes of international criminal law, Article 8 *bis* of the ICC Statute, in conformity with customary law, requires that the intensity of the use of force reaches the level of a limited war and that the use of force does not fall in one of the grey areas presently surrounding the prohibition of the use of force. Whether this or some other threshold of seriousness applies to the concept of act of aggression in Article 39 UN Charter, and to the concept of aggression in customary law, as restated in Articles 40 and 41 ARSIWA, cannot be stated with certainty at this point of legal development. It is fairly safe to predict that both the UNSC and the ICJ will continue to refrain from qualifying as (an act of) aggression a use of force which falls within one of the grey legal areas surrounding the prohibition of the use of force. Regarding the intensity dimension of the use of force, a further clarification is conceivable in the three following ways through future practice: First, the UNSC could consolidate its previous practice to apply a fairly lenient intensity threshold for an act of aggression similar to that posed by the ICJ for the concept of armed attack. The latter might adopt the same threshold for the concept of aggression under the customary law of State responsibility. Alternatively, the ICJ would not adopt such a fairly lenient threshold in construing the concept of aggression under the customary law of State responsibility, but would rather seek to devise a threshold in line with that contained in Article 8 *bis* of the ICC Statute and the underlying customary international criminal law. Finally, both the UNSC, in determining acts of aggression under Article 39 of the UN Charter, and the ICJ, in applying the customary law governing State responsibility for aggression, could be inspired by the international criminal law threshold.

F. A Look Ahead

To date, the frequency by which the concept of aggression is referred to in the political discourse stands in sharp contrast to its significance in the international legal practice. Not one single time has the UNSC made the determination that a State has committed an act of aggression under Article 39 UN Charter and not once has the ICJ found that a State has violated the customary law prohibition of aggression. With respect to international criminal law, the findings made by the Nuremberg and Tokyo Tribunals seemed like isolated events no longer resonating today—until the ICC's jurisdiction over the crime was activated in 2018. While this undoubtedly constitutes a noteworthy change in the landscape of international criminal justice, its practical significance is yet to be seen. Due to political controversies, the ICC's jurisdiction over the crime of aggression was narrowly defined. It is universal only on the basis of a UNSC referral of the relevant situation. Otherwise, the Court's jurisdiction is essentially consensual and confined to acts of aggression committed by one State Party against another.[116] The recent breakthrough regarding the crime of aggression has therefore been characterized by one observer as being largely devoid of any practical significance, as constituting, 'by and large (…) an act of symbolic international "legislation"'.[117] That said, it is also conceivable that the practice of States and the international community as a whole will shift in the future. Yet questions remain open as to whether and how this would in turn influence the practice of the UNSC in making determinations on the existence of acts of aggression and/or the practice of the ICJ to concretize the idea of aggravated responsibility for State aggression, and as to whether those UN organs will, irrespective of the future evolution in the field of international criminal justice, proceed in new directions in their application of the concept(s) of (act of) aggression. It has been the modest ambition of this chapter to set out with as much conceptual precision as possible the current international legal framework within which future practices may unfold.

[116] For an analysis of the jurisdictional regime, see the three relevant chapters written by Stefan Barriga and Niels Blokker in Kreß/Barriga (n 9) 621–74; for the ultimate part of the struggle, see Kreß (n 89).

[117] Andreas Zimmermann, 'A Victory for International Rule of Law? Or: All's Well that Ends Well? The 2017 ASP Decision to Amend the Kampala Amendment on the Crime of Aggression' (2018) 16 JICJ 19, 28.

CHAPTER 14

ARMED CONFLICTS, INTERNATIONAL LAW, AND GLOBAL SECURITY

JAKOB KELLENBERGER

A. Introduction

The invitation to contribute to this *Handbook* with a chapter on armed conflict started with the sentence 'security has become the dominant issue of the 21st century'. While today it is clear that protracted non-international armed conflicts (NIACs) are the prevalent type of armed conflict, international armed conflicts (IACs) seem likely to again become a major threat to global security in the future. This hypothesis is based, amongst other factors, on recent military confrontations involving a number of States in Syria, Russian involvement in Crimea, US tensions with Iran and North Korea, and broader regional tensions in the South China Sea. The present contribution will first provide an overview of the interrelation between armed conflicts and other threats to global security, and will then conduct a selective 'tour d'horizon' of armed conflicts currently raging in various geographical regions of the world, before taking a step back to consider the adequacy and effectiveness of the existing international regulatory framework governing armed conflicts in light of the broader challenges facing the contemporary world order.

B. Armed Conflicts in the Broader Global Security Environment

In examining armed conflicts, this chapter adopts the 'classic' dichotomy between IACs and NIACs as understood in international humanitarian law (IHL) and relevant international jurisprudence.[1] This being said, the author expects that non-State and sub-State actors with access to advanced instruments of war and new methods of destabilization are likely to play an increasingly important role in the future. While not necessarily leading to an escalation of armed conflicts, the resulting confrontations are expected to contribute to a widespread proliferation of violence, insecurity, and instability below the level of full-blown war. Indeed, in recent years, the prevalence of situations of violence other than armed conflict and their social, economic, political, and humanitarian impact has been increasing rapidly, including in the world's megacities, or in the various contexts affected by the so-called 'drug wars'.[2] In light of the number of people affected by such violent situations, these have to be considered a threat to global security similar to (or perhaps bigger than) armed conflicts. For example, violence in Brazil since 2001 has been reported to have cost more lives than the wars in Iraq and Syria put together; and there are no signs of changing trends in this regard.[3] The line between armed conflicts and other situations of violence is increasingly blurred,[4] and even countries which refuse to recognize the existence of a NIAC increasingly involve the armed forces in the fight against organized criminals and other armed non-State actors.[5]

In this chapter, no distinction is made between 'human' and 'State' security';[6] 'armed conflicts'[7] are assessed as a security threat and compared with other security threats. In analysing the legal framework relevant to armed conflicts from a global security perspective, the UN Charter will be prioritized, given that it is the main legal instrument

[1] On the classification of conflicts, Jan K Kleffner, 'Scope of Application of International Humanitarian Law' in Dieter Fleck (ed), *The Handbook of International Humanitarian Law* (3rd edn, OUP 2013); Dapo Akande, 'Classification of Armed Conflicts: Relevant Legal Concepts' in Elizabeth Wilmshurst (ed), *International Law and the Classification of Conflicts* (OUP 2012) 32; Marko Milanovic/Vidan Hadzi-Vidanovic, 'A Taxonomy of Armed Conflict' in Nigel D White/Christian Henderson (eds), *Research Handbook on International Conflict and Security Law: jus ad bellum, jus in bello, and jus post bellum* (Edward Elgar 2015); see also, *Prosecutor v Dusko Tadic aka 'Dule'* (Decision on the Defence Motion for Interlocutory Appeal on Jurisdiction) IT-94-1 (2 October 1995) para 70; but cf Emily Crawford, 'Unequal Before the Law: The Case for the Elimination of the Distinction between International and Non-International Armed Conflicts' (2007) 20 Leiden Journal of International Law 441.

[2] For various perspectives, Kees Koonings/Dirk Kruijt, *Megacities: The Politics of Urban Exclusion and Violence in the Global South* (Chicago UP 2009); Alejandro Rodiles, 'Law and Violence in the Global South: The Legal Framing of Mexico's "NARCO WAR"' (2018) 23 JCSL 269, 269–70; see the chapters by Cecily Rose, Chapter 8, and Pierre Hauck/Sven Peterke, Chapter 12 in this *Handbook*.

[3] Tjerk Brühwiller, 'Die Blutspur durch Lateinamerika' (*Frankfurter Allgemeine Zeitung*, 19 May 2018).

[4] Rodiles (n 2) 269.

[5] For example, then Mexican President Felipe Calderón sent '4260 soldiers and 54 members of the Mexican navy, along with 1400 federal police forces' as part of the 2006 *Operación Conjunta Michoacán* 'to fight criminal organizations in the state of Michoacán', Rodiles (n 2) 271.

[6] While nevertheless drawing the reader's attention to the UNDP, *Human Development Report* (OUP 1994); see also Nigel D White/Auden Davies-Bright, Chapter 1 in this *Handbook*.

[7] For the notion of 'armed conflict', Tristan Ferraro/Lindsey Cameron, 'Article 2: Application of the Convention' in Knut Dörmann et al (eds), *Commentary on the First Geneva Convention: Convention (I) for the Amelioration of the Condition of the Wounded and Sick in Armed Forces in the Field* (ICRC/CUP 2016) (Geneva Convention Commentary); Lindsay Cameron et al, 'Article 3: Conflicts Not of an International Character' in Dörmann et al (eds) ibid.

aiming to maintain international peace and security by regulating (and outlawing) the threat or use of force between States (the *jus ad bellum*), most notably through key provisions such as Articles 2(4), 2(7), 42, and 51.

In contrast to the rules governing the use of inter-State force, the role played by IHL in relation to global security is less evident. It certainly cannot be denied that IHL can contribute to global security, in that greater respect for its rules in the course of armed conflicts would result in significantly fewer victims and less destruction, and facilitate reconciliation as a consequence.[8] Moreover, better protection of civilian infrastructure would greatly help economic and social recovery after an armed conflict. It must be stressed, however, that the aim of IHL remains the regulation and mitigation of armed conflicts, and not their prevention.[9] It is widely recognized, thus, that more efforts should be invested in the prevention of armed conflicts. Recognition alone, however, is not sufficient.

As far as international criminal law is concerned, a serious and truly universal fight against impunity for international crimes committed during armed conflicts, resulting in a high likelihood of prosecution, would probably have a preventive effect with regard to serious violations of IHL.[10] The world is still far from this utopia, however, and not even the establishment of the International Criminal Court (ICC) changed the fact that, in reality, the impact of criminal law continues to depend mainly on the extent to which alleged war criminals are prosecuted at the national level.[11] For as long as the fight against impunity both at the national and the international level is subject to double standards and cannot rely on genuine political commitment, no major contribution of international criminal law to greater respect for IHL can be expected.

While both international and non-international armed conflicts undoubtedly have a significant impact on any security environment, their role should not be examined in isolation, but must always be understood in conjunction with a panoply of other, often related, security threats,[12] such as economic and social threats including poverty, the widening gap between rich and poor, infectious diseases,[13] and environmental degradation; genocide and other large-scale atrocities;[14] nuclear, radiological, chemical

[8] Cordula Droege/Helen Durham, Chapter 20 in this *Handbook*.

[9] Mary-Ellen O'Connell, 'Historical Development and Legal Basis' in Fleck (n 1) 10.

[10] For the relationship between international criminal justice and security, Olympia Bekou, 'International Criminal Justice and Security' in Mary E Footer et al (eds), *Security and International Law* (Hart Publishing 2016).

[11] cf Jelena Pejic, 'Accountability for International Crimes: From Conjecture to Reality' (2002) 84 International Review of the Red Cross 13, 31–2.

[12] eg UNGA 'Report of the High-Level Panel on Threat, Challenges and Change: A More Secure World—Our Shared Responsibility' (2 December 2004) UN Doc A/59/565.

[13] J Benton Heath, Chapter 32 in this *Handbook*.

[14] Adama Dieng, Chapter 19 in this *Handbook*.

and biological weapons;[15] terrorism;[16] transnational organized crime;[17] climate change;[18] and large-scale migration.[19]

Moreover, the broader security impact of armed conflicts can be exacerbated by mass exportation of sophisticated weapons systems to regions of war and high tension, the Gulf region currently being the most prominent example.[20] When economic or political interests are at stake, exporting States seem prepared to turn a blind eye to the political regimes and human rights records of destination countries, thus seriously undermining and weakening the authority and credibility of the relevant international legal frameworks.[21] As reported by the Stockholm International Peace Research Institute (SIPRI), the volume of international transfers of mayor weapons rose by 10 per cent between 2009 and 2013 and 2014 and 2018. The flow of the arms to the Middle East grew by 87 per cent between 2008 and 2013 and 2014 and 2018.[22]

According to the World Forum's 2020 Global Risk Report, four out of the five top global risks by likelihood are climatic and environmental. Cyberattacks are also in the top ten.[23] For example, cyberattacks, as distinct from cyberwarfare, are undisputed front runners in any ranking of global risks. Indeed, according to the Swiss Re Institute's 'New Emerging Risks Insights' report, periodic and escalating cyberattacks 'are already becoming a regular occurrence', while further novel forms of conflict are expected to arise, including quite possibly also military conflict, even between major powers.[24] One need only consider the NIAC in Syria with the military involvement of various global and regional powers on opposing sides, the massive armament of the Gulf States, and the

[15] Masahiko Asada, Chapter 18 in this *Handbook*.

[16] Helen Duffy/Larissa van den Herik, Chapter 11 in this *Handbook*.

[17] Hauck/Peterke (n 2).

[18] Joyeeta Gupta/Hilmer Bosch, Chapter 30 in this *Handbook*.

[19] Ben Saul, Chapter 23 in this *Handbook*.

[20] Brian Chang, 'By Weakening Arms Export Controls, Trump's National Security Strategy Will Create National and Global Insecurity' (*Just Security*, 20 December 2017) <https://www.justsecurity.org/49873/weakening-arms-export-controls-trumps-national-security-strategy-create-national-global-insecurity/> accessed 7 December 2019.

[21] Arms sales by Western States to Saudi Arabia, despite the reports for widespread violations of IHL and IHRL by the Saudi-led coalition in Yemen, are a pertinent example. See Alessandra Asteriti, 'The Use of Cluster Munitions by Saudi Arabia in Yemen and the Responsibility of the United Kingdom' (*EJIL:Talk!*, 7 March 2017) <https://www.ejiltalk.org/the-use-of-cluster-munitions-by-saudi-arabia-in-yemen-and-the-responsibility-of-the-united-kingdom/> accessed 7 December 2019; Ryan Goodman/Samuel Oakford, 'Did U.S. Provide Helicopter Used in Attack of Somali Refugees in Yemen?' (*Just Security*, 24 March 2017) <https://www.justsecurity.org/39210/united-states-implicated-helicopter-somali-refugees-yemen/> accessed 7 December 2019; cf German ban on arms sales to Saudi Arabia following the killing of journalist Jamal Khashoggi: Matthew Robinson/Nadine Schmidt, 'Germany Cuts Arms Exports by Quarter in Wake of Khashoggi Scandal' (*CNN*, 17 January 2019) <https://edition.cnn.com/2019/01/17/europe/germany-arms-sales-saudi-arabia-scli-ger-intl/index.html> accessed 9 November 2020.

[22] *SIPRI Yearbook: Armaments, Disarmaments and International Security* (OUP 2019) 8. See also the introduction to *SIPRI Yearbook: Armaments, Disarmaments and International Security* (OUP 2017) 4.

[23] World Economic Forum, 'Global Risk Report 2020' (WEF 2020) <https://www.weforum.org/reports/the-global-risks-report-2020> accessed 22 May 2020.

[24] Swiss Re Institute, 'SONAR: New Emerging Risk Insights' (May 2018) 22 <https://www.swissre.com/institute/research/sonar/sonar2018-a-peek-into-future-risk.html> accessed 4 November 2019.

conflict in Yemen, but also the festering tensions between the 'West'[25] and Russia, to spot obvious potential for escalation towards full-blown IACs.

Overall, both IACs and protracted NIACs pose serious risks to global security. With respect to the latter, and although they may seem quite distant in most cases, some of them have the potential to develop into full-blown international conflicts of regional dimension or worse. This is further aggravated by the fact that international actors are increasingly involved in NIACs without assisting to bring the conflict to an early end. Recent and current conflicts in Libya, Yemen, and Syria are some obvious examples.

As rightly observed by the US National Intelligence Council in January 2017,[26] 'the risks of conflicts, including inter-state conflict, will increase during the next two decades because of diverging interests among major powers (...)'.[27] Although according to the Council the risk of extensive military clashes between big powers is unlikely, it is today doubtful whether, as asserted, 'the presence of nuclear and advanced conventional weapons will contribute to deterring full-scale war among major powers, but lower level of security competition will continue or even increase'.[28]

C. A Selective 'tour d'horizon' of Contemporary Armed Conflicts

1. The Near East and the Middle East

The Near East and the Middle East, certainly one of the politically most sensitive regions worldwide, is currently affected by a number of armed conflicts carrying a significant potential for destabilization and escalation on a regional if not global level.

Most notably, at the time of writing, several non-international and international armed conflicts are taking place or have taken place in Syria.[29] As a matter of IHL,

[25] The term 'West' is still used despite the fact that it implies a level of cohesion that no longer exists, mostly because the USA has turned to unilaterally pursuing its own national interests in various fields—from defence to trade—without particular consideration even for its 'western' partners or allies. This is a theme running throughout The White House, 'National Security Strategy of the United States of America' (December 2017) <https://www.whitehouse.gov/wp-content/uploads/2017/12/NSS-Final-12-18-2017-0905.pdf> accessed 7 December 2019; see eg Heinrich August Winkler, *Geschichte des Westens* (CH Beck 2009); Bill Emmott, *The Fate of the West: The Battle to Save the World's Most Successful Political Idea* (*The Economist* 2017).

[26] National Intelligence Service, 'Global Trends: Paradox of Progress' (January 2017) <https://www.dni.gov/files/documents/nic/GT-Full-Report.pdf> accessed 7 December 2019.

[27] ibid 215. [28] ibid 216.

[29] For more details on the classification of the conflicts in Syria, see Dapo Akande, 'When Does the Use of Force Against a Non-State Armed Group Trigger an International Armed Conflict and Why Does This Matter?' (*EJIL:Talk!*, 18 October 2016) <https://www.ejiltalk.org/when-does-the-use-of-force-against-a-non-state-armed-group-trigger-an-international-armed-conflict-and-why-does-this-matter/> accessed 9 November 2020; Adil Ahmad Haque, 'The United States is at War with Syria (According to the ICRC's New Geneva Convention Commentary)' (*EJIL:Talk!*, 8 April 2016) <https://www.ejiltalk.

IAC-qualifications hold true regardless of the fact that Syria has not reacted to the military action taken against it by other States,[30] and that some of the relevant attacks were limited to isolated, punitive strikes. Arguably, a military reaction by Syria to the Turkish attacks, particularly on Turkish soil, could even have triggered Article 5 of the NATO Treaty on mutual assistance. The Turkish attacks and partial occupations are violating Article 2(4) of the UN Charter, while following an abusive interpretation of its Article 51. Until the first meting of the so called Constitutional Committee in 2019, there had been no direct talks between representatives of the Syrian Government and representatives of the armed opposition, either in the UN-led process in Geneva or in the Astana process. Russia, Iran, Turkey, the United States, and Hezbollah have all had boots on the ground.

Beyond the Syrian conflict, the Near East and Middle East are marked by protracted armed confrontations ranging from Israel/Palestine all the way to Yemen, rendering this region most vulnerable to international military escalation. Depending on the evolution of highly volatile circumstances on the ground, this may conceivably lead to IACs opposing, for example, Iran and an alliance between the United States, Israel, and possibly Saudi Arabia, or increasing tension between Russia and the United States with the Syrian conflict as a starting point. In light of mounting tensions and complex alliances moving across the region, the incessant supply of the most sophisticated weapons by various States to the parties involved certainly has done nothing to alleviate the risk of escalation. This is further exacerbated by powerful States, such as the US, applying double standards to their relations with regional powers, such as Saudi Arabia, on one hand, and Iran, on the other. The room to manoeuvre for arbitrary double standards would be more limited in a less unipolar world with more checks and balances. To apply double standards when taking decisions on weapons exports in regions of tension or conflict or when adopting sanctions is damaging to the reputation of those taking such decisions. The extraterritorial sanctions' policy applied by the US is increasingly perceived as an expression of imperialism. This is all the more so when sanctions seem arbitrary and motivated less by values and more by economic and political interests.

2. The South China Sea

The South China Sea is one of the main waterways of global trade. Despite the various competing territorial and maritime claims between China, Vietnam, the Philippines, Taiwan, Malaysia, and Brunei, however, it seems unlikely that any of these disputes could lead to a full-blown armed conflict.[31] The Chinese land claim of

org/the-united-states-is-at-war-with-syria-according-to-the-icrcs-new-geneva-convention-commentary/> accessed 7 December 2019; Adil Ahmad Haque, 'Whose Armed Conflict? Which Law of Armed Conflict?' (*Just Security*, 4 October 2016)<https://www.justsecurity.org/33362/armed-conflict-law-armed-conflict/> accessed 7 December 2019; cf Terry D Gill, 'Classifying the Conflict in Syria' (2016) 92 International Legal Studies 353.

[30] Geneva Convention Commentary (n 7) 81–2.

[31] For an overview of the competing claims of the various States in the South China Sea and relevant analysis, see the very helpful debate map created by Alexander Wentker/John Louth, 'Debate Map:

1947 certainly adds an additional element of tension to the China–US relations but, unless American interests are affected in a concrete manner, it is unlikely to trigger direct military confrontations.

Although China has ratified the UN Convention on the Law of the Sea (UNCLOS), it has made use of the facultative exceptions of Article 298, which allow for the exclusion of all disputes over sovereignty from the Convention's dispute settlement system,[32] including adjudication by the ICJ. This notwithstanding, the Philippines managed to bring at least some aspects of the dispute before an UNCLOS Annex VII Tribunal through claims of damage to the marine environment.[33] China did not participate in the proceedings and fiercely contested their outcome.[34] Nonetheless, China's use of civilian fishing boats, backed up by naval forces, to assert sovereignty claims in the South China Sea has been described as an example of 'hybrid conflict', which is neither exceptional nor unprecedented in the history of territorial expansion.[35]

The uncertain future of the 'one country, two systems' model between China and Hong kong and the China-Taiwan relationship are adding to regional uncertainties.

3. Europe

As far as Europe is concerned, the primary focus should be on the current tensions and the potential for future conflict between NATO and the Russian Federation in zones of high relevance to their respective security concerns. Current developments have strayed significantly from the solemn declarations made at the 2002 Rome Summit between NATO Members and Russia when the NATO–Russian Council was established. According to the declaration, 'NATO member States and Russia will work as equal partners in areas of common interest'.[36] It remains unclear whether Russia had received assurances against NATO enlargements during the negotiation process for

Disputes in the South and East China Seas' (*Oxford Public International Law*, last updated 23 March 2017) <http://opil.ouplaw.com/page/222/debate-map-disputes-in-the-south-and-east-china-seas> accessed 22 May 2020.

[32] United Nations Convention on the Law of the Sea 1833 UNTS 3 art 298.

[33] *The South China Sea Arbitration (Philippines v People's Republic of China)* PCA Case No 2013–19, Award on Jurisdiction and Admissibility (29 October 2015) and Final Award (12 July 2016).

[34] 'Position Paper of the Government of the People's Republic of China on the Matter of Jurisdiction in the South China Sea Arbitration Initiated by the Republic of Philippines' (2016) 15 Chinese Journal of International Law 431; and, Chinese Society of International Law, 'The South China Sea Arbitration Awards: A Critical Study' (2018) 17 Chinese Journal of International Law 207.

[35] Benjamin Wittes, 'What is Hybrid Conflict?' (*Lawfare*, 11 September 2015) <https://www.lawfareblog.com/what-hybrid-conflict> accessed 7 December 2019.

[36] NATO-Russia Council, 'Declaration by Heads of State and Government of NATO Member States and the Russian Federation' (Rome Summit, 28 May 2002) 6 <https://www.nato.int/docu/comm/2002/0205-rome/rome-eng.pdf> accessed 7 December 2019.

German Reunification. The first enlargement towards central-eastern Europe (Czech Republic, Hungary, and Poland) took place in 1999, followed by the accession of Bulgaria, Estonia, Latvia, Lithuania, Romania, Slovakia, and Slovenia in 2004. The NATO declaration at the 2008 Bucharest Summit welcomed 'Ukraine's and Georgia's Euro-Atlantic aspiration for membership in NATO' and 'agreed . . . that these countries will become members of NATO'.[37] Arguably, this declaration can be seen as a negative turning point in NATO–Russian relations and a trigger for a significantly more assertive military stance by Russia. This became particularly evident in its 2008 invasion of Georgia to prevent the forcible reintegration of South Ossetia, as well as in its invasion and annexation of Crimea and the support of secessionist movements in Eastern Ukraine after the Maidan protests in February 2014. In contrast to this prevalently Western reading, a plausible alternative interpretation of events would be that Russia intervened in Georgia after Georgia's attempt to reintegrate South Ossetia by force, and that Russia encouraged Crimea's secession from Ukraine and Crimea's integration into the Russian Federation and the support of secessionist movements in Eastern Ukraine in response to the Maidan protests and the coup d'état in February 2014. In the view of the author, it is at least conceivable that Russia's military interventions could have been avoided, had NATO Member States themselves in their expansion plans not been blind to Russian security concerns.

Today, NATO is by far the world's largest military alliance and is committed to the principle of collective defence. After the dissolution of the Warsaw Pact in 1991, NATO increasingly struggled to justify its continued existence and, in doing so, may have significantly contributed to resurrecting its old enemy, not least through its policy of territorial expansion. Arguably, future perspectives of cooperation and peace in Europe would have been perhaps better served if former Warsaw Pact Members had instead only become, through their EU membership, part of the European Common Security and Defence Policy (CSDP), a policy which itself has, admittedly, some way to go.

Numerous are those who underline Europe's (meaning mainly the EU's) dependence on the USA in defence and security matters. This is a fact. This is particularly odd against the background of the EU's economic power and the combined military capacities of EU Member States. An EU with a real CSDP would rank amongst the three largest military powers of the world with a military budget close to China's, but still less than one third of the US defence budget 2019. Even without the United Kingdom, the EU ranks third. The time may come to take more seriously the European will to gradually emancipate itself from US dominance, and achieve a more balanced relationship within NATO. Having reviewed the various latent and full-blown armed conflicts taking place in the various world regions, as well as their correlation to other security threats, the analysis will now turn to the applicable legal framework and its relevance to contemporary challenges.

[37] North Atlantic Council, 'Bucharest Summit Declaration' (Bucharest, 3 April 2008) para 23.

D. The Legal Framework and its Practical Relevance

1. *Jus ad bellum*

For the purposes of this contribution, a basic distinction should be made between the law on the (non-)use of force (*jus ad bellum*) and the law on the conduct of hostilities (*jus in bello*), which has already been considered in Section B above. The former is regulated mainly by the UN Charter, according to which the UN Security Council (UNSC) has the primary responsibility for the maintenance of international peace and security,[38] whereas the UN General Assembly (UNGA) has a complementary responsibility under Articles 10, 11, and 14 of the Charter.[39]

Under Article 2(4) UN Charter 'all Members shall refrain in their international relations from the threat of use of force against the territorial integrity or political independence of any state, (...)'. In practice, however, this provision does not command much respect. Governments routinely threaten others with force without being accused of violating this article, as illustrated, for example, by the constant exchange of threats between the US and North Korea or the threats made by the USA and Israel against Iran. Moreover, the last two decades have seen a significant erosion of the prohibition of the use of force itself, starting from the initiation of hostilities by NATO States against Yugoslavia without UNSC authorization in 1999, the manifestly unlawful invasion and occupation of Iraq by the United States and the United Kingdom in 2003, to the invasion and annexation of the Crimea by Russia in 2014.[40] More recently, in April 2018 reports about the use of chemical weapons by the Syrian Army triggered punitive air attacks by the USA, France, and the United Kingdom in Syria, even before the Organisation for the Prohibition of Chemical Weapons had carried out its investigation. At the same time, the growing de facto tolerance of the international community for the unilateral use of force against States has been accompanied by a clear increase in *prima facie* unlawful cross-border military operations against non-State actors, such as by the United States in Pakistan, Israel in Lebanon, Colombia in Venezuela, Kenya in Somalia, or Turkey in Syria and Iraq, to name just a few. It is clear that, from a global security perspective, these developments are extremely troubling and may well suggest nothing less than the impending implosion of the entire security edifice of the post-Cold War world order.

[38] Charter of the United Nations 1 UNTS XVI (UN Charter) art 24(1). See, also, *Certain Expenses of the United Nations (Article 17, paragraph 2, of the Charter)* (Advisory Opinion) [1962] ICJ Rep 151, 163.

[39] *Certain Expenses* (n 38); also Higgins et al, *Oppenheim's International Law: United Nations* (vol 2, OUP 2017) 963–73; Leserbrief von Dr Hansjörg Döpp (*FAZ*, 2 February 2018).

[40] For similar thoughts, see Thomas Franck, 'What Happens Now? The United Nations After Iraq' (2003) 97 AJIL 607; cf Anne Peters, 'Crimea: Does "The West" Now Pay the Price for Kosovo' (*EJIL:Talk!*, 22 April 2014) <https://www.ejiltalk.org/crimea-does-the-west-now-pay-the-price-for-kosovo/> accessed 7 December 2019; Marko Milanovic, 'Crimea, Kosovo, Hobgoblins and Hypocrisy' (*EJIL:Talk!*, 20 March 2014) <https://www.ejiltalk.org/crimea-kosovo-hobgoblins-and-hypocrisy/> accessed 7 December 2019.

Indeed, given the fundamental importance of Article 2(4) UN Charter for the contemporary world order, extreme caution should be used not to undermine the predominant consensus as to the very exceptional justifications for the threat or use of force as laid down in the UN Charter.[41]

Most importantly, apart from situations of armed attacks requiring immediate use of force in self-defence, the UNSC must retain the primary responsibility for the maintenance of international peace and security and the sole authority for authorizing individual or collective use of military force for that purpose. The only area where the existing framework would perhaps require moderate expansion to compensate for blockages within the UNSC is that of humanitarian disasters in line with the principles developed within the responsibility to protect (R2P) framework.[42]

If the existing rules of the Charter on the threat or use of force are not interpreted soberly, self-defence may soon routinely be used as a mere fig leaf for aggressive interventions and wars of aggression. The duty of States to interpret and execute their international duties in good faith[43] means that care must be taken already to avoid the corruption of language. For example, the High-level Panel on Threats, Challenges, and Change proposed in its Report an updated interpretation of Article 51 UN Charter,[44] permitting pre-emptive self-defence against an imminent or proximate threat provided the action is proportionate, whereas anticipatory self-defence without imminent threat was not admitted. These interpretations remain controversial, however, and, in the view of this author, with good cause.

The reality is that, under the guise of self-defence, unwarranted military force is increasingly used for the purposes of asserting political influence and preventing unfavourable shifts in regional power balance. Not surprisingly, therefore, such action rarely remains limited to what is necessary or proportionate to address the purported threat and often triggers a prolonged downward spiral marked by an implosion of civilian governance structures and a proliferation of violence. Today, violations of Article 2(4) of the UN Charter rarely entail adverse consequences beyond oral condemnations of different degrees, particularly where the aggressing State can count on support by one of the UNSC Permanent Five Members (P5).

[41] FAZ, 19.7. 2017. In that respect see also the symposium organized in the American Journal of International Law on Monica Hakimi, 'The *Jus Ad Bellum*'s Regulatory Form' (2018) 111 AJIL 151, with contributions by Ashley S Deeks, 'Introduction to the Symposium on Monika Hakimi "The *Jus Ad Bellum*'s Regulatory Form"' (2018) 112 AJIL Unbound 94; Theresa Reinold, 'Informal Regulation and the Hyper-Responsiveness of International Law' (2018) 112 AJIL Unbound 97; Tess Bridgeman, 'In Defense of the "Conventional Account" of the *Jus Ad Bellum*' (2018) 112 AJIL Unbound 102; Christian J Tams, 'Three Questions About "Informal Regulation"' (2018) 112 AJIL Unbound 108; Ian Johnstone, 'Condoning the Use of Force: The UN Security Council as Interpreter of the *Jus Ad Bellum*' (2018) 112 AJIL Unbound 113.

[42] Claus Kress, 'Wird die humanitäre Intervention strafbar?' (*Frankfurter Allgemeine Zeitung*, 9 November 2017) <http://www.kress.jura.uni-koeln.de/sites/iipsl/Home/FAZ131117.pdf> accessed 4 November 2019. ICISS, *The Responsibility to Protect* (International Development Research Center 2001); UNGA Res 60/1, '2005 World Summit Outcome' (24 October 2005) para 30; see also Simon Chesterman, Chapter 44 in this *Handbook*.

[43] Vienna Convention on the Law on Treaties 1155 UNTS 331 arts 26 and 31.

[44] High-level Panel Report (n 12) para 188.

Another argument with potentially far-reaching, harmful effects is that advanced by the UK in relation to the April 2018 airstrikes in Syria.[45] According to the UK, the use of force in that case did not violate the relevant Charter framework as the Syrian government had made use of illegal chemical weapons. Such statements are particularly significant as they demonstrate the emerging perception of powerful States that unilateral use of force on their part no longer requires a decision of the UNSC under Chapter VII of the UN Charter, or even a genuine motivation to maintain international peace and security, thus opening the door to wars or acts of aggression labelled as 'punitive' or 'just'. This fundamental erosion of the post-war world order is further exacerbated by the same States' weapons exports and the violations of IHL resulting from them in various conflicts around the world.

It would seem that this 'relaxation' of the UN Charter framework accelerated in parallel to the UNSC's push towards enlarging its own competences. More specifically, in 1992, the Council widened the concept of 'threat to international peace and security' under Chapter VII to encompass large-scale violations of international human rights and humanitarian law, and allow thus for the adoption of measures under Chapter VII.[46] Nonetheless, no action was taken during one of the worst civil wars in Africa, in South Sudan. The endorsement of the concept of R2P in the 2005 World Summit Outcome Document has also been viewed as adding an important element to the competences of the UNSC. However, there is pervasive suspicion of R2P by certain States, especially Russia. This can be mainly attributed to the overstepping of the mandate to use force given under UNSC Resolution 1973 (2011) in Operation Unified Protector.[47] Despite the fact that UNSC Res 1973 authorized the employment of 'all necessary measures' to protect the civilian population, the use of force employed by the coalition of intervening States and the support granted to the Libyan rebels was primarily aimed at overthrowing the Gaddafi regime.[48]

The foregoing analysis indicates that the rules on the prohibition of the use of force and the authorization of collective military action under Chapter VII of the UN Charter have been frequently breached. NATO Member States, Russia, and other States have repeatedly ignored the rules, while at the same time the United States and Russia remained the undisputed 'veto masters'.[49] The gradual erosion of the rules of the UN Charter, the lacking credibility of allegations coming from all sides, and the use of double standards depending on the interests of powerful States have significantly increased the

[45] See, similarly, the Opinion by Dapo Akande, 'The Legality of the UK's Air Strikes on the Assad Government in Syria' (16 April 2018) 1 <https://d3n8a8pro7vhmx.cloudfront.net/campaigncountdown/pages/2243/attachments/original/1523875290/Akande_Opinion_UK_Government's_Legal_Position_on_Syria_Strike_April_2018.pdf?1523875290> accessed 7 December 2019, calling the position taken by the UK Government as 'significantly flawed' and 'the military action taken [as] not in accordance with the United Nations Charter and international law'.

[46] Higgins (n 39) 988–90.

[47] For this point see, generally, Olivier Corten/Vaios Koutroulis, 'The Illegality of Military Support to Rebels in the Libyan War: Aspects of jus contra bellum and jus in bello' (2013) 18 JCSL 59.

[48] ibid.

[49] For an account of UNSC Resolutions passed and vetoed up to 2006, see Vaughan Lowe et al (eds), *The United Nations Security Council and War* (OUP 2008) 688 (Appendix 5); also, Higgins (n 39) 88–91.

risk of an impending resurgence of IACs. The increasing tolerance towards violations of Article 2(4) of the UN Charter and of the rules restricting collective action under Chapter VII is further exacerbated by the broadening interpretation of Article 51 governing the use of force in self-defence, which opens the door to additional potential for uncontrolled escalation and destabilization of the contemporary security environment.

2. *Jus in bello*

The relevant international legal standards for the conduct of hostilities and the protection of persons during armed conflicts are reflected primarily in the Hague Regulations of 1907,[50] the four Geneva Conventions of 1949,[51] their additional Protocols,[52] and the international conventions and other instruments prohibiting or restricting the use of certain weapons.[53] The main purpose of IHL is, as mentioned, to protect civilians and other persons who are not, or are no longer, taking a direct part in hostilities, and to regulate the conduct of hostilities, including through the prohibition or restriction of the use of certain weapons.[54] As new weapon technologies continue to emerge, additional rules may become necessary to safeguard that new weapons will conform to the core principles of IHL.

From a State security perspective, violations of IHL and international human rights law (IHRL) are sometimes perceived as a lesser threat to global security than violations of the *jus ad bellum*. In reality, however, especially widespread or systematic violations of IHL and HRL can have a significant destabilizing and escalatory potential, as can be illustrated, most notably, by the current conflicts in Syria and Libya, but also by the fact that a staggering 65 million persons are currently on the move worldwide due to forced displacement. Especially over a longer period of time, such violations may trigger additional wars and make reconciliation at the end of the conflict particularly complicated, if not impossible. Without any doubt, therefore, the devastating impact of armed conflict on the social and economic environment would be much smaller if core humanitarian

[50] Regulations Respecting the Laws and Customs of War on Land, annexed to the Convention Respecting the Laws and Customs of War on Land 205 CTS 277 (Hague Convention IV).

[51] Geneva Convention for the Amelioration of the Condition of the Wounded and Sick in Armed Forces in the Field 75 UNTS 31 (GC I); Geneva Convention for the Amelioration of the Condition of Wounded, Sick and Shipwrecked Members of Armed Forces at Sea 75 UNTS 85 (GC II); Geneva Convention relative to the Treatment of Prisoners of War 75 UNTS 135 (GC III); Geneva Convention relative to the Protection of Civilian Persons in Time of War 75 UNTS 287 (GC IV).

[52] Protocol Additional to the Geneva Conventions of 12 August 1949, and relating to the Protection of Victims of International Armed Conflicts 1125 UNTS 3 (AP I); Protocol Additional to the Geneva Conventions of 12 August 1949, and relating to the Protection of Victims of Non-International Armed Conflicts 1125 UNTS 609 (AP II); Protocol Additional to the Geneva Conventions of 12 August 1949, and relating to the Adoption of an Additional Distinctive Emblem 2404 UNTS 261 (AP III).

[53] The introduction by the editors Dietrich Schindler/Jiri Tomanto (eds), *The Laws of Armed Conflict: A Collection of Conventions, Resolutions and other Documents* (4th edn, Martinus Nijhoff 2004) provides a short and instructive introduction to the development of the laws of armed conflict.

[54] O'Connell (n 9).

law principles, such as the rule of distinction between combatants and civilians, and military objectives and civilian property were better respected.

The increasing reluctance of States to conclude legally binding agreements in the area of IHL is striking, particularly given that the law of international responsibility in case of violation of a State's international obligations has few, if any, tangible consequences.[55] Indeed, the International Committee of the Red Cross (ICRC) failed in its attempt to create legally binding or soft law procedures in order to promote compliance with IHL, especially in NIACs, or during efforts to fill the gaps in IHL, applicable mainly to detention of combatants in NIACs.

Unfortunately, the pervasive disrespect of the rules of IHL—in particular of the principles on the conduct of hostilities, such as distinction, proportionality, precaution—is a daily occurrence. The widespread disregard of the principle of proportionality reminds of the times of 'just war' when vengeance was considered acceptable. Humanitarian organizations tend to warmly welcome any new agreement that could be assimilated to a humanitarian agreement; in recent times these agreements refer mainly to weapons. However, this obscures the fact that most powerful States have failed to ratify these agreements and, therefore, do not consider themselves bound by them.

Issues relating to nuclear weapons are primarily dealt with in the framework of the Treaty on the Non-Proliferation of Nuclear Weapons (NPT).[56] The last NPT review conference in 2015 illustrated that proposals that are not favoured by nuclear powers tend not to be taken forward. Although non-proliferation and nuclear disarmament are the overarching goals of the regime established under the NPT, they are not necessarily pursued in every corner of this world.

Additionally, certain States, which are important exporters or importers of weapons, seem to benefit from the prolongation of armed conflicts and security threats. Similarly, many of those States are not champions of the fight against impunity and, correspondingly, have not ratified the Rome Statute. The world's biggest military powers, the US, China, and Russia, belong to that group. Amongst Western States themselves there is, however, a remarkable difference between the US on the one hand, and France and the UK on the other, the latter being more willing to be bound by IHL agreements.

3. International Criminal Law

International and national criminal law also constitutes part of the international legal framework relevant to armed conflicts. In principle, the systematic prosecution of war crimes, crimes against humanity, genocide and the crime of aggression, through its deterrent effect, certainly could significantly contribute to improving respect for international humanitarian law, human rights law, and the *jus ad bellum* and, thereby,

[55] ILC, 'Articles on the Responsibility of States for Internationally Wrongful Acts' (12 December 2001) UN Doc A/RES/56/83, Annex, arts 31 et seq.

[56] Treaty on the Non-Proliferation of Nuclear Weapons 729 UNTS 161.

contribute to international stability, peace and security.[57] However, the less efficient the fight against impunity for international crimes is in actual practice, the weaker the preventive dimension of the rules of national and international criminal law will be. From a global perspective, the fight against impunity still is not systematic enough today; and it certainly is neither broad nor efficient enough to contribute decisively to the prevention of armed conflicts and other major situations of violence, thereby, to global stability and security. Even the establishment of the ICC, which started its work in 2002, brought no major change but, from a historical perspective, certainly is an important step in the right direction, as was the initial recognition of international individual criminal responsibility after the Second World War.

The Rome Statute reminds us of a simple fact: the relevance of international legal instruments depends to a large extent on the States who have ratified them.

4. Human Rights Law

The same holds true for human rights treaties, applicable in times of peace and war, in particular the International Convention on Civilian and Political Rights (ICCPR).[58] Especially in the case that the applicability of IHL is contested by a State, human rights law becomes a precious safety network, even though it is not binding upon armed non-State actors, according to the majority view of experts. Moreover, as far as the obligations of States are concerned, the application of human rights law alongside IHL during armed conflicts can offer significant procedural advantages to victims, because human rights treaties generally provide them with direct legal remedies, including individual complaints and entitlements to compensation and redress. Thus, both the European and the Inter-American Human Rights Courts and Commissions have adjudicated numerous individual complaints relating to human rights violations which had occurred during armed conflicts and which also amounted to serious violations of IHL but which, in the absence of a competent international criminal court or tribunal, could not be prosecuted internationally as war crimes.

5. New Technologies

The 2019 Report on the International Humanitarian Law and the challenges of anticipating armed conflicts starts with two challenges in the conduct of hostilities: urbanization of armed conflicts and new technologies of warfare.[59] In recent years, cyberspace has

[57] Bekou (n 10).

[58] *Legality of the Threat or Use of Nuclear Weapons* (Advisory Opinion) [1996] ICJ Rep 226 [25]; *Legal Consequences of the Construction of a Wall in the Occupied Palestinian Territory* (Advisory Opinion) [2004] ICJ Rep 136 [106].

[59] ICRC, *International Humanitarian Law and the Challenges of Contemporary Armed Conflicts* (ICRC 2019).

posed distinct although not entirely novel challenges to global security. Cyber operations, when used as a means and method of warfare to initiate an armed conflict or during an armed conflict, amount to cyberwarfare. The main regulatory framework on cyber operations is currently the *Tallinn Manual on the International Law Applicable to Cyber Warfare*.[60] The latter encompasses both the *jus ad bellum* and the *jus in bello* rules applicable to cyberwarfare. Beyond this, as the UN Group of Governmental Experts in its 2015 report affirmed '[i]nternational law, and in particular the Charter of United Nation (*jus ad bellum*) is applicable' to cyber operations, along with 'established legal principles, including, where applicable, the principle of humanity, necessity, proportionality and distinction.'[61]

For its part, the ICRC had asserted early on, both in public statements and in its discussions with delegates and governments, the applicability of IHL to cyber operations in armed conflicts and it was largely successful in convincing a large part of the international community. The fundamental principles of IHL according to the ICRC, namely the principles of distinction, proportionality, and precaution, are applicable in the conduct of hostilities in the cyberspace. The principle of proportionality is particularly vulnerable in this context. According to art 51(5)(b) AP I:

> An attack which may be expected to cause incidental loss of civilian life, injury to civilians, damage to civilian objects, or a combination thereof, which could be excessive in relation to the concrete and direct military advantage anticipated.

In practice, the application of this principle in cyber operations would probably mean that attacks on computer infrastructure and networks used by both the military and the civilian population are prohibited. The ICRC constantly advocates broadening the circle of States that recognize the applicability of IHL to cyberwarfare. The EU, NATO and mostly Western States recognize today such applicability of IHL to cyberwarfare.[62] The reports of the ICRC on IHL and the challenges of contemporary conflicts presented to the International Conferences in 2011, 2015, and 2019 set out the reasons behind the ICRC position in quite some detail. A different question that remains to be answered is

[60] Michael N Schmidt (ed), *Tallinn Manual on the International Law Applicable to Cyber Warfare* (CUP 2013).

[61] See also Cordula Droege, 'Get Off My Cloud: Cyber Warfare, International Humanitarian Law and the Protection of Civilians' (2012) 94 International Review of the Red Cross 533.

[62] eg North Atlantic Council, Warsaw Summit Communiqué (NATO, Warsaw, 8–9 July 2016) <https://www.nato.int/cps/en/natohq/official_texts_133169.htm> accessed 7 December 2019; EU, 'Statement: United Nations 1st Committee—Thematic Discussion on Other Disarmament Measures and International Security' (New York, 26 October 2018) <https://eeas.europa.eu/delegations/un-new-york/52894/eu-statement---united-nations-1st-committee-thematic-discussion-other-disarmament-measures-and_en> accessed 7 December 2019; US DoD, Law of War Manual (Office of General Counsel, May 2016) <https://apps.dtic.mil/dtic/tr/fulltext/u2/1014128.pdf> accessed 7 December 2019; France Ministère des Armées, 'Droit international appliqué aux operations dans le cyberspace' (9 September 2019) <https://www.defense.gouv.fr/content/download/565895/9750877/file/Droit+internat+appliqué+aux+opérations+Cyberespace.pdf> accessed 7 December 2019.

whether existing rules on the conduct of hostilities are refined enough to deal with cyber operations.

To the challenges posed to IHL by cyber operations, the development of autonomous weapons systems should be added. According to the ICRC, an autonomous weapons system is 'any system with autonomy in its critical functions. That is, a weapons system that can select (that is, search for or detect, identify, track, select) and attack (namely, use force against, neutralize, damage or destroy) targets without human intervention.'[63] However, in order to ensure compliance with core humanitarian law principles, such as distinction, proportionality and precaution in attack, a certain level of human control over attacks is required. In its 2019 Challenges Report, the ICRC stated that it considers there to be an urgent need for agreement on the type and extent of human control necessary in practice to ensure both compliance with IHL and ethic acceptability. As Neil Davison puts it 'states should now begin to determine where internationally agreed limits must be placed by assessing the type and degree of human control required, in the use of weapons to carry out attacks, to ensure compliance with IHL.'[64] From another perspective, the development of autonomous weapons systems may significantly alter the global security landscape beyond IHL. To the extent they can facilitate the waging of war without risking human lives, the political, economic, and social cost of going to war may be lowered, deepening further the asymmetric nature of warfare. New weapon technologies are hence particularly relevant to *jus ad bellum* as well. The Group of Governmental Experts on Lethal Autonomous Weapons Systems, established in 2016 within the framework of the Convention on Prohibitions or Restrictions on the Use of Certain Conventional Weapons,[65] qualified opinions in the last session from 9 to 13 April 2018 as widely divergent.[66]

Overall, therefore, new weapon technologies are an important issue both under IHL and from a *jus ad bellum* perspective. Assuming that IHL-related questions are settled in a satisfactory way, the question remains as to what extent new weapon technologies increase the likelihood of wars being triggered or escalated and to what extent they deepen the asymmetric nature of armed conflicts.[67] Reflecting on this latter point, the question arises as to what the reaction of belligerents not possessing such advanced

[63] ICRC, 'Views of the ICRC on Autonomous Weapons Systems' (Meeting of Experts on Lethal Autonomous Weapons Systems (LAWS), Geneva, 11 April 2016) 1 <https://www.icrc.org/en/document/views-icrc-autonomous-weapon-system> accessed 7 December 2019.

[64] Neil Davison, 'A Legal Perspective: Autonomous Weapon Systems under International Humanitarian Law' in UNODA, *Occasional Papers No 30: Perspectives on Lethal Autonomous Weapon Systems* (UN 2017) 8.

[65] Group of Governmental Experts of the High Contracting Parties to the Convention on Prohibitions or Restrictions on the Use of Certain Conventional Weapons Which May Be Deemed to Be Excessively Injurious or Have Indiscriminate Effects, 'Report of the 2018 Session of the Group of Governmental Experts on Emerging Technologies in the Area of Lethal Autonomous Weapons Systems' (23 October 2018) UN Doc CCW/GGE.1/2018/3, para 27.

[66] ibid.

[67] See Eliav Lieblich/Owen Alterman, *Transnational Asymmetric Armed Conflict Under International Humanitarian Law: Key Contemporary Challenges* (INSS 2015) 54, 95, 111, 120.

weapons will be and how they would seek to compensate for their seemingly weaker military position.

E. Evaluating the Role of International Law

As the foregoing analysis indicates, the international legal frameworks mentioned above have hardly proven effective in preventing armed conflicts or the dramatic humanitarian consequences caused by them. Reflecting on countless images and reports of destroyed cities and civilian casualties, it seems obvious that the applicable international law and the work of the UNSC have not achieved their goal to 'save succeeding generations from the scourge of war'.[68] This notwithstanding, the negative impacts of armed conflicts certainly would have been far worse in the absence, in particular, of the relevant norms of IHL, and the tireless efforts and advocacy carried out by the ICRC and countless other humanitarian stakeholders.[69]

According to a survey carried out by WIN/Gallup International between June and September 2016, almost half of the people living in countries affected by armed conflict responded that the Geneva Conventions prevent wars from getting worse.[70] The broadening and intensification of the dissemination of IHL rules is one of the ICRC's core policies. The better its rules are known and the more broadly they are accepted and mainstreamed, the higher becomes the reputational and political risk of ignoring them and the less likely are parties to a conflict to claim that they were not aware of the consequences of their actions. Increased efforts are all the more important as proposals for the establishment of mechanisms and procedures aiming at ensuring more effective compliance with the law have not been particularly successful so far.

Serious breaches of IHL could be further decreased if the efforts to prosecute and convict perpetrators intensified both at the national and the international levels. Taking recent developments into consideration, however, this seems to remain a distant prospect.

The fact that an increasing number of States feel less bound today by the *jus ad bellum* rules of the UN Charter is particularly worrying. Although the rules may not be openly challenged, they are simply not respected or are interpreted in an excessively broad or arbitrary manner, thus paving the way for an emerging customary rule fundamentally undermining the stabilizing and de-escalatory edifice of the Charter. The more violations remain without decisive reaction on the part of the international community, the less respect will eventually be commanded by the relevant rules.[71]

[68] UN Charter (n 38) preamble.

[69] See Christina Binder, Chapter 56 in this *Handbook*.

[70] ICRC, 'People on War: Perspective from 16 Countries' (December 2016) <https://www.icrc.org/en/document/people-on-war> accessed 12 November 2020.

[71] Anthea Roberts, 'Syrian Strikes: A Singular Exception or a Pattern and a Precedent?' (*EJIL:Talk!*, 10

F. Outlook

As we have seen, armed conflicts continue to constitute one of the main threats to global security on all levels and, therefore, their prevention must be absolutely central to any sustainable global governance system. In light of this observation, current trends towards undermining the preventive and stabilizing legal order of the UN Charter are particularly worrying.

Today, after several decades of relative stability, IACs pose a resurging security risk of global scale. Arguably, the growing global volume of arms trade may serve as a realistic indicator for the crumbling level of confidence worldwide as to the prospect of a peaceful future. In light of these factors, and taking into consideration other key contributors to armed conflict, such as extreme poverty, unbearable socio-economic inequality, and other forms of discrimination, the coming decade is very likely to see an increase in armed conflicts and other situations of violence worldwide.

The achievement of the Sustainable Development Goals (SDGs)[72] by 2030 would address many of the most important causes of armed conflict. Indeed, the SDGs may be considered a large-scale conflict prevention programme. At the same time, ongoing armed conflicts and their devastating socio-economic impact may well constitute one of the primary threats to the realization of the SDGs. As declared already in the 2005 World Summit Outcome document, conflict prevention is of paramount importance,[73] and significantly more resources have to be invested to that end, especially taking into consideration the enormous difficulties of bringing armed conflicts to an end. To be successful, however, conflict prevention policies often would have to go far beyond responding to official political narratives and address fundamental socio-economic realities, such as discriminatory, exploitative, or otherwise dysfunctional governance systems in the effected contexts. In the short-term, reduction of weapon exports is crucial. In that respect, it is encouraging that various bodies, intergovernmental bodies included, have been examining at an early stage the potential consequences of new weapon technologies.

For its part, IHL faces challenges in promoting compliance with existing rules, in filling the gaps in the existing law, in taking on new initiatives like partnerships in order to promote the respect of IHL, as well as in adjusting to new developments. The rules of IHL need, more than anything else, the unequivocal and consistent support of civil society, not only within States affected by armed conflicts, but worldwide. The Ottawa Convention on the Ban of Anti-Personnel Mines and the Arms Trade Treaty are pertinent examples.[74] Additionally, it is crucial to reflect on whether new terms and regulatory

April 2017) <https://www.ejiltalk.org/syrian-strikes-a-singular-exception-or-a-pattern-and-a-precedent/> accessed 7 December 2019.

72 UNGA Res 66/288 (27 July 2012).

73 UNGA Res 60/1 (24 October 2005) para 74.

74 See Binder (n 69).

instruments are indeed necessary to address new realities, since they may confuse and deflate already existing duties and obligations.[75]

As the present analysis has illustrated, the post-Second World War order has established an ambitious international legal framework for the elimination of one of the greatest threats to international peace and security: inter-State war. Without any question, therefore, compliance with the UN Charter is key to global, national, and human security. The same holds true for IHL, its central goal being the mitigation of armed conflicts, most notably through the protection of persons who are not, or are no longer, taking a direct part in the hostilities, and through the prohibition or restriction of certain weapons and other means or methods of warfare. For that reason, any violation of these fundamental provisions requires decisive and effective reaction on the part of the international community. Similarly, any complacency with bad faith interpretations of the law, particularly concerning the exceptions to the strict prohibition of force established in the UN Charter, fundamentally undermine the authority of the international legal norms put in place to prevent such armed conflicts after the horrors of the Second World War. Given the exponentially multiplied potential of total destruction and annihilation which States have accumulated in the seven decades that have passed since then, no one ought even to contemplate what the collapse of this essential edifice would mean for the future of global peace and security and, indeed, for the human species as a whole.

[75] See Wittes (n 35); Hakimi (n 41) and the contributions to the AJIL Unbound Symposium (n 41).

CHAPTER 15

CONTESTED TERRITORY

CHRISTOPHER J BORGEN

A. Introduction: The Many Geographies of Contested Territory and the Modes of Acquisition

Territorial disputes are perhaps the quintessential problem of public international law. States clashing over borders; empires scrambling for land and encountering the people who already live there; populations struggling to break free from colonial domination; communities trying to separate from States to become new countries. The soil of contested territory is often blood-soaked. Such conflicts are a Gordian knot of geography, sovereignty, and nationality, of history, myth, and economics.[1] What role, then, for law, let alone for technical legal distinctions?

In its transformation from the ancient world, through feudalism, and into the Westphalian system of States, territory has been repeatedly reconceptualized and reorganized from an era of frontiers—'fuzzy' zones between communities—to a modern world segmented by borders.[2] This modern compartmentalization of territory emphasizes the concept of rightful ownership, of title.

Sir Robert Jennings, prior to becoming a judge on the International Court of Justice (ICJ), described title as the 'vestitive facts which the law recognizes as creating a right'.[3] The so-called 'modes of acquisition' in the analytical literature are an attempt to explain and classify how territory may be legally acquired and transferred and, thus, disentangle which States have legal title to which territory. Jennings described five of these modes, while concluding that the list must be incomplete:

[1] See eg William B Wood/George J Demko, 'Introduction: Political Geography for the Next Millennium' in George J Demko/William B Wood (eds), *Reordering the World: Geopolitical Perspectives on the 21st Century* (2nd edn, Westview Press 1999) 4.

[2] Alexander C Diener/Joshua Hagen, *Borders: A Very Short Introduction* (OUP 2012) 2, 4.

[3] Robert Jennings, *The Acquisition of Territory in International Law* (Manchester UP 1963) 17.

> (1) *occupation*, viz. of territory which is not under sovereignty of anyone; (2) *prescription*, by which title flows from an effective possession over a period of time; (3) *cession*, or the transfer of territory by treaty provision; (4) *accession* or *accretion*, where the shape of land is changed by the processes of nature; and finally (5) *subjugation* or, if you prefer the older terminology, *conquest*.[4]

This chapter addresses the theory and practice of territorial contestation, past, present, and possibly future. Section B will sketch the evolution of these modes and other concepts through different eras. The next two sections will then address methods of resolving territorial disputes: Section C will describe political and military responses to territorial contests and Section D will turn to judicial resolution. Section E will focus on the particular role that recognition plays in resolving territorial disputes. Section F will then reconsider the modes of territorial acquisition in light of these historical, methodological, and doctrinal discussions. Section G will look forward to emerging issues of contestation and the closing section will conclude the discussion.

B. Eras of Contestation and Eras of Doctrine

Although territory has been a source of conflict since the dawn of humanity, this chapter focuses on the relation of law to such disputes in the eras since the European expansion across the globe. This is an admittedly Eurocentric narrative because, as imperial powers, the States of Europe defined much of the modern international law of sovereignty and territorial title.

Prior to the so-called 'Age of Exploration', conflicting views of territorial dispositions in medieval Europe could be resolved by the Pope or by the Holy Roman Emperor (although there were disagreements as to which had the proper authority).[5] By the late 1600s, though, papal demarcations 'played almost no role' in the settlement of territorial disputes, except in the relations between the Spanish and Portuguese empires.[6]

During this period, European powers devised legal doctrines both to support their claims of title to lands already inhabited by indigenous populations and to defend such title against other European powers.[7] The act of so-called 'discovery' only provided inchoate title that could act as 'a temporary bar to occupation by another State'.[8] A subsequent act of effective occupation and extension of sovereignty was required to perfect title.

[4] ibid 20.

[5] Wilhelm G Grewe, *The Epochs of International Law* (Walter de Gruyter 2000) 119ff.

[6] ibid 396.

[7] Andrew Fitzmaurice, 'Discovery, Conquest, and Occupation of Territory' in Bardo Fassbender/Anne Peters (eds), *The Oxford Handbook of the History of International Law* (OUP 2012).

[8] Robert Jennings/Arthur Watts (eds), *Oppenheim's International Law: Volume I, Peace* (9th edn, Longman 1992) 690, para 252, quoting Hall (8th, edn 1924) 127.

Centuries later, in its *Western Sahara* advisory opinion, the ICJ stated that such lands had not been treated as *terrae nullius* by European States but rather that in their claims of territorial title those States emphasized agreements with local rulers.[9] However, European States took the position that, although the leaders of indigenous populations could transfer land to European States, those populations were not sovereign in the sense understood by international law (as defined by European States) and, thus, agreements with those leaders were not at the same level as treaties amongst European States.[10]

As for disputes amongst European powers over territory in central Africa, the States in the Berlin Conference of 1884–85 agreed to use effective occupation as a means to resolve territorial disputes.[11] However, as there were no definite criteria for effectiveness, the concept was loose in application.[12]

More generally, European States in the nineteenth and early twentieth centuries saw boundaries 'as fluid and changing phenomena, a concept clearly stemming from and supported by the incessant ebb and flow of the territorial expansion and contraction of States during that period'.[13] Conquest was an important—and accepted—method of territorial reordering.[14]

However, after the shock of the First World War, the establishment of the League of Nations and the Permanent Court of International Justice (PCIJ) emphasized the peaceful resolution of territorial disputes. Two cases from the inter-war period, one before the PCIJ (*Eastern Greenland*) and the other before a single arbitrator (*Island of Palmas*), would become particularly influential in parsing doctrines concerning contested territory.

A quarter-century later, in the years following the Second World War, States further developed the international law and institutions that would respond to a new era of territorial contestation. The UN cemented the legal doctrine that a State could no longer use force as a means to legally acquire territory.[15] The evolution of self-determination

[9] *Western Sahara* (Advisory Opinion) [1975] ICJ Rep 12 [80]; Malcolm Shaw, *Title to Territory in Africa: International Legal Issues* (OUP 1986) 37; Jennings/Watts (n 8) 687 fn 4. European powers often based their claims of title on agreements with African leaders: Anthony Anghie, *Imperialism, Sovereignty and the Making of International Law* (CUP 2004) 71.

[10] Judge Huber in *Island of Palmas Case (United States v the Netherlands)* (1928) 2 RIAA 829, 858; Joshua Castellino/Steve Allen, *Title to Territory in International Law: A Temporal Analysis* (Ashgate 2003) 98–9.

[11] Concerning, *inter alia*, the Berlin Conference of 1884–85: Matthew Craven, 'Colonialism and Domination' in Fassbender/Peters (n 7) 880; Daniel-Erasmus Khan, 'Territory and Boundaries' in Fassbender/Peters (n 7) 235; Anghie (n 9) 91.

[12] Martti Koskenniemi, *The Gentle Civilizer of Nations: The Rise and Fall of International Law 1870–1960* (CUP 2001) 123–4.

[13] Bradford L Thomas, 'International Boundaries: Lines in the Sand (and the Sea)' in Wood/Demko (n 1) 70.

[14] Shaw (n 9) 45.

[15] Georg Schwarzenberger, 'Title to Territory: Response to a Challenge' (1957) 51 AJIL 308, 309; Enrico Milano, *Unlawful Territorial Situations in International Law: Reconciling Effectiveness, Legality and Legitimacy* (Martinus Nijhoff 2006) 104ff; Hugh Thirlway, 'Territorial Disputes and Their Resolution in the Recent Jurisprudence of the International Court of Justice' (2018) 31 Leiden Journal of International Law 117, 128.

during the era of decolonization was intertwined with the renewed application of *uti possidetis*.[16] Originally invoked in the nineteenth century in Latin America, *uti possidetis* stood for the proposition that the pre-existing colonial boundaries would also mark the borders of the newly independent States.[17] The ICJ later wrote in *Burkina Faso v Mali* that *uti possidetis*:

> ... is not a special rule which pertains solely to one specific system of international law. It is a general principle which is logically connected with the phenomenon of the obtaining of independence, wherever it occurs.[18]

The end of the Cold War provided another moment of State formation and doctrinal evolution due to dissolutions of the USSR and of Yugoslavia, as well as other transitions around the world. The territorial implications of self-determination became all the more contentious in situations that did not involve decolonization. The Badinter Commission opinions concerning the break-up of Yugoslavia applied *uti possidetis* in a non-colonial context.[19] The expansion of the doctrine from colonial boundaries to using internal administrative divisions of a predecessor State remains controversial because, although colonial boundaries were 'external' claims delimiting sovereignty, administrative demarcations within a State may have been based upon reasons that have no relation to the considerations put into external boundaries.[20]

C. Non-judicial Responses to Territorial Disputes

Parties have used a variety of means, singly and in combination, in attempts to resolve territorial disputes. This section will consider strategies not involving the use of courts and tribunals and Section D will consider the role of courts and tribunals in interpreting, applying, and formalizing legal rules.

[16] The language is the same in International Covenant on Civil and Political Rights 999 UNTS 171 art 1; International Covenant on Economic, Social and Cultural Rights 993 UNTS 3 art 1; Declaration on Principles of International Law Concerning Friendly Relations and Cooperation among States in Accordance with the Charter of the United Nations, UNGA Res 2625 (XXV) (24 October 1970) Annex.

[17] John Dugard, *The Secession of States and their Recognition in the Wake of Kosovo* (Brill 2013) 124.

[18] *Case Concerning the Frontier Dispute (Burkina Faso/Mali)* [1986] ICJ Rep 554 [20]; Dugard (n 17) 126–7.

[19] Conference on Yugoslavia Arbitration Commission, Opinion No 2 (1992) 31 ILM 1497; Badinter Commission, Opinion No 2, Opinion No 3 (1992) 31 ILM 1499.

[20] eg Dugard (n 17) 128–32.

1. Military Action

As previously noted, although conquest had been an important and accepted method of territorial acquisition up through the nineteenth century, it is no longer considered a legally valid means of acquiring title. Nonetheless, States continue to attempt to use force to redistribute territory, such as Libya's seizure of the Aouzou strip, Iraq's invasion of Kuwait, and Russia's annexation of Crimea. While these actions are widely considered illegal, such territorial occupation or redistribution can nonetheless persist for decades. The legal ramifications of illegal situations existing for significant periods will be discussed below.

2. Treaty/Conferences

International agreements have been, and remain, one of the key methods of defining boundaries, ranging from bilateral treaties resolving disputes between two parties to system-defining instruments such as Westphalia[21] and the 1919 Versailles Treaty.

Due to their critical position in international security, treaties defining State boundaries are resilient to change. State succession does not end the applicability of a previous boundary treaty.[22] Similarly, the International Law Commission's (ILC) Draft Articles on the Effects of Armed Conflicts on Treaties lists 'treaties establishing or modifying land and maritime boundaries' as amongst the treaties which would be presumed to remain in effect during an armed conflict.[23]

3. Resolution through the UN or other International Organizations

While territorial dispositions until the early twentieth century were often decided by treaties amongst 'Great Powers', with the 1919 Treaty of Versailles as perhaps the apotheosis of this practice, today international organizations with global or regional memberships, such as the UN, the Organization for Security and Cooperation in Europe (OSCE), and the Organization for African Unity (OAU), play important roles in resolving territorial conflicts. In addition to formal adjudication through international courts and tribunals, discussed below, international organizations can sponsor mediation, as in the cases of Northern Cyprus, Kosovo, Transnistria, and Nagorno-Karabakh, amongst others.[24]

[21] Schwarzenberger (n 15) 310.

[22] Vienna Convention on the Succession of States in Respect of Treaties 1946 UNTS 3 art 11; Jennings/Watts (n 8) 663.

[23] ILC, 'Draft Articles on the Effects of Armed Conflicts on Treaties, with Commentaries' (2011) II(2) Yearbook of the International Law Commission 119.

[24] UNSC Res 1244 (1999) authorized a negotiation process concerning the status of Kosovo. Regarding the OSCE mediation of the conflict over the status of Transnistria: William H Hill, *Russia, the Near Abroad, and the West: Lessons from the Moldova-Transdniestria Conflict* (Johns Hopkins UP 2012).

The UN Security Council (UNSC) 'can direct the parties to a boundary dispute to solve it according to certain terms'[25] or deter the recognition of an aspirant State or of territorial change between two States. For example, it had declared illegal the attempted secession of Katanga from the Congo and has called upon States not to recognize any Cypriot State other than the Republic of Cyprus.[26] More generally, the ICJ found in the *Namibia* advisory opinion that when the UNSC 'adopts a decision under Article 25 in accordance with the Charter, it is for member States to comply with that decision, including those members of the Security Council which voted against it and those Members of the United Nations who are not members of the Council'.[27]

The UNSC can also require the international administration of a particular territory in the wake of a conflict as a step towards resolving questions of status and sovereignty.[28] The UNSC has authorized various forms of territorial administration in cases, such as East Timor, Bosnia-Herzegovina, and Kosovo.[29] In a study spanning from the years following the First World War to the aftermath of the 2003 Iraq War, Ralph Wilde concluded that, inasmuch as a State has the power to authorize an entity (such as the League of Nations or the UN) to administer part or all of that State's territory, the administration of the territory by that entity does not imply 'the enjoyment of sovereignty in the sense of title'.[30] However, '[t]o say that the exercise of sovereignty as administration did not operate in conjunction with the enjoyment of sovereignty-as-title is not to say that this arrangement did not sometimes play a constitutive role in the legal status of the territory concerned'.[31]

In addition to, or instead of, UNSC action, the UN General Assembly (UNGA) may pass a non-binding resolution. For example, in the case of Crimea, the UNGA called upon:

> all States to desist and refrain from actions aimed at the partial or total disruption of the national unity and territorial integrity of Ukraine, including any attempts to modify Ukraine's borders through the threat or use of force or other unlawful means...[32]

In sum, international organizations utilize a variety of tools to address territorial contestation, including overseeing a process of mediation, framing the terms of the settlement, calling on members either to recognize or not recognize an entity or a situation, and providing judicial resolution, such as through the ICJ.

[25] Steven R Ratner, 'Land Feuds and Their Solutions: Finding International Law Beyond the Tribunal Chamber' (2006) 100 AJIL 808, 811.

[26] Regarding Katanga: UNSC Res 169 (1961). Regarding Northern Cyprus: UNSC Res 541 (1983), which calls upon States not to recognize any Cypriot State other than the Republic of Cyprus; UNSC Res 550 (1984); Jennings/Watts (n 8) 190 fn 20.

[27] *Legal Consequences for States of the Continued Presence of South Africa in Namibia (South West Africa) Notwithstanding Security Council Resolution 276 (1970)* (Advisory Opinion) [1971] ICJ Rep 16 [116]; Koskenniemi (n 12) 232.

[28] For a discussion of international territorial administration: Ralph Wilde, *International Territorial Administration* (OUP 2008).

[29] Milano (n 15) 206–7; regarding Kosovo: UNSC Res 1244 (1999). [30] Wilde (n 28) 105.

[31] ibid 148. [32] Territorial integrity of Ukraine: UNGA Res 68/262 (27 March 2014).

D. Courts, Tribunals, and the Legal Framework for Territorial Contestation

Jennings opined that boundary delimitation 'is a matter which is perhaps particularly suitable for the settlement of disputes by adjudication or arbitration . . . .'[33] However, as Steven Ratner noted, an 'overwhelming number of territorial disputes have not been resolved by courts.'[34] These views are not actually in opposition—an issue area may lend itself to judicial resolution and yet the majority of these conflicts may be resolved by other means. Yet, this does lead one to reconsider the role of judicial decision-making.

While, theoretically, the modes of acquisition described in Section A should frame the arguments of the parties, tribunals often consider factors including 'recognition, acquiescence and preclusion; possession and administration; affiliations of inhabitants of the disputed territory; geographical considerations; economic considerations; [and] historical considerations.'[35] Ratner observed that '[t]he ICJ's judges themselves have gently traded barbs about whether the Court's rulings improperly favor political realities over legal principles.'[36]

Perhaps the most influential single decision regarding the acquisition of territory is Judge Huber's award as the sole arbitrator in the *Island of Palmas* arbitration. Judge Huber described the question as a technical legal issue concerning the comparative weight of the evidence of title:

> If a dispute arises as to the sovereignty over a portion of territory, it is customary to examine which of the States claiming sovereignty possesses a title—cession, conquest, occupation, etc.—superior to that which the other State may possibly bring against it.[37]

[33] Jennings (n 3) 26. ICJ cases concerning territorial disputes include: *Sovereignty Over Certain Frontier Lands (Belgium/Netherlands)* [1959] ICJ Rep 209; *Frontier Dispute* (n 18); *Land Island and Maritime Frontier Dispute (El Salvador/Honduras; Nicaragua intervening)* [1992] ICJ Rep 351; *Territorial Dispute (Libya/Chad)* [1994] ICJ Rep 6; *Kasikili/Sedudu Island (Botswana/Namibia)* [1999] ICJ Rep 1045; *Land and Maritime Boundary between Cameroon and Nigeria (Cameroon v Nigeria; Equatorial Guinea intervening)* (Preliminary Objections) [1998] ICJ Rep 275; *Sovereignty over Pulau Ligitan and Pulau Sipadan (Indonesia/Malaysia)* (Application by the Philippines for Permission to Intervene) [2001] ICJ Rep 575 and (Judgment) [2002] ICJ Rep 625; *Frontier Dispute (Benin/Niger)* [2005] ICJ Rep 90; *Territorial and Maritime Dispute between Nicaragua and Honduras in the Caribbean Sea (Nicaragua v Honduras)* [2007] ICJ Rep 659; *Sovereignty over Pedra Branca/Pulau Batu Puteh, Middle Rocks and South Ledge (Malaysia/Singapore)* [2008] ICJ Rep 12; *Maritime Delimitation in the Caribbean Sea and the Pacific Ocean* (*Costa Rica v Nicaragua*) and *Land Boundary in the Northern Part of Isla Portillos (Costa Rica v Nicaragua)* [2018] ICJ Rep 139. List in part adapted from Castellino/Allen (n 10) 122–55 and Thirlway (n 15) 119, fnn 8, 9.

[34] Ratner (n 25) 813. [35] Jennings/Watts (n 8) 710. [36] Ratner (n 25) 816.

[37] *Island of Palmas* (n 10) 838–9.

However, Huber underscored the importance of evidence of effective application of sovereignty, often called '*effectivités*', because 'practice, as well as doctrine, recognizes—though under different legal formulae and with certain differences as to the conditions required—that the continuous and peaceful display of territorial sovereignty (peaceful in relation to other States) is as good as a title'.[38]

The following subsections will consider how courts and tribunals attempt to resolve title based on treaty and on effective application of sovereignty, as well as certain related evidentiary issues.

1. Title, Treaties, and Succession

A State claiming existing title to territory has the initial burden of proof.[39] Hugh Thirlway has written that '[f]or long-established states, the original territory is practically a "given"; yet even for these there may be neglected boundary problems raising questions of title'.[40] A State with title only needs to show that it has not explicitly or tacitly abandoned its claim of title nor acquiesced to the claim of another.[41] Reference to a treaty is the most straightforward and possibly the most common support for a claim of title. The treaty may itself convey title or otherwise evidence which State the signatories considered sovereign over a particular area.

Absent a treaty, a State claiming sovereign title to territory may base its claims on State succession, *uti possidetis*, or effective control.[42]

2. Title Proven by Effective Displays of Sovereignty

However, the application of evidence of a peaceful display of sovereignty has been the most significant—if not malleable—doctrine applied by tribunals in the resolution of territorial disputes. This doctrinal flexibility was evident in *Island of Palmas*, where Judge Huber explained that although displays of sovereignty by the Netherlands were only sporadic, given the distance of the island from the Netherlands this was neither surprising nor was it 'necessary that the display of sovereignty should go back to a very distant period'.[43] Rather, he emphasized the importance of notice:

> It may suffice that such a display existed in 1898, and had already existed as continuous and peaceful before that date long enough to enable any Power who might have considered herself as possessing sovereignty over the island, or having

[38] ibid 839. [39] Thirlway (n 15) 136. [40] ibid 126.

[41] Jennings (n 3) 44; Castellino/Allen (n 10) 123–4 (discussing *Sovereignty over Certain Frontier Lands* (n 33)).

[42] See Michal Saliternik, 'Expanding the Boundaries of Boundary Dispute Settlement: International Law and Critical Geography at the Crossroads' (2017) Vanderbilt Journal of Transnational Law 113, 125.

[43] *Island of Palmas* (n 10) 867.

> a claim to sovereignty, to have, according to local conditions, a reasonable possibility for ascertaining the existence of a state of things contrary to her real or alleged rights.[44]

Evidence of *effectivités* superseded inchoate title based on discovery.[45]

With the PCIJ's subsequent use of *effectivités* in *Eastern Greenland*, the doctrine became an important component of the modern jurisprudence of territorial sovereignty.[46] In *Pulau Ligitan and Pulau Sipadan*, the ICJ quoted *Eastern Greenland* in explaining that:

> a claim to sovereignty based not on some particular act or title such as a treaty of cession but merely upon continued display of authority, involves two elements each of which must be shown to exist: the intention and will to act as sovereign, and some actual exercise or display of such authority.[47]

In *Pulau Ligatan/Pulau Sipadan*, Indonesia and Malaysia each submitted examples of what they claimed were acts of sovereignty, including acts by the States from which each litigant claimed to have received title. Indonesia gave evidence of Dutch patrols, followed by activities by Indonesia's Navy and fishing by Indonesian fisherman. Malaysia's examples of acts of sovereignty included British environmental regulations, the construction of lighthouses by British North Borneo colonial authorities, and then the regulation of tourism by the Malaysian government. In weighing these arguments, the ICJ found that none of the acts cited by Indonesia was of a 'legislative or regulatory character'.[48] By contrast, although the acts referenced by Malaysia were 'modest in number', they were nonetheless 'diverse in character and include legislative, administrative and quasi-judicial acts' over a 'considerable period of time and show a pattern revealing an intention to exercise State functions' with respect to the islands.[49]

One must also take into account the possibility of 'historical consolidation' or 'prescription' in which 'undisturbed continuous possession could under certain conditions produce a title for the possessor, if the possession has lasted for some length of time'.[50] In practice, States have been able to annex territory by use of force and then, over time, that acquisition has been effectively recognized by other States.[51]

However, that process is not just a question of time but of whether or not there has been broad recognition by other States of the territorial change. In some cases, many

[44] ibid.

[45] ibid 869 (stating '[a]n inchoate title however cannot prevail over a definite title founded on continuous and peaceful display of sovereignty').

[46] *Legal Status of Eastern Greenland (Denmark v Norway)* [1933] PCIJ, Ser A/B, No 53; eg *Territorial and Maritime Dispute* (n 33) [172]; Thirlway (n 15) 135.

[47] *Legal Status of Eastern Greenland* (n 46) 45–6, as quoted in *Pulau Ligitan and Pulau Sipadan* (n 33) [134].

[48] *Pulau Ligitan and Pulau Sipadan* (n 33) [137].

[49] ibid [148]; Thirlway (n 15) 137–8.

[50] Jennings/Watts (n 8) 706; Martti Koskenniemi, *From Apology to Utopia* (CUP 1989) 284.

[51] Ratner (n 25) 812 (citing Jennings (n 3)).

decades may pass in which effective occupation is still considered illegal and there is no international recognition of the factual change of territorial control.

3. Effectiveness Reconsidered: Self-Determination and *Uti Possidetis*

Decolonization and secession bring together the right of self-determination with questions of territorial status. Martti Koskenniemi explains that '[t]he very claim of self-determination is premised on the assumption that however long, mere possession cannot suffice to justify sovereignty'.[52] Numerous territorial disputes before the ICJ were contextualized in some way by colonialism, decolonization, or self-determination.[53]

State practice shows that a variety of entities have a right of self-determination. Depending on the circumstances, these 'self-determination units' include colonies, the total citizenry of a State itself, areas which are 'non-self-governing' such that the inhabitants have no say in how they may govern their own lives, or any entity if the parties involved in the dispute agreed that self-determination was an 'appropriate solution' for the situation.[54]

A right of self-determination is not a general right of secession. While there is international support for 'external self-determination' in the context of decolonization, whether there is a right of remedial secession outside of the colonial context is highly controversial and not well supported.[55]

Discussions of self-determination often turn to the issue of whether *uti possidetis* is in tension with self-determination: whether fidelity to colonial boundaries undercuts the ability of a people to determine their political future, or vice versa. The ICJ reframed the issue and described *uti possidetis* as supporting the peaceful implementation of decolonization because '[i]ts obvious purpose is to prevent the independence and stability of new States being endangered by fratricidal struggles provoked by the challenging of

[52] Koskenniemi (n 50) 285; for more on the interrelation of self-determination and territorial title: Shaw (n 9) 149ff.

[53] Examples of the ICJ addressing issues of territorial contestation within a broader context of colonialism and/or decolonization are: *International Status Of South West Africa Case (Advisory Opinion)* [1950] ICJ Rep 128; *Northern Cameroons (Cameroon v UK)* [1963] ICJ Rep 15; *Western Sahara* (n 9); *Frontier Dispute* (n 18); *Territorial and Maritime Dispute* (n 33) (which assessed the validity of 1906 arbitration by the King of Spain regarding frontier issues); *Island and Maritime Frontier Dispute* (n 33); *Legal Consequences of the Separation of the Chagos Archipelago from Mauritius in 1965* (Advisory Opinion) [2019] ICJ Rep 1. See also Thirlway (n 15) 139–42.

[54] James Crawford, *The Creation of States in International Law* (2nd edn, OUP 2006) 127 (describing the various 'self-determination units').

[55] See eg *Accordance with International Law of the Unilateral Declaration of Independence in Respect of Kosovo* (Advisory Opinion) [2010] ICJ Rep 403 [82] (*Kosovo*); and, generally, Christopher J Borgen, 'The Language of Law and the Practice of Politics: Great Powers and the Rhetoric of Self-Determination in the Cases of Kosovo and South Ossetia' (2009) 10 Chicago Journal of International Law 1.

frontiers following the withdrawal of the administering power'.[56] Given the artificiality of borders, this conception of *uti possidetis* in service to self-determination is not without critics, even within the ICJ itself.[57]

As explained by Enrico Milano, the development of the doctrine of self-determination, as well as *jus cogens* and *erga omnes* obligations (such as concerning the use of force) winnowed the breadth of application of effectiveness.[58] In regards to self-determination, this is a double-edged sword: while control by a pre-existing State can be undone by a claim of self-determination within the context of decolonization, in other situations effective control of territory by a secessionist entity is not legally dispositive. Outside of decolonization, very few attempted secessions that are contested by the pre-existing State receive support by the international community.[59]

4. Cartographic Evidence and Critical Dates

In addition to the substantive and interpretational issues set out previously in this section, disputes over territory often include discussions of cartographic evidence and of 'critical dates'. However, those tools may not actually put the matter to rest.

The ICJ has repeatedly noted that maps, in and of themselves, do not constitute a territorial title, although they can acquire legal force when they become an integral part of an official text.[60] Otherwise, 'maps are only extrinsic evidence of varying reliability or unreliability which may be used, along with other evidence of a circumstantial kind, to establish or reconstitute the real facts'.[61]

Judicial decision-making also attempts to simplify the tangle of history, myth, economics, culture, and strategic interest by means of bright line rules such as the 'critical date', the point after which actions of the parties can no longer affect the resolution of a particular issue in a case.[62] However, courts, including the ICJ in *Minquiers and Ecrehos*, have 'been reluctant to accept critical date arguments aimed at hampering their discretion to look at the whole of the evidence before coming to a decision'.[63]

[56] *Frontier Dispute* (n 18) [20]; Karen Knop, 'Statehood: Territory, People, Government' in James Crawford/Martti Koskenniemi (eds), *The Cambridge Companion to International Law* (CUP 2012) 104.

[57] eg *Territorial Dispute (Libya v Chad)* (n 33) [9], [53] (Sep Op of Judge Ajibola), as quoted by Dugard (n 17) 125 fn 326.

[58] Milano (n 15) 25, 43; Grewe (n 5) 629 (observing 'the general decline of the principle of effective occupation' in the twentieth century).

[59] For more on listing successful and unsuccessful secessions: Borgen (n 55) 9–10; but Crawford (n 54) 415 (stating that, at the time of writing, only Bangladesh was a successful secession).

[60] *Pulau Ligitan and Pulau Sipadan* (n 33) [88], quoting *Frontier Dispute* (n 18) [54]; *Kasikili/Sedudu Island* (n 33) [84].

[61] ibid. [62] Jennings (n 3) 46; Thirlway (n 15) 122–3.

[63] Jennings/Watts (n 8) 711. But, for an application of a critical date: *Frontier Dispute* (n 18) [33].

5. Conclusion

While the use of courts and tribunals is an important method of resolving territorial disputes, it is limited. At times, actual conflicts are papered over and left unresolved. Koskenniemi writes:

> What happens in dispute-solution is that *disputing States' positions are interpreted so as to lose the conflict between them*. Effective possession and general recognition are so interpreted as to point to the same solution. Either both are present or both are absent.[64]

Steven Ratner concluded that '[w]hile tribunals can significantly advance the conflict resolution process, compliance often requires close follow-up by regional actors and, in many cases, renewed negotiations. . . .'[65] Moreover, although boundary cases between States will continue to be an important part of the caseload of international courts and tribunals, other types of territorial contestation are not likely to be presented before tribunals. Conflicts with entities such as ISIL/Da'esh, the Revolutionary Armed Forces of Colombia (FARC) or secessionist groups do not lend themselves to judicialized dispute resolution. Either there is no jurisdiction or the litigants would not want to submit the issues to a tribunal.

Tribunals alone are not enough.

E. Recognition and State Action

In the absence of judicial resolution, questions of territorial control may transform into questions of recognition, either of Statehood or of territorial change. Recognition can be used to try to resolve questions of territorial control by setting forth the view of the recognizing State as to who is sovereign over the territory in question.[66] The 'moment of time at which independent Statehood is attained is unavoidably to be regarded as a root of title to territory'.[67] This, however, can impel a strategy of claiming and holding territory as part of a gambit for recognition.

Although States emphasize that recognition in its various forms is primarily a political decision by the recognizing State, it is nonetheless a political decision within a legal

[64] Koskenniemi (n 50) 288. [65] Ratner (n 25) 817.

[66] Jennings included in his monograph the role of recognition of statehood as a means by which a new State establishes sovereignty over territory: Jennings (n 3) 21–3, 28; Marcelo G Kohen, 'Introduction' in Robert Jennings, *The Acquisition of Territory in International Law* (reissue MUP 2017) 8; Jennings/Watts (n 8) 127 (stating recognition, in its broadest sense, 'involves the acceptance by a State of any fact or situation occurring in relation to other States').

[67] Jennings (n 3) 52.

framework and with legal effects.[68] One part of the legal context of the recognition of Statehood is the Montevideo Convention on the Rights and Duties of States (1933), which describes how 'the state as a person of international law should possess the following qualifications: (a) permanent population; (b) defined territory; (c) government; and (d) capacity to enter into relations with other States'.[69] Although these criteria have become customary international law, they are not the final word in defining what is, or is not, a State but rather supply common terms of discussion.[70]

Some jurists have argued that 'effectiveness', meaning, in the context of Statehood and recognition, the fact of exercising sovereign authority over a certain territory and population, is a better overall test than, or perhaps a summation of, the Montevideo criteria. However, there are limits to the usefulness of the concept of effectiveness and the practice of recognition as means of resolving questions of Statehood or territorial change.

Consider the conflicts over Abkhazia and South Ossetia, which Russia has recognized as independent States. Or Crimea, which Russia recognized as an independent State before signing a so-called treaty of merger, claiming that Crimea was not annexed, but rather chose sovereign merger with Russia.[71] Given Russia's intervention on behalf of the separatists in these regions, the argument that recognition has resolved these situations is not persuasive. According to Article 41(2) of the Articles on the Responsibility of States for Internationally Wrongful Acts (ARSIWA): 'No State shall recognize as lawful a situation created by a serious breach ... [of a legal obligation under a peremptory norm under international law], nor render aid or assistance in maintaining that situation.'[72] Thus, a State may be responsible for a wrongful act if it prematurely recognizes an entity as a State or a change in territory that is itself the result of a breach of an international obligation.

Conversely, a State may be responsible for an internationally wrongful act if an entity clearly meets the criteria of Statehood or if a territorial change is clearly legal, and that situation is recognized as such by a substantial majority of the international community, and yet the non-recognizing State ignores the basic obligations with that entity seeking recognition. For example, if a State treated an entity that clearly meets the requirements of Statehood as if it were *terra nullius*, its acts would likely be broadly viewed as violations of sovereignty.

[68] ILA, 'Fourth (Final) Report of the Committee on Recognition and Non-Recognition in International Law' (Sydney, 2018) 18 <https://www.ila-hq.org/images/ILA/DraftReports/DraftReport_Recognition.pdf> accessed 18 November 2020.

[69] Convention on the Rights and Duties of States 165 LNTS 19 art 1.

[70] Fourth (Final) Report of the Committee on Recognition and Non-Recognition in International Law' (n 68) 7.

[71] 'Ukraine Crisis: Putin Signs Russia-Crimea Treaty' (*BBC*, 18 March 2014) <https://www.bbc.com/news/world-europe-26630062> accessed 9 April 2020; Christopher J Borgen, 'Law, Rhetoric, Strategy: Russia and Self-Determination Before and After Crimea' (2015) 91 International Law Studies 216.

[72] James Crawford, *The International Law Commission's Articles on State Responsibility: Introduction, Text and Commentaries* (CUP 2002) art 41; Hersch Lauterpacht, *Recognition in International Law* (CUP 1947) 431 (describing non-recognition as resistance to illegal acts).

F. Reconsidering Doctrine

The conceptual toolbox of international lawyers holds more than the modes of conquest, cession by treaty, discovery and occupation, prescription, and accretion. Doctrines of recognition, effectivity, and *uti possidetis* interact with these classic techniques. The ICJ has tended to intertwine discussions of *effectivités* with assessments of one or more of the classic modes, in particular whether there was some form of conveyance by treaty. For example, effectivity can support the application of a treaty but it cannot be used to overcome title. When there is no title or title is unclear, then effectiveness may resolve the situation.[73] However, the mere fact of effective control will not overcome the prohibition of acquisition via conquest nor will effective control overcome the right of self-determination. Thus, in certain situations, *uti possidetis* is braided into the analysis.[74]

Even with this expanded toolkit, the standard view has been that 'international law has nothing to say on where a particular boundary *should* be, merely that the boundary is where the parties agree that it is'.[75] But the jurisprudence of territorial disputes has changed over time and some scholars now argue that it is in another period of change, going beyond simply an application of where a line is and giving greater thought to where a line should be. Referring to the Permanent Court of Arbitration's (PCA) *Abyei* arbitration and the ICJ judgments in *Frontier Dispute (Burkina Faso/Niger)* and the *Temple of Preah Vihear (Request for Interpretation)*, Michal Saliternik writes:

> These decisions look beyond the traditional inter-state perspective to identify the essential interests of the communities living in the border area as well as of other stakeholders that might be affected by the location of the border. The interests identified include collective self-determination, peacemaking, utilization of water resources, protection of pasture rights, and access to heritage sites. Of course, this does not mean that international adjudicators no longer care about the stability of boundaries. However, stability is gradually being transformed from the exclusive determinant of boundary lines into one among several considerations that should be taken into account when delineating boundaries.[76]

These new perspectives may become part of the panoply of approaches available to advocates, negotiators, judges, and scholars. And, as contestation continues to evolve, the full range of methods will be continually tested, not only by pre-existing problems, but also by new or re-emerging issues. Following are three such challenges: the role of territorial non-State actors; the set of territorial problems that have armed conflict and occupation as a nexus; and the new geography of contestation.

[73] Milano (n 15) 112–13. [74] See eg *Frontier Dispute* (n 18) 586–7 [63]. [75] Thirlway (n 15) 121.
[76] Saliternik (n 42) 135.

G. (Re-)Emerging Issues and Challenges

1. The Challenge of Territorial Non-State Actors

In addition to the contestation of the territory itself, some situations concern the application of legal regimes when the land is controlled by a non-State actor. Territorial non-State actors have included secessionist entities such as Transnistria and the Turkish Republic of Northern Cyprus, as well as organized armed groups, such as the FARC in Colombia. (And, there can also be overlaps amongst terrorism, gangsterism, and/or secessionism.) ISIL/Da'esh made taking and holding territory a key part of its strategy.[77] Regardless of whether or not, at the time of writing, ISIL/Da'esh is on the wane, the concern remains whether it signifies a trend of terrorist organizations emphasizing the acquisition and control of territory. These entities have different goals and strategies than States in 'classic' inter-State territorial conflicts.

As secessionist conflicts, in particular, and other struggles with territorial non-State actors are often primarily internal struggles within existing States, the role of international law may be narrower than in an inter-State context. For example, the ICJ in the *Kosovo* advisory opinion stated that 'the scope of the principle of territorial integrity is confined to the sphere of relations between States',[78] and, as will be discussed below, the full breadth of the law of armed conflict (LOAC) may not be applicable.

2. Contested Territory, Armed Conflict, and Occupation

Territorial contests are often armed conflicts. The broadest application of LOAC takes place in an armed conflict between two States. In an international armed conflict (IAC) between two signatories of the Geneva Conventions, the full corpus of LOAC based on those conventions is applicable. For a conflict between a State and a non-State actor to rise to the level of a non-international armed conflict (NIAC) requires both a certain level of organization of the non-State actor and intensity of the conflict.[79] If a NIAC does exist, then the parties are regulated by Common Article 3 of the Geneva Conventions and, under certain circumstances, including when some territorial control by the non-State actor exists, Additional Protocol II to the Geneva Conventions.[80] Any State involved in a

[77] eg 'Isis Rebels Declare "Islamic State" in Iraq and Syria' (*BBC*, 30 June 2014) <http://www.bbc.com/news/world-middle-east-28082962> accessed 9 April 2020.

[78] *Kosovo* (n 55) [80]; Dugard (n 17) 140.

[79] Vaios Koutroulis, 'The Fight Against the Islamic State and Jus in Bello' (2016) 29 Leiden Journal of International Law 827, 830–1 fn 27; *Prosecutor v Haradinaj et al* (Trial Judgment) ICTY-04-84 (3 April 2008) paras 39–60.

[80] See, generally, Geoffrey S Corn, 'Legal Classification of Military Operations' in Geoffrey S Corn et al (eds), *U.S. Military Operations: Law, Policy, and Practice* (OUP 2016) 74–5; Liesbeth Zegveld, *Accountability of Armed Opposition Groups in International Law* (CUP 2002) 9–14.

NIAC or other conflict also has obligations under human rights law.[81] However, if the situation is below the threshold of a NIAC, then it is unlikely that LOAC would apply and a State may approach the situation as a domestic criminal matter.[82] Moreover, Additional Protocol I applies to conflicts 'in which peoples are fighting against colonial domination and alien occupation and against racist régimes in the exercise of their right of self-determination.'[83]

Regarding the occupation of contested territory by military forces, such belligerent occupation during times of armed conflict is not the same as 'occupation' in the sense of modes of acquisition, which refers to a State taking and holding *terra nullius* and undertaking acts of sovereignty, such as settlement. The Hague Regulations explain that, in the context of an armed conflict, '[t]erritory is considered occupied when it is actually placed under the authority of the hostile army.'[84] The obligations of the occupier are set out in Geneva Convention IV, relevant sections of the First and Second Additional Protocols to the Geneva Conventions, as well as customary international law.[85]

The law of armed conflict prohibits a change of title through belligerent occupation.[86] However, modern occupants tend not to acknowledge the status of an occupation, in an attempt to give themselves more leeway.[87] Situations of long-term occupation lead to questions of whether the result will be a change of title, in which the occupation either becomes an annexation or assisted secession. The lack of widespread recognition of attempted territorial changes in Northern Cyprus, South Ossetia, Abkhazia, and Crimea have underscored the importance of international law as well as the difficulty of enforcing international law to the point of actually resolving the ongoing territorial disputes.

3. Once- and Future Contested Territories: Polar Regions and Celestial Objects

Besides the issues posed by non-State actors and armed conflict, there are new or re-emerging challenges related to certain types of territory.

Both polar regions are re-emerging areas of contestation. The Arctic has received the most attention, due to claims of Arctic States of sub-sea resources. Those disputes are

[81] Zegveld (n 80) 38–9.
[82] Nonetheless, even in a purely domestic dispute below the NIAC threshold, international law is still relevant due to the applicability of human rights obligations.
[83] Protocol Additional to the Geneva Conventions of 12 August 1949 and Relating to the Protection of Victims of International Armed Conflicts (Protocol I) 1125 UNTS 3 art 1(4); Crawford (n 54) 420.
[84] Regulations Respecting the Laws and Customs of War on Land, annex to Convention (IV) Respecting the Laws and Customs of War on Land 205 CTS 277 art 42 (Hague Regulations).
[85] Milano (n 15) 91ff, including 92 fn 138.
[86] Hague Regulations (n 84) arts 42–56; Geneva Convention (I) for the Amelioration of the Condition of the Wounded and Sick in Armed Forces in the Field 75 UNTS 31 art 2; Geneva Convention (IV) relative to the Protection of Civilian Persons in Time of War 75 UNTS 287 arts 2, 27–34, 47–78; Jennings/Watts (n 8) 700; Wilde (n 28) 308; Eyal Benvenisti, *The International Law of Occupation* (2nd edn, Princeton UP 2004) 3.
[87] Benvenisti (n 86) 5.

largely based on competing applications of maritime delimitations. This subsection will focus instead on claims over parts of the Antarctic continent.

Argentina, Chile, Britain, France, New Zealand, South Africa, and Norway all made territorial claims on Antarctica, using various modes, in the first half of the twentieth century.[88] At the time, Britain, France, and Norway even renewed the use of arguments of title by discovery.[89] These claims became dormant with the coming into force of the Antarctic Treaty.[90] Antarctica became a region defined by scientific exploration, not economic exploitation. However, Article IV states, in part, that '[n]othing contained in the present Treaty shall be interpreted as . . . a renunciation by any Contracting Party of previously asserted rights of or claims to territorial sovereignty in Antarctica . . . .'[91]

The Protocol on Environmental Protection, part of the Antarctic Treaty System, will be reviewed in 2048, possibly opening the way for mining in the Antarctic. Observers are concerned that this will spur renewed territorial claims, with States even using archaeology to try to support arguments of occupation, though such sparse evidence is unlikely to be persuasive.[92]

Another hypothesized argument is based on 'sector theory', in which States would 'assert a territorial claim along lines of latitude that run directly to the Pole, thereby effectively dividing up the region.'[93] However, this theory 'has never been the subject of final determination by an international court or tribunal, has never been officially relied upon by claimant states to polar lands, and has been subject to widespread critique from commentators.'[94]

In addition to re-emerging tensions over the polar regions, there are nascent disputes over celestial bodies, such as the Moon, Mars, and asteroids. The Outer Space Treaty states that '[o]uter space, including the moon and other celestial bodies, is not subject to national appropriation by claim of sovereignty, by means of use or occupation, or by any other means.'[95] However both private companies and States are interested in possibly mining or otherwise using resources found on celestial bodies. The question of whether a private entity or a State may extract resources either for their own use or place them into the stream of commerce is a topic that, at the time of this writing, generates debate across space agencies and private enterprise. The United States and Luxembourg have

[88] Grewe (n 5) 685. [89] ibid 629.

[90] Jennings/Watts (n 8) 694–6. [91] Antarctic Treaty 402 UNTS 71 art IV.1.a.

[92] Regarding the use of archaeology to support territorial claims, Martha Henriques, 'The Bones that Could Shape Antarctica's Fate' (*BBC*, 21 October 2018) <http://www.bbc.com/future/story/20181019-the-bones-that-could-shape-antarcticas-future> accessed 9 April 2020; Chris Borgen, 'Weaponized Archaeology and Sovereignty Disputes' (*Opinio Juris*, 12 December 2015) <http://opiniojuris.org/2015/12/19/weaponized-archaeology/> accessed 9 April 2020.

[93] Donald R Rothwell, 'Polar Territorial and Maritime Sovereignty in the Twenty-First Century' in Christine Chinkin/Freya Baetans, *Sovereignty, Statehood and State Responsibility: Essays in Honour of James Crawford* (CUP 2015) 113.

[94] ibid 114.

[95] Treaty on Principles Governing the Activities of States in the Exploration and Use of Outer Space, including the Moon and Other Celestial Bodies 610 UNTS 205 art 2.

passed domestic laws in which these governments will recognize the transfer of resources extracted from celestial bodies by private companies organized under their respective laws.[96] Other countries might also enact such domestic regulations. Detractors of these initiatives view them as de facto extensions of sovereignty over territory that is the heritage of all humanity. The implications of this regulatory competition remain to be seen.

H. Conclusion

Territory has been, is, and will continue to be, contested. The relevance of law to territorial disputes is about more than the location of title. Territorial contestation implicates a range of legal issues including self-determination, whether and when there are legal obligations of recognition or non-recognition, and the application of LOAC and human rights law.

This diversity of approaches can be expected to continue, if not widen, as what is being contested continues to evolve. Although territorial contestation has been about title to territory, the goals of recent and possible future disputes may be somewhat different. Today, non-State actors seize and hold territory without ever seeking any form of recognition. Tomorrow, States may claim the ability to exploit resources in the Antarctic or on celestial bodies. These are arguments about the use of territory, but not necessarily about title.

Inasmuch as territorial contests are a knot of geography, history, identity, and economics, no single technique can equitably resolve all such claims. But as the disputes continue to evolve, we can expect that the international legal toolbox will continue to expand, as well.

[96] In 2017, President Obama signed into law the Space Resource Exploration and Utilization Act of 2015 (H.R. 1508) and the Spurring Private Aerospace Competitiveness and Entrepreneurship (SPACE) Act of 2015, Pub. L.114-90 (25 November 2015); the Parliament of Luxembourg passed the Projet de loi sur l'Exploration et l'Utilisation des Ressources de l'Espace (Law of 20 July 2017 on the exploration and use of space resources).

CHAPTER 16

MARITIME SECURITY

DOUGLAS GUILFOYLE

A. Introduction

WHILE maritime security has attracted a substantial literature,[1] a satisfactory definition remains elusive.[2] Attempts encounter both normative and conceptual problems. Security for *whom* and from *what*?[3] The concept has certainly expanded beyond traditional military and national security concerns. But where to draw the boundaries remains uncertain. Indeed, authors frequently conclude that it is not capable of being given any unified meaning. Thus, Klein has written that maritime security is a term which, while

> widely used and understood in the day-to-day workings of naval and law-enforcement officials, (…) vessel owners and operators, as well as in the academic literature (…) is rarely defined in a categorical way, and instead tends to have a context-specific meaning. (…) the most useful approach (…) is to identify what are commonly perceived as existing or potential threats (…) and [to examine steps taken to address them].[4]

For example, within the UN, maritime security can encompass: food security and 'sustainable livelihoods'; protection and 'sustainable use' of the marine environment; climate change 'adaptation and mitigation'; energy security; terrorism, piracy, and other

[1] HeinOnline returns 220 law journal articles referring to 'maritime security' before 2001 and over 1700 since. See Douglas Guilfoyle, 'Maritime Security and Risk' in Monika Ambrus et al (eds), *Risk and the Regulation of Uncertainty in International Law* (OUP 2017) 59–60.

[2] Natalie Klein, *Maritime Security and the Law of the Sea* (OUP 2011) 2; James Kraska/Raul Pedrozo, *International Maritime Security Law* (Martinus Nijhoff 2013) 1.

[3] David A Baldwin, 'The Concept of Security' (1997) 23 *Review of International Studies* 5, 13–17 (adding a range of further questions). Compare: Christian Bueger, 'What is Maritime Security?' (2015) 53 Maritime Policy 159.

[4] Klein (n 2) 11.

transnational organized crime (including the smuggling of drugs, firearms and migrants); shipboard safety, including the use of armed guards; the vulnerability of submarine communication cables; and radioactive material transportation.[5] Such a pragmatic approach can yield useful insights. By its nature, however, it cannot offer a normatively coherent definition. For Bueger, such a 'laundry list' approach to maritime security as a collection of responses to a collection of problems renders the term a 'buzzword'.[6] Bueger, however, does not see this as necessarily a bad thing.[7] A buzzword allows mobilization of political capital and material resources to address problems, while also papering over differences between interested actors.[8] Simply put, use of a common term may give the impression that those involved are discussing the same thing and have the same interests. In Bueger's analysis, maritime security covers a matrix of issues. The four principal corners of the field are: the marine environment, economic development (the 'blue economy'), human security, and traditional national security concerns. Individual threats may then be situated. Smuggling of small arms, for example, is likely to fall somewhere along an axis between questions of national and human security; while the threat of pollution sits between environmental and economic security. This matrix approach allows us to map the terrain of maritime security. Even if a final definition is elusive, the contours of the field are knowable. A simplified version of Bueger's matrix may be represented as follows (Figure 16.1):

The utility of this 'four-cornered field' approach[9] is that it emphasizes the unified character of the oceans. The law of the sea has always had to balance competing rights

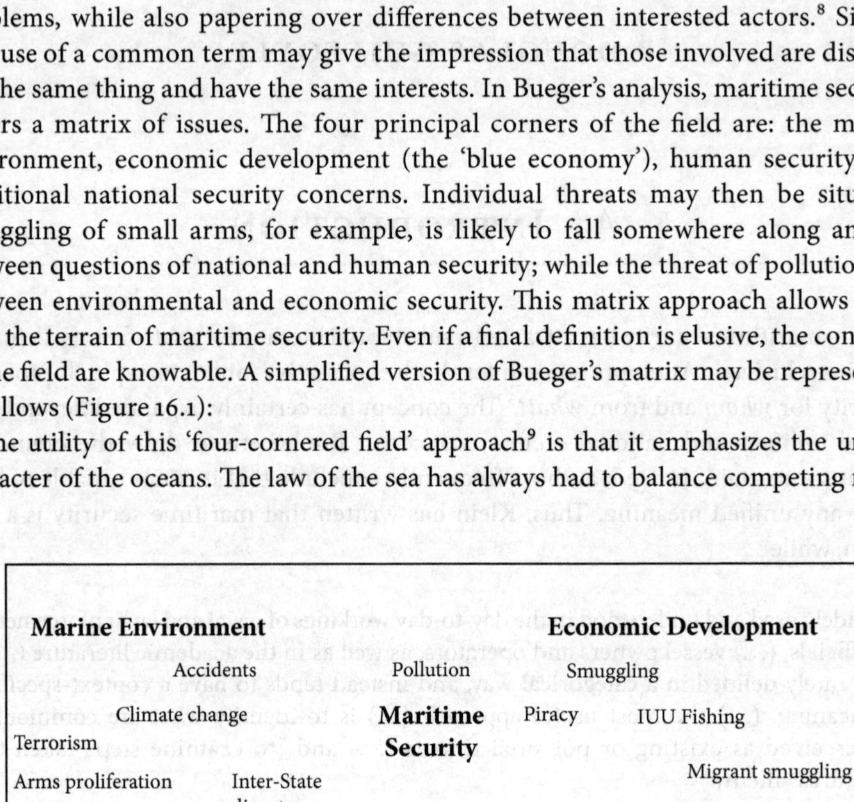

FIGURE 16.1 Maritime Security Matrix

Source: Based on Bueger 2015.

[5] 'Security' is used thirty-six times in the annual UNGA Resolution on Oceans and the Law of the Sea, UNGA Res 72/73 (5 December 2017), excluding references to 'Security Council'. See the preamble and paras 27, 28, 107–10, 118–20, 133, 135, 137, 143, 145–6, 154, 161, 172, 175, 181, 197, 232(b), 331.

[6] Bueger (n 3) 159–60. [7] ibid. [8] ibid.

[9] I borrow the metaphor from William Schabas, *Genocide in International Law: The Crime of Crimes* (2nd edn, CUP 2009) 129.

and interests in the use of an integrated commons.[10] While a threat-based approach to maritime security has tended to generate discrete silos of law and practice, there is increasing interest in questions which cut across them. This chapter will first consider a number of those 'siloed' concerns, before turning to common cross-cutting themes or challenges.

The chapter will therefore proceed as follows. First, some basic law of the sea concepts will be reviewed. The modern law of the sea encompasses both functional and zonal approaches: the question of the law applicable to any situation thus involves analysis of both the activity in question and where it is conducted. Several traditional law of the sea enforcement techniques are also being adapted to new challenges. Principal amongst these are the doctrines of port State jurisdiction and hot pursuit. The chapter will then briefly survey a number of challenges in the maritime domain, each of which is considered in more detail in other chapters: crimes of violence (piracy and terrorism); the smuggling of drugs, migrants, and weapons of mass destruction; environmental security; and military activities at sea.

Finally, this chapter will turn to three major themes cutting across these various silos. The first is Maritime Domain Awareness (MDA). If the law of the sea regulates who may do what and where, then a challenge for enforcement is *knowing* who is doing what and where. National policymakers have often been called 'sea-blind', but that blindness is often quite literal in terms of information available about conduct in maritime zones under, or beyond, their jurisdiction. The second theme is the turn to informality. Most new maritime security initiatives do not involve creating new organizations or legal instruments. Responses to collective or regional challenges tend now to occur through informal coalitions.[11] This has certain virtues, particularly efficiency and the potential to de-politicize security challenges by making them issues of technical cooperation. Informality can create, however, challenges of its own. These include how to facilitate information flows between partner States, and questions of legal fragmentation and accountability. Finally, the broadening of maritime security brings a wider range of non-State or 'grey zone' actors into the picture, including migrants, seafarers, transnational criminals, and hybrid private/State actors such as the Chinese maritime militia.

[10] Myres S McDougal/William T Burke, *The Public Order of the Oceans* (reissue of 1962 edn, New Haven 1987) ch 1; note, however, Gilbert Gidel, *Le Droit International Public de la Mer: Le Temps de Paix: La mer territorial et la zone contiguë* (vol III(i), Sire 1934) 168–9; Robin R Churchill/Alan V Lowe, *The Law of the Sea* (3rd edn, Manchester UP 1999) 81.

[11] Sarah Percy, 'Counter-Piracy in the Indian Ocean: A New Form of Military Cooperation' (2016) 1 Journal of Global Security Studies 270; Douglas Guilfoyle, 'Somali Pirates as Agents of Change in International Law-Making and Organisation' (2012) 1 Cambridge Journal of International and Comparative Law 81; Christian Bueger, 'Communities of Security Practice at Work? The Emerging African Maritime Security Regime' (2013) 6 African Security 297.

B. The Law of the Sea and the Sectoral Approach to Maritime Security

1. The Zonal and Functional Approach

International law divides the sea into jurisdictional zones and functional uses, which may overlap. This has consequences for maritime security as the powers available to States depend both upon the nature of the activity and where it is undertaken.

Briefly put, a coastal State is sovereign within its baselines and internal waters, an area effectively equated to land territory. Ocean space seaward of a coastal State's baselines is divided into: the territorial sea; the contiguous zone; the exclusive economic zone and continental shelf; and the high seas and the seabed area beyond national jurisdiction. In each of these zones coastal States and flag States may exercise varying degrees of sovereignty, sovereign rights, or jurisdiction. At its most basic, the law of the sea involves striking a balance between the different interests in uses of the oceans. The varying apportionment of rights in each zone reflects the legal balance struck. Thus, within the 12 nm territorial sea the coastal State, generally speaking, exercises full sovereignty subject to navigating States' right of innocent passage.[12] Beyond the territorial sea in a contiguous zone (out to 24 nm from a State's baselines), the coastal State has a limited jurisdiction to prevent or punish infringement of its fiscal, immigration, sanitary and customs laws.[13] In the exclusive economic zone (EEZ) (extending up to 200 nm) and in the continental shelf (which may extend still further), the coastal State exercises sovereign rights and jurisdictions over living and non-living resources.[14] The high seas constitutes a zone of freedoms beyond national jurisdiction, and its freedoms also apply within the EEZ to the extent they are not incompatible with coastal State rights. The freedoms of the high seas, including freedoms of navigation, fishing, and the right to lay submarine cables, are limited in number and subject to certain legal obligations.[15] The deep seabed beyond national jurisdiction is considered the common heritage of all mankind and is supervised by the International Seabed Authority.[16] Superimposed

[12] United Nations Convention on the Law of the Sea 1833 UNTS 3 (UNCLOS) arts 2, 17–28; and commentary in Alexander Proelß (ed), *United Nations Convention on the Law of the Sea: A Commentary* (Beck/Hart/Nomos 2017) 27–34, 176–241.

[13] UNCLOS (n 12) art 33; Proelß (n 12) 254–72.

[14] On offshore infrastructure see Stuart Kaye, 'The Protection of Platforms, Pipelines and Submarine Cables under Australian and New Zealand Law' in Natalie Klein et al (eds), *Maritime Security: International Law and Policy Perspectives from Australia and New Zealand* (Routledge 2010) 186; Assaf Harel, 'Preventing Terrorist Attacks on Offshore Platforms: Do States Have Sufficient Legal Tools?' (2012) 4 Harvard National Security Journal 131.

[15] UNCLOS (n 12) art 87; Proelß (n 12) 678–82.

[16] At least amongst the 168 UNCLOS parties: UNCLOS (n 12) art 136; Donald Rothwell/Tim Stephens, *The International Law of the Sea* (2nd edn, Hart 2016) ch 6.

upon this zonal approach are regimes dealing with functional uses of ocean space, especially the management of fisheries which straddle zonal boundaries.[17]

For all of this, the basic structures of the law of the sea would still be recognizable to nineteenth-century scholars. The two principles by which order at sea is maintained remain the regulatory powers of the coastal State and the exclusive jurisdiction of the flag State on the high seas. The latter is something of a misnomer, being an immunity from the enforcement jurisdiction of foreign government vessels rather than a guarantee that no other State may extend its prescriptive jurisdiction to events occurring on board a foreign-flagged vessel.[18] Regardless, a flag State bears special responsibility for social, technical, and administrative matters regarding ships flying its flag.[19]

High-seas enforcement actions are complex. Only a limited number of countries have the capability to conduct maritime law enforcement outside their territorial sea. Further, the exclusive jurisdiction of the flag State knows few exceptions in international law and enforcement action must often rely upon special treaty regimes or obtaining flag-State consent in real time. Malefactors thus have incentive to seek out 'flags of convenience', States with limited treaty commitments and inefficient governance. The most useful tool in the maritime security arsenal, therefore, is often port States' jurisdiction over vessels entering internal waters.[20] The doctrines of hot pursuit and constructive presence, which exceptionally extend a coastal State's enforcement jurisdiction onto the high seas for violations committed within its zones, also provide potentially useful exceptions to flag-State jurisdiction.[21]

Against this backdrop we can examine maritime security's 'silos': crimes of violence; smuggling drugs, migrants, and weapons of mass destruction (WMD); environmental security; and military activities.

2. Crimes of Violence

A key twentieth- and twenty-first-century maritime security concern has been violence at sea: armed robbery against ships; piracy; and acts covered by so-called 'suppression' (or 'terrorism') conventions. We may start with piracy. As presently defined, piracy consists of: any act of violence, detention or theft committed on the high seas; by a private vessel against another vessel (the 'two ships' requirement); committed for private ends.[22]

[17] UNCLOS (n 12) art 63; Proelß (n 12) 506–13; Yoshifumi Tanaka, *The International Law of the Sea* (2nd edn, CUP 2015) ch 7.

[18] *SS Lotus (France v Turkey)* (Judgment) [1927] PCIJ Ser A, No 10, 30–1; Douglas Guilfoyle, *Shipping Interdiction and the Law of the Sea* (CUP 2009) 7–10; Proelß (n 12) 702–3. Recent cases have taken a stricter view: *The MV "Norstar" Case (Panama v Italy)* Judgment of 10 April 2019, [225].

[19] UNCLOS (n 12) art 94; Proelß (n 12) 707–14.

[20] Z Oya Özçayir, *Port State Control* (2nd edn, Routledge 2004). See also UNCLOS art 25(2); Proelß (n 12) 255.

[21] Nicholas M Poulantzas, *The Right of Hot Pursuit in International Law* (2nd edn, Martinus Nijhoff 2002). See also UNCLOS (n 12) art 111; Proelß (n 12) 772–9.

[22] UNCLOS (n 12) art 101.

This definition has obvious limitations. First, it does not apply within the territorial sea. Similar offences within territorial waters are therefore commonly called 'armed robbery against ships'. Secondly, the 'two ships' requirement excludes acts of violence committed aboard a single vessel. The classic such incident which could not by definition constitute piracy was the *Achille Lauro* hijacking, discussed below. Thirdly, how widely or restrictively the 'private ends' element should be construed remains controversial.[23] A narrow view suggests that any act lacking State sanction is 'private'. A wider view holds that any subjective political motivation means an act cannot be for 'private ends'. It is sufficient to note that the trend of judicial and academic authority is towards the narrow view whereby, for example, vigilante violence by environmental protestors may be considered for private ends (either on the theory that the act lacks State sanction, or because a subjective political belief is a matter of private motivation).[24] Despite these limitations, the law of piracy has several attractions. Crucially, it forms a rule of customary international law providing permissive universal jurisdiction to all States. While States are not per se obliged to prosecute piracy, they do have a general duty to cooperate in its repression and can exercise universal jurisdiction over offenders.[25] Further, piracy is amongst the few exceptions to exclusive flag-State jurisdiction, allowing all States not merely to board and inspect vessels suspected of piracy but to arrest and prosecute suspects.[26]

The limitations of piracy law as a means for dealing with violent crime at sea were exposed by the *Achille Lauro* incident.[27] This involved members of the Palestinian Liberation Front posing as passengers in order to board an Italian cruise liner and then hijacking it and taking those aboard hostage, resulting in the death of one passenger. Eventually, the safe release of the surviving crew and passengers was negotiated by Egypt which allowed the hostage-takers to disembark, claiming it lacked jurisdiction to detain them. The incident led to the negotiation in 1988 of the Convention for the Suppression of Acts against the Safety of Maritime Navigation (SUA Convention), modelled on earlier conventions dealing with aircraft hijacking. The Convention applies to conduct aboard vessels navigating (or scheduled to navigate) outside any one State's territorial waters. States Parties are required to criminalize a range of SUA Convention offences which may endanger safe navigation, including seizing control of a ship by violence.[28] The Convention also creates a 'prosecute or extradite' regime applicable *inter partes*, meaning that when a person suspected of an SUA offence comes within a Party's territory it must

[23] Guilfoyle (n 18) 32–42.

[24] *Castle John and Nederlandse Stichting Sirius v NV Mabeco and NV Parfin* (Belgian Court of Cassation) (1986) 77 International Law Review 537; *Institute of Cetacean Research v Sea Conservation Society* (United States Court of Appeals for the Ninth Circuit) (No 12–35266, 25 February 2013, amended 24 May 2013) <http://caselaw.findlaw.com/us-9th-circuit/1632126.html> accessed 21 January 2020.

[25] UNCLOS (n 12) art 100; Robin Geiß/Anna Petrig, *Piracy and Armed Robbery at Sea: The Legal Framework for Counter-Piracy Operations in Somalia and the Gulf of Aden* (OUP 2011) 143–51.

[26] UNCLOS (n 12) arts 105, 110; Proelß (n 12) 749–53, 767–72.

[27] Larry McCullough, 'International and Domestic Criminal Law Issues in the *Achille Lauro* Incident: A Functional Analysis' (1986) 36 Naval Law Review 53.

[28] Convention for the Suppression of Unlawful Acts Against the Safety of Maritime Navigation 1678 UNTS 222 (SUA Convention) arts 3 and 6.

investigate the case and decide either to: prosecute the alleged offence; or, extradite the suspect to a Party willing to do so.[29] The SUA Convention is thus a 'suppression convention' designed to repress defined offences. While often called a 'terrorism convention', this is misleading. The Convention does not require its covered offences to be committed with a terrorist motive.

While the SUA Convention jurisdictional regime closes several gaps in the law of piracy, it notably: applies only amongst its parties; covers offences with different elements; and confers no right of intervention on the high seas. Nonetheless, it is accepted that certain piratical acts may nonetheless fall within the SUA Convention.[30]

3. Smuggling of Drugs, Migrants, and Weapons of Mass Destruction

Some 90 per cent of the world's trade moves by sea.[31] The oceans also provide a highway for illicit traffic in goods and services (hereafter 'trafficking' or 'smuggling'). Such trafficking can pose significant challenges for States of transit (not destination). For example, Seychelles' geographical position 'makes it an excellent centre for moving illicit drugs' between Africa and 'the sub-Indian continent' and there is a spillover into the local market, especially of heroin, leading to both addiction and HIV infection.[32] This can be disastrous for States with small populations.

The key model for intercepting high-seas smuggling has been provided by narcotics interdiction regimes. The critical problem in narcotics interdiction has, unsurprisingly, been the principle of exclusive flag-State jurisdiction. While the UN Convention on the Law of the Sea (UNCLOS) outlines a general duty for States to cooperate in the repression of such traffic,[33] it provided no mechanism to seek and receive foreign flag-State consent to high-seas law-enforcement boardings. That defect was remedied by several multilateral treaties, most notably the Vienna Narcotics Convention 1988.[34] Under the Convention, Parties agree to criminalize *inter alia* the production, manufacture, and transportation of certain drugs. Critically, Article 17(3) provides that where a State Party reasonably suspects a vessel on the high seas, flying the flag of another Party, is

[29] ibid art 7.

[30] See UNSC resolutions on Somali piracy: recently, UNSC Res 2383 (2017), preambular para 8; and other Resolutions listed in the preamble.

[31] eg International Chamber of Shipping, 'Shipping and World Trade' (undated) <https://www.ics-shipping.org/explaining/> accessed 27 November 2020.

[32] 'Seychelles National Drug Control Master Plan 2014–2018: National Coordination of the Seychelles Response to Drug Abuse and Trafficking' (The Government of Seychelles, March 2015) <http://www.aho.afro.who.int/networks/sites/default/files/national_drug_control_master_plan_2014-2018.pdf> accessed 28 February 2019.

[33] UNCLOS (n 12) art 108; Proelß (n 12) 759–63.

[34] UN Convention against Illicit Traffic in Narcotic Drugs and Psychotropic Substances 1582 UNTS 95.

> engaged in illicit traffic may so notify the flag State, request confirmation of registry and, if confirmed, request authorization from the flag State to take appropriate measures in regard to that vessel [including boarding, searching and other flag-State authorised action].

This basic model of seeking flag-State authorization to board and search a vessel, and even potentially prosecute the crimes discovered aboard, has been replicated in many other treaties, including an extensive network of bilateral interdiction arrangements entered between the United States and neighbouring countries. The same model underpins both the Protocol to the UN Transnational Organised Crime Convention dealing with migrant smuggling[35] and the 2005 Protocol to the SUA Convention dealing with the smuggling of biological, chemical nuclear weapons and their precursors (SUA 2005).[36] Over time, the new treaties in this field have developed innovative provisions addressing several practical problems. These have included: provisions on 'reverse hot pursuit', allowing the pursuit of suspects into a partner State's territorial sea; increasingly extensive use of 'safeguard clauses' governing how an interdiction should be conducted, including questions regarding the use of force;[37] and provision for the embarkation of law enforcement officials from a foreign jurisdiction aboard a patrolling coastguard or naval vessel (so-called 'ship riders').[38]

Nonetheless, for all the legal ingenuity in developing these subject-matter-specific regimes, little has been done to make such arrangements interoperable. For example, if a vessel is boarded following flag-State consent given on the basis of a suspicion it was engaged in drug smuggling, but was instead found to be smuggling material related to the proliferation of WMD, complications may arise. In particular, the boarding State might face difficulty in mounting a prosecution under SUA 2005, as it only contemplates a non-flag prosecution following a boarding conducted under SUA 2005 itself.[39] There may also be practical questions of mandate: what is a government vessel, tasked with counter-piracy, to do if it encounters migrant smuggling occurring aboard a vessel it boards and inspects?

Finally, one should note that, despite occasional suggestions to the contrary, thus far nothing in this treaty practice indicates a weakening of exclusive flag-State jurisdiction

[35] Protocol against the Smuggling of Migrants by Land, Sea and Air, Supplementing the United Nations Convention against Transnational Organized Crime 2241 UNTS 507 (Migrant Smuggling Protocol) art 8.

[36] Protocol to the Convention for the Suppression of Unlawful Acts against the Safety of Maritime Navigation IMO Doc LEG/CONF.15/21 (SUA Protocol 2005) art 8*bis*. Consolidated text in: Alan V Lowe/Stefan A G Talmon (eds), *Legal Order of the Oceans: Basic Documents on the Law of the Sea* (Hart 2009).

[37] SUA Protocol 2005 (n 36) art 8*bis* (9), (10); Migrant Smuggling Protocol (n 35) art 9.

[38] eg Agreement Concerning Co-Operation in Suppressing Illicit Maritime and Air Trafficking in Narcotic Drugs and Psychotropic Substances in the Caribbean Area arts 9 and 12; text in UNODC, 'Practical Guide for Competent National Authorities under Article 17 of the United Nations Convention against Illicit Traffic in Narcotic Drugs and Psychotropic Substances of 1988' (UN 2004) 161ff <https://www.unodc.org/documents/treaties/organized_crime/CNA%20Directory/English_ebook.pdf> accessed 21 January 2020.

[39] SUA Protocol 2005 (n 36) art 8bis (8).

or the emergence of new customary law rules allowing unilateral high-seas boarding and search of suspect vessels. Simply put, all these treaties are premised on the express consent of the flag State. It is hard to argue from such treaties to an emerging right to board without consent, no matter how desirable curtailing exclusive flag-State jurisdiction might appear.

4. Environmental Security

While coastal States have power to act regarding vessel-source pollution in their waters, and while treaties provide for high-seas inspection of fishing vessels, questions of environmental security are most frequently regulated by port State measures. All States have a duty to conserve marine living resources, to manage fisheries in their EEZ to maintain the 'maximum sustainable yield', and to cooperate in conserving fish stocks which 'straddle' jurisdictional boundaries, including through setting up regional fisheries management organizations (RFMOs) where appropriate.[40] These duties, however, can come into tension with the high-seas freedom to fish.[41] In respect of fisheries management, the usual concern is illegal, unreported, or unregulated fishing capable of undermining the conservation and management measures ('measures') adopted by coastal States or RFMOs.[42] While many RFMOs, especially those dealing with tuna, have at-sea boarding and inspection schemes, it is port State enforcement which may be most effective in deterring illegal, unreported, and unregulated (IUU) fishing. Port States may demand verifiable information from fishing vessels confirming that their catch was taken in an RFMO-compliant manner and can otherwise prohibit the landing or transshipment of fish in or through their ports.[43] Port States may also deny market access to vessels suspected of fishing in a manner undermining RFMO measures entered on fisheries agency 'black lists' (for example, if sighted fishing during a closed season). Such information can be shared amongst port States Parties to an RFMO and, indeed, between RFMOs.[44]

While IUU vessels can simply sail on to other ports, the ports an RFMO 'can effectively close' are usually those 'nearest the relevant fishing ground'.[45] Port State measures can thus 'widen the circumference of controls, effectively forcing IUU vessels to sail further to unload', thus decreasing their 'efficiency and profits'.[46] In recognition of this,

[40] UNCLOS (n 12) arts 61(3), 63(2), 64(1); Proelß (n 12) 485–6, 512–13, 517–18.

[41] UNCLOS (n 12) art 87(1)(e); Proelß (n 12) 682.

[42] For definitions see FAO, *International Plan of Action to Prevent, Deter and Eliminate Illegal, Unreported and Unregulated Fishing* (FAO 2001) paras 3.1–3.3. See, also, Agreement on Port State Measures to Prevent, Deter and Eliminate Illegal, Unreported and Unregulated Fishing, FAO Res 12/2009 (22 November 2009).

[43] ibid paras 55–6 and 63. [44] ibid para 64.

[45] Rachel Baird, 'CCAMLR Initiatives to Counter Flag State Non-Enforcement in Southern Ocean Fisheries' (2005) 36 Victoria University of Wellington Law Review 733, 740.

[46] ibid.

there has been a substantial push towards concluding port State control instruments as tools of regional fisheries enforcement.

Vessel-source pollution may also threaten maritime security.[47] The powers granted to coastal States to deal with pollution reflect a series of compromises between freedom of navigation and coastal protection. For example, in the territorial sea a coastal State may take enforcement action against a vessel suspected of violating its pollution laws where there are 'clear grounds for believing' it has committed such a violation.[48] However, in the EEZ coastal State powers of detention or arrest only follow from 'clear objective evidence' a vessel has committed a violation 'resulting in a discharge causing [or threatening] major damage'.[49] Lesser cases justify only measures of inspection[50] with the flag State taking follow-up action. The most effective powers thus remain those of port State control. A port State may act against any vessel voluntarily in port for pollution violations occurring anywhere in its territorial sea or EEZ, or upon request of another coastal State[51] and even prevent vessels posing pollution risks from sailing until repaired.[52] Measures to control pollution in straits used for international shipping are more problematic, given the principle that transit passage through such straits shall not be impeded. It remains contentious whether a port State may apply and enforce national measures intended to reduce pollution risks in an international strait against vessels subsequently in port.[53]

5. Military Activities

In the territorial sea, foreign military activities and intelligence gathering 'to the prejudice of the defence or security of the coastal State' are plainly illegal.[54] Whether such activities may be conducted in the EEZ is contentious. The key question is whether such activities constitute freedoms of the high seas applicable in the EEZ so long as they are

[47] The legal regime is complex. See UNCLOS (n 12) arts 211, 217 (on flag-State duties); and the major IMO treaties: International Convention for the Prevention of Pollution from Ships 1340 UNTS 184 (MARPOL 73/78), as amended; International Convention on Civil Liability for Oil Pollution Damage 973 UNTS 3; Protocol to the International Convention on the Establishment of an International Fund for Compensation for Oil Pollution Damage 1956 UNTS 255, and its Supplementary Fund Protocol; International Convention for the Control and Management of Ships' Ballast Water and Sediments IMO Doc BWM/CONF/36; and other instruments discussed in Tanaka (n 17) ch 8.

[48] UNCLOS (n 12) art 220(2); Proelß (n 12) 1505–12.

[49] UNCLOS (n 12) art 220(6).

[50] UNCLOS (n 12) art 220(5).

[51] UNCLOS (n 12) art 218; Proelß (n 12) 1487–96.

[52] UNCLOS (n 12) art 219; Proelß (n 12) 1496–505.

[53] See debate over the Australian approach to the Torres Strait: Robert C Beckman, 'PSSAs and Transit Passage: Australia's Pilotage System in the Torres Strait Challenges the IMO and UNCLOS' (2007) 38 Ocean Development and International Law 325; Sam Bateman/Michael White, 'Compulsory Pilotage in the Torres Strait: Overcoming Unacceptable Risks to a Sensitive Marine Environment' (2009) 40 Ocean Development and International Law 184.

[54] UNCLOS (n 12) art 19(2)(b) and (c). For arguments that innocent passage is not a precondition of lawful presence in the territorial sea: James Kraska, 'Putting Your Head in the Tiger's Mouth: Submarine Espionage in Territorial Waters' (2015) 54 Columbia Journal of Transnational Law 164, 222–9.

exercised with 'due regard' for the rights of the coastal State over resource exploration and exploitation.[55] In this context, intelligence gathering may take two forms: hydrographic surveying or electronic eavesdropping. The first involves surveys of the seabed which could have navigational/military uses (especially for submarines) or, depending on the type of data gathered, scientific or economic utility. If classed as a navigational activity, arguably such surveys are a high-seas freedom applicable in the EEZ. If, however, information is gathered as part of peaceful scientific research or the information 'is of direct significance' for natural resource exploration and exploitation such activities require coastal State consent.[56] While military survey data will generally not be released to the scientific community (and indeed the equipment used for navigational surveys tends to be different from other forms of marine research), the distinction between 'military' and 'commercial' data may largely be one of end-use rather than inherent character.[57] Indeed, given the utility of accurate hydrographic charts to a coastal State in exploiting its maritime natural resources, it has become very hard 'to identify any hydrographic data, including that collected by military surveying ships, which would not have some potential value to the coastal State' and thus fall within its EEZ jurisdiction.[58] Several States, notably China, thus consider that any form of EEZ surveying requires coastal State consent.

C. Contemporary Challenges

Cutting across these various pillars of maritime security are a number of common challenges. These include: Maritime Domain Awareness, the turn to informality in transnational governance, and non-State or 'grey zone' actors. Each is considered in turn below.

1. Maritime Domain Awareness

As discussed, exercising jurisdiction over the sea depends upon knowing who is doing what where. Accurate information is crucial. In this context, Maritime Domain Awareness (MDA) means:

> The effective understanding of any activity associated with the maritime environment that could impact upon (…) security, safety, economy or [the] environment.[59]

[55] Space prevents further discussion. See James Kraska, *Maritime Power and the Law of the Sea: Expeditionary Operations in World Politics* (OUP 2011) ch 5.

[56] UNCLOS (n 12) art 246(3) and (5); Proelß (n 12) 1649–64.

[57] Sam Bateman, 'Hydrographic Surveying in Exclusive Economic Zones: Jurisdictional Issues' (2004) 5 International Hydrographic Review 24, 30.

[58] ibid.

[59] See Amendments to the International Aeronautical and Maritime Search and Rescue (IAMSAR) Manual IMO Doc MSC.1/Circ.1415 <https://www.mardep.gov.hk/en/msnote/pdf/msin1242anx1.pdf> accessed 21 January 2020. Compare: National Security Presidential Directive NSPD-41/Homeland

Early approaches to MDA tended to see the issue as primarily technical. Indeed, often the necessary first step was enhancing coastal States' capacity to monitor their waters. An International Maritime Organization (IMO) capacity-building project in the Indian Ocean thus achieved notable successes in improving the interoperability of existing infrastructure within a coastal State and then assisting in plugging the gaps. To take Seychelles as an example, considerable improvements in its MDA capacity have been made since 2014 through creating, with international support, an IT platform which can fuse and display readily available sources of data.[60] This included information transmitted from vessels via automatic identification systems (AIS) or vessel monitoring systems (VMS), and data exchanged by regional States and international navies through mechanisms such as the Djibouti Code of Conduct (discussed below) and the Maritime Security Centre Horn of Africa. On a bigger scale, the IMO Long-Range Identification and Tracking (LRIT) system established in 2006 set up a data exchange on ship movements.[61] Under LRIT, which has force under the Safety of Life at Sea Convention 1974 (SOLAS), coastal States are given access to position data automatically generated by ships every six hours.

Such systems are useful, but those of us without operation experience may overestimate their reliability. Radar systems vary in terms of range, accuracy in measuring target locations, ability to distinguish one type of target from another, and ability to detect the desired type of target amongst 'echoes' generated by weather, atmospheric phenomena, and even birds.[62] Radar may also have difficulty detecting the small wooden-hulled vessels commonly used in various criminal enterprises. Further, LRIT coverage is limited. It applies only to passenger ships, cargo ships of at least 300 gross tons, and mobile offshore drilling units. By definition, it does not cover cargo or passenger ships under 300 tons, nor fishing vessels, nor small privately owned recreational craft. Yet it is precisely such vessels that may readily be used by 'smugglers of weapons of mass destruction (WMDs), narcotics, aliens, and other contraband, and other criminals; indeed, '[s]mall vessels have also been successfully employed (...) by terrorists to deliver Waterborne Improvised Explosive Devices (WBIEDs)'.[63]

Security Presidential Directive HSPD-13: Maritime Security Policy (US Executive Office of the President, 21 December 2004) 5.

[60] Contact Group on Piracy off the Coast of Somalia, 'Developing Maritime Domain Awareness and Law Enforcement Capacity in Seychelles' (UNODC, Trust Fund, Project Document, 10 June 2014) <http://mptf.undp.org/factsheet/project/00090817> accessed 21 January 2020.

[61] Adoption of Amendments to the International Convention for the Safety of Life at Sea, 1974, as amended (adopted 19 May 2006, Resolution MSC.202(81)) Regulation 19–1, para 5 in IMO Doc MSC 81/25/Add.1 (Annexe 2); Chris Rahman, 'Maritime Domain Awareness in Australia and New Zealand' in Natalie Klein et al (eds), *Maritime Security and the Law of the Sea* (OUP 2011) 211; Klein (n 2) 232.

[62] See eg Douglas Guilfoyle, 'The Gulf of Tonkin Incident—1964' in Tom Ruys/Olivier Corten (eds), *The Use of Force in International Law: A Case-Based Approach* (OUP 2018) ch 10. See further 'Factors Affecting Radar Performance' Encyclopedia Britannica, <https://www.britannica.com/technology/radar/Factors-affecting-radar-performance> accessed 21 January 2020.

[63] Department of Homeland Security, 'Small Vessel Security Strategy' (April 2008) (Foreword) <https://www.dhs.gov/sites/default/files/publications/small-vessel-security-strategy.pdf> accessed 10 August 2020.

Realistically, assembling any MDA picture at a national level involves a mix of technological solutions, human-source intelligence, and interagency cooperation. The state-of-the-art approach is to have 'an MDA centre that fuses data from sensors and human sources through a central database and is staffed with seconded personnel from each maritime agency'.[64] On this approach, MDA is a process not an end state, one of creating a 'culture of cooperation' between agencies.[65] Nonetheless, considerable barriers to sharing information can arise within a single State let alone between States within a region.[66] To take one example, within Australia military personnel may lack the right security clearance to view criminal intelligence data.

2. The Turn to Informality in Transnational Governance

Early studies of maritime security in international law tended to focus on formal legal structures, especially multilateral mechanisms including: the Caribbean Area Agreement to combat narcotics trafficking through jurisdiction-sharing measures such as 'ship riders' and 'reverse hot pursuit'; and the Regional Cooperation Agreement on Combating Piracy and Armed Robbery against Ships in Asia (ReCAAP) which established a multilateral information-sharing centre in Singapore.[67] Nonetheless, such treaty-law mechanisms have not provided the enduring model some anticipated.[68] Instead, there has been a turn to informal mechanisms. This is most apparent in the response to African piracy.

The Somali piracy crisis of 2008–13 prompted experiments in maritime security governance.[69] Chief amongst these were the UN-sponsored Contact Group on Piracy off the Coast of Somalia (CGPCS) and the Djibouti Code of Conduct.[70] (The Yaoundé Code of Conduct followed in respect of West African maritime crime.) The CGPCS was established in 2009 in response to UNSC Resolution 1851's call to 'all States and regional organizations fighting piracy and armed robbery at sea' off Somalia 'to establish an international cooperation mechanism'.[71] Why was a new forum to coordinate

[64] Christian Bueger/Timothy Edmunds, 'Mastering Maritime Security: Reflexive Capacity Building and the Western Indian Ocean Experience, A Best Practice Toolkit' (Safeseas 2018) 14 <http://www.safeseas.net/wp-content/uploads/2018/02/Mastering-Maritime-Security-final.pdf> accessed 21 January 2020.

[65] ibid. [66] ibid 15.

[67] See Guilfoyle (n 18) 57–61, 92–4; Klein (n 2) 136–7; Efthymios Papastavridis, *The Interception of Vessels on the High Seas. Contemporary Challenges to the Legal Order of the Oceans* (Hart 2013) 220–4; Agreement Concerning Co-Operation in Suppressing Illicit Maritime and Air Trafficking in Narcotic Drugs and Psychotropic Substances in the Caribbean Area (n 38) arts 9, 12; Regional Cooperation Agreement on Combating Piracy and Armed Robbery against Ships in Asia 2398 UNTS 199 art 4–9.

[68] eg Joseph E Kramek, 'Bilateral Maritime Counter-Drug and Immigrant Interdiction Agreements: Is this the World of the Future?' (2000) 31 University of Miami Inter-American Law Review 121.

[69] Christian Bueger, 'Responses to Contemporary Piracy: Disentangling the Organizational Field' in Douglas Guilfoyle (ed), *Modern Piracy: Legal Challenges and Responses* (Elgar 2013) 91.

[70] Percy (n 11); Guilfoyle (n 11); Bueger (n 11). [71] UNSC Res 1851 (2008).

counter-piracy outside UN or IMO auspices thought necessary? All existing organizations had mandates which were over- or under-inclusive, or expertise in only pieces of the problem be it the civilian or commercial, law enforcement, or military aspects. Thus, the CGPCS is

> not a UN or an IMO body. It is voluntary cooperation among states and organizations engaged in or with an interest in countering piracy off the coast of Somalia. The participants thus share a clear common goal and the work of the CGPCS has therefore been characterized (…) [by] specific and practical progress (…)[72]

The CGPCS functions through working groups tackling specific areas of common concern such as operational matters, legal issues, or financial flows. Typically, these working groups meet several times a year and involve representatives from governments, international organizations, and industry groups. While the CGPCS lacks any decision-making authority, it serves as a forum for sharing information and experience. Its working groups are thus more a co-operative forum than a standard-setting body. Such a mechanism clearly falls within Scott and Trubek's concept of 'new governance' which: 'accepts the possibility of coordinated diversity' amongst legal systems; 'brings actors from various levels of government' together with industry to generate 'open-ended standards, flexible and revisable guidelines, and other forms of "soft law"'; and does so to 'support and coordinate' policy rather than 'create uniformity'.[73]

Similarly, the Djibouti Code had its origins in IMO-sponsored meetings in 2008–09. Its goals include facilitating counter-piracy cooperation through establishing 'a system of national information centers', criminalizing piracy in national law, and making a common regional commitment to apprehend and prosecute piracy suspects.[74] Nonetheless, the Code is non-binding and functions as a coordinating 'soft law' instrument.[75] Indeed, successful implementation of the Djibouti Code does not require any new binding instruments, but rather closer coordination (and better implementation) of existing commitments. That is, of twenty-one signatories to the Djibouti Code, eighteen are already parties to UNCLOS, the SUA Convention, and the Hostage Taking Convention: the latter two treaties containing extensive provisions potentially applicable to maritime violence coupled with domestic implementation and 'prosecute or extradite' obligations.[76]

[72] Thomas Winkler, 'Foreword' in Bibi van Ginkel/Frans-Paul van der Putten (eds), *The International Response to Somali Piracy: Challenges and Opportunities* (Martinus Nijhoff 2010) vii, viii.

[73] Joanne Scott/David M Trubek, 'Mind the Gap: Law and New Approaches to Governance in the European Union' (2002) 8 European Law Journal 1, 6.

[74] Lucas Bento, 'Toward an International Law of Piracy Sui Generis: How the Dual Nature of Maritime Piracy Law Enables Piracy to Flourish' (2011) 29 Berkeley Journal of International Law 399, 427.

[75] Code of Conduct concerning the Repression of Piracy and Armed Robbery against Ships in the Western Indian Ocean and the Gulf of Aden IMO Doc C 102/14 (2009) art 15(a).

[76] J Ashley Roach, 'Global Conventions on Maritime Crimes Involving Piratical Acts Assessing Global Trends and Efforts to Combat Piracy' (2013) 46 Case Western Reserve Journal of International Law 91.

Following the containment of Somali piracy, international attention turned (or returned) to the Gulf of Guinea: an area perennially plagued by maritime crime, including 'piracy, armed robbery at sea, illegal, unreported and unregulated (IUU) fishing, trafficking of all sorts, dumping and other environmental crimes, and oil theft'.[77] Such activities were characterized as early as 2007 as 'undermin[ing] economic activity, hinder[ing] the movement of goods and services, and mak[ing] it difficult for [the littoral] countries to attain their development goals'.[78] The regional response which has emerged is the under-examined 2013 Yaoundé Code of Conduct,[79] closely modelled on the Djibouti Code. The Yaoundé Code addresses maritime crime as an issue with implications for peace, security, development, and environmental protection requiring a 'whole-of-government approach':

> This inter-ministerial approach to maritime security is, functionally, a human security approach, as it not only seeks to tackle the physical security matters, but addresses the legal, institutional, economic and societal conditions that can sustainably reduce the impetus for illicit activity.[80]

Amongst the Gulf of Guinea States, Cameroon, Gabon, São Tomé and Príncipe, and Equatorial Guinea have operationalized the Yaoundé Code under a 2009 Technical Accord supporting collective law-enforcement patrolling of the four States' combined maritime domain.[81]

Such informal mechanisms are not unique. European Union joint efforts in the Mediterranean to combat irregular migration and migrant smuggling rely not on formal legal mechanisms set up under the European Border and Coast Guard Agency (Frontex) Directive but on EU Naval Force (NAVFOR): a mission authorized by the UNSC in a manner echoing the response to Somali piracy.[82] The result is an ad hoc military deployment rather than an EU border agency coordinated response. This choice appears designed to avoid difficult questions of human rights law and EU principles regarding disembarkation of rescued persons. Similarly, an upsurge in maritime crime and violence in the Sulu-Celebes Sea has resulted in the littoral States, Malaysia, Indonesia, and Philippines, establishing a trilateral information-sharing and cooperative patrolling mechanism,[83] and in 2018 the establishment of a UN Office on Drugs and

[77] Ian M Ralby, 'A Human Security Approach to Maritime Security in the Gulf of Guinea' (*Comparative Jurist*, 31 August 2016) <https://comparativejurist.org/2016/08/31/a-human-security-approach-to-maritime-security-in-the-gulf-of-guinea/> accessed 21 January 2020.

[78] Raymond Gilpin, 'Enhancing Maritime Security in the Gulf of Guinea' (2007) 6 *Strategic Insights* <http://www.dtic.mil/dtic/tr/fulltext/u2/a520363.pdf> accessed 21 January 2020.

[79] Ken Ifesinachi/Chikodiri Nwangwu, 'Implementation of the Yaounde Code of Conduct and Maritime Insecurity in the Gulf of Guinea' (2015) 5 Research on Humanities and Social Sciences 54, 55.

[80] Ralby (n 77). [81] ibid.

[82] UNSC Res 2240 (2015). See Daniel Ghezelbash et al, 'Securitization of Search and Rescue at Sea: The Response to Boat Migration in the Mediterranean and Offshore Australia' (2018) 67 ICQL 315.

[83] Francis Chan/Wahyudi Soeriaatmadja, 'Indonesia, Malaysia, Philippines launch joint operations in Sulu Sea to tackle terrorism, transnational crimes' *The Straits Times* (Singapore, 19 June 2017); Prashanth Parameswaran, 'What's Next for the New Sulu Sea Trilateral Patrols?' *The Diplomat* (Tokyo, 20 June 2017).

Crime (UNODC)-sponsored Contact Group on Maritime Crime in the Sulu and Celebes Seas.

3. The Rise of Non-State and 'Grey Zone' Actors: The Chinese Maritime Militia

In one sense, maritime security has always focused upon non-State actors. The smuggling of drugs and migrants is largely conducted by profit-motivated transnational criminal groups.[84] An exception was the idea of 'States of proliferation concern' announced by the Proliferation Security Initiative in 2003 as part of its efforts to counter the transfer of WMD precursor technologies to States and non-State groups.[85] However, Somali piracy brought international attention back to the harms which could be inflicted by criminal groups at sea; and how such groups could operate as 'asymmetrical actors' using relatively unsophisticated technologies to inflict significant costs on world trade and human security, which were difficult to counter with conventional military means.[86]

A new challenge has arisen in the form of 'grey zone' actors whose status as non-State or State-sanctioned is deliberately blurred for strategic ends. US Special Operations Command defines 'gray zone challenges' as 'competitive interaction among and within state and non-state actors' falling between war and peace paradigms 'characterized by ambiguity about the nature of the conflict, opacity of the parties involved, or uncertainty about the relevant policy and legal frameworks'.[87] Grey zone tactics

> are mostly the province of revisionist powers—those actors that seek to modify some aspect of the existing international environment—and the goal is to reap gains (…) normally associated with victory in war.[88]

The US State Department's International Security Advisory Board classifies Chinese action in the South China Sea as involving a grey zone strategy, 'aggressively advancing its disputed maritime claims in the South and East China Seas, by both incremental establishment of "facts on the ground," [and] by construction and occupation of

[84] Andreas Schloenhardt, 'Organised Crime and the Business of Migrant Trafficking: An Economic Analysis' (1999) 32 Crime, Law and Social Change 203.

[85] Guilfoyle (n 18) 235.

[86] Guilfoyle (n 11); Martin N Murphy, *Small Boats, Weak States, Dirty Money: Piracy and Maritime Terrorism in the Modern World* (Columbia UP 2009).

[87] US Special Operations Command, 'White Paper: The Gray Zone' (USASOC 9 September 2015) <https://www.soc.mil/swcs/ProjectGray/Gray%20Zones%20-%20USSOCOM%20White%20Paper%209%20Sep%202015.pdf> accessed 27 November 2020.

[88] Hal Brands, 'Paradoxes of the Gray Zone' (Foreign Policy Research Institute, 5 February 2016) <https://www.fpri.org/article/2016/02/paradoxes-gray-zone/> accessed 21 January 2020; see also Michael J Mazarr, *Mastering the Gray Zone: Understanding a Changing Era of Conflict* (Strategic Studies Institute/US Army War College Press 2015).

disputed features'.[89] A key tool in pursuing these policies has been the use of a 'maritime militia'.

The most comprehensive examination of the Chinese maritime militia has been conducted by Kennedy and Erickson.[90] The Chinese armed forces consist of several branches including the conventional People's Liberation Army (and PLA Navy) and a parallel militia, being a reserve force. This reserve force now includes a maritime component. Most militia members are primarily mariners normally 'working in the civilian economy who are trained and can be mobilised' in support of PLA Navy or other government action, including defending or advancing Chinese maritime claims, rights, and interests.[91] Maritime militia units report to township-level Grassroots People's Armed Forces Departments. These Departments in turn report to district level authorities in both military and civilian chains of command. Militia units can be called upon to support operations reporting directly to the Navy, Border Security Forces, or the China Coast Guard.[92] Thus, the maritime militia also appears to have been involved, for example, in search and rescue operations.

Three emblematic Chinese maritime militia incidents are commonly discussed.[93] First, in 2009 the USNS *Impeccable* was confronted in the South China Sea by five Chinese vessels, including two maritime militia trawlers, during a hydrographic survey. The Chinese vessels engaged in aggressive manoeuvring, almost causing a collision, while attempting to snag the *Impeccable*'s towed acoustic array sonars. Secondly, in 2012 a Philippines naval surveillance aircraft spotted eight Chinese fishing vessels at anchor inside the contested Scarborough Shoal, and a frigate was dispatched to conduct a fisheries inspection.[94] When it attempted to arrest the Chinese vessels, a stand-off ensued with PLA Navy and maritime law-enforcement vessels. This apparently resulted from the Chinese fishing vessels carrying a communications suite fitted as part of a maritime militia unit. They had therefore been able to report their situation directly to a border defence control station which had then involved PLA Navy and maritime law-enforcement vessels. While it does not seem that the fishing vessels were deployed to the Scarborough Shoal as a deliberate provocation, what could have been resolved as a fisheries law-enforcement matter quickly escalated due to the integration of the vessels into Chinese law-enforcement and military communication networks. Thirdly, in 2014 The *Haiyang Shiyou 981* (*HS981*), a semi-submersible oil exploration platform owned by the China national offshore oil corporation, conducted exploration activity 17 nm from

[89] International Security Advisory Board, 'Report on Gray Zone Conflict' (US Department of State—ISAB, 3 January 2017) <https://2009-2017.state.gov/t/avc/isab/266650.htm> accessed 21 January 2020; compare Mazarr (n 88) 83ff.

[90] Conor M Kennedy/Andrew S Erickson, 'China's Third Sea Force, The People's Armed Forces Maritime Militia: Tethered to the PLA' (China Maritime Report No. 1, China Maritime Studies Institute—US Naval War College, March 2017) <http://www.andrewerickson.com/wp-content/uploads/2017/03/Naval-War-College_CMSI_China-Maritime-Report_No-1_People%E2%80%99s-Armed-Forces-Maritime-Militia-Tethered-to-the-PLA_Kennedy-Erickson_201703.pdf> accessed 21 January 2020.

[91] ibid. [92] ibid.

[93] The following discussion draws on: Kennedy/Erickson (n 90); Mazarr (n 88) 83–4.

[94] *The South China Sea Arbitration (The Philippines v China)* PCA Case No 2013–19, Award of 12 July 2016, paras 1046–58.

Triton Island in the south-western Paracel Islands, claimed by both Vietnam and China.[95] When twenty-nine Vietnamese ships moved to evict *HS981* from disputed waters, they met resistance from some eighty Chinese vessels including maritime militia vessels. Indeed, a cordon of maritime militia vessels, together with Chinese naval ships, prevented Vietnamese government vessels from approaching the *HS981*. This incident is taken as demonstrating China's capacity to rapidly mobilize specially equipped and trained civilian vessels in support of government operations.

The blurred status of the maritime militia arises in part from the uncertainty in any given context as to whether they are operating as a State organ. Kennedy and Ericson suggest that PLA leaders 'see value' in this ambiguity:

> It offers freedom to act in ways that would otherwise tarnish the PLA's professional image and heighten escalation risks (…) Having a third sea force that can keep a low profile and engage in deception while remaining subject to PLA command and control thus appears to be an essential motivation for China's retention of a body that might [otherwise] appear crude and unprofessional.[96]

It is not always clear whether vessels involved in confrontations are maritime militia units or not. However, the possibility that militia or government vessels may rapidly come to the rescue could embolden nationalistic behaviour and a willingness to confront the coastguard and maritime law enforcement forces of neighbouring States. Notably, there has been a series of clashes between Chinese vessels engaged in illegal fishing and the Republic of Korea Coast Guard. In 2016, a South Korean Coast Guard speedboat sank following a collision with a 100-ton Chinese fishing vessel; 2016 also saw UN-flagged Korean Coast Guard operations against Chinese fishermen operating illegally in the maritime component of the Korean Demilitarized Zone.[97] Thus, while there is a literature on the virtue of using civilian coastguards to conduct operations in defence of jurisdictional claims, which could escalate dangerously if conducted by warship,[98] the same is not necessarily true of 'gray zone' actors. Their lack of discipline or full integration into governmental chains of command inevitably risks escalation.

D. Outlook

The fundamental framework of the law of the sea remains sound and, while perhaps under pressure, is not under existential threat. UNCLOS has proven a

[95] See further: Carl Thayer, 'China's Oil Rig Gambit: South China Sea Game-Changer?' *The Diplomat* (Singapore, 12 May 2014).

[96] Kennedy/Erickson (n 90).

[97] Dan D Luce, 'Beijing Tells Seoul to Stay Calm and Carry On, after Chinese Fishermen Sink a South Korean Coast Guard Boat' *Foreign Policy* (Washington, 12 October 2016).

[98] Sam Bateman, 'Regional Navies and Coastguards: Striking a Balance between "Lawships" and Warships' in Geoffrey Till/Jane Chan (eds), *Naval Modernisation in South-East Asia: Nature, Causes and Consequences* (Routledge 2014) 245.

widely acceptable treaty precisely because it papered over certain disagreements with constructively ambiguous text.[99] It is unsurprising, therefore, that both tensions over differing interpretations remain and that certain anticipated threats to legal order have not materialized. UNCLOS is itself flexible enough to accommodate a degree of change.[100] Certainly, there is some risk of escalation over claims in the South China Sea. Much of that risk is, however, contained by China often acting through coastguard, fisheries inspectorate, or 'maritime militia' units rather than military vessels. Otherwise, however, the rise of maritime security has occurred within the existing legal framework and without demands for its fundamental revision.

The extent to which this is a good thing is debatable. The real challenges lie in the turn to informal governance and the policy pressure to sequester maritime security measures away from ordinary oversight or interaction with human rights norms. Informality has pragmatic, instrumental benefits. Coalitions spanning governmental, industry, and other actors can come together—often at a level of technical cooperation considered non-political—to engage in governance experiments directed at problems of common concern.[101] However, the very contingency of such experiments makes them fragile, and significant effort is required to maintain them.[102] There is also the risk that in operating at a purely 'technical' level other questions are pushed out of the frame, whether deliberately or otherwise. In the result, the burden of securitization in the maritime domain tends to fall disproportionately on marginal or transnational groups, especially seafarers and irregular migrants,[103] and there is a risk that aspects of the law of the sea—such as the duty of rescue—become 'instrumentalized for security purposes.'[104]

[99] Douglas Guilfoyle, 'The South China Sea Award: How Should We Read the UN Convention on the Law of the Sea?' (2018) 8 Asian Journal of International Law 51, 51–2.

[100] Alan Boyle, 'Further Development of the Law of the Sea Convention: Mechanisms for Change' (2005) 54 ICLQ 563.

[101] Christian Bueger, 'Territory, Authority, Expertise: Global Governance and the Counter-Piracy Assemblage' (2018) 24 European Journal of International Relations 614.

[102] ibid.

[103] Irini Papanicolopulu, *International Law and the Protection of People at Sea* (OUP 2018); Guilfoyle (n 1) 62–71.

[104] Ghezelbash et al (n 82) 336.

CHAPTER 17

INTERNATIONAL DISARMAMENT AND ARMS CONTROL

In the Middle of a Paradigm Shift?

MIRKO SOSSAI

A. Introduction

Disarmament and arms control were envisaged as an integral part of the collective security system set out in the UN Charter, which was designed to 'save succeeding generations from the scourge of war'.[1] Since 1945, disarmament efforts have been geared towards achieving a negotiated reduction in armaments amongst all States as a means to avoid recourse to the use of force in international relations. In practice, however, the maintenance and restoration of international peace and security has required the continued existence of efficient armed forces. As articulated by the UN Security Council (UNSC) in a 2008 Presidential Statement, it remains important to maintain 'appropriate levels of military expenditure, in order to achieve undiminished security for all at the lowest appropriate level of armaments'.[2]

Whereas disarmament is related to the reduction (or even the total abolition) of a category of weapons, arms control was developed in the context of nuclear deterrence, which characterized the bipolar confrontation of the United States and the USSR during the Cold War. Given that the goal of arms control conventions was the stabilization of the security environment, such agreements usually included measures such as mutually agreed limitations on certain armaments or freezing their number at a given level.

[1] Charter of the United Nations 1 UNTS XVI (UN Charter) preamble.
[2] UNSC Presidential Statement 43 (2008) UN Doc S/PRST/2008/43.

Cooperation, reciprocity, and inclusiveness[3] were the major features of an approach that promoted confidence-building amongst States as the most effective tool to prevent ambiguities, doubts and suspicions, and, as a consequence, reduce the risk of surprise or accidental attacks.[4] As such, the essential distinction between disarmament and arms control lies in what they seek to achieve.[5] This seems to be confirmed by the temporal application of relevant conventions in these areas. To elaborate, since disarmament is the outcome of a broad strategy for peace, as a rule, disarmament treaties tend to apply in perpetuity, and may not be subject to reservations. Conversely, most treaties on arms control are of a limited duration (although they may be indefinitely extended).[6]

International law on disarmament and arms control is in essence treaty law: hence, this chapter first identifies the distinctive features of the existing legal framework. In the post-Cold War era, the 1993 Chemical Weapons Convention (CWC)[7] has been seen as representing the most successful model for subsequent disarmament treaties, including those on antipersonnel landmines and cluster munitions. Such conventions, which also address humanitarian concerns, do not only include prohibitions on the development and production of weapons and a duty to destroy existing stockpiles, but also introduce a comprehensive ban on their use, 'under any circumstances'. The ban on chemical weapons and the indefinite extension of the Treaty on the Non-Proliferation of Nuclear Weapons (NPT)[8] in 1995 seemed to confirm that a legal framework on disarmament and arms control, based on a system of bilateral as well as multilateral treaties, would come to constitute an effective tool to preserve peace and to safeguard humanity in the new century.[9] However, since then, changes in the international security architecture have been of such a magnitude that, only a few years later, the question turned to whether the existing regime suffered structural deficits.[10]

Following that, the chapter focuses on current developments in both international politics and military technology and their impact on international security and arms

[3] Heike Krieger, 'A Nuclear Test for Multilateralism—Challenges to the Non-Proliferation Treaty as a Means of Arms Control' (2006) 49 German Yearbook of International Law 17.

[4] Kenneth W Abbott, '"Trust but Verify": The Production of Information in Arms Control Treaties and Other International Agreements' (1993) 26 Cornell International Law Journal 1.

[5] Adrian Loets, 'Arms Control' MPEPIL (OUP, July 2013).

[6] Gabriella Venturini, 'Control and Verification of Multilateral Treaties on Disarmament and Non-Proliferation of Weapons of Mass Destruction' (2011) 17 UC Davis Journal of International Law and Policy 346, 347; Felix Calderón, 'The Duration of Arms Control and Disarmament Treaties' in Julie Dahlitz/Detlev C Dicke (eds), *The International Law of Arms Control and Disarmament: Proceedings of the Symposium, Geneva, 28 February—2 March 1991* (UN 1991) 145.

[7] Convention on the Prohibition of the Development, Production, Stockpiling and Use of Chemical Weapons and on their Destruction 1975 UNTS 45 (CWC).

[8] 729 UNTS 161 (NPT).

[9] 1995 Review and Extension Conference of the Parties to the Treaty on the Non-Proliferation of Nuclear Weapons, 'Final Document: Part I, Organization and Work of the Conference' (11 May 1995) Doc NPT/CONF.1995/32, Annex, Decision 3: Extension of the Treaty on the Non-Proliferation of Nuclear Weapons.

[10] Serge Sur, 'L'entreprise du désarmement au péril du nouveau contexte international de sécurité' (2004) 5 Annuaire Français de Relations Internationales 727.

control efforts. In a post-9/11 world, the concept of counter-proliferation has been utilized to identify all the initiatives taken to ensure that weapons of mass destruction (WMD) do not fall into the hands of terrorist groups or irresponsible governments.[11] One of the driving forces behind this drastic change in approach has been the UNSC, particularly through the adoption of quasi-legislative decisions such as Resolution 1540 (2004) on WMD and terrorism, as well as the imposition of targeted sanctions. Moreover, to address the serious concerns raised by the use of chemical weapons in Syria, the UNSC closely cooperated with the Organization for the Prohibition of Chemical Weapons (OPCW) to implement a disarmament programme in that country.[12] Although the elimination of stockpiles and production facilities in 2014 should be regarded as a successful process under the difficult circumstances of a complex armed conflict, the UNSC was not able to prevent the use of chemical agents by all parties.

Since 2014, the re-emergence of strategic tensions between the major powers has marked a new period of arms competition.[13] The review conferences of both the NPT and CWC have revealed tensions which prevented the emergence of any consensus regarding a final outcome document. Whereas arms control efforts of both the US and Russia have so far been devoted to maintaining the legacy of the Cold War (which ensured a stable military balance and a platform for communications to defuse tensions), recent developments speak to the deterioration of the existing system based on legal and political commitments. The fate of the Intermediate-Range Nuclear Forces (INF) Treaty, the 1987 bilateral agreement on the elimination of intermediate-range and shorter-range missiles, is paradigmatic: the US decided first to suspend its obligations[14] and later to withdraw from the treaty,[15] due to Russia's material breach, on the basis of the *inadimplenti non est adimplendum* principle enshrined in Article 60 of the Vienna Convention on the Law of Treaties (VCLT).[16]

In addition, the pillars of the arms control architecture in Europe, namely the 1990 Treaty on Conventional Armed Forces in Europe (CFE Treaty)[17] and the 1992 Treaty on Open Skies,[18] together with the Vienna Document on Confidence and Security-Building Measures (CSBM),[19] are at risk. It is not only political and structural challenges which undermine the effectiveness, or indeed the very existence of such a system. Rapid advances in military technology contribute to limit the relevance of the global security

[11] Daniel H Joyner, *International Law and the Proliferation of Weapons of Mass Destruction* (OUP 2009); Michael Bothe, 'Weapons of Mass Destruction, Counter-Proliferation' MPEPIL (OUP, August 2016).

[12] UNSC Res 2118 (2013).

[13] UNODA, *Securing Our Common Future: An Agenda for Disarmament* (UN 2018).

[14] The White House, 'Statement from the President Regarding the Intermediate-Range Nuclear Forces (INF) Treaty' (1 February 2019) <https://www.whitehouse.gov/briefings-statements/statement-president-regarding-intermediate-range-nuclear-forces-inf-treaty/> accessed 19 September 2019.

[15] US Department of Defense, 'Statement From Secretary of Defense Mark T. Esper on the INF Treaty' (2 August 2019) <https://www.defense.gov/Newsroom/Releases/Release/Article/1924386/statement-from-secretary-of-defense-mark-t-esper-on-the-inf-treaty/> accessed 19 September 2019.

[16] 1155 UNTS 331. [17] (1991) 30 ILM 1. [18] UKTS No 27.

[19] OSCE 'Vienna Document 2011 on Confidence and Security-Building Measures' (30 November 2011) FSC.DOC/1/11.

system, insofar as the relevant instruments do not cover crucial contemporary capabilities, such as unmanned aerial vehicles (UAVs) and cyberwarfare assets.[20] In order to avoid further escalation in the growing military confrontation and the associated risks for the continent, a group of like-minded European countries have launched a structured dialogue within the framework Organization for Security and Cooperation in Europe (OSCE) for the modernization of arms control and confidence-building arrangements.[21]

B. The Legal Framework

Throughout the twentieth century, victorious States imposed prohibitions or restrictions on armaments in the construction of post-war arrangements as an essential tool to exercise control over the military capabilities of defeated parties. For instance, the 1919 Treaties of Versailles constrained the strength of Germany's armed forces and established a verification regime, though such restrictions were justified 'in order to render possible the initiation of a general limitation of armaments of all nations'.[22] In 1945, the post-surrender policy vis-à-vis Japan was the disarmament and demilitarization of the country.[23]

Since the end of the Second World War, a consistent number of peace-time agreements created the current disarmament and arms control framework. Such treaties reflected both the place that armaments regulation had within the UN system and the specific features of the bipolar order during the Cold War. It is not by chance that the preamble of the 1968 NPT establishes a bridge between its obligations and the maintenance of international peace and security, based on the ban on the use of force in international relations under the UN Charter.

1. Disarmament and Arms Control within the UN System

The UN Charter recognizes that a certain relationship exists between the level of armaments and the establishment of international peace and security. The focus, however, is most often on the regulation of arms rather than on disarmament as such.[24] The point has been made that the goal of disarmament in the UN framework does not have the

[20] Łukasz Kulesa, 'The Future of Conventional Arms Control in Europe' (2018) 60 Survival 75, 81.

[21] OSCE Ministerial Council, 'From Lisbon to Hamburg: Declaration on the Twentieth Anniversary of the OSCE Framework for Arms Control' (9 December 2016) OSCE Doc MC.DOC/4/16 (OSCE, 'From Lisbon to Hamburg').

[22] Treaty of Peace between the Allied and Associated Powers and Germany 112 BFSP 1 p V.

[23] Takako Ueta, 'Japan: A Case of a Non-Control Regime' in Fred Tanner (ed), *From Versailles to Baghdad: Post-War Armament Control of Defeated States* (UN 1992) 101.

[24] Hans Kelsen, *The Law of United Nations* (Praeger 1950) 104: The UN Charter 'does not impose upon the Members the obligation to reduce their armaments'.

central position it had held in the League of Nations Covenant,[25] Article 8 of which strongly emphasized that the maintenance of international peace required a reduction in armaments.[26] The content of Articles 11 and 26 of the UN Charter reflects the view of the founders of the UN that it was necessary to keep a certain level of armaments for the purposes of the collective security system envisaged in Chapter VII of the Charter. The former entrusts the UN General Assembly (UNGA) with the mandate of formulating general principles, while the latter envisages for the UNSC the task of submitting concrete plans. Although Article 26 has mostly remained a dead letter,[27] it has had a fundamental normative influence in giving expression to the principle of 'least diversion of the world's human and economic resources', which links regulation of armaments to socio-economic development issues.[28]

It follows that the UNGA has a position of monopoly in relation to disarmament matters. Its abundant practice has contributed to successes in specific areas but has also resulted in reduced efficacy of the numerous and often redundant resolutions, due to their lack of clarity and at times less than coherent messages.[29] Established by the UNGA as the 'single multilateral disarmament negotiating forum of the international community',[30] the Conference on Disarmament played an essential role in the drafting of most treaties addressing WMD. After almost two decades in which the body remained in a state of stagnation, attempts have been made to bring it back to substantive discussions: in 2018 the Conference created five subsidiary bodies on its agenda items 'to work on reaching an understanding on the areas of commonalities by taking into consideration all relevant views and proposals past, present and future; to deepen technical discussions and broaden areas of agreement; and to consider effective measures, including legal instruments for negotiations'.[31]

It is significant that arms control efforts under the auspices of the UN have also focused on certain conventional weapons with inhumane effects. Two sessions of a UN conference, held in 1979 and 1980, led to the adoption of the Convention on Prohibitions or Restrictions on the Use of Certain Conventional Weapons Which May be Deemed to be Excessively Injurious or to Have Indiscriminate Effects (CCW).[32] As a compromise solution, the CCW is an 'umbrella treaty', containing itself no substantive provisions,

[25] 108 LNTS 188; Hector Gross-Espiell, 'Article 26' in Jean-Pierre Cot et al (eds), *La Charte des Nations Unies: commentaire article par article* (3rd edn, Economica 2005) 922.

[26] Emmanuel Bourdoncle, 'Le désarmement dans le cadre de la SDN—Commentaire des articles 8 et 9' in Robert Kolb (ed), *Commentaire sur le Pacte de la Société des Nations* (Bruylant 2014) 385.

[27] Hans-Joachim Schütz, 'Article 26' in Bruno Simma et al (eds), *The Charter of the United Nations: A Commentary* (3rd edn, OUP 2012) 869.

[28] Annyssa Bellal/Gilles Giacca, 'Principle 25: Peace, Development and Environmental Protection' in Jorge E Viñuales (ed), *The Rio Declaration on Environment and Development: A Commentary* (OUP 2015) 593.

[29] Eckart Klein/Stefanie Schmahl, 'Article 11' in Simma et al (n 27) 497.

[30] UNGA Res S-10/2 (30 June 1978).

[31] Conference on Disarmament, 'Decision Adopted at the 1442nd plenary meeting at 16 February 2018' (19 February 2018) Doc CD/2119.

[32] 1342 UNTS 137 (CCW).

which are instead left to its five protocols. Each of these protocols addresses a category of weapons, combining various elements of international humanitarian law (IHL) and arms control. Ratifying States must become party to at least two of the protocols in existence at the relevant time.[33] Interestingly, Article 8 CCW provides for a procedure for the adoption of new protocols at review conferences, requiring consensus amongst parties.[34] However, although decision-making by consensus may in principle favour the subsequent ratification of an agreement by the widest possible number of parties, it has often meant the production of drafts which represent the minimum common denominator amongst competing national interests. The unsatisfactory results achieved within the framework of the CCW as to the content of Amended Protocol II[35] led a group of like-minded States, with the active support of the International Committee of the Red Cross (ICRC) and civil society actors, to seek an alternative forum in order to negotiate, under different voting procedures, a complete ban on the use of landmines. The 1997 Ottawa Convention was the successful outcome of that initiative.[36]

2. The Place of Customary International Law

It is commonly agreed that customary international law does not contain disarmament rules prohibiting the development, production, or possession of specific armaments.[37] The argument goes that international custom is not well suited for regulating a field where law needs to adapt itself to changing technologies, where the relevant legal rules must be clear and precise, and State implementation needs to be verified through international control.[38] Nevertheless, although the International Court of Justice (ICJ) did not decide the issue on the merits,[39] the customary nature of the obligation to pursue in good faith and bring to a conclusion negotiations leading to nuclear disarmament

[33] William J Fenrick, 'New Developments in the Law concerning the Use of Conventional Weapons in Armed Conflict' (1981) 9 Canadian Yearbook of International Law 229.

[34] In 1980, the UN Conference adopted the CCW and the first three protocols by consensus; cf CCW (n 32) art 8: 'Such a conference may agree, with the full participation of all States represented at the conference, upon additional protocols which shall be adopted in the same manner as this Convention.'

[35] Protocol II on Prohibitions or Restrictions on the Use of Mines, Booby-Traps and Other Devices 2048 UNTS 133.

[36] Convention on the Prohibition of the Use, Stockpiling, Production and Transfer of Anti-Personnel Mines and on their Destruction 2056 UNTS 211 (Ottawa Convention). Norway's initiative to convene an international conference in Oslo on the ban of cluster munitions was criticized because negotiations took place outside the framework of the CCW. See Karen Hulme, 'The 2008 Cluster Munitions Convention: Stepping Outside the CCW Framework (Again)' (2009) 58 ICLQ 219.

[37] cf *Case Concerning Military and Paramilitary Activities in and against Nicaragua (Nicaragua v USA)* (Merits) [1986] ICJ Rep 14 [135]: '[I]n international law there are no rules, other than such rules as may be accepted by the State concerned, by treaty or otherwise, whereby the level of armaments of a sovereign State can be limited.'

[38] Venturini (n 6) 346, quoting Julie Dahlitz, 'The Role of Customary Law in Arms Limitation' in Dahlitz/Dicke (n 6) 164.

[39] *Obligations Concerning Negotiations Relating to Cessation of the Nuclear Arms Race and to Nuclear Disarmament (Marshall Islands v Pakistan)* (Jurisdiction and Admissibility) [2016] ICJ Rep 552.

played an important role in the applications submitted by the Marshall Islands in the *Obligations concerning Negotiations relating to Cessation of the Nuclear Arms Race and to Nuclear Disarmament* cases. Legal scholarship appears divided on this issue.[40]

The point has been made that nuclear disarmament obligations are 'part of customary international law or at least evolving custom' and 'are valid *erga omnes*, as they affect the international community as a whole rather than a particular State or group of States.'[41] Those in disagreement with such arguments have observed that it is difficult to see how Article VI NPT can become customary international law without considering the practice and *opinio juris* of those States that possess nuclear weapons and to which the provision is primarily addressed.

3. A Typology of International Treaty Obligations

There are many bilateral, regional, and universal international conventions on disarmament and the control of armaments. A classification of the corpus of disarmament and arms control treaties must necessarily take into account different variables: the type of weapon, the scope of the prohibitions, the forum of negotiation, and the number of States Parties.

The first category comprises the substantive obligations related to the elimination or reduction of armaments. Those disarmament treaties, which are aimed at dismantling an entire category of weapons, contain specific prohibitions addressed to the parties as to the development, production, acquisition, stockpiling, retention, transfer, or use of them, and provide for their destruction. Along with the CWC, both the 1997 Ottawa Convention and the 2008 Convention on Cluster Munitions (CCM)[42] belong to this category. The terminology 'never under any circumstances' affirms the comprehensive approach of the ban: it covers non-international armed conflicts as well as use in acts of reprisal.

In contrast, arms control treaties are usually aimed at setting quantitative restrictions on the numbers of the regulated weapons.[43] The 1990 CFE Treaty is an example of arms limitation, as it binds groups of States Parties to reduce five categories of their conventional armaments and military equipment to agreed levels. The same goal of avoiding

[40] cf Daniel H Joyner 'The Legal Meaning and Implication of Article VI of the Non-Proliferation Treaty' in Gro Nystuen et al (eds), *Nuclear Weapons and International Law* (CUP 2014) 413–17; Daniel Rietiker, *Humanization of Arms Control Paving the Way for a World Free of Nuclear Weapons* (Routledge 2017).

[41] ILA, 'Second Report of the Committee on Nuclear Weapons, Non-Proliferation and Contemporary International Law: Legal Aspects of Nuclear Disarmament' (Washington, 2014) 7 <https://ila.vettoreweb.com/Storage/Download.aspx?DbStorageId=994&StorageFileGuid=3ca8870f-183c-40c5-930a-02a1285fb500> accessed 9 January 2020.

[42] 2688 UNTS 39.

[43] cf David A Koplow, 'Eve of Destruction: Implementing Arms Control Treaty Obligations to Dismantle Weaponry' (2017) 8 Harvard National Security Journal 158, 169.

the alteration of the power balance characterizes the non-proliferation effort, which is aimed at maintaining the status quo by preventing the spread of certain weapons.[44]

Other treaty obligations fall within the realm of transparency and confidence-building measures. This second category includes exchange of information as well as observation measures, such as the presence of foreign observers, which allow participating States to monitor each other's military facilities and activities. They do not strictly constitute a disarmament tool as they are not related to a restriction on, or ban of, any type of weapon. Their objective is to translate the prohibition of the threat or use of force in international relations into positive action. The 1992 Open Skies Treaty gives each State Party the right to conduct, and the obligation to accept, short-notice unarmed observation flights over their territory to promote openness of military forces and their activities.[45] The duty to provide information also characterizes both the Ottawa Convention and the CCM: their Article 7, significantly titled 'Transparency Measures', states that the Parties shall submit annual reports to the UN Secretary-General.

A third typology of obligations is the expression of the preventive approach of certain disarmament treaties vis-à-vis the activities of private individuals and entities. Article IV of the 1972 Biological and Toxin Weapons Convention (BTWC)[46] is a paradigmatic example: it contains the explicit duty for a State Party to take any necessary measures to proscribe and prevent the development, production, stockpiling, acquisition, or retention of such weapons, 'in accordance with its constitutional processes' and 'within the territory of such State, under its jurisdiction or under its control anywhere'. Although the treaty does not specify the domestic measures required to give effect to its provisions, the final documents adopted by the review conferences have recognized that the prohibitions under the BTWC require a range of different issues to be addressed at national level, including the criminalization of the prohibited activities, law enforcement measures, and export controls. In particular, States Parties are called upon to adopt legislative, administrative, judicial, and other measures designed to 'ensure the safety and security of microbial or other biological agents or toxins in laboratories, facilities, and during transportation, to prevent unauthorized access to and removal of such agents or toxins'.[47]

Finally, an increasingly common feature of disarmament obligations is the inclusion of 'measures for remediation', as they are referred to in the report of the UN Secretary-General,[48] which cover a range of activities, including explosive ordnance destruction and demining, repair of the natural environment, and assistance to victims and survivors.

[44] See Masahiko Asada, Chapter 18 in this *Handbook*.

[45] Hartwig Spitzer, 'The Open Skies Treaty: Entering Full Implementation at a Low Key' (2006) 17 Helsinki Monitor 83.

[46] Convention on the Prohibition of the Development, Production and Stockpiling of Bacteriological (Biological) and Toxin Weapons and on their Destruction 1015 UNTS 163 (BTWC).

[47] Eighth Review Conference of the States Parties to the Convention on the Prohibition of the Development, Production and Stockpiling of Bacteriological (Biological) and Toxin Weapons and on Their Destruction, 'Final Document' (11 January 2017) Doc BWC/CONF.VIII/4, para 11. See Treasa Dunworth et al 'National Implementation of the Biological Weapons Convention' (2006) 11 JCSL 141.

[48] See n 13.

In particular, Article 5 CCM has represented a major step forward compared to the Ottawa Convention, which was the first breakthrough in victim assistance in treaties governing weapons.[49] The provision establishes a link between disarmament and human rights by stating that States Parties, with respect to cluster munitions victims in areas under its jurisdiction or control, shall provide 'age- and gender-sensitive assistance, including medical care, rehabilitation and psychological support, as well as provide for their social and economic inclusion'.

4. The Nature of Disarmament Obligations and the Impact on Verification

The evolution of disarmament and arms control agreements evidences a shift from bilateralism to community interests in international law. Whereas bilateral arms control agreements are characterized by mutual reduction targets with a view to a reciprocal interchange of benefits, multilateral disarmament treaties have been recognized as containing integral (or interdependent) obligations.[50] For instance, as early as 1963 the Partial Test Ban Treaty included duties that 'are inextricably interrelated, form an indivisible whole'.[51]

Interestingly, obligations under the NPT reveal a degree of synthesis between the principle of peaceful coexistence in the mutual relations between the two superpowers at that time, and the emerging trends of the protection of certain fundamental values. The regime against the proliferation of nuclear weapons is concerned with the collective interests of the international community as a whole (namely international peace and security), while at the same time dealing with cardinal, particular interests of the major powers.[52] There is no doubt that the substantive obligations in this field cannot 'be brought under a bundle of bilateral relations'; rather, they are 'dominated by a sort of global reciprocity in the sense that each state disarms because the others do likewise'.[53]

It follows that '[o]ne state's non-compliance with its obligations under a treaty on arms control or disarmament may fundamentally and negatively affect the security of

[49] Markus Reiterer/Tirza Leibowitz, 'Article 5: Victim Assistance' in Gro Nystuen/Stuart Casey-Maslen (eds), *The Convention on Cluster Munitions: A Commentary* (OUP 2010) 328.

[50] The notion was developed by Gerald Fitzmaurice, 'Second Report on the Law of Treaties' (1957) II Yearbook of the International Law Commission 54.

[51] Treaty Banning Nuclear Weapon Tests in the Atmosphere, in Outer Space and Under Water 480 UNTS 43. See Bruno Simma, 'From Bilateralism to Community Interest in International Law' (1994-IV) 250 Recueil des Cours 217, 336.

[52] Andreas Paulus/Jörn Müller, 'Survival Through Law: Is there a Law Against Nuclear Proliferation?' (2007) 18 Finnish Yearbook of International Law 83.

[53] Linos-Alexander Sicilianos, 'The Classification of Obligations and the Multilateral Dimension of the Relations of International Responsibility' (2002) 13 EJIL 1127, 1134; see *Obligations concerning Negotiations relating to Cessation of the Nuclear Arms Race and to Nuclear Disarmament (Marshall Islands v UK)* (Preliminary Objections) [2016] ICJ Rep 885, Sep Op Tomka [35]: '[T]he performance of the obligation by a State is conditional on the performance of the same obligation by the other States'.

others'; and conversely 'continued compliance with such treaty obligations impacts positively on security'.[54] As a result, in both cases, 'credible verification to establish compliance or non-compliance is of major importance'.[55] The UNGA, for instance, has recognized that the ultimate objective of 'general and complete disarmament' could only be achieved 'under effective international control'.[56] The nature of disarmament obligations has had an impact on the choice of the specific forms and modalities of verification. This in turn individuates those supervisory mechanisms and procedures aimed at ensuring that States Parties are in compliance with the substantive rules of a convention. This having been said, occasionally individual States are given the right to 'verify through observations the activities of the other State Parties of the Treaty',[57] and multilateral treaties usually provide that each State Party may present a request to a competent verification body to assess the consistency of another Party's conduct with disarmament obligations or even make a complaint about alleged breaches.[58]

C. Current Developments

1. Chemical Weapons in Syria between Disarmament and Investigative Mechanisms

Recent disarmament and arms control efforts must be understood within a dynamic between coercion and consent. This is the case of the dismantlement programme regarding Syrian chemical weapons. While the US and its allies emphasized the coercive aspect of the disarmament process, Syria and Russia stressed its consent-based elements, rooted in the principle of State sovereignty. This is certainly due to the unique framework created for the purpose of chemical dismantlement.[59]

After reports confirmed the use of chemical agents during the civil war, Syria announced its intention to accede to the CWC on 12 September 2013 and, on that same day, the US and Russia reached a political agreement to ensure the elimination of

[54] Weapons of Mass Destruction Commission, *Weapons of Terror: Freeing the World of Nuclear, Biological and Chemical Arms* (WMDC 2006) 169.

[55] ibid.

[56] Final Document of the Tenth Special Session of the General Assembly, UNGA Res S-10/2 (30 June 1978).

[57] Treaty on the Prohibition of the Emplacement of Nuclear Weapons and Other Weapons of Mass Destruction on the Sea-Bed and the Ocean Floor and in the Subsoil Thereof 955 UNTS 115 (Seabed Treaty) art III(1).

[58] Matthew Happold, 'The "Injured State" in Case of a Non-Proliferation Treaty and the Legal Consequences of Such a Breach' in Daniel H Joyner/Marco Roscini (eds), *Nonproliferation Law as a Special Regime* (CUP 2012) 175.

[59] Ralf Trapp, 'Elimination of the Chemical Weapons Stockpile of Syria' (2014) 19 JCSL 7.

chemical weapons.[60] Two weeks later, the OPCW Executive Council adopted a decision on the matter,[61] which was subsequently endorsed by UNSC Resolution 2118 (2013). While the CWC constituted the overall legal foundation for subsequent actions, special procedures were nonetheless introduced given the exceptional circumstances in the country. Not only did the Joint UN-OPCW Mission have 'immediate and unfettered access to and the right to inspect, in discharging their functions, any and all sites' on the basis of Resolution 2118, but the OPCW decision also provided that it could 'inspect as soon as possible any other site identified by a State Party as having been involved in the Syrian chemical weapons programme': an ad hoc procedure that resembled the challenge inspections system under Article IX CWC.

The most relevant deviation from the CWC regime was the decision taken by the UNSC to remove chemical-warfare agents and precursors from the territory of Syria for their destruction outside that country. The operation was then successfully supported by various countries and coordinated with the help of the Joint UN-OPCW Mission.[62] In other terms, Resolution 2118 set aside the prohibition of transfer of chemical weapons under the CWC for the specific purpose of disarmament. This might be seen as a further manifestation of the UNSC practice of adapting binding treaty law to a particular situation on an ad hoc basis.[63] Beyond relying on Article 103 UN Charter to affirm the hierarchically superior character of a binding resolution over obligations under the CWC, the special procedures adopted for the Syrian chemical disarmament could be better understood within the framework of the bilateral cooperation agreement between the UN and the OPCW.[64]

Despite progress in dismantling chemical stockpiles and facilities, incidents involving the use of toxic chemicals as a weapon did not cease entirely. The UNSC initially succeeded in establishing an UN–OPCW Joint Investigative Mechanism (JIM), with the mandate 'to identify to the greatest extent feasible, individuals, entities, groups or governments who were perpetrators, organisers, sponsors or otherwise involved in the use of chemicals as weapons.'[65] However, the UNSC was ultimately divided on the issue of accountability: eventually, it failed to renew the mandate of the JIM. In an attempt to fill that vacuum, in April 2018 the Conference of States Parties of the CWC decided on the

[60] UNGA/UNSC 'Identical letters dated 19 September 2013 from the Permanent Representatives of the Russian Federation and the United States of America to the United Nations addressed to the Secretary-General' (24 September 2013) UN Doc A/68/398–S/2013/565.

[61] OPCW Executive Council, 'Decision: Destruction of Syrian Chemical Weapons' (27 September 2013) Doc EC-M-33/DEC.1.

[62] OPCW Executive Council, 'Note by the Director-General: Overall Report on the Elimination of the Syrian Chemical Weapons Programme' (4 July 2014) Doc EC-76/DG.16.

[63] Guido den Dekker, 'Absolute Validity, Absolute Immunity: Is There Something Wrong with Article 103 of the UN Charter?' in Cedric Ryngaert et al (eds), *What's Wrong with International Law? Liber Amicorum A.H.A. Soons* (Brill 2015) 247; Stefan Talmon, 'Security Council Treaty Action' (2009) 62 Revue Hellénique de Droit International 65.

[64] Agreement Concerning the Relationship Between the United Nations and the Organization for the Prohibition of Chemical Weapons, UNGA Res 55/283 (24 September 2001) Annex.

[65] UNSC Res 2235 (2015).

creation of the Investigation and Identification Team, a new mechanism within the OPCW Technical Secretariat 'to identify the perpetrators of the use of chemical weapons in the Syrian Arab Republic'.[66]

2. The Deterioration of the Foundations of Arms Control in Europe

As Cold War tensions appear to re-emerge, there is a concrete risk that the arms control framework that came into effect in the early 1990s is coming to an end. The legal edifice of cooperative security, aimed at avoiding an arms race through mutual confidence and reducing inadvertent escalation of tensions in and around Europe, is collapsing. Its conventional pillars are the CFE Treaty and the Open Skies Treaty. Since the beginning of the twenty-first century, relations between Russia and NATO have deteriorated, leading to mutual accusations of treaty breaches and initiatives aimed at suspending or terminating certain obligations contained therein.[67] The rules on suspension and termination of treaties are contained in Articles 54–64 of the 1969 VCLT. Although arms control and disarmament treaties usually include withdrawal clauses, contracting parties may invoke one of the two general grounds that are particularly relevant in this context: the principle *inadimplenti non est adimplendum* under Article 60 and the *rebus sic stantibus* clause under Article 62.[68]

Article IV of the 1963 Partial Test Ban Treaty has represented the model for the withdrawal clauses of most disarmament and arms control treaties.[69] Under Article XIX of the CFE Treaty, States have the right to withdraw, subject to a requirement to provide advance notice to all other parties, when supreme interests are jeopardized by extraordinary events related to the subject matter of the treaty. The notion of 'extraordinary events' has been intentionally left vague and its interpretation is not easy, given limited practice.[70] When announcing its withdrawal from the 1972 Anti-Ballistic Missile Treaty (ABM Treaty) in 2001, the US seemed to combine the standard withdrawal clause with

[66] OPCW Conference of the States Parties, 'Decision: Addressing the Threat from Chemical Weapons Use' (27 June 2018) Doc C-SS-4/DEC.3.

[67] Corentin Brustlein, *The Erosion of Strategic Stability and the Future of Arms Control in Europe* (Proliferation Papers, No 60, IFRI 2018).

[68] Daniel H Joyner/Marco Roscini, 'Withdrawal from Non-Proliferation Treaties' in Joyner/Roscini (n 58) 151.

[69] cf NPT (n 8) art X; BTWC (n 46) art XIII; CWC (n 7) art XVI.

[70] On 22 May 2020, the US provided notice of its decision to withdraw from the Open Skies Treaty, pursuant to its art XV, which does not oblige Parties to give reasons for the exercise of that right. The US administration nonetheless claimed that Russia was not adequately implementing the agreement. In a joint statement, twelve European states expressed 'regret' over the US decision and reaffirmed that the treaty 'remains functioning and useful'.

the general ground of *rebus sic stantibus*, as it also relied on a fundamental change of circumstances (those affecting national security).[71]

At the time of its adoption in 1990, the CFE Treaty was considered as being at the heart of security policy in Europe, due to the fact that it set limits on the types of conventional equipment that were considered to be the most useful in a surprise attack (such as battle tanks and other armoured vehicles, artillery, helicopters, and combat aircraft), and provided for the regular exchange of military information and the possibility of mutual verification. The CFE Adaptation Agreement, which was concluded in 1999 to reflect changing security realities (in particular NATO enlargement to the East) never entered into force due to the fact that NATO Members decided not to ratify it until Russia would honour its commitment to withdraw its military deployments in Moldova and Georgia. Subsequent reactions were justified by reciprocal allegations of non-compliance: Russia suspended its participation in the CFE Treaty in 2007, while NATO allies announced in 2011 that they would cease carrying out certain procedural obligations (those of information exchange and accepting on-site inspections) with regard to Russia.[72] Finally, although remaining a party to the agreement, Russia formally announced it was 'completely' suspending its participation in March 2015. While the US presented the suspension as a 'violation' of treaty obligations, the government of Russia has never invoked the withdrawal clause but it continues to justify the suspension with a combination of 'material breach' and 'fundamental change' arguments, claiming that the NATO efforts 'further change [...] the balance of forces in the European region in their favour, including in the direct vicinity of Russia's borders'.[73]

More generally, there is no doubt that withdrawal is not a tool at States' disposal in order to merely absolve themselves from their obligations. Given the essentially auto-interpretive nature of the criteria required for unilateral withdrawal,[74] it has been argued that the only limitation would appear to be the universal obligation to perform all treaty obligations in good faith.[75] Various proposals have been advanced to make withdrawal more difficult, such as providing the convening of a special Conference of the States Parties upon the announcement of an intent to withdraw; or obliging any State that seeks to withdraw to forfeit the right to retain or to use any of the technology or goods it acquired as a treaty party.[76] Finally, some commentators have raised questions relating to the effects of war on disarmament agreements: whether an armed conflict may cause

[71] Guido den Dekker/Tom Coppen, 'Termination and Suspension of, and Withdrawal from, WMD Arms Control Agreements in Light of the General Law of Treaties' (2012) 17 JCSL 25, 30.

[72] Mika Hayashi, 'Suspension of Certain Obligations of the CFE Treaty by NATO Allies: Examination of the Response to the 2007 Unilateral Treaty Suspension by Russia' (2013) 18 JCSL 131.

[73] The Ministry of Foreign Affairs of the Russian Federation, 'Russia's Assessment of the US Department of State's Report on Adherence to and Compliance with Arms Control, Nonproliferation, and Disarmament Agreements and Commitments' (24 April 2018) <http://www.mid.ru/en/foreign_policy/news/-/asset_publisher/cKNonkJE02Bw/content/id/3192916> accessed 9 January 2020.

[74] cf Natalino Ronzitti, 'Problems of Arms Control Treaty Interpretation' in Dahlitz/Dicke (n 6) 120.

[75] Daniel H Joyner, 'What if Iran Withdraws from the Nuclear Nonproliferation Treaty? Part I: Can They Do That?' (2012) 1 European Society of International Law Reflections 4.

[76] Weapons of Mass Destruction Commission (n 54) 51.

their suspension is not clear. Though the mere fact of the outbreak of a conflict would not be a sufficient reason for withdrawal, a State may invoke a grave breach of the treaty or even the acquisition of the relevant category of weapons by a hostile non-party neighbour.[77]

3. Arms Trade and Global Security

International arms transfers have increasingly become a concern for the international community. The terms 'arms trade' and 'traffic in arms' encompass all stages of transfers of weapons and military equipment, including parts, components, and ammunition between States, between non-State entities, or between States and non-State entities.[78] Whereas disarmament conventions usually prohibit transfers in absolute terms, as part of the specific aim of eliminating a category of weapons, the object of the 2013 Arms Trade Treaty is both improving the regulation of the international trade in conventional arms and eradicating illicit traffic for the purpose, amongst others, of contributing to international and regional peace and security: therefore, it belongs to the realm of international law of arms control.[79]

The main challenge for transfer controls is represented by the dual-use nature of items which could be diverted to weapons programmes. As a matter of fact, advances in science (including the convergence of chemistry and biology) might offer opportunities for malevolent exploitation including by non-State actors for terrorist purposes.[80] The lack of universal standards for trade controls was one of the reasons for the adoption of Resolution 1540 (2004), which imposes on all UN Member States the obligation '[to] establish, develop, review and maintain appropriate effective national export and trans-shipment controls over [WMD-related] items.'[81] As part of its task of facilitating the implementation of this resolution, the 1540 Committee developed a matrix in order to organize the information received by Member States.[82] Although such a reference tool is not meant to measure State compliance with Resolution 1540, it has nevertheless contributed to setting the standard for an effective export control system, which should include domestic legislation providing for a list of control items and a mechanism of authorizations and licences, industry outreach, and an enforcement system.

[77] cf Andrea Gioia, 'The Chemical Weapons Convention and its Application in Time of Armed Conflict' in Michael Bothe et al (eds), *The New Chemical Weapons Convention: Implementation and Prospects* (Kluwer 1998) 393.

[78] Anthony E Cassimatis et al, 'Arms, Traffic in' MPEPIL (OUP, August 2016).

[79] cf Tom Coppen, 'The Evolution of Arms Control Instruments and the Potential of the Arms Trade Treaty' (2016) 7 Göttingen Journal of International Law 353.

[80] David P Fidler, 'Nuclear, Chemical and Biological Terrorism in International Law' in Ben Saul (ed), *Research Handbook on International Law and Terrorism* (2nd edn, Edward Elgar 2020) 80.

[81] UNSC Res 1540 (2004).

[82] See the '1540 Matrix Template' adopted in 2005 by the 1540 Committee, established under UNSC Res 1540 (2004), '1540 Matrices' <http://www.un.org/en/sc/1540/national-implementation/1540-matrices.shtml> accessed 10 January 2020.

An increasing number of States have joined the various informal, voluntary, non-treaty-based arrangements, which are complementary to treaty regimes, to improve the export controls on dual-use materials related to WMD. Whereas the Australia Group covers biological and chemical agents,[83] the Zangger Committee and Nuclear Suppliers Group (NSG) establish standards and guidelines governing nuclear transfers.[84] Other relevant export control regimes, covering for instance WMD delivery systems, include the Missile Technology Control Regime,[85] and the Wassenaar Arrangement on Export Controls for Conventional Arms and Dual-Use Goods and Technologies.[86] One of the most pressing challenges facing these export control regimes is represented by their application not only to the transfer of physical items but also to intangible transfers of associated technologies. In particular, participating States fear that the rapid development of additive manufacturing processes, including three-dimensional printing, might pose a serious proliferation risk.[87]

Despite technological advances, the most commonly available weapons in situations of internal armed conflicts are light and rarely complex, such as handguns, assault rifles like the Kalashnikov, mortars and portable rocket launchers of the RPG-7 type. Over the last decade, there has been increasing awareness of the direct and indirect effects on the civilian population of poorly regulated arms trade and the illicit trafficking of arms.[88] The adoption and subsequent entry into force in 2014 of the landmark Arms Trade Treaty (ATT)[89] have represented significant steps towards effective regulation of transfers of conventional weapons, for the purposes of contributing to peace and security, reducing human suffering, promoting cooperation, transparency, and responsible action.[90]

The preamble of this Treaty recognizes 'the challenges faced by victims of armed conflict and their need for adequate care, rehabilitation and social and economic inclusion', and recalls that 'civilians, particularly women and children, account for the vast majority of those affected by armed conflict and armed violence'. The scope of application of the treaty, as defined in Article 2, includes the military equipment categories already covered by the UN Register on Conventional Arms.[91] The core of ATT is represented by Articles 6 and 7, which, respectively, establish prohibitions that prevent States Parties

[83] The Australia Group, 'Guidelines for Transfers of Sensitive Chemical or Biological Items' <https://australiagroup.net/en/guidelines.html> accessed 10 January 2020.

[84] See <http://zanggercommittee.org/our-mission.html> accessed 10 January 2020.

[85] Missile Technology Control Regime, 'Guidelines for Sensitive Missile-Relevant Transfers' <https://mtcr.info/guidelines-for-sensitive-missile-relevant-transfers/> accessed 10 January 2020.

[86] See <https://www.wassenaar.org/about-us/> accessed 10 January 2020.

[87] Kolja Brockmann/Robert Kelley, *The Challenge of Emerging Technologies to Non-Proliferation Efforts: Controlling Additive Manufacturing and Intangible Transfers of Technology* (SIPRI 2018).

[88] UN Coordinating Action on Small Arms, *The Impact of Poorly Regulated Arms Transfers on the Work of the United Nations* (UNODA Occasional Paper No 23, UN 2013).

[89] 3013 UNTS 3.

[90] Gilles Giacca, 'Article 1. Object and Purpose' in Andrew Clapham et al (eds), *The Arms Trade Treaty: A Commentary* (OUP 2015) 51.

[91] The UN Register was created by the UNGA Res 46/36 (L) (6 December 1991) in order to 'prevent excessive and destabilizing accumulation of arms, [...] to promote stability and strengthen regional or international peace and security'.

from authorizing a transfer in specified circumstances, including arms embargoes sanctioned by the UNSC, and impose upon them a duty to assess whether the transfer of conventional arms would either undermine peace and security or could be used to commit or facilitate a serious violation of IHL and international human rights law (IHRL).[92]

It is still too early to tell whether the ATT will change State behaviour. A test for the efficacy of arms trade regulations has been the initiative of a group of NGOs that successfully challenged the approval of licences for arms exports to Saudi Arabia before UK courts on the grounds, *inter alia*, that there was a clear risk that the items might be used in the commission of a serious violation of IHL.[93] Still, the impact of the ATT risks being seriously undermined by the position taken by the US administration 'to take [their] signature back',[94] namely the decision that the US will never ratify the treaty.

4. The Challenge of Emerging Technologies

In addition to political constraints, advances in science and technology also pose a range of risks and challenges for existing disarmament and arms control instruments. Mapping out the implications of new technologies for peace and security requires taking into account the impact of a variety of innovations on warfare.[95] There is no doubt that evolutions—particularly in the fields of artificial intelligence (AI), life sciences, and digital technology—enable new military capabilities: particular worry has been expressed with respect to the risks associated to the development of autonomous weapons systems, hypersonic weapons, cyber operations, and the military applications of biotechnology.[96]

Since 2014, negotiations with respect to the regulation of lethal autonomous weapons systems (LAWS) are being conducted within the framework of the CCW. The positions upheld by the delegations have differed as to whether existing and undisputed rules of IHL and arms control law are able to cope with the challenges arising from LAWS (and to define possible limits) or whether further regulations or clarifications were needed. In this context, the key issue is how to regulate the human–machine interaction, as demonstrated by the debate on the concept of 'human control', both as a fail-safe mechanism and as an accountability catalyst.[97] Some progress was made in the context of the Group

[92] Stuart Casey-Maslen et al, 'Article 7. Export and Export Assessment' in Clapham et al (n 90) 244.

[93] *The Queen (on the application of Campaign Against Arms Trade) v Secretary of State for International Trade and others* [2019] EWCA Civ 1020.

[94] See, also, The White House, 'Presidential Message to the Senate of the United States on the Withdrawal of the Arms Trade Treaty' (29 April 2019) <https://www.whitehouse.gov/briefings-statements/presidential-message-senate-united-states-withdrawal-arms-trade-treaty/> accessed 19 September 2019.

[95] William Boothby, 'So, What Do We Make Of All This?' in William Boothby (ed), *New Technologies and the Law in War and Peace* (CUP 2018) 427.

[96] Heiko Maas, Opening Speech at the Conference '2019. Capturing Technology. Rethinking Arms Control' (15 March 2019) <https://www.auswaertiges-amt.de/en/newsroom/news/maas-conference-2019-capturing-technology-rethinking-arms-control/2199902> accessed 27 November 2020.

[97] Daniele Amoroso/Guglielmo Tamburrini, 'What Makes "Meaningful" the Human Control over Weapons Systems?' in Giampiero Giacomello et al (eds), *Technology and International Relations: The New Frontier in Global Power* (Edward Elgar 2019).

of Governmental Experts (GGE), affirming eleven guiding principles: there is an emerging consensus that '[h]uman responsibility for decisions on the use of weapons systems must be retained since accountability cannot be transferred to machines'.[98] Should the CCW States Parties reach consensus on the adoption of a new protocol (or, alternatively, on a set of non-binding rules), there would be several options as for its specific content: either introducing a comprehensive ban on the development and use of weapons systems lacking human control or setting positive obligations to safeguard human control in the use of force.

Moreover, there is growing concern with respect to the impact of three specific emerging technologies—additive manufacturing, AI, and robotics—on the development and production of biological weapons and their delivery systems.[99] The UNSC has significantly called upon States 'to take into account developments on the evolving nature of risk of proliferation and rapid advances in science and technology in their implementation of Resolution 1540 (2004)'.[100]

D. Conclusion

The failure of the CWC States Parties to agree to a final consensus document at the Fourth Review Conference reflected in clear terms the new international tensions which risk undermining the legal framework on disarmament and arms control, developed at the end of the Cold War.[101] The main source of disagreement at the conference was the question of accountability for the use of chemical weapons in Syria. In a joint declaration, sixty-five countries called on all States Parties 'to mobilize and stand firm in defence of the Convention as an essential pillar of the international disarmament and non-proliferation architecture', urging them 'to join in a dedicated effort to reinforce the CW [Cold War] regime and to deter all use of chemical weapons'.[102]

The impression of a divided international community also characterized the unsuccessful outcome of the 2015 NPT review conference. The approval of the Treaty on the Prohibition of Nuclear Weapons (TPNW) in July 2017 has been accompanied by the enthusiasm of the proponents but also by harsh criticism of the nuclear weapons States

[98] Group of Governmental Experts on Emerging Technologies in the Area of Lethal Autonomous Weapons Systems, 'Report of the 2019 session' Annex IV (25 September 2019) UN Doc CCW/GGE.1/2019/3.

[99] Kolja Brockmann et al, *Bio Plus X: Arms Control and the Convergence of Biology and Emerging Technologies* (SIPRI 2019).

[100] UNSC Res 2325 (2016).

[101] OPCW Review Conference, 'Chairperson's Report of the Proceedings of the Fourth Special Session of the Conference of the States Parties to Review the Operation of the Chemical Weapons Convention' (30 November 2018) Doc RC-4/3/Rev.1.

[102] OPCW Review Conference, 'Joint Statement Delivered by H.E. Ambassador Philippe Lalliot Permanent Representative of France to the OPWC at the Fourth Special Session of the Conference of the State Parties to Review the Operation of the Chemical Weapons Convention' (30 November 2018) Doc RC-4/NAT.37.

and their allies. Significantly, the 2017 Nobel Prize has certified the role of NGOs in the adoption of the TPNW. In more general terms, one could easily foresee that civil society organizations will continue to promote transparency in disarmament and arms control, not only as a means to build confidence amongst States but also as an indispensable element of democratic oversight and public scrutiny.

Reciprocal allegations of treaty violations are increasingly eroding the legal architecture of conventional arms control in Europe. However, despite declining relevance of the CFE Treaty, its data exchange and its inspections remain meaningful tools. German attempts to create a dialogue aimed at de-escalating existing tensions between NATO and Russia led to the launch of the OSCE Structured Dialogue on confidence-building, risk reduction, and arms control.[103] It is far from certain that this multilateral forum for discussing political and military challenges in Europe will succeed: neither Russia nor the US have so far demonstrated much interest in the negotiations. Nevertheless, there is a clear need for a modernized regime which can also take into account new categories of conventional weapons.

Great expectations exist with regard to the initiative of the UN Secretary-General to launch a new agenda for disarmament. Based on four pillars, the 'Securing Our Common Future' report identifies forty practical steps, the implementation of which involves various actors both within and outside the UN system.[104]

[103] OSCE, 'From Lisbon to Hamburg' (n 21). [104] See n 13.

CHAPTER 18

NUCLEAR NON-PROLIFERATION AND DISARMAMENT UNDER INTERNATIONAL LAW

MASAHIKO ASADA

A. Introduction

EVER since its invention, the nuclear weapon has occupied a special place in the global security order, both militarily and politically, due to its extraordinary destructive power. No other type of weapon has so starkly divided opinion amongst States and people as nuclear weapons. They are seen as both the ultimate guarantor of State security and as weapons of evil. Nevertheless, no one denies (at least openly) the ultimate goal of the total elimination of nuclear weapons.

This picture is further complicated by the fact that nuclear material has both military and civilian uses. From a military perspective, nuclear weapons are the most well-known product of nuclear material. But they are not the only military application of nuclear energy. Non-explosive military use, such as in nuclear-powered aircraft carriers or submarines, is another example. However, nuclear-powered vessels, for example icebreakers, are also used for non-military purposes. Other civilian use of nuclear material includes generating electricity through nuclear reactors. Nuclear material also has medical, agricultural, and other peaceful applications, such as its use in the treatment of cancer.

It is against this complex background that regulating the use of nuclear energy and material has taken place. This chapter traces the history of such attempts and achievements, focusing on nuclear non-proliferation and disarmament, by first assessing such treaties as the Partial Test Ban Treaty (PTBT),[1] Treaty on the Non-Proliferation of

[1] Treaty Banning Nuclear Weapon Tests in the Atmosphere, in Outer Space and Under Water 480 UNTS 43.

Nuclear Weapons (NPT),[2] Comprehensive Nuclear-Test-Ban Treaty (CTBT)[3] and the Treaty on the Prohibition of Nuclear Weapons (TPNW),[4] followed by an examination of current challenges taking place in the Democratic People's Republic of Korea (DPRK) and Iran.

B. Legal Framework

1. Initial Attempts to Control Nuclear Energy for Peaceful Purposes

Attempts to regulate nuclear energy commenced almost immediately after the termination of the Second World War. The UN General Assembly's (UNGA) very first resolution aimed at dealing with the problems raised by the 'discovery of atomic energy'. It established an 'Atomic Energy Commission' which would *inter alia* ensure the use of atomic energy solely for peaceful purposes and the elimination of atomic weapons and all other major weapons of mass destruction.[5] However, the Commission failed to agree on any meaningful measures due to the different priorities of the US and the USSR when it came to the destruction of existing stocks and the establishment of a control system, as well as the application of the UN Security Council (UNSC) veto in the proposed enforcement mechanism.[6] The US proposal regarding international control, outlined in the 1953 'Atoms for Peace' address of President Eisenhower to the UNGA, eventually led to the establishment of the International Atomic Energy Agency (IAEA) in 1957.

2. Partial Test Ban Treaty

Atmospheric nuclear testing in March 1954 caused worldwide public concern. A large thermonuclear hydrogen bomb detonated by the US caused highly radioactive fallout in a large area surrounding the Bikini Atoll in the Pacific Ocean. A Japanese fishing boat, the *Daigo Fukuryu Maru*, and its crew members were heavily contaminated by it. The following month, Indian Prime Minister Jawaharlal Nehru proposed a ban on nuclear testing.

A series of nuclear tests carried out by the US, the UK, and the USSR in 1957–58 raised widespread concerns about their potential environmental effects. Beginning in

[2] 729 UNTS 161. [3] (1996) 35 ILM 1439.

[4] Treaty on the Prohibition of Nuclear Weapons UN Doc A/CONF.229/2017/8.

[5] UNGA Res 1(I) (24 January 1946) para 5.

[6] For details on the US 'Baruch Plan' of 14 June 1946: Department of State, *Documents on Disarmament 1945–1959*, vol I (Department of State Publication 1960) 7–16. For the Soviet 'Gromyko Plan' of 19 June 1946: ibid 20–2. The latter plan maintained that a control system should be enforced within the framework of the UNSC with its Permanent Members retaining veto power. Disarmament Affairs Division, *The United Nations and Disarmament: 1945–1970* (UN 1970) 15, 17–19.

November 1958, these three States observed a nuclear test moratorium for nearly three years (until September 1961). However, despite the many proposals for a comprehensive ban on nuclear tests,[7] disagreement concerning methods for the verification of the prohibition on underground testing (particularly regarding the number of on-site inspections and of seismic stations to be placed on each State's territory) prevented the US and the USSR from agreeing on a comprehensive nuclear test ban at that time.[8] It was only after the Cuban Missile Crisis of October 1962, and the resulting need for improved relations between the two States, that agreement was eventually reached.[9]

The PTBT,[10] the first major international treaty on nuclear weapons, entered into force in 1963. It prohibits 'any nuclear weapon test explosion, or any other nuclear explosion' in the three environments mentioned in the title of the Treaty (Article I, para 1(a)), but does not extend the ban to underground explosions, unless such explosion causes radioactive debris to spread outside the territorial limits of the State where the explosion is conducted (Article I, para 1(b)). This provision indicates that environmental concerns significantly influenced the drafting of the PTBT. India (a State Party) after conducting underground nuclear tests in May 1998, declared that '[m]easurements have also confirmed that there was no release of radioactivity into the atmosphere'.[11]

Because underground tests were excluded from its scope, the PTBT has been criticized as legalizing underground testing. But its practical effect was seen more broadly. While advanced nuclear States like the US, the UK,[12] and the USSR could continue to improve their nuclear arsenals by conducting underground tests,[13] latecomer nuclear States like France and China would have difficulties in doing so.[14] Perhaps for this reason, France and China have not acceded to the PTBT, although both States gave up atmospheric testing through unilateral statements: France in 1975 following the *Nuclear*

[7] UK/US, 'Draft Treaty on Discontinuance of Nuclear Tests' (21 March 1962) ENDC/9; USSR, 'Statement by the Soviet Government dated 27 November 1961 on connexion with the Resumption of Negotiations on the Discontinuance of Nuclear and Thermonuclear Tests' (22 March 1962) ENDC/11; UK/US, 'Draft Treaty Banning Nuclear Weapon Tests in all Environments' (27 August 1962) ENDC/58.

[8] Pierce S Corden, 'Historical Context and Steps to Implement the CTBT' in Mordechai Melamud et al (eds), *Banning the Bang or the Bomb? Negotiating the Nuclear Test Ban Regime* (CUP 2014) 19.

[9] George Bunn, *Arms Control by Committee: Managing Negotiations with the Russians* (Stanford UP 1992) 32; Glenn T Seaborg, *Kennedy, Khrushchev, and the Test Ban* (University of California Press 1981) 176.

[10] PTBT (n 1). PTBT has currently 125 States Parties, including non-NPT Parties such as India, Pakistan, and Israel, but excluding the DPRK.

[11] 'Letter Dated 11 May 1998 from the Permanent Representative of India Addressed to the Secretary-General of the Conference Transmitting a Press Statement Issued in New Delhi on 11 May' (12 May 1998) CD/1504; 'Letter Dated 13 May 1998 from the Permanent Representative of India Addressed to the Secretary-General of the Conference Transmitting a Press Statement Issued in New Delhi on 13 May' (13 May 1998) CD/1504/Add.1.

[12] The UK started conducting its nuclear tests jointly with the US at the Nevada Test Site in 1962. *SIPRI Yearbook 2018: Armaments, Disarmament and International Security* (OUP 2018) 301.

[13] For the annual number of underground nuclear tests by the US and the USSR: ibid 300.

[14] France and China conducted their first nuclear weapon test explosion in 1960 and 1964, while the US, the UK, and the USSR did so in 1945, 1949, and 1952, respectively.

Tests cases at the International Court of Justice (ICJ),[15] and China several years later as a result of a series of protests by neighbouring and distant States.[16] As such, the PTBT has been regarded as a first attempt to prevent the proliferation of nuclear weapons,[17] although the extent to which it has really served non-proliferation is questionable. For instance, India and Pakistan, both Parties to the PTBT, successfully conducted their first nuclear tests underground in 1974 and 1998, respectively.

3. Treaty on the Non-proliferation of Nuclear Weapons

In contrast to the PTBT, which aimed at both prevention of pollution from radioactive fallout and non-proliferation of nuclear weapons, the NPT pursues only the latter objective. The idea of the non-proliferation of nuclear weapons is based on the belief that 'the proliferation of nuclear weapons would seriously enhance the danger of nuclear war'.[18]

In response to UNGA Res 1665(XVI), negotiations led by the US and the USSR began in 1962, first within the framework of the draft treaties for general and complete disarmament, and from 1965 in the form of independent stand-alone draft treaties. The resulting NPT was signed in 1968 and entered into force in 1970.

a. *Basic Obligations under the NPT*

The Treaty distinguishes between two categories of States: nuclear-weapon States and non-nuclear-weapon States, imposing different obligations on each. Nuclear-weapon States are under the obligation not to transfer nuclear weapons or other nuclear explosive devices or control over them to any recipient (Article I). Non-nuclear-weapon States are obligated not to receive the transfer of such weapons or explosive devices or control over them and not to manufacture or otherwise acquire such weapons or explosive devices (Article II). While the Treaty places substantial obligations on non-nuclear-weapon States, nuclear-weapon States have, for their part, undertaken to 'pursue negotiations in good faith on effective measures relating to cessation of the nuclear arms race at an early date and to nuclear disarmament' (Article VI).

Article IX(3) NPT provides the criteria for distinguishing between nuclear-weapon and non-nuclear-weapon States. A nuclear-weapon State is considered a State 'which has manufactured and exploded a nuclear weapon or other nuclear explosive device prior to 1 January 1967'. This cut-off date (well before the Treaty's signing day) must have been chosen in order to avoid a last-minute attempt by any State to manufacture

[15] *Nuclear Tests Case (Australia v France)* [1974] ICJ Rep 253, 265–7.

[16] Jozef Goldblat, *Arms Control: The New Guide to Negotiations and Agreements* (2nd edn, Sage 2002) 50.

[17] United States Arms Control and Disarmament Agency, Documents on Disarmament 1962 (vol II, 1963) 813.

[18] NPT (n 2) preambular para 2; UNGA Res 1665(XVI) (1961); UNGA Res 1380(XIV) (1959); UNGA Res 1576(XV) (1960).

and explode a nuclear weapon so as to qualify as nuclear-weapon States under the Treaty.

A dispute concerning this definition arose following the dissolution of the USSR in 1991, questioning: which republic of the Union was to succeed to the USSR status as a nuclear-weapon State? Although Russia might have seemed the obvious successor, other republics like Kazakhstan based their claim to such status on the aforementioned definition of a nuclear-weapon State and sought to accede to the NPT as such.[19] Western States rejected such claims; according to NATO '[n]either the mere physical presence of nuclear weapons in these states [former Soviet republics] nor the locus of past Soviet nuclear testing activities constitute grounds for regarding these states as nuclear weapons states under the [NPT]'.[20] Although most Soviet nuclear weapon tests had been conducted at the Semipalatinsk Test Site in Kazakhstan, it was not Kazakhstan but the USSR that manufactured and exploded these weapons and, at that time, Kazakhstan was not itself a 'State'. By December 1994, all former Soviet republics, with the exception of Russia, had acceded to the NPT as non-nuclear-weapon States.[21] By November 1996, they had also transferred all nuclear weapons from their territories to Russia for dismantlement.[22]

b. *Verification of the Non-Manufacture Obligation*

Under Article III of the NPT, non-nuclear-weapon States Parties have, in relation to their obligation not to manufacture nuclear weapons, undertaken to accept verification measures, called 'safeguards', to be conducted by the IAEA. During its first fifteen years, the IAEA produced two major types of safeguards systems, one for NPT Parties (INFCIRC/153: comprehensive safeguards agreements or CSA) and another for non-NPT Parties (INFCIRC/66: item-specific safeguards agreements).[23] Both types of agreements are concluded between the non-nuclear-weapon State and the IAEA.

Under the CSA, States Parties undertake to accept safeguards on 'all source or special fissionable material [ie, nuclear material] in all peaceful nuclear activities' within their territories 'for the exclusive purpose of verifying that such material is not diverted to

[19] Daniel Sneider, 'Kazakhstan Seeks US Pact for Further Nuclear Cut' (*Christian Science Monitor*, 27 April 1992) <https://www.csmonitor.com/1992/0427/27012.html> accessed 2 April 2020; *SIPRI Yearbook 1992: World Armaments and Disarmament* (OUP 1992) 537.

[20] 'Text of NATO Statement on NPT' (21 April 1992) (on file with author). The statement also announced that Russia was 'to fulfil the role of the former Soviet Union as a depository and nuclear weapon state under the NPT'.

[21] Ukraine, which also claimed nuclear-weapon State status, acceded to the NPT as a non-nuclear-weapon State under the arrangements of the Budapest Memorandum (UNGA/UNSC 'Letter dated 7 December 1994 from the Permanent Representatives of the Russian Federation, Ukraine, the United Kingdom of Great Britain and Northern Ireland and the United States of America to the United Nations addressed to the Secretary-General' (19 December 1994) UN Doc A/49/765-S/1994/1399). It has been argued that Russia violated this commitment during the 2014 Crimea crisis.

[22] *SIPRI Yearbook 1993: World Armaments and Disarmament* (OUP 1993) 228; *SIPRI Yearbook 1997: Armaments, Disarmament and International Security* (OUP 1997) 368–70.

[23] A third kind of safeguards agreements, called 'voluntary offer agreements', are concluded between the IAEA and nuclear-weapon States.

nuclear weapons or other nuclear explosive devices'.[24] The basic modality of safeguards is (1) for the State to keep records and provide the IAEA with information concerning nuclear material subject to safeguards as well as operation of the relevant facilities, and (2) for the IAEA to conduct inspections to examine the records and verify that reports provided by the State are consistent with records.[25]

The effectiveness of such a declaration-reliant CSA system was called into question after the 1991 Gulf War. The IAEA, having conducted on-site inspections under UNSC Resolution 687 (1991), discovered that Iraq had been developing nuclear weapons in undeclared facilities adjacent to its declared facilities.[26] The IAEA had not hitherto pronounced Iraq to be in breach of its Safeguards Agreement.[27] This situation revealed a major weakness of the safeguards system based on the CSA, in that inspectors may routinely inspect only those facilities that the State has declared, regardless of whether unreported activities may be going on elsewhere.

In response, the IAEA Board of Governors affirmed that the scope of CSA was not limited to verification of the non-diversion of nuclear material actually declared by the State but included verifying the absence of undeclared nuclear material and activities in the State. In other words, the Agency had the right and obligation under the CSA to verify not only that State declarations are 'correct' but that they are also 'complete'.[28]

Such an interpretation of the CSA is, however, not unanimously shared.[29] Undeniably, a State has undertaken under its CSA to accept safeguards on 'all [nuclear material] in all peaceful nuclear activities'. Hence it would be a violation of the agreement if the State failed to declare any such material. The existence of the 'special inspection' system in the CSA, which allows IAEA inspectors to have access to undeclared sites,[30] also indicates that the agreements' scope covers not only declared but also undeclared nuclear material.[31] However, the IAEA may verify the absence of undeclared nuclear material only through

[24] IAEA, 'The Structure and Content of Agreements Between the Agency and States Required in Connection with the Treaty on the Non-Proliferation of Nuclear Weapons' (June 1972) Doc INFCIRC/153 (corrected) para 1.

[25] ibid paras 51–8, 59–69, 70–82.

[26] UNSC, 'Note by the Secretary-General' (8 October 1991) UN Doc S/23122, paras 3–6; David Albright/Mark Hibbs, 'Iraq's Quest for the Nuclear Grail: What Can We Learn?' (1992) 22(6) Arms Control Today 9.

[27] IAEA (28 October 1991) Doc GOV/OR.760, para 47.

[28] Laura Rockwood, *Legal Framework for IAEA Safeguards* (IAEA 2013) 19; IAEA, 'The Safeguards System of the International Atomic Energy Agency' para 6 <https://www.jaea.go.jp/04/iscn/iscn_old/resource/safeguards%20system.pdf> accessed 15 August 2018.

[29] cf IAEA (21 February 1995) Doc GOV/2784, para 110 in IAEA, GC(39)/17, Annex 1; Pierre-Emmanuel Dupont, 'Interpretation of Nuclear Safeguards Commitments: The Role of Subsequent Agreements and Practice' in Jonathan L Black-Branch/Dieter Fleck (eds), *Nuclear Non-Proliferation in International Law* (vol II, Asser 2016) 34.

[30] IAEA Doc INFCIRC/153 (n 24) para 73.

[31] A report on the drafting history of INFCIRC/153 states that '[t]here is . . . an unmistakeable record as to the obligation to accept safeguards on all nuclear material in all peaceful uses, *regardless of whether reported by the state*' (emphasis original). International Energy Associates Limited, *Review of the Negotiating History of the IAEA Safeguards Document INFCIRC/153: Final Report* (vol I, 1984) 35 <https://cgs.pnnl.gov/fois/doclib/IAEA_153_Negotiating_History.pdf> accessed 15 August 2018.

a special inspection, and the practical threshold for triggering such inspections is very high because of their accusatory overtones.[32]

Thus, a new, user-friendly legal tool was developed in the form of the Additional Protocol to the CSA, a model of which was adopted by the IAEA Board of Governors in 1997.[33] According to the Model Additional Protocol, IAEA inspectors under the 'complementary access' system would have access to '[a]ny location specified by the Agency…to carry out location-specific environmental sampling' (Article 5(c))[34] without the accusatory connotations which are associated with special inspections. Now that Additional Protocols are in force for as many as 136 States, complementary access seems for practical purposes to have almost displaced the need for special inspections, although some States in which significant nuclear activities occur are still to adopt the Additional Protocol,[35] and thus the important deterrent function of the special inspection system has hardly diminished.

c. *Duration of the Treaty and its Extension*

Unlike most disarmament treaties, the NPT was not concluded as a treaty with unlimited duration, as some of the negotiating States objected to giving up their nuclear ambitions forever at that time.[36] As a result, according to Article X(2), twenty-five years after the NPT had entered into force, a conference was to be convened to decide upon its potential extension. The 'NPT Extension Conference' was convened in April 1995 in conjunction with the fifth Review Conference of the Treaty. At the time, it was not certain that agreement would be reached for the indefinite extension of the Treaty. This was mainly due to the fact that certain Non-Aligned Movement (NAM) States were dissatisfied with the

[32] Only one case of special inspection has been invoked by the IAEA for DPRK in 1993. A special inspection in respect of Romania was triggered by the new government which invited the IAEA to undertake a special inspection to resolve matters that had occurred under the previous Romanian regime. John Carlson/Russell Leslie, 'Special Inspections Revisited' (INMM 2005 Symposium, Phoenix, July 2005) 1 <https://www.dfat.gov.au/sites/default/files/inmm2005_special_inspections.pdf> accessed 6 April 2020.

[33] The adoption of the Model Additional Protocol is part of a broader project called 'Programme 93+2', initiated in 1993. For Programme 93+2: IAEA Doc GC(39)/17 (22 August 1995) paras 1–2.

[34] IAEA, 'Model Protocol Additional to the Agreement(s) between State(s) and the International Atomic Energy Agency for the Application of Safeguards' (1 September 1997) Doc INFCIRC/540, art 5(c); Theodore Hirsch, 'The IAEA Additional Protocol: What It Is and Why It Matters' (2004) 11(3) The Nonproliferation Review 147, 147–52.

[35] They are Argentina, Brazil, Egypt, North Korea, Syria, and Venezuela. Mark Hibbs, 'Nuclear Suppliers Group and the IAEA Additional Protocol' (*Carnegie Endowment for International Peace*, 18 August 2010) <https://carnegieendowment.org/2010/08/18/nuclear-suppliers-group-and-iaea-additional-protocol-pub-41393> accessed 6 April 2020.

[36] It has been asserted that in the Eighteen-Nation Committee on Disarmament, Italy spoke for Germany, which was not a member of the Committee. George Bunn/Charles N Van Doren, 'Options for Extension of the NPT: The Intention of the Drafters of Article X.2' in George Bunn et al (eds), *Options and Opportunities: The NPT Extension Conference of 1995* (PPNN 1991) 1, 3.

extent of nuclear disarmament, and because the decision required a majority of all States Parties to the NPT and not of those present and voting.[37]

As most participating States Parties preferred a consensus decision over a majority decision, attempts were made to accommodate those who were dissatisfied with the lack of progress in nuclear disarmament. Ultimately, the decision on the indefinite extension of the Treaty was adopted without a vote (by consensus) along with two other decisions.[38] One of them was the decision entitled 'Principles and Objectives for Nuclear Non-Proliferation and Disarmament', which, amongst others, required '[t]he completion by the Conference on Disarmament [CD: the single multilateral disarmament negotiating forum] of the negotiations on a universal and internationally and effectively verifiable Comprehensive Nuclear-Test-Ban Treaty no later than 1996'.[39]

4. Comprehensive Nuclear-Test-Ban Treaty

A comprehensive nuclear test ban has always been a priority in Article VI NPT[40] and is also specifically mentioned in its preamble. In January 1991, States Parties to the PTBT held an Amendment Conference to discuss a proposal for two Protocols to the Treaty. Protocol I would prohibit nuclear testing underground or in any other environment; Protocol II would deal with verification of compliance with a comprehensive test ban.[41] The Conference did not vote on them, but decided to 'mandate the President of the Conference to conduct consultations with a view to…resuming the work of the Conference at an appropriate time',[42] which never occurred.

Instead, negotiations on a CTBT started at the CD in 1994 with the NPT Extension Conference scheduled for the following year,[43] and the CD finalized the text during its

[37] eg Jozef Goldblat, 'Issues Facing the 1995 NPT Extension Conference' (1992) 23(4) Security Dialogue 25, 25–6.

[38] The other decision was entitled 'Strengthening the Review Process for the Treaty'. See 1995 Review and Extension Conference of the Parties to the Treaty on the Non-Proliferation of Nuclear Weapons, 'Final Document' (1995) NPT/CONF.1995/32 (Part I) 8–13; '1995 NPT Review and Extension Conference: Verbatim Record of the 17th Plenary Meeting' (11 May 1995) NPT/CONF.1995/PV.17, 3. Separately, a resolution on the Middle East was also adopted without a vote.

[39] NPT/CONF.1995/32 (Part I) (n 38) 10, para 4(a).

[40] George Bunn/Roland M Timerbaev, 'Nuclear Disarmament: How Much Have the Five Nuclear Powers Promised in the Non-Proliferation Treaty?' in John B Rhinelander/Adam M Scheinman (eds), *At the Nuclear Crossroads: Choices about Nuclear Weapons and the Extension of the Non-Proliferation Treaty* (UP of America 1995) 26.

[41] PTBT/CONF/6 (12 December 1990); PTBT/CONF/8 (20 December 1990).

[42] By a vote of 74 to 2 (UK, US) with 19 abstentions. States Parties to the PTBT, 'Amendment Conference: Report' (7–18 January 1991) PTBT/CONF/13/Rev.1, 4–5, 330.

[43] Thomas Graham, Jr, *Disarmament Sketches: Three Decades of Arms Control and International Law* (University of Washington Press 2002) 239–42. It is said that a decision by the US to extend its nuclear test moratorium gave the final push to the CD in agreeing on a mandate to negotiate the CTBT: Rebecca Johnson, *Unfinished Business: The Negotiation of the CTBT and the End of Nuclear Testing* (UNIDIR 2009) 46.

1996 session.[44] Despite the fact that, due to an objection by India, the consensus-governed CD could not 'adopt' the final text in its own setting,[45] the CTBT was later adopted by the UNGA[46] and opened for signature on 24 September 1996.

a. *Comprehensive Test Ban*

Article I CTBT prohibits 'any nuclear weapon test explosion or any other nuclear explosion', without any limitation in terms of environment. On the other hand, the Treaty does not prohibit non-explosive nuclear testing, such as subcritical experiments (namely, nuclear tests involving nuclear material that purposely result in no yield). In fact, the US and other nuclear-weapon States have continued to conduct such tests even after signing the CTBT.[47] The Treaty does not cover such tests because of the difficulty involved in their verification.

Although the Treaty has not yet entered into force,[48] signatory and ratifying States are arguably bound by such prohibition in light of Article 18 of the Vienna Convention on the Law of Treaties (VCLT),[49] which provides that those States are obliged to 'refrain from acts which would defeat the object and purpose of a treaty' prior to its entry into force. While the exact content of this obligation is unclear, in the CTBT context it may be argued that it includes carrying out a nuclear test. This is supported by statements made by signatory and ratifying States to that effect,[50] and by a UNSC resolution co-sponsored by forty-five States and adopted without a negative vote which recognized that 'a nuclear-weapon test explosion or any other nuclear explosion would defeat the object and purpose of the CTBT'.[51]

However, under Article 18(a) VCLT the obligation of the signatory is terminated when it makes 'its intention clear not to become a party to the treaty'. In 1999, after the Senate rejected ratification of the CTBT, the US sent a letter to several States to reassure them of its intention to 'continue to act in accordance with its obligations as a signatory

[44] France and China continued nuclear testing until 1996, only shortly before they signed the CTBT. *SIPRI 1997* (n 22) 433.

[45] Ad Hoc Committee on a Nuclear Test Ban, 'Report to the Conference on Disarmament' (16 August 1996) CD/1425, 37. The Indian objection concerned the absence of a time-bound provision on nuclear disarmament and the requirement for it to sign and ratify the CTBT for the Treaty to enter into force: ibid 19–20.

[46] UNGA Res 50/245 (10 September 1996).

[47] One of the most recent instances of subcritical nuclear experiment was the US experiment conducted in December 2017. Garry R Maskaly, 'Vega and the Lyra Series' (2018) 8(1) NNSA Stockpile Stewardship Quarterly 6.

[48] The CTBT has been ratified by 168 States but has not yet entered into force due to its extremely strict entry into force clause, which requires the forty-four specific States listed in Annex 2 to the Treaty to ratify the Treaty before it enters into force.

[49] 1155 UNTS 331.

[50] They include Japan and the US. Masahiko Asada, 'CTBT: Legal Questions Arising from Its Non-Entry-Into-Force' (2002) 7 JCSL 85, 95–6.

[51] UNSC Res 2310 (2016) para 4. No divergent view was expressed on this point in the Council debate: UNSC Verbatim Record (23 December 2016) UN Doc S/PV.7776.

under international law'.[52] However, it subsequently revised its policy and declared that it 'will not become a party to [the CTBT]'.[53] Following that, it seems to have again revised its policy as, in a 2016 letter to the Senate Foreign Relations Committee Chairman, after referring to Article 18 obligations, Secretary of State John Kerry stated that '[a] future Administration could make clear that the United States no longer intends to become a party to the [CTBT], in which case the United States would no longer have such obligations'.[54] This illustrates the uncertainty that covers obligations under Article 18 VCLT.[55]

b. *Verification of the Ban*

In terms of verification, the CTBT provides for two processes: an international monitoring system (IMS) and an on-site inspection system. While the latter can only be activated after the Treaty enters into force, the former has already been virtually operating within the framework of the Comprehensive Nuclear-Test-Ban Treaty Organization's (CTBTO) Preparatory Commission (PrepCom). The PrepCom was established by the Text on the Establishment of a Preparatory Commission for the Comprehensive Nuclear-Test-Ban Treaty Organization (PrepCom Text), annexed to a resolution of the CTBT signatories adopted on 19 November 1996.[56] When completed, the IMS will be capable of detecting one kiloton of nuclear explosion conducted anywhere in the world. The system will consist of 337 stations to be established in some ninety countries around the world, of which 300 stations (nearly 90 per cent) have been certified by the Commission.[57]

The legal basis for constructing IMS stations can be found in provisions of the CTBT and the PrepCom Text. Article IV(1) of the Treaty provides that '[a]t entry into force of this Treaty, the verification regime shall be capable of meeting the verification requirements of this Treaty'. In order to meet the Treaty's verification requirements at entry into force, it is logically necessary to start preparations before its entry into force. This is one of the rare examples of substantive treaty provisions having legal force (in addition to procedural provisions such as those on entry into force or reservations) before the treaty's entry into force.[58]

However, this provision may not lead directly to such concrete action as the construction or operation of the IMS. The latter has been made possible by paragraphs 13 and 14

[52] 'The Imperial Presidency' *Washington Times* (5 November 1999).

[53] UNGA Verbatim Record (7 October 2003) UN Doc A/C.1/58/PV.3, 4.

[54] Letter from Secretary of State John Kerry to Senate Foreign Relations Committee Chairman Bob Corker (7 September 2016) (on file with author).

[55] Masahiko Asada, 'Article 18 of the Vienna Convention on the Law of Treaties Obligations and the Comprehensive Nuclear-Test-Ban Treaty' in Treasa Dunworth/Anna Hood (eds), *Disarmament Law* (Routledge forthcoming).

[56] States Signatories of CTBT, 'Resolution establishing the Preparatory Commission for the Comprehensive Nuclear-Test-Ban Treaty Organization' (19 November 1996) CTBT/MSS/RES/1.

[57] 'Home' (*CTBTO*) <https://www.ctbto.org/> accessed 15 April 2020.

[58] VCLT (n 49) art 24(4). That substantive provisions are also covered by this paragraph can be confirmed by its drafting history. *United Nations Conference on the Law of Treaties, First Session, Official Records* (UN 1969) 426, para 19.

of the PrepCom Text, which provides that the PrepCom 'shall undertake all necessary preparations to ensure the operationalization of the Treaty's verification regime at entry into force, pursuant to article IV, paragraph 1', and that the PrepCom 'shall supervise and coordinate ... the development, preparation, technical testing and, pending their formal commissioning, provisional operation as necessary of ... the [IMS]'. These provisions may be considered as an authentic interpretation of Article IV CTBT falling under Article 31(2) VCLT. In any case, the IMS has been provisionally operating and has already detected Indian, Pakistani, and North Korean nuclear test explosions.[59]

5. Nuclear Disarmament

a. *ICJ Nuclear Weapons Advisory Opinion*

While there should be no doubt concerning the devastating and inhumane effects of nuclear weapons use, different opinions exist on how to address the issue given the importance of nuclear deterrence for many States' security policies. In its 1996 advisory opinion, the ICJ stated that:

> [a] threat or use of nuclear weapons should ... be compatible with the requirements ... of the principles and rules of international humanitarian law, [and that] the threat or use of nuclear weapons would generally be contrary to ... the principles and rules of humanitarian law[60]

but declared that it

> cannot conclude definitively whether the threat or use of nuclear weapons would be lawful or unlawful in an extreme circumstance of self-defence, in which the very survival of a State would be at stake.[61]

Additionally, the Court found an 'obligation to pursue in good faith and bring to a conclusion negotiations leading to nuclear disarmament ... under strict and effective international control',[62] although no good explanation or justification was given for this conclusion, which diverged from the text of Article VI of the NPT (referring only to an obligation 'to pursue negotiations in good faith') and despite the fact that it was offered as an interpretation of that provision.[63]

[59] Committee on Technical Issues related to Ratification of the Comprehensive Nuclear Test Ban Treaty, *Technical Issues related to the Comprehensive Nuclear Test Ban Treaty* (National Academy Press 2002) 40 fn 10; 'Comparison of Seismic Signals (to Scale) of All Six Declared DPRK Nuclear Tests' (*CTBTO*) <https://www.ctbto.org/the-treaty/developments-after-1996/2017-sept-dprk/> accessed 5 January 2019.

[60] *Legality of the Threat or Use of Nuclear Weapons* (Advisory Opinion) [1996] ICJ Rep 226.

[61] ibid [105(2)E].

[62] ibid [105(2)F].

[63] ibid [99]–[100]; ibid Declaration Bedjaoui [23].

b. *Treaty on the Prohibition of Nuclear Weapons*

The Court's dictum on nuclear disarmament has provided the basis not only for annual UNGA resolutions on the subject[64] but also for a series of ICJ cases instituted in 2014 by the Marshall Islands against nine nuclear-armed States.[65] The Court only dealt with the cases against the UK, India, and Pakistan, because of a lack of jurisdiction over the other six States. In its almost identical judgments, the Court dismissed the claims against all three respondents on the ground of 'the absence of a dispute between the Parties'.[66]

For its part, the advisory opinion dictum concerning the application of international humanitarian law on nuclear weapons seems to have influenced later developments in nuclear disarmament. The 2010 NPT Review Conference in its Final Document 'express[ed]... deep concern at the catastrophic humanitarian consequences of any use of nuclear weapons and reaffirm[ed] the need for all States at all times to comply with applicable international law, including international humanitarian law'.[67] This statement, as well as a 2011 International Red Cross and Red Crescent Movement resolution, which found it 'difficult to envisage how any use of nuclear weapons could be compatible with the rules of international humanitarian law',[68] led to the delivery of a Joint Statement by sixteen States in the 2012 Preparatory Committee for the 2015 NPT Review Conference, which declared that: '[i]t is of utmost importance that these weapons never be used again, under any circumstances. The only way to guarantee this is the total, irreversible and verifiable elimination of nuclear weapons'.[69]

After the abortive 2015 NPT Review Conference, the UNGA, in response to the recommendation[70] of the Open-Ended Working Group meetings held in 2016,[71] decided to convene in 2017 a UN conference 'to negotiate a legally binding instrument to prohibit nuclear weapons, leading towards their total elimination'.[72] On 7 July 2017 the conference adopted a TPNW, the first treaty comprehensively prohibiting nuclear weapons

[64] The most recent is UNGA Res 73/64 (5 December 2018).

[65] This term is used to include not only nuclear-weapon States under the NPT but also other States which (are believed to) possess nuclear weapons, such as India, Pakistan, Israel, and North Korea.

[66] eg *Obligations Concerning Negotiations Relating to Cessation of the Nuclear Arms Race and to Nuclear Disarmament (Marshall Islands v United Kingdom)* (Preliminary Objections) [2016] ICJ Rep 833 [59].

[67] 2010 Review Conference of the Parties to the Treaty on the Non-Proliferation of Nuclear Weapons, 'Final Document' (2010) NPT/CONF.2010/50(Vol.I), 19, para I.A.v.

[68] Council of Delegates of the International Red Cross and Red Crescent Movement, 'Working Towards the Elimination of Nuclear Weapons' (26 November 2011) CD/11/4.1, para 2.

[69] 'Joint Statement on the Humanitarian Dimension of Nuclear Disarmament' (First Session of the Preparatory Committee for the 2015 Review Conference of the Parties to the Treaty on the Non-Proliferation of Nuclear Weapons, 2 May 2012) <https://unoda-web.s3-accelerate.amazonaws.com/wp-content/uploads/assets/WMD/Nuclear/NPT2015/PrepCom2012/statements/20120502/SwitzerlandOnBehalfOf.pdf> accessed 6 April 2020. This was the first such statement delivered in 2012. The follow-on statements and resolutions were essentially to the same effect with some variations.

[70] UNGA, 'Note by the Secretary-General: Taking Forward Multilateral Nuclear Disarmament Negotiations' (1 September 2016) UN Doc A/71/371, 19, para 67.

[71] The Group's meetings were held in accordance with UNGA Res 70/33 (7 December 2015) paras 2, 3, 5.

[72] UNGA Res 71/258 (23 December 2016) para 8.

and intended for universal application.[73] Under the Treaty, it is prohibited to develop, test, produce, manufacture, otherwise acquire, possess, stockpile, transfer, receive, use, or threaten to use nuclear weapons as well as to assist, encourage, or induce anyone to engage in any prohibited activity, to seek or receive any assistance to engage in any prohibited activity, or to allow stationing, installation, or deployment of nuclear weapons in the State Party's own territory (Article 1). The Treaty will enter into force ninety days after fifty States ratify it (Article 15, para 1).

No nuclear-armed State or any of their allies (so-called 'nuclear umbrella States') has signed the TPNW so far. This seems to be mainly due to the Treaty's prohibition of the threat of use of nuclear weapons as well as of assistance, encouragement, or inducement of prohibited activity, which conflict with the doctrine of nuclear deterrence. This was also the explanation given by the Netherlands at the 2017 UN conference, the only nuclear umbrella State participating in the negotiations[74] in which it cast a negative vote. It declared that '[t]he obligations in Article 1 are incompatible with [its] commitments as a NATO state'.[75] On top of this, the Netherlands characterized the treaty as 'in essence, not verifiable'.[76] Indeed, the question of verification of nuclear disarmament was postponed to a later stage, as was partly the case with the destruction of nuclear weapons themselves. Nuclear-armed States are allowed, if they so choose, to retain their nuclear weapons even after becoming a party to the Treaty, and are required to destroy such weapons before a deadline to be determined by the States Parties.[77] In terms of verification, the Treaty requires such irreversible elimination to be verified by an undetermined 'competent international authority'.[78]

Relatedly, it should also be noted that due to the opposition of some NAM States,[79] the verification requirement for non-nuclear-armed States Parties has become so moderate as to only be the conclusion or maintenance of CSA (Article 3). This is contrasted with the fact that CSA and Additional Protocol have long been recognized by many States as the '(current) verification standard' for non-nuclear-weapon States Parties to the NPT.[80]

[73] TPNW (n 4). The Treaty was adopted by a vote of 122 to 1 (Netherlands) with 1 abstention (Singapore).

[74] No nuclear-armed States participated.

[75] Kingdom of the Netherlands, 'Explanation of Vote of the Netherlands on Text of Nuclear Ban Treaty' (7 July 2017) <https://www.permanentrepresentations.nl/latest/news/2017/07/07/explanation-of-vote-of-ambassador-lise-gregoire-on-the-draft-text-of-the-nuclear-ban-treaty> accessed 1 January 2019.

[76] ibid. [77] TPNW (n 4) art 4(2). [78] ibid art 4(6).

[79] Argentina, Brazil, Egypt, and Iran opposed the Additional Protocol as part of the safeguards requirement under the TPNW: Gaukhar Mukhatzhanova, 'The Nuclear Weapons Prohibition Treaty: Negotiation and Beyond' (*Arms Control Association*, 1 September 2017) <https://www.armscontrol.org/act/2017-09/features/nuclear-weapons-prohibition-treaty-negotiations-beyond> accessed 3 April 2020.

[80] Masahiko Asada, 'The Treaty on the Non-Proliferation of Nuclear Weapons and the Universalization of the Additional Protocol' (2011) 16 JCSL 3, 5–20.

Additionally, the Netherlands argued that the TPNW placed itself 'above the NPT'[81] and that its review mechanism might overlap with the NPT one. Article 18 TPNW provides that: '[t]he implementation of this Treaty shall not prejudice obligations undertaken by States Parties with regard to existing international agreements, to which they are party, where those obligations are consistent with the Treaty'. Even without this provision, however, a State Party both to the NPT and the TPNW must abide by its TPNW obligations, which are stricter than the NPT ones. In other words, the aforementioned provision is not only unnecessary but may also be taken as indicating the TPNW's somewhat competing position vis-à-vis the NPT, and hence as potentially undermining the NPT process. On the other hand, TPNW proponents argue that the Treaty 'constitutes an essential contribution . . . towards the implementation of article VI of the [NPT]'.[82]

Whichever view is the correct understanding of the relationship between the two treaties, the question arises as to what the influence of the TPNW will be on the international law concerning nuclear weapons, and particularly whether it reflects a development of international law on the matter since the ICJ's 1996 advisory opinion. In this respect, on the same day that the TPNW was adopted, the three Western nuclear-weapon States issued a statement to the effect that they 'do not intend to sign, ratify or ever become party to it' and that they 'would not accept any claim that this treaty reflects or in any way contributes to the development of customary international law'.[83] This, along with similar statements made by the five nuclear-weapon States, India, and Pakistan,[84] makes it extremely difficult to conclude that customary international law has developed, or will emerge, to prohibit the threat or use of nuclear weapons. Should such a customary rule emerge, it would not bind these States as persistent objectors.[85]

[81] Stuart Casey-Maslen, *The Treaty on the Prohibition of Nuclear Weapons: A Commentary* (OUP 2019) 256, para 18.07.

[82] UNGA, 'Taking Forward Multilateral Nuclear Disarmament Negotiations' (6 October 2017) UN Doc A/C.1/72/L.6, preamble.

[83] Permanent Representatives to the United Nations of the United States, United Kingdom, and France, 'Joint Press Statement Following the Adoption of a Treaty Banning Nuclear Weapons' (7 July 2017) <https://usun.usmission.gov/joint-press-statement-from-the-permanent-representatives-to-the-united-nations-of-the-united-states-united-kingdom-and-france-following-the-adoption/> accessed 6 April 2020.

[84] China, France, Russian Federation, United Kingdom, and United States, 'Joint Statement' UNGA 73, First Committee: Thematic Debate (Nuclear Weapons) (22 October 2018) <https://www.mid.ru/en/foreign_policy/news/-/asset_publisher/cKNonkJE02Bw/content/id/3384609> accessed 6 April 2020; Ministry of External Affairs, Government of India, 'Response by the Official Spokesperson to a Media Query regarding India's View on the Treaty to Ban Nuclear Weapons' (18 July 2017) <https://www.mea.gov.in/media-briefings.htm?dtl/28628> accessed 6 April 2020; Ministry of Foreign Affairs, Government of Pakistan, 'Press Statement on the Treaty on the Prohibition of Nuclear Weapons (Nuclear Weapons Ban Treaty)' (7 August 2017) <http://mofa.gov.pk/press-statement-on-the-treaty-on-the-prohibition-of-nuclear-weapons-nuclear-weapons-ban-treaty/> accessed 6 April 2020.

[85] ILC, 'Draft Conclusions on Identification of Customary International Law, with Commentaries' (2018) II(2) Yearbook of the International Law Commission, Conclusion 15, para 1.

C. Current Challenges to the NPT Regime

Despite being a 'cornerstone of global security',[86] the NPT has faced many challenges. In addition to the unfulfilled Article VI obligation and the unachieved objective of universalization of the Treaty, it presently faces two main challenges: the DPRK and Iran.

1. DPRK

DPRK acceded to the NPT in 1985. It concluded the requisite CSA in early 1992, nearly five years later than the deadline provided in the NPT.[87] Moreover, after conducting ad hoc inspections in May 1992 to verify the DPRK's initial report, the IAEA detected certain inconsistences concerning plutonium production. Faced with a request by the IAEA's Director General to accept a special inspection, the DPRK rejected the request and declared on 12 March 1993 that it would withdraw from the NPT. Later DPRK 'suspend[ed]' the declared withdrawal one day before its effectuation,[88] but on 10 January 2003, after the disclosure of the existence of a DPRK nuclear weapons programme based on uranium in October 2002 and ensuing international condemnation, it declared that it would revoke the 'suspension' and withdraw from the NPT on the following day. It is not clear whether and, if so, when the DPRK withdrew from the Treaty.[89] The most plausible view is that it withdrew from the NPT in 2003.[90]

Despite efforts by the international community to make the DPRK retract its announced NPT withdrawal and resolve the North Korean nuclear issue, including through the six-party talks amongst China, DPRK, Japan, Republic of Korea, Russia, and the United States between August 2003 and April 2009, the DPRK continued its nuclear weapons development and on 9 October 2006 conducted its first nuclear weapon test. In response, the UNSC adopted Resolution 1718 (2006), demanding that 'the DPRK not conduct any further nuclear test' and that it 'return to the [NPT] and [IAEA] safeguards', and deciding that it 'shall abandon all nuclear weapons and existing nuclear programmes in a complete, verifiable and irreversible manner'[91] and 'shall act strictly in accordance with the obligations applicable to parties under the [NPT] and the terms

[86] UN Secretary-General, 'Statement: Non-Proliferation Treaty "Cornerstone" of Global Security But Conference Must Narrow Gap Between Performance, Promise' (2 May 2005) UN Doc SG/SM/9847-DC/2956.

[87] NPT (n 2) art III(4).

[88] According to ibid art X, a notice of withdrawal takes effect three months after giving such notice.

[89] Officially the status of DPRK is considered 'uncertain': Credentials Committee, 'Final Report: Credentials of representatives to the Conference' (3 June 2015) NPT/CONF.2015/CC/1/Rev.1, 2 fn 1.

[90] Masahiko Asada, 'Arms Control Law in Crisis? A Study of the North Korean Nuclear Issue' (2004) 9 JCSL 331.

[91] The demand for 'complete, verifiable and irreversible denuclearization (CVID)' is what the US had long maintained as its negotiating position within the framework of the six-party talks.

and conditions of its [IAEA] Safeguards Agreement'. The latter decision seems to have been the Council's fallback demand in case the DPRK refused (as it, in fact, did) to return to the NPT and IAEA safeguards. The Resolution also introduced a set of stringent sanctions. In response to repeated nuclear testing and ballistic missile launches, the sanctions have been strengthened many times by successive UNSC resolutions.[92]

In order to break the decade-long impasse, US President Donald Trump met with North Korean leader Kim Jong Un in Singapore on 12 June 2018 and signed a Joint Statement, according to which 'the DPRK commits to work toward complete denuclearization of the Korean Peninsula'.[93] While the DPRK has unilaterally suspended its nuclear testing and ballistic missile launch programmes (except for short-range missiles), little progress has been made in the denuclearization of the Korean Peninsula.

2. Iran

In 2002, an Iranian dissident group revealed the existence of two nuclear facilities under construction in Iran, which had not been reported to the IAEA.[94] Initially, Iran reacted favourably to the international demand to cooperate with the IAEA by signing and voluntarily implementing the Additional Protocol as well as by voluntarily suspending all uranium enrichment(-related) and reprocessing activities.[95] However, it subsequently resumed uranium conversion activity under new President Mahmoud Ahmadinejad in August 2005. In response, the IAEA Board of Governors adopted a resolution, finding that 'Iran's many failures and breaches' of its obligations under the Safeguards Agreement constitute 'non compliance'.[96] Another resolution was adopted in February 2006, reporting to the UNSC the steps that the IAEA Board required Iran to take, as well as all relevant documents and resolutions.[97] Shortly afterward, Iran informed the IAEA that

[92] UNSC Res 1874 (2009); UNSC Res 2087 (2013); UNSC Res 2094 (2013); UNSC Res 2270 (2016); UNSC Res 2321 (2016); UNSC Res 2356 (2017); UNSC Res 2371 (2017); UNSC Res 2375 (2017); and UNSC Res 2397 (2017). UNSC Res 2371 was described as 'the most stringent set of sanctions imposed on any country in a generation': UNSC Verbatim Record (5 August 2017) UN Doc S/PV.8019, 2 (US).

[93] President Donald J Trump/Chairman Kim Jong Un, 'Joint Statement' (Singapore Summit, 12 June 2018) <https://www.whitehouse.gov/briefings-statements/joint-statement-president-donald-j-trump-united-states-america-chairman-kim-jong-un-democratic-peoples-republic-korea-singapore-summit/> accessed 6 April 2020.

[94] Yaël Ronen, *The Iran Nuclear Issue* (Hart 2010) 1.

[95] Iranian Government/EU Foreign Ministers, 'Statement' (21 October 2003) <https://www.bits.de/public/documents/iran/Tehran_EU_Iran_Agreement03.pdf> accessed 7 April 2020; IAEA, 'Communication dated 26 November 2004 received from the Permanent Representatives of France, Germany, the Islamic Republic of Iran and the United Kingdom concerning the agreement signed in Paris on 15 November 2004' (26 November 2004) Doc INFCIRC/637, 3–4.

[96] IAEA, 'Implementation of the NPT Safeguards Agreement in the Islamic Republic of Iran' (24 September 2005) Doc GOV/2005/77, para 1. Under the IAEA Statute art XII.C, 'non-compliance' is to be reported to the UNSC and UNGA.

[97] IAEA, 'Implementation of the NPT Safeguards Agreement in the Islamic Republic of Iran' (4 February 2006) Doc GOV/2006/14, paras 1, 2.

all voluntary and non-legally binding measures, including the provisions of the Additional Protocol, would be suspended.[98]

The UNSC, for its part, adopted Resolution 1696 (2006) '[d]emand[ing]' that 'Iran shall suspend all enrichment-related and reprocessing activities' to be verified by the IAEA.[99] As the Resolution was adopted 'under Article 40 of Chapter VII of the Charter of the United Nations in order to make mandatory the suspension required by the IAEA' and in accordance with Article 103 of the UN Charter, this obligation took precedence over Iran's rights and obligations under the NPT, including those concerning the peaceful use of nuclear energy. Resolution 1696 (2006) also imposed sanctions, '[c]all[ing] upon all States' to 'prevent the transfer of any items, materials, goods and technology that could contribute to Iran's enrichment-related and reprocessing activities and ballistic missile programmes'.[100]

As a result of the successive strengthening of UN sanctions[101] and the autonomous sanctions imposed by the US and the EU, as well as the election of the more moderate President Hassan Rouhani in 2013, negotiations between the so-called E3/EU+3[102] and Iran reached a final agreement on a comprehensive solution to the Iranian nuclear issue on 14 July 2015. This so-called Joint Comprehensive Plan of Action (JCPOA)[103] has been described as 'the best possible model of successful diplomacy'.[104]

According to the JCPOA, Iran is supposed to keep its enrichment capacity of 5060 first-generation centrifuges for ten years, maintain a total enriched uranium stockpile of no more than 300 kg of up to 3.67 per cent enriched uranium hexafluoride for fifteen years,[105] not to engage in any spent fuel reprocessing for fifteen years, and to provisionally apply the IAEA Additional Protocol pending ratification.[106] Iran has also allowed the

[98] Ronen (n 94) 63. [99] UNSC Res 1696 (2006) para 2. [100] ibid para 5.

[101] ibid; UNSC Res 1737 (2006); UNSC Res 1747 (2007); UNSC Res 1803 (2008); UNSC Res 1835 (2008); UNSC Res 1929 (2010).

[102] Namely China, France, Germany, Russia, United Kingdom, and the United States, with the High Representative of the EU for Foreign Affairs and Security Policy.

[103] UNSC 'Annex to the letter dated 16 July 2015 from the Permanent Representative of the United States of America to the United Nations addressed to the President of the Security Council: Joint Comprehensive Plan of Action, Vienna, 14 July 2015' (16 July 2015) UN Doc S/2015/544 (JCPOA). cf UNSC 'Annex to the letter dated 16 July 2015 from the Permanent Representative of the United States of America to the United Nations addressed to the President of the Security Council: Statement' (16 July 2015) UN Doc S/2015/545.

[104] Daniel H Joyner, *Iran's Nuclear Program and International Law: From Confrontation to Accord* (OUP 2016) 244.

[105] This is so that Iran cannot amass enough weapons-grade uranium to create one nuclear weapon in less than one year. Daryl G Kimball, 'Why Congress Should Support the Iran Deal' (2015) 45(7) Arms Control Today 3.

[106] JCPOA (n 103) paras 2, 5, 7, 12, 13; ibid Annex I, paras 18, 19, 27, 28, 56, 64; ibid Annex V, para 8. The provisional application is in accordance with the Additional Protocol (n 34) art 17(b). Iran is legally bound to apply the provisions of the Protocol during its provisional application period, but it is not impossible for it to legally terminate such provisional application by notifying its intention not to become a party to the Protocol as the JCPOA is not legally binding. VCLT (n 49) art 25(2).

IAEA to monitor implementation of the JCPOA measures.[107] For their part, the EU, the US, and the UN terminated the sanctions against Iran, as specified in the relevant provisions of the JCPOA and its Annexes II and V.[108] Issues arising from the implementation of the JCPOA may be referred to the Joint Commission consisting of the E3/EU+3 and Iran.[109]

The JCPOA itself is not a legally binding document,[110] despite the fact that the UNSC endorsed the JCPOA by Resolution 2231 (2015) and '[c]all[ed] upon all Member States' to 'take such actions as may be appropriate to support [its] implementation'.[111] The decisions dealing with UNSC measures in the Resolution, however, are legally binding as indicated in its preamble referring to Article 25 of the UN Charter.[112] The Resolution contains a decision to terminate sanction measures imposed by previous UNSC resolutions and also a decision whereby the terminated measures would be resurrected if *a proposal for the termination to persist* is rejected by the Council.[113] Although no such thing has happened so far, the US under President Trump in May 2018 withdrew from the JCPOA and re-imposed its sanctions on Iran which had been lifted or waived under the JCPOA.[114] In response, Iran started to breach commitments under the JCPOA in May 2019, including limitations on uranium enrichment. Shortly after Iran announced the elimination of the last key operational restriction in January 2020, the three European parties to the accord triggered its dispute resolution mechanism to 'preserve the deal and address Iran's breaches'.[115]

[107] JCPOA (n 103) para 15; ibid Annex I, paras 67–81. For the latest report by the IAEA Director General concerning verification of JCPOA implementation: IAEA, 'Report by the Director General: Verification and Monitoring in the Islamic Republic of Iran in light of United Nations Security Council resolution 2231 (2015)' (3 March 2020) Doc GOV/2020/5.

[108] JCPOA (n 103) paras 18–33; ibid Annex II; ibid Annex V.

[109] ibid paras ix, 24, 36.

[110] In the opening sentence after the preamble the JCPOA declares that 'Iran and E3/EU+3 will take the following voluntary measures within the timeframe as detailed in this JCPOA and its Annexes'; Kristina Daugirdas/Julian Davis Mortenson (eds), 'Contemporary Practice of the United States Relating to International Law' (2015) 109 AJIL 407, 410–11.

[111] UNSC Res 2231 (2015) paras 1, 2.

[112] ibid preamble: 'Underscor[es] that Member States are obligated under Article 25 of the Charter of the United Nations to accept and carry out the Security Council's decisions'. UNSC Res 2231 was not adopted under ch VII of the Charter of the United Nations 1 UNTS XVI (UN Charter), but contains many 'decisions', including those on the termination of sanctions.

[113] UNSC Res 2231 (2015) para 12. This provision lasts 10 years, but according to the six foreign ministers' letter to the UN Secretary-General, there is a possibility to extend it for five years. Somini Sengupta, '"Snapback" is an Easy Way to Reimpose Iran Penalties' (*The New York Times*, 16 July 2015) <https://www.nytimes.com/2015/07/17/world/middleeast/snapback-is-easy-way-to-reimpose-iran-penalties.html> accessed 7 April 2020.

[114] The re-imposed sanctions are a robust combination of primary and secondary sanctions on domestic and foreign entities. Jean Galbraith (ed), 'Contemporary Practice of the United States Relating to International Law' (2018) 112 AJIL 486, 517.

[115] Kelsey Davenport, 'Europe Seeks to Avoid UN Iran Sanctions' (2020) 50(2) Arms Control Today 27.

D. Conclusion

In March 2020, the NPT celebrated its 50th anniversary. During this fifty-year period, it has been faced with a number of challenges: in 1991, it was confronted with the revelation that a non-nuclear-weapon State Party (Iraq) was developing nuclear weapons; it faced the dissolution of a nuclear-weapon State Party (the USSR) in the same year; and the question of how to extend the Treaty arose in 1995. The resolution of these issues eventually strengthened the NPT regime. Russia alone has continued the USSR nuclear-weapon State status, while the rest of the former Soviet republics all joined the NPT as non-nuclear-weapon States; the NPT was indefinitely extended in 1995; and the Model Additional Protocol strengthening the CSA was adopted in 1997.

The challenges the NPT regime faces today, however, cannot be dealt with adequately by what was achieved in the last century. Very little can be done for the DPRK's persistence to withdraw from the NPT. The Iranian issue is also difficult to resolve due to the fact that, as long as Iranian activities are claimed to be for peaceful purposes, the NPT regime cannot prohibit them without convincing evidence to the contrary. While sanctions have provisionally assisted in addressing these challenges, both situations are fragile.

When it comes to nuclear disarmament, the adoption of the TPNW in 2017 has been hailed as a great triumph by its proponents. Important stakeholders, however, see it as a source of complication. Growing concern exists in the NPT community that divisions between nuclear-weapon and non-nuclear-weapon States Parties may become exacerbated, making progress in disarmament even more difficult.

Amongst nuclear-weapon States, the notification by the US on 2 February 2019 of its withdrawal from the Intermediate-Range Nuclear Forces Treaty symbolizes the difficulty involved in maintaining the balance of nuclear forces amongst nuclear powers. The only remaining US–Russian nuclear arms control treaty, the New START, is on the verge of termination.

All these developments serve to illustrate how complex and difficult it is to deal with nuclear non-proliferation and disarmament, both of which go to the heart of national and international security.

HUMAN SECURITY

CHAPTER 19

ATROCITY CRIMES AND LARGE-SCALE HUMAN RIGHTS VIOLATIONS

ADAMA DIENG

A. Introduction

The prevention of conflicts and protection of populations from atrocity crimes and large-scale human rights violations remains a primary responsibility of States. Indeed, in the 2005 World Summit Outcome Document, UN Member States reaffirmed their responsibility to protect populations from genocide, war crimes, ethnic cleansing, and crimes against humanity.[1] They committed to assist each other to fulfil this responsibility and to act collectively when States 'manifestly failed' to protect their populations from these crimes. This was the first time States committed internationally to protect populations from atrocity crimes.[2]

In this contribution, I contend that the international community cannot undertake meaningful prevention without respect for human rights and fundamental freedoms universally recognized and guaranteed by the International Bill of Rights and other international and regional instruments.[3] If the international community is to achieve sustainable peace, States must reaffirm their commitment to the primacy of human dignity and human rights as reflected in the UN Charter[4] and other international and

[1] UNGA Res 60/1 (16 September 2005); see, generally, Adama Dieng, 'The Maintenance of International Peace and Security Through Prevention of Atrocity Crimes: The Question of Cooperation between the UN and Regional Arrangements' in Margaret M de Guzman/Diane M Amann (eds), *Arcs of Global Justice: Essays in Honour of William Schabas* (OUP 2018).

[2] Dieng (n 1).

[3] Christopher NJ Roberts, *The Contentious History of the International Bill of Human Rights* (CUP 2015).

[4] Charter of the United Nations 1 UNTS XVI (UN Charter).

regional human rights instruments. As underscored by the preamble to the Universal Declaration of Human Rights (UDHR), 'recognition of the inherent dignity and of the equal and inalienable rights of all members of the human family is the foundation of freedom, justice and peace'.[5] It is therefore crucial that respect of human rights is put at the heart of prevention of atrocity crimes.

B. Atrocity Crimes and Human Rights Violations

In recognition of the complexities of preventing atrocity crimes, and of the important responsibility of the UN in this regard, the UN Secretary-General pioneered an innovative approach aimed at putting human rights protection at the core of the work of the organization. The 'Human Rights up Front' initiative[6] is premised on an understanding that serious human rights violations, particularly when targeting a specific group, constitute one key early indicator of the risk of atrocity crimes. Experience has shown that, be it in Syria, Libya, Iraq, or Yemen, failure to address serious human rights violations often presages more serious acts such as atrocity crimes.

The 'Human Rights up Front' initiative recognizes the critical role and primary responsibility of Member States to protect their populations from atrocity crimes. The initiative is therefore meant to concretize what is already reflected in the UN Charter, the UDHR, and various UN General Assembly (UNGA) resolutions on the protection of human rights. It reaffirms the centrality of human rights to the objectives of the UN and calls upon the international community to address human rights violations before they escalate and result in the loss of human life. Amongst the key components of the 'Human Rights up Front' initiative are improved coordination between the Secretariat and UN offices in the field to strengthen human rights protection capacities, and enhanced engagement with the Member States.[7] The Secretary-General's 'Human Rights up Front' initiative complements State and regional initiatives that aim to improve the protection of populations who are at risk of genocide, war crimes, ethnic cleansing, and crimes

[5] UNGA Res 217(III) A (10 December 1948).

[6] UN Secretary-General, 'Rights up Front: A Plan of Action to Strengthen the UN's Role in Protecting People in Crises' (17 December 2013) <http://responsibilitytoprotect.org/2%20pager%20-%20RuFAP%20Summary%20-%20General%20Assembly%20-%2017%20Dec%202013%20-%20FINAL.pdf> accessed 16 October 2019. See also, Gerrit Kurtz, 'With Courage and Coherence: The Human Rights up Front Initiative of the United Nations' (Global Public Policy Institute, 2015) <https://www.gppi.net/media/Kurtz_2015_Courage_and_Coherence_UN_Human_Rights.pdf> accessed 10 January 2020.

[7] Ekkehard Strauss, 'The UN Secretary-General's Human Rights Up Front Initiative and the Prevention of Genocide: Impact, Potential, Limitations' (2018) 11 Genocide Studies and Prevention: An International Journal 48.

against humanity. Indeed, the examples of the Central Africa Republic[8] and South Sudan,[9] have demonstrated that when human rights violations and long-standing grievances remain unaddressed, they can easily lead to violence that may result in the commission of atrocity crimes and large-scale human rights violations.

To address large-scale human rights violations before becoming atrocity crimes, the UN established the Office of the Special Adviser on Prevention of Genocide (Office of the Special Adviser) in 2004.[10] This office continues to explore ways to enhance collaboration and coordination with individual States, UN offices in the field, civil society organizations, and others, ensuring that early warning information on the risk of atrocity crimes is shared with relevant stakeholders for timely action.[11] Working closely with these institutions has the potential to significantly enhance our collective ability to recognize and respond to risk factors and precursors to atrocity crimes.[12] To enhance its understanding of the factors that increase the risk of atrocity crimes, the Office of the Special Adviser has developed a Framework of Analysis for Atrocity Crimes, based on an assessment of historical cases and of international jurisprudence, which sets out and explains the risk factors for genocide, war crimes, and crimes against humanity, as well as the early indicators of risk.[13] The Framework is a set of fourteen risk factors with related indicators that can help to identify, in a consistent and systematic manner, the risk of genocide, crimes against humanity, and war crimes in any given situation.

The Framework of Analysis for Atrocity Crimes starts with six risk factors that are common to all crimes, recognizing that when there are the first signs of trouble, it is not necessarily true that a certain type of crime is more likely to occur. For example, before the conflict in South Sudan assumed an ethnic dimension, the tensions were largely political in nature. However, as time passed, and the situation deteriorated, an assessment

[8] Under Secretary-General and Special Adviser on the Prevention of Genocide Adama Dieng visited the Central African Republic between 17 and 21 December 2013 to assess the risk of genocide, war crimes and crimes against humanity (atrocity crimes) and to advocate with transitional authorities and other actors for a cessation of violence and enhanced protection of the civilian population.

[9] Under Secretary-General and Special Adviser on the Prevention of Genocide Adama Dieng visited South Sudan in April 2014 following brutal attacks against civilians in the northern town of Bentiu, where people were killed in places of worship, hospitals, and a UN base, where internally displaced people (IDPs) were sheltering.

[10] For comprehensive coverage of the Office of the Special Adviser on the Prevention of Genocide (Office of the Special Adviser) see, generally, Bertrand G Ramcharan, 'Historical Insights into the Establishment of the Position of Special Adviser on the Prevention of Genocide' and William Schabas, 'The Special Adviser on the Prevention of Genocide and his Inscrutable Mandate' in Charles R Majinge (ed), *The Rule of Law through Human Rights and International Criminal Justice: Essays in Honour of Adama Dieng* (Cambridge Scholars Publishers 2015).

[11] Adama Dieng, 'Preventing Genocide and Crimes Against Humanity: Reflection on Future Challenges and Opportunities' in Cherif Bassiouni (ed), *Globalization and Its Impact on the Future of Human Rights and International Human Rights* (Intersentia 2015) 349.

[12] ibid.

[13] UN, 'Framework of Analysis for Atrocity Crimes: A Tool for Prevention' (2014) <https://www.un.org/en/genocideprevention/documents/about-us/Doc.3_Framework%20of%20Analysis%20for%20Atrocity%20Crimes_EN.pdf> accessed 16 October 2019 (Framework of Analysis for Atrocity Crimes).

of specific risk factors associated with each of the crimes clearly pointed to a more specific direction.[14]

The resolution adopted by the Human Rights Council (HRC) on the prevention of genocide in 2015 made specific reference to the Framework of Analysis for Atrocity Crimes.[15] This tool has also been endorsed by the Secretary-General and has been issued as an official UN document.[16] It is being used to build the capacity of both UN staff and of the Member States and regional organizations to identify and respond to the risk of atrocity crimes at an early stage. However, it can be argued that risk does not equal inevitability. Even when several risk factors are present, a situation may not necessarily escalate to the point where atrocities are committed.[17] This could be due to the absence of a triggering event, such as a contested election or an irregular regime change, or the presence of mitigating elements, such as the activities of a peace operation or the support of regional organizations. The Framework was designed to reflect these considerations and evolving scenarios.

The presence of a strong, representative civil society is also an important mitigating factor for large-scale human rights violations. Experience over time has demonstrated the crucial role that civil society can play in prevention efforts relating to mass atrocity crimes and other large-scale human rights violations.[18] They do so through monitoring and reporting on local developments, advocating for action to protect populations and, crucially, holding national governments and the international community to account for their actions and omissions. Further, it can be argued that religious leaders have a special responsibility. In countries such as the Central African Republic, Iraq, or Myanmar, where such leaders have been shown to have influence over a large number of people, these actors can play a key role in fostering a culture of peace and acceptance rather than inflaming a culture of hatred and division.[19]

Experience from the work of the Office of the Special Adviser has demonstrated that the Framework Analysis noted above, if applied systematically, can assist in assessing concerning signs and sound the alarm both early and more consistently. This means assessing a range of factors related not only to the risk of armed conflict but also to other types of situations that put stress on a State and create an environment conducive to atrocity crimes. This means looking, for example, at the capacities and motivations of

[14] AU Assembly 'Interim Report of the African Union Commission of Inquiry on South Sudan' (26–27 June 2014) Assembly/AU/19(XXIII).

[15] HRC Res 28/34 (7 April 2015).

[16] Framework of Analysis for Atrocity Crimes (n 13).

[17] ibid.

[18] For example, see the work of the Office of the High Commissioner for Human Rights on civil society in OHCHR, 'Civil Society: UN Human Rights Resources for NGOs, Human Rights Defenders, and Other Actors in Civic Space' (2019) <https://www.ohchr.org/en/aboutus/pages/civilsociety.aspx> accessed 10 January 2020.

[19] See UN Office on Genocide Prevention and Responsibility to Protect, 'Plan of Action for Religious Leaders and Actors to Prevent Incitement to Violence that Could Lead to Atrocity Crimes' (UN 2017), developed under the auspices of Under-Secretary-General and Special Adviser Adama Dieng, <https://www.un.org/en/genocideprevention/documents/Plan%20of%20Action%20Advanced%20Copy.pdf> accessed 10 January 2020.

potential perpetrators, monitoring the human rights situation, assessing strengths and weaknesses of key State institutions, identifying gaps in societal resilience and sources of mitigation, and anticipating a variety of possible triggers.

It is critical that the international community moves from a reactive to a preventive approach for large-scale human rights violations. Achieving this objective requires readiness to act earlier when the first warning signs appear. Prevention is so much less costly (in all senses, but particularly in terms of human life) and provides many more options for action.[20] For example, who knows how different the situation in Syria would have been had the UN Security Council (UNSC) acted early on to prevent human rights violations from escalating into a deadly, complicated civil war? The consequences for the Syrian people and the wider region have been indeed devastating and will be felt for generations, as can already be seen in the massive displacement of persons and the proliferation of terrorist activities in the region.[21]

C. Legal Framework

1. United Nations and Prevention of Atrocity Crimes

To fulfil the commitment that the atrocities committed during the Second World War would never happen again, and one day before the adoption of the UDHR on 9 December 1948, the UNGA adopted the Convention on the Prevention and Punishment of the Crime of Genocide.[22] The adoption of the Convention, while to a large extent symbolic in nature, reaffirmed the gravity of the crime of genocide.[23] Further, it demonstrated the commitment of the international community to ensure both the prevention of genocide and the punishment of its perpetrators when it could not be prevented. The importance of this Convention is therefore twofold. First, it defines genocide as a crime under international law,[24] regardless of whether it is committed in times of peace or times of war. Secondly, it provides a definition of the elements of genocide, setting out clearly what genocide is and what it is not (at least for the purposes of the Convention).[25]

[20] See, generally, Dieng (n 1).

[21] Elizabeth Ferris/Kemal Kerisci, *The Consequences of Chaos: Syria's Humanitarian Crisis and the Failure to Protect* (Brookings Institution Press 2017).

[22] 78 UNTS 277 (Genocide Convention).

[23] See, generally, John Quigley, *The Genocide Convention: An International Law Analysis* (Routledge 2016).

[24] ibid 1–10.

[25] Genocide is defined in the Genocide Convention (n 22) art 2 as:

> [A]ny of the following acts committed with intent to destroy, in whole or in part, a national, ethnical, racial or religious group, as such: killing members of the group; causing serious bodily or mental harm to members of the group; deliberately inflicting on the group conditions of life calculated to bring about its physical destruction in whole or in part; imposing measures intended to prevent births within the group; [and] forcibly transferring children of the group to another group.

The role of the UN in the maintenance of international peace and security is grounded in its Charter. Indeed, the UN Charter is itself premised on the 'need to rid the world of the scourge of war'.[26] As such it can be argued that the UN Charter designates the protection of populations from atrocity crimes as a key function of the Organization. Within the Charter framework, the primary responsibility for maintaining international peace and security lies with the UNSC, under Article 24 and is underpinned by Article 39 of the Charter.[27]

The text of Article 39 allows for the Council to characterize any situation as constituting a threat to international peace and security—whether in a particular region of the world or within individual States. The Charter neither provides criteria for such determinations nor compels the UNSC to intervene in any particular situation; rather, it leaves decisions as to whether and on what basis to intervene within the prerogative of the Council. Nor does Article 39 specify the mechanisms to be used by the UNSC when intervening. Rather, this is also left to the discretion of the Council (subject, however, to the broad but non-exhaustive parameters set out in Articles 41 and 42). Throughout the years, the Council significantly expanded its interpretation of what may constitute a potential or generic threat to international peace and security, including in this category terrorist acts, the proliferation of weapons of mass destruction, and the proliferation and illicit trafficking of small arms and light weapons, amongst others.[28]

It is worth noting that the role of the Council in preventing atrocity crimes is not limited to military intervention. Rather, both Chapter VI and Chapter VII of the Charter encompass a wide range of enforcement measures to address possible threats to peace and security that do not necessarily involve military means. For example, the Council can resort to mediation between warring parties, support the good offices of the UN Secretary-General or establish judicial mechanisms in the form of referrals to the International Criminal Court (ICC) or through the creation of international or hybrid criminal tribunals. The latter mechanism can also be undertaken as a deterrence mechanism for future crimes. For example, the Council established criminal tribunals in the former Yugoslavia,[29] Rwanda,[30] Cambodia,[31] and Sierra Leone.[32] The latter two, while not directly accountable to the Council, were negotiated by the Secretary-General with the strong support of the Council. Similarly, the UNSC has supported the establishment of peacekeeping missions with strong mandates to protect civilians, after having

[26] UN Charter (n 4) preamble.

[27] Under UN Charter (n 4) art 24 'Members confer on the Security Council primary responsibility for the maintenance of international peace and security', while, under art 39, the UNSC shall 'determine the existence of any threat to the peace, breach of the peace, or act of aggression and... make recommendations, or decide what measures shall be taken... to maintain or restore international peace and security'.

[28] See UNSC, 'Repertoire of Security Council Practice: Actions with Respect to Threats to the Peace, Breaches of the Peace, and Acts of Aggression', art 39 <https://www.un.org/securitycouncil/content/repertoire/actions#rel1> accessed 12 February 2020.

[29] See UNSC Res 827 (1993).

[30] See UNSC Res 955 (1994).

[31] See, generally, Daniel Donovan, 'Joint UN–Cambodia Efforts to Establish a Khmer Rouge Tribunal' (2003) 44 Harvard International Law Journal 551.

[32] Charles Jalloh, *Consolidated Legal Texts for the Special Court for Sierra Leone* (Martinus Nijhoff 2007).

determined the existence of threats to international peace and security.[33] The Council has also supported the establishment of accountability mechanisms for ISIL/Da'esh.[34]

The UN General Assembly has also made efforts to prevent and protect populations against atrocity crimes. The adoption of the 'Responsibility to Protect' doctrine in the 2005 World Summit Outcome Document is one step in that direction. Paragraphs 138–40, which have been recalled in subsequent UNSC resolutions,[35] call for national and international action to prevent atrocity crimes and can be considered a positive step in the action of the UNGA and the Council to address the challenge of maintaining international peace and security. One can certainly argue that, since it was the UNGA that stipulated the principle in the World Summit Outcome Document, the Assembly itself maintains a specific responsibility in overseeing the implementation of the principle.

The UN Secretary-General also plays an extremely important role in advancing the Responsibility to Protect, not least in light of his mandate *ex* Articles 98 and 99 of the Charter.[36] Since the adoption of the Document, the Secretary-General has taken measures to ensure that the concept moves from an ideal to a concrete reality, capable of affording requisite protection to those in whose name it was adopted.[37] As mentioned above, in 2004 the Secretary-General established the Office of the Special Adviser on the Prevention of Genocide. These efforts of the Secretary-General are an acknowledgement of past failures and an attempt to create a better institutional framework within the organization to prevent and respond to protection needs of populations against atrocity crimes.

In this context, the role of the Secretary-General can be seen as twofold. First, it is to ensure that the principle of Responsibility to Protect is conceptualized within the framework envisaged under the World Summit Outcome Document to protect populations against atrocity crimes. Secondly, the Secretary-General is to engage in preventive

[33] See UNSC Res 1593 (2005) (referral of the situation in Darfur to the ICC); See also, *Prosecutor v Omar Hassan Ahmad Al Bashir ('Omar Al Bashir')* (Warrant of Arrest for Omar Hassan Ahmad Al Bashir) ICC-02/05-01/09 (4 March 2009).

[34] The UNSC adopted Resolution 2379 (2017) to establish the Office of the Special Adviser to collect evidence to be used to hold to account the terrorist group ISIL/Da'esh of acts that may amount to war crimes, crimes against humanity, and genocide.

[35] The responsibility to protect has been reaffirmed by the UNSC in its resolutions: UNSC Res 1674 (2006); UNSC Res 1894 (2009); UNSC Res 2117 (2013); UNSC Res 2150 (2014). Resolution 2150 (2014), adopted on the twentieth anniversary of the genocide in Rwanda, also recalled the important role of the Special Advisers on the Prevention of Genocide and on the Responsibility to Protect. The UNSC has continued to refer to the responsibility of States to protect their populations in country-specific resolutions and, in relation to some of these situations, has authorized action to assist the State to protect its populations from atrocity crimes.

[36] Article 98 of the UN Charter (n 4) provides that the Secretary-General, in addition to acting in that capacity as Secretary-General in all meetings of the UNGA, of the UNSC, of the ECOSOC, and of the Trusteeship Council, 'shall perform such other functions as are entrusted to him by these organs'. These often include functions in the field of the prevention and the peaceful settlement of disputes. Article 99 of the UN Charter (n 4) provides that the Secretary-General may 'bring to the attention of the Security Council any matter that in his opinion may threaten international peace and security'.

[37] In July 2012, the UN Secretary-General appointed Mr Adama Dieng as his Special Adviser on the prevention of Genocide and in July 2013, the Secretary-General appointed Professor Jennifer Welsh as his Special Adviser on the Responsibility to Protect.

diplomacy within the framework of Responsibility to Protect. The Secretary-General has indeed used his good offices to ensure that potential sources of conflict are addressed before they erupt into full-blown conflicts, and to encourage actors to fulfil their protection responsibilities.[38] Indeed, amongst the key roles of the Special Adviser is to advise the Secretary-General on the appropriate approach in addressing these challenges.

Nonetheless, in light of the primary responsibility assigned to it by the Charter for the maintenance of international peace and security, it is the UNSC that is inherently best placed to take measures within the Charter framework to address these challenges. It is therefore no surprise that since the adoption of the World Summit Outcome Document, the Council has taken various measures, including the authorization of the use of force in Libya, to protect populations against atrocity crimes.[39] The Council has also used other tools, such as sanctions and mediations, and has in some cases referred and supported referral of situations to the ICC, on the grounds that doing so advances the objective of protecting civilians and enhancing international peace. In some cases, including South Sudan,[40] Mali,[41] and the Central African Republic,[42] the Council acted at the request of the affected State. In others, like in the case of the international intervention in Libya in 2011,[43] the Council acted against the will of the domestic authorities at the time.

2. Regional Arrangements and Prevention of Atrocity Crimes

As already stated in the introductory part of this chapter, the role of preventing and protecting populations from atrocity crimes cannot be adequately fulfilled by the UN alone. It is this reality that calls for the greater involvement of regional institutions. The

[38] On the question of prevention see generally the agenda of the UN Secretary-General 'Priorities: Prevention' <https://www.un.org/sg/en/priorities/prevention.shtml> accessed 12 February 2020.

[39] Charles Majinge, 'The Use of Force in International Law and the UN Security Council Resolution 1970 and 1973 on Libya' (2011) 24 Hague Yearbook of International Law 153.

[40] In UNSC Res 1996 (2011) establishing the UN Mission in the Republic of South Sudan (UNMISS), the Council aimed at 'advising and assisting the Government of the Republic of South Sudan, including military and police at national and local levels as appropriate, in fulfilling its responsibility to protect civilians.'

[41] In UNSC Res 2085 (2012), which authorized the deployment of an African-led International Support Mission in Mali (AFISMA), the Council stated that it aimed at 'support(ing) the Malian authorities in their primary responsibility to protect the population.' See para 7(d) of the Resolution.

[42] In UNSC Res 2127 (2013), which complemented the mandate of the UN Mission in the Central African Republic with strong protection of civilian tasks, the Council underscored that 'the Transitional Authorities [of the Central African Republic] have the primary responsibility to protect the civilian population.'

[43] In UNSC Res 1973 (2011), the UNSC authorized Member States that have notified the Secretary-General, acting nationally or through regional organizations or arrangements, and acting in cooperation with the Secretary-General, to take all necessary measures, notwithstanding UNSC Res 1970 (2011) para 9, to protect civilians and civilian populated areas under threat of attack in the Libyan Arab Jamahiriya, while '[r]eiterating the responsibility of the Libyan authorities to protect the Libyan population and reaffirming that parties to armed conflicts bear the primary responsibility to take all feasible steps to ensure the protection of civilians.'

role of regional institutions in the maintenance of international peace and security is provided for under Chapter VIII of the Charter. While Chapter VIII authorizes the UNSC to delegate peace enforcement action to regional arrangements, it is important to note that Chapter VIII does not in and of itself delegate such power to regional arrangements.[44] Rather, context-specific delegation by the UNSC is needed. Article 53(1) of the Charter in particular provides that

> [t]he Security Council shall, where appropriate, utilize such regional arrangements or agencies for enforcement action under its authority. But no enforcement action shall be taken under regional arrangements or by regional agencies without the authorization of the Security Council . . .[45]

The World Summit Outcome Document recognizes the key role of regional institutions to prevent and protect civilians from atrocity crimes. While this recognition is not explicit, paragraph 139 of the Outcome Document requires the international community 'to use appropriate diplomatic, humanitarian and other peaceful means, in accordance with Chapter VIII to protect populations' on a case-by-case basis and in cooperation with relevant regional organizations. It can therefore be argued that this paragraph fully recognizes the role of regional institutions precisely because Chapter VIII covers the relationship between the UN and regional organizations. In 2011, the Secretary-General, in his annual report to the UNGA on the Responsibility to Protect, provided a detailed explanation of the role of regional and sub-regional arrangements in implementing the responsibility to protect populations from atrocity crimes.[46] From the Secretary-General's perspective, the role of regional institutions is well grounded in the Charter, which recognizes the indispensable role of these institutions in addressing challenges relating to international peace and security.

Indeed, it is because of this recognition of the role of regional institutions in the Charter, that regional and sub-regional institutions have often undertaken measures to protect civilians from atrocity crimes. These measures have included peacekeeping operations, supporting peace processes, and in some cases authorizing military intervention. It is worth noting that these measures have been undertaken within and outside the framework of the Charter.[47] Initial academic and independent policy formulations of the Responsibility to Protect seemed to imply that, under certain circumstances, regional organizations might be entitled to resort to the use of force even in the absence

[44] See for an analysis Christine Gray, *International Law and the Use of Force* (4th edn, OUP 2018) ch 8.

[45] UN Charter (n 4) art 53(1). See, also, Dieng (n 1).

[46] See UNGA/UNSC 'Report of the Secretary-General: The Role of Regional and Sub-regional Arrangements in Implementing the Responsibility to Protect' (28 June 2011) UN Doc A/65/877-S/2011/393.

[47] For example, while the intervention in Libya was sanctioned by the UNSC, the intervention in Kosovo was not. For a discussion of the latter conflict see Christine Chinkin, 'Kosovo: a "Good" or "Bad" War?' (1999) 93 AJIL 841.

of an explicit authorization by the UNSC.[48] These arguments built on the recognition that, at least in two instances in the 1990s (the interventions by the Economic Community of West African States Monitoring Group (ECOMOG) and ECOWAS respectively in Sierra Leone and Liberia in 1997), UNSC authorization came after the actual deployment of military troops by a regional organization.[49] It has further been argued that actions taken by regional organizations consistent with their mandate in their respective geographical scopes contain sufficient safeguards with respect to the legality and legitimacy of the use of force under international law, even in the absence of prior UNSC authorization.[50] From the perspective of this author, as already highlighted above, in the current state of international law, it is extremely hard to assess how these arguments could be reconciled with prevailing interpretations of the provisions of the Charter setting up the UN collective security mechanism.

Despite this state of affairs, it can be argued that the capability of some regional institutions remains far below their potential. While most of them recognize their role in preventing and protecting civilians from atrocity crimes, few can mount effective operations to fulfil this task without international assistance, both financially and technically, especially from members of the UNSC. It is this reality that continues to necessitate the involvement of the UNSC in protecting populations against atrocity crimes.

D. Challenges and Opportunities for the Future

There is a need to recognize that the international community has entered into an era in which the prevention of atrocity crimes constitutes a defining element of responses to

[48] See, in this respect, ICISS, *The Responsibility to Protect: Report of the International Commission on Intervention and State Sovereignty* (International Development Research Centre 2001) 54:

> The UN Charter recognizes legitimate roles for regional organizations and regional arrangements in Chapter VIII. In strict terms, as we have already noted, the letter of the Charter requires action by regional organizations always to be subject to prior authorization from the SC. But as we have also noted, there are recent cases when approval has been sought ex post facto, or after the event (Liberia and Sierra Leone), *and there may be certain leeway for future action in this regard*' (emphasis added).

For a comment, see Paul D Williams/Alex J Bellamy, 'The Responsibility to Protect and the Crisis in Darfur' (2005) 36 Security Dialogue 27, 37.

[49] For comprehensive coverage of this subject see Monica Hakimi, 'To Condone or to Condemn, Regional Enforcement Actions in the Absence of Security Council Authorization' (2007) 40 Vanderbilt Journal of Transnational Law 643. See also Ugo Villani, 'The Security Council's Authorization of Enforcement Action by Regional Organizations' (2002) 6 Max Planck Yearbook of United Nations Law 535, 543.

[50] See Hakimi (n 49) 666–75. Also Jean Allain, 'The True Challenge to the United Nations System of the Use of Force: The Failures of Kosovo and Iraq and the Emergence of the African Union' (2004) 8 Max Planck Yearbook of United Nations Law 237, 288.

crises around the world. The outcome of efforts to prevent and halt these crimes will be determined by the ability of States and international institutions to identify and respond to potential risks before they transform into fully fledged atrocity crimes.

For more than half a century, the UN and regional institutions have witnessed the development of a critical legal and institutional framework to protect human rights and prevent and punish atrocity crimes. However, this framework must evolve to reflect the realities of time. The Genocide Convention adopted seventy years ago is a powerful but imperfect document. In my view, it has two major flaws: lack of clarity regarding the obligation to prevent genocide and lack of enforcement mechanisms.

Regarding the first point, there is very little in the Genocide Convention to explain the type of actions that States should take to comply with the obligation to prevent genocide. Instead, the Convention tends to focus much more on the obligation to punish. The meaning of 'prevention' and the obligations it entails must be better defined. Some international tribunals have attempted to do this. The ICJ, in the 2007 *Bosnian Genocide* case, addressed the responsibility of third-party States to prevent genocide.[51] While such efforts are welcome, it is important to clarify the prevention obligations of States to better address the increasing challenges in this regard.

In relation to the second point, while the other key human rights conventions have established monitoring mechanisms, no such mechanism was established under the Genocide Convention and as such there is no systematic way of holding States to account for failure to meet their obligations under the Convention. One option for remedying this gap would be to include questions related to the domestic implementation of the Convention within the peer review mechanism of the Human Rights Council. Further, the question of which groups should be provided protection against potential crimes of genocide was vigorously debated in the process of drafting the Convention. The decision was made that protection should be limited to national, ethnic, racial, and religious groups, based on the fact that these aspects of an individual's identity are generally fixed. Some academics and activists have challenged what they see as limitations of the Convention and have argued for the expansion of the definition to include other groups that have been targeted on a massive scale, such as political groups. In Argentina, for example, human rights activists have argued that the civilians targeted during Argentina's 'dirty war' constituted a national group.[52] On this basis, they contend that the perpetrators of crimes committed during that period should be charged with genocide.[53]

There are other questions worth raising. I believe that the presence of non-State armed actors continues to pose serious challenges to our ability to prevent atrocity

[51] *Application of the Convention on the Prevention and Punishment of the Crime of Genocide (Bosnia and Herzegovina v Serbia and Montenegro)* (Judgment) [2007] ICJ Rep 43.

[52] Daniel Feierstein, *Juicios, Sobre la elaboración del genocidio II* (Fondo de Cultura Económica 2015) 288. From 2006 to 2015, nine different Argentine Tribunals recognized the definition of genocide for the Argentine case in twenty-six sentences with the qualification of the 'partial destruction of the Argentine national group' (ibid). For the theoretical debate and the reference of the judicial cases, see ibid.

[53] ibid.

crimes and large-scale human rights violations, especially because the nature and dynamics of conflict have evolved in such a way that most modern conflicts are now intra-State rather than inter-State.[54] The status of these groups, their role and the challenge of making them accountable for crimes committed are issues that the international community must address if it is to succeed in prevention efforts. Another challenge is related to how to engage with these groups in a constructive way that will contribute to preventing atrocity crimes and better protect populations, particularly when such groups control territories.[55] As the world is constantly changing, new conflict dynamics will emerge, and the methods perpetrators use to achieve their goals will evolve too. It is therefore crucial that strategies and means of responding to these threats and challenges are adapted.

Closely related to the preceding question is that of the increasing role of multinational corporations in conflict-prone areas. In a world of globalization, the presence of commercial actors or companies in locations where atrocity crimes are likely to occur or are ongoing can further contribute to the ability of perpetrators to commit crimes while weakening the institutions of governance through corruption and human rights violations. Such actors can serve as enablers by providing goods, services, or other forms of practical or technical support that help sustain perpetrators. How to make these actors responsible and accountable for their acts is a matter of profound concern.

It is also true that States are also challenged by the need to prevent the incitement of violence without violating the right to freedom of expression and opinion of their people.[56] At times, it is difficult to draw a line between an individual's right to express themselves freely and a State's responsibility to prevent incitement to violence based on ethnic or religious hatred, which is prohibited under international law and may lead to atrocity crimes. Where can the line be drawn between the enjoyment of fundamental rights and the duty not to abuse these rights? In a world of new technologies that facilitate communication at an unprecedented speed and with an incredible capacity to influence, how should these issues be addressed from a legal perspective? What should be permitted and what should be restricted?[57] Again, as the role of technology in the lives of individuals and States proliferates, there is a need for clarification of these issues because they are of profound relevance to prevention efforts.

[54] Sebastian von Einsiedel et al, *Civil War Trends and the Changing Nature of Armed Conflict* (Occasional Paper no 10, UN University 2017). See also, Adama Dieng, 'The Value of Customary International Law in the Light of the Recent Emergence of Non-State Actors as Subjects of International Law' (2007) African Yearbook of International Humanitarian Law 166.

[55] Claudia Hofmann/Ulrich Schneckener, 'Engaging Non-State Armed Actors in State and Peacebuilding: Options and Strategies' (2011) 93 International Review of the Red Cross 603.

[56] Adama Dieng/Simona Cruciani, 'When Media is used to Incite Violence: The UN, Genocide, and Atrocity Crimes' in Robin Andersen/Purnaka L de Silva (eds), *Routledge Companions to Media and Humanitarian Action* (Routledge 2017).

[57] On the intersection between technology and human rights, see, generally, OHCHR, 'Technology for Human Rights: UN Human Rights Office announces landmark partnership with Microsoft' (16 May 2017) <https://www.ohchr.org/EN/NewsEvents/Pages/DisplayNews.aspx?NewsID=21620&LangID=E> accessed 16 October 2019.

It is further argued that for effective prevention efforts, those who violate human rights, including those who perpetrate atrocity crimes, should be held accountable. Increasingly both at the international and the national level it is recognized that impunity is not an option, and that whoever commits atrocity crimes must be held to account. With the creation of the permanent ICC and the various ad hoc tribunals, international and national policymakers seem to have finally realized this fact. Despite these modest achievements on accountability for atrocity crimes, however, there is still need to translate the commitment to accountability into actual support for these institutions, which will enable them to discharge their mandates effectively. Their capacity to investigate and prosecute those who commit atrocity crimes, in particular the capacity of the ICC, will depend on the cooperation extended to them to fulfil this role. It is therefore crucial for the international community to provide the necessary support to the ICC and other related institutions established to exercise accountability for atrocity crimes, so that they can effectively perform their functions. In this context, strategic cooperation and accountability between individual nations through mutual legal assistance treaties can facilitate the prosecution of perpetrators of the crimes prosecuted by the Court.[58] The treaties, negotiated between individual States, ensure that all evidence and other relevant information relating to potential criminal prosecutions is shared between those States in a timely and forthright manner. This kind of cooperation would significantly contribute to the maintenance and strengthening of the national and international rule of law and human rights.

E. Conclusion

An assessment of historical cases shows that atrocity crimes are most likely to occur in situations of armed conflict. But genocide and crimes against humanity have also occurred outside of conflict situations. This fact underlines the importance of paying attention to, understanding, and reacting to the early warning signs of atrocity crimes. However, the international community, must move beyond early warning alone and insist on early action. Acting early not only increases the likelihood of being able to address a risk before it becomes a crisis, it is also more cost effective than responding once a crisis is ongoing, when the stakes are higher, and the options are fewer.

Ultimately, for an effective prevention strategy, there is a critical need to build the resilience of individual States to these crimes so that the assistance, or intervention, of the international community is not required. National institutions that are responsible for the protection of populations should be strengthened to ensure that they place the rights of the people at the forefront and operate with respect for the rule of law. These

[58] See, generally, Jeremy Sarkin, 'Reforming the International Criminal Court to Achieve Increased State Cooperation in Investigations and Prosecutions of International Crimes' (2020) 9 International Human Rights Law Review 27, 27–30.

institutions should manage diversity constructively so that there is no home for the kind of grievances that create tensions between communities, tensions that can result in threats to peace and security. In short, States must be willing and able to act to protect their populations when a warning is received.

The Office of the Special Adviser on the Prevention of Genocide continues to work closely with the Member States, regional organizations, and other partners to assist efforts to strengthen their preventive capabilities. For example, the Office continues to work closely with States to establish national mechanisms and initiatives aimed at the prevention of genocide, war crimes, and crimes against humanity. Within its limited resources, it continues to champion capacity-building, especially through support for the various initiatives undertaken by civil society organizations in different countries. The Office also conducts sensitization missions and works closely with policymakers to exchange knowledge and bring about change. Prevention is a collective responsibility. The involvement of everyone, whatever their role, will help humanity achieve its goal of a world without genocide and other atrocity crimes.

Acknowledgement

This chapter does not represent the views of the United Nations or the Office of the Special Adviser on the Prevention of Genocide. I would like to express my appreciation to Dr Charles Majinge for his excellent support during the research and drafting of this chapter.

CHAPTER 20

CIVILIAN PROTECTION IN ARMED CONFLICT

CORDULA DROEGE AND HELEN DURHAM

A. Introduction

Civilians bear the brunt of contemporary armed conflicts. While in the broader historical context the numbers of deaths during conflict have fallen in the last few decades,[1] the suffering of civilians in armed conflict is deeply concerning. The conflicts in the Middle East stand out as the most dramatic, with the humanitarian situations in Iraq, Syria, and Yemen amongst the worst in the world. Long-standing conflicts like those in South Sudan or the Democratic Republic of the Congo continue to generate suffering and to hamper development for millions of people. Direct deaths and injuries are only the tip of the iceberg. Indirect effects of conflicts often cause even higher rates of civilian deaths. Unmet medical needs, food insecurity, inadequate shelter, and water contamination have a significant impact upon communities across the globe. They are also clearly connected with the number of people fleeing fighting and violence.[2] It is estimated that there are 134.1 million people in need of humanitarian assistance, with the great majority living in countries at war or that have fled war.[3] Many contemporary conflicts are part of a conflict spiral, whereby existing or past conflicts engender further conflicts. They are of concern, not only because of the suffering they cause to the affected populations, but also because they create regional poles of instability and affect global security.

[1] Therése Petterson/Kristine Eck, 'Organized Violence, 1989–2017' (2018) 55 Journal of Peace Research 535; Steven Pinker, *Enlightenment Now: The Case for Reason, Science, Humanism, and Progress* (Viking 2018) 159–60.

[2] In 2017, 68.5 million people were forcibly displaced as a result of persecution, conflict, or generalized violence. Ten years ago, this number was 39.5 million. See UNHCR, 'Global Trends: Forced Displacement in 2017' (UNHCR, 2018) 2 <https://www.unhcr.org/5b27be547.pdf> accessed 22 May 2020.

[3] OCHA, 'Global Humanitarian Overview' (OCHA, 2018) <https://www.unocha.org/sites/unocha/files/GHO2019.pdf> accessed 22 May 2020.

Inevitably, all armed conflicts cause suffering for civilians. International humanitarian law (IHL) aims to reduce suffering but as a normative regime it cannot completely address the plight of civilians, which has much broader political, economic, and ideological dimensions. That said, considering that many of the hardships experienced by civilians appear to actually be a direct result of IHL violations, better respect for IHL would indeed lead to better protection for civilians. While contemporary armed conflicts pose a number of challenges to this body of law, the correct application, interpretation, and, where necessary, development of IHL is a valid starting point for increased civilian protection.

This chapter will first offer a brief historical overview of the areas of international law relating to the protection of civilians during times of armed conflict. It will then focus on a number of key challenges facing both the normative regime and the practical application of rules—from denial of civilian status, terrorism, the nature of warfare (asymmetric, urban, and protracted), and the impact of displacement to new technologies.

B. Historical Overview

Even before the adoption of the first IHL treaties, rules to protect certain parts of the population, and cultural and religious objects from warfare, had existed for centuries. In ancient codes, rules and religious ethics, there have always been elements of protective regimes, such as the prohibition to attack non-combatants, destroy crops, or attack religious sites.[4] Nevertheless, unlimited war destroying the enemy and civilians alike was regularly an accepted practice in wars.[5]

The first modern laws of war appeared in the nineteenth century with early legal frameworks mainly concerned with the protection of combatants. Civilian suffering, though widespread during the wars of the nineteenth century and before, was not addressed in many of the formal regulations. An exception was the Lieber Code of the Union Forces during the American Civil War.[6] These early rules conceptualized the balance to be found between 'military necessity' and 'humanity'. Today IHL remains fundamentally a balancing act between the two and it is clear that much of the protective value of IHL for civilians depends on how the scales tilt.

The massive civilian suffering in the First World War[7] and the coming of age of international humanitarian relief work made it increasingly obvious that legal protection should also cover civilians. From 1921 to 1925, each International Conference of the Red

[4] Mary Ellen O'Connell, 'Historical Development and Legal Basis' in Dieter Fleck (ed), *The Handbook of International Humanitarian Law* (3rd edn, OUP 2013) paras 105–25.

[5] Hugo Slim, 'Civilians, Distinction, and the Compassionate View of War' in Haidi Willmot et al (eds), *Protection of Civilians* (OUP 2016).

[6] Instructions for the Government of Armies of the United States in the Field, General Order N° 100 (adopted 24 April 1863).

[7] Tammy M Proctor, *Civilians in a World at War, 1914–1918* (NYU Press 2010).

Cross and Red Crescent adopted resolutions inviting the International Committee of the Red Cross (ICRC) to undertake action in this field. In response, a draft treaty covering civilians was adopted at the International Conference of the Red Cross in Tokyo in 1934. However, the Second World War broke out without the treaty having been accepted by States, leaving tens of millions of people without specific protection. In 1949, the Tokyo Draft was reconsidered and formed the basis for discussions, which led to the adoption of the Fourth Geneva Convention. This was the first international treaty to specifically protect civilians in times of international armed conflict (IAC). Further, common Article 3 to the four Geneva Conventions extended the protection for civilians and those hors de combat to those in non-international armed conflicts (NIACs).

The Additional Protocols of 1977 provided a second milestone in the protection of civilians in times of armed conflicts. For the first time, the rules on the conduct of hostilities were enshrined in an international treaty, with the core principles of distinction, proportionality, and precaution forming the cornerstones to spare civilians from the effects of military operations. These rules are also all based on the balance between military necessity and humanity. This has led to a discussion whether IHL should be seen as a permissive regime or a restrictive regime.[8] International humanitarian law neither outlaws war, nor forbids the use of force. Rather, it places limits on the conduct of belligerents aiming at reducing (not eradicating) suffering. Thus, at its core, IHL aims at providing for the protection of civilians and, importantly, also civilian objects.

International humanitarian law has also progressed in other ways, especially by banning a number of specific weapons. Increased awareness of civilian suffering, as highlighted by civil society, has encouraged the creation of new norms. The first weapons were banned in response to the suffering endured by soldiers, for example, chemical weapons in 1925 after the use of chlorine gas during the First World War.[9] The more recent prohibition of anti-personnel landmines[10] is a victory in particular for civilians, who were by far their greatest victim.[11] The 2017 Treaty on the Prohibition of Nuclear Weapons[12] is another milestone in banning weapons that have the potential to harm civilians in great numbers.

In addition to IHL, international human rights law (IHRL) evolved in the second part of the twentieth century to provide additional protection to individuals, including in times of armed conflict, as was acknowledged for the first time clearly in the 1968

[8] Marco Sassòli et al, *How Does Law Protect in War: Vol. I: Outline of International Humanitarian Law* (3rd edn, ICRC 2011); Nils Melzer, *International Humanitarian Law: A Comprehensive Introduction* (ICRC 2016) 8.

[9] Protocol for the Prohibition of the Use of Asphyxiating, Poisonous or Other Gases, and of Bacteriological Methods of Warfare 94 LNTS 65.

[10] Convention on the Prohibition of the Use, Stockpiling, Production and Transfer of Anti-Personnel Mines and on their Destruction 2056 UNTS 211.

[11] The Landmine Monitor has reported, year after year, that 70 to 85 per cent of casualties are civilians. See 'Arguments for the Ban' (*International Campaign to Ban Landmines*) <http://www.icbl.org/en-gb/problem/arguments-for-the-ban.aspx> accessed 10 January 2019.

[12] Treaty on the Non-Proliferation of Nuclear Weapons 729 UNTS 161.

Teheran Declaration.[13] The specific vulnerabilities and needs of certain categories of people have also been increasingly recognized. Additional treaties and soft law instruments have addressed specific vulnerabilities, such as for internally displaced people[14] or children.[15] The UN has also developed a number of mechanisms dedicated to specific sub-issues, in particular the protection of children in armed conflict[16] and women.[17]

Since 1999, with the first report on the protection of civilians by the Secretary-General,[18] the UN Security Council (UNSC) has regularly addressed the protection of civilians as a dedicated item on its agenda. The protection of civilians has become a central issue for the UN, with the Rights Up Front initiative seeking to bring the whole UN system together around human rights and the protection of civilians.[19] Today, many UN peace operations include a protection of civilians mandate.[20] As a result, we now have a rather comprehensive normative framework to protect civilians in times of armed conflict, and a fairly dense landscape of mechanisms.

C. Legal Framework

There are many excellent texts and reference books written on IHL.[21] Suffice to say for the purposes of this chapter, IHL can be described as a set of rules that seek to limit the humanitarian consequences of armed conflicts. It protects persons who are not, or are no longer, participating in hostilities and restricts the means and methods of warfare. It is therefore the main source of legal protection of civilians in armed conflict.

International humanitarian law protects civilians through a complex patchwork of rules that have evolved over time, as described above. A first critical set of norms are the rules on the conduct of hostilities—the rules limiting the use of force during fighting. It

[13] Final Act of the International Conference on Human Rights (Tehran, 22 April–13 May 1968) UN Doc A/CONF.32/41.

[14] UNCHR 'Guiding Principles on Internal Displacement' (11 February 1998) UN Doc E/CN.4/1998/53/Add.2, 5.

[15] Optional Protocol to the Convention on the Rights of the Child on the Involvement of Children in Armed Conflict 2173 UNTS 222; The Paris Commitments to Protect Children from Unlawful Recruitment or Use by Armed Forces or Armed Groups (5–6 February 2007) <https://www.icrc.org/en/doc/assets/files/other/pariscommitments_en.pdf> accessed 28 November 2020; UNICEF 'Principles and Guidelines on Children Associated with Armed Forces or Armed Groups' (February 2007) <https://www.unicef.org/mali/media/1561/file/ParisPrinciples.pdf> accessed 11 November 2019.

[16] UNSC Res 1612 (2005); UNSC Res 1882 (2009).

[17] UNSC Res 1325 (2000).

[18] UNSC 'Report of the Secretary-General on the Protection of Civilians in Armed Conflict' (8 September 1999) UN Doc S/1999/957.

[19] Inter-Agency Standing Committee, 'Human Rights up Front: An Overview' (2015) <https://interagencystandingcommittee.org/system/files/overview_of_human_rights_up_front_july_2015.pdf> accessed 28 November 2020.

[20] Nigel White, 'Peacekeeping or War-Fighting' in Nigel White/Christian Henderson (eds), *Research Handbook on International Conflict and Security Law* (Edward Elgar 2013) 592–6.

[21] Sassòli et al (n 8); Melzer (n 8); Jean Pictet, *Development and Principles of International Humanitarian Law* (Martinus Nijhoff 1985).

is based on three cardinal principles: distinction, proportionality, and precautions. The principle of distinction requires that parties distinguish civilian populations and objects from combatants and military objectives, and solely direct their operations against military objectives.[22] The principle of proportionality prohibits attacks which cause excessive incidental harm to civilians or civilian objects.[23] The principle of precaution obliges belligerents to take all feasible precautions to avoid or minimize incidental harm to civilians.[24]

Other rules protecting civilians include specifically prohibited methods of warfare, like starvation; specifically protected persons, such as medical and religious personnel; specifically protected objects, like cultural property or the natural environment; the prohibition of certain weapons; and certain fundamental guarantees, including the prohibition of ill-treatment, the requirement of humane conditions of detention, judicial guarantees for trials, and provisions relating to the dead, missing persons, and family reunification. While the law of IACs and NIACs evolved separately, most rules are by now part of customary international law for both types of armed conflict.[25] A critical exception, however, is the question of combatant status, which does not exist in NIAC. This has serious repercussions in such conflicts (which form by far the majority of conflicts today) and—by extension—affects the protection of civilians.

D. Recent Developments and Contemporary Challenges

To ensure the legal protection of civilians, the most important factor is that existing IHL is respected and applied in good faith. Yet, contemporary armed conflicts pose a number of challenges to the application and interpretation of IHL. First, there is a hardening of fronts in armed conflicts, in which the very concept of civilian is being challenged. Additionally, many conflicts are asymmetric and create negative spirals of non-compliance. In this space, acts of terrorism and responses to such acts put pressure on key principles of IHL. A second set of issues relate to the changing conflict landscape, including the complexity of conflicts, their protracted nature, and the urbanization of fighting. A third challenge to IHL comes from new technological developments.

[22] Protocol Additional to the Geneva Conventions of 12 August 1949, and relating to the Protection of Victims of International Armed Conflicts 1125 UNTS 3 art 48 (AP I); Jean-Marie Henckaerts/Louise Doswald-Beck, *Customary International Humanitarian Law, Volume 1: Rules* (ICRC/CUP 2005) 3 and 25 (rules 1 and 7).

[23] AP I (n 22) art 51(5)(b); Henckaerts/Doswald-Beck (n 22) 46 (rule 14).

[24] AP I (n 22) art 57.

[25] The Customary International Humanitarian Law study concluded that 136 (and arguably even 141) out of 161 rules of customary humanitarian law, many of which run parallel to rules of AP I applicable as a treaty to international armed conflicts, apply equally to non-international armed conflicts: Henckaerts/Doswald-Beck (n 22).

1. Denial of Civilian Status and Protection

While in legal terms the international community has agreed on the principle of distinction, in fact, beyond the circle of IHL lawyers, this fundamental principle is far from unquestioned. In every conflict, as popular opinion and political discourse harden towards the enemy, the frailty of the prohibition to target civilians becomes apparent. There is no shortage of comments to the effect that civilians can be attacked when they are in any way associated with 'terrorists'. Echoing this, there is much discussion amongst philosophers as to whether the absolute prohibition of directly attacking civilians is morally just or allows for exceptions, and this has a bearing also on the ethical thinking of armies.[26] Some parties to conflict even fundamentally reject IHL, and deny the very concept of protection of civilians, or the relevance of IHL as a reference framework. In the case of some, IHL violations can even be a propaganda tool. In legal terms, this translates into a long-standing dispute about the definition of the terms 'civilian' and 'direct participation in hostilities'.

The principle of distinction only allows for attacks to be directed against combatants and prohibits attacks against civilians, unless and for such time as they take a direct part in hostilities.[27] In IACs, civilians are defined as all those who are not combatants, namely not members of the armed forces of a State member of the armed forces, nor members of irregular armed forces belonging to a State, nor participants in a *levée en masse*.[28] In NIACs, however, combatant status is not foreseen, and there no treaty definition of 'civilian' exists. In short, three categories of people are liable to attack: members of a State's armed forces; members of organized armed groups; and civilians who directly participate in hostilities. No agreement exists as to the definition of these latter two categories.

The ICRC has sought to clarify the concept of civilian in NIAC as all persons who are not members of State armed forces or organized armed groups of a party to a conflict; and defined organized armed groups as consisting only of individuals who have a continuous combat function.[29] It has also sought to clarify the concept of direct participation in hostilities. While some States have accepted the ICRC's definition, others have rejected it, because they feel the definition of civilian is too broad and that of direct participation in hostilities is too narrow, not providing a symmetry between the State armed forces and non-State armed groups (NSAGs), and diminishing

[26] Michael Walzer, *Just and Unjust Wars: A Moral Argument with Historical Illustrations* (Basic Books 1977); Jeff MacMahan, *Killing in War* (OUP 2009); Asa Kasher/Amos Yadlin, 'Military Ethics of Fighting Terror: An Israeli Perspective' (2005) 4 Journal of Military Ethics 1, 15.

[27] AP I (n 22) art 51(3); Protocol Additional to the Geneva Conventions of 12 August 1949 and relating to the Protection of Victims of Non-International Armed Conflicts 1125 UNTS 609 (AP II) art 13(3); Henckaerts/Doswald-Beck (n 22) 3–25 (rules 1–6).

[28] AP I (n 22) art 50(1).

[29] Nils Melzer, *Interpretive Guidance on the Notion of Direct Participation in Hostilities under International Humanitarian Law* (ICRC 2009) 33.

the influence that some indirect contributions by civilians can have on the military capacity of the adversary.[30]

These controversies contribute to the dramatically differing numbers of civilian deaths and casualties that are reported from conflicts. In fact, the numbers not only depend on the factual information available, but also on who counts as a civilian. Political claims of 'zero civilian casualties' by some States have to be read in light of this debate and distract from a genuine analysis on the real impact of warfare on civilians in certain contexts.

2. Terrorism and Counter-terrorism

Counter-terrorism discourse has for a long time been one of the main challenges for IHL and IHRL. It was one of the divisive issues over the adoption of the Additional Protocols—which were seen by some States as legitimizing terrorist groups.[31] Just as today, most, if not all, counter-terrorism strategies in the 1970s, 1980s and 1990s (from Latin America to Algeria to Sri Lanka) were military and security responses to threats by NSAGs (sometimes operating in disregard of IHL), and relied on a discourse of exceptionalism. Their situation was portrayed as an exceptional and unprecedented fight against terrorists, and therefore allowing for exceptional deviations from the law.[32]

Counter-terrorism strategies and discourse have intensified since 9/11, national counter-terrorism legislation has proliferated, and the landscape of international mechanisms, especially at UN level, is now extremely dense. This has led to some attempts to question the relevance or application of IHL to these strategies, for instance by denying the existence of armed conflict (redefined as counter-terrorism measures), or by denying protections to certain civilians that are seen as associated with, or part of, 'terrorist groups', for example, women and children accompanying Islamic State fighters in Iraq and Syria even if not themselves participating in hostilities.[33]

The counter-terrorism landscape also reduces the space for humanitarian organizations to reach civilians in need, by criminalizing their engagement and dialogue with NSAGs, banning travel to certain areas where such groups are active, or putting excessive reporting and verification burdens on humanitarian organizations to avoid aid

[30] Stephen Pomper, 'Toward a Limited Consensus on the Loss of Civilian Immunity in Non-International Armed Conflict: Making Progress Through Practice' (2012) 88 US Naval War College International Law Studies 181, 188–90.

[31] eg *Official Records of the Diplomatic Conference on the Reaffirmation and Development of International Humanitarian Law Applicable in Armed Conflicts* (vol 5, Geneva, 1974–77) 57 (Israel) and 67 (South Africa).

[32] International Commission of Jurists, the Eminent Jurists Panel on Terrorism, Counter-Terrorism and Human Rights, *Assessing Damage, Urging Action* (International Commission of Jurists 2009) in particular the chapter entitled 'Learning from the Past', 26.

[33] Anne Barnard, 'Red Cross Warns of "Dehumanising" Rhetoric in ISIS Fight' (*The New York Times*, 26 October 2017) <https://www.nytimes.com/2017/10/26/world/middleeast/red-cross-islamic-state.html> accessed 9 November 2019.

diversion.[34] Understandably, States seek to reduce the risk that their support of humanitarian organizations inadvertently props up the military efforts of NSAGs or fuels war economies. However, it has been documented that the net effect of such policies can be counterproductive and, through limiting the activities of humanitarians, can be detrimental to the protection of civilians.[35]

3. Asymmetric Warfare

Asymmetric warfare refers to conflicts—mostly between States and NSAGs—in which the two opposing sides have unequal military strength. As the weaker side—often, but not always, NSAGs—has little chance to win the war by military means, it might deliberately resort to strategies and tactics that do not comply with IHL, by placing military assets in or amongst civilian structures, taking human shields, launching attacks amongst civilians, or preventing civilians from leaving areas that are under attack. Conversely, the civilian population is at risk of the overwhelming use of force by the stronger military power. The key to protecting civilians in such conflicts is to overcome the disincentives that asymmetric warfare creates for the parties.

The first disincentive is the normative asymmetry inbuilt into NIAC law. While IHL recognizes that both States and NSAGs can be parties to conflicts with ensuing rights and obligations, the so-called equality of belligerents is undermined de facto in NIAC because of the lack of combatant status. While in IACs, members of State armed forces are immune from prosecution for taking part in hostilities and are entitled to prisoner-of-war status, no such immunity is recognized for NSAGs in NIACs. International humanitarian law does not prohibit the criminalization of taking up arms by insurgents.[36]

Anecdotal evidence attests that this constitutes a disincentive for armed groups to respect IHL because they will be prosecuted (usually for belonging to a terrorist organization) even if they fight according to its rules.[37] Several avenues exist to overcome this. Additional Protocol II recognizes this asymmetry and encourages States to provide amnesty at the end of a conflict for the mere participation in hostilities,[38] trying to pave a way for reconciliation and peace. Further, there are many other ways to engage with NSAGs about respect for IHL, such as their interest in having the support of the civilian

[34] Kate Mackintosh/Patrick Duplat, 'Study of the Impact of Donor Counter-Terrorism Measures on Principled Humanitarian Action' (July 2013) <https://www.unocha.org/sites/unocha/files/CounterTerrorism_Study_Full_Report.pdf> accessed 9 November 2019. (Independent study commissioned by OCHA and the Norwegian Refugee Council); see Emanuela-Chiara Gillard/Nathalie Weizmann, Chapter 28 in this *Handbook*.

[35] ibid. [36] Melzer (n 8) 172–3.

[37] Olivier Bangerter, 'Reasons Why Armed Groups Choose to Respect International Humanitarian Law or Not' (2011) 93 International Review of the Red Cross 353, 377–8.

[38] AP II (n 27) art 6(5).

population; their ambition to be 'respectable' before the international community; and their own ethical, cultural, or religious references.[39]

The second challenge is the spiral of negative reciprocity and non-compliance. Much asymmetric warfare results in a high number of civilian casualties ensuing from the use of force by the more militarily powerful party. Those casualties tend to be 'attributed' to the enemy under the justification that the enemy 'held the civilians hostage'.[40] States are also increasingly reluctant to put their own troops at risk, and the imperative of 'force protection' risks detrimental effects for civilians.[41] From a legal perspective, this leads to controversies in particular over the prohibition of indiscriminate attacks and the principle of proportionality.[42]

No easy answers exist to this dilemma, but clearly both sides need to respect IHL for civilians to be protected. In many cases, the combination of the relative vagueness of principles on the conduct of hostilities (in particular, proportionality) and the difficulties to come by hard facts in the fog of war makes it difficult to assess the legality of the parties' conduct.

Nonetheless, breaking down the factual and legal issues can lead to concrete measures to better mitigate harm to civilians, especially precautionary measures. For instance, what were the exact rules of engagement? What measures were taken to distinguish civilians from fighters? How much effort was put into intelligence gathering?[43] What types of weapons were used? How was direct and indirect incidental civilian harm factored into the attack?

For better compliance with IHL in complex battlefields, much could be gained by more transparency on these questions, exchanges of lessons learnt amongst peers, and use of new technologies not only for better military results but also to better protect civilians.

[39] See eg ICRC, 'The Roots of Restraint in War' (June 2018) <https://www.icrc.org/en/publication/roots-restraint-war#> accessed 9 November 2019.

[40] See State of Israel, 'The 2014 Gaza Conflict, 7 July–26 August 2014, Factual and Legal Aspects' (May 2015) paras 39–45 <https://mfa.gov.il/ProtectiveEdge/Documents/2014GazaConflictFullReport.pdf> accessed 9 November 2019; Foreign Minister Sergey Lavrov, 'Statement and Answers to Media Questions at a News Conference following the 23rd OSCE Ministerial Council meeting, Hamburg, December 9, 2016' (9 December 2016) <https://osce.mid.ru/web/osce-en/-/foreign-minister-sergey-lavrov-s-statement-and-answers-to-media-questions-at-a-news-conference-following-the-23rd-osce-ministerial-council-meeting-ham?inheritRedirect=true> accessed 28 November 2020.

[41] Robin Geiß, 'The Principle of Proportionality: "Force Protection" as a Military Advantage' (2012) 45 Israel Law Review 71.

[42] Robin Geiß, 'The Conduct of Hostilities in Asymmetric Conflicts: Reciprocity, Distinction, Proportionality, Precautions' (2010) 23 Journal of International Law of Peace and Armed Conflict 122; Michael Schmitt, 'Asymmetrical Warfare and International Humanitarian Law' (2008) 62 Air Force Law Review 1.

[43] On the importance of intelligence gathering in asymmetric, and particularly urban warfare, see Nathalie Durhin, 'Protecting Civilians in Urban Areas: A Military Perspective on the Application of International Humanitarian Law' (2016) 98 International Review of the Red Cross 177, 179 and 189.

4. The Complexity of the Battlefield

Contemporary armed conflicts often involve a great number of parties. Armed groups multiply and splinter. Foreign powers intervene in conflicts abroad, frequently through partnered warfare and by resorting to a 'lighter footprint' and local proxies.[44] Conflicts become regional and 'globalized', and new technologies allow for 'remote' warfare.[45] This creates a number of legal challenges. The first pertains to the classification of such conflicts, with IACs and NIACs overlapping, and the legal regime applicable to specific belligerent relationships is not always easy to determine.[46]

Secondly, the support by States in its various forms—from transfer of weapons, to training, to joint military and capture operations—leads to complex questions of legal responsibility. Simply put, States will seek to have as much control over their allies and local partners as to have a maximum of military influence over them, but not as much control as would make them parties to the conflict or liable for possible violations committed by their partners. This creates a risk that responsibility for the respect of IHL is diluted. Conversely, it can also be seen as an opportunity by which supporting parties can use their influence to bring their partners to respect IHL. The legal underpinnings of the obligation to use their influence lies in common Article 1 to the Geneva Conventions (and corresponding customary IHL[47]), which requires States to 'respect and ensure respect' for IHL.[48]

As conflicts and parties morph over time, discussions over the applicability of IHL *ratione materiae*, *loci*, and *temporis*, but also over the legal and moral responsibility of States for their various interventions will remain critical, so that the legal protection of civilians is not undermined by more—and sometimes deliberate—confusion over the law.

[44] Cordula Droege/David Tuck, 'Fighting Together and International Humanitarian Law: Ensuring Respect for the Law and Assessing Responsibility for Violations' (*Humanitarian Law and Policy Blog*, 17 October 2017) <https://blogs.icrc.org/law-and-policy/2017/10/17/fighting-together-international-humanitarian-law-ensuring-respect-law-assessing-responsibility-violations-2-2/> accessed 9 November 2019.

[45] Which is not to say that there is a 'global war' or a 'global battlefield', see ICRC 'Report: International Humanitarian Law and the Challenges of Contemporary Armed Conflicts' (32nd International Conference of the Red Cross and Red Crescent, 8–10 December 2015) 32IC/15/11, 15 <https://www.icrc.org/en/document/international-humanitarian-law-and-challenges-contemporary-armed-conflicts> accessed 9 November 2019 (ICRC Report 2015).

[46] Droege/Tuck (n 44).

[47] Henckaerts/Doswald-Beck (n 22) 495 (rule 139), 498 (rule 140), 509 (rule 144).

[48] See Jean-Marie Henckaerts, 'Article 1: Respect for the Convention' in Knut Dörmann et al (eds), *Commentary on the First Geneva Convention: Convention (I) for the Amelioration of the Condition of the Wounded and Sick in Armed Forces in the Field* (ICRC/CUP 2016) paras 144–73. Some reject this interpretation of common Article 1: see John Reid, 'Ensuring Respect: the Role of State Practice in Interpreting the Geneva Conventions' (*ILA Reporter*, 2017) <http://ilareporter.org.au/2016/11/ensuring-respect-the-role-of-state-practice-in-interpreting-the-geneva-conventions-john-reid/> accessed 10 January 2019; *Turp v Canada (Foreign Affairs)* [2017] FC 84; Jann Kleffner, 'Transatlantic Workshop on International Law and Armed Conflict' (*Intercross Blog*, 26 September 2017) <https://intercrossblog.icrc.org/blog/transatlantic-workshop-on-international-law-and-armed-conflict-introduction-to-a-joint-blog-series> accessed 28 November 2020.

5. Urban Warfare

As the world urbanizes, so too do wars. Almost 50 million people are affected by conflict in urban areas.[49] Related to the asymmetry mentioned above, retreating into the density of the city is another military tactic of armed groups against the overwhelming military power—especially air power—of the enemy, as it is much easier to move and hide within the cities, and to blend in with the population. It is a common misperception that within urban warfare, the civilian population is an incidental issue. In fact, 'urban warfare is about civilians. Civilians are a crucial part of the equation: hurting them or protecting them is part of the strategy.'[50]

A significant reason for the devastating humanitarian consequences of warfare in urban environments is the combination of deaths and injuries and the degradation and destruction of infrastructures through the use of explosive weapons in such populated areas. This often leads to the collapse of vital systems, such as electricity, water, sanitation systems, and roads. The destruction of hospitals and shortages in medical personnel and supplies leads to the collapse of health systems, which can rapidly lead to epidemics.

In urban areas, belligerents tend to still use explosive weapons with a wide area effect, originally designed for open battlefields, such as large bombs or artillery and mortars. This raises a number of legal and policy questions.

First, there are divergent views on whether the use of explosive weapons in populated areas is compatible with the prohibition of indiscriminate attacks and the principle of proportionality. Further questions exist as to whether existing IHL rules sufficiently regulate such use of explosive weapons, or whether it is necessary to clarify their interpretation, develop new standards or rules, or ban (some of) them altogether. These questions are currently debated in the context of a number of initiatives by both civil society and States.[51]

Some point to the evidence about the devastating effects of such weapons, arguing that their use in populated areas is contrary to IHL, and call for a ban.[52] Others observe the high likelihood of indiscriminate effects and consider that despite the absence of an express legal prohibition for specific types of weapons, explosive weapons with a wide impact area should be avoided in densely populated areas.[53] However, contrary to the above, some point out that there is no specific prohibition of such weapons in IHL, and

[49] ICRC, *Urban Services during Protracted Armed Conflict: A Call for a Better Approach to Assisting Affected People* (ICRC 2015).

[50] Vincent Bernard/Ellen Policinski, 'Interview with Eyal Weizman' (2016) 98 International Review of the Red Cross 21, 32.

[51] For example, the Austrian-led process for a political declaration to address the harm from explosive weapons in populated areas; the UN Secretary-General Protection of Civilians Reports (n 18); the ICRC's engagement to discuss good practices; and the International Network on Explosive Weapons (INEW) Regional Conferences.

[52] eg 'The Use of Explosive Weapons in Populated Areas—It Is Time to Act' (*Handicap International/ Humanity Inclusion*, 2018) <https://hi.org/sn_uploads/document/L-utilisation-d-armes-explosives-en-zones-peuplees_il-est-urgent-d-agir_en_1.pdf> accessed 9 November 2019.

[53] ICRC Report 2015 (n 45) 48.

military necessity sometimes justifies their use, so that compatibility should be assessed on a case-by-case basis.[54]

The discussion depends, of course, on how the rules themselves are interpreted. The increase in hostilities conducted in urban environments is putting pressure on well-established IHL norms. To resolve these issues careful analysis is required, which factors in the fast developing capacity of parties to predict the effects of specific military operations and weapons in urban areas.

Beyond the law, and beyond the specific question of explosive weapons, urban warfare puts a renewed focus on the question of how much civilian harm is acceptable even when it is not in itself unlawful. Some instances, such as the operations of the International Security Assistance Force in Afghanistan, have shown that when there is political will, militaries have considerable scope to take measures to reduce the effects of their operations on civilians.[55]

6. The Protractedness of Armed Conflicts

Decades-long conflicts deplete resources, cause long-term damage to infrastructure, and severely erode the social fabric and the means of resilience of civilians.[56] During these long wars, civilians still need to go about their lives, find coping mechanisms, have lucrative employment, and send their children to school.[57]

International humanitarian law is not necessarily equipped to deal with all the consequences of such long-term armed conflicts. The rules governing the conduct of hostilities will remain just as relevant if and when hostilities break out amongst the warring parties, and the general rules on the protection of civilians too—interpreted, as appropriate, in light of contemporary realities. Moreover, IHL has relatively little to say about many fundamental aspects of life, such as freedom of movement, the right to work, healthcare beyond life-saving, education, and so forth. Human rights and other bodies of law, and soft law standards, will play a greater role.

[54] House of Commons, International Development Committee, 'Crisis in Yemen: Government Response to the Committee's Fourth Report of Session 2015–16' (14 July 2016) HC 557, Appendix.

[55] Camilla Waszink, 'Protection of Civilians under International Humanitarian Law: Trends and Challenges' (Norwegian Peacebuilding Resource Centre, August 2011) 13 <https://www.regjeringen.no/globalassets/upload/ud/vedlegg/hum/reclaiming_background.pdf> accessed 9 November 2019.

[56] Hugo Slim/Ariana Lopes Morey, *Protracted Conflict and Humanitarian Action: Some Recent ICRC Experiences* (ICRC 2016).

[57] ICRC, 'Report: International Humanitarian Law and the Challenges of Contemporary Armed Conflicts: Recommitting to Protection in Armed Conflict on the 70th Anniversary of the Geneva Conventions' (33rd International Conference of the Red Cross and Red Crescent, 9–12 December 2019) 33IC/19/9.7, 29–39 <https://rcrcconference.org/app/uploads/2019/10/33IC-IHL-Challenges-report_EN.pdf> accessed 12 December 2019 (ICRC Report 2019); More broadly on the 'humanitarian development nexus', Filipa Schmitz Guinote, 'A Humanitarian-Development Nexus that Works' (*Humanitarian Law & Policy Blog*, 21 June 2018) <https://blogs.icrc.org/law-and-policy/2018/06/21/humanitarian-development-nexus-that-works/> accessed 10 January 2019.

For example, a lot of attention has been given to the need to save generations of children from simply going without any education.[58] The destruction of schools, the storage of weapons in, and the general military use of, schools as well as the targeting of teachers and students, has a devastating impact upon communities and individuals. With education being identified as a humanitarian need, such attacks have consequences for systems of education, in the short and long term depriving the young of a future and societies of potential to develop. Various IHL provisions focus on securing access to education during armed conflict,[59] as do human rights provisions.[60] Recent policy developments, such as the Safe Schools Declaration,[61] are examples of the identification of 'new needs' being grappled with by frameworks that complement existing norms that are deemed insufficient.[62]

7. Displacement

According to UNHCR's *Global Trends* report, 68.5 million people were displaced as of the end of 2017. Refugees and asylum seekers fleeing their countries to escape conflict and persecution accounted for 28.5 million of the 68.5 million people. About two-thirds of displaced people, however, are internally displaced persons (40 million).[63]

Palestinian refugees constitute about one-fifth of the world's refugees. Of the remaining number, two-thirds come from just five countries: Syria, Afghanistan, South Sudan,

[58] Over 25 million children between six and fifteen years old are currently out of school in twenty-two conflict-affected countries, accounting for 22 per cent of children in that age group. UNICEF, 'Press Release: 25 Million Children out of School in Conflict Zones' (24 April 2017) <www.unicef.org/press-releases/25-million-children-out-school-conflict-zones> accessed 12 July 2018; UNGA/UNSC 'Report of the Secretary-General: Children and Armed Conflict' (16 May 2018) UN Doc A/72/865-S/2018/465.

[59] eg Convention relative to the Protection of Civilian Persons in Time of War 75 UNTS 287 arts 13, 24, 50, 94, 108 and 142 (GC IV); Convention relative to the Treatment of Prisoners of War (GC III) 75 UNTS 135 arts 38, 72 and 125; AP I (n 22) art 78; AP II (n 27) art 4(3)(a). Protection during the conduct of hostilities is offered by the general rules as schools and other education facilities are presumed to be civilian objects and students and educational personnel are presumed to be civilians. Special respect for children is provided for as well: see AP I (n 22) art 77; AP II (n 27) art 4(3).

[60] Universal Declaration of Human Rights, UNGA Res 217 A (III) (10 December 1948) arts 2 and 26; International Covenant on Civil and Political Rights 999 UNTS 171 art 2; International Covenant on Economic, Social and Cultural Rights 993 UNTS 3 arts 2, 13 and 14; Convention on the Elimination of All Forms of Discrimination against Women 1249 UNTS 13 art 10; Convention on the Rights of the Child 1577 UNTS 3 arts 2, 22, 28, 29, 38 and 39.

[61] 'New International Guidelines Address an Insidious Gap in Protecting Education during War' (*Global Coalition to Protect Education from Attack*, 16 December 2014) <https://protectingeducation.org/news/new-international-guidelines-address-an-insidious-gap-in-protecting-education-during-war/> accessed 28 November 2020.

[62] International Commission on Financing Global Education Opportunity, 'The Learning Generation: Investing in Education for a Changing World' (2016) <http://report.educationcommission.org/> accessed 12 July 2018.

[63] UNHCR (n 2).

Myanmar, and Somalia—in other words, from armed conflict situations. Similarly, the ten largest internally displaced people (IDP) populations are all in countries at war.[64]

While people move for a range of reasons (political, social, economic), the literature indicates that people flee more because of violence and conflict than any other cause.[65] In this respect, it is important to examine the protections provided within IHL and the wider context when reflecting on the massive global challenge of people displaced.

International humanitarian law provides that parties may not deport or forcibly transfer civilians from an occupied territory or order their displacement in NIACs, unless the security of the civilians or imperative military reasons so demands.[66] A recent ICRC study demonstrates that many acts of violence, constituting violations of IHL, directly or indirectly trigger displacement. Of course, some civilians would still flee from affected territories even if IHL were fully complied with during a conflict. Nevertheless, ICRC experience shows that disregarding IHL in the choice of weapons or in the methods of warfare impacts upon the patterns of displacement.[67] Encouraging compliance with IHL is thus one of several ways to pre-emptively address causes of displacement. Other findings relate to the decisive role respect for IHL plays in supporting humanitarian action, which can prevent displacement and the vital impact it has in creating an environment conducive to repatriation. These considerations are reminders of the wider benefits that respect for IHL can bring.

8. New Technologies

The fourth industrial revolution has brought challenges and solutions that we can only begin to understand. Belligerents, civilians, and humanitarian organizations have all started to use new technologies. It has allowed many civilians to remain better connected with the outside world[68] and enabled them to be more involved in influencing humanitarian responses. Humanitarian organizations are increasingly exploring the potential of new technologies to better protect and assist civilians, for instance by providing digital means to help people re-establish contact with relatives. Yet, not everyone is connected and this creates risks for those left behind.

[64] ibid 35 figure 12: Colombia, Syrian Arab Republic, DRC, Iraq, Somalia, Yemen, Sudan, South Sudan, Afghanistan, Ukraine.

[65] Emilie Combaz, 'Effects of Respect for International Humanitarian Law on Displacement' (*GSDRC*, 2 October 2016) 5 <http://gsdrc.org/wp-content/uploads/2016/10/HDQ1393.pdf> accessed 12 July 2018; Sean Healy/Sandrine Tiller, 'Be Near a Road: Humanitarian Practice and Displaced Persons in North Kivu' (2016) 35 Refugee Survey Quarterly 56, 65–78; Laura Hammond, 'History, Overview, Trends and Issues in Major Somali Refugee Displacements in the Near Region (Djibouti, Ethiopia, Kenya, Uganda and Yemen)' (2014) 13 Bildhaan: An International Journal of Somali Studies 55.

[66] GC IV (n 59) arts 49, 147; AP II (n 27) art 17; Henckaerts/Doswald-Beck (n 22) 457–75 (rules 129–33).

[67] ICRC, Displacement in Times of Armed Conflict: How International Humanitarian Law Protects in War, and Why it Matters (ICRC 2019).

[68] eg 'Raqqa is Being Slaughtered Silently' <https://www.raqqa-sl.com/en/> accessed 28 November 2020.

New technologies have always transformed warfare.[69] In some instances, this can lead to better respect for IHL.[70] Yet, technological development without corresponding considerations regarding the impact on civilians can have devastating consequences. Already during the negotiation process of the Additional Protocols, the drafters identified new technologies as an important consideration for civilian protection.[71] The inclusion of Article 36 of Additional Protocol I obliges States to put in place 'weapon review systems' to ensure that newly developed technologies can be employed as weapons, means and methods of warfare in conformity with existing IHL.[72] This fundamental guarantee is particularly crucial in light of today's rapid technological developments.

Two rapidly progressing areas are cyberwarfare and autonomous weapons.[73] While most cyberattacks are launched outside of armed conflict situations, the use of cyber weapons in conflict is already happening and likely to increase. Cyberattacks on electricity networks or essential services such as water supply and health systems could have extremely serious effects from a humanitarian perspective. Cyberwarfare poses several challenges to civilian protection.[74] This is mostly because cyberspace challenges some of the basic premises of IHL, and therefore application of the general rules might be more difficult in practice or controversial in law.[75]

First, States do not unanimously agree on the application of IHL in cyberspace.[76] This is seemingly because some States take the position that accepting the application of IHL in cyberspace amounts to militarization of this space, which should be avoided.[77] Yet, from a legal point of view, the trigger for the application of IHL is whether there is an armed conflict (international or non-international). As soon as this is the case, attacks, including cyberattacks, which are launched in the context of the conflict, are governed

[69] eg Martin van Creveld, *Technology and War: From 2000 BC to the Present: A Revised and Expanded Edition* (The Free Press 1991) 1 and 3.

[70] Michael Schmitt, 'Precision Attack and International Humanitarian Law' (2005) 87 International Review of the Red Cross 445.

[71] In particular, *Official Records of the Diplomatic Conference on the Reaffirmation and Development of International Humanitarian Law Applicable in Armed Conflicts* (vol 16, Geneva, 1974–77).

[72] AP I (n 23) art 36; Vincent Boulanin/Maaike Verbruggen, 'Article 36 Reviews: Dealing with the Challenges Posed by Emerging Technologies' (SIPRI 2017).

[73] About the potential benefits for civilians but also the risks of remote warfare and 'standoff' weapons, see David Whetham, 'Remote Killing and Drive-By Wars' in David Lovell/Igor Primoratz (eds), *Protecting Civilians During Violent Conflict: Theoretical and Practical Issues for the 21st Century* (Ashgate 2012).

[74] Cordula Droege, 'Get Off my Cloud: Cyber Warfare, International Humanitarian Law, and the Protection of Civilians' (2012) 94 International Review of the Red Cross 533, 541.

[75] For example, the meaning of 'attack'. See ICRC Report 2015 (n 45) 41–2.

[76] See UN Secretary-General António Guterres, 'Address at the Opening Ceremony' (Munich Security Conference, 16 February 2018) UN Doc SG/SM/18900.

[77] Michael Schmitt/Liis Vihul, 'International Cyber Law Politicized: The UN GGE's Failure to Advance Cyber Norms' (*Just Security*, 30 June 2017) <https://www.justsecurity.org/42768/international-cyber-law-politicized-gges-failure-advance-cyber-norms> accessed 23 July 2018.

by IHL.[78] However, whether and under what circumstances a cyberattack itself can trigger an armed conflict is a difficult legal question, subject to controversy.[79]

Secondly, as there is only one cyberspace shared by civilian and military users, its interconnectivity makes the fundamental principle of distinction between military and civilian objects very difficult. The key challenges are to ensure that attacks are directed against military objects only and that constant care is taken to spare the civilian population and civilian objects. Much of the digital infrastructure constitutes 'dual-use objects', which may be targeted. But even then, incidental harm to civilian infrastructure—including indirect but foreseeable harm caused by reverberating effects—must be anticipated and taken into account when assessing proportionality.

Besides IHL's protective role as a 'legal' firewall in cyberwarfare, we must also consider whether more clarification of the rules, or stronger, tailor-made rules, are necessary.[80] The *Tallinn Manual* on cyberwarfare goes a long way in clarifying how IHL rules apply to cyberwarfare.[81] However, many legal issues remain controversial and in need of further clarification at the international level. In the meantime, the digital industry is coming under pressure more broadly, and Microsoft is calling for a 'Digital Geneva Convention'.[82] Whether enough consensus will be found to advance the protection of civilians and civilian infrastructure in this politically highly divisive field remains to be seen.

In addition to the impressive growth of cyberspace, major innovations have also occurred in the field of artificial intelligence and robotics that have led to progress in the development of autonomous weapon systems. Autonomous weapons are weapon systems with autonomy in their critical functions—that is, weapon systems that can select and attack targets without human intervention.[83] Once activated by a human operator, the sensors, software, and weaponry take on the targeting functions that would otherwise be controlled by humans.

Autonomous weapons, like any new weapons, have to be compliant with IHL.[84] Some of the critical issues under discussion—many of which derive from the technological uncertainty surrounding these weapons—include the level of autonomy allowed, considering that accountability under international law is traditionally based on a certain

[78] eg Michael Schmitt (ed), *Tallinn Manual on the International Law Applicable to Cyber Warfare* (CUP 2013).

[79] ibid. [80] Droege (n 74) 578. [81] *Tallin Manual* (n 78).

[82] Brad Smith, 'The Need for a Digital Geneva Convention' (*Microsoft on the Issues*, 14 February 2017) <https://blogs.microsoft.com/on-the-issues/2017/02/14/need-digital-geneva-convention/> accessed 23 July 2018.

[83] ICRC, 'Views of the ICRC on Autonomous Weapons Systems' (Convention on Certain Conventional Weapons (CCW), Meeting of Experts on Lethal Autonomous Weapons Systems (LAWS), Geneva, 11 April 2016) 1 <https://www.icrc.org/en/document/views-icrc-autonomous-weapon-system> accessed 5 November 2019.

[84] Neil Davison, 'A Legal Perspective: Autonomous Weapon Systems under International Humanitarian Law' (2018) 30 UNODA Occasional Papers 5, 7.

level of control and foreseeability.[85] Much of the discussion revolves around the level of autonomy permissible or human control necessary, though some of this goes beyond the legal sphere and touches upon ethical issues.[86] There are also complex questions around liability regimes that should be applied when such weapons are deployed, as they appear to present—at this stage—a higher risk of failing and degree of unpredictability.[87] A number of international processes and initiatives exist, discussing the meaning and possible development of the applicable legal regime.[88] As with digital technologies, autonomous technologies are likely to remain the subject of legal, political, and ethical debate for the foreseeable future.

E. Outlook

While this chapter focused on protection of civilians in general, it is important to underline that civilians are not a homogeneous group of persons. In a sense, if civilian protection is to be taken seriously, it must start with the experience of civilians themselves, which varies widely.

International Humanitarian Law is not blind to the different experiences of civilians during armed conflict in light of their diverse identity and power relations.[89] Hence, several provisions protect particular categories of civilians such as children and women, the disabled, refugees and other groups with specific needs. Three categories of civilians have—rightly—been the focus of special attention by the international community, and made the subject of further norms and standards: women, children, and displaced persons.

Moreover, greater consideration should be given to the whole range of factors that influence a person's experience in armed conflict.[90] Factors creating singular or

[85] Robin Geiß, 'Autonomous Weapons Systems, Risk Management and State Responsibility' (Convention on Certain Conventional Weapons (CCW), Meeting of Experts on Lethal Autonomous Weapons Systems (LAWS) 11–15 April 2016, Geneva) <https://www.unog.ch/80256EDD006B8954/(httpAssets)/00C95F16D6FC38E4C1257F9D0039B84D/$file/Geiss-CCW-Website.pdf> accessed 28 November 2020; Nils Melzer, 'Study: Human Rights Implications of the Usage of Drones and Unmanned Robots in Warfare' (European Parliament Directorate General for External Policies, Policy Department, May 2013) EXPO/B/DROI/2012/12, PE 410.220.

[86] Davison (n 84); ICRC Report 2015 (n 45) 45; ICRC Report 2019 (n 57) 22–3. [87] Geiß (n 85).

[88] The States Parties to the Convention on Certain Conventional Weapons have, for example, convened an informal Meeting of Experts and subsequently a Group of Governmental Experts on Lethal Autonomous Weapons. See UNOG, 'Background on Lethal Autonomous Weapons Systems in the CCW' <https://www.unog.ch/80256EE600585943/(httpPages)/8FA3C2562A60FF81C1257CE600393DF6?OpenDocument> accessed 10 January 2018. See also 'The Problem, The Solution' (*Campaign to Stop Killer Robots*, 2018) <https://www.stopkillerrobots.org/learn/#problem> accessed 10 January 2019.

[89] Lindsey Cameron et al, 'Article 3: Conflicts not of an International Character' in Dörmann (n 48) para 553.

[90] Hugo Slim, 'Impartiality and Intersectionality' (*Humanitarian Law & Policy Blog*, 16 January 2018) <https://blogs.icrc.org/law-and-policy/2018/01/16/impartiality-and-intersectionality/> accessed 10 January 2019.

interconnected vulnerabilities, including gender, ethnicity, disability, race, religion, and ideological beliefs, need to be examined in a more sophisticated way to ensure that protections provided reflect the specific reality of the individual. For instance, in order to fully grasp the complexity of sexual crimes during armed conflict, one has to have consideration for different forms of human diversity and power relations of the specific situation—and how they affect women, men, girls and boys, or persons with disabilities differently. While women suffer in unacceptable numbers from sexual violence, the use of sexual abuse against men in conflict, in particular detention, needs a deeper examination. Simplistically classifying certain groups of civilians during conflict as exclusively 'vulnerable' can overlook capacities for resilience and the creation of some of the solutions to complex problems. Further analysis is necessary to better understand how to reduce chronic poverty and uphold socio-economic developments, during and after conflict and tensions.

Lastly, as the chapter has outlined, the protective value of IHL for civilians depends on several conditions. First, on basic respect for the rules—many of them are relatively clear, and if they were respected, much suffering could be avoided. Secondly, on the interpretation of IHL: how willing are belligerents to give due weight to the protection of civilians in the balance between military necessity and humanity? And, how much will public opinion, in the current climate, drive political leaders to strive towards ever more humanity? And thirdly, on the discussion about lacunae as regards the evolving nature of war—IHL grew over time, from the protection of soldiers, to the protection of civilians, cultural property, treaties on weapons, and numerous complementary standards. It 'stitches together diverse layers of the legal fabric in a patchwork manner... Patchwork, almost ineluctably, means gaps and lacunas'.[91] In the absence of any willingness of States to embark on a holistic review of IHL, it is likely that we will continue to witness more layers of legal fabric or other standards being stitched to the existing ones—on new technologies, on other subjects. In all these efforts, the protection of civilians must be a paramount consideration.

Acknowledgement

The authors would like to thank Paulien Vandendriessche and Jemma Arman for their assistance in the preparation of this chapter.

[91] Yoram Dinstein, 'Keynote Address: The Recent Evolution of the International Law of Armed Conflict: Confusions, Constraints, and Challenges' (2018) 51 Vanderbilt Journal of Transnational Law 701, 707.

CHAPTER 21

HUMAN TRAFFICKING AND SLAVERY

VLADISLAVA STOYANOVA

A. Introduction

The engagement of international law with the issues of slavery and human trafficking has not been straightforward and unambiguous. In the past, international law was used to authorize and also justify slavery.[1] It was only in the 1950s that all European societies prohibited slave trade.[2] In 1926, the first multilateral treaty that obliged its States Parties to prevent and suppress slave trade and 'bring about, progressively and as soon as possible, the complete abolition of slavery in all its forms' was signed.[3] This convention is still relevant today as it contains the definition of slavery used under international law, as will be explained below. From a contemporary perspective, the most important international legal instruments addressing slavery are the global and regional human rights treaties, all of which incorporate a right not to be subjected to slavery, servitude, or forced labour. The importance of this right will be also reviewed in the present contribution. This right, however, has not been used to address issues of human security. The right not to be subjected to slavery, servitude, and forced labour has remained, in that respect, silent. Rather, since the beginning of the twenty-first century the concept of human trafficking has become the dominant frame for addressing issues of human security.

[1] Seymour Drescher/Paul Finkelman, 'Slavery' in Bardo Fassbender/Anne Peters (eds), *The Oxford Handbook of the History of International Law* (OUP 2012) 897.

[2] ibid 907. For the prohibition of the African slave trade in the US, see Paul Finkelman, 'Slavery in the United States: Persons or Property?' in Jean Allain (ed), *The Legal Understanding of Slavery: From Historical to the Contemporary* (OUP 2012) 120–2.

[3] Slavery, Servitude, Forced Labour and Similar Institutions and Practice Convention 60 LNTS 253 (1926 Slavery Convention).

As regards human trafficking, it is important to observe first that human trafficking was the subject of a separate development in international law that resulted in separate legal instruments. More specifically, in the beginning of the twentieth century, trafficking in women, also referred to as 'white slavery',[4] became a subject of international law-making, due to concerns about the export of prostitutes from Europe to brothels in the colonial empires.[5] A series of international treaties was then adopted,[6] before being consolidated in 1949 with the adoption of the Convention for the Suppression of Traffic in Persons and the Exploitation of the Prostitution of Others.[7] The Convention obliges States Parties to criminalize trafficking for the purpose of prostitution, exploitation of prostitution, and keeping a brothel, all of which were indicative of the fact that the treaty reflected an abolitionist approach to prostitution.[8]

With the adoption in 2000 of the Protocol to Prevent, Suppress, and Punish Trafficking in Persons, Especially Women and Children (UNTOC Trafficking Protocol),[9] which supplements the UN Convention against Transnational Organized Crime (UNTOC),[10] human trafficking was explicitly defined in a way that is not limited to prostitution and sexual exploitation. This definition will also be discussed below. For now, it is important to observe the debates surrounding the different approaches to prostitution; the question whether all prostitution is necessarily exploitative animated the drafting of the Trafficking Protocol.[11] These debates continue to shape the responses to human trafficking today and the question of who should be a subject of protection.[12]

The contemporary salience of human trafficking and slavery as subjects of concern finds its roots, however, not so much in concerns about the protection of individuals,

[4] Elizabeth M Bruch, 'Models Wanted: The Search for an Effective Response to Human Trafficking' (2004) 40 Stanford Journal of International Law 1, 7–11.

[5] Ethan A Nadelmann, 'Global Prostitution Regimes: The Evolution of Norms in International Society' (1990) 44 International Organization 479.

[6] International Agreement for the Suppression of the White Slave Traffic 1 LNTS 83; International Convention for the Suppression of the White Slave Traffic 3 LNTS 254; International Convention for the Suppression of the Traffic in Women and Children 9 LNTS 416; International Convention for the Suppression of the Traffic in Women of Full Age 150 LNTS 431.

[7] Convention for the Suppression of the Traffic in Persons and of the Exploitation of the Prostitution of Others 96 UNTS 271.

[8] Jo Doezema, 'Forced to Choose Beyond the Voluntary v. Forced Prostitution Dichotomy' in Kamala Kempadoo/Jo Doezema (eds), *Global Sex Workers: Rights, Resistance and Redefinition* (Routledge 1998) 39. For the approaches to prostitution, see Heli Askola, *Legal Responses to Trafficking in Women for Sexual Exploitation in the European Union* (Hart 2007) 13–14.

[9] Protocol to Prevent, Suppress and Punish Trafficking in Persons, Especially Women and Children, supplementing the United Nations Convention against Transnational Organized Crime 2237 UNTS 319 (UNTOC Trafficking Protocol).

[10] United Nations Convention against Transnational Organized Crime 2225 UNTS 209 (UNTOC).

[11] Vladislava Stoyanova, *Human Trafficking and Slavery Reconsidered: Conceptual Limits and States' Positive Obligations in European Law* (CUP 2017) 62.

[12] See eg Erika Schulze et al, 'Sexual Exploitation and Prostitution and its Impact on Gender Equality' (European Parliament, Directorate-General for Internal Policies, Policy Department C: Citizens' Rights and Constitutional Affairs, EU 2014) <https://www.europarl.europa.eu/RegData/etudes/etudes/join/2014/493040/IPOL-FEMM_ET%282014%29493040_EN.pdf> accessed 21 May 2020.

but rather in Western States' concerns for the integrity of their national borders. The adoption of the UNTOC Trafficking Protocol and UN Protocol against the Smuggling of Migrants by Land, Sea, and Air (UNTOC Smuggling Protocol),[13] which also supplements UNTOC, was triggered by destination States' concerns regarding the problem of facilitation and organization of illegal immigration.[14] Although human trafficking is intended to refer to abusive processes that might lead to 'exploitation' and, accordingly, might not per se include illegal border crossing, on which basis it can also be distinguished from human smuggling, the migration control measures envisioned by the UNTOC Smuggling Protocol are mirrored in the UNTOC Trafficking Protocol.[15] Thus, securing the integrity of the destination States' borders and immigration legislation is effectively the main objective pursued. This immigration control rationale is supplemented with measures intended to facilitate State cooperation in the area of criminal law (such as facilitation of extradition, and police and judicial cooperation between States).[16] It is thus the security of the destination States that is at the core of the legal regime. The security of the individuals affected, and their assistance and protection needs, are effectively sidelined. Many of these individuals are asylum seekers who flee violence and insecurity; in the absence of legal migration channels to exercise their right to seek asylum,[17] these individuals find themselves blocked in countries of origin and transit.[18] To leave these countries, they are willing to risk their lives, including by undertaking dangerous sea crossings.[19] There is therefore a clear tension here between State security and individual security.

In light of these dynamics, this chapter will first clarify the applicable international legal framework on human trafficking and slavery. The main tension that permeates this framework concerns the security of the individuals who might be victims of human trafficking and slavery and the security of the borders of their desired States of destination. Given this tension, the last section of the chapter will discuss the main challenges that lie ahead in this area of international law.

[13] Protocol against the Smuggling of Migrants by Land, Sea and Air, supplementing the United Nations Convention against Transnational Organized Crime 2241 UNTS 480 (UNTOC Smuggling Protocol).

[14] Boister has clarified how transnational criminal law treaties, such as the UNTOC Trafficking Protocol and the UNTOC Smuggling Protocol, have been an attractive tool deployed by 'rich States to police in poorer States' since the former are vulnerable to certain activities that originate in the latter group of States. Neil Boister, *An Introduction to Transnational Criminal Law* (OUP 2012) 277.

[15] See UNTOC Trafficking Protocol (n 9) arts 11–13 and UNTOC Smuggling Protocol (n 13) arts 11–13.

[16] Neil Boister, '"International Criminal Law"?' (2003) 14 EJIL 953.

[17] Universal Declaration of Human Rights, UNGA Res 217A (III) (10 December 1948) art 14. See Catherine Briddick/Vladislava Stoyanova, 'Human Trafficking and Refugees' in Cathryn Costello et al (eds), *The Oxford Handbook of International Refugee Law* (OUP, forthcoming).

[18] Elspeth Guild/Vladislava Stoyanova, 'The Human Right to Leave Any Country: A Right to be Delivered' (2018) European Yearbook of Human Rights 373; Vladislava Stoyanova, 'The Right to Leave Any Country and the Interplay between Jurisdiction and Proportionality in Human Rights Law' (2020) 32 International Journal of Refugee Law (forthcoming).

[19] Thomas Spijkerboer, 'Wasted Lives. Borders and the Right to Life of People Crossing Them' (2017) 86 Nordic Journal of International Law 1; Vladislava Stoyanova, 'The Right to Life under the EU Charter and Cooperation with Third States to Combat Human Smuggling' (2020) 21 German Law Journal 436.

B. Legal Framework

The international law instruments of historical relevance in the area of human trafficking have already been mentioned in the introductory section;[20] this section will instead focus on the contemporary legal framework. Despite the fact that human rights treaties providing for a right not to be subjected to slavery were adopted prior to the adoption of the UNTOC Trafficking Protocol, this section starts with the human trafficking legal framework. The primary reason for this is that the latter has been the dominant way of framing the contemporary problems surrounding human mobility and exploitation.[21]

1. The Human Trafficking Legal Framework

Article 3(a) of the UNTOC Trafficking Protocol defines human trafficking as:

> the recruitment, transportation, transfer, harbouring or receipt of persons, by means of the threat or use of force or other forms of coercion, of abduction, of fraud, of deception, of the abuse of power or of a position of vulnerability or of the giving or receiving of payments or benefits to achieve the consent of a person having control over another person, for the purpose of exploitation. Exploitation shall include, at a minimum, the exploitation of the prostitution of others or other forms of sexual exploitation, forced labour or services, slavery or practices similar to slavery, servitude or the removal of organs.

A clarification is also added to the definition of human trafficking in the Protocol to the effect that the consent of a victim of trafficking to the intended exploitation shall be irrelevant, where any of these means mentioned in the provision have been used.[22]

As the definition suggests, human trafficking refers to a process that might or might not lead to exploitation as exploitation only needs to be intended.[23] In other words, human trafficking is 'the international supply chain into exploitation' rather than a type of exploitation itself.[24] In turn, 'slavery' is envisaged as an example of exploitative practices; but, 'exploitation' itself is left undefined, potentially encompassing a spectrum of exploitative practices. This renders the severity threshold of the definition undetermined and opens up the possibility for expansive interpretations.[25] Accordingly,

[20] See nn 6 and 7. [21] Stoyanova (n 11) 1.

[22] There is a separate definition of trafficking of children, an issue that will not be covered in this chapter.

[23] Stoyanova (n 11) 292.

[24] Jean Allain, *Slavery in International Law: Of Human Exploitation and Trafficking* (Martinus Nijhoff 2013) 355.

[25] See UNODC, 'The Concept of "Exploitation" in the Trafficking in Persons Protocol' (Issue Paper, UNODC 2015) <https://www.unodc.org/documents/congress/background-information/Human_Trafficking/UNODC_2015_Issue_Paper_Exploitation.pdf> accessed 21 May 2020.

'exploitation' can be interpreted as including any form of engagement with prostitution and, in this sense, any prostitution could be exploitative. More limitative interpretations of 'exploitation' are, however, also possible and, indeed, have been endorsed by some States.[26] A similar problem arises in the area of labour exploitation, where there is no uniform standard against which to measure whether certain abusive working conditions are sufficiently severe to pass the threshold of 'exploitation' for the purposes of the definition of human trafficking and for the purpose of the imposition of criminal law sanctions.[27] The same indeterminacy permeates the 'means' element of the definition (eg, 'deception', 'abuse of power or of a position of vulnerability').[28] These terms can be an object of more limitative or more expansive interpretations.[29] In that respect, Article 5(1) of the UNTOC Trafficking Protocol imposes an obligation upon States to establish human trafficking as a criminal offence at the national level. Once the definition of the crime of human trafficking is transposed to the national level, these definitional difficulties will have to be resolved by national criminal law.[30]

This definition of 'human trafficking' under the UNTOC Trafficking Protocol, including the uncertainties/ambiguities that accompany it, has been transferred to the regional European level.[31] The CoE Convention on Action against Trafficking in Human Beings[32] and the EU Directive on preventing and combating trafficking in human beings and protection of its victims[33] incorporate the same definition of human trafficking.[34] In contrast, the South Asia Association for Regional Cooperation Convention on Preventing and Combating the Trafficking in Women and Children for Prostitution adopted in 2002 defines trafficking as 'the moving, selling or buying of women and children for prostitution within or outside a country for monetary or other considerations with or without the consent of the person subjected to trafficking'.[35] This definition is reminiscent

[26] See Vladislava Stoyanova, 'The Crisis of a Definition: Human Trafficking in Bulgarian Law' (2013) 5 Amsterdam Law Forum 64; Jean Allain, 'No Effective Trafficking Definition Exists: Domestic Implementation of the Palermo Protocol' (2014) 7 Albany Governmental Law Review 111.

[27] Stoyanova (n 11) 66; Cathryn Costello, 'Migrants and Forced Labour: A Labour Law Response' in Alan Bogg et al (eds), *The Autonomy of Labour Law* (Hart 2015) 189.

[28] See UNODC, 'Abuse of a Position of Vulnerability and other "Means" within the Definition of Trafficking in Persons' (Issue Paper, UN 2013) <https://www.unodc.org/documents/human-trafficking/2012/UNODC_2012_Issue_Paper_-_Abuse_of_a_Position_of_Vulnerability.pdf> accessed 28 November 2020.

[29] For example, the EU Anti-trafficking Directive defines 'a position of vulnerability' as 'a position in which the person concerned has no real or acceptable alternative but to submit to the abuse involved'. European Parliament and Council Directive 2011/36/EU of 5 April 2011 on preventing and combating trafficking in human beings and protecting its victims, and replacing Council Framework Decision 2002/629/JHA OJ L 101/1 (Directive 2011/36/EU) art 2(1).

[30] Stoyanova (n 11) 77.

[31] Gregor Noll, 'The Insecurity of Trafficking in International Law' in Vincent Chetail (ed), *Mondialisation, migration et droits de l'homme: le droit international en question* (Bruylant 2007) 343.

[32] CoE Convention on Action against Trafficking in Human Beings ETS No 197.

[33] Directive 2011/36/EU (n 29).

[34] Directive 2011/36/EU (n 29) art 2(3) has included begging and 'exploitation of criminal activities' as additional examples of exploitative practices.

[35] SAARC Convention on Preventing and Combating Trafficking in Women and Children for Prostitution art 1(3) <https://www.saarc-sec.org/index.php/resources/agreements-conventions/50-

of the one contained in the 1949 Convention for the Suppression of Traffic in Persons and the Exploitation of the Prostitution of Others, which was mentioned in the introductory section of this chapter.[36]

From a definitional perspective, it is important to distinguish human trafficking from human smuggling. The latter is defined in the UNTOC Smuggling Protocol as 'the procurement, in order to obtain, directly or indirectly, a financial or other material benefit, of the illegal entry of a person into a State Party of which the person is not a national or a permanent resident'.[37] Unlike human trafficking, smuggling does not entail coercion or deception of the victim; smuggling is a voluntary act on the part of those smuggled. By contrast, the focus in cases of trafficking is on the abusive migration process and the intended exploitation. Another basis on which to distinguish the two is that the 'services' of smugglers end when those smuggled have reached their destination. To the contrary, trafficking results in people being exploited. Additionally, human smuggling entails international movements; it always has a transnational element, whereas human trafficking can take place both within and across national frontiers. Finally, smuggling entails illegal entry into a given State, while entry can both be legal and illegal in the case of trafficking. For example, a victim of human trafficking could have entered the destination country on a valid passport.

Despite these differences, the difficulties in drawing the distinction between the two phenomena must also be highlighted. More specifically, many migrants, including those who could be defined as victims of trafficking, in fact, agree to be transported and expect to be exploited. There could be different degrees of victimization and exploitation during the migration process and once the migrant is in the receiving State. The abovementioned uncertainties as to the severity thresholds demanded by the international law definition of human trafficking concerning the 'purpose' element (namely, exploitation) and the 'means' element (namely, 'abuse of power or of a position of vulnerability') further contribute to blurring the dichotomy. Given the fact that many migrants who use smuggling services are asylum seekers fleeing their countries and given that they likely have no alternative routes to access the territory of destination States, it is questionable whether we can actually definitively and conclusively say that asylum seekers consent to be smuggled. If they have no other reasonable alternatives but to resort to smuggling services,[38] it is questionable whether their consent to smuggling may be considered a valid one. The measures that States have agreed upon to counter human smuggling and human trafficking are very similar (criminalization, cooperation in the area of criminal justice, enhancement border control measures), which arguably further undermines the distinction.

saarc-convention-on-preventing-and-combating-trafficking-in-women-and-children-for-prostitution/file> accessed 28 November 2020. For a brief overview of this Convention see Anne T Gallagher, *The International Law of Human Trafficking* (CUP 2010) 129.

[36] See n 7. [37] UNTOC Smuggling Protocol (n 13) art 3(a).

[38] Vladislava Stoyanova, 'The Right to Life under the EU Charter and Cooperation with Third States to Combat Human Trafficking' (2020) 31 German Law Journal 436.

A possible benefit from separating the phenomenon of human smuggling from that of human trafficking could be that once a migrant is identified as a victim of human trafficking, he or she could benefit from certain forms of protection and assistance that are not extended to smuggled migrants. The UNTOC Trafficking Protocol indeed contains provisions addressing the issues of protection of, and assistance to, victims. Article 2(b) indicates in very general terms that one of the objectives of the Protocol is to 'protect and assist the victims of such trafficking, with full respect of their human rights'. Articles 6 to 8 outline in more concrete terms what this protection and assistance could imply: protecting 'the privacy and identity of victims of trafficking in persons, including, *inter alia*, by making legal proceedings relating to such trafficking confidential', providing victims with information on relevant court and administrative proceedings, 'appropriate housing', 'counselling and information', 'medical, psychological and material assistance', 'employment, educational and training opportunities'. However, it is important to note that all these provisions are hortatory and fall short of imposing binding legal obligations on States Parties.[39]

Hence, from another perspective, and given the absence of concrete and robust obligations for the protection of, and assistance to, victims of human trafficking, the value of identifying individuals as such victims, and of separating them from the category of smuggled migrants, may be seriously questioned. This further supports the concern that the engagement with human trafficking, including the drafting of international legal instruments addressing human trafficking, has barely served the interests of the individuals affected, but it has rather been a tool for Western States to enhance the security of their borders.[40]

2. The Right not to be Subjected to Slavery

As opposed to human trafficking, which has been a prominent issue on the international agenda for almost two decades now (particularly, since the adoption of the UNTOC Trafficking Protocol), and a subject of international lawmaking at both global and regional levels, the right not to be subjected to slavery as enshrined in the International Covenant on Civil and Political Rights (ICCPR)[41] Article 8, the European Convention on Human Rights (ECHR)[42] Article 4, the American Convention on Human Rights

[39] Contrast with the Council of Europe and the European Union anti-trafficking frameworks that impose concrete obligations upon States to assist and protect victims of human trafficking. See Stoyanova (n 11) 74.

[40] James Hathaway has argued that the engagement of international law with human trafficking has served as a pretext for the globalization of border control. See James C Hathaway, 'The Human Rights Quagmire of "Human Trafficking"' (2008) 49 Virginia Journal of International Law 1; for a response see Anne Gallagher, 'Human Rights and Human Trafficking: Quagmire or Firm Ground? A Response to James Hathaway' (2009) 49 Virginia Journal of International Law 789.

[41] International Covenant on Civil and Political Rights 999 UNTS 171 (ICCPR).

[42] European Convention on Human Rights and Fundamental Freedoms ETS No 5 (ECHR).

(ACHR)[43] Article 6, and the African Charter on Human and Peoples' Rights (ACHPR)[44] Article 5 has remained relatively silent. This is illustrated by the fact that there is comparatively limited engagement with this right by the bodies mandated to monitor and supervise the above-mentioned human rights treaties.[45] The UN Human Rights Committee has not so far issued a general comment on Article 8 of the ICCPR and no communication has ever been delivered by the committee concerning circumstances of private exploitation (namely, circumstances where not the State or a State agent, but rather a private party arguably exploits another individual).[46] In contrast, the Economic Community of West African States (ECOWAS) Court of Justice has delivered one relevant judgment, in which Niger was found responsible under Article 5 of the ACHPR for the violation of the prohibition of slavery. The case of *Hadijatou Mani Koraou v Republic of Niger* concerned Niger's practice of wahiya whereby 'a young girl, generally a slave [is acquired] to work as a servant as well as a concubine'.[47] Overall, the circumstances of *Hadijatou Mani Koraou* reveal a case of *de jure* slavery, in which the slave owner sought to vindicate his right of property on the woman before the national courts and the national judge recognized this right, namely the right of property over the woman.[48]

Similarly, the Inter-American Court of Human Rights (IACtHR) has issued only one judgment where it qualified the factual circumstances as slavery. To reach this conclusion, it utilized the international law definition of slavery under the 1926 Slavery Convention. Article 1(1) of this Convention defines slavery as 'the status or condition of a person over whom any or all of the powers attaching to the right of ownership are exercised'. The IACtHR applied this definition to the circumstances of the case of *Brasil Verde v Brazil*.[49] This case concerned workers recruited from poor communities and lured to work at a larger farm in Brazil. They were not paid, worked in deplorable

[43] American Convention on Human Rights 1144 UNTS 123 (ACHR).

[44] African Charter on Human and Peoples' Rights 1520 UNTS 217 (ACHPR).

[45] It has to be acknowledged here that international criminal law has made an important contribution to the understanding of the international law definition of slavery. See Stoyanova (n 11) 222–34; Harmen van de Wilt, 'Trafficking in Human Beings, Enslavement, Crimes against Humanity: Unravelling the Concepts' (2014) 13 Chinese Journal of International Law 297.

[46] For elaboration, see Vladislava Stoyanova, 'United Nations against Slavery: Unravelling Concepts, Institutions and Obligations' (2017) 38 Michigan Journal of International Law 359.

[47] *Hadijatou Mani Koraou v The Republic of Niger* No ECW/CCJ/JUD/06/08 (Judgment) Economic Community of West African States Community Court of Justice (27 October 2008) paras 77, 80; for an unofficial English translation see *Hadijatou Mani Koraou v The Republic of Niger* (refworld) para 9 <www.refworld.org/docid/496b41fa2.html> accessed 20 May 2020. For commentary, see Jean Allain, 'Hadijatou Mani Koraou v. Republic of Niger' (2009) 103 AJIL 311; Horace S Adjolohoun, 'The ECOWAS Court as a Human Rights Promoter? Assessing Five Years' Impact of the Koraou Slavery Judgment' (2013) 31 Netherlands Quarterly of Human Rights 342.

[48] Stoyanova (n 46) 416.

[49] *Case of the Hacienda Brasil Verde Workers v Brazil* (Preliminary Objections, Merits, Reparations and Costs) IACtHR Series C No 318 (Judgment of 20 October 2016) (*Brasil Verde*). For further discussion see Rebecca J Scott et al, 'How Does the Law Put a Historical Analogy to Work? Defining the Imposition of "Condition Analogous to that of a Slave" in Modern Brazil' (2017) 13 Duke Journal of Constitutional Law and Policy 1, 39; Carlos H B Haddad, 'The Definition of Slave Labor for Criminal Enforcement and the Experience of Adjudication: The Case of Brazil' (2017) 38 Michigan Journal of International Law 497.

conditions under constant supervision without freedom to leave. The Inter-American Court qualified these living and working conditions as slavery. The Court observed that the concept of slavery has evolved since the adoption of the 1926 Slavery Convention, and it is no longer limited to legal ownership of a person. It rather also encompasses situations of control of one person over another; the level of control implies that the victim is deprived of his or her own will, or that his or her personal autonomy is considerably reduced. The Court clarified that 'powers attaching to the right of ownership', an expression found in the definition of slavery,

> must be understood in the present day as the control exercised over a person that significantly restricts or deprives him of his individual liberty with intent to exploit through the use, management, profit, transfer or disposal of a person. This control is usually obtained and maintained through means such as the violence, deception and/or coercion.[50]

In contrast to the IACtHR that did not eschew to use the label of slavery in *Brasil Verde v Brazil*, the European Court of Human Rights (ECtHR) has never defined any factual circumstances as slavery. At the time of writing, the ECtHR has delivered nine judgments under Article 4 of the ECHR.[51] With the exception of *S M v Croatia*, all of them concerned migrants who were victims of severe forms of exploitation. In all of these judgments the factual circumstances were classified as either forced labour, servitude, or human trafficking;[52] the concept of slavery was found applicable in none of these cases. In fact, in the case of *Siliadin v France*, a girl from Togo arrived in France to work for a family under the promise that her immigration status would be regularized but, in

[50] *Brasil Verde* (n 49) para 271 (author's translation).

[51] *Siliadin v France*, App No 73316/01, 26 July 2005; *C N and V v France*, App No 67724/09, 11 October 2012; *C N v UK*, App No 4239/08, 13 November 2012; *Rantsev v Cyprus and Russia*, App No 25965/04, 7 January 2010; *L E v Greece*, App No 71545/12, 21 January 2016; *J and Others v Austria*, App No 58216/12, 17 January 2017; *Chowdury and Others v Greece*, App No 21884/15, 30 March 2017; *M and Others v Italy and Bulgaria*, App No 40020/03, 31 July 2012 (the complaint under Article 4 was found inadmissible in this case); *S M v Croatia* [GC], App No 60561/14, 25 June 2020. See also *G J v Spain* App No 59172/12, 21 June 2016 Decision (inadmissible).

[52] The concept of human trafficking was used in *Rantsev* (n 51), *M and Others v Italy and Bulgaria* (n 51), *L E v Greece* (n 51) and *J and Others v Austria* (n 51). In contrast in *C N and V v France*, the Court preferred the legal concepts specifically provided for in the text of the ECHR: 'It is true that in the case of *Rantsev v Cyprus and Russia* the Court affirmed that human trafficking itself falls within the scope of Article 4 of the Convention in so far as it is without doubt a phenomenon that runs counter to the spirit and purpose of that provision. However, it considers that, above all, the facts of the present case concern activities related to "forced labour" and "services", legal concepts specifically provided for in the Convention' (*C N and V v France* (n 51) para 88). In *S M v Croatia* (n 51) the Court did not determine whether the applicant was actually forced into prostitution since the finding was limited to the determination that the national authorities did not make sufficient efforts to themselves assess whether she was forced. See Vladislava Stoyanova, 'The Grand Chamber Judgment in S.M. v Croatia: Human Trafficking, Prostitution and the Definitional Scope of Article 4 ECHR' (*Strasbourg Observers*, 3 July 2020) <https://strasbourgobservers.com/2020/07/03/the-grand-chamber-judgment-in-s-m-v-croatia-human-trafficking-prostitution-and-the-definitional-scope-of-article-4-echr/> accessed 7 September 2020.

practice, became a domestic servant and was subjected to very abusive working conditions. However, in its judgment the Court rejected the contemporary relevance of the concept of slavery as defined in the 1926 Slavery Convention. More specifically, it observed that, according to this definition,

> slavery is the status or condition of a person over whom any or all of the powers attaching to the right of ownership are exercised. It [the Court] notes that this definition corresponds to the 'classic' meaning of slavery as it was practised for centuries. Although the applicant was, in the instant case, clearly deprived of her personal autonomy, the evidence does not suggest that she was held in slavery in the proper sense, in other words that Mr and Mrs B. exercised a genuine right of legal ownership over her, thus reducing her to the status of an 'object'.[53]

This reasoning suggests that the ECtHR seems to interpret the definition of slavery as requiring ownership sanctioned by the legal system. This interpretation, however, is not compatible with the plain wording of the definition of slavery as actually found in the 1926 Slavery Convention, which refers to 'powers attaching to the right of ownership'. If the Court's conservative interpretation were to be followed, the concept of slavery would lose its contemporary relevance since no legal system recognizes today the possibility that one human being exercises rights of legal ownership over another or more human beings.

Surprisingly, the ECtHR has used the definition of slavery for the purposes of defining human trafficking. More specifically, in *Rantsev v Cyprus and Russia*, in which a young Russian woman entered Cyprus on a specific type of visa (an artiste visa) to work as a dancer in clubs and arguably had been exploited in the context of prostitution by her employer, the ECtHR stated,

> trafficking in human beings, by its very nature and aim of exploitation, is based on the *exercise of powers attaching to the right of ownership*. It treats human beings as commodities to be bought and sold and put to forced labour, often for little or no payment, usually in the sex industry but also elsewhere. It implies close surveillance of the activities of victims, whose movements are often circumscribed. It involves the use of violence and threats against victims, who live and work under poor conditions. It is described by Interights and in the explanatory report accompanying the Anti-Trafficking Convention as the modern form of the old worldwide slave trade. The Cypriot Ombudsman referred to sexual exploitation and trafficking taking place 'under a regime of modern slavery'.[54]

The conflation of the concepts of human trafficking and slavery and the sidelining of the concept of slavery is a reason for concern since ultimately the minimum threshold for

[53] *Siliadin* (n 51) para 122.

[54] *Rantsev* (n 51) para 281 (emphasis added; references omitted). See Jean Allain, '*Rantsev v Cyprus and Russia*: The European Court of Human Rights and Trafficking as Slavery' (2010) 10 Human Rights Law Review 546.

triggering the application of Article 4 of the ECHR is rendered uncertain. The ambiguities that underpin the definition of human trafficking, as mentioned in Section B.1, further exacerbate this uncertainty.[55] More specifically, the definition of human trafficking has remained vague as to the minimum severity threshold required in order to determine that a person has been exploited. After *Rantsev v Cyprus and Russia*, this same uncertainty has been transposed to Article 4 of the ECHR.

From a different perspective, an argument could be made that this conflation and the possible lowering of the minimum threshold for triggering the application of Article 4 of the ECHR, given that 'exploitation' might imply a lower severity threshold than 'exercise of powers attaching to the right of ownership', is beneficial for individuals. This way it might be easier for them to invoke the protection of this provision and the positive obligations that it generates.[56] At the same time, however, we should be wary of any possible negative effects. In particular, when there is no clarity as to what is meant by the terms 'human trafficking' and 'slavery' and what definitional severity threshold is applied, States can more easily justify their coercive migration control measures with the argument that these are necessary for the purpose of preventing human trafficking and slavery. Coercive measures, including measures of containment and pre-departure controls,[57] are more easily legitimized once they are represented as anti-trafficking measures.[58] For example, combating human smuggling and human trafficking has been one of the flagships of the 'external dimension' of the EU immigration policy of imposing pre-departure controls and containment of migrants in host and transit States.[59] At the same time, these types of measures for migration control lead to containment of people in States (such as Libya), where they are subjected to severe forms of human rights law violations,[60] including conditions arguably amounting to slavery.[61] Thus, ultimately, it is the security, including the border security, of Western States that matters

[55] Vladislava Stoyanova, 'Dancing on the Borders of Article 4: Human Trafficking and the European Court of Human Rights in the *Rantsev* Case' (2012) 30 Netherlands Quarterly of Human Rights 163; see also the Dissenting Opinion of Judge Koskelo in *S M v Croatia*, App No 60561/14, 19 July 2018.

[56] On the positive obligations generated by ECHR (n 42) art 4, see Stoyanova (n 11) 319.

[57] Thomas Gammeltoft-Hansen/James C Hathaway, 'Non-Refoulement in a World of Cooperative Deterrence' (2015) 53 Columbia Journal of Transnational Law 235; Violeta Moreno-Lax, *Accessing Asylum in Europe: Extraterritorial Border Controls and Refugee Rights under EU Law* (OUP 2017) 323.

[58] Jean-Pierre Gauci/Vladislava Stoyanova, 'The Human Rights of Smuggled Migrants and Trafficked Persons in the UN Global Compacts on Migrants and Refugees' (2018) 4 International Journal of Migration and Border Studies 222.

[59] Commission and High Representative of the European Union for Foreign Affairs and Security Policy, 'Migration on the Central Mediterranean Route: Managing Flows, Saving Lives' JOIN(2017)4final, 5; see also Nora Markard, 'The Right to Leave by Sea: Legal Limits on the EU Migration Control by Third Parties'(2016) 27 EJIL 591; CoE Commissioner for Human Rights, *The Right to Leave a Country* (Issue Paper, Council of Europe 2013) <https://rm.coe.int/the-right-to-leave-a-country-issue-paper-published-by-the-council-of-e/16806da510> accessed 21 May 2020.

[60] See also UNCHR 'Report of the Special Rapporteur on Torture and Other Cruel, Inhuman or Degrading Treatment or Punishment' (26 February 2018) UN Doc A/HRC/37/50.

[61] Nima Elbagirm/Raja Razek et al, 'People for Sale: Where Lives are Auctioned for $400' (*CNN*, Tripoli) <www.edition.cnn.com/2017/11/14/africa/libya-migrant-auctions/index.html> accessed 10 January 2020.

and that is what is actually ensured through such anti-trafficking measures, rather than the security and the protection of the affected individuals.

The aforementioned judgment of the ECtHR in *Rantsev v Cyprus and Russia* may be used as a concrete illustration of this problem. After suggesting that Rantseva could have been a victim of human trafficking, the ECtHR proceeded to determine whether Cyprus had fulfilled its positive obligations to prevent human trafficking. In particular, from the perspective of States' positive obligations under Article 4 of the ECHR, the artiste visa regime was found problematic since, in practice, it enabled employers to exercise a high level of control over migrant women who entered the country under this regime. The Court held that,

> while an obligation on employers to notify the authorities when an artiste leaves her employment is a legitimate measure to allow the authorities to monitor the compliance of immigrants with their immigration obligations, responsibility for ensuring compliance and for taking steps in cases of non-compliance must remain with the authorities themselves. Measures which encourage cabaret owners and managers to track down missing artistes or in some other way to take personal responsibility for the conduct of artistes are unacceptable in the broader context of trafficking concerns regarding artistes in Cyprus... In the circumstances, the Court concludes that the regime of artiste visas in Cyprus did not afford to Ms Rantseva practical and effective protection against trafficking and exploitation. There has accordingly been a violation of Article 4 in this regard.[62]

To comply with the judgment of the Court, Cyprus, instead of modifying the conditions within the artiste visa regime so that it empowers migrant women against their employers and provides them with a more secure migration status,[63] eliminated the artiste visa regime altogether.[64] This way, a lawful channel for migration was eliminated. This situation fits well within the problematic logic that portrays the removal of possibilities for migration as contributing to the reduction of human trafficking.[65]

C. Contemporary Challenges

One of the most challenging problems relating to human trafficking and slavery concerns human mobility in the context of mass migration. The main objective of countries

[62] *Rantsev* (n 51) paras 292–3.

[63] On how insecure migration status produces vulnerabilities, see Gregor Noll, 'Why Human Rights Fail Undocumented Migrants?' (2010) 12 European Journal of Migration and Law 241.

[64] See Secretariat of the Committee of Ministers, 'Communication from the delegation of Cyprus in the case of Rantsev against Cyprus and the Russian Federation (Application No. 25965/06)' (12 August 2010) Doc DH–DD(2010)376E.

[65] Audrey Macklin, 'Dancing Across Borders: "Exotic Dancers", Trafficking, and Canadian Immigration Policy' (2003) 37 International Migration Review 464, 484 and 485; Stoyanova (n 55); Stoyanova (n 11) 393.

of destination is to limit such mobility to preserve the integrity of their borders and immigration legislation. This objective is usually pursued by the means of containment, which implies preventing the departure of persons from countries of origin and transit and the development of politics of *non-entrée*.[66] The latter aim at preventing the migrants from accessing the jurisdiction of States of destination[67] and thus falling under the protective scope of human rights instruments that these States are bound to observe.[68] Destination States have persistently argued that *non-entrée* policies and policies of containment serve to prevent human trafficking. The purported reasoning behind such assertions is that in light of these policies migrants are prevented from departing from their home States in the first place, and, even if they somehow manage to depart, they stand no chance of entering destination States. Pursuant to this logic, once migrants know that there is no chance of entry, this will act as a deterrent discouraging them from initiating their perilous journeys in the first place.

In developing these policies, States of destination have sought the cooperation of States of origin and transit. Willingness to cooperate by the latter group of States has been secured by, *inter alia*, the argument that cooperation serves the objective of preventing human trafficking and human exploitation.[69] Empirically, however, this is a questionable assumption for the following reasons. Given the protracted international and non-international armed conflicts, the civil wars, and instabilities in many parts of

[66] This term was first used in James Hathaway, 'The Emerging Politics of Non-Entrée' (1992) 91 Refugees 40–1.

[67] See eg *Hirsi Jamaa and Others v Italy*, App No 27765/09, 23 February 2012, paras 70–5, for the ECtHR's approach to the requirement of jurisdiction under ECHR (n 42) art 1.

[68] Samantha Besson 'The Extraterritoriality of the European Convention on Human Rights: Why Human Rights Depend on Jurisdiction and What Jurisdiction Amounts to' (2012) 25 Leiden Journal of International Law 857. See also Charles Heller et al, '"It's an Act of Murder": How Europe Outsources Suffering As Migrants Drown' (*The New York Times*) <www.nytimes.com/interactive/2018/12/26/opinion/europe-migrant-crisis-mediterranean-libya.html> accessed 10 January 2020.

[69] As Hathaway has framed it 'the developed world's goal of enlisting global participation in its migration control project at a decidedly minimum cost' has been ensured through the international human trafficking and human smuggling legal frameworks. See Hathaway (n 40) 30. A clarification is due here. More specifically, the objective of 'combating' human trafficking is only one of the incentives that countries of departure and transit pursue to control their own borders to contain movement. The demand to control borders and contain movements imposed by countries of destination upon countries of origin and transit comes as part of a larger package of financial assistance and other incentives. See eg the EU–Turkey Deal, where Turkey was promised visa liberalization. See Memorandum of Understanding on Cooperation in the Fields of Development, the Fight against Illegal Immigration, Human Trafficking and Fuel Smuggling and on Reinforcing the Security of Borders between the State of Libya and the Italian Republic (2 February 2017) <https://www.repubblica.it/esteri/2017/02/02/news/migranti_accordo_italia-libia_ecco_cosa_contiene_in_memorandum-157464439/?refresh_ce> accessed 10 January 2020. For an English translation see <https://eumigrationlawblog.eu/wp-content/uploads/2017/10/MEMORANDUM_translation_finalversion.doc.pdf> accessed 10 January 2020. Pursuant to art 1(B) of this Memorandum: 'the Italian party commits to provide technical and technological support to the Libyan institutions in charge of the fight against illegal immigration'. See also Commission, 'Communication on establishing a new Partnership Framework with third countries under the European Agenda on Migration' COM(2016)385final, 15; Commission, 'Fifth Progress Report on the Partnership Framework with third countries under the European Agenda on Migration' COM(2017)471final, 9; Commission, 'Progress Report on the European Agenda on Migration' COM(2017)669final, 8.

the world, individuals will continue to flee. In light of the absence of lawful channels for migration and in order to reach States of destination so as to be able to claim asylum, individuals will essentially continue to resort to the services of human smugglers,[70] which could then easily be transformed into human trafficking. Additionally, taking into consideration the absence of lawful channels for reaching and accessing the territories of States of asylum and that anti-trafficking and anti-smuggling measures block routes, thus pushing migrants to undertake even more dangerous journeys,[71] both the risks (including risks to the migrants' lives) and the fees that migrants have to pay to smugglers are increased.[72] This might, in turn, compel migrants to enter into exploitative agreements to secure their transportation (including debt bondage, amongst others), which may amount to human trafficking and slavery. As already mentioned above, it has been widely reported that the situation in States, such as Libya, where migrants are contained, is characterized by severe human rights law violations, including conditions amounting to slavery. Ultimately, affected individuals are left with the stark choice between war and conflict in States of origin, severe human rights violations (including slavery) in transit States and, in the (at times distant) hope of reaching safe shores, entering into exploitative and life-endangering agreements with smugglers or traffickers.

D. Conclusion

In our increasingly securitized, twenty-first-century world, the 'fight' against human smuggling and human trafficking has been used by destination States to primarily further their migration control interests and border security. This has happened with little consideration about the well-being of the affected individuals, who are often fleeing situations of extreme violence and instability. Anti-smuggling and anti-trafficking measures have been justified with the argument that they are in the interests of migrants themselves, given that they deter 'dangerous journeys' by undercutting the demand for

[70] It needs to also be kept in mind that international refugee law explicitly acknowledges that asylum seekers can use illegal means of entering countries of destination. See Convention relating to the Status of Refugees 189 UNTS 137 (1951 Refugee Convention) art 31. See Cathryn Costello et al, 'Article 31 of the 1951 Convention Relating to the Status of Refugees' (2017) UNHCR Legal and Protection Policy Research Series PPLA/2017/01. See also the saving clauses in the UNTOC Trafficking Protocol (n 9) art 14(1) and the UNTOC Smuggling Protocol (n 13) art 19: 'Nothing in this Protocol shall affect the other rights, obligations and responsibilities of States and individuals under international law, including international humanitarian law and international human rights law and, in particular, where applicable, the 1951 Convention and the 1967 Protocol relating to the Status of Refugees and the principle of non-refoulement as contained therein.'

[71] Tim Stokholm, 'Mediterranean Migrant Crisis: A Critical Challenge to Global Nation-States' (2016) Centre for Social Justice and Change Working Papers No 3 <https://repository.uel.ac.uk/item/852z4> accessed 10 January 2020.

[72] Gauci and Stoyanova (n 58).

the services of smugglers and traffickers. In reality though, these measures have led to the prevention of movement and the containment of migrants in countries with a record of widespread human rights violations and systemic insecurity. These anti-smuggling and anti-trafficking measures have also practically led to annihilation of the right to asylum since individuals have been prevented from reaching countries of destination and coming into contact with these countries' authorities. As the analysis in the present contribution has illustrated, today it can hardly be said that the anti-trafficking and, to a lesser extent, the anti-slavery legal framework are used to further the security of individuals. Rather, the interests and security of Western States are put once again front and centre.

CHAPTER 22

INSTITUTIONALIZED INHUMANITY

From Torture to Assassination

NATASA MAVRONICOLA

A. Introduction

There is, in one sense, nothing more human than the inhuman. Atrocity pervades human history. Individuals and groups have wielded their relative power over other persons in a variety of cruel ways, not least torture and assassination. The legal framework that gradually emerged to counter such abuse reflected a deontic humanity—humanity not as it is, but as it ought to be. This deontic vision of humanity was premised on human dignity, an egalitarian idea according to which every single human person is fundamentally worthy of a certain level of respect. The lines set by the law were meant to serve as a bulwark against the desecration of this deontic humanity. This chapter examines the legal framework on torture and other cruel, inhuman or degrading treatment or punishment and assassination, broadly conceived, and considers some of the main developments in this area. It reflects on key challenges arising or enduring in respect of the relevant law and the deontic humanity that underpins it, challenges at the heart of which are (national, global, or transnational) security structures, or appeals to security: from consequentialist arguments for abandoning the prohibition of torture, to the securitization of (groups of) persons in ways which contradict human dignity.

B. Legal Framework

1. The Prohibition of Torture

Following the unequivocal condemnation of torture and other cruel, inhuman, or degrading treatment or punishment in Article 5 of the Universal Declaration of Human

Rights (UDHR), the absolute prohibition of torture and ill-treatment[1] has been enshrined in various human rights instruments, such as the International Covenant on Civil and Political Rights (ICCPR)[2] Article 7, the European Convention on Human Rights (ECHR)[3] Article 3, the American Convention on Human Rights (ACHR)[4] Article 5, and the African Charter on Human and Peoples' Rights (ACHPR)[5] Article 5. The prohibition of torture, cruel, humiliating, and degrading treatment is also included in Common Article 3 of the 1949 Geneva Conventions,[6] reflecting 'elementary considerations of humanity'.[7] Moreover, torture or '[o]ther inhumane acts', when part of a widespread or systematic practice, amount to crimes against humanity, and during armed conflict to war crimes.[8]

In addition, a number of instruments elaborating specific safeguards against torture and ill-treatment have emerged out of the imperative to end torture and ill-treatment. With substantial mobilization by civil society in the face of persistent and widespread torture and brutality, in 1975 the UN General Assembly (UNGA) adopted the Declaration on the Protection of All Persons from Being Subjected to Torture and Other Cruel, Inhuman or Degrading Treatment or Punishment, which described torture and ill-treatment as 'an offence to human dignity' to be 'condemned as a denial of the purposes of the Charter of the United Nations'.[9] In 1984, the Convention against Torture and Other Cruel, Inhuman, or Degrading Treatment or Punishment (UNCAT) was adopted, which imposes a range of obligations on States, including the criminalization, investigation, and prosecution of allegations of torture,[10] the provision of redress and rehabilitation to victims,[11] and the adoption of various legislative and practical measures to prevent torture and related ill-treatment.

These instruments are complemented by a rich body of jurisprudence elaborating the substantive scope and demands of the prohibition of torture and ill-treatment in an array of settings,[12] as well as a range of relevant soft law instruments, such as the revised United Nations Standard Minimum Rules for the Treatment of Prisoners (Nelson Mandela Rules),[13] the Code of Conduct for Law Enforcement Officials (CCLEO),[14] the Basic Principles on the Use of Force and Firearms by Law Enforcement Officials

[1] The term 'ill-treatment' denotes cruel, inhuman, or degrading treatment or punishment, or a combination thereof.

[2] 999 UNTS 171. [3] ETS No 5. [4] 1144 UNTS 123. [5] 1520 UNTS 217.

[6] 75 UNTS 31 (GC I); 75 UNTS 85 (GC II); 75 UNTS 287 (GC III); 75 UNTS 135 (GC IV).

[7] *Military and Paramilitary Activities in and Against Nicaragua (Nicaragua v USA)* (Merits) [1986] ICJ Rep 14 [215], referring to *Corfu Channel Case (UK v Albania)* (Merits) [1949] ICJ Rep 4, 22.

[8] This is codified in the Rome Statute of the International Criminal Court 2187 UNTS 3 arts 7 and 8.

[9] UNGA Res 3452(XXX) (9 December 1975).

[10] Convention against Torture and Other Cruel, Inhuman, or Degrading Treatment or Punishment 1465 UNTS 85 (UNCAT) arts 4–7, 12–13, 15.

[11] UNCAT (n 10) art 14.

[12] On this, see OHCHR, 'Interpretation of Torture in the Light of the Practice and Jurisprudence of International Bodies' (2011) <https://www.ohchr.org/Documents/Issues/Torture/UNVFVT/Interpretation_torture_2011_EN.pdf> accessed 25 July 2019.

[13] UNGA Res 70/175 (17 December 2015) Annex.

[14] UNGA Res 34/169 (17 December 1979).

(BPUFF),[15] and the Istanbul Protocol on the Effective Investigation and Documentation of Torture and Other Cruel, Inhuman or Degrading Treatment or Punishment.[16]

Several bodies have been established to give effect to the prohibition.[17] The implementation of the UNCAT is overseen by the Committee Against Torture (CAT), which also elaborates on the Convention's demands through general comments.[18] The prevention of torture and related ill-treatment is now further facilitated, under the Optional Protocol to the Convention Against Torture of 2002 (OPCAT),[19] by the Subcommittee on Prevention of Torture and other Cruel, Inhuman, or Degrading Treatment or Punishment (SPT) and the requirement for States to set up a National Preventive Mechanism (NPM).[20] Furthermore, the mandate of the UN Special Rapporteur on torture and other cruel, inhuman, or degrading treatment or punishment (UN Torture Rapporteur), which does not hinge on treaty ratification, has contributed to the fight against torture and ill-treatment and to clarifying the contours of the prohibition since 1985.[21]

The prohibition of torture and other cruel, inhuman, or degrading treatment or punishment is part of customary international law[22] and is considered to be a peremptory norm of international law (jus cogens).[23] Furthermore, this prohibition is absolute: it cannot be lawfully infringed or derogated from, even in circumstances of emergency or war.[24] As a matter of international law, therefore, even the most (seemingly) compelling security imperative cannot render torture or ill-treatment acceptable. On the level of global governance and, indeed, morality, this position has been defended in the strongest terms by the UN Torture Rapporteur: 'abhorrent practices such as torture, slavery

[15] United Nations Congress on the Prevention of Crime and the Treatment of Offenders, Basic Principles on the Use of Force and Firearms by Law Enforcement Officials (27 August to 7 September 1990) and adopted without a vote by UNGA Res 45/166 (18 December 1990).

[16] OHCHR, *Istanbul Protocol: Manual on the Effective Investigation and Documentation of Torture and Other Cruel, Inhuman or Degrading Treatment or Punishment* (Professional Training Series No. 8/Rev.11, UN 2004).

[17] For a thorough account of these developments, see Nigel Rodley/Matt Pollard, *The Treatment of Prisoners under International Law* (3rd edn, OUP 2011) especially chs 1 and 5.

[18] eg CAT 'General Comment No 4 (2017) on the implementation of article 3 of the Convention in the context of article 22' (6 December 2017) UN Doc CAT/C/GC/4.

[19] 2375 UNTS 237.

[20] See further, Rachel Murray et al (eds), *The Optional Protocol to the UN Convention Against Torture* (OUP 2011).

[21] On the mandate, see <https://www.ohchr.org/en/issues/torture/srtorture/pages/srtortureindex.aspx> accessed 21 May 2020.

[22] See *Ahmadou Sadio Diallo (Republic of Guinea v Democratic Republic of the Congo)* (Merits) [2010] ICJ Rep 639 [87]; *Questions relating to the Obligation to Prosecute or Extradite (Belgium v Senegal)* (Judgment) [2012] ICJ Rep 422 [99]; HRC Res 8/8 (18 June 2008); and UNGA Res 70/146 (17 December 2015).

[23] See further, Erika de Wet, 'The Prohibition of Torture as an International Norm of *Jus Cogens* and its Implications for National and Customary Law' (2004) 15 EJIL 97.

[24] Natasa Mavronicola, 'What is an "Absolute Right"? Deciphering Absoluteness in the Context of Article 3 of the European Convention on Human Rights' (2012) 12 Human Rights Law Review 723; cf Steven Greer, 'Is the Prohibition against Torture, Cruel, Inhuman and Degrading Treatment Really "Absolute" in International Human Rights Law?' (2015) 15 Human Rights Law Review 101; but see Natasa Mavronicola, 'Is the Prohibition against Torture and Cruel, Inhuman and Degrading Treatment Absolute in International Human Rights Law? A Reply to Steven Greer' (2017) 17 Human Rights Law Review 479.

and genocide have been absolutely prohibited as a matter of universal jus cogens not because they never "work" in practice but because all of them irreparably destroy the humanity and integrity of the victims, the perpetrators and, ultimately, society as a whole.'[25]

Absoluteness entails an either–or approach—either there has been a breach of the prohibition, which is conclusively unlawful, or there has not. This means that the interpretation through which the content of the prohibition is concretized, which we might label the 'specification' of the standard, takes centre stage.[26] Specification determines the substantive scope of the absolute prohibition and has implications for a legal standard's capacity to guide behaviour. It is also an exercise which, unless undertaken in earnest good faith and in pursuit of arriving at and applying a principled understanding of the sorts of wrongs proscribed therein, can operate to displace the prohibition through the 'back door'.[27] As Jeremy Waldron instructively puts it:

> We are certainly not permitted to follow . . . a realist logic proceeding on the basis of modus tollens:
>
> 1. If X is inhuman then X is prohibited;
> 2. But because X is necessary [or widely popular and/or politically advantageous], it is unthinkable that X should be prohibited;
>
> therefore,
>
> 3. X cannot be regarded as inhuman.[28]

The content and demands of the prohibition are continually being specified by the bodies tasked with interpreting and applying it. A degree of fragmentation in the understanding of what amounts to torture or ill-treatment can be observed across different international legal regimes, along several axes, including for example whether State involvement is required for torture to be made out.[29] Nonetheless, the UN Torture Rapporteur has distilled the conceptual essence of the wrong of torture as being the deliberate infliction of pain or suffering on a person in someone's control for a particular purpose.[30] Usually, this purpose necessitates such pain or suffering to be experienced in a particularly physically and/or psychologically debilitating manner, in order to subvert the person's will.[31]

[25] UNGA 'Interim Report of the Special Rapporteur on Torture and Other Cruel, Inhuman or Degrading Treatment or Punishment' (20 July 2018) UN Doc A/73/207, para 48.

[26] Mavronicola, 'What is an "Absolute Right"?' (n 24) 739. For a critical take, see Stijn Smet, 'The "Absolute" Prohibition of Torture and Inhuman or Degrading Treatment in Article 3: Truly a Question of Scope Only?' in Eva Brems/Janneke Gerards (eds), *Shaping Rights in the ECHR: The Role of the European Court of Human Rights in Determining the Scope of Human Rights* (CUP 2014).

[27] Mavronicola, 'A Reply to Steven Greer' (n 24) 494.

[28] Jeremy Waldron, *Torture, Terror, and Trade-offs* (OUP 2012) 297.

[29] Nigel S Rodley, 'The Definition(s) of Torture in International Law' (2002) 55 Current Legal Problems 467.

[30] Report A/73/207 (n 25) para 7. But note that a discriminatory motivation can also make up the 'purposive' element of torture: see UNCAT (n 10) art 1.

[31] See David Sussman, 'What's Wrong with Torture?' (2005) 33 Philosophy and Public Affairs 1.

It is impossible to provide a comprehensive enumeration of the forms that torture and ill-treatment might take, but it is important to recognize that they cover substantial terrain: besides the interrogational torture scenario which may be viewed as paradigmatic (involving the infliction of suffering on someone for the purpose of extracting information from them which they are unwilling to share), torture, cruelty, inhumanity, and degradation can take a vast variety of forms,[32] ranging from police violence to detention of disabled persons in settings which are not adequately tailored to their condition, to the denial of access to vital reproductive care.[33]

2. The Prohibition of Assassination

The twentieth century saw international law coalesce against the arbitrary infliction of irreparable harm, most significantly the taking of life. It saw a proliferation of legal standards and institutional mechanisms aimed at protecting life, with the elaboration of stringent negative and positive obligations emanating from the right to life under human rights law, stringent standards on the legality of use of force, including the use of force between States, and an increasing focus on humanity over military necessity in the law regulating armed conflict.[34] Article 3 UDHR provided that '[e]veryone has the right to life, liberty and security of person', and the right to life has subsequently been enshrined in various human rights instruments, such as Article 6 ICCPR, Article 2 ECHR, Article 4 ACHPR, and Article 4 ACHR. The prohibition of murder and extrajudicial execution is also included in Common Article 3 of the Geneva Conventions, reflecting 'elementary considerations of humanity'.[35]

Instruments which focus on suppressing particular ways in which human life is destroyed or endangered include the 1948 Convention on the Prevention and Punishment of the Crime of Genocide[36] and the 1998 Rome Statute for the International Criminal Court,[37] as well as a range of norms of international humanitarian law enshrined in the 1949 Geneva Conventions[38] and the 1977 Additional Protocols.[39] These instruments are similarly complemented by relevant jurisprudence,[40] as well as a range of soft law

[32] For example, the non-exhaustive list in Cordula Droege, '"In Truth the leitmotiv": The Prohibition of Torture and Other Forms of Ill-Treatment in International Humanitarian Law' (2007) 89 International Review of the Red Cross 515, 537–8.

[33] On the denial of reproductive care, see UNHRC 'Views adopted by the Committee under Article 5(4) of the Optional Protocol, concerning communication No 2324/2013' (*Mellet v Ireland*) (17 November 2016) UN Doc CCPR/C/116/D/2324/2013. On the detention of persons with disabilities, see further, Manfred H Nowak/Adriana Zarraluqui, 'When Detainees have a Disability: Their Rights and Fundamental Freedoms (2009) 5 International Journal of Prisoner Health 113, esp 119–23. On the extra-custodial use of force by law enforcement officials, see UNGA 'Report of the Special Rapporteur on Torture and Other Cruel, Inhuman or Degrading Treatment or Punishment' (20 July 2017) UN Doc A/72/178.

[34] Christof Heyns/Sarah Knuckey, 'The Long-Term International Law Implications of Targeted Killing Practices' (2013) 54 Harvard International Law Journal 101, 101–2.

[35] See n 7. [36] 78 UNTS 277. [37] See n 8. [38] See n 6.

[39] 1125 UNTS 3 (Additional Protocol I) and 1125 UNTS 609 (Additional Protocol II).

[40] eg Ilias Bantekas/Lutz Oette, *International Human Rights Law and Practice* (CUP 2016) 340–53.

instruments, such as the Principles on the Effective Prevention and Investigation of Extra-legal, Arbitrary, and Summary Executions,[41] CCLEO, BPUFF, and the Minnesota Protocol on the Investigation of Potentially Unlawful Death.[42] A range of institutional mechanisms have been established or mobilized to safeguard human life, notably the UN Special Rapporteur on extrajudicial, summary, or arbitrary executions, whose mandate includes all violations of the right to life as guaranteed by international human rights law, and is universal and independent of treaty ratification.[43]

While the supreme importance of human life has been duly recognized,[44] the killing of human persons is not absolutely proscribed at international law.[45] Life can be lawfully taken in certain circumstances, which are delimited in distinct ways under different legal paradigms. Leaving aside, for present purposes, the contested issue of the legality of the death penalty,[46] even international human rights law, under which the right to life is non-derogable, restricts the prohibition on killing to proscribing the '*arbitrary*' deprivation of life.[47]

The discussion here will focus on a particular category of unlawful killing: assassination. Traditionally, 'assassination' was associated with politically motivated illegal killings,[48] or, in wartime, the targeted killing of a person by treacherous means.[49] Today, it is often taken to capture wider circumstances of the unlawful deployment of deliberately lethal force against targeted persons.

Significant efforts have been made to address a particularly cruel practice targeting persons considered to be 'enemies of the State' and variations thereof, often culminating in killing: enforced disappearances. The 2006 International Convention for the Protection of All Persons from Enforced Disappearance marked a concerted international mobilization against enforced disappearances, and the prohibition is today considered to have attained *jus cogens* status.[50] Sustained human rights litigation on enforced

[41] ECOSOC 'Effective Prevention and Investigation of Extra-Legal, Arbitrary and Summary Executions' Res 1989/65 (24 May 1989).

[42] OHCHR, *The Minnesota Protocol on the Investigation of Potentially Unlawful Death (2016)* (UN 2017).

[43] On the mandate, see <https://www.ohchr.org/en/issues/executions/pages/srexecutionsindex.aspx> accessed 21 May 2020.

[44] UNHRC 'General Comment No 6: Article 6 (Right to Life)' (30 April 1982) UN Doc CCPR/C/21/Add.1 (GC 6).

[45] Bertrand G Ramcharan, 'The Concept and Dimensions of the Right to Life' in Bertrand G Ramcharan (ed), *The Right to Life in International Law* (Martinus Nijhoff 1985) 15; Nils Melzer, *Targeted Killing in International Law* (OUP 2008) 91.

[46] But see Report A/73/207 (n 25) para 43; and see, generally, Roger Hood/Carolyn Hoyle, *The Death Penalty: A Worldwide Perspective* (5th edn, OUP 2015). The death penalty is now considered to violate the ECHR in all circumstances—see *Al Saadoon and Mufdhi v UK*, App No 61498/08, 2 March 2010.

[47] UNGA 'Report of the Special Rapporteur on Extrajudicial, Summary or Arbitrary Executions' (23 May 2011) UN Doc A/HRC/17/28, para 44.

[48] See the US approach to this, discussed in Michael N Schmitt, 'State-Sponsored Assassination in International and Domestic Law' (1992) 17 Yale Journal of International Law 610; and Melzer (n 45) 45–51.

[49] Schmitt (n 48) 632.

[50] 2716 UNTS 3. Jeremy Sarkin, 'Why the Prohibition of Enforced Disappearance Has Attained Jus Cogens Status in International Law' (2012) 81 Nordic Journal of International Law 537.

disappearances has also illuminated an important interconnection between the right to life and the right not to be subjected to torture or ill-treatment, with close relatives of disappeared persons having been found to have been subjected to ill-treatment where the State has forcibly disappeared their loved ones and/or shown callous disregard to their relatives' plight in the context of their disappearance.[51]

We must turn to 'targeted killings' to be apprised of the contours of contemporary assassination, understood thus as *unlawful* targeted killing. For this purpose, Nils Melzer's definition of 'targeted killing' will be adopted: 'the use of lethal force attributable to a subject of international law with the intent, premeditation and deliberation to kill individually selected persons who are not in the physical custody of those targeting them.'[52]

Targeted killings have gradually transitioned from being seen as illegal, or 'half-legal,'[53] and illegitimate, to being considered a legitimate means of conducting 'surgical'[54] warfare and countering terrorism.[55] This legitimation can partly be attributed to a sanitization by terminology: the label 'targeted killing' and its grounding in national security or counter-terrorism narratives or attenuated accounts of 'self-defence' can serve to distinguish such killings, at least rhetorically, from the traditional understanding of assassinations, which seem more readily to provoke condemnation.[56] While the rhetoric of legitimation has grown in the context of the global, or at least hegemonic, securitization of the persons (allegedly) targeted, particularly in the context of counter-terrorism,[57] international law itself permits targeted killings only in very narrow circumstances. It is instructive to approach the legality of targeted killings along two axes: under the law enforcement paradigm; and under the conduct of hostilities paradigm.[58] The following analysis concerns killings by State agents.

Under the law enforcement paradigm, the use of (potentially) lethal force is only lawful in narrow circumstances, generally where it is no more than absolutely necessary to protect human life or bodily integrity from serious threat. Killings that result from the

[51] eg *Serrano-Cruz Sisters v El Salvador* (Merits, Reparations and Costs Judgment) Inter-American Court of Human Rights Ser C No 120 (1 March 2003); *Varnava and others v Turkey*, App Nos 16,064/90, 16,065/90, 16,066/90, 16,068/90, 16,069/90, 16,070/90, 16,071/90, 16,072/90 and 16,073/90, 18 September 2009; see further, Alexander Murray, 'Enforced Disappearance and Relatives' Rights before the Inter-American and European Human Rights Courts' (2013) 2 International Human Rights Law Review 57.

[52] Melzer (n 45) 5. [53] ibid 9.

[54] The operation resulting in the killing of Osama Bin Laden, for example, was described as a 'surgical raid', see The White House, 'Press Briefing by Senior Administration Officials on the Killing of Osama bin Laden' (*Office of the Press Secretary*, 2 May 2011) <https://obamawhitehouse.archives.gov/the-press-office/2011/05/02/press-briefing-senior-administration-officials-killing-osama-bin-laden> accessed 25 July 2019.

[55] Melzer (n 45) 9. See also Susanne Krasmann, 'Targeted Killing and Its Law: On a Mutually Constitutive Relationship' (2012) 25 Leiden Journal of International Law 665.

[56] Krasmann (n 55) 665.

[57] See Michael C Williams, 'Words, Images, Enemies: Securitization and International Politics' (2003) 47 International Studies Quarterly 511.

[58] This is adopted in Melzer (n 45) and reflects the approach taken in a range of relevant materials, including Geneva Academy of International Humanitarian Law and Human Rights, *Use of Force in Law Enforcement and the Right to Life: The Role of the Human Rights Council* (Geneva Academy 2016).

use of force that exceeds what is absolutely, or strictly, necessary in the circumstances are considered 'arbitrary' and therefore unlawful. The term 'arbitrary' is found in Article 6 ICCPR, which provides that 'No one shall be arbitrarily deprived of his life'.[59] Explicit reference to the 'absolute necessity' test is made in Article 2(2) ECHR. 'Absolute necessity' is a demanding standard—it is more stringent than the 'necessary in a democratic society' criterion applicable to infringements upon rights such as privacy or freedom of expression.[60] It entails that such force can only be used as a last resort—if the threat can be otherwise neutralized then the use of (potentially) lethal force will not be considered lawful.[61] The principles applicable to the use of (potentially lethal) force are:

Sufficient legal basis: It must have a legal basis and pursue a lawful purpose.

Necessity: It must only be used when and to the extent it is absolutely necessary to achieve such lawful purpose.

Proportionality: The harm likely to be inflicted by the use of force must not be excessive compared to the benefit of the lawful purpose pursued.

Precaution: All practically possible precautions must be taken to minimize the likelihood of potentially lethal force becoming necessary, and, whenever use of force is strictly unavoidable, to minimize the harm caused.[62]

The application of these criteria to *deliberately* lethal force against a specific person or persons translates into a very narrow window of legality: deliberately lethal force can only be used when strictly unavoidable in order to protect human life from unlawful attack.[63] This renders unlawful any blanket shoot-to-kill policies,[64] as well as targeted killings in circumstances that do not render lethal force indispensable. For example, where the threat is attenuated rather than immediate, or where alternative means of averting such threat can be employed, or if the overall operation was not planned and overseen in such a way as to minimize the use of (potentially) lethal force,[65] targeted killings will be unlawful.

Conflict can fundamentally realign the normative framework, bringing to the fore the 'law of hostilities'.[66] The law of hostilities expands the window of legality but nonetheless imposes substantial constraints on targeted killing. Under the law of hostilities, the legality of using force is delineated by the principles of distinction, proportionality, and precaution, with the overarching standard of military necessity being both permissive and restrictive: permissive of action which is indispensable for achieving a legitimate

[59] For this wording, see also ACHR (n 4) art 4(1); ACHPR (n 5) art 4. On the contours of arbitrary killing, see UNHRC, 'General Comment No 36 (2018) on Article 6 of the International Covenant on Civil and Political Rights, on the Right to Life' (30 October 2018) UN Doc CCPR/C/GC/36, para 12 (GC 36).

[60] See *McCann v UK*, App No 18984/91, 27 September 1995, para 149.

[61] Melzer (n 45) 59. On absolute necessity, see Melzer (n 45) 115 fn 140, 227–9.

[62] See further, UN Human Rights Council 'Report of the Special Rapporteur on Extrajudicial, Summary or Arbitrary Executions' (1 April 2014) UN Doc A/HRC/26/36, paras 55–73; Stuart Casey-Maslen/Sean Connolly, *Police Use of Force under International Law* (CUP 2017) ch 3.

[63] Melzer (n 45) 233.

[64] eg UNCHR 'Report of the Special Rapporteur on Extrajudicial, Summary or Arbitrary Executions' (8 March 2006) UN Doc E/CN.4/2006/53, paras 45–54.

[65] GC 36 (n 59) paras 12–13.

[66] Melzer (n 45) ch 10.

military purpose and simultaneously prohibitive of force which is not indispensable[67] to achieve a legitimate military purpose.[68] In particular, in order to be lawful under the law of hostilities, a targeted killing must, on Melzer's sharp distillation of the relevant legal parameters:

- constitute 'an integral part of the conduct of hostilities';
- take place in a situation of international or non-international armed conflict;
- be 'likely to contribute effectively to the achievement of a concrete and direct military advantage without there being an equivalent non-lethal alternative';
- be 'directed against an individual not entitled to protection against direct attack';
- not 'be expected to inflict incidental death, injury or destruction on persons or objects protected against direct attack', which would be 'excessive' as against the military advantage to be achieved;
- be 'planned and conducted so as to avoid erroneous targeting, as well as to avoid, and in any event to minimize, the incidental infliction of death, injury and destruction on persons and objects protected against direct attack';
- be halted 'when the targeted individual surrenders or otherwise falls *hors de combat*';
- 'not be conducted by undercover forces feigning non-combatant status or otherwise by resort to perfidy', meaning action which invites the trust of an adversary in respect of the adversary's entitlement or duty to provide protection under international humanitarian law, carried out with intent to betray that trust; and
- not be conducted by resort to poison or weapons which are prohibited under international humanitarian law.[69]

This is a formidable set of cumulative criteria for legality, which are often not met in the contemporary practice of counterterrorist targeted killings in particular.[70] Targeted killings that do not fulfil these criteria amount to assassinations and are unlawful under international law.

It also bears emphasizing that the law of hostilities does not govern every situation within an armed conflict; rather, it encompasses the rules applicable to the conduct of military operations[71] against an adversary by a party to such conflict.[72] The law of hostilities only displaces the law enforcement paradigm where armed confrontations amount to 'hostilities' within the meaning of international humanitarian law and force

[67] See further, William G Downey Jr, 'The Law of War and Military Necessity' (1953) 47 AJIL 251.

[68] Melzer (n 45) 286–9; see, also, Henri Meyrowitz, 'The Principle of Superfluous Injury or Unnecessary Suffering: From the Declaration of St. Petersburg of 1868 to Additional Protocol 1 of 1977' (1994) 34 International Review of the Red Cross 98, 116.

[69] Melzer (n 45) 419, and chs 10–14 more broadly.

[70] Even commentators who support targeted killing in contexts that might not fulfil all the criteria set out by Melzer often find contemporary practice to be too loosely constrained—see eg Amos N Guiora, 'Targeted Killing: When Proportionality Gets all out of Proportion' (2012) 45 Case Western Reserve Journal of International Law 235.

[71] ICRC, *Handbook on International Rules Governing Military Operations* (ICRC 2013) para 2.3.1.1.

[72] Melzer (n 45) 275.

is being directed against a legitimate military target, based on the principle of *lex specialis generalibus derogat*.[73] The narrower criteria for the legality of lethal force applicable under the law enforcement paradigm subsist as *lex generalis*, and capture all residual situations in armed conflict where the use of force is not governed by the law of hostilities.[74]

C. Recent Developments and Contemporary Challenges

1. Recent Developments

The contours of the prohibition of torture and ill-treatment have, for many years, been a site of fruitful engagement and contestation, which has been conducive to elucidating the wrongs at issue. Research, experience, and mobilization by victims, human rights defenders and other bodies, both in a proactive fashion and in response to bad faith attempts to circumvent the prohibition, have helped illuminate the various forms the wrongs of torture and related ill-treatment can take. For example, psychological or mental suffering, whether inflicted intentionally and purposefully to break a person,[75] and/or as an effect of certain, often pervasive, practices such as solitary confinement,[76] has received increasing attention. Unfortunately, this process of illumination has often gone hand in hand with the growing 'refinement' of techniques to break persons, with many States favouring methods which are more difficult to detect,[77] focusing especially on causing psychological anguish, disorientation, or even 'learned helplessness', with techniques including mock executions, attacks on personal, religious, and cultural sensibilities, and cumulative methods involving the accumulation of what might otherwise be seen as minor annoyances and humiliations.[78]

[73] ibid 277.

[74] Gloria Gaggioli, 'Remoteness and Human Rights Law' in Jens D Ohlin (ed), *Research Handbook on Remote Warfare* (Edward Elgar 2017) 173–5.

[75] See, amongst others, Pau Pérez-Sales, *Psychological Torture: Definition, Evaluation and Measurement* (Routledge 2016); Hernán Reyes, 'The Worst Scars are in the Mind: Psychological Torture' (2007) 89 International Review of the Red Cross 591.

[76] eg UNGA 'Report of the Special Rapporteur on Torture and Other Cruel, Inhuman or Degrading Treatment or Punishment' (5 August 2011) UN Doc A/66/268; Elizabeth Vasiliades, 'Solitary Confinement and International Human Rights: Why the U.S. Prison System Fails Global Standards' (2005) 21 American University International Law Review 71.

[77] The ECtHR has expressed its concerns on this: '[D]ue regard must be had to the special difficulties in proving allegations of torture. Torture is (…) practiced in secret, often by experienced interrogators who are skilled at ensuring that it leaves no visible signs on the victim (…)', see *Othman (Abu Qatada) v UK*, App No 8139/09, 17 January 2012, para 276.

[78] See Rodley/Pollard (n 17) 103. See also John T Parry, 'The Shape of Modern Torture: Extraordinary Rendition and Ghost Detainees' (2005) 6 Melbourne Journal of International Law 516, 525; Reyes (n 75) especially 612.

The past decades have seen a growing focus on gender-based violence and on States' obligations to take measures to prevent and redress it.[79] This development has been spearheaded by the valuable critical work of feminist scholars, jurists, and activists who have challenged hegemonically distorted or skewed perceptions of the nature and domains of torture and ill-treatment, and confronted patriarchal norms such as the public–private divide, thus pushing norm-appliers to see torture and ill-treatment 'beyond the paradigmatic'[80] or indeed to shift the paradigms themselves.[81] Besides these transformative insights, which take the anti-torture norm beyond the traditional security-centred or securitized domains, there is increasing recognition by relevant international actors that fighting gender-based torture and ill-treatment requires closer linkages and synergies with other legal frameworks, notably those focused on combating discrimination.[82]

Another domain in which important insights are crystallizing and feeding into (our understanding of) the legal framework on torture and ill-treatment is States' extra-custodial use of force, which can be understood as the use of force by State agents outside the context of detention. While the key preventive mechanisms such as the SPT, CPT (European Committee on the Prevention of Torture), and NPMs are, in principle, mandated to engage in torture prevention only in places of deprivation of liberty,[83] the relevance of the prohibition of torture and ill-treatment to the extra-custodial use of force is confirmed by a body of jurisprudence of international and regional tribunals and other oversight bodies. For example, in *Rosendo Cantú et al v Mexico*, the Inter-American Court of Human Rights (IACtHR) found that 'rape may constitute torture even when it (…) takes place outside State facilities,'[84] while the CAT has repeatedly highlighted extra-custodial State brutality in its reports.[85] In *Cestaro v Italy* and *Bartesaghi Gallo and Others v Italy*, the ECtHR found that violence against a number of anti-globalization protestors for the purpose of intimidating, humiliating, or punishing them amounted to

[79] eg UNGA 'Report of the Special Rapporteur on Torture and Other Cruel, Inhuman or Degrading Treatment or Punishment' (5 January 2016) UN Doc A/HRC/31/57; also, Alice Edwards, *Violence against Women under International Human Rights Law* (CUP 2011) ch 5.

[80] Clare McGlynn, 'Rape, Torture and the European Convention on Human Rights' (2009) 58 ICLQ 565, 594.

[81] Edwards (n 79) chs 2 and 5. See also Lisa Davis, 'The Gendered Dimensions of Torture: Rape and Other Forms of Gender-Based Violence as Torture Under International Law' in Metin Başoğlu (ed), *Torture and Its Definition In International Law: An Interdisciplinary Approach* (OUP 2017).

[82] See eg Report A/73/207 (n 25).

[83] Arts 1 and 4 OPCAT (n 19) arts 1 and 4; European Convention for the Prevention of Torture and Inhuman or Degrading Treatment or Punishment ETS No 126 (ECPT) art 1.

[84] *Rosendo Cantú et al v Mexico* (Merits, Reparations, Costs) Inter-American Court of Human Rights Ser C No 216 (31 August 2010) para 118.

[85] eg UNGA 'Report of the Committee against Torture' (26 July 1995) UN Doc A/50/44 (Supp No 44) para 126; CAT 'Concluding Observations on the Combined Third and Fourth Periodic Reports of the Bolivarian Republic of Venezuela' (12 December 2014) UN Doc CAT/C/VEN/CO/3-4, para 12; CAT 'Concluding Observations on the Combined Third to Fifth Periodic Reports of the Republic of Korea' (11 May 2017) CAT/C/KOR/CO/3–5, para 13.

torture.[86] In 2017, the UN Torture Rapporteur produced a thematic report clarifying the application of the prohibition of torture and ill-treatment to the extra-custodial use of force.[87] A key element of the report is the finding that extra-custodial uses of force that do not comply with the standards of legality, necessity, and proportionality will likely amount to proscribed ill-treatment and, in some instances, may amount to torture;[88] another is the identification of a duty to regulate and review the development, acquisition, trade, and use of weapons and other means of deploying force,[89] including so-called 'less-lethal' weapons.[90]

The normative framework aimed at safeguarding persons from irreparable harm has also seen a renewed and growing impetus towards effective prevention, with prevention-orientated institutional oversight placed at the forefront of the fight against torture and ill-treatment especially. The European Convention for the Prevention of Torture and Inhuman or Degrading Treatment or Punishment,[91] for example, has seen the CPT conduct vital preventive work in places of deprivation of liberty over several years.[92] The OPCAT has played a decisive role in internationalizing this endeavour,[93] with the SPT undertaking preventive oversight in places of custody but also shaping domestic preventive efforts.[94] Moreover, the ongoing process of instituting and bolstering effective NPMs in signatory States, if neither universal nor without flaws, has enjoyed a degree of momentum.[95] As concerns the right to life, the revised 2016 UN Manual on the Effective Prevention and Investigation of Extra-Legal, Arbitrary, and Summary Executions (the Minnesota Protocol) now constitutes a vital tool towards accountability for unlawful killings. Compliance with its demands not only allows redress to be offered in respect of particular incidents, but can also lead to the identification and implementation of safeguards towards non-recurrence and prevention more broadly.

An important recent development in respect of the right to life is the Human Rights Committee's General Comment No 36, which clarifies the prohibition of the arbitrary

[86] *Cestaro v Italy*, App No 6884/11, 7 April 2015, paras 170–90; *Bartesaghi Gallo and Others v Italy*, App Nos 12131/13 and 43390/13, 22 June 2017, paras 114, 117.

[87] Report A/72/178 (n 33). See also UNGA, 'Joint Report of the Special Rapporteur on the Rights to Freedom of Peaceful Assembly and of Association and the Special Rapporteur on Extrajudicial, Summary or Arbitrary Executions on the Proper Management of Assemblies' (4 February 2016) UN Doc A/HRC/31/66. See further, Human Rights Council 'The Promotion and Protection of Human Rights in the Context of Peaceful Protests' (28 March 2014) UN Doc A/HRC/RES/25/38 and Human Rights Council 'The Promotion and Protection of Human Rights in the Context of Peaceful Protests' (24 March 2016) UN Doc A/HRC/RES/31/37.

[88] Report A/72/178 (n 33) para 62.

[89] ibid paras 58–61.

[90] On 'less lethal' weapons, Omega Research Foundation and Amnesty International, *The Human Rights Impact of Less Lethal Weapons and other Law Enforcement Equipment* (Amnesty International 2015).

[91] ECPT (n 83).

[92] On the work of the CPT, see Rodney Morgan/Malcolm Evans, *Combating Torture in Europe: The Work and Standards of the European Committee for the Prevention of Torture (CPT)* (Council of Europe 2001).

[93] See Murray et al (n 20).

[94] Elina Steinerte, 'The Changing Nature of the Relationship between the United Nations Subcommittee on Prevention of Torture and National Preventive Mechanisms: In Search for Equilibrium' (2013) 31 Netherlands Quarterly of Human Rights 129.

[95] See further, Murray et al (n 20) ch 6.

deprivation of life, the duty to protect life, the implications of the right to life in relation to the death penalty, the relationship between the right to life and other rights, and the duties surrounding the development, acquisition, and use of certain technologies and weapons capable of destroying or jeopardizing human life, including autonomous weapons.[96] While it does not definitively resolve all contentious matters—for instance, it proceduralizes the question of the legality of autonomous weapons[97]—it provides a considerably more extensive statement of the law than the previous relevant General Comments.[98]

2. Contemporary Challenges

While it is impossible to do so comprehensively, the discussion below considers some of the predominant contemporary challenges to the relevant norms.

a. *Implementation*

The perennial challenge to protecting persons against institutionalized inhumanity is the enduring chasm between rhetorical commitment to the demands of international law and the practical and political will to adhere to them. Many States have not expressly or adequately criminalized torture and lack provisions for the exercise of universal jurisdiction and the pursuit of redress without undue impediments.[99] States often fail to guarantee effective investigation, accountability, reparation, and rehabilitation in respect of instances of torture and ill-treatment.[100] There are widespread deficiencies in providing victims of torture with rehabilitation services.[101] Moreover, in spite of the progressive legal recognition of such harms as falling within the ambit of the anti-torture norm, there are chronic failings across most States in preventing racist and gender-based violence, including through an overhaul of repressive or disempowering legal regimes.[102]

[96] See GC 36 (n 59). [97] ibid para 65.

[98] GC 6 (n 44) and UNHRC 'General Comment No 14: Article 6 (Right to Life)—Nuclear Weapons and the Right to Life' (9 November 1984).

[99] REDRESS, *Justice for Torture Worldwide: Law, Practice and Agendas for Change* (Redress 2013). In relation to explicit criminalization, see UNGA 'Report of the Special Rapporteur on Torture and Other Cruel, Inhuman or Degrading Treatment or Punishment (Addendum)' (5 February 2010) UN Doc A/HRC/13/39/Add.5, paras 48–9. In relation to universal jurisdiction, see UNGA 'Report of the Special Rapporteur on Torture and Other Cruel, Inhuman or Degrading Treatment or Punishment' (15 January 2007) UN Doc A/HRC/4/33, paras 41–7.

[100] UNGA 'Interim Report of the Special Rapporteur on Torture and Other Cruel, Inhuman or Degrading Treatment or Punishment' (10 August 2010) UN Doc A/65/273, para 90; Report (Addendum) A/HRC/13/39/Add.5 (n 99) para 174.

[101] Report (Addendum) A/HRC/13/39/Add.5 (n 99) paras 167–85.

[102] See, *inter alia*, UNGA 'Report of the Special Rapporteur on Torture and Other Cruel, Inhuman or Degrading Treatment or Punishment' (9 February 2010) UN Doc A/HRC/13/39, para 62; UNGA 'Report of the Special Rapporteur on Torture and Other Cruel, Inhuman or Degrading Treatment or Punishment' (15 January 2008) UN Doc A/HRC/7/3, paras 44–58; Report A/HRC/31/57 (n 79) para 73.

Furthermore, while experts have highlighted the significance of operational safeguards, such as access to a lawyer and doctor,[103] towards preventing torture and ill-treatment, particularly in the first hours of custody,[104] such safeguards are too often absent or merely nominal. Their effective operation is often critically undermined by well-founded fear of reprisals,[105] delays,[106] or other impediments.

Across the world, many States fail to comply with, or actively seek to circumvent or undermine, their *non-refoulement* duties,[107] including through collective expulsion of migrants in irregular situations, through States' externalization of their borders and procedures, and through extra-territorial 'pushback' and 'pullback' operations, often in cooperation with other States or non-State actors.[108] Recently, both the Torture Rapporteur and the Rapporteur on extrajudicial, summary, or arbitrary executions issued damning condemnations of many States' practices in respect of migrants in irregular situations, including refugees and asylum seekers, whose plight has been distorted by the securitization of migration,[109] and of the resulting humanitarian crisis characterized by widespread unlawful deaths and exposure to torture and ill-treatment suffered by persons worldwide, solely on account of their migration status.[110]

Finally, the implementation of both the prohibition of torture and ill-treatment and the law in respect of the use of deliberately lethal force against targeted persons is plagued by transparency and accountability gaps, including through the operation of blanket immunities or limitation periods,[111] or as a product of the secrecy which particularly characterizes security operations in which such practices often occur.[112] What results is a vicious cycle of disregard for the legal framework,[113] which jeopardizes the

[103] Further, Rodley/Pollard (n 17) ch 11.

[104] Richard Carver/Lisa Handley, *Does Torture Prevention Work?* (Liverpool UP 2016) ch 3. See also *Kurt v Turkey*, App No 24276/94, 25 May 1998, para 123.

[105] eg Report A/HRC/13/39 (n 102) para 49; Report A/HRC/31/57 (n 79) para 35.

[106] eg Report (Addendum) A/HRC/13/39/Add.5 (n 99) para 86.

[107] eg REDRESS, *Torture in Asia: The Law and Practice* (Redress 2013) 19; REDRESS, *Legal Frameworks to Prevent Torture in Africa: Best Practices, Shortcomings and Options Going Forward* (2016) 37.

[108] See further, UNGA 'Report of the Special Rapporteur on Torture and Other Cruel, Inhuman or Degrading Treatment or Punishment' (26 February 2018) UN Doc A/HRC/37/50, paras 38–59.

[109] Philippe Bourbeau, *The Securitization of Migration: A Study of Movement and Order* (Routledge 2011).

[110] UNGA 'Report of the Special Rapporteur on Extrajudicial, Summary or Arbitrary Executions' (15 August 2017) UN Doc A/72/335; and Report A/HRC/37/50 (n 108) paras 38–59.

[111] Report A/73/207 (n 25) paras 22–3, 57; and eg UNGA 'Report of the Special Rapporteur on Extrajudicial, Summary or Arbitrary Executions (28 April 2014) UN Doc A/HRC/26/36/Add.1; see also Hannah Russell, *The Use of Force and Article 2 of the ECHR in Light of European Conflicts* (Hart Publishing 2017) ch 9.

[112] eg Report E/CN.4/2006/53 (n 64) para 37 (and footnotes).

[113] See Philip Alston, 'The CIA and Targeted Killings Beyond Borders' (2011) 2 Harvard National Security Journal 283; Carver/Handley (n 104) ch 3.

bodily and mental integrity of persons who find themselves on the wrong side of the 'friend–enemy' divide that broadly marks this domain.[114]

b. *Interpretation*

In the context of counter-terrorism in particular, and notably after 9/11, the notion that torture may be permissible or even necessary in a 'ticking bomb' situation has intermittently entered mainstream political and even academic debate, usually involving variations of short-sighted, and often security-driven, consequentialist reasoning, or sheer disregard for the rights of 'others'.[115] The ticking bomb scenario, and an increased preoccupation with security, has exposed a readiness in some quarters to imagine States' positive obligations, which have been vital in placing effective protection and prevention at the heart of human rights law, as demanding rights-infringing action—even demanding the infliction of torture in order to save lives.[116] In relation to the prohibition of torture, this has largely been resisted.[117] With the absolute character of the prohibition of torture remaining firm in the face of this debate, other methods have been employed to bypass it, notably through attempts to re-define the terms of the norm itself, or simply through the denial that certain torturous or cruel, inhuman, or degrading practices constitute torture or related ill-treatment. Such manoeuvres have included attempts to narrow the substantive scope of the norm, for example through requiring grave injury or long-term harm in order for torture or other ill-treatment to be established,[118] and blunting the inhumanity of coercive interrogation methods through terms such as 'enhanced interrogation'.[119] While such definitional contortions in no way alter the illegality, under international law, of such practices, they continue to be employed to give cruel, inhuman, degrading, or torturous practices the colour of law.

The anti-assassination norm has also been the subject of multiple interpretive manoeuvres, not least efforts to stretch beyond their limit or simply to circumvent the cumulative criteria that render targeted killing lawful. For instance, the twenty-first century has seen a push by the US towards recognizing a 'third' category of armed conflict, encompassing the global 'War on Terror'.[120] This has occurred even though there is little basis on which to assert a legal category besides 'international armed conflict' and 'non-international armed conflict', and every reason to reject such category—which, to boot,

[114] See, in this regard, the critical examination of the concept of terrorism in Jörg Friedrichs, 'Defining the International Public Enemy: The Political Struggle behind the Legal Debate on International Terrorism' (2006) 19 Leiden Journal of International Law 69.

[115] See the helpful overview in Michelle Farrell, *The Prohibition of Torture in Exceptional Circumstances* (CUP 2013); also Natasa Mavronicola, 'Torture and Othering' in Benjamin Goold/Liora Lazarus (eds), *Security and Human Rights* (2nd edn, Hart Publishing 2019).

[116] eg Greer (n 24).

[117] Mavronicola, 'A Reply to Steven Greer' (n 24).

[118] eg the critique in David Luban/Henry Shue, 'Mental Torture: A Critique of Erasures in U.S. Law' (2012) 100 Georgetown Law Journal 823.

[119] Report A/73/207 (n 25) para 45. See the interesting analysis in Jared Del Rosso, *Talking About Torture: How Political Discourse Shapes the Debate* (Columbia UP 2015).

[120] Melzer (n 45) 265.

was put forward while simultaneously denying the applicability of fundamental tenets of international humanitarian law to the 'enemies' involved in such conflict.[121] Importantly, there is reason to fear that substantial mobilization towards accommodating contemporary practices of targeted killing within the parameters of international law will have or is having a corrosive effect on the norms themselves and on the deontic humanity that drives them. Christof Heyns and Sarah Knuckey, for example, have warned of the latitude towards evolving targeted killing practices 'leaving everyone less secure';[122] Jeremy Waldron has highlighted not only the scope for abuse in this expansiveness, but the inherently abusive attitude behind the drive towards greater latitude for 'murder';[123] and Susanne Krasmann has taken the legal reasoning employed towards accommodating contemporary targeted killing practices to illustrate that nothing is fundamentally 'unlegalizable'.[124]

c. *Distribution of Protection/Harm*

There is, of course, no room for contemplating a 'healthy' distribution of assassinations or inflictions of torture or ill-treatment. Nonetheless, insofar as such practices remain, it is imperative to acknowledge who are ultimately the 'haves' and the 'have-nots' of the entitlement to live free from torture, ill-treatment, or assassination. As Malcolm Evans has observed, '[m]ost torture is the result of routine barbarity in systems which just cannot be bothered to address it'.[125] The 'banality'[126] of such barbarity has much to do with the positioning of its 'typical' victims on the margins of society's regard. Victims of torture and ill-treatment, for example, tend to experience vulnerability, marginalization, or even dehumanization not only during, but also prior to and subsequent to experiencing such ill-treatment. Former UN Torture Rapporteur Nigel Rodley put it as follows:

> [W]hen [torture] is part of an institutional practice (...) the victim is—must be—dehumanized, seen as an object. This is the traditional and inevitable means of considering "the enemy" (...) Whatever the group, its members must be stripped of their inherent dignity as human beings in order to mobilise the rest against them.[127]

Torture, ill-treatment, and unconstrained 'liquidation' is predominantly the fate of persons the value of whose life and dignity has already become demoted, usually not solely in the eyes of the perpetrators, but more systemically. This is not new. Studying practices of torture in ancient republics, Darius Rejali has highlighted that it was

[121] ibid 262–9.

[122] Heyns/Knuckey (n 34) 103.

[123] Jeremy Waldron, 'Justifying Targeted Killing with a Neutral Principle?' in Claire Finkelstein et al (eds), *Targeted Killings: Law and Morality in an Asymmetrical World* (OUP 2012).

[124] Krasmann (n 55) 682.

[125] Malcolm D Evans, 'Publication Review: The Prohibition of Torture in Exceptional Circumstances—Michelle Farrell' (2014) 63 ICLQ 507, 508.

[126] I borrow this term from Hannah Arendt: see Hannah Arendt, *Eichmann in Jerusalem: A Report on the Banality of Evil* (Penguin 2006).

[127] Rodley/Pollard (n 17) 14–15.

inflicted 'exclusively on noncitizens: slaves, barbarians and foreigners',[128] while Page DuBois has described it as 'an instrument of demarcation' which delineated 'the boundary between slave and free, between the untouchable bodies of free citizens and the torturable bodies of slaves'.[129] What is more palpable today, however, is that a process of securitization often underpins and informs this systemic or systematic demotion. As the UN Torture Rapporteur recently observed, the construction of 'suspect communities' and concomitant stigmatization, demonization and prejudice 'tend to create "black holes" of legal protection and are almost invariably accompanied by increasing tolerance of and widespread impunity for torture and ill-treatment'.[130]

The distribution of violability is at the heart of war and its laws, where torture and assassination often occur, with the rendering of some bodies—'enemies' or those in their proximity—more expendable than others. While the international legal framework on assassination has evolved since Grotius posited that 'by the law of nature but also by the law of nations (…) it is in fact permissible to kill an enemy in any place whatsoever; and it does not matter how many there are who do the deed, or who suffer',[131] a form of dehumanization of the 'enemy' arguably remains at its core.[132] Importantly, the attenuation of the value of some human lives is augmented in the context of ever more technologically advanced remote warfare,[133] and perhaps materializes most strongly in the advent of autonomous weapons, such as unmanned aerial vehicles, and the prospect that the decision to employ lethal force against a person or persons will be left to be determined by a purely algorithmic process.[134]

Ultimately, the distribution of violence and vulnerability to grave violence is shaped by an array of problematic features of the global and local order.[135] The progressive interpretation of the immediately relevant legal standards, such as the anti-torture norm, is not enough to eradicate the incidence of such wrongs against persons rendered vulnerable by a range of structural and systemic factors, not least the securitization of their bodies or very existence. It is necessary to look beyond the immediately relevant legal framework to establish how some 'bodies' are invariably placed on the front line of grave violations of bodily integrity and a wider structural and systemic endeavour is needed to address the mechanics of disempowerment, dehumanization, and violence

[128] Darius Rejali, *Torture and Democracy* (Princeton UP 2007) 56.

[129] Page DuBois, *Torture and Truth* (Routledge 1991) 63.

[130] Report A/73/207 (n 25) para 62.

[131] Hugo Grotius, *The Law of War and Peace* (1625) book 3, ch 4. For an overview of historical understandings of the normative framework, see Schmitt (n 48) 613–18.

[132] On 'disposable' human lives and 'topographies of cruelty' in different forms of warfare see further, Achille Mbembe, 'Necropolitics' (2003) 15 Public Culture 11; Jamie Allinson, 'The Necropolitics of Drones' (2015) 9 International Political Sociology 113.

[133] See, generally, Jens David Ohlin (ed), *Research Handbook on Remote Warfare* (Edward Elgar 2017).

[134] See the wider concerns set out in Michael Carl Haas/Sophie-Charlotte Fischer, 'The Evolution of Targeted Killing Practices: Autonomous Weapons, Future Conflict, and the International Order' (2017) 38 Contemporary Security Policy 281; see also Christof Heyns, 'Autonomous Weapons in Armed Conflict and the Right to a Dignified Life: An African Perspective' (2017) 33 South African Journal of Human Rights 46.

[135] eg Report A/73/207 (n 25) paras 60–74.

that pervade our societies. In this regard, it is to be hoped that both constructive critique and a progressive (re)interpretation and reshaping of international legal norms can be harnessed to redress the gendered, racialized, and otherwise unjust ways in which the deontic vision of humanity is challenged every day.

D. Outlook

Torture and assassination are two examples of acts that are antithetical to the deontic humanity reflected in the post-Second World War promise of a world order premised on human dignity. The current global landscape, and various ways in which security rhetoric is mobilized therein, offer little cause for complacency in the fight against these wrongs. It is vital for the law to be developed, interpreted, and implemented with renewed vigour in response to challenges old and new, and for sustained efforts to be made to root out inhumanity not only at the level of our force-wielding institutions, but also in the entrenched attitudes, practices, and normative standards which shape our securitized societies and crystallize into untold suffering and irreparable harm for the 'others' amongst us.

CHAPTER 23

MIGRATION, DISPLACEMENT, SECURITY, AND INTERNATIONAL LAW

BEN SAUL

A. Introduction

DESPITE populist alarmism about mass migration, globally the number of migrants has been fairly constant over the past four decades as a proportion of world population—between 2.8 per cent (in 1980) and 3.4 per cent (in 2017, amounting to 258 million people).[1] About two-thirds of international migrants are migrant workers,[2] many of whom—uncontroversially—are encouraged and authorized to move by receiving States keen to fill labour shortages and grow their economies. Unsurprisingly, around two-thirds of international migrants reside in high-income economies,[3] which also tend to be those most concerned about 'irregular' migration and possess the strongest border 'security' regimes to counter it. In addition, there are about 28.5 million refugees and asylum seekers—a record high since the Second World War—and 40 million internally displaced persons.[4] Most of these are hosted in developing States.

[1] Global Migration Data Portal, 'Data' (2019) <https://migrationdataportal.org/data?i=stock_abs_&t=2017> accessed 8 April 2019. On current numbers, data issues and definitions, see IOM, World Migration Report 2018 (IOM 2017) ch 2.

[2] IOM (n 1) 28. [3] ibid 20.

[4] UNHCR, 'Global Trends at a Glance: 2017' <www.unhcr.org/globaltrends2017> accessed 8 April 2019.

In absolute terms, these global numbers are well within the absorptive capacity of the international community. The 'crisis' of displacement is a political and responsibility-shifting one, not one involving a lack of capacity or resources, or any technical difficulty in formulating effective legal rules, coordination mechanisms, or governance institutions. In recent years, irregular migration and forced displacement have become more visible, and moved up the international policy and global cooperation agendas, not so much because of the raw numbers, but because irregular movement has increased to developed States—Europe and North America. In contrast, the 'warehousing' for many decades of many millions of displaced persons in developing countries—from Pakistan and Iran to the African Great Lakes to the Thai/Myanmar border—proved unable to animate comparable international concern.

It is very difficult to measure the prevalence of 'regular' versus 'irregular' migration, not least because States define regularity differently and have very variable capacities to measure it.[5] Perhaps a fifth of global migrants are irregular,[6] with the phenomenon proliferating since the 1980s, due to factors such as economic and other structural drivers, the increased ease of international travel, and the restriction of regular migration pathways into developed States. It concerns States because they have less capacity to control who is entering their territory, for what purposes, and under what conditions.

States and their populations may accordingly express legitimate (as well as illegitimate) security and other concerns about it. Similar anxieties are expressed about refugees, whose initial flight and onward movements are often unplanned. As Germany's reception of 1.4 million refugees from Syria from 2015 to 2018 suggests, even very wealthy and stable democracies have struggled to absorb large influxes in a way that is politically sustainable and preserves social cohesion. State attitudes to migration are often bound up in the inflammatory politics of identity, nationalism, and national security, which may result in virulently restrictive tendencies. In the New York Declaration for Refugees and Migrants in 2016, the UN General Assembly (UNGA) duly expressed concern about 'increasingly xenophobic and racist responses' to refugees and migrants, including religious stereotyping.[7]

The relationship between mass migration, security, and international law is not straightforward. The security implications of migration first depend on *what type of migration* is at issue and what international legal frameworks accordingly apply to it.

[5] See eg UN Economic Commission for Europe, 'Measuring Hard-to-Count Migrant Populations: Importance, Definitions, and Categories' (4 October 2012) Working Paper 9 <https://www.unece.org/fileadmin/DAM/stats/documents/ece/ces/ge.10/2012/WP_9_UNECE.pdf> accessed 21 May 2020; Albert Kraler/David Reichel, 'Measuring Irregular Migration and Population Flows—What Available Data Can Tell' (2011) 49 International Migration 97.

[6] Franck Duvell, 'Irregular Migration' in Alexander Betts (ed), *Global Migration Governance* (OUP 2011) 78 (citing the latest available statistics, from 2006).

[7] New York Declaration for Refugees and Migrants, UNGA Res 71/1 (19 September 2016) (New York Declaration) paras 13–14.

Migration encompasses many different types of movement—from voluntary to forced, to in-between categories such as 'economic migration' driven by poverty, as well as 'mixed flows'.[8] Migration can be individual or involve mass influxes (or 'large movements'[9]); internal or transboundary; regular or irregular (or 'documented' or 'undocumented, or 'lawful' or 'unlawful'); and its causes can be human-made, natural, or a combination of both.

The security implications of migration, and the international legal responses to them, also depend on *how security is defined*—whether as national, international, or 'human' security—a highly contested terrain, as the chapters in Part I of this book discuss. Thus, depending on one's perspective, migrants may be fleeing from conflict (such as the 1.8 million migrants caught up in Libya during the civil war from 2011[10]) or other 'hard' security threats such as terrorism; or they may move because of human insecurity risks, such as human rights violations, poverty, environmental degradation, natural disasters, or climate change.

In addition, the transit of migrants may threaten human security, as it may involve loss of life during perilous journeys at sea or during remote land crossings, and exploitative practices such as enslavement or human trafficking. The 'securitization' of migration in receiving States can itself be a further source of human insecurity, where stronger border protection forces migrants to take more dangerous and expensive routes and to engage exploitative people smugglers, rendering them vulnerable to loss of life, crime and violence, family separation, or trafficking.[11]

Further, migrants or displaced persons may themselves occasionally present hard or soft security threats. For example,[12] they may be radicalized or recruited for violence in displacement camps. They may infiltrate mass flows of people in order to carry out attacks abroad. Even when settled in a foreign country, individual and structural drivers of violent extremism have led to some migrants (and children born in the receiving country) engaging in terrorism or becoming 'foreign terrorist fighters' in conflicts in third countries such as Syria or Iraq. The UN's International Organization for Migration (IOM), however, cautions that:

> the risk is that isolated contemporary incidents, or distant historical examples, are taken out of context and then projected into the future and used as the basis for

[8] ibid para 6.

[9] ibid (defined by the number of people arriving, the economic, social, and geographical context, the capacity of the receiving State to respond, the impact of a movement that is sudden or prolonged, and its irregular nature).

[10] Christine Aghazarm et al, *Migrants Caught in Crisis: The IOM Experience in Libya* (IOM 2012).

[11] Pia Oberoi/Elanor Taylor-Nicholson, 'The Enemy at the Gates: International Borders, Migration and Human Rights' (2013) 2 Laws 169, 173.

[12] The following examples are drawn from IOM, *Report 2018* (n 1) ch 9 ('Migration, Violent Extremism and Social Exclusion').

> sweeping generalizations about the threat that large-scale migration and asylum flows may pose to national and regional security. This may in turn inform policy choices.[13]

Migration and refugee policy accordingly risks being unjustifiably affected by other national or international agendas, such as counter-terrorism or preventing violent extremism.

The 'securitization' of displacement has involved a variety of techniques to strengthen immigration control and border protection.[14] These include pre-screening; visa requirements; carrier sanctions; 'upstream' or extraterritorial controls in countries of origin; country of origin profiling; surveillance (from biometrics to aerial drones) and 'big data';[15] the building of border 'walls'; criminalization of irregular movement (as well as smuggling and trafficking); restrictions on due process and independent review; detention; naval interdiction; offshore processing; temporary protection; lower quality protection statuses; 'safe' third countries or 'internal flight' alternatives; and the use of intelligence, security, and military agencies against the 'threat' of migrants. Such techniques have often overshadowed more structural preventive measures, such as conflict prevention and resolution in source countries, addressing the effects of climate change, or adequately supporting human development in developing States.

International legal frameworks in relation to migration generally are relatively underdeveloped,[16] including in relation to its security dimensions. Instead, a patchwork of international norms (hard and soft), regimes, and institutions apply to different facets of the migration–security nexus. This chapter focuses on the security dimensions (including terrorism) of international laws governing refugees, complementary human rights protection, and due process in the expulsion of aliens (including disclosure of classified information). Along the way the chapter identifies gaps and challenges evident in the existing regimes, and charts contemporary developments through soft law initiatives.

[13] ibid 209.

[14] See eg Oberoi/Taylor-Nicholson (n 11); Idil Atak/Francois Crepeau, 'National Security, Terrorism and the Securitization of Migration' in Vincent Chetail/Celine Bauloz (eds), *Research Handbook on International Law and Migration* (Edward Elgar 2014). A high profile recent example is the restriction of European borders in the face of the Syrian crisis: see eg Antonis Vradis et al, *New Borders: Hotspots and the European Migration Regime* (Pluto Press 2019); Ruben Andersen, *Illegality, Inc.: Clandestine Migration and the Business of Bordering Europe* (University of California Press 2014).

[15] Ben Yahes, 'Migration and Data Protection: Doing No Harm in an Age of Mass Displacement, Mass Surveillance and "Big Data"' (2017) 99 International Review of the Red Cross 179.

[16] For an overview see eg Susan Martin, 'The Legal and Normative Framework of International Migration' (Global Commission on International Migration, September 2005) <https://www.iom.int/jahia/webdav/site/myjahiasite/shared/shared/mainsite/policy_and_research/gcim/tp/TP9.pdf> accessed 28 November 2020; Betts (n 6); IOM (n 1) ch 5; Francois Crepeau et al, 'International Migration: Security Concerns and Human Rights Standards' (2007) 44 Transcultural Psychiatry 311. Outside the scope of this chapter are other legal regimes relevant to the hard or human security aspects of movement, some of which are addressed in other chapters of this *Handbook*, including insurgency (Chapter 9), terrorism (Chapter 11), transnational organized crime (Chapter 12), armed conflict (Chapter 14), human trafficking (Chapter 21), humanitarian relief (Chapter 28), climate change (Chapter 30) and disaster response law (Chapter 31).

B. Lack of an International Migration Law Framework Addressing Security Risks

There is no specialized branch of 'international migration law,'[17] including addressing its security dimensions, in large part because States view immigration and border control, and associated security controls, as core attributes of sovereignty. As such, they are reluctant to cede domestic freedom of action to international legal regulation, at least outside of the few integrated supranational communities guaranteeing free movement such as the European Union. Regulation of a State's population is, indeed, a necessary incident of statehood, and States have long enjoyed a very wide discretion to admit—or refuse to admit—non-citizens.[18] Historically, that discretion has not always been exercised restrictively; migration control only became commonplace as recently as the early twentieth century.[19]

State sovereignty over migration control has been explicitly reaffirmed in recent international policy instruments whose purpose is to encourage greater cooperation—voluntary and non-binding—on irregular migration and displacement, including in the New York Declaration for Refugees and Migrants of 2016 and the Global Compact for Safe, Orderly and Regular Migration 2018.[20] The Declaration duly seeks to 'promote international cooperation on border control and management as an important element of security for States, including issues relating to battling transnational organized crime, terrorism, and illicit trade.'[21] It was also accepted that States 'are entitled to take measures to prevent irregular border crossings'.[22] The Global Compact on Migrants likewise identifies potential for greater cooperation on border control, including pre-screening of arriving persons, pre-reporting by carriers of passengers, and use of information and communication technology.[23] Paradoxically, greater international cooperation on migration and displacement can strengthen, rather than diminish, sovereign control of borders,[24] and unilateral action is not necessarily more effective.

[17] See the discussion in Brian Opeskin et al, 'Conceptualising Migration Law' in Brian Opeskin et al (eds), *Foundations of International Migration Law* (CUP 2015) 1.

[18] See Richard Perruchoud, 'State Sovereignty and Freedom of Movement' in Opeskin et al (n 17) 123.

[19] Catherine Dauverge, 'Irregular Migration, State Sovereignty and the Rule of Law' in Chetail/Bauloz (n 14) 79.

[20] New York Declaration (n 7) para 42; UNGA 'Global Compact for Safe, Orderly and Regular Migration' (13 July 2018) UN Doc A/Conf.231/3, Annex, para 15 (Global Compact on Migration).

[21] New York Declaration (n 7) para 24. [22] ibid.

[23] Global Compact on Migration (n 20) para 27(b).

[24] Susan Martin/Elizabeth Ferris, *Border Security, Migration Governance and Sovereignty* (IOM 2017) 2.

The New York Declaration pointedly qualifies the breadth of State sovereignty over migration by declaring that its exercise is 'subject to that State's international obligations'.[25] International law structures national discretion in relation to migration in a number of key ways. First, a State's freedom to refuse admission to or to expel a non-citizen is subject to its obligation not to return (*refoule*) a person to persecution (under refugee law) or certain other serious harms (under complementary human rights protections). These protections are in turn subject to exhaustively defined security exceptions. The Global Compact on Refugees 2018 duly acknowledges '[t]he legitimate security concerns of States' and affirms that '[t]he primary responsibility for safety and security lies with States', including by applying the refugee exclusion criteria, norms on human trafficking and smuggling, and the duty to separate fighters from refugees in mass displacement situations.[26]

States enjoy a freer hand in relation to the admission or expulsion of migrants who are not refugees or entitled to complementary protection, including in defining security exclusions. Nonetheless, where a migrant is lawfully present in a foreign State, human rights law guarantees due process in all types of expulsion proceedings (including criminal extradition) (discussed in Section F.1). There are also protections against arbitrary detention of migrants, against inhumane treatment, for family unity and child rights, and in relation to the presence and exit of migrant workers (including irregular ones).[27]

Beyond these minimum conditions, recent international policy instruments seek to strengthen 'global governance' of migration.[28] The New York Declaration does so by addressing drivers and structural factors (from poverty to conflict to climate change)[29] behind migration; protecting the safety, dignity, and human rights of migrants;[30] facilitating opportunities for safe, orderly, and regular migration (including employment creation, labour mobility, circular migration, family reunification, and educational opportunities);[31] and encouraging cooperation on returns of irregular migrants.[32] In a prevailing context of strong border sovereignty, it is a challenging agenda. Even though the Declaration and the two Compacts are non-binding, aspirational agendas for cooperation, with no hard targets or allocations of responsibility, a significant number of migrant-receiving States have still refused to endorse them—including, for example, the United States, various European countries, and Australia.

[25] New York Declaration (n 7) para 42.

[26] UNGA 'Report of the United High Commissioner for Refugees: Global Compact on Refugees, (Part II)' (2 August 2018) UN Doc A/73/12, paras 56–7, affirmed by UNGA Res 73/151 (2018).

[27] See eg International Covenant on Civil and Political Rights 999 UNTS 171 (ICCPR) arts 9 (freedom from arbitrary detention), 7 (freedom from torture and cruel, inhuman or degrading treatment or punishment), 10 (humane conditions of detention), 17 and 23 (family rights) and 24 (child rights); Convention on the Rights of the Child 1577 UNTS 3 arts 9 (non-separation of children from families) and 10 (entry for family reunification); and International Convention on the Protection of the Rights of All Migrant Workers and Members of Their Families 2220 UNTS 3.

[28] New York Declaration (n 7) para 49.

[29] ibid para 43; Global Compact on Migration (n 20) paras 12, 18.

[30] New York Declaration (n 7) para 41.

[31] ibid para 57; Global Compact on Migration (n 20) para 21.

[32] New York Declaration (n 7) para 58.

C. International Refugee Law

From amongst the disparate patchwork of norms regulating aspects of migration and displacement, international refugee law contains the most explicit and developed regime addressing security concerns. Whereas States are largely free to determine any security grounds for excluding migrants, under international refugee law these are exhaustively defined in relation to refugees. The 1951 Refugee Convention contains three relevant provisions: exclusion for certain serious (mostly criminal) acts under Article 1F; a security exception to *non-refoulement* (non-return) under Article 33(2); and expulsion of a lawfully resident refugee under Article 32. As will be shown, refugee law contains ample grounds for dealing with security threats, not least because the drafters in 1951 had recent memory of the grave and varied security risks during the Second World War.

1. Exclusion from Refugee Status

Article 1F of the Refugee Convention excludes certain persons from refugee status, such that there is no obligation not to return such persons to persecution (although complementary human rights protection, such as freedom from return to torture, may still apply, discussed below). Article 1F may thus permit a State to refuse entry to a person to its territory, although it will often be necessary to temporarily admit a person to adequately determine their refugee claim, including to investigate whether the exclusion clauses apply.

There are three specific exclusion clauses under Article 1F. Under Article 1F(a), exclusion from refugee protection is required where there are serious reasons for considering that a person has committed a crime against peace, a war crime, or a crime against humanity,[33] including where these are committed by terrorist organizations or other violent non-State actors. Under Article 1F(b), refugee status cannot be granted to a person if there are 'serious reasons' for considering that 'he has committed a serious non-political crime outside the country of refuge prior to his admission to that country as a refugee'.[34] A crime may be considered 'serious' where it is punishable by a 'very grave' penalty,[35] as for murder, rape, armed robbery, torture, hijacking, or other violent acts.

Article 1F(b) only applies, however, to 'non-political' offences, which potentially excludes its application to certain national security crimes—for instance, treason,

[33] See, generally, Jelena Pejic, 'Article 1F(a): The Notion of International Crimes' (2000) 12 International Journal of Refugee Law 11; Matthew Zagor, 'Persecutor or Persecuted? Exclusion under Article 1F(A) and 1F(B) of the Refugee Convention' (2000) 23 University of New South Wales Law Journal 164.

[34] See, generally, Walter Kälin/Jörg Künzli, 'Article 1F(b): Freedom Fighters, Terrorists and the Notion of Serious Political Crimes' (2000) 12 International Journal of Refugee Law 46.

[35] UNHCR, *Handbook and Guidelines on Procedures and Criteria for Determining Refugee Status* (UNHCR 2011) para 155 (UNHCR Handbook).

espionage, subversion, and rebellion. A crime will be regarded as 'non-political' when 'other motives (such as personal reasons or gain)' predominate.[36] Even where an act is politically motivated, however, it may still be treated as non-political if: there is no clear link between the crime and its political objective; the act is disproportionate to its objective;[37] the methods used are atrocious or indiscriminate;[38] or the political objective is inconsistent with human rights.[39] Such tests would cover most terrorist violence and thus exclude perpetrators from refugee protection.[40] Article 1F(b) does not, however, automatically exclude all 'terrorists' from protection; an assessment must always be made of the contribution made by the individual and its severity.[41]

Under Article 1(F)(c), refugee status cannot be granted to a person if there are 'serious reasons' for considering that 'he has been guilty of acts contrary to the purposes and principles of the United Nations'.[42] This is interpreted restrictively to only be 'triggered in extreme circumstances by [international] activity which attacks the very basis of the international community's coexistence'.[43] Examples include threats to international security, or serious and sustained violations of human rights by State or de facto State authorities.[44] United Nations Security Council (UNSC) resolutions have also deemed terrorist acts to threaten international security,[45] although exclusion will depend on the gravity of the act and the person's individual contribution to it.[46] Mere participation in combat[47] is not sufficient; nor is mere membership in a violent State or non-State

[36] UNHCR 'Guidelines on International Protection No 5: Application of the Exclusion Clauses: Article 1F of the 1951 Convention relating to the Status of Refugees' (4 September 2003) UN Doc HCR/GIP/03/05, para 15 (UNHCR Guidelines).

[37] ibid. [38] UNHCR Handbook (n 35) para 152.

[39] UNHCR, 'Background Note on the Application of the Exclusion Clauses: Article 1F of the 1951 Convention relating to the Status of Refugees' (4 September 2003), para 43 <https://www.refworld.org/docid/3f5857d24.html> accessed 13 November 2019 (UNHCR Background Note).

[40] ibid para 81; UNHCR Guidelines (n 36) paras 15 and 26. For example, where a violent Islamist political organization in Algeria indiscriminately killed civilians at an airport: *T v Secretary of State for the Home Department* [1996] 2 All ER 865 (HL).

[41] UNHCR Guidelines (n 36) para 26; UNHCR Background Note (n 39) paras 81–2 (low level terrorist financing) and 85–6 (hijacking to escape persecution).

[42] See, generally, Edward Kwakwa, 'Article 1F(c): Acts Contrary to the Purposes and Principles of the United Nations' (2000) 12 International Journal of Refugee Law 79.

[43] UNHCR Guidelines (n 36) para 17.

[44] ibid. See also *Pushpanathan v Canada (Minister of Citizenship and Immigration)* [1998] 1 SCR 982 (Supreme Court of Canada); UNHCR Background Note (n 39) para 59.

[45] UNSC Res 1373 (2001) para 4; UNSC Res 1269 (1999) para 3; UNSC Res 1377 (2001) Annex; and UNSC Res 1624 (2005) preamble.

[46] UNHCR Background Note (n 39) para 49; see also UNHCR Guidelines (n 36) para 17; UNHCR, 'Note on the Impact of Security Council Resolution 1624 (2005) on the Application of Exclusion under Article 1F of the 1951 Convention Relating to the Status of Refugees' (9 December 2005) paras 3–4 <https://www.refworld.org/pdfid/440ff6944.pdf> accessed 13 November 2019.

[47] *KJ (Sri Lanka) v Secretary of State for the Home Department* [2009] Imm AR 674.

group;[48] nor acts of lesser gravity such as providing logistical support (such as false passports)[49] or non-military support (including medical care[50] or minor financing) to a terrorist group.

2. The Exception to *Non-refoulement*

Under Article 33(2) of the Refugee Convention, *non-refoulement* 'may not . . . be claimed by a refugee whom there are reasonable grounds for regarding as a danger to the security of the country in which he is, or who, having been convicted by a final judgement of a particularly serious crime, constitutes a danger to the community of that country'. The exception to *non-refoulement* thus applies to a recognized refugee who may nonetheless be deprived of protection because he or she poses a verifiable future risk to the country of asylum.[51]

Because of the grave consequence of Article 33(2), namely return to persecution, it must be stringently interpreted. Article 33(2) imposes a high threshold of very serious danger, rather than lesser threats, and which target either national security or the 'community' (namely, the safety and well-being of the population as a whole, not ordinary criminal activities).[52] Acts which could come within its scope include those endangering the constitution, government, territorial integrity, independence, or the external peace of a country;[53] as well as espionage, sabotage, and terrorist acts targeting civilians.[54] The alternative threshold, of threats to the community, must be substantiated by a criminal conviction as well as evidence that the person presents an ongoing risk. Due process and standard of proof safeguards also apply.[55]

[48] Cour Nationale du Droit d'Asile, *MZM*, no 10004811 (5 April 2012) (France) (concerning Iranian State authorities); Conseil du Contentieux des Etranger, *x c le Commissaire général aux réfugiés et aux apatrides*, Arrêt No 54335 (13 January 2011) (Belgium) (involving a Moroccan terrorist organization); Joined Cases C-57/09 and C-101/09 *Bundesrepublik Deutschland v B and D* [2010] ECLI:EU:C:2010:661 (PKK in Turkey); UNHCR Background Note (n 39), paras 60 and 62 (but UNHCR suggests that voluntary membership of violent extremist groups may give rise to a rebuttable presumption that the person has contributed to the group's violence; see also UNHCR Guidelines (n 36) para 26).

[49] Conseil du Contentieux des Etrangers, *x c le Commissaire général aux réfugiés et aux apatrides*, Arrêt No 96933 (12 February 2013) (Belgium).

[50] *MH (Syria) v Secretary of State for the Home Department* [2009] EWCA Civ 226.

[51] UNHCR, 'Addressing Security Concerns without Undermining Refugee Protection: UNHCR's Perspective' (29 November 2001) Rev.1, para 22 <https://www.refworld.org/docid/3c0b880e0.html> accessed 13 November 2019 (UNHCR 'Addressing Security').

[52] Elihu Lauterpacht/Daniel Bethlehem, 'The Scope and Content of the Principle of *Non-refoulement*: Opinion' in Erika Feller et al (eds), *Refugee Protection in International Law: UNHCR's Global Consultations on International Protection* (CUP 2003) 87, paras 169 and 192.

[53] Atle Grahl-Madsen, *Commentary on the Refugee Convention: Articles 2–11, 13–37* (UNHCR 1997) Article 33, commentary para 8.

[54] Lauterpacht/Bethlehem (n 52) para 171.

[55] UNHCR 'Addressing Security' (n 51) para 21; Lauterpacht/Bethlehem (n 52) para 168.

3. Expulsion of a Lawfully Resident Refugee

Article 32 of the Refugee Convention provides for the expulsion of a refugee lawfully present in a State's territory only 'on grounds of national security or public order' (Article 32(1)). The main difference from Article 33(2) is that Article 32 is not an exception to *non-refoulement* and only permits expulsion to a State where the person is not at risk. The threshold for Article 32 is comparable to that under the first limb of Article 33(2), discussed above, and could extend to serious terrorist threats against the State of refuge. It would not, however, extend to ordinary criminal activities that lack any security dimension.[56] The drafting record indicates that it should be restrictively interpreted, such that a refugee should only be expelled as a last resort and as the only practicable means of protecting the State's legitimate security interests.[57] Unlike Article 33(2), Article 32 includes explicit due process guarantees in Article 32(2), elements of which may be restricted 'where compelling reasons of national security' require.

4. Mass Influxes of Refugees and Security

In principle, the above provisions (Articles 1F, 33(2) and 32) all apply to both individual assessments of refugees as well as mass influxes of refugees. In practice, however, refugee determination in a mass influx situation is often adapted to the realities of the large scale of arrivals. First, refugee status is often granted on wider grounds than a Convention-based fear of persecution, to protect victims of conflict or grave rights violations more generally, including where there are mixed flows of people.[58]

Secondly, refugee status may be positively recognized on a group basis, due to the impracticality and expense of individual procedures.[59] In contrast, denial of protection in mass influx situations may not, however, normally be made on a group basis, but must usually involve an individualized determination according to a fair procedure. Exclusion decisions may have to wait, however, until after the emergency phase of a new

[56] Ulrike Davy, 'Article 32' in Andreas Zimmermann (ed), *The 1951 Convention Relating to the Status of Refugees and its 1967 Protocol: A Commentary* (OUP 2011) 1310.

[57] UNHCR, 'Note on Expulsion of Refugees' (24 August 1977) EC/SCP/3, para 4 <https://www.unhcr.org/uk/excom/scip/3ae68cbf14/note-expulsion-refugees.html> accessed 13 November 2019; UNHCR, 'The Scope of International Protection in Mass Influx' (2 June 1995) EC/1995/SCP/CRP.3, para 8 <https://www.unhcr.org/uk/excom/scip/3ae68cc018/scope-international-protection-mass-influx.html> accessed 13 November 2019 (UNHCR 'Protection in Mass Influx').

[58] UNHCR 'Protection in Mass Influx' (n 57) paras 8–9; UNHCR, 'Guidelines on the Application in Mass Influx Situations of the Exclusion Clauses of Article 1F of the 1951 Convention relating to the Status of Refugees' (7 February 2006) para 1 <https://www.refworld.org/publisher,UNHCR,THEMGUIDE,,43f48c0b4,0.html> accessed 13 November 2019 (UNHCR 'Mass Influx Guidelines'). Regionally there may be specific legal grounds for wider protection, as under the Convention Governing the Specific Aspects of Refugee Problems in Africa 1001 UNTS 45 art 1(2) and the Cartagena Declaration on Refugees OAS Doc OEA/Ser.L/V/II.66/doc.10, rev.1, 190.

[59] UNHCR 'Protection in Mass Influx' (n 57) para 12; UNHCR 'Mass Influx Guidelines' (n 58) para 9.

influx, when the humanitarian situation has stabilized.[60] Once a person is excluded, they should be separated and removed from the refugee camp, while ensuring the safety of refugees and humanitarian personnel.[61]

Exceptionally, active combatants (or fighters in non-international armed conflict) do not enjoy the presumption of group-based refugee status[62] and are thereby excludable on a collective basis. Armed or military activities are incompatible with the civilian and humanitarian character of asylum,[63] which host States are obliged to guarantee.[64] The United Nations High Commissioner for Refugees (UNHCR) recommends that States should identify, disarm, separate, and intern combatants as early as possible, including through screening at point of arrival.[65] In addition, host States should locate refugee camps away from the border, maintain law, order, and security within camps, and prevent the flow of weapons into and recruitment inside camps.[66] Family members of combatants should, however, be treated as refugees. Former combatants who have genuinely and permanently renounced military activities may also be entitled to refugee status upon an individual determination in a fair procedure.[67] Former child soldiers should enjoy special protection, assistance, and rehabilitation.

Thirdly, protection may be provided on a temporary basis for mass influxes rather than on a permanent basis (as for individual arrivals), subject to a continuing requirement to seek durable solutions (including elsewhere),[68] because the scale of mass influxes overwhelms normal absorption capacity. Protection need not, however, be limited to temporary protection, and the duration of protection is relative to the capacity of receiving States vis-à-vis the scale and nature of the influx.[69] For example, even when over one million refugees and migrants arrived in Europe from the Syrian crisis and North Africa in 2015, the EU—with a population of 515 million people and an economy of almost US$19 trillion—still did not trigger its Temporary Protection Directive 2001, designed precisely to respond to a mass influx 'in particular if there is also a risk that the asylum system will be unable to process this influx without adverse effects for its efficient operation'.[70]

5. Excessive Securitization of Refugees

Despite the comprehensive provisions and procedures discussed above for accommodating any plausible security risks posed by refugees, particularly since 9/11, it has

[60] UNHCR 'Mass Influx Guidelines' (n 58) para 7. [61] ibid para 35.

[62] ibid para 10. [63] ibid.

[64] UNHCR EXCOM Conclusion No 94 (LIII) 'Civilian and Humanitarian Character of Asylum' (2002) paras (a)–(b).

[65] ibid para (c). [66] ibid paras (c) and (e).

[67] ibid; UNHCR 'Mass Influx Guidelines' (n 58) para 10.

[68] UNHCR 'Protection in Mass Influx' (n 57) para 15.

[69] See eg UNHCR EXCOM Conclusion No 100 (LV) 'International Cooperation and Burden and Responsibility Sharing in Mass Influx Situation' (2004) para (a).

[70] Council Directive 2001/55/EC of 20 July 2001 on temporary protection in the event of a mass influx of displaced persons OJ L 212/12, art 2(a).

become all too common for States to draw 'unwarranted linkages' between refugees and terrorism and to take additional security measures that impair (often unlawfully) access to refugee status.[71] The UNHCR has expressed concern that asylum seekers may be victimized by public prejudice and restrictive legal or administrative measures, and that refugee protection may be eroded.[72] It has emphasized that '[a]ny discussion on security safeguards should start from the assumption that refugees are themselves escaping persecution and violence, including terrorist acts, and are not the perpetrators of such acts'.[73] Racism and xenophobia against refugees has also increased.[74] The UNHCR further notes that States are required to bring terrorists to justice,[75] which may not be fulfilled by excluding a person or expelling them.

In addition to the over-expansive application of Articles 1F, 32 and 33(2) of the Refugee Convention (including based on excessively broad terrorism offences) refugees have been adversely affected by other security measures. These foremost include more restrictive border controls, such as penalties for illegal entry or lack of documentation; discriminatory ethnic or religious profiling; summary processing or rejection at the border; exclusion of families based on 'no fly lists'; non-confidential data-sharing (even with a country of persecution); and lack of gender sensitivity in immigration enforcement.[76] Relatedly, unjustified detention has increased, including mandatory, protracted, or indefinite detention where not necessary or proportionate in the individual's circumstances, or non-discriminatory.[77]

Thirdly, violations of *non-refoulement* have occurred[78] including through the use of accelerated procedures or unreliable diplomatic assurances,[79] limits on due process, or where expulsion decisions on security grounds lack sufficiently fair procedures.[80] Violations of *non-refoulement* can counterproductively create conditions conducive to terrorism if returnees face socio-economic exclusion and become vulnerable to terrorist recruitment.[81] Fourthly, refugees have been returned to 'extremely volatile security

[71] UNGA, 'Report of the UN Special Rapporteur (Martin Scheinin) on the Promotion and Protection of Human Rights and Fundamental Freedoms While Countering Terrorism' (15 August 2007) UN Doc A/62/263, paras 34, 78.

[72] UNHCR 'Addressing Security' (n 51) para 2. [73] ibid para 3. [74] ibid paras 28–30.

[75] ibid para 9.

[76] See eg ibid para 11; Scheinin (n 71) paras 36–49; UNGA, 'Report of the OHCHR on the Protection of Human Rights and Fundamental Freedoms while Countering Terrorism' (2 September 2009) UN Doc A/HRC/12/22, paras 30–1.

[77] Scheinin (n 71) paras 40–8. [78] ibid paras 49–53.

[79] UNCAT 'Decisions of the Committee against Torture under article 22 of the Convention against Torture and Other Cruel, Inhuman and Degrading Treatment or Punishment concerning communication No. 233/2003' (*Ahmed Hussein Mustafa Kamil Agiza v Sweden*) UN Doc CAT/C/34/D/233/2003 (20 May 2005) para 13.4; UNHRC 'Views of the Human Rights Committee under article 5, paragraph 4, of the Optional Protocol concerning communication No. 1416/2005' (*Mohammed Alzery v Sweden*) UN Doc CCPR/C/88/D/1416/2005 (25 October 2006) paras 11.4–11.5.

[80] UNHRC 'Views of the Human Rights Committee under the Optional Protocol considering communication No. 1051/2002' (*Mansour Ahani v Canada*) UN Doc CCPR/C/80/D/1051/2002 (29 March 2004) paras 10.7–10.8.

[81] Scheinin (n 71) paras 75–6.

and humanitarian situations', often affected by counter-terrorism operations, where returnees lack access to humanitarian needs.[82] There has, fifthly, been a reduced commitment to the proactive resettlement of refugees from abroad.[83] Finally, countering human trafficking has been increasingly linked to counter-terrorism, a policy that securitizes a human rights issue and can result in punishment of victims and even increase trafficking.[84]

D. Complementary Human Rights Protection

Where persons are not technically refugees at risk of persecution, international human rights law provides 'complementary' or 'subsidiary' protection against other serious harms.[85] The extended principle of *non-refoulement* protects against return to a country where there is a real and foreseeable risk of torture or cruel, inhuman, or degrading treatment or punishment;[86] arbitrary deprivation of life,[87] including the application of the death penalty to crimes which are not the 'most serious'; or the flagrant denial of other fundamental human rights,[88] such as the right to a fair trial,[89] liberty,[90] or freedom of thought, religion, or conscience.[91]

Unlike under the Refugee Convention, human rights conventions do not articulate express grounds for excluding from protection persons who pose security risks. While freedom from return to torture is absolute, human rights law otherwise permits necessary and proportionate restrictions to be placed on other entitlements to complementary protection. In practice, regional and national laws accordingly include security-based

[82] ibid para 73.

[83] UNHCR 'Addressing Security' (n 51) para 27.

[84] UNGA 'Report of the UN Special Rapporteur (Martin Scheinin) on the Promotion and Protection of Human Rights and Fundamental Freedoms While Countering Terrorism' (3 August 2009) UN Doc A/64/211, para 51.

[85] See, generally, Jane McAdam, *Complementary Protection in International Refugee Law* (OUP 2007). As a regional example, see EU Directive 2011/95/EU of 13 December 2011 on refugee status and subsidiary protection OJ L 337/9, art 15 (EU Directive 2011).

[86] ICCPR (n 27) art 7; Convention against Torture and Other Cruel, Inhuman or Degrading Treatment or Punishment 1465 UNTS 85 art 3.

[87] ICCPR (n 27) art 6 (including the application of the death penalty to crimes which are not the 'most serious'); or of the death penalty where the host State is a party to the Second Optional Protocol to the International Covenant on Civil and Political Rights, aiming at the abolition of the death penalty 1642 UNTS 414.

[88] UNHRC 'Views of the Human Rights Committee under article 5, paragraph 4, of the Optional Protocol concerning communication No. 692/1996' (*ARJ v Australia*) UN Doc CCPR/C/60/D/692/1996 (28 July 1997) para 6.9 (concerning ICCPR rights).

[89] *Othman v UK*, App No 8139/09, 9 May 2012.

[90] *Tomic v UK*, App No 17837/03, 14 October 2003.

[91] *Z and T v UK*, App No 27034/05, 28 February 2006.

exceptions to complementary protection, which may be modelled or influenced by those in refugee law.

For example, in EU law, a person is excluded from complementary protection if he or she has committed an international crime, a serious crime, or acts contrary to UN purposes or principles[92]—thus reflecting the substance of Article 1F of the Refugee Convention. Also excluded are those who constitute a danger to the community or security of the host State[93]—reflecting the exception to *non-refoulement* under Article 33(2) of the Refugee Convention, although the EU provision technically excludes the person from protection rather than (as under refugee law) still conferring protected status but permitting return to harm. Persons fleeing from punishment for prior crimes committed abroad are also excluded.[94]

E. Irregular Maritime Arrivals, Law of the Sea, and Offshore Processing

The irregular movement of migrants and refugees at sea has been a challenge for international coordination and protection at least since the exodus of the Indochinese 'boat people' after the end of the Vietnam War in 1975. Subsequent maritime flows of people have included Haitians and Cubans to the United States in the 1980s, mixed flows from the Middle East and Asia to Australia in the 1990s and 2000s, Rohingya refugees from Myanmar throughout Asia in the 2000s, and most recently movements from North Africa across the Mediterranean to Europe.

A number of intersecting legal regimes are relevant. Under the international law of the sea, a State's vessels have a fundamental duty to rescue persons in distress at sea[95] and shipmasters must 'do everything possible, within the capabilities and limitations of the ship, to treat the survivors humanely and to meet their immediate needs'.[96] Rescuees must be disembarked at a 'place of safety', with minimum further deviation from a ships' intended course.[97] A 'place of safety' is not, however, defined, resulting in disputes about where rescuees may be landed. There is some support in State practice that rescuees should normally be disembarked at the next port of call.[98] The International Maritime Organization (IMO) Guidelines 2004 suggest that a place of safety is a location where the rescue ends, the person's life is no longer in danger, their basic human needs (such as

[92] EU Directive 2011 (n 85) art 17(1)(a)–(c). [93] ibid art 17(1)(d). [94] ibid art 17(3).

[95] UN Convention on the Law of the Sea 1833 UNTS 3 art 98(1)(b).

[96] Resolution MSC 167(78), 'Annex 34: Guidelines on the Treatment of Persons Rescued at Sea' (20 May 2004) IMO Doc MSC 78/26/Add.2, principle 5.1.2 (IMO Guidelines); UNHCR EXCOM Conclusion No 97 (LIV) 'Protection Safeguards in Interception Measures' (2003) para (a)(ii) (UNHCR Conclusion 97).

[97] Resolution MSC 153(78), 'Annex 3: Adoption of Amendments to the International Convention for the Safety of Life at Sea, 1874, as amended' (20 May 2004) IMO Doc MSC 78/26/Add.1.

[98] UNHCR EXCOM Conclusion No 23 (XXXII) 'Problems related to the Rescue of Asylum-Seekers in Distress at Sea' (1981) para 3.

food, shelter, and medical needs) can be met, and their onward transport can be arranged.[99] Refugees and asylum seekers must not be disembarked in a place where they have a well-founded fear of persecution.[100]

Vessels carrying asylum seekers sometimes enter into distress because of the unsafe practices of people smugglers who have organized their voyage. While a treaty seeks to suppress the transnational crime of people smuggling, IMO standards additionally encourage States to improve maritime safety by taking steps to eliminate unsafe practices concerning the trafficking or transport of migrants by sea.[101]

Under international refugee law and human rights law, wherever a State exercises jurisdiction, including on the high seas or at the frontier, the State must not return a refugee or asylum seeker to a country where he or she is at risk of persecution or other serious harm.[102] The duty of *non-refoulement* extends to both direct and indirect return to harm;[103] the latter may include maritime transfer to a third country that lacks adequate protection safeguards to prevent onward return to a country of persecution. EU regulations on maritime operations explicitly preclude disembarking or transferring a person in breach of *non-refoulement*.[104]

At the procedural level, UNHCR identifies at least three types of 'on water' assessment procedures of rescuees: profiling or pre-screening; refugee status (or other protection) determination processing; and temporary protection grants.[105] UNHCR argues, however, that full refugee processing on board ships 'is generally not appropriate', nor even possible given that minimum standards of reception and fair asylum determination cannot be guaranteed.[106] IMO guidelines add that the masters of ships that rescue persons at sea should not participate in asylum processing on board other than to establish the identity, the name, age, gender, health and medical condition, and any special needs of a rescuee.[107]

Instead, UNHCR recommends that claims for protection should normally be processed in the territory of the intercepting State.[108] The IMO recommends that status assessment

[99] IMO Guidelines (n 96) para 6.12. [100] ibid, para 6.17.

[101] Protocol against the Smuggling of Migrants by Land, Sea and Air, supplementing the Convention against Transnational Organized Crime 2241 UNTS 507; IMO, 'Interim Measures for Combating Unsafe Practices Associated with the Trafficking or Transport of Migrants by Sea' (12 June 2001) IMO Doc MSC/Circ.896/Rev.1.

[102] UNHCR 'Advisory Opinion on the Extraterritorial Application of Non-Refoulement Obligations under the 1951 Convention relating to the Status of Refugees and its 1967 Protocol' (26 January 2007), paras 24–43 <https://www.unhcr.org/4d9486929.pdf> accessed 20 May 2020.

[103] UNHCR Conclusion 97 (n 96) para (a)(iv).

[104] EU Regulation No 656/2014 of 15 May 2014 on surveillance of the external sea borders OJ L 189/93, art 4.

[105] UNHCR, 'Protection Policy Paper: Maritime Interception Operations and the Processing of International Protection Claims: Legal Standards and Policy Considerations with respect to Extraterritorial Processing' (November 2010) para 14 <https://www.refworld.org/docid/4cd12d3a2.html> accessed 15 November 2019.

[106] ibid paras 55–6.

[107] IMO, 'Principles Relating to Administrative Procedures for Disembarking Persons Rescued at Sea' (22 January 2009) IMO Doc FAL.3/Circ.194, para 2.2.

[108] UNHCR (n 105) para 2.

should be carried out after disembarkation to a place of safety.[109] Third-country processing may also be appropriate in exceptional circumstances of responsibility-sharing, as long as it is accompanied by adequate protection safeguards.[110]

F. Other Human Rights Safeguards on Security Expulsion

Outside the contexts of refugee law and status and complementary protection, there is no duty on a State to admit a non-citizen. As such, the articulation of legal grounds for a refusal—whether based on security or other reasons—is unnecessary under international law. One outermost constraint may be that where a State admits non-citizens, admission may not be refused on prohibited grounds of discrimination under international human rights law.[111]

Where a person has been lawfully admitted, international law likewise does not stipulate the permissible substantive grounds upon which a non-citizen may be expelled. The issue is left to national law, which may define the circumstances in which security concerns may justify expulsion. International human rights law does, however, regulate certain other aspects of expulsion, including due process, family and child rights, and liberty and detention.

1. Due Process and Review in the Expulsion of Aliens

Article 13 of the ICCPR guarantees due process for non-citizens subject to any form of obligatory[112] expulsion, including extradition.[113] While it does not regulate the substantive grounds of expulsion, the purpose of Article 13 is to prevent arbitrary expulsions.[114] It is modelled on the due process guarantees in Article 32(2) of the Refugee Convention.[115] The provision contains four key protections. First, expulsion must be

[109] ibid. [110] ibid paras 3, 34–5.

[111] ICCPR (n 27) art 26 provides equal protection before the law in any field regulated by public authorities (UNHRC 'General Comment 18: Non-discrimination' (10 November 1989) CCPR/C/21/Rev.1/Add.1, para 12), including in relation to entry or residence of non-citizens: UNHRC 'General Comment 15: The Position of Aliens under the Covenant' (11 April 1986) UN Doc HRI/GEN/1/Rev.1, para 5 (GC 15).

[112] GC 15 (n 111) para 9; Manfred Nowak, *UN Covenant on Civil and Political Rights: CCPR Commentary* (NP Engel 2005) 293.

[113] UNHRC 'Views of the Human Rights Committee under article 5, paragraph 4, of the Optional Protocol concerning communication No. 193/1985' (*Pierre Giry v Dominican Republic*) UN Doc CCPR/C/39/D/193/1985 (20 July 1990) para 5.5.

[114] GC 15 (n 111) para 10. [115] Nowak (n 112) 291.

reached 'in accordance with law', including substantive and procedural law,[116] as interpreted 'in good faith and in a reasonable manner', and not abusively, by the national authorities.[117]

Secondly, under Article 13 a person subject to expulsion 'shall…be allowed to submit the reasons against his expulsion', which implies corollary rights to be given notice of the decision[118] and to be informed of the case against oneself[119] (such as the reasons and evidence upon which the decision is based), so as to enable the person to effectively respond.

Thirdly, Article 13 requires 'review' by a 'competent authority'[120] above, and sufficiently independent from, the original decision-maker,[121] although it need not be a court.[122] The remedy against expulsion must be effective[123] in that it is legally binding, not discretionary.[124] An appeal must be available prior to a person's expulsion and expulsion must be suspended pending its determination.[125] As the UN International Law Commission's Draft Articles on the Expulsion of Aliens recognizes, 'the right to challenge the expulsion decision'[126] is 'well established in international law'.[127] Finally, Article 13 provides a right to be represented on appeal.[128]

2. Due Process and Security

While expulsion decisions must always be reached in accordance with law, Article 13 enables the other three elements of due process in the expulsion of aliens to be adjusted

[116] UNHRC 'Views of the Human Rights Committee under article 5, paragraph 4, of the Optional Protocol concerning communication No. 58/1979' (*Anna Maroufidou v Sweden*) UN Doc CCPR/C/12/D/58/1979 (9 April 1981) para 9.3.

[117] ibid para 10.2.

[118] The same implication is drawn in respect of the Refugee Convention relating to the Status of Refugees 189 UNTS 137 art 32(2): Davy (n 56) 1317; ILC, 'Expulsion of Aliens: Texts and Titles of the Draft Articles adopted by the Drafting Committee on Second Reading' (30 May 2014) UN Doc A/CN.4/L.832, draft art 26(1)(a) (right to be notified).

[119] Guy Goodwin-Gill/Jane McAdam, *The Refugee in International Law* (3rd edn, OUP 2007) 523.

[120] ILC 'Expulsion of Aliens' (n 118) describe the principle as 'a right of access to effective remedies to challenge the expulsion decision': draft art 26(1)(d).

[121] See also Davy (n 56) 1318 (on the corresponding implication under the Refugee Convention (n 118) art 32(2)).

[122] Nowak (n 112) 297; see also Davy (n 56) 1317 (on Refugee Convention (n 118) art 32(2)).

[123] GC No 15 (n 111) para 10.

[124] UNGA, 'Report of the UNHRC: Consideration of Reports Submitted by States Parties under Article 40 of the Covenant: Concluding Observations: Syrian Arab Republic' (5 April 2001) UN Doc A/56/40, para 81.

[125] UNHRC 'Views of the Human Rights Committee under article 5, paragraph 4, of the Optional Protocol concerning communication No. 155/1983' (*Eric Hammel v Madagascar*) UN Doc CCPR/C/29/D/155/1983 (3 April 1987) para 19.2; see also Nowak (n 112) 298–9; ILC 'Expulsion of Aliens' (n 118) draft art 27.

[126] ILC 'Expulsion of Aliens' (n 118) draft art 26(1)(b).

[127] UNGA, 'Report of the International Law Commission of its 64th Session' (7 May–1 June and 2 July–3 August 2012) UN Doc A/67/10, 63.

[128] Nowak (n 112) 299–300 (based on the similar provision in the Refugee Convention (n 118) art 32(3)).

'where compelling reasons of national security otherwise require'. The UN Human Rights Committee accepts that a State enjoys a 'wide discretion' in the 'assessment of whether a case presents national security considerations bringing the exception contained in article 13 into play'.[129] However, it has found that where a domestic procedure *does* allow a person to provide limited reasons against his or her expulsion and to receive a degree of review of the case, it would be 'inappropriate' to accept that 'compelling reasons of national security' existed to exempt the State party from its obligation under Article 13 to provide procedural protections.[130] Thus where a procedure has been provided in national security cases, it must still be fair.

In addition, the non-derogable requirement that decisions be 'in accordance with law' arguably implies a qualitative dimension to legality, namely the prevention of arbitrariness.[131] As the European Court of Human Rights (ECtHR) stated when interpreting a very similar provision,[132] protection against arbitrariness requires independent review even of decisions involving national security, with 'some form of adversarial proceedings before an independent body competent to review the reasons for the decision and relevant evidence, if need be with appropriate procedural limitations on the use of classified information'.[133] In a number of national security cases, the ECtHR has found that expulsion decisions were not made 'in accordance with law' where the reasons were not disclosed to the person, their lawyer, or an independent body.[134] In such cases, where the authorities are in sole possession of the evidence, it is impossible for the affected person to present their case adequately in response to highly generalized allegations.[135]

Expulsions on security grounds raise difficult questions about the competing interests of the State in ensuring the secrecy of intelligence information and an affected person's right to receive a fair hearing by seeing, and being able to effectively challenge, the allegations. Even in some democratic States, non-citizens have been expelled with very limited disclosure of the allegations, resulting in a denial of due process, illegal detention, and lack of judicial protection.[136] In contrast, the ECtHR has guaranteed a minimum irreducible disclosure of security information, requiring 'sufficiently specific' allegations and precluding the State from relying on 'general assertions'.[137]

[129] *Alzery v Sweden* (n 79) para 11.10. [130] *Ahani v Canada* (n 80) para 10.8.

[131] *Lupsa v Romania*, App No 10337/04, 8 June 2006, para 55.

[132] Protocol No 7 to European Convention for the Protection of Human Rights and Fundamental Freedoms ETS No 117 art 1.

[133] *Al-Nashif v Bulgaria*, App No 50963/99, 20 June 2002, paras 123–4.

[134] ibid para 126.

[135] See eg *C G and Others v Bulgaria*, App No 1365/07, 24 April 2008.

[136] UNHRC 'Views of the Human Rights Committee under article 5, paragraph 4, of the Optional Protocol concerning communication No. 1937/2010' (*Mansour Leghaei and others v Australia*) (26 March 2015) UN Doc CCPR/C/113/D/1937/2010.

[137] *A and Others v UK*, App No 3455/05, 19 February 2009, paras 217–20.

G. Conclusion

Irregular migration and displacement intersect with international, national, and human security considerations, and the applicable international law, in complicated ways. The lack of any comprehensive international law on migration leaves States relatively free to define whom they wish to exclude for security reasons. International due process protections nonetheless apply to the expulsion of aliens, but are restricted to lawfully present aliens (leaving irregular migrants vulnerable) and may be restricted in other (but not all) respects if security requires. The protection of security information also presents special challenges for a fair hearing.

In the case of refugees or persons at risk of other serious harms, the principle of *non-refoulement* applies. Refugee law still accommodates States' security concerns, including in mass influx situations, but tightly defines the applicable substantive grounds and procedural protections. Complementary human rights protection is both stronger (in preventing return to torture) and more uncertain (in less prescriptively regulating the grounds and procedures of expulsion). Despite the higher protections for refugees than migrants, since 9/11 refugees and asylum seekers have been increasingly 'securitized', including as regards to maritime interdiction and the declining access to, and the quality of, protection. Paradoxically, however, unilateral national responses to the security challenges of irregular migration and displacement can intensify—not diminish—what are inevitably common security challenges in a globalized world.

CHAPTER 24

STATES AND NON-STATE ACTORS AND HUMAN SECURITY

MARKOS KARAVIAS

A. Introduction

ZYGMUNT Bauman, in *Community: Seeking Safety in an Insecure World*, notes that security is a quality, 'which the world we inhabit is ever less able to offer and ever more reluctant to promise'.[1] A fleeting glance at the news headlines validates this gloomy outlook. The number of people fleeing war, persecution, and conflict exceeded 70 million globally in 2018, the highest number recorded by UNHCR in almost seventy years of its operation.[2] Inequality has also increased, with sixty-two of the world's richest people owning as much wealth as half of the world's population in 2015.[3] Climate change continues unabated with the years 2014 to 2018 being the four hottest on record.[4] It should perhaps come as no surprise then that there has been a surge of inquiries into security with academics seeking to rethink, redefine, and revise the concept.[5]

[1] Zygmunt Bauman, *Community: Seeking Safety in an Insecure World* (Polity 2001) 145.

[2] UNHCR, 'Global Trends Report: Forced Displacement in 2018' (2019) 2 <https://www.unhcr.org/5d08d7ee7.pdf> accessed 26 April 2020.

[3] 'Inequality' (*UN Global Compact*) <https://www.unglobalcompact.org/what-is-gc/our-work/social/inequality> accessed 26 April 2020.

[4] 'WMO Climate Statement: Past 4 years warmest on record' (*WMO*, 29 November 2018) <https://public.wmo.int/en/media/press-release/wmo-climate-statement-past-4-years-warmest-record> accessed 26 April 2020.

[5] See Jessica Tuchman Matthews, 'Redefining Security' (1989) 68 Foreign Affairs 162; J Ann Tickner, 'Re-Visioning Security' in Ken Booth/Steve Smith (eds), *International Relations Theory Today* (Polity Press 1995) 175.

Security operates on a number of levels, from the individual to the global. In this sense, a one-size-fits-all approach is not workable. In its most basic form, according to Kelsen, 'security is the condition of being protected against, or not exposed to, a danger. It is an objective condition of man which, rightly or wrongly, man assumes to exist.'[6] Security thus connotes the protection of an object by minimizing the threat to its survival.[7] One could disaggregate security into its components, namely the referent object of protection, the actor of protection, the origin of threat, and the means of protection.[8]

The key question that emerges is that of the level of analysis. For international lawyers, the first port of call has been the security of the sovereign State, which is only natural considering the centrality of the State in the international legal system. In the aftermath of the Second World War, and in the context of the UN, the 'collective security' of States assumed a significance of nearly existential proportions. After all, the UN Charter established a system in which each State 'accepts that the security of one is the concern of all, and agrees to join in a collective response to threats to, and breaches of, the peace.'[9]

Still, this State-centred reading of security has come under increasing pressure over the last three decades.[10] In 1994, the United Nations Development Programme (UNDP) in its *Human Development Report* made extensive reference to the concept of 'human security'. The Report argued for a move 'from an exclusive stress on territorial security to a much greater stress on people's security'.[11] In this sense, human security encompasses 'economic security, food security, health security, environmental security, community security, political security'.[12] The concept of 'human security' was further refined in the Commission on Human Security's *Human Security Now*. Therein the Commission made the following key findings. First, that while the State remains 'the fundamental purveyor of security (...) it often fails to fulfill its security obligations'.[13] Secondly, that it is necessary to shift from the security of the State to the security of people, that is, from State security to human security.[14] Thirdly, the Commission underscored that 'human security complements state security, enhances human rights and strengthens human development'.[15] Fourth, it upheld the broader reading of the content of security envisaged by the UNDP by referring to threats such as 'environmental pollution, transnational terrorism, massive population movements (...) such infectious diseases as HIV/AIDS and long-term conditions of oppression and deprivation'.[16] And, finally, it affirmed that the State was no longer the sole actor in the context of guaranteeing the

[6] Hans Kelsen, *Collective Security under International Law* (US Government Printing Office 1957) 1.

[7] More generally: Barbara von Tigerstrom, *Human Security and International Law* (Hart 2007) 8–14.

[8] cf the elaborate analysis on referent objects, securitizing actors and functional actors in Barry Buzan et al, *Security: A New Framework for Analysis* (Lynne Rienner 1998) 35–42.

[9] Vaughan Lowe et al, 'Introduction' in Vaughan Lowe et al (eds), *The United Nations Security Council and War: The Evolution of Thought and Practice since 1945* (OUP 2008) 13.

[10] See Nigel White/Auden Davies-Bright, Chapter 1 in this *Handbook*.

[11] UNDP, *Human Development Report 1994* (OUP 1994) 24. [12] ibid 24–5.

[13] Commission on Human Security, *Human Security Now* (Commission on Human Security 2003) 2.

[14] ibid. [15] ibid. [16] ibid 6.

security of people, thus foreshadowing the weaving of non-State actors into discussions on human security.[17]

The revisiting of the concept of 'security' came full circle in the oft-discussed UN Secretary-General's High Level Panel on Threats, Challenges and Change Report, entitled 'A More Secure World: Our Shared Responsibility', which set forth as a central challenge 'to fashion a new and broader understanding... of what collective security means'.[18] The need for this broader understanding was said to stem from the fact that the actual threats that the world faces 'go far beyond States waging aggressive war'.[19] They include 'poverty; infectious disease and environmental degradation; war and violence within States; the spread and possible use of nuclear, radiological, chemical and biological weapons terrorism; and transnational organized crime'.[20] According to the Report '[t]hese threats emerge from non-state actors as well as States and they threaten human security as well as State security'.[21]

The above reports mark fundamental shifts in contemporary thinking on security. First, they highlight that threats to collective or global security are not solely driven by military force. Secondly, they refocus the attention on individuals as the ultimate beneficiaries of any collective—or global, for that matter—system. Finally, they open up the discourse on security beyond States and international organizations by recognizing the potential role of non-State actors in guaranteeing the security of individuals.

This chapter aims to further this thinking on non-State actors in the context of guaranteeing human security. Of course, 'human security' as a concept may be seen as methodologically over-inclusive. After all, threats to collective or international security, such as inter-State use of military force, necessarily imperil the security of individuals.[22] For the purposes of this chapter, threats to 'human security' are understood as threats to the fundamental human rights of individuals. It is posited that international practice has recognized the interlinking—and potential causal—pathways between gross violations of human rights and threats to international peace.[23]

The chapter starts by discussing the traditional dual role of States, as violators and guarantors of human rights. Security offered by States to individuals within their territory is crucial in terms of attaining security at an international level. Indeed, lack of security within the boundaries of a State can have debilitating effects on regional or

[17] ibid.

[18] UNGA 'Report of the High-level Panel on Threats, Challenges and Change: A More Secure World: Our Shared Responsibility' (2 December 2004) UN Doc A/59/565, 11.

[19] ibid. [20] ibid. [21] ibid.

[22] See in this respect the criticism offered by Roland Paris, 'Human Security: Paradigm Shift or Hot Air?' (2001) 26 International Security 87. In this context: eg UNHRC 'General Comment No 36 (2018) on article 6 of the International Covenant on Civil and Political Rights, on the right to life' (30 October 2018) UN Doc CCPR/C/GC/36 (GC 36), para 70, according to which:

> States parties engaged in acts of aggression as defined in international law, resulting in deprivation of life, violate ipso facto article 6 of the Covenant... States parties that fail to take all reasonable measures to settle their international disputes by peaceful means might fall short of complying with their positive obligation to ensure the right to life.

[23] UNSC Res 1072 (1996); GC 36 (n 22).

international peace. It then examines whether non-State actors can assume a corresponding dual role, looking into the role of multinational enterprises, de facto regimes, and clans through the lens of international human rights and refugee law. Finally, it reframes the category of 'non-State actors' more generally and posits that these actors may not be all that detached or different from States in the first place.

B. States and Security in International Law

States are presumed to effectively control portions of territory, and within such territory exercise public authority, assert a monopoly over the legal use of force, and maintain law and order.[24] Due to said effective control, States are the prime originators of threat to the well-being of individuals on their territory. Individuals have historically engaged in a struggle against the legal and socio-economic power that the sovereign wields over them. The product of this struggle is human rights rules. Human rights from a historical and normative point of view are concerned with the relations between individuals and power. The internationalization of human rights in the post Second World War era amounted to an effort to create a body of law that stands extraneous to power,[25] and is capable of safeguarding the freedoms of individuals against arbitrary State action.[26] In the words of European Court of Human Rights (ECtHR) Judge Loucaides, human rights countermand 'the possibility of imposing the will of the State on any person'.[27] At the same time, States on account of their effective control are the prime actors of protection vis-à-vis persons within their territory to the exclusion of other sovereigns. The State then has a dual role in relation to the security of individuals, namely as violator and guarantor.

This duality is captured in contemporary human rights law. Suffice here to make reference to Article 5 of the European Convention on Human Rights (ECHR), which proclaims the right to liberty and security of person.[28] On the one hand, the provision routinely applies to situations of deprivation of liberty as a result of coercive action by law enforcement agents of a State.[29] On the other hand, States have been held in violation of the same provision when they acquiesce in infringements on a person's liberty caused by private individuals.[30]

[24] Nico Schrijver, 'The Changing Nature of State Sovereignty' (2000) 70 British Yearbook of International Law 65, 71.

[25] Patrick Wachsmann, *Les droits de l'homme* (Dalloz 1993) 3.

[26] Thomas Buergenhta, 'International Human Rights in an Historical Perspective' in Janusz Symonides (ed), *Human Rights: Concepts and Standards* (Routledge 2000) 3.

[27] *Assandize v Georgia*, App No 71503/01, 8 April 2004, Concurring Opinion of Judge Loucaides, para 1.

[28] Convention for the Protection of Human Rights and Fundamental Freedoms ETS No 5 art 5.

[29] *Krupko and Others v Russia*, App No 26587/07, 17 November 2014, para 36; *Foka v Turkey*, App No 28940/95, 24 June 2008, para 78.

[30] *Rantsev v Cyprus and Russia*, App No 25965/04, 7 January 2010, paras 319–21.

Parallel to guaranteeing the life and liberty of individuals within the territorial boundaries of a State, namely the security within the State, it is imperative that the security of the State apparatus itself is safeguarded. State security covers the preservation by States of their territory, values, development, and the quality of life of their population from external threat.[31] The absence of danger to the integrity of a State emanating from another has been recognized as a precondition for international security. As succinctly put in a UN Group of Experts Report, '[i]nternational security is (…) the sum of the security of each and every State (…) international security cannot be reached without full international co-operation'.[32] The same point has been made in the African Union Declaration on the Common African Defence and Security Policy, wherein it is proclaimed that 'the security of one African country is inseparably linked to the security of other African countries and the African continent as a whole'.[33] States then emerge on the international level as referent objects of protection, actors of protection, and originators of threat. In refraining from acts endangering international security, States perform a 'public mission in the interest of international stability'.[34]

C. Multinational Enterprises as a Threat to Human Security

In an era of globalization, thought to erode State sovereignty and thus the centrality of States on the global plane, it has become trite to refer to multinational enterprises (MNEs)[35] as a threat to human rights. Multinational enterprises pose a challenge to sovereign States in three key ways. First, the annual revenue of MNEs such as Walmart or Royal Dutch Shell dwarves that of the majority of States.[36] Secondly, and more importantly, MNEs have entered 'what used to be in many countries "reserved" state businesses

[31] Alexander Orakhelashvili, *Collective Security* (OUP 2011) 4.

[32] UNGA 'Report of the Secretary-General: Study on Concepts of Security' (26 August 1985) UN Doc A/40/553, 10.

[33] AU, 'Solemn Declaration on the Common African Defence and Security Policy' (Sirte, 28 February 2004) <http://www.peaceau.org/uploads/declaration-cadsp-en.pdf> accessed 26 April 2020.

[34] Christian Tomuschat 'International Law: Ensuring the Survival of Mankind on the Eve of a New Century: General Course on Public International Law' (2001) 281 Recueil des Cours 94.

[35] In his seminal article on the issue, Vagts defined the MNE as 'a cluster of corporations of diverse nationality joined by ties of common ownership and responsive to a common management strategy': Detlev F Vagts, 'The Multinational Enterprise: A New Challenge for Transnational Law' (1970) 83 Harvard Law Review 740. Whereas the terms 'multinational enterprise' and 'transnational' or 'multinational corporation' have been employed by various authors and bodies to denote a variety of corporate structures, one could infer from the above definitions some of the key characteristics of the MNE from a legal point of view. First and foremost, an MNE owns and operates assets and controls their use across national frontiers. Secondly, this complex of discrete entities constitutes a single economic unit, responsive to the managerial direction of a sole decision-making centre.

[36] 'Global 500 List' (*Fortunes*) <https://fortune.com/global500/> accessed 26 April 2020.

in the "public service" fields',[37] such as electricity, gas transports, the operation of prisons, even the conduct of war. Finally, the multinational nature of their conduct clashes with territorially bounded conceptions of sovereignty. Multinational enterprises have the capacity to operate in a number of host countries through subsidiaries, while remaining responsive to the strategic decisions made by the parent company incorporated in the home State. Any proposal that the home State regulate the conduct of the corporation as a whole is bound to meet with criticism from the standpoint of sovereignty and interventionism.[38] Conversely, the regulation of corporations by the host State may not always result in guaranteeing corporate responsibility. Host States competing for foreign investment, the argument goes, often lower their domestic standards to attract corporate investors.[39] What is more, they may have weak enforcement mechanisms or may lack the capacity or resources to enforce regulatory standards in the first place.[40]

Indeed, there has been ample documentation of MNEs' conduct posing a threat to human security. Perhaps the most prominent case is that of Royal Dutch Shell's operation in Nigeria's Ogoniland. In this situation, the Nigerian-domiciled Shell Petroleum Development Company acted as shareholder in a consortium with the Nigerian State oil company, namely the Nigerian National Petroleum Company. The purpose of the consortium was to exploit oil reserves in the region of Ogoniland. As a response to the operations of the consortium, a protest group called the Movement for the Survival of the Ogoni People (MOSOP) engaged in a campaign bringing to public attention the nefarious environmental impact of said operations. In response to the protest, the Nigerian military and police forces resorted to attacks on the villages in the area, and nine MOSOP activists were tried by a special tribunal and executed.[41]

The Ogoni case was brought before domestic and international fora, shedding light on corporate conduct and its interlinking with the host State. The African Commission on Human and Peoples' Rights was called upon to hear a complaint against Nigeria turning *inter alia* on the violation of the right to life under Article 4 of the African

[37] August Reinisch, 'The Changing International Legal Framework for Dealing with Non-State Actors' in Philip Alston (ed), *Non-State Actors and Human Rights* (OUP 2005) 75.

[38] Francesco Francioni, 'Exporting Environmental Hazard through Multinational Enterprises: Can the State of Origin be Held Responsible?' in Francesco Francioni/Tullio Scovazzi (eds), *International Responsibility for Environmental Harm* (Graham and Trotman 1991) 275.

[39] Peter T Muchlinski, 'Human Rights and Multinationals: Is there a Problem?' (2001) 77 International Affairs 31, 44–7; Carlos M Vazquez, 'Direct vs. Indirect Obligations of Corporations under International Law' (2005) 43 Columbia Journal of Transnational Law 927, 931–2; Rebecca M Bratspies, '"Organs of Society": A Plea for Human Rights Accountability for Transnational Enterprises and Other Business Entities' (2005) 13 Michigan State Journal of International Law 9, 37.

[40] The differences between States with regard to their institutional and economic capacity pose a wider challenge in respect of the effectiveness of international law. Peter Sand, 'Institution-Building to Assist Compliance with International Environmental Law: Perspectives' (1996) 50 Zeitschrift für ausländisches öffentliches Recht und Völkerrecht 774, 780.

[41] Jędrzej George Frynas, 'Corporate and State Responses to anti-oil Protests in the Niger Delta' (2001) 100 African Affairs 27.

Charter on Human and Peoples' Rights.[42] The Commission found that the provision had been breached 'given the widespread violations perpetrated by the Government of Nigeria and by private actors (be it following its clear blessing or not)'.[43] Whereas the Commission noted that 'the intervention of multinational corporations may be a potentially positive force for development if the State and the people concerned are ever mindful of the common good and the sacred rights of individuals and communities',[44] it went on to stress that 'the Nigerian government has given the green light to private actors, and the oil companies in particular, to devastatingly affect the well-being of the Ogonians'.[45]

At the same time, the widows of the executed activists sought relief before US domestic courts under the Alien Tort Claims Act, claiming that Royal Dutch Petroleum Co., a subsidiary of Royal Dutch Petroleum domiciled in the United States, aided and abetted the Nigerian Government in committing violations of the law of nations in Nigeria, including the perpetration of extrajudicial killings. According to the Alien Tort Claims Act, 'district courts shall have original jurisdiction of any civil action by an alien for a tort only, committed in violation of the law of nations or a treaty of the United States'.[46] The case reached the US Supreme Court, which was called upon to decide whether a claim under the Alien Tort Statute 'may reach conduct occurring in the territory of a foreign sovereign'.[47] The Court answered the question in the negative, holding that a presumption against extraterritoriality applied to the statute. Justice Roberts, writing for the majority, opined that all the relevant conduct took place outside the US. He continued stating that, even

> where the claims touch and concern the territory of the United States, they must do so with sufficient force to displace the presumption against extraterritorial application (…) Corporations are often present in many countries, and it would reach too far to say that mere corporate presence suffices.[48]

The final act of the Ogoni saga is to play out in the Netherlands, where Esther Kiobel and three other widows of the deceased Ogoni activists sued Royal Dutch Shell. Whereas Shell argued that the jurisdictional requirements to enable the Dutch courts to hear the claim against the Nigerian subsidiary and the Dutch 'anchor defendant' had not been met, the District Court of the Hague, on 1 May 2019, allowed the case to go forward. More specifically, the Court granted leave to the claimants to prove that the defendant was involved in bribing witnesses in the trial of the Ogoni activists, as well as that the statements of the witnesses bribed played a role in the detention, arrest, and conviction of the activists.[49]

[42] 1520 UNTS 217.

[43] *Social and Economic Rights Action Center and the Center for Economic and Social Rights v Nigeria*, African Commission on Human and Peoples' Rights, Comm No 155/96 (27 May 2002) para 67.

[44] ibid para 58. [45] ibid para 69. [46] Alien Tort Claims Act 28 U.S.C. §1350.

[47] *Kiobel v Royal Dutch Petroleum Co.* 133 U.S. 1664 (2013). [48] ibid 1669.

[49] Rechtbank Den Haag, C/09/540872/HA ZA 17-1048 (2019).

One may resort to the Ogoni case to make a number of key remarks vis-à-vis MNEs and the threat they pose to human security. Corporations bring their economic power to bear upon developing States. Still, as accurately noted by Seidl-Hohenveldern as far back as 1977, 'even a very small State has sovereign powers, which even a powerful transnational corporation does not have'.[50] Therefore, it is not so much that MNEs flagrantly act in defiance of fundamental rules of the international legal order. Rather, they do so in the shadow of, or in collusion with, the State. The State, despite its purported demise, retains a key role in guaranteeing human security, not only in its relations with individuals, but also in relations between individuals themselves, as well as individuals and MNEs.[51] This role of the State becomes even more accentuated as it chooses to delegate public functions to private entities, such as MNEs, thus giving rise to 'new fragmented centres of power... [which means that] the individual now perceives authority, repression and alienation in a variety of new bodies, whereas it was only the apparatus of the States which was perceived in the doctrine to exhibit those characteristics'.[52] To the extent that threats to human security emanate from MNEs, acting in concert with the State, such threats can only be countered by the State retaining a firm regulatory grip over corporate actors entering the realm of exercising public authority.

D. De facto Regimes, Armed Groups, and Clans as 'Actors of Protection'

Nonetheless, it is not always the case that non-State actors act in cooperation or in the shadow of the State, as with the MNEs. In the context of internal conflicts, armed opposition groups act in a manner which is antagonistic to the territorial State, seeking to supplant its control over territory. In this context, a different conundrum emerges. International human rights law is traditionally seen as binding States alone.[53] Non-state armed groups are then let off the legal hook, in the sense that they cannot be held responsible under international law in respect of human rights abuses. The response to this conundrum follows two parallel tracks. On the one hand, it is argued non-State armed groups in non-international armed conflicts are nonetheless bound by common

[50] Ignaz Seidl-Hohenveldern, 'The United Nations and Transnational Corporations' in Kenneth Simmonds (ed), *Legal Problems of Multinational Corporations* (BIICL 1977) 49.

[51] This point has been made by the ECtHR in the celebrated *X and Y v the Netherlands*, where the Court held that the obligations of States under international human rights law, and in particular the right to respect for private and family life, may involve 'the adoption of measures designed to secure the respect for private life even in the sphere of the relations of individuals between themselves': *X and Y v the Netherlands*, App No 8978/80, 26 March 1985, para 23.

[52] Andrew Clapham, *Human Rights in the Private Sphere* (OUP 1993) 137.

[53] Liesbeth Zegveld, *The Accountability of Armed Opposition Groups in International Law* (CUP 2002) 53; Ben Saul, 'Enhancing Civilian Protection by Engaging Non-State Armed Groups under International Humanitarian Law' (2017) 22 JCSL 39.

Article 3 of the Geneva Conventions of 1949, which requires each 'party' to a conflict to respect minimum humanitarian obligations, and customary international humanitarian law.[54] On the other hand, there have been calls for a paradigm shift in the manner in which the function of international human rights law is perceived. Indeed, it has been put forward that non-State armed groups should be seen as bound by international human rights law, and that this shift is evidenced in international practice.[55] More importantly, non-State armed groups have unilaterally committed themselves through the adoption of codes of conduct to baseline obligations under international humanitarian and human rights law, thus recognizing the relevance of these obligations in the context of their operations.[56] In this vein, one may ponder whether non-State armed groups do not solely pose a threat to human security, but whether they can amount to actors of protection.

One may address this last point through the lens of international refugee law. International refugee law regulates a complex triangular relationship between the refugee, the State of their nationality, and the State of asylum.[57] The refugee, owing to a well-founded fear of persecution for the reasons enumerated in the 1951 Refugee Convention, finds themselves outside the State of their nationality while being unwilling or unable to obtain the protection of this State.[58] By crossing the border into a third State, the refugee seeks the protection of the latter. The definition of the 'refugee' thus builds on two key concepts; 'fear of persecution' and 'protection of the State of nationality'. These two key concepts are intertwined. The failure of a State to safeguard the security of its nationals constitutes an integral element of a finding on persecution.[59]

It becomes obvious then that the term 'protection' by the State of nationality in Article 1(A)(2) of the 1951 Refugee Convention refers to the protection of human rights normally available to individuals located within their State of origin. As analysed by Fortin,

[54] Saul (n 53).

[55] Andrew Clapham, *Human Rights Obligations of Non-State Actors* (OUP 2006) 280–5; Sandesh Sivakumaran, *The Law of Non-International Armed Conflict* (OUP 2012) 94–7; Katharine Fortin, *The Accountability of Armed Groups under Human Rights Law* (OUP 2017) 240–84.

[56] Marco Sassòli, 'Engaging Non-State Actors: The New Frontier for International Humanitarian Law' in PSIO/UNIDIR/Geneva Call (eds), *Exploring Criteria and Conditions for Engaging Armed Non-State Actors to Respect Humanitarian Law and Human Rights Law* (Université de Genève 2008); Cedric Ryngaert/Anneleen Van de Meulebroucke, 'Enhancing and Enforcing Compliance with International Humanitarian Law by Non-State Armed Groups: An Inquiry into some Mechanisms' (2011) 16 JCSL 443, 451–3.

[57] Christian Tomuschat,'State Responsibility and the Country of Origin' in Vera Gowlland-Debbas (ed), *The Problem of Refugees in the Light of Contemporary International Law Issues* (Martinus Nijhoff 1996).

[58] Convention relating to the Status of Refugees 189 UNTS 137 art 1(A)(2).

[59] Lord Hoffmann of the UK House of Lords summarized this state of affairs in the following formula: «Persecution = Serious Harm + The Failure of State Protection» in *R v Immigration Appeal Tribunal and Another, Ex parte Shah* [1999] 2 AC 629, 653. The interplay between persecution and protection has been affirmed in numerous other jurisdictions. In New Zealand: *Daniel Martin Butler v Attorney General and Refugee Status Appeals Authority* [1999] NZAR 205, 216–17. In Canada: *Zalzali v Canada (Minister of Employment and Immigration)* [1991] 3 FC 605, 609–10.

> [p]rotection within the territory is provided through measures and mechanisms designed to establish the rights of the person and at setting up mechanisms to ensure that these can effectively be claimed and exercised, prevent the violation of the person's rights, and provide remedies where such violations occur. Protection within the territory may, thus, be promotional, preventive or remedial in nature, and implies the existence and effective functioning of administrative and judicial structures, as well as the existence and effective functioning of mechanisms and procedures for the investigation, prosecution and punishment of violations of the person's rights.[60]

In case such protection becomes unavailable for an individual, who then opts for flight as the ultimate option of survival, international refugee law comes into play. As the House of Lords noted in *Horvath*, '[t]he general purpose of the [1951 Refugee Convention] is to enable the person who no longer has the benefit of protection against persecution (…) in his own country to turn for protection to the international community'.[61] Protection offered to individuals recognized as refugees under the 1951 Refugee Convention, in sum international protection, is considered subsidiary or surrogate in character and is triggered when the protection of the State of nationality is lacking.[62]

Whereas 'protection' in international refugee law can be interpreted to refer to that due by the State of nationality to its nationals or that due to the refugee by the asylum State, domestic courts have inquired into whether the protection can also be offered by non-State 'actors of protection'.[63] This proposition turns the traditional logic inside out. Apart from posing a risk to individuals' safety, non-State actors may also be thought of as offering protection from persecution. This line of reasoning has a significant implication: if protection is available to the applicant within his or her country of nationality, albeit by a non-State actor in control of territory, then the 'well-foundedness' of his or her fear of persecution is vitiated. By implication, the said applicant is not in need of international protection under the 1951 Refugee Convention.[64]

One of the more interesting—and peculiar for that matter—cases, where courts have held that a non-State actor is in the position to offer protection, has been that of the de facto regime of Somaliland. Once a British protectorate, Somaliland attained independence on 26 June 1960, but was later united with the Trust territory of Somalia, which had gained independence from Italy, with a view to forming a 'Greater Somalia'. Following the fall of the Somali government in 1991, Somaliland participated briefly in the ensuing intra-clan hostilities before retreating to the former colonial borders and declaring

[60] Antonio Fortin, 'The Meaning of "Protection" in the Refugee Definition' (2000) 12 International Journal of Refugee Law 548, 552.

[61] *Horvath v Secretary of State for the Home Department* [2000] 3 All ER 577.

[62] James Hathaway/Michelle Foster, *The Law of Refugee Status* (2nd edn, CUP 2014) 289; cf Guy Goodwin-Gill/Jane McAdam, *The Refugee in International Law* (3rd edn, OUP 2007) 10–12.

[63] eg *Canaj v Secretary of State for the Home Department* [2001] INLR 342 (Eng CA); *Dyli . Secretary of State for the Home Department* [2000] Imm AR 652 (UKAIT).

[64] *DM (Majority Clans Entities can protect) Somalia* [2005] UKAIT 00150.

independence.[65] Ever since the Declaration of Independence, 'Somaliland has morphed into a de facto state exhibiting all the quintessential features of a state' but for recognition by third States.[66]

In a case turning on the dismissal of an asylum claim of a Somali on account of available 'protection' in Somaliland, the UK Immigration Appeal Tribunal held that

> [t]he administration in Somaliland operates the main functions of a government and spends a large proportion of its annual budget on security and law and order. Whilst it is not recognized as an independent state... nevertheless there has been appreciation from the United Nations for what they have achieved.[67]

On the basis of these considerations, the Tribunal held that under the circumstances of the case, there was sufficient protection within Somaliland and dismissed the appeal. The Swiss *Asylrekurskommission* has followed a similar logic. While recognizing the chaotic situations in the South of Somalia, it has noted the 'constant progress, especially in terms of stability of institutions and security, in the north of the country, which is made up of Somaliland and Puntland'.[68] It therefore has concluded that Somali claimants hailing from Somaliland clans can be reasonably returned to Somaliland and Puntland, unless they belong to vulnerable groups, such as unaccompanied minors, or they do not have a family network to turn to for support in Somaliland.[69]

Another category of non-State actors found to be able to offer protection equal to that of the State of nationality is clans. The leading case in this respect is *DM*, in which the UK Asylum and Immigration Tribunal held that majority clans in Somalia can serve as actors of protection. According to the reasoning of the Tribunal:

> All that is essential for Refugee Convention... purposes, therefore, is that as a matter of fact an entity within a country or state affords effective protection. Plainly, an entity which relies for its law an [sic] order functions on drug barons or armed militias may be less able to provide effective protection than one which can rely on those functions being performed by properly trained, properly resourced and accountable police or army personnel whose standards of human conduct are exemplary.[70]

The Tribunal then went on to analyse the operation of clans in Somalia and held that it is beyond dispute that three major clans in Somalia each control a substantial part of its territory. It then held:

[65] James Crawford, *The Creation of States in International Law* (2nd edn, OUP 2006) 413–14.

[66] Jackson Maogoto, 'Somaliland: Scrambled by International Law?' in Duncan French (ed), *Statehood and Self-Determination: Reconciling Tradition and Modernity in International Law* (CUP 2013) 209.

[67] *HF (Persecution-Discrimination-Yibir-Occupation-Caste) Somalia CG* [2002] UKAIT 05520.

[68] Commission suisse de recours en matière d'asile, Case no 2006/2, §7.1–7.2 (author's translation).

[69] ibid §7.2.

[70] *DM (Majority Clan Entities Can Protect) Somalia* (n 64) para 22.

> we see no logical difficulty with clan militiamen and other majority clan personnel performing quasi-governmental functions being considered as state actors (as opposed to non-state actors)...there will be a continuum of circumstances spanning the state agency/non-state actor divide.[71]

A similar line of reasoning was adopted by the Federal Court of Canada in *Elmi*, which concerned the refusal of refugee status to a Somali applicant. The Federal Court allowed the application for judicial review and set aside the initial judgment, finding that it erred in law. Yet, it refused to find an error in law as regards the reliance on behalf of the Immigration and Refugee Board on specialized knowledge. The Board had based its finding on the experience gathered by the Board in dealing with cases on Somalia. Specifically, the Board held that 'it is one's clan that is the de facto government and therefore the de facto agent of protection in the various regions controlled by one's clan; it is the clan that is the social welfare agency in that region.'[72]

The above analysis from the perspective of refugee law lends credence to the proposition that non-State actors such as de facto regimes, armed groups, and clans may for the purposes of the 1951 Refugee Convention be conceived as actors of protection, thus validating the aforementioned paradigm shift vis-à-vis the manner in which we perceive the relationship between non-State actors and human security.

E. Revisiting Non-State Actors in the Context of Human Security

The role of non-State actors with respect to the security of individuals can be multifaceted, as non-State actors assume a variety of forms and functions. Non-State actors may have a positive role as guarantors of human security or a detrimental one as violators of human rights, just as States do. It is then imperative to revisit and lay bare the concept of 'non-State' actors and seek to understand what it is about these actors that differentiates them from States, and to what extent.

Discussions on 'non-State' actors have become a key *leitmotiv* in international legal scholarship ever since the end of the Cold War. At first, international lawyers were overwhelmed by the 'demise' or 'waning' of the State,[73] the basic building block of the international legal order throughout the positivist twentieth century. Subsequently, they

[71] ibid para 31.

[72] *Elmi v the Minister of Citizenship and Immigration* [1999] FC IMM-580-98, para 8.

[73] Oscar Schachter, 'The Decline of the Nation State and its Implications for International Law' (1997) 36 Columbia Journal of Transnational Law 7; Christoph Schreuer, 'The Waning of the Sovereign State: Towards a New Paradigm of International Law' (1993) 4 EJIL 447; Martii Koskenniemi, 'The Future of Statehood'(1991) 32 Harvard International Law Journal 397.

sought to come to terms with the advent of the 'non-State', understand its workings and examine how it fits within the corsetry of international law.

It has been argued that 'non-state actors can be any actor on the international plane other than a sovereign state'.[74] Still, using a term that does not contain a single positive attribute, leads to an analytical oversimplification. Alston has in this respect spoken of the 'not-a-cat' syndrome, whereby his daughter would describe a rabbit, a mouse or a kangaroo as a 'not-a-cat'.[75] The same goes for international lawyers. According to Alston, reference to the 'non-State' has the 'ability to obfuscate any debate', yet insistence upon defining all actors in terms of what they are not may not stem from 'language inadequacies' but may seek to reinforce 'the assumption that the State is not only the central actor, but also the indispensable and pivotal one around which all the other entities revolve'.[76] From an international law point of view, 'key actors are divided into two categories: states and the rest'.[77]

Nonetheless, the State is neither the sole entity with the capacity to act on the international plane nor the sole entity bestowed with international legal personality. Today, international organizations and individuals are routinely considered subjects of international law.[78] Interestingly, references to 'non-State' actors seem to go beyond individuals, who form the backbone of States, and international organizations, whose backbone are States. It is as if the 'non-State' label is reserved for those assemblages of individuals, which have not yet been woven into the fabric of contemporary international law.

The traditional, State-centred account of the international legal order builds on a number of fallacies that one needs to dispel prior to engaging in any meaningful discussion of specific non-State actors in the context of human security.

First and foremost, the juxtaposition of States to non-State actors suggests that the latter do not possess the ontological attributes of the former, and therefore the two do not conceptually overlap. In short, an entity is either State or non-State. What appears to set the two apart is *effectiveness*, on which the traditional criteria of statehood were almost entirely based.[79] It is often presumed that what sets States apart from individuals, international organizations, and the rest is the capacity of States to effectively exercise governmental power with respect to some area and population, to the exclusion of the exercise of similar power by another State. This in turn means, as stated above, that the State is the prime guarantor of human security within its boundaries. Conversely, this should mean that non-State actors operate within the territory of a State or across national borders, always presumably finding themselves under the control of one or more sovereign States.

[74] Mary Ellen O'Connell, 'Enhancing the Status of Non-State Actors through a Global War on Terror' (2005) 43 Columbia Journal of Transnational Law 435, 437.

[75] Philip Alston, 'The 'Not-a-Cat Syndrome: Can the International Human Rights Regime Accommodate Non-State Actors?' in Alston (n 37) 3.

[76] ibid. [77] ibid.

[78] James Crawford, *Brownlie's Principles of Public International Law* (9th edn, OUP 2019) 106–11.

[79] ibid 97.

Of course this is not always the case. Or to be more precise, this has rarely been the case. The idea that the globe can be wholly apportioned into swaths of land, over each of which there actually exists effective control by a sovereign State, is fiction. Political scientists have increasingly engaged with the question of 'areas of limited statehood', that is 'areas where central state authorities do not control the territory, do not possess the monopoly over the means of violence, and/or have limited capacities to enforce and implement decisions'.[80] Limited statehood is not just limited to 'failed' States. On the contrary, many developing and transition States contain such areas.

The lack of a State, or to be more precise, the lack of effective control by a State over given territory does not necessarily give rise to a vacuum, anarchy or chaos: '[r]ather, we do find governance—both rule-making and the provision of collective goods—in areas of limited statehood which is both legitimate and effective under certain conditions'.[81] This ultimately leads to the contestation of the assumption above, namely that effective control over territory is intrinsically bound with statehood. Groups of individuals other than the State, such as armed groups or even de facto regimes may exercise effective control over territory. Verhoeven has noted with respect to Somalia, the paradigmatic example of State failure, that whereas it resembled a 'terrifying war zone' to outsiders, it was in reality a 'complex mosaic of traditional and imaginative informal mechanisms and pacts [which provided] a reasonable degree of stability'.[82]

This equally means that the centrality of the State in respect of guaranteeing security is only part of the story. Non-State actors who exercise effective control over territory may be in the position to deliver security to individuals in a measure comparable to that of States:

> [B]y creating structures, procedures and norms related to governance provision, violent and criminal non-state actors learn to speak the "language of stateness". This goal can be especially important to groups with clearly political and governance-based objectives, including secession or government replacement.[83]

In short, State and non-State entities may not be as radically different as imagined. State and non-State are not mutually exclusive, but form the opposite ends of the spectrum. An entity not constituting a State may still be an entity that could become a State, thus being of considerable significance from the perspective of security.

[80] Tanja Börzel/Thomas Risse, 'Governance without a State: Can it Work?' (2010) 4 Regulation and Governance 113, 119.

[81] Thomas Risse, 'Governance Configurations in Areas of Limited Statehood: Actors, Modes, Institutions, and Resources' (2012) SFB-Governance Working Paper Series No 32, 5 <https://www.sfb-governance.de/en/publikationen/sfb-700-working_papers/wp32/SFB-Governance-Working-Paper-32.pdf> accessed 26 April 2020.

[82] Harry Verhoeven, 'The Self-Fulfilling Prophecy of Failed States: Somalia, State Collapse and the Global War on Terror' (2009) 3 Journal of Eastern African Studies 405, 411 and 412, as referred to in Fortin (n 55) 41.

[83] Benedetta Berti, 'Violent and Criminal Non-State Actors' in Thomas Risse et al (eds), *The Oxford Handbook of Governance and Limited Statehood* (OUP 2018) 276–7.

The State/non-State conundrum can further be read from a functional perspective. International lawyers have deplored the retreat of the State and the assumption by non-State actors of functions closely linked to sovereignty.[84] The idea is that the more the non-State expands, the more the State wanes. Private corporations today run prisons, provide health services, wage wars. Non-governmental organizations are instrumental in the running of reception facilities for asylum applicants. Nonetheless, one needs to keep in mind that the increase in the regulatory space occupied by the non-State is not a natural occurrence, but the result of political choices. Thus, the privatization of the provision of public goods is the result of State policies, often deliberated in national parliaments, and proceeding on the basis of national laws. In sum, non-State actors may act as functional extensions of the State. In these cases, the State and the non-state are in a cooperative relationship.

This in turn raises the question of which is the entity responsible for guaranteeing human security in any given context. International legal scholarship has focused entirely on the need to submit non-State actors to international law as a means of guaranteeing respect for the human rights of individuals.[85] This logic stems from a belief that non-State actors in their various guises act as autonomous centres of power that need to be restrained, a power which stands above that of the sovereign State. Still, as argued above and as exemplified by the Ogoni case, the power exercised by corporations is often power delegated to them by the sovereign or power to the exercise of which the sovereign has acquiesced. The more the sovereign State delegates powers to non-State actors, such as corporations, the more vigilant it should be towards guaranteeing human security. As the ECtHR has notably held, '[t]he State cannot completely absolve itself of its responsibility by delegating its obligations in this sphere to private bodies or individuals.'[86]

F. Conclusion

Discussions on security have witnessed a widening in terms of actors and a broadening in terms of themes. As such, we have now moved past the traditional analytical frame of the threats to security owing to the use of military force by sovereign States. In the context of human security, the individual, and its fundamental rights, have emerged as referent objects of protection. The actors of protection and actors from the conduct of which the threat originates may be both States and the wide variety of non-State actors. To insist on non-State actors as a uniform set of actors does not make sense analytically. One needs to inquire into the actual configuration of power within which the actor

[84] Schreuer (n 73); Schachter (n 73) 7–23.
[85] See Clapham, *Human Rights Obligations of Non-State Actors* (n 55).
[86] *Storck v Germany*, App No 61603/00, 16 June 2005, para 103.

operates. A non-State actor, such as an armed group or a de facto regime, may itself aim to become the territorial State. Conversely, a non-State actor, such as a multinational enterprise, may act as the functional extension of the territorial State, in the sense that the latter has delegated public functions to the former. In both cases, the non-State actor emerges as a source of authority, and thus is in the position to both undermine and uphold human security.

ECONOMIC AND RESOURCE SECURITY

CHAPTER 25

ENERGY SECURITY IN INTERNATIONAL LAW

TIBISAY MORGANDI AND JORGE E VIÑUALES

A. Introduction

ENERGY is an essential requirement of modern society, and this has given rise to the concept of 'energy security', understood as the 'uninterrupted availability of energy resources at an affordable price'.[1] Importantly, according to this definition, the 'availability' of energy resources is measured against existing energy demand, and threats to energy security are therefore threats to the supply of enough energy to meet existing energy demand.

Such threats have been addressed in different ways: some through policies focusing on energy supply (such as investment in increased energy supply, diversification of energy sources relied upon, diversification of energy imports); and others on energy demand (including energy efficiency policies and policies aimed at changing consumer behaviour).

It is not always possible to clearly distinguish between domestic and international aspects of energy (in)security, due to the fact that energy security is a function of both (domestic) demand and (domestic and/or international) threats. To put it simply, energy supply depends upon both domestic and international factors (eg, resource availability as opposed to geopolitical stability), which are so interconnected that it is difficult to distinguish where one starts and the other ends. What is clear, however, is that international law plays a fundamental role in addressing many threats to energy security.

[1] International Energy Agency (IEA), 'Energy Security' <https://www.iea.org/topics/energysecurity/> accessed 12 January 2020.

This chapter provides an overview of existing threats to energy security and the international legal frameworks that have been established in response. The first section discusses several important challenges to energy security, including an exponential increase in world energy demand, shortages of national oil and gas deposits, the need to reduce dependence on fossil fuel production in order to counteract climate change, along with risks of geopolitical instability. The next section outlines the main domestic and international legal responses to these challenges, focusing on the mechanisms aimed to ensure that the flow of energy remains uninterrupted and at an affordable price as well as on those mechanisms aimed at increasing access to energy resources. The last section concludes the analysis with some observations on how energy security could be enhanced.

B. Challenges to Energy Security

1. World Energy Demand and Fossil Fuel Reserves

Since the Industrial Revolution in the late eighteenth century, economic development and social welfare have been largely built upon the availability and use of fossil fuels (namely coal, oil, and natural gas).

While in the seventeenth century worldwide energy demand was satisfied by firewood, wind power, and hydropower, alongside animal and manpower, the invention and diffusion of the coal-fired steam engine progressively reduced reliance on those forms of energy, which came to be replaced with coal. The expansion in the use of coal was facilitated by abundant and easily recoverable reserves exploited first in England and later in other countries in Europe, such as Germany. From the end of the eighteenth and throughout the nineteenth century, coal became the predominant source of energy in these countries, fuelling their rapid economic development and their military and political ambitions.

With the invention of modern drilling processes for onshore deep oil wells and oil refining techniques in the mid-nineteenth century, oil entered the scene. Refined oil began to be used for the purpose of lighting and increasingly also in internal combustion engines. At the end of the nineteenth century, the oil industry had expanded from Pennsylvania to Texas and California and US oil companies were exporting crude oil to England and Europe, covering one-third of worldwide energy demand. Following this trend, in the 1950s States started exploiting a third kind of fossil fuel, natural gas, which by then, together with coal and oil, covered the majority of global energy demand. At the same time, global energy demand continued to increase exponentially along with significant increases in world economic development. Nuclear energy, the energy released by nuclear fission, was seen by some as the next major source of energy, succeeding coal and oil. However, this prediction only materialized in some specific countries, such as

France or Japan, which invested heavily in nuclear energy for reasons of energy security. At the global level, the energy matrix became significantly diversified, including fossil fuels, nuclear energy and [some share of] hydroelectricity. Fossil fuels remained—and still are—the main source of energy for the main energy services, thermal services, transportation, and electricity.

There have long been fears that, as they are finite, hydrocarbon resources are at risk of depletion. This fear found expression in a debate over whether we have reached 'peak oil'.[2] At a worldwide level, it is unclear whether this will happen in the foreseeable future, given that technological development (specifically the shale oil and gas revolution) is constantly redefining the size of domestic reserves. Nonetheless, at the national level, fossil fuel production has decreased substantially in many countries, either due to depletion of local reserves or because it is more economical to import fossil fuels from other countries.

Since the early twentieth century, this has increasingly led to the internationalization of the energy industry. This trend has also been enhanced by other factors, including the possibility of developing fossil fuel reserves located offshore. The Truman Declaration, after the Second World War, asserting jurisdiction over the US continental shelf was a clear manifestation of this enhanced ability to develop offshore fossil fuel resources, and it triggered a race which eventually led to the recognition of States' sovereign rights over their continental shelves. This has potential for both conflict and cooperation, as jurisdiction over the areas in which these reserves are found has to be delimited and, even when this is possible, the deposits often straddle the continental shelves of several States. The resources underneath the Arctic provide a good example of complexities involved in such processes.

Worldwide energy demand continues to increase. At the same time, there is increasing evidence that the energy matrix is undergoing a profound 'transformation' from high- to low-carbon sources, due to the need to combat climate change, shifting public perceptions and, perhaps above all, major changes in the demand for fossil fuels driven by technological change.[3] This transformation has deep geopolitical implications, as emphasized by a 2019 Report from the Global Commission on the Geopolitics of the Energy Transformation, chaired by Iceland's former President, Ólafur Ragnar Grímsson.[4] It is important to note, however, that the bulk of international law relating to energy security was built with a different landscape in view, modelled on the causes and consequences of the oil crisis of 1973, when the Arab members of the Organization of the Petroleum Exporting Countries (OPEC) imposed an oil embargo on the United States

[2] See eg Tyler Priest, 'Hubbert's Peak: The Great Debate over the End of Oil' (2014) 44 Historical Studies in the Natural Sciences 37.

[3] Jean-François Mercure et al, 'Macroeconomic Impact of Stranded Fossil-Fuel Assets' (2018) 8 Nature Climate Change 588.

[4] International Renewable Energy Agency, Global Commission on the Geopolitics of the Energy Transformation, *A New World: The Geopolitics of the Energy Transformation* (IRENA 2019).

and other countries supporting Israel in the Yom Kippur War.[5] This basic feature must be kept in mind in order to understand the international legal frameworks addressing energy security, which may otherwise appear ill-suited for the ongoing process of energy transformation.

2. Supply-side Threats: Geopolitical Considerations

Energy security is affected by geopolitical considerations in several ways. The most basic one is that energy resources, such as coal, oil, gas, and uranium, are stocks, and they are unevenly distributed around the world amongst energy resource-rich and energy resource-scarce countries.[6] Some States, such as Gulf countries or Russia, hold significant reserves of fossil fuels, whereas other States (for example China, India, and Japan) and State organizations (such as the EU) are net importers of some of these resources. Reliance on imports to satisfy domestic energy demand makes these actors dependent upon their international partners. However, these sources of supply can be unstable for several reasons.

First, importers can be put under coercive pressure by exporters. Aside from the 1973 oil embargo, one example in this regard is Ukraine, which imports Russian gas.[7] When, in summer 2014, Russia turned off the taps and stopped providing Ukraine with its agreed supply of gas, Ukraine was faced with the threat of gas shortages during a cold winter. The EU, as a major importer of Russian energy resources through Ukraine, played a key role in this situation and brokered a temporary resolution to the crisis.[8] The three parties signed a trilateral agreement which led to the resumption of Russian gas exports to Ukraine as well as to the sale of reverse flow volumes of gas from Europe, placed at a more competitive price ($30–40 million cubic metres lower than Russian gas).[9]

Secondly, downstream energy importers can be vulnerable to political tension between exporters and transit countries. Again, Ukraine serves as an example, because it is not just a consumer of Russian gas, but also a transit country for Russian gas exports to Europe.[10] Over the last fifteen years, Europe's gas supply has been affected by the increasing tension between Ukraine and Russia, exacerbated by the war in Eastern Ukraine and Russia's annexation of Crimea.[11] On three occasions, Russia has interrupted gas supply

[5] G John Ikenberry, 'The Irony of State Strength: Comparative Responses to the Oil Shocks in the 1970s' (1986) 40 International Organization 105.

[6] Arghyrios A Fatouros, 'An International Legal Framework for Energy' (2007) 332 Recueil des Cours 373.

[7] Simon Pirani/Katja Yafimava, 'Russian Gas Transit across Ukraine Post-2019: Pipeline Scenarios, Gas Flow Consequences, and Regulatory Constraints' (Oxford Institute for Energy Studies (OIES) Paper NG 105, 2016) 16 <https://www.oxfordenergy.org/wpcms/wp-content/uploads/2016/02/Russian-Gas-Transit-Across-Ukraine-Post-2019-NG-105.pdf> accessed 20 May 2020.

[8] ibid. [9] ibid. [10] ibid 8. [11] ibid 9–10.

to Ukraine (in 2006, 2009, and 2014),[12] leading to a drop of up to 30 per cent in gas pressure in the pipelines of countries such as Austria, France, Germany, Hungary, Italy, and Poland.[13] This has cast doubt on Russia's reliability as a gas supplier, and has, as a result, led European countries increasingly to turn to other partners, such as Qatar and the United States, who are now major exporters of Liquefied Natural Gas (LNG) worldwide.[14] Recently, Germany announced the construction of two LNG terminals through which US LNG could reach the German market and, from there, the European gas market.[15]

Thirdly, security of imports can also be threatened by factors that are beyond the immediate control of the exporting countries. For example, a crash in oil prices can affect countries whose revenues are highly dependent on oil exports and even lead to the reduction of their production capacity. Indeed, lower revenues may lead to under-investment in production capacity and thereby curtail future export prospects. This can be illustrated by the case of Venezuela, which was the fourth largest producer of crude oil and became a country whose 'oil exports are headed toward zero'.[16]

Conflict or political instability in an exporting country can also undermine the energy security of importers. For example, in June 2018, one of the two main Libyan factions, the Libyan National Army, froze oil exports, purportedly in response to corruption in the industry, leading to a sharp increase in global oil prices, with adverse—albeit transitory—effects on EU oil imports.[17] Indeed, in some countries, the presence of valuable resources can itself be a 'curse' and generate domestic political instability[18] when the normal political order breaks down. At its worst, exporting countries can also become subject to sanctions preventing them from exporting their resources, as illustrated by sanctions adopted against Iraq, Iran, and Libya.

It is important to note that the internationalization of energy markets is a double-edged sword. Dependence on foreign resources may create insecurity but the diversification of foreign sources, which is a key dimension of internationalization, can offset such insecurity. This can be illustrated again by reference to Libya's oil exports in 2018:

[12] ibid 18–20.

[13] John Henley, 'Is Europe's Gas Supply Threatened by the Ukraine Crisis' (*The Guardian*, 3 March 2014) <https://www.theguardian.com/world/2014/mar/03/europes-gas-supply-ukraine-crisis-russsia-pipelines> accessed 12 January 2020.

[14] Pirani/Yafimava (n 7) 9.

[15] Guy Chazan, 'US Welcomes Germany's Announcement of New Gas Terminals' (*Financial Times*, 12 February 2019) <https://www.ft.com/content/fb07c374-2ece-11e9-ba00-0251022932c8?desktop=true&segmentId=d8d3e364-5197-20eb-17cf-2437841d178a#myft:notification:instant-email:content> accessed 12 January 2020.

[16] Robert Rapier, 'Venezuela's Oil Exports are Headed toward Zero' (*Forbes*, 8 June 2018) <https://www.forbes.com/sites/rrapier/2018/06/08/venezuelas-oil-exports-are-headed-toward-zero/#7f9a56bb6876> accessed12 January 2020.

[17] Scott Belinski, 'The Real Reason Europe Finally Attempts to Stabilize Libya' (*Oil Price*, 27 October 2018) <https://oilprice.com/Geopolitics/International/The-Real-Reason-Europe-Finally-Attempts-To-Stabilize-Libya.html> accessed 12 January 2020.

[18] An in-depth analysis of the correlation between oil-exporting countries and authoritarian regimes has been carried out by Leif Wenar, *Blood Oil: Tyrants, Violence and the Rules that Run the World* (OUP 2016). See also Jorge E Viñuales, 'The Resource Curse: A Legal Perspective' (2011) 17 Global Governance 197.

> Libya's growing output has...been able to stave off some unexpected production declines—such as the 150,000 barrels per day drop in Iranian production that was offset by Libya's 100,000 barrels per day jump. Saudi Arabia boasts that its total spare capacity is in excess of 1.3 million barrels per day, but that won't cover the almost 2 million barrels per day Iran exported in August. With the Trump administration's Iran sanctions kicking back in November 5, Libya's importance to the stability of the global oil markets will only increase in importance.[19]

Besides geopolitical factors, other important factors have a bearing on energy (in)security, as discussed next.

3. Demand-side Threats: Stranded Fossil Fuel Assets and Insufficient Planning

One might think that measures relating to the transition to a low-carbon economy, such as efficiency measures, renewable energy mandates, and the like, could have no adverse impact on energy security. This is because such measures are designed to reduce reliance on foreign stocks of energy resources. This is certainly true to some extent. Efficiency and renewable energy policies adopted as part of efforts to curb climate change can be seen as a means to be less dependent on fossil fuels, either because energy demand is lower (buildings, equipment, and appliances use less energy to perform the same task) or because it is satisfied in another form (such as electricity generated from renewable sources). On closer inspection, however, the energy transformation driven by the need to respond to climate change can have significant adverse effects on energy security, at least if no suitable plan anticipating these effects is put in place.

First, there is now a vast body of climate change law at the international,[20] transnational,[21] and domestic levels,[22] which, if properly enforced, may place limits on the use of fossil fuels. Countries which do not plan for a more diversified energy matrix may face the insecurity arising from 'transitional risks', such as the risk of adverse impact on the fossil fuel industry (and other industries exposed to it) resulting from laws and regulations to limit emissions. Such risks may arise both from the economic collapse of the domestic energy industry (thus exposing a country to the risks of importing energy) or from mismatches between energy demand and domestic capacity. There has been much debate about 'stranded' fossil fuel resources, namely resources which cannot be

[19] Belinski (n 17).

[20] Pierre-Marie Dupuy/Jorge E Viñuales, *International Environmental Law* (2nd edn, CUP 2018) ch 5.

[21] Harriet Bulkeley et al, *Transnational Climate Change Governance* (CUP 2014).

[22] Justin Gundlach/Michael Gerrard, 'Climate and Energy Transition Policies' in Emma Lees and Jorge E Viñuales (eds), *The Oxford Handbook of Comparative Environmental Law* (OUP 2019).

extracted and used due to climate change targets.[23] The debate typically pits against each other two perspectives, that is, a 'moralistic' perspective and a 'cynical' perspective, with attempts at bridging the gap between the two by 'timeframe' arguments. In short, requiring that fossil fuel resources stay underground in order to comply with climate change legislation (the moralistic view) has been criticized by those who believe that no State, faced with energy shortages, would allow that (the cynical view). In fact, the latter view holds that climate legislation remains vague and its implementation weak. Between these two extremes, some argue that the reasons why fossil fuel reserves can be extracted and used is that the timeframe of climate change policies allows for that, at least transitionally. In this debate, the question of whether fossil fuel resources will remain unused (stranded) or not seems to depend almost entirely on the stringency and enforcement of climate change policies.

Yet, there is a subtler and, in our view, much stronger reason why energy transition policies may have an adverse effect on energy security. As shown by a study published in Nature Climate Change in 2018, existing investments in renewable technologies, energy efficiency, and electric vehicles are already driving a decline in demand for fossil fuels.[24] In the scenarios analysed by this study, demand for fossil fuels will peak around 2040, leading to the stranding of fossil fuel assets in high-cost producers, such as Canada, the United States, and Russia. The study argues that this will be the case 'even if major fossil fuel producers (such as the US) refrain from adopting climate change mitigation policies'.[25] If further policies to reach the targets set by the Paris Agreement are also adopted, the decline in demand for fossil fuels is likely to be more sudden and steeper.[26] The security of energy supply would then be affected unless policies to avert this scenario are adopted, such as a reduction in the current rates of investment in fossil fuels and, more generally, divestment from them.

Thirdly, climate change can also lead to disruptions in energy supply, and as such to energy insecurity more generally, through a range of extreme weather events which climate change makes much more likely. These include not only hurricanes (also called typhoons or cyclones), with direct impact on the operation of the electric grid, but also heat- (and cold-) waves, which dramatically increase energy consumption and may lead to supply interruptions, as well as slow onset events which may require far more energy to be produced (for example substantial increases in average high temperatures in some regions, which require much more energy to provide thermal services, such as air conditioning).

Both supply- and demand-side threats are well-known and relatively well anticipated. However, as discussed in the following section, whereas the energy transition has led to significant changes at the level of domestic policy, most notably through diversification

[23] eg James Leaton, Unburnable Carbon: Are the World's Financial Markets Carrying a Carbon Bubble? (Carbon Tracker 2011) <https://www.banktrack.org/download/unburnable_carbon/unburnablecarbonfullrev2.pdf> accessed 12 January 2020.

[24] Mercure et al (n 3). [25] ibid. [26] ibid.

policies, at the level of international law the main prism through which energy security is approached remains based on fossil fuel stocks.

C. Legal Responses to Energy Security

1. Domestic Approaches

At the domestic level, the main responses to energy security threats have traditionally focused on (a) diversification policies (of energy sources and foreign suppliers) and, more recently, (b) efficiency policies (relating to buildings, equipment and appliances, and vehicles and transport systems). Each of these policies will be discussed in turn.

Regarding diversification, some States have addressed these threats by investing in the production of alternative energy resources, such as nuclear energy. This is the case, for instance, for countries such as France where the production of nuclear energy supports most of its domestic energy demand.[27] The decision to invest in nuclear power plants in France pre-dated discussions on climate change and was mainly driven by energy security reasons (reliability of the supply at a low cost).[28] Nuclear energy production has been economically beneficial in France, as suggested by a pro-nuclear think tank,[29] but the environmental impact of the industry is more controversial.[30]

Other States have opted to increase their reliance on a more traditional source of energy, namely hydropower, which exploits the water flow of a watercourse, and as such is a renewable source. Hydropower plants are certainly not a panacea. A 2016 study demonstrated that they are responsible for significant greenhouse gas emissions.[31] Moreover, the construction of large dams to operate a hydropower plant, besides requiring large investments, can pose serious risks to the health and safety of the people living in their vicinity (such as indigenous communities) and to the environment (including biodiversity of a region). The collapse of a hydroelectric dam in Laos in 2018 provides a concrete reminder of this risk.[32] Furthermore, the use of a watercourse to produce hydroelectricity can conflict with other existing (or potential) uses, such as fishing and irrigation, as well as with the interests of downstream and upstream States. There is an

[27] World Nuclear Association, 'Nuclear Power in France' (updated October 2019) https://www.world-nuclear.org/information-library/country-profiles/countries-a-f/france.aspx accessed 12 January 2020.

[28] ibid. [29] ibid.

[30] Abdullah Al Faruque, *Nuclear Energy Regulation, Risk and the Environment* (Routledge 2019) 1–16.

[31] Bridget Deemer et al, 'Greenhouse Gas Emissions from Reservoir Water Surfaces: A New Global Synthesis' (2016) 66 Bioscience 949.

[32] Hannah Ellis-Petersen, 'Laos Dam Collapse: Work Continues on Huge Projects Despite Promise Halt' (*The Guardian*, 21 August 2018) <https://www.theguardian.com/world/2018/aug/21/laos-dam-collapse-work-continues-on-huge-projects-despite-promised-halt> accessed 12 January 2020.

extensive body of case law showing that watercourses used for hydropower generation can be a source of conflict, especially at the international level.[33] More recently, there has been massive investment in non-hydro renewable energy technologies, such as solar panels and wind turbines. Schemes incentivizing these energy sources are commonplace, with countries from Germany to South Africa, China, and the United States having set targets and established promotion schemes. India and the United States offer two good illustrations. In India, the Electricity Act was amended in 2003 to introduce targets for renewable energy generation and requires the State Electricity Regulatory Commissions to pursue such targets (8 per cent share by 2022[34]) through a system of Renewable Purchase Obligations (RPOs) imposed on utilities under their jurisdictions.[35] In the United States, the 1992 Energy Policy Act[36] provided tax incentives for facilities producing electricity from renewable sources, such as the 'Renewable Electricity Production Tax Credit' (PTC) or the 'Business Energy Investment Tax Credit' (ITC). The first provides a tax rebate for part of the electricity produced by renewable facilities whereas the second provides a rebate based on the amounts of investment in new renewable energy facilities. These investments have not yet resulted in a non-hydro renewable energy industry capable of providing the bulk of energy needs. All in all, diversification is about striking a country-specific balance amongst different sources of energy.

With regard to energy efficiency policies, most countries rely on a patchwork of laws to manage the energy transition.[37] Importantly, these patchworks are not necessarily coherent, with policies to support both renewable energy and fossil fuels coexisting, sometimes even in the same instrument, as in the United States.[38] Energy efficiency is addressed through instruments focusing on buildings, equipment, appliances and vehicles, either separately or in combination. The EU offers a good illustration of how this is handled. In addition to some object-specific instruments, such as the 2010 Energy

[33] eg, *Lac Lanoux Arbitration (Affaire du Lac Lanoux) (France v Spain)* (1957) 12 RIAA 281. See also more recently Kishenganga arbitration: *In the matter of the Indus Waters Kishenganga Arbitration between the Islamic Republic of Pakistan and the Republic of India (Pakistan v India)* (Partial Award) (2013) 31 RIAA 55; *In the matter of the Indus Waters Kishenganga Arbitration between the Islamic Republic of Pakistan and the Republic of India (Pakistan v India)* (Final Award) (2013) 31 RIAA 309.

[34] Ministry of Power of India, 'Tariff Policy' Gazette of India p I s I, Resolution No 23/2/2005-R&R (Vol III) (6 January 2006) <http://www.orierc.org/documents/National%20Electricity%20Tariff%20Policy.pdf> accessed 12 January 2020.

[35] Ministry of New and Renewable Energy of India, 'Jawaharlal Nehru National Solar Mission Phase II: Policy Document' (December 2012) 18–19 <http://www.euindiacoop.org/el/phase_ii_of_solar_mission_india.pdf> accessed 12 January 2020.

[36] US Energy Policy Act 42 USC §13201 et seq (1992) s 1212.

[37] The following discussion is based on Gundlach/Gerrard (n 22) and Jorge E Viñuales, *The Architecture of Environmental Law: A Comparative Analysis* (OUP 2020, forthcoming) ch 3.

[38] See US Energy Policy Act 42 USC §13201ff (2005) section 202 (renewable energy production incentive) and Title III (oil and gas), subtitle E (production incentive).

Performance of Buildings Directive (EPBD),[39] the 2017 Energy Labelling Regulation (ELR),[40] or the 2009 Clean Vehicles Directive (CVD),[41] it adopted a more general instrument in the form of a 2012 Energy Efficiency Directive.[42] The latter requires States to set 'indicative national energy efficiency targets' in their national plans and pursue them through a range of measures from the energy demand (or 'use') and supply sides. Energy use measures[43] include requirements in renovation of buildings, public procurement of energy efficient products, services, and buildings, an 'energy efficiency obligation scheme' for energy distributors or retail energy sales companies, energy audits, and metering and billing information for end consumers (for them to track their energy consumption more clearly). Energy supply measures[44] are organized according to activity segments, namely heating and cooling, as well as transformation, transmission, and distribution.

Domestic energy diversification and efficiency policies are closely connected to international legal frameworks relating to energy security. As discussed in the following section, international law touches upon energy security in various ways, whether directly (such as through establishing a buffer system to address sudden shortages, or creating and securing routes for energy resources and products to move across boundaries) or indirectly (creating the general conditions for investment in energy, joint production, and trade).

2. International Legal Frameworks

a. *Direct Response: The International Energy Agency Sharing System*

Perhaps the most direct and specific approach to respond to energy security threats in international law was the so-called 'Sharing System' of the International Energy Agency (IEA), established in 1974 in response to the oil crisis of October 1973.[45] This crisis resulted from the oil embargo instituted by some Arab OPEC members against the United States and other industrialized countries in response to measures adopted by the US government (including offering military support to Israel in the Yom Kippur War).

[39] Directive 2010/31/EU of the European Parliament and of the Council of 19 May 2010 on the Energy Performance of Buildings OJ L153/13 (which applies to 'energy-related products' and expressly excludes from its scope 'means of transport for persons or goods', see art 1).

[40] Regulation (EU) 2017/1369 of the European Parliament and of the Council of 4 July 2017 setting a Framework for Energy Labelling and Repealing Directive 2010/30/EU OJ L198/1 (this instrument repealed the previous Energy Labelling Directive).

[41] Directive 2009/33/EC of the European Parliament and of the Council of 23 April 2009 on the Promotion of Clean and Energy-Efficient Road Transport Vehicles OJ L120/5.

[42] Directive 2012/27/EU of the European Parliament and of the Council of 25 October 2012 on Energy Efficiency OJ L 315/1.

[43] ibid ch II. [44] ibid ch III.

[45] Rudolf Dolzer, 'International Co-operation in Energy Affairs' (2014) 372 Recueil des Cours 395, 472–3.

As a result of the embargo, global oil prices quadrupled, rising from $2.90 per barrel to $11.65 per barrel.[46] The effects of this crisis were widespread and long lasting. Indeed, the crisis affected energy demand worldwide, by making oil prices remain at unprecedented high levels even after the embargo ended. This very crisis is what prompted the international community to establish an intergovernmental organization such as the IEA, which represents the interests of oil-importing countries to counterbalance the market power wielded by oil-exporting countries acting through OPEC.[47]

The IEA's original mission was to devise cooperative strategies to respond to future oil crises or other energy security emergencies.[48] The first and foremost strategy developed consisted of requiring IEA member States to hold emergency oil reserves which could be released to the market to respond to oil supply shocks or any other form of oil shortage. These emergency stocks, in the form of government stocks, industry stocks, agency stocks, or a combination thereof, need to be 'equivalent to at least ninety days of net oil imports'.[49] This is the most important condition that acceding States need to fulfil in order to become IEA members.[50] The decision on funnelling oil into the market rests with the IEA Secretariat in consultation with the IEA member States, and it is based on an assessment of the impact on the oil market of the emergency in question.[51] The potential release of emergency stocks is, however, a short-term measure, as it is not aimed at adjusting the oil price but rather buffering the impact of such an emergency. Further, it is a collective measure involving all IEA members, as each of them is called to contribute proportionately in accordance with its 'share of total oil consumption among IEA member countries'.[52] In addition to the release of oil stocks, there are a number of other measures that members can adopt, such as restraining demand or substituting oil with other energy resources. All of these measures are summarized in Figure 25.1 below.[53]

The IEA resorted to this collective mechanism on three occasions, namely (i) before the Gulf War (1991); (ii) after hurricanes Katrina and Rita in the Gulf of Mexico (2005); and (iii) after the Libyan Civil War (2011). Besides oil, the IEA is developing mechanisms to respond to challenges arising in relation to the secure supply of other energy resources, such as natural gas[54] and electricity.[55]

[46] Michael Corbett, 'Oil Shock of 1973–4' (*Federal Reserve History*, 22 November 2013) <https://www.federalreservehistory.org/essays/oil_shock_of_1973_74> accessed 12 January 2020.

[47] IEA, 'Our Mission' <https://www.iea.org/about/ourmission/> accessed 12 January 2020.

[48] ibid.

[49] Agreement on an International Energy Program 1040 UNTS 271 art 2. See also IEA, 'Oil Security', Web Archive 2019 <https://web.archive.org/web/20190528230904/https://www.iea.org/topics/energysecurity/oilsecurity/> accessed 12 January 2020.

[50] IEA, 'IEA Membership' <https://www.iea.org/countries/members/> accessed 12 January 2020.

[51] IEA, 'Oil Security' (n 49). [52] ibid. [53] ibid.

[54] IEA, 'Natural Gas Security' <https://www.iea.org/topics/energysecurity/naturalgassecurity/> accessed 12 January 2020.

[55] IEA, 'Electricity Security' <https://www.iea.org/areas-of-work/ensuring-energy-security/electricity-security> accessed 12 January 2020.

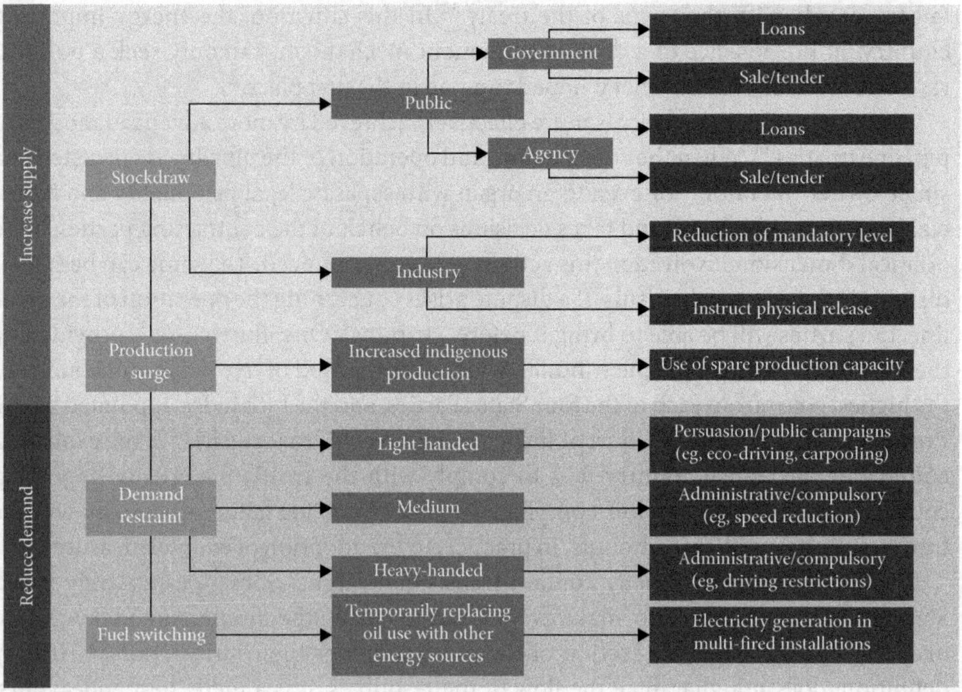

FIGURE 25.1 Summary of measures that IEA member countries can adopt to respond to oil shortages

b. *Facilitation of Energy Flows: Pipeline Treaties*

Another important approach to address energy security is to facilitate the conditions through which energy flows move across boundaries. This can follow two main perspectives, namely the organization of the movement as such (through pipeline agreements) and the underlying liberalization of energy flows (through trade and, to some extent, investment agreements). Here we discuss the first perspective. The second is discussed in the following section.

Pipeline agreements govern the construction and/or operation of pipelines across territorial and/or maritime boundaries. The extent to which these treaties can enhance energy security depends upon two factors: (i) the centralized ownership and operation of the pipeline system, and (ii) the existence of a dispute settlement mechanism.[56] Basic models of pipeline treaties where there is no single owner or operator of the pipeline may enable an uninterrupted flow so long as there is no disagreement between the contracting parties.[57] In this framework, each owner or operator is responsible, individually, for the construction and operation of the pipeline section under its jurisdiction; issues arise when either the energy-exporting country or the transit country

[56] Tibisay Morgandi, *Bilateral Energy Governance: State Practice in International Law* (CUP forthcoming).

[57] ibid.

fail to comply with the terms of the treaty.[58] In this situation, the energy-importing country, in the absence of a dispute settlement mechanism, can only seek a political resolution, which is often what it hoped to avoid in the first place.[59]

Conversely, energy security is more effectively achieved by more advanced models of pipeline treaties.[60] When the construction and operation of the pipeline is entrusted to a single owner/operator,[61] or even to an organ with separate legal personality and financial autonomy, which acts and takes decisions on behalf of the contracting parties,[62] the political dimension involved in this activity is less pronounced. The same can be said of dispute settlement mechanisms. If a dispute arises concerning the operation of the pipeline, the parties will be able to bring it before a tribunal. One illustration is provided by the West African Gas Pipeline tribunal, which is composed of five judges (one judge of the highest court from each of the four States Parties, and the fifth judge appointed by the President of the ECOWAS Court of Justice from judges of that court).[63] If the exporting country or the transit country fails to comply with the treaty, the energy-importing country can challenge the non-compliant Member State for failure to comply with its transit obligations.[64] This amounts, in practice, to the adoption of countermeasures.[65]

Pipeline agreements usually contain transit obligations. Some are relatively weak. States Parties are required to 'make every effort to ensure the uninterrupted flow' of oil or natural gas through the section of the pipeline under their jurisdiction.[66] This, by definition, does not guarantee the flow of the resources; it is a mere 'best endeavours' obligation.[67] In other pipeline agreements, States Parties undertake, instead, an obligation to achieve a certain outcome and, thus, an obligation of result.[68] One example is the Baku-Supsa Pipeline Agreement, where States Parties are required not to interrupt or

[58] ibid.

[59] eg, Agreement among the Hellenic Republic, the Republic of Turkey and the Italian Republic concerning the Development of the Turkey–Greece–Italy Gas Transportation Corridor (Turkey–Greece–Italy) (26 July 2007) art 5 <http://www.energybilaterals.org/agreements/469> accessed 12 January 2020.

[60] Morgandi (n 56).

[61] eg, Agreement between the Government of the State of Qatar and the Government of the United Arab Emirates Relating to the Transmission of Gas by Pipeline between the State of Qatar and the United Arab Emirates (Qatar–United Arab Emirates) (26 September 2004) art IV(1) <http://www.energybilaterals.org/agreements/465> accessed 12 January 2020. (Dolphin Gas Pipeline Agreement).

[62] eg, Treaty on the West African Gas Pipeline Project between the Republic of Benin and the Republic of Ghana and the Federal Republic of Nigeria and the Republic of Togo (Republic of Benin–Republic of Ghana–Federal Republic of Nigeria–the Republic of Togo) (31 January 2003) arts IV(1) and IV(2) <http://www.energybilaterals.org/agreements/463> accessed 12 January 2020 (West Gas Pipeline Agreement).

[63] ibid arts IV(15)(1) and VI(5)(1).

[64] ibid art VII(3)(1)(c).

[65] Danae Azaria, *Treaties on Transit of Energy via Pipelines and Countermeasures* (OUP 2015) 190.

[66] eg, Turkey–Greece–Italy Gas Transportation Corridor Agreement (n 59) art 2(11). See also Agreement between the Hellenic Republic and the Italian Republic for the Development of the Interconnection Greece–Italy (IGI) Project (Greece–Italy) (4 November 2005) art 2(3) <http://www.energybilaterals.org/agreements/466> accessed 12 January 2020.

[67] Azaria (n 65) 75. [68] ibid 74.

impede the flow of petroleum through the pipelines located under their jurisdiction.[69] This is a stronger obligation as the flow of energy resources has to be guaranteed. Non-compliance with this obligation can be challenged by the energy-importing country and the latter can take action against the party in breach.[70]

There is an important exception to the obligation relating to the transit of oil and gas through pipelines.[71] States may interrupt or impede the transit of oil and gas in circumstances where the operation of the facilities may create a threat to public health, safety, property, or the environment.[72] In these circumstances, however, the State in whose territory the interruption of flow has taken place must give immediate notice, including notice of any justification to the other contracting party.[73] Likewise, the State must also use its best endeavours to eliminate the reasons underlying the interruption and restore the flow at the earliest opportunity.[74]

One interesting case study of the legal complexities surrounding the laying of pipelines and their operation is provided by the Nord Stream gas pipeline project connecting Russia and Germany, passing entirely through the Baltic Sea.[75] Increasing tensions between Ukraine and Russia led to the construction of two lines between 2011 and 2012. Subsequently, a project to double the carrying capacity of Nord Stream was envisaged (Nord Stream 2 or NS2). Construction of these two additional lines is almost complete but it has come under criticism in Europe and in the US.[76] The major concerns raised in relation to NS2 relate to Russia's role as an exporting country. Some European countries and the United States argue that these new lines would increase the strategic role already played by Russia and the giant Russian gas company, Gazprom. In turn, this could threaten Europe's gas security by making it even more dependent on Russia's gas exports, and further isolating Ukraine.[77] This would also increase Europe's vulnerability to the Russian supplier Gazprom, which would be the owner/operator of the pipeline.[78] In the absence of a pipeline agreement regulating potential energy security issues, the completion and operation of the NS2 pipeline could prove problematic. One possibility would be to have Nord Stream 2 governed by EU law. Germany has opposed this option on the grounds that it would make the project uneconomical and unviable. In early February 2019, however, an understanding was reached amongst EU countries whereby they would allow the project to be completed but brought under the rules (including competition rules) governing the EU internal energy market. In exchange, Germany would

[69] eg, Agreement between the Azerbaijan Republic and Georgia relating to the Development and Refurbishment of Certain Existing Petroleum Transportation Facilities, the Development of New Petroleum Transportation Facilities, and the Transportation of Petroleum via Such Facilities beyond the Territory of Georgia (Azerbaijan Republic–Georgia) (8 March 1996) art 2(1) <http://www.energybilaterals.org/agreements/459> accessed 12 January 2020 (Baku–Supsa Pipeline Agreement).

[70] eg, West African Gas Pipeline Agreement (n 62) arts VII(3) and VIII(3).

[71] Morgandi (n 56).

[72] eg, Baku–Supsa Pipeline Agreement (n 69) art 2(1).

[73] eg, ibid art 2(2). [74] eg, ibid.

[75] For further information on the NordStream pipeline see <https://www.nord-stream.com/the-project/construction/> accessed 12 January 2020.

[76] Chazan (n 15). [77] ibid. [78] ibid.

remain the lead negotiator of the project.[79] In accordance with this approach, (i) Russia would continue exporting gas to Europe via Ukraine, and (ii) Gazprom's control over the pipeline would be limited.[80] EU law rather than ad hoc pipeline treaties would be the controlling framework. What seemed to be an adequate compromise has, however, proved to be insufficient. The completion of the project has recently been slowed down by a set of sanctions approved by US President Trump targeting companies involved in pipe-laying for the construction of NS2. These sanctions, which were adopted on 20 December 2019 by the US Senate as part of their annual defence bill (the National Defense Authorization Act or NDAA),[81] had an immediate effect on the finalization of the Nord Stream 2 project. One day after the National Defense Authorization Act became law, one of the companies involved, Allseas, issued a statement announcing that it suspended its Nord Stream 2 pipelaying activities in 'anticipation of the enactment of the . . . NDAA'.[82] Allseas also declared that it would wind down operations in compliance with the terms of the National Defense Authorization Act[83] and wait to receive 'guidance comprising of the necessary regulatory, technical and environmental clarifications from the relevant US authority'.[84] It is too soon to say what long-term consequences these sanctions will have on the completion of the Nord Stream 2 project. There is no doubt, however, that, in the absence of EU countermeasures, they will at best delay completion. These sanctions, which are arguably aimed to protect US national security and Europe's energy security,[85] were labelled by Germany's Finance Minister Olaf Scholz 'a severe intervention in German and European internal affairs'.[86] This shows that, even when EU law operates as the controlling framework, EU energy security may be endangered or enhanced—depending on whether one adopts the EU or the US interpretation—by exogenous factors such as the sanctions in question.

c. *Facilitation of Energy Flows: Setting the Playing Field*

Aside from the more operational matters of transit, international law plays an important role in connection with the liberalization of energy markets and, more specifically, market access for energy resources, products and services, and non-discrimination disciplines. Two major multilateral frameworks can be referred to as illustrations: the system of treaties under the aegis of the World Trade Organization (WTO) and the Energy Charter Treaty[87] (ECT).

[79] 'Nord Stream 2: EU Agrees Tighter Rules for Russian Pipeline' (*BBC News*, 8 February 2019) <https://www.bbc.co.uk/news/world-europe-47170420> accessed 12 January 2020.

[80] Chazan (n 15).

[81] US Public Law 116–92 (2019) s 1790—National Defense Authorization Act for Fiscal Year 2020.

[82] 'Allseas Suspends Nord Stream 2 Pipelay Activities' (*Allseas News*, 21 December 2019) <https://allseas.com/news/allseas-suspends-nord-stream-2-pipelay-activities/> accessed 12 January 2020.

[83] The NDAA provides for an exemption from the sanctions for those companies which, within a 30-day period from the enactment of the Act, engage in good faith efforts to wind down operations on Nord Stream 2. See US Public Law 116–92 (n 81).

[84] 'Allseas Suspends Nord Stream 2 Pipelay Activities' (n 82).

[85] See US Bill (2019) s 1441.

[86] 'Trump Sanctions Halt Russia–Germany Pipeline Work' (*DW News*, 21 December 2019) <https://www.dw.com/en/trump-sanctions-halt-russia-germany-pipeline-work/av-51762117> accessed 29 November 2020.

[87] Energy Charter Treaty 2080 UNTS 95 (ECT).

Under the WTO agreements, WTO members may not discriminate against each other in relation to trade in goods, except in some cases by way of import and export duties. The application of non-discrimination standards to energy-related services is more limited, as it is conditioned on the inclusion of a service sector in the schedule of commitments of the relevant country (under the General Agreement on Trade in Services (GATS)). Oil, natural gas, and electricity count as goods for these purposes, whereas the transmission of oil, gas, and electricity count as services.[88] WTO energy-importing members can challenge other members by requesting the establishment of a panel, which is in practice automatic, to determine whether the respondent is in violation of its obligations under WTO agreements.[89] If the claimant is successful, the respondent WTO member has to comply with the relevant trade disciplines, and if it does not, the claimant is entitled to retaliate by suspending WTO obligations owed to that member.[90] One difficulty with this arrangement is that, since many energy-exporting countries do not have diversified economic sectors, it might be difficult for an energy-importing country to find a sector against which it can retaliate.[91] It is notable that OPEC members, which are also WTO members, have not been challenged, for example, in relation to their price-stabilization policies that affect exports and appear to be illegal *prima facie* under WTO law.[92] This has been explained partly in terms of political considerations[93] and shows that the existence of the WTO dispute settlement mechanism is not necessarily sufficient to guarantee energy security. In addition, WTO rules only apply to WTO members. In the energy sector, this may be problematic since some important energy-producing countries are not WTO members (such as Libya). To some extent, this gap is filled by the ECT, which regulates various energy-related issues for European States as well as former Soviet Union countries. The ECT incorporates WTO rules on trade in goods by reference,[94] which apply to non-WTO members.[95]

The ECT gives its signatories (many of which are energy-importing countries) a tool to enforce compliance with trade-related provisions. Annex D of the ECT deals with trade-related disputes where at least one party is not a WTO member.[96] It establishes a

[88] Gabrielle Marceau, 'The WTO in the Emerging Governance Debate' (2012) 106 American Society of International Law Proceedings 385.

[89] WTO Dispute Settlement Understanding 1869 UNTS 401 art 6. There is also a right of appeal to the WTO Appellate Body, although the WTO Appellate Body is currently in a deadlock. Since 10 December 2019, the Appellate Body does not have the minimum number of members to function, as a result of the US ongoing veto on the appointment of new members.

[90] For a comprehensive overview of the trade regime in relation to energy goods and services under the WTO, see Sanam Salem Haghighi, *Energy Security: The External Legal Relations of the European Union with Major Oil- and Gas-Supplying Countries* (Hart 2007) 237–20.

[91] Marceau (n 88) 389.

[92] Melaku Geboye Desta, 'The Organization of Petroleum Exporting Countries, the World Trade Organization, and Regional Trade Agreements' (2003) 37 Journal of World Trade 523, 535 (also noting some possible public policy justifications).

[93] ibid 535; Haghighi (n 90) 254.

[94] The Trade Amendment of the ECT (adopted 24 April 1998, entered into force 21 January 2010) <https://energycharter.org/fileadmin/DocumentsMedia/Thematic/Trade_Amendment_Explanations-EN.pdf> accessed 16 July 2019.

[95] ECT (n 87) arts 4 and 29.

[96] ECT (n 87) art 29(7). See also Haghighi (n 90) 301.

mechanism similar to the WTO dispute settlement mechanism, where the complainant, under certain circumstances, can request the Energy Charter Secretariat to establish a panel and adjudicate the matter.[97] The ECT panel functions in accordance with rules of procedure 'as close as possible to those of the GATT [General Agreement on Tariffs and Trade]' and must take into consideration and be guided by the interpretations given to the GATT by WTO panels.[98] As with WTO-related disputes, once the panel report is adopted, if the non-compliant party does not remove the non-compliant measure, the complainant is entitled, subject to a specific procedure, to retaliate bilaterally by suspending trade-related obligations owed to that ECT party.[99] The same concerns raised above in relation to countermeasures adopted in response to WTO obligations apply here. Establishing energy partnerships can be a long and complex operation, involving politics, money, as well as infrastructure, and energy-importing countries will consider carefully before endangering an existing relationship with an energy-exporting country.

The WTO system and the ECT also cover questions of transit, although only as a matter of principle rather than in connection with the specific development and operation of pipelines. Article V of GATT 1994 requires WTO members to ensure freedom of transit through the territories of WTO members, and specifies that charges and other regulations applicable to goods in transit must be reasonable and non-discriminatory in terms of the origin of the transit traffic. The ECT follows the same system. Article 7 requires the ECT parties to 'take the necessary measures to facilitate the transit of energy materials and products'. Whether the reference to 'facilitation' makes this obligation weaker than Article V of GATT 1994 is somewhat debated.[100] On other points, Article 7 is rather more detailed. In particular, Article 7(6) requires any ECT parties involved in a dispute about transit not to 'interrupt or reduce... the existing flow of [e]nergy [m]aterials and [p]roducts' (unless this is permitted by a relevant agreement) but instead to engage in dispute settlement procedures set out in Article 7(7).

In addition to the WTO Agreements and the ECT, numerous Free Trade Agreements (FTAs) contain rules relevant for energy. But the overall logic is comparable. Their focus is to establish a level playing field for the liberalization (within specifically negotiated bounds) of energy resources, products, and services. Liberalization is not directly a response to an energy security threat, but it certainly lays the ground for energy to circulate more freely and, thereby, for energy-importing countries to have facilitated access to it.

D. Concluding Observations

As discussed in this chapter, the international legal framework relevant to energy security considerations is largely focused on the idea of energy as a 'stock' (eg, resources

[97] ECT (n 87) Annex D(2)(a).
[98] ibid.
[99] ECT (n 87) Annex D(5)(b).
[100] Haghighi (n 90) 324.

of coal, oil, gas, uranium), which is unevenly distributed across countries and thereby creates vulnerabilities for energy-importing countries. This picture may be slowly changing as a result of the energy transformation, namely the increasing role played by renewable energies, particularly non-hydro energies, in the energy matrix. Indeed, such energies rely on 'flows' (wind and sunlight) rather than stocks and, as a result, their political configuration is entirely different. This has been recognized in the aforementioned 2019 Report of the Global Commission on the Geopolitics of the Energy Transformation.

This being said, the international legal frameworks governing energy security have certainly not lost their relevance. Fossil fuels remain, at present, the main underlying source of thermal services, transportation, and electricity. Secure and continued access to them remains therefore very important. This is the case even if the redistribution of energy resources implied by the shale oil and gas revolution is taken into account. As a general matter, international law responds to energy security threats by establishing specific collective mechanisms (for instance under the IEA) and by facilitating the flows of energy resources across countries through pipelines and pipeline agreements, as well as through foundational instruments liberalizing energy resources, products, and services.

Over time, as the energy transformation reduces the demand for fossil fuels, the economic and strategic configuration of energy security will likely change, and quite significantly so. Energy security may then become much more a question of access to the relevant technologies to generate it from 'flow' sources. Contemporary international law also addresses some aspects of what energy security may become in the future, for example through agreements relating to trade, investment, and intellectual property. As long as energy markets remain internationalized, international law will have a significant role to play.

CHAPTER 26

FINANCIAL CRISES

JASPER FINKE

A. Introduction

The possible impacts of financial crises can be devastating. They do not merely affect the financial industry nationally, regionally, or globally. They can create spillover effects to the real economy, thus causing a long-lasting economic downturn, as happened, for example, during the Great Depression that unfolded after the so-called 'Black Monday' and 'Black Tuesday'.[1] Prolonged economic recessions or depressions in turn impede the State's ability to provide public goods. Especially sovereign debt crises force States to reduce public spending, which requires cuts in the public health and education system, a decrease in social welfare benefits generally, lower salaries and pensions for public employees, and fewer public employees. In short, States lose the capacity to act, which may even include the ability to uphold public safety. Both a decline in public safety and higher poverty rates can cause mass migration, which can destabilize neighbouring States or even entire regions. While financial crises do not necessarily have all these consequences, they do have a destructive potential beyond the individual State.

It might therefore be unsurprising that we can observe structural and conceptual similarities in how States respond to situations that are more broadly perceived as security crises and financial crises. This chapter will demonstrate how an 'emergency mindset' is present in debates on what role law has played and should play in responding to financial crises. Since modern economic history has experienced many financial crises, two case studies will be used to illustrate the presence of an 'emergency mindset' in such situations, which is conceptually similar to traditional security crises: the 2008 global

[1] Whether the financial turmoil that ensued after 'Black Monday' caused the Great Depression or whether the financial crisis was itself the result of an initial economic downturn and then prolonged by other factors is contested. While the former reflects conventional wisdom, the latter view is advanced, amongst others, by Milton Friedman/Anna J Schwartz, *A Monetary History of the United States, 1967–1960* (Princeton UP 1963) 299ff.

financial crisis and the still unresolved multilevel financial crisis in the Eurozone.[2] First, the term 'emergency mindset' will be explained in more detail before illustrating how it has shaped not only economic responses but has also influenced the legal perspective on the 2008 Global Financial Crisis and the Eurozone Crisis. In lieu of a conclusion, an outlook will stress the importance for a more phenomenological and less normative approach to financial crises.

B. Emergency Mindset

'Emergency mindset' is not a technical or legal term. It is rather used to describe a general framing that influences and informs debates on crises from a legal perspective.[3] It establishes the parameters and limits for such debates without indicating or prescribing specific results, even though it affects the arguments that will be heard. In the following, I will briefly explain why an emergency mindset features so prominently in debates on security crises and how the debate, due to the inbuilt biases of this frame, pays too little attention to the transforming power of crises; why it assumes that crises are temporary deviations from normality and that solving a crisis will restore this normality without taking into account what has changed as a consequence of a crisis.

1. Emergency Powers

The perception of crises as temporary deviations from normality is the main reason why concepts of emergency powers figure so prominently in legal debates on crises. Their history is closely connected to the archetypal security crises, that is war, rebellion and, to

[2] While the term 'Euro-Crisis' is incorrect insofar as it implies a currency crisis that is characterized by a sharp decline in the currency's external value, it also misleadingly reduces the crisis to a sovereign debt crisis. While it is undisputed that unsustainable debt is one of the causes and in the Greek case, possibly the main cause, several other factors combined nearly caused the collapse of the Euro currency zone. The institutional design of the Eurozone was one of them. This chapter will thus use the term 'Eurozone Crisis' to capture this complex situation; on its causes see, amongst others, Karloo Tuori/Klaus Tuori, *The Eurozone Crisis—A Constitutional Analysis* (CUP 2014) 3ff, 61ff; Ashoka Mody/Damiano Sandri, 'The Eurozone Crisis: How Banks and Sovereigns Came to Be Joined at the Hip' (2012) 27 Economic Policy 199, 212ff; Torben Iversen/David Soskice, 'A Structural-Institutional Explanation of the Eurozone Crisis' in Philip Manow et al (eds), *Welfare Democracies and Party Politics* (OUP 2018) 257.

[3] The term 'framing' is used consciously. Cognitive science has shown that the use of certain words and concepts has an immediate effect on how we absorb and process information. While information that fits the existing frame is overstated in its relevance, other information that cannot be reconciled with the overall frame is neglected. The underlying reason is simple and obvious: concepts and words are never neutral, but convey a certain meaning; see Erving Goffman, *Frame Analysis: An Essay on the Organization of Experience* (Harvard UP 1974) 9ff. How frames influence the interpretation of international law norms has been analysed by Martin Wählisch, 'Cognitive Frames of Interpretation in International Law' in Andrea Bianchi et al (eds), *Interpretation in International Law* (OUP 2015) 338.

a lesser extent, riots.[4] Traditionally, emergency powers enlarge the power of the executive vis-à-vis other actors, especially the parliament and the judiciary for the duration of the crisis so that the executive can effectively respond to the challenges and restore security and stability.[5] With the advent of human rights, a new dimension of emergency powers emerged: the constraint or suspension of individual freedoms.[6] Still, their legal or constitutional design varies significantly.

It is possible to distinguish two fundamentally different concepts: models of extra-legality and models of accommodation, especially constitutional accommodation of emergency powers.[7] While extra-legality rests on the assumption that law is suspended during times of crisis, either factually because it is disregarded or through a formal act of suspension, most constitutions feature some kind of emergency powers clause.[8] At their core all these models have a self-defence hypothesis. A State, like an

[4] For historical concepts of emergency powers see Oren Gross/Fionnuala Ní Aoláin, *Law in Times of Crisis: Emergency Powers in Theory and Practice* (CUP 2006) 17ff; Karin Loevy, *Emergencies in Public Law: The Legal Politics of Containment* (CUP 2016) 17.

[5] In modern political and constitutional thought John Locke was amongst the first to advance the view that the executive is best suited to react swiftly, decisively, and thus efficiently to a crisis; John Locke, *Second Treatise of Government* (Crawford B Macpherson ed, Hackett Publishing 1980) 160. This view has persisted over time, even though it could be argued that technological developments have changed the operation of government to such an extent that it could call the traditional assumptions into question; see Deborah N Pearlstein, 'Form and Function in the National Security Constitution' (2009) 41 Connecticut Law Review 1549, 1552, and 1586ff.

[6] While the Roman dictatorship is often cited as a prime example for the argument that the organization of government has to be adjusted so as to address violent crises, the suspension of habeas corpus rights under English law beginning in the seventeenth century is often referred to in support for the widespread belief that efficient crisis response is incompatible with the unrestrained guarantee of human rights; on the English tradition of suspending the habeas corpus writ, see Albert V Dicey, *Introduction to the Study of the Law of the Constitution* (8th edn, Macmillan 1915) 139ff who also points out that the writ was not generally suspended, but only in cases in which individuals were accused of treason. The assumption that human rights impair efficient crisis response is also reflected in the derogation clause that can be found in major human rights conventions; see eg European Convention on Human Rights and Fundamental Freedoms ETS No 5 (ECHR) art 15 and International Covenant on Civil and Political Rights 999 UNTS 171 (ICCPR) art 4, which refer to situations of war or other public emergency which threatens the life of the nation.

[7] Gross/Aoláin (n 4) 17ff and 110ff; Karin Loevy, 'An Introduction to the Theory of Crisis Containment: The Problem of Emergency and Its Paradigmatic Solutions' (2011) 27 Yearbook of Research in English and American Literature 3, 6ff.

[8] The US Constitution, for example, does not confer explicit emergency powers on the President. It follows the English law tradition allowing for the suspension of the habeas corpus privileges in cases of rebellion and invasion if public safety requires it (art I s 9 cl 2). However, much ink has been spilled on the implicit war powers of the President or (hidden) elements of an emergency constitution; eg Harold H Koh, *The National Security Constitution: Sharing Power after the Iran-Contra Affair* (Yale UP 1990) 67ff; Michael S Paulsen, 'The Constitution of Necessity' (2004) 79 Notre Dame Law Review 1257; critically, Jules Lobel, 'Emergency Power and the Decline of Liberalism' (1989) 98 Yale Law Journal 1385. A quite different approach was adopted in the Weimar Constitution. According to art 48, the German Reich President could take the measures necessary to re-establish law and order, including if necessary the use of armed forces, and to suspend a number of civil rights either partially or in their entirety. Since art 48 Weimar Constitution was instrumental to overthrowing the democratic order in 1933 and to the establishment of a totalitarian regime by the Nazi Party, it has been deemed as an example of a too broadly and thus badly designed emergency powers clause conferring unrestrained powers to the executive without proper checks and balances; see Gross/Aoláin (n 4) 83–4; Frederick M Watkins, *The Failure of Constitutional Emergency Powers under the German Republic* (Harvard UP 1939) 16ff.

individual, may take the means necessary to defend itself against its enemies if its existence is at risk.[9] Not only do efficiency considerations trump other concerns, it is also assumed that a State must be able to act swiftly and that the executive is best situated to provide such a resolute and prompt response. Whether this requires the (partial) suspension of the legal order or whether this can be dealt with through constitutional emergency provisions, has been, and will continue to be, discussed anew with every major big security crisis. It is therefore not very surprising that the 9/11 terrorist attacks revived the debate on emergency powers and on how these should be designed to avoid abuse.[10]

Emergency power provisions are, however, not restricted to national constitutions or domestic laws. International treaties also contain provisions that enlarge the power of certain organs in times of crisis. The most prominent examples are the powers of the UN Security Council (UNSC) under Chapter VII of the UN Charter. Their similarity to constitutional emergency powers is striking for several reasons. For one, the Charter has been likened to a constitution, not a domestic, but an international or a global one.[11] Secondly, Chapter VII confers very broad powers on an organ that has been described as executive-like.[12] And thirdly, apart from the veto power of the P5, there is little constraint on the UNSC's use of its Chapter VII powers.[13]

[9] When 'its very survival [of the State] would be at stake' not even the use of otherwise prohibited nuclear weapons has been deemed as outright prohibited. See *Legality of the Threat or Use of Nuclear Weapons* (Advisory Opinion) [1996] ICJ Rep 226 [96]–[97].

[10] See, amongst others, Bruce Ackerman, 'The Emergency Constitution' (2004) 113 Yale Law Journal 1029. A radically different view is taken by liberal representatives of an extra-legal approach who are concerned that integrating emergency powers into the constitutional or legal order would impair law's function to provide individual freedoms; see eg Oren Gross, 'Extra-Legality and the Ethics of Political Responsibility' in Victor V Ramraj (ed), *Emergencies and the Limits of Legality* (CUP 2008) 64ff and Mark Tushnet, 'The Political Constitution of Emergency Powers' in ibid 151ff, who both argue for either ex-post or political responsibility as an alternative means of providing what they consider to be more efficient constraints and accountability on political actors in times of crisis.

[11] Charter of the United Nations 1 UNTS XVI (UN Charter). Originally, Humphrey Waldock, 'General Course on Public International Law' (1962-II) 106 Recueil des Cours 20 categorized the UN Charter as a Constitution of an Organization, which was already an important distinction to the then prevailing and technical perspective which qualified the Charter as a mere multilateral treaty. Since then the idea of the UN Charter as a constitution has developed, first to be a world constitution and then a global one; see, amongst others, Ronald St J Macdonald, 'The Charter of the United Nations as World Constitution' 75 International Legal Studies 263, 264ff; Bardo Fassbender, *The United Nations Charter as the Constitution of the International Community* (Brill 2009) 52ff; critically Michael W Doyle, 'Dialectics of a Global Constitution: The Struggle over the UN Charter' (2011) 18 European Journal of International Relations 601, 602ff.

[12] That the UNSC enjoys wide discretion regarding when and how to exercise its Chapter VII powers is commonplace in international law; see eg Erika de Wet, *Chapter VII Powers of the Security Council* (Hart 2004) 5; Stefan Talmon, 'The Security Council as World Legislature' (2005) 99 AJIL 175, 180.

[13] On the constraints on the UNSC see, amongst others, de Wet (n 12) 133ff; and, generally, Antonios Tzanakopoulos, *Disobeying the Security Council: Countermeasures Against Wrongful Sanctions* (OUP 2011).

2. Dynamics of Crisis as a Challenge to Law

The 'emergency mindset' is pertinent beyond (constitutional) emergency powers. It also manifests itself in the clash between the dynamics that crises trigger and the impact that these dynamics have on law as a static system. To illustrate this relationship, it is helpful to start by stating the obvious: most crises are not legal crises. Instead, law is a tool to implement strategies to combat a crisis, to achieve thus non-legal goals.[14] To that end, States either implement new laws or use existing laws as the basis for their crisis response measures.

At the same time, even though crisis response measures take the form of law, they are also frequently perceived as being unlawful. In many cases, it is contested whether the laws that are invoked as the legal basis can actually sustain these measures since this would require a reinterpretation and a usually more expansionist reading of these provisions. This also applies to situations, in which crises response measures are thought to be incompatible with constitutional provisions and human rights. Yet, reinterpretations in light of the new realities stemming from a crisis are always met with considerable scepticism.

In this regard, the debate on the expansionist reading of Chapter VII powers of the UNSC is again very informative. In response to the many security crises and other challenges after the end of the Cold War, these powers have been given a continuously broader understanding. This is why some authors now apply an extra-legality model of emergency powers to conceptualize the legal dynamics that security crises triggered.[15] Reinterpretation in response to security crises is, however, not confined to the debate on the Chapter VII powers of the UNSC, but includes also the right to self-defence after the 9/11 terrorist attacks. The proclaimed 'war on terror' that followed was also accompanied by attempts to reinterpret central provisions of international humanitarian law. Amongst the most contested questions are the requirements for direct participation of civilians in hostilities[16] and the spatial and temporal limits of 'armed conflict'.[17]

[14] Victor V Ramraj, 'No Doctrine More Pernicious? Emergencies and the Limits of Legality' in Ramraj (n 10) 3.

[15] See Devon Whittle, 'The Limits of Legality and the United Nations Security Council: Applying the Extra-Legal Measure Model to Chapter VII Action' (2015) 26 EJIL 671, 677ff; similarly, Jared Schott, 'Chapter VII as Exception: Security Council Action and the Regulative Ideal of Emergency' (2008) 6 Northwestern Journal of International Human Rights 24, 26ff.

[16] eg Nils Melzer, *Interpretive Guidance on the Notion of Direct Participation in Hostilities under International Humanitarian Law* (ICRC 2009).

[17] eg Noam Lubell, 'The War (?) against Al-Qaeda' in Elizabeth Wilmshurst (ed), *International Law and the Classification of Conflicts* (OUP 2012) 421; Michael N Schmitt, 'Classification in Future Conflicts' in ibid 455—the notion of 'complex battle spaces' is particularly striking and significant.

C. Emergency Mindset in the 2008 Global Financial Crisis and the Eurozone Crisis

This emergency mindset in its different manifestations can also be observed during financial crises. These are also perceived as times of emergency, and are experienced as threats to the stability and security of global financial markets that, if not contained in time, could spread and infect other parts of the economy and cause a comprehensive economic crisis.[18] In that respect, we can also observe how the dynamics of a crisis challenge how lawyers conceptualize law's functioning, turning to concepts of necessity, extra-legality and efficiency to provide legitimacy, even if these measures do not adhere to 'normal' standards of legality.[19] To illustrate this emergency mindset, it is necessary to provide a brief summary of the events that led to the 2008 Global Financial Crisis and the Eurozone Crisis and highlight some of the responses to it. Given their complexity, this summary remains essentially compact. Still, it is sufficient to illustrate why a security mindset is prevalent also in the legal debates on financial crises and why this mindset is too narrow as it turns a blind eye to the transforming power of such crises.

1. The 2008 Global Financial Crisis

Most crises start long before they are perceived as such. This is also true for the 2008 global financial crisis[20] that already began to unfold in 2007 with a crisis in the US subprime housing market.[21] Despite all efforts to contain it, the crisis spread, causing a full-

[18] Even though financial markets are part of the larger economy, they are also independent of the rules and dynamics of the real economy (goods market). At the same time, many links between the two exist. Thus, a financial crisis may affect the real economy, while a downturn in production may have impacts on the financial industry. For a brief account of how the 2018 global financial crisis and the Eurozone Crisis affected the real economy see Sections C.1 and C.2.

[19] More generally William E Scheuerman, 'The Economic State of Emergency' (2000) 21 Cardozo Law Review 1869; specifically addressing the Eurozone Crisis, see Jan Christoph Suntrup, 'From Emergency Politics to Authoritarian Constitutionalism? The Legal and Political Cost of EU Financial Crisis Management' (2018) 19 German Law Journal 375.

[20] While some had warned that certain developments such as excessive subprime lending and the ongoing securitization might lead to a financial crisis, few if any had foreseen the implications and consequences of the global financial crisis: The Financial Crisis Inquiry Commission, *The Financial Crisis Inquiry Report: Final Report of the National Commission on the Causes of the Financial and Economic Crisis in the United States* (Government Printing Office 2011) 3 (FCIC, *The Financial Crisis Inquiry Report*).

[21] Frederic S Mishkin, 'Over the Cliff: From the Subprime to the Global Financial Crisis' (2011) 25 Journal of Economic Perspectives 49, 50ff; FCIC, *The Financial Crisis Inquiry Report* (n 20) 233ff.

blown global financial crisis. Several factors combined were responsible for creating this 'perfect storm'.[22]

One major problem was excessive mortgage lending and borrowing that was, at least partially, politically driven. The declared political will to continuously increase home-ownership meant that banks had to provide more loans and mortgages at relatively low interest rates. The two governmentally supported banks, Freddie Mac and Fannie Mae, were crucial in finding a solution to the problem.[23] They bought and redistributed mortgages through securitization in the form of mortgage backed securities (MBS).[24] The mortgages were, however, not pooled and the MBS issued by the banks themselves. Instead, so-called special purpose vehicles (SPV) were created,[25] which operate off-balance sheet, meaning that risks associated with these activities are not included in a bank's balance sheet.[26] Nevertheless, if the SPV is about to default, the parent company still faces real economic consequences since it either has to provide equity or accept losses in the liquidation process of the SPV. Before the crisis such a scenario was believed to be very unlikely since MBS combined mortgages of different risk categories and were therefore considered to be exposed to very little risk.[27]

When defaults due to decreasing housing prices started to rise, insecurity about risk exposure spread throughout the market. The combination of mortgages of different risk categories turned into a means to spread the risk from the sub-prime market to other sectors of the US real estate market since the composition of MBS and thus the amount of sub-prime mortgages was far from transparent.[28] Positive ratings that were designed to counteract the lack of transparency could not fulfil this function since they were mistrusted due to lack of transparency themselves. As the exposure to risk was difficult to assess, suspicion grew with regard to the credit standing amongst banks and other

[22] Robert Bestani, 'Understanding the Current Financial Crisis—The Perfect Financial Storm' (2009) Collaboratory for Research on Global Projects Working Paper No 44 <https://gpc.stanford.edu/sites/default/files/wp044_0.pdf> accessed 10 January 2020; James Crotty, 'Structural Causes of the Global Financial Crisis: A Critical Assessment of the "New Financial Architecture"' (2009) 33 Cambridge Journal of Economics 563, 564ff.

[23] On the relevance of Fannie Mae and Freddie Mac see Viral V Acharya et al, *Guaranteed to Fail: Fannie Mae, Freddie Mac and the Debacle of Mortgage Finance* (Princeton UP 2011) particularly 31ff; Helen Thompson, 'The Political Origins of the Crisis: The Domestic and International Politics of Fannie Mae and Freddie Mac' (2009) 80 The Political Quarterly 17.

[24] For a description of the complex mortgage securitization industry, see Neil Fligstein/Alexander F Roehkasse, 'The Cause of Fraud in the Financial Crisis of 2007: Evidence from the Mortgage-Backed Securities Industry' (2016) 81 American Sociological Review 617, 619ff.

[25] For more details on the securitization process, see Gary Gorton/Andrew Metrick, 'Securitization' (2012) National Bureau of Economics Research Working Paper 18,611 <www.nber.org/papers/w18611.pdf> accessed 10 January 2020.

[26] See Anthony J Amoruso/Jonathan Duchac, 'Special Purpose Entities and the Shadow Banking System: The Backbone of the 2008 Financial Crisis' (2014) 18 Academy of Accounting and Financial Studies Journal 107, 108 according to whom off-balance sheet financing is the primary purpose of an SPV.

[27] The role of rating agencies for the mortgage-backed securities business should not be underestimated even though it is only briefly mentioned here; see the analysis of FCIC, *The Financial Crisis Inquiry Report* (n 20) particularly 118ff.

[28] ibid 119–21.

financial actors. Banks started to mistrust other banks to such an extent that they were unwilling to lend to them in the short term.[29]

The extensive use of credit default swaps (CDS) further accelerated the crisis. CDS function as an insurance on bonds,[30] and since bond issuers usually do not default, the risk for those who offer CDS seemed to be very limited. Investors in MBS often purchased CDS.[31] With the real estate market under pressure, many MBS received lower ratings, which meant that the issuer of the CDS had to provide additional equity as lower ratings indicate higher risks of default. Because of the necessity to provide additional equity, the largest issuer of CDS, the American Insurance Group (AIG), faced bankruptcy in September 2008.[32] What had been meant to further eliminate risks for individual investors, turned into a fire accelerant of the crisis, which, due to globalized financial markets, spread throughout the financial markets worldwide.[33]

Furthermore, the crisis was not restricted to the financial industry. During the crisis, banks decreased their lending activities with an immediate effect on the real economy. In 2009, international trade collapsed to an even larger extent than global economic performance. The 2008 global financial crisis was therefore accompanied and partially succeeded by the Great Recession.[34] In response, States had to heavily intervene in the financial markets to prevent key actors that were considered 'too big to fail' from collapsing. At the same time, recession caused less tax revenue and higher social spending. Further, the teetering economy put pressure on States to provide economic stimulus packages that strained public spending and thus additional public deficit.

2. The Eurozone Crisis

The Eurozone Crisis is best characterized as a comprehensive banking, sovereign debt, and economic crisis linked to the 2008 global financial crisis with diverse manifestations

[29] Markus K Brunnermeier, 'Deciphering the Liquidity and Credit Crunch 2007–2008' (2009) 23 Journal of Economic Perspectives 77, 85ff.

[30] FCIC, *The Financial Crisis Inquiry Report* (n 20) 50.

[31] According to Eric Arentsen et al, 'Subprime Mortgage Defaults and Credit Default Swaps' (2015) 70 *Journal of Finance* 689, 690, MBS market participants were less concerned about the decline in credit quality because CDS allowed them to limit their risk exposure.

[32] It is interesting to note that '[t]he enormous risk taking at AIG and its potential to blow up the financial system had been largely unrecognized by government officials, regulators, and markets', Mishkin (n 21) 54.

[33] Enrique G Mendoza/Vincenzo Quadrini, 'Financial Globalization, Financial Crises and Contagion' (2009) National Bureau of Economics Research Working Paper Series 15,432, 1 <www.nber.org/papers/w15432.pdf> accessed 10 January 2020; Dimitrios Dimitriou/Theodore Simos, 'Contagion Channels of USA Subprime Financial Crisis: Evidence from USA, EMU, China and Japan Equity Markets' (2013) 5 Journal of Financial Economic Policy 61.

[34] For a more detailed analysis of the causes and effects see, amongst others, the contributions in Richard Baldwin (ed), *The Great Trade Collapse: Causes, Consequences and Prospects* (Centre for Economic Policy Research 2009).

in Eurozone countries.[35] Spain and Ireland, for example, had to address the collapse of their real estate market, which had driven and sustained economic growth for a considerable period of time.[36] Banks in these countries faced two problems: as borrowers defaulted on their debt, property that served as a guarantee decreased in value. Bad loans required additional equity, which had to be provided by the State to save banks from bankruptcy and the financial system from collapsing. Thus, Spain and Ireland were exposed to a vicious circle of macroeconomic difficulties, a failing financial system, and rising public debt,[37] while unsustainable public and private debt lay at the core of the Greek crisis.[38]

While the causes of the crisis differ for each affected State, structural problems stemming from the Eurozone's institutional design also played an important role in prolonging and deepening the Eurozone Crisis. Following the Euro's introduction as common currency, Member States lost their ability to counteract macroeconomic shocks through an individual expansive monetary policy and increase their economy's competitiveness through a devaluation of their currency.[39] Irrational capital flows since 2002, namely capital flows (especially investments) not supported by fundamental economic data, into Members that were most affected, contributed to the worsening of the crisis.[40] These capital flows not only reflected an overly optimistic assessment of the economic situation in these States, they also resulted in very low interest rates within and for these States. The Great Recession put a sudden stop to these capital flows.

In reaction to the crisis, a host of different measures was adopted. When it became evident that first Greece and then Ireland needed financial assistance, the European Commission, the European Central Bank (ECB) and the IMF granted a three-year loan worth €110 billion after the Greek government had committed to a number of austerity measures and economic adjustment programmes.[41] These measures, however, were hardly sufficient to contain the crisis. Thus, only a few months later, the European Financial Stability Mechanism and the European Financial Stability Facilities were

[35] On the causes see, amongst others, Tuori/Tuori (n 2) 3ff, 61ff; Mody/Sandri (n 2) 212ff; Iversen/Soskice (n 2) 257ff.

[36] On Spain, see Francisco Carballo-Cruz, 'Causes and Consequences of the Spanish Economic Crisis: Why the Recovery is Taken so Long?' (2011) 3 Panoeconomicus 209; on Ireland, see K P V O'Sullivan/Tom Kennedy, 'What Caused the Irish Banking Crisis?' (2010) 18 Journal of Financial Regulation and Compliance 224, 225.

[37] For an illustration of this vicious circle see Jay C Shambaugh, 'The Euro's Three Crises' (2012) Brookings Papers on Economic Activity 157, 159.

[38] Antimo Verde, 'The Greek Debt Crisis: Causes, Policy Responses and Consequences' in Pompeo D Posta/Leila S Talani (eds), *Europe and the Financial Crisis* (Palgrave Macmillan 2011) 144ff.

[39] Leila Simona Talani, *The Political Economy of Italy in the Eurozone Crisis: Between Credibility and Competitiveness* (Palgrave Macmillan 2017) 77ff.

[40] Jeffry Frieden/Stefanie Walter, 'Understanding the Political Economy of the Eurozone Crisis' (2017) 20 Annual Review of Political Science 371, 373ff.

[41] For a brief summary of the events surrounding the first Greek economic adjustment programme, see Prodromos Vlamis, 'Greek Fiscal Crisis and Repercussions for the Property Market' (2014) 32 Journal of Property Investment and Finance 21, 24ff.

created as the Euro-rescue fund.[42] Together with funds from the IMF they could provide financial support of up to €750 billion. It is important to note that both mechanisms were created as temporary emergency measures to provide financial stability in the Eurozone.[43] This emergency rationale changed, however, with the establishment of the European Stability Mechanism (ESM), an intergovernmental organization aiming to act as a permanent firewall for the Eurozone.[44] Recipient States of all these funds had to agree to economic adjustment programmes and austerity policies.[45]

In addition, the ECB played an important role throughout the crisis, providing liquidity when banks became increasingly reluctant to lend to one another, by implementing what it calls 'non-standard measures' to enhance credit support, and by introducing programmes such as the Long-Term Refinancing Operation (LTRO) and the Outright Monetary Transactions (OMT).[46] To combat at least some of the underlying structural and institutional problems, the European Fiscal Compact was adopted.[47] It binds all EU Member States, except the UK and the Czech Republic, and provides stricter rules on budget deficit, government debt-to-GDP ratio, and economic cooperation.[48]

3. The Use of Emergency Powers in Financial Crisis

The use of emergency powers or exceptional rules can be observed throughout the 2008 Global Financial Crisis and the Eurozone Crisis.

[42] For details see Ledina Gocaj/Sophie Meunier, 'Time Will Tell: The EFSF, the ESM, and the Euro Crisis' (2013) 35 Journal of European Integration 239, 240ff.

[43] ibid 239: 'The European Financial Stability Facility (EFSF) was the "shock and awe" solution created in May 2010 to stop the possible contagion of the crisis and convince markets that euro area leaders would stand behind the common currency.'

[44] ibid 247ff.

[45] See art 12 of the Treaty Establishing the European Stability Mechanism T/ESM 2012-LT/en (ESM-Treaty) <https://www.esm.europa.eu/sites/default/files/20150203_-_esm_treaty_-_en.pdf> accessed 10 January 2020, according to which '... the ESM may provide stability support to an ESM Member subject to strict conditionality...' While in particular Germany insisted on the implementation of austerity measures in exchange for rescue funds, this insistence has been widely criticized. Especially post-Keynesian economists have provided theoretical as well as empirical evidence that austerity policies are counterproductive; see eg Alberto Botta/Daniele Tori, 'A Critique of Expansionary Austerity: Theoretical Weakness and Empirical Counter Evidence' (2015) Post-Keynesian Economic Society Working Paper 1511 (revised 2017) 1 <www.postkeynesian.net/working-papers/1511/> accessed 10 January 2020. For an unorthodox illustration of two competing economic theories, see Emergent Order, 'Fear the Boom and the Bust: Keynes v. Hayek—The Original Economic Rap Battle' (*YouTube*, 23 January 2010) <www.youtube.com/watch?v=donERTFo-Sk> accessed 10 January 2020; Emergent Order, 'Fight of the Century: Keynes v. Hayek—Economics Rap Battle Round Two' (*YouTube*, 27 April 2011) <www.youtube.com/watch?v=GTQnarzmTOc> accessed 10 January 2020.

[46] On the role of the ECB in the Eurozone Crisis, see Amy Verdun, 'Political Leadership of the European Central Bank' (2017) 39 Journal of European Integration 207, 209ff.

[47] Treaty on Stability, Coordination, and Governance in the Economic and Monetary Union T/SCG/en <www.consilium.europa.eu/media/20399/stootscg26_en12.pdf> accessed 10 January 2020.

[48] The Compact's focus on more efficiently limiting deficits and debts has been criticized as 'turning a policy instrument into a policy objective', see Jérôme Creel et al, 'The European Fiscal Compact: A Counterfactual Assessment' (2012) 27 Journal of Economic Integration 537.

a. *Emergency Powers in the USA during the 2008 Global Financial Crisis*

The US Federal Reserve System (Fed), for example, committed to lend up to US$200 billion to banks and certain non-bank institutions through the newly created Term Securities Lending Facility in early March 2008, shortly before the investment bank Bear Stearns faced the modern equivalent of a bank run.[49] The Fed invoked section 1(3) of the Federal Reserve Act (FRA)[50]—a provision that applies to 'unusual and exigent circumstances', last used in 1934.[51] Only a few days after this innovative response to the already developing crisis, the Fed had to rely on section 13(3) FRA again to authorize an emergency credit to Bear Stearns via JP Morgan to prevent its imminent bankruptcy on 14 March 2008.[52] Since the decision had to be taken overnight and required the vote of at least five board members, even though two seats were vacant and one board member was unavailable, the Fed used yet another emergency provision (section 11(r)(2) FRA) which allows decisions by fewer than five members if they are taken unanimously and if they are necessary to 'prevent...serious harm to...stability of the financial system'. A few months later, section 13(3) FRA was again instrumental in rescuing AIG just one day after the bankruptcy of Lehman Brothers on 15 September 2008.

Shortly after AIG's bailout, then Treasury Secretary Paulson requested Congress to sign into law the Emergency Economic Stabilization Act, which conveyed broad discretionary powers to the executive in order to respond efficiently and swiftly to the not yet contained financial crisis.[53] At first, the House of Representatives refused Paulson's request. After certain amendments improving oversight and accountability, though, and in light of the market crash following the first refusal, the Senate approved the Act and the House reconsidered its original vote.[54]

The Federal Deposit Insurance Corporation (FDIC) used a different emergency tool. Relying on the Federal Deposit Insurance Act (FDIA), it invoked its powers under the 'systemic risk exception'. The provision allows the FDIC to implement emergency measures under certain procedural and substantive requirements.[55] In October 2008, the provision served as the legal basis for the establishment of the Temporary Liquidity Guarantee Program, issuing liability guarantees that amounted at its peak to more than US$500 billion.[56] Even though efficient in containing the crisis, there was considerable doubt whether the FDIC had statutory authority to issue such extensive guarantees,[57] even under the exceptional rules of the FDIA, especially since the FDIC lacked direct accountability. This highlights the democratic deficit problem inherent in all concepts of

[49] For details, see Michael J Fleming et al, 'The Term Securities Lending Facility: Origin, Design, and Effects' (2009) 15 Current Issues in Economics and Finance 1.

[50] Federal Reserve Act, 12 USC ss 221–522.

[51] Philip A Wallach, *To the Edge: Legality, Legitimacy, and the Responses to the 2008 Financial Crisis* (Brookings Institution Press 2015) 46.

[52] John L Walker, 'Emergency Tools to Contain a Financial Crisis' (2016) 35 Review of Banking and Financial Law 672, 683ff.

[53] For details, see Archit Shah, 'Emergency Economic Stabilization Act of 2008' (2009) 46 Harvard Journal on Legislation 569.

[54] Wallach (n 51) 86ff. [55] Walker (n 52) 686ff. [56] Wallach (n 51) 98ff.

[57] Walker (n 52) 689 with further references.

emergency powers since they empower the executive to the detriment of the legislative and the judiciary. It is therefore interesting to note that the Dodd–Frank Wall Street Reform and Consumer Protection Act, which was enacted in response to the 2008 Global Financial Crisis in January 2010, restricted the availability of emergency powers that, at least in the view of some commentators, were crucial to contain that crisis.[58] Unsurprisingly, the curtailment of these emergency powers caused concerns that neither the Fed nor the FDIC will now be able to efficiently respond to the next financial crisis.[59]

b. *Emergency Powers during the Eurozone Crisis*

Similarly, the EU in its efforts to deal with and contain the Eurozone Crisis utilized emergency provisions or at least an emergency rationale. Of particular importance was Article 122(2) of the Treaty on the Functioning of the European Union (TFEU),[60] which allows for financial assistance to a Member State if it is in, or is threatened with, severe difficulties that have been caused by exceptional occurrences beyond its control.[61] While there was little doubt that the crisis qualified as an exceptional occurrence,[62] the more technical problem was whether the financial problems of individual Member States were indeed beyond their control.[63] While this problem could have been resolved with reference to the discretionary powers of EU institutions to interpret and apply the exceptional provision in the absence of previously established case law, the provisions that limit these emergency powers, especially Article 125(1) TFEU—the so-called bailout prohibition—presented a more fundamental problem. In its relevant parts, it

[58] On the restrictions introduced by the Dodd–Frank Act, see Hal S Scott, *Connectedness and Contagion: Protecting the Financial System from Panics* (MIT Press 2016) 93ff.

[59] Group of Thirty, *Managing the Next Financial Crisis* (Group of Thirty 2018) 16; Stijn Claessens/ Laura Kodress, 'The Regulatory Response to the Global Financial Crisis: Some Uncomfortable Questions' (2014) IMF Working Paper 14/46, 15 <www.imf.org/external/pubs/ft/wp/2014/wp1446.pdf> accessed 10 January 2020; See also Hal S Scott, 'Connectedness and Contagion: A Global Perspective' (IMF, IMF HQ, 7 November 2016) 1 <www.imf.org/external/np/seminars/eng/2016/contagionrisk/110716.pdf> accessed 10 January 2020.

[60] OJ C326/47 (TFEU).

[61] While this is not a typical emergency provision, it neatly fits the rule–exception paradigm due to its reference to exceptional circumstances. It reflects characteristic elements contained in provisions precluding wrongfulness in the law of international responsibility, such as force majeure or necessity; see ILC, 'Articles on Responsibility of States for Internationally Wrongful Acts' UNGA Res 56/83 (12 December 2001) Annex, arts 23 and 25.

[62] Critically Alan Greene, 'Questioning Executive Supremacy in an Economic State of Emergency' (2015) 35 Legal Studies 594, 606.

[63] Council Regulation (EU) 407/10 of 11 May 2010 establishing a European Financial Stabilization Mission OJ (L 118) 1 characterized the crisis as exceptional circumstances beyond the Member States' control and thus confirmed TFEU (n 60) art 122(2) as the legal basis for the EFSF. In its reasoning, the regulation refers to the 'serious deterioration in the international economic and financial environment'. For a critique see Boris Ryvkin, 'Saving the Euro: Tensions with European Law in the European Union's Efforts to Protect the Common Currency' (2012) 45 Cornell Journal of International Law 227, 235ff; Bruno de Witte, 'Treaty Games—Law as Instrument and as Constraint in the Euro Crisis Policy' in Franklin Allen et al (eds), *Governance in the Eurozone—Integration and Disintegration* (Wharton Financial Institution Center Press 2012) 148.

states that the EU 'shall not... assume the commitments' of any EU Member State. None of the emergency measures provided by the EU or its Members directly assumed any commitments. The individual Member States remained liable for their own debt. However, bilateral loans, guarantees by Members necessary to establish the Euro-rescue fund, and haircuts that affect public debtors can have a similar effect and could thus be qualified as a 'factual' assumption of commitments and thus a circumvention of the bail-out prohibition.[64] The emergency rationale prevailing during the Eurozone Crisis and the fear that a sovereign default within the Eurozone would threaten the existence of the Euro and possibly the EU itself, heavily influenced the discussion on whether Article 125(1) TFEU should be construed narrowly or broadly.

The emergency mindset was also visible in the foundations of the first temporary Euro-rescue fund. A more permanent structure would have required a different legal basis since emergency measures are inherently required to be temporary. As the establishment of the Euro-rescue fund already faced many legal challenges, its temporary character was deemed necessary to provide additional legal justification. At the same time, by amending Article 136(3) TFEU, EU Member States provided the legal basis for a more permanent solution.[65]

All crises have long-term implications. It is, however, notable that the EU used the Eurozone Crisis and the prevailing emergency rationale to transform initially temporary emergency measures into permanent institutional changes. This is understandable and shows that the crisis revealed deficits in the institutional design of the Eurozone itself that had contributed to causing, worsening, and prolonging the crisis.[66] At the same time, there has been considerable unease about this process as it required an unusual amount of legal flexibility. This already indicates that the Eurozone Crisis illustrates how economic and political dynamics clash with the perception of law as a static system that is meant to provide stability and predictability for all participating actors.

4. Legal Dynamics during Financial Crises

Legal stability and predictability require that the meaning of legal provisions remains unaffected from the factual dynamics that any crisis may trigger. At the same time,

[64] See Hannes Hofmeister, 'To Bail Out or Not to Bail Out—Legal Aspects of the Greek Crisis' (2011) 13 Cambridge Yearbook European Legal Studies 113, 119ff; Rainer Palmstorfer, 'To Bail Out or Not to Bail Out? The Current Framework of Financial Assistance for Euro Area Member States Measured Against the Requirements of EU Primary Law' (2012) 37 European Law Review 771, 775ff; on the relevance of TFEU (n 60) art 125 in case of a 'haircut' involving public creditors see Armin Steinbach, 'The "Haircut" of Public Creditors under EU Law' (2016) 12 European Constitutional Law Review 223, 225ff.

[65] Alberto Merino, 'Legal Developments in the Economic and Monetary Union during the Debt Crisis: The Mechanisms of Financial Assistance' (2012) 49 Common Market Law Review 1613, 1628ff.

[66] Greene (n 62) 606, who criticizes the use of the emergency paradigm since the 'old' normalcy is part of the problem and a return to this 'normalcy' is not at all desirable.

interpretations adapt to the changing facts and challenges that financial crises pose. Thus, the factual dynamics result in legal dynamics—a phenomenon visible in the US responses to the 2018 global financial crisis and, even more distinctly, in the EU response to the Eurozone Crisis. While the Fed and the FDIA, for example, were able to rely on existing emergency powers, their extensive use was at that point unprecedented.[67] The question whether the existing legal provisions supported the emergency measures adopted was seriously raised. Thus, contrary to popular belief, it cannot be said that law was shunted aside in the name of economic necessity,[68] even though the emergency rationale influenced the interpretative approach.

The same applies to the Eurozone Crisis, which triggered legal dynamics resulting in what could be considered as reinterpretations of existing legal provisions. This does not only apply to Articles 122(2) and 125 TFEU that were discussed above, albeit briefly. Many of the measures adopted by the ECB, for example, especially the LTRO or the OMT programmes, can be challenged as either not falling within its mandate or as violating Article 123 TFEU, which prohibits monetary financing.[69] In addition, no provision exists that would allow the ECB to deviate, at least temporarily, from either its primary responsibility to maintain price stability or the prohibition of monetary financing, even though Article 127(1) TFEU allows some flexibility since it permits the ECB to support the EU's general economic policies if this does not endanger the price stability objective. It could, of course, be argued that due to the financial and economic crisis the impact of the ECB measures on price stability was different and lesser than in what one might call normal economic times. Still, the ECB itself invoked the rule–exception paradigm that is inherent in the emergency mindset, stressing that it was necessary to take these 'unconventional' measures in light of the exceptional economic situation.[70]

In this context the reference to exceptional rules and circumstances is utilized to provide legitimacy for the 'unusual' or 'unconventional' measure. Labelling the measure as 'unusual' or 'unconventional' implies that it will not be used in normal times and is

[67] Lawrence H White, 'The Federal Reserve and the Rule of Law' (Cato Institute, 12 September 2012) 2 <www.cato.org/publications/testimony/federal-reserve-rule-law> accessed 10 January 2020; Alexander Mehra, 'Legal Authority in Unusual and Exigent Circumstances: The Federal Reserve and the Financial Crisis' (2010) 13 University of Pennsylvania Journal of Business Law 221, 226ff.

[68] See eg Wallach (n 51) 48ff who points out the decision to invoke and interpret s 13(3) FRA 'creatively' was not taken lightly.

[69] Particularly the OMT programme has not only been subject to academic debates but has also been challenged in court. The German Constitutional Court asked the ECJ for a preliminary ruling on the OMT programme. In its decision, the ECJ demanded certain safeguards, but did not find that the programme violated the TFEU as such; see Case C-62/14 *Gauweiler et al v German Bundestag* [2015] ECLI:EU:C:2015:400. The German Constitutional Court followed the reasoning of the ECJ; BVerfG, Judgment of the Second Senate of 21 June 2016 (2 BvR 2728/13) para 175ff, English version <https://www.bundesverfassungsgericht.de/SharedDocs/Entscheidungen/EN/2016/06/rs20160621_2bvr272813en.html> accessed 10 January 2020.

[70] For the difference between the ECB's conventional and unconventional monetary policies, see Horst Tomann, *Monetary Integration in Europe: The European Monetary Union after the Financial Crisis* (Palgrave Macmillan 2017) 55ff (conventional monetary policies) and 135ff (unconventional monetary policies).

limited to the duration of the crisis. Also, the emergency rationale provides a justification, why changing facts influence the interpretation and application of legal provisions even though legal orthodoxy upholds a top-down approach, according to which facts are not relevant in determining the meaning of law. As this reasoning does not follow the formal rules of legal interpretation, it is little surprise that it was widely criticized. In lack of an alternative explanation, either reference is either made to models of extra-legality or crises are portrayed as times in which the proper function of law is suspended.

D. Outlook

The emergency mindset frames financial crises as exceptional situations to which emergency powers are the paradigmatic response. The exceptional measures adopted in response to crises aim at restoring normality. Due to the binary structure of this conceptual approach, long-term changes tend to be neglected or played down as it is suggested that crises disrupt an otherwise unchanged normality. What is, however, inherent to crises is their transformative power, which has been particularly noticeable in the case of the Eurozone Crisis. In this regard, financial crises are no different than other crises, particularly security crises. They, too, have long-term effects. Most of these effects concern the interpretation of specific legal provisions. Yet, their underlying implications are anything but technical. The interpretative changes concerning the right to self-defence and the spatial and temporal limits of 'armed conflict',[71] for example, have far-reaching effects since they continuously blur the limits for the use of force and the classification of conflict.

If legal analysis and the design of crisis response measures want to escape the blind spot of the emergency mindset, a more phenomenological approach to crises in general, and financial crises in particular, needs to be developed. Crises should not be understood as times that are fundamentally different to normality, but as times in which change occurs at a much faster pace. It is therefore important to analyse how these changes will in fact transform the normality after the crisis. If the long-term consequences are not addressed, it is likely that a crisis, after some time of perceived calm, will surface again. Thus, the predominant emergency mindset and its focus on short-term and temporary solutions might well be the reason for the next crisis, either because some of the causes of the last crisis are still present or because the adopted crisis response measures created a 'new normal' that in itself is considered to constitute another crisis. Due to a new level of intergovernmentalism during the Eurozone Crisis,[72] fundamental concerns about the limits of further European integration have been voiced. Thus, the

[71] See n 17.

[72] Sergio Fabbrini, 'Intergovernmentalism and Its Limits: Assessing the European Union's Answer to the Euro Crisis' (2013) 46 Comparative Political Studies 1003, 1013ff.

Eurozone Crisis evolved into what could be called a general legitimacy crisis, to which prevailing legitimacy models provide no satisfactory solution.

Again, similar observations can be made with regard to international security crises. While applying Article 51 of the UN Charter to non-State actors appears plausible in light of the 9/11 terrorist attacks, it does little to confine the use of force, which, in turn, may cause the next crisis. Similarly, the UNSC's smart sanctioning practice, while providing a short-term solution, raises fundamental problems with regard to judicial review and human rights protection—as does the 'war on terror' in general. Also, the extensive interpretation of Chapter VII powers upsets the institutional set-up of the UN and thus causes legitimacy concerns that could affect the entire organization. Neither the emergency rationale nor models of extra-legality can offer sufficient explanation with regard to the long-term effects caused by specific crisis response measures as they maintain and even legitimize the existing legal and institutional framework, even though the crisis has created a new and different reality.

Note

The views expressed in this chapter are those of the author and do not necessarily reflect the position of the German Federal Ministry of Justice and Consumer Protection.

CHAPTER 27

FOOD SECURITY

HILAL ELVER

A. Introduction: Food Insecurity as a Threat to Global Security

In August 2017, the President of the UN Security Council (UNSC) expressed 'grave concern' about the unprecedented level of global humanitarian need and the threat of famine facing more than 30 million people in Yemen, Somalia, South Sudan, and north-eastern Nigeria.[1] Such widespread, catastrophic hunger should have been an issue of the past; yet, the current food crises engulfing these nations indicate that we still live in a world without peace and stability. In fact, the world we live in is one where mass starvation and famine, or 'food insecurity' at its most severe levels, pose an insurmountable threat to global security.

Though 'food security' is not a legal concept and does not impose rights or responsibilities, it is a necessary precondition to the full enjoyment of the right to food. The right to food is enshrined in Article 25 of the Universal Declaration of Human Rights (UDHR) as an integral part of the right to an adequate standard of living.[2] It is further elaborated as a legally enforceable right, namely a legal entitlement for right holders that is owed by States, the primary duty-bearers, in Article 11 of the International Covenant on Economic, Social and Cultural Rights (ICESCR).[3] As this right is indivisible, interrelated, and interdependent with all other fundamental freedoms,[4] it is ultimately essential for a secure, safe, and harmonious world.

Global security will therefore remain threatened so long as one billion people go to bed hungry and twice as many experience the triple burden of malnutrition. Even with global food production reaching historic heights, hunger has risen for the third year in a

[1] UNSC 'Statement by the President of the Security Council' (9 August 2017) UN Doc S/PRST/2017/14.

[2] Universal Declaration of Human Rights, UNGA Res 217 A(III) (10 December 1948) art 25.

[3] International Covenant on Economic, Social and Cultural Rights 993 UNTS 3 art 11.

[4] CESCR, 'General Comment No 12: The Right to Adequate Food (Art 11)' (12 May 1999) UN Doc E/C.12/1999/5, para 4 (GC 12).

row, affecting 821 million people, and killing more people each year than malaria, tuberculosis, and AIDS combined.[5] 'Hidden hunger', or micronutrient deficiencies, affects millions of people, including the 151 million children under five who experience stunted growth.[6] Conflicts and climate change-induced weather events further intensify human suffering, create unprecedented displacement, including the 68.5 million people who are forcibly displaced, a record high in 70 years.[7]

It is no exaggeration to say that hunger is by far the most widespread pandemic that the world faces and a major threat to global security and the enjoyment of all human rights. This threat is most severe when access to adequate food is compromised. Food security refers to the state in which 'all people, at all times, have physical, social and economic access to sufficient, safe and nutritious food that meets their dietary needs and food preferences for an active and healthy life'.[8] Further, the Integrated Food Security Phase Classification (IPC) classifies the severity of food insecurity into five distinct categories: minimal,[9] stress,[10] crisis,[11] emergency,[12] and famine.[13] The latter occurs when food is absolutely inaccessible to an entire population or subgroup of a population, potentially causing death in the short term.

According to the 2019 Global Report on Food Crises, 113 million people in fifty-three countries are currently experiencing food security at the crisis phase (IPC Phase 3) or worse.[14] The worst food crises as of 2018 are in Yemen, DRC, Afghanistan, Ethiopia, the Syrian Arab Republic, Sudan, South Sudan, and northern Nigeria, where two-thirds of the total number of people or nearly 72 million people face acute food insecurity. An additional 143 million people in forty-two countries are reportedly living in a 'stressed' condition (IPC Phase 2), at risk of a 'crisis', or worse. Not only are these countries impacted by food insecurity, but they tend to be embroiled in conflicts that undermine national, regional, and global security.

Together with climate change and economic turbulence, conflict is the main driver of most recent hunger. Along with other factors, such as poor governance, economic slow-

[5] FAO et al, *The State of Food Security and Nutrition in the World: Building Climate Resilience for Food Security and Nutrition* (FAO 2018) 2.

[6] UNICEF/WHO/World Bank, 'Levels and Trends in Child Malnutrition: Key Findings of the 2018 Edition' (2018) WHO/NMH/NHD/18.9. <https://www.who.int/nutgrowthdb/2018-jme-brochure.pdf> accessed 26 March 2020.

[7] UNHCR, 'Global Trends—Forced Displacement in 2017' (UNHCR 2018) 2 <https://www.unhcr.org/globaltrends2017/> accessed 20 May 2020.

[8] FAO, *The State of Food Insecurity in the World 2001* (FAO 2001).

[9] More than 80 per cent of households can meet basic food needs.

[10] At least 20 per cent of households have reduced food consumption and cannot protect their livelihoods.

[11] At least 20 per cent of households have significant food consumption gaps leading to high levels of acute malnutrition.

[12] An accentuated version of the first three categories.

[13] In order to reach famine status, at least 20 per cent of households in a given group will face extreme food deficit, without the ability to cope; acute malnutrition will exceed 30 per cent; and mortality rate will exceed 2 people per 10,000 inhabitants per day.

[14] Food Security Information Network, '2019 Global Report on Food Crises: Joint Analysis for Better Decisions' (2019) 2 <http://www.fsinplatform.org/sites/default/files/resources/files/GRFC_2019-Full_Report.pdf> accessed 26 March 2020 (2019 Report on Food Crises).

down, and natural disasters, food insecurity significantly destabilizes societies and causes tensions that may escalate into conflict. The impacts of conflict extend far beyond physical violence, transforming and often destroying economies, social networks, and household support systems. Conflict also compromises the right to adequate food and nutrition, with 80 per cent of the world's malnourished population living in conflict, protracted crises, and post-conflict countries.[15] Women, youth, and vulnerable groups are disproportionately impacted, as conflicts often reinforce existing inequalities and destabilize social balance. The legacy of conflict outlasts the violence itself, affecting the likelihood of return and success of reintegration and reconciliation long after stability is re-established.[16] Conversely, food insecurity might be an early indicator of conflict.

In 2018, three conflict-ridden countries, Yemen, the Democratic Republic of Congo, and Afghanistan, collectively accounted for almost 40 million people experiencing food insecurity at a 'crisis' level or worse.[17] While the nature of food insecurity in these countries differs greatly, they are all closely related to ongoing conflicts. Yemen has ranked highest amongst the most severe food crises in the Middle East since the onset of its civil war in 2015. The most recent estimates suggest that there are 17 million people living in food insecurity, with 60 per cent of the population in need of urgent assistance, and 8 million people at risk of famine and acute food insecurity.[18] Creating stability and security in the region remains a challenge, as pervasive hunger has weakened Yemen's agricultural production, social fabric, and governing institutions.

The cyclical relationship between food insecurity and conflict has become apparent elsewhere: the Syrian Arab Republic and Iraq similarly have highly food-insecure populations.[19] The fragile food security situation in South Sudan was severely compounded by the outbreak of civil war in 2013. In the latter half of 2018, 6.1 million people were in 'crises' or worse, including roughly 47,000 people who faced 'catastrophic' levels of food insecurity (IPC Phase 5).[20] Protracted war between the Nigerian army and the extremist group Boko Haram has forced 50,000 civilians into famine-like conditions in North Nigeria.[21] In Somalia, the ongoing presence of the terrorist group Al-Shabaab, as well as prolonged drought and water shortages, has intensified food insecurity since 2017.[22]

[15] FAO et al, *The State of Food Security and Nutrition in the World: Building Climate Resilience for Food Security and Nutrition* (FAO 2017).

[16] Concern Worldwide, 'Breaking the Cycle of Conflict, Hunger and Human Suffering' (2018) <https://www.concern.net/insights/breaking-cycle-conflict-hunger-and-human-suffering> accessed 28 November 2020.

[17] 2019 Report on Food Crises (n 14) 15.

[18] FAO, 'Yemen: Situation Report' (4 July 2017) <https://reliefweb.int/sites/reliefweb.int/files/resources/FAOYemen_sitrep_July2017.pdf> accessed 29 March 2020.

[19] 2019 Report on Food Crises (n 14) 78–81 for Iraq and 136–41 for the Syrian Arab Republic.

[20] ibid.

[21] Sam Loewenberg, 'Famine Fears in Northeast Nigeria as Boko Haram Fight Rages' (2017) 389 The Lancet 352.

[22] FAO, 'Somalia: Situation Report' (14 June 2017) <www.fao.org/emergencies/resources/documents/resources-detail/en/c/896083/> accessed 26 March 2020; 'Intensified Efforts and Investments Needed to Keep Famine at Bay' (FAO, 6 July 2017) <www.fao.org/news/story/en/item/903719/icode/> accessed 26 March 2020.

For their part, climate and other natural disasters drove 29 million people into situations of acute food insecurity in 2018.[23] More than 80 per cent of natural disasters are weather related while, due to climate change, they are becoming more frequent and intense. On average, there are now 355 disaster events each year, almost double the annual rate of the previous decade. In 2017 alone, extreme weather events, such as prolonged drought, were major triggers of the most severe crises in twenty-three countries with over 39 million food-insecure people in need of urgent assistance.[24] In Afghanistan and Myanmar, the heightened risk of acute food insecurity resulted from the combination of conflict and natural disasters. In Africa, nearly 23 million people in twenty countries 'were acutely food insecure' as a result of climate-related shocks.[25]

The impacts of El Niño in the past few years have intensified, severely affecting crop production, livestock, and agricultural livelihoods. Following prolonged droughts and catastrophic floods in 2016, an estimated 12 million people were food insecure in Southern Africa.[26] Due to climate change, prolonged and intensified El Niño has severely affected more than 60 million people around the world and led twenty-three countries to appeal for international humanitarian assistance in East and Southern Africa, Central America, the Caribbean, and the Pacific.[27] Such 'frequent and intense weather events will also necessarily complicate the logistics of food distribution during emergencies'.[28] Meanwhile, industrialized agricultural practices producing greenhouse gases and the heavy release of carbon dioxide into the atmosphere, may further compromise food security as crops might carry fewer nutrients, like zinc and iron, necessary for combatting malnutrition. These deficiencies will have a greater and more immediate impact on the poorest people.[29] According to the World Bank, natural disasters push 26 million people into poverty each year, and over 56 million people in more than twenty countries and territories affected by protracted conflicts are currently suffering from severe undernourishment and emergency levels of food insecurity.[30]

Even in the face of armed conflict and natural disasters, however, States are legally obligated to overcome hunger and malnutrition and to realize the right to food for all.[31]

[23] 2019 Report on Food Crises (n 14) 24. [24] ibid. [25] ibid 15.

[26] Vhusomuzi B Sithole, 'El Nino Impact on Southern Africa: Highlights from the 2015/16 season' (Southern Africa Regional Climate Services Workshop, 29 November–2 December 2016) <https://gfcs.wmo.int/sites/default/files/Sithole_El%20Nino%20Impacts%20in%20Southern%20Africa.pdf> accessed 25 March 2020.

[27] ibid.

[28] UNGA 'Interim Report of the Special Rapporteur on the Right to Food, Hilal Elver' (5 August 2015) UN Doc A/70/287, para 8.

[29] Taylor Kubota, 'Stanford Researchers Explore the Effects of Climate Change on Hunger' (*Stanford News*, 19 March 2019) <https://news.stanford.edu/2019/03/19/climate-change-hunger/> accessed 29 March 2020.

[30] Stephane Hallegatte et al, *Unbreakable: Building the Resilience of the Poor in the Face of Natural Disasters* (WHO 2017); FAO/WFP, 'Press Release: Protracted Conflicts Causing Alarming Spikes in Severe Hunger' (Rome, 29 July 2016) <www.fao.org/news/story/en/item/427423/icode/> accessed 24 March 2020.

[31] OHCHR, 'Fact Sheet No 34: The Right to Adequate Food' (April 2010) 5 <https://www.ohchr.org/Documents/Publications/FactSheet34en.pdf> accessed 20 May 2020.

In light of ongoing food crises and rising hunger and malnutrition, it is apparent that States are either unable or unwilling to take the steps necessary to progressively realize the right to food in accordance with this obligation. This contribution demonstrates that severe food insecurity continues to inflict massive casualties, and create and prolong conflicts and states of emergency, despite well-established rules of international law, international humanitarian law (IHL), and international human rights law (IHRL).

In light of all this, this chapter focuses on the international law principles protecting food security with the aim to diffuse emergency situations that create instability, inequality, and unrest, including those resulting from conflicts and natural disasters. The chapter concludes with suggestions for enforcing and enhancing existing laws and for the adoption of a new international convention which will set out clear duties and obligations for States and non-State actors with a view to eliminating food insecurity and preventing violations of the right to food for a safer, more secure world.

B. Legal Framework

1. International Human Rights Law

The right to adequate food is essential to global security and indispensable to the full enjoyment of all other human rights recognized under international law. It is also an unrestricted right regardless of state of emergency and conflict. Article 25 UDHR established the foundation for the right to food as we know it, declaring that 'everyone has the right to a standard of living adequate for the health and well-being of himself and his family' and identifying food as an element of this right.[32] Without legally binding force, however, the UDHR and its provisions are purely aspirational, although they are often deemed as having achieved the status of customary international law.[33]

The 1966 ICESCR drew heavily from the UDHR to codify economic, social, and cultural rights, including the right to food. Article 11 ICESCR obligates States to ensure that everyone has the right to an adequate standard of living for himself and his family, including adequate food, clothing, and housing. Article 11 further guarantees the right to be free from hunger and imposes an obligation on States to ensure 'the satisfaction of, at the very least, [the] minimum essential level' of this right under all circumstances.[34] Irrespective of whether a State is party to the Covenant, freedom from hunger is an accepted part of customary law and is owed to every individual at all times.[35]

[32] UDHR (n 2) art 25(1).

[33] Hurst Hannum, 'The Status of the Universal Declaration of Human Rights in National and International Law' (1996) 25 Georgia Journal of International and Comparative Law 287.

[34] CESCR, 'General Comment No 3: The Nature of States Parties' Obligations (Art 2, Para 1)' (14 December 1990) UN Doc E/1991/23, para 10.

[35] FAO, *The Right to Food Guidelines: Information Papers and Case Studies* (FAO 2006) 103–6.

Based on the language of the ICESCR, the right to food has been defined in terms of its critical elements: availability, accessibility, and adequacy as well as sustainability.[36] States have an obligation to 'respect existing access' to adequate food and to 'not take any measures that result in preventing such access' for current and future generations; States have an obligation to protect the right to food by ensuring 'that enterprises or individuals do not deprive individuals of their access to adequate food'; and States have an obligation to fulfil—both facilitate and provide for—the right to food.[37]

To date, 169 States have signed and ratified the ICESCR, agreeing to take steps to maximize available resources to progressively achieve the full realization of the right to adequate food, both nationally and internationally. The right to food is perpetually subject to criticism because of its indefinable, undeliverable and non-justiciable nature; however, it is undeniably a fundamental human right. Despite the various global targets and policy documents,[38] States have not delivered a zero-hunger result. Nevertheless, this unacceptable outcome does not change the fact that States are the proper duty-bearers and that the right to food is a justiciable entitlement for rights-holders.[39]

The Committee on Economic, Social and Cultural Rights published General Comment No 12 in 1999 to help explain the right to food in general terms: the right is realized when 'every man, woman and child, alone or in community with others, has physical and economic access at all times to adequate food or means for its procurement'.[40] General Comment No 12 provided principles for identifying corresponding obligations and responsibilities of State and non-State actors in its implementation, and set the foundation for the next phase of advancing the right to food: operationalizing the right at the national level.

In 2000, the UN Commission of Human Rights established a Special Rapporteur on the Right to Food, while the FAO established a Right to Food unit. These two efforts strengthened the basis for alliance between the right to food and the food sovereignty movements.[41] Under pressure from civil society, the 2002 World Food Summit tasked the FAO Council with coordinating amongst non-State actors 'a set of voluntary guidelines to support Member States' efforts to achieve the progressive realization of the right to adequate food in the context of national food security'. In 2004, the FAO adopted

[36] Fact Sheet No 34 (n 31) 2–3. [37] GC 12 (n 4) para 15.

[38] eg UN, 'Goal 2: Zero Hunger' (*UN Sustainable Development Goals*) <https://www.un.org/sustainabledevelopment/hunger/> accessed 25 March 2020.

[39] The Optional Protocol to the International Covenant on Economic, Social and Cultural Rights UN Doc A/RES/63/117, Annex enables those who experience violations of their economic, social, and cultural rights, including the right to food, to present complaints at the international level. Unfortunately, the 45 signatories and 24 parties that have ratified it, have been reluctant to implement the complaint mechanism, and thus, the protocol remains mostly dormant.

[40] GC 12 (n 4) para 6.

[41] For the concept of food sovereign and the relationship between the food sovereignty movement, especially as expressed through the IPC, and international institutions: Michael Fakhri, 'Third World Sovereignty, Indigenous Sovereignty, and Food Sovereignty: Living with Sovereignty Despite the Map' (2018) 9 Transnational Legal Theory 218, 239–50.

the Voluntary Guidelines to Support the Progressive Realization of the Right to Adequate Food in the Context of National Food Security (Right to Food Guidelines).[42]

Despite these efforts, the 2007/8 food price crisis following the global financial crisis confirmed that the right to food was far from realized. More specifically, this crisis revealed that the financialization of food systems presented a real danger to food security, especially in developing countries. As a result, in 2009 the Committee on World Food Security (CFS) was reborn as a progressive and inclusive, multistakeholder global policy platform to promote food and nutrition security.[43] The reformed CFS went beyond the usual protocol of UN institutions to include both civil society and private sector actors as well as government representatives in the decision-making process.[44]

Although the ultimate duty to realize the right to food is vested in States, these new partnerships and initiatives have supported a participatory, and inclusive human rights-based approach to food system governance. Promoting food security requires not just strategic policies but corresponding mechanisms for monitoring and accountability. International human rights law provides several mechanisms for monitoring State compliance with human rights obligations, like the Special Procedures of the Human Rights Council, including universal periodic reviews (UPR), and Special Rapporteurs, as well as individual complaint procedures. Still, it is up to States to adhere to IHRL and to create an enabling environment for the progressive realization of the right to food.

2. Protection of the Right to Food during an Emergency

Ensuring the right to food during emergencies requires proactive action by States to not only protect and respect this right, but to also fulfil the normative content of IHRL norms. The obligation to 'fulfil' requires States to take affirmative steps to facilitate the capacity of their people to feed themselves. This also requires identifying the most vulnerable segments of the population and ensuring their access to food, and directly supplying food when individuals or groups are unable, for reasons beyond their control, to secure adequate food (such as natural disasters or armed conflict).[45] This obligation may warrant the adoption of pre-emptive measures, such as insurance schemes like crop or natural disaster insurance, or other support to victims of disaster.[46]

States must further protect the right to food from interference by third parties, including armed groups, and refrain from interfering with individuals' enjoyment of

[42] FAO Council, 'Voluntary Guidelines to Support the Progressive Realization of the Right to Adequate Food in the Context of National Food Security' (November 2004) <http://www.fao.org/3/a-y7937e.pdf/> accessed 25 March 2020.

[43] Committee on World Food Security, 'Agenda Item III: Reform of the Committee on World Food Security—Final Version' (Rome, 14–17 October 2009) CFS: 2009/2 Rev.2.

[44] But see Fakhri (n 41) 244–7.

[45] UNGA 'Interim Report of the Special Rapporteur on the Right to Food, Hilal Elver' (21 July 2017) UN Doc A/72/188, paras 47–61.

[46] CESCR, 'General Comment No 19: The Right to Social Security (Art 9)' (4 February 2008) UN Doc E/C.12/GC/19, paras 29–51.

their right, such as withholding food as a political manoeuvre. Consistent with the principle of progressive realization, States cannot simply disregard or postpone their obligation to ensure that adequate food is accessible and available during times of conflict. Rather, States must continue to take deliberate and targeted steps, using all appropriate means to fulfil their obligations. They must also adhere to the prohibition of discrimination, even when taking regressive measures in response to an emergency situation.[47]

Over recent decades, international humanitarian aid has served an essential role in addressing barriers to the access, adequacy, and availability of food in emergency settings. As described below, the humanitarian legal framework and international assistance is necessary to fill gaps in situations where States are unable or unwilling to meet the needs of their populations. However, it is widely recognized that IHRL applies both in situations of normality and situations of conflict and disaster relief. The ICESCR, in particular, does not contain a derogation clause to suspend State obligations pertaining to the right to food in times of emergency. Rather, it remains, first and foremost, the responsibility of States to take appropriate measures to guarantee the right to food even in contexts of conflict, disaster, and acute food insecurity.[48]

Obligations of States during an emergency situation are further elaborated in several non-binding human rights instruments, including the Right to Food Guidelines. The Guidelines reiterate that food should never be used as an instrument of political and economic pressure, and that States should seek to provide access to food even in situations of armed conflict.[49] Guideline 15 elaborates on the concept of international food aid in times of emergency, regardless of whether the emergency results from human-made conflict or natural disaster. The Framework for Action for Food Security and Nutrition in Protected Crises, which was developed by the CFS and endorsed by FAO's Member States in October 2015, was the first formulation of a global consensus to mitigate threats to food security and nutrition during protracted crises.[50]

3. International Humanitarian Law

International humanitarian law (IHL) and IHRL are mutually reinforcing in the protection of the right to food in situations of armed conflict. Unlike IHRL, humanitarian law—set forth in the 1949 Geneva Conventions and the 1977 Additional Protocols[51]—

[47] UNGA 'Report of the United Nations High Commission for Human Rights' (19 May 2015) UN Doc E/2015/59, paras 31–2.

[48] OHCHR, *International Legal Protection of Human Rights in Armed Conflict* (UN 2011).

[49] FAO, 'Voluntary Guidelines' (n 42).

[50] CFS, 'Framework for Action for Food Security and Nutrition in Protracted Crises' (13 October 2015) <http://www.fao.org/3/a-bc852e.pdf> accessed 25 March 2020.

[51] 75 UNTS 31 (GC I); 75 UNTS 85 (GC II); 75 UNTS 135 (GC III); 75 UNTS 287 (GC IV); Protocol Additional to the Geneva Conventions of 12 August 1949 and relating to the Protection of Victims of International Armed Conflicts (Protocol I) 1125 UNTS 3 (AP I); Protocol Additional to the Geneva Conventions of 12 August 1949 and relating to the Protection of Victims of Non-International Armed Conflicts 1125 UNTS 609 (AP II).

clearly binds both State and non-State actors, and further obliges conflicting parties to implement the relevant rules immediately and not progressively.

International humanitarian law should, therefore, be treated as a special legal framework in times of armed conflict, protecting peoples' livelihoods and their access to food.[52] While IHL does not mention the 'right to food' as such, many of its provisions are intended to prevent food insecurity during armed conflict. For example, it explicitly prohibits purposeful destruction of crops, foodstuffs, wells, and other items essential for the survival of civilians. It also prohibits forced displacement and, importantly, the use of starvation as a weapon of war.[53] If prevention fails and malnutrition and hunger become widespread, rules governing humanitarian assistance become applicable, as their primary purpose is the safeguarding of relief undertakings for people in need.

a. *Prohibition of Starvation of Civilians as a Method of Warfare*

Starvation of civilians as a method of warfare is unconditionally prohibited in international and non-international conflicts.[54] Under IHL, States are prohibited from

> attack[ing], destroy[ing], remov[ing] or render[ing] useless, for that purpose, objects indispensable to the survival of the civilian population, such as foodstuffs, agricultural areas for the production of foodstuffs, crops, livestock, drinking water installations and supplies and irrigation works.[55]

As with many provisions of IHL, these prohibitions are generally considered part of customary international law, and are applicable to all types of armed conflict.[56] A study by the International Committee of the Red Cross (ICRC) confirmed that humanitarian rules are violated when deprivation of food sources and supplies causes hunger, and when hunger results from denial of access to food in violation of human rights law.[57]

b. *Prohibition of Forced Displacement*

Displacement is a major factor contributing to hunger and starvation in times of armed conflict. Forced displacement is prohibited under Article 49 of GC IV and under Article 17 AP II. All possible measures must be taken to ensure that civilians are provided with satisfactory conditions of shelter, hygiene, health, safety, and nutrition and that members of a family are not separated. Unlawful displacement constitutes a war crime

[52] Jelena Pejic, 'The Right to Food in Situations of Armed Conflict: The Legal Framework' (December 2001) 83 International Review of the Red Cross 1097.

[53] GC IV (n 51) arts 23, 30 and 142; AP I (n 51) art 70(1).

[54] AP I (n 51) art 54; AP II (n 51) art 14. [55] ibid.

[56] Jean-Marie Henckaerts/Louise Doswald-Beck, *Customary International Humanitarian Law, Volume 1: Rules* (ICRC/CUP 2005) 186 (rule 53): The use of starvation of the civilian population as a method of warfare is prohibited and 189 (rule 54): Attacking, destroying, removing, or rendering useless objects indispensable to the survival of the civilian population are prohibited.

[57] ibid rule 53.

under the Rome Statute of the International Criminal Court (Rome Statute) in both international and non-international armed conflict.[58]

c. *Denying or Blocking Humanitarian Assistance*

The principles and rules governing humanitarian assistance are fundamental to protecting the right to food in situations of armed conflict. According to UNGA Resolution 46/182, 'humanitarian assistance must be provided in accordance with the principles of humanity, neutrality and impartiality'.[59] Parties to an armed conflict bear the primary duty to meet the needs of the population under their control. If parties to the conflict cannot meet those needs, they must allow and facilitate efforts by impartial humanitarian agencies to provide relief without interference.

States maintain an obligation to address potential food insecurity during armed conflict by ensuring the free flow of humanitarian aid. The GC IV requires States to grant free passage of humanitarian assistance for specific categories of people, such as pregnant women and children, who are particularly vulnerable to hunger and malnutrition, regardless of whether those persons belong to an adversary State or enemy non-State party. Article 70 (l) of AP I extends this requirement to all civilians.

States cannot refuse permission to deliver food, except in exceptional conditions, such as a credible claim of 'military necessity'. This claim may be invoked only to regulate, not prohibit, humanitarian access, and can only restrict access temporarily and within a specific location. Wilfully impeding relief supplies constitutes a war crime under Article 8, paragraph 2 (b) (xxv) of the Rome Statute.

4. International Criminal Law: Famine as an International Crime

Individual criminal responsibility is fundamental in ensuring accountability for violations of IHRL and IHL. Certain gross violations of IHRL and IHL are regulated under international criminal law, potentially triggering individual criminal responsibility. Article 5 of the Rome Statute provides the most complete and updated definition of relevant international crimes, namely genocide, crimes against humanity, and war crimes.

Under international criminal law, famine becomes a crime if there is sufficient evidence of an intentional or reckless effort to block certain groups from access to food under conditions of conflict or hardship.[60] The crime of famine could result from acts of omission, but also from indirect action such as blocking humanitarian assistance, failing to uphold the relevant laws of war or failing to provide international relief systems with the necessary resources in the context of famine conditions.

[58] 2187 UNTS 3 art 8(2)(a)(vii) and (b)(viii). [59] UNGA Res 46/182 (19 December 1991) para 2.

[60] For some thoughtful contributions on this issue: Antonio Coco et al (eds), 'Special Issue: Starvation in International Law' (2019) 17 JICJ 673.

In recent years the international community seems to be taking steps towards holding States accountable for violations of the right to food during times of war. In 2018, UNSC Resolution 2417 unanimously condemned using hunger as a weapon of war or unlawfully denying humanitarian access to civilians in need of aid, and pointed to the need for early warning, early action and investments in resilience by safeguarding agriculture-based livelihoods. Moreover, the resolution identified a series of actions and measures that can be undertaken to address IHL violations.

However, it is important to acknowledge the gap between what the law prescribes and the feasibility of its implementation, and what steps need to be taken to close this gap. In Afghanistan, the Central African Republic, Iraq, South Sudan, the Syrian Arab Republic, and Yemen, warring factions are undermining food security and the right to food on a daily basis.[61] Establishing that crimes of famine have been committed depends upon showing that the actions of those responsible are either intentional or reckless. In that respect, proving specific intent is quite difficult as death from starvation is slow and may result from other contributory factors.[62]

Formal codification of individual responsibility pertaining to famine and severe food insecurity would clarify the conditions of criminality. At present, legal authority is scattered and fragmented. The coherent formulation of the content of the crime in an authoritative text would significantly contribute to the development of international law in this setting, where the most fundamental human rights are currently subject to massive abuse without the activation of accountability procedures. The establishment of the International Criminal Court (ICC) was an important step forward, but its potential remains unrealized at present. Thus, it is theoretically possible to bring to justice States that allow their populations or those of their adversaries to starve to death during an armed conflict, but the political will to do so is not clearly manifested nor consistently present.[63] Recently, the States Parties of the ICC in December 2019 unanimously agreed to amend the Rome Statute to include the intentional starvation of civilians during non-international armed conflicts. This is a step towards enabling the court to redress the heinous practice of starving civilians during internal armed conflicts.[64]

[61] FAO/WFP, 'Monitoring Food Security in Countries with Conflict Situations: A Joint FAO/WFP Update for the United Nations Security Council' (July 2016) <http://www.fao.org/3/a-c0335e.pdf> accessed 25 March 2020.

[62] David Marcus, 'Famine Crimes in International Law' (2003) 97 AJIL 245; Catriona Murdoch/ Wayne Jordash, 'Clarifying the Contours of the Crime of Starvation' (*EJIL:Talk!*, 27 June 2019) <https://www.ejiltalk.org/clarifying-the-contours-of-the-crime-of-starvation/> accessed 25 March 2020.

[63] Interim Report of the Special Rapporteur 2017 (n 45) conclusion.

[64] 'IBA Welcomes Decision to Include Starvation in Non-International Armed Conflicts in Rome Statute' (IBA, 10 December 2019) <https://www.ibanet.org/Article/NewDetailPreview.aspx?ArticleUid=a9a2c0bf-ce29-49cf-a8c5-f654621347e7> accessed 1 April 2020.

5. Natural Disaster Response

a. *Refining the Human Rights System Approach*

Although various UN Charter-based and treaty-based mechanisms address the link between human rights and disasters, the UN human rights system did not address natural disasters in a systematic manner until 2013, when HRC Resolution 22/16 was passed. In the resolution, the Human Rights Council (HRC) called for research on best practices and challenges in the promotion and protection of human rights in post-disaster and post-conflict situations.[65] With other branches of law also addressing the impacts of disasters on human rights, the legal landscape remains fragmented and uncertain.

Due to the absence of comprehensive, binding legal mechanisms, discrepancies amongst various interpretations of 'disaster', and the increased number of disaster situations worldwide due to climate change, the International Law Commission (ILC) has produced twenty-one Draft Articles on subjects ranging from the role of the affected State in coordinating an international response to the recognition of human rights in the context of natural disasters. These articles explicitly adopt a human rights-based approach, including the affirmation of human dignity, to address vulnerability in emergencies.[66]

The Draft Articles primarily cover the rights and obligations of States, but also remind the international community of the responsibilities of external actors towards disaster-affected people.[67] This position is largely at odds with the international community's dominant view that disaster relief is based on voluntarism, which often leads to unreliable, politically partisan, and arbitrary results.[68]

b. *Food Assistance and the Role of the International Community*

Although the immediate obligation to provide food, water, shelter, and medical aid is the duty of State governments, the international community has the responsibility to help countries in times of disaster. This responsibility is universal, normative, and ethical, and is also essential to sustainable world peace, which can only be achieved when hunger and malnutrition are eliminated. In recent decades, the international humanitarian response system has been essential in reducing the negative effects of

[65] UNGA 'Promotion and Protection of Human Rights in Post-Disaster and Post-Conflict Situations' (18 March 2013) UN Doc A/HRC/22/L.23, para 1.

[66] ILC, 'Report of the International Law Commission on its 68th session' (2 May–10 June and 4 July–12 August 2016) UN Doc A/71/10, para 48.

[67] Dug Cubie/Marlies Hesselman, 'Accountability for the Human Rights Implications of Natural Disasters: A Proposal for Systemic International Oversight' (2015) 33 Netherlands Quarterly of Human Rights 9.

[68] Therese O'Donnell/Craig Allan, 'Identifying Solidarity: The ILC Project on the Protection of Persons in Disasters and Human Rights' (2017) 49 George Washington International Law Review 53. The HRC Advisory Committee, 'Final Research-Based Report on Best Practices and Main Challenges in the Promotion and Protection of Human Rights in Post-Disaster and Post-Conflict Situations' (10 February 2015) UN Doc A/HRC/28/76, also does not refer to the International Law Commission's work on this issue or to that of the Commission's Special Rapporteur (n 66).

conflict and natural disasters on food security in lowering death tolls. The World Food Programme (WFP) estimates that food aid expenditure more than doubled between 2009 and 2016, from US$2.2 billion to US$5.3 billion.[69]

Due to the recent increase in disasters and conflicts, the humanitarian emergency system is currently experiencing a US$3 billion funding gap, and there are significant challenges in leadership, coordination, functionality, and efficiency. There remains a tendency to earmark food aid for short-term relief operations rather than invest in longer-term agricultural development, social protection programs, and rural infrastructure. Such investments would raise the quality of food security and build resilience in regions vulnerable to climate change and natural disasters. In addition, the humanitarian structure has evolved from fragmentary endeavours and is now composed of a multitude of autonomous entities with separate governance and accountability structures that lack effective, flexible coordination and clear leadership.[70]

(I) FOOD ASSISTANCE CONVENTION OF 2012 AND RIGHT TO FOOD APPROACH

The 2012 Food Assistance Convention is the only legally binding international treaty addressing 'the food and nutritional needs of the most vulnerable populations' in emergency situations.[71] First enacted in 1967, it has been continuously reformulated over the years; in 2012, the Convention's title changed from 'aid' to 'assistance', reflecting a shift towards longer-term development assistance by preventing distortions of local markets and generating benefits for local producers, thereby combining emergency responses with broader food security goals in recipient countries. The Convention also contains an explicit reference to the right to food and draws from the Right to Food Guidelines, consistent with emerging endorsement generally amongst donor States, of a human rights-based approach to food insecurity.[72]

(II) WORLD HUMANITARIAN SUMMIT

In May 2016, the first World Humanitarian Summit (WHS) was convened by the UN to develop a more global, accountable, and robust humanitarian system, and to reform the humanitarian aid industry.[73] The WHS has been groundbreaking, as it has encouraged more flexible funding, greater local ownership and greater accountability. Agreements were made to use less earmarking, to make greater use of cash transfers, and to raise the ceiling of the Central Emergency Response Fund. Some critics argue, however, that the limits of possible reform have been reached, given the structural

[69] WFP, 'World Food Assistance 2017: Taking Stock and Looking Ahead' (July 2017) <https://docs.wfp.org/api/documents/WFP-0000019564/download/?_ga=2.76488913.532296476.1584170004-238389434.1501478750> accessed 25 March 2020.

[70] Active Learning Network for Accountability and Performance in Humanitarian Action (ALNAP), *The State of the Humanitarian System* (ALNAP 2015) 19.

[71] Food Assistance Convention 2884 UNTS 3. Ratified by Austria, Canada, Denmark, Finland, Japan, Switzerland, and the United States, and by the European Union, in 2012.

[72] ibid preamble, art 2(a)(ii), (iv), (v), and (c)(i).

[73] 'World Humanitarian Summit' (*Agenda for Humanity*) <https://www.agendaforhumanity.org/summit> accessed 1 April 2020.

limitations of the current humanitarian framework, and condemned the Summit for failing to agree on meaningful structural reform.[74]

C. Contemporary Challenges to Global Food Security

Despite the various international law regimes and institutions designed to prevent populations from experiencing the most severe forms of food insecurity, new and prolonged conflicts as well as climate change continue to increase hunger and malnutrition and to put the normative framework under strain. From this perspective, the loss of available, adequate, and accessible food is one of the main barriers to achieving food security.

The agricultural sector plays a critical role in promoting the resilience of populations and ensuring secure, stable societies, particularly for rural populations, who rely on farming, livestock and horticulture for sustenance and income. Although the impact may vary in each specific context, as demonstrated in the Introduction, both armed conflict and natural disasters inevitably disrupt food production and distribution, increasing the risks of food insecurity and poverty.

1. Disruption of Agricultural Sector and Deterioration of Sustainable Food Systems (Availability)

During protracted armed conflict and following natural disasters, crops may be destroyed and serious damage may be inflicted on agricultural infrastructure. Farmers may have restricted access to land, may be displaced, or may be forcibly recruited into armed forces or militias. Fisheries and livestock are also vulnerable to shocks. As a result of the conflict in Yemen, the country experienced a 30 per cent decrease in agricultural output and a 70 per cent decrease in fish product in 2016 due to disrupted access to farmland and extension services, and blockades of land, air, and marine ports by armed groups.[75]

In developing countries, the total percentage of losses and damage absorbed by the agriculture sector following natural disasters is estimated at 22 per cent.[76] While crops are susceptible to floods and storms, livestock is usually affected by droughts, and fisheries

[74] UNGA 'Report of the Special Rapporteur on the Right to Food' (25 January 2018) UN Doc A/HRC/37/61, para 101.

[75] FAO, 'FAO in the 2016 Humanitarian Appeals: Saving Livelihoods Saves Lives' (2016) <www.fao.org/3/a-i5320e.pdf> accessed 26 March 2020; 'Yemen: Situation Report' (n 18).

[76] FAO, *The Impact of Natural Hazards and Disasters on Agriculture, Food Security and Nutrition* (FAO 2015) 11.

are often destroyed by storms, hurricanes, and cyclones. During Hurricane Matthew in Haiti (2016) and Hurricane Maria in Puerto Rico (2017), close to 100 per cent of the crops in impacted areas were destroyed, creating immediate food shortages and long-term infrastructural damage.[77] Recent droughts in Ethiopia have resulted in a high rate of livestock morbidity and mortality, as well as modification of animals' migration patterns.[78] Similarly, in Malawi, drought induced by El Niño impacted the production of various cereals, including maize, rice, sorghum, and millet, leading to below-average crop productions in 2015 and 2016.[79]

Climate change has not only intensified these natural disasters, both in terms of their frequency and impact, but has also altered the geography of food production and trade, which has serious ramifications for food security. As a result, climate change is anticipated to force more that 100 million people into extreme poverty by 2030.[80]

Even after these conflicts and disasters subside, key resources and ecosystems that are vital for sustainable food production may suffer long-term damage. In protracted crises, agricultural assets may be so eroded that households lack the capacity to resume farming activities or lack the resources and equipment. Following a natural disaster, contamination of soil and water may negatively impact food quality, and salinization of water bodies affects the fertility of agricultural lands, which reduces crop yields. Damage to natural buffers, such as forests and mangroves may also increase exposure of certain areas to natural hazards in the future.

2. Economic Deterioration and Physical Barriers (Accessibility)

Disaster and conflict can also create barriers to accessing adequate food, thus perpetuating food insecurity particularly amongst rural and isolated communities. Mass unemployment or loss of income and the breakdown of social services limit the ability to afford adequate food, while currency devaluation, price inflation, market disruptions, and reliance on costly food imports owing to shortages may render basic food items prohibitively expensive. Disasters and fighting may also lead to the destruction of infrastructure and market access points. During armed conflict, warring groups may

[77] WFP Americas, 'A Timeline of WFP's Response to Hurricane Matthew in Haiti' (*WFP Americas*, 28 December 2016) <https://wfp-americas.exposure.co/a-timeline-of-wfps-response-to-hurricane-matthew-in-haiti> accessed 2 April 2020; 'Puerto Rico: Human Rights Concerns Mount in Absence of Adequate Emergency Response' (OHCHR, 30 October 2017) <https://www.ohchr.org/EN/NewsEvents/Pages/DisplayNews.aspx?NewsID=22,326&LangID=E> accessed 2 April 2020.

[78] FAO, 'FAO in Ethiopia: El Niño Response Plan 2016' (January 2016) 10 <http://www.fao.org/emergencies/resources/documents/resources-detail/en/c/380012/> accessed 26 March 2020; FAO, 'Ethiopia: Situation Report' (April 2016) <http://www.fao.org/emergencies/resources/documents/resources-detail/en/c/410229/> accessed 26 March 2020.

[79] Food Security Information Network, 'Global Report on Food Crises' (2017) 83 <http://www.fao.org/3/a-br323e.pdf> accessed 2 April 2020 (FSIN Report).

[80] 'Climate Change' (The World Bank) <https://www.worldbank.org/en/topic/climatechange/overview> accessed 2 April 2020.

deliberately undermine the food security of civilians for political or strategic reasons by intentionally targeting markets and ports.

In Yemen, for example, the poverty rate doubled to 62 per cent during ongoing conflict, and three-quarters of all households are experiencing substantially reduced purchasing power.[81] Public salaries and social support mechanisms have stalled, and restrictions on movement are further depriving individuals from earning income. Conflict has also created physical barriers to staple food items. Prior to conflict, 90 per cent of Yemen's staple foods were imported into the country. The creation of a naval blockade, fighting around the port of Aden, and air strikes on the port of Hudayah, however, interfered with imports, causing a loss of food stock and led to alarming price inflation for basic food products.[82] The Ministry of Agriculture and Irrigation also found that farms, livestock and irrigation infrastructure, food stores, agriculture markets, and food trucks were amongst identified bombing targets.

In Nigeria, currency devaluation as a result of the scarcity of agricultural produce, aggravated by conflict and the drop in global oil prices, caused food prices almost to double.[83] Producers are also struggling to access markets due to the destruction of transportation infrastructure and risk of ambush, and fishers are similarly unable to access water due to military operations and the appropriation of the fishing industry by Boko Haram. Across the Lake Chad region, conflict has led to the closure of some of the largest markets in Africa and disruption of cross-border trade in cattle, dried fish, and agricultural products.[84] There are additional reports that Boko Haram denies access to vehicles transporting food aid and steals humanitarian supplies.[85] Cyclical droughts and floods have further exacerbated the challenges presented by the conflict.[86]

Even without armed conflict interfering with access, natural disasters threaten food storage, sale, and distribution. In Pakistan in 2010, intense monsoons induced floods, which affected more than 20 million people and seriously impacted the circulation of food commodities inside the country as both roads and the rail network had been damaged.[87] In 2016, El Niño-related drought disturbed the harvest season in Lesotho, leading to low production and food price inflation. Similarly, the drought impacted

[81] FAO/UNICEF/WFP, 'As Yemen Food Crisis Deteriorates, UN Agencies Appeal for Urgent Assistance to Avert a Catastrophe' (WFP, 10 February 2017) <https://www.wfp.org/news/yemen-food-crisis-deteriorates-un-agencies-appeal-urgent-assistance-avert-catastro> accessed 2 April 2020; WFP, 'Special Focus Yemen: What Does the Conflict-Induced Public Sector Crisis Mean for Food Security in Yemen?' (November 2016) <https://documents.wfp.org/stellent/groups/public/documents/ena/wfp288497.pdf?_ga=2.40335393.2014126783.1585835607-238168873.1585246212> accessed 2 April 2020.

[82] FAO, 'Counting the Cost: Agriculture in Syria after Six Years of Crisis' (2017) <http://www.fao.org/emergencies/resources/documents/resources-detail/en/c/878213/> accessed 29 November 2020.

[83] Oxfam, 'Lake Chad's Unseen Crisis: Voices of Refugees and Internally Displaced People from Niger and Nigeria' (19 August 2016) <https://policy-practice.oxfam.org.uk/publications/lake-chads-unseen-crisis-voices-of-refugees-and-internally-displaced-people-fro-618488> accessed 2 April 2020.

[84] ibid.

[85] 'UN: World Facing Greatest Humanitarian Crisis since 1945' (*BBC News*, 11 March 2017) <https://www.bbc.co.uk/news/world-africa-39238808> accessed 29 November 2020.

[86] FAO, 'Lake Chad Basin: Situation Report' (April 2017) <http://www.fao.org/emergencies/resources/documents/resources-detail/en/c/879537/> accessed 26 March 2020.

[87] WFP, 'Pakistan Flood Impact Assessment' (September 2010) 8 <http://documents.wfp.org/stellent/groups/public/documents/ena/wfp225987.pdf> accessed 26 March 2020.

small-scale farmers in Ethiopia, forcing many to sell off livestock and agricultural assets for short-term relief.[88] Such coping strategies have long-term consequences on achieving the right to food.

3. Adequacy

Food in conflict and post-disaster settings may also not satisfy the dietary needs of the affected population, or may not be culturally acceptable and nutritious. Indeed, with limited availability and access, there are often fewer food choices and less dietary diversity in conflict and post-disaster settings. Food may also be unsafe or contaminated, particularly after disasters. Poor sanitation, lack of clean water, destruction of infrastructure and lack of suitable conditions for preparing food create higher risks of mass outbreaks of food-borne diseases. As discussed below, vulnerable populations, including children, may suffer from malnutrition and deficiencies if the only available and accessible food is inadequate to satisfy dietary needs.

4. Populations at Heightened Risk of Food Insecurity

The aforementioned threats to available, accessible, and adequate food tend to have a disproportionate impact on the most disadvantaged and marginalized groups, as threats to global security, such as natural disasters and conflict, often reinforce existing social inequalities. Amongst these groups are elderly persons, persons with disabilities, people living with HIV/AIDS, minorities, women and girls, children, and migrants, including refugees and internally displaced persons. For pastoralists, nomadic peoples, and traditional communities, conflict and disasters disproportionately impact their access to land, fishing, and hunting resources, as well as access to adequate and culturally acceptable foods. Subsistence farmers, peasants, and indigenous peoples are also disproportionately impacted. These populations are often dependent on the least-resilient landscapes, such as hillsides, deserts, and floodplains, and often already suffer from chronic food insecurity, even in times of peace and stability.

D. Conclusion

The interdependence of food insecurity and global insecurity, particularly as a result of armed conflict and natural disasters exasperated by climate change, has become clearer in recent years. Ending conflicts, empowering women, nourishing and educating children, improving rural infrastructure, and reinforcing social safety nets are essential for a

[88] FSIN Report (n 79).

resilient, stable, and hunger-free world. Investments in conflict prevention and disaster mitigation and response will help sustain peace, save lives and livelihoods, reduce structural vulnerabilities, and address the root causes of hunger.

Considering the increased hunger and malnutrition in recent years, the current situation of famine in protracted conflict and post-conflict areas, and the lack of political interest and funding to respond to climate change, there is a need for a global convention that gives States and the international community clear legal mandates to prevent famine and protect peoples' right to adequate food. This protection cannot be reliably achieved on a voluntary basis. If the international community is serious about the imperative character of the right to food and the eradication of serious food insecurity, steps must be taken to encourage the implementation of existing standards and codify and elaborate new international rules.

First, a binding agreement with a human rights-based approach to food security should be put in place to cover essential elements of conflict prevention, prohibitions associated with famine and starvation, and post-conflict rehabilitation of the agricultural sector. International legal standards should be developed that strongly reinforce the norm that deliberate action taken to cause starvation is a war crime or a crime against humanity, and that in the most serious cases these should be referred to the ICC for investigation and prosecution. Formal recognition of famine as a crime will impede the tendency of Governments 'to hide behind a curtain of natural disasters and state sovereignty to use hunger as a genocidal weapon.'[89]

Secondly, steps should be taken to maximize local and regional sourcing of food for aid, including increasing developmental assistance for long-term recovery. In times of emergency, simultaneous action across the humanitarian–development nexus is necessary to deliver a hunger-free world in the twenty-first century. In the last ten years, humanitarian assistance and spending needs have grown by around 127 per cent—approximately 40 per cent was directed to the food and agriculture subsectors.[90] The surge in humanitarian need, as well as the potential for agricultural development and rural resilience-building to provide a buffer against crises, highlights the need for a new response to food insecurity.

Thirdly, the right investments in agriculture should be made in pre- and post-disaster and post-conflict periods in order to avert or mitigate severe food insecurity. Even at the earliest stages of disaster response, it is crucial to strengthen the resilience of affected communities and to deploy a range of humanitarian, economic, political, and even military tactics. This is only possible with coordinated political and financial commitments by developed countries. Following a conflict, interventions to support peasants, smallholder farmers, and marginal fishers are needed with priority for decommissioned combatants and women. These groups constitute the largest segments of the workforce in current conflict zones, and the capacity of these workers to jump-start their livelihoods

[89] Marcus (n 62) 281.

[90] Development Initiatives, 'Global Humanitarian Assistance Report 2019' (2019) <http://devinit.org/wp-content/uploads/2019/09/GHA-report-2019.pdf> accessed 26 March 2020.

could be greatly enhanced by providing them with an understanding of how markets work, facilitating their access to improved production systems, and making their farms more resilient.

Finally, long-term policies that recognize the right to food as a collective right, as well as an individual right, are essential if the international community is to avoid the periodic recurrence of famine and promote greater peace and stability. It is necessary to think holistically about improving food systems, and to provide legal protections for communities to access resources and assets at all times. Only by fully recognizing famine as a complete and enforceable violation of the right to food, and only by achieving a convergence of emergency food aid, food assistance, and development cooperation, will we ensure the security of food and of societies around the world.

CHAPTER 28

HUMANITARIAN RELIEF IN SITUATIONS OF ARMED CONFLICT

EMANUELA-CHIARA GILLARD AND NATHALIE WEIZMANN

A. Introduction

In many modern wars, more civilian deaths and suffering occur as a result of humanitarian crises prompted or exacerbated by the conflicts than from actual hostilities. In addition to those who die as a result of lack of food, water, access to medical care, or adequate sanitation, hundreds of thousands are obliged to leave their homes and sources of livelihoods, thereby heightening their vulnerability to a range of attacks, food insecurity, and losing access to basic services.

'Freedom from want' is one of the two constituent dimensions of human security articulated by the UN Development Programme (UNDP) in its landmark 1994 'Human Development Report'.[1] The report breaks down the notion of human security further into seven categories, two of which are particularly relevant to humanitarian relief in situations of armed conflict: food security and health security. Recently, the UN Security Council (UNSC) has addressed this dimension of human security in a thematic resolution drawing a connection between its primary responsibility for the maintenance of international peace and security and its 'commitment to address conflict-induced food insecurity, including famine, in situations of armed conflict'.[2] The UNSC has also indicated that the denial of safe and unimpeded access of humanitarian personnel to civilians in armed conflicts may constitute a threat to international peace and security.[3] This

[1] UNDP, *Human Development Report* (OUP 1994) ch 2. [2] UNSC Res 2417 (2018) preamble.
[3] ibid para 4; UNSC Res 1296 (2000) para 8.

suggests that, rather than competing, human security and international security converge when it comes to meeting the needs of civilians in extreme situations.

Without entering here into an analysis of the content and evolution of the notion of 'human security', it suffices to note that international humanitarian law (IHL), the body of law applicable in armed conflict that regulates the conduct of hostilities and protects those not or no longer taking direct part in hostilities, includes an important body of rules aimed at ensuring that the basic needs of civilians caught up in conflict are met. While these protections can be considered as a manifestation of the 'freedom from want' dimension of human security, it is essential to bear in mind that the relevant rules of IHL are well established, binding on States and, in case of non-international armed conflict, also organized armed groups.

The present contribution consists of two sections. The first outlines the rules of IHL regulating collective humanitarian relief operations, with a particular focus on how they balance the dictates of belligerents' security interests and civilians' 'human security' needs and entitlements. The second section focuses on one particular way in which a pressing national and international security objective—countering terrorism—interacts with, and adversely impacts, the capacity of humanitarian actors to operate in a principled manner, and thus impairs the human security of populations in need.

B. The Rules of International Humanitarian Law Regulating Collective Humanitarian Relief Operations for Civilians

In situations of armed conflict, the delivery of collective humanitarian relief for civilians in need raises some important and competing security concerns relating to both national security and human security. Humanitarian relief operations have the aim of distributing articles of prime necessity for subsistence and health[4] according to need alone.[5] Precisely what constitute items essential for survival will depend on the local

[4] Geneva Convention (IV) Relative to the Protection of Civilian Persons in the time of War 75 UNTS 287 art 59; Protocol Additional to the Geneva Conventions of 12 August 1949, and relating to the Protection of Victims of International Armed Conflicts 1125 UNTS 3 (AP I) arts 69, 70.

[5] Relief operations must be impartial and conducted without adverse distinction, refraining from diverting consignments or favouring certain persons on any grounds other than need (such as race, religion or political opinion). AP I (n 4) art 70; Protocol Additional to the Geneva Conventions of 12 August 1949, and relating to the Protection of Victims of Non-International Armed Conflict (AP II) 1125 UNTS 609 art 18.

conditions, and typically include water, food, medical supplies, clothing, bedding, means of shelter, fuel for heating, and objects needed for religious worship.[6]

Yet, despite the narrowly circumscribed aim of providing civilians in need with items of prime necessity for their subsistence and health, belligerents may have reservations about allowing humanitarian relief operations. They may worry, for instance, that humanitarian relief destined for a population under the control of the enemy may indirectly favour the enemy and enhance the latter's chances of success,[7] or that humanitarian convoys are delivering weapons, not humanitarian assistance.[8]

As with all of IHL, the specific rules governing humanitarian relief operations in armed conflict aim to strike a balance between competing considerations of humanity and military necessity.[9] Humanity has been described as 'a complex motive in which kindred elements such as kindness, pity, gentleness, generosity, patience, and mercy are present in varying degrees',[10] while military necessity commonly reflects belligerents' security concerns. It is

> the claim that, because of extreme circumstances, security concerns override competing considerations... Though the term *military necessity* can be used to describe any instance in which political, social, or economic calculations are superseded by reasons of war, it is most commonly employed in situations in which security considerations are said to trump ethical restraints on the conduct of war.[11]

One expert has explained the balancing act in IHL, as follows:

[6] The 2016 ICRC Commentary distinguishes humanitarian relief from broader assistance activities, which include 'all activities, services and the delivery of goods carried out primarily in the fields of health, water, habitat... and economic security': Lindsey Cameron et al, 'Article 3: Conflict not of an International Character' in Knut Dörmann et al (eds), *Commentary on the First Geneva Convention: Convention (I) for the Amelioration of the Condition of the Wounded and Sick in Armed Forces in the Field* (CUP 2016) paras 819–20 (Commentary GC I). Nevertheless, in situations of protracted occupation, it has been suggested that the 'protective scope of IHL can only be fully realised... by providing, and facilitating the provision of, assistance aimed at meeting the deeper, longer-term needs of the occupied population'. Diakonia International Humanitarian Law Resource Centre, *The Humanitarian—Development Divide: A False Dichotomy?* (Diakonia 2018) 6.

[7] Michael Bothe, 'Relief Actions: The Position of the Recipient State' in Frits Kalshoven (ed), *Assisting the Victims of Armed Conflict and Other Disasters: Papers Delivered at the International Conference on Humanitarian Assistance in Armed Conflict, The Hague, 22–24 June 1988* (Martinus Nijhoff 1989); Non-State armed groups share similar concerns: some groups, such as the Yekîneyên Parastina Gel (People's Protection Units) (YPG) and the Popular Front for the Liberation of Saguia el-Hamra and Rio de Oro (Polisario Front) have stated that 'access would be denied if aid were seen to benefit or explicitly support the enemy'. Geneva Call, *In Their Words: Perceptions of Armed Non-State Actors on Humanitarian Action* (Geneva Call 2016) 20.

[8] UNSC Verbatim Record (13 December 2018) UN Doc S/PV.8423.

[9] Michael Bothe et al, *New Rules for Victims of Armed Conflicts: Commentary on the Two 1977 Protocols Additional to the Geneva Conventions of 1949* (2nd edn, Martinus Nijhoff 2013) 432–3.

[10] Jean Pictet, 'Red Cross Principles' (1955) 37(440) International Review of the Red Cross 483, 497.

[11] Ron Hassner, 'Military Necessity' *Encyclopedia Britannica* (26 November 2014).

> If military necessity were to prevail completely, belligerent parties would have full freedom of action, with a view to winning a war. If humanitarian considerations were the only guide to the conduct of hostilities, the waging of war would become impossible by dint of the death, injury, and suffering that unavoidably accompany it. The law [...] therefore takes a middle road, rendering unto military necessity what is due to it, while protecting and respecting at least a minimal level of humanitarianism even in the midst of hostilities.[12]

Without defining the terms 'security' or 'military necessity', IHL, including its body of rules regulating humanitarian relief operations, reflects a compromise between a range of security concerns, from State sovereignty and belligerents' military interests,[13] to people-centred human security interests focused on 'freedom from want and freedom from fear',[14] aspects of which include food security,[15] adequate shelter,[16] and security against threats to human dignity.[17] While a compromise between security concerns underlies each rule of IHL, at times these concerns also appear explicitly as exceptions that authorize some deviation from the general rule, often with broad discretion when it relates to the security of the State. For instance, in cases of 'imperative military necessity' the activities of the relief personnel may be limited or their movements may be temporarily restricted.

This section of the chapter will explore the interplay between competing security concerns—for States and non-State armed groups (whose security considerations are analogous to those of States even if their motivations clash), civilians in need, and humanitarian personnel and assets—within the rules of IHL governing collective relief operations for civilians in armed conflict.

[12] Yoram Dinstein, 'Military Necessity' MPEPIL (OUP, September 2015) MN 2; Toni Pfanner, 'Asymmetrical Warfare from the Perspective of Humanitarian Law and Humanitarian Action' (2005) 87 International Review of the Red Cross 149, 164.

[13] eg AP I (n 4) art 52 limiting attacks to military objectives.

[14] UNDP (n 1). The report identified two key components of human security: 'freedom from fear' and 'freedom from want', outlining seven facets of human security: economic security, food security, health security, environmental security, personal security, community security, and political security. On the evolution and scope of the concept of human security; Avril McDonald/Hanna Brollowski, 'Security' MPEPIL (OUP, May 2011) MN 11–13.

[15] eg AP I (n 4) art 54, which prohibits starvation of civilians as a method of war and protecting objects indispensable to the survival of the civilian population.

[16] eg GC IV (n 4) art 49 on evacuation of civilians if the security of the population or imperative military reasons so demand, but with the obligation to transfer persons back to their homes as soon as hostilities in the area have ceased.

[17] eg ibid art 41 on safeguards for persons who are *hors de combat*, and, more generally, Geneva Convention (I) for the Amelioration of the Condition of the Wounded and Sick in Armed Forces in the Field 75 UNTS 31 (GC I) art 3; Geneva Convention (II) for the Amelioration of the Wounded, Sick and Shipwrecked Members of Armed Forces at Sea 75 UNTS 85 (GC II) art 3; Geneva Convention (III) Relative to the Treatment of Prisoners of War 75 UNTS 135 (GC III) art 3; GC IV (n 4) and AP I (n 4) art 75 on humane treatment and other protections of persons in the power of a party to the conflict.

1. Offers to Carry Out Humanitarian Activities

Each State has the responsibility to meet the needs of persons in its territory or under its control.[18] In armed conflict, organized armed groups also have the responsibility to meet the needs of civilians under their control when the State has not done so.[19] There are times, however, when the relevant parties fail to meet these needs. In such circumstances, humanitarian organizations and other actors can play a key role in the provision of relief to persons in need. States may expressly seek outside help, or impartial humanitarian organizations may offer to carry out assistance activities.

Today, a range of actors—States, as well as international and non-governmental organizations—may offer to carry out humanitarian relief operations in both international and non-international armed conflicts.[20] At times, however, belligerents may perceive such offers as an unfriendly act, interference in their internal affairs, or as a way to support or legitimize the enemy. In other words, many of these reservations relate to preserving the State's sovereignty, that is, its 'independence and exclusive authority over its territory and those residing upon it'.[21] Sovereignty is understood to be a central component of national security,[22] which experts have explained as follows: 'The affinity between sovereignty and national security is ... readily evident; indeed, the latter can be viewed, in many respects, as being a simple expansion of the former.'[23]

For instance, in situations of non-international armed conflict (necessarily involving non-State armed groups), the concern has been expressed as follows:

> In a civil war the lawful Government, or that which so styles itself, tends to regard its adversaries as common criminals. This attitude has sometimes led governmental

[18] This is an element of the generally recognized principle of sovereignty; eg UNGA Res 46/182 (19 December 1991) principle 4.

[19] This can be derived from the obligation of humane treatment under GC I-IV (n 17) common art 3 and AP II (n 5) art 4; Dapo Akande/Emanuela-Chiara Gillard, 'Oxford Guidance on the Law Relating to Humanitarian Relief Operations in Situations of Armed Conflict' (2016) paras 14–15 <https://reliefweb.int/sites/reliefweb.int/files/resources/Oxford%20Guidance%20pdf.pdf> accessed 9 January 2020; Geneva Call (n 7) 22: '[Armed Non-State Actors (ANSAs)] diverge considerably on [...] their own obligations to provide relief to affected populations (depending on their degree of territorial control, objectives, and other factors). Many ANSAs refer to their concern and responsibility for civilian populations and a desire to see them receive assistance and protection.'

[20] GC I-IV (nn 4, 17) common art 3; AP I (n 4) art 70; AP II (n 5) art 18 (also GC I–IV (nn 4, 17) arts 9, 9, 9 and 10 respectively; AP II (n 5) art 3).

[21] Christian Henderson, 'The Arab Spring and the Notion of External State Sovereignty in International Law' (2014) 35 Liverpool Law Review 175, 175–6, referring to James Crawford, 'Sovereignty as a Legal Value' in James Crawford/Martii Koskenniemi (eds), *The Cambridge Companion to International Law* (CUP 2012) 131.

[22] '[L]egal rules concerning property and territory, including sovereignty and the use of force to protect possessions, have been central to the development of the concept of security and the pursuit of a state of security.' McDonald/Brollowski (n 14) MN 4.

[23] Euan MacDonald/Philip Alston, 'Sovereignty, Human Rights, Security: Armed Intervention and the Foundational Problems of International Law' in Euan MacDonald/Philip Alston (eds), *Human Rights, Intervention, and the Use of Force* (OUP 2008) 3.

> authorities to look upon relief given by the Red Cross to war victims of the other Party to the conflict as indirect aid to those who are guilty. Applications by a foreign Red Cross or by the International Committee of the Red Cross have more than once been treated as unfriendly attempts to interfere in the internal affairs of the country concerned.[24]

Nevertheless, under international law, an offer of humanitarian relief that is impartial and conducted without adverse distinction is not considered as interference in an armed conflict or an unfriendly act.[25] In contrasting humanitarian assistance with paramilitary activities in the case of *Military and Paramilitary Activities in and against Nicaragua*, the International Court of Justice (ICJ) found that '[t]here can be no doubt that the provision of strictly humanitarian aid to persons or forces in another country, whatever their political affiliations or objectives, cannot be considered as unlawful intervention...'[26] This is also captured in UN General Assembly (UNGA) Resolution 2675 (XXV), which states, '(t)he provision of international relief to civilian populations is in conformity with the humanitarian principles of the Charter of the United Nations, the Universal Declaration of Human Rights and other international instruments in the field of human rights.'[27]

The position is valid in both international and non-international armed conflict. With respect to international armed conflict, the International Committee of the Red Cross (ICRC) 2016 Commentary to the First Geneva Convention (GC I) states that '[w]hen an offer of services is made, it may be regarded neither as an unfriendly act, nor as an unlawful interference in a State's domestic affairs in general or in the conflict in particular. Nor may it be regarded as recognition of or support to a Party to the conflict.'[28] According to the 1987 Commentary to Article 70 of the First Additional Protocol (AP I), the expressions 'interference in the armed conflict or as unfriendly acts' entail that 'the offer or action cannot be seen as a hostile act, let alone as an act of war.'[29]

[24] Jean Pictet (ed), *Commentary: Convention (I) for the Amelioration of the Condition of the Wounded and Sick in Armed Forces in the Field* (ICRC 1952) 39. The same Commentary (ibid 58) adds: 'Although the International Committee of the Red Cross has been able to do a considerable amount of humanitarian work in certain civil wars, in others the doors have been churlishly closed against it, the mere offer of charitable services being regarded as an unfriendly act—an inadmissible attempt to interfere in the internal affairs of the State.'

[25] This is true in international and non-international armed conflict. For international armed conflict, AP I (n 4) art 70; For non-international armed conflict, AP II (n 5) art 3(2) and Yves Sandoz et al (eds), *Commentary on the Additional Protocols of 8 June 1977 to the Geneva Conventions of 12 August 1949* (Martinus Nijhoff 1987) paras 4502–3 (Commentary AP I and Commentary AP II).

[26] *Military and Paramilitary Activities in and against Nicaragua (Nicaragua v United States of America)* (Merits) [1986] ICJ Rep 14 [242] (*Nicaragua*).

[27] UNGA Res 2675(XXV) (9 December 1970).

[28] On GC I (n 17) art 9 (the equivalent of which can be found in GC II (n 17) art 9, GC III (n 17) art 9, and GC IV (n 4) art 10): Bruno Demeyere, 'Article 9—Activities of the ICRC and Other Impartial Humanitarian Organizations' in Commentary GC I (n 6) para 1133.

[29] Commentary AP I (n 25) para 2812.

As for non-international armed conflict, the 2016 ICRC Commentary to Common Article 3 explains:[30]

> When an offer of services is made, it may be regarded neither as an unfriendly act nor as an unlawful interference in a State's domestic affairs in general or in the conflict in particular.[31] Nor may it be regarded as recognition of or support to a Party to the conflict. Therefore, an offer of services and its implementation may not be prohibited or criminalized, by virtue of legislative or other regulatory acts.[32]

A recurring concern of States that is specific to non-international armed conflict is that humanitarian offers of services to, and engagement with, organized non-State armed groups will amount to their political legitimization and recognition, thereby interfering with the State's political aim or enhancing the armed group's authority. In fact, some armed groups have been perceived as seeking legitimization through their engagement with humanitarian organizations. As explained by Geneva Call, there is a tendency for armed groups to use institutions, commissions, or committees, including those responsible for engagement with humanitarian bodies, for political propaganda purposes.[33] In 2015 in eastern Ukraine, the de facto authorities controlling parts of Donetsk and Luhansk introduced an 'accreditation' process for humanitarian actors to operate, which some considered to be a political manoeuvre by the de facto authorities to acquire international recognition.[34]

Concerns about legitimization and recognition arise even though Common Article 3 to the Geneva Convention states that the right of an impartial humanitarian body to offer its services 'shall not affect the legal status of the Parties to the conflict'. The Commentary of 1952 states:

> This clause [...] meets the fear—always the same one—that the application of the Convention, even to a very limited extent, in cases of civil war may interfere with the de jure Government's lawful suppression of the revolt, or that it may confer belligerent status, and consequently increased authority, upon the adverse Party. [...] It makes it absolutely clear that the object of the Convention is a purely humanitarian one, that it is in no way concerned with the internal affairs of States, and that it merely ensures respect for the few essential rules of humanity which all

[30] Commentary GC I (n 6) paras 804–5. [31] *Nicaragua* (n 26) [242].

[32] Commentary GC I (n 6) paras 804–5; Commentary AP II (n 25) para 4892: 'Consequently the ICRC continues to be entitled to offer its services to each party without such a step being considered as interference in the internal affairs of the State or as infringing its sovereignty, whether or not the offer is accepted'.

[33] Geneva Call (n 7) 19.

[34] Veronique Barbelet, 'Humanitarian Access and Local Organisations in Ukraine' (*Humanitarian Policy Group*, September 2017) <https://www.odi.org/sites/odi.org.uk/files/resource-documents/11746.pdf> accessed 18 February 2019.

civilized nations consider as valid everywhere and under all circumstances and as being above and outside war itself.[35]

The UNSC has also recognized the importance of humanitarian engagement with all parties to conflict, including armed groups.[36]

2. State Consent to Humanitarian Relief Operations

Whenever offers of humanitarian relief are made in situations of international armed conflict, consent is required from the State Party in whose territory the humanitarian relief is carried out, as well as from other States Parties if the relief must transit through territory under their effective control, and from other States in whose territory the relief is initiated or must transit.[37] This consent requirement aims to protect the concerned State's sovereignty, an important aspect of its national security.[38]

On offers of humanitarian relief that are made in non-international armed conflict, Common Article 3 to the Geneva Conventions is silent on the question of consent. This has led to some debate as to whether the consent of the State Party to the conflict in whose territory the humanitarian relief is carried out is required in all cases, or only when the State is exercising effective control over the area in which the relief must transit or is destined. Some experts consider that Common Article 3 allows relief operations by impartial humanitarian bodies as long as the State or non-State Party receiving the offer consents to it and the relief operation does not have to cross the territory controlled by the opposing side. However, if only the consent of a non-State Party were obtained, this would entail an important infringement on the territorial State's sovereignty.[39] Article 18 of Additional Protocol II is more explicit on the question as it requires the consent of the State Party 'concerned'. Nevertheless, here, too, there is some debate as to whether a State Party should be considered 'concerned' under this provision even when

[35] ICRC Commentary of 1952 (n 24) 60; The 2016 Commentary adds:

> An offer of services by the ICRC or another impartial humanitarian organization has no bearing on the international legal status of the entity to which the offer is made. As is clear from common Art. 3(4), the fact that an offer of services is made to a non-State Party to the armed conflict has no impact on that Party's legal status. Likewise, an offer of services may not be interpreted as endorsement of the reasons for which the entity is engaged in an armed conflict.

Commentary GC I (n 6) para 805.

[36] UNSC Res 1296 (2000) para 12; UNSC Res 1894 (2009) para 14; UNSC 'Statement by the President of the Security Council' (12 February 2013) UN Doc S/PRST/2013/2.

[37] AP I (n 4) art 70.

[38] Commentary AP I (n 25) para 2805. Maurice Torrelli, 'From Humanitarian Assistance to Intervention on Humanitarian Grounds?' (1992) 32 International Review of the Red Cross 228, 232: 'Consent—the expression of sovereignty—is hence a basic principle in the exercise of the right to humanitarian assistance in armed conflicts.'

[39] Dapo Akande/Emanuela-Chiara Gillard, 'Cross-Border Relief Operations—A Legal Perspective' (2014) 12–19 <https://www.unocha.org/sites/unocha/files/dms/Documents/Legal%20Perspective%20 Cross-border%20relief%20operations.pdf> accessed 10 January 2020.

it does not have effective control over the territory in which the humanitarian relief operations are intended or transit.

An interpretation that gives due weight to a State's territorial sovereignty and to its responsibility towards the civilian population is to always require the consent of the State in whose territory the humanitarian relief operations are intended or transit, regardless of its effective control over the area. In any event, as a matter of practice in order to ensure a safe and unimpeded relief operation, the consent of all parties to an armed conflict, including non-State armed groups,[40] will be required when the humanitarian relief is intended for or passing through territory under their effective control.[41]

3. Withholding of Consent

With regard to the question of when consent might be lawfully withheld, a leading commentator on the question has written, '[i]n many situations, legitimate military considerations will compete with humanitarian ones. A balancing of different values will then be required which makes it extremely difficult to precisely draw the line between a lawful and an unlawful refusal of consent.'[42] While the requirement of consent is rooted in a concern to protect a State's sovereignty as an element of its national security, this does not imply that the State has absolute and unlimited discretion to refuse the relief operations.

Consent may only be withheld for valid and compelling reasons.[43] These can include imperative considerations of military necessity (for example where foreign relief personnel might hamper military operations[44]), but consent should not be withheld beyond what military necessity demands.[45]

[40] eg Geneva Call (n 7) 16 and 20:

> However much they express a willingness to facilitate humanitarian access, none of these ANSAs favour humanitarian access without prior consultation and/or their consent. [...] Failure to obtain consent from ANSAs or to abide by the conditions they impose are seen as the most likely factors to lead to the expulsion of or harm to aid workers and their property. Both Hamas and the KNPP refer to instances where they expelled actors who had not sought prior permission to work.

[41] In non-international armed conflict, IHL does not explicitly address the consent of States in whose territory the relief is initiated or must transit.

[42] Bothe (n 7) 95.

[43] In situations of occupation, if the civilian population, in whole or in part, is not adequately provided with supplies essential to its survival, the occupying power has an *unconditional* obligation to consent to impartial humanitarian relief operations. The same absolute obligation binds States in whose territory the relief operation is initiated or passes through. GC IV (n 4) art 59.

[44] Bothe (n 7) 93.

[45] Dapo Akande/Emanuela-Chiara Gillard, 'Arbitrary Withholding of Consent to Humanitarian Relief Operations in Armed Conflict' (21 August 2014) 10 <https://www.unocha.org/sites/unocha/files/dms/Documents/Arbitrary%20Withholding%20of%20Consent.pdf> accessed 16 January 2020; Bothe (n 7) 95; The ICRC has expressed a contrary view: 'Military necessity is no valid ground under humanitarian law to turn down a valid offer of services or to deny in their entirety the humanitarian activities proposed by impartial humanitarian organizations'; see Commentary GC I (n 6) para 838.

When the following cumulative conditions are met, a State must not withhold its consent arbitrarily:[46] (a) civilians are inadequately provided with essential supplies; (b) the party responsible for meeting their needs does not provide the necessary assistance; and (c) offers of services have been made by actors capable of carrying out relief operations that are exclusively humanitarian and impartial in character, and are conducted without any adverse distinction.[47]

Consent is withheld arbitrarily if it is withheld in three situations. First, if it is withheld in circumstances that would result in a violation of obligations under international law with respect to the civilian population in question, including obligations under IHL and international human rights law (IHRL).[48] For instance, withholding consent to humanitarian relief operations would be arbitrary in situations where the civilian population is inadequately supplied and the State intends to cause, contribute to, or perpetuate starvation.[49] The Commentary to the Additional Protocols states:

> If the survival of the population is threatened and a humanitarian organization fulfilling the required conditions of impartiality and non-discrimination is able to remedy this situation, relief actions must take place. In fact, they are the only way of combating starvation when local resources have been exhausted. The authorities responsible for safeguarding the population in the whole of the territory of the State cannot refuse such relief without good grounds. Such a refusal would be equivalent to a violation of the rule prohibiting the use of starvation as a method of combat as the population would be left deliberately to die of hunger without any measures being taken.[50]

The second circumstance is when consent is withheld in violation of the principles of necessity and proportionality, which find expression in IHRL in the context of the right to life and the right to liberty.[51] In order not to be arbitrary, withholding of consent must be necessary, no more than necessary, and proportionate to the end sought. For instance, where consent to relief operations is withheld because of imperative considerations of military necessity that go beyond what military necessity demands, such a withholding would violate the principle of necessity.[52] Or, as an expert has written, '[t]he principle of proportionality may also be helpful […], for instance, to outlaw a refusal where the

[46] Commentary AP I (n 25) paras 2805 and 4885; Bothe et al (n 9) 434; Akande/Gillard (n 45) 10; UNGA 'Report by Special Rapporteur on extrajudicial, summary or arbitrary executions, Agnes Callamard' (6 August 2018) UN Doc A/73/314, para 23.

[47] Akande/Gillard (n 19) s E.

[48] ibid paras 50–1.

[49] AP I (n 4) art 54(1) and AP II (n 5) art 14. Commentary AP I (n 25) para 2808; Bothe (n 7) 94; Dapo Akande/Emanuela-Chiara Gillard, 'Conflict-induced Food Insecurity and the War Crime of Starvation of Civilians as a Method of Warfare' (2019) 17 JICJ 753.

[50] Commentary AP I (n 25) para 4885. The prohibition on starvation of the civilian population as a method of warfare is set out in ibid.

[51] Akande/Gillard (n 45); Akande/Gillard (n 19) para 52.

[52] ibid.

legitimate military considerations are relatively unimportant, but the suffering of the civilian population particularly poignant'.[53]

Finally, consent is withheld arbitrarily if it is withheld in a manner that is unreasonable, or that may lead to injustice or lack of predictability, or that is otherwise inappropriate, such as withholding of consent simply because of 'State sovereignty, the internal legal order, national pride and/or interests, political orientation, the interests of the regime in power, and similar arguments'.[54] Another example would be a total failure to provide reasons for withholding consent, giving rise to a lack of predictability and making it impossible to assess the underlying reasons. As the International Law Commission (ILC) has noted in relation to humanitarian assistance in natural disasters, '[t]he provision of reasons is fundamental to establishing the good faith of the affected State's decision to withhold consent. The absence of reasons may act to support an inference that the withholding of consent is arbitrary.'[55]

Interestingly, upon determining in 2014 that the deteriorating humanitarian situation in Syria constituted a threat to peace and security in the region and recalling the UN Secretary-General's view that 'arbitrarily withholding consent for the opening of all relevant border crossings is a violation of international humanitarian law', the UNSC, for the first time, overrode the requirement of State consent and decided to authorize UN humanitarian agencies and their implementing partners to use routes across conflict lines and certain border crossings in order to ensure that humanitarian assistance reached people in need throughout the country.[56] In this instance, human security considerations appear to have outweighed sovereignty and other national security considerations.

4. The Obligation to Allow and Facilitate Passage and to Respect and Protect Personnel and Assets

In any situation of armed conflict, once consent to an offer of humanitarian relief has been obtained, the parties must allow and facilitate rapid and unimpeded passage—over land, water, or by air—of humanitarian relief consignments, equipment, and personnel.[57] Measures to allow and facilitate passage can include waiving or simplifying and expediting entry procedures for humanitarian personnel; waiving, reducing, or expediting customs inspection requirements; exemptions from taxes, duties, and fees; simplified

[53] Bothe (n 7) 95. [54] Akande/Gillard (n 45) 12.

[55] ILC, 'Report of the International Law Commission on the Work of its 63rd Session' (26 April–3 June and 4 July–12 August 2011) UN Doc A/66/10, 270, para 8; Akande/Gillard (n 45); Akande/Gillard (n 19) paras 53–4.

[56] UNSC Res 2165 (2014).

[57] In international armed conflict, including situations of occupation, this obligation to allow and facilitate also applies to States in whose territory relief operations are initiated or transit. In non-international armed conflict, IHL does not explicitly address the role of States in whose territory the relief is initiated or transits.

procedures for humanitarian organizations to acquire legal personality; issuing permits for the passage of humanitarian relief, equipment, and personnel; ensuring adequate staffing and schedules in order to meet formalities efficiently and expeditiously; and allowing telecommunications equipment to be imported for its exclusive use in humanitarian relief operations, except as required for imperative reasons of security.[58] Guidance on the range of legal facilities that States may adopt for both entry and operations can be drawn from the 'Guidelines for the domestic facilitation and regulation of international disaster relief and initial recovery assistance', which apply in disasters arising from accident, nature or human activity, but not to armed conflict.[59] Non-State armed groups also have structures in place to coordinate, facilitate, and monitor humanitarian action.[60]

Except in cases of urgent necessity in the interests of the civilian population concerned (and not for military considerations), relief supplies must not be delayed or diverted from their intended destination.[61] Delays are permitted if they are necessary to ensure the safe passage of relief and to prevent its loss or destruction when the situation might endanger its safe passage.[62] Moreover, it is only in case of 'imperative military necessity' that the activities of the relief personnel may be limited or their movements may be temporarily restricted. For instance, movement may be restricted to prevent relief operations from interfering with military operations; this could affect the belligerents' security but also endanger humanitarian relief personnel.[63] This explicit 'military necessity' exception is intended to allow the parties 'to make quick decisions to take into account the development of hostilities'.[64] While the commander is afforded a 'great deal of latitude', he or she must nevertheless exercise this discretion in good faith.[65] Restrictions should not last longer than necessary; they must be temporary, and 'sound reasons' must be given to justify prolonging them.[66] Here, the parties' security interests can temporarily override human security concerns.

With the approval of the State on whose territory the humanitarian relief operation is intended, personnel may participate in a humanitarian relief operation, typically for the

[58] Akande/Gillard (n 19) para 64. For examples of practice to facilitate passage, UNSC 'Report of the Secretary-General on the Protection of Civilians in Armed Conflict' (29 May 2009) UN Doc S/2009/277, Annex, paras 50–61.

[59] IFRC, Introduction to the Guidelines for the Domestic Facilitation and Regulation of International Disaster Relief and Initial Recovery Assistance (IFRC 2011) part V; it is also useful to note that in the context of disasters, ILC, 'Draft Articles on the Protection of Persons in the Event of Disasters' (2 May–10 June and 4 July–12 August 2016) UN Doc A/71/10, art 15 requires that the affected State take the necessary measures to facilitate the prompt and effective provision of external assistance, in particular regarding visas, work permits, tariffs, taxation, and that the State ensure that its relevant legislation and regulations are readily accessible in order to facilitate compliance with national law.

[60] Geneva Call (n 7). [61] GC IV (n 4) art 60; AP I (n 4) art 70(3)(c).

[62] Bothe et al (n 9) 436.

[63] Jean-Marie Henckaerts/Louise Doswald-Beck, *Customary International Humanitarian Law, Volume I: Rules* (ICRC/CUP 2005) 200 (rule 56).

[64] Commentary AP I (n 25) para 2896. [65] Dinstein (n 12) para 28.

[66] Commentary AP I (n 25) para 2896.

transportation and distribution of relief consignments. The parties must ensure the freedom of movement of humanitarian personnel that is essential to the exercise of their functions.[67] Of course, personnel must behave in a manner consistent with their humanitarian mission and must respect the law and security requirements of the Party in whose territory they are operating.[68] These requirements can include routes, schedules, and curfews imposed by the parties, however they must not aim to obstruct relief operations.[69]

Parties to an armed conflict must respect and protect humanitarian relief personnel during military operations.[70] It is prohibited to direct attacks against them. Practice indicates that it is also prohibited to harass, intimidate, or arbitrarily detain them.[71] The parties must also respect and protect objects that are used for humanitarian relief operations, such as supplies, installations, material, units, or vehicles; their destruction, misappropriation, and looting are also prohibited.[72] Intentionally directing attacks against personnel, installations, material, units, or vehicles involved in a humanitarian assistance mission is considered a war crime in both international and non-international armed conflicts, as long as they are entitled to the protection given to civilians or civilian objects under IHL.[73]

To protect their security interests, parties to an armed conflict and States in whose territory relief operations are initiated or transit also have the right to prescribe measures of control for the passage of humanitarian relief. They can impose technical arrangements such as the search of consignments to verify that relief consignments are exclusively humanitarian (for example, that they do not contain equipment that could be used for military purposes), the use of prescribed routes at specific times so that relief convoys do not interfere with and are not endangered by military operations, or measures to ensure that medical supplies and equipment comply with health and safety standards.[74] Technical arrangements must be applied in good faith, and their nature, extent, and impact must not prevent the rapid delivery of humanitarian relief in a principled manner. Their imposition or effect must not be arbitrary.[75] In addition, the parties to an armed conflict may make passage of humanitarian relief consignments conditional on their distribution under the local supervision of an impartial organization or on other measures to ensure that the supplies will reach their intended beneficiaries.[76] At times, humanitarian organizations will make their own arrangements to monitor distribution

[67] GC IV (n 4) art 59; AP I (n 4) arts 70, 71; Henckaerts/Doswald-Beck (n 63) 193–203 (rules 55–6).

[68] AP I (n 4) 71; Bothe et al (n 9) 439. [69] Commentary AP I (n 25) para 2902.

[70] AP I (n 4) arts 69, 71; Henckaerts/Doswald-Beck (n 63) 105 (rule 31).

[71] Henckaerts/Doswald-Beck (n 63) 105 (rule 31).

[72] AP I (n 4) art 70; Henckaerts/Doswald-Beck (n 63) (rule 32).

[73] Rome Statute of the International Criminal Court 2187 UNTS art 8(2)(b)(iii), (e)(iii).

[74] GC IV (n 4) art 59; AP I (n 4) art 70(3)(a). [75] Akande/Gillard (n 19) para 56.

[76] AP I (n 4) art 70(3)(b).

and confirm that relief items reach their intended beneficiaries. This has happened, for instance, in 2018 in Yemen[77] and Syria.[78]

As the ICRC Commentary to Article 70 of Additional Protocol I explains, the right of a State to prescribe technical arrangements is designed to protect security interests, 'including the military interests of an adverse Party through whose territory, area of control or blockade relief consignments are to pass'. The condition of local supervision is also meant to provide an additional guarantee that relief actions are humanitarian and impartial in character, conducted without any adverse distinction, and with priority to those persons who under IHL are to be afforded privileged treatment or special protection, such as children, expectant mothers, maternity cases, and nursing mothers.[79]

The regulation of humanitarian access for security reasons is not exclusive to States. As explained by Geneva Call, '[j]ust like many recognized governments, the [armed non-State actors (ANSAs)] consulted believe they are entitled to control and regulate humanitarian activities, [for instance] by coordinating the logistical and security conditions for access to be viable'.[80] Armed groups have analogous security concerns to those of States, even though they obviously run contrary to them. IHL factors into its rules the security interests of all parties—State and non-State alike. Humanitarian personnel must comply with technical arrangements prescribed by the parties, such as routes, schedules, and curfews.[81] If humanitarian personnel exceed the terms of their mission, their assignment may be terminated and they may be compelled to leave the country,[82] however this would not necessarily call into question the entire relief operation.[83] The ICRC Commentary to Article 71 adds:

> [t]he possibility of prosecuting personnel participating in a relief action by the receiving Party is not explicitly excluded. However, it should be avoided as much as possible, in view of the disastrous consequences this could have on the action as a whole. Moreover, it is desirable to provide in the framework of the agreement concerning such action that personnel participating in relief action should enjoy immunity before the courts.[84]

[77] OCHA, 'Statement of the Under-Secretary General for Humanitarian Affairs and Emergency Relief Coordinator, Mark Lowcock' (Briefing to UNSC, New York, 9 January 2019) <https://reliefweb.int/sites/reliefweb.int/files/resources/ERC_USG%20Mark%20Lowcock%20Statement%20to%20the%20SecCo%20on%20Yemen%20-%2009January2019%20-%20as%20delivered.pdf> accessed 13 January 2020.

[78] OCHA, 'Statement of the Under-Secretary General for Humanitarian Affairs and Emergency Relief, Mark Lowcock' (Briefing to UNSC, New York, 13 December 2018) <https://reliefweb.int/report/syrian-arab-republic/under-secretary-general-humanitarian-affairs-and-emergency-relief-87> accessed 13 January 2020.

[79] Bothe et al (n 9) 436.

[80] Geneva Call (n 7) 17.

[81] Commentary AP I (n 25) para 2902.

[82] AP I (n 4) art 71; Bothe et al (n 9) 439; Commentary AP I (n 25) para 2903.

[83] Akande/Gillard (n 19) 76–7; Commentary AP I (n 25) para 2904.

[84] Commentary AP I (n 25) paras 2906–7.

Despite their obligation to allow and facilitate rapid and unimpeded passage, parties to conflict—States and non-State armed groups alike—often impede humanitarian relief operations, resulting in delayed delivery, decreased effectiveness, increased operational costs, and, ultimately, prolonged suffering of people in need.[85] Bureaucratic impediments are reported to be amongst the most severe constraints on humanitarian access.[86] They are frequently imposed upon entry into the country, in the form of cumbersome procedures for visas, permits, or the import of supplies. Inside the country, they also take the form of detailed limitations relating to certain locations, amounts and types of relief items, or modes of transportation. Parties might require long notice periods before any movement is allowed. Multiple checkpoints, roadblocks, and searches often delay or impede the movement of relief personnel and items. Restrictions are often imposed in an inconsistent or unpredictable fashion and at multiple levels, ranging from central to local.[87]

Refusing the passage of humanitarian relief intended for civilians in need, including by deliberately impeding humanitarian relief or restricting the freedom of movement of humanitarian relief personnel, may constitute a violation of the obligation to allow and facilitate rapid and unimpeded passage and of the prohibition of starvation. It may also be a war crime.[88] However, it is not so straightforward to determine at what point the effect of constraints, impediments or delays to humanitarian relief operations is of such a nature and extent as to amount to a violation of the obligation to allow and facilitate the rapid and impeded passage of relief consignments, personnel, and equipment. To determine when impediments amount to a violation, the principal factor to consider is the impact of the impediments on the needs of the civilian population:

> If they are such as to leave the civilian population as whole, or segments thereof—either in specific locations or particular groups—without essential relief items or specific services for prolonged periods of time, then the party can be considered to have violated the obligation to allow and facilitate rapid and unimpeded passage of relief operations and, therefore, to have unlawfully impeded humanitarian relief operations.[89]

5. Concluding Reflections on IHL Rules Regulating Collective Humanitarian Relief Operations for Civilians

Through each of its rules governing collective humanitarian relief operations, IHL strikes a compromise between belligerents' security interests and human security aims.

[85] eg UNSC 'Report of the Secretary General: Protection of Civilians in Armed Conflict' (14 May 2018) UN Doc S/2018/462, para 21; UN Doc S/2009/277 (n 58) Annex, 18.

[86] UN Doc S/2018/462 (n 85) para 20.

[87] eg UN Doc S/2009/277 (n 58) Annex, 18.

[88] AP I (n 4) art 54(1) and AP II (n 5) art 14; Henckaerts/Doswald-Beck (n 63) 186 (rule 53); ICC Statute (n 73) art 8(2)(b)(xxv).

[89] Dapo Akande/Emanuela-Chiara Gillard 'Promoting Compliance with the Rules Regulating Humanitarian Relief Operations in Armed Conflict: Some Challenges' (2017) 50 Israel Law Review 119.

Only in narrow circumstances can the former lawfully restrict the latter: consent to impartial humanitarian relief operations may not be arbitrarily withheld when civilians' essential needs are not being met; parties may impose measures of control on the passage of humanitarian relief, but these must be applied in good faith, and must not prevent the rapid delivery of impartial relief; belligerents may limit the movement of humanitarian personnel on the grounds of imperative military necessity, but restrictions must be temporary. In extreme cases, as the UNSC has shown, human security can become a matter of international peace and security and outweigh a State's national security interests.

C. Counter-terrorism Measures and Humanitarian Action

International terrorism is currently one of the greatest threats to many States' national security, and to international security. In the aftermath of the attacks of 11 September 2001, the UNSC has systematically affirmed that international terrorism constitutes a threat to international peace and security.[90] Terrorism does not just pose a threat to States and to the international community. It is also a significant threat to human security, and the response to terrorism has given rise to serious violations of fundamental human rights, IHL, and refugee law.[91] While efforts have been made in recent years, particularly at the international level, to ensure that counter-terrorism responses comply with these bodies of law,[92] the reality in practice remains that national and international security has taken precedence over considerations of human security—and in so doing has violated binding obligations and fundamental rights.[93]

Counter-terrorism measures have adversely affected the rights of individuals in numerous ways. The present chapter focuses on one dimension: the impact of such

[90] eg UNSC Res 1373 (2001); and most recently UNSC Res 2178 (2014); UNSC Res 2396 (2017). On these occasions the Council qualified 'international terrorism' as such, without reference to particular situations, as a threat to international peace and security. Before 2001 the Council had determined that specific acts of international terrorism amounted to such a threat. Christian Walter, 'Terrorism' MPEPIL (OUP, April 2011).

[91] Ben Saul (ed), *Research Handbook on International Law and Terrorism* (Edward Elgar 2020).

[92] eg Alice Debarre, *Safeguarding Medical Care and Humanitarian Action in the UN Counter-terrorism Framework* (IPI 2018). As noted by Debarre (ibid 10) as of 2004 terrorism-related resolutions adopted by the UNSC and UNGA started noting that measures adopted to combat terrorism must comply with States' obligations under international law, noting in particular 'international human rights, refugee, and humanitarian law'.

[93] eg Carla Ferstman, 'The Human Security Framework and Counter-Terrorism: Examining the Rhetoric Relating to "Extraordinary Renditions"' in Alice Edwards/Carla Ferstman (eds), *Human Security and Non-Citizens: Law, Policy and International Affairs* (CUP 2010); Reports of successive Human Rights Council Special Rapporteurs on the Promotion and Protection of Human Rights and Fundamental Freedoms while Countering Terrorism from 2005 to date: <https://www.ohchr.org/en/issues/terrorism/pages/srterrorismindex.aspx> accessed 14 January 2020.

measures on humanitarian action.[94] The expression 'humanitarian action' is used here to refer to various exclusively humanitarian activities conducted in accordance with the humanitarian principles of impartiality, neutrality, and independence. It is broader in scope than the provision of humanitarian relief discussed in the preceding section.

1. Counter-terrorism Prohibitions on Assistance to Designated Groups

Choking the financing of groups designated as terrorist organizations by the UNSC, regional intergovernmental organizations, or individual States, is a key element of international and national counter-terrorism strategies. As a matter of law, this is achieved by two principal means: financial sanctions against such groups; and criminal counter-terrorism measures that criminalize a range of activities that may provide financial assistance or other forms of material support directly or indirectly to such groups.

a. *Sanctions*

Financial sanctions can be imposed by intergovernmental organizations like the UN or the EU, or autonomously by individual States. These sanctions are principally asset freezes that impact humanitarian action and usually consist of two elements: an obligation to freeze the assets owned or controlled directly or indirectly by designated groups;

[94] For a recent analysis of the legal challenges and recommendations for reducing the tensions between counter-terrorism measures and humanitarian action: Emanuela-Chiara Gillard, 'Humanitarian Action and Non-State Armed Groups: the International Legal Framework' (2017) Chatham House Research Paper <https://www.chathamhouse.org/sites/default/files/publications/research/2017-02-02-humanitarian-action-non-state-armed-groups-gillard.pdf> accessed 14 January 2020 (Gillard, Humanitarian Action and Non-State Armed Groups); Emanuela-Chiara Gillard, 'Recommendations for Reducing Tensions in the Interplay between Sanctions, Counter-terrorism Measures and Humanitarian Action' (2017) Chatham House Research Paper <https://www.chathamhouse.org/sites/default/files/publications/research/CHHJ5596_NSAG_iv_research_paper_1708_WEB.pdf> accessed 28 November 2020 (Gillard, Recommendations for Reducing Tensions). The issue has received considerable attention in academic and policy writings: eg Harvard Program on Humanitarian Policy and Conflict Research, 'Humanitarian Action under Scrutiny: Criminalizing Humanitarian Engagement' (2011) HPCR Working Paper <https://reliefweb.int/sites/reliefweb.int/files/resources/Full_report_169.pdf> accessed 14 January 2020; Sara Pantuliano et al, *Counter-Terrorism and Humanitarian Action: Tensions, Impact and Ways Forward* (October 2011) HPG Policy Brief 43 <https://www.odi.org/sites/odi.org.uk/files/odi-assets/publications-opinion-files/7347.pdf> accessed 14 January 2020; Naz Modirzadeh et al, 'Humanitarian Engagement under Counter-Terrorism: A Conflict of Norms and the Emerging Policy Landscape' (2011) 93 International Review of the Red Cross 623; Kate Mackintosh/Patrick Duplat, 'Study of the Impact of Donor Counter-Terrorism Measures on Principled Humanitarian Action' (July 2013) <https://www.unocha.org/sites/unocha/files/CounterTerrorism_Study_Full_Report.pdf> accessed 14 January 2020; Victoria Metcalfe-Hough et al, 'UK Humanitarian Aid in the Age of Counter-terrorism: Perceptions and Reality' (2015) HPG Working Paper <https://www.odi.org/sites/odi.org.uk/files/odi-assets/publications-opinion-files/9479.pdf> accessed 14 January 2020; Phoebe Wynn-Pope et al, 'Legislating against Humanitarian Principles: A Case Study on the Humanitarian Implications of Australian Counter-terrorism Legislation' (2016) 97 International Review of the Red Cross 235.

and an obligation to ensure that funds, financial assets, or other economic resources are not made available to or for the benefit of designated groups. As elaborated below, it is this second dimension that can be problematic for humanitarian action.

b. *Criminal Counter-terrorism Measures*

States have assumed numerous obligations to prevent and suppress acts of terrorism under international conventions or pursuant to binding UNSC decisions. In terms of treaties, the 1999 International Convention for the Suppression of the Financing of Terrorism is of particular relevance for humanitarian action. This treaty makes it an offence to provide or collect funds by any means, directly or indirectly, unlawfully and wilfully, with the intention that they should be used, or in the knowledge that they are to be used, in full or in part, in order to carry out an act of terrorism.[95]

In terms of binding UNSC decisions, landmark Resolution 1373 (2001) was the first in a series of thematic resolutions aimed at strengthening the international community's counter-terrorism response by requiring Member States to take a number of measures to enhance their legal and institutional ability to prevent and criminalize terrorist activities. Of particular relevance to humanitarian action, Resolution 1373 required States to prevent and suppress the financing of terrorist acts, including by:

> [p]rohibit[ing] their nationals or any persons and entities within their territories from making any funds, financial assets or economic resources or financial or other related services available, directly or indirectly, for the benefit of persons who commit or attempt to commit or facilitate or participate in the commission of terrorist acts, of entities owned or controlled, directly or indirectly, by such persons and of persons and entities acting on behalf of or at the direction of such persons.[96]

The effect of these measures is essentially identical to asset freezes in sanctions. However, unlike sanctions, the regime established by Resolution 1373 does not include a list of designated persons or entities. It is left to States to establish their own lists.

The counter-terrorism framework established by Resolution 1373 is constantly evolving. In 2014, for example, the UNSC adopted Resolution 2178 on 'foreign terrorist fighters'. Amongst other things this requires Member States to criminalize travel by their nationals 'who travel or attempt to travel to a State other than their States of residence or nationality… for the purpose of the perpetration, planning, or preparation of, or participation in, terrorist acts, or the providing or receiving of terrorist training'.[97] As the areas to which 'foreign terrorist fighters' are likely to travel are frequently areas of conflict to which people also travel to conduct humanitarian activities, this provision has led to greater scrutiny by investigators and courts of the activities of staff of humanitarian organizations.

[95] International Convention for the Suppression of the Financing of Terrorism 2178 UNTS 197 art 2.

[96] UNSC Res 1373 (2001) para 1(d).

[97] UNSC Res 2178 (2014) para 6(a).

2. The Interplay with Humanitarian Action

The groups designated under sanctions and counter-terrorism measures have frequently included organized armed groups that are parties to armed conflicts and have control over civilian populations in severe need. These include Al Shabaab in Somalia, Al-Qaeda in the Arab Peninsula in Yemen, and Boko Haram in Nigeria—three countries identified as at risk of famine in 2017. Other examples are ISIS in Syria, and Hamas in Gaza.

Problems arise because the prohibited provision of 'material support'[98] has been interpreted extremely broadly. A real risk exists that transactions and activities carried out by humanitarian actors may fall within the scope of the restrictions. These can include incidental payments that humanitarian actors may have to make to designated groups as part of their humanitarian operations; or relief consignments that may be diverted and end up in the hands of the designated groups. More alarmingly, individuals have been listed under UN sanctions for, amongst other things, having provided medical care to members of designated groups, and criminal investigations have been conducted in a number of States on these grounds.[99] This is a particularly troubling development as the entitlement of the wounded and sick in armed conflict—including fighters—to receive medical care and the protection of those providing such care is a foundational principle of IHL.

3. The Consequences on Principled Humanitarian Action

The approach States have adopted to give effect in national law to their obligations under counter-terrorism measures is by no means uniform. Some States have followed the language of the 1999 Terrorist Financing Convention more closely and criminalized the provision of resources with the knowledge or intent that they will be used to commit an act of terrorism. Others have taken a broader approach, criminalizing support to a terrorist group more generally. This latter approach is more problematic for humanitarian actors, as the offences are defined broadly enough to capture payments made to designated

[98] The term 'material support' is taken from 18 US Code 2339A, where it is defined as:

> currency or monetary instruments or other financial securities, financial services, lodging, training, expert advice or assistance, safehouses, false documentation or identification, communications equipment, facilities, weapons, lethal substances, explosives, personnel, transportation, and other physical assets, except medicine or religious materials.

While this is the definition of 'material support' for the purposes of relevant US measures, it is essential to bear in mind that although the expression 'material support' is used colloquially to refer to the prohibited support under other measures, the actual prohibitions are *not* defined this broadly.

[99] Dustin Lewis et al, 'Medical Care in Armed Conflict: International Humanitarian Law and State Responses to Terrorism' (2015) Legal Briefing HLS PILAC, 110–11 <https://dash.harvard.edu/handle/1/22508590> accessed 14 January 2020; Marine Buissonnière et al, 'The Criminalization of Healthcare' (2018) <https://www1.essex.ac.uk/hrc/documents/54198-criminalization-of-healthcare-web.pdf> accessed 18 February 2019.

groups in order to operate, or relief supplies that are diverted to such groups.[100] Moreover, States have designated different persons and groups and some have granted their courts extraterritorial jurisdiction over these offences, meaning that more than one State's laws may be applicable.

These restrictions give rise to an extremely complex legal landscape that humanitarian organizations and their staff must navigate to avoid civil or criminal liability. Concerns about violating the prohibitions have frequently led to over-compliance with the law and have led organizations to place unwarranted limits on humanitarian operations. Some have curtailed their operations in certain areas, despite the existence of severe needs. This opens up humanitarians to allegations of not operating in a principled manner, and may leave people in severe need without assistance.

Until recently, investigations and proceedings against humanitarian organizations and their staff had not been numerous. The adverse impact was described principally as a 'chilling effect'. However, in the past few years there has been an increase in investigations, frequently against people who provided medical assistance—or claimed to have done so.[101] There are a number of possible reasons for this. First, many of the investigations have been brought pursuant to measures aimed at suppressing the phenomenon of 'foreign fighters'. States are likely to be more vigilant and less willing to accept risks in relation to people who return from areas of fighting who are potentially 'radicalized' and perceived as posing a more direct and immediate threat to national security than designated groups based overseas who might be receiving 'material support'. A second possible reason is that this is a manifestation of the broader and systematic erosion of the protections afforded to the wounded and sick and to those providing medical care.[102]

4. Banking Sector Restrictions

The problem is aggravated by the fact that it is not just humanitarian actors that must comply with sanctions and counter-terrorism measures. Banks must also do so, freezing the assets of designated individuals and groups, and not providing material support to them, directly or indirectly, including *via* the humanitarian organizations to whom they provide banking services.

Fears of violating these measures, coupled with a perception—fuelled to a significant degree by the Financial Action Task Force (FATF)—that the 'not-for profit' sector as a whole is vulnerable to abuse, the reality that humanitarian organizations are rarely

[100] Gillard, 'Humanitarian Action and Non-State Armed Groups' (n 94) 14.

[101] TMC Asser Institute, International Crimes Database: <http://www.internationalcrimesdatabase.org/> accessed 18 February 2019.

[102] Lewis et al (n 99); Buissonnière et al (n 99).

profitable clients, and the 'derisking' conducted by banks has led to a significant restriction in the financial services they provide to such organizations.[103]

Humanitarian actors operating in what banks consider 'high-risk jurisdictions', in or near areas where designated groups are based or operate, or faith-based, mainly Muslim, humanitarian organizations have been particularly affected. They are experiencing significant difficulties in accessing the financial services that are crucial to their capacity to fundraise and disburse funds, and thus operate. There has been an increase in regulatory compliance and disclosure requirements, with banks demanding increasingly detailed information about the organizations, their transactions, and their programmes. More damagingly, organizations have been unable to open accounts, receive donations, or transfer funds; have experienced delays or significantly increased charges; or have had their accounts closed.

5. Reducing the Tensions

Normatively, the tensions between sanctions, counter-terrorism measures and humanitarian action can be avoided by including exemptions in sanctions, and exceptions in criminal counter-terrorism measures. Such measures would reduce the risk of liability and provide reassurance to banks.

At present, however, at the UN level only one country-specific sanction regime (Somalia) includes an exemption for humanitarian action.[104] There is no substantive justification for this, as the same problems can arise in all contexts where asset freezes have been imposed on designated groups that exercise effective control over people in need. What is required is a concerted effort to raise awareness of the problem and to press for the systematic inclusion of exemptions.[105]

One might assume that concerns about material support would be less significant in country-specific rather than counter-terrorism sanctions, as terrorism is perceived as posing a more serious threat to international security than groups listed in country-specific sanctions, who may be designated for a range of grounds, and, consequently, that the UNSC would be more amenable to considering exemptions in the former regimes. Interestingly, however, it was the ISIL (Da'esh)/Al-Qaeda sanctions panel of experts that reached out to humanitarian actors for information on the adverse impact of the sanctions. The panel also indicated its concern that asset freezes, and banks' consequent restriction of services to humanitarian organizations with operations in areas where

[103] Tom Keatinge/Florence Keen, 'Humanitarian Action and Non-State Armed Groups: The Impact of Banking Restrictions on UK NGOs' (2017) Chatham House Research Paper <https://www.chathamhouse.org/sites/default/files/publications/research/2017-04-28-nsags-banking-restrictions-ngo-keatinge-keen.pdf> accessed 14 January 2020; Sue Eckert et al, *Financial Access for U.S. Nonprofits* (Charity and Security Network 2017).

[104] First introduced by UNSC Res 1916 (2010) para 5; and renewed most recently in UNSC Res 2444 (2018) para 48.

[105] For recommendations Gillard, 'Recommendations for Reducing Tensions' (n 94).

designated entities are based, have led to resort to informal and unregulated channels to transfer the funds necessary to operate. This makes it more difficult to monitor such funds, and increases the risk of the very abuse the sanctions are trying to prevent.[106]

As is the case with sanctions, the most effective way of ensuring that assets, or other support that reaches designated groups in the course of humanitarian operations, do not violate criminal counter-terrorism measures would be to include an express exception to this effect in the relevant international or domestic instruments. Neither the 1999 Terrorist Financing Convention nor UNSC Resolution 1373 refer to, let alone exclude, humanitarian action. This is not surprising, as both instruments were adopted before the impact of such measures on humanitarian action was identified. In recent years, the UNGA has started highlighting the potential adverse impact of counter-terrorism measures on humanitarian action[107] and has urged States to ensure that such measures 'do not impede humanitarian and medical activities or engagement with all relevant actors as foreseen by international humanitarian law'.[108]

The inclusion of these provisions in UNGA resolutions is a positive development, that shows States' increasing awareness of the potential adverse impact of counter-terrorism measures, and suggests a willingness to begin to address these tensions. However, the resolutions are not binding and to date none of the binding UNSC decisions on counter-terrorism have excluded humanitarian action from counter-terrorism measures.

At present, change is more likely to occur when States adopt legislation implementing their international obligations in domestic law. At this stage, tensions can be addressed in a number of ways. The clearest is inserting express exceptions for humanitarian action in the offences of providing support to designated entities. Such exceptions are rare;[109] one of the reasons for this is that many States adopted legislation implementing the 1999 Terrorist Financing Convention and UNSC Resolution 1373 before the potential adverse impact of counter-terrorism measures on humanitarian action was identified, so did not consider the issue. While understandable, this is unfortunate, because

[106] Author interviews, New York, Geneva and Rome (October 2016–May 2017).

[107] For example, in December 2015, in its resolution on the protection of human rights and fundamental freedoms while countering terrorism, UNGA 70/148 (17 December 2015) para 7 urged States, 'while undertaking counter-terrorism activities, to respect their international obligations regarding humanitarian actors and to recognize the key role played by humanitarian organizations in areas where terrorist groups are active'. The call was reiterated in UNGA Res 72/180 (19 December 2017) para 7.

[108] UNGA Res 70/291 (1 July 2016) para 22. The call was reiterated in UNGA Res 72/284 (26 June 2018) para 79.

[109] For example, the Australian Criminal Code includes two exceptions. The first is the offence of associating with terrorist organizations when this is only for the purpose of providing aid of a humanitarian nature (Australia, Criminal Code Act 1995, Division 102.8). A second terrorism-related offence, entering or remaining in a 'declared area'—namely, an area declared by the foreign minister as one where a listed entity is engaging in hostile activity—is not committed if a person enters, or remains in, the area solely for legitimate purposes, including the provision of aid of a humanitarian nature (Australia, Criminal Code Act 1995, Division 119.2(3)(a)); Gillard, 'Humanitarian Action and Non-State Armed Groups' (n 94).

amending existing legislation is much more difficult than including exceptions from the outset.[110]

States have a further opportunity to insert exclusions in existing counter-terrorism legislation when revising it to give effect to new international obligations, such as those under UNSC Resolution 2178 on foreign terrorist fighters. At this juncture, they could either insert a general exception for humanitarian action, or, as a minimum, include one in relation to the new offences.

The UK has taken this approach in the 2019 Counter-Terrorism and Border Security Act. Amongst other things, this implements obligations pursuant to UNSC Resolution 2178 on foreign fighters. The Act introduces a new provision giving the Home Secretary the power to 'designate' a country, or region thereof, and making it an offence for UK nationals and residents to enter or remain in this area. The government accepted an amendment to the draft law creating an exception to the offence for those entering or remaining in a designated area for a number of purposes, including 'providing aid of a humanitarian nature'.[111]

A second approach is framing counter-terrorism offences narrowly to make it less likely that they would cover support provided in the course of humanitarian action.[112]

There have also been some positive developments at the EU level. In 2017 a safeguard clause for humanitarian action was included in the preamble to the 2017 EU Directive on Combating Terrorism. This notes that:

> The provision of humanitarian activities by impartial humanitarian organisations recognised by international law, including international humanitarian law, do [sic] not fall under the scope of this Directive, while taking into account the case law of the Court of Justice of the European Union.[113]

[110] For example, the experience in the UK. In 2015 a parliamentary committee recommended that the Government consider introducing exceptions to counter-terrorism legislation for humanitarian activities. The Home Office and Treasury Office of Financial Sanctions Implementation replied that doing so would 'create a loophole that could be exploited by unscrupulous individuals and leave NGOs vulnerable to abuse'. No explanation was given of the basis for this assessment, nor why the risk of exploitation could not be reduced by inclusion of a suitably worded intention requirement: cited in Kate Jones, 'Humanitarian Action and Non-State Armed Groups: The UK Regulatory Environment' (2017) Chatham House Research Paper, 12 <https://www.chathamhouse.org/sites/default/files/publications/research/2017-02-17-humanitarian-action-non-state-armed-groups-uk-jones.pdf> accessed 14 January 2020. In 2019, the UNSC adopted resolution 2462, urging 'States, when designing and applying measures to counter the financing of terrorism, to *take into account the potential effect of those measures on exclusively humanitarian activities*, including medical activities, that are carried out by impartial humanitarian actors in a manner consistent with international humanitarian law' (emphasis added).

[111] Counter-Terrorism and Border Security Bill [as amended on report], HL Bill (2018) 153, ch 1 s 4 <https://publications.parliament.uk/pa/bills/lbill/2017-2019/0153/18153.pdf> accessed 18 February 2020.

[112] Gillard, 'Humanitarian Action and Non-State Armed Groups' (n 94) 14.

[113] Directive (EU) 2017/541 of 15 March 2017 on Combating Terrorism OJ L88/6, preambular para 38.

6. The Way Forward

In order to reduce the tensions, concerted action is required at the global, EU, and national level. At the global level, and in particular at the UN level, a significant amount of awareness-raising is still necessary to systematically highlight the problem, and to persuade Member States to, equally systematically, include exemptions for humanitarian action in sanctions.[114]

Much of the attention to date has focused on the UN, however the same problems also arise at the EU level, when the EU adopts sanctions or counter-terrorism measures. Recent developments give cause to believe that EU Member States and institutions are receptive to the challenges faced by humanitarian actors, and are willing to explore ways to reduce the tensions. Sustained engagement should be conducted with policymakers in Brussels to build upon this.

Finally, the same issues need to be tackled with States at the domestic level when they are giving effect to UN and EU measures. By way of example, EU Member States should be encouraged to expressly include the safeguard clause when giving effect to the 2017 EU Directive in domestic law.

7. Concluding Reflections on Counter-terrorism Measures and Humanitarian Action

The adverse impact of counter-terrorism on humanitarian action does not appear to be an intentional undermining of human security, unlike in other areas where counter-terrorism has been used as a justification for the severe curtailing of individual rights and undermining of human security.[115] The impact might have been unintended and unexpected, when the issue first came to the fore during the famine in Somalia in 2010, when Al Shabaab, a designated group, was in control of many of the people in severe need. Although, since, the problem has received considerable attention, not enough has been done to address the problem. While States are now occasionally referring to the issue, all too frequently this remains mere lip-service.

Numerous government departments are involved in the adoption of counter-terrorism decisions: ministries of foreign affairs, home affairs, justice, finance, and overseas aid and development.[116] Often, these departments are not working on the different dimensions of this issue in a coordinated and coherent manner. Priorities can clash and when decisions need to be taken, national security concerns still prevail over reducing the adverse impact on humanitarian action.

[114] Gillard, 'Recommendations for Reducing Tensions' (n 94) 8–9. [115] Ferstman (n 93) 535.
[116] Jones (n 110) 10.

D. Conclusion

In situations of armed conflict, humanitarian relief operations give rise to competing security concerns, ranging from State sovereignty and belligerents' military interests to civilians' food and health security. The well-established and binding rules of IHL governing humanitarian relief operations reflect a delicate compromise between these concerns. They aim to ensure that civilians receive articles of prime necessity for their survival while admitting narrow circumstances in which belligerents' security interests may restrict human security aims. In practice, these interests are in constant tension, such that relief operations are fundamentally a matter of negotiation between those carrying them out and the parties to the conflict.

International and national counter-terrorism measures are frequently also applicable in situations of armed conflict and can pose challenges for humanitarian action. Unless efforts are made to reduce the tensions between counter-terrorism measures and humanitarian action, there is very real risk that, as a matter of practice, the rules of IHL governing relief operations will not come into play. Humanitarian actors may simply be forced to refrain from operating in contexts where the risk of liability is too high, or may effectively be prevented from doing so as banking sector restrictions make it impossible to access funds.

Unless national security and human security interests are properly balanced in both law and practice, principled humanitarian action can be severely compromised, leaving civilians without the essentials they need to survive. In turn, this may, in extreme situations, even pose a threat to international peace and security.

Note

The views expressed herein are those of the authors and do not necessarily reflect the views of the United Nations. The research leading to these results has received funding from the European Research Council under the European Union's Seventh Framework Programme (FP/2007-2013) / ERC Grant Agreement No [340956 - IOW].

CHAPTER 29

WATER SECURITY

PIERRE THIELBÖRGER

A. Introduction

WATER security is a contested normative concept, without clear definitions, meanings, or interpretations.[1] Water[2] can save a man or kill him. With this in mind, the term 'water security' must be understood in two distinct ways: security *through* water (meaning individuals' access to water to sustain their lives and livelihoods) and security *against* water (meaning the absence of water-related threats, both natural and man-made).[3] In this way water security is different from food or energy security as these two terms mainly describe reliable access to sufficient supplies to meet basic needs of individuals or groups.[4] Contrariwise, not only the absence of water but also its presence can pose a threat, given water's dual life-generating and destructive qualities.[5]

The first lens of security through water implies a human rights approach. While security had traditionally been understood as a State-centred concept relating to the national security of State territory in international law, the ideas of environmental

[1] Jeremy Allouche et al, 'Water Security: Towards the Human Securitization of Water?' (2011) 12 Whitehead Journal of Diplomacy and International Relations 153.

[2] If not referred to otherwise, 'water' in this chapter refers to freshwater/potable water.

[3] Similarly, Gutierrez argues that water security must be based on three pillars: freedom from want, freedom of fear, and freedom to live with human dignity, see Eric Gutierrez, 'Boiling Point: Issues and Problems in Water Security and Sanitation' (August 1999) Water Aid Briefing Paper <http://citeseerx.ist.psu.edu/viewdoc/download?doi=10.1.1.581.8862&rep=rep1&type=pdf> accessed 29 May 2020.

[4] See eg World Food Summit, 'Rome Declaration on Food Security' and 'World Food Summit Plan of Action' (FAO, 13–17 November 1996) <http://www.fao.org/WFS/> accessed 11 September 2019; and for the term energy security, see *World Energy Assessment: Energy and the Challenge of Sustainability* (UNDP 2000) 11.

[5] David Grey/Claudia W Sadoff, 'Sink or Swim? Water Security for Growth and Development' (2007) 9 Water Policy 545, 547.

security,[6] and later of human security,[7] entered the international arena in the last few decades and have materially broadened the concept. The concept of water security as security through water is a tool to guarantee certain minimum standards of water for individuals (for drinking, hygiene, and other basic purposes). This aspect of water security is closely related to the idea of a human right to water as derived from, and related to, other human rights such as the right to life (Article 6 of the International Covenant on Civil and Political Rights (ICCPR)),[8] an adequate standard of living (including housing and food) (Article 11 International Covenant on Economic Social and Cultural Rights (ICESCR)),[9] and the right to the highest attainable standard of health (Article 12 ICESCR). The right to water has extensively occupied international legal scholars over the last decades.[10] Nonetheless many questions remain open and the right itself can still be considered 'new' in international law.[11]

The second lens through which water security can be understood is that of security *from* water. Water can pose essentially two threats. First, given its outstanding political and economic significance, the likelihood of 'water wars'[12] has been discussed in international law and politics for some time. Given its economic value as a resource—some authors refer to water as 'blue gold'[13]—many observers contend that future wars would be fought over water, rather than land or other resources, such as oil and gas. Secondly, scientific research has shown that water systems are particularly affected by climate change.[14] Not only are we witnessing already rising sea levels posing existential security risks to low-lying coastal regions and islands; we also know that natural disasters such as floods and tsunamis will become more common, both in number and severity.[15]

[6] Jessica T Mathews, 'Redefining Security' (1989) 68 Foreign Affairs 162.

[7] UNGA 'Report of the World Summit for Social Development' (19 April 1995) UN Doc A/CONF.166/9, Annex II; Wolfgang Benedek, 'Human Security and Human Rights Interaction' (2008) 59(s1) International Social Science Journal 7.

[8] International Covenant on Civil and Political Rights 999 UNTS 171 (ICCPR).

[9] International Covenant on Economic, Social and Cultural Rights 993 UNTS 3 (ICESCR).

[10] eg Pierre Thielbörger, *The Right(s) to Water: The Multi-Level Governance of a Unique Human Right* (Springer 2014); Inga Winkler, *The Human Right to Water: Significance, Legal Status and Implications for Water Allocation* (Hart 2012); Silke Laskowski, *Das Menschenrecht auf Wasser* (Mohr Siebeck 2010).

[11] Danwood M Chirwa, 'Access to Water as a New Right in International, Regional and Comparative Constitutional Law' in Andreas von Arnauld et al (eds), *The Cambridge Handbook of New Human Rights* (CUP 2019); Pierre Thielbörger, 'Something Old, Something New, Something Borrowed and Something Blue: Lessons to be Learned from the Oldest of the "New" Rights—The Human Right to Water' in Andreas von Arnauld et al (eds), *The Cambridge Handbook of New Human Rights* (CUP 2019).

[12] Aaron T Wolf, ' "Water Wars" and Water Reality: Conflict and Cooperation Along International Waterways' in Stephen C Lonergan (ed), *Environmental Change, Adaption, and Security* (NATO ASI Series: Environment, vol 65, Springer 1999) 251–65; Muhammad Rahaman, 'Water Wars in 21st Century: Speculation or Reality?' (2012) 4 International Journal of Sustainable Society 3.

[13] Maude Barlow/Tony Clarke, *Blue Gold: The Battle Against Corporate Theft of the World's Water* (Routledge 2002); Violeta Petrova, 'All the Frontiers of the Rush for Blue Gold: Water Privatization and the Human Right to Water' (2006) 31 Brooklyn Journal of International Law 577.

[14] Valérie Masson-Delmotte et al (eds), *Global Warming of 1.5°C: Summary for Policymakers* (Intergovernmental Panel on Climate Change 2018) 10ff (IPCC, *Summary for Policymakers*). For the case of water, see also the Section C.2 of this chapter.

[15] IPCC, *Summary for Policymakers* (n 14) 10.

B. Legal Frameworks

As with the two conceptions of the term 'water security', the applicable legal framework is likewise subdivided into the two categories of security *through* water and security *from* water.

1. Security *through* Water—Legal Framework

In 1994, the Human Development Report defined security as 'safety from such chronic threats as hunger, disease and repression (…) and protection from sudden and hurtful disruptions in the patterns of daily life—whether in homes, in jobs or in communities'.[16] As an extension of this definition, UN Water defines water security as:

> [T]he capacity of a population to safeguard sustainable access to adequate quantities of acceptable quality water for sustaining livelihoods, human well-being, and socio-economic development, for ensuring protection against water-borne pollution and water-related disasters, and for preserving ecosystems in a climate of peace and political stability.[17]

a. *The Human Right to Water in International Treaties and Interpretations Thereof*

One way to achieve water security in this sense is by means of recognizing a right that grants all individuals a legal claim to water access to realize their basic human needs.

In 1979, the right to water was recognized in Article 14(2)(h) of the Convention on the Elimination of all Forms of Discrimination Against Women[18] (CEDAW), which provides that 'States parties shall (…) ensure to (…) women the right: (…) To enjoy adequate living conditions, particularly in relation to (…) sanitation, (…) and water supply (…)'. Given CEDAW's very high ratification rate,[19] Article 14(2)(h) CEDAW was a milestone for the universal recognition of the right to water. As in many societies women and girls are tasked with fetching water, sometimes from distant sources, recognizing the need for physical accessibility of water for every household is an indispensable condition for guaranteeing women's and girls' physical safety.

[16] UNDP, *Human Development Report 1994* (OUP 1994) 23.

[17] UN Water, *Water Security and the Global Water Agenda: A UN-Water Analytical Brief* (UN University—Institute for Water, Environment and Health 2013) vi.

[18] 1249 UNTS 13 (CEDAW).

[19] For the current ratification status, see <https://treaties.un.org/Pages/ViewDetails.aspx?src=TREATY&mtdsg_no=IV-8&chapter=4&lang=en> accessed 24 September 2020. One of the few non-member States is the USA.

In 1989, Article 24(2) of the Convention on the Rights of the Child[20] (CRC) stated that 'States Parties shall (. . .) take appropriate measures (. . .) to combat disease and malnutrition (. . .) through, inter alia, the provision of adequate nutritious foods and clean drinking water'. Being the most widely ratified international treaty,[21] the CRC plays a key role in not only promoting the right to water for vulnerable groups, but also in paving the way for its future universal recognition.

In 2002, the Committee on Economic Social and Cultural Rights (CESCR) released General Comment No 15 on 'The Right to Water'. Therein it described the normative content of the right and emphasized that, while not included in the ICESCR explicitly, it must be understood as being derived from the right to an adequate standard of living.[22] The experts also saw it as being closely related to the right to the highest attainable standard of health[23] and the right to life (without using these rights explicitly as to life as a core right for derivation).[24]

Despite its non-binding nature, General Comment No 15 is a landmark document in the establishment of the right to water.[25] General Comments are generally accepted as authoritative interpretations of the ICESCR,[26] and General Comment No 15 was met with broad support from the very beginning, with only few exceptions.[27]

b. *The Human Right to Water as Part of International Customary Law*

Political declarations, while not legally binding per se, can certainly reflect customary law, and in particular *opinio juris*.[28] Support for the right has provided substantial *opinio juris* over recent years, as expressed in many political declarations.

Already in 1977 the Action Plan of the UN Water Conference in Mar del Plata proclaimed for the first time that access to water should be a right, demanding that '[a]ll peoples [..] have the right to have access to drinking water in quantities and of a quality equal to their basic needs'.[29]

In 2000, States committed themselves to a new global partnership to reduce global poverty, setting out eight targets to be achieved by 2015 (the Millennium Development

[20] 1577 UNTS 3 (CRC).

[21] See <https://treaties.un.org/pages/ViewDetails.aspx?src=IND&mtdsg_no=IV-11&chapter=4&lang=en> accessed 24 September 2020.

[22] CESCR, 'General Comment No 15 (2002): The Right to Water (arts. 11 and 12 of the ICESC)' (20 January 2003) UN Doc E/C.12/2002/11, para 3 (GC 15).

[23] ibid. [24] ibid para 11. [25] Thielbörger (n 10) 67.

[26] ECOSOC Res 1987/5 (26 May 1987), containing no authorization for legally binding comments; also see Emilie Filmer-Wilson, 'The Human Rights-Based Approach to Development: The Right to Water' (2005) 23 Netherlands Quarterly of Human Rights 213.

[27] Stephen Tully, 'A Human Right to Access Water? A Critique of General Comment No 15' (2005) 23 Netherlands Quarterly of Human Rights 35; Stephen Tully, 'Flighty Purposes and Deeds: A Rejoinder to Malcolm Langford' (2006) 24 Netherlands Quarterly of Human Rights 461.

[28] *Case Concerning the Military and Paramilitary Activities in and Against Nicaragua (Nicaragua v USA)* (Merits) [1986] ICJ Rep 99–100 [188].

[29] United Nations Water Conference, 'Mar del Plata Action Plan' (Mar del Plata 14–25 March 1977) UNST/DPI/DESI(063.1)/M2, 63.

Goals (MDGs)). MDG 7c demanded that by 2015, the proportion of the population without sustainable access to safe drinking water and basic sanitation should have been halved.[30] By 2015 significant progress had indeed been achieved with regard to these targets.[31]

In July 2010, the UN General Assembly adopted a declaration entitled 'The human right to water and sanitation,'[32] in which it declared water and sanitation to be human rights. While UNGA Resolution 64/292 was met with significant reluctance by some States[33] (mostly more disgruntled by the drafting process than the substance of the resolution),[34] a few months later Human Rights Council (HRC) Resolution 15/9 was accepted without a vote. The HRC therein again emphasized that the right to water derived from other Covenant rights, in particular the right to an adequate standard of living.[35]

Fifteen years after the MDGs, the UNGA unanimously proclaimed the Sustainable Development Goals (SDGs),[36] a collection of seventeen broad and interdependent goals, further specified in 169 targets. SDG 6 demands the availability and sustainable management of water and sanitation for all, subdivided in eight targets and measured against eleven indicators.[37] In its latest report in mid-2018,[38] the UN was partially optimistic about SDG 6 in light of the fact that the global population using at least basic drinking water services increased by 9 per cent between 2000 and 2015.[39]

Despite this overwhelmingly strong expression of *opinion juris*, States and legal academics have in the past been reluctant to accept the right to water as part of customary

[30] UNGA Res 55/2 (18 September 2000) para 19.

[31] For all these numbers, see UN, The Millennium Development Goals Report 2015 (UN 2015) 7, 52ff (MDGs Report); much less progress, however, has been achieved in the field of sanitation.

[32] UNGA Res 64/292 (3 August 2010).

[33] UN, 'General Assembly Adopts Resolution Recognizing Access to Clean Water, Sanitation as Human Right, by Recorded Vote of 122 in Favour, None against, 41 Abstentions' (28 July 2010) UN Doc GA/10967.

[34] Thielbörger (n 10) 79–80. [35] GC 15 (n 22) paras 3, 41.

[36] UNGA Res 70/1 (25 September 2015).

[37] While targets break down the overall goal in several sub-categories, indicators represent the quantifiable metrics by which to track whether these different targets are met. Specifically on water, it sets out the targets to achieve universal and equitable access to safe and affordable drinking water for all (target 6.1), to significantly improve water quality (target 6.3), to increase water-use efficiency to address water scarcity (target 6.4), to improve integrated water resources management and transboundary cooperation (target 6.5), to protect and restore water-related ecosystems (by 2020) (target 6.6), to expand international water cooperation and capacity-building for developing countries (target 6.6a), as well as to strengthen the participation of local communities in improving water management (target 6.6b): UNGA Res 70/1 (25 September 2015).

[38] UN Water, *Sustainable Development Goal 6: Synthesis Report 2018 on Water and Sanitation* (UN 2018) <https://www.unwater.org/app/uploads/2018/12/SDG6_SynthesisReport2018_WaterandSanitation_04122018.pdf> accessed 11 September 2019.

[39] ibid 39.

law, mainly due to incoherent State practice. In the conclusions on its work on the identification of customary international law, the International Law Commission (ILC) has emphasized the importance of both elements of custom, State practice and *opinio juris*, which are to be ascertained separately.[40] However, the International Court of Justice (ICJ) has in the past been rather flexible in identifying norms of customary law. In some cases, it has relied almost exclusively on *opinio juris*[41] and has been less preoccupied with simultaneously showing consistent State practice. There seems to be some flexibility regarding the intensity with which both elements must exist: 'less' of the one can be made up for by 'more' of the other.[42]

Such (even if limited) State practice supporting a customary right to water becomes apparent when looking at the monitoring of MDG 7c and SDG 6. Recent monitoring accounts state that the targets with regard to water have been met prematurely or will be met within the envisaged timeframe of the goals.[43] This clearly indicates that broadening access to water is a priority in most States' public policies. Not making efforts in this regard is no longer acceptable State practice within the international community. Together with the abundant *opinio juris* evidenced through numerous political declarations and treaties over the last forty years, it is at least arguable that the right to water has by now crystallized into a norm of customary international law.[44]

c. *The Normative Content of the Human Right to Water*

General Comment No 15 is the best guide when determining the normative content of the right to water. The CESCR drew upon its previous work, as parts of the normative content of the right to water had been previously elaborated in General Comment No 4 (on the right to housing),[45] General Comment No 12 (on the right to food)[46], and

[40] ILC 'Report of the International Law Commission on the work of its 70th session' (30 April–1 June and 2 July–10 August 2018) UN Doc A/73/10, para 65.

[41] ibid paras 184 and 188.

[42] Anthea E Roberts, 'Traditional and Modern Approaches to Customary International Law: A Reconciliation' (2001) 95 AJIL 757, referring back also to well-known approaches by Frederic L Kirgis, 'Custom on a Sliding Scale' (1987) 81 AJIL 146 and John Tasioulas, 'In Defence of Relative Normativity: Communitarian Values and the Nicaragua Case' (1996) 16 Oxford Journal of Legal Studies 85.

[43] See eg the recent report by WHO/UNICEF, Progress on Drinking Water, Sanitation and Hygiene—2017 Update and SDG Baselines (WHO and UNICEF 2017) 58ff <https://washdata.org/report/jmp-2017-report-final> accessed 24 September 2020.

[44] Pierre Thielbörger, 'Re-Conceptualizing the Human Right to Water: A Pledge for a Hybrid Approach' (2015) 15 Human Rights Law Review 225, 234–43.

[45] CESCR, 'General Comment No 4: The Right to Adequate Housing (Art. 11 (1) of the Covenant)' (13 December 1991) UN Doc E/1992/23, para 8(b).

[46] CESCR, 'General Comment No 12: The Right to Adequate Food (Art. 11 of the Covenant)' (12 May 1999) UN Doc E/C.12/2000/4, paras 7–13.

General Comment No 14 (on the right to health).[47] After 2002, later General Comments have equally reinforced the existence of a human right to water under the ICESCR.[48]

As with all economic, social, and cultural rights, States obligations are to respect, protect, and fulfil the human right to water.[49] General Comment No 15 summarizes that '[t]he human right to water entitles everyone to sufficient, safe, acceptable, physically accessible and affordable water for personal and domestic uses'.[50] This essentially leads to the three main requirements of water availability, water quality, and water accessibility (both physical and economic accessibility). These elements of the right in turn explain the right's origin in different core rights. In other words, if water is not available for drinking and other basic uses, the right to life (Article 6 ICCPR) is at stake; if water is not of the required quality, it endangers consumers' right to health (Article 12 ICESCR); and if water is out of proportionate physical or financial reach, it jeopardizes the fulfilment of the right to an adequate standard of living (Article 11 ICESCR). Given its basis in both civil and political and socio-economic rights the right to water has been termed a 'hybrid right'.[51]

2. Security *from* Water—Legal Framework

Turning to security *from* water, water has always been a point of contention between States. This is a highly political topic, hence the coining of the term hydro-politics as a branch of international politics and diplomacy in the late 1970s.[52] Hydro-politics in this way deals with inter-State conflict and cooperation in the field of international freshwater sources, such as rivers, lakes, or aquifers.

a. *Water Scarcity as a Driver for Armed Conflict?*

Water scarcity was perceived in the past as a potential driver for armed conflict. The rather inadequate term 'water wars' has been used in the literature and the media alike.[53]

[47] CESCR, 'General Comment No 14: The Right to the Highest Attainable Standard of Health (Art. 12 of the Covenant)' (11 August 2000) UN Doc E/C.12/2000/4, paras 4, 11, 12a, 15, 34 and 51.

[48] CESCR, 'General Comment No 16: The Equal Right of Men and Women to the Enjoyment of All Economic, Social and Cultural Rights (Art. 3 of the Covenant)' (11 August 2005) UN Doc E/C.12/2005/4, para 4; CESCR, 'General Comment No 19: The Right to Social Security (Art. 9 of the Covenant)' (4 February 2008) UN Doc E/C.12/GC/19, para 59; CESCR, 'General Comment No 20: Non-Discrimination in Economic, Social and Cultural Rights (Art. 2, para. 2, of the International Covenant on Economic, Social and Cultural Rights)' (2 July 2009) UN Doc E/C.12/GC/20, para 25; CESCR, 'General Comment No 21: Right of Everyone to take Part in Cultural Life (Art. 15, para. 1a of the Covenant on Economic, Social and Cultural Rights)' (1 December 2009) UN Doc E/C.12/GC/21, para 16(e); CESCR, 'General Comment No 24: on State Obligations under the International Covenant on Economic, Social and Cultural Rights in the Context of Business Activities' (10 August 2017) UN Doc E/C.12/GC/24, paras 2, 26.

[49] GC 15 (n 22) para 20.

[50] ibid para 2; see the different definitions in para 12(a–c).

[51] Thielbörger (n 44) 225–49.

[52] eg John Waterbury, *Hydropolitics of the Nile Valley* (Syracuse UP 1979).

[53] See 'Special Issue on Water Wars in 21st Century along International Rivers Basins: Speculation or Reality?' (2012) 4 International Journal of Sustainable Society.

However, this term is both misleading and superficial as both water scarcity and armed conflict require further specification.

'Water scarcity' must be subdivided into different categories to distinguish between the different causes for water shortage. The literature suggests a subdivision into demand-driven water scarcity (typically caused by population growth),[54] supply-driven water scarcity (caused by decreasing amounts of the overall available potable water, acerbated by climate change),[55] and water scarcity as a result of structural inequality (such as power inequalities between different groups). Armed conflict relating to water scarcity may appear in the form of either scarcity-induced inter-State conflicts or severe intra-State conflict between the State and different social or ethnic groups (or amongst these groups themselves).[56]

Existing empirical studies show that inter-State water conflicts are the less likely form of violent water conflicts. Most water conflicts take place within States.[57] The empirical findings on these intra-State conflicts are not all consistent, however. Some researchers have claimed that aggravating water scarcity, amongst other consequences of climate change, has a direct positive effect on the incidence of civil war;[58] other researchers, however, found that resource scarcity had no effect on State failure and civil war.[59] Some studies have shown that increased precipitation volatility, including more frequent floods and droughts, has a negative effect on economic development and increases the risk of civil war,[60] while other studies found precipitation patterns and water scarcity to have no robust effect on inter-group conflicts such as civil war.[61] Some authors even claim the reverse effect, namely that population density combined with renewable resource wealth (including improved access to water) can increase, rather than decrease, the risk of civil war.[62]

The UN Security Council (UNSC) itself has increasingly considered the effects of climate change as a threat to international peace and security. In 2011, it emphasized the

[54] Irna van der Molen/Antoinette Hildering, 'Water: Cause for Conflict or Co-operation?' (2005) 1 ISYP Journal on Science and World Affairs 133; Halvard Buhaug et al, *Implications of Climate Change for Armed Conflict* (Social Development Department—The World Bank 2008) 16ff.

[55] Fulu Tao et al, 'Future Climate Change, the Agricultural Water Cycle, and Agricultural Production in China' (2003) 95 Agriculture, Ecosystems and Environment 203; Ragab Ragab/Christel Prudhomme, 'Climate Change and Water Resources Management in Arid and Semi-arid Regions: Prospective and Challenges for the 21st Century' (2002) 81 Biosystems Engineering 3.

[56] Thomas Homer-Dixon, *Environment, Scarcity, and Violence* (Princeton UP 1999); van der Molen/Hildering (n 54).

[57] Homer-Dixon (n 56) 12–27.

[58] Wenche Hauge/Tanja Ellingsen, 'Beyond Environmental Scarcity: Causal Pathways to Conflict' (1998) 35 Journal of Peace Research 299.

[59] Daniel C Esty et al, *State Failure Task Force Report: Phase II Findings* (McLean VA: Science Application International Corporation 1998).

[60] Edward Miguel, 'Economic Shocks and Civil Conflict: An Instrumental Variables Approach' (2004) 112 Journal of Political Economy 4, 725–53.

[61] Ole Magnus Theisen/Kristian Brandsegg, 'The Environment and Non-State Conflicts' (48th Annual Convention of the International Studies Association, 2007).

[62] Indra de Soysa, 'Paradise is a Bazaar? Greed, Creed, and Governance in Civil War 1989–1999' (2002) 39 Journal of Peace Research 395.

importance of including security implications of climate change, as a possible driver of conflict, in conflict analysis and contextual information.[63] In 2017, it highlighted the security risks of water stress vis-à-vis several regions in light of, *inter alia*, water scarcity, drought, desertification, and land degradation.[64] The Council has also recently emphasized water-related security risks for specific countries and regions (mainly on the African continent), such as West Africa and the Sahel region,[65] Somalia,[66] Sudan,[67] and Mali.[68] Accordingly, water scarcity is becoming increasingly important for the international security agenda and the UNSC needs to make this an area of priority.[69]

b. *Watercourse Convention*

In parallel with the aforementioned UNSC activities, and in order to avoid future water conflicts and expand water cooperation, an increasing number of bilateral and multilateral water agreements have been concluded in the last few decades. According to UN Water and the UN Economic Commission for Europe (UNECE), between the late 1940s and mid-2010s, around 300 international water agreements were concluded.[70] Nevertheless, according to the Stockholm International Water Institute (SIWI) around two-thirds of the world's transboundary rivers are not governed by a cooperative management framework.[71]

The most general (and relevant) of these treaties is the 1997 UN Convention on the Law of Non-Navigational Uses of International Watercourses (Watercourses Convention).[72] It aims to regulate the uses, as well as the conservation, of all transboundary waters above and below the surface.[73] Notably, the Convention took almost twenty years to enter into force, due to the lack of the necessary ratifications by States.[74] This illustrates further that water, and specifically States' sovereign rights over water sources within their territory, remains a highly controversial topic. Even today only

[63] UNSC Presidential Statement 15 (2011) UN Doc S/PRST/2011/15. [64] UNSC Res 2349 (2017).

[65] UNSC Presidential Statement 3 (2018) UN Doc S/PRST/2018/3.

[66] UNSC Res 2408 (2018); UNSC Res 2431 (2018). [67] UNSC Res 2429 (2018).

[68] UNSC Res 2432 (2018).

[69] Pierre Thielbörger, 'Climate Change and International Peace and Security: Time for a "Green" Security Council?' in Hans-Joachim Heintze/Pierre Thielbörger (eds), *From Cold War to Cyber War, The Evolution of the International Law of Peace and Armed Conflict over the Last 25 Years* (Springer 2016).

[70] See 'Transboundary Waters' (*UN Water*) <http://www.unwater.org/water-facts/transboundary-waters/> accessed 11 September 2019, in connection with 'Good Practices in Transboundary Water Cooperation' (*UN Water*, March 2015) <http://www.unece.org/fileadmin/DAM/env/water/publications/WAT_Good_practices/2015_PCCP_Flyer_Good_Practices__LIGHT_.pdf> accessed 24 September 2020.

[71] See Stockholm International Water Institute, 'Cooperation over Shared Waters' (SIWI) <http://www.siwi.org/priority-area/transboundary-water-management/> accessed 24 September 2020.

[72] 36 ILM 700 (Watercourses Convention). Very instructive on the Convention's drafting history and background: Stephen McCaffrey/Mpazi Sinjela, 'The 1997 United Nations Convention on International Watercourses' (1998) 92 AJIL 97.

[73] Watercourses Convention (n 72) preamble and art 1.

[74] The necessary number of thirty-five States ratifications (ibid art 36(1)) was only reached in 2014 with the ratification by Côte d'Ivoire.

thirty-six States have ratified the treaty,[75] with key actors such as the US, Canada, Russia, and Brazil remaining outside the treaty regime.

For the regulation of inter-State water usages, the treaty relies on two main principles: the principle of equitable use of shared resources (Articles 5 and 6) and the no-harm principle (Article 7). These principles have a long history in international environmental law. For instance, the *Trail Smelter* arbitration established in the early 1940s that a State may not cause transboundary damage to the environment of another State as 'under the principles of international law (…) no State has the right to use or permit the use of its territory in such a manner as to cause injury by fumes in or to the territory of another or the properties or persons therein (…)'.[76] This principle was re-affirmed in the Stockholm Declaration (Principle 21) and is now reflected in Article 7 of the Watercourse Convention, in relation to transboundary water harm specifically.

Similarly, according to the *Lac Lanoux* arbitration 'there does exist a duty of consultation and of bringing into harmony the respective actions of the two States when general interests are involved in matters concerning waters'.[77] This essentially means that in the case of shared resources, such as lakes, the use of one State's sovereign rights shall not result in the deprivation of rights of other States. Article 5 of the Watercourse Convention confirmed this principle. When finding an adequate balance of shared resources, geographical characteristics as well as socio-economic needs in the affected States have to be taken into account under Article 6 of the Convention.

c. *Important Regional Treaties and Initiatives on Shared Waters*

In the absence of a widely ratified global treaty, regional treaties and initiatives have gained particular importance. In 1816, the Central Commission for the Navigation on the Rhine, which is often referred to as the oldest international organization, was created. This emphasizes that the need for cooperation on shared water resources became apparent early in the history of international relations.

A regional initiative of particular political importance is the 1960 Indus Water Treaty.[78] The treaty regulates the use of water from the Indus river and its tributaries: Pakistan is allowed to use the three western (water-rich) rivers, while India may use the three eastern rivers. As India's intensive use of water contributed to the eastern rivers on Pakistani territory drying up, Pakistan received financial support to supply water from other sources to these lower reaches. Since the treaty's ratification, there have been no military conflicts between India and Pakistan over the water; most disputes have

[75] See <http://treaties.un.org/pages/ViewDetails.aspx?src=TREATY&mtdsg_no=XXVII-12&chapter=27&lang=en> accessed 24 September 2020.

[76] *Trail Smelter Case* (*United States v Canada*) (1938 and 1941) 3 RIAA 1905, 1965.

[77] *Affaire du lac Lanoux* (*Espagne v France*) (1957) 12 RIAA 281, 310.

[78] Indus Waters Treaty 1960 between the Government of India, the Government of Pakistan and the International Bank for Reconstruction and Development (India–Pakistan) 419 UNTS 126; Hamir Sahni, 'The Politics of Water in South Asia: The Case of the Indus Waters Treaty' (2006) 26 SAIS Review 153; Majed Akhter, 'The Hydropolitical Cold War: The Indus Waters Treaty and State Formation in Pakistan' (2015) 46 Political Geography 65.

been settled via legal procedures. The most pertinent case has been the Indus Waters Kishenganga Arbitration.[79] The case concerned the Kishenganga Hydro-Electric Project (KHEP) located on the Kishenganga/Neelum River ruling that India, the upstream State, may under the Indus Water Treaty use water from the river for power generation, but that a minimum flow of water in the river must always be maintained for the downstream regions.

Other regional initiatives of particular relevance are the Nile Basin Initiative (NBI),[80] an intergovernmental partnership of ten Nile Basin countries established in 1999 to provide a forum for consultation and coordination for the sustainable management and development of the shared water, as well as the 1973 treaty between Brazil and Paraguay, concerning the hydroelectric utilization of the water resources of the Parana River, including the Iguazu region.[81]

Water-sharing is also particularly crucial in Central Asia,[82] and has led to a variety of agreements, such as in the Syr Darya Basin[83] between Kazakhstan, Kyrgyzstan, and Uzbekistan, as well as the rivers Chu and Talas between Kazakhstan and Kyrgyzstan.[84] Competition for water has often been a source of tensions, particularly between Uzbekistan and its upstream neighbours, but the situation has recently been more relaxed,[85] *inter alia* because of the successful regional water-sharing agreements.

3. Hybrid Matters of Security through and Security from Water

In some instances, the dimensions of security through water and security from water are inextricably linked. This is particularly so in the cases of international humanitarian law (IHL) and international criminal law (ICL), and has also become apparent in the most prominent water-related ICJ cases.

[79] *Indus Waters Kishenganga Arbitration (Pakistan v India)* (2013) 31 RIAA 1, 358.

[80] For further information, see Nile Basin Initiative (Nile-Sec) <http://www.nilebasin.org> accessed 11 September 2019.

[81] Treaty concerning the Hydroelectric Utilization of the Water Resources of the Parana River Owned in Condominium by the Two Countries, from and including the Salto Grande de Sete Quedas or Salto del Guaira, to the mouth of the Iguassu River (Brazil, Paraguay) 923 UNTS 57 (Brazil–Paraguay Treaty).

[82] Aibet Zhupankhan et al, 'Water in Kazakhstan, a Key in Central Asian Water Management' (2018) 63 Hydrological Sciences Journal 752; Barbara Janusz-Pawletta, 'Current Legal Challenges to Institutional Governance of Transboundary Water Resources in Central Asia and Joint Management Arrangements' (2015) 73 Environmental Earth Sciences 887.

[83] Agreement on the Use of Water and Energy Resources of the Syr Darya Basin (adopted 17 March 1998) <https://iea.uoregon.edu/treaty-text/1998-waterenergyresourcessyrdaryabasinentxt> accessed 11 September 2019.

[84] Agreement on the Use of Water Management Facilities of Intergovernmental Status on the Rivers Chu and Talas (adopted 21 January 2000).

[85] Martin Russell, 'Water in Central Asia: An Increasingly Scarce Resource' (*European Parliamentary Research Service PE 625.181*, EU 2018) <https://www.europarl.europa.eu/thinktank/en/document.html?reference=EPRS_BRI(2018)625181> accessed 29 November 2020.

a. *Water-related Provisions in International Humanitarian Law*

Under Article 54(2) Additional Protocol I (AP I), applicable to international armed conflicts (IACs), it is 'prohibited to attack, destroy, remove or render useless objects indispensable to the survival of the civilian population, such as (…) drinking water installations and supplies (…)'.[86] Protection of these objects is restricted for a select number of cases under Article 54(3) and (4) AP I, when objects are solely used for members of the armed forces or in direct support of military activity and if the civilian population can survive without them.

Additional Protocol II (AP II), applicable to non-international armed conflicts (NIACs), provides in Article 14 that 'it is (…) prohibited to attack, destroy, remove or render useless (…) objects indispensable to the survival of the civilian population, such as (…) drinking water installations and supplies and irrigation works'.[87] There are no restrictions to this rule for AP II comparable to AP I. The norms do not specify whether the water sources themselves (rather than water installations) are indispensable objects in the sense of the norm. This could potentially include lakes, rivers, and even aquifers, which would broaden the protection of water under AP I and AP II extensively,[88] and even electricity-generating plants that supply power to water pumping and water purifying installations.[89]

In IACs, under Article 56(1) AP I, dams and dykes may not be attacked, if such an attack would unleash dangerous forces. This special protection ends according to Article 56(2a) AP I if dams or dykes are used for other than their normal functions in regular, significant, and direct support of military operations, and if the attack is the only way to stop such support. For NIACs, Article 15 AP II states that dams and dykes may not be attacked, even where they are military objectives, if the attack would cause the release of dangerous forces and consequent severe losses in civilian population.

These provisions show that water shall never be used as a target or weapon during IACs or NIACs. International humanitarian law recognizes the vital role of water simultaneously with its tragically great potential as a weapon in warfare.

b. *Water-related Provisions in International Criminal Law*

The International Criminal Court (ICC) Statute offers several connections to water-related crimes. Genocide can be committed by causing serious harm to members of the group (Article 6(b) ICC Statute) or by deliberately inflicting on the group conditions of life calculated to bring about its physical destruction in whole or in part (Article 6(c) ICC Statute).[90] Both alternatives are well imaginable through water deprivation or

[86] 1125 UNTS 3. [87] 1125 UNTS 609.

[88] Mara Tignino, 'Water, International Peace, and Security' (2010) 92 International Review of the Red Cross 647, 659.

[89] ibid; Toni Pfanner, 'Editorial' (2010) 92 International Review of the Red Cross 541, 542.

[90] 2187 UNTS 3.

inflicting a temporary drought on a population.[91] The notion of an ecocide, understood as the killing of nature itself,[92] has so far remained outside the scope of the ICC Statute.

Article 8(b)(iv) ICC Statute declares a war crime to be *inter alia* 'an attack in the knowledge that such attack will (…) [cause] widespread, long-term and severe damage to the natural environment which would be clearly excessive in relation to the concrete and direct overall military advantage anticipated'. This is, in fact, the one provision in which the ICC Statute addresses crimes resulting in environmental damage explicitly.

Crimes against humanity (Article 7 ICC Statute) is the broadest category of crimes under the ICC Statute.[93] The definition of 'widespread or systematic attack directed against any civilian population' certainly encompasses possible crimes relating to water as target or weapon. Interestingly, in 2016 the Prosecutor announced that it would consider, in the selection of crimes to be submitted to the ICC's jurisdiction, crimes that were either committed through, or resulting in, the destruction of the environment or the illegal exploitation of natural resources.[94] This proposal has been criticized harshly in the literature and by States,[95] and in light of the ICC's ongoing legitimacy crisis,[96] it remains to be seen whether the Prosecutor goes through with this ambitious agenda.

c. *Disaster Response Law*

International humanitarian law and ICL are accompanied by international disaster response law (IDRL), a form of soft law as pronounced by the Red Cross,[97] UNGA[98] and by the Task Force on Ethical and Legal Issues in Humanitarian Assistance (Mohonk

[91] Office of the UN Special Adviser on the Prevention of Genocide, 'Analysis Framework' (2009) <http://www.un.org/ar/preventgenocide/adviser/pdf/osapg_analysis_framework.pdf> accessed 24 September 2020.

[92] Polly Higgins et al, 'Protecting the Planet: A Proposal for a Law of Ecocide' (2013) 59 Crime, Law and Social Change 251; Martin Crook/Damien Short, 'Marx, Lemkin and the Genocide-Ecocide Nexus' (2014) 18 International Journal of Human Rights 298.

[93] Pierre Thielbörger, 'International Criminal Law' in Hans-Joachim Heintze/Pierre Thielbörger (eds), *International Humanitarian Action* (Springer 2018) 189.

[94] Office of the Prosecutor, 'Policy Paper on Case Selection and Prioritisation' (15 September 2016) para 41 <https://www.icc-cpi.int/itemsDocuments/20160915_OTP-Policy_Case-Selection_Eng.pdf> accessed 11 September 2019.

[95] For a good overview see Nadia Bernaz, 'An Analysis of the ICC Office of the Prosecutor's Policy Paper on Case Selection and Prioritization from the Perspective of Business and Human Rights' (2017) 15 JICJ 527; Jessica Durney, 'Crafting a Standard: Environmental Crimes as Crimes Against Humanity Under the International Criminal Court' (2018) 24 Hastings Environmental Law Journal 413.

[96] Burundi declared its withdrawal in October 2016, the Philippines in March 2018. See ICC, 'Situation in the Republic of Burundi' <https://www.icc-cpi.int/burundi> accessed 11 September 2019; ICC, 'ICC Statement on The Philippines' Notice of Withdrawal: State Participation in Rome Statute System Essential to International Rule of Law' (20 March 2018) <https://www.icc-cpi.int/Pages/item.aspx?name=pr1371> accessed 11 September 2019.

[97] See IFRC, 'Introduction to the Guidelines for the Domestic Facilitation and Regulation of International Disaster Relief and Initial Recovery Assistance' (2011).

[98] UNGA Res 63/139 (5 March 2009); UNGA Res 63/141 (10 March 2009).

criteria).[99] While water is in most cases not mentioned directly, the guidelines provide that where a government is unable or unwilling to provide life-sustaining aid itself, the international community has the right and obligation to protect and provide relief to affected and threatened civilian populations, in conformity with international law principles.[100] Such life-sustaining aid is largely understood to encompass water[101] as a key component of such help.

d. *Settlement of Water Disputes at the International Court of Justice*

The ICJ has often had to deal with cases relating to water security, the three most influential of which were *Gabčíkovo-Nagymaros*,[102] *Pulp Mills*,[103] and the *Construction of a Road in Costa Rica along the San Juan River*.[104] The Court emphasized in *Gabčíkovo-Nagymaros* that the protection of the environment is an 'essential interest' of a State and could substantiate a state of environmental necessity (Article 33 of the Articles on the Responsibility of States for Internationally Wrongful Acts).[105] The ICJ also stated that, when weighing different values against each other, for instance within a proportionality test, environmental considerations, like the protection of water, can play a particularly important role.[106] The ICJ's findings on environmental impact assessment (EIA) in *Pulp Mills* are of particular relevance. The Court recognized the need to conduct an EIA as forming part of customary international law, whenever there is risk of pollution with transboundary effects (as is the case with shared watercourses).[107] This was upheld in the *Construction of a Road* case, where the ICJ determined the threshold for (illegal) transboundary harm to be that of 'significant' or 'substantial' character.[108] Furthermore, the ICJ is currently confronted with another prominent water dispute in the pending case between Chile and Bolivia relating to the use of shared waters, in which Chile relies on the Watercourses Convention as part of customary international law (as neither State is party to the Convention).[109]

[99] Jon M Ebersole, 'The Mohonk Criteria for Humanitarian Assistance in Complex Emergencies: Task Force on Ethical and Legal Issues in Humanitarian Assistance' (1995) 17 Human Rights Quarterly 192.

[100] ibid 197, principle II.4.

[101] J Benton Heath, 'Disasters, Relief, and Neglect: The Duty to Accept Humanitarian Assistance and the Work of the International Law Commission' (2011) 43 NYU Journal of International Law and Policy 419, 463.

[102] *Gabčíkovo-Nagymaros Project* (*Hungary v Slovakia*) (Judgment) [1997] ICJ Rep 7.

[103] *Pulp Mills on the River Uruguay* (*Argentina v Uruguay*) (Judgment) [2010] ICJ Rep 14.

[104] *Certain Activities Carried Out by Nicaragua in the Border Area* (*Costa Rica v Nicaragua*) *and Construction of a Road in Costa Rica along the San Juan River* (*Nicaragua v Costa Rica*) (Judgment) [2015] ICJ Rep 665.

[105] *Gabčíkovo-Nagymaros Project* (n 102) [53]. [106] ibid [140].

[107] *Pulp Mills* (n 103) [204].

[108] *Nicaragua v Costa Rica* (n 104) [104], [112], [143], [155] and especially [187] et seq.

[109] *Dispute over the Status and Use of the Waters of the Silala* (*Chile v Bolivia*) (Application Instituting Proceedings) [2016] ICJ <https://www.icj-cij.org/files/case-related/162/162-20,160,606-APP-01-00-EN.pdf> accessed 24 September 2020.

C. Recent Developments and Contemporary Challenges

While many important issues and challenges exist with regard to water security, the present analysis will focus on three: the privatization of water; water stress aggravated by climate change, and the global sanitation crisis.

1. Privatization of Water

Water is one of the most financially valuable goods worldwide. Publicly run water services are a noble but naive idea. Engaging the private sector offers access to financial resources otherwise unavailable to States. Such resources can be used for better and faster realization of the human right to water, if sufficiently regulated by State authorities.

Unsurprisingly, investment law has gained importance over the years in water management, particularly in cases of (failed) water privatization. Certain water disputes before investment tribunals have attracted attention since the 1990s. These include *Aguas del Tunari*[110] (dubbed as the 'water war of Cochabamba' by the media), *Azurix*,[111] and *Aguas del Aconquija*[112]—often with favourable results for investors.[113] The most important arbitral awards of the recent past relating to water privatization include *Biwater v Tanzania*,[114] *Suez v Argentina*,[115] *Saur v Argentina*,[116] and *Pac Rim Cayman LLC v Republic of El Salvador*.[117] Whether ICSID (International Centre for Settlement of Investment Disputes) tribunals should refer to human rights as part of the applicable law when addressing water-related investment disputes,[118] and to what extent they have

[110] *Aguas del Tunari, S.A. v Republic of Bolivia* (Decision on Jurisdiction) [2005] ICSID Case No ARB/02/3.

[111] *Azurix Corp. v The Argentine Republic* (Award) [2006] ICSID Case No ARB/01/12.

[112] *Compañiá de Aguas del Aconquija S.A. and Vivendi Universal S.A. v Argentine Republic* (Annulment Decision) [2010] ICSID Case No ARB/97/3.

[113] For more detail, Pierre Thielbörger, 'The Human Right to Water Versus Investor Rights: Double-Dilemma or Pseudo-Conflict?' in Pierre-Marie Dupuy et al (eds), *Human Rights in International Investment Law and Arbitration* (OUP 2009).

[114] *Biwater Gauff (Tanzania) Ltd v United Republic of Tanzania* (Award) [2008] ICSID Case No ARB/05/22.

[115] *Suez, Sociedad General de Aguas de Barcelona, S.A. and Vivendi Universal, S.A. v Argentine Republic* (Decision on Liability) [2010] ICSID Case No ARB/03/19.

[116] *SAUR International SA v Republic of Argentina* (Award) [2014] ICSID Case No ARB/04/4.

[117] *Pac Rim Cayman LLC v Republic of El Salvador* (Award) [2016] ICSID Case No ARB/09/12.

[118] ibid.

done so in the past, remains an open question.[119] A case pertinent to water security is *Urbaser v Argentina*,[120] in which the arbitral tribunal directly referred to the right to water[121] and also discussed the possibility of holding the investor responsible for a possible human rights violation. Argentina had filed a counterclaim to Urbaser's original claim, emphasizing the investor's lack of investment in promoting the human right to water.[122]

It will be interesting to see whether discussions on the human rights obligations of corporations, currently under review by several UN-led initiatives,[123] will also reach the realm of investment arbitration. This pertains to the broader question of interactions between different water-related legal regimes.[124]

2. Climate Change as Catalyst for Global Water Stress

Climate change will put further strain on a world already in ecological distress. This is particularly pertinent when it comes to water. In the 2018 IPCC report,[125] experts emphasized the dramatic climate change-related vulnerability of water systems. The report explicitly warns, *inter alia*, of the imminence of long-term sea-level rise,[126] in particular marine ice sheet instability in Antarctica or loss of the Greenland ice sheet;[127]

[119] Instructive in this regard, Silvia Steininger, 'What's Human Rights Got to Do With It? An Empirical Analysis of Human Rights References in Investment Arbitration' (2018) 31 Leiden Journal of International Law 33.

[120] *Urbaser S.A. and Consorcio de Aguas Bilbao Bizkaia, Bilbao Biskaia Ur Partzuergoa v The Argentine Republic* (Award) [2016] ICSID Case No ARB/07/26.

[121] ibid, eg paras 720–1, 1193 et seq.

[122] For more information, see Kevin Crow/Lina L Escobar, 'International Corporate Obligations, Human Rights, and the Urbaser Standard: Breaking New Ground' (2018) 36 Boston University International Law Journal 87; Stefanie Schacherer, *International Investment Law and Sustainable Development: Key Cases from the 2010s* (International Institute for Sustainable Development 2018); Edward Guntrip, 'Private Actors and Public Goods and Responsibility for the Right to Water in International Investment Law: An Analysis of *Urbaser v Argentina*' (2018) 1 Brill Open Law 37.

[123] See Open-ended Intergovernmental Working Group on Transnational Corporations and Other Business Enterprises with respect to Human Rights, 'Legally Binding Instrument to Regulate, in International Human Rights Law, the Activities of Transnational Corporations and Other Business Enterprises' (16 July 2018) <https://www.ohchr.org/Documents/HRBodies/HRCouncil/WGTransCorp/Session3/DraftLBI.pdf> accessed 29 November 2020. For a critical appraisal, Pierre Thielbörger/Tobias Ackermann, 'A Treaty on Enforcing Human Rights Against Businesses: Closing the Loophole or Getting Stuck in a Loop' (2017) 24 Indiana Journal of Global Legal Studies 43.

[124] No general international regime concerning wastewater exists, only bilateral agreements. The most important ones include the US–Mexico agreement concerning an international wastewater treatment plant near San Diego developed by the International Boundary and Water Commission (IBWC), see Conceptual Plan for the International Solution to the Border Sanitation Problem in San Diego, California, Tijuana, Baja California (USA–Mexico) 2203 UNTS 105.

[125] Intergovernmental Panel on Climate Change, 'Special Report SR1.5, Global Warming of 1.5°C' (IPCC, 2018) <https://www.ipcc.ch/sr15/> accessed 24 September 2020.

[126] IPCC, *Summary for Policymakers* (n 14); for more details see chs 1.2 (56–67), 3.3 (186–211).

[127] ibid ch B.2.2.

irreversible impacts of climate change on oceanic ecosystems;[128] a regional increase in intensity or frequency of droughts;[129] the exposure of small islands, low-lying coastal areas, and deltas to rising sea levels and increased saltwater intrusion into freshwater systems;[130] increased risks to human health and water supply;[131] and overall the climate change-induced increase in water stress.[132] It continuously emphasizes the dramatic difference for water security between a 1.5°C versus a 2°C global warming scenario.

Other prominent global reports echo the IPCC's warning of climate change-induced water-distress in the future. The 2016 edition of the Global Risks Report, published by the World Economic Forum, states that climate change (and the failure to prevent and to adapt) as well as water crises are perceived as two of the three biggest future global challenges, as a large-scale survey of business, academia, civil society, and the public sector representatives has shown.[133]

3. The Sanitation Gap

Finally, if water features on the international agenda—sanitation does much less so.[134] In contrast to water, the international community is clearly failing on sanitation as recent monitoring of the MDGs indicates.[135] Apart from the doctrinal question whether water and sanitation should be treated as one or separate human rights,[136] the world is indeed facing a sanitation crisis.

This crisis persists for several reasons. Most prominent amongst these is the unease associated with publicly discussing toilets, putting them on the political agenda or raising private funds to improve the realization of the right to sanitation.[137] To raise awareness for the topic, the UN declared 2008 as the 'Year of Sanitation'.[138] Former Special Rapporteur, Catarina de Albuquerque, rightly focused on sanitation as one of the first

[128] ibid chs A.3.1 and A.3.2. [129] ibid ch B.1.1. [130] ibid ch B.2.3.
[131] ibid ch B.5. [132] ibid ch B.5.4.
[133] WEF, Global Risk Report 2016 (11th edn, 2016) 6 <http://www3.weforum.org/docs/GRR/WEF_GRR16.pdf> accessed 11 September 2019.
[134] For a good overview over the right to sanitation, see Inga T Winkler, 'The Human Right to Sanitation' (2016) 37 University of Pennsylvania Journal of International Law 1331.
[135] See eg the MDGs Report (n 31) 7, 58, according to which 'globally, 147 countries have met the drinking water target', and only '95 countries have met the sanitation target', meaning that in 2015, 2.4 billion people were still using unimproved sanitation facilities, including 946 million people who were still practising open defecation. This makes the MDG target on sanitation one lagging behind most other MDGs.
[136] Thielbörger (n 10) 120ff.
[137] See Catarina de Albuquerque, *On the Right Track: Good Practices in Realising the Rights to Water and Sanitation* (UNESCO WWAP 2012) 73ff, especially 78.
[138] UNGA Res 61/192 (6 February 2007).

topics during her mandate.[139] Nonetheless, the numbers remain depressing: according to most recent estimations, 4.5 billion people lack access to safely managed sanitation and 892 million people still practise open defecation.[140] This becomes even more dramatic if one considers that this lack of safe sanitation closely relates to high child mortality rates in developing countries.[141] It remains to be seen whether and when the international community will take up this most severe sanitation challenge.

D. Conclusion

The human right to water has been a success story of the last twenty years, a story which other 'new' human rights could use as a model.[142] Equally, the entry into force in 2014 of the Watercourse Convention gives reason for optimism with regard to the peaceful settlement of inter-State water disputes. Nonetheless, as the foregoing analysis revealed, significant challenges with regard to water security, both in terms of security *through* water and security *from* water, remain.

The work does not end with the establishment of a (legally binding) norm—rather, the focus needs to shift. The bare establishment of the human right to water does not stop global thirst; equally, the entry into force of the Watercourse Convention does not mark the end of water conflicts. Academic and political focus now has to shift from fighting for acceptance of the new norms to ensuring their implementation.

With regard to the Watercourse Convention, we are now barely above the necessary number of thirty-five ratifications. Since its entry into force only one new State (Palestine) has acceded to the Convention. The Convention is thus far from being globally accepted and from making the difference that so many observers hope it would make.

Similarly, the numerical improvement vis-à-vis the realization of the right to water has been reached by improving the situation in certain countries (such as China and India), but there has not been a global improvement yet. Additionally, huge disparity exists between realizing access to water in urban and rural areas. The divide has arguably become even greater in recent years as urban populations have disproportionally benefited from the expansion of water services. This is due to the fact that expansion in cities is more profitable than building water services in rural areas.

[139] Ms de Albuquerque chose the topic of sanitation as her focus in 2009, culminating in UNGA 'Report of the Independent Expert on the issue of Human Rights Obligations related to Access to Safe Drinking Water and Sanitation' (1 July 2009) UN Doc A/HRC/12/24.

[140] UNGA Res 39/8 (5 October 2018) preamble.

[141] Günther Fink et al, 'The Effect of Water and Sanitation on Child Health: Evidence from the Demographic and Health Surveys 1986–2007' (2011) 40 International Journal of Epidemiology 1196.

[142] Thielbörger (n 11).

If water security on a global scale is to be realized, this requires (almost all) States to accept the basic rules on sharing watercourses, as laid down in the Watercourse Convention, and a universal realization of the human right to water expanding beyond a privileged part of the global population.

Acknowledgement

Thanks to Rouven Diekjobst, Vanessa Bliecke, and Maximilian Bertamini for help with editing and research for this chapter.

ENVIRONMENTAL SECURITY

CHAPTER 30

CLIMATE CHANGE AND SECURITY

JOYEETA GUPTA AND HILMER BOSCH

A. Introduction

It is almost two centuries since the greenhouse gas problem was signalled and thirty years since negotiations on the climate change problem began in earnest.[1] The window for keeping climate change within manageable limits is closing soon; existing policy within the Paris Agreement on Climate Change seems to be on track towards a world where the average temperatures rise by more than 3°C in relation to pre-industrial times, considerably exceeding the considered 'safe' limit of 1.5-2°C.[2] Although there are ongoing negotiations to accelerate measures to reduce the emissions of greenhouse gases, the delay in taking measures implies that the measures needed to reduce emissions in line with the Paris Agreement will be themselves very drastic.

Successive reports of the Intergovernmental Panel on Climate Change (IPCC) have provided growing evidence of the impacts of climate change—including melting glaciers, melting polar regions, rising sea levels, rising global temperatures, and extreme weather events.[3] These impacts can lead to changing precipitation patterns and affect global water and food availability, while putting coastal and river basin regions under considerable pressure. Extreme weather events are increasing in intensity and number and are displacing and killing people and animals. The outbreak of fires in the US, Spain, and more recently in Australia (causing the death of more than 1 billion animals) have

[1] Joyeeta Gupta, *The History of Global Climate Governance* (CUP 2014).

[2] UNEP, 'Emissions Gap Report 2019: Global Progress Report on Climate Action' (26 November 2019) <https://www.unenvironment.org/interactive/emissions-gap-report/2019/> accessed 9 April 2020.

[3] Rajendra K Pachauri et al (eds), *Climate Change 2014: Synthesis Report* (Intergovernmental Panel on Climate Change 2015).

left large areas devastated and affected human lives, livelihoods, and property.[4] Super storms could even trigger nuclear disasters, through earthquake-like movements and flooding—not least because many nuclear power stations have been built on or near the sea shores.[5] Climate change can affect human well-being in terms of access to water, food, energy, and land (especially in coastal areas), as well as in terms of risks to human health.[6] Thus, climate change is seen as a driver of all other socio-ecological problems worldwide.[7] Climate change is also seen as a risk and threat multiplier,[8] as it can exacerbate existing challenges faced by States including the challenge of poor governance institutions and existing poverty. However, climate change policy could potentially be a 'threat minimizer' if mitigation and adaptation measures are integrated into the development paradigm.

A key question is—is climate change a security issue? Climate change has been on the political agenda since the 1980s and its security implications have been discussed since the early days. Early on in 1988, climate change was seen as 'second only to a global nuclear war'.[9] In 2009, the UN General Assembly (UNGA) adopted a Resolution on Climate Change and its possible security implications.[10] This led to a report prepared by the UN Secretary-General on the subject.[11] This report identifies five pathways of reduced security:

(a) *Vulnerability*: climate change threatens food security and human health, and increases human exposure to extreme events;

[4] Tom Jeffrey et al, '2019 Wildfire Risk Report' (*CoreLogic*, 2019) <https://www.corelogic.com/downloadable-docs/wildfire-report_0919-01-screen.pdf> accessed 13 December 2019; John Henly, 'Spain Battles Biggest Wildfires in 20 Years as Heatwave Grips Europe' (*The Guardian*, 27 June 2019) <https://www.theguardian.com/world/2019/jun/27/hundreds-of-firefighters-tackle-blaze-in-north-east-spain> accessed 13 December 2019; Jessie Yeung, 'Australia's Deadly Wildfires are Showing No Signs of Stopping. Here's What You Need To Know' (*CNN*, 10 January 2020) <https://edition.cnn.com/2020/01/01/australia/australia-fires-explainer-intl-hnk-scli/index.html> accessed 30 November 2020.

[5] Frédéric Moreau, 'Climate Change and Nuclear Risk: The Forthcoming (Un)Natural Disasters' (*Facing Future. Earth*) <https://www.facingfuture.earth/climate-change-and-nuclear-risk-the-forthcoming-unnatural-disasters/> accessed 30 November 2020.

[6] Paul Ekins et al (eds), Global Environment Outlook—GEO-6: Healthy Planet Healthy People (CUP 2019).

[7] ibid.

[8] Climate change recognized as 'threat multiplier', 'UN Security Council Debates its Impact on Peace' (*UN News*, 25 January 2019) <https://news.un.org/en/story/2019/01/1031322> accessed 22 December 2019; European Council, 'Paper from the High Representative and the European Commission: Climate Change and International Security' (14 March 2008) S113/08; Simon Dalby, 'Climate Change and the Insecurity Frame' in Shannon O'Lear/Simon Dalby (eds), *Reframing Climate Change: Constructing Ecological Geopolitics* (Routledge 2015).

[9] WMO/UNEP, 'Statement: The Changing Atmosphere: Implications for Global Security' (Toronto, June 1988) 292 <http://cmosarchives.ca/History/ChangingAtmosphere1988e.pdf> accessed 20 November 2019.

[10] UNGA Res 63/281 (3 June 2009).

[11] UNGA 'Report of the Secretary General: Climate Change and its Possible Security Implications' (11 September 2009) UN Doc A/64/350 (Secretary-General Report).

(b) *Development*: if climate change results in slowing down or reversing the development process, this will exacerbate vulnerability and could undermine the capacity of States to maintain stability;
(c) *Coping and security*: migration, competition over natural resources, and other coping responses of households and communities faced with climate-related threats could increase the risk of domestic conflict as well as have international repercussions;
(d) *Statelessness*: there are implications for rights, security, and sovereignty of the loss of statehood because of the disappearance of territory;
(e) *International conflict*: there may be implications for international cooperation from climate change's impact on shared or undemarcated international resources.'[12]

Against this background, this chapter addresses the following issue: What is the nature of the security debate raised by the climate change issue and how is this being addressed within scholarly, as well as policy and legal fora? This chapter looks at the different ways in which security has been defined in the literature and its diverse implications for law and policy. The chapter first discusses the current status of the debate, turning then to recent developments and outlooks for the future.

B. Current Status of the Debate

1. Introduction

In assessing whether climate change has security implications, we first need to look at when the nature of the impacts qualifies as having security implications. What does the term 'security' mean in law and policy? Does a security definition enhance or aggravate the way in which climate change is addressed? A literature review in preparation for this chapter revealed that the security aspects of climate change are discussed broadly in a wide variety of disciplines and take on a wide variety of meanings. This chapter has therefore chosen not to interpret security in a narrow sense but to reflect on the diverse meanings of security in the literature.

While some divide the security debate into 'traditional' (or armed conflict-related) security challenges and non-conventional or human security-related risks,[13] others look at security issues in terms of the level at which they manifest themselves—from local to global, and yet others look also at the security implications for ecosystems.[14] In trying to make sense of this, this section looks at climate change security challenges in

[12] ibid.

[13] Ben Saul, 'Climate Change, Conflict and Security: International Law Challenges' (2009) 9 New Zealand Armed Forces Law Review 1.

[14] eg Matt McDonald, 'Climate Change and Security: Towards Ecological Security?' (2018) 10 International Theory 153.

terms of their local dimensions, national dimensions, inter-State dimensions, and global dimensions. Although there are multiple security dimensions that cut across these issues, we focus on migration as a key cross-cutting issue and deal with that separately. Each of these dimensions are explained briefly below.

2. Human Security

The United Nations Development Programme (UNDP) popularized the notion of human security; this gives the problem of climate and environmental impacts a human face.[15] Climate change is expected to have a huge impact on lives and livelihoods. Growing heat can lead to premature deaths but also affect agricultural productivity, water and food security, and livelihoods. Coral bleaching can affect fish populations, also affecting food security and livelihoods. In fact, thousands of humans have died prematurely because of the impacts of climate change—the World Health Organization (WHO) calculates this to be at around 150,000 in the period from mid-1970 to 2000.[16] The difference between 1.5 and 2°C may mean that several hundred million more people will face extreme poverty and climate impacts and the latest IPCC report expands on the degree to which people may suffer as a consequence. More people will be displaced by rising sea levels.[17]

An impact on human security can be addressed in legal terms through discussions on human rights and climate change:

> Thinking of climate change as a human rights issue can help us see that it is not just a matter of aggregate costs and benefits but of winners and losers—of the powerful few preventing the political system from acting to protect the powerless many. But perhaps even more importantly, treating climate change as a human rights issue simply begins to imbue it with a sense of gravity and moral urgency that communicates to all of us: this is something different; this is an issue that must be understood to stand apart from the normal clatter and noise of day-to-day politics and to demand attention from our best selves.[18]

Although there has been slow progress to develop the human rights agenda over the last thirty years,[19] the UN Human Rights Council has stated that 'climate change poses an

[15] Oscar A Gómez/Des Gasper, *Human Security: A Thematic Guidance Note for Regional and National Human Development Report Teams* (UNDP, 2013).

[16] 'Climate and Health: Fact Sheet, July 2005' (WHO, July 2005) <https://www.who.int/globalchange/news/fsclimandhealth/en/> accessed 23 November 2019.

[17] Valérie Masson-Delmotte et al (eds), *Global Warming of 1.5°C: An IPCC Special Report on the Impacts of Global Warming of 1.5°C above Pre-Industrial Levels and Related Global Greenhouse Gas Emission Pathways, in the Context of Strengthening the Global Response to the Threat of Climate Change, Sustainable Development, and Efforts to Eradicate Poverty* (IPCC 2019).

[18] Amy Sinden, 'Climate Change and Human Rights' (2008) 27 Journal of Land, Resources and Environmental Law 1, 17.

[19] Gupta (n 1).

immediate and far-reaching threat to people and communities around the world and has implications for the full enjoyment of human rights',[20] while the United Nations High Commissioner for Human Rights[21] recognized growing 'climate injustice' for the poor but did not go so far as to say that climate change violated human rights and hence was a breach of legal obligations. The adoption of a resolution on the Human Right to Water and Sanitation in 2010 by the UNGA linked water access to climate change.[22] The debate is on whether human rights approaches should be expanded to include a clear recognition of conditions under which human rights are violated by climate change. In the *Urgenda* case,[23] brought against the Netherlands for breach of its duty to reduce Greenhouse Gas emissions, the Court of Appeals of The Hague referred to the European Convention on Human Rights (ECHR) in its judgment, citing the violation of Articles 2 (right to life) and 8 (right to respect for private and family life).[24] This judgment has been upheld by the Supreme Court of the Netherlands.[25] At the other end of the spectrum—the right to development, and the right to promote sustainable development—are used to discuss the nature of mitigation issues.[26] The latest report of the UN Special Rapporteur on Human Rights and the Environment discusses how human rights are violated by climate change and comes with strong recommendations.[27]

[20] HRC Res 7/23, 'Human Rights and Climate Change' (28 March 2008) 1.

[21] UNGA 'Annual Report of the United Nations High Commissioner for Human Rights and Reports of the Office of the High Commissioner and the Secretary-General' (15 January 2009) UN Doc A/HRC/10/61.

[22] UNGA Res 64/292 (28 July 2010).

[23] This case inspired cases in Belgium, Canada, Colombia, France, Germany, Ireland, India, New Zealand, Norway, Pakistan, Switzerland, US, the UK, and against the EU. 'Global Climate Litigation' (*Urgenda*) <https://www.urgenda.nl/en/themas/climate-case/global-climate-litigation/> accessed 5 January 2020; for a mapping of the climate change related litigation: 'Climate Change Litigation Databases' (*Climatechangechart*) <http://climatecasechart.com/> accessed 14 January 2020.

[24] Ingrid Leijten, 'Human Rights v Insufficient Climate Action: The Urgenda Case' (2019) 37 Netherlands Quarterly of Human Rights 112; Johannes Fahner, 'Climate Change Before the Courts: Urgenda Ruling Redraws the Boundary between Law and Politics' (*EJIL: Talk!*, 16 November 2018) <https://www.ejiltalk.org/climate-change-before-the-courts-urgenda-ruling-redraws-the-boundary-between-law-and-politics/> accessed 14 January 2020.

[25] For a comment: André Nollkaemper/Laura Burgers, 'A New Classic in Climate Change Litigation: The Dutch Supreme Court Case in the Urgenda Litigation' (*EJIL:Talk!*, 6 January 2020) <https://www.ejiltalk.org/a-new-classic-in-climate-change-litigation-the-dutch-supreme-court-decision-in-the-urgenda-case/> accessed 14 January 2020; 'Dutch State to Reduce Greenhouse Gas Emissions by 25% by the End of 2020' (*De Rechtspraakt*, 20 December 2019) <https://www.rechtspraak.nl/Organisatie-en-contact/Organisatie/Hoge-Raad-der-Nederlanden/Nieuws/Paginas/Dutch-State-to-reduce-greenhouse-gas-emissions-by-25-by-the-end-of-2020.aspx> accessed 14 January 2020.

[26] Joyeeta Gupta/Karin Arts, 'Achieving the 1.5°C Objective: Just Implementation Through a Right to (Sustainable) Development' (2018) 18 International Environmental Agreements: Politics, Law and Economics 11.

[27] UNEP, 'Safe Climate: A Report of the Special Rapporteur on Human Rights and the Environment' (1 October 2019) UN Doc A/74/161.

3. National Security and State Survival

National security aggregates the challenges faced by humans within the national context in terms of statistical data and societal trends and climate change is often described in the literature as a challenge for national security.[28] This can be in terms of an existential crisis for some States; it can be in terms of the potential for great suffering including violent conflict; and it can be in terms of the security consequences for other States where it borders on inter-State security issues.

For small island States such as Tuvalu and the Maldives, the question of physical survival is serious.[29] The potential loss of national territory with resulting statelessness and displacement are critical challenges for these States.[30] Although there is an increasing amount of research on the impacts of climate change, the UNGA notes that '[t]here is little empirical research on the fourth channel, as it is one that poses truly unprecedented challenges to States and to the international community'.[31] A special element of this is the issue of statelessness. If the land where people live disappears, the State in theory ceases to exist. How can stateless people then be addressed? Who can be held responsible for causing such statelessness and who can provide relief to the people who become stateless? In the legal literature, securitization has been linked to possible court cases. The potential for small island States to seek international legal redress has been extensively discussed in the literature but some argue that this may face challenges of causality and responsibility, not least because most States have now ratified the Paris Agreement on Climate Change.[32] However, many of these small island States have clearly stated, while ratifying, that such ratification does not imply that other States are exempt from responsibility. For example, the Cook Islands have specified in its declaration upon ratification as follows:

> *Declaration*: The Government of the Cook Islands declares its understanding that acceptance of the Paris Agreement and its application shall in no way constitute a renunciation of any rights under international law concerning State responsibility for the adverse effects of climate change and that no provision in the Paris Agreement can be interpreted as derogating from principles of general international law or any claims or rights concerning compensation due to the impacts of climate change.
>
> The Government of the Cook Islands further declares that, in light of the best available scientific information and assessment on climate change and its impacts, it considers the emissions reduction obligations in the aforesaid Paris Agreement to be inadequate to prevent a global temperature stabilisation level at or above

[28] Joshua W Busby, 'Who Cares About the Weather? Climate Change and US National Security' (2008) 17 Security Studies 468.

[29] Marc Limon, 'Human Rights and Climate Change: Constructing a case for Political Action' (2009) 33 Harvard Environmental Law Review 439.

[30] Saul (n 13) para 17.

[31] Secretary-General Report (n 11) para 20 s 17.

[32] Paris Agreement UNTC No 54113, 187.

> 1.5 degrees Celsius relative to pre-industrial levels and as a consequence, such emissions will have severe implications for our national interests.[33]

For many other States, the impacts of climate change can exacerbate problems of drought and floods, high temperatures, and have health impacts. About 70 per cent of States who produce a national security report have discussed climate security in their reports.[34] About thirty-three States are at risk of political destabilization as a consequence of rising prices of food and about thirty-six States house people who may suffer from lack of access to food and water within the next five years.[35] According to some scholars, about half the world population may be at risk of violent conflict:

> There are 46 countries—home to 2.7 billion people—in which the effects of climate change interacting with economic, social and political problems will create a high risk of violent conflict. There is a second group of 56 countries where the institutions of government will have great difficulty taking the strain of climate change on top of all their other current challenges.[36]

Although there is debate as to whether conflicts are driven by climate change alone, one historical study of 8000 conflicts between the years 1400 and 1900 shows that climate change is linked to an increase in conflict especially through the impacts on crops, food prices and access, and relative food scarcity was a key reason for this.[37]

Such conflict is not only a challenge for the individual State, but can be seen as raising security concerns for other States too. Intelligence agencies in the US are warning their government that '[g]lobal environmental and ecological degradation, as well as climate change, are likely to fuel competition for resources, economic distress, and social discontent through 2019 and beyond.'[38]

One of the international legal and policy solutions to the potential rise of ecological disasters is the law and policy on disaster risk management. At the international level,

[33] 'Status of Treaties: Paris Agreement' (*United Nations Treaty Collection*) <https://treaties.un.org/Pages/ViewDetails.aspx?src=TREATY&mtdsg_no=XXVII-7-d&chapter=27&clang=_en#EndDec> accessed 18 November 2019.

[34] Andrew Holland/Xander Vagg, 'The Global Security Defense Index on Climate Change: Preliminary Results National Security Perspectives on Climate Change from Around the World' (American Security Project, 21 March 2013) <https://www.americansecurityproject.org/ASP%20Reports/Ref%200121%20-%20Global%20Security%20Defense%20Index%20P-Results.pdf> accessed 21 December 2019, cited in Shirley V Scott, 'Implications of Climate Change for the UN Security Council' (2015) 91 International Affairs 1317.

[35] US National Intelligence Council, *Global Trends 2025: A Transformed World* (US Government Printing Office 2008).

[36] Dan Smith/Janani Vivekananda, *A Climate of Conflict: The Links between Climate Change, Peace and War* (International Alert 2007).

[37] David D Zhang et al, 'Global Climate Change, War, and Population Decline in Recent Human History' (2007) 104 Proceedings of the National Academy of Sciences of the United States of America 19, 214.

[38] Daniel R Coats, 'Worldwide Threat Assessment of the US Intelligence Community' (29 January 2019) 23 <https://www.dni.gov/files/ODNI/documents/2019-ATA-SFR---SSCI.pdf> accessed 19 November 2019.

the UN Office for Disaster Risk Reduction, created in December 1999, 'works towards the substantial reduction of disaster risk and losses to ensure a sustainable future'.[39] At the heart of disaster risk reduction, amongst others, are climate change, displacement, and the collapse of financial systems. More recently, the International Organization for Migration (IOM) became a related organization of the UN, focusing on 'promoting humane and orderly migration for the benefit of all'.[40] Many other UN agencies and organizations are committed to reducing disaster risks.[41] The EU increasingly incorporates disaster risk reduction in its development cooperation policies.[42]

4. Interstate Dimensions: The United Nations Framework Convention on Climate Change versus the Security Council

Apart from the larger consequences for humanity and ecosystems as a whole, climate change will have serious impacts on people within States and on inter-State relations. Since 1990, the climate change problem has been subject to negotiations. These negotiations have been conducted within the auspices of the UNGA and within the regime of the United Nations Framework Convention on Climate Change (UNFCCC). Unlike other international environmental issues, within two years of negotiations a universal Convention on Climate Change was adopted in 1992, which came into force in 1994. The Convention set out a long-term qualitative objective, principles for the allocation of responsibility, targets for industrialized States listed in Annex 1, and mechanisms for implementing the Convention. As the targets were seen as falling short of what was necessary, the Kyoto Protocol was adopted in 1997 with quantified targets for industrialized States listed in Annex B. Although the Kyoto Protocol entered into force significantly later in 2005, its ultimate success was marred as the whole of North America (the US and Canada) did not participate in implementing the targets for the first commitment

[39] 'About UNDRR' (UN Disaster Risk Reduction, 2019) <https://www.undrr.org/about-undrr> accessed 28 December 2019.

[40] UNGA, 'Note by the Secretary-General: Agreement concerning the Relationship between the United Nations and the International Organization for Migration' (8 July 2016) UN Doc A/70/976; 'About IOM' (*IOM UN Migration*) <https://www.iom.int/about-iom> accessed 27 December 2019.

[41] Including the: World Meteorological Organization, UNESCO, Food Agricultural Organization, World Food Programme, International Atomic Energy Authority, International Labour Organization, International Telecommunication Union, UN Office for the Coordination of Humanitarian Affairs, Office of the High Commissioner for Human Rights, UN Centre for Regional Development, UN Development Operations Coordination Office, UNDP (Bureau for Crisis Prevention and Recovery), UN Economic Commission for Europe, UN Environment Programme, and many others.

[42] eg Commission of the European Union, 'EU Strategy for Supporting Disaster Risk Reduction in Developing Countries' (23 February 2009) COM(2009)84final; Commission of the European Union, 'The EU Approach to Resilience: Learning From Food Security Crises' (3 October 2010) EC(2012)586final; Commission of the European Union, 'Action Plan for Resilience in Crisis Prone Countries 2013-2020' (19 June 2013) SWD(2013)227final.

period (2008–12) in the Protocol, while the follow-up Doha Amendment for the period (2012–20) with quantified targets for States never entered into force. Jubilation regarding the 2015 Paris Agreement may be a little short-sighted, as although the Agreement quantified the long-term objective by specifying that global temperatures should not rise above 2°C and should if possible stay as low as 1.5°C with respect to pre-industrial levels, the US has already notified its withdrawal from the Paris Agreement (on 4 November 2019—withdrawal takes effect a year from the date of notification),[43] while the EU has voted in favour of a resolution declaring a climate and environmental emergency (29 November 2019)[44] and presented the Green Deal on 11 December 2019 aiming to be climate neutral by 2050.[45] The Paris Agreement includes a long-term objective but relies on ambitious Nationally Determined Contributions which some see as vague and voluntary; others, however, argue that the Agreement is legal even if it is weak in enforcement.[46] The issue of compensating States for the loss and damage they face may have received greater attention through security framing, but whether it will lead to major change is not clear.[47]

The Climate Change Convention regime is remarkable in that despite the huge, and sometimes perceived as contradictory, stakes involved in terms of economic, social, and ecological goals, it has been a centralized and active regime bringing 193 States together regularly for three decades. The problem is that the initial idea, that the industrialized States would take the lead in showing the developing world that it was possible to develop without major greenhouse gas emissions, failed as North America has not participated in implementing the quantitative targets and developing States have thus continued to follow a carbon-intensive production process, although many of them have significantly altered their energy production patterns to actively invest in renewables, including China and India. China, for example, is the biggest investing country, having committed US$758 billion between 2010 and mid-2019 to renewable energy; this is more than Europe as a whole, which invested US$698 billion in the same period.[48] Costa Rica is expecting that more than 99 per cent of its electricity will be generated from renewables

[43] Michael R Pompeo, 'Press Statement on the US Withdrawal from the Paris Agreement' (4 November 2019) <https://www.state.gov/on-the-u-s-withdrawal-from-the-paris-agreement/> accessed 30 November 2020.

[44] European Parliament, 'Resolution: Climate and Environmental Emergency' (28 November 2019) 2019/2930(RSP).

[45] Commission of the European Union, 'The European Green Deal' (11 December 2019) COM(2019)640final.

[46] Daniel Bodansky, 'The Legal Character of the Paris Agreement' (2016) 25 Review of European, Comparative and International Environmental Law 142.

[47] Francesco Sindico, 'Climate Change and Security' (2017) 3 Carbon and Climate Law Review 187.

[48] Frankfurt School-UNEP Centre/BNEF, 'Global Trends in Renewable Energy Investment 2019' (2019) <https://wedocs.unep.org/bitstream/handle/20.500.11822/29752/GTR2019.pdf?sequence=1&isAllowed=y> accessed 20 January 2020.

in 2019.[49] As a result of growing investments in renewables, the costs of solar photovoltaics and offshore wind went down by 81 per cent and 46 per cent respectively in the past decade.[50] Furthermore, 'a record 167GW of renewable power capacity (excluding large hydro) started production in 2018, up from 160GW in 2017. This made up almost 68% of all the net new generating capacity (fossil fuel, nuclear and renewable) added last year.'[51]

The problem with the Climate Change Convention and its follow-up Protocols, like all other international treaties, is that it is based on State consent and States can withdraw if they like based on their perception of their own national interest. The regime is subject to the idea of State sovereignty and hence when States feel threatened by the nature of the measures, they can opt out. The idea of not causing harm to other States was not included in the five principles governing the climate change regime and the international law on State responsibility is unable to address the issue of harm caused to others through the emissions of greenhouse gases.[52] The progressive development of law seems to have been unable to address issues where there are many emitters, where it is difficult to identify causal links, and where there are complex temporal dimensions.

The recurring question is whether securitizing the issue of climate change and bringing it to the attention of the UN Security Council (UNSC) can somehow bypass State unwillingness to take the climate change problem seriously. Scholars and policymakers have pushed the security agenda, thinking that this may be more influential.[53] Since the early days and particularly since 1992, there have been ongoing discussions in the scholarly literature to address climate change within the UNSC.[54] In 2007, the UNSC actually dealt with the issue, as a result of a number of factors, including: the leadership role taken on by the United Kingdom, the definition of the issue as a human security issue, and the need for sustainable development and the prevention of conflicts.[55] While many industrialized States and small island States have been interested in securing UNSC engagement, other developing States have been sceptical—seeing the UNSC as less democratic than other UN agencies.[56] Nevertheless, the UNSC has tabled the climate change issue in 2007, 2011, 2015, 2017—resulting in it adopting resolution 2349[57]—and

[49] Instituto Costarricense de Electricidad (Costa Rican Institute of Electricity), 'Costa Rica Superará 99 % de Generación Eléctrica Renovable en 2019' (*Grupo ICE*, 16 December 2019) <https://grupoicecr.com/costa-rica-superara-99-generacion-electrica-renovable-2019/> accessed 20 January 2020.

[50] Frankfurt School-UNEP Centre/BNEF (n 48).

[51] ibid 20.

[52] Florentina Simlinger/Benoit Mayer, 'Legal Responses to Climate Change Induced Loss and Damage' in Reinhard Mechler et al (eds), *Loss and Damage from Climate Change: Climate Risk Management, Policy and Governance* (Springer 2019).

[53] Peter H Gleick, 'Water, Drought, Climate Change, and Conflict in Syria' (2014) 6 Weather Climate and Society 331; Aryn Baker, 'How Climate Change is Behind the Surge of Migrants to Europe' (*Time Magazine*, 7 September 2015) <https://time.com/4024210/climate-change-migrants/> accessed 28 November 2019.

[54] Catherine Tinker, 'Environmental Security in the United Nations: Not a Matter for the Security Council' (1992) 59 Tennessee Law Review 787.

[55] Francesco Sindico, 'Climate Change: A Security (Council) Issue?' (2007) 1 Carbon and Climate Law Review 26.

[56] Sindico (n 47).

[57] UNSC Res 2349 (2017).

2018, by allowing States to discuss this more openly. Resolution 2349 stated that the UNSC:

> *Recognises* the adverse effects of climate change and ecological changes among other factors on the stability of the Region, including through water scarcity, drought, desertification, land degradation, and food insecurity, and *emphasises* the need for adequate risk assessments and risk management strategies by governments and the United Nations relating to these factors (original emphasis).

However, it remains unclear as to how the UNSC could perhaps address this problem.[58] Chapters VI and VII of the UN Charter highlight the different ways in which the UNSC can engage or not in such a discussion and whether such engagement could lead to conflict resolution or binding or non-binding responses.[59] Some non-response options are evident in Presidential statements[60] and UNSC resolutions.[61] Since the UNSC has the primary responsibility to maintain international peace and security under Article 24 of the UN Charter, it arguably has the power to adopt binding measures under Article 39 in combination with Articles 25 and 48(1) of the UN Charter. The obvious problem with this is the veto power of the Permanent Members of the UNSC. To avoid this, the literature suggests that a resolution under Article 39 should be so worded to avoid a veto, but nevertheless provide the gravity of the situation such that it has a strong impact on States even if it is formally non-binding.[62] By continuously citing data from IPCC which shows the urgency of the issue, and calling on States to take action without being too specific on what action States should take and thus avoid encroaching on sovereignty—the voting procedure would not be necessary.[63]

Having gone through the extensive literature on the possible role of the UNSC, it seems to us that the problem of climate change is so important that all UN agencies need to be engaged and to that extent the engagement of the UNSC is important. But we are not convinced that the UNSC is in a position to take appropriate decisions to mitigate the problem or to adapt to it.

58 Ken Conca et al, 'Climate Change and the UN Security Council: Bully Pulpit or Bull in a China Shop?' (2017) 17 Global Environmental Politics 1.

59 Shirley V Scott, 'Climate Change and Peak Oil as Threats to International Peace and Security: Is it Time for the Security Council to Legislate?' (2008) 9 Melbourne Journal of International Law 495.

60 UNSC 'Statement by the President of the Security Council' (20 July 2011) UN Doc S/PRST/2011/15; UNSC 'Statement by the President of the Security Council' (30 January 2018) UN Doc S/PRST/2018/3.

61 UNSC Res 2349 (2017); UNSC Res 2408 (2018).

62 Ash Murphy, 'The United Nations Security Council and Climate Change: Mapping a Pragmatic Pathway to Intervention' (2019) 13 Carbon and Climate Law Review 50.

63 ibid.

5. Planetary Security and Tipping Points

The 2019 Global Environment Outlook-6 defined the already manifested and expected impacts of climate change as a driver of other social, ecological, and economic problems.[64] With major impacts on coral reefs, the polar regions, and the oceans, climate change is likely to exacerbate existing problems with ocean fisheries; with rising temperatures and their impacts, planetary security is impacted. Together with other ecological problems, scholars expect that planetary security will be affected and tipping points will be passed.[65] On biodiversity loss, the literature sees that we are in the midst of a mass extinction crisis with repercussions on the rest of the world's life support systems.[66] The literature also proposes the notion of ecological security and the need to maintain basic ecosystem functions[67] not only so that life on earth is protected but also the future of the human race itself. As a consequence, Future Earth has now set up an Earth Commission to assess how best to stay within planetary boundaries.[68]

6. Migration (Domestic, Regional, Transboundary, and Global)

A cross-cutting feature of climate security is the issue of displacement and migration. While Norman Myers was one of the first to predict that hundreds of millions of people would be forced to migrate as a consequence of climate change,[69] recent literature shows that both slow onset disasters (eg, increasing drought) and fast onset disasters (eg, floods and storms) could lead to major internal and external displacements.[70] However, the

[64] Tariq Banuri et al, 'Drivers of Environmental Change' in Paul Ekins et al (eds), *Global Environment Outlook—GEO-6: Healthy Planet Healthy People* (CUP 2019).

[65] Timothy M Lenton et al, 'Tipping Elements in the Earth's Climate System' (2008) 105 Proceedings of the National Academy of Sciences 1786; Johan Rockström et al, 'A Safe Operating Space for Humanity' (2009) 461 *Nature* 472.

[66] The Intergovernmental Science-Policy Platform on Biodiversity and Ecosystem Services (IPBES), 'Summary for Policymakers of the Global Assessment Report on Biodiversity and Ecosystem Services of the Intergovernmental Science-Policy Platform on Biodiversity and Ecosystem Services' (2019) IPBES/7/10/Add.1 <https://ipbes.net/global-assessment-report-biodiversity-ecosystem-services> accessed 17 November 2019.

[67] McDonald (n 14).

[68] 'Earth Commission: A Compass for Humanity' (*Earth Commission*) <https://earthcommission.org/> accessed 9 April 2020.

[69] Norman Myers, 'Environmental Refugees: A Growing Phenomenon of the 21st Century' (2002) 357 Philosophical Transactions of the Royal Society of London 609; Norman Myers/Jennifer Kent, *Environmental Exodus: An Emergent Crisis in the Global Arena* (Climate Institute 1995).

[70] Michael Berlemann/Max F Steinhardt, 'Climate Change, Natural Disasters, and Migration—A Survey of the Empirical Evidence' (2017) 63 CESifo Economic Studies 353.

causality between climate impacts and displacement is not straightforward; displacement may be caused by multiple reasons combined. At the same time, climate change may also entrap people by reducing their ability to move.[71] A meta analysis concludes that the literature is diverse in its conclusions regarding whether climate change leads to displacement or not.[72] Estimates range from 50 to 350 million by 2050; these estimates focus on displacements where climate change could play a role in exacerbating the existing situation of local people.[73] Climate change-related relocations are already taking place in the small island States of Vanuatu, the Federated States of Micronesia, Papua New Guinea, Tuvalu, and the Solomon Islands,[74] and in low-lying States like Bangladesh.

From a security perspective, a key issue is whether climate change and its impacts on displacement affect radicalization. Some authors argue that:

> [h]ere there is a two-fold risk of radicalisation: first, within communities faced with receiving large numbers of 'climate refugees' and secondly, within displaced communities frustrated by the unwillingness of the international community to adequately respond to their plight.[75]

Migration can enhance conflict by competition, ethnic tensions, distrust, fault lines, and auxiliary problems and it is vital to address these problems before they become too large.[76] Environmental change including climate change may exacerbate displacement through extreme weather events that require temporary to permanent relocation; reduced food and water availability that forces people to move; exposure to sea level rise which leads to coastal squeeze; and increased competition over natural resources.[77]

While the idea of migration as a consequence of climate change was seen as an issue raised by alarmists, many lawyers who were afraid that the term 'climate refugee' would be used loosely, began to join the camp of the sceptics.[78] According to the IOM definition:

> Environmental migrants are persons or groups of persons who, for compelling reasons of sudden or progressive change in the environment that adversely affects their lives or living conditions, are obliged to leave their habitual homes, or choose to do so, either temporarily or permanently, and who move either within their country or abroad.[79]

[71] Richard Black et al, 'The Effect of Environmental Change on Human Migration' (2011) 21 Global Environmental Change S3.

[72] Michel Beine/Lionel Jeusette, 'A Meta-Analysis of the Literature on Climate Change and Migration' (2018) CESifo Working Paper No 7417 <https://papers.ssrn.com/sol3/papers.cfm?abstract_id=3338771> accessed 30 November 2020.

[73] Saul (n 13) para 54.

[74] ibid para 57. [75] ibid 7.

[76] Rafael Reuveny, 'Climate Change-Induced Migration and Violent Conflict' (2007) 26 Political Geography 656; Susan Martin, 'Climate Change, Migration, and Governance' (2010) 16 Global Governance 397.

[77] Martin (n 76). [78] ibid.

[79] IOM, 'Discussion Note: Migration and the Environment' (1 November 2007) MC/INF/288, 1–2.

Although the issue of migration has been on the global legal agenda for a few decades, international law has not yet progressed to deal with the issue of climate-induced displacement and migration. Climate and environmental refugees are not yet recognized as 'refugees' who are entitled to legal protection and recognition of their human rights as such. They are possibly more likely to be treated as 'economic migrants'.[80] However, some States like Sweden and Finland are making provisions for environmental migrants.[81]

The only instrument to address this issue is the National Adaptation Plans of Action under the climate change regime which requires least-developed States to prepare such Plans and hopefully incorporate elements to address domestic displacement.[82] Under the Universal Declaration of Human Rights, 'everyone has the right to freedom of movement and residence within the borders of each state'[83] but displaced people may not have the resources and jobs to finance such moves. And resources to finance such plans remain limited.

7. Inferences

Climate change affects the survival of individuals—especially those who are poor and those who live on marginalized and/or vulnerable lands. In an effort to survive, these people may either suffer, migrate, or engage in conflictive behaviour to gain access to resources. This is the human dimension of climate insecurity. Scaled up to the national level, this can lead to large-scale human suffering, displacement and/or social conflict—which can potentially lead to political destabilization, or even loss of statehood. Scaled up to the international level, this can lead to major transboundary migrations and conflict—which can also aggravate radicalization. Scaled up to the global level, this can imply major damage to global bio-physical systems with a potential risk for global collapse. Much of the literature tries to frame solutions in win-win language where the scholarly literature argues in favour of prevention, adaptation, aid, and peacebuilding in order to address such problems,[84] but the bottom line is that the world is facing an intractable problem of unprecedented nature.

While the legal system is struggling to deal with this through a range of policy and legal instruments ranging from human rights law, environmental law, disaster law, and the UNSC, it may be that law in this case is not able to compensate for political

[80] Saul (n 13). [81] Martin (n 76).

[82] LDC Expert Group, 'National Adaptation Plans: Technical Guidelines for the National Adaptation Plan Process' (UNFCCC, December 2012) <https://unfccc.int/files/adaptation/cancun_adaptation_framework/application/pdf/naptechguidelines_eng_high__res.pdf> accessed 8 April 2020.

[83] UNGA Res 217(III)A (10 December 1948).

[84] Charlotte Collins, 'Climate Change and Global Security: Planning for Potential Conflict' (Climate Institute, 25 September 2019) <http://climate.org/climate-change-and-global-security-planning-for-potential-conflict/> accessed 11 December 2019.

unwillingness. This is hence a chicken and egg situation: what comes first, political willingness followed by legal measures or legal measures that require political action?

C. Recent Developments and Contemporary Challenges: Securitization versus Security

In this section, we move beyond the multilevel analysis of different security dimensions to discuss whether climate change should be securitized or not. We also reflect on three ongoing 'security' debates: the nexus approach which links climate change to energy security, food security, and water security, amongst others; climate security and financial security—especially in terms of the problem of stranded assets; and climate security and environmental security and its implications for the growth paradigm and hence economic security.

Any risk that is existential, that affects human security, can lead to the securitization of an issue. In general, an issue is considered a high politics issue when it affects the survival of a State in physical or even economic terms. Such high politics issues have always been prioritized over low politics issues (such as the environment), which concern issues of importance, but not necessarily those that are seen as existential. However, many scholars and policymakers have seen climate change as an existential threat and have wanted to thus securitize the issue by discussing it within the UNSC. This is also true for the small island States. Many national scholars and policymakers have also looked at climate security as an issue that needs to be dealt with within the military establishments.[85] This is an attempt to securitize the issue. The risk with securitizing an issue is that it can also lead to a suspension of the rule of law. In the context of climate change, this could imply that countries refuse to collaborate on greenhouse gas emission reduction in the international context (eg, withdrawal of the US from the Paris Agreement); it could imply that countries refuse to acknowledge and accept climate refugees with attendant consequences for these migrants (cf global discussions on environmental migrants); and it could imply that countries refuse to share transboundary waters affected by the changing hydrological system and melting glaciers and even threaten or go to war to protect their perceived national interests. When extreme events happen, this often justifies rapid emergency measures—which may themselves create new or reproduce existing injustices within and between States. Within the domestic context, displacement often means that people move to more hospitable land, but the people who live in these areas may not welcome them. How will the needed redistribution at local to global level then be organized—through a legal and just procedure, or in an ad hoc manner? This is, of course, speculation, but given some of the expected

[85] Saul (n 13).

impacts of climate change, especially on reduced resources where land is increasingly eroded by a rising sea level, fresh water supplies become increasingly variable, food productivity is affected, and temperatures rise beyond the ability of the body to survive in—this is not unthinkable. We anticipate that many parts of the world will become so hot that people cannot conduct their agricultural practices and survive there. Will this lead to civil conflict? How will this civil conflict manifest itself—will it lead to ethnic violence as some groups protect themselves against others, or to violence between States as some countries protect themselves against others? How will governments choose between whom to protect? How will they deal with the expropriation of land and water rights in order to make life possible for others? Who will they choose for? And are governments more generally easier to trust than the military? Some authors have therefore argued against securitization, stating that treating climate change as an economic and ethical issue is perhaps more important.[86]

Climate security is closely linked to energy security,[87] food security,[88] and water security.[89] There is a growing debate which links climate change to access to energy and energy security, with access to food and food security, and access to water and water security—at once both broadening the security dimension of climate change in terms of the number of interlinked issues and in terms of the interlinked levels of discussion from local to global level. For example, addressing energy security urgently might mean increasing cheap supplies of energy for poor people, or relying on national supplies of fossil fuel, which would hinder the application and potentially violate the obligations under the Climate Change Convention regime, which requires us to move away from fossil fuels towards renewable energy. The nexus issue becomes all the more important with the adoption of Agenda 2030 and its requirement to meet the seventeen Sustainable Development Goals simultaneously and not some at the cost of others.[90] Climate change is mentioned several times in the Sustainable Development Goals, and has its own Goal 13, requiring urgent action to combat climate change and its impacts. There are also goals on energy, water, and food.

Another relevant issue—is the relationship between climate change and financial security. Given that the fossil fuel sector is a five trillion-dollar industry, phasing this industry out is likely to lead to a major disruption to the global economy and to all those whose savings, investments, and lifestyles are built around the fossil fuel industry. The risk of stranded assets can be a huge financial security challenge facing the global

[86] McDonald (n 14); Joyeeta Gupta et al, 'Water Sovereignty and Security, High Politics and Hard Power: The Dangers of Borrowing Discourses!' in Claudia Pahl-Wostl et al (eds), *Handbook on Water Security* (Edward Elgar 2016).

[87] Tibisay Morgandi and Jorge E Viñuales, Chapter 25 in this *Handbook*.

[88] Hilal Elver, Chapter 27 in this *Handbook*.

[89] Pierre Thielbörger, Chapter 29 in this *Handbook*.

[90] UNGA Res 70/1 (25 September 2015).

community in the near future, not only for rich States but also for the poorer ones who have large quantities of, as yet unexploited, oil and gas reserves.[91]

A more fundamental debate that is also taking place is the issue of what climate insecurity and environmental insecurity more broadly mean for the 'growth' paradigm. Globally, there are two schools of thought on the relationship between climate security and growth. The dominant school argues that climate risks can negate the progress achieved by growth and that:

> [a] halt to or significant slowdown of growth caused by climate change could pose a serious security threat to developing countries, not least by worsening poverty and desperation. Growth is seen as important to strengthening resilience, maintaining political stability, increasing the attractiveness of cooperation and providing hope to underprivileged populations.[92]

Many current reports and governments feel that 'growth' is necessary to address climate change and that the problem with climate change is that it undermines 'growth'. The IPCC also uses scenarios where growth patterns are built into the models.

At the same time, there is a growing movement that argues that the nature of growth has to change radically if it is to be consistent with climate mitigation and environmental problem solving. Climate change is not so much undermining 'growth' as human well-being, and the very forces of economic growth are responsible for the problem of climate change. So more growth to address climate change and other environmental problems is an oxymoron. The rise of de-growth or post-growth, and alternative development schools of thought question the current way of life and the dominant neo-liberal capitalist framework. This can have also larger security implications as it threatens the very premise upon which many national and international security frameworks are built.[93]

D. Outlook

Climate change has brought the world to face an unprecedented problem. It has major existential characteristics—it can affect the life of an individual who lives in a coastal region or a rain dependent farmer; it can affect national security by disrupting the lives, livelihoods, and property of the people and the economy and safety of a nation; it can affect international security by disrupting people's lives, displacement and migration, and exacerbating conflict over limited resources; and it can affect the security of the

[91] Joyeeta Gupta/Kyra Bos, 'Stranded Assets and Stranded Resources: Implications for Climate Change Mitigation and Global Sustainable Development' (2019) 56 Energy Research and Social Science 1.

[92] Secretary-General Report (n 11).

[93] Gabriel E Eckstein, 'Water Scarcity, Conflict, and Security in a Climate Change World: Challenges and Opportunities for International Law and Policy' (2009) 27 Wisconsin International Law Journal 409.

planet itself and the various ecosystems that need to function to make life for humans and other species possible. The literature on the security dimensions of climate change addresses the issue of security (namely, the existential nature of the problem) in vastly different ways and promotes a range of policy and legal instruments to address this, ranging from human rights approaches, disaster risk reduction, environmental law, and security law. This is on the impact side. But mitigating climate change is also challenging and can raise existential issues of a different nature—it can affect energy access, it can affect the global financial system, and it calls into question our current 'growth' models and possibly the right to (sustainable) development of people and States.[94] In this context, we stand by those who argue in favour of addressing the problem democratically and rationally and argue against 'securitizing' the debate which risks the suspension of the rule of law in addressing an urgent problem. We are not convinced that engaging the UNSC and national militaries will provide democratic and legitimate approaches to solving the problem of climate change, but recognize that other scholars, and especially many Western governments, think differently on this issue.

[94] Gupta/Arts (n 26) 11.

CHAPTER 31

INTERNATIONAL DISASTER LAW

ARNOLD N PRONTO

A. Introduction

Every year the onset of disasters causes significant harm to large numbers of individuals and damage to property. Natural hazards such as hurricanes, cyclones, tornadoes, tsunamis, earthquakes, wild fires, floods, epidemics, heatwaves, ice storms, prolonged drought, can cause widespread damage and harm. While smaller-scale, localized events might result in less widespread damage, their relative frequency (in relation to major disasters) significantly magnifies their impact over time. Natural hazards are nothing new, especially on a geologically active planet. Conceptually, a natural hazard is not a disaster. The 'disaster' is the consequential harm arising from the hazard, whether natural or man-made. Understood as such, the extent of the harm caused is intrinsically linked to the degree of vulnerability of the affected person.[1] Historical records are replete with references to disruptive events. What is different today is the exposure to risk.[2]

[1] Peter Macalister-Smith, 'Disaster Relief: Reflections on the Role of International Law' (1985) 45 Heidelberg Journal of International Law 25; Victoria Bannon, 'International Disaster Response Law and the Commonwealth: Answering the Call to Action' (2008) 34 Commonwealth Law Bulletin 843; Boniface Okere/Ernest M Makawa, 'Global Solidarity and the International Response to Disasters' in David D Caron/Charles Leben (eds), *The International Aspects of Natural and Industrial Catastrophes* (Martinus Nijhoff 2001) 431–6; David D Caron et al (eds), *The International Law of Disaster Relief* (CUP 2014); Dug Cubie, *The International Legal Protection of Persons in Humanitarian Crises: Exploring the Acquis Humanitaire* (Hart 2017); Oliver Rubin/Rasmus Dahlberg, *A Dictionary of Disaster Management* (OUP 2017); Andrea de Guttry et al (eds), *International Disaster Response Law* (Asser Press 2018); UNGA, 'Protection of Persons in the Event of Disasters: Memorandum by the Secretariat' (11 December 2007) UN Docs A/CN.4/590 and Add.1–Add.3 (Secretariat Memorandum).

[2] Jim Chen, 'Modern Disaster Theory: Evaluating Disaster Law as a Portfolio or Legal Rules' (2011) 25 Emory International Law Review 1121; see also Peter Hough, Chapter 6 in this *Handbook*.

As human settlements continue to expand, including into disaster-prone areas, so has the exposure to the risk of harm increased.

The effect of disasters, whether widespread or localized, poses a major threat to human security, as it places significant strain on human support systems. What is more is that disasters invariably have a disproportionately harmful impact on the particularly vulnerable, who typically subsist at the margins of society, usually in harm's way. For many States, the impact of specific disasters can be measured in terms of setbacks to human development. Economic and social gains can be reversed overnight, sometimes quite literally. Looking back at the period 2005–15, the *Sendai Framework for Disaster Risk Reduction 2015–2030* observes that:

> disasters have continued to exact a heavy toll and, as a result, the well-being and safety of persons, communities and countries as a whole have been affected . . . Overall, more than 1.5 billion people have been affected by disasters in various ways, with women, children and people in vulnerable situations disproportionately affected. The total economic loss was more than $1.3 trillion. In addition, between 2008 and 2012, 144 million people were displaced by disasters. Disasters, many of which are exacerbated by climate change and which are increasing in frequency and intensity, significantly impede progress towards sustainable development. Evidence indicates that exposure of persons and assets in all countries has increased faster than vulnerability has decreased, thus generating new risks and a steady rise in disaster-related losses, with a significant economic, social, health, cultural and environmental impact in the short, medium and long term, especially at the local and community levels.[3]

The impact of a disaster is also a function of the level of the efforts marshalled in anticipation thereof and response thereto. Modern States allocate significant resources to providing relief assistance immediately following the onset of disasters. Be it the immediate need to save lives and rescue the stranded, or to provide shelter, food, and comfort to those affected by a disaster, humanitarian assistance efforts typically require a sustained effort by a range of actors. Increasingly, such activities are also being undertaken at the international level, especially in cases of major disasters with transboundary effects. The imperative to provide aid and assistance is increasingly viewed as a key interest of the international community. The UN devotes significant resources to the coordination of efforts at the international level, aimed at facilitating cooperation in the provision of humanitarian assistance. The organization has also become the central locus for contemplation at the global level on best practices in disaster risk reduction.[4] This chapter seeks to describe the outlines of an emerging international disaster law, motivated in large part by a growing awareness of the role law can play in efforts to reduce vulnerability

[3] The Sendai Framework for Disaster Risk Reduction 2015–2030, adopted by the Third United Nations World Conference on Disaster Risk Reduction, and endorsed in UNGA Res 69/283 (23 June 2015) Annex II, para 4 (footnote omitted).

[4] United Nations Office for Disaster Risk Reduction (UNDRR).

to, and mitigate the impact of, disasters. Such sentiments are, in turn, driven by an appreciation of the potential deleterious consequences for global security arising from the widespread dislocation brought about by major disasters (especially, but not limited to, major disasters of a transboundary nature).

B. Legal Framework

1. Sources

A striking feature of international disaster law is that there exists a significant body of hard-law already in place.[5] Research by the International Federation of the Red Cross and Red Crescent Societies (IFRC) and the UN Secretariat in the early 2000s, uncovered hundreds of directly applicable bilateral treaties, as well as a number of multilateral agreements, mostly at the regional level.[6] In addition, there exists a penumbra of rules formulated with disasters in mind, located in conventions dealing with broader topics (such as trade, customs regulations etc). Those conventions typically establish exceptions or special dispensations in the event of the occurrence of a disaster. This body of rules is in turn buttressed by a third layer of soft law, emanating from a range of authoritative sources.

a. *Treaties*

At present, the only global treaty dedicated specifically to disasters is the 1998 Tampere Convention on the Provision of Telecommunication Resources for Disaster Mitigation and Relief Operations (Tampere Convention).[7] Although focusing on a specific aspect arising in the context of the immediate recovery and response phase, the convention nonetheless provides useful legal guidance on several core concepts (such as the legal definition of a 'disaster').[8] A further key multilateral instrument is the 2000 Framework Convention on Civil Defence Assistance,[9] which seeks to foster cooperation between national civil defence teams in providing emergency relief and assistance in the wake of a disaster.[10]

At the regional level, a particularly prominent treaty is the ASEAN Agreement on Disaster Management and Emergency Response, adopted in 2005.[11] To a certain extent,

[5] See Andrea de Guttry, 'Surveying the Law' in Guttry et al (n 1).

[6] See the online database of the IFRC <http://www.ifrc.org/en/publications-and-reports/idrl-database/> accessed 28 February 2019; as well Secretariat Memorandum (n 1) UN Doc A/CN.4/590/Add.2.

[7] 2296 UNTS 5 (Tampere Convention). [8] ibid art 6(1). [9] 2172 UNTS 213.

[10] Examples of multilateral agreements concerned with specific types of disasters include the Convention on Early Notification of a Nuclear Accident 1439 UNTS 275; and the Convention on Assistance in the Case of a Nuclear Accident or Radiological Emergency 1457 UNTS 133.

[11] ASEAN Agreement on Disaster Management and Emergency Response. Reprinted in *ASEAN Document Series 2005* (ASEAN Secretariat 2006) 157 (AADMER).

the ASEAN treaty reflects the current state of the art in the thinking about disaster law. While covering some traditional aspects of emergency response, the treaty places a strong emphasis on the management and reduction of the risk of disasters.[12]

In addition, there exist literally dozens of bilateral treaties, throughout the world, establishing mutual cooperation and assistance arrangements between neighbouring States. As in South East Asia and the European Union, some such agreements exist within the broader framework of regional arrangements.[13]

b. *Non-Binding Statements of Principle and Policy*

The real ferment in the thinking about disaster law has taken place in the non-binding and policy spheres. There exist numerous non-binding instruments purporting to offer guidance on a variety of aspects of disaster law.[14] One of the most prominent, and authoritative, examples of recent guidance is that of the IFRC in its Guidelines for the Facilitation and Regulation of International Disaster Relief and Initial Recovery Assistance,[15] adopted in 2007 (the International Disaster Response Laws (IDRL) Guidelines). That instrument contains a number of recommendations aimed primarily at governments to help them prepare their regulatory systems for international disaster response. It reflects the *acquis* of the IFRC's extensive experience on the ground in confronting the challenges (including legal) faced by humanitarian assistance actors in offering assistance to States and populations affected by disasters.

In a similar vein, the International Law Commission (ILC) adopted the draft articles on the protection of persons in the event of disasters in 2016.[16] The draft articles seek to establish an international legal framework to 'facilitate the adequate and effective response to disasters and reduction of the risk of disasters, so as to meet the essential needs of the persons concerned, with full respect for their rights'.[17]

The draft articles are also best understood within the context of broader efforts within the UN. They draw on, *inter alia*, a seminal resolution adopted by the General Assembly in 1991,[18] which established the current policy framework for the organization's mandate as the global coordination point for emergency humanitarian assistance. The set of Guiding Principles annexed to that resolution also provide a framework for the basic legal parameters within which international disaster law operates today.

To these sources should be added a series of major statements by the international community concerning disaster risk reduction. The most recent, the Sendai Framework

[12] eg ibid art 4(a). [13] Secretariat Memorandum (n 1) UN Doc A/CN.4/590/Add.2, pt I–IV.

[14] For a selected list of such texts, see ibid pt V.B.

[15] International Federation of Red Cross and Red Crescent Societies, 'Introduction to the Guidelines for the Domestic Facilitation and Regulation of International Disaster Relief and Initial Recovery Assistance' (IFRC 2011) (IDRL Guidelines). See also David Fisher, 'Law and Legal Issues in International Disaster Response: A Desk Study' (International Federation of Red Cross and Red Crescent Societies 2007).

[16] ILC 'Draft Articles on the Protection of Persons in the Event of Disasters' (2016) UN Doc A/71/10 13–17 (ILC Draft Articles), as well as the commentaries to the draft articles (ibid 17–73) (ILC Commentary).

[17] ILC Draft Articles (n 16) art 2. [18] UNGA Res 46/182 (19 December 1991).

for Disaster Risk Reduction 2015–2030,[19] was adopted in 2015. The Framework sets an ambitious agenda for disaster risk management throughout the world, with a view to enhancing resilience and reducing vulnerability to the adverse effects of disasters.

2. The Scope of International Disaster Law

a. *Ratione materiae*

The scope *ratione materiae* of international disaster law is determined by the legal definition of the concept of 'disaster'.[20] At least two approaches exist. The first, more traditional, conceptualizes a disaster as the occurrence of an event. An example can be found in the definition contained in the draft articles of the ILC:

> 'disaster' means a calamitous event or series of events resulting in widespread loss of life, great human suffering and distress, mass displacement, or large-scale material or environmental damage, thereby seriously disrupting the functioning of society (…)[21]

There the focus is on causation ('events resulting in'), linking the required threshold of harm to the occurrence of an event.

The alternative, more contemporary, approach is to focus on the consequence of the onset of an event, so that what constitutes a 'disaster' is understood as a function of the exposure to risk. An example is to be found in the IDRL Guidelines, which were inspired by the definition contained in the Tampere Convention:

> 'Disaster' means a serious disruption of the functioning of society, which poses a significant, widespread threat to human life, health, property or the environment, whether arising from accident, nature or human activity, whether developing suddenly or as the result of long-term processes, but excluding armed conflict.[22]

As such, the occurrence of the event is not as legally significant as the consequential serious disruption of the functioning of society.

Where the emphasis is placed is significant for understanding the range of activities that implicitly fall within the scope of international disaster law. The focus on the occurrence of an event is traditionally associated with response-related activities aimed at initial recovery assistance. Conversely, a definition focusing on the fact of the existence of harm is more permissive of an analysis focused on the exposure to risk. The key insight is that two similar events of comparable magnitude affecting urban areas of comparable

[19] UNGA Res 69/283 (23 June 2015).

[20] Generally Michael H Hoffman, 'What is the Scope of International Disaster Response Law?' in *International Disaster Response Laws, Principles and Practice: Reflections, Prospects, and Challenges* (IFRC 2003) 13–20.

[21] ILC Draft Articles (n 16) art 3(a).

[22] IDRL Guidelines (n 15) s 2(1).

density of population may result in significantly different levels of loss, owing to differences in exposure to risk. Seen in such light, international disaster law has a broader scope, covering also risk reduction activities aimed at prevention, preparedness, and mitigation of potential harm.

Equally important are the thresholds of harm envisaged in the definitions, as those trigger the application of international rules. The ILC sought to set a high threshold for the application of the draft articles, of 'widespread loss of life, great human suffering and distress, mass displacement, or large-scale material or environmental damage, thereby seriously disrupting the functioning of society'. This was done on purpose, both to exclude other types of serious events, such as those arising from serious political or economic crises, as well as to set a high threshold for the triggering of various international legal obligations.

In fact, the high threshold for the application of international rules is also to be understood as being driven by the structure of the rules which proceed from the assumption of the primacy of role of the affected State.[23] In the traditional conception of international disaster law, it is only once the national response capacity of the affected State has been overwhelmed that international humanitarian assistance activities (and rules) are triggered.[24] The underlying assumption therefore being that this would only be the case in truly calamitous situations. In other words, the high threshold in the definition of 'disaster' under international law is in a sense a relic of the traditional structure of the interplay between national and international rules.

However, such considerations continue to evolve in line with the dynamic nature of activities undertaken on the ground. The national response capacities of States vary significantly, with the resultant implication that, in practice, the threshold for the triggering of international assistance fluctuates, sometimes below the intensity threshold recognized by instruments such as the ILC's draft articles. This is, for example, likely the case when coming to small-scale disasters, whose intensity does not normally meet the international threshold, but whose frequency in aggregate may cause a similar level of serious disruption to the functioning of society. In other words, the definitions of disaster at the international level, to the extent they serve as thresholds for the triggering of assistance, as a matter of law, need to be understood and applied flexibly.

Two further points merit consideration. First, humanitarian assistance provided in the context of armed conflict is, *a priori*, excluded from the scope *ratione materiae* of international disaster law (as it typically falls within the scope of international humanitarian law).[25] Secondly, it is not uncommon to see the distinction drawn between

[23] ILC Draft Articles (n 16) art 10 (2); and IDRL Guidelines (n 15) s 10(1). Generally, Toshiya Ueki, 'Natural Disasters and the Theory of International Law' in Caron et al (n 2) 21–8.

[24] ILC Draft Articles (n 16) art 11; IDRL Guidelines (n 15) s 3(2); Institute of International Law, 'Humanitarian Assistance' (Resolution adopted by the Institute of International Law, Bruges Session 2003) art III.3.

[25] ILC Draft Articles (n 16) art 18; Daniela Gavshon, 'The Applicability of IHL in Mixed Situations of Disaster and Conflict' (2009) 14 JCSL 243; Gabriella Venturini, 'Disaster and Armed Conflict' in de Guttry et al (n 1).

natural disasters (namely those arising from natural hazards, such as earthquakes and weather-related phenomena) and human caused disasters. However, generally speaking, international disaster law does not draw such a distinction. The emphasis is on the provision of assistance to those in need, regardless of the origin.

b. *Ratione personae*

The scope *ratione personae* of international disaster law is at the same time relatively well defined and potentially extensive. The key entity of concern is the State affected by the disaster. It is the actions (or inaction) of the affected State that will trigger the application of international disaster law. Most States have internal processes for the legal ascertainment of the existence of a disaster, for example by means of the issuance of an official declaration. At the level of international law, the affected State has a legal obligation to protect persons on its territory from the effects of the disaster.[26] This is the key inflection point within international disaster law around which a number of other rights and obligations are structured.

The counterparts to the affected State are the assisting States. Sometimes the assistance is provided at the bilateral or regional levels. In other cases, typically the more severe, assisting States might act in concert, including under the auspices of an international organization. In such cases, it is common to speak of assistance being provided by, or on behalf of, the international community.[27] This depiction, however, does not necessarily change the applicable legal construction. Rights and duties are imposed at the level of assisting States (or international organizations) themselves, not the collective.

There exists a further periphery of States that may be involved in the response to the onset of a disaster. These include, for example, third States from which assistance provided by international organizations, such as the UN, originates. There are transit States through which aid or assistance might be transported. There are States under whose flag assistance by sea is transported. There are States through which monetary assistance intended for disaster relief operations flows, or States from which financial backing (including insurance) for the provision of assistance is secured. There are States of nationality of both legal (such as non-governmental organizations registered in their territories) and natural (such as humanitarian assistance personnel) persons, and which maintain a legal interest in the protection of their nationals. There are also States which participate in cooperative arrangements, for example for the maintenance of early warning systems. There are also States that are parties to regional mutual assistance agreements, which may not be providing direct assistance, but which retain a legal interest in ensuring the implementation of the obligations under the agreement.

International organizations are also extensively involved in the provision of assistance, and bear rights and obligations of their own. The role of the UN is of particular significance, given its central coordination mandate. To these might be added the role

[26] ILC Draft Articles (n 16) art 10(1). Blaise Knapp, 'La responsabilité de l'État en cas de catastrophes naturelles' (1986) Revue de droit Suisse 589.

[27] Okere/Makawa (n 1).

played by the Red Cross Movement, and in particular the role of the IFRC. Despite possessing a *sui generis* character, its level of integration into the existing international framework for the provision of assistance, positions it closer to international organizations, even if not all of the same legal obligations under international law are opposable to it.

Finally, it is a particular hallmark of the field of disaster relief assistance that a significant number of private actors, primarily non-governmental organizations, are involved. The range of their activities varies tremendously. The more institutional such actors typically participate in cooperation arrangements with the UN and other international organizations, or even with States, including directly with affected States. In principle, such entities are subject to the national law of the State in which they are registered and that of the State in whose territory they operate. They are not subjects of international law, and accordingly cannot bear rights and obligations arising from international law. However, in some cases, international organizations such as the UN carry out their humanitarian assistance activities through non-governmental actors, for example by sub-contracting to them aspects of the actions to be undertaken.[28] Such circumstances may give rise to questions of the legal attribution of the acts of those private actors to the contracting international organization.[29]

c. *Ratione temporis*

The traditional focus on initial recovery and response meant that the overriding concern of the law was the facilitation of assistance in the immediate wake of the onset of a disaster. While this is still largely the case, the scope *ratione temporis* of international disaster law has been extended backwards to also cover pre-disaster activities aimed at risk reduction. At present, the post-disaster rehabilitation and rebuilding phase has largely been left to other actors and other rules.

It is worth pointing out that the temporal scope is actually quite important for the application of the law in the context of disaster response. For affected States, the onset of a disaster is an unusual occurrence which, *inter alia*, triggers the operation of an extraordinary legal regime, typically establishing exceptions and opt-outs from existing national laws. For the lawyer engaged in this work, therefore, it is important to know precisely when, as a matter of law, the special regime has commenced, and when it terminates. For international actors, the timing of the request for assistance is similarly critical, as it triggers a process, and the consequential rights and obligations under international law.

d. *Ratione loci*

It goes without saying that the scope *ratione loci* of international disaster law extends primarily over the area affected by the disaster. At the same time, no specific restriction

[28] See Christina Binder, Chapter 56 in this *Handbook*.

[29] See ILC, 'Draft Articles on the Responsibility of International Organizations' (2011) UN Doc A/66/10, 54ff, art 6.

is placed on the geographic extent of the harm. While truly calamitous events (such as massive hurricanes or significant tsunamis) do, on occasion, have a transboundary component, no such *a priori* requirement is established. In other words, international disaster law is equally applicable to disasters occurring entirely with the territory of the affected State. It also applies to other geographic areas, including States where assistance originates, and transit States, and States where assistance material destined for a particular disaster is staged.

Furthermore, the geographic scope of the application of the law may be different and even broader when coming to pre-disaster risk reduction activities. For example, the establishment of a tsunami early warning system may span an entire ocean, far from the location of the actual event, were it to happen. Similarly, legal cooperation in prevention and mitigation of harm may extend also to downstream riparian States which may be adversely affected by a flood, or failed dam.

3. General Rules and Principles

Broadly speaking, international disaster law operates at different degrees of generality. There is the set of rules which applies residually at the level of core obligations and rights, or as general principles. Parallel to these is the 'lawyer's law' set of rules and recommendations concerned with the practicalities of ensuring effective and prompt relief.

a. *Duty to Cooperate*

International disaster law is about international cooperation.[30] The legal duty to cooperate in the provision of disaster assistance, and in risk reduction, is central to the effective implementation of international disaster law, and is drawn from principles well known to international law.[31] The framework of international legal rules and obligations arising from international disaster law is, accordingly, intended to provide a legal basis for such cooperation. The ILC's draft articles are organized around this central purpose.

The ILC employed the imperative 'shall', in draft Article 7, so as to establish the duty at the level of international law. The obligation is also reflected in a number of instruments concerned with disaster relief, including the ASEAN Declaration for Mutual Assistance on Natural Disasters,[32] the Framework Convention on Civil Defence Assistance,[33] and the Tampere Convention.[34]

[30] Generally, Bogdan Babović, 'The Duty of States to Cooperate with One Another in Accordance with the Charter' in Milan Šahović (ed), *Principles of International Law Concerning Friendly Relations and Cooperation* (Oceana Publications 1972).

[31] It is listed as one of the seven fundamental principles of international law elaborated in the Friendly Relations Declaration, UNGA Res 2625(XXV) (24 October 1970) Annex, para 1.

[32] ASEAN Declaration for Mutual Assistance on Natural Disasters (Manila, 26 June 1976) art 1 <https://asean.org/?static_post=asean-declaration-on-mutual-assistance-on-natural-disasters-manila-26-june-1976> accessed 20 May 2020.

[33] Framework Convention on Civil Defence Assistance (n 9) art 4.

[34] Tampere Convention (n 7) art 3(4)(d).

Draft Article 7 has a three-fold purpose. First, to confirm the existence of a legal obligation. Secondly, to indicate the role of international law. Since the obligation is embedded within international law, international cooperation should be implemented in accordance with international law, which includes with full respect for the sovereignty and territorial integrity of the affected State. Finally, to confirm the entities to whom the obligation is owed, namely other States, the UN, the components of the Red Cross and Red Crescent Movement, as well as 'other assisting actors', which are defined as competent intergovernmental organizations, or relevant non-governmental organizations or entities, providing assistance to an affected State with its consent.[35]

At the same time, the provision has to be understood within the broader structure of the entire draft articles. Since the affected State has the primary duty to protect its population, international assistance in fulfilling such imperative is essentially supportive in character. In other words, the obligation to cooperate is without prejudice to the primary role of the affected State in protecting persons on its territory.[36]

Cooperation can take many forms. In the context of response, the ILC, in a non-exhaustive manner, identified as typical actions, 'humanitarian assistance, coordination of international relief actions and communications, and making available relief personnel, equipment and goods, and scientific, medical and technical resources'.[37] As regards risk reduction, the main types of cooperation identified are the conducting of risk assessments, the collection and dissemination of risk and past loss information, and the installation and operation of early warning systems.[38] All of these are, by nature, context-specific and reflect the prevailing state of the art. It is in the nature of the activities being covered that new forms of assistance may emerge over time.

b. *Duty to Reduce Disaster Risk*

One of the innovations of the ILC's draft articles is the recognition, at the level of international law, of an obligation on all States to 'reduce the risk of disasters by taking appropriate measures, including through legislation and regulations, to prevent, mitigate, and prepare for disasters'.[39] As discussed earlier, disaster risk reduction is increasingly a key area of focus for international disaster law.[40] Nonetheless, its inclusion within the scope of application of the topic implies an expansion of the types of obligations that arise, and the range of actors that are involved. The consequential obligations are not structured around a binary relationship, between affected State and assisting actor, as in the case of disaster response. The international law obligation is instead directed to each State, individually, to act at the national level. This is without prejudice to the general obligation on all States to cooperate, including with regard to disaster risk reduction.

[35] ILC Draft Articles (n 16) art 3(d). [36] ILC Commentary (n 16) 38, para 4.

[37] ILC Draft Articles (n 16) art 8. [38] ibid art 9(2). [39] ibid art 9.

[40] Abdelkhaleq Berramdane, 'L'obligation de prévention des catastrophes et risques naturels' (1997) 113 Revue du droit public et de la science politique en France et à l'étranger 1717; Stephen J Green, 'Expanding Assistance for National Preparedness and Prevention Programs' in Lynn H Stephens/ Stephen J Green (eds), *Disaster Assistance: Appraisal, Reform and New Approaches* (NY UP 1979).

A key issue of consideration is whether it is feasible to impose such an obligation on all States, regardless of economic development and available capacity. The solution found was to qualify the obligation with the reference to 'taking appropriate measures'. By 'appropriate' the ILC meant not only measures that were relevant in the context of the State in question, but also measures that reflect the respective capacities of States.[41] In the words of the ILC, '[t]he duty being envisaged is one of conduct and not result; in other words not to completely prevent or mitigate a disaster, but rather to reduce the risk of harm potentially caused thereby'.[42]

c. *Duty to Ensure the Protection of Persons*

The legal obligation to ensure the protection of persons at risk of, or affected by, disasters on its territory is the core obligation underlying the *raison d'être* of the draft articles. In principle, the obligation falls on the affected State.[43] It arises primarily as a consequence of sovereignty, as conceptualized under contemporary international law.[44] It also emerges from the basic legal obligations binding on States under international human rights law.[45] Furthermore, it is commonly reflected in obligations imposed by national law on the State, including, on occasion, at the constitutional level. As such, it imports all the obligations under international human rights law[46] and national law implied in the concept of 'protection' of persons. In the context of international disaster law, such obligations may extend not only to the protection of life, but also to that of livelihood.

The further implication of such obligation is that the affected State, in turn, has the primary role in directing, controlling, coordinating, and supervising the provision of relief assistance on its territory.[47] In the words of the ILC, '[t]he primacy of an affected State is (…) grounded in the long-standing recognition in international law that the State is best placed to determine the gravity of an emergency situation and to frame appropriate response policies'.[48] It should also be understood as reflecting a basic bargain with the affected State, where on the one hand an obligation to protect is imposed by international law, while on the other, its primacy is expressly recognized by the law. Such primacy is not entirely absolute, since it is subject to the general duty of the affected State to cooperate with other actors. In principle, under international law, the obligation on the State extends to all persons on its territory (or territory under the jurisdiction or control of the State).

41 ILC Commentary (n 16) 47, para 9.
42 ibid 47–8, para 10.
43 ILC Draft Articles (n 16) art 10(1).
44 See the opinion of Judge Alvarez in the *Corfu Channel Case* (*UK v Albania*) (Merits) [1949] ICJ Rep 4.
45 Generally Flavia Z Giustiniani et al (eds), *Routledge Handbook of Human Rights and Disasters* (Routledge 2018).
46 See CESCR, 'General Comment No 12: The Right to Adequate Food' (12 May 1999) UN Doc E/C.12/1999/5; generally, Cubie (n 1) pt 5.
47 ILC Draft Articles (n 16) art 10(2). See also UNGA Res 46/182 (19 December 1991) Annex, para 4.
48 ILC Commentary (n 16) 52, para 7.

d. *Duty to Seek External Assistance*

The affected State, faced with a disaster which has overwhelmed its national response capacity, has an obligation to reach out to the international community and seek assistance.[49] Doing so may in fact be required as a means of fulfilling its obligations under international human rights law. Such recognition of an obligation at the level of international law represents the culmination of the evolution in the thinking about how States may best respond in the wake of a disaster, and what the role of the international community should be. It also reflects an appreciation of the interest the international community retains in addressing the potential threat to broader regional and global security posed by the instability arising following a major disaster.

As formulated in the ILC's draft articles, the concept of 'seeking' assistance 'implies a broad, negotiated approach to the provision of international aid'.[50] The affected State retains the discretion to choose from amongst which offers of assistance, made in response, are the most appropriate to its specific needs.[51]

As discussed earlier, the notion that international assistance may only be sought when the national response capacity of the affected State has been overwhelmed, is not an absolute requirement. Such a threshold requirement serves only to trigger the legal obligation to seek assistance. It, however, does not preclude the possibility of the affected State seeking external assistance in the context of smaller-scale disasters.[52]

e. *Right to Offer Assistance*

The ILC draft articles recognize the right ('may') of States, the UN, and other potential assisting actors to 'offer assistance to the affected State'.[53] In the words of the ILC, the provision:

> acknowledges the interest of the international community in the protection of persons in the event of disasters, which is to be viewed as complementary to the primary role of the affected State enshrined in draft article 10. It is an expression of the principles of solidarity and cooperation, highlighted in the preamble, which underlie the whole set of draft articles on the topic (...)[54]

What emerges is an interplay of rights, organized around the process of offer and acceptance.[55] So, while the provision recognizes a 'right' to offer, it deliberately falls short of proclaiming a legal duty to do so. The prevailing view within the ILC (and the Sixth Committee of the UN General Assembly (UNGA)) was that 'offers, whether made unilaterally or in response to a request, are essentially voluntary and should not be

[49] ILC Draft Articles (n 16) art 11.
[50] ILC Commentary (n 16) 55, para 6.
[51] Katja Luopajärvi, 'Is there an Obligation on States to Accept International Humanitarian Assistance to Internally Displaced Persons under International Law?' (2003) 15 International Journal of Refugee Law 678.
[52] ILC Commentary (n 16) 56, para 9.
[53] ILC Draft Articles (n 16) art 12(1).
[54] ILC Commentary (n 16) 57, para 1.
[55] Secretariat Memorandum (n 1) paras 51–65, 41–50.

construed as recognition of the existence of a legal duty to assist'.[56] Conversely, an offer of assistance does not establish for the affected State a corresponding obligation to accept it.[57]

f. *Duty to Give Due Consideration to Requests for Assistance*

A State, the UN, or other potential assisting actor, which has received a request for assistance from an affected State, is obliged to 'expeditiously give due consideration to the request and to inform the affected State of its reply'.[58] Such procedural obligation was included to mitigate the discretionary nature of the right of the international community to offer assistance. The obligation arises as a matter of international law, for States, the UN and those other potential actors which are subjects of international law. For non-governmental organizations, which cannot incur obligations under international law, the provision should be understood as a recommendation of best practice.

The obligation is triggered by a request from the affected State, which may be presented simply in the form of appeal for ('seeking') assistance. For the countervailing obligation to give due consideration to be triggered, there must be a level of specificity in the request for assistance sufficient for the obligation to be opposable to the recipient State, international organization, or other entity.[59]

As already indicated, there is no duty on the recipients to actually 'provide' assistance in response to a request. Nonetheless, when coming to the UN, which it singled out for 'special mention given the central role it plays in receiving requests for assistance', as well as other intergovernmental organizations, the ILC felt it necessary to indicate that:

> [t]he United Nations and intergovernmental organizations not only are entitled, as mandated by their constituent instruments, but are also encouraged to make offers of assistance to the affected State.[60]

g. *The Role of Consent*

Consent provides the legal basis for what are essentially voluntary acts. The consent of international actors to provide assistance is balanced by the consent of the affected State to the provision of such assistance.[61] The ILC draft articles clearly proclaim that '[t]he provision of external assistance requires the consent of the affected State'.[62] Such requirement flows as a consequence of the legal recognition that the affected State retains the primary role in the direction, control, coordination, and supervision of relied assistance.[63] This is as much a statement of law as it is a reflection of the practical reality of disaster relief assistance. The vast majority of external assistance provided following the onset of a disaster is done on the basis of the consent of the affected State. In practice, it makes little sense to do otherwise.

[56] ILC Commentary (n 16) 57, para 2; Michael Eburin, 'International Law and Disaster Response' (2010) 36 Monash University Law Review 162.

[57] ILC Commentary (n 16) 56.

[58] ILC Draft Articles (n 16) art 12(2).

[59] ILC Commentary (n 16) 58, para 8.

[60] ibid 57, para 4.

[61] Milena C Trascasas, 'Access to the Territory of a Disaster-Affected State' in de Guttry et al (n 1).

[62] ILC Draft Articles (n 16) art 13(1).

[63] ibid art 10(2).

Consent establishes legality. Without it, the provision of external assistance may be viewed as a form of unlawful intervention in the internal affairs of the State. Without it, relief goods and personnel present on the territory of the affected State do not, in principle, enjoy the protections and preferential treatment of the international legal regime, which are triggered by the onset of the disaster. Assisting States, international organizations such as the UN,[64] and entities such as the IFRC and reputable non-governmental organizations are typically reluctant to provide assistance in the absence of the consent of the affected State.[65]

However, consent is a flexible concept which may require different reactions in different contexts, usually depending on the internal law and distribution of authority within the affected State.[66] It is thus possible for general consent to be sufficient, or in other circumstances for specific consent to specific consignments of relief assistance to be required. Part of the motivating concern for the establishment of international rules and guidance on the provision of relief assistance has been precisely the desire to minimize and streamline internal consent procedures. In principle, however, it is for the affected State to determine such requirements and to specify, in accordance with its laws, which authorities have the legal competency to provide the necessary consent.

Consent does not always have to be express. Consent might also, in some (usually rare) circumstances, be constructed. In the case of overwhelming disasters where the very functioning of central governmental authority has been disrupted, it is not uncommon for international actors to rely on the consent of local authorities at the point of admission into the State, for example. Formal consent may also be provided *ex post*. It might be conveyed orally, or be given in writing. Consent could also be provided in advance, in the form of an existing agreement. Such legal arrangements are quite common. It is also relatively common for non-international actors, such as non-governmental organizations involved in the provision of relief assistance, to have their own standing arrangements with States. Putting such arrangements into place in advance, particularly in relation to areas prone to natural hazards, is in itself a form of disaster risk reduction.

Consent can be denied. That is, in fact, the point of the requirement, and reflects the underlying voluntarist nature of the process. It is no exaggeration that such guarantee (of the freedom to deny) is of central importance for all States. It flows as a consequence of their assertion of sovereignty, and their expectation that such sovereignty be respected by others.[67] Such confidence on the part of affected States is foundational to the success

[64] On occasion, the UNSC has authorized the provision of humanitarian assistance in the absence of the formal consent of the one whose territory the assistance was to be provided; eg UNSC Res 2139 (2014). Such actions are rare and have been limited to the context of the provision of humanitarian assistance to persons affected by armed conflict (not disasters per se).

[65] Arthur C Helton, 'The Legality of Providing Humanitarian Assistance without the Consent of the Sovereign' (1992) 4 International Journal of Refugee Law 373.

[66] Elizabeth Katchka, 'Challenges for "Affected States" in Accepting International Disaster Aid: Lessons from Hurricane Katrina' (2015) 48 Vanderbilt Journal of Transnational Law 921, 927–30.

[67] See eg Kofi N Awoonor, 'The Concerns of Recipient Nations' in Kevin M Cahill (ed), *A Framework for Survival: Health, Human Rights and Humanitarian Assistance in Conflicts and Disasters* (Routledge 1993).

of international disaster law. Suspicions that external assistance is merely foreign intervention in another guise can significantly retard the provision of assistance. Nonetheless, there is an increased awareness in the international community as to the implications of the unfettered application of the requirement of consent, both for the protection of the persons affected and as regards the impact on broader security interests. Contemporary thinking, therefore, has focused on how best to qualify the requirement of consent.

In the view of the ILC, the legal affirmation of the centrality of the affected State's consent to external assistance is balanced by two legal obligations placed on the affected State. First, the denial of consent has to be valid. It may not be withheld arbitrarily.[68] Such qualification proved to be the most controversial provision in the ILC's draft articles. The ILC sought to attenuate the implications of the prohibition on arbitrary withholding of consent through the second requirement, namely that the affected State shall, whenever possible, make known its decision regarding the offer in a timely manner.[69] Such further obligation is both intended to establish a procedural basis for the determination of the valid denial of consent, and to ground the offer and acceptance dynamic in the concept of good faith. An offer of assistance made in good faith gives rise to the legitimate expectation of a good faith response. The lack of such response leads to the inference that the affected State may be acting arbitrarily, in violation of its obligations under international law.[70] At the same time, such process is qualified by the phrase 'whenever possible'. This alludes to the context-driven nature of the assessment taking place, and calls for the evaluation of the circumstances, and for the application of a margin of appreciation.

h. *Conditionality*

The right to impose conditions on the provision of assistance[71] is a further consequence of the primary role attributed to the affected State in the direction, control, coordination, and supervision of relief assistance. All States assert the right to do so. The function of international law in this context, therefore, is to place certain limits on the imposition of conditions. The ILC identified at least three qualifiers:

First, '[s]uch conditions shall be in accordance with the (…) draft articles, applicable rules of international law, and the national law of the affected State'.[72] This confirms the requirement of a legal basis for the imposition of conditions. It further suggests the applicable legal framework. In referring to both international and national rules, the ILC sought to reflect the subtle interplay between both sets of rules which takes place in practice.

Secondly, '[c]onditions shall take into account the identified needs of the persons affected by disasters and the quality of the assistance'.[73] Modern international disaster law takes a 'needs-based' approach to the provision of humanitarian assistance to persons affected by disasters. This has both positive and negative dimensions. The affected

[68] ILC Draft Articles (n 16) art 13(2). Matias Thomsen, 'The Obligation Not To Arbitrarily Refuse International Disaster Relief: A Question of Sovereignty' (2015) 16(2) Melbourne Journal of International Law 484.

[69] ILC Draft Articles (n 16) art 13(3). [70] ILC Commentary (n 16) 62, para 10.

[71] ILC Draft Articles (n 16) art 14. [72] ibid. [73] ibid.

State has to link the conditions it imposes on an assessment of the actual needs of the persons in question, including the special needs of women, children, the elderly, persons with disabilities,[74] and vulnerable or disadvantaged persons and groups.[75] Conversely, the implication is that the affected State retains the right to assess the nature of the assistance being offered, and to reject unwanted or unneeded assistance, and to determine what and when assistance is appropriate.[76]

Thirdly, '[w]hen formulating conditions, the affected State shall indicate the scope and type of assistance sought'.[77] In principle, it is for the affected State to assess and then indicate its needs. While, in practice, this may be undertaken in collaboration with its humanitarian assistance partners, the provision is intended to confirm that the initiative lies with the affected State. What is envisaged is a conversation taking place between the affected State seeking assistance and the assisting actor(s) offering it. The provision was also motivated by a growing concern about the phenomenon of the unsolicited delivery of inappropriate or unnecessary assistance or relief goods. What is expected is that assisting actors would tailor their assistance to that requested by the affected State.

i. *Duty to Protect Humanitarian Personnel, Equipment, and Goods*

A further key component of contemporary international disaster law is the recognition of the legal obligation on the affected State to ensure the protection of relief personnel and of equipment and goods present in its territory (or territory under its jurisdiction or control).[78] As recognition of the legal significance of the consent of affected States is central to their confidence in the process, so too is the protection of the personnel and goods sent by assisting actors key to their participation.

Protection implies, in the negative, protection from the organs of the affected State itself. It also implies a positive duty to protect personnel, equipment, and goods from, for example, the illicit activities of non-State actors.[79] In the version contained in the ILC draft articles the duty to protect is qualified by the phrase 'appropriate measures', so as to allow a margin of discretion to the affected State in deciding what actions to take.[80]

j. *Duty to Facilitate Assistance*

The concurrence of the affected State to receive external assistance triggers a further obligation on it, under international law, namely to facilitate the prompt and effective provision of such assistance.[81] Facilitation of external assistance relates primarily to relief personnel, and to equipment and goods.

[74] Akiko Ito, 'Disasters, International Law, and Persons with Disabilities' in Caron et al (n 2) 208–14.

[75] ILC Commentary (n 16) 65, para 8.

[76] ibid 64–5, para 7; Katchka (n 67) 930–4.

[77] ILC Draft Articles (n 16) art 14.

[78] ibid art 16; Lena M Ulrich, 'The Customary International Law Obligation to Protect Foreign Disaster Relief Personnel and Their Equipment'(2015) 22 Willamette Journal of International Law and Dispute Resolution 343; Stefano Silingardi, 'The Status of Emergency Workers' in de Guttry et al (n 1).

[79] ILC Commentary (n 16) 68, paras 4 and 5.

[80] ibid para 5.

[81] ILC Draft Articles (n 16) art 15.

The core of the obligation is the requirement to 'take the necessary measures' with a view to facilitating the 'prompt and effective' provision of assistance. The concept of 'necessary measures' includes legislative, executive, or administrative measures. This might even extend to temporary non-compliance with national law.[82]

The obligation is essentially one of conduct, namely to seek to improve existing, or put into place new, procedures and practices that will ensure the effectiveness of the provision of assistance.[83] In the context of response following the onset of a disaster, such effectiveness is also a function of the timeliness ('prompt') of the provision of assistance.

4. Practical Rules for the Facilitation of Disaster Relief Assistance

International disaster law is also very much about the day-to-day practicalities of disaster relief assistance.[84] In fact, the origins of the contemporary work in the area, as exemplified by the IDRL Guidelines, was the realization that law could make a practical difference. Preparedness, as a component of disaster risk reduction, also includes legal preparedness. As just discussed, all States have the duty to put into place the necessary legislative and administrative frameworks to facilitate the prompt and effective provision of assistance. These relate primarily to the provision of legal facilities for entry and operations.

With regard to personnel, facilitation includes, *inter alia*, the granting of visas and necessary work permits, ideally without cost. Those visas and permits should be renewable locally (i.e. no requirement to leave the territory of the affected State in order to renew the visa). In the immediate period of initial recovery following the onset of a disaster, the requirement of visas and work permits should be waived or their grant should be significantly expedited. Procedures ought to be put into place for the expedited consideration of the temporary recognition of professional qualifications for foreign medical personnel, as well as of drivers' licences and other types of licences and certificates.[85]

Freedom of access to and movement in and from the disaster-affected area needs to be ensured.[86] This implies, for example, the temporary recognition of foreign car registrations and plates.[87] Likewise, permission should be granted, without undue delay, for the speedy passage of land, marine and air vehicles operated by an assisting State, organization, or entity, for the purpose of transporting disaster relief assistance and any applicable fees should be waived.[88] Similarly, permission should be granted for overflight, landing, and departure of aircraft. Such aircraft should also be authorized to operate within the territory of the affected State as required for the delivery of assistance.[89]

[82] ILC Commentary (n 16) 66, para 2.

[83] Elyse Mosquini, 'Are Lawyers Unsung Disaster Heroes? The Importance of Well-prepared Domestic Legal and Regulatory Frameworks for Effective Disaster Response' (2011) 25 Emory International Law Review 1217.

[84] Giovanni D Servo, 'Actors, Activities, and Coordination in Emergencies' in de Guttry et al (n 1).

[85] IDRL Guidelines (n 15) s 16(1). [86] ibid. [87] ibid s 18(1).

[88] ibid s 19(1). [89] ibid s 19(2).

The privileges and immunities of humanitarian assistance personnel, where applicable, should likewise be respected and upheld,[90] and their legal status should be respected. This would include the recognition of their distinctive emblems and identity cards.[91] Assisting entities should, upon entry or as soon as possible thereafter, be granted at least temporary authorization to legally operate on the territory of the affected State so as to enjoy the rights, *inter alia*, to open bank accounts, enter into contracts and leases, acquire and dispose of property, and initiate legal proceedings, for the purpose of providing disaster relief assistance. Assisting States, organizations and entities should also be granted the right to freely bring the necessary funds and currencies in or out of the affected State through legal means and to obtain legal exchange rates. Assisting States, organizations, and entities should be permitted to legally hire and terminate the contracts of local personnel.[92]

Concerning equipment and goods, facilitation would include establishing exemptions from all customs duties, taxes, tariffs, or fees; exemptions from all export, transit, or import restrictions; streamlining of documentation requirements for export, transit, and import; and placing no limitations on re-exportation of equipment or unused goods which the assisting State, organization, or entity owns and wishes to retain.[93] Inspection requirements should be waived or reduced, and clearance procedures expedited, including outside of business hours. Assisting States, organizations, and entities can themselves facilitate such streamlined procedures by appropriately packing, classifying, and marking disaster relief goods, according to agreed international standards. They should also assume the responsibility for removing or disposing of unwanted and unused goods, particularly if they pose a threat to health or safety, or to the environment.[94]

Affected States should further waive or expedite the granting of any applicable licences and reduce any other barriers to the use, import, or export of telecommunications and information technology equipment by assisting States, organizations, and entities.[95] Likewise, originating, transit and affected States should reduce legal and administrative barriers to the exportation, transit, importation, and re-exportation of medications and medical equipment by assisting States, organizations, and entities, to the extent consistent with public safety and international law.[96]

C. Conclusion

The impulse to protect persons in need is not new. What is new is the expansion of international law, during the twentieth century, from a law focused on regulating the interactions of States to one increasingly concerned with the plight of individuals. This shift in emphasis has been manifested in the expansion of international rules relating to the

[90] ibid s 21(1). [91] Secretariat Memorandum (n 1) paras 120–56.
[92] IDRL Guidelines (n 15) s 20(2)–(3). [93] ibid s 17(1). [94] ibid s 17(2)–(4).
[95] ibid s 18(2). [96] ibid s 18(3).

protection of human rights, and the minimization of the deleterious impact of armed conflict. By definition those rules apply to the interaction between States and their nationals and other persons on their territory (and sometimes the territories of other States), both in peacetime or in the context of armed conflict—the two classic scenarios in which persons may find themselves in harm's way. There is, however, a third such scenario, namely that of persons affected by the onset of disasters.

While human rights law and international humanitarian law provide a certain measure of legal coverage, there has been a growing realization that a more specific set of rules, dedicated to the exigencies of disasters, is required to adequately respond to the difficulties that arise. In fact, as has been explained, such insight is not necessarily new. There is ample evidence of States providing, in instruments binding on them as a matter of international law, for specific and typically complex rules on how to regulate international cooperation in response to the onset of disasters. In recent times, this has expanded to cooperation in the pre-disaster phase on measures for disaster risk reduction. What is different is the conceptualization of that body of rules as a distinct field of international law—as international disaster law. The two most prominent recent international statements in the area have emerged from the work of the IFRC and of the ILC. Both have asserted a series of best practices framed within a patchwork of international rules, some drawn from existing general principles or rules but fine-tuned to the special context of disaster risk reduction and response.

Notwithstanding these developments, two general considerations would seem to apply. First, we are by no means at the end of the normative phase in the development of international disaster law. Much work still remains to be done in fleshing out the legal framework, particularly in the relatively new area of disaster risk reduction. Secondly, while the development of a legal framework might, in principle, be a laudable exercise, for a rule, regardless of how carefully crafted, to contribute to the goal of protecting persons it needs to make a discernible difference on the ground. A legal framework that is simply unworkable, or ignored, or treated as merely discretionary, has limited impact. The challenge therefore exists in continuing to seek ways in which the law might prove relevant to the specific needs of persons affected by disasters.

Note

The views expressed in this chapter do not necessarily reflect those of the United Nations.

CHAPTER 32

PANDEMICS AND OTHER HEALTH EMERGENCIES

J BENTON HEATH

A. Introduction

In the early months of 2020, the novel coronavirus now known as COVID-19 spread from China across the globe, infecting nearly 1.5 million people and killing more than 80,000 by early April.[1] The outbreak initially met with optimistic forecasts, along with outright denialism and suppression of information.[2] But within weeks the initially sunny global outlook gave way to increasingly draconian policies, including travel restrictions, quarantine and isolation measures, and nationwide lockdowns.[3] While researchers rushed to develop and test treatments for COVID-19,[4] governments scrambled to seize, manufacture, and stockpile necessary supplies like masks and ventilators.[5]

[1] Johns Hopkins University Center for Systems Science and Engineering, 'Coronavirus COVID-19 Global Cases' <https://gisanddata.maps.arcgis.com/apps/opsdashboard/index.html> accessed 21 April 2020.

[2] eg Laurie Garrett, 'How China's Coronavirus Incompetence Endangered the World' (*Foreign Policy*, 15 February 2020) <https://foreignpolicy.com/2020/02/15/coronavirus-xi-jinping-chinas-incompetence-endangered-the-world/> accessed 21 April 2020; David Leonhardt, 'A Complete List of Trump's Attempts to Play Down Coronavirus' (*The New York Times*, 15 March 2020) <https://www.nytimes.com/2020/03/15/opinion/trump-coronavirus.html> accessed 21 April 2020.

[3] Oxford University, 'Covid-19 Government Response Tracker' <https://www.bsg.ox.ac.uk/research/research-projects/oxford-covid-19-government-response-tracker> accessed 21 April 2020 (COVID-19 Response Tracker).

[4] 'Information for Clinicians on Therapeutic Options for Patients with COVID-19' (*Centers for Disease Control and Prevention*, last updated 25 April 2020) <https://www.cdc.gov/coronavirus/2019-ncov/hcp/therapeutic-options.html> accessed 30 April 2020.

[5] eg 'Presidential Memorandum on Allocating Certain Scarce or Threatened Health and Medical Resources to Domestic Use' (3 April 2020) <https://www.whitehouse.gov/presidential-actions/memorandum-allocating-certain-scarce-threatened-health-medical-resources-domestic-use/>

Eventually, nearly everyone's life was touched by the virus, as schools, workplaces, and universities shut down,[6] hospital systems were overwhelmed,[7] and 'essential' workers—including grocery store clerks, mail carriers, and warehouse employees—found themselves on the front lines.[8] As the pandemic spread, it touched off a global crisis, shaking the foundations of the international economic, political, and legal order.[9]

At the centre of the international public health response to COVID-19 sits the World Health Organization (WHO). Founded in 1946, the WHO has matured during a time when many feared air travel, mass migration, and the pace of globalization enabled diseases to cross the globe at previously unknown speeds.[10] Today, the organization remains 'the directing and co-ordinating authority on international health work'[11] and it administers the International Health Regulations (IHR),[12] a binding international agreement that is 'the key global instrument for the protection against the international spread of disease'.[13] The Regulations provide a basis for the WHO to exercise leadership in public health emergencies, and they purport to restrain States from overreacting to health threats with unnecessary restraints on travel, trade, and human rights.[14] After years of near-irrelevance, the IHR were thoroughly revised in 2005 and were thereafter

accessed 4 May 2020; Commission Implementing Regulation (EU) 2020/402 of 14 March 2020 making the exportation of certain products subject to the production of an export authorization OJ L77 I, 1–7.

[6] COVID-19 Response Tracker (n 3).

[7] Shalini Ramachandran et al, 'Coronavirus Cases Strain New York City Hospital' (*Wall Street Journal*, 20 March 2020) <https://www.wsj.com/articles/coronavirus-cases-strain-new-york-city-hospitals-were-getting-pounded-11584719908> accessed 21 April 2020.

[8] Abha Bhattarai, 'Grocery Workers are Beginning to Die of Coronavirus' (*Washington Post*, 6 April 2020)s <https://www.washingtonpost.com/gdpr-consent/?next_url=https%3a%2f%2fwww.washingtonpost.com%2fbusiness%2f2020%2f04%2f06%2fsupermarket-workers-deaths-coronavirus-%2f> accessed 21 April 2020; Max Zahn, '"This Is Blood Money": Amazon Warehouse Workers Stage Second Walkout Over Coronavirus Fears' (*Yahoo! Finance*, 6 April 2020) <https://uk.finance.yahoo.com/news/amazon-warehouse-workers-second-walkout-one-week-over-coronavirus-fears-195814468.html?soc_src=social-sh&soc_trk=ma> accessed 21 April 2020.

[9] Anthea Roberts/Nicolas Lamp, 'Will the Coronavirus End Globalization? There Is No One Answer' (*Barron's*, 15 March 2020) <https://www.barrons.com/articles/is-the-virus-killing-globalization-theres-no-one-answer-51584209741> accessed 21 April 2020.

[10] For perspectives throughout the post-war era: Gian Luca Burci/Jakob Quirin, 'Ebola, WHO, and the United Nations: Convergence of Global Public Health and International Peace and Security' (2014) 18 ASIL Insights <https://www.asil.org/insights/volume/18/issue/25/ebola-who-and-united-nations-convergence-global-public-health-and> accessed 28 February 2019; P Dorolle, 'Old Plagues in the Jet Age: International Aspects of Present and Future Control of Communicable Disease' (1968) 4 British Medical Journal 789; International Health Agency, 'Memorandum Submitted by the Brazilian Delegation, May 14, 1945' UNCIO X, 107.

[11] Constitution of the World Health Organization 14 UNTS 185 art 2(a).

[12] International Health Regulations 2509 UNTS 79 (IHR 2005).

[13] World Health Assembly, 'Revision of the International Health Regulations' (23 May 2005) WHA58.3, preamble.

[14] eg Lawrence O Gostin, *Global Health Law* (Harvard UP 2014) 177–204; David P Fidler/Lawrence O Gostin, 'The New International Health Regulations' (2006) 34 Journal of Law, Medicine and Ethics 85; Barbara von Tigerstrom, 'The Revised International Health Regulations and Restraint of National Measures' (2005) 13 Health Law Journal 35.

touted as establishing an innovative and comprehensive framework for global health security in the twenty-first century.[15]

Today, the status of the WHO and the IHR is once again in doubt. A series of widely criticized responses to the 2009 global H1N1 pandemic, the 2014 outbreak of Ebola in West Africa, and the COVID-19 pandemic led observers to question whether the organization has the mandate, capacity, expertise, or political independence to address global outbreaks.[16] Lack of funding, both for national capacity-building and for global surveillance and response, has raised serious questions about the promise and future of the Regulations and the organization.[17] Further, recent years have witnessed an increasing number of institutional competitors—whether the UN, international financial institutions, public–private partnerships, national governments, or private entities—seeking a role in global health security.[18] These issues are becoming perennial, with major outbreaks presenting themselves not only as health and security crises, but as existential crises for the health security regime.[19]

This chapter traces the normative challenges underlying the legal framework for health security. Today's challenges can be understood as the result of three successive stages of development in global health law.[20] First was the securitization of global public health, whereby a diffuse group of international and national health officials, outside experts, and advocates worked to redefine infectious disease outbreaks as a critical national and international security issue.[21] Secondly, this concept of global health security was inscribed in law through the 2005 revisions to the IHR, which adopted a governance framework that appeared to be deliberately modelled on domestic emergency powers regimes.[22]

Thirdly, this development, rather than settling the WHO's authority in health emergencies, has in turn set off waves of contestation that concerns the nature of global health security and how it should be institutionalized. In this way, the WHO experience provides a crucible for studying the emergence of global security regimes more broadly. Security discourses exist in ambiguous relation to both politics and technical expertise.[23]

[15] David P Fidler, 'From International Sanitary Conventions to Global Health Security' (2005) 4 Chinese Journal of International Law 325; WHO, *A Safer Future: Global Public Health Security in the 21st Century* (WHO 2007) 8–14.

[16] eg J Benton Heath, 'Global Emergency Power in the Age of Ebola' (2016) 57 Harvard International Law Journal 1, 26–36.

[17] eg Yves Beigbeder, *The World Health Organization: Achievements and Failures* (Routledge 2018) 9–19.

[18] ibid 10–19.

[19] From different perspectives: Lawrence O Gostin, 'New Ebola Outbreak in Africa is a Major Test for the WHO' (2018) 320 Journal of the American Medical Association 125; 'The Ebola Twilight of Public Institutions' (*Wall Street Journal*, 16 October 2014) <https://www.wsj.com/articles/the-ebola-twilight-of-public-institutions-1413415407> accessed 28 February 2019.

[20] For helpful consideration of this development from a security studies perspective: Tine Hanrieder/Christian Kreuder-Sonnen, 'WHO Decides on the Exception?' (2014) 45 Security Dialogue 331.

[21] Generally, Sara E Davies et al, *Disease Diplomacy* (Johns Hopkins UP 2015).

[22] eg Heath (n 16) 9–10; Hanrieder/Kreuder-Sonnen (n 20) 338.

[23] Barry Buzan et al, *Security: A New Framework for Analysis* (Lynne Rienner 1998) 21–48.

When an issue is treated as a 'security' matter, it is, in a sense, hyper-politicized, because security issues are understood to be matters of public imperative, usually requiring intervention by national and increasingly international institutions.[24] But, in another sense, security is 'opposed to politics' in that security discourses present matters as urgent, existential, and best dealt with decisively by leaders and their expert advisers, without the 'normal haggling' of political debate.[25] As this chapter shows, this ambiguity destabilizes the claims to normative authority that organizations like the WHO rely on to secure coordination, compliance, and trust, thereby contributing to the waves of contestation we have observed.[26] It is hoped that a close investigation of the normative challenges facing institutions like the WHO can identify potential tools for controlling emergency power at the international level and for shoring up emergency authority where it is desirable to do so.[27]

This chapter's focus on the Regulations and their emergency powers framework does not—and cannot—represent an exhaustive study of global institutions related to health security. Some observers have noted a 'significant governance shift' in public health away from formal organizations, as public and private transnational networks of health professionals, laboratories, and other actors have emerged to monitor and respond to disease outbreaks.[28] Recent years have also seen renewed controversy over virus-sharing and access to vaccines, along with the development of new governance frameworks to address these issues.[29] The COVID-19 outbreak, moreover, demonstrates that other areas of international and global law—including trade, human rights, environment, and the law of international organizations—are also very much in play during a pandemic.[30] Nevertheless, a focus on the IHR and the emergency powers framework is warranted not least because the IHR continue to be 'the only international rules governing global health security'.[31]

This chapter proceeds in three further sections. Section B discusses the developments that led to the current controversies surrounding global health governance, focusing on the securitization of infectious disease and the resulting legal developments at the WHO. Section C then sketches three layers of contestation that have emerged since the adoption of the revised IHR. These layers comprise conflicts over governance arrangements within the WHO, conflicts of jurisdiction between the WHO and other institutions, and disagreement about the *normative* orientation and scope of the WHO's emergency power. Section D concludes.

[24] ibid 23, 29. [25] ibid 29. [26] Heath (n 16) 12–13.

[27] ibid 36–46; Hanrieder/Kreuder-Sonnen (n 20) 343–4.

[28] Margaret P Karns/Karen A Mingst, *International Organizations* (2nd edn, Lynne Rienner 2010) 75.

[29] Lawrence O Gostin et al, *The Global Health Law Trilogy* (2017) 390 The Lancet 1918, 1922–4.

[30] Generally, Barrie Sander et al (eds), 'Covid-19 and International Law' (*Opinio Juris*, Symposium March–April 2020) <http://opiniojuris.org/wp-content/uploads/B.-Sander-J.-Rudall-eds-COVID-19-and-International-Law-Opinio-Juris-Symposium-copy-1.pdf> accessed 21 April 2020.

[31] Gostin (n 14) 177.

B. Emergency Law and Power at the World Health Organization

The emergence of a global regime for health security was a remarkable and historic development for international law.[32] At the end of the twentieth century, the international legal framework for controlling infectious diseases was effectively non-existent, and the WHO was largely sidelined when it came to managing disease outbreaks.[33] Yet, by 2005, the international community had adopted a comprehensive, universal agreement governing States' obligations to identify, report, and respond to disease outbreaks. Perhaps even more surprising, the authority to manage a global response to these outbreaks was placed directly and explicitly in the hands of the WHO Secretariat.[34]

These rapid changes in the global governance of disease outbreaks were made possible in large part by broader efforts to reframe health as a matter of national and international 'security'. Throughout the 1990s, WHO and national health officials, outside experts, and advocates worked to present infectious disease surveillance and control as a critical global security issue, and to develop legal responses. These efforts ultimately resulted in the adoption by nearly all States of the revised IHR—a new legal framework for global health security.

1. The Securitization of Disease Outbreaks

The revision of the IHR came about during a period when the relationship between public health and security was undergoing a rapid transformation.[35] The end of the Cold War had brought about a wave of new thinking about the meaning of 'national' and 'global' security, and about the security dimensions of traditionally non-military threats, such as environmental degradation, food scarcity, crime, and disease.[36]

These developments quickly worked their way into international law and institutions. The most striking example is the transformation of the UN Security Council's (UNSC) mandate to maintain and restore 'international peace and security'.[37] In what is now considered a milestone, the UNSC in January 2000 held a debate on the impact of

[32] Guy Fiti Sinclair, *To Reform the World: International Organizations and the Making of Modern State* (OUP 2017) 3–4.

[33] David P Fidler, 'Return of the Fourth Horseman: Emerging Infectious Diseases and International Law' (1997) 81 Minnesota Law Review 771, 775.

[34] David P Fidler, 'Constitutional Outlines of Public Health's "New World Order"' (2004) 77 Temple Law Review 247, 268; Benedict Kingsbury/Lorenzo Casini, 'Global Administrative Law Dimensions of International Organizations Law' (2009) 6 International Organizations Law Review 319, 336.

[35] Davies et al (n 21) 18–23.

[36] eg Alexandra Gheciu/William C Wohlforth, 'The Future of Security Studies' in Alexandra Gheciu/William C Wohlforth (eds), *The Oxford Handbook of International Security* (OUP 2018) 4–5.

[37] UN Charter 1 UNTS XVI arts 24, 39.

HIV/AIDS on international peace and security, explicitly linking the two concepts.[38] Opening that debate, then-US Vice President Al Gore insisted on a 'new agenda for world security', which would address, *inter alia*, 'the new pandemics laying waste to whole societies; and the emergence of new strains of old diseases that are horrifyingly resistant to the antibiotics that protected the past three generations.'[39]

Against this backdrop, officials within the WHO began in 1995 to lay the groundwork for a new set of international regulations to comprehensively address infectious diseases.[40] Over the next several years, a team of WHO officials and their allies acted as 'norm entrepreneurs', attempting to sell State governments on a concept of global health security that contrasted sharply with earlier visions of both military security and international disease control.[41] This included a view of diseases as threats to national and global security, a recognition that States could no longer rely on border barriers and quarantines to keep their populations safe, and an emphasis on the WHO as a central authority in coordinating the response to international health emergencies.[42] The revised IHR adopted in 2005 incorporated each of these elements, framing infectious disease as 'a particular *kind* of security threat that required a particular kind of cooperative and (…) institutionalized international response.'[43]

2. Legalizing Global Health Security

This international, institutionalized concept of global health security is reflected in the structure of the new IHR in at least three ways.[44] These include the broad scope given to the new regime; the role of State governments that is envisioned in the revised IHR; and the rather elaborate institutional framework established for the exercise of emergency power by the WHO secretariat. That these elements were set out in an international legal instrument binding all WHO members was all the more striking at the time.[45]

a. *Scope: Defining Global Health Security*

The 2005 IHR contained relatively few limitations on the types of emergent health threats they could address. Their purpose is to prevent and respond to the 'international spread of disease' and to public health risks 'in ways that are commensurate with and restricted to public health risks, and which avoid unnecessary interference with international traffic and trade.'[46]

[38] Burci/Quirin (n 10). [39] UNSC Verbatim Record (10 January 2000) UN Doc S/PV/4087.
[40] Davies et al (n 21) 27. [41] ibid 40–2. [42] ibid 39–40. [43] ibid 56.
[44] Guénaël Rodier et al, 'Global Public Health Security' (2007) 13 Emerging Infectious Diseases 1447.
[45] The International Health Regulations are binding on all WHO Members under international law, unless a Member opts out within a specified period. WHO Constitution (n 11) arts 21, 22. As of April 2013, there were 196 States Parties to the revised Regulations: 'States Parties to the International Health Regulations (2005)' (WHO, 16 April 2013) <http://www.who.int/ihr/legal_issues/states_parties/en/> accessed 28 February 2019.
[46] IHR 2005 (n 12) art 2.

The core subject of these IHR—'disease' and 'public health risks'—are defined broadly. 'Disease' means 'an illness or medical condition, *irrespective of origin or source*, that presents or could present significant harm to humans'.[47] The definition of 'public health risk' mirrors this flexibility.[48] This is in significant contrast to earlier WHO regulations, which specifically targeted certain diseases such as cholera and smallpox.[49] This breadth reflects the uncertainty underlying the global health security frame, which is particularly concerned with emerging pathogens like the 2003 outbreak of Severe Acute Respiratory Syndrome (SARS) that could not have been predicted in advance.[50] The effect of this broad scope is to delegate to the WHO secretariat significant discretion to decide when and under what circumstances to declare a health emergency.

Another scoping issue concerns the values that are meant to be protected and promoted in responding to health threats. The above-quoted provision establishes a link between public health threats and the free movement of 'international traffic and trade', which is a long-standing concern of the international public health regime.[51] Here, however, the relationship between public health measures and international trade is re-conceptualized to incorporate an expectation of rationality in domestic and international regulatory measures, similar to the principles adopted in trade and investment agreements of the 1990s.[52] And the IHR espouse other values like human rights and human dignity.[53] This has led some commentators to argue that the IHR require 'balancing' between trade, health security, and human rights,[54] or that 'the WHO is at least now in part a human rights organization'.[55] This mixture of values can pull in opposite directions: as the emphasis on scientific rationality seeks to depoliticize the regulation of disease, the introduction of human rights into this framework brings with it a more ambiguously political dimension.[56]

b. *The Roles and Obligations of States*

From the perspective of the revised IHR, States are treated as constituent parts of an internationalized response to public health emergencies. States are expected to monitor health threats, report outbreaks, and then accordingly implement their obligations under the IHR, and they are obligated to build the capacity necessary to meet these expectations. In practice, State compliance with these obligations is uneven at best, and the ability of the WHO to effectively coordinate an international response has also been

[47] ibid art 1. [48] ibid. [49] eg International Health Regulations 764 UNTS 3.

[50] Mary Whelan, 'Negotiating the International Health Regulations' (2008) Graduate Institute, Global Health Programme Working Paper No 1 <https://repository.graduateinstitute.ch/record/4066?ln=en> accessed 28 February 2019.

[51] WHO, *International Health Regulations* (3rd annotated edn, WHO 1983) 5.

[52] eg Agreement on the Application of Sanitary and Phytosanitary Measures 1867 UNTS 493 art 2.2; Fidler (n 15) 383; von Tigerstrom (n 14) 59–61.

[53] IHR 2005 (n 12) art 3(1). [54] Gostin (n 14) 183–4.

[55] José E Alvarez, *The Impact of International Organizations on International Law* (Brill 2016) 215.

[56] cf Matthias Goldmann, 'Contesting Austerity: Genealogies of Human Rights Discourse' (2020) MPIL Research Paper Series No 2020–09 <https://papers.ssrn.com/sol3/papers.cfm?abstract_id=3561660> accessed 21 April 2020.

called into question. But, by design, the IHR envision a hub-and-spoke model, where an international organization coordinates the response to international health emergencies, even if States are the prime movers within their own jurisdictions.[57]

The IHR require that Member States develop the capacity to 'detect, assess, notify and report' potential health emergencies in all areas within their territory and to respond 'promptly and effectively'.[58] Each State must also establish a 'National Focal Point' for coordination with the WHO.[59] As a result of these provisions, the Regulations reflect a kind of administrative law, with significant implications for how States structure their primary health systems.[60]

States must notify the WHO of a potential public health emergency in their territory within twenty-four hours.[61] In deciding whether to notify, States shall consider a range of factors including the cause of the outbreak, the seriousness of the public health impact, whether the event was unexpected, the risk of international spread, and the risk of States adopting travel or trade restrictions.[62] While certain diseases—smallpox, poliomyelitis, SARS, and new subtypes of influenza—must always be notified,[63] 'any event of potential international public health concern, including those of unknown causes or sources', can constitute an international emergency.[64]

State compliance with both the capacity-building and notification requirements has been uneven. As to capacity-building, the only mechanism for compliance in the IHR is a horizontal one, whereby States can review each other based on annual reports to the World Health Assembly.[65] The IHR also do not impose any specific, binding obligations on States to give funding or technical assistance to countries that may struggle to meet their capacity obligations.[66] As of 2016, only one-third of States Parties to the IHR had declared that they meet the core capacity requirements.[67]

States also have significant incentives to avoid complying with their notification obligations.[68] The failure of States to report outbreaks was a significant factor driving the revision of the IHR in 1995.[69] Nevertheless, the new IHR contain no mechanism for enforcing the obligation to report potential emergencies, beyond the risk that the WHO decides to declare an emergency in the absence of the affected State's cooperation.

[57] Fidler (n 34) 267–9; Alvarez (n 55) 208–33.

[58] IHR 2005 (n 12) arts 5(1)–(2), 13(1)–(2) and Annex 1, s A(4). [59] ibid art 4(1)–(2).

[60] Alvarez (n 55) 215. [61] IHR 2005 (n 12) art 6(1). [62] ibid Annex 2. [63] ibid.

[64] ibid.

[65] Gian Luca Burci/Jakob Quirin, 'Implementation of the International Health Regulations (2005): Recent Developments at the World Health Organization' (2018) 22 ASIL Insights <https://www.asil.org/insights/volume/22/issue/13/implementation-international-health-regulations-2005-recent-developments> accessed 28 February 2019.

[66] Fidler/Gostin (n 14) 88.

[67] UNGA, 'Protecting Humanity from Future Health Crises: High-level Panel on the Global Response to Health Crises' (9 February 2016) UN Doc A/70/723.

[68] Arielle Silver, 'Obstacles to Complying with the World Health Organization's 2005 International Health Regulations' (2008) 26 Wisconsin International Law Journal 229, 234–7.

[69] Adam Kamradt-Scott, 'The WHO Secretariat, Norm Entrepreneurship, and Global Outbreak Control' (2010) 1 Journal of International Organizations Studies 72.

c. *International, Institutional Emergency Power*

Once a serious health risk is detected, the WHO Director-General[70] must decide whether to declare a public health emergency.[71] The IHR use a flexible definition of 'emergency'.[72] The Director-General must consider certain categories of information in deciding whether these criteria are met, including information provided by the affected State, available scientific evidence, and assessments of the risks posed by the disease.[73] No particular piece of information is dispositive.

The Director-General is not limited to official State reports when deciding whether to declare a health emergency. This was a critical element of the 2005 reforms, and a transformation from prior practice.[74] Prior to the revised Regulations, the WHO's most notable use of unofficial sources was in 2003, when it relied on information gained from an internet-based early warning system to challenge the Chinese government's official narrative of events.[75] At the time, WHO officials thought of that action, and other measures taken in response to SARS, to be an early 'roll out' of the IHR, then in draft form.[76] The final revised IHR later imposed some disciplines on this use of non-governmental information: the information must be assessed according to established epidemiological principles; the WHO must consult with, make the information available to, and attempt to obtain verification from, the affected State; and the organization may withhold the source of the information from the affected State 'only where it is duly justified'.[77]

The WHO Director-General's decision whether to declare a public health emergency is ordinarily made in consultation with an 'Emergency Committee' selected from a pre-existing 'roster' of experts.[78] Upon the emergency declaration, the WHO Director-General issues so-called 'temporary recommendations' to members, such as proposed health measures relating to travel, medical examination, vaccination, quarantine, and exit screening.[79] Recommendations are meant to apply on a 'time-limited, risk-specific' basis, and must be calibrated 'to prevent or reduce the international spread of disease and minimize interference with international traffic'.[80] 'Travel advisories' issued by the WHO during the SARS crisis, warning individuals to avoid non-essential travel to Toronto, China, and other locations, were the prototypical examples of a temporary

[70] The WHO Director-General is the head of the WHO Secretariat, essentially the administrative arm of the organization. WHO Constitution (n 11) arts 30–7.

[71] IHR 2005 (n 12) art 12(1).

[72] ibid art 1(1) provides:

public health emergency of international concern' means an extraordinary event which is determined, as provided in these Regulations:
(i) to constitute a public health risk to other States through the international spread of disease and
(ii) to potentially require a coordinated international response[.]

[73] ibid art 12(4). [74] eg Kamradt-Scott (n 69) 76–7.

[75] Jennifer Shkabatur, 'A Global Panopticon?' (2011) 33 Michigan Journal of International Law 160, 192–4.

[76] Fidler/Gostin (n 14) 85. [77] IHR 2005 (n 12) art 9(1).

[78] ibid arts 12, 47–8. The IHR also require that the Director-General attempt to consult with the affected State prior to declaring an emergency (ibid art 12).

[79] ibid arts 1, 15, 18. [80] ibid art 1.

recommendation.[81] After the 2005 revisions, WHO recommendations have included that Pakistan, Cameroon, and Syria ensure that all residents and long-term visitors receive polio vaccinations;[82] that States affected by the 2014 Ebola outbreak declare a national emergency;[83] and that States *not* restrict travel or trade during the H1N1 pandemic of 2009,[84] and, more controversially, as COVID-19 was spreading worldwide.[85]

Although the IHR provide that these recommendations are 'non-binding advice,'[86] they may have substantial legal and practical effects.[87] As a legal matter, 'additional' emergency health measures that go beyond WHO recommendations shall not be more restrictive of travel or trade, or more invasive to persons, than 'reasonably available alternatives.'[88] If a State's additional health measures 'significantly' interfere with international traffic, the State shall provide the public health rationale and relevant scientific information to the organization, which will share that information with other States Parties.[89] The State must also review those measures within three months of their implementation, and must enter into consultations with any State impacted by such measures at the impacted State's request.[90] These provisions suggest a duty to 'comply or explain' deviations from WHO recommendations,[91] thus complicating the IHR's suggestion that such recommendations are mere non-binding advice.[92]

In practice, State implementation of WHO recommendations, and compliance with their obligations regarding 'additional' health measures, has also been uneven.[93] As with

[81] WHO, 'Update 92: Chronology of Travel Recommendations, Areas with Local Transmission' (1 July 2003) <http://www.who.int/csr/don/2003_07_01/en/index.html> accessed 28 February 2019.

[82] WHO, 'Statement on the meeting of the International Health Regulations Emergency Committee concerning the international spread of wild poliovirus' (5 May 2014) <http://www.who.int/mediacentre/news/statements/2014/polio-20,140,505/en/> accessed 28 February 2019.

[83] WHO, 'Statement on the 1st Meeting of the IHR Emergency Committee on the 2014 Ebola Outbreak in West Africa' (8 August 2014) <http://www.who.int/mediacentre/news/statements/2014/ebola-20,140,808/en/> accessed 28 February 2019.

[84] WHO Director-General, 'Statement Following the Fifth Meeting of the Emergency Committee' (24 September 2009) <http://www.who.int/csr/disease/swineflu/5th_meeting_ihr/en/> accessed 28 February 2019.

[85] WHO, 'Statement on the Second Meeting of the Emergency Committee regarding the Outbreak of Novel Coronavirus' (30 January 2020) <https://www.who.int/news/item/30-01-2020-statement-on-the-second-meeting-of-the-international-health-regulations-(2005)-emergency-committee-regarding-the-outbreak-of-novel-coronavirus-(2019-ncov)> accessed 30 November 2020.

[86] IHR 2005 (n 12) art 43(1). [87] eg von Tigerstrom (n 14).

[88] IHR 2005 (n 12) art 43(1); ibid art 1: 'Health measures (…) [are] procedures applied to prevent the spread of disease or contamination; a health measure does not include law enforcement or security measures.'

[89] ibid art 43(3). [90] ibid art 48(6)–(7).

[91] Armin von Bogdandy/Pedro A Villareal, 'International Law on Pandemic Response: A First Stocktaking in Light of the Coronavirus Crisis' (2020) MPIL Working Paper No 2020–07, 15 <https://papers.ssrn.com/sol3/papers.cfm?abstract_id=3561650> accessed 21 April 2020.

[92] Gian Luca Burci, 'The Outbreak of COVID-19 Coronavirus: Are the International Health Regulations Fit for Purpose?' (*EJIL Talk!*, 27 February 2020) <https://www.ejiltalk.org/the-outbreak-of-covid-19-coronavirus-are-the-international-health-regulations-fit-for-purpose/> accessed 21 April 2020.

[93] Bradly J Condon/Tapen Sinha, 'The Effectiveness of Pandemic Preparations: Legal Lessons from the 2009 Influenza Epidemic' (2010) 22 Florida Journal of International Law 1.

notification and capacity-building, the IHR lack a formal legal mechanism to enforce compliance, relying instead on the same types of horizontal controls, such as reporting and reason-giving requirements.[94] They provide for arbitration of disputes thereunder, but only with the agreement of both parties.[95] States do retain any rights to challenge burdensome health measures in other fora.[96]

The practical impacts of WHO recommendations can also be significant and sometimes difficult to control.[97] Recommendations by the WHO can impact travel and trade patterns,[98] create domestic demand for vaccinations or other public health measures,[99] or even have unintended negative consequences for traveller or consumer behaviour.[100] States are also free to amplify the legal effects of WHO recommendations, such as by concluding procurement contracts with drug manufacturers that are triggered automatically upon a declaration of emergency by the organization. But this technique can be politically costly, as demonstrated during the 'swine flu' crisis of 2009, when some States were unable to cancel contracts for unused doses of flu vaccines.[101]

In light of these potential effects, the IHR establish a procedure for channelling and checking this emergency power. The Director-General must consult with the aforementioned Emergency Committee of outside experts before issuing any temporary recommendations.[102] The committee prepares a report summarizing its deliberations and any advice given to the WHO.[103] Although the Director-General makes the final call, the committee's report is published along with her decision.[104] Therefore, if the Director-General disagrees with the Emergency Committee, she must, as a practical matter, either explain her disagreement or change her position to avoid embarrassment. In practice, the committee and the Director-General have frequently avoided potential conflict by speaking with one voice.[105] Once the Director-General decides that an

[94] WHO Director-General, 'Report: Public Health Preparedness and Response' (11 April 2018) WHO Doc A71/8, paras 22–3.

[95] IHR 2005 (n 12) art 56(3).

[96] ibid art 56(4). On the possibility of bringing challenges under trade agreements: von Tigerstrom (n 14) 71 fn 172.

[97] Heath (n 16) 23.

[98] Colleen M Flood/Anthea Williams, 'A Tale of Toronto: National and International Lessons in Public Health Governance from the SARS Crisis' (2004) 12 Michigan State Journal of International Law 229, 242–3.

[99] Sheryl Gay Stolberg, 'Shortage of Vaccine Poses Political Test for Obama' (*The New York Times*, 28 October 2009) <https://www.nytimes.com/2009/10/29/us/politics/29shortage.html> accessed 30 April 2020; Ulrich Beck, 'World at Risk: The New Task of Critical Theory' (2008) 37 Development and Society 1, 15–18.

[100] eg 'The Butcher's Bill' (*The Economist*, 30 April 2009) <https://www.economist.com/briefing/2009/04/30/the-butchers-bill> accessed 30 November 2020.

[101] Nick Triggle, 'Swine Flu Vaccine Contracts "Lacked Get Out Clauses"' (*BBC News*, 1 July 2010) <https://www.bbc.com/news/10474155> accessed 20 May 2020; Social, Health and Family Affairs Committee, Paul Flynn, 'The Handling of the H1N1 Pandemic: More Transparency Needed' (Parliamentary Assembly of the Council of Europe, 7 June 2010) Doc 12,283, para 46.

[102] IHR 2005 (n 12) arts 47–9. [103] ibid art 49. [104] ibid. [105] Heath (n 16) 25.

emergency has ended, the Regulations provide a mechanism for reviewing the emergency response through the establishment of another body of outside experts.[106]

C. Challenges to the Health Security Framework

The implementation of the WHO's emergency powers has come with significant challenges. After initial enthusiasm following the defeat of SARS in 2003, the organization was seen by many critics to have bungled the responses to H1N1 ('swine flu'), Ebola, and COVID-19.[107] The 2014 Ebola outbreak, in particular, spurred a new round of soul-searching within and outside the organization, and at least four independent panels (including a Review Committee) were organized to make recommendations for reforming and reorganizing the international response to disease.[108] These criticisms addressed a wide range of issues, including the organization's inability to ensure compliance with all aspects of the Regulations, and many propose detailed structural reforms. But the criticisms arising out of these events also raise deeper questions about the basic structure of the emergency powers framework.

1. Security between Expertise and Politics: Decision-Making Inside the World Health Organization

The WHO experience in the swine flu, Ebola, COVID-19, and other outbreaks demonstrates the tension between politics and expertise in a newly securitized regime. WHO officials and experts have in the past expressed some discomfort with the political dimensions of the organization's emergency power.[109] It has been observed that the

[106] IHR 2005 (n 12) art 50.

[107] eg Kumanan Wilson et al, 'Strengthening the International Health Regulations: Lessons from the H1N1 Pandemic' (2010) 25 Health Policy and Planning 505; Lawrence O Gostin/Eric A Friedman, 'Ebola: A Crisis in Global Health Leadership' (2014) 384 The Lancet 1323; Oyewale Tomori, 'Ebola in an Unprepared Africa' (2014) 349 British Medical Journal 5597; Robert Wright, 'Trump Isn't Wrong About Investigating WHO' (*Wired*, 10 April 2020) <https://www.wired.com/story/trump-isnt-wrong-about-investigating-who/> accessed 21 April 2020.

[108] eg WHO, 'Report of the Ebola Interim Assessment Panel' (July 2015) <https://www.who.int/csr/resources/publications/ebola/report-by-panel.pdf?ua=1> accessed 28 February 2019; Suerie Moon et al, 'Will Ebola Change the Game? Ten Essential Reforms Before the Next Pandemic: Harvard-LTSM Independent Panel on the Global Response to Ebola' (2015) 386 The Lancet 2204; WHO, 'Report of the Review Committee on the Role of the International Health Regulations (2005) in the Ebola Outbreak and Response' (13 May 2016) WHO Doc A69/21, Annex (WHO Report); UN High-Level Panel Report (n 67).

[109] eg WHO, 'Report of the Review Committee on the Functioning of the International Health Regulations (2005) in Relation to Pandemic (H1N1) 2009' (5 May 2011) WHO Doc A64/10, para 69.

WHO has a 'technical, normative culture', and that the organization may be averse to challenging national governments regarding domestic health measures or the extent of a health emergency on their territories.[110] The collision of expertise and politics results in policymaking compromises that reflect 'a conflation of politics and science where both end up getting disfigured'.[111]

This collision is readily apparent in the frequently controversial decisions by the WHO secretariat on whether to declare a public health emergency. A declaration of emergency is an inherently political exercise that requires broad discretion, but the complexity of such decisions also demands extensive expert advice.[112] This duality is reflected in the Regulations' criteria for declaring a public health emergency, which require consideration of scientific principles, scientific evidence, and expert advice,[113] but which ultimately leave the decision to the discretion of the WHO Director-General.[114] For a self-consciously technical organization like the WHO, this tension becomes especially problematic when the science points to a rapidly spreading and deadly disease, while extrinsic factors appear to counsel discretion.

In such cases, the WHO has often sought to legitimize its exercise of political discretion by reference to malleable legal criteria, often focusing on the definition of an 'emergency' as involving the 'international spread' of disease.[115] The organization justified its five-month delay in declaring an emergency with respect to the 2014 Ebola outbreak by explaining that it did so only when the disease spread by air travel to Lagos, notwithstanding the fact that Ebola had been circulating amongst a three-country region in Western Africa for some time.[116] The definition of 'international spread' once again became a flashpoint between the WHO and its critics when Ebola emerged in the Democratic Republic of Congo in 2018.[117] The initial decision not to declare an emergency for COVID-19 was again justified in these terms, with some members of the Emergency Committee reportedly arguing in January 2020 that there were not yet any reported cases of human-to-human transmission outside China.[118] To many observers, this restraint seemed like undue deference to China, consistent with the WHO's continued praise for the country's authoritarian response domestically.[119] This perception was only compounded by the fact that actual instances of cross-border spread are not

[110] WHO, 'Report of the Ebola Interim Assessment Panel' (n 108) para 23 and 'Box' after para 22.

[111] William E Scheuerman, 'Executive and Exception' in Anthony F Lang/Antje Wiener (eds), *Handbook on Global Constitutionalism* (Edward Elgar 2017) 324.

[112] cf J Benton Heath, 'National Security and Economic Globalization: Toward Collision or Reconciliation?' (2019) 42 Fordham International Law Journal 1431, 1445–8.

[113] IHR 2005 (n 12) art 12(4). [114] ibid arts 12(2), 49(5).

[115] Heath (n 16) 27–30. [116] WHO Report (n 108) para 103.

[117] David P Fidler, 'To Declare or Not to Declare: The Controversy Over Declaring a Public Health Emergency of International Concern for the Ebola Outbreak in the Democratic Republic of the Congo' (2019) 14 Asian Journal of WTO and International Health Law and Policy 287, 301.

[118] Mark Eccleston-Turner, 'The Declaration of a Public Health Emergency of International Concern in International Law' in Sander et al (n 30).

[119] Garrett (n 2).

necessary elements of a public health emergency, either in the text of the IHR or in WHO practice.[120]

In these cases, the resort to unsustainable legal criteria appears to reflect the WHO's reluctance to be identified as a political, rather than technical, actor. In both the 2014 Ebola outbreak and the COVID-19 pandemic, the WHO's delay in declaring a global emergency may be explained by a desire to defer to local and regional authorities.[121] Such a policy may even be justified, given that an emergency declaration can entail dire and unmanageable economic consequences.[122] But there is no principle of deference or subsidiarity amongst the IHR criteria for declaring a health emergency, and exercising such a principle would be difficult to square with the organization's self-conception as a technical, not political, body.[123] The demands of the IHR 'global health security' frame thus create a problem for the WHO in nearly every outbreak, as it continues to struggle to reconcile its technical expertise with its irreducibly political role.

The same struggle can be seen in the selection of expert advisers and the procedure for emergency decision-making under the IHR. Initially, members of WHO emergency committees were nearly all public health professionals and scientists, and their work was treated as that of any other expert advisory committee. This meant that emergency committees met in secret—and still do as of this writing—with only limited summaries of their deliberations and decisions made available to the public afterward.[124] In making emergency declarations and setting policy, the WHO Director-General and the emergency committees have tended to speak with 'one voice', presenting their decisions as emerging from scientific consensus rather than political debate.[125] Initially, the WHO even kept secret the identities of emergency committee members, out of concern that the members would be subject to political pressure, 'potentially compromising their advice'.[126] During the H1N1 pandemic, this raised concerns that costly and politically difficult decisions were being made by a cabal of anonymous experts—a perception that became inflamed when it was discovered that some committee members had ties to drug companies.[127]

[120] Eccleston-Turner (n 118). [121] Heath (n 16) 27–30.

[122] ibid 28. [123] ibid 30.

[124] Mark Eccleston-Turner/Adam Kamradt-Scott, 'Transparency in IHR Emergency Committee Decision Making: The Case for Reform' (2019) 4 British Medical Journal Global Health 1; Lawrence O Gostin/Rebecca Katz, 'The International Health Regulations' (2016) 94 Millbank Quarterly 264, 304.

[125] Heath (n 16) 44–6; von Bogdandy/Villareal (n 91) 13. In this respect, the recent declaration of emergency regarding COVID-19 was a rare and partial exception, which involved public discussion of divisions within the emergency committee over the appropriateness of this decision: Eccleston-Turner (n 118).

[126] 'The International Response to the Influenza Pandemic: The WHO Responds to the Critics' (WHO, 10 June 2010) <https://www.who.int/csr/disease/swineflu/notes/briefing_20100610/en/> accessed 21 April 2020.

[127] eg Abigail C Deshman, 'Horizontal Review between International Organizations' (2011) 22 EJIL 1089; Deborah Cohen/Philip Carter, 'WHO and the Pandemic Flu 'Conspiracies' (2010) 340 British Medical Journal 2912; Helen Epstein, 'Flu Warning: Beware the Drug Companies!' (*New York Review of Books*, 12 May 2011) <https://www.nybooks.com/articles/2011/05/12/flu-warning-beware-drug-companies/> accessed 21 April 2020; H1N1 Review Committee (n 109) 277–8.

The WHO has made halting steps to address some of these issues, but there appears to be some persisting discomfort with the political dimensions of global health security. The organization now publishes upfront the names, affiliations, and any disclosed conflicts of all committee members,[128] but meetings of the committees still take place behind closed doors and are subject to only limited disclosures after the fact.[129] The WHO has also slowly adjusted the composition of its emergency committees to include experts from outside traditional public health and medical fields, such as anthropology, risk communication, and sustainable development.[130] This development suggests some recognition on the WHO's part that broader political contexts cannot be neatly excised from the day-to-day administration of global health security.[131]

In 2019, the WHO took a new approach to applying the IHR that arguably represented a dramatic break from the past. When Ebola emerged in the Democratic Republic of the Congo (DRC) in late 2018, the organization quickly convened an emergency committee to consider the outbreak, but repeatedly declined to declare a public health emergency under the Regulations.[132] The Emergency Committee and the Director-General both emphasized the severity of the outbreak and made a plea for resources and international cooperation.[133] But the committee stated that declaring an emergency would produce 'no added benefit' to the response.[134] Members feared that an emergency declaration would trigger unnecessary trade and travel restrictions from third States, hampering the response, further damaging affected communities, and likely increasing local resistance to international health workers.[135] These fears were not unfounded—prior experience had shown that States suffer disproportionate economic consequences when they report outbreaks, and it was at least plausible that emergency declarations would only exacerbate this problem. Even so, disproportionate trade and travel restrictions are exactly the kinds of measures that WHO emergency powers were supposed to prevent. If the WHO

[128] Emily A Bruemmer/Allyn L Taylor, 'Institutional Transparency in Global Health Lawmaking: The World Health Organization and the Implementation of the International Health Regulations' in Andrea Bianchi/Anne Peters (eds), *Transparency in International Law* (CUP 2013) 286.

[129] Eccleston-Turner/Kamradt-Scott (n 124).

[130] 'IHR Committees and Expert Roster' (WHO) <http://www.who.int/ihr/procedures/ihr_committees/en/> accessed 28 February 2019.

[131] For one example of cross-cutting issues of politics and power in recent health crises: Sara E Davies/Belinda Bennett, 'A Gendered Analysis of Ebola and Zika: Locating Gender in Global Health Emergencies' (2016) 92 International Affairs 1041, 1049–55.

[132] Fidler (n 117) 297–315.

[133] WHO, 'Statement on the Meeting of the Emergency Committee for Ebola Virus Disease in the Democratic Republic of the Congo' (Geneva, 12 April 2019) <https://www.who.int/news-room/detail/12-04-2019-statement-on-the-meeting-of-the-international-health-regulations-(2005)-emergency-committee-for-ebola-virus-disease-in-the-democratic-republic-of-the-congo-on-12th-april-2019> accessed 21 April 2020.

[134] ibid.

[135] Helen Branswell, 'Could an Emergency Declaration Over Ebola Make a Bad Situation Worse?' (*Statnews*, 14 May 2019) <https://www.statnews.com/2019/05/14/could-an-emergency-declaration-over-ebola-make-a-bad-situation-worse/> accessed 21 April 2020.

was accepting that an emergency declaration would *create* those conditions, it was effectively acknowledging that the Regulations were not fit for purpose.[136]

In taking this approach, the WHO suggested a modest, but potentially transformative, rethinking of the institution's role in global health security. On the one hand, the WHO was able to recognize and be responsive to the broader political and economic consequences of its decisions.[137] The decision not to declare an emergency almost explicitly recognized the limitations of the WHO's power, as well as the vulnerability of developing countries to harsh trade restrictions, and modulated the organization's response accordingly. At the same time, the very act of creating an emergency committee created a centralized mechanism for monitoring the outbreak response, evaluating State policies, and providing technical and policy advice, even if not styled as 'recommendations' under the Regulations. This approach to 'managed decentralization' has the advantage of recognizing the political limitations of the WHO's role while leveraging its position as the central actor for international public health.[138]

Unfortunately for the WHO, this approach backfired, drawing intense criticism from public health advocates.[139] The organization was accused of 'playing politics', and of 'favouring local protectiveness over global galvanizing'.[140] Critics argued that, by premising its decision on the presumed effects on commerce or the relative weakness of the Regulations—rather than on scientific evidence—the Emergency Committee and the Director-General had abused their discretion and acted *ultra vires*, damaging the WHO's legitimacy and arguably incurring international responsibility.[141] The WHO ultimately relented, declaring a public health emergency in July 2019, despite little change in the facts on the ground.[142] If the DRC Ebola outbreak had been a trial run for a reconfigured, more politically sensitive application of the IHR, it was a failure.

This was the State in which the WHO found itself in early 2020, when it was called upon to decide whether COVID-19 constituted another public health emergency. Once again, the WHO has been accused of playing politics, offering undue deference to the government at the centre of the outbreak, and ignoring the scientific evidence.[143]

This backlash is likely to demand significant rethinking of the WHO's emergency powers framework and governance structure. Following COVID-19, the organization stands at a crossroads. Some—including this author—have argued that the WHO will have to develop institutional structures that openly acknowledge and respond to the broader political dimensions of disease outbreaks, if the organization is to maintain its role as the central actor for global health security.[144] But this is not the only path.

[136] Fidler (n 117) 306.

[137] Johan Giesecke, 'The Truth About PHEICs' (*The Lancet*, 5 July 2019) <https://www.thelancet.com/journals/lancet/article/PIIS0140-6736(19)31566-1/fulltext> accessed 21 April 2020.

[138] Heath (n 16) 37–41. [139] Fidler (n 117). [140] ibid 309.

[141] ibid 320–6. [142] ibid 315–19.

[143] Kai Kupferschmidt, 'Mission Impossible? WHO Director Fights to Prevent a Pandemic Without Offending China' (*Science*, 10 February 2020) <https://www.sciencemag.org/news/2020/02/mission-impossible-who-director-fights-prevent-pandemic-without-offending-china> accessed 21 April 2020.

[144] Heath (n 16) 36–47.

Longtime WHO counsel Gian Luca Burci has suggested, instead, that the IHR's emergency powers framework be revised in favour of a more varied and 'context-sensitive approach that avoids altogether the fraught concept of emergency'.[145] This approach might emphasize the WHO's 'softer' normative functions—such as guidance documents, technical coordination, and so forth—over the more dramatic use of something that looks like emergency power.[146]

2. International Peace and (Health) Security: Pandemics in the United Nations System

The transformation of the global health security regime also has broader implications for the design of the international system as a whole. In 1996, the International Court of Justice determined that the WHO's responsibilities, as a 'specialized agency' of the United Nations,[147] 'are necessarily restricted to the sphere of public "health" and cannot encroach on the other responsibilities of the United Nations system', such as the UN's competence concerning nuclear disarmament.[148] It is questionable whether this distinction can be maintained today.[149] The developments of the past two decades have created new linkages amongst international institutions, leading at once to new operational challenges and new possibilities for the enforcement of States' international health obligations.

One consequence has been the proliferation of potential competitors and allies in outbreak preparedness and response.[150] In 2014, the UNSC declared Ebola a threat to 'international peace and security', activating its powers under Chapter VII and marking the first time it had ever made this declaration for a disease outbreak.[151] The UN Secretary-General subsequently activated the first-ever UN emergency health mission—the UN Mission for Ebola Emergency Response (UNMEER)—to provide a 'singular, UN system-wide approach in responding to Ebola'.[152] The mission was credited with bringing high-level political and donor attention to the outbreak, but drew criticism for its own operational response, which bypassed existing organizational frameworks.[153]

The coordination of these proliferating organizations has become a significant problem in health emergencies. Whereas the response to humanitarian crises is orchestrated through a UN system that engages relevant international agencies and non-governmental

[145] Burci (n 92). [146] ibid. [147] WHO Constitution (n 11) art 69.

[148] *Legality of the Use by a State of Nuclear Weapons in Armed Conflict* (Advisory Opinion) [1996] ICJ Rep 66 [26].

[149] Alvarez (n 55) 214.

[150] Tine Hanrieder, 'WHO Orchestrates? Coping with Competitors in Global Health' in Kenneth W Abbott et al (eds), *International Organizations as Orchestrators* (CUP 2015) 191.

[151] Burci/Quirin (n 10).

[152] 'UN Mission for Ebola Emergency Response (UNMEER)' (*Global Ebola Response*) <https://ebolaresponse.un.org/un-mission-ebola-emergency-response-unmeer> accessed 28 February 2019.

[153] WHO Report (n 108) para 78.

organizations,[154] there has been no similar structure for outbreak response.[155] And the WHO historically has not maintained the capacity to implement an on-the-ground humanitarian-style response to outbreaks, despite having the legal mandate to do so.[156] These issues led to severe organizational problems in the Ebola response, with some arguing that 'the whole response system [was] begging for a McKinsey & Company, or some other troubleshooter, to rush in and problem solve'.[157] WHO members have since established a new Health Emergencies Programme to develop operational capabilities and coordinate outbreak response.[158]

The linkage with the UNSC also creates new—though largely untapped—possibilities for enforcement. Some observers have seen the Council's power as a means towards increasing compliance with the IHR, including through the threat of UNSC sanctions.[159] Others have argued that sanctions would be counter-productive in health emergencies.[160] And tying the global health security regime even more closely to the UNSC's powers under Chapter VII of the UN Charter could further politicize pandemic response and bring even greater legitimacy challenges to these institutions.

Others have sought enforcement mechanisms through cooperation with other international organizations. For example, it has been argued that international financial institutions such as the World Bank and the International Monetary Fund could 'condition' certain health-related funding on meeting capacity-building targets or otherwise complying with the IHR.[161] And, given the close link between the Regulations and international trade, it may be possible to enforce the regulations indirectly through litigation under the auspices of the World Trade Organization,[162] though this remains only a theoretical possibility.

3. What Will Global Health Security Become? Borders, Humanitarianism, Development, Equity

Underlying all of these challenges are lingering questions about the nature of global health security today. The International Sanitary Conferences of the nineteenth century—the forerunners of today's IHR—were concerned with ensuring 'Europe's protection against epidemic diseases of exotic origin' while minimizing the interference with

[154] J Benton Heath, 'Managing the "Republic of NGOs": Accountability and Legitimation Problems Facing the U.N. Cluster System' (2014) 47 Vanderbilt Journal of Transnational Law 239.

[155] WHO Report (n 108) para 67. [156] ibid paras 28–9.

[157] Jeffrey Gettleman, 'As Ebola Rages, Poor Planning Thwarts Efforts' (*The New York Times*, 6 December 2014) <https://www.nytimes.com/2014/12/07/world/africa/as-ebola-rages-in-sierra-leone-poor-planning-thwarts-efforts.html> accessed 3 May 2020.

[158] 'WHO's New Health Emergencies Programme' (WHO, 31 October 2016) <http://www9.who.int/features/qa/health-emergencies-programme/en/> accessed 3 May 2020.

[159] WHO Report (n 108) para 19. [160] WHO Report (n 108) para 77.

[161] eg Gostin/Katz (n 124) 302.

[162] WHO Report (n 108) para 84; WHO, 'Preparedness and Response' (n 94) para 24.

international commerce.[163] It is still unclear whether, and if so, to what extent, the new conception of global health security embodied in the 2005 IHR truly departs from this Western slant.[164] And critics argue that the 'securitization' of public health steers policy responses towards military solutions, quarantines, and border barriers, which are not conducive to achieving lasting defence against health threats.[165] The challenge, then, is to identify a conception of global health security that is capable of weathering these criticisms.

One recently suggested approach is to better integrate a concept of 'medical humanitarianism' into the global health security architecture.[166] From this perspective, the IHR can be unduly centred on surveillance and protection against cross-border transmission, ultimately working for the benefit of high-income States.[167] The response, it is argued, should be to recognize the role that humanitarian actors play in delivering global health security, through day-to-day, ground-level provision of services, and to integrate those organizations into the governance framework for health security.[168] On this view, the treatment of the 2014 Ebola outbreak exclusively as an international public health crisis, rather than also as a humanitarian emergency, led to many of the observed operational failures.[169] These critics welcome the WHO's recognition that it must build operational capacity into the global health security framework, but question the organization's decision to establish a new Health Emergencies Programme rather than to focus on 'coordinating or strengthening the actors which already exist'.[170]

Another approach is to reframe global health security to refocus on developing primary health care systems and infrastructure in vulnerable and disadvantaged countries. This approach would recast global health security to focus on security against the 'structural violence' of chronically underdeveloped domestic health institutions, which renders States in the Global South significantly more vulnerable to massive and lethal outbreaks.[171] One focus of this frame is to reform the rules to 'provide greater carrots for States to comply voluntarily' with their capacity-building requirements, including by obliging wealthier States to provide technical assistance, capacity-building, and financing.[172]

A final question concerns the extent to which States in the Global South will exert their leverage to demand greater control over global health security institutions. In

[163] Yves Beigbeder, *The World Health Organization* (Martinus Nijhoff 1998) 1.

[164] For perspectives: Sara E Davies, 'Securitizing Infectious Disease' (2008) 84 International Affairs 295; David P Fidler, 'Public Health and National Security in the Global Age: Infectious Diseases, Bioterrorism, and Realpolitik' (2003) 35 George Washington International Law Review 787; Andrew Lakoff, 'Two Regimes of Global Health' (2010) 1 Humanity 59.

[165] Susan Peterson, 'Epidemic Disease and National Security' (2002–03) 12 Security Studies 43.

[166] Sophie Harman/Clare Wenham, 'Governing Ebola: Between Global Health and Medical Humanitarianism' (2018) 15 Globalizations 362.

[167] Lakoff (n 164) 75. [168] Harman/Wenham (n 166) 365.

[169] ibid 367–9. [170] ibid 369.

[171] Matiangai Sirleaf, 'Ebola Does Not Fall from the Sky: Structural Violence & International Responsibility' (2018) 51 Vanderbilt Journal of Transnational Law 477.

[172] ibid 525.

2006, Indonesia stunned the global health community by announcing that it would not share samples of an avian flu virus unless it received assurances that a vaccine would be available to its citizens, setting off years of political contestation.[173] This episode saw Indonesia and its allies leveraging 'viral sovereignty' to demand new multilateral frameworks for ensuring open access to vaccines, even as developed countries accused Indonesia of 'jeopardising global health security'.[174] The fallout led to the adoption of the Pandemic Influenza Preparedness framework for virus- and benefit-sharing, a non-binding instrument that applies only to a limited subset of flu viruses.[175] It remains unclear how established practices of virus- and benefit-sharing should interact with the 2014 Nagoya Protocol to the Convention on Biodiversity, which affirms State sovereignty over genetic resources and contemplates access and benefit-sharing on the basis of prior, informed consent and mutually agreed terms.[176] The tension between these frameworks has the potential to revive debates over viral sovereignty and global health security.[177]

D. Conclusion

The aftermath of COVID-19 is sure to spark a reconsideration of the international legal regime for responding to health emergencies. In its first few months, the outbreak had already highlighted many of the difficulties with 2005 IHR. China's underreporting of the virus's spread once again revealed the WHO's limited ability to force States to publicize potentially damaging information about infectious diseases. Once the disease's true threat was realized, the WHO's advice to avoid restricting travel to essential areas came into tension with States' domestic policies, highlighting the organization's limited enforcement capacity in times of crisis. And the perennial tension between politics and expertise has once again emerged in criticism that the WHO was 'playing politics' by being unduly deferential to China, culminating most dramatically in the United States' stated intent to withdraw from the organization in 2021.

[173] Eyal Benvenisti, 'Sovereigns as Trustees of Humanity: On the Accountability of States to Foreign Stakeholders' (2013) 107 AJIL 295, 325.

[174] Peter K Yu, 'Virotech Patents, Viropiracy, and Viral Sovereignty' (2013) 45 Arizona State Law Journal 1563, 1604–18.

[175] WHO, *Pandemic Influenza Preparedness Framework for the Sharing of Influenza Viruses and Access to Vaccines and Other Benefits* (WHO 2011); David P Fidler/Lawrence O Gostin, 'The WHO Pandemic Influenza Preparedness Framework: A Milestone in Global Governance for Health' (2011) 306 Journal of the American Medical Association 200.

[176] Nagoya Protocol on Access to Genetic Resources and the Fair and Equitable Sharing of Benefits Arising from their Utilization to the Convention on Biological Diversity UN Doc UNEP/CBD/COP/10/L.43/Rev.1; WHO Secretariat, 'Implementation of the Nagoya Protocol and Pathogen Sharing: Public Health Implications' (2017) <https://www.who.int/influenza/pip/2016-review/NagoyaStudyAdvanceCopy_full.pdf?ua=1> accessed 28 February 2019; UN High-Level Panel Report (n 67) paras 196–8.

[177] Daniel Cressey, 'Treaty to Stop Biopiracy Threatens to Delay Flu Vaccines' (2017) 542 Nature 148.

Even so, it would be a missed opportunity for these discussions to focus too narrowly on learning lessons from COVID-19. As the foregoing discussion has shown, the global health security regime is already engaged in a long period of adjustment and reconfiguration, especially after successive large-scale Ebola outbreaks in Africa. These outbreaks raised critical questions about the normative foundations of global health security, the structure of the WHO, and its links with other international institutions involved in pandemic response. The COVID-19 outbreak provides a high-profile opportunity to direct resources and energy to reimagining the architecture of global health security, but it remains unclear whether there is political will to address some of the foundational questions identified in this chapter.

CHAPTER 33

WILD FAUNA AND FLORA PROTECTION

GUS WASCHEFORT

A. Introduction

MOST of the world's wildlife is under significant pressure as a result of numerous factors including, for example, natural loss of habitat due to desertification and climate change. However, wildlife's greatest threat comes from interaction with humans. For a large number of species, ranging from pangolin to elephant, this threat is greatly exacerbated through poaching and the illicit trade in wild fauna and flora, fuelled by an almost insatiable international demand.[1] While a number of international legal instruments have been adopted to regulate transnational trade in wild fauna and flora, trade in high-value species persists in significant numbers. Sustainable Development Goal 15, providing for 'life on land', specifically requires that biodiversity loss be halted, and target 15.7, under the 2030 Agenda for Sustainable Development, requires that we 'take urgent action to end poaching and trafficking of protected species of flora and fauna and address both demand and supply of illegal wildlife products'.[2]

Recently the UN Security Council (UNSC), which bears 'primary responsibility for the maintenance of international peace and security',[3] has adopted a number of resolutions regarding the security situations in the Democratic Republic of the Congo (DRC), and the Central African Republic (CAR), in which a nexus is recognized between the poaching and associated illicit trade in wild fauna and flora (particularly elephant ivory) and international peace and security. The supply chain of ivory poached in the CAR and DRC is rather complex and provides for a number of entry points from an international law perspective. Traditionally, the broader imperative was the need to preserve biodiversity (the conservation imperative). This imperative is given effect to through a range of

[1] eg UNODC, *World Wildlife Crime Report: Trafficking in Protected Species* (UNODC 2016) 65–9.

[2] UNGA Res 70/1 (25 September 2015) 25.

[3] UN Charter 1 UNTS XVI art 24(1).

measures, including, at the national level, conservation policy and legislative frameworks that provide for conservation management—here the militarization of conservation poses serious questions in the context of international human rights law (IHRL) and international humanitarian law (IHL); and, at the international level, regulation of international trade in wildlife and wildlife products (hereinafter reference to wildlife will include wildlife products). The 1973 Convention on Illegal Trade in Endangered Species of Wild Fauna and Flora (CITES), the apex instrument for the regulation of trade in wild fauna and flora, expressly recognizes that wild fauna and flora 'are an irreplaceable part of the natural systems of the earth which must be protected for this and the generations to come'.[4] Nevertheless, the contemporary international law conservation regime remains largely anthropocentric, as it is premised on the need for sustainable development, with an emphasis on intergenerational equity.[5] The Stockholm Declaration provides that fauna and flora 'must be safeguarded for the benefit of present and future generations'.[6] Yet, in the conservation context, the threat to the sustainability of the species remains still a primary consideration.[7] As such, issues such as the number of specimens poached, and the deterioration of habitat are of primary importance.

During the past decade, greater emphasis has also been placed on the suppression of transnational crime imperative. In this regard, the focus is on suppressing conduct that amounts to serious crimes, which is transnational in nature, and is perpetrated by an organized criminal group. The nature of the commodity in question is largely immaterial. Now the peace and security imperative has entered the fray, here the emphasis is on taking measures to ensure the maintenance of international peace and security, in terms of the UN Charter. While the conservation imperative directly recognizes the inherent value of the object in question, and indeed, is premised precisely on its conservation, the transnational crime imperative does so only indirectly—the fact that poaching and illicit trade is regarded as a 'serious crime' is due, in large part, to the national legislative frameworks established in terms of the conservation imperative. The peace and security imperatives, on the other hand, are not at all premised on the conservation imperative.

This chapter focuses on elephant poaching for purposes of the trade in ivory in the DRC and CAR, as this is the context in which the UNSC has recognized the link between

[4] Convention on Illegal Trade in Endangered Species of Wild Fauna and Flora 993 UNTS 243 preamble.

[5] Edith Brown Weiss, *In Fairness to Future Generations: International Law, Common Patrimony, and Intergenerational Equity* (Transnational Publishers Inc. 1989) 24.

[6] 'Declaration of the United Nations Conference on the Human Environment' (June 1992) UN Doc A/CONF.48/14/Rev.1, principle 2; UNGA 'United Nations Conference on the Human Environment' (15 December 1972) UN Doc A/RES/2994.

[7] The term 'conservation' is not a technical term in international law, even though a number of conventions identify conservation as a key objective. Definitionally, a distinction is to be made between conservation premised on the intrinsic value of the species, or conservation premised on the value of a species as a human-exploitable resource. Regardless of the preferred approach, a common element in defining conservation is the sustainability of the species or natural environment. See eg Patricia Birnie et al, *International Law and the Environment* (3rd edn, OUP 2009) 588–93.

poaching and international peace and security. While this chapter is concerned specifically with the link between the protection of wild fauna and flora and global security, the international legal regime geared towards such protection is most developed in the context of conservation and trade. As such, the subsequent section, dealing with the applicable legal framework, will introduce the broader conservation framework, with particular emphasis on the regime created by CITES. In this section, focus is on wild fauna and flora in the broad sense (that is, not linked to security). Focus then shifts to recent developments and contemporary challenges, focusing specifically on elephant poaching in the DRC and CAR. Finally, the emerging UNSC practice with regard to wild fauna and flora is scrutinized and discussed.

B. Legal Framework

Modern efforts at international regulation of conservation first emerged during the latter parts of the nineteenth century. These were of a fragmented character and were focused on issues, where industry and consumerism impacted on nature and wildlife. Early examples of such international regulation included the water resources in the Rhine and the Danube, and the fur seal trade.[8] It was the 1972 Stockholm Declaration that constituted a watershed moment in formalizing a coherent international environmental law and policy framework. A number of significant developments preceded Stockholm, but these formed part of a patchwork of uncoordinated efforts, influenced by disparate and wide-ranging considerations, as they related to particular settings in particular times. While the substance and impact of the Stockholm Declaration goes far beyond the protection of wild fauna and flora, the momentum that had been generated leading up to, and following, the Stockholm Declaration contributed to the recognition that the commodification of wild fauna and flora represented one of the core challenges to their protection. CITES, adopted shortly after, and the licensing scheme it created, is the primary means through which such trade is restricted and regulated on the international plane.

Together with CITES, the Convention for the Protection of the World's Cultural and Natural Heritage (World Heritage Convention)[9] and the Convention on Biological Diversity (Biodiversity Convention)[10] form the apex of international law's protection of wild fauna and flora. The World Heritage Convention is rather unique in that it aims to protect the 'world heritage of mankind as a whole', comprising both nature as well as culture.[11] In this instrument, the emphasis is very much on intergenerational obligations

[8] Michael Bowman et al, *Lyster's International Wildlife Law* (2nd edn, CUP 2010) 3–6.

[9] Convention for the Protection of the World's Cultural and Natural Heritage 1037 UNTS 151 (World Heritage Convention).

[10] Convention on Biological Diversity 1760 UNTS 79 (Biodiversity Convention).

[11] World Heritage Convention (n 9) preamble.

of conservation. In the context of nature, the focus is not on the protection of specific species or taxa, but instead on 'natural features', 'geological and physiographical formations', and 'natural sites'.[12] That is to say, the protection is aimed at the environment in which wild fauna and flora are to flourish. The objectives of the Biodiversity Convention are the conservation of biological diversity; the sustainable use of its components; and the fair and equitable sharing of benefits arising from genetic resources.[13] The first two objectives are shared in common with CITES. The Biodiversity Convention aims to achieve its goals through wide-ranging measures that depend heavily on influencing planning and policy at the national level.

A number of regional developments are also relevant to the conservation of wild fauna and flora. The African Convention on the Conservation of Nature and Natural Resources (African Convention on Conservation) is of particular relevance to the present contribution, as to date the linkages between illicit exploitation of wild fauna and flora and threats to global security have been limited to the African continent.[14] While the African Convention on Conservation was first adopted in 1968, a substantially revised convention was adopted in 2003.[15] The Revised African Convention aims to 'enhance environmental protection'; 'foster conservation and sustainable use of natural resources'; and 'harmonize and coordinate policies in these fields'.[16] Three principles guide States in achieving these goals: all people have a right to a satisfactory environment favourable to their development; States have an individual and collective duty to ensure the right to development; and States must ensure that developmental and environmental needs are met in a sustainable, fair, and equitable manner.[17] Similar to the Biodiversity Convention, the Revised African Convention provides for wide-ranging measures, but does so in a manner that responds to the African context specifically.

The legal framework applicable to wild fauna and flora protection in the context of global security consists of the international law regimes relevant to the conservation and trade in wild fauna and flora, transnational organized crime, and global security. While the World Heritage and Biodiversity Conventions play an important role in the conservation of wild fauna and flora, emphasis is placed on the regulation of trade, as it is precisely the commodification of species that fuels demand, which in turn leads to illicit trade. The CITES regime is augmented by developments in the law on transnational organized crime, facilitating possible criminal prosecution for illicit trade in wildlife.[18]

[12] ibid art 2. [13] Biodiversity Convention (n 10) art 1. [14] 1001 UNTS 3.

[15] AU, Revised African Convention on the Conservation of Nature and Natural Resources (adopted 11 July 2003, entered into force 23 July 2016). Article XXXIV of the Revised Convention provides that as between State Parties to the Revised Convention, it will supersede the 1968 Convention.

[16] ibid art II. [17] ibid art III.

[18] See Pierre Hauck/Sven Peterke, Chapter 12 in this *Handbook*.

1. International Law on Conservation and Trade in Wild Fauna and Flora

The central aim of CITES is to protect certain species of wild fauna and flora from over-exploitation through international trade.[19] Technically, CITES regulates trade in specimens, and not in species as such—as regards animals, specimens include the animal (alive or dead), as well as 'any readily recognizable part or derivative thereof' (for the purposes of CITES Appendix III the parts or derivatives of the animal have to be expressly included in the appendix).[20] Trade includes 'export, re-export, import and introduction from the sea'.[21] Protected species are included in one of three appendices, which, in total, includes approximately 5,600 species of animals and 30,000 species of plants.[22] Appendix I is aimed squarely at the protection of species threatened with extinction, which may be affected by trade.[23] Trade in such species is authorized only in exceptional circumstances, and as such, Appendix I serves mostly to prohibit trade, and not so much to regulate it. Appendix II includes species which are not currently threatened with extinction, but which may become so threatened should trade not be regulated to avoid utilization incompatible with their survival.[24] Finally, through Appendix III CITES created a mechanism for States to self-identify species subject to regulation within the State in question.[25] By allowing States to include species in Appendix III, CITES facilitates cooperation amongst States Parties in controlling trade in these species.

CITES regulates trade through a permit scheme. Trade in species listed in appendices I and II requires an export permit, or re-export certificate (where the specimen was previously imported). The conditions for such an export permit, which are applicable to both appendices I and II, are set out in Articles III(2) and IV(2) of the Convention.

Export permits for Appendix I species have the additional requirement that the export State's management authority be satisfied that an import permit has already been generated for the specimen.[26] It is thus primarily the required import permit that distinguishes the trade provisions of Appendix I species from those of Appendix II species. The requirements for an import permit are set out in Article III(3) of the Convention. Those species included in Appendix I are deemed 'threatened with extinction which are or may be affected by trade'.[27] Therefore, the requirement that the import will be certified as being for 'purposes which are not detrimental to the survival of the species involved'[28], together with the exclusion of imports primarily for commercial purposes, severely restricts the lawful trade in Appendix I specimens.

[19] CITES (n 4) preamble. [20] ibid art I. [21] ibid.

[22] Hennie Strydom, 'Transnational Organized Crime and the Illegal Trade in Endangered Species of Wild Fauna and Flora' in Pierre Hauck/Sven Peterke (eds), *International Law and Transnational Organized Crime* (OUP 2016) 270.

[23] CITES (n 4) art II. [24] ibid. [25] ibid. [26] ibid art III(2). [27] ibid art II.

[28] ibid art III(3).

In addition to this more mechanical dimension of the operation of the CITES regime, CITES also provides for a number of State obligations, including: Parties must penalize trade and possession of specimens procured in violation of the Convention;[29] provision must be made for the confiscation and return to State of export of such specimens;[30] Parties must ensure minimum delays in specimens passing through trade formalities, such as customs procedures;[31] Parties must ensure that specimens are properly cared for during transit and holding;[32] Parties must maintain records of trade in specimens reflected in each of the three appendices;[33] Parties must report annually to the CITES Secretariat on the number and type of permits and certificates granted, and biennially on the legislative, regulatory, and administrative measures that it has taken to enforce the provisions of the Convention.[34] States may also provide for internal reimbursement for expenses incurred as a result of the confiscation of a specimen as provided for in the Convention.[35] Finally, States Parties are free to adopt legislative measures that are more restrictive in the trade of CITES species than the Convention, and to provide for trade restrictions in respect of species not regulated under CITES. In the latter case, States have the option of including such species in Appendix III.[36]

The success of CITES depends heavily on the implementation of robust systems at the national level. This is so due to two primary reasons: the day-to-day scientific decision-making is delegated to national authorities, and, as Sand explains:

> CITES implementation illustrates a legal phenomenon known as '*dédoublement fonctionnel*', in the terms coined by Georges Scelle. Rather than imposing a supranational regulatory mechanism of its own, the regime relies on reciprocal recognition of national regulatory decisions, provided that these are made in accordance with mutually agreed standards. It is then left up to designated national 'Management Authorities' . . . to operate the system on behalf of the international community.[37]

The Convention mandates the designation of at least one management and one scientific authority in each State Party, and requires States to enact domestic legislation to give effect to the Convention.[38] The CITES Secretariat organizes regular meetings of the Conference of the Parties (CoP) with the purpose of reviewing the implementation of the Convention. At CoP 15 a resolution was adopted mandating the Secretariat to identify Parties who have not implemented sufficient domestic measures to: (1) designate a management and scientific authority; (2) prohibit trade in specimens in violation of the Convention; (3) penalize trade conducted in violation of the Convention; and (4) provide for the confiscation of specimens illegally traded or possessed.[39] As of December 2019,

[29] ibid art VIII(1)(a). [30] ibid art VIII(1)(b). [31] ibid art VIII(3). [32] ibid.
[33] ibid art VIII(6). [34] ibid art VIII(7)(a)–(b). [35] ibid art VIII(2).
[36] ibid art XIV.
[37] Peter H Sand, 'The Whither CITES—The Evolution of a Treaty Regime in the Borderland of Trade and Environment' (1997) 8 EJIL 29, 47.
[38] CITES (n 4) arts VIII(7)(b) and IX(1).
[39] CITES, 'Resolution: National Laws for Implementation of the Convention' Doc Conf.8.4 (Rev. CoP15) para 1.

of the 183 States Parties, 102 (55.7 per cent) are regarded as meeting all four requirements for effective implementation; 44 (24 per cent) are regarded as meeting one to three of the four requirements for effective implementation; 29 (15.9 per cent) are regarded as not meeting any of the four requirements for effective implementation; and eight States have recently acceded to the Convention, and are not yet included in the statistical analysis.[40] Both the DRC and CAR are long-standing Parties to CITES.[41] The domestic legislation implementing CITES in the DRC is regarded as being fully compliant with all four requirements;[42] on the other hand, the implementing legislation in the CAR is deemed at present not to meet any of the four requirements.[43]

Although these figures are generally positive, the transnational nature of trade in wild fauna and flora requires that all States relevant to a given transaction, including the State of origin, transit States and the States of destination, have adequate legislation and institutions in place to ensure compliance with the Convention regime. Where one State relevant to the supply chain of a given transaction has a shortcoming in implementation, it compromises the process as a whole. There is no doubt that the insecurity, general breakdown of law and order, and corruption that is rampant in States such as the CAR and Eastern DRC makes for an environment in which criminal networks involved in poaching and illicit wildlife trade thrive. Considering that armed groups often have significant control over areas in which poaching is rife, that they are well armed, and that such groups need to create revenue in order to secure their continued existence, it is not surprising that they may capitalize on such illicit trade. Moreover, the mere implementation of measures does not speak to the effectiveness of those measures.

The CoP has shown a willingness to address compliance issues as they manifest. Recently, much emphasis has been placed on the transnational organized crime dimensions of the illicit trade in wild fauna and flora. To this end, the CoP has facilitated cooperation between States Parties and wildlife law enforcement agencies and developed strategies for border control and investigations.[44] Most significantly, in 2010 CITES together with Interpol, the UN Office on Drugs and Crime (UNODC), the World Bank and the World Customs Organization established the International Consortium on Combating Wildlife Crime (ICCWC).[45] The ICCWC's 'Strategic Programme 2016–2020' aims to substantially reduce poaching and trafficking in wildlife and forest products through a programme of five focus areas with a number of planned activities and expected outcomes attached to each. These are to:

(1) Provide institutional support and strengthen cooperation and coordination;
(2) Facilitate analysis of national capacity to strengthen law enforcement responses and help guide investment;

[40] CITES, 'National Legislation Project' <https://cites.org/eng/legislation/National_Legislation_Project> accessed 21 August 2018.

[41] The DRC acceded to the Convention in 1976, and the CAR in 1980: <https://www.cites.org/eng/disc/parties/chronolo.php> accessed 24 August 2018.

[42] CITES National Legislation Project (n 40). [43] ibid.

[44] eg CITES, 'Resolution: Compliance and Enforcement' Doc Conf.11.3 (Rev.CoP16).

[45] See <https://cites.org/eng/prog/iccwc.php> accessed 21 August 2018.

(3) Develop or enhance criminal justice and preventive capacity across institutions;
(4) Increase awareness and support for measures to combat wildlife and forest crime;
(5) Expand the use of knowledge, technology, and innovation.[46]

Beyond this, the UN Convention against Transnational Organized Crime (UNTOC) serves generally to 'promote cooperation to prevent and combat transnational organized crime more effectively'.[47] To achieve this goal, the Convention applies to the prevention, investigation, and prosecution of conduct that amounts to serious crimes (offences punishable by a 'maximum deprivation of liberty of at least four years'), which are transnational in nature and perpetrated by an organized criminal group ('a structured group of three or more persons... acting in concert with the aim of committing one or more serious crimes... in order to obtain, directly or indirectly, a financial or other material benefit').[48] As mentioned, CITES requires States to penalize trade that violates the Convention. Such unlawful trade is, by definition, transnational in nature (as CITES regulates international 'trade'), and is very often perpetrated by organized criminal groups. Traditionally, the international law response to illicit trade in wildlife was largely limited to trade regulation (CITES); however, the emerging regime of transnational organized crime provides for a further layer of protection—the potential criminal prosecution for those responsible for such trade.[49] The link between organized crime and illicit trade in wildlife is very well established. Indeed, Interpol suggests that the illicit trade in wildlife is worth up to US$20 billion annually, and ranks among the five most lucrative illicit trades internationally (together with the trade in drugs, small arms, counterfeit goods, and human trafficking).[50] Moreover, the UNODC has emphasized the organized criminal nature of illicit trade in wildlife.[51] However, law enforcement agencies and prosecutorial authorities have been slow to adopt an organized crime approach to the investigation and prosecution of poaching. For example, in South Africa, the country most affected by rhino poaching internationally, prosecutions have focused almost exclusively on those responsible for the actual poaching, and not on those higher up in the supply chain.[52]

In conclusion, trade in wild fauna and flora is regulated by a relatively mature regime within international law, which is augmented by a range of international law instruments aimed at nature conservation.

[46] ICCWC, 'Strategic Programme 2016–2020' (July 2016) <https://cites.org/sites/default/files/eng/prog/iccwc/ICCWC_Strategic_Programme_2016-2020_final.pdf> accessed 21 August 2018.

[47] 2225 UNTS 209. [48] ibid art 3 read with art 2. See also Hauck/Peterke (n 18).

[49] For more academic commentary on the organized crime dimensions of illicit trade in wildlife and wildlife products: Strydom (n 22).

[50] Interpol, 'Global Wildlife Enforcement: Strengthening Law Enforcement Cooperation Against Wildlife Crime' (March 2018) 3.

[51] *World Wildlife Crime Report* (n 1) 65–9.

[52] eg Robert Doya Nanima, 'Prosecution of Rhino Poachers: The Need to Focus on Prosecution of the Higher Echelons of Organised Crime Networks' (2016) 9 African Journal of Legal Studies 221.

C. Recent Developments and Contemporary Challenges

The notion that matters affecting natural resources and the environment may constitute a threat to peace and security is not novel. Trade in so-called 'conflict diamonds', as well as other minerals such as columbite-tantalite, has received widespread attention since the late 1990s. With respect to diamonds, this attention led to the establishment of the famed Kimberley Certification Scheme in 2000. On 17 April 2007, the UNSC first debated the nexus between climate change and international security,[53] an issue it has revisited on a number of occasions since.[54] In light of this, and considering the long-standing practice of ivory poaching in fragile, often war-torn, African States, fuelled by an increasing international demand, it is perhaps surprising that the UNSC only acknowledged the link between wildlife poaching and international peace and security in 2013. During that year the UNSC condemned 'the devastation of natural heritage and not[ed] that poaching and trafficking of wildlife are among the factors that fuel the crisis in the CAR'.[55]

The next section considers the dynamics of poaching and illicit trade in wildlife, specifically in the context of the CAR and the DRC. It is beyond the scope of this contribution to analyse the conflict landscape in these States. The CAR has experienced significant insecurity since 2004 with the start of the CAR Bush War, after which a number of successive armed conflicts have plagued the CAR and the region more generally. For its part, the DRC has experienced significant insecurity, and multiple successive armed conflicts since the end of the Second World War. There are ongoing UN Peace Support Operations in both States: the UN Multidimensional Integrated Stabilisation Mission in the Central African Republic (MINUSCA); and the UN Organisation Stabilisation Mission in the Democratic Republic of the Congo (MONUSCO). Following the discussion of poaching and illicit trade in wildlife in the CAR and DRC, focus will shift to the nexus between poaching and such illicit trade in wildlife and international peace and security.

1. Elephant Poaching in the CAR and DRC

The illicit trade in wildlife encompasses many species, with the most trafficked animal being the pangolin, which is in high-demand for their scales, used both in traditional medicine as well as for ornaments; their meat, which is a delicacy in parts of Asia; and for their leather.[56] With regard to trade in wildlife products procured through poaching,

[53] UNSC, 'Press Release: Security Council Holds First-Ever Debate on Impact of Climate Change on Peace, Security, Hearing over 50 Speakers' (17 April 2007) UN Doc SC/9000.

[54] UNSC, 'Press Release' (20 July 2011) UN Doc SC/10332.

[55] UNSC Res 2121 (2013) preamble.

[56] *World Wildlife Crime Report* (n 1) 65–9.

the most lucrative trade relates to ivory, rhino horn and lion bones. South East Asia, particularly Vietnam, and China are the largest market for rhino horn and lion bone products, where they are used in a range of traditional medicines and other products.[57] Lion bones have no historic role in any specific culture in Asia, but with the increased unavailability of tiger bones, due to intensified conservation measures, and the lack of availability of tigers, as a result of the near extinction of most sub-species of tigers, lion bones are commonly used as a substitute. Despite the fact that both rhino and lion poaching are a significant concern from a conservation perspective, they constitute less of a threat to international peace, as things currently stand; hence, it is ivory trade that is most relevant to the present discussion. It is worth mentioning though that the wild rhino populations of both the DRC and CAR have been completely wiped out due to poaching; indeed, the northern white rhino sub-specie (*ceratotherium simum cottoni*) that occurred naturally in the DRC and CAR is believed to be extinct in the wild, following the poaching of the last four known wild animals in the Garamba National Park of north-eastern DRC around 2008. While there are currently lion populations in both the CAR and DRC, demand for lion bones is largely met from lions bred in captivity.

Ivory trade has been so devastating that it has been estimated that between 1979 and 1989 half of Africa's entire elephant population succumbed to poaching.[58] In 1989, CITES elevated the protection status of elephant by including the species in Appendix I, thereby introducing an international ban on commercial ivory trade, which came into force in 1990 and showed early results.[59] There was a significant lull in elephant poaching for more than a decade following the ban on commercial trade in ivory. However, with increased demand for ivory and its escalated value in Asia, particularly China, fuelled by the buying power of a massively expanding middle class, elephant poaching has again significantly increased during the past decade.[60]

There are three recognized species of elephant, two of which are found in sub-Saharan Africa: the African Bush Elephant (*loxodonta africana*) and the African Forrest Elephant (*loxodonta cyclotis*). In the context of links between international security and poaching, the poaching of forest elephants is particularly relevant. Forrest elephants produce a denser ivory than bush elephants, for which there is a premium in the market place. In a leading study Maisels et al concluded that between 2002 and 2011 the African forest elephant population dwindled by 62 per cent.[61] Ninety-five per cent of the DRC forests

[57] Willow Outhwaite, 'The Legal and Illegal Trade in African Lions: A Study in Support of Decision 17.241 e)' (*Traffic*, 29 June 2018) 21–3 submitted to the Thirtieth meeting of the Animals Committee of CITES <https://cites.org/sites/default/files/eng/com/ac/30/Inf/E-AC30-Inf-15x.pdf> accessed 24 August 2018; Bryan Christie, 'Special Investigation: Inside the Deadly Rhino Horn Trade' National Geographic (October 2016).

[58] 'Statistics' (*Save the Elephants*) <http://www.savetheelephants.org/about-elephants-2-3-2/statistics/> accessed 24 August 2018.

[59] CITES (n 4) Appendix I.

[60] eg CITES, 'Control of Trade in Ivory in China' (2012) SC62 Inf. 8, 3 <http://www.savetheelephants.org/wp-content/uploads/2014/02/E62i-08.pdf> accessed 24 August 2018.

[61] Fiona Maisels et al, 'Devastating Decline of Forest Elephants in Central Africa' (2013) PLoS ONE <https://journals.plos.org/plosone/article?id=10.1371/journal.pone.0059469> accessed 10 February 2020.

are now empty of elephants—this is the country believed historically to have held the greatest number of forest elephants.[62] Half of the surviving forest elephants are in Gabon, with a fifth in the DRC, and this is while Gabon only represents 13 per cent and the DRC a staggering 62 per cent of the total central African forest area.[63]

Wasser has pioneered a method through which DNA samples, extracted from elephant dung, have been used to create a geo-profile of elephant DNA mutations across Africa.[64] This geo-profile can be used to determine from where ivory originated, after it is seized, through cross-referencing the DNA reference samples with DNA extracted from the tusks. This method also allows for a much better understanding of the supply chain involved in the ivory trade. In a recent study, Wasser et al tested samples of major ivory shipments that had been seized during three periods: 1996–2005; 2006–11; and 2012–14.[65] The analysis is based on 1350 reference samples (349 of which are for forest elephant) originating from seventy-one locations across twenty-nine African countries. The 1996–2005 seizures included five consignments of forest elephant ivory, all of which came from eastern DRC.[66] For the period 2006–14 six of seven forest elephant consignments originated from the Tri-National Dja-Odzala-Minkébé protected ecosystem (TRIDOM) spanning Cameroon, the Republic of Congo and Gabon and the adjacent Dzanga Sangha Reserve in southwestern CAR; as mentioned elsewhere, the UNSC has specifically referenced poaching and ivory trade emanating from this reserve. Accordingly, forest elephant ivory enters the market that originates from each of the five States in which they occur. This has a range of implications; for example, from a conservation perspective, it means that poaching threatens forest elephant across their range. More pertinent to the present discussion, the shift in poaching numbers from the DRC to TRIDOM raises the question to what extent do non-State armed groups (NSAGs), who engage in poaching, operate across border between these States. While this information is not available, it is evident that such cross-border poaching operations have the potential to seriously threaten peace and security in the region. The borders in question are porous, and mobility, and an ability to operate across borders, is a key characteristic of some NSAGs in the central African region that have been implicated in poaching, for example the Lord's Resistance Army (LRA).

While Wasser's data is scientifically accurate, and of immense significance, tests can only be performed on seized consignments. Customs authorities estimate that around 10 per cent of contraband is detected and seized.[67] This means that, while no ivory was seized emanating from the DRC after 2005, it is very likely that such ivory still enters the market place in significant quantities. This is supported by the fact that national parks in the DRC with forest elephant populations, particularly the Garamba National Park,

[62] ibid. [63] ibid.

[64] Samuel K Wasser et al, 'Genetic Assignment of Large Seizures of Elephant Ivory Reveals Africa's Major Poaching Hotspots' (2015) 349 Science 84.

[65] ibid 84. [66] ibid.

[67] Samuel K Wasser et al, 'The Ivory Trail' (2009) Scientific American 72.

which serves frequently as a base for the LRA, remain amongst the places that are most heavily affected by elephant poaching.[68]

2. Poaching and Illicit Trade in Wildlife as a Threat to International Peace and Security

The suggested nexus between poaching and illicit trade in wildlife and threats to international peace and security occurs in two contexts. First, poaching and illicit trade may fuel regional instability; secondly, it may provide NSAGs with a source of financing. Both these issues were recognized in a 2013 Secretary-General Report to the UNSC, which asserted that the illegal trade in ivory may be a source of funding for armed groups, in particular the LRA, and that:

> [p]oaching and its potential linkages to other criminal, even terrorist, activities constitute a grave menace to sustainable peace and security in Central Africa. In this regard, I urge Governments of the subregion to consider the issue of poaching as a major national and subregional security concern requiring their concerted and coordinated action.[69]

Poaching is an activity for which NSAGs are well placed, as the training, weapons, and tactics required for poaching overlap significantly with those required for guerrilla warfare. Moreover, high-value species occur in the environment in which NSAGs operate both in the CAR and the DRC. However, the underlying evidence linking NSAGs to poaching is often more tentative than may be thought. The militarized nature of weapons and tactics used in poaching is evidenced through the response to poaching—anti-poaching units are routinely armed with military assault rifles, they are increasingly trained in military tactics, and indeed, State armed forces are increasingly deployed as part of anti-poaching operations.[70] States are also adopting increasingly sophisticated military equipment for anti-poaching purposes, including manned and unmanned aerial vehicles for surveillance, etc.[71] There is a strong body of scholarship critical of the militarization of conservation. Much of the critical literature centres around, as Duffy puts it, the questions '...who we are protecting wildlife from, what we are protecting

[68] eg Gervais Ondoua Ondoua et al, *An Assessment of Poaching and Wildlife Trafficking in the Garamba-Bili-Chinko Transboundary Landscape* (Traffic, December 2017).

[69] UNSC 'Report of the Secretary-General on the Activities of the United Nations Regional Office for Central Africa and on the Lord's Resistance Army-affected areas' (20 May 2013) UN Doc S/2013/297, paras 9 and 74.

[70] Natasha White, 'The "White Gold of Jihad": Violence, Legitimisation and Contestation in Anti-Poaching Strategies' (2014) 21 Journal of Political Ecology 452, 454.

[71] Elizabeth Lunstrum, 'Green Militarization: Anti-Poaching Efforts and the Spatial Contours of Kruger National Park' (2014) 104 Annals of the Association of American Geographers 816, 817 and 825–6.

wildlife for and what methods we deem acceptable'.[72] While conservation policy is at the periphery of the present discussion, it is important to note that approaching anti-poaching operations from the perspective of peace and security likely results in the further militarization of conservation. The Panel of Experts on the CAR has reported that 'poaching and wildlife trafficking have provided income to local ex-Séléka forces in the past, especially in the north-east and south-east of the country',[73] and:

> Poaching and wildlife trafficking around the Dzanga Sangha Special Reserve ... continues. Poachers do not belong to organized armed groups but are rather related to criminal networks ... representatives of the CAR local authorities, and in particular internal security forces, are at times supporting, if not actively participating in, such activities.[74]

On the other hand, the NGO Traffic has produced a compelling, and very detailed report, which concludes that a range of NSAGs, including the LRA and the Janjaweed, are significantly involved in elephant poaching in the Garamba National Park of north-eastern DRC. The evidence suggests that these groups are involved with the actual poaching of the animals, following which they trade the ivory for supplies and funds.[75] It was further found that 'the LRA has put unprecedented pressure on wildlife since they arrived in the Uélé provinces in 2005'.[76] Moreover, the extent to which poaching and illicit wildlife trade is a source of financing to terrorist groups is hotly contested. It has been estimated that al-Shabaab secures up to 40 per cent of their 'base payroll' through poaching.[77] On the other hand, Lawson and Vines note that the link between poaching and terrorist groups is 'largely unverified by published literature on the illegal wildlife trade'.[78]

In December 2013, the UNSC formally condemned the devastation of natural heritage and noted 'that poaching and trafficking of wildlife are among the factors that fuel the crisis in the CAR'.[79] Acting under Chapter VII, in Resolution 2127 (2013) it imposed

[72] Rosaleen Duffy, 'Waging a War to Save Biodiversity: The Rise of Militarized Conservation' (2014) 90 International Affairs 819, 823. For a further critical perspective on the militarization of conservation: Lunstrum (n 71).

[73] UNSC 'Letter dated 6 December 2017 from the Panel of Experts on the Central African Republic extended pursuant to Resolution 2339 (2017) addressed to the President of the Security Council' (6 December 2017) UN Doc S/2017/1023, para 174.

[74] UNSC 'Letter dated 23 July 2018 from the Panel of Experts on the Central African Republic extended pursuant to Resolution 2399 (2018) addressed to the President of the Security Council' (23 July 2018) UN Doc S/2018/729, para 121.

[75] Ondoua (n 68) 4. [76] ibid 40.

[77] Andrea Crosta/Kimberly Sutherland 'The White Gold of Jihad: al-Shabaab and the Illegal Ivory Trade' (*Elephant Action League*, 2016) 8 and 28 <https://elephantleague.org/wp-content/uploads/2016/02/Report-Ivory-al-Shabaab-Oct2016.pdf> accessed 24 August 2018.

[78] Katherine Lawson/Alex Vines, *Global Impacts of the Illegal Wildlife Trade: The Costs of Crime, Insecurity and Institutional Erosion* (Chatham House February 2014) 8.

[79] UNSC Res 2127 (2013) preamble.

sanctions on the CAR that apply to military arms, equipment, ammunition, and services.[80] Amongst the exclusions to the sanction's regime are small arms and related equipment intended solely for 'international patrols providing security in the Sangha River Tri-national Protected Area to defend against poaching, smuggling of ivory and arms . . .'[81] As mentioned, the Sangha River Tri-national Protected Area is one of the hotbeds of supply of forest elephant ivory.

Two months after Resolution 2127 was adopted, the UNSC took another significant step forward. Again, acting within its Chapter VII powers, it mandated Member States to impose travel and transit sanctions, as well as financial sanctions (including freezing of assets and economic resources, and prevention of financing) in respect of 'individuals and entities designated by the [Sanctions] Committee as . . . providing support for armed groups or criminal networks through the illicit exploitation of natural resources, including diamonds and wildlife and wildlife products', in the CAR.[82]

By imposing sanctions targeting those who support armed groups through the illicit trade in wildlife and wildlife products, the UNSC de facto recognized such illicit trade as a threat to international peace and security.[83] This marked a significant development, as Resolution 2127 had merely recognized that poaching and trafficking of wildlife products 'are among the factors that fuel the crisis in the CAR'. Nonetheless, even at the time, by excluding from the sanctions regime arms and equipment intended for international anti-poaching and smuggling patrols, the UNSC acknowledged the importance of such operations and that they had to not be impacted.

Similar measures were adopted for the DRC. Resolution 2136 recognized the 'linkage between the illegal exploitation of natural resources, including poaching and illegal trafficking of wildlife, illicit trade in such resources, and the proliferation and trafficking of arms as one of the major factors fuelling and exacerbating conflicts in the Great Lakes region of Africa'.[84] The focus on the Great Lakes region, as opposed to focusing on the individual State, is significant in that it brings the issue more squarely into the mandate of the UNSC as one which affects international peace and security. This resolution further called on the DRC and other States in the Great Lakes region to improve control on exports of wildlife and wildlife products through their customs agencies, and to ensure regional cooperation in the suppression of wildlife poaching and trafficking.[85] Finally, the resolution extended an existing sanctions regime, including travel and financial sanctions, to apply to 'individuals or entities supporting armed groups in the DRC through illicit trade of natural resources, including gold or wildlife as well as wildlife products'.[86]

[80] ibid para 54. [81] ibid para 54(d).

[82] UNSC Res 2134 (2014) para 37(d). This was the first resolution in which the UNSC included poaching in an operative paragraph of a Chapter VII resolution.

[83] Anne Peters, 'Elephant Poaching and Ivory Trafficking as a Threat to the Peace' (2014) 108 AJIL Unbound 162.

[84] UNSC Res 2136 (2014) preamble.

[85] ibid para 24. [86] ibid paras 3–4.

UNSC Resolution 1373 (2001) requires States to criminalize and prohibit the direct or indirect financing of terror groups and activities.[87] Accordingly, where terrorist groups benefit financially from involvement in any part of the ivory supply chain, the relevant States will be duty-bound to take positive action to disrupt such funding.

The recognition of poaching and illicit trade in wildlife as a threat to international peace and security is as much attributable to an evolving understanding by the UNSC of what amounts to such threats as it is to shifts in the dynamics of the illicit wildlife trade. Alvarez has stated that Resolution 2127 (2013) addresses:

> not only those who are alleged to have engaged in acts that are themselves threats to the peace but also those who are seen as contributing to such threats... Resolution 2027... connects the dots between threats to the peace and law and order associated with stable governments.[88]

Similarly, Peters traces the evolution of the UNSC's understanding of threats to the peace starting with Resolution 688 on Northern Iraq.[89] She concludes that while the UNSC has adopted a much more expansive understanding since the end of the Cold War, during which threats to the peace were narrowly construed as inter-State armed conflict, a requirement of a trans-boundary feature remains.[90] This is further confirmed by the fact that in the context of the resolutions regarding both the CAR and DRC, the UNSC emphasized the impact of the country situations on regional instability.

While the UNSC sanctions regimes and the CITES regime are premised on significantly different considerations, they have a common goal in combating poaching and illicit trade in wildlife in contexts where they threaten international peace and security. If the effectiveness of CITES, and the law on transnational organized crime, in intercepting consignments in transit or at the State of destination is enhanced, the feasibility of poaching will diminish. On the other hand, if the sanctions regimes put in place by the UNSC more effectively curb poaching and illicit trade at the source of the wildlife product, that would disrupt the supply chain as a whole. It was acknowledged earlier that the regulation of trade through CITES is often compromised by the weakest State (as regards customs processes, etc) in a given supply chain, yet, it is currently unrealistic for trade regulation to be effective in ivory supply States such as the CAR and DRC. The deterioration of law and order in such States and the porous nature of their borders mean that there can be no real confidence in the border control and customs processes relevant to curbing illicit trade. However, the evidence shows that the ivory supply chain is such that consignments pass through a number of intermediary transit States, in attempts to hide the State of origin to avoid suspicion.[91] If the customs authorities and

[87] UNSC Res 1373 (2001) para 1.

[88] José E Alvarez, *The Impact of International Organizations on International Law* (Brill 2017) 107.

[89] Peters (n 83) 163.

[90] ibid.

[91] Fiona M Underwood et al, 'Dissecting the Illegal Ivory Trade: An Analysis of Ivory Seizures Data' (2013) PLoS ONE <https://journals.plos.org/plosone/article?id=10.1371/journal.pone.0076539> accessed 10 February 2020.

other agencies involved in enforcing CITES are better able to identify and seize ivory in transit, and at the point of destination, the feasibility of the trade, and thus of the poaching itself, will be impacted.[92] Any approach to the economic analysis of law will conclude that, if, hypothetically, all poached ivory was intercepted, there would be no incentive for poaching and trafficking. Holistically, the supply chain, which begins with the taking of the wildlife product and ends with the end-consumer of the product, is intricate, and proper enforcement of trade restriction in transit and destination States will impact the feasibility of trade, and thus the poaching itself.

The UNSC sanctions regimes regarding poaching in the CAR and DRC, on the other hand, are aimed specifically at the State at hand and the regional level. Primary responsibility for the implementation of the measures adopted rests with government agencies, such as the interior and finance ministries, and customs authorities.[93] While the same issues that plague the effectiveness of CITES at the State level will have an impact on the effectiveness of such authorities to implement the sanctions regimes, UN institutions play a much more far-reaching role in State engagement and monitoring on the ground in the CAR and DRC than CITES ever will. Thus, the sanctions regimes' strength compensates for the weakness of the CITES regime in tackling trade in the source State.

D. Outlook

Global Animal Law (GAL) is an emerging research field in international legal scholarship, aimed at 'fleshing out a new branch of law and legal research', providing for effective international regulation in the advancement of animal welfare.[94] Poaching and illicit trade in wildlife impact dramatically on animal welfare, and as such, undoubtedly form part of GAL. The GAL project has gained considerable momentum in a short space of time, and may well have significant impact on international law and the protection of wildlife in the near future. However, in the context of *lex lata*, the corpus of international law that contributes to the suppression of poaching, and associated illicit trade in wildlife, does not consist of an identifiable sub-regime of international law, but instead draws from a range of sub-regimes, including international environmental law, international trade law, transnational criminal law, and now also, global security law and, potentially, the counter-terrorism regime.

Historically, the protection of wildlife occurred in the context of the conservation imperative. The applicable international law, particularly CITES, has resulted in significant protection for wildlife—this is well illustrated by the immediate impact of the 1989 ban on lawful commercial ivory trade. However, the fact that the value of ivory has skyrocketed on the illicit market, largely due to substantial increases in consumer buying

[92] Sand (n 37). [93] Peters (n 83) 162.

[94] Anne Peters, 'Global Animal Law: What It Is and Why We Need It' (2016) 5 Transnational Environmental Law 9, 9–10.

power, has driven the global ivory trade underground. Restrictions on lawful trade are not adequate to respond to the growing illicit trade in wildlife. In this regard, there is urgent need for transnational criminal law to play a more significant role in the suppression of poaching and illicit wildlife trade. The recognition of illicit trade in wild fauna and flora as a threat to international peace and security, that is, the peace and security imperative, marks a significant paradigm shift. It is intuitive to suggest that, regardless of the imperative at play, such a patchwork approach may create layers of protection for wildlife—as long as the net result includes the suppression of illicit wildlife trade, conservation will be enhanced (as was indeed argued above). However, it remains vital that conservation of wildlife, as opposed to the human security dimension, not get muffled.

It is fallacious to suggest that any form of suppression of poaching and illicit wildlife trade necessarily furthers the goals of conservation. For example, from a peace and security perspective, the overall reduction of poaching by NSAGs in a given area may be regarded a as a positive outcome, while the protection of highly endangered sub-species may be irrelevant to the peace and security imperative. From a conservation perspective, the protection of sub-species is central to preservation of biodiversity—this is again well illustrated by the recent functional extinction of the northern white rhino, as a consequence of poaching. Classifying poaching and illicit wildlife trade as a threat to peace and security has already very likely led to the further militarization of conservation in some regions, which raises acute IHRL and IHL issues regarding the use of lethal force, etc. This is not to say that the peace and security imperative in regards to poaching and illicit wildlife trade is not an important development—it certainly is. Where factually poaching and illicit wildlife trade does indeed threaten international peace and security, the peace and security architecture provide appropriate response apparatus, including potential coercive measures under the UN Charter, as well as, the inclusion of the suppression of such illicit trade in the mandate of Peace Support Operations. However, it is essential to ensure that no 'creep' occurs, in terms of which the responses reserved for threats to peace and security impact upon the broader conservation responses to poaching and wildlife trade, emanating from the conservation imperative. It is equally essential to ensure that the conservation imperative does not get lost in efforts to legitimately suppress poaching in the context of peace and security.

Considering that the UNSC first recognized the nexus between poaching and illicit wildlife trade, and international peace and security recently, and that there is little information on the practical implications of the emerging UNSC practice on poaching and illicit wildlife trade at this stage, there is significant need for further research to be done on a number of issues. These include: the extent of involvement in, and benefit derived from, poaching and illicit wildlife trade by NSAGs, and particularly terrorist groups; the contribution that poaching by NSAGs and terrorist groups makes to the global market; and the extent to which poaching and trade in species other than elephant may threaten international peace and security. There is equally a need for further research on issues such as the legal regulation of anti-poaching operations where these operations are carried out in areas where NSAGs, who are party to an armed conflict, are active in poaching.

TECHNOLOGICAL SECURITY

CHAPTER 34

ARTIFICIAL INTELLIGENCE AND ROBOTIZATION

MARTINA KUNZ AND SEÁN Ó HÉIGEARTAIGH

A. Introduction

THE aim of this chapter is to give an overview of international law governing applications of artificial intelligence and robotics that affect global security, highlighting challenges arising from technological developments and how international regulators are responding to them. Contrary to popular belief, international governing bodies are actively addressing impacts of advances in artificial intelligence and robotics within their remit, such as risks and opportunities from increasingly autonomous transport by air, land, and sea.

First, a few terminological clarifications are in order. 'Artificial intelligence' (AI) is an umbrella term including both logic-based, symbolic AI, such as expert systems and theorem provers, as well as data-driven approaches typically called 'machine learning' (ML). Within ML, the sub-field of 'deep learning',[1] which uses neural networks with multiple layers of artificial neurons to learn complex functions, has received significant attention in recent years.[2] 'Artificial general intelligence' (AGI) denotes a property ascribed to hypothetical future systems, which would have the ability to achieve goals in a wide range of environments.[3] This is typically contrasted with 'narrow' or 'specialized' AI systems built thus far, but the distinction is not clear-cut and more of a spectrum than a binary categorization. As for robotics, the term will be used here in a broad sense as

[1] Yann LeCun et al, 'Deep Learning' (2015) 521 Nature 7553, 436.

[2] Stuart J Russell/Peter Norvig, *Artificial Intelligence: A Modern Approach* (3rd edn, Prentice Hall 2016) for a canonical introduction to AI.

[3] Shane Legg/Marcus Hutter, 'Universal Intelligence: A Definition of Machine Intelligence' (2007) 17 Minds and Machines 391.

'embodied AI'. Thus, AI systems can be purely virtual (eg, algorithmic trading systems or personal digital assistants), whereas robotic systems always have a physical component.

As AI is increasingly applied to all kinds of human activity, no security issue is left untouched. Much of the international law literature thus far has focused on the implications of increasingly autonomous weapons systems. Our contribution instead seeks to cover a broader range of global security risks resulting from large-scale diffuse or concentrated, gradual or sudden, direct or indirect, intentional or unintentional, AI- or robotics-caused harm. While some overlap with other chapters in this volume is unavoidable, we aim to focus on challenges either unique to, or greatly exacerbated by, the development and deployment of AI and robotics applications.

While the hype around AI may see peaks and troughs, as has happened throughout the history of its development, the phenomenal increases in computing power and its affordability suggest that present-day developments are going to continue apace. Moreover, even if scientific progress were to slow down drastically, the technology available today already has major security implications. We consider it important to distinguish between the impacts of current technologies and that of future, more speculative developments. Scholarly, policy, and media debates on the subject often conflate the two, thereby potentially leading to inadequate prioritization of effort while preventing alternative futures from being envisaged and realized. We would be the last to dismiss long-term concerns over emerging technologies. However, when examining and designing legal and policy responses, it is best to consider a range of potential scenarios unfolding over time, taking into account possible interventions and their likely costs and benefits.

Accordingly, the present chapter is divided into two parts: the first and more substantial is concerned with global security governance of contemporary technology, whereas the second briefly considers governance of potential future AGI.

B. Global Security Governance of Contemporary Robotics and Artificial Intelligence

1. Preventing Large-Scale Harms from Robotics

Robotic systems, used for automation of tasks requiring some degree of physical labour and outfitted with ever more complex software, can both intentionally and unintentionally be the cause of disasters on various scales. At the risk of oversimplification, the four main sources of harm are (i) hardware faults, such as exploding batteries, (ii) data-related harm including data corruption, theft, and manipulation, (iii) software malfunction or misuse, including AI software components, and (iv) human operator mistakes or deliberate attacks, such as military drone strikes. The scale of potential harm from a robotic device or system depends on how widely deployed a vulnerable device or system is and how many people and resources could come to harm if a given system were to fail beyond recovery. For instance, if a large fleet of driverless vehicles operating in dense urban environments were to simultaneously suffer from a steering-system failure, many lives would be at risk. Issues relating to data and software across application domains will be discussed in Section B.2 on AI risks.

Lethal and other harms caused by both stationary and mobile robotic systems are not novel[4] and are governed by a number of international treaties and technical standards, some of which are under review for amendment or further development. A comprehensive treatment of all existing and emerging international hard and soft law governing robotic applications as diverse as space robots and medical robots, or cleaning robots and military robots, would fill an entire volume. Hence, we will limit the scope of this section to international law governing transborder mobile robotics, with a focus on safety and security risk management.

Mobile robots able to move across borders arguably include highly automated or autonomous aerial, space, ground, surface, and underwater vehicles with or without people or cargo on board and with varying degrees of human oversight during operation. While much of the initial development during the first half of the twentieth century occurred in the military domain, peaceful applications have since taken off, and nowhere more vigorously than in aviation,[5] spurring economic growth and globalization. Automation of maritime and road transport is lagging far behind that of aviation but has received considerable financial investment and regulatory attention in recent years. However, with increased global mobility and automation come greater risks, such as cyber-hijacking, or misusing commercial vehicles for terrorism or illicit trafficking of biological, chemical, and radiological weapons. In the civilian domain this has led to stricter international rules and audit mechanisms, whereas in the military domain relevant technology transfer is increasingly restricted, but the international law on development and use of autonomous weapons has not yet been updated, at least not by way of treaty amendment or new legal instruments. The examination of a potential evolution of customary international law is beyond the scope of this contribution.

a. *Civil Aircraft Safety and Security*

A crucial actor in the phenomenal growth of the aviation industry is the International Civil Aviation Organization (ICAO), a UN specialized agency with a clear focus on safety and security. ICAO's constitutional treaty, the 1944 Chicago Convention on International Civil Aviation, recognizes in its preamble that while international civil aviation can promote cooperation and peace in the world, 'its abuse can become a threat to general security' and coordination is therefore needed to develop it in a 'safe and

[4] See eg the case of Robert Williams, a Ford Motor Company factory worker killed by an industrial robot in 1979: Associated Press, 'Around the Nation: Jury Awards $10 Million In Killing by Robot' *The New York Times* (New York, 11 August 1983).

[5] For a brief history of aerial robotics, see Robert Mahony et al, 'Modeling and Control of Aerial Robots' in Bruno Siciliano/Oussama Khatib (eds), *Springer Handbook of Robotics* (Springer 2016) 1307–9.

orderly manner'.[6] The Convention also already contains a provision on 'pilotless aircraft', prohibiting its unauthorized entry into the airspace of another contracting party and stipulating that parties shall obviate any danger to civil aviation through appropriate controls.[7] More recently, ICAO has amended relevant annexes to the Chicago Convention and has issued various guidance documents in an ongoing process to facilitate the development of a globally harmonized, comprehensive regulatory framework for dealing with drone safety and security, including issues such as identification and tracking, aided by a proposed online global aircraft registration network,[8] communication systems for traffic management, and geofencing-like systems to prevent drones from approaching restricted areas such as airports, nuclear facilities, and prisons.[9] ICAO has also developed a strong focus on cybersecurity over the past decade, leading, *inter alia*, to the inclusion of preventive measures relating to cybersecurity in Annex 17 on security,[10] compliance with which is audited in the context of ICAO's Universal Security Audit Programme, which started in the aftermath of the terrorist attacks of 11 September 2001.[11]

In addition to the comprehensive risk management and capacity-building approach of the Chicago Convention's annexes and related guidance materials, a number of aviation security treaties and amendments thereto have been adopted under the auspices of ICAO since the 1960s, some of which are directly relevant for preventing and prosecuting transnational aerial robot-enabled crime, such as cyber-hijacking of commercial aircraft and terrorist drone attacks. In particular, the 1970 Hague Convention for the Suppression of Unlawful Seizure of Aircraft[12] was amended by a supplementary protocol in 2010[13] to include the criminalization of remote seizure or exercise of control of an

[6] Convention on International Civil Aviation 15 UNTS 295 (Chicago Convention), preambular paras 1 and 3. See generally Brian F Havel/Gabriel S Sanchez, 'The International Law Regime for Aviation Safety and Security' in Brian F Havel/Gabriel S Sanchez (eds), *The Principles and Practice of International Aviation Law* (CUP 2014).

[7] Chicago Convention (n 6) art 8.

[8] ICAO, 'Implementation' *Annual Report of the Council* (2017) <www.icao.int/annual-report-2017/Pages/global-priorities-all-strategic-objectives-nclb-initiatives-implementation.aspx> accessed 30 October 2018. The aircraft registration network aims to include all civil aircraft, from small drones to large airliners.

[9] ICAO, 'Unmanned Aerial System Traffic Management (UTM)', *Annual Report of the Council* (2017) <www.icao.int/annual-report-2017/Pages/new-emerging-activities-unmanned-aerial-system-traffic-management.aspx> accessed 30 October 2018.

[10] Chicago Convention (n 6) Annex 17 paras 4.9.1 (requiring the identification of critical ICT systems and data used for civil aviation purposes and, in accordance with a risk assessment, the implementation of appropriate measures to protect them from unlawful interference) and 4.9.2 (recommending that the measures implemented include 'security by design, supply chain security, network separation, and the protection and/or limitation of any remote access capabilities' as appropriate, depending on the risk assessment).

[11] For a recent status update on the Programme and associated targets, see the working paper prepared by the ICAO Secretariat for the Second High-Level Conference on Aviation Security (Montreal, 29–30 November 2018), 'Status of the Global Aviation Security Plan' HLCAS/2-WP/3 Rev.1 11/10/18. In a nutshell, as of 21 August 2018 (by which date 180 out of 192 parties had been audited), 116, or 64 per cent of the parties audited had reached or surpassed 65 per cent effective implementation of the critical elements of an effective aviation security system as defined by ICAO.

[12] Convention for the Suppression of Unlawful Seizure of Aircraft 860 UNTS 105.

[13] Protocol Supplementary to the Convention for the Suppression of Unlawful Seizure of Aircraft (2011) 50 ILM 153 (Beijing Protocol).

aircraft 'by any technological means'.[14] Moreover, the 1971 Montreal Convention for the Suppression of Unlawful Acts Against the Safety of Civil Aviation[15] was replaced by the 2010 Beijing Convention on the Suppression of Unlawful Acts Relating to International Civil Aviation[16] in the relations between the parties to both treaties.[17] The Beijing Convention builds upon the Montreal Convention but also explicitly recognizes that civil aircraft can be used as a weapon and as a delivery platform for weapons. It thus establishes as an offence the intentional use of a civil aircraft 'for the purpose of causing death, serious bodily injury, or serious damage to property or the environment'.[18] The release or discharge from an aircraft of a biological, chemical, or nuclear weapon, or explosive, radioactive, or similar substances in a manner that is likely to cause harm is also criminalized.[19] However, the Montreal Convention will still remain relevant for some time to come, as it enjoys nearly global ratification with 188 parties, whereas the Beijing Convention has only twenty-six parties to date.[20]

b. *Autonomous Shipping and Maritime Security*

For waterborne robots, unlike in the air and space domains, the regulatory landscape is more fragmented. The main fault line lies between international maritime law and freshwater law, the former having the benefit of a dedicated UN specialized agency, the International Maritime Organization (IMO), which has taken leadership in monitoring and facilitating treaty implementation, complementing hard law with soft law. Its main focus is on safety and security of shipping as well as the prevention of pollution from ships, and it is currently conducting a regulatory scoping exercise to identify legal barriers and gaps hindering the safe development of remote-controlled, autonomous, or semi-autonomous surface ships.[21] The issuance of a circular precluding the operation of autonomous ships in international waters pending the entry into force of an international regulatory framework was considered but did not receive sufficient support.[22] Instead, Member States and international organizations were invited to submit proposals for interim guidelines for autonomous shipping trials.[23] Some of the outcomes of these

[14] ibid art 1(1).

[15] Convention for the Suppression of Unlawful Acts Against the Safety of Civil Aviation 974 UNTS 177 (Montreal Convention).

[16] Convention on the Suppression of Unlawful Acts Relating to International Civil Aviation (2011) 50 ILM 144 (Beijing Convention).

[17] ibid art 24(a). [18] ibid art 1(f). [19] ibid art 1(g).

[20] Unless otherwise specified, any factual statements in the present chapter regarding numbers of treaty participants and depositary notifications were last updated on 30 October 2018 and were drawn from either the United Nations Treaty Collection (<https://treaties.un.org>) or from the official website of the relevant organization, in this case from ICAO's 'Current lists of parties to multilateral air law treaties' <www.icao.int/secretariat/legal/Lists/Current%20lists%20of%20parties/AllItems.aspx> accessed 20 May 2020.

[21] For the initial decision and mandate, see IMO, 'Report of the Maritime Safety Committee on its Ninety-Eighth Session' (28 June 2017) Doc MSC 98/23, para 20.2. The target completion date is 2020.

[22] IMO, 'Report of the Maritime Safety Committee on its Ninety-Ninth Session' (5 June 2018) Doc MSC 99/22, para 5.22.1.

[23] ibid para 5.27.2.

regulatory activities may also serve as templates or inspiration to govern the operation of autonomous vessels on international inland waterways.

Pending the widespread commercial deployment of autonomous ships, perhaps the largest robot-related threat to global security from civil waterborne vehicles is as a means of transport for terrorist drone swarms carrying explosives or biological, chemical, or radioactive ('dirty') bombs, given that many large cities are situated along coasts or rivers. Hence, it is worth mentioning that the international maritime security regime was considerably strengthened after the 9/11 terrorist attacks. A series of amendments to the annex of the widely ratified International Convention for the Safety of Life at Sea[24] were adopted in 2002, including a new chapter XI-2 'Special Measures to Enhance Maritime Security',[25] which refers to a comprehensive International Ship and Port Facility Security Code adopted on the same occasion.[26] Similar to the aviation domain, the 1988 Convention for the Suppression of Unlawful Acts against the Safety of Maritime Navigation was overhauled to criminalize additional terrorist acts as well as the transport on board a ship of certain dangerous materials, such as biological, chemical, or nuclear weapons or their precursor materials (Article 3bis), or of a fugitive of a treaty crime (Article 3ter), and introduced detailed cooperation and enforcement mechanisms, including ship-boarding and inspection procedures (Article 8bis).[27]

c. *Ground Vehicle Safety and Security*

Regarding autonomous ground vehicles, recent amendments to the 1968 Vienna Road Traffic Convention[28] allow for vehicle systems that are either in conformity with relevant international legal instruments or which can be overridden or switched off by the driver.[29] The amendments entered into force for all parties in 2016 through the tacit acceptance procedure of Article 49 of the Convention.[30] Similar amendments were unsuccessfully proposed for the 1949 Geneva Convention on Road Traffic[31] in 2015.[32]

[24] International Convention for the Safety of Life at Sea 1184 UNTS 278, as amended (SOLAS).

[25] 'Consideration and Adoption of Amendments to the International Convention for the Safety of Life at Sea, 1974' (12 December 2002) IMO Doc SOLAS/CONF.5/32, Annex, para 7. The amendments were adopted under the tacit acceptance procedure of art VIII of the Convention and entered into force on 1 July 2004.

[26] International Code for the Security of Ships and of Port Facilities (17 December 2002) IMO Doc SOLAS/CONF.5/34, Annex 1.

[27] Convention for the Suppression of Unlawful Acts against the Safety of Maritime Navigation 1678 UNTS 221, as amended by the Protocol to the Convention for the Suppression of Unlawful Acts against the Safety of Maritime Navigation IMO Doc. LEG/CONF.15/21.

[28] Convention on Road Traffic 1042 UNTS 17 (Vienna Road Traffic Convention).

[29] ibid, as amended, arts 8(5bis) and 39(1).

[30] Vienna Road Traffic Convention depositary notification C.N.529.2015.TREATIES-XI.B.19 (Acceptance of amendments to articles 8 and 39 of the Convention), 6 October 2015.

[31] Convention on Road Traffic 125 UNTS 3 (Geneva Road Traffic Convention). This Convention was replaced by the Vienna Road Traffic Convention (n 28) as between the parties to both treaties, but it has ninety-seven parties whereas the Vienna Convention has only seventy-eight.

[32] Geneva Road Traffic Convention depositary notification C.N.91.2016.TREATIES-XI.B.1 (Proposal of amendments to articles 8 and 22), 22 March 2016.

The World Forum for the Harmonization of Vehicle Regulations, hosted by the UN Economic Commission for Europe (UNECE), has been working on automated driving for several years,[33] adopting amendments to relevant UN regulations and formalizing its efforts institutionally by setting up a new Working Party on Automated/Autonomous and Connected Vehicles in June 2018, addressing a wide range of issues such as human machine interfaces, cybersecurity, software updates, data storage systems, automatically commanded steering functions, and testing procedures, amongst other issues.[34]

These standardization and regulatory oversight efforts are all the more pressing from a road safety perspective as vehicles with automated controls have already been involved in fatal crashes.[35] Unfortunately, despite UNECE efforts to promote global cooperation, participation in vehicle regulation is nowhere near that seen in the aviation and maritime transport domains, perhaps because the latter benefit from specialized agencies with global reach.

d. *Cross-Domain Counter-terrorism and Arms Control*

In addition to sector-specific approaches, the global counter-terrorism and arms control regimes are also relevant to the extent that robotic systems such as autonomous aerial, waterborne, or ground vehicles are used in attacks or for illicit trafficking of weapons. In particular, the 1997 Convention for the Suppression of Terrorist Bombings[36] covers 'explosive[s] or other lethal device[s]' that are delivered, placed, discharged, or detonated in, into, or against 'a place of public use, a State or government facility, a public transportation system or an infrastructure facility'.[37] Notably, this includes a 'device that is designed, or has the capability, to cause death, serious bodily injury or substantial material damage through the release, dissemination or impact of toxic chemicals, biological agents or toxins or similar substances or radiation or radioactive material'.[38] Thus, for example, terrorist use of agricultural drones repurposed to spray toxic chemicals onto crowds would also qualify as an offence under the Convention.

Alongside other treaties relating to terrorism and Weapons of Mass Destruction (WMD), a number of binding UN Security Council (UNSC) resolutions adopted under Chapter VII of the UN Charter are also relevant. Most notable for present purposes are

[33] For a timeline of activities see UNECE, 'Relevant UNECE Activities on Automated Driving' <www.unece.org/trans/themes/transtheme-its/selfdriving/automated-driving.html> accessed 30 October 2018.

[34] See UNECE, Inland Transport Committee, 'Report of the Working Party on Automated/Autonomous and Connected Vehicles on its first session' (23 October 2018) ECE/TRANS/WP.29/GRVA/1.

[35] For example, a test drive by Uber Inc. caused a pedestrian fatality in the US State of Arizona in 2018, see National Transportation Safety Board, 'Preliminary Report Highway HWY18MH010' (24 May 2018) <www.ntsb.gov/investigations/AccidentReports/Pages/HWY18MH010-prelim.aspx> accessed 30 October 2018.

[36] International Convention for the Suppression of Terrorist Bombings 2149 UNTS 256 (Terrorist Bombings Convention).

[37] ibid art 2(1). 'Infrastructure facility' is defined in art 1(2) as 'any publicly or privately owned facility providing or distributing services for the benefit of the public, such as water, sewage, energy, fuel or communications'.

[38] ibid art 1(3)(b).

UNSC Res 1373 (2001) on preventing and suppressing terrorist acts, and Res 1540 (2004) on non-proliferation of WMDs and their means of delivery,[39] both of which established a committee to monitor and promote implementation with the respective resolution.[40] It is in this context of renewed efforts to prevent terrorism and limit State and non-State actors' access to WMDs that the scope of maritime and aviation security conventions was broadened, both with regard to substantive and procedural provisions.

Of course, some mobile robotic systems fall under conventional arms control regimes and weapons law. States have long used the leeway granted under international treaties to restrict export of security-related technology and have coordinated such actions through voluntary regimes such as the 1987 Missile Technology Control Regime,[41] covering, *inter alia*, drones which are either long range (greater than 300km) or which incorporate an aerosol-dispensing system or mechanism with a capacity greater than 20 litres.[42] Another such regime is the 1996 Wassenaar Arrangement,[43] which covers a wide range of relevant hardware and software, including both military and civil unmanned aerial and submersible vehicles exceeding certain performance thresholds.[44] These non-binding regimes with restricted membership are complemented by the more inclusive 2013 Arms Trade Treaty[45] regulating international trade in conventional arms, including unmanned combat aerial vehicles, attack helicopters, warships, and armoured combat vehicles (Article 2(1)). National definitions for all but one category covered by the Treaty are required to be at least as extensive as the descriptions used in the UN Register of Conventional Arms[46] at the time of entry into force of the Treaty.[47]

Apart from trade restrictions and associated reporting requirements, the legality of the development and use of increasingly autonomous military mobile robotics has also been the focus of much attention but has yet to crystallize into international regulatory action. Initial discussions at the international level were stimulated by the reports of two successive Special Rapporteurs on extrajudicial, summary, or arbitrary executions to the UN General Assembly (UNGA) and the Human Rights Council in 2010 and 2013 respectively, focusing on the legal, ethical, and policy implications of emerging lethal

[39] 'Means of delivery' (of WMDs) are defined for the purpose of the resolution as 'missiles, rockets and other unmanned systems capable of delivering nuclear, chemical, or biological weapons, that are specially designed for such use'. See UNSC Res 1540 (2004) para 1 and fn.

[40] See, respectively, UNSC Counter-Terrorism Committee, 'The United Nations Security Council Counter-Terrorism Committee' <www.un.org/sc/ctc> accessed 30 October 2018, and 1540 Committee, '1540 in Focus' <www.un.org/en/sc/1540> accessed 30 October 2018.

[41] See Missile Technology Control Regime <http://mtcr.info> accessed 30 October 2018.

[42] Category II, Item 19.A.3, not including model aircraft specially designed for recreational or competition purposes, see Missile Technology Control Regime, 'Equipment, Software and Technology Annex' (22 March 2018) MTCR/TEM/2018/Annex, 75.

[43] Wassenaar Arrangement on Export Controls for Conventional Arms and Dual-Use Goods and Technologies <www.wassenaar.org> accessed 30 October 2018.

[44] Wassenaar Arrangement (n 43) Public Documents Vol II (December 2017), List of Dual-Use Goods and Technologies, entries 9.A.12.a (UAVs) and 8.A.1.d (unmanned untethered submersible vehicles).

[45] Arms Trade Treaty (2013) 52 ILM 988 (ATT).

[46] See UN Register of Conventional Arms <www.unroca.org> accessed 30 October 2018.

[47] ATT (n 45) art 5(3).

robotic technologies used in armed conflicts and law enforcement contexts.[48] The parties to the Convention on Conventional Weapons (CCW)[49] in turn started holding informal expert meetings in 2014, and at their fifth Review Conference in 2016 decided to establish an open-ended Group of Governmental Experts (GGE) on emerging technologies in the area of lethal autonomous weapons systems (LAWS). The GGE was tasked to explore and agree on possible recommendations on options in the context of the Convention, considering not only the issue of compliance of LAWS with international humanitarian law (IHL) and international human rights law (IHRL), but also potential effects on regional and global security and stability, effects on the threshold for armed conflicts, risk of an arms race, proliferation risks, and risks posed by cyber operations in relation to LAWS.[50] While international support for a ban on LAWS is growing, major military powers are still blocking progress towards a new legal instrument, arguing that existing international law is sufficient. Scholarship is split on both the issue of legality of envisaged LAWS under current international law and on the desirability of a ban.[51]

2. Governing Artificial Intelligence Risks across Application Domains

AI can be used for automating cognitive tasks, either purely virtually or as part of a cyber–physical system, including robotic systems. Even without robotics, some AI systems may directly or indirectly cause lethal harm by providing information[52] that humans act upon or by otherwise manipulating (non-robotic) cyber–physical systems.

As for advisory systems causing lethal harm, a rather straightforward example is AI-based fatal medical advice that a suitably trained human would not have given, such as advising a patient with stroke symptoms to stay at home instead of going to the hospital, or recommending lethal combinations of medicines. The reason for the detrimental information output by an AI system in any given case could be an innocent mistake, negligence by the engineers training and testing the application, or an intentional

[48] UNGA 'Interim Report of the Special Rapporteur on Extrajudicial, Summary or Arbitrary Executions, Philip Alston' (23 August 2010) UN Doc A/65/321; UNGA 'Report of the Special Rapporteur on Extrajudicial, Summary or Arbitrary Executions, Christof Heyns' (9 April 2013) UN Doc A/HRC/23/47.

[49] Convention on Prohibitions or Restrictions on the Use of Certain Conventional Weapons Which May Be Deemed to Be Excessively Injurious or to Have Indiscriminate Effects 1342 UNTS 137 (CCW).

[50] Decision 1 of the Fifth Review Conference of the High Contracting Parties to the CCW, see 'Final Document of the Fifth Review Conference' (23 December 2016) UN Doc CCW/CONF.V/10, 9; in conjunction with the recommendations contained in 'Report of the 2016 Informal Meeting of Experts on Lethal Autonomous Weapons Systems (LAWS)' (10 June 2016) UN Doc CCW/CONF.V/2, Annex.

[51] See, generally, Nehal Bhuta et al (eds), *Autonomous Weapons Systems: Law, Ethics, Policy* (CUP 2016).

[52] 'Information' is used in a broad sense here, including both structured and unstructured data, such as the estimated coordinates of a person's location, the classification of a person as criminal, a recommendation to join a terrorist group on a social media platform, a medical diagnosis, or a generated picture, video, text, or audio sequence based on relevant samples which may incite to engage in violence.

criminal act targeting either a specific individual or any person with certain characteristics such as a particular ethnicity, belief, gender, sexual orientation, or disability. In some cases, deaths may result from AI applications used voluntarily by individuals, whereas in others lethal harm could be caused by AI-based advice acted upon by third parties, including State or non-State actors. Aside from fatalities due to malfunctioning or subverted AI software in otherwise beneficial health and safety-relevant domains, AI may also increasingly be used to identify and select targets for intentional State or non-State killing. More indirectly, the role of commercial AI-based recommender systems in the spread of incitements to terrorism, genocide, ethnic cleansing, and other violent crimes on social media is also a growing concern. Such systems would arguably qualify as causing lethal harm if they were instrumental in recruiting new perpetrators or in securing resources necessary for violent attacks resulting in deaths. By way of example, the Independent International Fact-Finding Mission on Myanmar highlighted the role of hate speech on social media, in particular Facebook, in the atrocities committed in Myanmar.[53] The Mission reported a number of cases in which widely circulated inflammatory Facebook posts immediately preceded outbreaks of violence against the Rohingya and called for an independent and thorough examination of the 'extent to which the spread of messages and rumours on Facebook has increased discrimination and violence in Myanmar' as the social media giant had unfortunately been 'unable' to provide it with country-specific data about the spread of hate speech on its platform.[54]

Regarding other AI-involving manipulation of cyber-physical systems with potentially lethal consequences, a growing threat category is AI-based cyberattacks compromising the availability or integrity of computer networks critical for the provision of public services such as energy, healthcare, water, telecommunications, and public transport. For instance, even a preventable and relatively easy-to-stop ransomware attack like WannaCry in May 2017 led to five hospitals in the UK being unable to provide emergency care for several days because they were locked out of devices.[55]

Perhaps the most extreme scenario with present-day technology is AI being misused to spark a nuclear war by launching weapons directly if nuclear control systems were digitized and insufficiently secured, or in combination with social engineering techniques, for instance by using AI to forge a military command or escalate tensions.[56]

Short of lethality, certain types of AI systems, with or without criminal manipulation, may exacerbate risks of unlawful discrimination and other harms in whichever area

[53] UNGA 'Report of the Detailed Findings of the Independent International Fact-Finding Mission on Myanmar' (17 September 2018) UN Doc A/HRC/39/CRP.2, especially 320–45 (on the issue of hate speech), and 428–9 (recommendations addressed to Facebook and other social media active in Myanmar).

[54] ibid 340–3.

[55] UK National Audit Office, 'Investigation: WannaCry Cyber Attack and the NHS' HC 414 Session 2017–19 (25 April 2018) paras 1.7, 1.8, 1.10, 1.13 <https://www.nao.org.uk/wp-content/uploads/2017/10/Investigation-WannaCry-cyber-attack-and-the-NHS.pdf> accessed 30 October 2018.

[56] See description of scenarios and risk assessment in Page O Stoutland/Samantha Pitts-Kiefer, 'Nuclear Weapons in the New Cyber Age' *Nuclear Threat Initiative* (26 September 2018) <www.nti.org/analysis/reports/nuclear-weapons-cyber-age> accessed 30 October 2018.

they are applied to, including important domains such as criminal justice, education, healthcare, employment, finance, social security, and so forth.[57]

AI applications are governed by a wealth of international hard and soft law, the introduction of which would require a book-length treatment. Thus, in the following we will focus on two cyber-specific international legal regimes aimed at the prevention of harm across economic sectors by governing (i) AI-based processing of personal data, and (ii) AI as a target and tool for crime. On cybersecurity and cyberwarfare, readers are referred to Chapter 36 of this *Handbook* for a national and collective security perspective complementary to the human security perspective taken here.

a. *Artificial Intelligence-Based Data Processing*

A pioneering multilateral treaty in this domain is the 1981 Convention for the Protection of Individuals with regard to Automatic Processing of Personal Data.[58] Although concluded under the auspices of the Council of Europe (CoE), it was elaborated in close collaboration with the OECD and is open for accession by non-Member States (Article 23). About half a dozen Latin American and African countries have joined in recent years, leading to a total of fifty-three parties to date.[59] While this treaty is usually discussed under the heading of the right to privacy or data protection, it can also be seen as an AI treaty. Indeed, the definition of automatic data processing under the Convention is wide enough to encompass data processing by both symbolic AI and machine learning,[60] and personal data defined as 'any information relating to an identified or identifiable individual'[61] includes not only inputs to an AI system but arguably also outputs thereof, such as an inferred personality profile, consumer classification, and behaviour prediction. The object and purpose of the Convention, set forth in Article 1, is to secure 'respect for [the] rights and fundamental freedoms' of every individual, 'and in particular his [or her] right to privacy', with regard to automatic processing of personal data. Thus, the right to privacy is certainly a key, but by no means the sole, focus of the Convention.

The basic principles enshrined in the Convention include lawfulness, fairness, transparency, and data security of automatic processing.[62] Data security obligations as per

[57] For a general introduction, see Cathy O'Neil, *Weapons of Math Destruction: How Big Data Increases Inequality and Threatens Democracy* (Crown Books 2016); Andrew Guthrie Ferguson, *The Rise of Big Data Policing: Surveillance, Race, and the Future of Law Enforcement* (NYU Press 2017). For a recent overview of the implications of AI technologies for human rights in the information environment, see UNGA 'Report of the Special Rapporteur on the Promotion and Protection of the Right to Freedom of Opinion and Expression' (29 August 2018) UN Doc A/73/348; and for the impact of AI and robotics on the elderly, see UNGA 'Report of the Independent Expert on the Enjoyment of All Human Rights by Older Persons' (21 July 2017) UN Doc A/HRC/36/48, 4–16.

[58] Convention for the Protection of Individuals with regard to Automatic Processing of Personal Data 1496 UNTS 65 (Automatic Processing Convention).

[59] See CoE, 'Chart of signatures and ratifications of Treaty 108' <www.coe.int/en/web/conventions/full-list/-/conventions/treaty/108/signatures> accessed 30 October 2018.

[60] Automatic processing as defined in art 2(c) of the Convention includes the 'carrying out of logical and/or arithmetical operations' on data by automated means which are the building blocks of AI.

[61] Automatic Processing Convention (n 58) art 2(a).

[62] ibid arts 5, 7–8.

Article 7 of the Convention include not only guarding against accidental or unauthorized access, destruction, and dissemination of personal data, but also unauthorized alteration thereof, such as attacks causing a modification in an AI system's decisions, recommendations, or predictions about an individual. With regard to both the input and output of an AI system, subject to certain exceptions and restrictions,[63] individuals have the right to obtain a copy of its content 'in an intelligible form' (Article 8(b)) and to have it rectified or erased if inaccurate, out of date, not obtained or processed fairly or lawfully, or if the data are inadequate, irrelevant, or excessive in relation to the specified and legitimate purposes for which they are stored, which are to be communicated to the data subject.[64] Most notable from a global perspective is that (i) these protections are offered to 'every individual, whatever his [or her] nationality or residence' as long as the data processing falls under the jurisdiction of a State party,[65] and that (ii) parties have a duty to assist persons living abroad in the exercise of their rights under the domestic law implementing the Convention.[66] This includes the right to a remedy if requests for confirmation, communication, rectification, or erasure are not complied with by data controllers (Article 8(d)).

Moreover, the Convention has undergone a modernization process culminating in the adoption of a protocol amending it in May 2018. This introduced further safeguards against negative AI impacts, such as the right of every individual 'not to be subject to a decision significantly affecting him or her based solely on an automated processing of data without having his or her views taken into consideration',[67] the right to 'obtain, on request, knowledge of the reasoning underlying data processing where the results of such processing are applied to him or her',[68] and an obligation for data controllers and, where applicable, data processors, to conduct a prior impact assessment of the intended data processing on the rights and fundamental freedoms of data subjects.[69] In the EU, the General Data Protection Regulation,[70] revised in tandem with the Convention, already implements and amplifies the provisions of the modernized version

[63] Such as for the protection of national security, public safety, criminal justice, or the rights and freedoms of others, see Automatic Processing Convention (n 58) art 9.

[64] ibid art 8(c) in conjunction with art 5–6 as and to the extent implemented in domestic law ('if these have been processed contrary to the provisions of domestic law giving effect to the basic principles set out in Articles 5 and 6 of this Convention').

[65] ibid art 1.

[66] ibid art 14(1) ('Each Party shall assist any person resident abroad to exercise the rights conferred by its domestic law giving effect to the principles set out in Article 8 of this Convention').

[67] Convention for the Protection of Individuals with regard to Automatic Processing of Personal Data 1496 UNTS 65, as modified by the Protocol amending the Convention for the Protection of Individuals with regard to Automatic Processing of Personal Data ETS No 223 (Modernized Automatic Processing Convention) art 9(1)(a).

[68] ibid art 9(1)(c).

[69] ibid art 10(2), subject to certain restrictions under the domestic law implementing the Convention in accordance with art 10(4).

[70] Regulation (EU) 2016/679 of the European Parliament and of the Council of 27 April 2016 on the protection of natural persons with regard to the processing of personal data and on the free movement of such data, and repealing Directive 95/46/EC (General Data Protection Regulation) OJ L119/1.

of the Convention, but entry into force of the amendments to the Convention will be important for their scope to extend to data processing under the jurisdiction of non-EU parties to the Convention.

b. *Artificial Intelligence as a Target and Tool for Crime*

AI systems, like other information technologies, can simultaneously be a target of, and tool for, criminal activity, both of which are within the scope of a second major international treaty governing AI risks—the 2001 Budapest Convention on Cybercrime,[71] also elaborated within the CoE framework with active participation of non-Member States from the outset.[72] Thus far, sixty-one States have become party to the Convention, including all but four CoE Member States,[73] and the growth rate outside of the CoE area is accelerating. While universal ratification may be unattainable for political reasons, one of the main aims of the treaty is to harmonize domestic substantive and procedural criminal law as a pre-condition for more effective international cooperation given dual criminality requirements.[74] As the first and most widely ratified multilateral treaty on cybercrime, it may achieve this aim even without formal global participation, simply by serving as a model instrument.[75]

AI-targeted crime is covered by Articles 2–6 of the Convention on offences against the confidentiality, integrity, and availability of computer data and systems. '[C]omputer system' is defined in a relatively technology-neutral way as 'any device or a group of interconnected or related devices, one or more of which, pursuant to a program, performs automatic processing of data' (Article 1(a)). '[C]omputer data', in turn, is construed broadly as 'any representation of facts, information or concepts in a form suitable for processing in a computer system, including a program suitable to cause a computer system to perform a function' (Article 1(b)). AI applications can thus fall under both definitions, depending on whether only the software or also the hardware layer is considered. The hindering of an AI system's proper functioning could qualify as system interference under Article 5, rather than, or in addition to, data interference under Article 4. Data interference refers to intentional unauthorized 'damaging, deletion, deterioration, alteration or suppression of computer data'[76] (Article 4(1)), and parties

[71] Convention on Cybercrime 2296 UNTS 167 (Budapest Convention).

[72] In particular Canada, Japan, South Africa, and the USA, all of which are signatories and three of which are parties (South Africa has yet to ratify the Convention).

[73] Ireland, San Marino, and Sweden have signed but not yet ratified, and Russia has neither signed nor ratified (as of 1 November 2018).

[74] CoE, 'Explanatory Report to the Convention on Cybercrime' (23 November 2001) <https://rm.coe.int/CoERMPublicCommonSearchServices/DisplayDCTMContent?documentId=09000016800cce5b> accessed 11 July 2018 (Budapest Convention Explanatory Report) paras 16 and 33.

[75] UNODC, 'Comprehensive Study on Cybercrime (Draft)' (2013) 74–6 <https://www.unodc.org/documents/organized-crime/cybercrime/CYBERCRIME_STUDY_210213.pdf> accessed 30 October 2018.

[76] The term used in the Convention is 'without right', which according to the Explanatory Report was deliberately left open for parties to interpret, but 'may refer to conduct undertaken without authority (whether legislative, executive, administrative, judicial, contractual or consensual)'. See Budapest Convention Explanatory Report (n 74) para 38.

may require that the conduct result in serious harm (Article 4(2)). System interference is the intentional 'serious hindering without right of the functioning of a computer system', either via data interference as defined in Article 4(1), or by inputting or transmitting computer data, such as in denial-of-service attacks.[77] In line with the preventive approach of the Convention, illegal access to computer systems and illegal interception of non-public transmissions of computer data to, from, or within computer systems, including electromagnetic emissions from a computer system carrying computer data, are also to be established as criminal offences subject to certain conditions.[78] These provisions have been elucidated by Guidance Notes issued by the Cybercrime Convention Committee in accordance with Article 46(1) in order to facilitate the effective use and implementation of the Convention. Topics covered by Guidance Notes include botnets, phishing, distributed denial-of-service attacks, critical information infrastructure attacks, spam, new forms of malware, and terrorism.[79]

As for AI as a tool for crime, Article 6 stipulates that the mere production, possession and distribution, or otherwise making available of 'a device, including a computer program, designed or adapted primarily for the purpose of committing any of the offences established in accordance with Articles 2 through 5' is to be criminalized under certain conditions (Article 6(1)). The Convention also describes a few specific offences which raise particular challenges or gain new proportions when committed through the use of computer systems, namely computer-related forgery (Article 7), computer-related fraud (Article 8), offences related to child pornography (Article 9), and offences related to infringements of copyright and related rights (Article 10). Other offences considered for inclusion in the Convention were racist and xenophobic threats, insults and propaganda, as well as denial, gross minimization, approval, or justification of genocide or crimes against humanity committed through computer systems. However, these were ultimately relegated to an additional protocol that entered into force less than two years after the Convention.[80] Note that all of the offences contained in the Convention require criminal intent that may be difficult to prove. Nonetheless, the data used to train a given machine learning system could be an indicator of the developer's intent in certain cases. More importantly, most of the procedural provisions of the Convention apply not only to the offences established in accordance with its substantive law section, but also to other criminal offences committed by means of a computer system (Article 14(2)(b)), as well as to the collection of evidence in electronic form of any criminal offence (Article 14(2)(c)). The procedural mechanism of the Convention is being revisited in the context of the drafting process of a second additional protocol to the Convention, which started

[77] Budapest Convention (n 71) art 5; Budapest Convention Explanatory Report (n 74) para 67.

[78] Budapest Convention (n 71) arts 2 and 3 respectively.

[79] CoE, 'Guidance Notes' (2012) <www.coe.int/en/web/cybercrime/guidance-notes> accessed 30 October 2018.

[80] Additional Protocol to the Convention on Cybercrime, Concerning the Criminalization of Acts of a Racist and Xenophobic Nature Committed Through Computer Systems 2466 UNTS 205. As compared to the Convention, this Additional Protocol has only about half the number of parties thus far (thirty-one as of 1 November 2018).

in 2017 and aims to enhance cooperation against cyberterrorism and clarify the legal framework of transborder data access and direct cooperation with service providers in other jurisdictions, as well as strengthening legal safeguards such as data protection requirements.[81]

Other regional treaties include the Commonwealth of Independent States' Agreement on Cooperation in Combating Offences related to Computer Information (2001), the Shanghai Cooperation Organization's Agreement on Cooperation in the Field of International Information Security (2010), the League of Arab States' Arab Convention on Combating Information Technology Offences (2010), and the African Union Convention on Cyber Security and Personal Data Protection (2014, not yet in force), but these have a much smaller geographical scope to date.[82]

Prospects for a global treaty remain slim, but discussions on the merits and scope of a UN instrument resumed with renewed intensity in 2017.[83] Pending progress towards a global agreement, the UN Convention on Transnational Organized Crime[84] provides a legal basis for global cooperation amongst States not party to a cyber-specific instrument in the many cases where cybercrime activities constitute transnational organized crime. At the law enforcement level, the International Criminal Police Organization supports transnational cybercrime investigations and operations amongst its 192 Member States.[85]

C. Mitigating Risks from Potential Future Artificial General Intelligence

In addition to concerns surrounding increasingly powerful domain-specific AI, there are also ongoing debates about risks from the development of artificial general intelligence, including the potential that it may threaten the survival of the human species itself.[86] Even the best engineers working on the most high-stakes technologies occasionally

[81] CoE Cybercrime Convention Committee (T-CY), 'Terms of Reference for the Preparation of a Draft 2nd Additional Protocol to the Budapest Convention on Cybercrime' (9 June 2017) T-CY (2017) 3. Unilateral transborder access to data has been controversial since the negotiation of the Convention and an additional protocol has long been contemplated, but drafting only started in 2017.

[82] For an in-depth analysis of both regional and global treaties and non-binding mechanisms see UNODC (n 75) ch 3.

[83] See eg ECOSOC, Commission on Crime Prevention and Criminal Justice, 'Report on the Meeting of the Expert Group to Conduct a Comprehensive Study on Cybercrime' (13 April 2018) UN Doc E/CN.15/2018/12, paras 1–6, 15–20.

[84] United Nations Convention against Transnational Organized Crime 2225 UNTS 209.

[85] See INTERPOL, 'Cybercrime' <www.interpol.int/Crimes/Cybercrime> accessed 30 October 2018.

[86] See, generally, Nick Bostrom, *Superintelligence: Paths, Dangers, Strategies* (OUP 2014); Murray Shanahan, *The Technological Singularity* (MIT Press 2015).

make mistakes. Moreover, thus far the technology built has not had much autonomy and the negative consequences of human errors have been relatively contained, whereas with AGI this may not be the case. It is still highly uncertain if and when general intelligence comparable to that of humans might be achieved in artificial systems, but taking into account the magnitude of the consequences and a certain degree of inertia and path dependency of international governance, it is worth considering potential risks and mitigation strategies early on.

AGI systems with human-level or super-human capabilities in most cognitive domains could hypothetically exploit existing infrastructure and other resources, develop new technologies, manipulate people, and produce new generations of ever more capable AGI systems.[87] Even if the goals of such systems were set by well-intentioned humans, it is conceivable that pursuing these goals could inadvertently have catastrophic consequences and that it may be very difficult to intervene in the process once set in motion.[88]

A key difficulty in engaging with AGI risks from a policy perspective, as with most emerging or speculative technologies, is uncertainty regarding the development trajectory and timeline. Expert surveys suggest that there is not much disagreement as to *whether* it is theoretically possible to build AGI, but there is no consensus as to *when* it could happen, with estimates ranging from the technology being a decade out to centuries away.[89] A crucial question in this regard is how much advance notice policymakers will have before the technology becomes an acute global catastrophic risk, namely whether late-stage development will move in slow increments or in sudden leaps. Spending time negotiating a new treaty now if AGI is only developed in a hundred years would be a waste of resources and might even be counterproductive, but neglecting the danger until it is too late would also be irresponsible. Thus, it is a topic well-suited for academic exploration at this point, before the need for a solution arises.

To some extent this work is relevant to current efforts dealing with specialized AI and robotics, even if most of its benefit will accrue in the longer term. For instance, improving cybersecurity is important for both near-term and long-term uses of AI and robotics, and discussions about global inequality and labour displacement might also be usefully informed by a longer-term perspective. Moreover, any progress towards more preventive, effective, and agile global governance is likely to benefit AGI governance, especially if late-stage development occurs rapidly.

D. Outlook

Effective international governance of AI and robotics is certainly a formidable challenge. Applications of these technologies permeate almost every domain of human

[87] Bostrom (n 86) 94. [88] Russell/Norvig (n 2) 1036–40.

[89] Katja Grace et al, 'Viewpoint: When Will AI Exceed Human Performance? Evidence From AI Experts' (2018) 62 Journal of Artificial Intelligence Research 729.

activity and thus unsurprisingly have an equally wide range of risk profiles, from a discriminatory algorithmic decision causing financial distress to an AI-sparked nuclear war collapsing global civilization. Hence, it is only natural that much of the international regulatory activity takes place in domain-specific fora. Many of these fora coordinate with each other, both within and beyond the UN system, spreading insights and best practices on how to deal with common concerns such as cybersecurity, licensing, monitoring, and reliability, so as to prevent accidents and misuse.

Much of this activity seems to occur below the radar of generalist scholarly, media, and NGO attention thus far, at times leading to an under-recognition of international treaties and other governance mechanisms relevant to AI and robotics given that efforts to ban or curb autonomous weapons systems and cyberwarfare have not yet been successful. Our contribution has attempted to counter this perception by showing how wide-ranging international governance of these technologies is. International regulators are actively engaging with existing and emerging safety and security challenges relating to AI and robotics. Our overview is by no means exhaustive. It merely provides a few pointers for exploring the international regulatory landscape, which will play a critical role in navigating present and future global security challenges from AI and robotization.

CHAPTER 35

BIOSECURITY

JAMES REVILL AND ANNA ROESSING

A. Introduction

The term 'biosecurity' remains a relatively new addition to the global security lexicon. Moreover, it is a term that has been disparately conceptualized by different actors operating in different contexts. Notwithstanding such conceptual difficulties, biosecurity has become an important topic in twenty-first-century security discourse as multilateral and national security policymaking organs have recognized the potential security-related risks associated with contemporary biotechnology and have sought to mitigate such risks.[1]

This chapter seeks to elaborate on what is meant by the term biosecurity, what has been achieved in terms of building a biosecurity architecture, and what challenges are faced making this architecture both effective and enduring. The chapter begins by looking at the origins and evolution of the concept of biosecurity, drawing attention to drivers of interest in biosecurity and the linguistic, cultural, and political challenges to cohesively defining this concept. The chapter then proceeds to look at the current status of the biosecurity debate, drawing on examples from the patchwork of biosecurity measures undertaken across the globe to illustrate how this is an area that has made considerable progress over the course of the last two decades.

The chapter proceeds to look at the contemporary and future challenges facing biosecurity, attending to, first, the challenge of homogenizing biosecurity provisions in circumstances where no one-size-fits-all; secondly, the implications of advances in life

[1] See, for example, the G7's work on 'The Global Partnership Biological Security Working Group' (*Global Partnership Against the Spread of Weapons and Materials of Mass Destruction*, 2017) <https://www.gpwmd.com/bswg> accessed 4 October 2019; Council of the European Union, 'EU Strategy Against Proliferation of Weapons of Mass Destruction' (10 December 2003) Doc No 15708/03; UK Government, 'UK Biological Security Strategy' (*The Home Office*, July 2018) <https://assets.publishing.service.gov.uk/government/uploads/system/uploads/attachment_data/file/730213/2018_UK_Biological_Security_Strategy.pdf> accessed 4 October 2019.

sciences and biotechnology for building a sustainable and robust biosecurity architecture; and thirdly, the difficulties in quantitative risk-assessment modelling to inform the development of a biosecurity architecture. The chapter concludes by arguing that biosecurity is a work in progress which will become increasingly salient in the global security discourse as life science and biotechnology continues to advance in a changing geostrategic context.

1. Origins and Evolution of Biosecurity

Early references to the term biosecurity in the academic literature began to emerge in the late 1980s and early 1990s. Unlike many contemporary framings of biosecurity, much of the early literature focused on efforts to prevent intrusive pest species and infectious diseases from threatening agriculture, crops, or the environment.[2] Around the turn of the century, however, growing concerns over how non-State actors might exploit the ever-advancing capacity of the life sciences for hostile purposes resulted in the fragmentation of conceptualization of what constituted 'biosecurity' in the academic literature, as well as the policies of some States. Thus, while a body of academic (and policy) literature continued to conceptualize biosecurity in relation to 'activities designed to keep out new pests',[3] there emerged a growing body of, primarily Western, literature focused on preventing non-State actors from gaining access to materials and equipment that could be used in support of bioterrorist activities.[4]

The terrorist attacks of 9/11 and the subsequent anthrax letter attacks in the US can be seen as focusing events that highlighted a pressing need to prevent non-State actors from gaining access to dangerous pathogens.[5] The latter series of events, which involved the dissemination of anthrax spores through the US mail system, resulted in the deaths of five individuals and the infection of seventeen others, as well as generated considerable economic damage with the decontamination process alone estimated at costing 'about $320 million'.[6] The event demonstrated how 'the malicious releases of dangerous pathogens, once unthinkable, ha[d] become a reality'.[7] Moreover, it did so at the dawn of

[2] eg D H Gifford et al, 'Evaluation of Biosecurity in Broiler Breeders' (1987) 31 Avian Diseases 339; Camille Moore, 'Biosecurity and Minimal Disease Herds' (1992) 8 Veterinary Clinics of North America: Food Animal Practice 461.

[3] eg Tiakina Aotearoa, *Protect New Zealand: The Biosecurity Strategy for New Zealand* (Bio Security Council 2003) 5: '[F]reedom from major pests and diseases is critical to producing efficiently and trading freely.'

[4] In October of 1999, the Centers for Disease Control and Prevention (CDC) published a Notice of Proposed Rulemaking (NPRM) seeking both to revise the biosafety standards that facilities must follow when handling select agents and to provide new biosecurity standards for such facilities.

[5] Caitríona McLeish/Paul Nightingale, 'Biosecurity, Bioterrorism and the Governance of Science: The Increasing Convergence of Science and Security Policy' (2007) 36 Research Policy 1635.

[6] Ketra Schmitt/Nicholas A Zacchia, 'Total Decontamination Cost of the Anthrax Letter Attacks' (2012) 10 Biosecurity and Bioterrorism: Biodefense Strategy, Practice, and Science 98.

[7] US National Research Council, *Life Sciences and Related Fields: Trends Relevant to the Biological Weapons Convention* (National Academies Press 2011).

what some have labelled the 'biotechnology revolution', in which ever greater capacity of the life sciences to manipulate fundamental life processes was being increasingly diffused around the globe.[8] The outcome was that bioterrorism became a 'priority concern of American security policy as a result of the anthrax letters of 2001'.[9]

Concerns over bioterrorism were further heightened over the coming decade by incidents of what became known as 'Dual Use Research of Concern' (DURC); that is 'research that, based on current understanding, can be reasonably anticipated to provide knowledge, information, products, or technologies that could be directly misapplied to pose a significant threat (…)'.[10] Early examples of DURC include: the chemical synthesis of the polio virus in 2002, a step that illustrated how it was theoretically possible for those with hostile intent to acquire dangerous pathogens through chemical synthesis;[11] and research on the 1918 flu virus[12] which demonstrated the possibility of acquiring pathogens that do not otherwise exist in nature. All these experiments were undertaken for legitimate reasons, yet in each case the nature of the research nonetheless generated concerns because of the potential for hostile exploitation by States or non-State actors (both terrorist and criminal).[13]

2. Biosecurity Goes Global

The experience with the anthrax letter attacks, combined with concerns over how changes in both the capacity and geography of the life sciences could facilitate bioterrorism, resonated across many countries in the Western world, to the extent that discussion around 'biosecurity' as a policy response to concerns over bioterrorism, became salient in the wider international security discourse in the early twenty-first century. This was certainly evident in discussions under the auspices of the 1972 Biological and Toxin Weapons Convention (BTWC). This disarmament treaty addresses national implementation under Article IV; however, the language remains rather vague, with States Parties committing to 'take any necessary measures to prohibit and prevent the development,

[8] US National Research Council, *Biotechnology Research in an Age of Terrorism* (National Academies Press 2004).

[9] Elisa D Harris/John D Steinbruner, 'Scientific Openness and National Security After 9-11' (2005) 67 The CBW Conventions Bulletin 1.

[10] National Institute of Health—Office of Science Policy (NIH-OSP), 'Dual Use Research of Concern' (*NIH-OSP*, 2018) <https://osp.od.nih.gov/biotechnology/dual-use-research-of-concern/> accessed 4 October 2019.

[11] Jeronimo Cello et al, 'Chemical Synthesis of Poliovirus CDNA: Generation of Infectious Virus in the Absence of Natural Template' (2002) 297 Science 1016.

[12] Terence M Tumpey et al, 'Characterization of the Reconstructed 1918 Spanish Influenza Pandemic Virus' (2005) 310 Science 77.

[13] James Revill et al (Rapporteurs), *Governance of Dual Use Research in the Life Sciences: Advancing Global Consensus on Research Oversight* (National Academies Press 2018) 14–17.

production, stockpiling, acquisition or retention' of biological weapons 'within the territory of such State, under its jurisdiction or under its control anywhere'.[14]

Nonetheless, States Parties have sought to attend to biosecurity in response to the growing salience of the perceived threat from bioterrorism through the BTWC. In 2003, States Parties addressed the topic of 'national mechanisms to establish and maintain the security and oversight of pathogenic microorganisms and toxins' as part of a new programme of work following the collapse of discussion around a protocol intended to strengthen the BTWC. As Tibor Tóth, the Chair of the first intersessional meeting in 2003, noted, the discussion around biosecurity was, for some States, 'their first exposure to such a concept'[15] and Japan remarked that 'the number of countries which have taken measures specifically, from the point of view of biosecurity, remains small'.[16]

The internationalization of measures to respond to concerns over bioterrorism has been leant succour through other mechanisms. For example, measures corresponding closely with some framings of biosecurity were employed through the use of Chapter VII of the Charter of the United Nations, in UN Security Council (UNSC) Resolution 1540 (2004), which obligates UN Member States to *inter alia*, '(...) develop and maintain appropriate effective measures to account for and secure' material related to biological weapons development.

In addition, the integration of laboratory biosecurity into the third edition of the WHO's Laboratory Biosafety Manual in 2004 can be seen as further internationalizing biosecurity as a response to concerns over bioterrorism.[17]

Notably, the manual further includes a definition of 'Laboratory biosecurity' as referring to 'institutional and personal security measures designed to prevent the loss, theft, misuse, diversion (...)';[18] however, this was only one interpretation of biosecurity.

3. Linguistic Difficulties

The promulgation of biosecurity as laboratory biosecurity in the early twenty-first century was not without challenges. One immediate challenge with efforts to promulgate biosecurity more widely across the globe lies in the linguistic barriers that exist outside the English-language realm. In many other languages the distinction between the concepts of biosecurity and biosafety did not exist prior to the early 2000s and subsequent attempts to engineer distinctions have not always proved entirely successful. For example, in the German language the term '*Biosicherheit*' is used in two senses describing

[14] Convention on the Prohibition of the Development, Production and Stockpiling of Bacteriological (Biological) and Toxin Weapons and on their Destruction 1015 UNTS 163 (BTWC) art IV.

[15] Tibor Tóth, 'Chairman's Closing Remarks' (Meeting of the State Parties to the BTWC, Report of the Meeting of Experts, 18 September 2003) Doc BWC/MSP.2003/MX/4 (Part II), 151.

[16] Japan, 'Possible Measures for Strengthening Biosecurity' (Meeting of the State Parties to the BTWC, 28 July 2003) UN Doc BWC/MSP.2003/MX/WP.11, 2.

[17] World Health Organization, *Laboratory Biosafety Manual: Third Edition* (WHO 2004).

[18] ibid 47.

both biosafety and biosecurity concerns and refers to 'the protection of human life or health, the environment or other important legal interests against unintentional harm caused by working with microorganisms'.[19] Similarly, in Spanish, Portuguese, and French the respective terms *bioseguridad, biossegurança*, and *biosécurité* do not readily correspond to the emerging Western-led notion of biosecurity.[20] Although there have been efforts to engineer distinctions in translations[21] it is unclear the extent to which the English distinction between biosafety and biosecurity has resonated in other languages. Certainly in some linguistic context, in cases where a clear distinction is necessary, reference is found to the English terms 'biosafety' and 'biosecurity'.[22]

4. Contextual Difficulties

In addition to linguistic challenges, it also became apparent that 'biosecurity does not seem to have a standardized meaning across human, animal and plant health sectors'.[23] As Australia remarked in 2003 'the FAO use (...) [biosecurity] in terms of securing food supplies (...) within Australian agriculture (...) [biosecurity] also means protecting the country from exotic pests and diseases through quarantine, surveillance and early detection measures'.[24]

Nor is it necessarily standardized across different national institutions. In the German context '*Biosicherheit*' is invoked by the Federal Ministry of Defence and the Foreign Office to describe risks resulting from dangerous toxins and pathogens and the threat of their direct misuse,[25] whereas the *Bernhard-Nocht-Institut for Tropical Medicine (BNITM)* associates '*Biosicherheit*' also with (global) health emergencies, such as the 2016 Ebola crisis.[26] Confusion around the concept of 'biosecurity' might then arise from the different ways it is used across different institutional and disciplinary contexts.

[19] German Ethics Council, *Biosecurity—Freedom and Responsibility of Research: Opinion* (Deutscher Ethikrat 2014).

[20] See eg the different translations of the background document Implementation Support Unit, 'Biosafety and Biosecurity' (Meeting of State Parties to the BTWC, 24 June 2008) Doc BWC/MSP/2008/MX/INF.1 <https://www.unog.ch/__80256ee600585943.nsf/(httpPages)/8c24e93c19bdc8c4c12574f60031809f?OpenDocument&ExpandSection=1#_Section1> accessed 4 October 2019.

[21] In translations of UN background materials into Spanish, for example, 'bioseguridad' was translated to correspond with biosafety, and 'biocustodia' was used to reflect biosecurity.

[22] German Ethics Council (n 19). [23] Implementation Support Unit (n 20) 2.

[24] UN, 'Report of the Meeting of the States Parties: Statements, Presentations and Contributions made available to the Chairman' (Meeting of States Parties, 10–14 November 2003) BWC/MSP/2003/4 (Vol II) Annex II, 125.

[25] See eg Interview with Lieutenant Colonel Kai Hoberg (adviser for arms control: Bundesministerium der Verteidigung), 'Biosicherheit: Das Risiko unter Kontrolle halten' (*BMVg*, 12 May 2017) <https://www.bmvg.de/de/aktuelles/biosicherheit-11320> accessed 4 October 2019; Auswärtiges Amt, 'Das Deutsche Biosicherheitsprogramm' (*AA*, 2017) <https://www.auswaertiges-amt.de/de/aussenpolitik/themen/abruestung-ruestungskontrolle/uebersicht-bcwaffen-node/biosicherheit> accessed 4 October 2019.

[26] Bernhard-Nocht-Institute for Tropical Medicine, 'Ausbruch des Ebola-Fiebers in der Demokratischen Republik Kongo' (BNITM, 2018) <https://www.bnitm.de/aktuelles/mitteilungen/7408-ausbruch-des-ebola-fiebers-in-der-demokratischen-republik-kongo/> accessed 4 October 2019.

5. 'Narrow' versus 'Wide' Biosecurity

Beyond the challenges posed by linguistic and contextual differences lies a more fundamental division over the value of what some saw as a 'narrow' approach to biosecurity as akin to the World Health Organization's (WHO) 'laboratory biosecurity', versus a broader approach to biosecurity which addresses deliberate threats from terrorists *and* naturally occurring biological threats. This difference was clearly articulated by representatives of Indonesia who suggested that 'biosecurity is not limited to protecting laboratory-based pathogens and toxins from theft (...) [S]uch a narrow strategy has limited value in Indonesia, where dangerous pathogens are not only located in laboratories, but can also be found readily in nature'.[27]

Indeed, for States relatively untroubled by bioterrorism, but ravaged by natural outbreaks of disease, the narrow approach to biosecurity as a means to prevent terrorists from acquiring pathogens is understandably less of a priority. As was bluntly stated in the BTWC context, 'in a country such as South Africa the utility of spending $1 million on biosecurity still fails to prevent an individual going into Kruger National Park and digging up anthrax spores'.[28] In contrast, for States with a comparatively low burden of infectious disease, but significant concerns over bioterrorism and the spread of high-containment biological laboratories around the world (and the maintenance and personnel management within such laboratories), biosecurity was much more narrowly focused on what the WHO has termed 'laboratory security',[29] which aims to prevent people from deliberately removing materials from the laboratory for malign usage. For such States, in which pathogenic agents of concern are located primarily within the laboratory, the context is different and, as such, the discourse is logically focused on improving laboratory security. Under such circumstances, biosecurity was considered as being comprised of some variant[30] of the following principles of practice: physical security, personnel security, material control and accountability, transfer security, information security, and, underlying in many of the above principles, some form of program management.[31] In this context, in the early stages of the twenty-first century at

[27] Franciscus Halim, 'Biological Threats and Biosecurity Efforts in Indonesia' in Sandia National Laboratories, 'International Biosecurity Symposium: Securing High Consequence Pathogens and Toxins—Symposium Summary' (Sandia Report, SAND2004-2109, *SNL* 2004) 11 <https://digital.library.unt.edu/ark:/67531/metadc891445/m2/1/high_res_d/919184.pdf> accessed 4 October 2019.

[28] Jez Littlewood, *The Biological Weapons Convention: A Failed Revolution* (Ashgate Publishing 2005) 236.

[29] WHO, 'Biorisk Management: Laboratory Biosecurity Guidance' (WHO/CDS/EPR/2006.6, *World Health Organization*, September 2006) <http://www.who.int/csr/resources/publications/biosafety/WHO_CDS_EPR_2006_6.pdf> accessed 4 October 2019.

[30] The exact terminology used by States varies, however most Western approaches largely included components which fell within these overarching categories.

[31] These principles are derived from the work of Sandia National Laboratories, Biosecurity project. For an excellent discussion with a range of views on this issue see Sandia National Laboratories (n 27).

least, definitions of biosecurity were disparately constructed in a manner that, not unreasonably, reflected the differing interests and priorities of States. This may, however, be changing in the wake of natural disease outbreaks, such as the Ebola outbreak in West Africa.

B. Current Status of the Debate

While considerable definitional issues with the notion of biosecurity remain, in the context of international security discourse, the biosecurity-as-laboratory-biosecurity model has largely 'won out', with biosecurity becoming hegemonically (re)conceptualized in background materials to the BTWC, indicating that 'in the setting of the BWC [biological weapons convention], it is most commonly used to refer to mechanisms to establish and maintain the security and oversight of pathogenic microorganisms, toxins and relevant resources'.[32]

Moreover, this is an area that has seen considerable advances over the course of the twenty-first century, with a number of initiatives developed in support of what can loosely be termed (laboratory) biosecurity governance. Such measures have often been funded by developed States in the EU and G7 Global Partnership.[33] Funding from these and other bodies and wider interest in the concept of biosecurity has fed into the development of several components of biosecurity governance. These range from hard measures designed to ensure the physical security of laboratory facilities, to measures focused on particular phases of the life science research life cycle—such as the screening of publications for security sensitive content—to 'softer' approaches, including the development and promulgation of biosecurity educational materials and codes of conduct for life scientists. Illustrative examples of some more novel areas of biosecurity activity are outlined below.

1. Education

Over the course of the last decade there has been considerable attention paid to the idea of education and awareness-raising for scientists, with projects undertaken in a range of countries, including Denmark, Morocco, Japan, Pakistan, Switzerland, and the US. Thus, Morocco, for example, has developed a programme of dual-use education, which notably includes a biosecurity and biosafety 'caravan', in order to minimize the risks of misuse of life science research as well as minimizing 'constraints on research through

[32] Implementation Support Unit (n 20).

[33] See eg the work done under the EU Chemical, Biological, Radiological and Nuclear Risk Mitigation Centres of Excellence Initiative (CBRN CoE).

self- or government-imposed censorship'.[34] In the UK, the Department of Peace Studies at Bradford University developed an Educational Module Resource for life science lecturers and 'train the trainer' programmes which have been used in several countries.[35]

2. Codes of Conduct

A second element of biosecurity governance is the notion of developing codes of conduct for life scientists. Following a discussion under the BTWC on Codes of Conduct for Life Scientists in 2005, there have been many code-type initiatives. For example, in 2005, the Inter Academy Panel issued a statement on biosecurity which contained a number of principles that represented 'fundamental issues that should be taken into account when formulating codes of conduct';[36] in 2008, the Netherlands developed a Code of Conduct for Biosecurity intended 'to prevent life sciences research or its application from directly or indirectly contributing to the development, production or stockpiling of biological weapons';[37] whereas the 2011 European DIYbio Congress produced a Draft DIYbio Code of Ethics which includes the stipulation that 'Biotechnology must only be used for peaceful purposes'.[38]

3. Development of Life Science Funding Criteria

A third development is the integration of biosecurity components into the criterion for applying for funding with a view to raising awareness of biosecurity concerns and steering life science research away from unnecessarily risky activities. In 2005, three prominent UK funders of life science research, the Biotechnology and Biological Sciences Research Council (BBSRC), the Medical Research Council (MRC) and the Wellcome Trust (WT), issued a statement that established changes to policies, including the introduction of questions related to biosecurity in funding application forms. More recently, the White House Office of Science and Technology Policy (OSTP) has issued a policy

[34] Fatima Lamchouri, 'Role and Importance of Education and Awareness in the Implementation of the Biological Weapons Convention: Moroccan Experience' (*International Workshop on Cooperation and Assistance under Article X of the Biological Weapons Convention*, 22 June 2018) <https://www.unog.ch/80256EDD006B8954/(httpAssets)/05A9A1055998EBA4C12582B80040F0EB/$file/Prof.+Fatima+LAMCHOURI+-+Morocco+-+for+upload.pdf> accessed 30 November 2020.

[35] Masamichi Minehata et al, 'Implementing Biosecurity Education: Approaches, Resources and Programmes' (2013) 19 Science and Engineering Ethics 1473.

[36] The InterAcademy Panel, 'IAP Statement on Biosecurity' (*IAP*, 7 November 2005) <https://www.interacademies.org/statement/iap-statement-biosecurity> accessed 30 November 2020.

[37] Royal Netherlands Academy of Arts and Sciences, *A Code of Conduct for Biosecurity: Report of the Biosecurity Working Group* (Royal Netherlands Academy of Arts and Sciences 2008).

[38] European DIYbio Congress, 'Draft DIYBio Code of Ethics from European Congress' (*DIYBio*, 2011) <https://diybio.org/codes/draft-diybio-code-of-ethics-from-european-congress/> accessed 4 October 2019.

guidance calling for a 'pre-funding review mechanism for certain research proposals' dealing with potentially pandemic pathogens.[39]

4. Publication Screening

The twenty-first century has also seen the emergence of initiatives intended to prevent the proliferation of biosecurity-sensitive information in academic publications. In 2003, leading journal editors issued a joint statement which 'recognized that on occasion an editor may conclude that the potential harm of publication outweighs the potential societal benefits' and added that '[u]nder such circumstances, the paper should be modified, or not be published'.[40] Similarly, the Council of Science Editors has recognized that '[i]n rare cases, some information needed to reproduce the experiment should be eliminated or the manuscript itself should not be published' and, in a 2012 update of a White Paper, argued that '[e]ditors should develop guidelines and procedures to allow the scientific evaluation as well as the evaluation of the possible risk of communicating information with dual use potential'.[41] This effort represents a laudable step on the part of journal editors to incorporate biosecurity considerations into editorial reviews and, where necessary, modify content to minimize dual-use risks. However, in reality, as discussed subsequently, it has become increasingly difficult to prevent the proliferation of potentially sensitive information.

5. Institutional Risk Assessment

One further measure that has received considerable attention is risk assessment (and mitigation). This has led to the emergence of institutional committees designed to address biosecurity risks of particular research proposals in advance and potentially provide binding recommendations on the design or conduct of dual-use research as well as stipulations for particular biosecurity measures to be employed in any future research programme.[42] Such institutions have been established in a number of Western organizations. For example, the University of Chicago has established Institutional Biosafety

[39] The White House—Office of Science and Technology Policy, 'Recommended Policy Guidance for Departmental Development of Review Mechanisms for Potential Pandemic Pathogen Care and Oversight (P3CO)' (The White House, 9 January 2017) <https://obamawhitehouse.archives.gov/sites/default/files/microsites/ostp/p3co-finalguidancestatement.pdf> accessed 4 October 2019.

[40] Journal Editors and Authors Group, 'Statement on Scientific Publication and Security' (2003) 299 Science 1149.

[41] Council of Science Editors, 'White Paper on Promoting Integrity in Scientific Journal Publications' (CSEs, 2018) <http://www.councilscienceeditors.org/resource-library/editorial-policies/white-paper-on-publication-ethics/> accessed 4 October 2019.

[42] Personal notes from international workshop organized by the InterAcademy Panel on the Governance of Dual Use Research in the Life Sciences: Advancing Global Consensus on Research Oversight, in Zagreb, Croatia.

Committees (IBC) tasked with reviewing research proposals and, where necessary, applying security and safety conditions for biological research on certain pathogenic agents.[43]

6. Reflections on the Emergence of Biosecurity Governance

While there has been considerable biosecurity-related activity around the globe, there is little consistency between the measures undertaken around the world for different reasons: first, there is little cohesive agreement over exactly what is required of States seeking to build biosecurity while, unlike the sphere of chemical weapons, where the Chemical Weapons Convention has developed matrices of measures for national implementation, exactly what is required to 'prevent' biological weapons at the national level is less clear-cut. Secondly, yet still related to the above, biosecurity-related measures remain context specific and dependent upon the local culture, language, and priorities. Indeed, it has become widely accepted that there is no one-size-fits-all approach to biosecurity around the world. Thirdly, such measures have been undertaken with different objectives, a trend that perhaps reflects rather mixed assessments of the nature of the risks posed by biological weapons and the differences in the purpose of some biosecurity measures. As Rappert noted in 2010, with regard to biosecurity education, this has multiple functions, including: as a prerequisite 'for other security-related activities to be undertaken'; and a deficiency-correcting tool designed to 'correct' the ignorance of life scientists in relation to biosecurity risks.[44]

It is also difficult to determine the extent to which biosecurity governance measures work and there is little empirical evidence of what works (best), with regards to measures such as education and codes. Moreover, this is something very difficult to determine empirically across a range of contexts and cultures.[45] Measures to better scrutinize the funding of dual-use research may well have served to raise awareness and minimize some obvious risks. However, it is unclear the extent to which the necessary time and expertise are available to all those reviewing funding bids to do so thoroughly and scrutinize all research proposals for biosecurity issues.

Similarly, although editorial controls have flagged a small number of controversial scientific papers prior to publication, seemingly all have eventually been published, in some cases with only minor modifications. Moreover, it remains difficult to prevent the dissemination of materials at this late stage in the research life cycle for three reasons: (i) by the point of formal publication, information pertaining to research will likely already have been circulated; (ii) because of the lack of time, resources and biosecurity-related expertise of reviewing bodies to identify sensitive content; and (iii) because of the

[43] The University of Chicago Institutional Biosafety Committee (IBC) and Select Agent (SA)-IBC Policy and Procedure Manual.

[44] Brian Rappert (ed), *Education and Ethics in the Life Sciences Strengthening the Prohibition of Biological Weapons* (The Australian National University 2010).

[45] Richard R Nelson, 'The Moon and the Ghetto Revisited' (2011) 38 Science and Public Policy 681.

pressure on researchers to publish their results, which makes intervention at this point 'significantly harder'.[46]

Furthermore, even the most advanced systems in developed Western States are likely to remain problematic, if experience with biosafety incidents is any guide. In 2014, staff in US labs were accidently exposed to live anthrax as a result of multiple protocol breaches in an episode Ebright described as 'not an isolated incident, but instead is part of a continuing pattern of biosafety and biosecurity problems at the [US Center for Disease Control]'.[47] As the CDC remarked, the lapse showed:

> a lack of standard operating procedures, a lack of lab-adequate laboratory oversight, a lack of an approved study plan, use of unapproved sterilization techniques for anthrax, the transfer of material that wasn't confirmed to be inactive. In fact, the use of anthrax at all for this experiment should not have been done. It was not appropriate.[48]

Some have argued that underlying these events is a deeper problem with the organizational culture of those working on research in the life sciences and certainly some researchers view biosecurity measures as unnecessary box-ticking exercises that impede progress.[49] This is compounded by very different perceptions of the risks and benefits of dual-use biology, something evident in a number of recent scientific developments, as discussed further below.

C. Recent Developments and Contemporary Challenges

Over recent years the convergence of different scientific disciplines ranging from biology and chemistry to engineering, mathematics, as well as computer science, is revolutionizing the life science research. With this process, biology's focus has moved from solely reading the genetic code of biological systems to rewriting it, thereby transforming cells into small chemical factories. Facilitated by so-called 'enabling technologies', such as genome editing and synthetic biology, the human capacity for engineering genomes throughout a wide variety of taxonomies has plausibly enlarged. With the

[46] NASEM, *Governance of Dual Use Research in the Life Sciences* (National Academies Press 2018).

[47] Sharon Begley/Julie Steenhuysen 'Multiple Protocol Breaches Behind Anthrax Exposure at US Federal Labs' (*Reuters*, 21 June 2014) <https://www.reuters.com/article/us-usa-anthrax-insight/multiple-protocol-breaches-behind-anthrax-exposure-at-u-s-federal-labs-idUSKBN0EW0TJ20140621> accessed 4 October 2019.

[48] Centers for Disease Control and Prevention, 'Press Conference on Laboratory Quality and Safety after Recent Lab Incidents' (*CDC Newsroom Releases*, 11 July 2014) <https://www.cdc.gov/media/releases/2014/t0711-lab-safety.html> accessed 4 October 2019.

[49] Revill et al (n 13).

increasing automatization of key laboratory processes and the accumulation and digitization of large DNA sequence databases, access to knowledge and enabling technologies has proliferated around the globe.[50] While unquestionably promising great economic, medical, and political benefits, the collective scientific and technological breakthroughs also have raised profound concerns over how they overcome past technological limitations and enable a next generation of more reliable and dangerous biological weapons that could be pursued by States and perhaps even non-State actors.[51]

1. CRISPR

Of particular note is the emergence of 'clustered regularly interspaced short palindromic repeats' or 'CRISPR'-based systems[52] as a method for site-directed genome and base editing used to investigate and manipulate genetic functions and interactions. Often described as 'gene scissor', it allows one to deliberately insert or delete DNA sequences and bases at specific genetic loci.[53] Although genomic alterations have been possible for many years (for instance, in order to replace defective genes), CRISPR has increased the precision and pace of modifications while also expanding its application to a wide variety of organisms. Since CRISPR-Cas9, other CRISPR-endonucleases systems such as Cpf1 have become a routine and facilitating instrument for research with utilities in numerous medical and agricultural applications.[54]

Yet while CRISPR is fundamentally widening the possibilities of genetic engineering, it has simultaneously raised profound ethical, legal *and* biosecurity-related concerns. Significant ethical and legal concerns over CRISPR erupted in late 2018 in response to the controversial 'CRISPR Babies' research reportedly conducted by Professor He Jiankui in China.[55] More specific to biosecurity is the concern over the dual-use potential of CRISPR as a relatively inexpensive and easy-to-use tool, to facilitate the development of biological weapons—a concern expressed by the then Director of US National

[50] Federal Department of Defence, Civil Protection and Sports et al (FDDCPS), 'Spiez CONVERGENCE Report on the Second Workshop' (Spiez Laboratory, October 2016) <https://www.labor-spiez.ch/pdf/en/Report_on_the_second_workshop-5-9_September_2016.pdf> accessed 4 October 2019.

[51] NASEM, *Biodefense in the Age of Synthetic Biology* (National Academies Press 2018).

[52] CRISPR stands for 'clustered, regularly interspaced, short palindromic repeats' that function together with several endonuclease, for instance Cas9 (CRISPR-associated protein9).

[53] See only Martin Jinek et al, 'A Programmable Dual-RNA Guided DNA Endonuclease in Adaptive Bacterial Immunity' (2012) 337 Science 816.

[54] See eg European Academies Science Advisory Council, *Genome Editing: Scientific Opportunities, Public Interests and Policy Options in the European Union* (EASAC Policy Report 31, German National Academy of Sciences Leopoldina 2017); Royal Netherlands Academy of Arts and Science, 'Genome Editing: Position Paper of Royal Netherlands Academy of Arts and Science' (Royal Netherlands Academy of Arts and Science, November 2016) <https://www.knaw.nl/en/news/publications/genome-editing> accessed 4 October 2019.

[55] David Cyranoski, 'First CRISPR Babies: Six Questions That Remain' (*Nature News*, 30 November 2018) <https://www.nature.com/articles/d41586-018-07607-3> accessed 4 October 2019.

Intelligence[56] that has been echoed by several scientists.[57] Pointing to its enabling misuse by potential terrorists, Bill Gates remarked at the Munich Security Conference in 2016, 'the next epidemic could originate on the computer screen of a terrorist intent on using genetic engineering to create a synthetic version of the smallpox virus'.[58]

In reaction to those statements, some members of the scientific community reported more general unease about the transformative nature of the technology,[59] accompanied by the rapid and broad distribution of knowledge and resources, as well as the lowering of costs and accelerated pace of scientific developments. Some have also mentioned a general lack of caution over gene-editing's societal implications 'for which the alarm about how it could go wrong has largely lagged behind the hype of what good it could achieve'.[60]

Yet for all the legitimate concern and careful attention there is a need for caution with regard to the hype surrounding CRISPR and the biosecurity implications it presents. The Swiss Defence Laboratory at Spiez for instance reported that 'from an arms control perspective, the implications [of CRISPR] are probably modest'.[61] Other biological arms control experts such as Invernizzi have noted that CRISPR 'does not enable things previously impossible (…), it rather renders the already possible less cumbersome, less time-consuming and less expensive', although as he further notes 'it cannot be excluded that CRISPR will find its way into a biological weapons program'.[62]

2. Synthetic Biology

Synthetic biology, a field that strives to 'make the engineering of biology easier and more predictable'[63] similarly has become an ideograph for the unease about what specific technologies and applications might enable in the future and how they might shape research trajectories at large. A recent report by the US National Academics of Science, Engineering and Medicine, for instance, noted that it might 'even expand (…) what is

[56] James R Clapper, 'Statement for the Record: Worldwide Threat Assessment of the US Intelligence Community' (*Senate Armed Services Committee*, 9 February 2016) <https://www.armed-services.senate.gov/imo/media/doc/Clapper_02-09-16.pdf> accessed 4 October 2019.

[57] Tim Trevan, 'Biological Research: Rethink Biosafety' (2015) 527 Nature 155.

[58] Bill Gates, 'Opening Speech to the Panel Discussion "Health Security: Small Bugs, Big Bombs" at the 53rd Munich Security Conference' (Munich Security Conference, 17–19 February 2017) <https://securityconference.org/mediathek/suche/?tx_solr%5Bq%5D=bill+gates> accessed 4 October 2019.

[59] Nature International Journal of Science, 'CRISPR Everywhere' (2016) 531 Nature 155.

[60] Nature International Journal of Science, 'Gene Intelligence: The Risks and Rewards of Genome Editing Resonate beyond the Clinic' (2016) 531 Nature 140.

[61] FDDCPS (n 50) 24.

[62] Cédric Invernizzi, 'CRISPR and the Hype Cycle' in Quentin Ladetto (ed), *Defence Future Technologies: What We See on the Horizon* (Federal Department of Defence, Civil Protection and Sport DDPS 2017).

[63] The Royal Academy of Engineering, *Synthetic Biology: Scope, Applications and Implications* (The Royal Academy of Engineering 2009) 6.

possible in creating new weapons.'[64] Due to its 'de-skilling' capacities along with the extended online access to large DNA data libraries and the decreasing costs for DNA synthesis, it is regularly claimed to enable a growing range of actors operating outside professional laboratories, including mal-intended individuals. Additionally, synthetic biology has created new pathways to create and synthesize pathogenic viruses 'from scratch'. This raises concern as it can evade the control of agents through traditional export-control instruments.[65] Synthetic biology works in concert with other (technological) trends such as 3D printing that facilitate the international shipment of goods and complicate their control. It indicates a shift in how goods such as virus samples can move between national borders, sometimes in discarding their materiality and transcending to the data points of their genetic code. By implication, control approaches that have been designed in view of the steadiness of materiality itself are experiencing a growing challenge.

Demonstrating the relevance of such concerns, an experiment published in 2018, the *de novo* synthesis of horsepox virus,[66] served as a striking example of both synthetic biology's potential and the significant biosecurity implications therein.[67] Some feared the techniques and acquired knowledge might be transferable or even directly applicable to the re-creation of the horsepox-related smallpox-causing variola virus. By decreasing existing technical barriers, this research was perceived by some as a 'gamechanger' for biosecurity that enables the re-creation of smallpox in the future with only 'little specialized knowledge' necessary.[68]

Yet, despite the legitimate concern voiced over such progress and its potential misuse, synthesizing variola and other poxviruses remains a substantial challenge, even for trained scientists, due to the specialized expertise required to conduct this type of research. Some therefore suggested the significance of this experiment rather depends on the degree to which the use of poxviruses as a vector system becomes a routine means of conducting biomedical research, which might increase the danger of its unintentional, accidental release.[69] The controversy effectively highlighted still unsolved issues related to biosecurity and the regulation and assessment of dual-use research in heterogeneous national approaches while also scrutinizing the effectiveness of scientific self-governance and self-constraint by the scientific community.

[64] NASEM (n 51) 155.

[65] Michele Garfinkle/Lori Knowles, 'Synthetic Biology, Biosecurity, and Biosafety' in Ronald L Sandler (ed), *Ethics and Emerging Technologies* (Palgrave Macmillan 2014).

[66] Ryan S Noyce et al, 'Construction of an Infectious Horsepox Virus Vaccine from Chemically Synthesized DNA Fragments' (2018) 13 PLOS ONE <http://dx.plos.org/10.1371/journal.pone.0188453> accessed 4 October 2019.

[67] Gregory D Koblentz, 'The *De Novo* Synthesis of Horsepox Virus: Implications for Biosecurity and Recommendations for Preventing the Reemergence of Smallpox' (2017) 15 Health Security 620.

[68] Kai Kupferschmidt, 'How Canadian Researchers Reconstituted an Extinct Poxvirus for $100,000 Using Mail-Order DNA' (*Science*, 6 July 2017) <http://www.sciencemag.org/news/2017/07/how-canadian-researchers-built-poxvirus-100000-using-mail-order-dna> accessed 4 October 2019.

[69] Koblentz (n 67).

3. Gain-of-Function Research

So-called 'Gain-of-Function' (GoF) research is another example that prompted international biosecurity concern following attempts to publish experiments that altered 'respiratory pathogens with pandemic potential' using widely available and accessible knowledge and technologies.[70] According to the principal investigators, the research was prompted by concerns that naturally occurring mutations in the avian influenza H5N1 virus genome could result in its (increased) transmissibility amongst humans, who in the rare cases of an infection showed a relatively high mortality rate. A particular concern was that the H5N1 virus could acquire the ability to be transmitted by aerosol or respiratory droplet between humans. To investigate a possible airborne transmission of H5N1 viruses, a research team surrounding Ron A. M. Fouchier genetically modified the virus in a 'Gain-of-Function' study in ferrets. The modified H5N1 virus acquired the ability to be airborne transmissible in ferrets.[71] The publication process of these results, however, spurred a greater controversy over the scope and detail the documentation of steps leading to the airborne H5N1 virus would make publicly accessible. Whereas the scientists claimed their research was in the interest of public health and pandemic preparedness objectives,[72] reports of laboratory safety and security lapses highlighted the risks of an accidental release of such a pathogen.[73]

Moreover, the ensuing public controversy unleashed over GoF raised questions over how to assess the risks and benefits of experiments that potentially create novel, highly virulent pathogens with no existing human immunity.[74] Differing views about the value of such research within the scientific community complicated finding a consensus on this issue. As a result, the US National Science Advisory Board for Biosecurity (NSABB) formulated, for the first time, a recommendation to redact a scientific publication to mitigate its misuse potential.

However, the debate about the H5N1 virus studies was as much a substantial question of whether they should have been conducted at all, as about how to engage with their misuse risks, yet both such aspects expanded the NSABB's (political and legal) mandate.[75] The institutional shortcomings in the existing oversight and biosecurity risk management brought forth in the debate, together with growing biosafety concerns over laboratory lapses, resulted in a US Government-initiated one-year deliberative

[70] See eg European Academies Science Advisory Council, *Gain of Function: Experimental Applications Relating to Potentially Pandemic Pathogens* (EASAC 2015).

[71] Ron AM Fouchier et al, 'Airborne Transmission of Influenza A/H5N1 Virus Between Ferrets' (2012) 336 Nature 1534.

[72] Ron AM Fouchier et al, 'Pause on Avian Flu Transmission Studies' (2012) 481 Nature 443.

[73] Kupferschmidt (n 68).

[74] See eg Marc Lipsitch/Alison P Galvani, 'The Case Against "Gain-of-Function" Experiments: A Reply to Fouchier and Kawaoka' (*CIDRAP*, 19 June 2014) <http://www.cidrap.umn.edu/news-perspective/2014/06/commentary-case-against-gain-function-experiments-reply-fouchier-kawaoka> accessed 4 October 2019.

[75] Ruth R Faden/Ruth A Karron, 'The Obligation to Prevent the Next Dual-Use Controversy' (2012) 335 Science Policy Forum 802.

process that also instituted a pause for some experiments involving influenza, SARS, and MERS viruses.[76]

Equally concerned, the European Commission instructed the European Academies Science Advisory Council (EASAC) to investigate the issue.[77] The deliberation process resulted in the development of a policy governing the funding and conduct of future GoF research, with both the US National Institutes of Health and the EASAC concluding on the necessity of a robust assessment and prior special consideration of dangerous experiments in a multidisciplinary review process.[78]

4. Gene Drive Systems

The discussion on how to evaluate potential environmental, societal, and security risks also extends to ecological engineering systems. In recent years, some of the most contentious debates unfolded in the forum of the Convention on Biological Diversity (CBD) surrounding synthetic biology and so-called 'gene drive systems'.[79] With the help of advances in genome editing, especially CRISPR systems, gene drive systems allow scientists to steer a genetic modification or desirable genetic traits through the population of a sexually reproducing organism over many generations with greater efficiency compared to normal inheritance.[80] Its potential application is often thought in the context of global health challenges, for instance, to suppress wild populations of malaria-carrying Anopheles mosquitos via gene drives that 'drive' a 'sterility trait' through a population.

However, others have sounded a note of caution related to the broad scope of gene drive applications,[81] including their uptake for military programs,[82] and the uncertainty of tinkering with ecosystems that 'will likely impact everyone living within the target region'.[83] Identifying and addressing potential biosecurity and biosafety risks is even

[76] Institute of Medicine and National Research Council, *Potential Risks and Benefits of Gain-of-Function Research* (National Academies Press 2015).

[77] European Academies Science Advisory Council (n 70).

[78] The review process has been formalized in the 'Framework for Guiding Funding Decisions about Proposed Research Involving Enhanced Potential Pandemic Pathogens' (US Department of Health and Human Services, 2017) <https://www.phe.gov/s3/dualuse/Documents/p3co.pdf> accessed 4 October 2019.

[79] Convention on Biological Diversity—AHTEG, 'Report of the Ad Hoc Technical Expert Group on Synthetic Biology' (9 December 2017) CBD/SYNBIO/AHTEG/2017/1/3, para 25.

[80] Kevin M Esvelt et al, 'Emerging Technology: Concerning RNA-Guided Gene Drives for the Alteration of Wild Populations' (2014) 3 eLife <https://elifesciences.org/articles/03401> accessed 4 October 2019.

[81] Dorian Moro et al, 'Identifying Knowledge Gaps for Gene Drive Research to Control Invasive Animal Species: The Next CRISPR Step' (2018) 13 Global Ecology and Conservation.

[82] Robert G Reeves et al, 'Agricultural Research, or a New Bioweapon System?' (2018) 362 Science 35.

[83] Devora A Najjar et al, 'Driving towards Ecotechnologies' (2017) 111 Pathogens and Global Health 448.

more complicated in those countries and regions in which test fielding and the release of gene drive modified organisms is likely to occur, as the regulatory landscapes are fragmented and scope for public dialogue and engagement more limited.[84] Non-governmental organizations such as the ETC Group, therefore, argued for an international research and field test moratorium, as was discussed in the frame of the CBD in 2016[85] and 2018.[86] The Member States eventually rejected such a moratorium, leaving only the rather vague treaty requirements, which call for further risk assessments on a case-by-case basis, precaution in field tests, and consultation with affected local communities and indigenous groups.[87]

The 'transboundary movement' of living genetically modified organisms (LMOs) has also entered the agenda of export-control discussions[88] and prompted liability considerations in light of potential adverse effects and damages that such LMOs could cause to humans and the environment. The CBD's Cartagena Biosafety Protocol, as well as its Supplementary Nagoya-Kuala Lumpur Protocol, can be seen as part of an emerging international regulatory framework that incorporates gene drive applications, although its scope is limited to environmental and biodiversity issues. The supplementary protocol introduces international rules on liability, redress, and actions ('response measures') to be taken in case of damages caused by a released LMO[89] and may function within international confidence-building measures to support the responsible development and application of modern biotechnology amongst affected communities and innovators. Yet while its formulation includes non-State actors as 'operators' of LMOs (Article 2)—and thereby may extend beyond the traditional State-centred governance—activities to implement this treaty are primarily the responsibility of States Parties who are obliged to develop suitable domestic rules and procedures.[90] Also, central States for the development of gene drive systems like the US are non-signatory to the CBD[91] and are only indirectly affected through potential policies of its trading partners.[92]

[84] NASEM, *Gene Drives on the Horizon: Advancing Science, Navigating Uncertainty, and Aligning Research with Public Values* (National Academies Press 2016).

[85] Ewen Callaway, '"Gene Drive" Moratorium Shot Down at UN Biodiversity Meeting' (*Nature News*, 21 December 2016) <http://www.nature.com/doifinder/10.1038/nature.2016.21216> accessed 4 October 2019.

[86] Ewen Callaway, 'UN Treaty Agrees to Limit Gene Drives but Rejects a Moratorium' (*Nature News*, 29 November 2018) <https://www.nature.com/articles/d41586-018-07600-w> accessed 4 October 2019.

[87] ibid.

[88] Kenneth A Oye et al, 'Regulating Gene Drives' (2014) 345 Science Policy Forum 626.

[89] Secretariat of the Convention on Biological Diversity, 'Unintentional Transboundary Movements and Emergency Measures' (SCBD, 17 November 2014) <http://bch.cbd.int/protocol/cpb_art17.shtml> accessed 4 October 2019.

[90] Nagoya—Kuala Lumpur Supplementary Protocol on Liability and Redress to the Cartagena Protocol on Biosafety UN Doc UNEP/CBD/BS/COP-MOP/5/17.

[91] Marcy E Gallo et al, 'Advanced Gene Editing : CRISPR—Cas9' (Congressional Research Service, 7 December 2018) <https://fas.org/sgp/crs/misc/R44824.pdf> accessed 4 October 2019.

[92] Sam W Evans/Megan J Palmer, 'Anomaly Handling and the Politics of Gene Drives' (2018) 5sup(1) Journal of Responsible Innovation 223.

5. 'DIYBio' and Biosecurity

Concerns over changes in science and technology are exacerbated by changes in the human geography of the life sciences, including the emergence of actors outside the traditional laboratory system. For example, the emergence of DIY biology or 'basement biology' communities is sometimes associated, rather unfairly, with the increasing biosecurity risks posed by 'rogue actors'.[93] While the DIYbio community has grown significantly over the last decade, from one group to more than eighty groups around the world, the attention allotted to DIYbio groups has not always contributed to a nuanced and balanced analysis of either their capabilities or their limitations, with some speculative scenarios about the future conduct of scientific research in professional as well as in DIY laboratories presenting misleading assumptions about such groups and neglecting the importance of human practices and tacit knowledge.[94] Such knowledge and skill is acquired by experiences, 'learning by doing' as well as professional networks, and is institutionalized in laboratory 'cultures'. It cannot be easily codified or made available for those operating outside of such networks—for instance, bioterrorists but also DIY scientists.[95]

6. Biosecurity Risks and Uncertainties

The above experiments provide insights into some of the contemporary biosecurity-related challenges posed by changes in the capacity and geography of life science research. Dealing with such biosecurity challenges in the future will require careful consideration of the risks and benefits in order to develop balanced biosecurity strategies. Unfortunately, existing approaches to risk, particularly those applying quantification and/or ranking mechanisms to risks based on the probability and impact of an event, may be difficult to apply to assess contemporary biosecurity challenges.

This is, in part, because of the limitations in existing datasets. Although reasonable probabilities can be deduced for laboratory accidents and accidental release of such pathogens based on past data, where available, such data is less clear-cut when it comes to bioterrorism. While there are datasets pertaining to the cases of biological terrorism, such datasets often contain considerable gaps and even spin which renders an accurate assessment of the past a poor crystal ball for informing the future. The limitations in reliable data also complicate attempts to validate the underlying arguments guiding a probability estimation.[96]

[93] Emily Baumgaertner, 'As DIY Gene Editing Gains Popularity, "Someone is Going to Get Hurt"' (*The New York Times*, 14 May 2018) <https://www.nytimes.com/2018/05/14/science/biohackers-gene-editing-virus.html> accessed 4 October 2019.

[94] Catherine Jefferson et al, 'Synthetic Biology and Biosecurity: Challenging the "Myths"' (2014) 2 Frontiers in Public Health 115.

[95] ibid; James Revill/Catherine Jefferson, 'Tacit Knowledge and the Biological Weapons Regime' (2013) 41 Science and Public Policy 597.

[96] Toby Ord et al, 'Probing the Improbable: Methodological Challenges for Risks with Low Probabilities and High Stakes' (2010) 13 Journal of Risk Research 191.

Moreover, quantifications of risks cannot ignore the issue of agency and the capacity of terrorist groups; this is difficult to gauge given the hype around technologies, such as CRISPR, and their role in the wider array of technical requirements for developing significant biological weapons. In isolation, such technologies are of limited risk and this points to necessary contextual analysis and the reasonable communication of risks to prevent disproportionate reactions from public and governmental stakeholders.[97]

Risk assessment is also limited in part because of the considerable uncertainty and complexity surrounding the future of many emerging biotechnologies. For example, as research on gene drives moves towards the development of self-propagating systems that are anticipated to spread autonomously through the target species, there remains the possibility of unintended effects of tinkering with ecosystems, a step that could have profound implications for biosecurity more widely understood. The substantial risk of the unintended spread of a few organisms thereby prevents the conduct of field trials for gathering essential information about their safety and in order to address such concerns.[98]

The limitations in data and the challenges in dealing with emerging biotechnologies that are of high complexity has led to questions with respect to the suitability of existing risk assessment considerations and methodologies. As was pointed out by the Ad Hoc Technical Expert Group (AHTEG) installed by the Convention of Biological Diversity: 'existing risk assessment considerations and methodologies might not be sufficient or adequate to assess and evaluate the risks that might arise from organisms containing engineered gene drives due to limited experience and the complexity of the potential impacts on the environment.'[99]

D. Conclusion and Outlook

Biosecurity remains a relatively new concept that continues to have different meanings depending on the context in which it is being used. As perceptions of biological risk and threats have changed, the concept has evolved over time and with it so have the tools and practices for biosecurity governance.

While there has been considerable biosecurity-related activity around the globe, the existence and concurrent application of various distinct biosecurity and biosafety concepts in international and domestic models constitute a hurdle to the effective overall governance of scientific and technological developments and there is little cohesive agreement amongst States of the specific requirements for building biosecurity. Indeed, the context as well as cultural and linguistic differences inherent to biosecurity prevent a universal one-size-fits-all approach and impede efforts towards international standardization and harmonization processes for the regulation of work with pathogens and

[97] FDDCPS (n 50) 8. [98] Najjar et al (n 83).

[99] Convention on Biological Diversity—AHTEG, 'Report of the Ad Hoc Technical Expert Group on Synthetic Biology' (9 December 2017) CBD/SYNBIO/AHTEG/2017/1/3.

toxins, leaving somewhat of a patchwork approach to biosecurity. This is compounded by different objectives and purposes of biosecurity measures as well as limitations in empirical evidence of what works (best), with regards to biosecurity, particularly in relation to self-governance measures, such as education and codes of conduct.

Yet as the discussion on certain scientific experiments in recent years highlights, the power of the life sciences is increasing significantly and with it there is greater scope for accidental and deliberate releases of harmful agents. Although many of these technologies offer little in the way of relative advantage to many terrorist groups seeking to cause harm, some State and non-State actors could decide to exploit developments for hostile purposes. As such there is a need to guard against the hostile exploitation of the life sciences through biosecurity-related provisions designed to ensure life science research is steered towards public goods and away from efforts to weaponize biology.

Efforts, therefore, are needed to develop more globally coherent biosafety and biosecurity standards and overcome the gaps in the existing hotchpotch of national and international regulations that not only increase the risk of accidental releases of dangerous pathogens but also provide room for the intentional misuse of biotechnology. Such a step could serve as a confidence-building measure amongst States that facilitates greater exchange of (dual-use) information, materials, and technologies within the international research community while also creating trust and transparency amongst the different stakeholders and shaping a norm against biological weapons.

CHAPTER 36

CYBERSECURITY AND INTERNATIONAL LAW

MICHAEL N SCHMITT

At just over two decades old, the international law of cybersecurity remains in a relative state of infancy. This is despite the fact that the period has seen extraordinary advances in cyber capabilities, the exponential growth of societal cyber dependence and a corresponding rise in vulnerabilities to hostile cyber operations.

Indeed, States continue to struggle with such basic issues as sovereignty in cyberspace. In great part, the challenge is that many States are conflicted over the application and interpretation of key aspects of international law in the cyber context. After all, although international law can serve as a normative firewall against hostile cyber operations, the principle of sovereign equality means that protective norms also can act as barriers to a State's own cyber operations, some of which may be deemed essential to the State, especially with respect to national security. These differences of normative perspective often play out domestically in disagreements between ministries with different roles vis-à-vis cyberspace and internationally between States wielding offensive cyber capability and those that see themselves primarily as victims thereof.

To examine the relationship between cybersecurity and international law, this chapter begins by cataloguing the development of the international law of cyberspace. It then turns to the substantive legal issues, paying particular attention to those matters that presently are the source of contention amongst States. Discussion concludes with the author's brief thoughts as to the journey ahead.

A. Development of the International Law of Cyber Operations

Attention turned to the relationship between international law and cyber operations only in the late 1990s, well after significant cyber capabilities had been employed. At the international level, the Russian Federation took the lead by introducing a UN General Assembly (UNGA) draft resolution on the subject, which noted that 'the dissemination and use of information technologies and means affect the interests of the entire international community and that optimum effectiveness is enhanced by broad international cooperation', and which expressed 'concern that these technologies and means can potentially be used for purposes that are inconsistent with the objectives of maintaining international stability and security'. No mention was made of international law, although the resolution, which was adopted, tasked States with informing the Secretary-General of their views on 'developing international principles' to address the situation.[1]

At the national level, however, few States were considering how international law applied in this new theatre of conflict. An exception was the United States, for in 1999 the Department of Defense's General Counsel produced a working paper on the subject that was widely circulated.[2] The paper operated from the premise that the existing international law applied to cyber operations; the challenge lay in determining how it did so. It concluded:

> If information operations techniques are seen as just another new technology that does not greatly threaten the nations' interests, no dramatic legal developments may occur. If they are seen as a revolutionary threat to the security of nations and the welfare of their citizens, it will be much more likely that efforts will be made to restrict or prohibit information operations by legal means.[3]

Paradoxically, the international community today plainly sees hostile cyber operations as a significant threat to their security and their citizens' welfare, but efforts to legally prohibit or restrict them have borne little fruit.

With the attacks of 9/11 and ensuing wars in Afghanistan and Iraq, government and academic lawyers turned away from cyber matters to counter-terrorism and armed conflict. Nevertheless, in 2003 the UNGA tasked the Secretary-General to bring together government experts to consider cyberthreats and assess cooperative measures to combat them,[4] although this first Group of Governmental Experts (GGE) failed to produce a substantive report.[5] Of particular importance in the security context was disagreement amongst the States represented over whether to deal with the employment of cyber means for military and national security purposes.[6]

[1] UNGA Res 53/70 (4 December 1998).

[2] US DoD, 'An Assessment of International Legal; Issues in Information Operations' (Office of the General Counsel, May 1999) <https://fas.org/irp/eprint/io-legal.pdf> accessed 8 December 2019.

[3] ibid 2. [4] UNGA Res 58/32 (8 December 2003) 4.

[5] UNGA 'Group of Governmental Experts on Developments in the Field of Information and Telecommunications in the Context of International Security: Report by the Secretary-General' (5 August 2005) UN Doc A/60/202.

[6] UNODA, 'Fact Sheet: Developments in the Field of Information and Telecommunications in the Context of International Security' (July 2015) <https://unoda-web.s3-accelerate.amazonaws.com/wp-content/uploads/2015/07/Information-Security-Fact-Sheet-July2015.pdf> accessed 18 March 2019.

In 2007, global attention was instantly drawn to the threat posed by hostile cyber operations when NATO member Estonia was targeted by a nationwide distributed denial of service campaign launched from over 175 States, primarily Russia. Although the attacks could not be reliably attributed to Russia, the incident sparked a sea change in perspectives. In particular, the questions of whether the operations violated the UN Charter Article 2(4) prohibition on the use of force and, perhaps, justified action in collective self-defence pursuant to Article 51, came into sharp focus for the international lawyers and governmental decision makers.

The essentiality of forging an understanding of how international law applied to cyber operations was heightened the following year during the international armed conflict between Russia and Georgia. In the lead-up to hostilities and throughout the conflict, cyber operations targeted both government and civilian infrastructure. The issue of how international humanitarian law (IHL) constrained the conduct of hostilities during armed conflict was vividly engaged.

NATO States responded by establishing the Cooperative Cyber Defence Centre of Excellence (CCD COE) in Tallinn, Estonia, that year. The CCD COE quickly launched a major project to assess the international law applicable in cyberspace. An International Group of Experts (IGE) established to explore the subject produced the *Tallinn Manual on the International Law Applicable to Cyber Warfare* (*Tallinn Manual 1.0*) in 2013.[7] As the work only addressed the *jus ad bellum* (the law governing resort to force by States) and IHL, in 2014 the CCD COE commissioned a follow-on project to examine peacetime cyber operations. The result was the publication in 2017 of the *Tallinn Manual on the International Law Applicable to Cyber Operations* (*Tallinn Manual 2.0*).[8]

The UN also stepped up efforts to address the now evident cyberthreat. In 2009, a second GGE was established. Although the Secretary-General's foreword to its 2010 Report observed that 'we have only begun to develop the norms, laws and modes of cooperation needed for this new information environment',[9] there was no mention of international law in the Report itself.

A follow-on GGE convened in 2011. In its 2013 Report, the group did address international law. Confirming that 'international law, and in particular the Charter of the United Nations, is applicable and is essential to maintaining peace and stability and promoting an open, secure, peaceful and accessible ICT [information and communications technology] environment', it highlighted State sovereignty and international human rights law (IHRL), insisted that States not 'use proxies to commit internationally wrongful acts', and asserted that States should not allow their territory to be used for hostile cyber operations by non-State actors, a hortatory reference to the norm of due

[7] Michael N Schmitt (ed), *Tallinn Manual on the International Law Applicable to Cyber Warfare* (CUP 2013).

[8] Michael N Schmitt (ed), *Tallinn Manual 2.0 on the International Law Applicable to Cyber Operations* (CUP 2017).

[9] UNGA 'Report of the Group of Governmental Experts on Developments in the Field of Information and Telecommunications in the Context of International Security' (30 July 2010) UN Doc A/65/201, 4.

diligence.[10] While these legal conclusions and recommendations appear self-evident, the GGE, which included all five permanent members of the UN Security Council (UNSC), finally had begun to consider discrete elements of international law in the cyber context. Seeking to build on this progress, a fourth GGE was quickly established.

International law again occupied a place of prominence in the resulting 2015 Report.[11] In addition to reiterating the points made in 2013, this GGE cited the principle of sovereign equality, the duty to attempt peaceful settlement of certain disputes, the prohibition on the threat or use of force, the principle of non-intervention, and the obligation to protect human rights. It also emphasized the jurisdiction States enjoy over cyber infrastructure on their territory. Although it did not use the term 'self-defence', the Report 'noted the inherent right of States to take measures consistent with international law and as recognized in the Charter', a clear reference to that right. Similarly, the Report highlighted the IHL principles of humanity, necessity, proportionality, and distinction without direct mention of that body of law.

In light of this progress, a fifth GGE convened in 2015.[12] Unfortunately, it was unable to achieve further agreement. In particular, Russia and China objected to textual reference to 'self-defence' and 'international humanitarian law' in the prospective report, despite the fact that the previous report had contemplated their applicability. Additionally, an effort to include text dealing with the right to take countermeasures (actions that would be unlawful but for the fact that they are in response to another State's unlawful act and designed to put an end to it) failed.

The US expert summed up the view of liberal democracies regarding the inability to achieve consensus:

> ...I heard repeated assertions on the part of some participants that a discussion of certain bodies of international law, including the *jus ad bellum*, international humanitarian law, and the law of State responsibility, would be incompatible with the messages the Group should be sending regarding the peaceful settlement of disputes and conflict prevention. That is a false dichotomy that does not withstand scrutiny. A report that discusses the peaceful settlement of disputes and related concepts but omits a discussion of the lawful options States have to respond to malicious cyber activity they face would not only fail to deter States from potentially destabilizing activity, but also fail to send a stabilizing message to the broader community of States that their responses to such malicious cyber activity are constrained by international law.[13]

[10] UNGA 'Report of the Group of Governmental Experts on Developments in the Field of Information and Telecommunications in the Context of International Security' (24 June 2013) UN Doc A/68/98 (GGE Report 2013).

[11] UNGA 'Report of the Group of Governmental Experts on Developments in the Field of Information and Telecommunications in the Context of International Security' (22 July 2015) UN Doc A/70/174 (GGE Report 2015).

[12] UNGA Res 70/237 (23 December 2015).

[13] Michele Markoff, 'Remarks: Explanation of Position at the Conclusion of the 2016–2017 UN Group of Governmental Experts (GGE) on Developments in the Field of Information and Telecommunications in the Context of International Security' (New York, 23 June 2017) <https://usun.state.gov/remarks/7880> accessed 18 March 2019.

Reaction to the Russian and Chinese intransigence came in part through a 2017 G-7 Declaration issued prior to the GGE's conclusion.[14] The Declaration confirmed the applicability of international law, specifically citing IHL and self-defence, and acknowledged the right to take countermeasures, an endorsement of the right that had heretofore not appeared in any multilateral statement.

Regional International Governmental Organizations (IGOs) were active during this period as well. In 2013, the EU issued a Cybersecurity Strategy that confirmed 'the same laws and norms that apply in other areas of our day-to-day lives apply also in the cyber domain', specifically singling out IHL and IHRL.[15] In 2018, it reconfirmed this view and echoed the position on the use of proxies and due diligence contained in the 2015 GGE Report.[16]

NATO took a stance on international law's applicability to cyber operations in its 2014 Wales Summit Declaration.[17] The Alliance expressly endorsed the applicability of international law, including IHL, and noted that the 'impact of [cyber attacks] could be as harmful to modern societies as a conventional attack'. In the latter regard, the Declaration 'affirm[ed] that cyber defence is part of NATO's core task of collective defence', a position reiterated in its 2016 Warsaw Communiqué, in which NATO designated cyberspace a domain of operations.[18]

Other regions likewise moved towards acceptance of international law's role in providing stability and security in cyberspace. In 2012, the Organization of American States issued a declaration expressing its commitment to act in compliance with 'obligations under national and international law, including international human rights law, international humanitarian law, and international refugee law',[19] a commitment reaffirmed three years later.[20] In 2018, the leaders of the Association of Southeast Asian Nations released a statement on cybersecurity cooperation that incorporated language from the 2013 and 2015 GGE Reports.[21] Similarly, the Commonwealth Heads of Government acknowledged the applicability of international law the same year.[22]

[14] G7, 'Declaration on Responsible States Behavior in Cyberspace' (Lucca, 11 April 2017) <https://www.mofa.go.jp/files/000246367.pdf> accessed 18 March 2019.

[15] Commission/High Representative of the European Union for Foreign Affairs and Security Policy, 'Cybersecurity Strategy of the European Union: An Open, Safe and Secure Cyberspace' (Joint Communication to the European Parliament, the Council, the European Economic and Social Committee and the Committee of the Regions) JOIN(2013)1final.

[16] Council of the European Union, 'Council Conclusions on Malicious Cyber Activities' (16 April 2018) Doc 7925/18 (Annex).

[17] North Atlantic Council, 'Wales Summit Declaration' (5 September 2014) Press Release (2014)120.

[18] North Atlantic Council, 'Warsaw Summit Communiqué' (9 July 2016) Press Release (2016)100.

[19] Inter-American Committee Against Terrorism, 'Declaration: Strengthening Cyber-Security in the Americas' (7 March 2012) CITCE/DEC.1/12 rev.1.

[20] Inter-American Committee Against Terrorism, 'Declaration: Protection of Critical Infrastructure from Emerging Threats' (20 March 2015) CITCE/doc.1/15.

[21] ASEAN, 'ASEAN-United States Leaders' Statement on Cybersecurity Cooperation' (Singapore, 15 November 2018) <https://asean.org/storage/2018/11/ASEAN-US-Leaders-Statement-on-Cybersecurity-Cooperation-Final.pdf> accessed 18 March 2019.

[22] The Commonwealth, 'Commonwealth Cyber Declaration' (London, 20 April 2018) <https://www.chogm2018.org.uk/sites/default/files/Commonwealth%20Cyber%20Declaration%20pdf.pdf> accessed 18 March 2018.

Of course, not all States see cybersecurity from the same perspective. Liberal democracies reject the need for a broad cyber-specific treaty, preferring to focus on narrower issues, such as cybercrime. In this regard, the Council of Europe adopted the Convention on Cybercrime (Budapest Convention) in 2001;[23] a 2006 Protocol addresses racism and xenophobia online.[24] Open to accession by non-member States, it seeks harmonization of domestic laws, enhanced investigation techniques, and cross-border cooperation. China, India, and Russia have not acceded to the instrument, partly because they see certain provisions as an intrusion on their sovereignty.

Despite opposition to the Budapest Convention, Russia and China have long taken the position that a treaty regime to govern cyberspace is a better approach than relying on customary law and non-cyber-specific treaties. Accordingly, in 2009 the Shanghai Cooperation Organization (SCO: China, Russia, Kazakhstan, Kyrgyzstan, Tajikistan, Uzbekistan) adopted the Agreement on Cooperation in the Field of International Information Security.[25] In a veiled swipe at Western States, the treaty identified the '[d]evelopment and use of information weapons, preparation for and waging information war', the '[u]se of the dominant position in the information space to the detriment of interest and security of other States', and '[d]issemination of information harmful to social and political, social and economic systems, as well as spiritual, moral and cultural spheres of other States', as 'main threats'.[26]

In 2011, four of the SCO States, later joined by the remaining two, submitted an International Code of Conduct for Information Security to the UNGA.[27] The Code appears to have been designed, in part, to safeguard a State's control over activities on its territory and preclude external interference by cyber means with that control. For instance, it prohibited 'use [of] information and communications technologies and information and communications networks to interfere in the internal affairs of other States or with the aim of undermining their political, economic and social stability' and emphasized the need for 'protection of … public order [and] public health or morals'.[28]

[23] Convention on Cybercrime 2296 UNTS 167. For two regional agreements on cybercrime, see African Union Convention on Cyber Security and Personal Data Protection EX.CL/846(XXV); Arab Convention on Combating Information Technology Offences <https://www.asianlaws.org/gcld/cyberlawdb/GCC/Arab%20Convention%20on%20Combating%20Information%20Technology%20Offences.pdf> accessed 20 May 2020.

[24] Additional Protocol to the Convention on Cybercrime concerning the Criminalisation of Acts of a Racist or Xenophobic Nature Committed Through Computer Systems ETS No 189.

[25] Shanghai Cooperation Organization, Agreement Between the Governments of the Member States of the Shanghai Cooperation Organization on Cooperation in the Field of International Information Security (16 June 2009) <https://ccdcoe-admin.aku.co/wp-content/uploads/2018/11/SCO-090616-IISAgreement.pdf> accessed 11 July 2019.

[26] ibid art 2.

[27] UNGA 'International Code of Conduct for Information Security: Annex to the Letter dated 9 January 2015 from the Permanent Representatives of China, Kazakhstan, Kyrgyzstan, the Russian Federation, Tajikistan and Uzbekistan to the United Nations Addressed to the Secretary-General' (13 January 2015) UN Doc A/69/723, para 2(12).

[28] ibid paras 2(3), (7)(b).

Viewed as contrary to the free and open Internet championed by liberal democracies, the Code was never adopted.

However, in December 2019, the UNGA approved a Russian-sponsored and Chinese-supported resolution establishing an expert committee 'to elaborate a comprehensive international convention on countering the use of information and communications technologies for criminal purposes'.[29] The move was opposed by the United States and European countries on the grounds that it could be used to stifle free expression on the Internet, including criticism of the government. Human rights organizations have also expressed concern along the same lines.

B. Unsettled Aspects of the Law

During the preparation of the *Tallinn Manuals*, it became apparent that existing disagreements over how international law applies in the non-cyber context carry over into the examination of its application to cyber activities. As an example, disagreement over the existence of an 'unwilling or unable' test in the law of self-defence also rears its head with respect to cyber armed attacks. These and other international law points of contention apply *mutatis mutandis* to cyber activities and shall not be considered further. Rather, discussion will zero in on issues that are unique in the cyber context and that represent the greatest challenges for States. It must be cautioned that those set forth below in no way exhaust the field of unsettled issues.[30]

1. Sovereignty

The most important controversy deals with sovereignty. Sovereignty is a fundamental principle of international law that, as noted in the 1928 *Island of Palmas* arbitration, 'signifies independence. Independence in regard to a portion of the globe is the right to exercise therein, to the exclusion of any other State, the functions of a State'.[31] This right is complemented by corresponding obligations, the most important being the obligation to respect other States' sovereignty by, for example, refraining from using force against them or intervening in their internal affairs.

Early on, it was sometimes asserted that cyberspace is a global common, analogous to the high seas and outer space, over which no State could claim sovereignty. This position has been rejected on the basis that cyberspace is territorial in the sense that cyber infrastructure must be located somewhere, as must the persons involved in cyber operations and cyber activities themselves. When in a State, that infrastructure and those persons

[29] UNGA Res 74/247 (27 December 2019) para 2.

[30] Most have been catalogued in *Tallinn Manual 2.0* (n 9).

[31] *Island of Palmas (Netherlands v USA)* (1928) 2 RIAA 829, 838.

and activities are subject to the State's sovereign prerogatives like most other property, persons, and activities therein.

The application of the principle of sovereignty to cyber activities was until recently uncontroversial. For instance, the 2015 GGE Report provided that 'State sovereignty and international norms and principles that flow from sovereignty apply to the conduct by States of ICT-related activities'.[32] Despite agreement over the principle's applicability, States viewing it from divergent perspectives have come to different conclusions as to its practical application. Authoritarian States see it as a useful shield against information transmitted from abroad into their territory or made available therein from external sources. The paradigmatic example is the so-called Great Firewall of China, a reference to China's use of legislation and technology to control the Internet domestically, for instance through censorship, by requiring foreign companies to comply with strict domestic regulations, and using technical means to block information from abroad, including Internet tools like Google Search, Facebook and Twitter. [33]

Liberal democracies respond that sovereignty is not absolute. For example, in a 2016 speech setting forth US views, former State Department Legal Advisor Brian Egan observed:

> Any regulation by a State of matters within its territory, including use of and access to the Internet, must comply with that State's applicable obligations under international human rights law... The Internet must remain open to the free flow of information and ideas. Restricting the flow of ideas also inhibits spreading the values of understanding and mutual respect that offer one of the most powerful antidotes to the hateful and violent narratives propagated by terrorist groups.[34]

This approach has been echoed by other influential bodies and individuals. As an illustration, in 2016 the UN Human Rights Council affirmed 'that the same rights that people have offline must also be protected online, in particular freedom of expression, which is applicable regardless of frontiers and through any media of one's choice'.[35] It also recognized 'the global and open nature of the Internet as a driving force in accelerating progress towards development'.[36]

[32] GGE Report 2015 (n 11) para 27; eg the ASEAN–United States Leaders' Statement (n 21).

[33] Paul Mozur, 'Twitter Users in China Face Detention and Threats in New Beijing Crackdown' (*The New York Times*, 10 January 2019) <https://www.nytimes.com/2019/01/10/business/china-twitter-censorship-online.html> accessed 15 March 2019; Elizabeth C Economy, 'The Great Firewall of China: Xi Jinping's Internet Shutdown' (*The Guardian*, 29 June 2018) <https://www.theguardian.com/news/2018/jun/29/the-great-firewall-of-china-xi-jinpings-internet-shutdown> accessed 15 March 2019.

[34] Brian J Egan, 'International Law and Stability in Cyberspace' (2017) 35 Berkeley Journal of International Law 169, 176.

[35] HRC Res 32/13 'The Promotion, Protection and Enjoyment of Human Rights on the Internet' (1 July 2016) UN Doc A/HRC/RES/32/13, para 1; UNGA 'Report of the Special Rapporteur on the Promotion and Protection of the Right to Freedom of Opinion and Expression' (30 March 2017) UN Doc A/HRC/35/22.

[36] HRC Res 32/13 (n 35) para 2.

Nevertheless, there was general understanding that sovereignty was not only a principle from which various rights and obligations emanated, but also a binding rule of international law. As set forth in *Tallinn Manual 2.0*, it held that '[a] State must not conduct cyber operations that violate the sovereignty of another State'. Brian Egan correctly noted that the unfinished business was determining '[p]recisely when a non-consensual cyber operation violates the sovereignty of another State'.[37] *Tallinn Manual 2.0* suggests that whether a cyber operation by one State against another violates the latter's sovereignty depends on the degree of infringement on territorial integrity or whether there had been interference with, or usurpation of, an inherently governmental function, such as elections.[38] While the IGE agreed that a violation ensues whenever a State's remote cyber operation causes damage (including permanent loss of cyber infrastructure functionality) or injury in another State, consensus eluded them over operations not having those consequences. As an example, disagreement existed over causing cyber infrastructure to operate contrary to its intended purpose or destroying data.[39]

In 2017, the status of sovereignty as a rule of law began to be questioned. The argument that it was merely a principle from which rules such as intervention flowed surfaced in unofficial presentations and writings by several serving and former US government officials.[40] The following year the UK Attorney General, Jeremy Wright, announced:

> I am not persuaded that we can currently extrapolate from that general principle [of sovereignty] a specific rule or additional prohibition for cyber activity beyond that of a prohibited intervention. The UK Government's position is therefore that there is no such rule as a matter of current international law.[41]

In a positive vein, this position opens the door to taking robust measures short of intervention or the use of force to safeguard national security. Yet, it also dramatically lowers the normative firewall against hostile operations conducted into a State's territory. For instance, intervention requires a coercive intent with respect to a State's *domaine réservé* (areas ungoverned by international law and therefore left to the State to regulate, such as choice of government). Many hostile cyber operations are merely malicious, disruptive, or criminal, but lack coercive effect and therefore would not be encompassed in the prohibition. Nor would they likely fall within the scope of the use of force prohibition, which requires grave consequences, such as physical damage.

This reality was illustrated in 2018 when the UK's National Cyber Security Centre took the position that numerous Russian cyber campaigns had violated international

[37] Egan (n 34) 174.

[38] *Tallinn Manual 2.0* (n 9) rule 4, para 10. [39] ibid rule 4, para 14.

[40] Gary P Corn/Robert Taylor, 'Sovereignty in the Age of Cyber' (2017) 111 AJIL Unbound 207; For the opposing position: Michael N Schmitt/Liis Vihul, 'Sovereignty in Cyberspace: Lex Lata Vel Non?' (2017) 111 AJIL Unbound 213.

[41] Attorney General Jeremy Wright QC, 'Cyber and International Law in the 21st Century' (Chatham House, 23 May 2018) <https://www.gov.uk/government/speeches/cyber-and-international-law-in-the-21st-century> accessed 18 March 2019.

law.[42] However, it provided no legal rationale for the assertions and it is questionable that a number of them would hold water absent a rule prohibiting violations of sovereignty.[43]

Whether other States will follow the British lead remains to be seen. States might take the position that sovereignty, if a rule, poses an unacceptable obstacle to operations they need to conduct in order to safeguard national security, although none has endorsed the UK position openly as of January 2020. Alternatively, States could conclude the better approach is to focus on identifying the optimal threshold for a breach of sovereignty, one affording protection to key activities while permitting a degree of manoeuvre room to conduct their own operations. France and the Netherlands, *inter alia*, publicly adopted this position in 2019. The French Ministry of Defence took a particularly broad view of sovereignty, suggesting that '[a]ny cyberattack against French digital systems or any effects produced on French territory by digital means by a State organ, a person or an entity exercising elements of governmental authority or by a person or persons acting on the instructions of or under the direction or control of a State constitutes a breach of sovereignty'.[44]

In deciding which track to follow, States would be well advised to consider the response options international law already affords them. Even if a State's response to unlawful cyber operation would otherwise violate sovereignty or another rule of law, the wrongfulness of that violation will be precluded if the operation qualifies as a countermeasure, is consistent with the plea of necessity, or is an act of self-defence.[45] Therefore, the argument that adopting the sovereignty as a rule position leaves a nation defenceless is wrong as a matter of law.

2. Due Diligence

The issue of a rule of due diligence for cyberspace has been under careful consideration since the 2016 'Hague Process' meetings between representatives of the *Tallinn Manual 2.0* IGE and State representatives.[46] According to the *Manual*, '[a] State must exercise

[42] UK National Cyber Security Centre, 'Reckless Campaign of Cyber Attacks by Russian Military Intelligence Service Exposed' (4 October 2018) <https://www.ncsc.gov.uk/news/reckless-campaign-cyber-attacks-russian-military-intelligence-service-exposed> accessed 18 March 2019.

[43] Jeffrey Biller/Michael Schmitt, 'Un-Caging the Bear? A Case Study in Cyber Opinio Juris and Unintended Consequences' (*EJIL:Talk!*, 24 October 2018) <https://www.ejiltalk.org/un-caging-the-bear-a-case-study-in-cyber-opinio-juris-and-unintended-consequences/> accessed 18 March 2019.

[44] Ministère des Armées, 'Droit International Appliqué aux Operations dans le Cyberspace' (9 September 2019) <https://www.defense.gouv.fr/content/download/565895/9750877/file/Droit+internat+appliqué+aux+opérations+Cyberespace.pdf> accessed 8 April 2020; Government of the Netherlands, 'Letter to the Parliament on the International Legal Order in Cyberspace' (5 July 2019) <https://www.government.nl/documents/parliamentary-documents/2019/09/26/letter-to-the-parliament-on-the-international-legal-order-in-cyberspace> accessed 8 April 2020.

[45] *Tallinn Manual 2.0* (n 9) rules 20–6, 71–5.

[46] The Netherlands convened the meetings in 2016–17 to facilitate State input into the IGE's work.

due diligence in not allowing its territory, or territory or cyber infrastructure under its governmental control, to be used for cyber operations that affect the rights of, and produce serious adverse consequences for, other States'.[47] To meet this obligation, a State must 'take all measures that are feasible in the circumstances to put an end' to such operations.[48]

The obligation derives from the principle of sovereignty. As noted by the International Court of Justice (ICJ) in *Corfu Channel*, 'it is every State's obligation not to allow knowingly its territory to be used for acts contrary to the rights of other States'.[49] Two decades earlier, Judge Huber had similarly observed in *Island of Palmas* that a State must 'protect within the territory the rights of other States'.[50]

The GGE considered the principle in its 2013 Report, noting that 'States should seek to ensure that their territories are not used by non-State actors for unlawful use of ICTs'.[51] This exhortation was repeated in the 2015 Report,[52] which added 'States should not knowingly allow their territory to be used for internationally wrongful acts using ICTs', which extended its application to hostile cyber operations by States.[53] It is significant that the norm was expressed in hortatory (should), rather than binding, verbiage ('must'), thereby indicating an inability to forge consensus on its obligatory character.

During the Hague Process, some States expressed concern over the burden such an obligation would impose. However, the IGE representatives pointed out that the obligation is subject to key limitations. First, the hostile cyber operation must affect a right of the 'injured' State under international law. For instance, if a State makes another State's classified documents available via a server located in a third State, no right has been violated because States do not enjoy a right to have their confidential materials remain secret. Accordingly, the State where the server is located has no due diligence obligation to stop publication of the documents. By contrast, if a State takes control of cyber infrastructure in another State and uses it to cause damage in a third State, for instance by causing an oil pipeline to burst, the cyber operation would breach sovereignty and possibly be a use of force. In this case, the State in which the server is located bears an obligation to put an end to the operation.

Secondly, the due diligence obligation attaches only when 'serious adverse consequences' result from hostile cyber operation. This standard, drawn from international environmental law,[54] is of particular importance in the cyber context because it would exclude application of the rule to incidents that cause irritation, inconvenience, or minor disruption. Website defacement and temporary denial of service, as examples, would fall short of this threshold.

The third limitation is that the State concerned need only act to terminate the harmful activity that is emanating from its territory. There is no requirement to take preventive measures. Correspondingly, once the hostile cyber operations have ended, and the State

[47] *Tallinn Manual 2.0* (n 9) rule 6. [48] ibid rule 7.
[49] *Corfu Channel (UK v Albania)* (Merits) [1949] ICJ Rep 4, 22. [50] *Island of Palmas* (n 31) 839.
[51] GGE Report 2013 (n 10) para 23. [52] GGE Report 2015 (n 11) para 13(c).
[53] ibid para 28(b). [54] *Trail Smelter Case (United States, Canada)* (1941) 3 RIAA 1905, 1965.

reasonably concludes that they were not part of a continuing campaign from its territory, the due diligence obligation no longer attaches.

To illustrate, States need not monitor cyber activity on or through their territory to identify hostile cyber operations that affect other States, nor need they impose a regulatory framework that serves to preclude such operations, as in the case of mandating cyber hygiene measures. The only time a State must take measures in advance of a hostile cyber operation conducted from or through its territory is when that State knows of the hostile operation, a material step has been taken to conduct it, and execution of the operation is imminent. For instance, if a State intelligence agency has infiltrated a closed online forum and discovered a destructive operation about to be launched against another State, it would need to act to block that operation. But even in such cases, a number of the *Tallinn Manual 2.0* experts disagreed with this notion of 'anticipatory' due diligence.

Last, the State from or through which the operation is being conducted need only take measures that are feasible in the circumstances. The determination of feasibility may consider such matters as technical, intellectual, financial, and institutional capacity. If remedial means are beyond a State's reach, it need not act. Moreover, the State need not suffer unreasonably in order to terminate the operation. As an example, if the only way to terminate a hostile cyber operation from a State's territory is to isolate networks from the Internet, thereby causing self-denial of service with significant financial consequences, doing so is not feasible.

Importantly, the due diligence obligation can open the door to actions by States in response to hostile cyber operations that might not otherwise be available. Take the case of a non-State group that is conducting remote cyber operations from a State sympathetic to its cause but that is not directing or controlling the group's operations such that they are attributable under law to that State.[55] If the State fails to put an end to the operations, as in arresting group members, it is in breach of its due diligence obligation to the target State. The target State may, as a result, take a countermeasure involving cyber operations against the group. Absent the territorial State's breach, the operations might violate that State's sovereignty or other legal rule; however, because it qualifies as a countermeasure, the wrongfulness of the responsive operations is precluded as a matter of law.[56]

The Netherlands and France publicly endorsed the existence of a rule of due diligence in late 2019, while a number of other States have unofficially indicated their support of the obligation. For them, the rule is protective in that it obligates other States to put an end to remote harmful cyber operations in situations where there is no basis in international law for the target State itself to take extraterritorial measures terminating the hostile cyber operations into their territory. Additionally, as explained, the dynamic

[55] ILC, 'Articles on Responsibility of States for Internationally Wrongful Acts' (12 December 2001) UN Doc A/RES/56/83, art 8.

[56] Explanation in Michael N Schmitt, 'In Defense of Due Diligence in Cyberspace' (2015) 125 Yale Law Journal Forum 68.

described in the previous paragraph is appealing to States facing non-State actors operating from sanctuary territory.

Finally, the principle of due diligence to some extent mitigates the problem of attribution. Consider a case in which a remotely conducted hostile cyber operation cannot be reliably attributed but can be geolocated. The State from or through which the operation is being conducted would nevertheless be obligated to put an end to the operation because there is no requirement that the identity of the hostile operation's initiator be known.

3. Use of Force

The issue of how to apply the use of force rules to cyber operations has been a thorn in the side of States since the applicability of international law to such operations was first considered. The questions are simple. When does a cyber operation breach the prohibition in Article 2(4) of the UN Charter and customary international law and when may a State resort to force in response to cyber operations that rise to the level of an armed attack under Article 51 of the Charter and its customary international law counterpart?

Article 2(4) provides that '[a]ll Members [of the United Nations] shall refrain in their international relations from the threat or use of force against the territorial integrity or political independence of any state, or in any other manner inconsistent with the Purposes of the United Nations'. There is widespread agreement that the prohibition applies in the cyber context. For instance, the 2015 GGE Report and the G-7 Declaration cited above confirmed as much. The challenge is determining when a cyber operation qualifies as a 'use of force'.

It is self-evident that destructive or injurious cyber operations qualify, for it would be incongruous to suggest that a kinetic operation having such consequences would be a use of force but a cyber operation generating similar, or more severe, consequences would not. States are comfortable with this conclusion.[57] As an example, in 2012 the then US Department of State Legal Advisor, Harold Koh suggested that cyber operations that '(1) trigger[ed] a nuclear plant meltdown; (2) open[ed] a dam above a populated area, causing destruction; or (3) disable[d] air traffic control services, resulting in airplane crashes' were uses of force.[58]

[57] Advisory Council on International Affairs and the Advisory Commission on Issues of Public International Law, 'Advisory Report No 77, AIV/No. 22, CAVV: Cyber Warfare' (December 2011) endorsed by Government in 'Government Response to the AIV/CAVV Report on Cyber Warfare' (26 April 2012) 5 <http://docplayer.net/25408344-Government-response-to-the-aiv-cavv-report-on-cyber-warfare.html> accessed 27 March 2019; Office of the Legal Adviser, 'Applicability of International Law to Conflicts in Cyberspace' (2014) *Digest of United States Practice in International Law* ch 18, s A(3)(b), 734.

[58] Harold Koh, 'International Law in Cyberspace' (2012) 54 Harvard International Law Journal (Online) 1. The same examples were included in US DoD, 'Law of War Manual' (Office of the General Counsel, December 2016) para 16.3 <https://dod.defense.gov/Portals/1/Documents/pubs/DoD%20Law%20of%20War%20Manual%20-%20June%202015%20Updated%20Dec%202016.pdf?ver=2016-12-13-172036-190> accessed 9 April 2020.

Whether cyber operations having non-destructive or non-injurious consequences breach the prohibition is highly unsettled. In this regard, the ICJ concluded in *Nicaragua* that arming and training guerrilla forces engaged in hostilities against another State is a use of force.[59] This suggests by analogy that cyber activities such as providing destructive malware or training insurgents to conduct destructive cyber operations might qualify even though the State's actions are not themselves destructive or injurious and the insurgent operations are not attributable under law to the State.

No State has, to date, articulated a bright line threshold against which to judge non-destructive cyber operations in the context of the use of force prohibition. The severity of resulting non-physical effects does, however, appear to be one touchstone in making this determination. To illustrate, the UK Ministry of Defence's *Cyber Primer* offers 'a sustained attack against the UK banking system, which could cause severe financial damage to the State leading to a worsening economic security situation for the population' as an example of a use of cyber force.[60] The Netherlands similarly noted in 2019 that 'it cannot be ruled out that a cyber operation with a very serious financial or economic impact may qualify as a use of force'.[61] While these characterizations seem sensible, international consensus on appropriate criteria remains elusive. This is likely driven more by the difficulty of identifying reliable criteria than disagreement over whether non-destructive or non-injurious operations ever can amount to uses of force.

The *Tallinn Manual 2.0* IGE was similarly unable to set forth definitive criteria. Instead, it highlighted certain non-exclusive factors that States are likely to consider when assessing whether a cyber operation is a use of force. They include the severity, immediacy, directness, and measurability of the consequences; the operation's invasiveness; the extent of State involvement in an operation conducted by a non-State actor whose actions are attributable to the State; the prevailing political environment; and whether the operation is military in character. These and other factors are to be considered in concert when assessing a cyber operation and no factor, with the exception of severity, would alone qualify it as a use of force. For instance, a highly invasive, but temporary, denial of service operation against an intelligence agency would not qualify.

In 2019, France adopted the multi-factor approach suggested by the IGE. After confirming that 'France does not rule out the possibility that a cyber operation without physical effects may also be characterised as a use of force', a Ministry of the Armies position paper pointed to the relevance of factors such as the origin of the hostile operation, whether it was conducted by the military, the extent of penetration into the targeted system, and the resulting effects.[62] The same year, the Netherlands also endorsed the *Tallinn Manual*'s multi-factored approach to the matter. These are important first steps, but until progress is made in identifying consensus use of force criteria to apply to

[59] *Case Concerning Military and Paramilitary Activities in and against Nicaragua (Nicaragua v United States of America)* [1986] ICJ Rep 14 [228] (*Nicaragua*).

[60] UK Ministry of Defence, 'Cyber Primer' (2nd edn, Development, Concepts and Doctrine Centre 2016) 12.

[61] Government of the Netherlands (n 46).

[62] Ministère des Armées (n 44).

non-destructive or non-injurious cyber operations, characterization of a particular operation as a use of force will generally be controversial.

The situation with respect to the law of self-defence is only slightly clearer. Article 51 provides that 'nothing in the present Charter shall impair the inherent right of individual or collective self-defence if an armed attack occurs'. The premise that the right of self-defence applies in the cyber context is indisputable. It would defy logic to assert that a State could suffer widespread destruction or death produced by cyber means, but not enjoy the right of individual or collective self-defence against a State or non-State actor launching the attack.[63] Indeed, the 2015 GGE Report emphasized that 'the Charter applies in its entirety' vis-à-vis cyber activities and 'noted the inherent right of States to take measures consistent with international law'.[64] Given that the right of self-defence is codified in the Charter, and in light of the fact that the 'inherent right' text is lifted from Article 51, no other conclusion is possible. The dilemma lies in identifying the threshold at which a cyber operation qualifies as an 'armed attack'.

Again, there are no agreed-upon criteria. Most States view the armed attack threshold as higher than that of a use of force, as is the case in the cyber context for both the Netherlands and France. Their conclusions are informed by the ICJ's description of armed attacks as the 'most grave forms of the use of force', although the extent of difference between the thresholds is unclear. Suggesting that the answer lies in the 'scale and effects' of the action, the Court has distinguished an armed attack from a 'mere frontier incident'.[65] This distinction is neither very useful in drawing cyber analogies nor uncontroversial.

Some States even reject the premise of differing thresholds. Notably, the US has long held the view that all uses of force equally qualify as armed attacks, including with regard to cyber operations.[66] In principle, States adopting this approach might be expected to consider responding with force to hostile cyber operations at a lower level of severity than States that see a gap between the thresholds. In practice, however, the lack of consensus as to where the use of force threshold lies, as well as the absence of express national positions on the matter, means that it will be difficult to predict when any State would believe itself entitled to act in self-defence against a cyber operation.

Unquestionably, a cyber operation resulting in significant death, injury, physical damage, or destruction would be an armed attack. Whether States will be willing to characterize those causing lesser damage or injury—as in the case of a loss of functionality of cyber infrastructure that does not result in significant destructive or injurious knock-on effects, or no damage or injury at all—as an armed attack remains to be seen. It is, however, likely that victim-States would consider some such operations as activating their right to self-defence.

[63] eg Wales Summit Declaration (n 17) para 72.

[64] GGE Report 2015 (n 11) para 28(c).

[65] *Nicaragua* (n 59) [191], [195].

[66] eg DoD Manual (n 58) para 16.3.3.1; Abraham Sofaer, 'International Law and the Use of Force' (1988) 82 ASIL Proc 420, 422.

In this regard, Dutch Minister of Defence, Ank Bijleveld has publicly pointed to cyber operations causing 'serious disruption with long-lasting consequences'. She explained, '[f]or instance, if a cyber-attack targets the entire Dutch financials system . . . or if it prevents the government from carrying out essential tasks such as policing or taxation . . . it would qualify as an armed attack . . . and . . . trigger a state's right to defend itself even by force'.[67] The Minister is the first senior national leader to express a position on the matter. It would seem inevitable that other States will follow the Dutch lead and begin to consider self-defence against cyber operations in the context of the severity of their consequences generally, rather than solely their physical consequences.

4. International Humanitarian Law

The final body of law regarding which significant uncertainty over key issues exists is IHL. As noted earlier, and despite the controversy over inclusion of the term 'international humanitarian law' in the aborted 2017 GGE Report, there is little doubt that IHL governs cyber operations during an armed conflict. Nevertheless, myriad issues remain unsettled. Two have drawn the most attention from States as they attempt to translate them into guidance such as military manuals and rules of engagement.

The first is identifying when cyber operations qualify as an 'attack' in IHL. This terminological quandary is fundamental because many key IHL prohibitions are framed in terms of attacks. Most important in the cyber context is that set forth in Additional Protocol I, Article 52: 'Civilian objects shall not be the object of attack or of reprisals.'[68] If a cyber operation does not qualify as an attack, the prohibition does not apply even if the target is civilian cyber infrastructure. Other important rules that depend on qualification of the underlying cyber operation as an attack include the prohibitions on indiscriminate attack or those directed at persons or objects enjoying special protection, the rule of proportionality, and the requirement to take precautions to minimize harm to civilians and civilian objects.

Article 49(1) of Additional Protocol I defines attacks as 'acts of violence against the adversary, whether in offense or in defence'. The notion is universally understood to extend to violence against civilians and civilian objects. Consensus also exists that although cyber operations do not release kinetic force having destructive effect, the definition can be understood as including cyber operations with violent consequences, such as damage to objects or injury of persons. The problematic issue is whether the term encompasses operations' other consequences.

[67] Ank Bijleveld, Dutch Minister of Defence, 'Keynote Address: We Have to Steer the Cyber Domain before it Steers Us' (Diplomacy and Defense in Cyber Space Cyber Seminar, The Hague, 21 June 2018) <https://english.defensie.nl/downloads/speeches/2018/06/21/keynote-address-by-the-minister-of-defence-ms.-ank-bijleveld-marking-the-first-anniversary-of-the-tallinn-manual-2.0-on-the-20th-of-june-2018> accessed 3 July 2019.

[68] Protocol Additional to the Geneva Conventions of 12 August 1949 and Relating to the Protection of Victims of Non-International Armed Conflicts1125 UNTS 609 arts 1(2), 52(1).

During the *Tallinn Manual 1.0* deliberations, 'loss of functionality' was adopted as satisfying the damage criterion.[69] Thus, a cyber operation that causes cyber infrastructure to permanently cease working or necessitates repair is an 'attack' subject to the prohibitions and limitations on attacks. No consensus could be achieved on whether other effects, like a temporary loss of functionality or causing cyber infrastructure to operate improperly, would so qualify.

France has now embraced the functionality test. But broadly speaking the issue remains unresolved. It is a particularly important dilemma because States sensibly may want to conduct cyber operations not having the aforementioned effects against civilian infrastructure, the paradigmatic example being psychological operations designed to undercut support for the enemy war effort or creating a less hostile environment for friendly force operations. At the same time, though, a high threshold for qualification as an attack leaves key civilian cyber infrastructure and the activities that rely upon it at risk, as in the case of manipulation of a system upon which the national social systems rely.

A related issue is whether data qualifies as an 'object' that, if civilian, enjoys protection against attack. If so, alteration or destruction of civilian data would violate IHL. Two schools of thought have emerged.[70] The first is that data is not an object because it is intangible and therefore treatment as an object would be contrary to the plain meaning of the word. Irrespective of its legal merit, the approach is unsatisfactory because it permits a party to the conflict to dramatically disrupt civilian life by targeting civilian data without restriction, and therefore runs contrary to IHL's humanitarian underpinnings. As an example, cyber operations targeting data upon which a nation's educational system relies would be allowable, even if the operation offered no direct military advantage.

Yet, if data is characterized as an object, most cyber operations directed at civilian infrastructure would be unlawful because they have some effect on data. This would preclude military operations that have been a feature of armed conflict for centuries. Again, the paradigmatic example is psychological operations conducted by cyber means. This interpretation runs counter to the practical military considerations that must also be considered when interpreting IHL.[71]

Neither of these issues admits of an easy solution, for the approaches set forth above skew the humanitarian considerations—military necessity balance that underpins respect for IHL in one direction or the other. Thus, IHL is one area of international law that merits consideration of new law either by treaty or through State practice combined with *opinio juris* that matures into customary law over time. Recommendations

[69] *Tallinn Manual 2.0* (n 9) rule 92, paras 10–12.

[70] Kubo Macak, 'Military Objectives 2.0: The Case for Interpreting Computer Data as Objects under International Humanitarian Law' (2015) 48 Israel Law Review 55; Michael N Schmitt, 'The Notion of "Objects" during Çyber Operations: A Riposte in Defence of Interpretive Precision' (2015) 48 Israel Law Review 81.

[71] Michael Schmitt, 'Military Necessity and Humanity in International Humanitarian Law: Preserving the Delicate Balance' (2010) 50 Virginia Journal of International Law 795.

along these lines are starting to surface as States struggle with such fundamental IHL predicaments.[72]

C. Quo Vadis?

The question is where the international law of cyber space is headed. As explained, States are making only halting progress in interpreting and developing this body of law. However, they clearly realize the importance of making further progress. Recently, the UN has agreed to not only convene a sixth GGE but also to establish an Open-Ended Working Group in which all States may participate. The first initiative will enjoy the benefit of a smaller size and therefore be more efficient in seeking consensus, whereas the second has the benefit of inclusivity, which is to be valued because of the entire global community's growing reliance on cyber activities.

Additionally, attempts to forge progress on norms are underway outside the strict confines of the State system. In some cases, States are teaming-up with the private sector and academia. Noteworthy in this regard is the Global Commission on the Stability of Cyberspace and the Paris Call. In some cases, the private sector is going it alone, as in the case of Microsoft's Digital Geneva Convention and Siemens' Charter of Trust.

But ultimately, only States make international law, either through treaty action or by engaging in activities that crystallize into customary law. And while academics, non-governmental organizations and others may opine on how the extant international law should be interpreted in the cyber context, only the interpretation by States of that body of law in the cyber context has determinative effect.

As a result, it will be left primarily to States to assess whether prospective interpretations or proposed norms foster or frustrate their national interests. At the macro level, they must reflect their national values and support their broad national interests. And at the operational level, the interpretation or proposed norm in question has to serve as a normative firewall against harmful cyber operations while permitting cyber operations necessary for their national security. The challenge will be, as it has been since the beginning of this journey, that all States are not similarly situated with respect to cyberspace and the activities that occur therein; what they see in cyberspace very much depends on where they stand.

[72] eg Michael Schmitt, 'Wired Warfare 3.0: Protecting the Civilian Population during Cyber Operations' (2019) 101 International Review of the Red Cross 333.

CHAPTER 37

OUTER SPACE SECURITY

STEVEN FREELAND AND ELISE GRUTTNER

A. Introduction

Since the dawn of the space age, security has been a driving force in the development of technical capabilities in outer space. The launch of the small Soviet space object called Sputnik I in 1957 occurred in the midst of the Cold War, a period when States' primary focus was on national security. Since that time, security has been the prevailing issue at the core of both State and international space law regimes. Over the last sixty years, the development of space-related technology has been inextricably linked to military capability—both real and perceived. The space race emerged at a time when both the United States and the Soviet Union sought to demonstrate their respective technological strengths.

It has now been more than sixty years since the very beginning of humankind's undertakings into orbital space.[1] Today, space is more accessible and depended upon than ever envisaged. Most military leaders regard space-related technology as an integral element of their strategic battle platform and State security. This is a reflection of the evolving technological nature of armed conflict, which challenges many aspects of international law, including the regulation of warfare. The continuing development and reliance on commercial and military space technology challenges the core principle of the 'peaceful purposes' doctrine that underpins the current international legal regulation of outer space. This chapter explores the development of activities in outer space, the regulation of national and global space security and the practical capabilities of leading spacefaring nations. It also highlights some of the critical issues that impact upon security-related concerns for States when it comes to the regulation of armed

[1] We have also recently celebrated the 50th anniversary of the Treaty on Principles Governing the Activities of States in the Exploration and Use of Outer Space, including the Moon and Other Celestial Bodies 610 UNTS 205 (Outer Space Treaty), which sets out a series of fundamental principles relating to the legal regulation of outer space.

conflict in outer space. The use of outer space for military purposes gives rise to difficult international law issues relating to use of force. What is not straightforward is precisely how various aspects of these activities are to be regulated at the international level should they transcend outer space and result in armed conflict.

In 2020, the regulation of outer space could not be more topical with regard to global security and international law. We are now engaged in a multitude of space activities far beyond the contemplation of those originally involved at the time of Sputnik. The utilization of space technology now forms a crucial part of everyday society across the globe. Outer space capabilities assist with Earth observation and weather forecasting, which plays an increasingly pivotal role in monitoring climate change and extreme weather events.[2] This reliance is illustrated by the reality that the world would cease to function in many respects without constant and unimpeded access to space. Space-based communication services have radically transformed everyday communications, banking, and navigation, allowing the world to be more interconnected than ever before.[3] This dependency has been driven both by the growth of the commercialization of outer space, but also its increasingly important strategic, security, and military significance. Government and military officials have acknowledged the indispensable role military capabilities in outer space now have in State security. It is understood that a 'day without space'[4] would represent a national security and commercial catastrophe.

From a security-related perspective, the law will continue to play an integral role in the opportunities and challenges the future uses of outer space offer.[5] At its core, international space security, as per the Outer Space Treaty, is concerned with undertaking activities in outer space in a way that is 'in the interest of maintaining international peace and security and promoting international cooperation and understanding'.[6] Unfortunately the United Nations Space Treaties were concluded in relatively general terms and have sometimes been the subject of divergent interpretation as to what they do (and do not) prohibit with regard to issues relating to security.

The role of key international players in this evolving field is vital to the development of the legal regulation of outer space. Leading actors like the US, China, and Russia have all announced and shown significant commitment to developing their outer space capabilities both militarily and scientifically.[7] This represents a major challenge in relation

[2] eg Jeff Greenblatt/Al Anzaldua, 'How Space Technology Benefits the Earth' (*The Space Review*, 29 July 2019) <http://www.thespacereview.com/article/3768/1> accessed 10 October 2019.

[3] ibid.

[4] eg, David Logsdon, 'A Day without Space' (*Space News Magazine*, 6 June 2016) <http://www.spacenewsmag.com/commentary/a-day-without-space/> accessed 30 August 2018.

[5] One of these developments is the increasing use of so-called small satellites, which also offer both considerable opportunities and some significant regulatory challenges. Steven Freeland, 'NewSpace, Small Satellites and Law: Finding a Balance between Innovation, a Changing Space Paradigm and Regulatory Control' in M Tanveer Ahmad/Jinyuan Su (eds), *NewSpace Commercialisation and the Law* (McGill University 2017).

[6] Outer Space Treaty (n 1) art III.

[7] eg NASIC, 'Competing in Space' (December 2018) <https://www.nasic.af.mil/Portals/19/documents/Space_Glossy_FINAL--15Jan_Single_Page.pdf?ver=2019-01-23-150035-697> accessed 26 February 2020.

to the ongoing development of effective legal principles and the use of outer space during the course of armed conflict.

Ultimately, clarification can only be achieved by multilateral agreement amongst the major stakeholders. Others have called for guidance on this issue of the extent to which international law principles of *jus in bello* apply to outer space activities[8] but, in the end, the engagement of all relevant States, and the conclusion of high level (and preferably binding) accountable instruments, will be the only way to address these uncertainties and the inherent risks associated with them.

B. Legal Framework

1. Principles of the International Regulation of Outer Space

Launched at the height of the Cold War, the Sputnik mission immediately caused concern amongst the international community about the use of outer space for military purposes.[9] Suddenly, one of the greatest threats to State and global security was the potential for outer space to become the next theatre of war, operating in a largely unregulated legal environment. The target for space technological prowess at the time was as much motivated by military considerations as a wish to explore and use space for other purposes. The international community had to find a balance between the wishes of the existing two space superpowers and a sense of uncertainty and apprehension on what the future of these military-driven achievements in space may hold.

Shortly after Sputnik, the UN established a new committee to take primary responsibility for the development and codification of the fundamental rules relating to outer space, the UN Committee on the Peaceful Uses of Outer Space (UN COPUOS). An ad hoc Committee on the Peaceful Uses of Outer Space, with eighteen initial Member States, was established in 1958,[10] and it subsequently became a permanent body in 1959.[11] UN COPUOS is now regarded by many as the principal multilateral body involved in the development of international space law.[12]

One of the major questions that was put to UN COPUOS was the legal status of outer space.[13] Although the Soviet Union had not sought the permission of other States to

[8] eg UN COPUOS, 'Report of the Legal Subcommittee on its fifty-seventh session, held in Vienna from 9 to 20 April 2018' (30 April 2018) UN Doc A/AC.105/1177, para 42.

[9] eg Francis Lyall/Paul B Larsen, *Space Law: A Treatise* (Ashgate 2009) 3–9.

[10] UNGA Res 1348 (XIII) (13 December 1958) passed barely two months after the launch of Sputnik, where the UNGA recognized 'the common interest of mankind in outer space' and that it is 'the common aim that outer space should be used for *peaceful purposes only*' (emphasis added).

[11] UNGA Res 1472(XIV) (12 December 1959).

[12] See UNOOSA, 'UNISPACE+50' (Vienna, 18–21 June 2018) <http://www.unoosa.org/oosa/en/ourwork/unispaceplus50/index.html> accessed 30 August 2018.

[13] eg UNGA Res 2222(XXI) (19 December 1966) preamble on 'the importance of developing the rule of law in this new area of human endeavour'.

undertake the Sputnik mission, there were no significant protests asserting that it had infringed on a country's sovereign territory as it circled the Earth. This confirmed an acknowledgement by States that this new frontier did not possess the elements of sovereignty that had already been well established under the international law principles regulating land, sea, and air space[14] and that outer space was to be regarded as being similar to a *res communis omnium*.[15] It was clear that specific international binding rules would be required to address the specific characteristics and legal categorization of outer space.

Since that time, a substantial body of law dealing with various aspects of the use and exploration of outer space has arisen. This includes and is manifested by the UN Space Treaties, UN General Assembly (UNGA) resolutions, bilateral arrangements, determinations by intergovernmental organizations, national legislation, and decisions of national courts.

The UNGA has adopted a number of space-related principles, which include the following:

1. Declaration of Legal Principles Governing the Activities of States in the Exploration and Use of Outer Space;[16]
2. Principles Governing the Use by States of Artificial Earth Satellites for International Direct Television Broadcasting;[17]
3. Principles Relating to Remote Sensing of the Earth from Outer Space;[18]
4. Principles Relevant to the Use of Nuclear Power Sources in Outer Space; and[19]
5. Declaration on International Cooperation in the Exploration and Use of Outer Space for the Benefit and in the Interest of All States, Taking into Particular Account the Needs of Developing Countries.[20]

These bolster the application of international law and promote international cooperation and understanding in space activities,[21] the dissemination and exchange of information through transnational direct television broadcasting via satellites[22] and remote satellite observations of Earth,[23] and general standards regulating the safe use of nuclear power sources required for the exploration and use of outer space.[24] More recent 'guidelines'

[14] There has, however, been one notable exception in this regard: In 1976, a number of equatorial States—including Brazil, Colombia, the Congo, Ecuador, Indonesia, Kenya, Uganda, and Zaire—issued the Bogota Declaration, in which they claimed sovereign rights over segments of geostationary synchronous orbit above their respective territories. They asserted their claims principally because of the lack of an accepted delimitation between airspace and outer space. Such assertions were strenuously opposed by other States and have not been successful.

[15] Antonio Cassese, *International Law* (2nd edn, OUP 2005) 95.

[16] UNGA Res 1962(XVIII) (13 December 1963) (Legal Principles Declaration).

[17] UNGA Res 37/92 (10 December 1982).

[18] UNGA Res 41/65 (3 December 1986).

[19] UNGA Res 47/68 (14 December 1992).

[20] UNGA Res 51/122 (13 December 1996).

[21] eg Legal Principles Declaration (n 16) principle 4.

[22] eg UNGA Res 37/92 (n 17) principles A and D.

[23] eg UNGA Res 41/65 (n 18) principles II or V.

[24] eg UNGA Res 47/68 (n 19) principle 3.

have also been agreed upon relating to various other important issues, including the problem of space debris.[25] Space debris poses a significant risk to operations in outer space as on-orbit collisions can have catastrophic repercussions and lead to further creation of debris. Related to the issue of space debris is the issue of maintaining the integrity of space assets, both in terms of adhering to measures on debris control and mitigation as well as remediation,[26] but also by minimizing the possibility that a State would destroy another State's satellite (and in the process almost certainly create additional space debris).[27]

The unplanned re-entry of the Chinese space station, Tiangong-1, in April 2018 is one recent example of the practical repercussions of the lack of regulation is this area.[28] Moreover, the Kessler Syndrome predicts a scenario in which space debris collisions generate more debris that overtime grows exponentially and creates a cascading effect, which could eventually eliminate humanity's capacity to utilize Earth's orbit.[29] While this level may never be reached, space debris remains a considerable threat to a nation's operations in outer space and their national security interests.

In the context of the regulation of the exploration and use of outer space, the aforementioned five sets of principles have largely been considered as constituting 'soft law',[30] however a number of specific provisions may now represent customary international law. Despite all of these developments, it is clear that the existing legal and regulatory regime has not kept pace with the remarkable technological and commercial progress of space activities in the twenty-first century.

2. Space Security Law

a. *International Peace and Security*

A number of fundamental legal principles relating to the exploration and use of outer space quickly emerged after 1957 through a combination of practice and discussion

[25] Inter-Agency Space Debris Coordination Committee, 'IADC Space Debris Mitigation Guidelines' (2007) <https://www.iadc-online.org/index.cgi?item=docs_pub> accessed 30 August 2018; UNGA Res 62/217 (22 December 2007) para 26; Ulrike Bohlmann/Steven Freeland, 'The Regulation of Space Activities and the Space Environment' in Shawkat Alam et al (eds), *Routledge Handbook of International Environmental Law* (Routledge 2013).

[26] Rada Popova/Volker Schaus, 'The Legal Framework for Space Debris Remediation as a Tool for Sustainability in Outer Space' (2018) 5 Aerospace 55.

[27] The year 2009 was the first known instance that two satellites collided in space and created a cloud of space debris. Maya Wei-Haas, 'Space Junk is a Huge Problem—and It's Only Getting Bigger' (*National Geographic*, 25 April 2019) <https://www.nationalgeographic.com/science/space/reference/space-junk/> accessed 10 October 2019.

[28] UN COPUOS Report (n 8) para 163.

[29] Donald J Kessler et al, 'The Kessler Syndrome: Implications to Future Space Operations (AAS 10-016)' (2010) 137 Advances in the Astronautical Sciences.

[30] Steven Freeland, 'The Role of "Soft Law" in Public International Law and its Relevance to the International Legal Regulation of Outer Space' in Irmgard Marboe (ed), *Soft Law in Outer Space: The Function of Non-Binding Norms in International Space Law* (Böhlau Verlag 2012).

within the UNGA. The Outer Space Treaty and the subsequent four treaties that followed are security documents that strive to limit actors' use of space for activities adverse to peace and security.[31] Issues such as the 'common interest', 'freedom', and 'non-appropriation' principles were incorporated into the terms of the UN Space Law Treaties and, in particular, the Outer Space Treaty,[32] thus codifying what many commentators believe were existing customary international law principles.[33]

Article II of the Outer Space Treaty encompasses the non-appropriation principle.[34] In general terms, it confirms that outer space (which includes the Moon and other celestial bodies) is not subject to ownership rights and prohibits *inter alia* any sovereign or territorial claims to outer space. Outer space therefore is not to be regarded as 'territorial', a principle that was already well accepted in practice virtually from the commencement of the space race.[35] This was an important proactive step designed to protect outer space from the possibility of conflict driven by territorial or colonizing ambitions. In this respect, therefore, Article II represents an important security-related principle for the conduct of space activities, which distinguishes it from territorial security-related concerns. As a result, the thrust of Article II was relatively uncontroversial at the time it was included in the Outer Space Treaty.[36]

The non-appropriation principle is set out immediately following an elaboration of the common interest and freedom principles set out in Article I. That provision confirms that the exploration and use of outer space is to be undertaken 'for the benefit and in the interests of all countries' and freely 'by all states without discrimination of any kind, on a basis of equality and in accordance with international law'.

[31] These treaties include: Agreement on the Rescue of Astronauts, the Return of Astronauts and the Return of Objects Launched into Outer Space 672 UNTS 119; Convention on International Liability for Damage Caused by Space Objects 961 UNTS 187; Convention on Registration of Objects Launched into Outer Space 1023 UNTS 15 and Agreement Governing the Activities of States on the Moon and other Celestial Bodies 1363 UNTS 3 (Moon Agreement).

[32] eg Outer Space Treaty (n 1) arts I and II.

[33] This issue is further elaborated in Ram Jakhu/Steven Freeland, 'The Relationship between the Outer Space Treaty and Customary International Law' in P J Blount et al (eds), *Proceedings of the International Institute of Space Law 2016* (Eleven International Publishing 2017).

[34] For a detailed analysis of article II of the Outer Space Treaty: Steven Freeland/Ram Jakhu, 'Article II' in Stephan Hobe et al (eds), *Cologne Commentary on Space Law, Volume I—Outer Space Treaty* (Carl Heymanns Verlag 2009).

[35] This is to be compared with Antarctica, which had seen a series of sovereign claims by several States in the period leading up to the finalization of the Antarctic Treaty 402 UNTS 71. ibid art IV has the effect of suspending all claims to territorial sovereignty in Antarctica for the duration of that instrument, as well as prohibiting any 'new claim, or enlargement of an existing claim'. The Protocol on Environmental Protection to the Antarctic Treaty 2941 UNTS 3 augments the Antarctic Treaty by protecting Antarctica from commercial mining for a period of fifty years.

[36] That said, the interpretation of article II, particularly as it relates to possible exploitation by non-governmental entities of the natural resources *in situ* on celestial bodies such as asteroids, has in recent times become highly contentious. See Steven Freeland, 'Common Heritage, not Common Law: How International Law Will Regulate Proposals to Exploit Space Resources' (2017) 35 Questions of International Law 19.

Through its Article III, the Outer Space Treaty affirms that activities in space are to be undertaken 'in accordance with international law'.[37] However, the fact that most existing international law at the time and even now has been largely developed for 'terrestrial' purposes means that it is not necessarily appropriate or directly applicable in every respect to all space activities. This also applies to the conduct of armed hostilities in and/or through space. Additionally, assessing such applicability must take into account the unique principles that space law presents.

Space capabilities do, however, play an important role in monitoring treaty verification. Specifically, remote sensing capabilities give States a unique mechanism for verification of disarmament agreements.[38] Additionally, remote sensing data has been employed by both State and non-State actors to monitor other security-related issues posed, such as human rights obligations, climate change, and humanitarian and disaster relief efforts.[39]

b. *National Security*

Current international space law does not prohibit States from enacting and following their own national security regime and targets, provided that they do not impose upon international peace and security or violate their international obligations. This freedom allows nations to advance their military capabilities in outer space. By investing in military space technology, States are striving to protect their own national interest against external threats. As the definition of national security evolves, so does the role of space systems in protecting national security.[40] National security issues presented to States include disarmament, protection of space assets in orbit, and the security of space technology from proliferation. Even if States are pre-emptively striving to maintain peace and security in the space domain, this will still accelerate the threat of an arms race in outer space. Ultimately, States will always have their own interests at heart when determining national strategic policy or security balances.

c. *Global Security*

The interconnected nature of space affairs is both a blessing and a curse. If well managed, the heavy reliance by States on their outer space capabilities for both civilian and military purposes can prove indispensable for global security. However, as States rely on their space systems, they become more vulnerable to various threats. The weaponization of outer space is a global security threat that is demonstrated by the proliferation of anti-satellite weapons, jamming, cyberthreats, kinetic-energy weapons, and laser weapons.[41]

[37] Outer Space Treaty (n 1) art III.

[38] eg Sven Nussbaum/Gunter Menz, *Object-Based Image Analysis and Treaty Verification: New Approaches in Remote Sensing—Applied to Nuclear Facilities in Iran* (Springer 2008).

[39] eg Jun Yang et al, 'The Role of Satellite Remote Sensing in Climate Change Studies' (2013) 3 Nature Climate Change 875.

[40] eg Todd Harrison et al, 'Space Threat Assessment 2019' (*CSIS*, 4 April 2019) <https://www.csis.org/analysis/space-threat-assessment-2019> accessed 10 October 2019.

[41] ibid.

As individual nations' space capabilities continue to grow, the risk of escalating an arms race becomes more likely. The increase in individual States' national security indirectly threatens that of global security.[42] While collective security allows States to work collaboratively to combat issues that are a risk to all nations, such as working together to enforce or establish modern international frameworks with an objective of collective security, individual States may seek to improve their own technical capabilities and compete against each other.

As such, the relationship between national security and global security does not go hand in hand, and overemphasis on the former impacts negatively the latter. This can be primarily observed by the steady weaponization of the space domain and the growing arms race in outer space. This impending risk of space warfare once again calls for an international regime that regulates and mitigates this threat. Unless concrete steps are taken to arrest this trend—which will require a significant shift in political will, particularly amongst the major powers—it is likely that space will increasingly be utilized to further the military and strategic aims of specific countries, particularly as military and space technology continues to evolve and develop.[43]

3. Main Principles Relevant to 'Military' Uses of Outer Space

The conventional obligations and restrictions that were codified in the major UN Space Treaties addressed, in part, specific military and weapons-related aspects of space activities. However, they were neither entirely clear nor sufficiently comprehensive to meet all of these challenges. While the Moon and other celestial bodies were to be used 'exclusively for peaceful purposes,'[44] there was no express reference as regards to what one might refer to as 'void outer space'. While most commentators would subsequently interpret the relevant provisions as prohibiting military space activities in outer space, this was not the practice of the military of those countries that actually had space capabilities.[45]

With the further technological development since that time, the situation has become increasingly more complex. Just as the major spacefaring nations have been undertaking what might be termed 'passive' military activities in outer space for many years, space is increasingly now being used as part of 'active' engagement in the conduct of armed

[42] eg Brian Weeden/Victoria Samson, 'Global Counterspace Capabilities: An Open Source Assessment' (*Secure World Foundation*, April 2019) <https://swfound.org/counterspace/> accessed 10 October 2019.

[43] eg US DoD, 'Annual Report to Congress: Military and Security Developments Involving the People's Republic of China 2019' (2019) <https://media.defense.gov/2019/May/02/2002127082/-1/-1/1/2019_CHINA_MILITARY_POWER_REPORT.pdf> accessed 15 February 2020; US DoD, 'United States Space Force' (February 2019) <https://media.defense.gov/2019/Mar/01/2002095012/-1/-1/1/UNITED-STATES-SPACE-FORCE-STRATEGIC-OVERVIEW.PDF> accessed 10 October 2019.

[44] Outer Space Treaty (n 1) art IV.

[45] Linda Johanna Friman, 'War and Peace in Outer Space: A Review of the Legality of the Weaponization of Outer Space in the Light of the Prohibition on Non-Peaceful Purpose' (2005) 16 Finnish Yearbook of International Law 285; Joint Chiefs of Staff, '3–14 Joint Publication: Space Operations' (10 April 2018) <https://www.jcs.mil/Portals/36/Documents/Doctrine/pubs/jp3_14ch1.pdf?ver=GfzdjuluCyyHDS9D_RtkNA%3D%3D> accessed 30 November 2020.

conflict.[46] Not only is information gathered from outer space—through, for example, the use of remote satellite technology and communications satellites—used to plan military engagement on Earth, but space assets now also direct military activity and represent an integral part of the military hardware of the major powers.[47] Increasingly, given the importance of this space-located military infrastructure, the security of the major countries becomes more vulnerable to an 'attack' against their space assets. We once again find ourselves facing the possibility that outer space may itself become a theatre of warfare.

By 1961, the UNGA had recommended that international law and the UN Charter should apply to 'outer space and celestial bodies'.[48] The prohibition on the threat and use of force under Article 2(4) of the UN Charter represents a crucial element in the regulation of international relations and has been argued by some commentators as being equally applicable to the use of outer space.[49] The sentiments underlying the UN Charter were strengthened further by the restrictions imposed in relation to nuclear weapons and weapons of mass destruction by Article IV of the Outer Space Treaty, although, as has been well documented, this provision in and of itself does not represent a complete restriction on the placement of weapons in outer space, nor of their use.[50] From time to time, proposals have been put forward to amend Article IV in order to enhance these restrictions, but these have not been successful.[51]

As noted, Article IV also provides that '[t]he moon and other celestial bodies shall be used by all States Parties to the [Outer Space] Treaty *exclusively for peaceful purposes*'.[52] There is a debate amongst space law commentators whether this is directed against

[46] eg Jackson Maogoto/Steven Freeland, 'The Final Frontier: The Laws of Armed Conflict and Space Warfare' (2007) 23 Connecticut Journal of International Law 165; David Simonds, 'China Anti-Satellite Test: A New Arms Race in Space?' (*The Economist*, 25 January 2007) <https://www.economist.com/leaders/2007/01/25/a-new-arms-race-in-space> accessed 15 February 2020; Thomas Ricks, 'Space is Playing Field for Newest War Game' (*The Washington Post*, 29 January 2001) <https://www.washington-post.com/archive/politics/2001/01/29/space-is-playing-fieldfor-newest-war-game/938e9674-0c3b-4d66-b67b-e3195b1275fd/> accessed 17 February 2020.

[47] eg Michael Sheetz/Amanda Macias, 'China and Russia are Militarizing Space with "Energy Weapons" and Anti-Satellite Missiles: Pentagon' (*CNBC*, 13 February 2019) <https://www.cnbc.com/2019/02/13/pentagon-warns-of-weaponization-of-space-by-china-russia-report.html> accessed 10 October 2019.

[48] UNGA Res 1721(XVI) (20 December 1961) para 1(a).

[49] United Nations Charter 1 UNTS XVI (UN Charter) art 2(4). See eg Jackson Nyamuya Maogoto/Steven Freeland, 'Space Weaponization and the United Nations Charter Regime on Force: A Thick Legal Fog or a Receding Mist?' (2007) 41 The International Lawyer 1091; Arjen Vermeer, 'The Laws of War in Outer Space: Some Legal Implications for the Jus ad Bellum and the Jus in Bello of the Militarisation and Weaponisation of Outer Space' in Bob Brecher (ed), *The New Order of War* (Brill 2007); Icho Kealotswe-Matlou, 'The Rule of Law in Outer Space—A Call for International Cooperation' (March 2018) <https://www.law.upenn.edu/live/files/7811-kealotswethe-rule-of-law-in-outer-spacepdf> accessed 17 February 2020.

[50] For a detailed analysis of the Outer Space Treaty (n 1) art IV: Kai-Uwe Schrogl/Julia Neumann, 'Article IV' in Hobe et al (n 34).

[51] eg Vladimir Bogomolov, 'Prevention of an Arms Race in Outer Space: The Deliberations in the Conference on Disarmament in 1993' (1993) 21 Journal of Space Law 141, where the author refers to a failed Venezuelan proposal to amend article IV.

[52] Outer Space Treaty (n 1) art IV. See also Moon Agreement (n 31) art 3(1) (emphasis added).

'non-military' or merely 'non-aggressive' activities.[53] In reality it is undeniable that, in addition to the many commercial, civilian, and scientific uses, outer space has been used for an expanding array of military activities.

If one were to adopt a hard-line pragmatic view, it seems that the 'non-military/non-aggressive' debate relating to the peaceful purposes requirement is a redundant argument, even though it represents an extremely important issue of interpretation of the strict principles of international space law. In one sense, this accepts that the militarization of space is a given, even though many international and space lawyers are at pains to admit this. The distinction between the 'militarization' and 'weaponization' of outer space is necessary to understanding the critical issues of armed conflict in outer space. Militarization refers to the enhancement of capabilities in a conventional setting, for instance the systems of intelligence, surveillance, and communications.[54] Alternatively, the physical deployment of weapons in outer space, or in a ground mode that can be used to attack and destroy targets in orbit, represents a weaponization of space.[55]

Article 51 UN Charter, which confirms the 'inherent right' to self-defence, is also applicable to the legal regulation of outer space.[56] Under general international law, this right remains subject to express legal limitations, the requirements of necessity, and proportionality.[57] Even where the right to self-defence is lawfully exercised, the State so acting will remain subject to the principles of international law. While this is, in theory, uncontroversial, the difficulty is to determine precisely whether (and how) these fundamental principles can be applied to the unique legal and technological context of outer space. This is particularly relevant given that the use of satellite technology already represents an integral part of the military strategy and the conduct of many armed conflicts.[58] As this technology continues to develop, national and global security will likely be directed towards a greater incorporation of satellite technology in outer space as part of the course of warfare.

[53] eg Patrick Gleeson, Legal Aspects of the Use of Force in Space (LLM thesis, Institute of Air and Space Law McGill University 2005).

[54] Anel Ferreira-Snyman, 'Selected Legal Challenges Relating to the Military Use of Outer Space, with Specific Reference to Article IV of the Outer Space Treaty' (2015) 18 Potchefstroom Electronic Law Journal 488.

[55] Harsh Vasani, 'How China is Weaponizing Outer Space' (*The Diplomat*, 19 January 2017) <https://thediplomat.com/2017/01/how-china-is-weaponizing-outer-space/> accessed 30 August 2018.

[56] eg Vermeer (n 49); Rajeswari Pillai Rajagopalan, 'Space Code Debate and the Right to Self-Defence under Article 51' (*Observer Research Foundation*, 31 July 2013) <https://www.orfonline.org/research/space-code-debate-and-the-right-to-self-defence-under-article-51/> accessed 10 October 2019.

[57] *The Caroline Case* (1837) 29 BFSP 1137–8; 30 BFSP 195–6, which also referred to a requirement of immediacy, although this was not mentioned in *Oil Platforms (Iran v USA)* (Merits) [2003] ICJ Rep 161.

[58] Ricky Lee/Sarah Steele, 'Military Use of Satellite Communications, Remote Sensing, and Global Positioning Systems in the War on Terror' (2014) 79 Journal of Air Law and Commerce 69; Michel Bourbonnière, 'Law of Armed Conflict (LOAC) and the Neutralisation of Satellites or "Ius in Bello Satellites"' (2004) 9 JCSL 43.

C. Current Challenges

1. Addressing the Risks of 'Space Warfare'

Since the beginning of the millennium, governments around the world have embarked on policies designed to enhance their domination of the space dimension of military operations. The use of space technology has become ever more sophisticated, as illustrated by the fact that, during the Gulf War in 1990, the military value of space assets for the conduct of warfare was utilized to a significant degree.[59] 'Operation Desert Storm' is regarded as 'the first space war'.[60] The announcement from the current Trump administration of a plan for a sixth branch of the US military 'Space Force' furthers the development of space technology for military uses and escalates the risk of an arms race in space.[61] The US is responding to the perceived threat posed by Russia and China, along with nations such as North Korea, to its military capabilities based on its dependence on space.[62] As all major powers dedicate more resources towards the militarization of space, this gives rise to resource exploitation and potential attempts by nations to ascertain means to protect themselves against their security weaknesses by denying access to space for others. The European Union has also identified outer space as 'a key component for its European Defense and Security Policy'[63] and China and Russia regard space as a vital part of their military infrastructure.

Ballistic missiles play an increasingly important role in any sophisticated national security structure, and the development of defensive systems 'is both a result of and additional factor driving' a global arms race.[64] In this complex geopolitical context, several commentators have opined that space warfare is, in fact, inevitable and cannot be avoided.[65] If these assertions turn out to reflect reality, various aspects of the laws of war may apply, in addition to international space law rules. It is not at all clear whether, and

[59] Peter Anson/Dennis Cummings, 'The First Space War: The Contribution of Satellites to the Gulf War' (1991) 136 The Rusi Journal 45; Larry Greenemeier, 'GPS and the World's First "Space War"' (*Scientific American*, 8 February 2016) <https://www.scientificamerican.com/article/gps-and-the-world-s-first-space-war/> accessed 10 October 2019.

[60] Maogoto/Freeland (n 49) 1107.

[61] Steven Freeland, 'The US Plan for a Space Force Risks Escalating a "Space Arms Race"' (*The Conversation*, 10 August 2018) <https://theconversation.com/the-us-plan-for-a-space-force-risks-escalating-a-space-arms-race-101368> accessed 30 August 2018.

[62] Joe Gould, 'Think Space Force is a Joke? Here Are Four Major Space Threats to Take Seriously' (*Defense News*, 9 August 2018) <https://www.defensenews.com/space/2018/08/09/think-space-force-is-a-joke-here-are-four-major-space-threats-to-take-seriously/> accessed 30 August 2018.

[63] Regina Hagen/Jürgen Scheffran, 'International Space Law and Space Security: Expectations and Criteria for a Sustainable and Peaceful Use of Outer Space' in Marietta Benkö/Kai-Uwe Schrogl (eds), *Space Law: Current Problems and Perspectives for Future Regulation* (Eleven International Publishing 2005) 273.

[64] ibid.

[65] eg Iole De Angelis, 'Legal and Political Implications of Offensives Actions from and against the Space Segment' (2002) 45 Proceedings of the Colloquium on the Law of Outer Space 197.

to what extent, these principles can coexist seamlessly, and what the correct legal position might be in a situation where they might conflict. What appears to be emerging is a divergence of views as to the interplay between the relevant principles that might apply to an armed conflict in space, as between the international laws of space and the existing *jus in bello* principles.[66] The lack of clarity gives rise to a heightened sense of uncertainty and (perceived) threats to security.

An additional complicating factor is the increasing prevalence of 'dual-use' satellites. The concept of a dual-use facility or resource—typically a commercial facility or resource that is also utilized by the military—has become a common feature of contemporary technological society.[67] This presents particular difficulties for those conducting armed conflict, since an asset that could *prima facie* be regarded as a legitimate military target on the basis of military objectives might also—even at the same time—be providing civilian/commercial services. It is sometimes very difficult, or indeed impossible, to 'quarantine' what is the civilian or commercial aspect of a functioning asset from the military component. Further, military 'customers' are now regularly utilizing commercial satellites to undertake military activities.[68] In this regard, the language of the international law instruments relating to space has not hampered the increasing utilization of satellite technology for an expanding array of military activities.

Yet, the testing exercise of the destruction by both China and the United States of their satellites highlights the dangers posed by the advent of this technology.[69] This, coupled with the 'dual-use' nature of satellites makes any attempt to apply the *jus in bello* principles to a 'space war' fraught with difficulty, highlighting the overly simplistic assumptions behind Article III of the Outer Space Treaty.

To continue to rely solely on existing international rules regulating warfare that were developed in a previous technological era, as important as they are, is akin to applying twentieth-century rules to twenty-first-century technology. In the absence of some additional protections, terrestrial international (humanitarian) law will most likely not be completely appropriate to adequately regulate all armed conflict-related contingencies of outer space.[70] Consequently, apart from the general rules provided by the *lex specialis*

[66] Steven Freeland, 'The Laws of War in Outer Space' in Kai-Uwe Schrogl et al (eds), *Handbook of Space Security: Policies, Applications and Programs* (Springer 2015) 102; Kubo Macak, 'Silent War: Applicability of the *Jus in Bello* to Military Space Operations' (2018) 94 International Law Studies 1.

[67] eg Abdul Rehman Khan, 'Space Wars: Dual-Use Satellites' (2017) 14 Rutgers Journal of Law and Public Policy 314.

[68] Peter de Selding, 'US Military Rebounding as a Commercial Satellite Customer' (*Space News*, 8 November 2016) <https://spacenews.com/u-s-military-rebounding-as-a-commercial-satellite-customer/> accessed 10 October 2019.

[69] William Broad/David Sanger, 'Flexing Muscle, China Destroys Satellite in Test' (*The New York Times*, 19 January 2017) <https://www.nytimes.com/2007/01/19/world/asia/19china.html> accessed 10 October 2019; Brian Weeden, 'Through a Glass, Darkly: Chinese, American, and Russian Anti-Satellite Testing in Space' (*The Space Review*, 17 March 2014) <https://www.thespacereview.com/article/2473/1> accessed 12 April 2020.

[70] Steven Freeland, 'Legal Regulation of the Military Use of Outer Space: What Role for International Humanitarian Law?' (2011) 41 Proceedings of the Bruges Colloquium: Technological Challenges for the Humanitarian Legal Framework 87.

of space law, there exists considerable uncertainty as to what rules regulate (and thus serve to deter) the use of outer space technology in the conduct of a conflict.

However, there is reluctance amongst the major powers to address this question through the use of binding treaty instruments. A voluntary soft-law approach has been preferred, utilizing transparency and confidence-building measures (TCBMs). A principal TCBM in the area of space security had been the (draft) International Code of Conduct for Outer Space Activities (CoC), which was initially developed as a European initiative but has since become broader in scope.[71] Discussions in 2015 intended to facilitate agreement on this instrument failed, with the instrument now not seriously referred to in relevant fora. Another soft-law approach that the international community has endeavoured to regulate is the build-up of weapons in outer space through the Prevention of an Arms Race in Outer Space (PAROS). The PAROS treaty negotiation process was originally raised through a UN established ad hoc committee in 1981, however after pushback from the United States, the committee was dissolved in 1994.[72]

While there are obvious benefits in developing greater trust between the space powers in issues relating to space security, the danger is that non-binding TCBMs are, for all practical purposes considered as the 'end game' on this issue, so that the formalization of binding obligations may *never* eventuate. At its core, the draft CoC provisions, for example, are merely guidelines or recommendations that do not have the force of law,[73] unless they are to be regarded as reflecting rules of customary international law, itself a very difficult assertion to substantiate in the absence of, say, a ruling by the International Court of Justice (ICJ). This approach appears inadequate to meet the complex risks associated with the continued development of space-related weapons.

2. Practical Capabilities of Spacefaring Nations

The modern space age no longer involves just the two major superpowers, but sees a new space race amongst existing and emerging powers. These emerging spacefaring nations are working towards increasing their presence in outer space through both military and scientific explorative avenues.[74] Investment of military capabilities in outer space has become a recent priority for many nations around the world, with nations

[71] The latest version of the draft CoC (Draft CoC) (31 March 2014) can be found at <http://www.eeas.europa.eu/non-proliferation-and-disarmament/pdf/space_code_conduct_draft_vers_31-march-2014_en.pdf> accessed 30 August 2018. Since meeting in 2015 there has been no progress.

[72] PAROS discussions and negotiations are still occurring in the Conference on Disarmament: 'Proposed Prevention of an Arms Race in Space (PAROS) Treaty' (*Nuclear Threat Initiative*, 29 September 2017) <https://www.nti.org/learn/treaties-and-regimes/proposed-prevention-arms-race-space-paros-treaty/> accessed 10 October 2019.

[73] Wolfgang Rathgeber et al, 'Space Security and the European Code of Conduct for Outer Space Activities' (2009) 4 Disarmament Forum 33, 34.

[74] International Space University, 'A Roadmap for Emerging Space States: Final Report' (Space Studies Program, 2017) <https://isulibrary.isunet.edu/doc_num.php?explnum_id=1350> accessed 10 October 2019; Brian Weeden, *Space Security Index 2019* (16th edn, Waterloo Printing 2019).

such as China and North Korea rapidly increasing their abilities and joining the ranks with the United States and Russia. The prospect of a global space race reflects the broader geopolitical competition amongst these powers and the changing balance of power from a bipolar system to a multipolar system. This is enhanced by nations such as North Korea building up their space capabilities in an unregulated environment.

a. *United States*

The US, the superpower that was once one of two spacefaring nations that participated in space exploration and outer space military development, is still 'maintaining the military high ground' on the world stage.[75] Since the mid-twentieth century, the US has held an unparalleled command of outer space. By leading the world with its outer space capabilities, it has maintained an immeasurable national security advantage. Its approach to strategic warfare has now become heavily reliant upon space capabilities. The US monopoly over surveillance facilities, precision weaponry, information dominance and command of strategic commons are all made possible by its political and financial investment in space. The Trump Administration announcement on establishing a 'Space Force' purports to further contribute to safeguarding American interests in the newest war-fighting domain. The Space Force aims to protect the US through the deterrence of malicious activities, improving foundational capabilities and strengthening deterrence and war-fighting options.[76]

In the unclassified summary of the National Security Space Strategy released in 2011, it was recognized that space was vital to US national security. The domain is utilized by the US for anticipating emerging threats, conducting military operations, projecting power internationally and enabling global economic sustainability.[77] The latest national Strategy for Space released by the Trump Administration notes that it is 'imperative that the United States adapts its policies, doctrine, and capabilities to protect [national] interests', while the President declared that 'it is not enough to merely have an American presence in space, we must have American dominance in space'.[78] The Space Force has the ultimate goal of accelerating the integration of space capabilities into other war-fighting forces. While the United States retains strategic and tactical dominance over its spacefaring challengers, old adversaries like Russia and rising players such as China compete for technical and strategic superiority in outer space.

[75] Bill Posey, 'Space: The Ultimate High Ground' (*Space News*, 24 February 2014) <https://spacenews.com/39613space-the-ultimate-high-ground/> accessed 30 August 2018.

[76] US DoD, 'Final Report on Organizational and Management Structure for the National Security Space Components of the Department of Defense' (*USNI News*, 9 August 2018) <https://news.usni.org/2018/08/09/report-congress-u-s-space-force-official-pentagon-announcement> accessed 30 August 2018.

[77] US DoD, 'National Security Space Strategy: Unclassified Summary' (January 2011) <http://archive.defense.gov/home/features/2011/0111_nsss/docs/NationalSecuritySpaceStrategyUnclassifiedSummary_Jan2011.pdf> accessed 30 August 2018.

[78] 'Remarks by President Trump at a Meeting with the National Space Council and Signing of Space Policy Directive-3' (The White House, 18 June 2018) <https://www.whitehouse.gov/briefings-statements/remarks-president-trump-meeting-national-space-council-signing-space-policy-directive-3/> accessed 17 February 2020.

b. *Russia*

Since the triumph of the Sputnik mission, the Soviet Union, and subsequently the Russian Federation has been one of the most powerful actors in outer space. Today, Russia has maintained its technical dominance in space, particularly in space launch technology. The US still uses a Russian rocket engine on the Atlas V, one of the nation's major space launch systems.[79] The Russian Federal Space Agency and the United Rocket and Space Corporation combined in 2015 into the Russian megacorporation known as Roscosmos.[80] The end of the United States Space Shuttle schedule in 2011 resulted in Russia being the sole launching State that transports astronauts to and from the International Space Station until only very recently.[81] Nonetheless, Russia has not continued to make advancements in its space capabilities the way the Soviet Union once did. Many of its technical assets have deteriorated over time and have not been reinvested in. Despite this, Russia remains a major actor in military space with decades of expertise in space operations. Like the US, Russia acknowledges that the militarization of outer space is a security threat and has reorganized its military forces to account for this progression. The Russian military doctrine approved in 2010 states that 'the securing of supremacy on land, at sea, and in the air and outer space will become decisive factors in achieving objectives'.[82] The legacy of the Soviet Union's ASAT technology has given Russia a substantial advantage in developing kinetic physical counter-space systems. Russia's capabilities also boast non-kinetic systems including directed-energy counter-space weapons, ground-based lasers, electronic attack, and cyber capabilities.[83]

c. *China*

One of the largest players in space technology, alongside the US and Russia, is China. China's national space programme and private commercial space companies have set a rigorous plan for their future role in space relations. Other nations are responding to

[79] Todd Harrison et al, 'Beyond the RD-180' (*Center for Strategic and International Studies*, March 2017) <https://aerospace.csis.org/beyond-rd-180/> accessed 17 February 2020; Matthew Bodner, 'Can SpaceX and Blue Origin best a decades-old Russian rocket engine design' (MIT Technology Review, June 2019) <https://www.technologyreview.com/2019/06/26/134490/spacex-blue-origin-russian-rd180-rocket-engine-design/> accessed 12 April 2020.

[80] Brian Garino/Jane Gibson, 'Space System Threats' in Air Command and Staff College (ed), *AU-18: Space Primer* (2nd edn, Air UP 2009).

[81] The US has only recently begun to regain the capability of transporting astronauts to and from the International Space Station through commercial space companies such as SpaceX and Boeing; Mike 'NASA Astronauts Launch from America in Historic Test Flight of SpaceX Crew Dragon' (NASA Press Release 20-057, 31 May 2020) <https://www.nasa.gov/press-release/nasa-astronauts-launch-from-america-in-historic-test-flight-of-spacex-crew-dragon> accessed 1 November 2020; Todd Harrison/Nahmyo Thomas, 'NASA in the Second Space Age: Exploration, Partnering, and Security' (Winter 2016) 10 Strategic Studies Quarterly 3.

[82] President of the Russian Federation, '2010 Military Doctrine of the Russian Federation' (5 February 2010) <https://carnegieendowment.org/files/2010russia_military_doctrine.pdf> accessed 20 February 2020.

[83] Todd Harrison et al, 'Space Threat Assessment 2018' (*Center for Strategic and International Studies*, April 2018) <https://aerospace.csis.org/wp-content/uploads/2018/04/Harrison_SpaceThreatAssessment_FULL_WEB.pdf> accessed 30 August 2018.

this impending threat and are collaborating on developing their commercial and military capabilities in outer space in response to China's dominance in the field.

China's technical capability in space mirrors its surge in global influence over the last thirty years. China launched its first satellite in 1970 and since then has become a major space power.[84] The country has successfully crewed space flights, two space stations, lunar orbiters and has a programme to put Chinese 'taikonauts' on the Moon in the next fifteen years.[85] In 2016, China set a national record of twenty-two launches and completed 2017 with eighteen launches.[86] China had the second highest budget dedicated to its space industry in 2018 behind the United States.[87] To improve its space capabilities and compete with the US' progression in the space industry, China is focusing on rapid development and launch of intelligence, surveillance, and reconnaissance satellites, as well as positioning, navigation, and timing satellites.[88] This will decrease its reliance on the US GPS constellation for both commercial and military applications.

In 2015, China published its first Defence White Paper on Military Strategy, which emphasized the strategic competition amongst all parties in outer space.[89] Highlighting the importance of military dominance in outer space, the People's Liberation Army has created the Strategic Support Force dedicated to space and cyberspace.[90] This strategy and the practical reality it represents contrasts with the White Paper's underlying intention to advocate for the peaceful uses of outer space, the opposition of weaponization, and the country taking an active role in encouraging international space cooperation.[91] China is rapidly making advances in its anti-satellite systems and progressing with its counter-space programme.[92] The first ASAT (anti-satellite) weapons test conducted by China occurred in 2005 and has had significant advancement over the last decade. Infamously, in 2007 China carried out a successful ASAT test, destroying its own redundant weather satellite, proving it can target and destroy space systems in low Earth orbit.

[84] Louis de Gouyon Matignon, 'Dong Fang Hong I, The First Chinese Satellite' (*Space Legal Issues*, 20 March 2019) <https://www.spacelegalissues.com/space-law-dong-fang-hong-i-the-first-chinese-satellite/> accessed 10 October 2019.

[85] Andrew Jones, 'Launch of First Chinese Space Station Module Delayed to 2020' (*GB Times*, 5 March 2018) <https://gbtimes.com/launch-of-first-chinese-space-station-module-delayed-to-2020?cat=chinas-space-program> accessed 30 August 2018.

[86] This was the third highest number of launches for a country's space programme, after the US (29) and Russia (20).

[87] Simon Seminari, 'Global Government Space Budgets Continues Multiyear Rebound' (*Space News*, 24 November 2019) <https://spacenews.com/op-ed-global-government-space-budgets-continues-multiyear-rebound/> accessed 12 April 2020.

[88] Todd Harrison et al, 'Space Threat 2018: China Assessment' (*Aerospace*, 12 April 2018) <https://aerospace.csis.org/space-threat-2018-china/> accessed 30 August 2018.

[89] The State Council Information Office of the People's Republic of China, 'China's Military Strategy' (May 2015) <http://english.www.gov.cn/archive/white_paper/2015/05/27/content_281475115610833.htm> accessed 17 February 2020.

[90] Bill Gertz, 'Chinese Military Revamps Cyber Warfare, Intelligence Forces' (*The Washington Free Beacon*, 27 January 2016) <https://freebeacon.com/national-security/chinese-military-revamps-cyber-warfare-intelligence-forces/> accessed 30 August 2018.

[91] China's Military Strategy (n 89) part IV.

[92] Vasani (n 55).

This test contributed to the dangerous debris that the Draft CoC and the Space Debris Mitigation Guidelines[93] are concerned with.

d. *North Korea*

While North Korea lags far behind the spacefaring leaders, its space and counter-space capabilities are progressing as a result of technological transfers from other countries and the country's ballistic missile program.[94] Despite a comparative lack of resources, it still poses a threat in the realm of non-kinetic forms of attack, such as cyber-attacks, jamming, and spoofing.[95] In 2018, reports claimed that North Korea has the intention of launching an advanced reconnaissance satellite with a high-resolution scanning capability that would allow it to transmit information down to the ground for the first time.[96] North Korea's unstable and unknown military capabilities in space elicit a reaction on the international stage that contributes to the brewing international space race.

The culture of increasing each country's space capabilities for the purpose of national security directly contributes to both the militarization and weaponization of outer space. The need for regulation of this trend is paramount to ensuring global security and thereby no future risk of an armed conflict in outer space.

D. Conclusion—Perspectives on the Way Forward

This discussion highlights that the international regulation of the military uses of outer space warrants very careful and rigorous consideration. Other technological areas that equally pose a threat to global security due to an even greater lack of regulation are the advancements in cyberspace and artificial intelligence. Similar to outer space, these evolving sectors also share the nexus between new technologies and their effect on warfare in the twenty-first century.

Unfortunately with regard to outer space, legal conversations increasingly assert that there is a growing trend that outer space will not only be used to facilitate armed conflict (as it already is), but might ultimately be a theatre of war, despite the efforts of the

[93] 'Space Debris Mitigation Guidelines' (n 25).

[94] Gordon G Chang, 'Did North Korea just Launch a Chinese Missile?' (*The National Interest*, 15 February 2017) <http://nationalinterest.org/feature/did-north-korea-just-launch-chinese-missile-19459> accessed 30 August 2018; Krishnadev Calamur, 'How Did North Korea's Missile and Nuclear Tech Get So Good So Fast?' (*The Atlantic*, 6 September 2017) <https://www.theatlantic.com/international/archive/2017/09/north-korea-tech/538959/> accessed 30 August 2018.

[95] Harrison et al (n 83).

[96] Asia Times, 'North Korea's Possible Satellite Launch Can Only Mean One Thing' (*The National Interest*, 8 January 2018) <https://nationalinterest.org/blog/the-buzz/north-koreas-possible-satellite-launch-can-only-mean-one-23979> accessed 30 August 2018.

international community.[97] The proliferation of military space assets means that, from a security standpoint, the disabling or destruction of satellites used by another country may be perceived as giving rise to very significant advantages. The issue of the military uses of outer space, and its possible weaponization, represents one of the most politicized and complex issues of our generation.[98]

It is incumbent on all stakeholders to find a path forward, in order to meet the challenges of the twenty-first century. The existing international regulatory framework, while important, cannot alone stand up to the strains and unknowns that military-related space technology imposes upon us. The framework that was created when humankind first went to outer space is no longer able to keep up with the scientific and military technological developments that exist in the twenty-first century. The current legal framework was born in the political climate of the Cold War, which, at the time, only had a few States with space capabilities.

The twenty-first century has not only brought about new spacefaring, but now companies and individuals have the capacity to utilize space technologies without the confines of a regulated industry. It is imperative that an appropriate and acceptable regulatory regime is established: however, the form and adherence this might take is still unclear. Over time, this regulation may manifest itself through more mandatory soft-law agreements between States. The long-term development of customary international law in relation to space-specific principles however, would create more binding obligations and decrease the current threat that space assets pose to global security. In the short term, States are taking it upon themselves to create national laws that regulate State space technologies. These are however mostly focused upon commercial development as opposed to military uses of outer space. Ultimately, in order to effectively implement laws that govern outer space, this regulation would need to be executed by States themselves to create an international standard on the regulation of outer space. Until this occurs, we must remain conscious of, and continue to hold onto, the fundamental sentiment of 'humanity' that underpins space law in order to avoid inconceivable scenarios.

[97] eg UNGA Res 69/32 (2 December 2014) para 5 which: '[e]ncourages all States, especially spacefaring nations, to consider the possibility of upholding as appropriate a political commitment not to be the first to place weapons in outer space'.

[98] Currently, leading space law experts are endeavouring to navigate this complex field to create international standards for States to follow when operating within the realm of international space law. eg Manual on International Law Applicable to Military Uses of Outer Space (MILAMOS) Project (McGill Centre for Research in Air and Space Law) <https://www.mcgill.ca/milamos/> accessed 10 October 2019; the Woomera Manual on the International Law of Military Space Operations Project (The University of Adelaide) <https://law.adelaide.edu.au/woomera/> accessed 10 October 2019.

PART III

SECURITY GOVERNANCE TOOLS

CHAPTER 38

NATIONAL SECURITY, SURVEILLANCE, AND HUMAN RIGHTS

THÉODORE CHRISTAKIS AND KATIA BOUSLIMANI

A. Setting the Scene: A National Security/Surveillance Psychosis in the Post 9/11 World?

THE Snowden leaks regarding the existence of mass electronic surveillance programmes operated for 'national security' purposes by the US and other States, revealed the impressive extent of bulk-data collection in our 'digital' world. According to the leaked information, governmental agencies such as the US National Security Agency or Britain's Government Communications Headquarters, allegedly monitored millions of individuals and a variety of targets in more than 60 countries.[1]

Programmes such as 'Prism' or 'Tempora' were, however, just the tip of the 'National Security Iceberg': in the post-9/11 world, we have witnessed a kind of psychosis concerning security policies. And the US is not the only democracy running a strong surveillance programme. Such programmes have also been used in, amongst others, France, Germany, and Britain, the latter having been described as 'one of the most heavily surveilled countries in the world'.[2] Governments often brag about how many terrorist attacks they were able to counter through their surveillance arsenal.

[1] eg James Glanz/Andrew W Lehren, 'NSA Spied on Allies, Aid Groups and Businesses' (*The New York Times*, 20 December 2013) <https://www.nytimes.com/2013/12/21/world/nsa-dragnet-included-allies-aid-groups-and-business-elite.html> accessed 20 May 2020; Glenn Greenwald, *No Place to Hide* (Penguin 2014) 90ff.

[2] Neil Richards, 'The Dangers of Surveillance' (2013) 126 Harvard Law Review 1938.

It must be emphasized from the beginning that it is perfectly legitimate and even essential for any legal regime to allow for security exceptions and considerations. Law, including human rights law, cannot regulate every single situation in detail. Both the domestic and international legal orders thus include 'safety valves' which allow States to evade the application of a rule in a particular case, or to mitigate its effects, in order to safeguard their own legitimate interests. Consequently, exceptions, reservations, derogations, restrictions, and other similar mechanisms are both necessary and beneficial: they encourage States to accept international obligations and thereby to contribute to the universality of international law, while tempering the excesses of law and allowing the legal system to 'breathe'. National security is one of the most important legitimate aims used to protect the State and should be given pre-eminence. The right of any State to protect its essential security interests, especially in times of crisis, by employing otherwise unavailable means is a 'bedrock feature of the international legal system'.[3] The possibility to adopt restrictive measures in case of threats to national security (such as the fight against terrorism) is thus an essential component of the legal system and one of those 'adjustment variables' that allow international human rights law (IHRL) to accommodate and ascertain its social functions.

The abuse of these mechanisms, however, is also a major threat to the legal order, judicial security, and the rule of law. History has revealed that national security is a concept with significant potential for abuse. Indeed, domestic rulers and security agencies have often used 'national security' as a pretext to violate human rights and fundamental freedoms; to monitor political opponents; to conceal embarrassing or illegal behaviour; to bypass investigation by independent and democratic bodies; or to suppress political and social unrest. Extraordinary circumstances, such as those following a terrorist attack, may be used to obtain massive public support in order to limit the application of legal frameworks for the protection of human rights and, therefore, to enable governments to use far-reaching measures legally unavailable in normal circumstances. To convince their population to accept restrictions on human rights, States not only brag about the efficiency of surveillance measures, but also use the 'nothing to hide' argument. Even if the intentions of governments within democratic States are honest, the possibility that they may overreact is ever-present.[4] This can undermine democratic governance and threaten the effectiveness of international human rights treaties. In France, Christian Estrosi, mayor of Nice, claimed recently that the massive deployment of facial recognition surveillance is an 'unavoidable means' to fight 'all types of barbarism'.[5]

[3] Hans L Schloemann/Stefan Ohlhoff, 'Constitutionalization and Dispute Settlement in the WTO: National Security as an Issue of Competence' (1999) 93 AJIL 426.

[4] A study of the history of US responses to situations that threaten national security concludes that Americans 'have a long history of *overreacting* to the perceived dangers [...]. Time after time, we have allowed our fears to get the better of us. Having discovered this tendency, we need to guard against such overreactions in the future.' Geoffrey R Stone, 'Free Speech and National Security' (2009) 84 Indiana Law Journal 955.

[5] Christian Estrosi, 'Interview' (*FranceTVInfo.fr*, 12 November 2019) <https://www.francetvinfo.fr/replay-radio/8h30-fauvelle-dely/laicite-reconnaissance-faciale-dans-les-lycees-affaire-polanski-le-8h30-franceinfo-de-christian-estrosi_35.html> accessed 26 April 2020.

In a democracy, surveillance must be balanced with public liberties, and especially with privacy. In this context, privacy corresponds to the classical definition proposed by Samuel Warren and Louis Brandeis: 'the right to be left alone'.[6] Surveillance is an intrusion on the intimacy of people, which became more and more sophisticated with the technological evolutions; from protecting people's houses from unwarranted searches, privacy today has evolved to also regulate the use of CCTV, facial and voice recognition, collection of personal data, etc. A lot of public liberties other than the right to privacy may also be affected by surveillance. Recently, in a report on facial recognition, the EU Fundamental Rights Agency stressed that 'people may feel uncomfortable going to public places under surveillance', affirming that if surveillance has a wide scope, it can affect people's 'capacity to live a dignified life'.[7] Widespread surveillance can also violate people's ability to exercise their democratic rights, such as freedom of expression and freedom to protest. The recent Chinese surveillance activities during the Hong Kong protests, where protesters were obligated to counter facial recognition surveillance using masks and other means in order to be able to exercise their political rights, is a reminder of such issues. The effect of surveillance on political rights does not happen exclusively in undemocratic States. Many privacy advocates address the 'chilling effect on [people's] rights to assemble and to free speech, because people may not want to exercise these rights if it means they will end up on a watchlist'.[8]

The Snowden revelations have raised public awareness about the potential abuses in cyber-surveillance. They have shown the limits of the 'trust us to protect you' argument often used by governments and have sparked a global debate about protection of privacy and the need for enhanced transparency and oversight of intelligence activities. They have also led to several policy changes and legal reforms and an improvement on the overall control and oversight of surveillance in democratic States. For example, the United States introduced the USA Freedom Act, which provided for more checks and balances in the government's domestic surveillance activities. From this point of view the impact of the Snowden revelations cannot be neglected.

On the other hand, the intrusive government surveillance programmes around the world not only remain largely intact but are also supported by new legal frameworks. Indeed, governments worldwide have enacted new intelligence and surveillance laws providing adequate legal cover to cyber-surveillance activities. As *The Guardian*, which published the initial Snowden revelations, stated, 'the principal change on the agenda is

[6] Samuel D Warren/Louis D Brandeis, 'The Right to Privacy' (1890) 4 Harvard Law Review 193.

[7] European Union Agency for Fundamental Rights (FRA), 'Facial Recognition Technology: Fundamental Rights Considerations in the Context of Law Enforcement' (FRA Focus, 2019) 20 <https://fra.europa.eu/sites/default/files/fra_uploads/fra-2019-facial-recognition-technology-focus-paper-1_en.pdf> accessed 20 May 2020.

[8] Stephanie Hare, 'Facial Recognition is Now Rampant: The Implications for our Freedom are Chilling' (*The Guardian*, 18 August 2019) <https://www.theguardian.com/commentisfree/2019/aug/18/facial-recognition-is-now-rampant-implications-for-our-freedom-are-chilling> accessed 20 May 2020.

granting the intelligence agencies formal licence to continue doing what they were caught doing'.[9]

It is of course far beyond the scope of this chapter to examine in detail the content of each national surveillance law enacted after the 9/11 terrorist attacks and its compatibility with IHRL. We will focus instead here on the situation in Europe and, more precisely, on the case law of the European Court of Human Rights (ECtHR). This focus on the ECtHR is justified by the fact that the Court was the only one at the international level that has had the opportunity to analyse on numerous occasions relevant domestic laws and to proceed to a balancing of interests in such detail.

We will start with an overview of the case law of the ECtHR in this field (Section B); we will continue with a successive presentation of the three main criteria used by the Court to assess the compatibility of surveillance laws with the European Convention of Human Rights (ECHR) (Section C); and we will end with some thoughts on the way forward (Section D).

B. The European Court of Human Rights and Domestic Surveillance Laws: An Overview

Since its first judgment concerning surveillance laws, in the 1978 *Klass v Germany*[10] case, the ECtHR has developed a solid case law about secret surveillance. This case law now seems to be at a crossroads.

The ECtHR's consistent position has been that surveillance measures can be essential in the fight against terrorism. In the 2016 *Szabó and Vissy v Hungary* judgment, for instance, the Court emphasized that 'it is a natural consequence of the forms taken by present-day terrorism that governments resort to cutting-edge technologies in pre-empting such attacks, including the massive monitoring of communications susceptible to containing indications of impending incidents'.[11] On the other hand, it has also constantly emphasized that 'a system of secret surveillance designed to protect national security entails a risk of undermining or even destroying democracy on the ground of defending it'.[12] The big issue at stake, at the moment of drafting this chapter, is how far the ECtHR is ready to go in the direction of controlling bulk surveillance activities and how robust its scrutiny of such laws could be.

[9] Edward Snowden, 'Opinion: The Guardian View on Surveillance after Snowden: An Outlaw Rewrites the Law' (*The Guardian*, 1 June 2015) <https://www.theguardian.com/commentisfree/2015/jun/01/guardian-view-on-surveillance-after-edward-snowden-outlaw-rewrites-law> accessed 20 May 2020.

[10] *Klass and Others v Germany*, App No 5029/71, 6 September 1978.

[11] *Szabó and Vissy v Hungary*, App No 37138/14, 12 January 2016, para 68.

[12] *Rotaru v Romania*, App No 28341/95, 4 May 2000, para 59.

Since 2001, the Court has found that the surveillance laws of several countries (including Hungary,[13] Russia,[14] Romania,[15] Bulgaria,[16] Moldova,[17] and Turkey[18]) did not meet ECHR requirements. In its important 2016 *Szabó* judgment[19] the Court went even further, considering that the margin of appreciation of States in deploying massive surveillance techniques is limited by a 'strict necessity' test. However, two more recent judgments, rendered in 2018 in the *Centrum för Rättvisa*[20] and *Big Brother Watch*[21] cases, caused some doubt in this regard. In these two cases the Court seemed to abandon the 'strict necessity' test and endorsed the policy of bulk surveillance as a 'valuable means' to protect national security.

These two decisions have been challenged by the applicants and are now pending before the ECtHR Grand Chamber. The Grand Chamber held hearings in these two cases in July 2019,[22] with the judgments being expected in 2020. These will be particularly important in understanding the direction of the future case law of the Court on surveillance. At the same time several other important applications are pending in the ECtHR, including that against the Austrian Police Powers Act,[23] one challenging the UK Intelligence Services Act,[24] and fourteen applications[25] challenging the new French Intelligences Laws passed in July 2015 after the Paris terrorist attacks.[26]

[13] *Szabó* (n 11).

[14] *Shimovolos v Russia*, App No 30194/09, 21 June 2011; *Roman Zakharov v Russia*, App No 47143/06, 4 December 2015.

[15] *Rotaru* (n 12); *Dumitru Popescu v Romania*, App No 71525/01, 26 April 2007; *Haralambie v Romania*, App No 21737/03, 27 October 2009; *Association '21 December 1989' and Others v Romania*, App Nos 33810/07 and 18817/08, 24 May 2011.

[16] *Association for European Integration and Human Rights v Bulgaria*, App No 62540/00, 28 June 2007.

[17] *Iordachi and Others v Moldova*, App No 25198/02, 10 February 2009.

[18] *Cemalettin Canli v Turkey*, App No 22427/04, 18 November 2008; *Mustafa Sezgin Tanrikulu v Turkey*, App No 27473/06, 18 July 2017.

[19] *Szabó* (n 11) paras 57–67.

[20] *Centrum för Rättvisa v Sweden*, App No 35252/08, 19 June 2018, para 112.

[21] *Big Brother Watch and Others v UK*, App No 58170/13, 62322/14 and 24960/15, 13 September 2018, para 385.

[22] Grand Chamber Hearings, *Centrum för Rättvisa v Sweden* (n 20) <https://www.echr.coe.int/Pages/home.aspx?p=hearings&w=08_019&language=en&c=&py=2019> ('*Centrum för Rättvisa* hearings'); Grand Chamber Hearings, *Big Brother Watch* (n 21) <https://www.echr.coe.int/Pages/home.aspx?p=hearings&w=13_019&language=en&c=&py=2019> ('*Big Brother Watch* hearings').

[23] *Tretter and Others v Austria*, 6 May 2013, App No 2599/10 (Communicated Case); *Ringler v Austria*, App No 2309/10, 6 May 2013 (Communicated Case).

[24] *Privacy International and Others v UK*, App No 46259/16, 19 November 2018 (Communicated Case).

[25] *Association confraternelle de la presse judiciaire v France* and 11 other cases, App Nos 49526/15, 49615/15, 49616/15, 49617/15, 49618/15, 49619/15, 49620/15, 49621/15, 55058/15, 55061/15, 59602/15 and 59621/15, 26 April 2017 (Communicated Case); *Follorou v France* and 1 other case, App Nos 30635/17 and 30636/17, 4 July 2017, (Communicated Case).

[26] In the aftermath of the first terrorist attacks in Paris, in particular the *Charlie Hebdo* shooting of January 2015, the French Government introduced to the Parliament new laws granting additional powers to the French intelligence services, regarding the interception of communications and data. The first new Intelligence law, concerning domestic communications, was adopted in July 2015 and was followed in November 2015 by another law concerning the international dimension of surveillance activities. The

Such surveillance laws raise several issues in relation to the rights guaranteed by the ECHR. Setting aside other rights that might be affected, like freedom of expression or the right to a fair trial, we will focus here on the right to privacy as guaranteed by Article 8 ECHR.

The ECtHR has adopted a very flexible approach on legal standing allowing a great variety of persons to challenge the different surveillance laws. The Court has held that an applicant can claim to be the victim of a violation of the Convention if they fall within the scope of the legislation permitting secret surveillance measures either because they belong to a group of persons targeted by the legislation or because the legislation directly affects everyone and they are potentially at risk of being subjected to such measures.[27]

C. Criteria Used to Assess the Compatibility of Surveillance Laws with the ECHR

The Court has little difficulty in finding that surveillance laws interfere with the right to privacy contained in Article 8(1). Secret surveillance of an individual can then only be justified under Article 8(2) if the following three criteria are cumulatively met:

- Surveillance must pursue one or more of the 'legitimate aims' to which Article 8(2) refers;
- Surveillance must be 'necessary in a democratic society' in order to achieve such legitimate aims—which means that a necessity and proportionality test is essential;
- Surveillance must be 'in accordance with the law'—which means that it must be provided for by domestic law meeting certain quality requirements.

As such, it is necessary to examine how the ECtHR interprets these three criteria.

two laws modified the French Code of Internal Security and were implemented by a series of administrative decrees adopted after the second Paris attacks of 13 November 2015 which also led the French Government to declare a State of emergency and request a derogation under the European Convention of Human Rights ETS No 5 (ECHR) art 15 and the International Covenant on Civil and Political Rights UNTS 999 UNTS 171 (ICCPR) art 4. For an analysis of these laws under the prism of the requirements of the ECHR, see Theodore Christakis, 'National Security, Terrorism and The Legality of Secret Surveillance: The Case of France' in Maura Conway et al (eds), *Terrorists' Use of the Internet: Assessment and Response* (NATO ARW, IOS Press 2017) 327–37.

[27] In general, the Court accepts to analyse an interference caused by the law as such (and not just its application) when there is no effective remedy available at the domestic level. See eg *Zakharov* (n 14) paras 170–2; *Szabó* (n 11) paras 32–9.

1. Legitimate Aims that Justify Secret Surveillance

This is the easiest requirement to meet for any surveillance law. Indeed, it has never happened and, as explained below, it might never happen that a surveillance law has been struck down for failure to meet this requirement.

Surveillance activities can be undertaken in pursuance of either the legitimate aims of 'public safety' and 'the prevention of disorder or crime' or for 'national security' reasons. Depending on the situation, surveillance can be targeted (eg, wiretapping of an accused in a drug trafficking case); or untargeted, as may be the case during the first steps of counter-terrorism operations where intelligence agencies use techniques of massive acquisition and examination of a large volume of communications to detect potential threats. While this distinction might be relevant to the two other criteria for assessing the admissibility of restrictions to Article 8, it makes no difference when it comes to the 'legitimate aim' criterion.

An interesting issue concerns cases where a domestic surveillance statute provides for legitimate aims other than those mentioned in Article 8(2). The 2015 French surveillance law is a good example. This law identifies in Article 2 the seven legitimate 'aims to protect' justifying extrajudicial surveillance:

1. National independence, territorial integrity, and national defence;
2. Major interests in foreign policy, enforcement of European and international commitments of France, and prevention of all forms of foreign interference;
3. Major economic industrial and scientific interests of France;
4. Prevention of terrorism;
5. Prevention of harm to the republican form of institutions; prevention of collective violence likely to cause serious harm to the public order; and actions against the maintenance or reconstitution of dissolved groups;
6. Prevention of organized crime;
7. Fight against the proliferation of weapons of mass destruction.

As stated above, normally, only those aims listed under Article 8(2) of the ECHR can be invoked to justify restrictions to the right to privacy. Arguably the French law goes beyond these legitimate aims by including additional categories such as 'enforcement of European and international commitments of France' or 'major economic industrial and scientific interests'. For this reason, those opposing the 2015 French law have argued that it is too vague and exceeds the objective of the fight against terrorism.[28]

[28] eg Amnesty International, France, 'New Surveillance Law a Major Blow to Human Rights' (24 July 2015) <https://www.amnesty.org/en/press-releases/2015/07/france-new-surveillance-law-a-major-blow-to-human-rights-2/> accessed 20 May 2020.

On the other hand, Article 8(2), and especially the undefined and open-ended concept of 'national security',[29] is broad enough to authorize an extensive interpretation of the legitimate aims to protect. Indeed, the ECtHR case law confirms this, as States have almost always managed to convince the Court that they were acting in support of a proper legitimate purpose. It would thus be hard to conceive how the French law could be struck down by the Court on this basis.

2. The Battle over 'Strict Necessity' and Proportionality

Contrary to the previous requirement (the existence of 'legitimate aims'), the requirement that surveillance must be 'necessary in a democratic society' in order to achieve such legitimate aims is absolutely central to any evaluation of the compatibility of a specific surveillance regime with Article 8 of the ECHR. What is at stake here is how the control of necessity and proportionality of the surveillance measures will be operated and what should be, in this field, the State's margin of appreciation. As the Court stated in *S and Marper*, 'the breadth of this margin varies and depends on a number of factors, including the nature of the Convention right in issue, its importance for the individual, the nature of the interference and the object pursued by the interference'.[30] Hence, the ECtHR adopts a case-by-case assessment, considering the tension between two opposite interests: on the one hand, the importance of the legitimate aim served by a specific restrictive measure, and on the other hand the importance of the interference and the specific right affected by such restrictive measure.

It is crucial to understand how the Court performs this delicate act of balancing between the importance of the interference and the importance of the legitimate aim pursued. The following analysis will show why, at the time of the drafting of this chapter (December 2019), we are at a real crossroads in this respect and why the Grand Chamber's judgments in *Centrum för Rättvisa* and *Big Brother Watch* are eagerly expected.

For years the ECtHR had given the impression of recognizing a considerable margin of appreciation in favour of States adopting surveillance measures. This seemed to change in 2016,[31] due to several factors, including the more robust necessity and proportionality test proposed by some other European bodies and the impressive technological developments since the *Klass and Others* case. Such developments have given States cutting-edge surveillance techniques to invade citizens' privacy and undertake mass surveillance and bulk collection of data in a scale unimaginable a few years ago.

[29] This concept has never been defined by the ECtHR, which nonetheless hinted in some cases that care must be 'taken not to stretch the concept of "national security" beyond its natural meaning'. See *Association for European Integration* (n 16) para 84.

[30] *S and Marper v UK*, App Nos 30562/05 and 30566/04, 4 December 2008, para 102.

[31] For a detailed analysis of this change, see François Dubuisson, 'La Cour européenne des droits de l'homme et la surveillance de masse' (2016) 108 Revue Trimestrielle des Droits de l'Homme 855.

For the Court of Justice of the European Union (CJEU), the indiscriminate and very general nature of the bulk collection and processing of personal data, even if for the purpose of protecting people against serious crimes, entails significant risks for human rights and freedoms and requires that 'derogations and limitations in relation to the protection of personal data must apply only in so far as is strictly necessary'.[32]

In the 2015 *Schrems* decision that invalidated *Safe Harbor*, the CJEU clearly stated that 'legislation permitting the public authorities to have access on a generalised basis to the content of electronic communications must be regarded as compromising the essence of the fundamental right to respect for private life, as guaranteed by Article 7 of the Charter'.[33]

Similarly, the 'Article 29 Working Party', which used to bring together the European Data Protection Authorities (and which has become, since the entry into force of the General Data Protection Regulation (GDPR), the 'European Data Protection Board' or EDPB), published in December 2017 its first review report on Privacy Shield where it 'recalled its long-standing position that massive and indiscriminate surveillance of individuals can never be considered as proportionate and strictly necessary in a democratic society, as is required under the protection offered by the applicable fundamental rights'.[34]

In 2016, the ECtHR gave the impression of following a similar path. In *Szabó* it condemned Hungary for its legislation on secret anti-terrorist surveillance and noted that 'both the Court of Justice of the European Union and the United Nations Special Rapporteur require secret surveillance measures to answer to strict necessity—*an approach it considers convenient to endorse*'.[35]

An analysis of the *Szabó* judgment seems to indicate that this 'strict necessity' and proportionality control includes several steps. The Court noted that in order for a State to adopt a specific surveillance measure, it must be shown that such a measure 'is strictly necessary, as a general consideration, for the safeguarding of the democratic institutions and, moreover, if it is strictly necessary, as a particular consideration, for the obtaining of vital intelligence in an individual operation'.[36] In the Court's view, 'any measure of secret surveillance which does not correspond to these criteria will be prone to abuse by the authorities with formidable technologies at their disposal'.[37] If this strict necessity requirement is met, the Court should then weight the consequences of such surveillance measures, which affect 'the most intimate aspects of citizens' lives' and 'may result in particularly invasive interferences with private life'.[38] This 'threat to privacy must be subjected to very close scrutiny'[39] and would also require, logically, an examination of whether less intrusive means might be used in order to achieve the same legitimate aim.[40]

[32] C-293/12 *Digital Rights v Ireland* [2014] ECLI:EU:C:2014:238, para 52.

[33] C-362/14 *Maximilian Schrems* [2015] ECLI:EU:C:2015:650, para 94.

[34] Article 29 Data Protection Working Party, 'Opinion 01/2016 on the EU–US Privacy Shield Adequacy Decision' (13 April 2016) Doc 16/EN/WP/238, 4.

[35] *Szabó* (n 11) para 73 (emphasis added).

[36] ibid para 73.

[37] ibid.

[38] ibid para 70.

[39] ibid.

[40] Dubuisson (n 31) 882.

It is against this background that two different Chambers of the Court examined, in 2018, the compatibility with Article 8 of the Swedish legislation permitting the bulk interception of electronic signals in Sweden for foreign intelligence purposes (*Centrum för Rättvisa* case[41]) and the *Big Brother Watch and others*[42] applications, lodged by journalists, individuals, and rights organizations after the Snowden revelations about programmes of surveillance and intelligence-sharing between the USA and the United Kingdom.

In the first case, the Court found that there was no violation of Article 8. In the *Big Brother Watch and others* cases, the Court condemned the United Kingdom for its mass surveillance programme. This was, however, a 'pyrrhic victory' for the NGOs involved,[43] as what the Court condemned were mainly certain techniques used by the British intelligence agency, including the fact that, in some respects, the United Kingdom did not match its monitoring system with sufficient safeguards and adequate oversight mechanisms. In reality, in both these cases the Court abandoned the 'strict necessity' test and recognized a very wide margin of appreciation in favour of the State adopting surveillance measures. This contrasted with both the position of the CJEU and the EDPB but also its own jurisprudence in *Szabó*. Far from considering that bulk surveillance cases are subjected to a 'strict necessity' test (the term is not even mentioned in the two Chamber judgments) and require a more robust scrutiny, the Court openly accepted the policy of mass surveillance.

Indeed, in *Rättvisa*, the Chamber stated that 'the decision to operate a bulk interception regime in order to identify hitherto unknown threats to national security is one which continues to fall within States' margin of appreciation.'[44] In *Big Brother Watch*, the Court went even further by saying that: 'It is clear that bulk interception is *a valuable means* to achieve the legitimate aims pursued, particularly given the current threat level from both global terrorism and serious crime.'[45]

The Chamber's conclusion in *Big Brother Watch* has been challenged by the applicants before the Grand Chamber. The Grand Chamber is invited to give more robust scrutiny to the necessity and proportionality of bulk surveillance and to go back to the 'strict necessity' test used by other European bodies and endorsed in *Szabó*.

The applicants have highlighted that 'not everything that is useful to a secret intelligence service is permissible in a democratic society. Just because the State can do something, and it is useful in combating crime or other threats, doesn't mean that it should.'[46] They recall, in this respect, that in *S and Marper* the UK argued that the retention of

[41] *Rättvisa* (n 20). [42] *Big Brother Watch* (n 21).

[43] Theodore Christakis, 'A Fragmentation of EU/ECHR Law on Mass Surveillance: Initial Thoughts' (*European Law Blog*, 20 September 2018) <https://europeanlawblog.eu/2018/09/20/a-fragmentation-of-eu-echr-law-on-mass-surveillance-initial-thoughts-on-the-big-brother-watch-judgment/>.

[44] *Rättvisa* (n 20) para 112. [45] *Big Brother Watch* (n 21) para 386 (emphasis added).

[46] Amnesty International, 'Applicants' Written Observation in Big Brother Watch and others v the United Kingdom' para 82 <https://www.amnesty.org/download/Documents/EURENGLISH.PDF> ('AI, Applicants Written Observation').

DNA samples from people who had not been charged or convicted of a criminal offence was of 'inestimable value' and produced 'enormous' benefits in the fight against crime and terrorism.[47] The Grand Chamber nonetheless held that the retention of such profiles was a 'disproportionate interference' with those individuals' private lives.[48]

It is thus important how the Grand Chamber will deal with these issues. Will the Court go back to *Szabó* and the 'strict necessity' test? Or will the Grand Chamber ignore this test, as did the Chambers in the *Rättvisa* case and *Big Brother Watch*, by recognizing a '*wide* margin of appreciation' in favour of States introducing bulk interception regimes?

3. Thinking about the 'Quality' of Surveillance Laws

A third criterion for assessing the compatibility of restrictions with the requirements of Article 8(2) is that surveillance must be 'in accordance with the law'. This means that it must have some basis in domestic law and that such law must meet certain quality requirements. The Court has explained on several occasions that such law must be 'accessible' to the persons concerned and 'foreseeable as to its effects'.[49] In the context of surveillance it is important to have clear, detailed rules, so as to avoid arbitrary interference. The Court has explained that the law must be sufficiently clear to give citizens an adequate indication as to the circumstances in which, and the conditions on which, public authorities are empowered to resort to any such secret measures.[50]

In the 2006 *Weber and Saravia* case (in which the applicants had challenged the 1994 German surveillance law) the Court tried to explain what 'quality' meant by designing six 'minimum safeguards' (the so-called '*Weber and Saravia* safeguards') 'that should be set out in statute law in order to avoid abuses of power'.[51] Thus, the law must provide *a minima*:

- The nature of the offences which may give rise to an interception order;
- A definition of the categories of people liable to be monitored;
- A limit on the duration of the surveillance measure;
- The procedure to be followed for examining, using, and storing the data obtained;
- The precautions to be taken when communicating the data to other parties;
- The circumstances in which [the data obtained] may or must be erased.

When assessing the quality of law, the Court always analyses meticulously whether those 'minimum safeguards' are present.

Furthermore, in cases where the legislation permitting secret surveillance is itself contested by the applicants (such as in the *Big Brother Watch*), the Court considers that

47 *S and Marper* (n 30) paras 91–4. 48 ibid para 125.

49 eg *Amann v Switzerland*, App No 27798/95, 16 February 2000, para 50; *Rotaru* (n 12) para 52.

50 *Zakharov* (n 14) para 229; *Association for European Integration* (n 16) para 75.

51 *Weber and Saravia v Germany*, App No 54934/00, 29 June 2006, para 95.

the lawfulness of the interference is closely related to the question whether the 'necessity' test has been complied with. As a consequence, the Court took the habit of examining jointly the 'in accordance with the law' and the 'necessity/proportionality' requirements. In other terms, the Court examines not only if the 'minimum safeguards' are set out in the domestic surveillance statute, but also if they are set out and applied in a satisfactory way in order to meet the necessity/proportionality requirements. While this makes sense and permits to avoid repetitions, the authors of this chapter consider that this practice is not necessarily the most appropriate from a methodological point of view. An examination of the *Big Brother Watch* judgment, for instance, shows that the mixing of the two criteria creates some confusion and that the assessment of proportionality has been sometimes neglected in favour of the 'quality of the law' criterion. In other terms, it seems to us that it is useful to distinguish between, on the one hand, the existence/quality of a surveillance statute law and, on the other hand, its applicability in practice and its capacity to achieve a balanced solution between the interests at stake. It might be better if the Court first assesses if the letter of the law meets the necessary accessibility/foreseeability requirements; and then proceeds to the necessity/proportionality test taking into consideration all the elements, including the application of the law in practice.

In the *Big Brother Watch* case, however, the applicants did not challenge the mixture between the 'in accordance with the law' and the 'necessity/proportionality' requirements. Instead, they asked the Court to 'update' and 'enhance' the '*Weber and Saravia* safeguards' in the light of the 'sea change' that had occurred in the technological field since that case.[52]

Other courts, such as the CJEU, have considered, in judgments such as *Digital Rights Ireland* or *Tele2/Watson*, that the severity of interference with private life rendered possible by today's technology, required extensive standards of protection. Similarly, the US Supreme Court, in its landmark 2017 Carpenter decision, extended the protections of the Fourth Amendment to ensure that the prohibition on unreasonable searches and seizures remains effective in the modern world. The ECtHR itself, in the *Szabó* judgment, emphasized that 'the techniques applied in such monitoring operations have demonstrated a remarkable progress in recent years and reached a level of sophistication which is hardly conceivable for the average citizen'.[53]

However, in its *Big Brother Watch* judgment the Chamber rejected the request to 'update' the '*Weber and Saravia* safeguards', saying that:

> while the Court does not doubt the impact of modern technology on the intrusiveness of interception, [...] it would be wrong automatically to assume that bulk interception constitutes a greater intrusion into the private life of an individual than targeted interception, which by its very nature is more likely to result in the acquisition and examination of a large volume of his or her communications.[54]

Of course, the *Big Brother Watch* judgment attempts to strike the right balance between, on the one hand, deferring to national security considerations and endorsing

[52] *Big Brother Watch* (n 21) para 316.
[53] *Szabó* (n 11) para 68.
[54] *Big Brother Watch* (n 21) para 316.

the policy of mass surveillance and, on the other hand, the need to effectively protect human rights, by insisting on a series of conditions and safeguards that States should meet in order to limit the risks of abuse. However, one could note here a certain paradigm shift in the case law of the Court. The endorsement of the policy of mass surveillance seems to lead the Court to 'adjust' the conditions and requirements of its own case law not in the direction wished by the applicants but, instead, towards a more flexible and permissive regime. This could be the case, for instance, in relation to the following matters:

a. *Notification of the Surveillance Target*

In previous judgments, the Court has held that:

> the question of subsequent notification of surveillance measures is inextricably linked to the effectiveness of remedies and hence to the existence of effective safeguards against the abuse of monitoring powers, since there is in principle little scope for any recourse by the individual concerned unless the latter is advised of the measures taken without his or her knowledge and thus able to challenge their justification retrospectively... [hence] as soon as notification can be carried out without jeopardizing the purpose of the restriction after the termination of the surveillance measure, information should be provided to the persons concerned.[55]

The CJEU has also recognized the importance of this safeguard.[56] Even more interestingly, the requirement of notice to the data subject (when possible and if necessary with delay so as not to hinder the effectiveness of a criminal investigation) appears as an important safeguard in the E-Evidence draft regulation (concerning access by law enforcement agents to digital evidence).[57]

In the *Big Brother Watch* judgment, though, the Court says that the very idea of notification is logically incompatible with a mass surveillance system (which, by definition, is not targeted) and must therefore be discarded.[58] This appears a little bit like a short-cut and seems to fail to distinguish between the moment of the initial bulk interception of data and the subsequent storage, processing, and use of information.

b. *Objective Evidence of Reasonable Suspicion in Relation to the Persons about Whom Data is Sought*

According to the Court, the domestic law must define the categories of people liable to be monitored. This condition is linked to the necessity criterion: a secret surveillance

[55] *Szabó* (n 11) para 86.

[56] C-203/15 *Tele2 Sveridge* AB [2016] ECLI:EU:C:2016:970, para 121.

[57] See Theodore Christakis, 'E-Evidence in a Nutshell: Developments in 2018, Relations with the Cloud Act and the Bumpy Road Ahead' (*Crossborder Data Forum*, 14 January 2009) <https://www.crossborderdataforum.org/e-evidence-in-a-nutshell-developments-in-2018-relations-with-the-cld-act-and-the-bumpy-road-ahead/>.

[58] *Big Brother Watch* (n 21) para 317.

measure must be limited, and the definition of the categories of people liable to be monitored is supposed to prevent States from monitoring all its population.

Indeed, to monitor an individual, law enforcement and intelligence agencies shall normally demonstrate that there is a reasonable suspicion on this individual, or on a category of people that this individual is part of. In order to do so, 'it is essential to have clear, detailed rules on the subject, especially as the technology available for use is continually becoming more sophisticated'.[59] For instance, as regards wiretapping, the Court found that the convention was violated because the domestic law did 'not elaborate *on the degree of reasonableness of the suspicion against a person* for the purpose of authorising an interception'.[60] In 2015, in *Zakharov*, the Grand Chamber held that the authorization procedure:

> must be capable of verifying the *existence of a reasonable suspicion against the person concerned*, in particular, whether there are factual indications for suspecting that person of planning, committing or having committed criminal acts or other acts that may give rise to secret surveillance measures, such as, for example, acts endangering national security.[61]

Similarly, in *Szabó* it noted the requirement of '*a sufficient factual basis for the application of secret intelligence gathering measures [...] on the basis of an individual suspicion* regarding the target person' as critical for 'the authorising authority to perform an appropriate proportionality test'.[62] The Court sanctioned the Hungarian surveillance regime, because the lack of definition of the categories of people liable to be monitored meant that the surveillance 'might include [...] any person and be interpreted as paving the way for the unlimited surveillance of a large number of citizens'.[63]

In the *Big Brother Watch* judgment, though, the Court held that 'bulk interception is by definition untargeted, and to require "reasonable suspicion" would render the operation of such a scheme impossible'.[64] This duplicates the argument previously mentioned concerning notice to the subject of surveillance and indicates, once again, that we have, henceforth, at the ECtHR two separate legal regimes: a 'classic' one, for targeted surveillance, where the '*Weber and Saravia* minimum safeguards' plainly apply; and a second one, designed for mass surveillance, where the previous case law on these criteria should be interpreted in a 'flexible', 'logical' and 'realistic' way. Of course, nobody could challenge the Chamber's idea that the requirement of 'reasonable suspicion' makes little sense *prima facie* in relation with bulk surveillance. However, once again, the argument has been criticized as failing to make the distinction between two different stages in the surveillance operation: the stage of the initial interception of data (when, logically, there can be no 'reasonable suspicion' requirement); and the stage of subsequent processing and examination of intercept material where, according to the applicants, selectors could be applied so that masses of irrelevant data of no legitimate interest should be

[59] *Association for European Integration* (n 16) para 75.

[60] *Iordachi* (n 17) para 51 (emphasis added). The Court also specified that '*only very serious reasons based on a reasonable suspicion that the person is involved in serious criminal activity should be taken as a basis for authorising it*'.

[61] *Zakharov* (n 14) para 260 (emphasis added).

[62] *Szabó* (n 11) para 71 (emphasis added).

[63] ibid para 67.

[64] *Big Brother Watch* (n 21) para 317.

deleted and the existence of 'reasonable suspicion' could sometimes be relevant in the processing of data.[65]

c. *No ex-ante Authorization by an Independent Authority for Mass Surveillance Measures?*

The issue of *ex-ante* authorization is another example of the 'more flexible' minimum safeguards recognized by the *Big Brother Watch* Chamber in relation to bulk surveillance.

In previous judgments (eg, *Zakharov*[66] or *Szabó*[67]) the Court held that authorization to conduct surveillance should be given (except in exceptional cases) either by a judge (preferable option) or an administrative authority independent from the executive. This is a procedural requirement intending to avoid abuses and has proved useful in the structuring of intelligence laws in Europe. Moreover, the Court monitors not only the respect of this procedural condition but also whether it is effective: in the case of *Zakharov*, it condemned Russia because, while *ex-ante* judicial review was provided by law, the Court considered that this control did not function effectively and therefore did not prevent the risk of abuse.[68]

It is interesting to note that the procedural requirement of judicial authorization also lies at the heart of both the EU E-Evidence draft regulation (mentioned above), which insists heavily on the requirement that an order for production of transactional and content data 'may be issued *only by* a judge, a court or an investigating judge competent in the case concerned'[69], and the negotiation mandate given to the European Commission by the EU Council to negotiate an EU/US Agreement on access to digital evidence, which requires the issuance of such orders by 'judicial authorities'.[70]

In *Big Brother Watch*, however, the Court neglects this procedural requirement. It states that while in the United Kingdom the authorization to carry out mass surveillance was given neither by a judge nor by an independent administrative authority, there is no problem because some elements show that there is no abuse by the executive.[71]

As one of the authors of this chapter has previously observed:

> For the Court, then, substance prevails over form. But we might lose in terms of legal certainty and predictability: it is one thing to lay down a clear procedural condition that States should respect—and then check of course whether it works effectively as in the *Zakharov* case; and it is another to remove this procedural requirement by saying that 'what is relevant is whether or not there was abuse'. How will the Court evaluate this and according to what criteria? Is there not a risk of a two-speed control? On the one hand there are Eastern European countries (Hungary, Russia, Romania, Croatia, Bulgaria, Moldova, Turkey etc.), whose surveillance laws the Court has found to be in violation of the Convention; and on the other, there are

[65] Amnesty International, Applicants' Written Observation (n 46) para 137.

[66] *Zakharov* (n 14) para 258. [67] *Szabó* (n 11) para 77.

[68] *Zakharov* (n 14) paras 259–302.

[69] Council of the European Union, Regulation of the European Parliament and of the Council on European Production and Preservation Orders for Electronic Evidence in Criminal Matters—General Approach (30 November 2018) Doc 15020/18 art 4(2).

[70] ibid. [71] *Big Brother Watch* (n 21) para 381.

> Western countries (Sweden, United Kingdom, possibly France in the future) who could benefit from a more 'flexible' evaluation because their democratic systems as such would be a pledge against abuse?[72]

d. *Dealing with Intelligence-Sharing*

Big Brother Watch was the first time that the Court has been asked to consider whether an intelligence-sharing regime has complied with the Convention, namely by evaluating the exchange practices between the GCHQ and the National Security Agency (NSA). The Court eventually considered that these practices did not violate the Convention and that the interference with human rights 'was kept to that which was "necessary in a democratic society" '.[73] However, we should notice that the Court is almost exclusively concerned with the question of whether the sharing of information was 'in accordance with the law' of the United Kingdom—and devotes only two very brief paragraphs (paras 445–6) to the crucial question of *proportionality*. This part of the judgment could have been more analytical and the Court could have discussed further the issue of *how* the intelligence-sharing took place in practice, what were the risks, the issue of prior authorization by an independent authority and that of the *effectiveness* of controls, safeguards, and remedies.

D. The Way Forward: From *Big Brother Watch 2* to New High-tech Cases?

This chapter revealed how much the ECtHR struggles with mass surveillance—and how the Court is trying to adapt itself to this evolving issue. The year 2020 will be important in assessing the Court's future direction on these issues. The Chambers' decisions in both *Big Brother Watch* and *Rättvisa* have been challenged in front of the Grand Chamber. The judgments of the Grand Chamber in these two cases will be particularly important and will answer many of the questions discussed in this chapter. Moreover, other important judgments are expected, including those concerning the fourteen applications filed against the new French surveillance laws.[74]

Beyond these cases challenging existing surveillance laws, one could expect that a new generation of cases will progressively arrive at the Court, concerning the use of even more sophisticated technologies for surveillance purposes. While the 'traditional' surveillance cases mainly concerned the interception and analysis of communications

[72] Christakis (n 43). [73] *Big Brother Watch* (n 21) para 446.

[74] *Association confraternelle de la presse judiciaire* (n 25); *Follorou* (n 25). In these cases, the applicants challenge, amongst other things, the proportionality of automated algorithm devices ('black boxes') used by the French authorities in order to analyse the metadata collected on the Internet.

and metadata (using increasingly cutting-edge technologies), this new generation of cases might concern the use, by States, of facial recognition technologies (FRTs) in order to monitor their own population and detect/arrest more easily terrorists and other criminals. The use of FRTs and biometric data, which are particularly sensitive data, raises extremely important new questions concerning the risks for human rights, including the right to privacy, freedom of association, freedom of expression, prohibition of discrimination and other protections. The French Data Protection Authority (CNIL) tried to raise public awareness on these issues in a recent opinion[75] where it highlights the risks stemming from FRTs: the monitoring could occur without the knowledge of the individual; the paradigm of surveillance could shift from targeted surveillance to mass surveillance for the purpose of identifying specific individuals; there are risks of technological biases and failures leading to errors and discrimination and risks of interference with the right to a private life, the right to protest, the freedom of expression and so on. The European Union Agency for Fundamental Rights (FRA) also raised several concerns including in relation to the right to human dignity,[76] the lack of accuracy of current FRTs,[77] the risk of discriminations,[78] and the existence of effective remedies.[79]

These risks are not just theoretical as shown by the deployment of FRTs for surveillance purposes in some States. China is currently using mass facial recognition surveillance on its own population. Besides the monitoring of the Hong Kong protests,[80] facial recognition is also used in the context of daily surveillance, for instance to arrest criminals,[81] to monitor the use of communication devices[82] or in public transportation.[83] The use of facial recognition to identify and profile the Uighurs, a Muslim minority, has also raised serious concerns.[84]

[75] Commission Nationale de l'Informatique et des Libertés (CNIL), *Reconnaissance Faciale. Pour un débat à la hauteur des enjeux* (15 November 2019) 7.

[76] FRA (n 7) 20. [77] ibid 9–10. [78] ibid 27–8. [79] ibid 31–2.

[80] Emma Graham-Harrison, 'Hong Kong: Clashes as First Charges Brought under Face Mask Ban Law' (*The Guardian*, 7 October 2019) <https://www.theguardian.com/world/2019/oct/07/hong-kong-protests-charges-anti-face-mask-laws> accessed 20 May 2020; Paul Mozur/Lin Qiqing, 'Hong Kong Takes Symbolic Stand against China's High-Tech Controls' (*The New York Times*, 3 October 2019) <https://www.nytimes.com/2019/10/03/technology/hong-kong-china-tech-surveillance.html> accessed 20 May 2020.

[81] 'Chinese Man Caught by Facial Recognition at Pop Concert' (*BBC News*, 13 April 2018) <https://www.bbc.com/news/world-asia-china-43751276> Louise Moon, 'China's Facial Recognition Cameras Apprehend Third Fugitive Jacky Cheung Concertgoer in Two Months' (*South China Morning Post*, 22 May 2018) <https://www.scmp.com/news/china/society/article/45/chinas-facial-recognition-cameras-apprehend-third-fugitive-jacky>.

[82] Brenda Goh, 'China's Facial Recognition Rollout Reaches into Mobile Phones, Shops and Homes' (*Reuters*, 2 December 2019) <https://www.reuters.com/article/us-china-technology-explainer/chinas-facial-recognition-rollout-reaches-into-mobile-phones-shops-and-homes-idUSKBN1Y60MN> accessed 20 May 2020.

[83] 'Beijing to Use Facial Recognition Technology in Metro Security Checks—State Media' (*Hong Kong Free Press*, 31 October 2019) <https://www.hongkongfp.com/2019/10/31/beijing-use-facial-recognition-technology-metro-security-checks-state-media/>.

[84] Paul Mozur, 'One Month, 500,000 Face Scans: How China Is Using A.I. to Profile a Minority' (*The New York Times*, 14 April 2019) <https://www.nytimes.com/2019/04/14/technology/china-surveillance-artificial-intelligence-racial-profiling.html> accessed 20 May 2020.

In Europe, the use of FRTs for surveillance purposes is much more moderate: States are experimenting and beginning to enable their law enforcement agencies to use such technologies at selected events or strategic places (such as train stations).[85] There are no pending cases about FRTs at the ECtHR, but some domestic cases are beginning to appear in Europe.

The most emblematic facial recognition case has been examined by the High Court of England and Wales, where police have 'been the most active in experimenting with live facial recognition technologies'.[86] In this case, the South Wales Police used an automated facial recognition device to monitor two events occurring in Cardiff in December 2017 and March 2018. Edward Bridges, a civil liberties campaigner, brought a claim in front of the High Court arguing that he had been submitted without permission to this surveillance on at least two occasions and that this interference into his private life was unlawful.[87] The device used by the police collected facial images of people, and then compared these images to a watchlist.[88] Once the comparison was done, if there was no match with the watchlist, the facial image was immediately deleted from the automated facial recognition system.[89] The High Court applied the ECtHR criteria and concluded that, while there was an interference into the right to a private life, this interference was 'in accordance with the law', and was necessary and proportionate to the legitimate aim of national security.[90] The Court found in particular that 'the fact that a technology is new does not mean it is outside the scope of existing regulation, or that it is always necessary to create a bespoke legal framework for it'.[91] Edward Bridges appealed this ruling,[92] claiming that the use of FRTs in this case constituted 'disproportionate government surveillance'.[93]

This case, or other similar cases, might one day arrive in Strasbourg and it will be interesting to see how the ECtHR will deal with these new technological developments. The European Data Protection Supervisor (EDPS) recently suggested that any assessment on the use of FRTs for surveillance purposes should start with a preliminary question: 'whether—if ever—facial recognition technology can be permitted in a democratic society. If the answer is yes, only then do we turn questions of how and safeguards and accountability to be put in place.'[94] In the United States some cities like San Francisco, Oakland, Somerville, and Berkeley have banned the use of FRTs for surveillance purposes

[85] FRA (n 7) 13. [86] ibid 11.

[87] *Edward Bridges v The Chief Constable of South Wales Police and Secretary of State for the Home Department* [2019] EWHC 2341 paras 8–16.

[88] ibid 7. [89] ibid 16. [90] ibid 47–158. [91] ibid 84.

[92] Nick Dermody, 'Facial Recognition Technology: Ed Bridges Appeals Human Rights Ruling' *BBC News* (21 November 2019) <https://www.bbc.co.uk/news/uk-wales-50495575> accessed 30 November 2020.

[93] Liberty, 'Liberty Fights for Facial Recognition Ban Following Court Ruling' (4 September 2019) <https://www.libertyhumanrights.org.uk/news/press-releases-and-statements/liberty-fights-facial-recognition-ban-following-court-ruling> accessed 20 May 2020.

[94] Wojciech Wiewiórowski, 'Facial Recognition: A Solution in Search of a Problem?' (*EDPS*, 28 October 2019) <https://edps.europa.eu/press-publications/press-news/blog/facial-recognition-solution-search-problem_en> accessed 20 May 2020.

by the police[95] and Portland is discussing an even more far-reaching measure.[96] In Europe, the case law of the ECtHR (and the CJEU, as far as the EU Member States are concerned) could be a very useful starting point in order to assess the compatibility of particularly intrusive new surveillance technologies, such as FRTs, with human rights. The case law of the two courts will unavoidably need to be adjusted to the challenges posed by such new surveillance technologies.

Note

This work has been supported by the Institut Universitaire de France and by the French National Research Agency in the framework of the 'Investissements d'avenir' programme (ANR-15-IDEX-02). The present chapter covers developments till December 2019.

[95] Matthew Guariglia, 'Victory! Berkeley City Council Unanimously Votes to Ban Face Recognition' (*Electronic Frontier Foundation*, 16 October 2019) <https://www.eff.org/fr/deeplinks/2019/10/victory-berkeley-city-council-unanimously-votes-ban-face-recognition> accessed 20 May 2020.

[96] Kristin Lam, 'Portland, the Largest City in Oregon, Plans to Propose First Facial Recognition Ban Affecting Private Companies' (*USA Today*, 3 December 2019) <https://eu.usatoday.com/story/tech/2019/12/03/facial-recognition-portland-oregon-ban/2601966001/> accessed 30 November 2020.

CHAPTER 39

PEACE DIPLOMACY AND CONFLICT PREVENTION

KIMBERLEY N TRAPP AND PRIYA URS

A. Introduction

Boutros Boutros-Ghali's 'Agenda for Peace'[1] was the first comprehensive UN engagement with conflict prevention and peace following the end of the Cold War, and continues to serve as an important starting point for discussion. The UN Secretary-General divided his agenda into preventive diplomacy, peacemaking and peacekeeping. But given the interconnectedness of global challenges, and the changing face of threats to international peace and security and armed conflict, a comprehensive approach calls for blurring the lines between these temporally defined elements of the architecture of peace. In particular disputes, the toolkit deployed in respect of one aspect of maintaining or securing peace may well be relevant or even critical in respect of another. Flexibility and responsiveness to the particular context is essential. While it remains true that international efforts towards peace and security operate on the sequential conflict cycle paradigm suggested by the Secretary-General, stakeholders increasingly seek to 'bridge the divides that…beset this discussion, between security and development, between crisis response and capacity building' in order to 'encompass our new conception of violence in a variety of environments'.[2]

[1] UNGA 'Report of the Secretary-General: An Agenda for Peace—Preventive Diplomacy, Peacemaking, and Peace-Keeping' (17 June 1992) UN Doc A/47/277 (UNSG, Agenda for Peace), followed up by UNGA/UNSC 'Report of the Secretary-General: Prevention of Armed Conflict' (7 June 2001) UN Doc A/55/985-S/2001/574 (UNSG, Prevention of Armed Conflict) and UNGA 'Report of the Secretary-General: Progress Report on Prevention of Armed Conflict' (18 July 2006) UN Doc A/60/891 (UNSG, Progress Report on Prevention of Armed Conflict).

[2] Andrew Tomlinson, 'Putting the Pieces Together: Towards a Unified Approach to Prevention at the United Nations' in Achim Wennmann (ed), '*20 Years of "An Agenda for Peace": A New Vision for Conflict Prevention?*' (2012) Geneva Peacebuilding Platform Paper No 5, 19.

This contribution approaches this vast subject area in keeping with its title—prevention (Section B.1) and peace (Section B.2) as the headlines, with diplomacy as a strategy interwoven throughout. That prevention and peace are addressed in different sections, however, should not be understood as suggesting that they are separate, or separable, endeavours. Indeed, the opposite is true—conflict prevention and post-conflict peacebuilding are two sides of the same coin. Section C outlines new developments and challenges, mapping onto the structure of Section B—but without endorsing a linear conflict cycle approach to the maintenance of international peace and security.

B. Legal Framework

1. Conflict Prevention

In his 'Agenda for Peace', Boutros Boutros-Ghali defines 'conflict prevention' as 'action to prevent disputes from arising between parties, to prevent existing disputes from escalating into conflicts and to limit the spread of the latter when they occur'.[3] This definition—still relevant today—highlights the twin dimensions of conflict prevention: systemic conflict prevention and conflict management.

a. *Systemic Conflict Prevention*

In terms of systemic conflict prevention, the 'Agenda for Peace' definition draws on both a structural approach and a particularized or operational approach. First, systemic conflict prevention should seek to develop the conditions for peaceful coexistence from a structural perspective.[4] These depend on the context and nature of the parties to a dispute (particularly, whether the dispute is between States or between States and non-State actors). For inter-State disputes, the legal standards and frameworks for the peaceful settlement of disputes (including the UN Charter obligation of peaceful settlement,[5] the potential role of the UN Security Council (UNSC),[6] the availability of

[3] UNSG, Agenda for Peace (n 1) 45.

[4] See Carnegie Commission on Preventing Deadly Conflict, 'Preventing Deadly Conflict: Final Report' (Carnegie Corporation of New York, 1997) xix <https://www.carnegie.org/publications/preventing-deadly-conflict-final-report/> accessed 30 November 2020 (Carnegie Commission); ICISS, *The Responsibility to Protect: Report of the International Commission on Intervention and State Sovereignty* (International Development Research Centre 2001) paras 3.7–3.9.

[5] See Charter of the United Nations 1 UNTS XVI (UN Charter) art 2(3) and ch VI. See, further, UNSG, Prevention of Armed Conflict (n 1) para 27.

[6] UN Charter (n 5) arts 34 and 36. Historically, the UNSC has not engaged overly in conflict prevention, instead focusing on addressing conflicts after they emerge, and this imbalance has long been on the UN agenda. See UNSG, Prevention of Armed Conflict (n 1) paras 31–2; UNSC Res 1625 (2005); UNSG, Progress Report on Prevention of Armed Conflict (n 1) para 77–8; UNGA/UNSC 'Report of the High-level Independent Panel on Peace Operations on Uniting our Strengths for Peace: Politics, Partnership and People' (17 June 2015) UN Doc A/70/95-S/2015/446, para 72 (HIPPO Report); UNGA/UNSC 'Report

the International Court of Justice (ICJ),[7] and the Secretary-General's good offices[8]), and the disarmament and arms control regimes[9] are of obvious relevance.

In respect of intra-State and trans-national disputes, systemic prevention focuses on addressing the underlying causes of grievance or the 'deep drivers of conflict in underlying economic, social, or political conditions, and the patterns and precipitants of escalation that can convert grievances into violent encounters'.[10] This dimension of conflict prevention includes promoting respect for human rights, the right to self-determination, the rule of law and good governance; State-building (eg, creating State capacity which adequately provides for human security and development); and fair and equitable resource management and sustainable development strategies.[11] These efforts are multifaceted and spread across a number of international, regional, and local organizations, often without coordination or a coherent and systemic prevention strategy. One response to this fragmented approach has been the International Dialogue on Peacebuilding and Statebuilding, working on implementing the 'New Deal for Engagement in Fragile States' which seeks to 'develop and support one national vision and one plan to transition out of fragility'.[12] While the UN has long emphasized that principal responsibility for systemic conflict prevention lies with territorial States,[13] it also acknowledges the important role it has to play in capacity-building. And there have been some important UN efforts to tackle the fragmented approach to its mandate for

of the Advisory Group of Experts on the Review of the Peacebuilding Architecture: Challenge of Sustaining Peace' (30 June 2015) UN Doc A/69/968–S/2015/490, para 125 (Challenge of Sustaining Peace Report).

[7] See UN Charter (n 5) ch XIV; UNSG, Agenda for Peace (n 1) paras 38–9; UNSG, Prevention of Armed Conflict' (n 1) paras 46–50.

[8] UNSG, Progress Report on Prevention of Armed Conflict (n 1) paras 57–8.

[9] See, generally, UNSG, Agenda for Peace (n 1) para 5; UNSG, Prevention of Armed Conflict (n 1) paras 86–93; UNSG, Progress Report on Prevention of Armed Conflict (n 1) para 19; Stuart Casey-Maslen/Tobias Vestner, *A Guide to International Disarmament Law* (Routledge 2019).

[10] Timothy D Sisk, 'The Agenda for Peace Twenty Years On: Scholarly Perspectives on the United Nations and Intrastate Conflicts' in Wennmann (n 2) 11. See, further, UNSG, Prevention of Armed Conflict (n 1) para 7.

[11] ICISS (n 4) paras 3.21–3.23 address these root causes in terms of political needs and deficiencies, economic deprivation and lack of economic opportunities, and legal protections and institutions. See, further, Carnegie Commission (n 4); UNSG, Prevention of Armed Conflict (n 1) paras 7–11, 94–6; UNSG, Progress Report on Prevention of Armed Conflict (n 1) paras 46, 50; Challenge of Sustaining Peace Report (n 6) para 15; UNGA Res 70/1 'Transforming Our World: The 2030 Agenda for Sustainable Development' (25 September 2015), para 35; UNGA Res 70/262 'Review of the United Nations Peacebuilding Architecture' (27 April 2016), para 16 (Review of the United Nations Peacebuilding Architecture). See, also, UNSG, Progress Report on Prevention of Armed Conflict (n 1) paras 15–30.

[12] International Dialogue on Peacebuilding and Statebuilding, 'The New Deal' (4th High Level Forum on Aid Effectiveness, 30 November 2011) <http://www.pbsbdialogue.org/en/new-deal/about-new-deal/> accessed 16 February 2020. Other international initiatives addressing fragile and conflict-affected States include the International Network on Conflict and Fragility of the OECD Development Assistance Committee (<http://www.oecd.org/dac/conflict-fragility-resilience/conflict-fragility/> accessed 16 February 2020), and the Geneva Peacebuilding Platform (<http://gpplatform.ch/> accessed 16 February 2020).

[13] UNSG, Agenda for Peace (n 1) para 17; UNSG, Prevention of Armed Conflict (n 1) para 6; UNSG, Progress Report on the Prevention of Armed Conflict' (n 1) para 7.

conflict prevention.[14] Nevertheless, as discussed in Section C.1.a, there is a prevailing focus on crisis intervention over systemic prevention, with recent reports calling for the development of more coherent, coordinated, and effective systemic conflict prevention.[15]

Of increasing relevance are efforts to address transnational criminal organizations.[16] These tend to apply a criminal law enforcement paradigm, but also include obligations of States to prevent the conduct they address, and consequently form part of the conflict prevention narrative.[17] Finally, there is increasing recognition of an environmental and climate change dimension to conflict prevention, but still relatively limited engagement between the two processes.[18] Some developments in this respect are discussed in Section C.1.a.

The second feature of systemic conflict prevention involves operational prevention efforts focused on a particularized risk of violence—seeking to prevent the outbreak of violence where efforts to address underlying causes have been unsuccessful. Early warning mechanisms (identifying disputes with potential to erupt into violence) have proliferated—some are UN processes focused on particular kinds of violence (such as atrocity crimes),[19] regions or States,[20] and others are undertaken within regional

[14] See UNDP/UNDPA 'Joint Programme on Building National Capacities for Conflict Prevention—Annual Report 2017' (UNDP, 23 May 2018) <https://www.undp.org/content/undp/en/home/librarypage/democratic-governance/conflict-prevention/joint-undp-dpa-programme-annual-report-2017.html> accessed 16 February 2020. The Joint Programme's expansion, however, is limited by funding uncertainties (Challenge of Sustaining Peace Report (n 6) para 69). The UN Peacebuilding Commission (<https://www.un.org/peacebuilding/> accessed 16 February 2020) was created a year later to bridge the pillars of UN activity: peace and security, development and human rights, but has had limited success in transcending the traditional division of labour between the UNSC, UNGA, and ECOSOC (see Challenge of Sustaining Peace Report (n 6) para 97). See, further, Review of the United Nations Peacebuilding Architecture (n 11) paras 2, 4. Finally, the UN System Chief Executives Board for Coordination has also been created with a view to coordinate efforts (<http://www.unsceb.org/> accessed 16 February 2020).

[15] See eg Challenge of Sustaining Peace Report (n 6) paras 61–7; HIPPO Report (n 6) paras 74–81.

[16] UNSG, Prevention of Armed Conflict (n 1) para 136; UNSG, Progress Report on Prevention of Armed Conflict (n 1) para 20. Organized criminal activity is not infrequently accompanied by a sustained campaign of violence potentially reaching relevant thresholds for armed conflict in otherwise stable States.

[17] See eg United Nations Convention against Transnational Organized Crime 2225 UNTS 209 art 1. See, for more detail, Pierre Hauck/Sven Peterke, Chapter 12 in this *Handbook*.

[18] UNSG, Progress Report on Prevention of Armed Conflict (n 1) para 22; Challenge of Sustaining Peace Report (n 6) paras 15–16.

[19] In particular, the Office of the Special Adviser to the Secretary-General on the Prevention of Genocide (OSAPG) was established under UNSC Res 1366 (2001). See Payam Akhavan, 'Report on the Work of the Office of the Special Adviser of the United Nations Secretary-General on the Prevention of Genocide' (2006) 28 Human Rights Quarterly 1043. Following the UNGA's adoption of the World Summit Outcome Document (UNGA Res 60/1 (16 September 2005)), the Secretary-General also designated a Special Adviser on the Responsibility to Protect. The mandate overlaps with that of the OSAPG insofar as early warning is concerned but has a wider remit—and both now operate under the auspices of the Office on Genocide Prevention and the Responsibility to Protect. See UN Office on Genocide Prevention and the Responsibility to Protect, 'Mandate' (UN, 2019) <http://www.un.org/en/genocideprevention/office-mandate.shtml> accessed 18 October 2019. See, for more detail, Adama Dieng, Chapter 19 in this *Handbook*.

[20] See eg UNSG, Prevention of Armed Conflict (n 1) para 74; UNDP/UNDPA 'Joint Programme on Building National Capacities for Conflict Prevention—Annual Report 2016' (UNDP, 13 June 2017) 32 <https://www.undp.org/content/undp/en/home/librarypage/democratic-governance/conflict-prevention/joint-undp-dpa-programme-on-building-national-capacities-for-con.html> accessed 18 October 2019.

organizations.[21] In addition, there are UN human rights treaty monitoring mechanisms[22] and international commissions of inquiry (with mandates from the UN General Assembly (UNGA), UNSC, the Human Rights Council, the Secretary-General and the High Commissioner for Human Rights)[23]—all of which add layers of information and analysis on potential conflict situations. It has long been said, however, that the conflict prevention challenge 'is less one of early warning than of early action'.[24] With the sources of early warning information ubiquitous, the challenge lies in developing better capacity to use this vast body of information effectively, and for there to be early and concerted action by prevention actors to address identified conflict triggers.[25] Where early warning information and analysis is appropriately channelled, it can provide a basis for the UN's deployment of good offices (eg, Special Envoys), mediation, and peace and development advisers.[26]

b. *Conflict Management*

Once a dispute erupts into violence, conflict management and efforts to restore peace (discussed in Section B.2) become the more immediately applicable frameworks—though systemic and structural elements should continue to inform the international community's engagement. Conflict management seeks to prevent ongoing conflicts from escalating or spreading by denying 'belligerents the ability to resupply arms, ammunition, and hard currency, combined with humanitarian operations that provide relief for innocent victims'.[27] There are a number of standards and legal frameworks relevant to managing and decreasing the severity of conflicts, or protecting civilian victims

[21] See eg the European Commission, 'EU Conflict Early Warning System: Objectives, Process and Guidance for Implementation—2017' (EU, 27 July 2017); AU, 'Continental Early Warning System (CEWS)' (AU Peace and Security, 15 May 2018) <http://www.peaceau.org/en/page/28-continental-early-warning> accessed 16 February 2020.

[22] See eg OHCHR, 'Monitoring the Core International Human Rights Treaties' (OHCHR, 2019) <https://www.ohchr.org/EN/HRBodies/Pages/Overview.aspx> accessed 16 February 2020; Review of the United Nations Peacebuilding Architecture (n 11) para 11.

[23] For a list of such commissions and missions, see UNHRC, 'International Commissions of Inquiry, Commissions on Human Rights, Fact-Finding Missions and other Investigations' <https://ohchr.org/EN/HRBodies/HRC/Pages/COIs.aspx> accessed 16 February 2020. See, further, UNSG, Prevention of Armed Conflict (n 1) paras 38, 54–5.

[24] Carnegie Commission (n 4) xxii.

[25] UNSG, Progress Report on Prevention of Armed Conflict (n 1) paras 90–2; Review of the United Nations Peacebuilding Architecture (n 11) paras 13–14, 30.

[26] UNSG, Progress Report on Prevention of Armed Conflict (n 1) paras 31–4; UN Political and Peacebuilding Affairs, 'Prevention and Mediation' <https://dppa.un.org/en/prevention-and-mediation> accessed 16 February 2020. The UN has established a mediation support unit and regional offices to support 'good offices' activities, preventive diplomacy and mediation (see UN Peacemaker, 'Mediation Support Activities and Services' <https://peacemaker.un.org/mediation-support/activities-and-services> accessed 16 February 2020). A High-Level Advisory Board on Mediation was established in 2017 to further support the Secretary-General (UN Peacemaker, 'SG's High-Level Advisory Board on Mediation' (UNDPPA, 13 September 2017) <https://peacemaker.un.org/mediation-support/SGHLABM> accessed 16 February 2020).

[27] Carnegie Commission (n 4) xviii.

during military operations. As with systemic conflict prevention, the relevance of a particular standard or framework depends in part on the context and nature of the parties to the conflict.

The newest of these legal frameworks, framed principally in counter-terrorism terms but equally aimed at preventing the escalation of armed conflicts, takes the form of the UNSC Foreign Terrorist Fighters (FTF) regime.[28] Acting under Chapter VII, the UNSC required States to prevent and criminalize 'travel or attempt[ed] travel to a State other than their States of residence or nationality' for terrorist purposes.[29] The UNSC, however, defines FTF not only by reference to terrorism, but also participation in armed conflicts.[30] Applied to 'fighters' *tout court*, as participants in foreign armed conflicts, this regime is potentially an important conflict management tool insofar as it prevents the influx of foreign fighters who may intensify ongoing conflict. But it is not without its challenges—particularly its conflation of counter-terrorism and armed conflict management paradigms, as discussed in Section C.1.a.

A significantly older regime, with potential to limit the escalation of armed conflicts and protect civilians from military operations, is Common Article 1 (CA1) to the Geneva Conventions (1949) and Additional Protocol I (1977).[31] Under CA1, States Parties 'undertake to respect and to ensure respect for' the Conventions. The second part of this provision is understood to extend to third States intervening in non-international armed conflicts, however the scope of their obligations remains obscure. The ICJ in *Nicaragua* defined this obligation narrowly, suggesting that it prohibits States Parties from 'encouraging' breaches of international humanitarian law (IHL) through their support,[32] but the law has developed since 1986. On one view, CA1 requires States Parties to ensure respect for IHL by the parties to an armed conflict, wherever and between whomever.[33] A more restrictive (and arguably more realistic) interpretation requires States actively supporting one or more of the belligerents in an armed conflict (financially, materially, or technically) to use the influence resulting from their support to encourage them to respect IHL, or to cease providing such support where there is a risk that the recipients will use it to breach IHL.[34] This shift from the *Nicaragua 'encouragement'* standard is also reflected in the 2013 Arms Trade Treaty (ATT), which imposes on

[28] UNSC Res 2178 (2014); UNSC Res 2396 (2017); see Helen Duffy/Larissa van den Herik, Chapter 11 in this *Handbook*.

[29] UNSC Res 2178 (2014) para 6(a); UNSC Res 2396 (2017) para 1.

[30] UNSC Res 2178 (2014) preambular para 8 and para 1.

[31] The 'revitalization' of CA1 obligation is in part due to the most recent ICRC, *Commentaries on the Geneva Conventions* (see n 33).

[32] *Military and Paramilitary Activities in and against Nicaragua (Nicaragua v USA)* (Merits) [1986] ICJ Rep 14 [255].

[33] See ICRC, *Commentary on the First Geneva Convention: Convention (I) for the Amelioration of the Condition of the Wounded and Sick in Armed Forces in the Field* (CUP 2016); ICRC, *Commentary on the Second Geneva Convention: Convention (II) for the Amelioration of the Condition of Wounded, Sick and Shipwrecked Members of Armed Forces at Sea* (CUP 2017).

[34] Kimberley N Trapp/Edmund Robinson, 'Extra-Territorial "Fiduciary" Obligations and "Ensuring" Respect for International Humanitarian Law' (2018) 63 McGill Law Journal 677.

States Parties exporting arms an obligation to assess *inter alia* their potential to undermine peace and security and their use in the commission of serious violations of IHL. States Parties must undertake measures to mitigate these risks, and, where the risk is 'overriding', are obliged not to export.[35] Widespread compliance with the CA1 and ATT obligations would evidently be an important contributor to conflict management, particularly insofar as civilian protection is concerned. The potential of this framework in the conflict management toolkit is discussed further in Section C.1.b.

Following the end of the Cold War and the UNSC's re-engagement with its primary responsibility to maintain and restore international peace and security, the UNSC has principally engaged in conflict management (as distinguished from prevention) activities.[36] Measures in this regard have taken a number of forms, including the imposition of arms embargoes[37] or financial sanctions[38] to encourage relevant actors to negotiate and to discourage them from activities which further threaten peace or endanger civilians.[39] These measures have not gone unchallenged; concerns include the unintended consequences of UNSC measures (eg, in the case of the territorial arms embargo applicable to Bosnia in its conflict with Serbia) and the human rights implications of sanctions regimes. The UNSC has also adopted Article 42 UN Charter enforcement measures in response to conflict, including authorizing force with a view to restoring a State's sovereignty (eg, following Iraq's invasion of Kuwait)[40] and uses of military force aimed at the protection of civilians as an instantiation of the responsibility to protect doctrine (eg, in the case of the Libyan intervention).[41] With the changing nature of armed conflicts, peacekeeping missions—requiring offensive capabilities—are also increasingly deployed where there is no peace to keep, and so the debate about whether Chapter VII enforcement measures are appropriate in respect of conflict prevention (including conflict management) continues in a new context.[42] Finally, the UNSC has relied on the logic of deterrence through the creation of international criminal tribunals, most notably in respect of the conflicts in the former Yugoslavia and in Rwanda.[43]

2. Peace

In many senses, peace processes aimed at resolving violent conflicts are preventive, as they seek to prevent the re-emergence of conflict. Various frameworks address different

[35] 3013 UNTS art 7(1)–(3). [36] See n 6. [37] eg UNSC Res 1970 (2011). [38] ibid.

[39] See UNSG, Progress Report on Prevention of Armed Conflict (n 1) paras 37, 104–5.

[40] UNSC Res 678 (1990).

[41] UNSC Res 1973 (2011). See, further, Simon Chesterman, Chapter 44 in this *Handbook*. Protecting civilians during military operations is also an important element of peace processes in that it 'preserves the chance of meaningful recovery and non-recurrence of the conflict'. UNSG, Progress Report on Prevention of Armed Conflict (n 1) para 36.

[42] HIPPO Report (n 6) para 109.

[43] ICISS (n 4) para 3.29. See, further, UNSG, Prevention of Armed Conflict' (n 1) para 97. The possibility of individual criminal responsibility may also prevent international crimes at a systemic level. See UNSG, Progress Report on Prevention of Armed Conflict (n 1) para 41.

features of this enterprise: disarmament, demobilization, and reintegration;[44] peacekeeping missions (with a view to monitoring ceasefires, disarmament, and disengagement);[45] and peacebuilding strategies, which include the markers for systemic conflict prevention.[46] Peace is also, of course, its own endeavour—through negotiated settlement of conflict.

In respect of negotiated settlement, the approach must be comprehensive,[47] requiring that mediation and facilitation efforts move 'beyond securing a ceasefire and [focus] on achieving comprehensive settlements, which deal with a broad range of issues such as, *inter alia*, power-sharing, wealth-sharing, constitutions, justice, human rights and security issues'.[48] In this sense, and to the extent that a *jus post bellum* or *lex pacificatoria* is emerging,[49] the legal standards which may apply are substantive, and mirror, in the post-conflict context, those which inform systemic conflict prevention.[50]

The practice in respect of negotiated peace agreements is vast,[51] and there are success stories. Nevertheless, many peace negotiations continue to operate on the basis of a narrow focus on immediate results, too often excluding relevant stakeholders and failing to properly address the underlying issues which contributed to the conflict. Injecting international criminal justice elements into peace negotiation, as discussed in Section C.2, raises particular challenges. The traditional divide between peacemaking and peacebuilding, operating on the basis of a linear, temporally defined conflict cycle paradigm, continues to inform efforts to secure an agreed peace.[52]

Peacekeeping operations were defined in 'Agenda for Peace' as 'the deployment of a UN presence in the field, *hitherto* with the consent of all the parties concerned, normally involving UN military and/or police personnel and frequently civilians as well'.[53] Modern peacekeeping missions, however, often have mandates going beyond keeping an agreed or existing peace, and can operate in conflict situations, including asymmetric conflicts where the threat to the mission (and the peace) emanates from non-State actors

[44] See UN Peacekeeping, 'Disarmament, Demobilization and Reintegration' <https://peacekeeping.un.org/en/disarmament-demobilization-and-reintegration> accessed 16 February 2020.

[45] See UN Peacekeeping, 'Action for Peacekeeping' <https://peacekeeping.un.org/en> accessed 16 February 2020. At the time of writing, there are fourteen UN peacekeeping missions deployed around the world, equally split between Africa and the rest of the world.

[46] Carnegie Commission (n 4) vii; Challenge of Sustaining Peace Report (n 6) para 34.

[47] Challenge of Sustaining Peace Report (n 6) para 22. Christine Bell, 'Peace Settlements and International Law: From *lex pacificatoria* to *jus post bellum*' in Christian Henderson/Nigel D White (eds), *Research Handbook on International Conflict and Security Law: Jus ad Bellum, Jus in Bello and Jus post Bellum* (Edward Elgar 2012) 1.

[48] UNGA Res 66/811 (25 June 2012) 5.

[49] The innovative 'Legal Tools for Peace Making Project' is investigating 'to what extent regulation of particular issue areas in peace agreements is consolidating towards the establishment of novel normative expectations'. See Lauterpacht Centre for International Law, 'Legal Tools for Peace-Making Project' (University of Cambridge) <https://www.lcil.cam.ac.uk/legal-tools-peace-making-project> accessed 16 February 2020.

[50] See n 11 and accompanying text.

[51] See the UN Peacemaker, 'Peace Agreements Database' <https://peacemaker.un.org/document-search> accessed 16 February 2020.

[52] Challenge of Sustaining Peace Report (n 6) paras 31–3.

[53] UNSG, Agenda for Peace (n 1) para 20.

who are not actively participating in any political settlement of the conflict.[54] As a result, the line between traditional peacekeeping and military counter-terrorism missions or Chapter VII enforcement measures is blurred. This potentially endangers the necessary impartiality of peacekeeping operations.[55] On the other hand, the High-level Independent Panel on Peace Operations calls for a more nuanced approach to 'peace-operations', eschewing the traditional approach to peacekeeping with a view to 'deliver[ing] more flexibly tailored "right fit" and not "template" missions' which respond to the particular context of a conflict.[56]

In respect of peacebuilding, there has been increasing focus on the necessity for sustained engagement in post-conflict States, in keeping with the markers of systemic conflict prevention.[57] Peacebuilding is strongly preventive—nurturing peace and structurally addressing conflict triggers, to avoid relapse. In 2005, the UN created the Peace Commission[58] with a broad mandate, including a focus on 'reconstruction and institution-building efforts necessary for recovery from conflict' in post-conflict States.[59] While sustained engagement by the UN in peacebuilding has long been identified as urgently in need of energy and resources,[60] moving from a culture of reaction to a culture of prevention, the High-level Independent Panel on Peace Operations reports that such a 'culture has yet to materialize ... [e]xpectations raised at the time of the creation of the Peacebuilding Commission that its focus would encompass prevention have not been met'.[61] The challenges to sustained and coordinated peacebuilding activities are well known, including resourcing and a lack of political will in respect of prevention over 'cure' (defined narrowly as intervention after a crisis has emerged).[62] This is not to understate what has been accomplished, institutionally through the creation of the Peace Commission, and politically in calling attention to the imperative for a change of perspective. But the 'momentum that carried the process forward up to and including December 2005 was not sustained'.[63]

C. Developments and Challenges

Faced with constantly evolving threats to international peace and security, and in the absence of a comprehensive or coherent system of conflict prevention,[64] international

[54] Challenge of Sustaining Peace (n 6) paras 109–10. [55] ibid paras 121–30.

[56] HIPPO Report (n 6) paras 49–52. [57] See n 11 and accompanying text.

[58] See UN Peacebuilding Commission <https://www.un.org/peacebuilding/commission> 16 February 2020. The Peacebuilding Commission is supported by the Peacebuilding Fund but remains underfunded. See UN Peacebuilding Fund <https://www.un.org/peacebuilding/fund> accessed 16 February 2020. See HIPPO Report (n 6) para 145.

[59] See UN Peacebuilding Commission, 'Mandate' <https://www.un.org/peacebuilding/commission/mandate> accessed 16 February 2020.

[60] UNSG, Agenda for Peace (n 1) para 15. [61] HIPPO Report (n 6) para 64.

[62] Challenge of Sustaining Peace (n 6).

[63] Review of the United Nations Peacebuilding Architecture (n 11) para 10; HIPPO Report (n 6) para 64.

[64] Alex J Bellamy, 'Conflict Prevention and the Responsibility to Protect' (2008) 14 Global Governance 136.

responses to the emergence of conflict are often ad hoc, and legal developments are, as a result, fragmented. Since the Agenda for Peace, systemic conflict prevention has gained traction, with greater attention being paid to the underlying structural causes of conflict. In practice, however, conflict management has remained the key focus of conflict prevention, owing in part to the absence of political will before the emergence of a conflict. As noted above, the armoury of conflict management includes, but is not limited to, measures aimed at coercion, such as the imposition of sanctions, the use of force, and peacekeeping missions. These are discussed in other chapters of Part III of this *Handbook*. In addition to systemic approaches to prevent the outbreak of conflict, and conflict management tools, the systemic conflict prevention toolkit is equally if not more important in post-conflict situations—to prevent the resurgence of conflict. Expanding peacebuilding mandates, facilitating the disarmament, demobilization and reintegration of combatants, and the lasting resolution of conflicts through participatory peace negotiations all work towards securing enduring peace. The following sections elaborate on some of the recent developments and challenges in respect of conflict prevention and peace processes in achieving these aims.

1. Conflict Prevention

a. *Systemic Conflict Prevention*

In Chapter 44 of this *Handbook*, Simon Chesterman discusses the responsibility to protect, noting the inclusion in the 2001 ICISS Report of a section addressing the less discussed 'responsibility to prevent'.[65] The emphasis of the latter is on systemic conflict prevention measures that precede conflict management, reaffirming the commitment in Article 55 UN Charter to 'the creation of conditions of stability and well-being which are necessary for the peaceful and friendly relations among nations'. The underlying causes identified by the ICISS encompass the broad range of political, economic, and legal considerations discussed in Section A.1.a.[66] It, too, recognizes the primary responsibility of States to alleviate the root causes of conflict, with UN and other international support.

The international responsibility to prevent through early assistance is particularly important in preventing conflicts in fragile States, and costs far less than intervention during conflict.[67] As the Commission observed, however, States' resources earmarked for prevention 'remain dwarfed by the resources devoted…to preparation for war, to warfighting, to coercive intervention, to humanitarian assistance, to the victims of conflict and catastrophe, to post-intervention reconstruction, and to peacekeeping'.[68] A lack of

[65] ICISS (n 4) para 3.1. [66] ibid paras 3.21–3.24.

[67] See, generally, Carnegie Commission (n 4).

[68] ICISS (n 4) para 3.7; UNSG, Progress Report on Prevention of Armed Conflict (n 1) para 35; Report of the Advisory Group of Experts on the Review of the Peacebuilding Architecture (n 6) 3, paras 5–7; HIPPO Report (n 6) 9.

political will to carry out the responsibility to prevent,[69] combined with the inability to quickly adapt to evolving threats, has limited the effectiveness of the responsibility to prevent framework, and remains a key challenge in respect of the future of the UN architecture. Political will is the answer, but short-termism and populist isolationism remain a feature of the modern political landscape—neither of which lends itself to properly resourcing long-term prevention.

A different 'resource' concern is the conflict potential that accompanies the scarcity and management of natural resources, a topic that has been on the agenda of the UNSC in recent years. The strategic use of natural resources as a means of warfare is not new. Water, oil, and extractive industries have been at the heart of several conflicts, with non-State armed groups seeking control of specific industries to finance and fuel conflict.[70] On a global scale, the environmental impacts of climate change are also being felt by farming, fishing, and other local communities, and the Intergovernmental Panel on Climate Change is working to identify the impacts of desertification, degradation of land, and food insecurity.[71] In this context, the equitable distribution of resources is as much a challenge as availability.

While engagement between peace and climate change processes remains relatively light, there are some important developments in this regard. The Food and Agriculture Organization (FAO) and the World Food Programme (WFP) play an important role in drawing the link between the availability of resources and conflict. Their 2019 Report 'Monitoring Food Security in Countries with Conflict Situations' attempts to quantify the impact of ongoing conflicts on food security. In the Democratic Republic of the Congo, for example, they found that 13.1 million people required urgent food, nutrition, and livelihood in 2017–18 alone.[72] Ongoing conflict is a key causal factor, resulting in mass displacement, the disruption of farming activities, and limited access to food.[73] Recognizing food shortage as a further contributing factor to the conflict and an impediment to its resolution remains a challenge. Ultimately, giving effect to the responsibility to prevent requires an awareness not only of the impact of environmental factors on communities, but also the effectiveness of the institutions they depend on for assistance.[74]

[69] Bellamy (n 64).

[70] Marie-Claire Cordonnier Segger, 'Keynote Speech: Resources of Conflict—Conflicts over Resources' (2011) 3 Göttingen Journal of International Law 16–17.

[71] IPCC, 'Decision and Outline of the Special Report on Climate Change, Desertification, Land Degradation, Sustainable Land Management, Food Security, and Greenhouse Gas Fluxes in Terrestrial Ecosystems' (28–31 March 2017) <https://www.ipcc.ch/site/assets/uploads/2018/04/Decision_Outline_SR_LandUse.pdf> accessed 18 October 2019.

[72] FAO and WFP, 'Monitoring Food Security in Countries with Conflict Situations' (Issue No 5, 2019) 9–10 <http://www.fao.org/3/ca3113en/CA3113EN.pdf> accessed 16 February 2020.

[73] FAO and WFP, 'Monitoring Food Security in Countries with Conflict Situations' (Issue No 4, 2018) 7–8 <http://www.fao.org/3/ca3113en/CA3113EN.pdf> accessed 18 October 2019.

[74] Ben Saul, 'Climate Change, Conflict and Security: International Law Challenges' (2009) 9 New Zealand Armed Forces Law Review 6.

b. *Conflict Management*

Non-international armed conflicts pose a particular challenge in terms of both systemic conflict prevention and conflict management strategies. Within the limits of Article 2(7) UN Charter, systemic conflict prevention measures, if any, are undertaken by or with the consent of the territorial State. At the early stages of conflict, a State may be unwilling to accept international assistance, perhaps wary of full-scale intervention or the legitimization of non-State armed groups.[75] This is often true of secessionist conflicts, and the absence of international involvement may fuel the conflict rather than resolve it.[76]

Once the threshold for a non-international armed conflict has been satisfied, conflict management becomes the immediately relevant framework. The limited scope of IHL in non-international armed conflicts is itself a challenge in this regard.[77] Nevertheless, IHL provides a framework which protects civilians from the dangers of military operations and prohibits the worst excesses of war. This is, of course, conditioned on compliance. The challenge for conflict management strategies lies in incentivizing belligerents to comply, and these efforts are potentially undermined by the applicability of terrorism suppression regimes. In particular, the criminalization of acts of terrorism pursuant to the Terrorism Suppression Conventions (TSCs) limits the role of IHL as a regime for conflict management. Terrorism is widely recognized as 'one of the most serious threats to international peace and security', evidenced by the monitoring and enforcement role of the UNSC.[78] However, where States Parties to the TSCs criminalize conduct that is either already addressed in IHL, or where IHL does not otherwise prohibit such conduct, the label of terrorism, combined with the absence of combatant privilege for members of non-State armed groups, leaves little incentive for compliance with IHL.[79] The Syrian government's incorporation of harsher penalties for terrorist offences is a case in point.[80] When addressing this regime interaction, incentivizing non-State armed groups to comply with IHL by excluding the application of anti-terrorism legislation could be an important conflict management tool. Indeed, a number of the TSCs do precisely that.[81] The FTF phenomenon that characterized the conflict in Syria and Iraq, discussed in Section A.1.b, is a recent manifestation of this problem. Security Council Resolution 2178 (2014)[82] conflates terrorism and armed conflict, ignoring the conceptual

[75] ICISS (n 4) para 3.34; Bellamy (n 64).

[76] Marc Weller, 'Settling Self-Determination Conflicts: Recent Developments' (2009) 20 EJIL 112.

[77] Sandesh Sivakumaran, 'Re-Envisaging the International Law of Internal Armed Conflict' (2011) 22 EJIL 219.

[78] UNGA Res 60/1 (16 September 2015) paras 81, 90.

[79] Kimberley N Trapp, 'The Interaction of the International Terrorism Suppression Regime and IHL in Domestic Criminal Prosecutions: The UK Experience' in Derek Jinks et al (eds), *Applying International Humanitarian Law in Judicial and Quasi-Judicial Bodies* (Asser Press 2014) 179; Tom Ruys, 'The Syrian Civil War and the Achilles' Heel of the Law of Non-International Armed Conflict' (2014) 50 Stanford Journal of International Law 270.

[80] Ruys (n 79).

[81] eg International Convention for the Suppression of Terrorist Bombings 2149 UNTS 256 art 19.

[82] In UNSC Res 2178 (2014) para 1, the conduct of 'foreign terrorist fighters' is characterized as both 'terrorist acts and participation in armed conflict'.

differences between the applicable legal regimes,[83] with the potential to undermine IHL as the governing paradigm for conflict management.

A further recurring challenge for conflict management is the indirect involvement of third States through the provision of funding, weapons, technical, and other support to one or more parties to the conflict. While CA1 of the Geneva Conventions and the ATT contribute to conflict management by imposing obligations on third States to cease supporting belligerents who are endangering civilians, the precise contours of the 'respect and ensure respect' obligation in CA1 remain contested,[84] and State support to belligerents known to be committing serious IHL breaches continues. State responsibility, in light of the *erga omnes* nature of the CA1 obligation, might usefully be deployed in this respect. Domestic processes may also be relevant in reviewing the compliance of States with their CA1 and ATT obligations and in holding governments to account for their role in exacerbating foreign armed conflicts.[85]

A related challenge to effective conflict management is non-compliance with other arms control obligations, including those imposed by the UNSC. Security Council Resolution 1970, adopted unanimously under Chapter VII UN Charter in relation to the conflict in Libya, illustrates the extent of States' non-compliance. The arms embargo imposed by the UNSC therein required States Parties to 'take the necessary measures to prevent the direct or indirect supply, sale or transfer' of weapons to and from Libya.[86] The 2017 Final Report of the Panel of Experts on Libya documents a wide range of violations of the arms embargo since 2011, including airstrikes, the provision of arms, military training and technical assistance.[87] Where non-compliance with UNSC-imposed arms embargos is the result of P-5 intervention in an armed conflict, the Chapter VII apparatus will not be available to address non-compliance.

[83] See eg Sandra Kraehenmann, *Foreign Fighters under International Law* (Geneva Academy of International Humanitarian Law and Human Rights 2014) 42; Jessica Burniske et al, 'Suppressing Foreign Terrorist Fighters and Supporting Principled Humanitarian Action: A Provisional Framework for Analyzing State Practice' (Harvard Law School Program on International Law and Armed Conflict, 14 October 2015) <https://papers.ssrn.com/sol3/Delivery.cfm/SSRN_ID2673502_code1186248.pdf?abstractid=2673502&mirid=> accessed 18 October 2019.

[84] Carlo Focarelli, 'Common Article 1 of the 1949 Geneva Conventions: A Soap Bubble?' (2010) 21 EJIL 125; Ryan Goodman, 'Two US Positions on the Duty to Ensure Respect for the Geneva Conventions' (*Just Security*, 26 September 2016) <https://www.justsecurity.org/33166/u-s-positions-duty-ensure-respect-geneva-conventions/> accessed 18 October 2019; Oona Hathaway/Zachary Manfredi, 'The State Department Advisor Signals a Middle Road on Common Article 1' (*Just Security*, 12 April 2016) <https://www.justsecurity.org/30560/state-department-adviser-signals-middle-road-common-article-1/> accessed 18 October 2019.

[85] The UK House of Lords International Relations Committee examining the situation in Yemen concluded that the UK is 'narrowly on the wrong side [of IHL]: given the volume and type of arms being exported to the Saudi-led coalition, we believe they are highly likely to be the cause of significant civilian casualties in Yemen, risking the contravention of international humanitarian law.' House of Lords/International Relations Committee, 'Yemen: Giving Peace a Chance' (*UK Parliament*, 16 February 2019) <https://publications.parliament.uk/pa/ld201719/ldselect/ldintrel/290/29003.htm#_idTextAnchor013> accessed 16 February 2019.

[86] UNSC Res 1970 (2011) para 9.

[87] UNSC 'Final Report of the Panel of Experts on Libya' (1 June 2017) UN Doc S/2017/466, 22–50.

In the absence of UNSC Article 41 or Article 42 measures, an important contribution to conflict management has been the 'third wave' of fact-finding as a means of documenting serious human rights violations during or after a conflict.[88] Historically, the fact-finding mandates of commissions of inquiry were characterized as a means of peaceful dispute settlement, but as noted in Section A.1.a, they may also contribute to conflict prevention by feeding into early warning mechanisms. Increasingly, fact-finding also feeds into accountability mechanisms, potentially encouraging parties to an ongoing conflict to halt IHL and human rights violations.[89] A huge step in this direction has been the use of new technologies, in particular social media.[90] In the long term, a fact-finding mission may even catalyse institutional change and provide the basis for 'renewed focus on structures to prevent the recurrence of atrocities'.[91] The ability of commissions of inquiry to meet these objectives, however, continues to be hampered by insufficient resources, one-sided mandates, and absence of political will. The Independent International Commission of Inquiry on Syria is only the most recent example, suffering the resignation of Carla Del Ponte, who cited a lack of political will within the UNSC to pursue accountability.[92]

There is an increasing tendency to perceive fact-finding as a precursor to individual criminal responsibility, and to define fact-finding mandates accordingly.[93] The mandate of the International Commission of Inquiry on Darfur serves as a good illustration.[94] Indeed, it was upon the Commission's recommendation that the UNSC referred the situation in Darfur to the International Criminal Court (ICC).[95] This focus on after-the-fact accountability has received mixed reviews. While some contend that it sidelines the prevention function of fact-finding,[96] others recognize that fact-finding may serve a signalling function to those responsible for the violations while also improving early warning systems in furtherance of the international responsibility to protect.[97] While acknowledging their

[88] Robert Miller, 'United Nations Fact-Finding Missions in the Field of Human Rights' (1973) 5 Australian Yearbook of International Law 40; Federica D'Alessandra, 'The Accountability Turn in Third Wave Human Rights Fact-Finding' (2017) 33 Utrecht Journal of International and European Law 59.

[89] Agnieszka Jachec-Neale, 'Human Rights Fact-Finding into Armed Conflict and Breaches of the Laws of War' (2011) 105 ASIL Proc 85, 88.

[90] Philip Alston, 'Third Generation Human Rights Fact-Finding' (2013) 107 ASIL Proc 61.

[91] Steven R Ratner, 'The Political Dimension of International Human Rights Fact-Finding' (2013) 107 ASIL Proc 70, 72; Philip Alston, 'Commissions of Inquiry as Human Rights Fact-Finding Tools' (2011) 105 ASIL Proc 81, 84.

[92] UNGA 'Report of the Human Rights Council on its Seventeenth Special Session' (18 October 2011) UN Doc A/HRC/S-17/2, para 13.

[93] See eg Shane Darcy, 'Laying the Foundations: Commissions of Inquiry and the Development of International Law' in Christian Henderson (ed), *Commissions of Inquiry: Problems and Prospects* (Hart 2017); Micaela Frulli, 'Fact-Finding or Paving the Road to Criminal Justice: Some Reflections on United Nations Commissions of Inquiry' (2012) 10 JICJ 1323.

[94] UNSC Res 1564 (2004) para 12.

[95] International Commission of Inquiry on Darfur, 'Report to the Secretary-General' (25 January 2005) <https://www.un.org/ruleoflaw/files/com_inq_darfur.pdf> accessed 16 February 2020, 145–6.

[96] D'Alessandra (n 88).

[97] Larissa van den Herik/Catherine Harwood, 'Commissions of Inquiry and the Charm of International Criminal Law: Between Transactional and Authoritative Approaches' in Philip Alston/Sarah Knuckey (eds), *The Transformation of Human Rights Fact-Finding* (OUP 2016) 238.

contribution to criminal investigations, effectively pursuing the prevention function of fact-finding requires that mandates are not restricted to the requirements of international criminal law.[98] Ensuring that they feed into early warning with a view to prevention, however, is only half the challenge—early warning information and analysis still needs to be put to effective preventive use.

2. Peace

The tension between conflict prevention and accountability is not limited to fact-finding. The competing pulls of peace and justice are discussed extensively post-conflict, particularly in the context of the UNSC's establishment of the ad hoc tribunals as a means of restoring international peace and security in the former Yugoslavia and in Rwanda. The 2019 peace agreement between the government of the Central African Republic and fourteen armed groups is a current example.[99] The negotiation of the agreement took place parallel to the establishment of the *Cour Pénale Spéciale*, which held its inaugural session on 22 October 2018,[100] and also witnessed the transfer of two anti-Balaka leaders to the ICC at the end of that year.[101] On the one hand, pursuing international criminal justice 'may simply result in prolonging a war of civilian atrocities',[102] defeating the prevention function that international criminal justice claims to perform.[103] Viewed in the long term, however, accommodating individual criminal responsibility into efforts aimed at preventing the recurrence of conflict may not only promote post-conflict peacebuilding but also gradually erode the culture of impunity that permitted the commission of the violations in the first place.[104] Ensuring that international criminal justice aims feed into

[98] ibid.

[99] 'Central African Republic—Signing of a Peace Agreement in Bangui' (*France Diplomatie—Ministry for Europe and Foreign Affairs*, 6 February 2019) <https://www.diplomatie.gouv.fr/en/country-files/central-african-republic/events/article/central-african-republic-signing-of-a-peace-agreement-in-bangui-06-02-19> accessed 16 February 2020.

[100] Ministère de la Justice et des Droits de l'Homme, 'Session inaugurale de la Cour Pénale Spéciale du 22 octobre 2018' (*Ministère de la Justice et des Droits de l'Homme de la République Centrafricaine*, 22 October 2018) <http://minjusticedh.cf/fr/session-inaugurale-de-la-cour-penale-speciale-du-22-octobre-2018> accessed 16 February 2020.

[101] Office of the Prosecutor, 'Statement of the Prosecutor of the International Criminal Court, Fatou Bensouda, on the Transfer of Suspect, Alfred Yekatom: "The Cause of Justice in the Central African Republic has been Strengthened by Today's Surrender"' (ICC, 17 November 2018) <https://www.icc-cpi.int/Pages/item.aspx?name=181,117-otp-stat> accessed 16 February 2020; Office of the Prosecutor, 'Statement of the ICC Prosecutor, Fatou Bensouda, on the Arrest of the Second Suspect in the Situation of the Central African Republic (CAR), Mr Patrice-Edouard Ngaïssona: "Our Quest for Justice in the CAR Continues"' (ICC, 12 December 2018) <https://www.icc-cpi.int/Pages/item.aspx?name=181,212-stat-prosecutor> accessed 16 February 2020.

[102] Anthony D'Amato, 'Peace vs Accountability in Bosnia' (1994) 88 AJIL 500, 502.

[103] See eg Rome Statute of the International Criminal Court 2187 UNTS 3, preambular para 5, which suggests that criminal prosecutions 'contribute to the prevention of such crimes'. See, further, n 45.

[104] Payam Akhavan, 'Beyond Impunity: Can International Criminal Justice Prevent Future Atrocities' (2001) 95 AJIL 7, 7–8.

post-conflict peacebuilding in a way that accounts for the particular context of the conflict and relevant stakeholders, however, remains a challenge.

Another significant development has been the acknowledgement of gender as an element of broader peace processes.[105] At least formally, women are recognized as not only victims of conflict but also contributors to conflict prevention, resolution, and post-conflict reconstruction.[106] Security Council Resolution 1325 (2000) was the first big step in this direction, emphasizing the need for an increased role for women 'in the prevention and resolution of conflicts' and in 'all efforts for the maintenance and promotion of peace and security'.[107] It calls on States to increase the participation of women in decision-making at all institutional levels.[108] The UNGA reaffirmed this commitment in its 2005 World Summit Outcome document,[109] and subsequent UNSC resolutions and Secretary-General reports attempt to spell out more clearly the forms of participation this may entail. These include, for instance, incorporating the views of local women's groups into early warning systems and in fact-finding.[110] The role of women in 'people to people' diplomacy is indeed a vital contribution to local capacity-building as a means of proactively preventing conflict.[111]

In practice, the implementation of these commitments by States has produced limited results, and, overall, the participation of women in conflict prevention remains low.[112] Nevertheless, where governments have expressed the political will to act, consultation with women has helped narrow in on specific causes of conflict. In 2015, for instance, the Afghan government took the initiative to publish an action plan on UNSC Resolution 1325 (2000), which included as a strategic objective the participation of women in drafting peace strategies and policies.[113] Its publication catalysed further consultation with Afghan women, leading to the recognition by the Secretary-General in his 2017 report

[105] Margaret E McGuinness, 'Women as Architects of Peace: Gender and the Resolution of Armed Conflict' (2007) 15 Michigan State University College of Law Journal of International Law 65. See, for more detail, Gina Heathcote, Chapter 5 in this *Handbook*.

[106] Thania Paffenholz, 'Beyond the Normative: Can Women's Inclusion Really Make for Better Peace Processes?' (Policy Brief, The Graduate Institute Geneva, 2015) <https://www.peacewomen.org/sites/default/files/Graduate%20Insitute%20of%20Geneva-%20Beyond%20the%20Normative.pdf> accessed 24 August 2020, outlining the results of a four-year study 'Broadening Participation in Political Negotiations and Implementation' conducted by the Graduate Institute of International and Development Studies' Centre on Conflict, Development and Peacebuilding.

[107] UNSC Res 1325 (2000) preambular para 5.

[108] ibid para 1.

[109] UNGA Res 60/1 (16 September 2005) para 116.

[110] UNSC 'Report of the Secretary-General on Women, Peace and Security' (16 October 2002) UN Doc S/2002/1154, para 34.

[111] UNSC 'Report of the Secretary-General on Women and Peace and Security' (13 October 2004) UN Doc S/2004/814, para 12.

[112] Christine Bell/Catherine O'Rourke, 'Peace Agreements or Pieces of Paper? The Impact of UNSC Resolution 1325 on Peace Processes and their Agreements' (2010) 59 ICLQ 941, 964–5, 968.

[113] Ministry of Foreign Affairs, 'Afghanistan's National Action Plan on UN Security Council Resolution 1325—Women, Peace and Security' (Directorate of Human Rights and Women's International Affairs, June 2015) <https://unama.unmissions.org/sites/default/files/wps-afghanistan_national_action_plan_1325_0.pdf> accessed 16 February 2020.

that women serve as 'a direct link to preventing violent extremism'—a key contributor to violence in Afghanistan and elsewhere.[114]

D. Conclusion

This chapter has canvassed various measures that comprise the conflict prevention and peace diplomacy architecture as it exists today, including systemic prevention and management as two elements of conflict prevention, as well as efforts aimed at peace. While the major focus of international attention has been on conflict management and resolution, systemic conflict prevention techniques are increasingly sophisticated, and greater recognition of their role in preventing conflict is, at least in some contexts, accompanied by the political will to implement them. Owing to the pervasiveness of current threats to international peace and security, a consolidated effort is warranted, and yet, the importance of adaptability in addressing different kinds of conflicts cannot be overstated. This requires ensuring the availability, adequate resourcing and effective application of various tools for systemic conflict prevention at relevant stages of a conflict.

From an international law perspective, this requires the alignment of applicable legal regimes to effectively further the objectives of conflict prevention and peacebuilding. The patchwork of legal regimes that apply to different kinds of conflicts and to other threats, and the competing interests each represents, pose a challenge to conflict prevention. This is evident from past and ongoing debates about the applicability of anti-terrorism regimes in competition with IHL during non-international armed conflict, but also in the definition of fact-finding mandates, which increasingly take on an accountability-based flavour, as well as in the peace versus justice debates that have come to characterize post-conflict resolution. None of these issues are easy. The challenges they pose, however, are dwarfed by the patent absence of political will to prioritize prevention over crisis intervention. While relevant prevention and peacebuilding stakeholders do extraordinary things with limited resources, progress requires a sea change in perspective: prevention and peacebuilding must not be an afterthought which is 'underprioritized, underresourced and undertaken only after the guns fall silent'.[115]

[114] UNSC 'Report of the Secretary-General on Women and Peace and Security' (16 October 2017) UN Doc S/2017/861, para 44.

[115] Report of the Advisory Group of Experts on the Review of the Peacebuilding Architecture (n 6) 3. See, also, UNGA/UNSC 'Report of the Secretary-General: Peacebuilding and Sustaining Peace' (18 January 2018) UN Doc A/72/707-S/2018/43, para 3.

CHAPTER 40

INTERNATIONAL COURTS AND TRIBUNALS AND VIOLENT CONFLICT

CHRISTIAN J TAMS

A. Introduction: Optimism at Vevey (1872)

It happened 150 years ago, on 'a fine warm autumn evening in Vevey in the year 1872', on the shores of Lake Geneva, in the 'little pension Le Cèdre'. A German lieutenant, von Bleichroden, and his wife share dinner with other guests: a 'melancholy Frenchman' grieving over the loss of Alsace-Lorraine, an Englishman, two Russians, a Spanish family and two ladies from Tyrol. Their conversation flows, touching some of the 'burning questions of the day': could war be stopped? (It is inevitable, thinks the Spaniard.) Might Alsace-Lorraine become part of a Confederation of European States, neither German nor French? (The Frenchman smiles, but his is 'the smile of pessimism and despair'.) Could 'Switzerland [be] the little miniature model after which the Europe of the future will be built up?' (Von Bleichroden is not sure: he certainly hopes so, but, 'formerly a pessimist', he remains scarred by the atrocities of the Franco-German war, during which he ordered the execution of irregular fighters, the francs-tireurs.) Throughout these big debates, the 'conversation proceeded... quietly and peacefully'—until suddenly, the Englishman receives a telegram, which he reads 'with visible emotion'. And then the spectacle unfolds:

> [T]he dark, steel-blue evening sky was cut through by a streak of light, and above the low-lying Savoy shore there rose a rocket of enormous size. It rose high...; it hung suspended as though it were looking round on the beautiful earth outspread beneath it... before it exploded with a report which took two minutes to reach Vevey. Then there spread out something like a white cloud which assumed a four-cornered

> rectangular shape, a flag of white fire; a moment after there was another report, and on the white flag appeared a red cross. All the party sprang up and hastened into the veranda. 'What does that mean?' exclaimed Herr von Bleichroden, startled. No one could or would answer, for now there rose a whole volley of rockets... and scattered a shower of fire which was reflected in the gigantic mirror of the lake. 'Ladies and gentlemen!' said the Englishman, raising his voice, while a waiter placed a tray with filled champagne glasses on the table. 'Ladies and gentlemen!' he repeated, 'this means, according to the telegram which I have just received, that the first International Tribunal at Geneva has finished its work; this means that a war between two nations, or what would have been worse—a war against the future, has been prevented; that a hundred thousand Americans and as many Englishmen have to thank this day that they are alive. The Alabama Question has been settled not to the advantage of America, but of justice, not to the injury of England, but for the good of future generations. Does our Spanish friend still believe that wars are unavoidable? When our French friend smiles again, let him smile with the heart and not with the lips only. And you, my German pessimist friend, do you believe now that the franc-tireur question can be settled without... fusillades, but also only in this way?... To-day, as an Englishman, I ought to feel depressed, but I feel proud on account of my country.... I have a right to be so, for England is the first European Power which has appealed to the verdict of honourable men, instead of to blood and iron. And I wish you all many such defeats as we have had to-day, for that will teach us to be victorious. Raise your glasses, ladies and gentlemen, for the Red Cross, for in this sign we will certainly conquer.'

* * *

The little scene appears near the end of one of August Strindberg's novellas, The German Lieutenant.[1] Its emphatic celebration of an arbitral decision (the settlement of the *Alabama* claims[2]) offers a useful perspective on key themes of this chapter: the promise of international adjudication and arbitration ('the verdict of honourable men' instead of 'blood and iron'); the need for States to accept intrusive forms of dispute settlement, and their traditional reluctance to do so; the audacity and the naivety of hope—with an internationally minded group sojourning in Switzerland toasting a billion dollar award as a gateway to a better world.

One hundred and fifty years on, the cause endures, and the hope lives on. The *Alabama* arbitration has become a landmark. States have over time established international courts and tribunals; today, quite frequently they do 'appeal to the verdict of honorable men [and women]' to settle disputes. And yet, were Strindberg's party to meet again today, the Englishman's optimism would probably be mixed with more than a dose of von Bleichroden's pessimism: for international courts and tribunals (ICaTs) produce decision upon decision, but hardly ever prevent 'wars between nations'. Their mandates have been expanded, but typically only cover aspects of violent conflicts.

[1] August Strindberg, *The German Lieutenant and Other Stories* (Claud Field tr, T. Werner Laurie 1915) 64–5.

[2] *Alabama claims* (*United States of America v Great Britain*) (1871) XXIX RIAA 125.

While such aspects are today increasingly submitted to arbitration or adjudication, 'conflict litigation' remains controversial and challenges the authority of ICaTs.

The purpose of this chapter is to offer a condensed account of these developments, and to assess the diverse roles of ICaTs in relation to violent conflicts. As will be shown, the significance of arbitration and adjudication over questions of violent conflict has varied over time and forms part of the general history of international dispute resolution. To reveal as much, Section B sketches out the evolving legal framework governing courts and conflicts. On the basis of this general account, Section C zooms in to discuss what aspects of violent conflicts are addressed by ICaTs under contemporary international law and highlights current challenges of 'conflict litigation'. Section D concludes by asking what Strindberg's Englishman and his friends would make of developments since their celebration of the *Alabama* award on that 'fine warm autumn evening in Vevey in the year 1872'.

B. Courts and Conflicts: The Evolving Legal Framework

The Englishman's enthusiasm at the time rested on a straightforward proposition. Britain and the US had done what States were meant to do: to settle conflicts not on the basis of blood and iron, on the battlefield—but by accepting the decision of impartial decision makers applying standards of law and justice. Peace, in other words, was sought through arbitration or adjudication. The idea no doubt is powerful, but it is clear that it is a particularly ambitious form of ensuring 'peace through law', which requires conflicting parties to be willing, not only to accept legal limits on their conduct, but to entrust sensitive disputes over such limits to an international court or tribunal.

Over time, the appeal of 'peace through arbitration and adjudication' (PtAA)[3] has varied. For the purposes of a summary account, the complex developments since the *Alabama* affair are condensed into three sections, which highlight crucial waypoints in the international community's approach: an idealist vision that viewed ICaTs as central guardians of world peace; a realist turn that saw ICaTs relegated to the margins of international affairs; and the more recent renaissance of international arbitration and adjudication.

1. Grand Schemes: World Courts as Guardians of World Peace?

When von Bleichroden's party met at Vevey in 1872, PtAA was on the verge of breaking through, at least as an intellectual force. The half-century until the end of the First

[3] In the following, 'PtAA' is used as shorthand to describe the movement towards binding resolution of armed conflicts. A fuller discussion would distinguish between earlier attempts to achieve 'peace through arbitration' and the later efforts to move from arbitration to adjudication.

World War may be seen as its heyday.[4] PtAA reflected trust in a rational mode of decision-making based on the power of argument. Compared to alternative visions of transforming world order (world government, disarmament, renunciation of war, etc), it seemed eminently practical and had wide appeal: amongst religious groups, pacifists, workers' movements—all of which came to embrace the cause. It certainly appealed to international lawyers, organized in new associations, for whom the move towards legal process was an obvious sign of progress. These groupings made for a broad church, but they all shared, in David Caron's words, a 'profound and widespread nineteenth-century faith in the peacekeeping ability of an international court'.[5] Into the early twentieth century, that faith remained strong: by 1914, as Mark Mazower observes, 'the campaign for international arbitration' was 'probably the single most influential strand of internationalism'.[6]

For present purposes, the close link between 'peace' and 'adjudication/ arbitration' is crucial. In the dreams and schemes of activists, as in the mind of Strindberg's Englishman, ICaTs were to be the central guardians of peace; arbitration and adjudication were considered to be 'substitutes for war'. Conversely, to substitute for war was their central rationale: in the debates of the nineteenth and early twentieth century, international courts appeared as, in Yuval Shany's terms, 'war-prevention tools'.[7]

That the reality lagged behind such ambitious visions should not come as a surprise. ICaTs could not be dreamed into being, they had to be established by inter-State treaties; their jurisdiction had to be based on consent. The *Alabama* affair suggested that even great powers might be willing to grant such consent—and just like Strindberg's Englishman, the PtAA movement celebrated the *Alabama* precedent as a model. States remained cautious, though, and did not view arbitration or adjudication as a vademecum. Adjudication remained an elusive ideal, as States disagreed on the composition or competence of a permanent international court.[8] As for arbitration, attempts to reach agreement on a multilateral treaty requiring the submission of all disputes to ad hoc tribunals proved unsuccessful. And States that, in principle, were willing to accept a duty to submit to arbitration frequently insisted on exceptions for questions of national honour or vital interests.

[4] The following draws on Christian J Tams, 'World Peace through International Adjudication?' in Heinz Gerhard Justenhoven et al (eds), *Peace Through Law: Can Humanity Overcome War?* (Nomos/Bloomsbury 2016) 215–54.

[5] David D Caron, 'War and International Adjudication: Reflections on the 1899 Peace Conference' (2000) 94 AJIL 1, 9.

[6] Mark Mazower, *Governing the World: The History of an Idea* (Penguin 2013) 83.

[7] Yuval Shany, 'No Longer a Weak Department of Power? Reflections on the Emergence of a New International Judiciary' (2009) 20 EJIL 73, 77.

[8] This was the main obstacle hindering the establishment of a Court of Arbitral Justice at the second Hague Peace Conference of 1907: Mary E O'Connell/Lenore VanderZee, 'The History of International Adjudication' in Cesare P Romano et al (eds), *The Oxford Handbook of International Adjudication* (OUP 2014) 50. By contrast, a Convention for the Establishment of an International Prize Court was agreed—but never entered into force. On the regional level, States did set up the Central American Court of Justice in 1908: ibid 51; Christian J Tams, 'Die Zweite Haager Konferenz und das Recht der friedlichen Streitbeilegung' (2007) 82 Friedens-Warte 119.

Yet to emphasize all this is to miss the central aspect: that in the aftermath of the *Alabama* affair, the PtAA movement seemed firmly on the rise—a rise reflected in the regular conclusion of bilateral (as opposed to multilateral) arbitration treaties; the growing number of cases submitted to arbitration; the increasing use of international commissions to redress reparations claims after violent conflicts; the first serious debates about international courts; and the centrality of binding dispute settlement at the two Hague Conferences of 1899 and 1907. The optimism of Vevey, in other words, was widely shared. Forty years after the *Alabama* award, Elihu Root, a central figure in the PtAA movement, used his 1912 Nobel Peace Prize lecture to look ahead: '[t]he next advance is to pass on from an arbitral tribunal … to a permanent court', whose establishment deserved 'the best efforts of those who wish to promote peace'.[9] Peace seemed in sight, and courts would be at the centre of the peace project—for Root and others, like Luis Drago, it was but a question of time until the 'civilization … supported by weapons [was replaced by] a civilization founded on arbitration of justice'.[10]

2. 'Realistic Horizons': International Courts on the Margins

The decision to present Elihu Root with the 1912 Nobel Prize was taken retrospectively, in 1913. Root was to deliver his acceptance speech in September 1914; perhaps ironically, the outbreak of the war prevented this—and it ushered in a new era, in which the 'realistic horizons' for international courts shrunk.[11] More importantly, the outbreak of the war made Root's words ring hollow. Arbitration had proved powerless to stop countries from sleepwalking into war, and could not restrain them from fighting it with unprecedented intensity.[12] The outbreak of war did not mean the end of law. As has been noted, at least in the official documents of Allied countries, the conflict appeared very much as a 'war about international law';[13] but its outcome (including the fate of Alsace-Lorraine, which had so concerned von Bleichroden's party four and a half decades earlier) was determined, not by the 'verdict of honourable men', but by 'blood and iron'.[14]

[9] Elihu Root, 'Nobel Lecture: Towards Making Peace Permanent' (1914) <https://www.nobelprize.org/prizes/peace/1912/root/lecture/> accessed 14 April 2020.

[10] Luis Drago, as quoted in William I Hull, *The Two Hague Conferences and Their Contributions to International Law* (Ginn and Company first published 1908) 340–1.

[11] Richard A Falk, 'Realistic Horizons for International Adjudication' (1971) 11 Virginia Journal of International Law 314.

[12] As Matheson notes, on the brink of the war, the Tsar had proposed to submit the Austro-Serbian dispute about Franz Ferdinand's murder to arbitration in The Hague, but Austria was unwilling: Michael J Matheson, *International Civil Tribunals and Armed Conflicts* (Martinus Nijhoff 2012) 19.

[13] Marcus Payk, '"What We Seek Is the Reign of Law": The Legalism of the Paris Peace Settlement after the Great War' (2018) 29 EJIL 809, 810.

[14] Tams (n 8).

a. *The 'Primacy of Politics': The Inter-War Experience*

How did this affect the role of ICaTs in the post-war order? In many ways, debates and developments at the end of the First World War foreshadowed future developments. In the immediate post-war period, the victorious powers sought to have the German Emperor tried, before a 'special tribunal' composed of foreign judges.[15] Their efforts were abandoned relatively quickly, but they marked a first attempt to use courts for a particular function, viz. to impose criminal sanctions on individuals. Another particular function they did exercise, and not just on paper: building on the examples of earlier claims commissions, States in the post-war period set up mixed arbitral tribunals to scrutinize wartime measures affecting private economic interests. No less than thirty-six (typically bilateral) such tribunals were in operation, rendering a total of 70,000 decisions, covering requisitions, damages, intellectual property rights, and much more.[16]

None of this commanded much attention at the time; the focus of debates was on a court of general competence. And indeed, with only a little delay, exactly half a century after the *Alabama* award, a permanent court was becoming a reality.[17] Envisaged in the League of Nations Covenant, the Permanent Court of International Justice (PCIJ)—the first 'world court'—was set up in 1922. Ostensibly, this was 'the next advance'[18] expected by Root, and some observers echoed the optimism voiced fifty years earlier by Strindberg's Englishman. Root's long-term ally James Brown Scott was chief amongst them; his editorial in the *American Journal* encouraged readers to 'fall upon our knees and thank God that the hope of ages is in process of realization'[19]—a world court born of a world war. Yet the grand rhetoric could not mask the fact that the World Court now created was to have a rather modest brief: whereas in the earlier debates, ICaTs had played a central role, in the post-war order they occupied the margins of the new 'peace machinery'.[20] The League's founders were idealist, too, but theirs was not the idealism of Strindberg's Englishman; they did not primarily rely on arbitration or adjudication, but on collective decision-making within international organizations: not the force of law, but the strength of political action backed by public opinion, was to ensure the League's success.[21]

[15] Treaty of Peace with Germany (Treaty of Versailles) 225 CTS 18 art 227; Kirsten Sellars, 'The First World War, Wilhelm II and Article 227: The Origin of the Idea of "Aggression" in International Criminal Law' in Claus Kreß/Stefan Barriga (eds), *The Crime of Aggression: A Commentary* (CUP 2017).

[16] For details see Marta Requejo Isido/Burkhard Hess, 'International Adjudication of Private Rights: The Mixed Arbitral Tribunals in the Peace Treaties of 1919–1922' in Michel Erpelding et al (eds), *Peace Through Law* (Nomos 2019).

[17] The following draws on Christian J Tams, 'Peace Through International Adjudication: The Permanent Court of International Justice and the Post-War Order' in Erpelding et al ibid.

[18] Root (n 9).

[19] James Brown Scott, 'The Permanent Court of International Justice (1921) 15 AJIL 52, 55.

[20] Philip C Jessup, 'A Half-Century of Efforts to Substitute Law for War' (1960) 99 Recueil des Cours 1, 18.

[21] Payk (n 13) 821 makes the point forcefully: 'Wilson's concept of world peace had little room for legal mechanisms, inflexible treaty arrangements or even a court-like institution'.

In line with this, the League's political organs (Council and Assembly) were the key actors of the post-war order, and the PCIJ—just as the various mixed arbitral tribunals doing the groundwork of redressing economic consequences—a useful sidekick. Elihu Root's assessment of the League Covenant reflected a sense of disappointment: '[n]othing has been done to provide for the reestablishment and strengthening of a system of arbitration or judicial decision... We are left with a program which rests the hope of the whole world for future peace in a government of men, and not of laws, following the dictates of expediency, and not of right.'[22]

Perhaps curiously, then, 'the next advance'[23] came at a price of a setback: plans to vest the World Court with automatic jurisdiction were (unlike in 1907) resisted by all major powers, so consensualism continued to dominate. For the World Court to become involved, States had to submit disputes to it, notably by special agreement, through compromissory clauses identifying particular categories of disputes suitable for adjudication, or by a voluntary commitment under the so-called optional clause. Questions of jurisdiction aside, the Court was embedded in, and limited by, a collective security system that 'enshrined the primacy of politics over international law institutionally within the powerful organ of the Council'.[24] The ambitious vision of a world court guarding peace was giving way to a more sober perspective on the role of adjudication and arbitration.

By and large, this more sober perspective was to dominate the second half-century since the *Alabama* award, and perhaps it has never really gone away. That peace should be sought through arbitration or adjudication has no doubt remained a postulate, but it never regained the prominence and wide support it had before the First World War.[25] The experience of the PCIJ confirmed the new realism: while the Court's systematic and solid approach to judicial dispute resolution, and its role as an agent of international legal development, are widely (and justly) praised, States made sparing use of the new institution. Even for disputes that could have been submitted to adjudication on the basis of compromissory clauses or the optional clause, and certainly for the major disputes of the day, States relied on other means of dispute settlement (or preferred not to settle). If compared to the hopes of Strindberg's Englishman, the PCIJ's figures are indeed sobering: over two decades of active existence, the Court addressed around three disputes per year, and few if any of them could be said to implicate major conflicts. As Ole Spiermann notes, '[i]n the political history of the League of Nations, the Permanent Court [was] but a footnote, partly because it did not address the main political issues of the day'.[26]

22 Root, as cited in Stephen Wertheim, 'The League of Nations: A Retreat from International Law?' (2012) 7 Journal of Global History 210, 228.

23 Root (n 9).

24 Jochen von Bernstorff, *The Public International Law Theory of Hans Kelsen: Believing in Universal Law* (CUP 2010) 195.

25 Mazower (n 6) 83–4.

26 Ole Spiermann, *International Legal Argument in the Permanent Court of International Justice* (CUP 2005) 132.

b. *De-Coupling Adjudication from War Prevention*

Perhaps surprisingly, the dramatic upheavals of the Second World War did not immediately affect this general picture. When, following another world war, a new generation of diplomats came to design a new post-war order, they corrected some of the League's design failures. However, they did not revisit the basic division of roles, between an institutionalized 'peace machinery', with 'primary responsibility for international peace and security',[27] on the one hand, and courts and tribunals on the other. Just as they had been after the First World War, ICaTs were part of the post-war settlement, but not central to it. In one respect, to be sure, their role was upgraded: the victorious powers set up international military tribunals to prosecute leaders of defeated nations for their role in the war—a 'creative precedent'[28] and a move from words to deeds, compared to the settlement after the First World War. By contrast, as regards individual reparations claims, the movement was in the opposite direction, as the economic consequences of the war were primarily redressed through inter-State treaties. While a number of dispute settlement bodies were set up, 'usage of mixed claims commissions [and mixed arbitral tribunals] declined after World War II' to the point where 'this model of dispute settlement appeared to have become extinct'.[29]

Outside these particular fields, and notwithstanding the ruptures of the Second World War, the picture is one of relative continuity. The UN, too, was to have a world court, but attempts to 'upgrade' its role stood no realistic chance of success. The World Court's 'second incarnation', the International Court of Justice (ICJ), was closely modelled on the PCIJ; its jurisdiction remained consent-based (with jurisdiction based on either *compromis*, compromissory clause, or optional clause), and its link with the UN's peace and security machinery tenuous.

At least during the first decades of its existence, the role of ICaTs in questions of armed conflict remained limited.[30] The impetus of Nuremberg and Tokyo faded in Cold War stagnation. As Claus Kress observes, for decades 'no real progress was made with respect to international criminal law in general or regarding the codification and enforcement of the crime of aggression in particular'.[31] Communist States resisted the principle of binding dispute settlement and were very cautious not to expand the ICJ's jurisdiction. Many newly independent States shared that scepticism and, in the wake of the *South West Africa* judgment,[32] viewed the ICJ with much reservation. All this affected the role of ICaTs generally, but it applied particularly to sensitive disputes relating to violent conflict, which many States considered ill-suited to judicial assessment.

[27] UN Charter 1 UNTS XVI art 24; and cf Jessup (n 20).

[28] Claus Kreß, 'Introduction: The Crime of Aggression and the International Legal Order' in Kreß/Barriga (n 15) 3.

[29] Rudolf Dolzer, 'Mixed Claims Commissions' MPEPIL (OUP, May 2011) para 8.

[30] *Corfu Channel* (*UK v Albania*) (Merits) [1949] ICJ Rep 4—brought after British warships were damaged by mines off the Albanian coast—is the main exception to this general trend.

[31] Kreß (n 28) 5.

[32] *South West Africa* (*Ethiopia v South Africa; Liberia v South* Africa) (Judgment) [1966] ICJ Rep 6.

Jurisdictional limitations aside, 'States remained reluctant to accept international adjudication of their conduct during wartime'.[33]

Unsurprisingly, many assessments of international courts during the 1950s to the 1970s reflect a growing sense of resignation. 'At present the Court has very little to do with the enforcement of peace', noted Lissitzyn in an early work on the ICJ.[34] Hersch Lauterpacht (perhaps the twentieth century's most influential advocate of international adjudication) thought it 'an exaggeration to assert that the Court has proved to be a significant instrument for maintaining international peace'.[35] According to an influential German study, the idea of arbitration as a substitute for war had been 'completely shipwrecked'.[36] In 1971, the World Court seemed as 'having fallen to perhaps its lowest position of international prestige'.[37] The question was not whether it would prevent wars—but whether it would have any role at all in international relations. A century after the *Alabama* claims, little seemed left of the Englishman's optimism.

3. An 'Age of Adjudication'? International Courts Renascent

A further fifty years on, the landscape of ICaTs has been transformed. In the third half-century since *Alabama*, and notably since the end of the Cold War, the general significance of international adjudication and arbitration has much increased, to the point where international lawyers have begun to speak of an 'age of adjudication'.[38] This age of adjudication is not primarily (this much may be given away) an age of adjudicating violent conflicts; the role of ICaTs in relation to this field requires a nuanced assessment.[39] However, the starting point for that assessment is clear: compared to the gloomy assessments cited at the end of the preceding section, international arbitration and adjudication have seen a renaissance. The trend has been described in detail elsewhere,[40] but for present purposes the main lines of development can be summarized in three steps.

[33] Matheson (n 12) 31.

[34] Oliver J Lissitzyn, *The International Court of Justice: Its Role in the Maintenance of International Peace and Security* (Carnegie Endowment 1951) 103.

[35] Hersch Lauterpacht, *The Development of International Law by the International Court* (Stevens and Sons 1958) 4.

[36] Hans von Mangoldt, *Die Schiedsgerichtsbarkeit als Mittel internationaler Streitschlichtung* (Springer 1974) 83 ('hat totalen Schiffbruch erlitten').

[37] Falk (n 11) 314–15.

[38] cf the title of a lecture by Judge Christopher Greenwood, 'International Law in the Age of Adjudication' (*UN Audiovisual Library of International Law*) <http://legal.un.org/avl/ls/Greenwood_CT.html> accessed 25 March 2020

[39] Section C.

[40] Notably Benedict Kingsbury, 'International Courts: Uneven Judicialization in Global Order' in James Crawford/Martti Koskenniemi (eds), *The Cambridge Companion to International Law* (CUP 2012); Shany (n 7); Cesare P Romano, 'Progress in International Adjudication: Revisiting Hudson's Assessment of the Future of International Courts' in Russel A Miller/Rebecca M Bratspiess (eds), *Progress in International Law* (Martinus Nijhoff 2008).

a. *Growth and Diversification of Fora*

The most obvious development in dispute resolution over the past half-century is the 'enormous growth of fora'.[41] Beginning in the 1970s, and picking up speed during the 1990s, States have established a whole range of new ICaTs. The number of standing international courts has increased from six at the end of the Cold War to the high 30s today, and many frameworks envisaging binding dispute settlement by ad hoc bodies have been activated.[42] As Kingsbury observes, in a number of fields (notably human rights, investment and trade) a '[n]ew paradigm of routinized [international] litigation and judicial governance [is] being layered alongside the traditional paradigm of episodic international (inter-state) dispute settlement by international tribunals'.[43]

Routine litigation, in turn, involves a more inclusive set of actors. While inter-State dispute settlement remains the standard, many of the new institutions have opened up. Individuals are the natural claimants before human rights courts and typically have some role before courts of economic integration. Investment arbitration is driven by investors. Since Nuremberg, the fact that '[c]rimes against international law are committed by men, not by abstract entities'[44] has meant that criminal justice is imposed on individuals. A look at the quantitative output reflects the speed and extent of change. By 2014, standing international courts 'ha[d] collectively issued over 37,000 binding legal judgments, more than 90 percent of which were issued since the fall of the Berlin Wall'.[45]

b. *Specialization and Regionalization*

The enormous growth and diversification of fora has been facilitated by two interrelated trends, those of specialization and regionalization. When Strindberg's Englishman, or participants at the Hague Conferences, reflected on arbitration and adjudication, their debates focused on global institutions with potentially unlimited, general jurisdiction.[46] Reflecting such a globalist, generalist mindset, the PCIJ and ICJ, just like arbitral tribunals established under the Hague system, could potentially address disputes covering international law in its entirety: all that mattered was for them to be vested with jurisdiction. They remain generalist, but the recent growth of fora has been driven by a very different approach.[47] The more recent binding dispute settlement regimes are specialized: particular courts or tribunals are set up to address disputes under a particular treaty, or class of treaties (the Rome Statute; regional economic integration treaties; the African,

[41] Romano (n 40) 435.

[42] For many details: Karen J Alter, 'The Multiplication of International Courts and Tribunals after the End of the Cold War' in Romano et al (n 8).

[43] Kingsbury (n 40) 210.

[44] International Military Tribunal, Judgment and Sentences (1947) 41 AJIL 172, 223.

[45] Alter (n 42) 64.

[46] This was not absolute: some of the early projects were specialized (individual claims tribunals, international military tribunals) and the first-ever international court was regional (CACJ); but at the time these were exceptional.

[47] Shany (n 7) 80.

Inter-American, and European human rights conventions; Bilateral Investment Treaties (BITs); the World Trade Organization (WTO) covered agreements; the UN Convention on the Law of the Sea (UNCLOS) etc), often as an indispensable part of an integrated regime that States wanting to be part of have to accept. Jurisdiction, in other words, is more narrowly defined, but has deepened. Moreover, as many of these deep, but narrow treaties are negotiated by States of geographic proximity, there has also been a move from global towards regional dispute settlement.[48]

Specialization and regionalization have permitted groups of States to carve out greater room for binding dispute settlement where global or general solutions lack support. At the same time, they have made the landscape of international dispute settlement more diverse: systems of international adjudication and arbitration today are tailor-made to meet the demands of specialized sub-systems and regional audiences. The 'honourable men [and women]' to whose 'verdict' litigants submit are an increasingly diverse group and function within highly particular social settings.

c. *Diverse Islands of Judicialization*

These developments have indeed 'dramatically transformed the field of international dispute settlement'.[49] That ICaTs have gained in relevance seems difficult to dispute: according to most plausible parameters (numbers of decisions, their impact on State governance, newspaper coverage, academic interest, etc) they matter a lot more today than at any point since the *Alabama* award. Judicialization is extremely 'uneven'[50] though. To every particular field that has been judicialized (trade, investment, human rights, etc), one can easily think of three that have not, or not directly (migration, climate change, finance, and most significantly disputes over *jus ad bellum* and *jus in bello*). As importantly, in a system based on consent, and relying on specialized regimes, the role of courts and tribunals varies from region to region and State to State. While the overall trend is clear—ICaTs have gained in relevance—the picture is significantly more messy than Strindberg's Englishman might have expected: many islands of judicialization have emerged in the sea of international relations, but they are of widely diverging size and scope.

C. Litigating Conflicts Today: Status Quo and Current Challenges

Do these islands of judicialization cover matters of conflict and security? Are the existing (and now numerous) ICaTs competent to address the questions that Strindberg's Englishman wanted them to address? A short response might be along the lines of 'anything but completely; but partly, and increasingly'.

[48] Alter (n 42) 65. [49] Shany (n 7) 79.
[50] cf the title of Kingsbury's excellent account (n 40).

The 'anything but completely' part of the response is straightforward: regimes of arbitration and adjudication remain islands in the sea of dispute settlement, after all, surrounded by water. The remainder of this section expands on the 'partly, and increasingly' part. It offers a highly condensed overview of the limited, but gradually expanding, roles of ICaTs in relation to violent conflict. It does so by identifying conflict-related questions that are submitted to binding dispute settlement with some measure of regularity and points to factors affecting the impact of exercises in conflict litigation. As will be shown, the involvement of ICaTs with questions of conflict and security mirrors the messy reality of uneven judicialization described above: there is great diversity, and different courts play very different roles. Seeking to reflect this, the subsequent section distinguishes between three forms of involvement: (1) the purposeful reliance on courts and tribunals to address discrete aspects of violent conflict; (2) increasing attempts to seek ICJ decisions during or after such conflicts; and (3) diverse attempts to have specialist ICaTs address violent conflicts from the particular perspective of their respective mandates. Needless to say, these distinctions are not clear-cut; in fact, particular conflicts have prompted litigation before generalist and specialist ICaTs. However, the distinction hopefully goes some way towards explaining the impact and limits of conflict litigation and it is believed may help structure the still nascent academic debate.

1. Judicialization by Design: Discrete Aspects of Violent Conflicts Entrusted to Binding Settlement

It is clear from the general account offered above that international adjudication and arbitration have largely been de-coupled from the task of war prevention.[51] Nevertheless, certain aspects of violent conflicts are today regularly entrusted to binding settlement. This remains exceptional, and the respective mandates of international courts are quite particular. Yet in two fields, something approaching a general pattern has emerged.

a. *Binding Resolution of Individual Reparation Claims*

The binding resolution of individual claims for reparation is the first example in point. Recent practice seems to reclaim the 'legacy' of early claims commissions and/or mixed arbitral tribunals.[52] No general reparations claims tribunal has ever been set up; the decision to establish commissions has always been ad hoc (or rather post hoc), taken in the aftermath of a particular crisis, and depending on the political will of the parties involved.[53] However, the practice of the last four decades shows a clear trend.

[51] cf Shany (n 7). [52] Sections B.1 and B.2.

[53] This is in contrast to developments in the field of international criminal justice, where the international community has moved from ad hoc, particular solutions to a general mechanism (in the form of the International Criminal Court): see Section C.1.b.

Most commentators view the Iran–US Claims Tribunal—set up to 'clea[r] away the economic debris following [the] large disruptions of human, economic and political relations' in US–Iranian relations during 1979–81[54]—as a pioneer.[55] Since then, there has been a (modest but significant) resurgence. Mechanisms to address reparation claims were established in the wake of the second Gulf War (the UNCC)[56] and the Eritrea–Ethiopia war of 1998–2000 (the EECC),[57] as well as to deal with more limited aspects of the Yugoslav civil war of 1991–95 and the Kosovo war of 1999.[58] Belatedly, from the end of the twentieth century onwards, a number of States, including Germany and Austria, also set up commissions to deal with reparations claims of victims of the Holocaust.[59]

The aggregate effect of these initiatives need not be overstated: far more often than not, the impact of violent conflicts on individuals remains un-remedied. However, reliance on ad hoc bodies established to 'right wrongs after conflict'[60] has clearly increased, and their output is significant.[61] As a recent study notes, this 'creation of a heterogeneous system of claims commissions complements the proliferation of international courts and tribunals as one further option for post-conflict reparations'[62]—an option that is now regularly on the agenda.

b. *Criminal Sanctions for Grave Infractions of International Law*

The second example is of more recent vintage; and unlike individual reparation claims, it has attracted an enormous amount of interest: this is the project of international(ized) criminal justice, based on the proposition that individuals responsible for certain grave breaches of international law have to answer for their conduct before a particular type of ICaT.[63] Perhaps more so than with reparation claims, the mandate of such courts or tribunals is particular: they scrutinize the conduct of individuals from a very limited angle and with a view to imposing a particular form of (criminal) liability.

[54] David D Caron/John R Crook, *The Iran-United States Claims Tribunal and the Process of International Claims Resolution* (Brill 2000) 363.

[55] Algiers Accords (1981) 20 ILM 224; and for an assessment Caron/Crook, ibid.

[56] UNSC Res 687 (1991) paras 16–19; and the clear account in Lea Brilmayer et al, *International Claims Commissions: Righting Wrongs after Conflict* (Edward Elgar 2017) 18–20.

[57] Agreement for the Resettlement of Displaced Persons, as well as Rehabilitation and Peacebuilding in both Countries (Eritrea-Ethiopia) 2138 UNTS 93 art 5; Brilmayer et al (n 56) 20–2.

[58] Namely the Bosnia-Herzegovina Commission for Real Property Claims of Displaced Persons and Refugees and the Housing and Property Directorate and Claims Commission (Kosovo). For comment and references: Leopold von Carlowitz, 'Settling Property Issues in Complex Peace Operations: The CRPC in Bosnia and Herzegovina and the HPD/CC in Kosovo' (2004) 17 Leiden Journal of International Law 599.

[59] Dolzer (n 29) MN 12.

[60] cf the subtitle of Brilmayer et al (n 56).

[61] To illustrate, the Iran–US Claims Tribunal has awarded *circa* \$2.5 billion to US claimants; the UNCC has addressed *circa* 2.7 mio claims; the Bosnian commission restored property rights in *circa* 200,000 instances.

[62] Brilmayer et al (n 56) 25–6.

[63] For a fuller discussion of developments barely sketched out here, see Claus Kreß, Chapter 13 in this *Handbook*.

The role and record of the various international(ized) criminal courts is controversial. Nearly all of them have been criticized as ineffective or slow, and few of them are immune from the charge of double standards. The International Criminal Court (ICC) in particular seems to bear the weight of the world upon its shoulders. In 2018, the twentieth anniversary of the Rome Statute was celebrated in a rather subdued mood.[64] All this is properly explored in specialist contributions, which abound. For present purposes, the main takeaway is that, since the 1990s, the notion that certain infractions of international law should attract criminal sanctions imposed by an international(ized) criminal court has gained momentum. A large majority of the States of the world are prepared to recognize a role of international courts to hold accountable individuals responsible for a narrowly defined set of international crimes—and demands for perpetrators to be held accountable have become part of the 'arsenal' of conflict management. This is the most high-profile aspect of violent conflicts to have been judicialized.

2. 'Oblique Paths': Conflict Litigation before the World Court

Beyond the two fields just described, the role of ICaTs in relation to violent conflict is more complex. To speak of 'judicialization by design' would be an overstatement: as Kingsbury notes, 'the ICJ's [and other courts'] route into major security-related issues has in recent decades often been through oblique paths'.[65] What is more, jurisdictional strictures have typically limited the impact of judicial pronouncements. Nevertheless, more and more litigants have chosen to explore the 'oblique paths'.

a. *Once Neglected, Now in Regular Use*

The case law of the World Court reflects both the limits and increasing appeal of conflict litigation. Since the 1980s, States have, on frequent occasions, brought before the Court questions of violent conflict. Nicaragua's suit against the United States, intended to end US support for Contra rebels, is widely seen as the beginning of a trend: in two 'epochal judgments'[66] the ICJ affirmed its jurisdiction to scrutinize US conduct and held that this

[64] *Pars pro toto*, see Theodore Meron/Maggie Gardner, 'Introduction to the Symposium on the Rome Statute at Twenty' (2018) 112 AJIL Unbound 155 (considering it 'undeniable that the Rome project still falls short of the expectations of the participants at the groundbreaking conference in Rome'); and a joint op-ed authored by four ex-presidents of the ICC Assembly of States Parties urging institutional reform: Zeid Raad Al Hussein et al, 'The International Criminal Court Needs Fixing' (*Atlantic Council*, 24 April 2019) <https://www.atlanticcouncil.org/blogs/new-atlanticist/the-international-criminal-court-needs-fixing> accessed 25 March 2020.

[65] Kingsbury (n 40) 211.

[66] Fernando L Bordin, 'The Nicaragua v United States Case: An Overview of the Epochal Judgments' in Edgardo Sobenes Obregon/Benjamin Samson (eds), *Nicaragua Before the International Court of Justice: Impact on International Law* (Springer 2018) 59.

conduct violated the prohibitions against the use of force and intervention.[67] This was widely perceived at the time as a remarkable victory of the 'David versus Goliath' type.[68] At the same time, the case tested, and shook, the Court's authority:[69] the US withdrew from the optional clause system, and it refused to comply with the judgment. Whether this judgment influenced the gradual phasing out of US support for the Contras remains disputed.[70]

Since *Nicaragua*, the ICJ has regularly been asked to pronounce on aspects of international conflicts. Its conflict-related cases can broadly be grouped into three[71] categories: First, in a range of conflicts applicants have, following the 'Nicaragua example', seised the Court while a conflict was ongoing, often requesting interim protection alongside.[72] This has, for example, resulted in litigation prompted by Burundi's, Rwanda's, and Uganda's involvement in the Congo wars and Honduras' involvement in the Nicaraguan civil war; and a range of cases arising from the wars between former Yugoslav Republics during the 1990s, between Serbia/Montenegro and NATO Member States during the Kosovo campaign, between Georgia and Russia during the 'July war' of 2008 and more recently between Ukraine and Russia. Secondly, applicants have occasionally instituted proceedings before the Court to challenge particular actions that were considered to escalate an ongoing conflict. Cases brought by Iran against the United States and by Pakistan against India, following attacks on civilian aircraft and on oil platforms, fit this pattern of more limited conflict litigation. Thirdly, on a number of occasions, the Court has been asked to pronounce on the validity of competing territorial claims at a time when violent conflicts had provisionally been contained: cases between Burkina Faso and Mali, Libya and Chad, Nigeria and Cameroon, are examples in point.

b. *Varying Degrees of Influence*

This briefest of summaries suggests that conflict litigation before the World Court has become a regular feature. However, to focus on the number of proceedings risks ignoring the fact that the Court's impact on conflict resolution has varied considerably. Jurisdictional strictures are chiefly responsible for this. Unlike in the *Nicaragua* case,

[67] *Military and Paramilitary Activities in and against Nicaragua* (*Nicaragua v USA*) (Jurisdiction and Admissibility) [1984] ICJ Rep 392; (Merits) [1986] ICJ Rep 14.

[68] Pierre d'Argent, 'Conclusions' in Sobenes Obregon/Samson (n 66) 430.

[69] James R Crawford, 'Military and Paramilitary Affairs in and against Nicaragua Case' MPEPIL (OUP, January 2019) MN 41.

[70] Constanze Schulte, *Compliance with Decisions of the International Court of Justice* (OUP 2004) 197–211.

[71] Advisory opinions—in which the ICJ has, for example, addressed the use of nuclear weapons (*Legality of the Threat or Use of Nuclear Weapons* (Advisory Opinion) [1996] ICJ Rep 226) and Israel's construction of a security wall/fence (*Legal Consequences of the Construction of a Wall in the Occupied Palestinian Territory* (Advisory Opinion) [2004] ICJ Rep 136)—could be viewed as a fourth category; for reasons of space, and as they are advisory rather than binding in nature, they are left aside here.

[72] For information about the cases referred to in the following: 'List of All Cases' (*International Court of Justice*) <https://www.icj-cij.org/en/list-of-all-cases> accessed 22 April 2020.

most cases falling into the first and second category mentioned above were brought on the basis of compromissory clauses covering only limited aspects of the conflict. This forced applicants to restrict their claims and, at times, to clutch at jurisdictional straws. It has also affected the character of the proceedings, many of which, notwithstanding their origin in a conflict, have been dominated by debates about procedural matters or detailed argument about discrete technical issues.

To illustrate, in the majority of Iran's cases against the United States, armed incidents have had to be rationalized as breaches of a bilateral friendship, commerce and navigation (FCN) treaty (the only plausible source of ICJ jurisdiction).[73] The Democratic Republic of the Congo (DRC), in the *Armed Activities* case, portrayed Rwanda's involvement in the Congo war as breaching various multilateral conventions, amongst them the Constitution of the World Health Organization and the Convention on the Elimination of All Forms of Discrimination against Women.[74] Similarly, the case between Bosnia-Herzegovina and Serbia and Montenegro (brought in the middle of the Bosnian war 'in order to prevent a human catastrophe of dimensions unprecedented since the Second World War'[75]), eventually turned on technical, arguments about the statehood of Serbia and Montenegro and its membership in the United Nations.[76] As regards the merits, the ICJ was limited to looking at the Bosnian war through the prism of the Genocide Convention (this being the only jurisdictional basis): for the purposes of the case, the only question was whether Serbia and Montenegro had breached its obligations regarding genocide. Other atrocities (war crimes, crimes against humanity, human rights violations) were irrelevant: as the Court's President observed at the time, 'we had no jurisdiction to make findings in that regard'.[77]

As this statement indicates, in dealing with conflict-related cases, the Court has approached even dramatic cases (which in the view of applicant States and well-meaning observers may have cried out for some judicial assessment) from a consensualist perspective.[78] The careful handling by the Court, coupled with the time requested by parties to prepare their pleadings, has lengthened proceedings, to the point where eventual judgments have turned into retrospective assessments, typically rendered at a time when the conflict had long cooled down, or its character changed.

[73] eg *Oil Platforms* (*Iran v USA*) [2001] ICJ Rep 568 (based on the 1955 Treaty of Amity).

[74] *Armed Activities on the Territory of the Congo* (*DRC v Rwanda*) (Jurisdiction and Admissibility) [2006] ICJ Rep 6.

[75] ICJ, 'Application Instituting Proceedings: Application of the Republic of Bosnia and Herzegovina' (20 March 1993) General List No 91, para 137 <https://www.icj-cij.org/files/case-related/91/7199.pdf> accessed 22 April 2020.

[76] *Application of the Convention on the Prevention and Punishment of the Crime of Genocide* (*Bosnia and Herzegovina v Serbia and Montenegro*) (Judgment) [2007] ICJ Rep 43.

[77] Rosalyn Higgins, 'Statement to the Press' (26 February 2007) <https://www.icj-cij.org/files/press-releases/7/13757.pdf> accessed 16 April 2020.

[78] Conversely, the ICJ has rejected attempts, by respondents, to portray disputes as non-justiciable because they concerned only an aspect of a broader, and sensitive, conflict: notably *Border and Transborder Armed Actions* (*Nicaragua v Honduras*) (Jurisdiction and Admissibility) [1988] ICJ Rep 69 [51], [54].

This does not mean that the Court's decisions in the cases falling within the first and second category mentioned above have been irrelevant—far from it. But their impact has been different from the one Strindberg's Englishman foreshadowed at Vevey: ICJ proceedings have been one means of keeping conflicts on the international agenda, for example with a view to facilitating a negotiated or mediated settlement. Merits judgments, if and when rendered, may have vindicated the position of victim States; they have on occasion helped establish a historical record; they have determined the legality of particular acts committed during ongoing conflicts; and have forced parties to spell out their position in legal terms.[79] However, the ICJ's jurisprudence hardly fits the initial idea of arbitration and adjudication as an alternative to war: the Court has 'at best had mixed results in attempting to end or constrain ongoing armed conflicts.'[80]

Conversely, where conflicts had been contained, the Court has at times played a decisive role in addressing underlying territorial disputes (the third category of cases mentioned above), thereby paving the way for a settlement. To illustrate, its decisions in the Burkina Faso–Mali and Libya–Chad disputes were complied with promptly[81] and are considered to have been 'important in securing peace'.[82] In the high-stake Bakassi dispute, the Court's judgment[83] (largely recognizing Cameroon's claims to a peninsula occupied by Nigeria) has defined the parameters for all subsequent attempts to solve the dispute.[84] Where the Court has been 'brought into' a conflict resolution process with the particular task of assessing territorial claims, without urgency, it has been at its most influential.

The overall experience of conflict litigation before the World Court is ambivalent. States, since *Nicaragua*, have regularly brought violent conflicts before the Court: unlike in the PCIJ's time, or during the Cold War, these cases comprise a significant part of the Court's docket. The Court's role however is typically limited: limited to particular legal aspects that often only tangentially relate to the underlying violent conflict; or limited in time in that the Court is asked to assess the validity of claims to territory once a conflict has been contained already. What is more, claimant States tend to seise the Court while pursuing other avenues alongside: conflict litigation is part of a broader strategy at dispute settlement, which regularly involves the UN's political organs, regional actors, and traditional inter-State diplomacy. In that sense, the Court often performs a

[79] For a more nuanced list, Matheson (n 12) 7–9. [80] ibid 363.

[81] *Territorial Dispute (Libyan Arab Jamahiriya v Chad)* (Judgment) [1994] ICJ Rep 6 (awarding the disputed Azouzou strip to Chad); *Frontier Dispute (Burkina Faso v Republic of Mali)* (Judgment) [1986] ICJ Rep 554 (dividing the Agacher strip between Burkina Faso and Mali); further Schulte (n 70) 232–4 and 183–4.

[82] Aloysius P Llamzon, 'Jurisdiction and Compliance in Recent Decisions of the International Court of Justice' (2008) 18 EJIL 815, 832.

[83] *Land and Maritime Boundary between Cameroon and Nigeria (Cameroon v Nigeria; Equatorial Guinea intervening)* (Judgment) [2002] ICJ Rep 303.

[84] Notably: Republic of Cameroon/Federal Republic of Nigeria, Agreement concerning the modalities of withdrawal and transfer of authority in the Bakassi Peninsula 2542 UNTS 13; and further Llamzon (n 82) 835–8.

'separate but complementary function', but as Rosenne notes, it typically has 'an auxiliary or supporting role'.[85]

3. Linkages and Creeping Jurisdiction: Conflict Litigation before Specialist Courts

When looking beyond reparations claims, international criminal justice and the record of the World Court, the picture becomes fuzzier still. What have other specialist ICaTs had to say on questions of violent conflict? Specialist ICaTs have made at least occasional forays into the terrain of violent conflict. The character and impact of these forays has varied considerably, reflecting the particularities of each individual dispute settlement regime. For the purposes of the present survey, the experience of the more prominent ICaTs can be summarized in two steps.

a. *Too Early to Tell: Litigation Based on World Trade Law, Investment Treaties, and the United Nations Convention on the Law of the Sea*

In three judicialized fields—international trade, investment, and the law of the sea—experience with conflict litigation has so far remained limited. Early attempts, by Nicaragua and Argentina, to challenge trade sanctions imposed during conflicts of the 1980s (the Falklands war and the Nicaraguan civil war, respectively) under the General Agreement on Tariffs and Trade (GATT) system did not go very far.[86] The treatment of investments during Sri Lanka's civil war prompted the first BIT-based investment case, but that initially remained a relatively isolated episode.[87] Early cases based on UNCLOS did see tribunals pronounce on the use of force, but mostly in the course of law enforcement operations of a limited scope.[88]

Over the course of the last decade, conflict litigation before these specialized ICaTs seems to have gained momentum. The Ukrainian practice is noteworthy: since 2016, Ukraine has challenged trade restrictions imposed by Russia before the WTO and instituted proceedings over a maritime incident in the Kerch strait on the basis of UNCLOS;[89] In addition, a number of Ukrainian investors are seeking compensation

[85] Shabtai Rosenne, 'A Role for the International Court of Justice in Crisis Management?' in Gerard Kreijen et al (eds), *State, Sovereignty, and International Governance* (OUP 2002) 217.

[86] Details in Michael J Hahn, 'Vital Interests and the Law of the GATT: An Analysis of GATT's Security Exception' (1991) 12 Michigan Journal of International Law 558.

[87] *AAPL v Sri Lanka*, ICSID Case No ARB87/3, Award (27 June 1990). Writing in 2013, Christoph Schreuer noted that 'the known effects of armed conflicts on investment protection have been few and far sporadic': 'The Protection of Investment in Armed Conflict' in Freya Baetens (ed), *Investment Law Within International Law* (CUP 2013) 20.

[88] eg *The M/V 'Saiga' (No 2) (Saint Vincent and The Grenadines v Guinea)* (Judgment) [1999] ITLOS Reports 10 and *In the Matter of an Arbitration between Guyana v Suriname*, PCA Case No 2004-04, Award (17 September 2007); Matteo Tondini, 'The Use of Force in the Course of Maritime Law Enforcement Operations' (2017) 4 Journal of the Use of Force in International Law 253.

[89] *Russia—Measures Concerning Traffic in Transit* (26 April 2019) WTO DS512; *Case concerning the Detention of Three Ukrainian Naval Vessels (Ukraine v Russian Federation)* (Order) [2019 ITLOS Reports.

from Russia for measures taken in Crimea.[90] At the WTO, Gulf States have followed suit and brought a string of proceedings challenging restrictive measures adopted in the standoff between Qatar, on the one hand, and Saudi Arabia and its allies on the other.[91] This may not be 'a new era',[92] but perhaps it reflects a trend—of parties to conflicts increasingly petitioning specialist ICaTs in the way they have, since *Nicaragua*, petitioned the ICJ: as a forum before which aspects of major conflicts can be raised, in the hope that the even limited judicial scrutiny of the respondent's conduct will further the claimants' cause.

Whether this new trend will yield tangible results, is too early to tell. Experience so far suggests that much will depend on the proper construction of treaty-based security exceptions. In the WTO context, the Panel in *Russia—Traffic in Trade*[93] recognized that Member States enjoy much discretion in taking measures 'consider[ed] necessary for the protection of... essential security interests'.[94] Should this reading become accepted, it would severely limit the potential for WTO litigation during 'situation[s] of armed conflict, or latent armed conflict, or of heightened tension or crisis, or of general instability engulfing or surrounding a state'.[95] Similar security clauses feature in many investment treaties, but their application to violent conflicts has yet to be tested.[96] Under UNCLOS, parties can exempt 'disputes relating to military measures' from the mandatory jurisdiction of UNCLOS dispute settlement bodies; while the International Tribunal for the Law of the Sea (ITLOS) in a recent interim decision has adopted a restrictive interpretation of that exception, its approach has been criticized and will certainly not be the last word.[97]

All this makes it very difficult to predict whether specialist ICaTs will ever play a significant role in relation to violent conflict. Recent practice certainly suggests that States involved in conflicts are exploring specialist litigation as an option; however, based on the ICJ's (slightly more reliable) experience, one should perhaps not expect WTO, UNCLOS, or investment dispute settlement bodies to play more than 'an auxiliary or supporting role'.[98]

[90] Useful information about the first nine proceedings is provided by Serhii Uvarov, 'Investment Disputes Related to Crimea: Overview' (*Arbitration Journal*, 22 January 2019) <https://journal.arbitration.ru/reviews/investment-disputes-related-to-crimea-overview/> accessed 24 March 2020.

[91] For details: 'Chronological List of Disputes Case' (*WTO*) (disputes DS526, DS527, DS528, DS567 and DS576) <www.wto.org/english/tratop_e/dispu_e/dispu_status_e.htm> accessed 22 April 2020.

[92] But cf Tania Voon, 'The Security Exception in WTO Law: Entering a New Era' (2019) 113 AJIL Unbound 45.

[93] *Russia—Measures Concerning Traffic in Transit*, Panel Report (5 April 2019) (WT/DS512/R).

[94] General Agreement on Tariffs and Trade 64 UNTS 187 art XXI(b)(iii).

[95] Panel Report (n 93) para 7.76.

[96] By contrast, in the Crimean cases brought by investors, tribunals seem to agree that investments made in Crimea are protected under the Russia–Ukraine 1998 BIT, which covers investments in 'the territory of the Russian Federation' (art 1(4)); G Matteo Vaccaro-Incisa, 'Crimea Investment Disputes: Are Jurisdictional Hurdles Being Overcome too Easily?' (*EJILTalk!*, 9 May 2018) <https://www.ejiltalk.org/crimea-investment-disputes-are-jurisdictional-hurdles-being-overcome-too-easily/> accessed 25 March 2020.

[97] *Case Concerning the Detention Of Three Ukrainian Naval Vessels* (n 89).

[98] Rosenne (n 85).

b. *Many Cases, Unclear Impact: Human Rights Litigation*

Of the various specialist institutions, human rights courts are the only ones to have frequently, and over a relevant period, engaged with questions of violent conflict.[99] Today, they regularly scrutinize State conduct during such conflicts from the perspective of human rights law, in response to individual and State claims. This has resulted in an amalgamation of human rights and rules of international humanitarian law (IHL) prescribing limits of State conduct during conflict—an amalgamation facilitated by international jurisprudence, which has freed human rights law from two potential shackles. To elaborate, human rights courts, as well as other human rights bodies, have recognized that human rights, while primarily meant to apply in peacetime, remain applicable in armed conflict, and that they are not derogated by special rules of IHL.[100]

Freed from these shackles, '[t]he main human rights bodies created under international law … have all repeatedly been confronted with situations of armed conflict'.[101] From their 'vast jurisprudence',[102] three main propositions would seem to emerge.

First, the reach of human rights protection during armed conflict may depend on the *locus* of the impugned measure. Human rights remain applicable in principle, but the jurisdiction of human rights courts is typically limited geographically: for measures taken in conflicts outside a State's territory, some sustained form of control over the human rights victim seems required.[103] Secondly, when determining the precise scope of human rights obligations during violent conflict, human rights courts have typically construed human rights obligations in light of applicable rules of IHL. This has resulted in a (challenging) context-specific reading that 'imports' considerations developed in the context of armed conflicts into human rights language: human rights have not only transformed discussions about armed conflict, but have also been transformed in the process. Thirdly, the 'vast jurisprudence' covers the field very unevenly. Human rights jurisprudence has notably accentuated remedial rights of victims, and emphasized the need for breaches to be investigated. By contrast, the debate about economic and social rights during violent conflict is at an early stage. All this suggests that, as noted by Lubell in 2005, 'the focus of the arguments [has] now shift[ed] from the question of if human rights law applies

[99] See Adama Dieng, Chapter 19 in this *Handbook*.

[100] For prominent statements reflecting the move towards amalgamation: eg the ICJ's *Wall* opinion (n 71) para 25; UNHRC 'General Comment No 29: Derogation during a State of Emergency (Article 4)' (31 August 2001) UN Doc CCPR/C/21/Rev.1/Add.11, para 3; Gerd Oberleitner, *Human Rights in Armed Conflict Law, Practice, Policy* (CUP 2015) chs 5–7.

[101] Oberleitner (n 100) 239.

[102] Cordula Droege, 'The Interplay Between International Humanitarian Law and International Human Rights Law in Situations of Armed Conflict' (2007) 40 Israel Law Review 310, 313.

[103] The precise degree of control is disputed and varies from regime to regime: for example, the ECtHR has exercised jurisdiction over extraterritorial conduct if the State concerned exercised 'effective overall control' over an area (eg, *Cyprus v Turkey*, App No 25781/94, 10 May 2001), but dismissed complaints brought by victims of an airstrike (*Banković v Belgium*, App No 52207/99, 12 December 2001). For details: Fons Coomans/Menno T Kamminga (eds), *Extraterritorial Application of Human Rights Treaties* (Intersentia 2004).

during armed conflict to that of how it applies, and to the practical problems encountered in its application.'[104]

Fifteen years later, these practical problems are far from addressed. In a 2015 study, Oberleitner struck a fairly cautious note: given the 'uneven . . . impact' of human rights decisions, he saw 'not very strong grounds for positioning human rights bodies as guardians of humanitarian law.'[105] If looked at from the comparative angle adopted in the present overview, this may, however, be too cautious a view: of the various specialized ICaTs, those operating in the field of human rights have the most sustained record of scrutinizing State conduct during violent conflict. Their jurisprudence cannot make up for the absence of an international 'IHL court', or more generally the deficiencies of the particular systems of ensuring respect for State conduct during violent conflict. However, their involvement can be seen as a 'second-best . . . option to ensure respect for humanitarian law.'[106]

D. Concluding Thoughts

What would von Bleichroden's party make of developments surveyed in the last sections? In some respects, the 'quiet and peaceful' conversation that took place 150 years ago has a modern feel. At enlightened dinner parties, at least those of the progressive–pacifist kind, whether war is inevitable remains a live question. Something more than a 'Confederation of European States'—a rather fanciful thought in 1872—has come to exist and some indeed view it, as Strindberg's Englishman anticipated, as a 'Switzerland writ large.'[107]

Yet when it comes to the role of ICaTs, von Bleichroden and his guests seem to have got it wrong. What they hoped for has proved illusory; while what has happened, they did not foresee. Nothing in their discussion hints at the massive growth of international arbitration and adjudication: presumably even Strindberg's Englishman would be amazed by the industrial scale of 'judgment production' that characterizes the current era. Conversely, his hope that ICaTs would regularly prevent wars has not materialized. They typically have neither the mandate nor the means to do so; neither States nor guests at dinner parties today view ICaTs as central guardians of world peace: the various 'wars against the future' waged in the course of the past 150 years have not led States to rally to the PtAA cause.

Nevertheless, one might hope that Strindberg's Englishman would see the developments of the last 150 years not just as a betrayal of an ideal, but rather as an adjustment of an initial plan: an adjustment that has seen ICaTs cede the centre stage to other actors and

[104] Noam Lubell, 'Challenges in Applying Human Rights Law to Armed Conflict' (2005) 87 International Review of the Red Cross 737, 738.

[105] Oberleitner (n 100) 322, 321. [106] ibid 320.

[107] Zbigniew Brzezinski, 'Living with a New Europe' (2000) 60 The National Interest 17, 20.

mechanisms of dispute resolution, notably to political organs of collective security organizations which, for a century, have been at the forefront of the international community's effort to maintain peace and security. But an adjustment that, especially in the past decades, has seen ICaTs perform a number of diverse functions in relation to violent conflicts. They have become fora for (often retrospective) debates about matters of war and peace, tools for mobilizing public opinion and recorders of history; they occasionally impose sanctions on individuals; they regularly enforce individual claims to reparation following major upheavals; and they undertake an often highly detailed scrutiny of particular aspects of State conduct on the basis of conventions containing compromissory clauses—from bilateral FCN treaties to human rights treaties. As the preceding discussion illustrates, these functions are not integrated into any master plan: the overall impression is of 'bric-à-brac', not coherent 'system'.[108] But the trend is clear: as Matheson notes, '[t]he involvement of international civil tribunals in situations of armed conflict over the past two decades stands in sharp contrast with what came before'.[109] If one adds to this observation (focused as it is on 'civil' tribunals) the gradual 'coming of age' of international criminal justice, then perhaps the picture is not altogether bleak. International courts and tribunals have a lesser role than anticipated by Strindberg's Englishman, but perform a range of functions and are increasingly asked to scrutinize State conduct during violent conflict.

[108] Jean Combacau, 'Le droit international: bric-à-brac ou système?' (1986) 31 Archives de philosophie du droit 85.

[109] Matheson (n 12) 61.

CHAPTER 41

CRIMINAL PROSECUTION

FAUSTO POCAR

A. The International Prosecution of International Crimes

Traditionally, in domestic law, criminal prosecution has been regarded as a tool capable of contributing to peaceful and secure governance. Although its role and effectiveness have sometimes been challenged, no State has ever excluded such a tool from its legislation and practice. Under international law, however, recourse to criminal prosecution as a safeguard for maintaining international peace and security is very recent and still limited, and in many respects disputed. This is the case both when international rules are intended to be applied by international jurisdictions and when they are directed at soliciting the exercise of criminal prosecution by domestic courts.

Except for some initiatives to engage the criminal responsibility of the German Kaiser for aggression against Belgium by Germany in the First World War,[1] it was only in the aftermath of the Second World War that a need was definitively perceived for international criminal prosecution to contribute to the establishment or maintenance of international peace and security. However, addressing this need implied the acceptance of two 'firsts' in international law: on one hand, that individuals and not only States could be personally responsible for the violation of international law, and, on the other hand, that serious violations of international law may entail individual criminal responsibility under international law, irrespective of the criminalization of such behaviour under domestic law. These legal implications explain why, unlike at the domestic level where the range of criminal conduct is frequently rather wide (depending on the public policy of a government), the prudent introduction of criminal prosecution in the

[1] Simeon E Baldwin, 'The Proposed Trial of the Former Kaiser' (1919) 29 Yale Law Journal 75; William A Schabas, *The Trial of the Kaiser* (OUP 2018).

international context was accompanied by its restriction to limited categories of serious crimes capable of affecting the whole international community.

With regard to international criminal prosecution, this approach was reflected in the 1945 London Charter of the International Military Tribunal (IMT Charter) and the 1946 Charter of the International Military Tribunal for the Far East,[2] which identified the categories of crimes against peace, war crimes, and crimes against humanity as crimes under international law. By identifying these categories of international crimes, the IMT Charter comprised both violations of the *jus ad bellum* (crimes against peace) and of the *jus in bello* (war crimes), with the addition of the category of crimes against humanity, provided that they were perpetrated 'in execution of or in connection with' any crime within the first two categories.[3] Later, domestic criminal prosecution of grave breaches of international humanitarian law was equally invoked in the four 1949 Geneva Conventions (GCs),[4] and in the subsequent 1977 Additional Protocol I (AP I).[5]

A similar approach inspired, almost fifty years later, the drafting by the UN Security Council (UNSC) of the Statute of the International Criminal Tribunal for the Former Yugoslavia (ICTY).[6] Although this Statute restricted the scope of international jurisdiction by dropping the category of crimes against peace, it reaffirmed jurisdiction over war crimes committed in international armed conflicts and crimes against humanity committed in armed conflict, whether international or internal. The addition of genocide as an international crime did not represent a proper increase in the scope of international jurisdiction, as the conduct constituting this crime was in fact categorized in the previous instruments under the label of crimes against humanity and was singled out as a specific crime only later, in the Convention on the Prevention and Punishment of the Crime of Genocide (Genocide Convention).[7] Equally, the Statute of the International Criminal Tribunal for Rwanda (ICTR) retained the same categories of crimes, but adapted the notion of war crimes to the events in the country concerned, where only a non-international conflict occurred, by introducing a grave breaches regime for violations of Common Article 3 of the GCs and AP II.[8]

[2] Respectively Agreement for the Prosecution and Punishment of the Major War Criminals of the European Axis, and Charter of the International Military Tribunal 82 UNTS 279 and Special Proclamation by the Supreme Commander for the Allied Powers at Tokyo (19 January 1946) TIAS 1589, 20.

[3] Yoram Dinstein, 'The Distinctions between War Crimes and Crimes against Peace' (1994) 24 Israel Yearbook of Human Rights 1.

[4] Geneva Convention (I) for the Amelioration of the Condition of the Wounded and Sick in Armed Forces in the Field 75 UNTS 31 art 49 (GC I); Geneva Convention (II) for the Amelioration of the Wounded, Sick and Shipwrecked Members of Armed Forces at Sea 75 UNTS 85 art 50 (GC II); Geneva Convention (III) Relative to the Treatment of Prisoners of War 75 UNTS 135 art 129 (GC III); Geneva Convention (IV) Relative to the Protection of Civilian Persons in Time of War 75 UNTS 287 art 146 (GC IV).

[5] Protocol Additional to the Geneva Conventions of 12 August 1949 and relating to the Protection of Victims of International Armed Conflicts (Protocol I) 1125 UNTS 3 art 85 (AP I).

[6] Adopted by UNSC Res 827 (1993).

[7] 78 UNTS 277; Paola Gaeta (ed), *The UN Genocide Convention: A Commentary* (OUP 2009).

[8] Statute of the International Criminal Tribunal for the Prosecution of Persons Responsible for Genocide and Other Serious Violations of International Humanitarian Law Committed in the Territory

The same categorization has also guided the drafting of the Rome Statute of the International Criminal Court (ICC Statute),[9] which expressly provides that the jurisdiction of the Court 'shall be limited to the most serious crimes of concern to the international community as a whole', and identifies these crimes as the crime of genocide, crimes against humanity, war crimes and the crime of aggression.[10] It has to be mentioned, in this context, that the ICC Statute aims at a complete codification of the crimes that deserve to be submitted to an international jurisdiction, and that the list of the crimes provided therein is far longer and more specific than the list contained in previous documents.[11]

A catalogue of the categories of crimes regarded as international by nature would not be complete without a reference to the statutes of other criminal courts and tribunals established with international participation.[12] Such ad hoc courts and tribunals are generally regarded as mixed or hybrid due to their composition, with chambers consisting of national judges of the country concerned and judges appointed by an international authority. They present different features and cannot be regarded as homogeneous from a legal point of view, and frequently their jurisdiction encompasses the prosecution of individuals for violations of national as well as international law. The scope of their jurisdiction is not uniform and may vary according to the exigencies of each situation. However, except for dealing with domestic crimes, reference is generally made to all, or limited to some, of the categories of international crimes described above. For these reasons, it is not necessary to go more into detail as to the features of these mixed jurisdictions, or domestic jurisdictions with international participation, except to underline that they make a substantial contribution to the application of international criminal law by domestic courts, in line with the general understanding that the implementation

of Rwanda and Rwandan Citizens Responsible for Genocide and Other Such Violations Committed in the Territory of Neighbouring States, between 1 January 1994 and 31 December 1994, adopted by UNSC Res 955 (1994) art 4 (ICTR Statute); Yoram Dinstein, *Non-International Armed Conflicts in International Law* (CUP 2014) 175–7.

[9] 2187 UNTS 3 (ICC Statute). [10] ibid art 5.

[11] Additionally, unlike in the Statutes of the ad hoc Tribunals, the list of crimes contained in the ICC Statute is supplemented by the *Elements of Crimes*, adopted by the Assembly of State Parties.

[12] The international community and the UN in particular have supported the institution of many judicial bodies, as it is illustrated by the establishment of the Mixed Panels by the UN Administration in Kosovo: Regulation No 2000/64 on Assignment of International Judges/Prosecutors and/or Change of Venue (15 December 2000) UNMIK/REG/2000/64; the Special Court for Sierra Leone (SCSL) UNSC Res 1315 (2000); United Nations Transitional Administration, Regulation No 2000/15 on the Establishment of Panels with Exclusive Jurisdiction over Serious Criminal Offences (6 June 2000) UNTAET/REG/2000/15; the Extraordinary Chambers in the Courts of Cambodia (ECCC), Agreement between the UN and the Royal Government of Cambodia Concerning the Prosecution Under Cambodian Law of Crimes Committed During the Period of Democratic Kampuchea (6 June 2003); the Special War Crimes Chamber of the State Court Bosnia and Herzegovina (BWCC) instituted in 2005 with the support of the European Communities; the Special Tribunal for Lebanon (STL) UNSC Res 1757 (2007); and the Kosovo Specialist Chambers and Specialist Prosecutor's Office, instituted in 2015 by the Kosovo Assembly following an exchange of letters between the President of Kosovo and the High Representative of the European Union for Foreign Affairs and Security Policy: Law No 05/L-053 on Specialist Chambers and Specialist Prosecutor's Office (2015) Official Gazette of the Republic of Kosovo, No 27 (31 August 2015) 1–46.

of international criminal law should be primarily a matter for domestic rather than for international courts.[13]

In short, the current notion of international crimes represents a limited development of the principles affirmed after the Second World War and is consolidated in international law, subject to the enlargement of the categories initially identified with the addition of specific new crimes, especially in the ICC Statute. However, while the notion of international crimes and their classification is not substantially disputed in international law, attention must be drawn to the differences that have occurred in their interpretation and application by international courts and tribunals, depending on whether they relied on customary international law or on their statutes. It must be recalled that ad hoc tribunals were created in the aftermath of armed conflict or of a crisis during which the crimes subjected to their jurisdiction had been committed. In light of this, their statutes could not dictate the applicable law, as this would constitute a violation of the general principle of non-retroactivity of criminal law. The lists of crimes contained in their statutes could only be regarded as governing the jurisdiction of the tribunal concerned, while the applicable law had to be drawn from customary international law existing at the time when the crimes had been perpetrated.[14] The same approach had to be followed with respect to the principles of individual criminal responsibility, except where a statute, like the ICC Statute, provides for the prosecution of crimes committed subsequent to its entry into force.[15] Only in this case may its provisions constitute the materially applicable law in full compliance with the principle of legality.

In this context, given that the ICC Statute does not merely codify customary international law, but also partially develops or restricts it, its adoption has produced some degree of fragmentation of international criminal law, which further impacts on the existing international case law. Paradoxically, such fragmentation is due to the creation of a court which is meant to be universal, thus arguably applying common international legal standards. It will be for the ICC to resolve the possible shortcomings of this fragmentation of the applicable law, by duly taking into account customary international law, as it can do under its statute,[16] as well as the abundant international case law based on customary law, with a view to enhancing a dialogue amongst international criminal courts and promoting the development of a consistent and coherent system of international criminal law.[17]

[13] GC I (n 4) art 49; GC II (n 4) art 50; GC III (n 4) art 129; GC IV (n 4) art 146, providing for domestic universal jurisdiction over war crimes; as well as ICC Statute (n 9) art 17 recognizing under certain conditions the priority of domestic prosecution over the Court's jurisdiction.

[14] However, reference could also be made to previous treaties applicable with no doubt to the concerned situation, like the GCs. These conventions, however, did not prescribe all the elements of the crimes constituting grave breaches. Consequently, these elements could only be assessed under customary law.

[15] ICC Statute (n 9) art 11(1). [16] ibid art 21(1)(b).

[17] Fausto Pocar, 'International Criminal Justice and the Unifying Role of Customary Law' (2016) 21 Uniform Law Review 171; Fausto Pocar, 'Transformation of Customary Law through ICC Practice' (2018) 112 AJIL Unbound 182.

B. International Crimes and their Connection with an Armed Conflict: War Crimes

Most of the aforementioned international legal instruments established criminal jurisdiction principally with respect to individual responsibility for infringing laws and customs of war or violating humanitarian principles in connection to an armed conflict. Indeed, although they also envisaged crimes against humanity, their international or domestic adjudication was initially provided only when such crimes were connected to an armed conflict or committed in wartime. Furthermore, States have traditionally been inclined to protect their sovereign prerogatives, particularly in terms of public policy and security, and their consequent reluctance to accept international or foreign investigation for purposes of prosecution with respect to events which have occurred on their territory during a domestic armed conflict or in peacetime. This has meant that only those international crimes which had occurred in connection with international armed conflicts had been considered international, and for a long time prevented the adoption of a more liberal approach which would include international crimes committed in non-international armed conflicts or peacetime.[18]

In this context, it is telling that the grave breaches regime set up in the GCs for serious violations of the obligations laid down in the conventions did not encompass violations of Common Article 3, which is the sole provision dealing with minimum humanitarian requirements in non-international armed conflicts. Even more telling is that no grave breaches regime was introduced in AP II almost thirty years later, notwithstanding the more detailed legislation on non-international armed conflicts provided therein. Therefore, such legal instruments only regarded criminal prosecution as a tool contributing to international security in special circumstances, namely when an international armed conflict required the prosecution of international crimes to establish or restore the rule of law in countries torn by the conflict, aiming at preventing the commission of such crimes in the future.

A similarly prudent approach guided the establishment of the first international criminal tribunal by the UN many years later. As already mentioned, the ICTY Statute entrusted the Tribunal with jurisdiction to adjudicate war crimes, genocide, and crimes against humanity, but mentioned expressly only the grave breaches regime of the GCs[19] and some violations of the laws and customs of war that reflected behaviour banned under the 1907 Hague Convention (IV) Respecting the Laws and Customs of War on

[18] Ken Roberts, 'The Contribution of the ICTY to the Grave Breaches Regime' (2009) 7 JICJ 743, 745.

[19] ICTY Statute (n 6) art 2 which essentially reproduces, with minor drafting changes, the list of grave breaches as contained in GC IV (n 4) art 147.

Land and the Regulations thereto.[20] Thus, it explicitly referred only to jurisdiction over war crimes committed in an international armed conflict.

However, the armed conflict in the Balkans was partly international and partly non-international, depending on the area in which belligerent acts took place, especially in Bosnia and Herzegovina where the regular army of the State was also fighting against non-State actors, or different groups of non-State actors were fighting against each other. Given this complexity, the ICTY had to define the scope of its jurisdiction over the war crimes committed in the region, either to restrict the notion of war crimes to violations committed in the situations where the conflict could be characterized as international, or to extend it to all violations of the same kind committed anywhere during the conflict. The ICTY chose the second option following a twofold approach.

On the one hand, it reaffirmed in *Tadic*[21] that a conflict is international not only where the belligerents are different States, but also where there is an internal armed conflict with a foreign State intervening, as held by the International Court of Justice (ICJ) in the *Nicaragua* case.[22] However, it departed from the ICJ's position that 'effective control' of a foreign State over an organized armed group fighting against the State is necessary to transform the internal armed conflict into an international one and to trigger State responsibility. The Tribunal rather held that 'overall control' by a foreign government is sufficient to conclude that a conflict is international in nature,[23] broadening the notion of an international armed conflict for the purposes of exercising criminal jurisdiction under the GCs and AP I grave breaches regime.

On the other hand, in a previous *Tadic* decision,[24] it interpreted Article 3 of the ICTY Statute—with respect to the clause indicating that the list of the violations contained therein is not exhaustive—as including, amongst the violations of the laws and customs of war, the 'serious violations' of Common Article 3 GCs, provided that certain conditions were met as to the gravity of the violation concerned. The *Tadic* Jurisdiction Decision constituted a 'breakthrough' in international humanitarian law and criminal law.[25] In explicitly stating that 'at least with respect to the minimum rules in Common Article 3 CGs, the character of the conflict is irrelevant',[26] it opened the door to going beyond Common Article 3 and concluding that all acts constituting war crimes in international conflicts also constitute war crimes when committed in non-international armed conflicts. It thus unified the regime of war crimes under customary international law, also bearing in mind that the GCs are generally regarded as reflecting customary

[20] ICTY Statute (n 6) art 3. It has to be noted, however, that the list of violations of the laws and customs of war contained ibid is not exhaustive.

[21] *Prosecutor v Tadic* (Appeal Judgement) ICTY Case No IT-94-1-A (15 July 1999) paras 115–45.

[22] *Case concerning Military and Paramilitary Activities in and Against Nicaragua (Nicaragua v United States of America)* (Merits) [1986] ICJ Rep 14 [115].

[23] *Tadic*, Appeal Judgment (n 21) paras 130–45.

[24] *Prosecutor v Tadic* (Decision on the Defence Motion for Interlocutory Appeal on Jurisdiction) ICTY Case No IT-94-1-AR72 (2 October 1995) paras 74, 88, 143–4.

[25] eg Michael Bothe, 'War Crimes' in Antonio Cassese et al (eds), *The Rome Statute of the International Criminal Court: A Commentary* (vol I, OUP 2002) 417.

[26] *Tadic*, Jurisdiction Decision (n 24) para 102.

international law.[27] From that decision on, the issue of assessing the nature of the conflict to exercise criminal jurisdiction became less critical in the case law of the ICTY.[28]

Notwithstanding this jurisprudential development, which is not challenged in international practice, the distinction between war crimes committed in international and non-international armed conflicts continued to be followed in international documents and instruments, including in the Draft Code of Crimes, adopted by the International Law Commission (ILC)[29] only a few months later, as well as in the ICC Statute, which did not formally unify the grave breaches regime. Article 20 of the Draft Code of Crimes, however, explicitly recognizes as war crimes the serious violations of international humanitarian law 'applicable in armed conflicts not of an international character', as contained in Common Article 3 GCs and Article 4(2) AP II.[30] Additionally, with respect to some crimes, it refers to violations of international humanitarian law in general terms, without distinguishing between the two types of conflict.[31]

Although the negotiations for the ICC Statute relied to a large extent on the Draft Code of Crimes, the Statute demonstrated a more traditional approach to the classification of war crimes in terms of the distinction between international and non-international armed conflicts. After referring to the grave breaches of the GCs[32] and describing a long list of other serious violations of the laws and customs applicable in international armed conflicts, within the established framework of international law,[33] the ICC Statute considers as war crimes, in the case of a non-international armed conflict, 'serious violations of article 3 common to the four Geneva Conventions',[34] without mentioning Article 4(2) of AP II. However, a long list of war crimes applicable in non-international armed conflicts was added in the ICC Statute, including most of the provisions in Article 4(2) of AP II.[35] This may be surprising in light of the jurisprudential trend towards minimizing the role of conflict characterization in defining war crimes under customary international law. However, the ICC Statute is an international treaty and the contracting States were concerned with adopting precise and exhaustive obligations on which all of them could agree, namely an extension of the GCs' grave breaches regime to non-international armed conflicts, rather than engaging in an introduction of such a regime for AP II, which does not enjoy the same general international support.[36]

[27] cf Fausto Pocar, 'Protocol I Additional to the 1949 Geneva Conventions and Customary International Law' (2001) 31 Israel Yearbook of Human Rights 145.

[28] The nature of the conflict continued to be brought before the ICTY especially for characterizing the victims as protected persons in international conflicts under the GCs.

[29] ILC, 'Draft Code of Crimes against the Peace and Security of Mankind, with Commentary' (1996) II(2) Yearbook of the International Law Commission 15 (Draft Code of Crimes).

[30] ibid art 20(f). This sub-paragraph is drawn from ICTR Statute (n 8) art 4, and has been considered by the ILC to be 'of particular importance in view of the frequency of non-international armed conflicts in recent years': see Draft Code of Crimes (n 29) art 20 and commentary (para 14).

[31] Draft Code of Crimes (n 29) art 20(d) and (g). [32] ICC Statute (n 9) art 8(2)(a).

[33] ibid art 8(2)(b). [34] ibid art 8(2)(c). [35] ibid art 8(2)(e).

[36] This prudent approach of the ICC Statute is confirmed by the simultaneous rigid definition of the threshold necessary for the existence of a non-international armed conflict: ibid art 8 (2)(d).

C. International Crimes Independent from an Armed Conflict: Crimes against Humanity

While the attention of criminal prosecution was initially focused on war crimes and crimes against humanity presenting a link with a conflict, that link was gradually abandoned after the Nuremberg experience. As early as 1948 the Genocide Convention,[37] which encompasses conduct that was in fact considered at Nuremberg under the category of crimes against humanity, affirmed that genocide could be committed 'in time of peace or in time of war'.[38] Except for genocide, however, a link with an armed conflict was considered necessary for criminal prosecution of crimes against humanity until the establishment of the ICTY. Although the ICTY Statute gave the tribunal the power to prosecute persons responsible for crimes against humanity 'when committed in armed conflict, whether international or internal in character',[39] the latter reduced the weight of this *nexus*, stating that it constituted only a jurisdictional requirement.[40] The link with an armed conflict also for jurisdictional purposes had already been omitted in the ICTR Statute, as it was later from the statutes of subsequent international or hybrid tribunals, including the ICC Statute, so that it cannot be regarded any longer as warranted under customary international law.[41]

In light of this, the common element that qualifies a criminal act as a crime against humanity under international law is its commission as part of a widespread or systematic attack against a civilian population, with knowledge of the attack. This approach is shared by the statutes and the case law of all existing international or hybrid tribunals, but has been sometimes restricted through additional qualifications of the attack, which in any event does not necessarily have to be an armed attack. Thus, the ICTR Statute indicates that the attack must be 'on national, political, ethnic, racial or religious grounds'.[42] The ICC Statute further restricts the scope of the provision by stating that the attack must occur 'pursuant to or in furtherance of a State or organizational policy to commit such attack'.[43] While the first restriction may stem from the consideration that crimes against humanity were committed in the 1994 Rwandan crisis in connection to genocide, the qualification introduced in the ICC Statute has a wider scope and aims to exclude the characterization of criminal acts as crimes against humanity even where they are part of a widespread or systematic attack against a civilian population, should the prosecution not prove that the attack is driven by a State or an organization. This restriction has not been identified by the ad hoc tribunals as required under customary international law, and should be regarded as a limitation introduced by the ICC Statute.

[37] See n 7. [38] Genocide Convention (n 7) art 1. [39] ICTY Statute (n 6) art 5.

[40] *Tadic*, Jurisdiction Decision (n 24) paras 141–2.

[41] Guido Acquaviva/Fausto Pocar, 'Crimes against Humanity' MPEPIL (OUP, June 2008) MN 13.

[42] ICTR Statute (n 8) art 3. [43] ICC Statute (n 9) art 7(2)(a).

While it is impossible to analyse here all criminal acts that could potentially qualify as crimes against humanity under the aforementioned circumstances, it is worth mentioning 'genocide' and 'persecution' as typical examples. According to the Genocide Convention, genocide means any of several criminal acts listed in the convention,[44] 'committed with intent to destroy, in whole or in part, a national, ethnical, racial or religious group, as such'.[45] The crime is therefore characterized by the special intent to destroy a qualified group, in addition to the general intent to commit the underlying criminal act. Persecution, in turn, means the intentional and severe deprivation of fundamental rights contrary to international law due to the identity of a group on political, racial, national, ethnic, cultural, religious, gender, or other grounds that are universally recognized as impermissible under international law.[46] Persecution, too, is therefore characterized by the special intent to target the victim because of his or her belonging to a qualified group. Thus, the special intent element associates the two crimes, although they are distinct because the range of the qualified groups is wider with respect to persecution. These two crimes were the typical offences adjudicated by the ICTY and the ICTR, where genocide was normally referred to in the context of Rwanda and persecution generally captured the situation in the former Yugoslavia, which was characterized by ethnic cleansing.

Despite their significance, or maybe just because of it, the debate is still open as to the precise scope of these two crimes. With respect to genocide, while the 1948 Convention certainly conforms to customary international law, it is unclear whether it currently codifies it entirely.[47] With regard to persecution, it is debated whether its underlying act (namely, the denial of a fundamental right) ought to be a crime as such or could be a violation of serious gravity but not necessarily constituting a crime under international law. The IMT Charter had taken the first option by stating that persecution should be punished only if associated with a crime under the statute.[48] By contrast, the ICTY Statute left the question open, and the Tribunal consistently expressed itself in favour of the second option, referring to customary international law.[49] The ICC Statute reverted to the first option,[50] arguably derogating from customary law. However, while a derogation is certainly admissible for purposes of ICC jurisdiction, it may still be challenged whether it has an impact on the construction of the legal elements of the crime concerned.[51]

[44] Genocide Convention (n 7) art 2. [45] ibid.

[46] *Prosecutor v Kupreskic et al* (Judgment) ICTY Case No IT-95-16-T (14 January 2000) para 621.

[47] *Prosecutor v Krstic* (Appeal Judgment) ICTY Case No IT-98-33-A (19 April 2004) para 16.

[48] IMT Statute (n 2) art 6.

[49] *Kupreskic* (n 46) para 621; *Prosecutor v Kvocka* (Appeal Judgment) ICTY Case No IT-98-30/1-A (28 February 2005) para 323.

[50] ICC Statute (n 9) art 7(1)(h).

[51] Fausto Pocar, 'Persecution as a Crime under International Criminal Law' (2008) 2 Journal of National Security Law and Policy 355.

D. International and Domestic Prosecution of International Crimes

In considering the classification of crimes under international law and their description, reference has been made primarily to statutes of international and hybrid criminal courts and tribunals. However, domestic courts are also required to exercise criminal jurisdiction over international crimes. In light of international practice—which records the occurrence of high numbers of international crimes—it is evident that internationally established courts cannot be given exclusive jurisdiction over all such crimes, unless this is strictly and narrowly provided.[52] A concurrence of international and domestic prosecution is therefore unavoidable, and distribution of competence cannot be based solely on the international or domestic nature of the crimes involved. It is therefore appropriate to consider the principles governing this concurrent jurisdiction under international law.

No common, rigid criteria have been followed in the existing statutes, although current practice seems to assert that international jurisdiction should be exercised only or primarily over high-ranking accused persons or significant cases of collective responsibility, while lower ranking accused persons and less significant cases should be left to domestic adjudication. This approach was evident already in the IMT Charter, which dealt primarily with the high-ranking Nazi leaders, ascribing to the IMT the power to declare that group criminal, leaving it to national, military, or occupation courts to bring individuals to trial for membership thereof. The understanding was that the criminal nature of the group would be considered proved and could not be further questioned.[53]

By contrast, no such approach inspired the ICTY and ICTR Statutes. They allocated jurisdiction to the respective tribunal over any alleged perpetrator of the crimes listed therein, without restrictions. While recognizing that domestic courts had concurrent jurisdiction over such crimes, they declare the priority of international over domestic jurisdiction, and provide that 'at any stage of the procedure, the International Tribunal may formally request national courts to defer to the competence of the International Tribunal'.[54] Thus, they left it to the ICTY and to the ICTR to decide, even on a case by case basis, on the distribution of their concurrent jurisdiction with domestic courts.[55] However, soon it became apparent that the high number of persons indicted and apprehended would not have permitted the two ad hoc tribunals to complete their work within a reasonable time under such circumstances. Thus, upon a recommendation of the UNSC,[56] a decision was taken to amend their rules of procedure and evidence to allow them to refer a case to the authorities of a State 'in whose territory the crime was

[52] This has been, for example, the case of the STL, whose statute specifically indicates the cases that may be brought before the Tribunal, though reserving an enlargement of its jurisdiction should the contracting Parties indicate additional cases.

[53] IMT Statute (n 2) art 10. [54] ICTY Statute (n 6) art 9(2) and ICTR Statute (n 8) art 8(2).

[55] *Tadic*, Jurisdiction Decision (n 24) paras 49–64. [56] UNSC Res 1534 (2004) paras 4 and 5.

committed; or in which the accused was arrested; or having jurisdiction and being willing and adequately prepared to accept such a case'. In determining whether a case should be referred to domestic courts, consideration had to be given to 'the gravity of the crimes charged and the level of responsibility of the accused'.[57] Thus, their practice was adapted to the principle that international jurisdiction should be reserved to high rank accused or to significantly serious cases.

The ICC Statute, in turn, seems to follow the same principle.[58] However, Article 5 does not deal with the concurring jurisdiction of domestic courts, and may simply indicate that the list therein comprises precisely the most serious international crimes. Furthermore, the rules on admissibility of cases show that the approach followed on concurrent jurisdiction partially diverges from previous practice.[59] Under the ICC Statute, as a general rule the Court shall declare a case inadmissible where it is being investigated or prosecuted by a State which has jurisdiction over it, or it has been investigated by a State which has jurisdiction over it and the State has decided not to prosecute the person concerned, unless the State is unwilling or unable genuinely to carry out the investigation or prosecution.[60] This approach gives priority to domestic jurisdiction, and is commonly referred to as an application of the principle of complementarity, as declared in the preamble of the Statute.[61] In other terms, the ICC has jurisdiction over a crime listed in the ICC Statute only if such a crime is not prosecuted at the national level by the courts of a State which has jurisdiction over it.[62]

This priority of the domestic jurisdiction is not applicable when a State is unable or unwilling to investigate or prosecute the case. A State is to be regarded as unwilling if the domestic proceedings were undertaken for the purpose of shielding the person concerned from criminal responsibility for crimes within the jurisdiction of the Court. This is also the case when there is an unjustified delay or the domestic proceedings are not being conducted independently or impartially, in a manner which, in the circumstances, is inconsistent with an intent to bring the person concerned to justice.[63] A departure from the priority of domestic jurisdiction may also apply where a case has already been adjudicated before a domestic court, but proceedings were conducted with the purpose of shielding the person concerned from criminal responsibility, or in a manner which was inconsistent with an intent to bring that person to justice.[64] As to inability, it may

[57] ICTY, 'Rules of Procedure and Evidence (as amended)' (8 July 2015) Doc IT/32/Rev. 50, rule 11*bis*, paras A and C.

[58] ICC Statute (n 9) art 5.

[59] As in previous practice, it is however possible for the ICC to determine that a case is inadmissible where the case is not of sufficient gravity to justify further action by the Court. ibid art 17 (1)(d).

[60] ICC Statute (n 9) art 17(1)(a) and (b).

[61] ibid para 10 of the preamble.

[62] Since ibid art 17 simply refers to a State 'which has jurisdiction' over the case and does not mention any ground for the exercise of national jurisdiction, arguably the principle of complementarity should also work when their competence is grounded on a provision allowing universal jurisdiction over international crimes, as provided, for example, in the GCs with respect to the grave breaches thereof.

[63] ibid art 17(2).

[64] ibid art 20(3), providing for a derogation from the general principle of *ne bis in idem*. Similarly, arts 10(2) and 9(2) of the ICTY (n 6) and ICTR (n 8) Statutes respectively.

depend on a substantial collapse or unavailability of the national judicial system, entailing the impossibility to obtain the accused or the necessary evidence to carry out fair judicial proceedings.[65]

E. Criminal Prosecution and Maintenance of Peace and Security

The foregoing description of the jurisdiction of international and hybrid criminal courts and tribunals, as well as of the obligations imposed on States parties by the GCs and AP I to exercise jurisdiction over international crimes, have been certainly inspired by humanitarian considerations, particularly in the aftermath of the Second World War and during subsequent conflicts at the end of the twentieth century and the beginning of the twenty-first. However, when new courts and tribunals were established, political considerations led to the selection of the situations which deserved international action according to such a humanitarian approach, but frequently ignored other situations where violations were equally egregious. Furthermore, it has already been pointed out that on most occasions emphasis has been put on war crimes or crimes against humanity connected with an armed conflict. In light of this, it seems clear that the humanitarian inspiration has only been one of the grounds for initiating criminal prosecution. The prevailing approach instead has been to contribute to, through criminal prosecution, maintaining peace and security either during an armed conflict or when hostilities have ceased and a secure environment can be achieved only by doing justice with respect to conduct regarded as seriously criminal under international law.

This approach has been manifest since the decision of the UN to establish the first international criminal tribunal, even if it may be odd that such a decision (the only one where an ad hoc tribunal has been established during an armed conflict) did not contain the conferral of jurisdiction over crimes against peace.[66] The UNSC resolution that adopted the ICTY Statute declared in its operative part that the tribunal was established 'for the sole purpose of prosecuting persons responsible for serious violations of international humanitarian law',[67] thus stressing the merely judicial function of the Court. However, the preamble of the Resolution repeatedly referred to the creation of a judicial body for the purpose of contributing to the restoration and maintenance of international peace and security.[68] Admittedly, the UNSC was obliged to adopt such a language because it could only act and impose obligations on Member States under Chapter VII of the UN Charter within its competence to take measures to maintain or restore international peace and security, including measures not involving the use of armed force to give effect to its decisions.[69] However, the link to the restoration of peace is also confirmed by the

[65] ICC Statute (n 9) art 17(3).

[66] See n 6.

[67] UNSC Res 827 (1993) para 2.

[68] ibid preambular paras 3, 4, 6, 7. Also the previous UNSC Res 808 (1993) preambular para 9.

[69] UN Charter 1 UNTS XVI arts 39 and 41.

attribution of jurisdiction to the ICTY on violations occurring 'between 1 January 1991 and a date to be determined by the Security Council upon restoration of peace'.[70]

The same approach, aiming at building a peaceful and secure environment through the prosecution of heinous crimes, has been largely followed in the establishment of most criminal international courts in the aftermath of international or non-international armed conflicts. Thus, the UNSC resolution adopting the ICTR Statute adopted the same language and expressed the view that criminal prosecution of the persons responsible for serious violations of international humanitarian law would 'contribute to the process of national reconciliation and to the restoration of peace and security'.[71] Similarly, the link between criminal prosecution and international peace and security was expressly mentioned when establishing the Special Court for Sierra Leone, which was created under an agreement between the UN and the Government of Sierra Leone. The UNSC resolution that promoted it recognized that a credible system of justice and accountability for the very serious crimes committed in the country 'would end impunity and would contribute to the process of national reconciliation and to the restoration and maintenance of peace'.[72] Here, too, the achievement of a durable peace appears to be the primary consideration for creating a new jurisdiction as a tool for generating a stable and secure environment with no place for egregious violations of international law.

The ICC Statute refers to peace to a more limited degree by recognizing in general terms that the grave crimes that deeply shock the conscience of humanity 'threaten the peace, security and well-being of the world', and affirms that 'the most serious crimes of concern of the international community as a whole must not go unpunished' through the creation of 'an independent permanent International Criminal Court', thus stressing the primary judicial function of the newly established institution for the purpose of putting an end to impunity and contributing to the prevention of such crimes. That said, the ICC Statute was not drafted with a specific country situation in mind, as was the case with the ad hoc tribunals. Moreover, the Statute is concerned with the prosecution of crimes against humanity also committed in peacetime, irrespective of their connection with an armed conflict, even if the, albeit limited, practice of the Court has mainly dealt so far with situations which were intimately connected with armed conflicts or with post-conflict restoration of peace and security.

The foregoing consideration of the goals to be achieved by international criminal prosecution according to the resolutions and statutes establishing international criminal courts and tribunals, as well as by domestic prosecution of international crimes, especially within the framework of the ICC Statute, posits the question of a precise definition of the mandate of these international judicial institutions. Their mandate appears indeed to pursue two goals at the same time: fighting impunity for serious criminal conduct affecting the international community as a whole, and contributing to maintaining or restoring peace and security. But are these two goals inextricably linked? Is there an automatic cause–effect relationship between the respect for the rule of law and international peace and security, so that the implementation of a mandate to prosecute alleged criminals

70 UNSC Res 827 (1993) para 2.
71 UNSC Res 955 (1994) preamble.
72 UNSC Res 1315 (2000).

will in and of itself contribute to international peace and security? In other terms, is the international criminal tribunals' purpose of bringing about security and stability strictly limited to the impact of its primary judicial function, or does it comprise also other tasks that the tribunals have been entrusted with for achieving that goal?

Generally, there is no doubt, as the UNSC resolutions discussed imply, that the exercise of the judicial function to fight impunity for crimes of concern to the entire international community (including the respect for the rule of law that it pursues) contributes to security and stability in international relations, and should prevent the recurrent commission of such crimes. The issue is, however, to what extent it offers such a contribution. It has often been maintained that international criminal courts and tribunals are mandated to reconcile a civil society torn by a conflict, to provide reparation to victims, and establish or re-establish governance inspired by the rule of law. All these objectives no doubt contribute to the establishment of peace and security. But do these goals fall within the competence of an international tribunal as far as they entail additional activities beyond the strict exercise of its judicial function?

There is no yes or no answer to these questions. A negative answer would result in a too restrictive reading of the role and competence of an international criminal jurisdiction. Certain statements, sometimes made even by members of the international judiciary, that administering justice is the only task of an international criminal court while reconciliation is a matter for the national community and its institutions, appear too radical in tracing a mutually exclusive separation of competence. They neglect the fact that a tribunal, notwithstanding its independence and impartiality, is not an abstract entity, but operates within the social environment under which laws it was established. This applies not only to domestic criminal courts but more importantly to international ones, which are accountable both to the international community which established it and to the domestic community of the State that would have been otherwise competent to prosecute the cases. In this context, it should be recalled that criminal justice cannot be shifted entirely from the domestic to the international level, and that the primary responsibility for prosecution rests with States and their judiciaries. Thus, if international courts are a temporary and objectively limited replacement of domestic jurisdictions, which ultimately bear the primary responsibility for re-establishing the rule of law and restoring security and stability in the national society, they too must contribute to reaching these goals. How far this contribution can go is a matter for each court to assess and may depend on the concrete situation in which the Court is operating. However, this dual accountability of an international court should not be forgotten and the significance of its role in achieving security at the domestic level should not be underestimated.

Nevertheless, it must be recognized that the answer to the question cannot be entirely positive either as the contribution of an international jurisdiction to the above-mentioned goals is limited in several respects. For example, reconciliation requires systematic review of the causes of the conflict or of the authoritarian rule under which criminal acts were perpetrated. Criminal prosecution, especially if exercised by a court established far away from the place of the crime, can hardly contribute to this effectively. First, a criminal court is bound to restrict its consideration to events alleged in the indictments, and its judicial record does not necessarily cover the whole truth of the events. Secondly, it cannot build a collective memory of the events based on an open discussion that may be shared by all individuals in the country or the region concerned; a truth and reconciliation commission is better suited to achieve this goal. In this context, the experience of Sierra Leone, where a truth and reconciliation commission was established alongside the Special Court for Sierra Leone, illustrates the limits of judicial prosecution, notwithstanding its significant results in successfully prosecuting a head of State.[73] Finally, providing reparation to victims with respect to mass crimes may perhaps be better served if administered by a special body, like the ICC's Trust Fund, rather than by criminal prosecution.[74]

F. The Impact of International Criminal Prosecution in the Countries Concerned

A consideration of the role of international criminal prosecution in contributing to peace, security and stability in countries torn by conflict or by authoritarian rule where mass and widespread crimes have been committed, cannot conclude without addressing the impact of such prosecution on the countries concerned. This is particularly relevant when inquiring how the exercise and the results of criminal prosecution have been perceived by the States concerned as well as by the people living in those countries and affected by the criminal events. A positive perception and acceptance of the role played by an international tribunal, of its performance and its outcomes, may substantially contribute to ensuring security and stability, and greater respect for the law, including by discouraging a recurrent commission of crimes. This should be the case both in the aftermath of and during a conflict. It is clearly impossible to examine here in detail all the situations considered by international justice so far, also because a limited number of studies have been conducted in this respect.[75] However, it can easily be affirmed that the impact of criminal prosecution has been controversial, especially in societies that suffered a non-international armed conflict based on ethnic or religious grounds. On the one hand, victims and survivors have welcomed the creation of an international jurisdiction mandated to deal with the crimes committed, and appreciated the efforts made to try the alleged perpetrators. However, they also frequently complained that such efforts have not been sufficient to meet their expectations and repair the violations, that sanctions imposed were too lenient, that some acquittals were not justified, and that

[73] Abdul Tejan-Cole, 'A Big Man in a Small Cell: Charles Taylor and the Special Court for Sierra Leone' in Ellen L Lutz/Caitlin Reiger (eds), *Prosecuting Heads of State* (CUP 2009).

[74] Sigall Horowitz, 'The Role of Victims' in Linda Carter/Fausto Pocar (eds), *International Criminal Procedure: The Interface of Civil Law and Common Law Legal Systems* (Edward Elgar 2013).

[75] For example, with respect to the recent conflict in the Balkans, Diane F Orentlicher, *Shrinking the Space of Denial. The Impact of the ICTY in Serbia*, and *That Someone Guilty Be Punished. The Impact of the ICTY in Bosnia* (Open Society Institute 2008).

international procedures have been too lengthy to bring effective closure to the individuals concerned. On the other hand, groups from which individuals have been investigated and tried frequently do not accept responsibility, or do so only to a limited extent, sometimes even regard the accused and convicted persons as heroes, and frequently claim that the International Court was biased against them for political purposes.

More generally, the establishment of an international criminal tribunal is not easily accepted in the countries concerned, while its location in a foreign country distant from the place of commission of the crimes has been frequently criticized for not allowing sufficient participation of the interested people in the judicial process. This has been even more so for the ICC, despite its permanent nature and its basis in a treaty, that has been voluntarily accepted by States parties, presumably after a ratification process accompanied by at least some public debate. That said, the main criticism of the ICC concerns its prosecutorial policy, described as biased against alleged African perpetrators,[76] and to its inefficiency because of its limited judicial activity resulting in only several judgments in more than fifteen years since its inception, a very low number if compared with the performance of the ad hoc tribunals.[77]

Finally, the question of the impact of criminal prosecution as a deterrent to the commission of grave breaches of international humanitarian and human rights law still cannot receive a clear answer, both as concerns specific situations and more generally in international practice. As to specific situations, the genocide perpetrated in Srebrenica in 1995, notwithstanding the establishment of the ICTY two years earlier, as well as the crimes subsequently committed during the Kosovo war in 1999, may invite a negative response. However, the limited number of cases dealt with by the ICTY during its very first years of activity and the even more limited publicity that they received were probably insufficient to eradicate the culture of impunity deeply rooted in the exercise of power in wartime, leading us thus to reserve final judgment on the matter. The same approach may guide us in considering the value of criminal prosecution as a deterrent tool more generally following the creation of a permanent international jurisdiction like the ICC. The recurrent commission of crimes under international law in recent years, since the adoption of the ICC Statute, needs no detailed description. Here, too, the aforementioned limited number of cases dealt with so far, their concentration in one continent, the unsuccessful referral of situations—even in that continent—by the UNSC to the Court, the failure of the Court to address situations worldwide, are unlikely to deter potential perpetrators from engaging in criminal conduct under international law. Hence, a final assessment of the impact of the ICC as a tool to deter high-ranking officials or other individuals from committing violations should for the time being be reserved, and will only be possible in the light of more consistent international practice in the future.

[76] eg Nadia Shamsi, 'The ICC: A Political Tool? How the Rome Statute is Susceptible to the Pressures of more Power States' (2016) 24 Willamette Journal of International Law and Dispute Resolution 85; Valérie Arnoud, 'A Court in Crisis? The ICC in Africa, and Beyond?' (2017) Egmont Paper 93 <http://www.egmontinstitute.be/content/uploads/2017/05/EP93.pdf?type=pdf> accessed 19 December 2019; Margaret M deGuzman, 'Is the ICC Targeting Africa Inappropriately? A Moral, Legal and Sociological Assessment' (2018) Temple University Legal Studies, Research Paper No 2018-17.

[77] eg William A Schabas, 'The International Criminal Court at Ten' (2011) 22 Criminal Law Forum 493.

CHAPTER 42

WE WHO ARE NOT AS OTHERS*

Sanctions and (Global) Security Governance

ANTONIOS TZANAKOPOULOS

A. Introduction

The concept of security is inextricably linked with the concept of threat. Security is needed to protect from something 'external', from some existential threat.[1] In that, it is a defining and inherent, if non-legal, characteristic of the State. 'The fact that every people feels itself threatened by the others gives the state its definite unifying power; it depends upon the instinct of self-preservation of society itself; the latent external crisis enables it to get the upper hand in internal crises.'[2] In that, any threats to the status quo are simply externalized and presented as an 'other'—and security serves to protect from that 'other'.[3] In the context of a self-organizing society based on voluntary cooperation rather than coercion, however, 'security' ought to be seen either as attained, or, more likely, as redundant: there ought to be no existential threat to protect from either external or externalized.[4]

The global outbreak of SARS-CoV-2, the coronavirus that causes the COVID-19 disease, which could be seen as such an external existential threat,[5] demonstrates the

* M Cavalera, 'We Who Are Not as Others' in Sepultura, *Chaos* AD (Roadrunner 1993).

[1] cf Keith Krause/Michael Williams, 'Security and "Security Studies": Conceptual Evolution and Historical Transformation' in Alexandra Gheciu/William C Wohlforth (eds), *The Oxford Handbook of International Security* (OUP 2018) 21–2 (discussing securitization).

[2] Martin Buber, 'Society and the State (1951)' in Maurice Friedman (ed and tr), *Pointing the Way: Collected Essays by Martin Buber* (Routledge and Kegan Paul, 1957) 172.

[3] Carl Schmitt, *Der Begriff des Politischen* (Hanseatische Verlaganstalt 1933) 28–9. [4] ibid 35–6.

[5] In the sense that 'the object of immune defence is the foreign as such. Even if it has no hostile intentions, even if it poses no danger, it is eliminated on the basis of its *Otherness*.' See Byung-Chul Han, *The Burnout Society* (Erik Butler tr, Stanford UP 2015) 2 (emphasis original).

point. Here the 'other' is not some group of people, but a faceless, non-sentient entity: a virus. And yet, even in that context, some States sought to give a face to that non-sentient 'other'—the face of children, our neighbours, our colleagues, and friends; or in some States the face of refugees and migrants or that of another State constructing the virus or allowing it to spread.[6] Everyone became an 'other' in the event. Measures to curb the spread of the virus, entailing serious limitations of rights, such as the right of movement, were adopted nationally, not globally, and were voluntarily complied with by large numbers of people around the world. This was a choice, a national choice—a choice which was made against the background of chronic underfunding of public health, a choice combined with the decision by some States not to 'test, test, test' as recommended by the World Health Organization (WHO),[7] and a choice that some States did not even make. This led Agamben to note, in a piece that provoked strong reactions, that 'we . . . accepted without too many problems, solely in the name of a *risk* that was not possible to specify, limiting to an extent that had never happened before . . . our freedom of movement'.[8]

This means that the concept of security in the highly centralized—and exclusive—method of organization that is the State is a *sine qua non*. In contrast, the loose, decentralized, international community should have no or little need for the concept. What external existential threat is there for the world to protect itself from?[9] Global warming and the climate emergency we did well to create for ourselves, as we did in the case of the coronavirus crisis, which, in its iteration was nothing but the result of targeted disinvestment in public health in late capitalism, whether due to privatization or poverty. Neither of those crises can be adequately dealt with by recourse to 'global security' measures, by the way. And no such measures were taken in the coronavirus example. Beyond that, and short of asteroids, solar flares, the arrival of locust-like alien species, or the death of our sun (the latter still a few billion years away) the world is not currently under any external threat—it is only under threats from itself, that is, threats of self-destruction.

And yet we treat threats that are internal to (parts of) the world as somehow being external to it and we unite to defeat them through the tools of global security. This is because the international community is primarily an international community of States,

[6] See eg Daniel Trilling, 'Migrants Aren't Spreading Coronavirus—But Nationalists Are Blaming Them Anyway' (*The Guardian*, 28 February 2020) <https://www.theguardian.com/commentisfree/2020/feb/28/coronavirus-outbreak-migrants-blamed-italy-matteo-salvini-marine-le-pen> accessed 4 May 2020; Maanvi Singh/Helen Davidson/Julian Borger, 'Trump Claims to Have Evidence Coronavirus Started in Chinese Lab But Offers No Details' (*The Guardian*, 1 May 2020) <https://www.theguardian.com/us-news/2020/apr/30/donald-trump-coronavirus-chinese-lab-claim> accessed 4 May 2020.

[7] WHO, 'WHO Director-General's Opening Remarks at the Media Briefing on COVID-19' (16 March 2020) <https://www.who.int/dg/speeches/detail/who-director-general-s-opening-remarks-at-the-media-briefing-on-covid-19---16-march-2020> accessed 4 May 2020.

[8] Giorgio Agamben, 'Una domanda' (*Quodlibet*, 13 April 2020) <https://www.quodlibet.it/giorgio-agamben-una-domanda> accessed 4 May 2020. English translation by Adam Kotsko <https://itself.blog/2020/04/15/giorgio-agamben-a-question/> accessed 4 May 2020.

[9] Schmitt (n 3) 36.

no matter what terminological or conceptual gloss we might try to put on it.[10] And States as the (prime) members of that community and its lawmakers will naturally project their own unifying characteristic upon that community. National security becomes international (or global) security if only to allow for the use of more effective tools for its attainment—never mind that 'security' may in fact be ultimately unattainable precisely because it is meant to be unattainable.[11]

Law is an obvious tool for 'security governance', and 'sanctions' are but an inextricable element of law. This chapter thus deals with sanctions as a (global) security governance tool. Section B discusses the terms—the meaning of sanctions and (global) security. Sections C and D trace the historical trajectory in the use of collective and unilateral sanctions in the service of security. Section E concludes. The point that the chapter makes is relatively simple: global security is nothing but national security projected onto the international plane. When a hegemonic concept of security, that is to say, of the existential threats 'we' need to protect against, is imposed and accepted,[12] for as long as it is accepted, collective sanctions rule supreme, and can be particularly effective.[13] When there is fragmentation and antagonism as to what the threats are, when there is no hegemonic national security accepted as synonymous to international security, there is a return to unilateral sanctions and a concomitant sidelining of collective security mechanisms.

B. Terms and Concepts

For the lawyer, a 'sanction' is *not* primarily a tool to govern security,[14] but rather one of the necessary elements of a legal rule—that is, if we are to accept the definition of a legal rule as provided by Kelsen, namely a command backed by a coercive sanction.[15] Commands backed by coercive sanctions, legal rules, aim to achieve something. It may be difficult to generalize what legal rules aim to achieve; and it may be even more

[10] Vienna Convention on the Law of Treaties 1155 UNTS 331 art 53, with UNGA, 'Articles on the Responsibility of States for Internationally Wrongful Acts' (2001) UN Doc A/RES/56/83, Annex, arts 33, 42, 48 (ARSIWA).

[11] Schmitt (n 3) 36: *plena securitas in hac vita non expectanda.*

[12] According to Krause/Williams (n 1) 21, 'in securitization theory, security represents a "speech act", involving the naming of particular phenomena as "existential threats", and having that declaration accepted by a relevant audience'.

[13] Schmitt (n 3) 37, also paraphrasing Pierre-Joseph Proudhon in writing the (in)famous line 'wer Menschheit sagt, will betrügen' ('whoever invokes humanity wants to cheat').

[14] Though, of course, it is so if one approaches the concept of 'sanctions' beyond the law, as a matter of international relations: eg David S Cohen/Zachary K Goldman, 'Like It Or Not, Unilateral Sanctions Are Here to Stay' (2019) 113 AJIL Unbound 146, where the first section of the work is entitled 'A Flexible *Security Tool* For All' (emphasis added).

[15] Hans Kelsen, *Introduction to the Problems of Legal Theory: A Translation of the First Edition of the Reine Rechtslehre or Pure Theory of Law* (Bonnie Litschewski Paulson/Stanley L Paulson trs, OUP 1997) 29–30 on the 'reconstructed legal norm'.

difficult to agree on what they aim to achieve were we to generalize it successfully. But there can be little doubt that overall they aim to achieve some political goal, to secure a particular status quo, to put their subjects into a particular line so as to maintain order.

The political ends that legal rules aim to achieve are basically determined by the dominant mode of production, and essentially refer to the 'constant reproduction' of its 'fundamental relations'.[16] Law is part of the superstructure; the base ('structure') is the relations of production, and it is this base that determines (and is reflected in) the superstructure.[17] In that sense, the proximate function of the sanction is to ensure compliance with a command, but the more distant or remote function is essentially to 'secure' that the dominant mode of production remains what it is and continues to operate effectively. To provide security for the system through coercion. To thwart threats to the system.

All this may seem trite to some and, equally, provoke violent objections in others. The point is that understanding sanctions in this manner sheds some light on their function as security tools, and allows for their assessment, both in terms of their unilateral and their collective format in international law. This section now turns to this matter.

* * *

In international law, the traditional sanctions before the advent of the UN Charter were, simply put, reprisals and war.[18] They were (or ought to have been) legal tools available to each State to attain national security from external threats by enforcing basic rules of the legal order—primarily non-interference. This was before the emergence of any notion of 'collective' or global security.

[16] Karl Marx, *Capital—An Abridged Edition* (David McLellan ed, OUP 1995) 461:

> here as always it is in the interest of the ruling section of society to sanction the existing order as law and to legally establish its limits given through usage and tradition. Apart from all else, this, by the way, comes about of itself as soon as the constant reproduction of the basis of the existing order and its fundamental relations assumes a regulated and orderly form in the course of time. And such regulation and order are themselves indispensable elements of any mode of production, if it is to assume social stability and independence from mere chance and arbitrariness.

[17] Karl Marx, *A Contribution to the Critique of Political Economy* (Nahum Isaac Stone tr, Charles H Kerr and Company 1904) 11–12 (Preface):

> In the social production which men carry on they enter into definite relations that are indispensable and independent of their will; these relations of production correspond to a definite stage of development of their material powers of production. The sum total of these relations of production constitutes the economic structure of society—the real foundation, on which rise legal and political superstructures and to which correspond definite forms of social consciousness. The mode of production in material life determines the general character of the social, political and [intellectual] processes of life. It is not the consciousness of men that determines their existence, but, on the contrary, their social existence determines their consciousness. At a certain stage of their development, the material forces of production in society come into conflict with the existing relations of production, or—what is but a legal expression of the same thing—with the property relations within which they had been at work before. From forms of development of the forces of production these relations turn into their fetters. Then comes the period of social revolution. With the change of the economic foundation the entire immense superstructure is more or less rapidly transformed.

[18] Kelsen (n 15) 119; Hans Kelsen, *Reine Rechtslehre* (2nd edn, Franz Deuticke 1960) 324–8.

Even the creation of the League of Nations did not alter this structure. The League of Nations Covenant merely subjected war to procedural requirements and put decentralized reprisals under the umbrella of an 'obligation' of Member States to take them in the event of violations of the Covenant rules regarding these procedural requirements.[19] There was, however, no collective organ to determine the existence of a violation of these requirements, and no collective organ to decide on the reprisals to be adopted. Up to this point the sanctions of international law are simply being put to the service of the national security of each State.

The paradigm shift came in the aftermath of the Second World War with the adoption of the UN Charter. International peace and security became the first purpose of the new organization,[20] to be secured through collective action for the removal of 'threats' to the peace. Even the organ that in the League of Nations was simply called the 'Council' became the 'Security' Council, a detail that is important beyond semantics. The International Court of Justice (ICJ) in *Certain Expenses* proclaimed international peace and security as the 'natural' priority in the UN Charter, 'since the fulfilment of the other purposes will be dependent upon the attainment of that basic condition'.[21]

First, it must be noted that there is nothing 'natural' about this priority at all. International peace and security are made into a primary purpose by those drafting the Charter and designing the UN system because this was their political priority. It is not a natural priority but a political decision and a political priority like any other, and as such it is a child of its time. One could easily imagine food and shelter and work (ie, the well-being of individuals), or the environment (ie, the well-being of the planet), as the basic condition *upon which* the attainment of *international* peace and security is dependent.

But the UN was the organization of the victorious allies after a world war. The threats they wanted to guard against were those that had just plunged them into that war. The 'other' was there, and was clear, though now defeated. The new organization was meant to ensure that it would not rise again, though of course it could not possibly be foreseen what other 'others' may emerge or be constructed. As the product of a wartime alliance, the UN's principal purpose of international peace and security was understood as security of one alliance of States from the threat posed by another, now defeated, alliance.[22] The only problem is, of course, that such a set-up requires two things to function: (a) a coherent alliance characterized by solidarity and consensus; and (b) an enemy (or many).

Sections C and D in this chapter discuss how the set-up actually worked over the many decades that the UN has been in existence. In this section, however, it must still be clarified what the understanding of sanctions in international law ought to be. In pursuit of their principal (if not natural) priority to maintain and restore international peace and security, the drafters of the UN Charter sought, to a considerable extent, to emulate the centralized structure of domestic legal orders with respect to the monopoly of coercion. This had considerable repercussions on the understanding of the traditional coercive sanctions of international law, reprisals and war.

[19] League of Nations Covenant 225 CTS 195 art 16(1). [20] UN Charter 1 UNTS XVI art 1(1).

[21] *Certain Expenses of the United Nations* (Advisory Opinion) [1962] ICJ Rep 151, 168.

[22] Hence also the UN Charter (n 20) provisions on 'enemy' States: arts 53, 107.

The first move was to emulate domestic legal orders with respect to physical coercion, to wit: war. The UN Charter flat out prohibits States from resorting to the threat or use of force in Article 2(4), and seeks to completely centralize recourse to force to the UN Security Council (UNSC) under Chapter VII. It is the UNSC that has sole[23] power to determine the existence of threats to the peace under Article 39,[24] and it is the UNSC that has the monopoly of the use of force under Articles 42 et seq (however that may have played out in practice, in view of the lack of Article 43 agreements). What remains for States is a limited power to resort to force unilaterally in cases of self-defence, under Article 51.

The second move was to partially centralize the power to resort to reprisals, or rather what, since 1945, ought to be called countermeasures (and retorsion).[25] Countermeasures are breaches of international obligations by one State towards another in response to the latter State's previous breach of an international obligation injuring the reacting State, and aiming to induce compliance.[26] The fact that they are taken in response to such a previous violation precludes their wrongfulness. In that, countermeasures are decentralized reactions to illegality,[27] the only means available to States in the decentralized legal order to seek to induce compliance with secondary international obligations of the responsible State, and thus to implement the responsibility of that State and enforce international law. They are thus means of exercising lawful coercion, politely called inducement. Relatedly, acts of retorsion are unfriendly but perfectly lawful acts[28] resorted to in order to put pressure on a State with a view to 'inducing' it to change its position or policy on some matter. They are meant to signify displeasure, but, being lawful, they can be resorted to at any time and not solely in response to some previous internationally wrongful act by the target State (though they are sometimes referred to as 'sanctions' as well, especially by lay people).

[23] UN Charter (n 20) art 24(1) provides that the UNSC has 'primary responsibility' for the maintenance of international peace and security, the implication being that the plenary organ, the UN General Assembly (UNGA) has residual authority in this respect, subject to the restriction in art 12 as interpreted through the practice of the UNGA: *Legal Consequences of the Construction of a Wall in the Occupied Palestinian Territory* (Advisory Opinion) [2004] ICJ Rep 136 [26]. However, it is the UNSC alone that can act under UN Charter (n 20) ch VII, and this is what is meant by 'sole' here.

[24] Also 'breaches of the peace' and 'acts of aggression', though the UNSC has very rarely determined the existence of a 'breach of the peace' and never that of an 'act of aggression'—which makes sense; this is a political organ which has the exact same powers under UN Charter (n 20) ch VII whatever determination it makes under Article 39. Achieving consensus over 'threat to the peace' is easier, and enough for the UNSC to act under ch VII: Dapo Akande/Antonios Tzanakopoulos, 'The International Court of Justice and the Concept of Aggression' in Claus Kreß/Stefan Barriga (eds), *The Crime of Aggression—A Commentary* (CUP 2016) 219.

[25] This is because the term 'reprisals', according to the ILC, has forcible overtones, which makes it inapposite in the context of an international legal order that prohibits recourse to force except in self-defence. ILC, 'Draft Articles on Responsibility of States for Internationally Wrongful Acts, with Commentaries' (2001) II(2) Yearbook of the International Law Commission 31, 75 (para 3) and 128 (para 3) (ARSIWA Commentary).

[26] This is a much-simplified definition. Generally on countermeasures, ARSIWA Commentary (n 25) 128ff.

[27] Linos Alexandre Sicilianos, *Les réactions décentralisées à l'illicite: des contre-mesures à la légitime défense* (LGDJ 1990).

[28] ARSIWA Commentary (n 25) 128 (para 3).

Essentially all references to unilateral 'sanctions', whether by international lawyers or others, are to be qualified legally: either (a) as lawful (if unfriendly) acts (such as severance of diplomatic relations or trade relations when there is no obligation to maintain such trade relations);[29] or (b) as countermeasures (when they are wrongful acts whose wrongfulness is excluded because they qualify as countermeasures); or finally (c) simply as internationally wrongful acts (when they are breaches of international law that cannot be otherwise justified).

The UN Charter preserves the power of States to resort to such measures unilaterally, given that there is no prohibition of any other form of 'force' in the UN Charter other than armed force. It does, however, partially centralize the use of retorsions[30] and countermeasures in response to threats to the peace: this is what is customarily (though non-technically) called 'UN sanctions'. They are 'measures not involving the use of armed force' adopted by the UNSC in response to a threat to the peace, in accordance with Articles 39 and 41. The taking of such measures constitutes an obligation for all Member States of the UN in accordance with Article 25 of the UN Charter. And being an 'obligation under the UN Charter', the obligation to take such measures prevails over obligations of the Member States under 'other' international agreements in the event of a conflict, in accordance with Article 103 of the Charter.[31]

In that sense, Article 41 measures are centralized collective reactions to illegality (the breach of international law in the instance being that an entity is posing a threat to the peace).[32] These 'collective sanctions' taken by the UNSC have far more coercive potential than decentralized sanctions taken unilaterally by a State. This is because UNSC Article 41 measures are to be implemented by every UN Member State, whereas unilateral measures are obviously only implemented by the State that decides to resort to them. According to the International Law Commission (ILC), the term 'sanctions' ought to be reserved for such collective reactions, and the term 'countermeasures' (along with retorsion) is to be used for unilateral reactions.[33]

Sections C and D will survey the use of 'sanctions' in governing security as discussed in this section. The use of the term 'collective or UN sanctions' is meant to indicate measures not involving the use of armed force under Article 41 UN Charter (or proper 'sanctions' as per the ILC), while the term 'decentralized or unilateral sanctions' is used to indicate, essentially, countermeasures.

[29] *Military and Paramilitary Activities in and against Nicaragua (Nicaragua v US)* (Merits) [1986] ICJ Rep 14 [245] and [276] (*Nicaragua*).

[30] UN Charter (n 20) art 41 contains an indicative (thus clearly non-exhaustive) list of such measures, some of which constitute acts of retorsion: the severance of diplomatic relations for example (as there is no obligation to maintain diplomatic relations with any State).

[31] eg *Questions of Interpretation and Application of the 1971 Montreal Convention Arising from the Aerial Incident at Lockerbie (Libya v UK)* (Provisional Measures) [1992] ICJ Rep 3 [39]. Antonios Tzanakopoulos, 'Collective Security and Human Rights' in Erika de Wet/Jure Vidmar (eds), *Hierarchy in International Law: The Place of Human Rights* (OUP 2012) 63–6.

[32] Antonios Tzanakopoulos, *Disobeying the Security Council: Countermeasures Against Wrongful Sanctions* (OUP 2011) 76–9, 176.

[33] ARSIWA Commentary (n 25) 75 (para 3); ILC, 'Report of the Commission to the General Assembly on the work of its thirty first session' (1979) II(2) Yearbook of the International Law Commission 121.

C. The Use of Collective Sanctions (as a Projection of Specific State Interests)

The 'alliance' that was the UN at its inception quickly splintered: the advent of the Cold War and the antagonism of the two superpowers, the United States and the Soviet Union, quickly consigned the 'collective security' part of the UN Charter to irrelevance, if not quite to the proverbial dustbin of history.[34] For almost forty-five years, between 1945 and 1990, the UNSC managed to agree to sanctions only twice, and that with great difficulty and on a matter on which agreement should not have been that hard to procure if the benchmark was as low as basic decency: racial segregation. The UNSC managed to impose sanctions on Rhodesia in 1966,[35] and on South Africa in 1977,[36] in the aftermath of the Soweto uprising. The Council did not even manage to agree on more stringent mandatory economic sanctions against South Africa, with Resolutions 558 (1984) and 591 (1986) using ambivalent language.

The end of the Cold War and the concomitant collapse of the Soviet Union and the Eastern Block may have signalled to some the 'end of history',[37] perhaps prematurely. What it certainly did do was to usher in a period of hegemonic consensus, with the United States-led 'West' now reigning supreme. In that context, the UNSC became the focal point of security, now 'collective' security, and UN sanctions saw unprecedented proliferation.[38] The 1990s were called, and rightly so, 'the sanctions decade'.[39] In that

[34] A phrase that is used often and in many variations but famously attributed to Trotsky during the October Revolution in 1917, referring to the Mensheviks: Bertrand M Patenaude, 'Trotsky and Trotskyism' in Silvio Pons/Stephen A Smith (eds), *The Cambridge History of Communism: Volume I: World Revolution and Socialism in One Country* (CUP 2017) 195 with further references. He was quite wrong on this one, as is the case with many who do not shy away from the hubris that is the attempt to declare the end of someone else's significance in the course of history, let alone the end of the course of history itself—see text at n 37.

[35] UNSC Res 232 (1966). For contemporary comment: Charles Rabinowitz, 'UN Application of Selective, Mandatory Sanctions Against Rhodesia: A Brief Legal and Political Analysis' (1967) 7 Virginia Journal of International Law 147; Rosalyn Higgins, 'International Law, Rhodesia, and the UN' (1967) 23 The World Today 94.

[36] UNSC Res 418 (1977).

[37] Francis Fukuyama, 'The End of History?' (1989) 16 The National Interest 3.

[38] Chesterman and Pouligny note, somewhat euphemistically, that the increased recourse to sanctions 'appears to have had less to do with a consensus on their utility *than with the more general political consensus* that emerged within the Council after the Cold War': Simon Chesterman/Béatrice Pouligny, 'Are Sanctions Meant to Work? The Politics of Creating and Implementing Sanctions Through the United Nations' (2003) 9 Global Governance 503, 504 (emphasis added). Chesterman is less restrained in his 'The Security Council as World Legislator? Theoretical and Practical Aspects of Law-making by the Security Council' (Institute for International Law and Justice, 2004), where s 2 is entitled 'The Imperial Security Council' <https://www.iilj.org/wp-content/uploads/2017/03/The-Security-Council-as-World-Legislator.pdf> accessed 24 April 2020.

[39] David Cortright/George A Lopez, *The Sanctions Decade: Assessing UN Strategies in the 1990s* (Lynne Rienner 2000).

decade alone, sanctions were imposed in over a dozen situations involving Iraq,[40] the former Yugoslavia,[41] Somalia,[42] Libya,[43] Liberia,[44] Haiti,[45] Angola,[46] Rwanda,[47] Sudan,[48] Sierra Leone,[49] Afghanistan,[50] Eritrea and Ethiopia,[51] and responding to threats to the peace as diverse as classical invasion and annexation, terrorism, human rights violations, and defence of democracy.[52] More sanctions followed in the 2000s, most prominently against North Korea,[53] and Iran,[54] but also against Lebanon.[55]

This ought to come as little surprise. At the time when superpower antagonism left little space for 'consensus' (meaning, essentially, domination of the interests of one State or bloc of States over all others), everyone just went off and did as they always did: they employed unilateral sanctions (in the guise of either acts of retorsion or countermeasures) whenever there was a 'security need' (in the sense of some political objective to deal with a perceived threat), while the UNSC lay dormant. Examples abound: from the UK taking measures against Iran in response to the nationalization of the Anglo-Iranian Oil Company in the 1950s,[56] to the US taking measures against Cuba in the 1960s,[57] and then Nicaragua,[58] amongst others, to the Arab boycott of Israel,[59] and other measures.

From amongst the many UN sanctions regimes that were imposed during this period of flourishing of collective sanctions, some examples are discussed here in order to demonstrate three aspects. First, how hegemonic consensus was at work in the UNSC. Secondly, how awesomely powerful UN sanctions can be in such cases. And thirdly, how this awesome power might in fact scare States into reacting to UN sanctions and to seek to reassert their position in a hegemonically homogeneous international environment.

The sanctions imposed on Libya in the aftermath of the Lockerbie incident serve as a glaring example of the hegemonic use of sanctions during the period under discussion. The explosion of a bomb on board a TWA flight out of Heathrow while the aircraft was flying over Lockerbie in Scotland led to the deaths of all passengers and crew. Two Libyan nationals (who were also claimed to be Libyan agents) were accused, primarily by the US and the UK, as being responsible for placing the bomb on the aircraft, and the US and the UK demanded that Libya extradite them. Eventually the two States got the UNSC to demand the handover of the agents, essentially echoing the demand of the US and the UK, and to impose sanctions on Libya in 1992.[60] For a number of years Libya,

[40] UNSC Res 661 (1990). [41] eg UNSC Res 713 (1991). [42] UNSC Res 733 (1992).
[43] UNSC Res 748 (1992). [44] UNSC Res 788 (1992).
[45] UNSC Res 873 (1993); UNSC Res 917 (1994). [46] UNSC Res 864 (1993).
[47] UNSC Res 918 (1994). [48] UNSC Res 1054 (1996). [49] UNSC Res 1132 (1997).
[50] UNSC Res 1267 (1999). [51] UNSC Res 1298 (2000).
[52] Chesterman/Pouligny (n 38) 504. [53] UNSC Res 1718 (2006).
[54] UNSC Res 1737 (2006). [55] UNSC Res 1636 (2005).
[56] Makio Miyagawa, *Do Economic Sanctions Work?* (Palgrave Macmillan 1992) 30–3.
[57] Margaret P Doxey, *Economic Sanctions and International Enforcement* (2nd edn, Macmillan Press 1980) 35ff.
[58] *Nicaragua* (n 29) 14.
[59] Preston L Greene, 'The Arab Economic Boycott of Israel: The International Law Perspective' (1978) 11 Vanderbilt Journal of Transnational Law 77.
[60] UNSC Res 748 (1992); UNSC Res 883 (1993).

through the mediation of the (then) Organisation of African Unity (OAU) (now African Union), sought to bring this situation to an end, suggesting various arrangements that would lead to the two accused facing justice, but not in the US or the UK, where—to be fair—an unbiased trial would have been about as possible as it would have been in Libya. The recalcitrance of the US and the UK, viz. the UNSC, in agreeing to any of the many proposals, led in June 1998 to a decision by the OAU, at the time counting fifty-three Member States, to stop complying with the UN sanctions with effect from September 1998.[61] A few days before the expiry of that deadline, in late August 1998, the suggestion of the OAU for the trial of two suspects by a Scottish court sitting in the Netherlands had been miraculously accepted and the UNSC had provided for the suspension of the sanctions.[62]

This is not to say that all instances of imposition of UN sanctions during this period were as glaringly one-sided as the Lockerbie debacle. But all of them did reflect primarily the perceived national interest of the US and its allies, many other States being simply unable or too weak to raise serious objections. The sanctions on (and subsequently intervention in) Haiti is yet another example of an essentially US/Western agenda being pushed globally under the guise of defence of democracy,[63] especially with the events in Grenada and Panama having taken place within the decade prior to the Haiti situation. The irony and hypocrisy are particularly evident when one considers that a number of shockingly undemocratic States are close allies of those very same States pushing the particular agenda. Already at that early stage commentators were noting the dangers of exclusive Western control of the UNSC, even foreboding a 'return to the veto-induced paralysis of the Cold War'.[64]

The terrorist attacks of 9/11 gave new impetus (or at least a new lease of life) to the hegemonic consensus of the 1990s. Terrorism, undefined as it is,[65] became the new threat to which the collective security system needed to respond. For the West, it was Islamic terrorism that needed to be targeted by the collective measures, and so it was. The 1267 sanctions regime against Osama Bin Laden, Al-Qaeda, and the Taliban introduced in 1999 was strengthened after the 2001 attacks and is still in operation some twenty years later, though now split into two regimes, one targeting the Taliban and one targeting ISIL/Da'esh.[66] A related anti-terrorism regime was introduced by the UNSC in Resolution 1373 (2001).[67] These sanctions regimes allowed States to pursue, whether

[61] OUA, 'The Crisis between the Great Socialist People's Libyan Arab Jamahiriya and the United States of America and the United Kingdom' (8–10 June 1998) Doc AHG/Dec.127 (XXXIV), paras 1–2.

[62] UNSC Res 1192 (1998). The sanctions were suspended a few months later, in April 1999, upon notification by the UN Secretary-General that the two accused had arrived in the Netherlands for trial, as provided for in UNSC Res 1192. The sanctions were finally lifted only in 2003: UNSC Res 1504 (2003).

[63] Justin Morris, 'Force and Democracy: UN/US Intervention in Haiti' (1995) 2 International Peacekeeping 391.

[64] ibid 408–9 with further references.

[65] eg Gilbert Gillaume, 'Terrorism and International Law' (2004) 53 ICLQ 537; Ben Saul, *Defining Terrorism in International Law* (OUP 2008).

[66] UNSC Res 1988 (2011); UNSC Res 1989 (2011) and UNSC Res 2253 (2015).

[67] For a discussion Stefan Talmon, 'The Security Council as World Legislature' (2005) 99 AJIL 175.

through the UNSC or autonomously, all kinds of objectives that had little to do with fighting terrorism, as discussed below.

As White and Davies-Bright argue in Chapter 1 of this *Handbook*, terrorism, though lacking a universally accepted definition, has a unifying function: 'all States can identify threats from groups that can be labelled as terrorist'.[68] This, of course, also works the other way around: all States can label as terrorist any groups from which they identify threats (and they do).[69] Thus, the 'general consensus that terrorism is a threat that must be countered'[70] comes as little surprise: it is entirely self-serving and almost akin to a blank cheque when viewed against the background of the lack of an accepted definition.[71] And as White and Davies-Bright rightly go on to suggest, this means that States 'securitizing terrorism' simply include 'any sociopolitical element that…threatens to disturb the status quo under the banner of terrorism'.[72] Given the status quo that is considered protection-worthy, however, and given the identity of those that get to decide it, this is not only unsurprising, but indeed the whole point of '(global) security'.

This is evident when considering in particular the 1267 sanctions regime and, to a somewhat lesser extent, the 1373 sanctions regime. Under the 1267/(1988)/1989/2253 regime it is the UNSC, through the relevant Sanctions Committee(s) that identifies persons and entities associated with Osama Bin Laden (until his death), the Taliban, Al-Qaeda, and since 2011 also ISIL/Da'esh, who are then put on a 'blacklist', and who are subject to asset freezes, travel bans, and arms embargoes by all Member States of the UN. But the process of putting such an entity on the list was initially completely obscure and based on nefarious evidence besides the will of particular States on the Council (sometimes acting on information provided by other States) that an entity should be subjected to sanctions.[73] Needless to say, the motives of States for including entities in the blacklist were not always the purest. To add insult to injury, there was also no process for getting a blacklisted entity removed from the list, up until the establishment of the Office of the Ombudsperson.[74]

Under the 1373 sanctions regime, UN Member States were made to subject to sanctions similar to those of the 1267 regime any entities associated with terrorism writ large. While the UNSC would not identify the entities to be sanctioned under this regime, it

[68] See Nigel White/Auden Davies-Bright, Chapter 1 in this *Handbook*, Section C.1.

[69] For example, during the Apartheid struggle, Nelson Mandela and the African National Congress (ANC) had been variously labelled as 'terrorist' by the white minority government of South Africa: in fact Mandela in his autobiography recalls how his wife Winnie was arrested and detained for some time under the 1967 Anti-Terrorism Act: Nelson Mandela, *Long Walk to Freedom* (Abacus 2013) 529. Beyond that, however, the ANC had been famously characterized by UK Prime Minister Margaret Thatcher a 'typical terrorist organisation': HC Deb 13 November 1987, vol 122, cols 701, 719.

[70] White/Davies-Bright (n 68).

[71] Robert Skidelsky, 'The Terrorism Paradox' (*Project Syndicate*, 20 January 2020) <www.project-syndicate.org/commentary/western-terrorism-fear-inversely-proportional-to-risk-by-robert-skidelsky-2020-01> accessed 25 March 2020.

[72] White/Davies-Bright (n 68).

[73] Antonios Tzanakopoulos, 'Transparency in the Security Council' in Andrea Bianchi/Anne Peters (eds), *Transparency in International Law* (CUP 2013) 372–3 with further references.

[74] UNSC Res 1904 (2009).

did 'authorize' States to do so, allowing them to impose sanctions on various entities without necessarily following the processes required under domestic law for adopting such far-reaching restrictive measures against individuals or legal entities.

After some years of operation, both regimes started coming under attack—though not from State executives, which were not too bothered about wielding such a powerful tool against their enemies, real or imagined, but by domestic (and regional international) courts to which individuals and legal entities subjected to sanctions under these regimes sought recourse. A detailed analysis of the developments that followed has been undertaken elsewhere.[75] Suffice it here to say that domestic (and regional international) court decisions such as *Kadi* in the Court of Justice of the European Union,[76] *Ahmed* in the UK Supreme Court,[77] and others, forced States to choose between disobeying the UNSC or forcing it to adopt at least some review mechanisms at the UN level. In other decisions, such as *OMPI*,[78] courts required evidence and guarantees as prescribed in domestic legal orders for those sanctioned under the 1373 regime.

The sanctions practice of the UNSC under the dominance of the United States and its allies during that period was not the only worrying development. It was coupled with the abuse of Council authorizations of the use of force, be it in Haiti or Libya, and with an increased assertion of unilateral power to use force in the name of the international community by the hegemonic powers of the era, be it in Kosovo or Iraq. All this served as an alarm bell for States like Russia and China, who would question the consensus in an organ they could scarcely control, and opt for a return to unilateral action—action that would no longer have any mantle of acting in the name of the international community by virtue of emanating from a collective organ. This would leave every State powerful enough to try to act unilaterally, all the while maintaining that it is fighting against some global threat.

D. The Resurgence of Countermeasures

While a good number of sanctions regimes introduced by the UNSC in the late 1990s and the early to mid-2000s remain in force, there is a notable tapering off of new UN sanctions towards the end of the 2000s and the 2010s. This, as foreshadowed in the last

[75] Antonios Tzanakopoulos, 'Domestic Court Reactions to UN Security Council Sanctions' in August Reinisch (ed), *Challenging Acts of International Organisations before National Courts* (OUP 2010) and 'The *Solange* Argument as a Justification for Disobeying the Security Council in the *Kadi* Judgments' in Matej Avbelj et al (eds), *Kadi On Trial: A Multifaceted Analysis of the Kadi Trial* (Routledge 2014).

[76] Joined Cases C-405/05P and C-415/05P *Yassin Abdullah Kadi and Al Barakaat International Foundation v Council of the European Union and Commission of the European Communities* [2008] EU:C:2008:461.

[77] *HM Treasury v Mohammed Jabar Ahmed and ors* [2010] UKSC 2.

[78] Case T-228/02 *Organisation des Modjahedines du peuple d'Iran v Council of the European Union* [2006] EU:T:2006:384.

section, was not due to disenchantment with UN sanctions because of any of their inherent features. If anything, collective sanctions are far more effective than unilateral sanctions, even if the latter are taken by a superpower. Rather, the problem was precisely the fact that hegemonic consensus in the UNSC started crumbling right around the mid- to late-2000s, with the resurgence of Russia, the rise of China, and the general crisis of the 'new world order' of the early 1990s. These events were also coupled with increasing (legal) challenges to UN sanctions starting in the early to mid-2000s and culminating in the early 2010s, which in fact revealed themselves as an awesomely powerful but ill-regulated tool at the hands of States happy to evade domestic and international legal constraints in taking such far-reaching action.

The natural corollary of the dip in the ability of the UNSC to achieve consensus and to operate effectively in a climate of renewed, and indeed multipolar, antagonism, was of course the resurgence of countermeasures, of unilateral sanctions, which had never really gone away, but had just receded into the background. This is nicely captured in the following excerpt from an article by Cohen and Goldman, pointing out the relevant policy considerations:

> The fact that sanctions are a core foreign policy tool has two important implications for the relationship between multilateral and unilateral sanctions. First, different countries will perceive a need to impose sanctions in different situations *because* they perceive their national security interests differently. Second, even when several countries agree on the need to impose sanctions, they will often differ on the targets, types, and duration of sanctions that need to be imposed. If countries were forced to abandon this tool for use exclusively through a multinational mechanism, *they would surrender the flexibility sanctions provide to address different kinds of risks*, not to mention an important aspect of sovereignty.[79]

States may perceive their national security interests differently. But when they are too weak to project them onto the international plane, they just fall into line with what the powerful States consider to be the appropriate security interests. And when the powerful States disagree on that, then the collective sanctioning system is cast aside in favour of everyone pursuing their own interests, globally or regionally. So, indeed, collective and unilateral sanctions exist side-by-side: both in legal reality (as described in Section B) and in actual reality. In actual reality, however, collective sanctions completely overshadow unilateral ones in cases where consensus can be achieved, while unilateral sanctions are resorted to when antagonism and balance of power considerations prevent the use of collective mechanisms.

Russia can be seen as receiving the first wake-up call with the Kosovo intervention in 1999.[80] Its strategy of promoting action through the UNSC, by occasionally making

[79] Cohen/Goldman (n 14) 147 (emphasis added).

[80] On the different eras of Soviet/Russian practice in the Security Council: Antonios Tzanakopoulos, 'La Russie et le Conseil de sécurité des Nations Unies: les trois époques de la pratique' (2019) 123 Revue Générale de Droit International Public 91.

painful concessions while it was still reeling from the dissolution of the Soviet Union, worked for it to maintain some disproportionate semblance of power for a while.[81] But the moment its interests diverged sharply (or insufferably) from those of the West in a matter of supreme national importance, an intervention in its old back yard against a close ally, it was not taken seriously by its partners in the UNSC: the whole Council was merely circumvented in the end.

Despite Russia's interest in exercising any influence that it may have in the UNSC, the intervention in Libya authorized by the UNSC in 2011[82] was yet another nail in the coffin of its (and China's) consensual approach. The way the use of force, authorized to 'protect civilians and civilian areas under imminent threat of attack',[83] played out, leading to regime change and the plunging of Libya into chaos to this day, served as an excellent excuse not only for Russia to withhold consensus over Syria,[84] but even purportedly to undertake its own unilateral action against Ukraine in Crimea, all the while 'trolling' the West. It cannot escape us that the language used by Russia with respect to Crimea is heavily reminiscent of the arguments used by NATO for its intervention in Serbia in 1999 over Kosovo.[85]

The US and the EU imposed then unilateral sanctions on Russia over Crimea,[86] seeing as how the UNSC would not be available for action against a Permanent Member. To the extent that such measures constitute breaches of international obligations owed by the US and the EU (or its Member States) to Russia, they would need to be qualified as countermeasures for the reacting entities to escape international responsibility. And, given that the violation claimed on their part is essentially the invasion and annexation of Crimea, the argument would be that these are countermeasures 'in the general interest', that is, countermeasures against the violation of an *erga omnes* obligation taken by 'States other than the injured State' in the sense of Article 48 of the Articles on State Responsibility.[87]

The resurgence of unilateral sanctions in the face of the loss of consensus in the Council is not solely due to the recalcitrance of Russia and increasingly China. The United States can be seen as taking the same route under President Trump. Its 'withdrawal'

[81] Nico Krisch, 'The Great Powers and the Security Council' in Vaughan Lowe et al (eds), *The United Nations Security Council and War* (OUP 2008) 141–4.

[82] UNSC Res 1973 (2011). [83] ibid para 4.

[84] For example, the statement by Russia in the UNSC: UNSC Verbatim Record (4 October 2011) UN Doc S/PV.6627, 4: 'The situation in Syria cannot be considered in the Council separately from the Libyan experience. The international community is alarmed by statements that compliance with Security Council resolutions on Libya in the NATO interpretation is a model for the future actions of NATO in implementing the responsibility to protect. It is easy to see that today's "Unified Protector" model could happen in Syria.'

[85] President of the Russian Federation, 'Address' (Kremlin, 18 March 2014) <http://en.kremlin.ru/events/president/news/20603> accessed 24 March 2020.

[86] 'Ukraine/Russia-related Sanctions' (*US Department of the Treasury*) <https://www.treasury.gov/resource-center/sanctions/Programs/Pages/ukraine.aspx> accessed 24 April 2020 and 'EU Restrictive Measures in Response to the Crisis in Ukraine' (*European Council/Council of the EU*) <https://www.consilium.europa.eu/en/policies/sanctions/ukraine-crisis/> accessed 24 April 2020.

[87] ARSIWA (n 10) art 48.

from the Joint Comprehensive Plan of Action (JCPoA),[88] which led to the suspension of UN sanctions against Iran, was swiftly followed by the (re-)imposition of unilateral sanctions against that State. Iran, of course, did challenge a number of these measures as breaches of the 1955 Treaty of Amity between itself and the US before the International Court of Justice.[89] But the most problematic part of such unilateral sanctions is, in the practice of the US at least, who is also the State most frequently resorting to significant such sanctions, their purported extraterritorial effects. These extraterritorial sanctions, often branded 'secondary sanctions' or 'secondary boycotts', aim at universalizing the effects of a sanctions regime by seeking to avoid the flouting of the unilateral sanctions by States and entities not bound by the sanctioning State's law: in essence, such sanctions regimes aim at emulating the effect that collective sanctions would have.[90] This makes it clear that unilateral sanctions can never achieve results similar to collective sanctions without exorbitant claims to jurisdiction. But it also makes it clear that when consensus is not present, powerful States will not shy away from adopting such sanctions in the interests of 'security'.

E. Conclusion

When there were still (only) two superpowers around, and indeed two with competing and contrasting politico-economic systems, international (peace and) security was just not a 'thing'—beyond avoiding 'mutually assured destruction'. The whole debate was about the security of each and every State and the maintenance of its internal status quo. Since the end of the Cold War, however, the concept of international security, and the process of 'securitization', has taken off. For a while this operated under the unchallenged dominance of the United States and its allies, all others being (or feeling) too weak to offer anything except occasional (and rather muted) opposition.

Once States like Russia and China started asserting themselves more forcefully in the international scene, the process of securitization did not stop—having been given a mantle of propriety by almost two decades of UN sanctioning practice. What did prove elusive though was any further consensus at the international level, with States now returning to pursuing their own interests through unilateral sanctions, while still purporting to some extent to act in the pursuit of global security from superficially accepted, but in reality ill-defined, threats such as 'terrorism'. This makes sense: in the vacuum left once again by the UNSC, the powerful appoint themselves as the protectors of all against real or perceived or even imaginary threats.

[88] UNSC Res 2231 (2015).

[89] *Alleged Violations of the Treaty of Amity, Economic Relations, and Consular Rights (Islamic Republic of Iran v United States of America)* (Application Instituting Proceedings) (16 July 2018) <https://www.icj-cij.org/files/case-related/175/175-20,180,716-APP-01-00-EN.pdf> accessed 25 March 2020.

[90] Antonios Tzanakopoulos, 'State Responsibility for "Targeted Sanctions"' (2019) 113 AJIL Unbound 135, 138–9 with further references.

But despite the recurrence of big power struggles, we have not returned to the same situation that we were in during the Cold War in all respects: while antagonism is back, no real alternative political configuration is on offer. Whatever the differences in the perception of threats to security, we are now operating under an absolutely dominant economic model, prevalent in almost all States even if with local adjustments and minor differences. We are thus witnessing a hegemonic mode of production, with the concomitant 'pariah-ization' of the few that do not conform. This allows the national security of each powerful State to lay claim to global radiance, under accepted 'categories', such as, primarily, terrorism. Security, national or global, thus becomes nothing other than the security of the current, hegemonic, and ultimately deadly, mode of production. To end, as I began, with a quote: 'Threat is urgent! Existential! With patience wearing thin. But the danger's elemental; it's chaos from within'.[91]

Acknowledgement

Thanks are due to Eleni Methymaki for her extremely valuable assistance, to Catherine Redgwell, Dapo Akande, Miles Jackson, and Christian J Tams for comments on earlier drafts, and to Robin Geiß for that and his endless patience. The usual disclaimer applies.

[91] Greg Graffin/Brett Gurewitz, 'Chaos from Within' in Bad Religion, *Age of Unreason* (Epitaph 2019).

CHAPTER 43

UNITED NATIONS PEACEKEEPING

A View from the Ground

BENJAMIN F KUSI

A. Introduction

According to the Preamble to the Charter of the United Nations (UN Charter)—the foundational document for all work undertaken by the Organization—'the Peoples of the United Nations' were 'determined to save succeeding generations from the scourge of war', 'to reaffirm faith in fundamental human rights', and 'to establish conditions under which justice and respect for the obligations arising from treaties and other sources of international law can be maintained'.[1] In pursuance of the lofty ideals set out therein, UN Member States pledged to unite their strength 'to maintain international peace and security'.[2] In practice, and in order to live up to this ideal of maintaining international peace and security in a world where conflict is rampant, the UN has had to creatively use the powers granted by its Member States under Chapters VI and VII of the UN Charter. In the early years of its existence, examples of such 'creative' action can be seen in the Organization's response to the conflict between Israel and its neighbouring States in 1948, to the Kashmir crisis in 1949, and the Suez Crisis in 1956.[3] Out of the need to deal with situations like these, and to bypass the Cold War paralysis of the UN Security Council (UNSC), the concept of 'peacekeeping' was born.[4] In doing so, and

[1] Charter of the United Nations 1 UNTS XVI (UN Charter) preamble. [2] ibid.

[3] Other early examples are observer missions in the Balkans (UNSCOB), Indonesia (UNCI) and Lebanon (UNOGIL), see Michael Bothe, 'Peacekeeping' in Bruno Simma et al (eds), *The Charter of the United Nations: A Commentary* (vol I, 3rd edn, OUP 2012) 1176–7.

[4] Christine Gray, *International Law and the Use of Force* (4th edn, OUP 2019) 270. As Gray has observed, 'a wide variety of types of operation . . . came to share the name of peacekeeping', ibid. According to Nigel D White, 'Peacekeeping and International Law' in Joachim A Koops et al (eds), *The Oxford*

given that the UN Charter neither contains any legal framework on peacekeeping nor does it envisage the idea of peacekeeping as such, it was very much necessary to 'think outside the box'. The original, and rather straightforward, idea of peacekeeping was to interpose an unarmed or lightly armed force in between feuding States on the basis of consent and cooperation to create a mutually accepted buffer zone while diplomatic attempts were made to find a solution to the conflict through any of the peaceful means prescribed under Chapter VI of the Charter.[5]

The first peacekeeping missions authorized by the UNSC were unarmed missions: the United Nations Truce Supervision Organization (UNTSO) in 1948, where unarmed military observers were deployed to supervise the armistice agreement between Israel and neighbouring Arab States, and the United Nations Military Observer Group in India and Pakistan (UNMOGIP) to monitor the conflict in Kashmir in 1949.[6] These were followed in 1956 by the first armed peacekeeping operation, the First UN Emergency Force (UNEF I), which was mandated to deal with the Suez Crisis.[7] The initial success of these innovative actions encouraged the UN to adopt peacekeeping operations as one of its main tools for the maintenance of international peace and security. Since 1948,

> more than 70 peacekeeping operations have been deployed by the UN. Over the years, hundreds of thousands of military personnel, as well as tens of thousands of UN police and other civilians from more than 120 countries have participated in UN peacekeeping operations. More than 3,000 UN peacekeepers from some 120 countries have died while serving under the UN flag.[8]

In the decades since its creation, peacekeeping has undergone several transformations. The traditional form of peacekeeping, where UN peacekeeping forces consisted of lightly armed troops deployed to serve in a neutral capacity, has evolved into multidimensional operations, largely as a result of the changing dynamics of conflict from inter-State to intra-State conflicts.[9] Thus, from traditional peacekeeping, the nomenclature has changed to Peace Support Operations (PSOs) which are multidimensional in nature and scope, 'encompassing', in the words of a former United Nations General Assembly (UNGA) President, 'conflict prevention, peacemaking, post-conflict peace-building, and assistance to the activities of international tribunals in bringing war criminals to

Handbook of United Nations Peacekeeping Operations (OUP 2015) 44: '[p]eacekeeping is a product of the restricting effects of the Cold War'.

[5] Alex J Bellamy et al, *Understanding Peacekeeping* (Polity Press 2004).

[6] These two peacekeeping operations are still ongoing today. Similar observer missions were the UNSCOB, UNCI, and UNOGIL, see Bothe (n 3).

[7] UNGA Res 998 (4 November 1956) and UNGA Res 1000 (5 November 1956).

[8] United Nations Peacekeeping, 'Our History' <https://peacekeeping.un.org/en/our-history> accessed 16 April 2020. A list of past and present UN peacekeeping operations (up to 2019) can be found here: <https://peacekeeping.un.org/sites/default/files/unpeacekeeping-operationlist_3_1_0.pdf> accessed 16 April 2020.

[9] Patryk I Labuda, 'Peacekeeping and Peace Enforcement' MPEPIL (OUP, September 2015) MN 29.

justice'.[10] Such multidimensional operations include both military and civilian components.[11] As UNSC Res 2086 (2013) recognized, 'peacekeeping ranges from traditional peacekeeping missions, which primarily monitor ceasefire to complex multidimensional operations, which seek to undertake peacekeeping tasks and address root causes of conflict'.[12] Additionally, and as a parallel development, the weapons and equipment used by the missions have, by and large, also changed and become more sophisticated.[13]

There is no doubt that peacekeeping operations have made a positive contribution to global security, for instance, by assisting the restoration of peace in war-torn countries and communities. Nevertheless, there have also been major downsides, with certain operations doing more harm than good.[14] Such successes and failures are to be assessed in light of each specific operation, its mandate, and from the perspective of all relevant stakeholders.[15] Without exception, however, peacekeeping operations have given rise to a wide range of legal and policy challenges. Examples include the ambiguous legal basis for the use of force by the missions, the quest for accountability for human rights abuses by peacekeepers, and the increasing use of private security companies and other subcontractors.

The purpose of this contribution is to examine the role of UN peacekeeping operations in an extraordinarily complex and rapidly evolving global security environment.[16] The chapter focuses in particular on lessons learned from peacekeeping taking place in African countries and its perspective is shaped by the author's own experience as a Brigade Staff Officer who launched the first Ghanaian troops into the ECOMOG operations (later serving as a Battalion Deputy Commanding Officer) in Liberia, and as Deputy Force Commander of the military component of the United Nations Operation in Côte d'Ivoire (UNOCI). The chapter starts by exposing the applicable legal framework and the role of the UNSC, particularly that of the five Permanent Members (P5) in authorizing peacekeeping operations. It then turns to recent developments in contemporary multidimensional operations and, finally, explores the outcomes of peacekeeping missions in terms of their pacifying but also at times destabilizing role in conflict situations.

[10] Russell Taylor, 'The Chronicle Interview: The Peaceful Resolution of Crises' (June–August 2001) 38 UN Chronicle 58. See also Michael Bothe, 'Peacekeeping Forces' MPEPIL (OUP, August 2016) MN 15–16; Labuda (n 9) MN 30.

[11] Nigel D White, 'The Use of Weapons in Peace Operations' in Stuart Casey-Maslen (ed), *Weapons Under International Human Rights Law* (CUP 2014) 201–2.

[12] UNSC Res 2086 (2013) preamble; see, also, ibid paras 5 and 8.

[13] See White (n 11) 225ff.

[14] See Section E.2.

[15] Paul Diehl/Daniel Druckman, 'Evaluating Peace Operations' in Joachim A Koops et al (n 4).

[16] Although the chapter is focused on UN peacekeeping operations as the archetypical peacekeeping, it should be noted that regional organizations have played a significant role in contributing personnel, resources, and setting up their own peacekeeping missions often in collaboration with the UN, especially in the African continent. See Bothe (n 10) MN 22–4.

B. Legal Framework, the United Nations Security Council, and Power Politics

1. Legal Framework

Although the institution of peacekeeping is not envisaged as such in the UN Charter, a legal and normative framework regulating it has developed through the practice of the relevant UN organs and participating and host States over the course of the past seventy years. Primarily mandated through UNSC resolutions, the basis of most peacekeeping operations is found in Chapters VI and VII of the UN Charter, depending on the circumstances of each case and the wording of the relevant resolutions.[17] In that respect, some authors have referred to the legal basis of peacekeeping as 'Chapter VI-and-a-half'.[18] In 1962, in the *Certain Expenses* advisory opinion, the International Court of Justice (ICJ) recognized that both the UNGA and the UNSC have the competence to authorize the deployment of peacekeeping operations,[19] but since the establishment of the UN Temporary Administration (UNTEA) and Security Force (UNSF) in West Irian in 1962 by the UNGA,[20] peacekeeping operations have been exclusively constituted by the UNSC.[21] Leaving aside authorization, the UN Secretary-General plays a central role in the constitution, overall management, and deployment of peacekeeping operations.[22]

In fact, it was UN Secretary-General Dag Hammarskjold who, in his appraisal of UNEF I, set out the three fundamental principles that underlie peacekeeping operations: host State consent; impartiality; and use of force only in (personal) self-defence.[23] When it comes to the requirement of consent by the host State, strictly speaking, when a peacekeeping operation is authorized under Chapter VII of the UN Charter, consent is not legally required. However, in practice, both for the success of the peacekeeping operation and the safety of the forces themselves, the consent of the host State (and of other main parties to the conflict) is instrumental and the UNSC has customarily sought to obtain it.[24] In terms of 'impartiality', the principle has been progressively interpreted to mean 'impartiality in the implementation of the mandate', given the changing nature of conflicts and the shift from traditional peacekeeping to fully fledged peace operations.[25] Finally, the principle of defensive use of force has been expanded over the

[17] Rosalyn Higgins et al, *Oppenheim's International Law: United Nations* (OUP 2017) 1039–56; Bothe (n 3) MN 1185–6. But see Gray (n 4) 270.

[18] Higgins et al (n 17) 1040.

[19] *Certain Expenses of the United Nations (Article 17, paragraph 2, of the Charter)* (Advisory Opinion) [1962] ICJ Rep 151, 163.

[20] UNGA Res 1572 (21 September 1962).

[21] Bothe (n 3) 1186; Higgins et al (n 17) 1030; Labuda (n 9) MN 16.

[22] White (n 4) 46.

[23] Labuda (n 9) MN 8; Gray (n 4) 271. See, also, White (n 4) 47–52.

[24] Higgins et al (n 17) 1056–7.

[25] White (n 4) 50.

years, especially in the context of operations that have been tasked to protect civilian populations.[26]

Beyond these fundamental legal principles and the somewhat nebulous but nevertheless settled constitutional basis of UN peacekeeping, the institution is further regulated by numerous other international agreements and ad hoc arrangements with the host State and Troop Contributing Countries (TCCs), such as the Status of Forces Agreement (SOFA) or the Convention on the Privileges and Immunities of the United Nations.[27] Peacekeepers also have to comply with international human rights law, while international humanitarian law is also applicable when they participate in hostilities.[28] Additionally, over the years, a host of high-level reports and other documents—with the Brahimi Report being a milestone[29]—have further developed the applicable normative framework, introduced reforms, and expanded on the legal and policy principles that underlie UN peacekeeping.

2. United Nations Security Council and Power Politics

According to a wise African saying, you cannot bypass the thumb and expect to tie a solid knot. Given that, in most cases, UN peacekeeping operations are mandated by the UNSC, it is necessary to examine how the UNSC operates when it comes to the authorization of peacekeeping missions, giving particular emphasis to the approach of the P5. Amongst the P5, Britain and France once controlled vast empires, and while their former colonies have now regained their independence, close ties remain between the former colonial powers and the formerly colonized States. The remaining three Permanent Members, namely the US, Russia, and China, have significant control over and interest in world affairs due to their size and (over the last decades) increasing economic power. As Nico Krisch has pointed out, the 'institutionalized privilege' of the P5 is stronger today than it has ever been, entrenching the 'Great Power' status of these States.[30] By and large, it is they who shape the outcomes of UN peacekeeping operations anywhere in the world, determining whether a peacekeeping operation will be authorized and constituted in the first place.[31] Even plainly in terms of realpolitik, it is inconceivable that the P5 would take decisions which would not in one way or another accommodate their national interests. And this has serious systemic implications for UN peacekeeping as a whole.

[26] White (n 11) 213–16, 232.

[27] David Scheffer, 'The Security Council and International Law on Military Occupations' in Vaughan Lowe et al (eds), *The United Nations Security Council and War* (OUP 2008) 588. See, also, UNGA Res 52/247 'Third Party Liability: Temporal and Financial Limitations' (17 July 1998).

[28] White (n 11) 206–7.

[29] UNGA/UNSC 'Report of the Panel on UN Peace Operations' (21 August 2000) A/55/305-S/2000/809.

[30] Nico Krisch, 'The Security Council and Great Powers' in Lowe et al (n 27) 136.

[31] Mats Berdal, 'The Security Council and Peacekeeping' in Lowe et al (n 27) 202.

In the introduction to his book, *UN Peacekeeping in Africa—From the Suez Crisis to the Sudan Conflicts*, Adekeye Adebajo cites former UN Secretary-General Boutros Boutros-Ghali who described the dilemma of the UN as follows:

> As Secretary-General I was duty-bound to carry out the resolutions of the Security Council to the letter. But as a lifelong student of international law, I lamented this situation, which both disparaged international law and displayed the United Nations not as an organisation of sovereign states equal under the Charter but as a political tool of the major powers.[32]

And as 'a political tool of the major powers', the UN, due to the ambivalent role played by the P5, and its peacekeeping operations have often served only as a palliative; dressing the wound and leaving it festering underneath to resurface years later.

In that, one cannot but agree with Adebajo, according to whom '[t]he games that these powers [P5] play... must always be placed at the center of any analysis of UN peacekeeping missions, for it is often these games that help determine the course and outcome of these interventions'.[33] The Suez Crisis, which led to the first armed peacekeeping mission UNEF I, authorized by the UNGA and deployed with Egypt's consent in its territory[34] in 1956, cannot be easily separated from the '[t]he colonial legacy and continuing interference by the Great Powers in the Middle East'.[35] Similarly, ONUC, which was deployed by the UNSC to deal with the Congo Crisis in 1960[36] came in the aftermath of a Belgian intervention which cooperated to an extent with the pro-Western secessionist forces at the expense of the pro-Soviet government.[37]

Such power politics have not been evident solely in the context of UN peacekeeping action stricto sensu but, rather, concern enforcement action too, which often precedes (as in Libya) or accompanies peacekeeping operations (as in Somalia). The Second Gulf War is a good illustration of how the P5 have often attempted to use UN institutions as proxy to further their own national interests. The US (and its allies), under the pretext of the presence of weapons of mass destruction (WMDs), tried to use the UN to carry out its own strategic national agenda, which has since greatly destabilized Iraq and the entire region.[38] In that case, the UN under the uncompromising leadership of late Secretary-General Kofi Annan refused to give in to those pressures, but this has not necessarily always been the case.

[32] Adekeye Adebajo, *UN Peacekeeping in Africa: From Suez Crisis to the Sudan Conflicts* (Lynne Rienner 2011) 1.

[33] ibid 2.

[34] UNGA Res 998 ES-I and UNGA Res 1000 ES-I (n 7).

[35] Charlotte Peevers, *The Politics of Justifying Force: The Suez Crisis, the Iraq War, and International Law* (OUP 2013) 70. In fact, for that reason it 'had been agreed that the UN force should not include troops from the permanent members of the Security Council or of any other country which for geographical or other reasons might have a special interest in the conflict', see Gray (n 4) 271.

[36] See particularly UNSC Res 143 (1960) and 161 (1961).

[37] Robert Kolb, 'The Belgian Intervention in the Congo—1960 and 1964' in Olivier Corten et al (eds), *The Use of Force in International Law: A Case-Based Approach* (OUP 2018) 78.

[38] For a discussion see Marc Weller, 'The Iraq War—2003' in Corten et al (n 37) 655ff.

From a different perspective, power politics and veto power often hinder operations where they are most needed, the genocide in Sudan being an illustrative example. According to Brendan January:

> In 2004 Colin Powell told the [Senate] committee on foreign affairs that a genocide had been carried out in Darfur, that the Sudanese government and the Janjaweed were responsible, and that the genocide may still be ongoing. Powell stated that having reviewed the evidence which had been compiled by the State Department and having compared it to information which was freely available throughout the international community he came to the conclusion that genocide had been carried out in Darfur.[39]

This weight of evidence had been preceded by reports of Amnesty International, the International Crisis Group, and humanitarian workers about 'escalating violence' and 'atrocities' in Darfur.[40] However, and until the deployment of a small AU mission (AMIS) in June 2004, the situation was not the subject of any sophisticated or coordinated response.[41] According to Lanz,

> non-consensual military intervention in Darfur did not occur because Western states had no appetite for another military intervention in a Muslim country one year after the invasion of Iraq... Policymakers and Western activists around the Save Darfur Coalition therefore settled for what they deemed to be the second best option: sending peacekeepers.[42]

Eventually the AU–UN Hybrid Operation in Darfur was deployed, but with limited success.[43]

A different issue can be identified in the NATO intervention in Libya with UN authorization under UNSC Resolution 1973 (2011) and on the basis of the Responsibility to Protect (R2P).[44] 'Operation Unified Protector', which was authorized by the UNSC 'to protect civilians and civilian populated areas', soon became a regime-change intervention.[45] This conduct, which resulted once again in the estrangement of Russia, China, and many other States,[46] has affected the ability of the UNSC to take any meaningful action in Syria, where civilians have been repeatedly attacked and continue to live under the most dire of circumstances.

[39] Brendan January, *Genocide: Modern Crimes against Humanity* (Twenty-First Century Books 2007) 114–15.

[40] David Lanz, 'African Union–United Nations Hybrid Operation in Darfur (UNAMID)' in Koops et al (n 4) 780.

[41] ibid 780–1. [42] ibid. [43] UNSC Res 1769 (2007); Lanz (n 40) 783–7.

[44] UNSC Res 1973 (2011) preamble.

[45] Higgins et al (n 17) 1023–4; for an appraisal, see Olivier Corten/Vaios Koutroulis, 'The Illegality of Military Support to Rebels in the Libyan War: Aspects of *jus contra bellum* and *jus in bello*' (2013) 18 JCSL 59. Later, under UNSC Res 2009 (2011) the United Nations Support Mission in Libya (UNSML) was established. For its mandate, see ibid para 12.

[46] For reactions, see Corten/Koutroulis (n 45) 74–7.

Of particular significance to African countries is the role played by France, who intervened militarily in its former colonies nineteen times between 1962 and 1995.[47] In the process of gaining independence in the 1960s, former colonies were forced to sign bilateral defence treaties with France, agreeing to various degrees of military cooperation and aid, while also depositing between 50 and 65 per cent of their national reserves to the French Treasury as a kind of collateral for the support of the West African CFA franc imposed on them.[48] Additionally, the *pacte colonial* is said to have contained secret clauses that granted France the right to militarily intervene in its former colonies and which were often construed at will to bring those considered erring or recalcitrant back into line.[49] Because of international outcry, successive French administrations since Jacques Chirac have sought to distance themselves from this interventionist approach instigated by Françafrique policies. In fact, Sarkozy declared in 2008, during a visit to South Africa, that France would no longer play the role of gendarme in Africa.[50] However, France's disengagement from Africa has not yet materialized to any satisfactory extent, and UN peacekeeping operations have sometimes been caught up in these messy political affairs.

By and large, the P5 have not been considered an honest broker when it comes to using peacekeeping operations as a tool for furthering international peace and security. The Rwandan genocide provides a tragic illustration: the 1994 genocide of the Tutsi minority and moderate Hutus took place with a UN peacekeeping force (UNAMIR) present in the country.[51] UNAMIR's inaction has partly been attributed to its strained resources and reduced personnel following the withdrawal of peacekeepers by Belgium and other TCCs. At the same time, France—a supporter and ally of the majority Hutu government—has been accused of, amongst other actions, enabling the Hutu *génocidaires*, and for allowing its UNSC-authorized 'Operation Turquoise' to be used by them to flee the country.[52] Against this background, and keeping in mind the role played by

[47] Andrew Hansen, 'Backgrounder: The French Military in Africa' (*The New York Times*, 9 February 2007) <https://archive.nytimes.com/www.nytimes.com/cfr/world/slot2_20070209.html?pagewanted=print> accessed 20 May 2020.

[48] On information about the CFA franc as a currency in the 'Franc Zone' see <https://www.diplomatie.gouv.fr/en/country-files/africa/franc-zone/> accessed 27 April 2020; for a critique, see Ndongo Samba Sylla, 'The CFA Franc: French Monetary Imperialism in Africa' <http://roape.net/2017/05/18/cfa-franc-french-monetary-imperialism-africa> accessed June 2018.

[49] Blandine Sixdenier, 'Stability Spectrum: The Battle for Stabilization in the Central African Republic' IRSEM Research Paper No 42 (July 2017) <https://www.irsem.fr/data/files/irsem/documents/document/file/1197/NR_IRSEM_42.pdf> accessed 27 April 2020. 2–3. Interestingly, Nicolas Sarkozy attempted and managed to re-negotiate most of these treaties, see <http://news.bbc.co.uk/2/hi/africa/8639874.stm> accessed June 2018.

[50] Paul Melly/Vincent Darracq, 'A New Way to Engage? French Policy in Africa from Sarkozy to Hollande' (Chatham House, Africa 2013/01, May 2013) 7–8.

[51] Labuda (n 9) MN 52.

[52] Jina Moore, 'Rwanda Accuses France of Complicity in 1994 Genocide' (*The New York Times*, 13 December 2017) <https://www.nytimes.com/2017/12/13/world/africa/rwanda-france-genocide.html> accessed 20 May 2020. France's 'Operation Turquoise' was authorized by UNSC Res 929 (1994) with a 'strictly humanitarian character' (ibid preamble) partly as a temporary solution until UNAMIR could be 'brought up to the necessary strength' (ibid para 1) and be redeployed. It is only 25 years after the genocide

power politics in this field, some recent developments in UN peacekeeping will now be examined.

C. Recent Developments in United Nations Peacekeeping

In an ever-changing world, UN peacekeeping has had to adapt and respond to the changing dynamics of conflict and societal reform, as well as to the multiplication of actors and organizations addressing these at the international level. This has led to a number of developments—with accompanying challenges—which can be grouped into the following four categories.

The first is the changing strategic context of peacekeeping and the emphasis on robust mandates to protect civilians. The dynamics of conflict have shifted from conventional warfare, which was experienced in the two World Wars (and which was essentially inter-State in nature), to asymmetric, low intensity warfare and protracted civil wars which are mostly intra-State in nature.[53] These intra-State conflicts have been further complicated by the increasing threat of violent extremism, terrorism, and transnational organized crime, including drug, human, and weapons trafficking.[54] This changing nature of conflict has shaped the new environment in which peacekeepers are deployed as well as the structure and composition of UN missions. Most UN missions today, whether in Mali, the Central African Republic (CAR), South Sudan or the Democratic Republic of Congo (DRC), have been deployed in environments in which there is little or no peace to keep and where violent extremism and terrorism pose a major threat to the peace process. This has made the protection of civilians (POC) a major focus of peacekeeping and many missions have a mandate to protect them, in particular when under threat of physical harm.[55]

that French President Macron established a panel of experts to examine France's role in it, see 'Rwanda Genocide: Macron Orders Probe of France's Role' (*BBC News*, 5 April 2019) <https://www.bbc.co.uk/news/world-europe-47826841> accessed 27 April 2020. In April 2020, the panel of experts released an initial report detailing its method of research, see Pierre Lepidi/Gaïdz Minassian, 'Génocide des Tutsi au Rwanda: la commission de recherche détaille sa méthode et ses moyens' (*Le Monde*, 7 April 2020) <https://www.lemonde.fr/afrique/article/2020/04/07/genocide-des-tutsi-au-rwanda-la-commission-de-recherche-detaille-sa-methode-et-ses-moyens_6035848_3212.html> accessed 27 April 2020.

[53] On the changing dynamics of conflict see Steven Haines, 'The Nature of War and the Character of Contemporary Armed Conflict' in Elizabeth Wilmshurst (ed), *International Law and the Classification of Conflicts* (OUP 2012) 16–27.

[54] See Helen Duffy/Larissa van den Herik, Chapter 11, and Pierre Hauck/Sven Peterke, Chapter 12 in this *Handbook*.

[55] Higgins et al (n 17) 1073–4; Lisa Hultman, 'Robust Peacekeeping: A Desirable Development' (*E-International Relations*, 2 September 2014) <https://www.e-ir.info/2014/09/02/robust-peacekeeping-a-desirable-development/> accessed 2 May 2020.

To effectively discharge their mandates, such peacekeeping missions are vested with robust powers under Chapter VII UN Charter and are authorized to use 'all means necessary' to protect civilians.[56] Examples of such missions are the United Nations Stabilization Mission in the Democratic Republic of the Congo (MONUSCO),[57] the United Nations Multidimensional Integrated Stabilization Mission in Mali (MINUSMA),[58] the United Nations Multidimensional Integrated Stabilization Mission in the Central African Republic (MINUSCA),[59] and UNAMID.[60] In MONUSCO, for instance, an Intervention Brigade had to be deployed with a robust mandate to carry out offensive operations, either unilaterally or jointly with the Congolese armed forces, to disrupt the activities of the M23, the Democratic Forces for the Liberation of Rwanda (FDLR), the Lord's Resistance Army (LRA), and all other armed groups in the DRC.[61]

Secondly, there is increasing demand for accountability for human rights violations. On the one hand, peacekeepers have been scrutinized for engaging in human rights abuses, especially those involved in sexual exploitation and abuse. To that end, a zero tolerance for Sexual Exploitation and Abuse policy has been developed,[62] with the UN Secretary-General regularly reporting on the efforts the UN is making towards ensuring protection from sexual exploitation and abuse.[63] Such reforms at the UN level have followed extensive criticism of the UN's activities as well as its lack of accountability due to the privileges and immunities it enjoys.[64] On the other hand, warring factions have come under scrutiny with regard to the prohibition of the use of child soldiers in conflict and conflict-related sexual violence (CRSV).[65]

Thirdly, the current peacekeeping environment involves a number of multiple organizational actors, including regional organizations and bilateral partners, all working together to promote international peace and security.[66] In particular, the African Union (AU) and the Economic Community of West African States (ECOWAS) have played an active role in deploying emergency missions in many African countries, such as Côte d'Ivoire and Darfur, while they have also expanded their political

[56] Bothe (n 3) 1179–80.

[57] UNSC Res 1925 (2010) para 11.

[58] UNSC Res 2100 (2013) para 17.

[59] UNSC Res 2149 (2014) para 29.

[60] UNSC Res 1769 (2007) para 15.

[61] UN Press Release, '"Intervention Brigade" Authorized as Security Council Grants Mandate Renewal for United Nations Mission in Democratic Republic of Congo' (28 March 2013) UN Doc SC/10964.

[62] UN Secretariat, 'Secretary-General's Bulletin: Special Measures for Protection from Sexual Exploitation and Abuse' (9 October 2013) UN Doc ST/SGB/2003/13.

[63] See, most recently, UNGA 'Report of the Secretary-General: Special Measures for Protection from Sexual Exploitation and Abuse' (17 February 2020) UN Doc A/74/705; see also UN Action for Peacekeeping, 'Fact Sheet: Sexual Exploitation and Abuse: Peacekeeping Initiatives in Action' (18 December 2019) <https://peacekeeping.un.org/sites/default/files/sea_fact_sheet_1.pdf> accessed 27 April 2020.

[64] Kristen Boon, 'The United Nations as Good Samaritan: Immunity and Responsibility' (2016) 16 Chicago Journal of International Law 341; August Reinisch, 'Privileges and Immunities' in Jacob Katz Cogan et al (eds), *Oxford Handbook of International Organizations* (OUP 2016) 1048; Rosa Freedman 'UN Immunity or Impunity? A Human Rights Based Challenge' (2014) 25 EJIL 239.

[65] See UNSC, 'Report of the Secretary-General on Conflict-Related Sexual Violence' (15 April 2017) UN Doc S/2017/249.

[66] Commission on Global Security, Justice and Governance, 'Report: Confronting the Crisis of Global Governance' (June 2017) 27–8 <http://www.platformglobalsecurityjusticegovernance.org/wp-content/uploads/2015/06/Commission-on-Global-Security-Justice-Governance-A4.pdf> accessed 2 May 2020.

missions.[67] The EU has also substantially contributed in Africa with a mission currently ongoing in Mali.[68] A strategic partnership between the UN and these organizations is crucial: according to Bothe, '[t]here are no hard and fast rules on the division of the respective roles of the UN and regional organisations… [t]he resources of the EU or the geographic proximity of regional organisations are important considerations.'[69]

Finally, due to the complex peacekeeping environments that feature asymmetric and unconventional threats, the UN has deployed technology in the field in order to assist its missions with monitoring efforts.[70] In the DRC and Mali, the introduction of unmanned aerial vehicles (UAVs) has had an immediate impact in gathering intelligence for swift response to emerging situations on the ground. GIS data is also being used to help find water sources for missions to limit their dependence on the limited local supply.[71] Efforts are also being made to explore alternative sources of energy such as solar panels as well as the introduction of waste water treatment plants to reduce the need for water and the generation of disposable waste.[72]

D. The Pacifying Role of United Nations Peacekeeping

There is no doubt that after the failure of the League of Nations to prevent the Second World War, the establishment of the UN—'an organization that reveals great imagination

[67] AU missions include the African Union Mission in Burundi (AMIB), African Mission in Sudan I (AMIS I), African Union Mission in Sudan II (AMIS II), African Union Mission for Support to the Elections in the Comoros (AMISEC), African Union Mission in Somalia (AMISOM) (2007), African Union Mission in the Comoros (MAES) (2007), Africa-led International Support Mission in Mali (AFISMA) (2013), African led Support Mission to the Central African Republic (MISCA) (2013), United Nations/African Union Hybrid Mission in Darfur (UNAMID). See, further, AU Commission, Peace Support and Operations Division, 'Silencing the Guns, Sustaining Peace' <http://www.peaceau.org/uploads/02-au-psod-brochure-23sep16.pdf> accessed 27 April 2020. For an example of ECOWAS action, see Section E.3.a on Liberia.

[68] See EUCAP Sahel Mali <https://eeas.europa.eu/csdp-missions-operations/eucap-sahel-mali_en> accessed 27 April 2020; Bothe (n 3) 1180 and fn 31.

[69] Both (n 3) 1180.

[70] UNGA/UNSC 'Report of the High-level Independent Panel on Peace Operations on Uniting our Strengths for Peace: Politics, Partnership and People' (17 June 2015) UN Doc A/70/95–S/2015/446, paras 310–13.

[71] UN ECOSOC, 'Geospatial Support for UN Operations' (Eighteenth United Nations Regional Cartographic Conference for Asia and the Pacific, 26–29 October 2009) E/CONF.100/IP.20, 11 <https://unstats.un.org/unsd/geoinfo/RCC/docs/rccap18/IP/18th_UNRCCAP_econf.100_IP20.pdf> accessed 27 April 2020.

[72] UN, 'Technology Boost for UN Peacekeepers "Essential" in Rapidly Evolving, Complex World—UN Experts' <https://news.un.org/en/story/2015/02/491752-technology-boost-un-peacekeepers-essential-rapidly-evolving-complex-world-un> accessed 2 June 2018; UNGA/UNSC 'Report of the Secretary-General: The Future of United Nations Peace Operations: Implementation of the Recommendations of the High-level Independent Panel on Peace Operations' (2 September 2015) UN Doc A/70/357–S/2015/682, para 128.

and profound shortcomings'[73]—with its collective security system and the absolute prohibition of the threat or use of force in international relations under Article 2(4) UN Charter, has come a long way to bring peace and stability worldwide. Indeed, the 1988 award of the Nobel Peace Prize to the UN Peacekeeping Forces is testament to the fact that 'the Peacekeeping Forces through their efforts have made important contributions towards the realization of one of the fundamental tenets of the United Nations. Thus, the world organization has come to play a more central part in world affairs and has been invested with increasing trust.'[74] This pacifying role of UN peacekeeping has many aspects, varies between missions, and has found expressions in the different functions of peacekeeping operations.[75] In this section, two key peacekeeping functions will be addressed: conflict resolution and governance strengthening along with security sector reform.

1. Conflict Resolution

To begin with, successful deployment of UN peacekeeping interventions has settled many conflicts, saving thousands of lives as a result. From Cambodia, El Salvador, Guatemala, Mozambique, Namibia to Sierra Leone, Côte d'Ivoire, Timor-Leste, Liberia, and Kosovo, the UN has helped to end conflicts by promoting dialogue and reconciliation amongst warring parties.[76] Many of these countries have transitioned to peace and socio-economic development after many years of internal conflict. The UN's operations in Sierra Leone, for instance, have been hailed as a success due to the role peacekeepers played in successfully implementing the peace agreement after the country's devastating civil war. Before its closure, the UN Mission in Sierra Leone (UNAMSIL) helped to disarm more than 75,000 ex-combatants, including child soldiers, and destroyed more than 40,000 weapons.[77] Similarly, the peaceful transfer of political power from the then incumbent government of Ellen Johnson Sirleaf to an opposition party led by George Weah (a former professional footballer) after the December 2017 elections showed the impact of the UN mission in the country.[78] Indeed, unlike previous elections, the 2017 election was solely handled by Liberians themselves with minimal support from the UN. Despite the lack of euphoria regarding the possibilities associated with UN peacekeeping in the early 1990s, the fact that there are currently close to 100,000 UN peacekeepers operating across thirteen different missions indicates

[73] Higgins et al (n 17) 3.

[74] See <https://www.un.org/en/sections/nobel-peace-prize/united-nations-peacekeeping-forces/index.html> accessed 30 November 2020.

[75] Higgins et al (n 17) 1068–74.

[76] See 'UN Peacekeeping—Our Successes' <https://peacekeeping.un.org/en/our-successes> accessed 2 May 2020.

[77] Adebajo (n 32).

[78] Clair MacDougall/Helene Cooper, 'George Weah Wins Liberia Election' (*The New York Times*, 28 December 2017) <https://www.nytimes.com/2017/12/28/world/africa/george-weah-liberia-election.html> accessed 2 May 2020.

that the UN, and in particular the UNSC, continues to see a role for UN peacekeeping in conflict resolution.[79]

2. Strengthening Governance and Implementing Security Sector Reform

More significantly, military, police, and civilian personnel serving in UN missions have helped to build and reform institutions of governance and security in war-torn countries, and in some instances, have taken over the interim political administration of territories,[80] as in the case of Kosovo[81] and Timor-Leste.[82] Peacekeeping missions have implemented and assisted in the implementation of security sector reforms in post-conflict States, such as Liberia, Rwanda, and Sierra Leone, with respect to the armed forces, the police, and especially the criminal justice system to improve their efficiency and independence. Such reforms of security institutions have in turn helped to prevent relapse into conflict.

More significantly, UN peacekeepers have also, through their peacebuilding interventions, addressed some of the underlying causes of conflict in many of the countries where they have been deployed. In particular, missions have been engaged in minimizing the threats posed by governance issues (such as corruption), political exclusion, and marginalization, as well as socio-economic challenges. In many conflict zones today, like Sudan, South Sudan, and the CAR, the presence of the UN has prevented further violence against civilians and widespread human rights abuses.[83]

E. The Destabilizing Role of United Nations Peacekeeping

As another African proverb goes, 'it is the same person who goes for water who is likely to break the water pot'. Despite the successes of the UN, there have been some major failures, too. In many instances, UN peacekeepers have failed to protect civilians in

[79] UN, 'Peacekeeping Data' <https://peacekeeping.un.org/en/data> accessed 27 April 2020; Berdal (n 31) 202.

[80] See Richard Caplan, 'The Security Council and the Administration of War-Torn and Contested Territories' in Lowe et al (n 27) 563.

[81] See the various reports of the UN Secretary-General on the UNMIK: <https://unmik.unmissions.org/sg-reports> accessed 27 April 2020; see further Berdal (n 31) 198.

[82] See, further, the reports of the UN Secretary-General on UNMIT: <https://unmit.unmissions.org/reports-secretary-general> accessed 27 April 2020; more generally, Daisaku Higashi 'The Challenge of Constructive Legitimacy in Peacebuilding: Case of Timor-Leste' (2009) CIR Working Paper No 48 <https://www.files.ethz.ch/isn/104635/WP48.pdf > accessed 27 April 2020.

[83] Berdal (n 31) 192, 203.

imminent danger:[84] Somalia, Rwanda, and the former Yugoslavia in the early 1990s are prominent examples. These setbacks have affected the credibility of the UN. In other cases, UN peacekeeping operations have left in their wake conduct and discipline issues, health and environmental issues, as well as 'unfinished business' and lingering controversies. Some of these failings are discussed in the following sections.

1. Conduct and Discipline

Although peacekeepers are expected to adhere to the highest standards of behaviour and conduct in a professional and disciplined manner during missions, plenty of cases of misconduct involving UN peacekeeping personnel have been reported. In the South Sudan, CAR, DRC, and Haiti, UN peacekeepers have been accused of both rape and of paying women (primarily, but also men) and children for sex.[85] A report by the UN showed that in the first seven months of 2017 alone at least fifty-five UN peacekeepers were accused of sexual exploitation and abuse of civilians across UN missions around the world.[86] Although measures, such as the 'zero tolerance' policy, have been put in place, the UN's reputation for protecting civilians has suffered due to these recurring cases of abuse by peacekeepers, while actual enforcement of accountability is also presently lacking.[87]

2. Health and Environmental Issues

Even though there are strict standards of health screening before deployment, peacekeepers have been unwitting 'vectors' in the spread of disease in their areas of

[84] Richard Spencer, 'UN at 70: Five Greatest Successes and Failures' (*Daily Telegraph*, 15 September 2015) <https://www.telegraph.co.uk/news/worldnews/europe/switzerland/11700969/UN-at-70-Five-greatest-successes-and-failures.html> accessed 28 May 2018.

[85] See UN, 'Preventing Sexual Exploitation and Abuse: Data on Allegations—UN System-wide' <https://www.un.org/preventing-sexual-exploitation-and-abuse/content/data-allegations-un-system-wide> accessed 2 May 2020; also, Human Rights Watch, 'UN: Stop Sexual Abuse by Peacekeepers' (4 March 2016) <https://www.hrw.org/news/2016/03/04/un-stop-sexual-abuse-peacekeepers> accessed 2 May 2020. See, generally, Martina Vandenberg, 'Peacekeeping, Human Trafficking, and Sexual Abuse and Exploitation' in Fionnuala Ní Aoláin et al (eds), *The Oxford Handbook of Gender and Conflict* (OUP 2018); Sabine Lee/Susan Bartels, '"They Put a Few Coins in your Hands to Drop a Baby in You"—265 Stories of Haitian Children Abandoned by UN Fathers' (*The Conversation*, 17 December 2019) <https://theconversation.com/they-put-a-few-coins-in-your-hands-to-drop-a-baby-in-you-265-stories-of-haitian-children-abandoned-by-un-fathers-114854> accessed 20 May 2020; Sienna Merope-Synge, 'Seeking Child Support from UN Peacekeepers—A View from Haiti' (*Opinio Juris*, 16 August 2019) <http://opiniojuris.org/2019/08/16/emerging-voices-seeking-child-support-from-un-peacekeepers-a-view-from-haiti/> accessed 20 May 2020.

[86] Azad Essa, 'UN Peacekeepers Hit by New Allegations of Sex Abuse' <https://www.aljazeera.com/news/2017/07/peacekeepers-hit-allegations-sex-abuse-170701133655238.html> accessed 1 June 2018.

[87] Vandenberg (n 85) 412–14.

operation. The cholera outbreak in Haiti, which was imported in 2010 by the Nepalese contingent of the UN peacekeeping force sent to stabilize the country after a destructive earthquake, is a prime example.[88] The outbreak turned into an epidemic which has devastated the country and has claimed more than 10,000 lives.[89]

On top of that, UN missions have also been considered responsible for half of the greenhouse gas emissions of the entire UN system.[90] According to the International Peace Institute, missions deployed to 'arid, land-locked countries have considerable resource requirements and can cause significant, if unintended, environmental damage to countries the UN is seeking to assist'.[91] United Nations peacekeepers have also on some occasions added stress to the already vulnerable ecosystems of host States as they are often deployed 'in complex and fragile ecosystems, where resources are scarce and the government is not responsive to the needs of its people'.[92]

3. Unfinished Business and Lingering Controversies

Earlier in this chapter, reference was made to the fact that while UN peacekeeping has been a force for good, the interference of the P5 in the internal affairs of other States has often tainted peacekeeping missions or excessively complicated the effective discharge of their mandates and functions. This will be illustrated through the representative examples of two conflict-ridden African States, where the contribution of the UN peacekeeping missions to their long-term stability and security (and to those of the region) has been fervently contested: Liberia and Côte d'Ivoire. The analysis will draw from the author's own experience and involvement in those missions.

a. *Liberia*

The Liberian crisis has been one of the cases that was left unresolved, only to re-emerge later. When civil war broke out in December 1989, ECOWAS stepped in to halt the carnage inflicted on unarmed civilians, especially West African nationals, through the

[88] Kristen E Boon, 'Haiti Cholera Update' (*Opinio Juris*, 20 September 2016) <http://opiniojuris.org/2016/09/20/haiti-cholera-update/> accessed 20 May 2020; UN 'Secretary-General Apologizes for United Nations Role in Haiti Cholera Epidemic, Urges International Funding of New Response to Disease' (1 December 2016) UN Doc SG/SM/18323-GA/11862; UNGA 'Report of the Special Rapporteur on Extreme Poverty and Human Rights' (26 August 2016) UN Doc A/71/367, paras 13–43.

[89] Jacob Kushner, '"It Became Part of Life": How Haiti Curbed Cholera' (*The Guardian*, 16 March 2020) <https://www.theguardian.com/global-development/2020/mar/16/it-became-part-of-life-how-haiti-curbed-cholera> accessed 2 May 2020.

[90] UN Peacekeeping, 'Our Approach' <https://peacekeeping.un.org/en/our-approach> accessed 27 April 2020.

[91] International Peace Institute, 'The Environmental Impact of UN Peace Operations' (18 April 2018) <https://www.ipinst.org/2018/04/environmental-impact-un-peace-operations> accessed 2 May 2020.

[92] ibid. See, for more detail, Lucile Maertens/Malkit Shoshan, 'Greening Peacekeeping: The Environmental Impact of UN Peace Operations' (International Peace Institute, Providing for Peace No 17, April 2018) <https://www.ipinst.org/wp-content/uploads/2018/04/1804_Greening-Peacekeeping.pdf> accessed 2 May 2020.

(hurriedly) assembled Ceasefire Monitoring Group (ECOMOG) comprised of troops from The Gambia, Ghana, Guinea, Nigeria, Mali, and Sierra Leone. ECOMOG forces were, by and large, able to stabilize the situation between 1990 and 1993 until the UN stepped in with the establishment of the UN Observer Mission in Liberia (UNOMIL).[93] UNOMIL was in fact the first UN mission established to support an already deployed regional operation.[94]

In February 1997, after four years on the ground, a joint assessment made by UNOMIL and ECOMOG forces concluded that the country had been sufficiently stabilized and pacified for elections to be held.[95] This followed the completion of a rushed disarmament process.[96] Elections were held and Charles Taylor, who had projected himself as the most militarily and financially endowed, won them. This proved a pyrrhic victory: barely two years later, in 1999, fighting broke out again amongst the dissatisfied factions who alleged that Charles Taylor had won the elections by intimidating the Liberian electorate. The fighting persisted, turning into a full-blown war from 2000 onwards, until ECOMOG forces landed in Monrovia in September 2003 to a rousing welcome and popular acclaim.[97] A new UN mission, the United Nations Mission in Liberia (UNMIL) was established[98], heralding the second entry of the Organization into the Liberian crisis. This mission only ended in March 2018 after fifteen years on the ground to ensure that this time peace would endure.

In the run up to the second deployment of ECOMOG/UN operations in Liberia, the present author was appointed as leader of a Joint Verification Team (JVT)[99] which was set up following the Comprehensive Peace Agreement (CPA) signed in Accra in June 2003 to monitor the ceasefire agreement. This team was moved from Accra to Freetown in July to await deployment into Liberia but for weeks nothing seemed to be moving. The understanding reached between the UN and ECOWAS was that the UN would use its helicopters to deploy the team if ECOWAS could guarantee an extraction force to stand by to recover the team in case of difficulties. ECOWAS was unable to provide this force. Although it was a great relief when the JVT was eventually moved to Abuja to accompany the hurriedly assembled ECOWAS force in its 'triumphant re-entry' into Liberia by air in September 2003, JVT's function to monitor the ceasefire had by this point been rendered moot.

[93] UNSC Res 866 (1993).

[94] Kathleen Jennings, 'United Nations Observer Mission in Liberia (UNOMIL)' in Koops et al (n 4) 456.

[95] See <https://peacekeeping.un.org/en/mission/past/unomilFT.htm#DECEMB> accessed 27 April 2020.

[96] For more detail, see Jennings (n 94) 456–9.

[97] Sarah Left, 'War in Liberia' (*The Guardian*, 4 August 2003) <https://www.theguardian.com/world/2003/aug/04/westafrica.qanda> accessed 27 April 2020.

[98] UNSC Res 1509 (2003).

[99] GhanaWeb, 'Joint Verification Team to leave for Liberia on Sunday' (20 June 2003) <https://www.ghanaweb.com/GhanaHomePage/NewsArchive/Joint-Verification-Team-to-leave-for-Liberia-on-Saturday-38029> accessed 27 April 2020.

Having learned their lesson, during their second stay in Liberia, both ECOMOG and UNMIL made sure that comprehensive steps were taken to avoid similar pitfalls.[100] Disarmament of factions commenced in December 2003 and ended in October 2004 with more than 100,000 combatants disarmed and demobilized.[101] Elections were held on schedule in October (first round) and November (second round) 2005 with UN security protection, ushering in Africa's first elected female President in the person of Ellen Johnson Sirleaf. A slowly and deliberately executed security sector reform, which saw the creation of a new army, was effected, and the UN finally withdrew in March 2018, hoping for no violent comebacks.[102]

b. *Côte d'Ivoire*

The 2011 events in Côte d'Ivoire, taking place at the same time as the intervention by the NATO-led coalition in Libya, caused controversy and raised many legal and policy questions regarding the role of UN peacekeeping operations, the authorization of use of force by the UNSC, and the role played by the P5 (in this case France). The aftermath of the events has left many States and individual observers concerned about key aspects of peacekeeping, particularly its impartiality.[103] This (perhaps justified) perception cannot be separated from the role France played in the crisis and the fall from power of the then incumbent President Laurent Gbagbo.

UNOCI was established under UNSC Resolution 1528 (2004) to succeed the UN Mission in Côte d'Ivoire (MINUCI)—a political mission established under UNSC Resolution 1479 (2003) to 'facilitate the implementation by the Ivorian parties of the Linas-Marcoussis Agreement' along with a military component to complement 'the operations of the French forces'[104]—and the ECOWAS forces in the country.[105] UNOCI was dispatched to monitor the ceasefire between the warring parties, supervise disarmament and demobilization, contribute to the protection and promotion of human rights, and support the peace process, including the conduct of free, fair, and transparent elections, amongst others.[106]

When the time came for the 2010 elections to take place, violence erupted and far-reaching human rights abuses took place.[107] The reason for this breakdown was that the two frontrunners, Laurent Gbagbo (then incumbent President) and Alassane

[100] For an assessment see Kathleen Jennings, 'United Nations Mission in Liberia (UNMIL)' in Koops et al (n 4).

[101] ibid 697.

[102] UN, 'UNMIL Completes its Mandate in a Now Peaceful Liberia' (30 March 2018) <https://unmil.unmissions.org/unmil-completes-its-mandate-now-peaceful-liberia?> accessed 27 April 2020.

[103] Dire Tladi, 'The Intervention in Côte d'Ivoire—2011' in Olivier Corten et al (eds), *The Use of Force in International Law: A Case-Based Approach* (OUP 2018).

[104] UNSC Res 1479 (2003) para 2. [105] UNSC Res 1528 (2004) para 1.

[106] UNSC Res 1528 (2004) para 6 and UNSC 1765 (2007) para 6.

[107] UNSC Res 1975 (2011) para 1. Former President Laurent Gbagbo subsequently faced criminal proceedings at the International Criminal Court (ICC) for crimes against humanity allegedly committed during the post-election violence in 2010–11. He was acquitted of all charges by the Trial Chamber I on 15 January 2019, but at the time of writing the case was pending before the ICC Appeals Chamber following the Prosecutor's appeal against the acquittal decision. See <https://www.icc-cpi.int/cdi/gbagbo-goude> accessed 30 November 2020.

Ouattara, and their supporters disagreed on the outcome of the second electoral round held in November 2010.[108] UNOCI was implicated in this as the Head of the Mission and the UN Special Representative of the Secretary-General confirmed the results of the Independent Elections Commission, which had declared Ouattara as the winner. The competence of UNOCI to certify the result of the elections was disputed and arguments were voiced that this power belonged to the Constitutional Council instead, which had in fact proclaimed Gbagbo as the winner. However, the international community, including the ECOWAS and the UNSC, recognized Ouattara as the elected President and called for Gbagbo to step down.[109]

In view of the subsequent violence, UNSC Resolution 1975 authorized 'UNOCI, while impartially implementing its mandate, to use all necessary means to carry out its mandate to protect civilians under imminent threat of physical violence'.[110] In pursuance of their mandate, UNOCI, along with French forces, whose presence predated UNOCI in Côte d'Ivoire, 'bombarded Gbagbo forces, leading to his eventual defeat and capture'.[111] Whether UNOCI's mandate encompassed the capture and eventual ousting of Gbagbo in favour of Ouattara under UNSC Resolution 1975, and in light of the principle of impartiality of peacekeeping operations, is doubtful. Indeed, many States expressed concerns about the legality of UNOCI's implication in this operation and its collaboration with the French forces to that end.[112] Matters were further complicated by the fact that France was the penholder in the UNSC for the relevant resolutions and 'was particularly keen to promote robust action'.[113] According to Novosseloff, 'France's presence and interests left the UN in the back seat both in the mediation . . . and security areas'.[114]

Since the 2010–11 events, the security situation in the country, although improved, can hardly be considered stable. In June 2012, seven peacekeepers, two civilians and at least one FRCI (Forces Républicaine de Côte d'Ivoire) soldier were killed in an ambush mounted by Liberian mercenaries and former pro-Gbagbo fighters from the Liberia side of the border.[115] The present author's advice as the outgoing Deputy Force Commander of the military component of UNOCI that the eastern border with Liberia was the one that merited increased police and military presence (and not the western one with Ghana) was not heeded. According to Human Rights Watch (HRW), between July 2011 and 9 June 2012, when the latest incident took place, more than forty people had lost their lives as a result of cross-border incursions from Liberia.[116] The situation was most precarious in July 2017, when a mutiny broke out from amongst the ranks of former rebels now serving in the army, demanding bonus payments. According to

[108] Tladi (n 103) 783–4. [109] ibid 784–6. [110] UNSC Res 1975 (2011).

[111] Tladi (n 103) 787. For the events, see also Alexandra Novosseloff, 'United Nations Operation in Côte d'Ivoire (UNOCI)' in Koops et al (n 4) 713–14.

[112] Tladi (n 103) 787–92. Tladi observes that the circumstances of Gbagbo's arrest remain somewhat obscure to the present day (ibid).

[113] ibid 788. [114] Novosseloff (n 111) 716.

[115] For more information, see <https://www.telegraph.co.uk/news/worldnews/africaandindianocean/cotedivoire/9321366/Seven-UN-peacekeepers-killed-in-Ivory-Coast.html> accessed 2 May 2020.

[116] For more information, see <https://www.hrw.org/news/2012/06/06/liberia-ivorian-government-foes-wage-plot-attacks> accessed 2 May 2020.

Amnesty International, at least ten people were killed and dozens wounded in violence in January 2018.[117]

All this notwithstanding, according to UNOCI's webpage, it 'successfully completed its mandate on 30 June 2017'.[118] However, the Presidential elections scheduled to take place in October 2020 will be the real test for Côte d'Ivoire's fragile stability.[119] According to HRW, '[i]nadequate progress in addressing a longstanding culture of impunity, reforming the security forces, and strengthening rule of law institutions threaten the country's long-term prospects for peace and development'.[120] In more diplomatic terms, during Côte d'Ivoire's Third Cycle of Universal Periodic Review at the Human Rights Council, amongst the conclusions and recommendations made by the Working Group and other States were the adoption of guarantees safeguarding the independence of the judiciary, investigation of all human rights abuses, especially those committed during 2010 to 2011, and the adoption of measures guaranteeing that the 2020 elections will be held in a credible and transparent manner.[121]

F. Conclusion

In its quest to safeguard international peace and security—'to save succeeding generations from the scourge of war'—the UN has faced limitations, but there have also been some notable successes. The Organization, through peacekeeping and other operations, has helped to stabilize a number of war-torn countries and led them to a path of sustainable peace and economic development. Nevertheless, the challenges that confront UN missions are enormous and concerted efforts are required to address them. The issue of sexual exploitation and abuse by peacekeepers has plagued peacekeeping operations; the only way to address this is enhanced training of the participating personnel, accountability for the human rights abuses committed by them, and redress for the victims. Adequate resources and personnel, as well as a clear mandate, are also necessary for the effective protection of civilians from armed groups and for the general effective discharge of the missions' mandate. Even though today the perception of the disproportionately privileged P5 and their interference in world affairs is still prevalent, the fact remains that peacekeeping is a useful tool of the UN in achieving its goals, and as such it should be strengthened and supported to be able to rapidly adapt to a changing global security landscape.

[117] For more information, see <https://www.reuters.com/article/us-ivorycoast-un-peacekeepers/u-n-closes-ivory-coast-mission-security-remains-fragile-idUSKBN19L1VK> accessed 2 May 2020.

[118] See <https://peacekeeping.un.org/mission/past/unoci.shtml> accessed 27 April 2020.

[119] Loucoumane Coulibaly, 'Ivory Coast's Ouattara Says He Won't Run for Re-Election' (*Reuters*, 5 March 2020) <https://www.reuters.com/article/us-ivorycoast-politics-idUSKBN20S1IZ> accessed 27 April 2020.

[120] See, for more information, <https://www.reuters.com/article/us-ivorycoast-un-peacekeepers/u-n-closes-ivory-coast-mission-security-remains-fragile-idUSKBN19L1VK> accessed 27 April 2020.

[121] UNGA 'Report of the Working Group on the Universal Periodic Review: Côte d'Ivoire' (3 July 2019) UN Doc A/HRC/42/6.

CHAPTER 44

RESPONSIBILITY TO PROTECT AND HUMANITARIAN INTERVENTION

From Apology to Utopia and Back Again

SIMON CHESTERMAN

A. Introduction

Despite the title of this chapter, the responsibility to protect (R2P[1]) was developed precisely as an alternative to humanitarian intervention—the notion that unilateral force can be used to protect human rights in another State. The term was coined by a commission established by the Canadian government after the controversial NATO airstrikes against the former Yugoslavia over its actions in Kosovo in 1999.[2] Though humanitarian intervention was the most plausible legal justification for the airstrikes,[3] the report avoided that language completely.[4] The rhetorical shift was useful, moving debate away from whether 'kind-hearted gunmen'[5] have a right to use force and onto

[1] Within the argot of the UN, the abbreviation 'RtoP' is also common.

[2] International Commission on Intervention and State Sovereignty (ICISS), *The Responsibility to Protect* (International Development Research Centre 2001); see also Thomas G Weiss, *Global Governance: Why? What? Whither?* (Polity 2013) 93–6.

[3] Simon Chesterman, *Just War or Just Peace? Humanitarian Intervention and International Law* (OUP 2001) 211–18. This chapter draws on some material first published in that book, as well as Simon Chesterman, '"Leading from Behind": The Responsibility to Protect, the Obama Doctrine, and Humanitarian Intervention After Libya' (2011) 25 Ethics and International Affairs 279.

[4] The report makes occasional reference to humanitarian intervention in 'scare quotes': ICISS (n 2) 9.

[5] Ian Brownlie, 'Thoughts on Kind-Hearted Gunmen' in Richard B Lillich (ed), *Humanitarian Intervention and the United Nations* (UP of Virginia 1973).

how the causes that might inspire such uses of force can be prevented or handled more peacefully. In the event that prevention and peaceful means fail, R2P does allow for action by the UN Security Council (UNSC) under existing rules. But it neatly dodges the more difficult question—epitomized by the Kosovo case—of what rules should govern a humanitarian crisis when both the State in question and the UNSC are unwilling or unable to act.

The sections that follow first examine the legal framework of humanitarian intervention and how R2P came to be adopted and endorsed by UN Member States in general and the UNSC in particular. The speed with which the language of R2P permeated the UN and the wider global system has been extraordinary, though this has been primarily in the nature of a political rather than a legal transformation. A later section highlights the present challenges faced by R2P, evident in the partially successful operation in Libya and the dismally ineffective response to the ongoing crisis in Syria. A final section makes some tentative projections about the future—in which the language of R2P appears likely to continue its spread, but weariness of intervention on the part of Western States and the rise of Asian States defending a conservative notion of sovereignty will dampen the conversion of words to action.

B. Legal Framework

The use of force generally is discussed by Elizabeth Wilmshurst in Chapter 45 of this *Handbook*. In brief, under the UN Charter, Member States forswore the right to use force except in two circumstances: when exercising their inherent right of self-defence under Article 51 of the Charter, or where the UNSC authorizes a State or group of States to respond to a threat to international peace and security under Chapter VII.[6] Beyond these exceptions, the language agreed by States at the San Francisco conference of 1945 was broad in its scope: 'All Members shall refrain in their international relations from the threat or use of force against the territorial integrity or political independence of any state, or in any other manner inconsistent with the Purposes of the United Nations.'[7]

From time to time it has been argued that certain limited uses of force might not contravene this provision. For example, Anthony D'Amato argued that the US invasion of Panama in 1989 was consistent with the UN Charter because 'the United States did not intend to, and has not, colonialized [*sic*], annexed or incorporated Panama.'[8] As Oscar Schachter archly observed, this demands an Orwellian construction of the terms 'territorial integrity' and 'political independence'.[9] It also runs counter to various statements by the UN General Assembly (UNGA) and the International Court of Justice

[6] Charter of the United Nations 1 UNTS XVI (UN Charter) art 42. [7] ibid art 2(4).

[8] Anthony D'Amato, 'The Invasion of Panama was a Lawful Response to Tyranny' (1990) 84 AJIL 516, 520.

[9] Oscar Schachter, 'The Legality of Pro-Democratic Invasion' (1984) 78 AJIL 645, 649.

(ICJ) concerning the meaning of non-intervention,[10] as well as UNSC practice, which has condemned and declared illegal the unauthorized use of force even when it is 'temporary'.[11] This is consistent with the drafting history of the provision, which, the US delegate to the San Francisco conference (amongst others) emphasized, left 'no loopholes'.[12]

The two exceptions to the general prohibition offer case studies of how norms concerning the use of force have a tendency to expand.[13] Self-defence, for example, has been invoked in ever-wider circumstances to justify military actions including a pre-emptive strike against a country's nuclear program[14] and in 'response' to a failed assassination attempt in a third country,[15] as well as against States that allegedly 'harbour' terrorists.[16]

UNSC-authorized actions have expanded even further, mandating actions in Somalia and Haiti in the 1990s that would never have been contemplated by the founders of the UN in 1945 because they would have been seen as matters that were purely 'domestic'.[17] Many such actions by the Council are considered in the same breath as true 'humanitarian interventions', but it is important to distinguish between humanitarian crises that have expanded the notion of a 'threat to international peace and security' under Chapter VII and the creation of an entirely new justification for the use of force without that authorization.[18] (As we shall see, the blurring of that line in cases like Libya gives rise to controversy and may, perversely, undermine the willingness of some States to support humanitarian operations under well-established law.)

A possible loophole is sometimes seen in the role the UNGA played during the Korean War in 1950. At a time when a Soviet veto threatened to block action by the Council, Western States turned to the UNGA and adopted the Uniting for Peace Resolution. In the case of a breach of the peace or act of aggression, measures available to the UNGA are said to include the use of armed force.[19] The legality of the UNGA

[10] eg a similar argument was advanced by the UK in the *Corfu Channel* case *(UK v Albania)* (Merits) [1949] ICJ Rep 4, 33–4 but rejected outright by the ICJ, ibid 35.

[11] See eg UNSC Res 332 (1973); UNSC Res 455 (1979); UNSC Res 545 (1983).

[12] UNCIO (1945) vol VI, 335.

[13] cf Monica Hakimi, 'The *Jus Ad Bellum*'s Regulatory Form' (2018) 112 AJIL 151, and the recent AJIL Unbound symposium organized around this article with contributions by Theresa Reinold, 'Informal Regulation and the Hyper-Responsiveness of International Law' (2018) 112 AJIL Unbound 97; Tess Bridgeman, 'In Defense of the "Conventional Account" of the *Jus Ad Bellum*' (2018) 112 AJIL Unbound 102; Christian J Tams, 'Three Questions about "Informal Regulation"' (2018) 112 AJIL Unbound 108; Ian Johnstone, 'Condoning the Use of Force: The UN Security Council as Interpreter of the *Jus Ad Bellum*' (2018) 112 AJIL Unbound 113.

[14] Timothy L H McCormack, *Self-Defense in International Law: The Israeli Raid on the Iraqi Nuclear Reactor* (St Martin's Press 1996).

[15] Dino Kritsiotis, 'The Legality of the 1993 US Missile Strike on Iraq and the Right of Self-Defence in International Law' (1996) 45 ICLQ 162.

[16] Christian J Tams/James G Devaney, 'Applying Necessity and Proportionality to Anti-Terrorist Self-Defence' (2012) 45 Israel Law Review 91.

[17] UN Charter (n 6) art 2(7).

[18] Generally, see Chesterman (n 3) 163–218.

[19] UNGA Res 377 A (V) (3 November 1950).

doing more than authorize peacekeeping with the consent of parties is dubious, however. The Uniting for Peace resolution was used with such consent during the Suez crisis in 1956 and in the Congo in 1960, but the procedure subsequently fell into desuetude beyond providing an occasional forum for rhetorical debate.[20] In particular, though well-meaning academics suggested that it might have been an appropriate mechanism to invoke during the Kosovo crisis, the Uniting for Peace Resolution appears not to have been seriously contemplated by the States themselves—apparently due to fears that NATO would have been unable to muster the necessary two-thirds majority support of the UN to invoke it.[21] The mechanism was floated more recently as a possible means of avoiding UNSC deadlock over Syria—that is, avoiding another Russian veto.[22]

The only other possible legal basis for action in situations like Kosovo is the argument that a new norm has developed, creating a discrete right of humanitarian intervention. There is no treaty to this effect, but the creation of such norms under customary international law is possible through the evolution of 'constant and uniform'[23] or 'extensive and virtually uniform'[24] State practice when accompanied by the necessary *opinio juris*—the belief that a practice is legally obligatory, and that instances of inconsistent conduct are treated as breaches of a rule.[25] Some writers have argued that there is evidence of both in the case of humanitarian intervention, typically pointing to the Indian action to stop the slaughter in East Pakistan in 1971, Tanzania's actions against Idi Amin in neighbouring Uganda in 1978–79, and Vietnam's intervention in Kampuchea in 1978–79.[26] In none of these cases, however, were humanitarian concerns invoked as a justification for the use of force. Rather, self-defence was the primary justification offered in each case, with humanitarian (and other) justifications being at best secondary considerations.[27]

The fact that States continue to rely on traditional justifications—most notably self-defence—undermines arguments that the law has changed. Indeed, it is striking that

[20] Andrew J Carswell, 'Unblocking the UN Security Council: The Uniting for Peace Resolution' (2013) 18 JCSL 453, 455. Increased activity in the UNSC following the end of the Cold War also contributed to the Uniting for Peace resolution falling into long hibernation. For a brief commentary on the resolution, see Rosalyn Higgins et al, *Oppenheim's International Law: United Nations* (OUP 2017) 57–61.

[21] UK House of Commons—Foreign Affairs Committee, 'Fourth Report: Kosovo, Minutes of Evidence, Examination of Witnesses' (Volume II, HC 28-II, 18 January 2000) Question 178 (Professor Adam Roberts) <https://publications.parliament.uk/pa/cm199900/cmselect/cmfaff/28/0011806.htm> accessed 28 February 2019.

[22] See eg Patrick Wintour, 'Syria: Western Nations Seek to Bypass Russian Veto at UN' *The Guardian* (London, 24 April 2018).

[23] *Asylum Case (Colombia/Peru)* (Judgment) [1950] ICJ Rep 266, 276.

[24] *North Sea Continental Shelf (Federal Republic of Germany v Denmark; Federal Republic of Germany v Netherlands)* (Merits) [1969] ICJ Rep 3, 43.

[25] *Case Concerning the Military and Paramilitary Activities in and Against Nicaragua (Nicaragua v United States of America)* (Merits) [1986] ICJ Rep 14, 98.

[26] See eg Fernando R Tesón, *Humanitarian Intervention: An Inquiry into Law and Morality* (2nd edn, Transnational 1997).

[27] Chesterman (n 3) 63–86. See also Gray, *International Law and the Use of Force* (4th edn, OUP 2018) 40ff.

despite the efforts by some scholars to argue for the existence of a right of humanitarian intervention, States themselves are very reluctant to follow suit[28]—even in defence of their own actions. This was particularly true in the case of NATO's intervention in Kosovo. Reluctance appears to have stemmed in part from the dubiousness of the legal argument, but also from the knowledge that if any such right were embraced it might well be used by other States in other situations. These concerns are well founded: when invading and annexing Crimea in 2014, Russian President Vladimir Putin made explicit comparisons with Kosovo in attempting to justify the military action.[29]

The wariness of establishing precedent was evident in the proceedings brought by the Federal Republic of Yugoslavia against ten NATO members before the ICJ, beginning in 1999. In hearings on provisional measures, only Belgium presented an elaborate legal justification for the action, relying variously on UNSC resolutions, a doctrine of humanitarian intervention (as compatible with Article 2(4) of the UN Charter or based on historical precedent), and the argument of necessity.[30] The United States, by contrast, emphasized the importance of UNSC resolutions, and, together with four other delegations (Germany, the Netherlands, Spain, and the United Kingdom) made reference to the existence of a 'humanitarian catastrophe'.[31] Four delegations did not offer any clear legal justification (Canada, France, Italy, and Portugal). The phrase 'humanitarian catastrophe' recalled the doctrine of humanitarian intervention, but some care appears to have been taken to avoid invoking the doctrine by name. The formulation was first used by the United Kingdom as one of a number of justifications for the no-fly zones over Iraq, but no legal pedigree had been established beyond this. The Court ultimately ruled against Yugoslavia for technical reasons concerning its jurisdiction, never discussing the merits of the case.[32]

Reticence about embracing a clear legal position was repeated in two major commissions that investigated the question of humanitarian intervention. The Kosovo Commission, headed by Richard Goldstone, concluded somewhat confusingly (from an international legal perspective) that NATO's Kosovo intervention was 'illegal but legitimate'.[33] The International Commission on Intervention and State Sovereignty

[28] The UK is an arguable exception. See 'UK Materials on International Law' (1986) 57 British Yearbook of International Law 487, 618ff, as subsequently repeated in (1992) 63 British Yearbook of International Law 615, 824–8, and (1999) 70 British Yearbook of International Law 387, 580ff. cf Article 4(h) of the Constitutive Act of the African Union 2158 UNTS 3 and Belgium's argumentation in the Provisional Measures phase of the *Legality of the Use of Force (Serbia and Montenegro v Belgium)* (n 30).

[29] Vladimir Putin, 'Address by President of the Russian Federation' (Duma, Moscow, 18 March 2014) <http://en.kremlin.ru/events/president/news/20603> accessed 28 February 2019.

[30] See *Legality of the Use of Force (Serbia and Montenegro v Belgium)* (Provisional Measures) (Oral Proceedings) Verbatim Records 1999/15 [1999] 7ff.

[31] ibid pleadings of the United States, Verbatim Records 1999/24 [1999] para 1.7; pleadings of Germany, Verbatim Records 1999/18 [1999] para 1.3.1; pleadings of the Netherlands, Verbatim Records 1999/20 [1999] para 40; pleadings of Spain, Verbatim Records 1999/22 [1999] para 1; pleadings of the United Kingdom, Verbatim Records 1999 [1999] paras 17–18.

[32] *Legality of the Use of Force (Serbia and Montenegro v United Kingdom)* (Prelimininary Objections) [2004] ICJ Rep 279.

[33] Independent International Commission on Kosovo, *The Kosovo Report* (OUP 2000) 4.

(ICISS), chaired by Gareth Evans and Mohamed Sahnoun, acknowledged that, as a matter of 'political reality', it would be impossible to find consensus around any set of proposals for military intervention that acknowledged the validity of any intervention not authorized by the UNSC or the UNGA:

> But that may still leave circumstances when the Security Council fails to discharge what this Commission would regard as its responsibility to protect, in a conscience-shocking situation crying out for action. It is a real question in these circumstances where lies the most harm: in the damage to international order if the Security Council is bypassed or in the damage to that order if human beings are slaughtered while the Security Council stands by.[34]

Key elements of the ICISS report, *The Responsibility to Protect*, were adopted by the UN World Summit in a 2005 resolution of the UNGA, which acknowledged that a State's unwillingness or inability to protect its own population from genocide, war crimes, ethnic cleansing, or crimes against humanity may give rise to an international 'responsibility to protect'. This was limited to peaceful means, however, except in extreme circumstances where the provisions of Chapter VII of the UN Charter may be invoked if the UNSC members agree to act:

> *Responsibility to protect populations from genocide, war crimes, ethnic cleansing and crimes against humanity*
>
> 138. Each individual State has the responsibility to protect its populations from genocide, war crimes, ethnic cleansing and crimes against humanity. This responsibility entails the prevention of such crimes, including their incitement, through appropriate and necessary means…
>
> 139. The international community, through the United Nations, also has the responsibility to use appropriate diplomatic, humanitarian and other peaceful means, in accordance with Chapters VI and VIII of the Charter, to help to protect populations from genocide, war crimes, ethnic cleansing and crimes against humanity. In this context, we are prepared to take collective action, in a timely and decisive manner, through the Security Council, in accordance with the Charter, including Chapter VII, on a case-by-case basis and in cooperation with relevant regional organizations as appropriate, should peaceful means be inadequate and national authorities are manifestly failing to protect their populations from genocide, war crimes, ethnic cleansing and crimes against humanity.[35]

The report and the UN Resolution were carefully silent about what happens if the Council does *not* agree. Subsequent proponents of the doctrine were at pains to emphasize that the use of force is only one aspect of R2P.[36] In the World Summit Outcome Document,

[34] ICISS (n 2) 54–5.

[35] UNGA Res 60/1 (24 October 2005) (World Summit Outcome Document) paras 138–9.

[36] For an interesting account of non-coercive precursors to R2P, see Luke Glanville, 'The Responsibility to Protect Beyond Borders in the Law of Nature and Nations' (2018) 28 EJIL 1069.

R2P embraces the responsibility to prevent, to react, and to rebuild. The language routinely now invoked is of pillars: protection by the State (Pillar 1), assistance in prevention by the international community (Pillar 2) and intervention by the UNSC (Pillar 3).[37] Given the role ascribed to the Council by the World Summit Outcome Document, the extent to which that body itself embraced the language of R2P was generally seen as crucial to measuring its impact.[38]

Initial progress was slow. After mentioning R2P in passing in Resolution 1653 (2006) on the Great Lakes Region,[39] the text of the World Summit Outcome Document was explicitly reaffirmed by the UNSC in Resolution 1674 (2006) on the protection of civilians in armed conflict[40]—though this was, once again, a diplomatic agreement on the theory of R2P rather than its application in practice. Subsequent Council endorsement for the next five years was confined to preambular mentions of R2P in resolutions dealing with Darfur in 2006,[41] and then a series of resolutions in 2011 on Côte d'Ivoire,[42] South Sudan,[43] Yemen,[44] and Libya.[45]

It was in Libya that R2P moved from preamble to operational paragraphs, when the Council '*underscore*[d] the Libyan authorities' responsibility for the protection of its population, including foreign nationals and African migrants'.[46] It was also in Libya, arguably, that the invocation of R2P moved from theory to practice. That operation showed the potential of the doctrine to shape debate over an issue—as well as, some said, the limitations of what could be achieved on the ground.

C. Recent Developments and Contemporary Challenges

R2P has inspired dozens of books, hundreds of articles, a handful of research centres, and at least two specialist journals. Yet its content remains imprecise. It is common to see it hailed variously as a new 'fully-fledged international norm',[47] an 'international *ethical* norm',[48] or an 'international *legitimacy* norm',[49] while others dismiss it as a mere

[37] Report of the Secretary-General, 'Implementing the Responsibility to Protect' (12 January 2009) UN Doc A/63/677.

[38] eg Andreas S Kolb, *The UN Security Council Members' Responsibility to Protect: A Legal Analysis* (Springer 2018).

[39] UNSC Res 1653 (2006) para 10 (the Council '*Underscores* that the governments in the region have a primary responsibility to protect their populations').

[40] UNSC Res 1674 (2006). See also UNSC Res 1894 (2009).

[41] UNSC Res 1706 (2006).

[42] UNSC Res 1975 (2011).

[43] UNSC Res 1996 (2011).

[44] UNSC Res 2014 (2011).

[45] UNSC Res 1970 (2011); UNSC Res 1973 (2011).

[46] UNSC Res 2016 (2011).

[47] Jason Ralph/James Souter, 'Is R2P a Fully-Fledged International Norm?' (2015) 3 Politics and Governance 68.

[48] Pınar G Ercan, 'R2P: From Slogan to an International Ethical Norm' (2014) 11 Uluslararası İlişkiler 35.

[49] Michael W Doyle, 'The Politics of Global Humanitarianism: The Responsibility to Protect Before and After Libya' (2016) 53 International Politics 14, 16.

slogan or 'political catchword'.[50] Efforts by the UN to flesh out and operationalize its content have taken place through the appointment of a special adviser to the Secretary-General on R2P and the publication of reports annually on the topic since 2009.[51] Proponents of R2P point to the Libya and Côte d'Ivoire actions in 2011 as examples of the principle shaping the UNSC's response and thereby reflecting a new sensibility in global politics.[52]

In Libya, as mentioned earlier, R2P featured in UNSC resolutions both as preambular and operational text. The willingness of the Council to act was driven in part by the unusually clear manner in which Muammar Gaddafi's government threatened large numbers of civilians and the unanimity of the international opprobrium that it attracted—importantly including the Arab League, the African Union, and the Organization of the Islamic Conference, condemnation by which was cited in each of the key resolutions. Resolution 1973 (2011) in particular authorized Member States to use all necessary means—that is, use force—'to protect civilians and civilian populated areas'.[53]

A similar dynamic was evident in Côte d'Ivoire. Debated in the Council less than two weeks after the Libyan authorization, Resolution 1975 (2011) unanimously reaffirmed that it was Côte d'Ivoire's responsibility to protect civilians, but also recalled its authorization for the UN Operation in Côte d'Ivoire (UNOCI) 'to use all necessary means to carry out its mandate to protect civilians under imminent threat of physical violence, within its capabilities and its areas of deployment'.[54]

Alex Bellamy concludes that these resolutions, adopted with some abstentions but no negative votes, 'clearly demonstrated the Council's determination to act on its responsibility to protect populations, including through the use of force when necessary and possible. They signalled a new phase in the Council's history from which there could be no return.'[55] The Secretary-General was no less effusive in his assessment:

[50] Carsten Stahn, 'Responsibility to Protect: Political Rhetoric or Emerging Legal Norm?' (2007) 101 AJIL 99, 120. See generally Ramesh Thakur/William Maley (eds), *Theorising the Responsibility to Protect* (CUP 2015).

[51] Report of the Secretary-General (n 37); UNGA 'Report of the Secretary-General: Early Warning, Assessment and the Responsibility to Protect' (14 July 2010) UN Doc A/64/864; UNGA/UNSC 'Report of the Secretary-General: The Role of Regional and Sub-Regional Arrangements in Implementing the Responsibility to Protect' (28 June 2011) UN Doc A/65/877–S/2011/393; UNGA/UNSC 'Report of the Secretary-General: Responsibility to Protect: Timely and Decisive Response' (25 July 2012) UN Doc A/66/874–S/2012/578; UNGA/UNSC 'Report of the Secretary-General; Responsibility to Protect-State Responsibility and Prevention' (9 July 2013) UN Doc A/67/929–S/2013/399; UNGA/UNSC 'Report of the Secretary-General: Fulfilling our Collective Responsibility: International Assistance and the Responsibility to Protect' (11 July 2014) UN Doc A/68/947–S/2014/449; UNGA/UNSC 'Report of the Secretary-General; A Vital and Enduring Commitment-Implementing the Responsibility to Protect' (13 July 2015) UN Doc A/69/981–S/2015/500; UNGA/UNSC 'Report of the Secretary-General: Mobilizing Collective Action-The Next Decade of the Responsibility to Protect' (22 July 2016) UN Doc A/70/999–S/2016/620; UNGA/UNSC 'Report of the Secretary-General: Implementing the Responsibility to Protect-Accountability for Prevention' (10 August 2017) UN Doc A/71/1016–S/2017/556.

[52] See text at paras 55–6. [53] UNSC Res 1973 (2011) para 4.

[54] UNSC Res 1975 (2011) para 6 (echoing language in UNSC Res 1528 (2004) para 6(i)).

[55] Alex J Bellamy, 'The Responsibility to Protect: Towards a "Living Reality" ' (London, United Nations Association-UK 2013) 19 <http://www.una.org.uk/sites/default/files/The%20Responsibility%20to%20Protect%20Towards%20a%20Living%20Reality%20-%20Professor%20Alex%20Bellamy.pdf> accessed 28 February 2019.

> In 2011, history took a turn for the better. The responsibility to protect came of age; the principle was tested as never before. The results were uneven, but at the end of the day, tens of thousands of lives were saved. We gave hope to people long oppressed. In Libya, Côte d'Ivoire, South Sudan, Yemen and Syria, by our words and actions, we demonstrated that human protection is a defining purpose of the United Nations in the twenty-first century.[56]

Yet a closer reading offers a more sceptical interpretation. In both the language of the resolutions and the statements of representatives, the emphasis is clearly on the responsibility of the State in question to protect its population. No reference is made, in particular, to the international community's residual responsibility when the State fails to act. Resolution 1970 (2011) stressed that it was 'the Libyan authorities' responsibility to protect its population'; Resolution 1973 (2011) reiterated that responsibility and reaffirmed that 'parties to armed conflicts bear the primary responsibility to take all feasible steps to ensure the protection of civilians'. Similarly, Resolution 1975 (2011) on Côte d'Ivoire—though it reiterated the limited mandate to protect civilians—merely reaffirmed the 'primary responsibility of each State to protect civilians'.

In the language of pillars, the emphasis was clearly on Pillar 1 (protection) and perhaps Pillar 2 (prevention), with Pillar 3 (intervention) looming large but silent in the background. The narrowness of the shared ground was on display when the military action in Libya was perceived by some to have gone far beyond the mere protection of civilians.[57]

Libya, then, appears to illustrate that R2P can provide supporting language when a State or group of States is willing to lead action against a common foe. Normatively, there is nothing new here: the Council authorizations in the case of Libya followed templates worked out in the course of the 1990s. Indeed, Michael Doyle has argued that R2P should both legitimize such actions and delegitimize exploitative or self-serving ones—acting as a '*license for* and a *leash against* forcible intervention'.[58]

A better test is whether R2P encouraged action even when the well of political will was running dry. Here, Syria offers a depressing counterpoint. Despite clearly satisfying any notional threshold for action, the failure to respond meaningfully to the unfolding Syrian crisis can only partly be explained by Russian ties to Assad's regime. China joined

[56] UN Secretary-General Ban Ki-moon, 'Address to the Stanley Foundation Conference on the Responsibility to Protect' (New York, 18 January 2012) <https://www.un.org/sg/en/content/sg/speeches/2012-01-18/address-stanley-foundation-conference-responsibility-protect> accessed 20 May 2020.

[57] Gareth Evans, 'The Evolution of the Responsibility to Protect: From Concept and Principle to Actionable Norm' in Ramesh Thakur/William Maley (eds), *Theorising the Responsibility to Protect* (CUP 2015) 32–4 (describing this period as R2P's 'mid-life crisis'). See also Olivier Corten/Vaios Koutroulis, 'The Illegality of Military Support to Rebels in the Libyan War: Aspects of *Jus Contra Bellum* and *Jus In Bello*' (2013) 18 JCSL 59. On the history of UN commitments to protect civilians, including in more traditional peacekeeping operations, see Mats Berdal, 'United Nations Peacekeeping and the Responsibility to Protect' in Ramesh Thakur/William Maley (eds), *Theorising the Responsibility to Protect* (CUP 2015).

[58] Michael W Doyle, *The Question of Intervention: John Stuart Mill and the Responsibility to Protect* (Yale UP 2015) 110 (emphasis original).

with Russia in vetoing several resolutions, with Libya casting a shadow over these debates insofar as resolutions explicitly renouncing regime change as a goal had been used to achieve exactly that.[59] Perhaps of more interest for present purposes is that the States agitating for action tended not to use the language of R2P—either wary of raising the spectre of Libya or, perhaps, because that language tends to be used in support of foreign policy objectives rather than to create those objectives.[60] If the latter is true, this would be consistent with the more cynical accounts of humanitarian intervention, which posit that the volume of a State's outrage at a humanitarian crisis varies directly with its willingness to act in response to that crisis.

Much as triumphalism at R2P's influence in Libya tended to overstate the case, reports of the death of R2P after Syria were greatly exaggerated.[61] Subsequent years saw continued mixed blessings for R2P. Russia and China vetoed at least four resolutions with R2P language over Syria,[62] while the Council as a whole was manifestly unable to deal with the crises in Central African Republic, Yemen, and elsewhere.

When States chose to act unilaterally against Syria—as the United States did on its own with airstrikes in 2017[63] and again together with France and the UK in 2018[64]—the justifications focused on punishing Syria for the use of chemical weapons and deterring future such use.[65] The UK published an elaborate legal justification for its role, including a statement that the UK was permitted under international law to take measures to alleviate overwhelming humanitarian suffering:

> The legal basis for the use of force is humanitarian intervention, which requires three conditions to be met:

[59] Justin Morris, 'Libya and Syria: R2P and the Spectre of the Swinging Pendulum' (2013) 89 International Affairs 1265.

[60] This was the conclusion, for example, of the German parliamentary research service on the 2018 strikes in Syria, see Wissenschaftliche Dienste, 'Völkerrechtliche Implikationen des amerikanisch-britisch-französischen Militärschlags vom 14. April 2018 gegen Chemiewaffeneinrichtungen in Syrien' (WD 2 - 3000 - 048/18, Deutscher Bundestag 2018) <https://www.bundestag.de/blob/551344/f8055abob-baoced333ebcd8478e74e4e/wd-2-048-18-pdf-data.pdf> accessed 28 February 2019.

[61] Alex J Bellamy, 'Making RtoP a Living Reality: Reflections on the 2012 General Assembly Dialogue on Timely and Decisive Response' (2013) 5 Global Responsibility to Protect 109; Abiodun Williams, 'The Responsibility to Protect and Institutional Change' (2017) 23 Global Governance 537.

[62] Eileen F Babbitt, 'Responsibility to Protect: Time to Reassess' (2017) 9 Journal of Human Rights Practice 431, 433.

[63] Dan Lamothe et al, 'US Strikes Syrian Military Airfield in First Direct Assault on Bashar al-Assad's Government' (*Washington Post*, 7 April 2017) <http://www.derechos.org/peace/syria/doc/syr8367.html> accessed 20 May 2020.

[64] Julian Borger/Peter Beaumont, 'Syria: US, UK and France Launch Air Strikes in Response to Chemical Attack' (*The Guardian*, 14 April 2018) <https://www.theguardian.com/world/2018/apr/14/syria-air-strikes-us-uk-and-france-launch-attack-on-assad-regime> accessed 20 May 2020.

[65] See eg 'Transcript and Video: Trump Speaks About Strikes in Syria' (*The New York Times*, 6 April 2017) <https://www.nytimes.com/2017/04/06/world/middleeast/transcript-video-trump-airstrikes-syria.html> accessed 20 May 2020; Helene Cooper et al, 'Trump Orders Strikes on Syria over Suspected Chemical Weapons Attack' (*The New York Times*, 13 April 2018) <https://web.archive.org/web/20180414012221/https://www.nytimes.com/2018/04/13/world/middleeast/trump-strikes-syria-attack.html> accessed 20 May 2020.

(i) there is convincing evidence, generally accepted by the international community as a whole, of extreme humanitarian distress on a large scale, requiring immediate and urgent relief;

(ii) it must be objectively clear that there is no practicable alternative to the use of force if lives are to be saved; and

(iii) the proposed use of force must be necessary and proportionate to the aim of relief of humanitarian suffering and must be strictly limited in time and in scope to this aim (i.e. the minimum necessary to achieve that end and for no other purpose).[66]

It was striking that virtually no mention was made of R2P. Germany, for its part, initially supported the air strikes as 'necessary and appropriate',[67] though a report commissioned by the Bundestag's Research Service concluded that the air strikes were an 'armed reprisal cast in the veil of humanitarianism' and a violation of international law.[68]

There were also some indications of a more principled opposition to R2P. Although China's former Minister for Foreign Affairs, Qian Qichen, was a commissioner on the body that came up with the concept of R2P, there are signs that it is rethinking its support. In a 2014 speech on the international rule of law, the current Foreign Minister Wang Yi highlighted some of the ongoing difficulties: 'Hegemonism, power politics and all forms of "new interventionism" pose a direct challenge to basic principles of international law including respect for sovereignty and territorial integrity and non-interference in other countries' internal affairs.'[69] Though China's rise sometimes inspires fears that it will seek to establish an alternative model of international order—an 'Eastphalian' system,[70] for example, opposed to the 'Westphalian' one that now dominates—such statements actually appear more consistent with a traditionally conservative approach to sovereignty that dominated for most of the twentieth century.[71]

The preceding account is consistent with the analysis of the foreign policy of China, Japan, and other States that continue to engage with the debates on R2P—with an eye,

[66] Prime Minister's Office, 'Syria Action—UK Government Legal Position' (14 April 2018) <https://www.gov.uk/government/publications/syria-action-uk-government-legal-position/syria-action-uk-government-legal-position> accessed 28 February 2019.

[67] 'Germany Backs Airstrikes in Syria as "Necessary and Appropriate"' (*Deutsche Welle*, 14 April 2018) <https://www.dw.com/en/germany-backs-airstrikes-in-syria-as-necessary-and-appropriate/a-43386145> accessed 20 May 2020.

[68] Dennis Schmidt, 'Germany's Research Report on the Syria Strikes: Unlawful Acts of Reprisal' (*Just Security*, 10 May 2018) <https://www.justsecurity.org/55852/germanys-research-report-syria-strikes-unlawful-acts-reprisal/> accessed 20 May 2020, quoting Wissenschaftliche Dienste (n 60).

[69] 'Full Text of Chinese FM's Signed Article on Int'l Rule of Law' (*Xinhua*, 24 October 2014) <http://en.people.cn/n/2014/1024/c90883-8,799,769.html> accessed 28 February 2019.

[70] Tom Ginsburg, 'Eastphalia and Asian Regionalism' (2010) 44 University of California at Davis Law Review 859, citing the unpublished 2009 doctoral thesis of Sungwon Kim, who appears to have first used the term.

[71] Tom Ginsburg, 'Eastphalia as the Perfection of Westphalia' (2010) 17 Independent Journal of Global Legal Studies 27; Simon Chesterman, 'Asia's Ambivalence About International Law and Institutions: Past, Present and Futures' (2016) 27 EJIL 945. For a more optimistic account, see Onuma Yasuaki, *International Law in a Transcivilizational World* (CUP 2017) 656–60.

however, not to expanding its scope but containing its effects. Bae, Infanzon, and Abbe have termed this partial engagement 'active in not being active'.[72]

It is undeniable, however, that R2P has changed the language of diplomacy. In the period up to 2012, for example, the UNSC made reference to R2P in its resolutions a total of a dozen times. In the years 2016 and 2017, it was passing that many resolutions each year that included the language.[73] Nevertheless, it is also striking that the vast majority of those resolutions still make no reference to Pillar 3—essentially using R2P as a means of pushing responsibility onto States rather than asserting it for the international community.[74] In one sense, this is entirely in keeping with the driving force of R2P from its origins: to emphasize the prevention of future Rwandas, rather than the authorization of future Kosovos. Yet at the same time this has replicated the divisions long seen in arguments about a traditional right of humanitarian intervention, with much academic ink spilt in the face of virtually no practice on the part of States.

In the language of International Relations and drawing on Finnemore and Sikkink's analytical framework of the 'norm life-cycle',[75] R2P has clearly emerged as a norm and arguably become embedded at the international level—but it has yet to become internalized in the practice of States.[76] The adoption of R2P after Kosovo was, arguably, a final nail in the coffin of absolute sovereignty. Though the UN Charter expressly disavows interference in the domestic jurisdiction of States (except where the UNSC authorizes action), no State today seriously argues that widespread human rights violations or humanitarian suffering do not at least belong on the agenda of the international community. What the international community can and should do in response to such crises remains a subject of intense debate. Responsibility to Protect has sharpened that debate, but it does not provide a clear answer; it shapes the discourse, but it does not yet shape behaviour.

[72] Sangmin Bae et al, 'Active in Not Being Active (AINBA): How East Asian Powers Accept R2P' (2018) 26 Asian Journal of Political Science 16. On the Western origin of much of human rights, including R2P, see Stephen Hopgood, 'Human Rights on the Road to Nowhere' in Stephen Hopgood et al (eds), *Human Rights Futures* (CUP 2017).

[73] Data compiled from <www.responsibilitytoprotect.org>.

[74] Aidan Hehir, '"Utopian in the Right Sense": The Responsibility to Protect and the Logical Necessity of Reform' (2017) 31 Ethics and International Affairs 335, 342.

[75] Martha Finnemore/Kathryn Sikking, 'International Norm Dynamics and Political Change' (1998) 52 International Organisation 887.

[76] Graham Melling, 'Beyond Rhetoric? Evaluating the Responsibility to Protect as a Norm of Humanitarian Intervention' (2018) 5 Journal on the Use of Force and International Law 78. There have been various attempts to determine the factors that are more likely to correlate with success if R2P is invoked by the UNSC. Genser, for example, posits three: (i) no government obstruction by the target state, or sufficient political will on the part of the P5 to overcome such obstruction; (ii) cooperation between regional organizations and the UNSC; (iii) adequate capacity for the UNSC to respond rapidly. See Jared Genser, 'The United Nations Security Council's Implementation of the Responsibility to Protect: A Review of Past Interventions and Recommendations for Improvement' (2018) 18 Chicago Journal of International Law 420.

D. Outlook

The rhetorical embrace of R2P by Member States of the UN and its UNSC within the space of two decades of the term being coined is remarkable. Yet there is something utopian about claims that this amounts to a major normative transformation. Such claims are easily contradicted by events—what I once termed the prevalence of 'inhumanitarian non-intervention'[77]—and confuse rhetorical support with changed behaviour.[78]

Although R2P may not create rights or impose legal obligations, it may amount to more than rhetoric if it is understood as a means of determining jurisdiction, as Anne Orford has argued.[79] Seen through that lens, the vague formulations embraced by the 2005 World Summit do not invoke 'responsibility' in the strict legal sense of an obligation to act in a specific way, but rather in the sense of an allocation of responsibility to respond to a situation. This may be compared to the function played by Article 99 of the UN Charter, which allows the UN Secretary-General to bring to the attention of the UNSC 'any matter which in his opinion may threaten the maintenance of international peace and security'. It is no coincidence that much of the energy behind the adoption and, now, implementation of R2P has come from the office of the Secretary-General.[80] Much like Article 99, the true significance of R2P may not be the creation of new rights or obligations to do 'the right thing'; rather, it is in making it harder to do the wrong thing or do nothing at all.[81]

[77] Chesterman (n 3) 219. [78] See eg Hehir (n 74).

[79] Anne Orford, *International Authority and the Responsibility to Protect* (CUP 2011) 22–7.

[80] eg Gareth Evans, *The Responsibility to Protect: Ending Mass Atrocity Crimes Once and for All* (Brookings Institution 2008) 46–51.

[81] cf James Pattison, *Humanitarian Intervention and the Responsibility to Protect: Who Should Intervene?* (OUP 2010) 247–50.

CHAPTER 45

THE USE OF FORCE

ELIZABETH WILMSHURST

A. Introduction

THE collective security system established by the UN Charter came on the heels of the failure of the League of Nations. One of the aims of the League had been to 'achieve international peace and security by the acceptance of obligations not to resort to war',[1] although the Covenant establishing the League included only very limited obligations in that area. Subsequently, in the Kellogg-Briand Pact of 1928, States agreed to renounce war 'as an instrument of national policy in their relations with each other'. That obligation did not, of course, prevent the outbreak of the Second World War.

The vision of the founders of the UN—'determined to save succeeding generations from the scourge of war'—was to make the preservation of international peace a collective responsibility and to locate that responsibility in the UN and, in particular, the UN Security Council (UNSC). Not only were States obliged to refrain from the use of force in their international relations, but they would contribute armed forces to the Council when called upon for the purpose of maintaining international peace and security. There would be no resort to armed force except 'in the common interest', declared the preamble to the Charter.

The obligation to contribute armed forces was not implemented and that aspect of the Charter is a dead letter. But the framework of the legal regulation of the use of force laid down in the Charter remained.

It was soon, however, being argued that the legal rules were to some extent 'already obsolescent by the time the Charter came into operation'.[2] And on many occasions more

[1] Covenant of the League of Nations 108 LNTS 188 preamble.

[2] Thomas Franck, 'Who Killed Article 2(4)' (1970) 64 AJIL 809, written as early as twenty-five years after the adoption of the Charter. He gave the view that the rules 'appeared to address themselves to preventing conventional military aggression at the very moment in history when new forms of attack

recently, including in the debates following the military intervention in Kosovo in 1999, and in Iraq in 2003, doubts were being expressed about the efficacy of the law.[3] But: '[w]e reaffirm that the relevant provisions of the Charter are sufficient to address the full range of threats to international peace and security', declared the Heads of State and Government in the 2005 World Summit Outcome Document.[4]

Those were confident words. Contemporary security threats, however, such as global terrorism and the proliferation of weapons of mass destruction (WMD) continue to give rise to questions about whether the law is indeed 'sufficient'.

This chapter outlines very briefly the international legal framework and discusses some of the difficulties in interpreting or applying aspects of the law in the context of recent challenges to the international legal order. The chapter considers whether this legal framework is still appropriate to deal with current security threats—threats to the security of the State as well as to the security of individuals—and whether the efficacy of the law is still recognized in the practice of States.

B. Legal Framework

Although the collective security system envisaged by the founders of the UN did not develop in quite the way that they had intended, the provisions of the UN Charter on the use of force remain at the heart of the international legal order. Article 2(4) of the Charter lays down a comprehensive prohibition on 'the threat or use of force against the territorial integrity or political independence of any State, or in any other manner inconsistent with the Purposes of the United Nations'.

The prohibition is subject to two exceptions. Force may be used, first, if authorized by the UNSC acting under Chapter VII of the Charter and thus in the common interest, as the preamble states. Secondly, under Article 51 of the Charter, force is lawful in the exercise of the 'inherent right of individual or collective self-defence if an armed attack occurs against a Member of the United Nations, until the Security Council has taken measures necessary to maintain international peace and security'.

There is a further possible exception, which remains controversial: the use of force to avert an overwhelming humanitarian catastrophe (or so-called 'humanitarian

were making obsolete all prior notions of war and peace strategy. And the Charter itself provided enough exceptions and ambiguities to open the rules to deadly erosion.' In response, see Louis Henkin, 'The Reports of the Death of Article 2(4) are Greatly Exaggerated' (1971) 65 AJIL 544.

[3] For debate after Kosovo 1999, see eg Michael Glennon, *Limits of Law, Prerogatives of Power: Interventionism after Kosovo* (Palgrave Macmillan 2001). For an overview of debate after Iraq 2003, see eg Andreas Paulus, 'The War Against Iraq and the Future of International Law: Hegemony or Pluralism?' (2004) 25 Michigan Journal of International Law 691.

[4] UNGA Res 60/1 (24 October 2005) para 79.

intervention'). While not provided for in the Charter, it is claimed that the right is found in the subsequent practice of States and in customary international law.[5]

The rules of international law on the use of force (or the *jus ad bellum*) have been subject to more analysis, critique, and criticism than almost any other branch of international law.[6] Nearly every aspect of the law has raised difficulties of interpretation or application. These cannot be dealt with here in anything like a comprehensive manner.[7] But a few points on the prohibition and the exceptions to it are in order.

1. The Prohibition of the Use of Force

The prohibition in Article 2(4) applies expressly to States 'in their international relations'. There is no reference to force used by a government within its own territory and against its own population; indeed, the Charter is notably reticent as to the extent to which the UN may interfere in a State's internal affairs (Article 2(7)). The protection of human rights, however, including within a State's own borders, is accepted as one of the concerns of the UN, and a government's violence against its own people has now become the subject of international collective concern and action.

The nature of the force prohibited in the Charter is generally recognized to be 'armed force'—not economic or other kinds of coercive measures.[8] Nevertheless, the question whether cyber operations by, or attributable to, a State, and causing damage to another State, come within Article 2(4) is the subject of debate. At least in the West, there is increasingly the view that in certain limited circumstances cyber operations may be regarded as an unlawful use of force and, again under certain conditions, may be regarded as an 'armed attack' sufficient to trigger the right to use force in self-defence.[9]

[5] See further Simon Chesterman, Chapter 44 in this *Handbook*.

[6] As a result, footnotes in publications on the use of force, making reference to other publications, can become very lengthy; this chapter will confine itself to a small number of references, geographically limited, while by no means excluding the value of all unreferenced publications.

[7] For an overview, and discussion of some of the many controversies, see International Law Association, 'Use of Force Committee, Final Report on Aggression and the Use of Force' (Sydney Conference, 2018) <https://ila.vettoreweb.com/Storage/Download.aspx?DbStorageId=11391&StorageFileGuid=6a499340-074d-4d4b-851b-7a56871175d6> accessed 23 August 2020 (ILA Report).

[8] Proposals to include economic pressure were not accepted during the negotiations on the UN Charter (UNCIO VI (1945) 334, 609; UNCIO III (1945) 253). The examples of prohibited use of force given in the Declaration on Principles of International Law concerning Friendly Relations and Co-operation amongst States in accordance with the Charter of the United Nations, UNGA Res 2625 (XXV) (24 October 1970) support the interpretation of armed or physical force (or arming others).

[9] A non-exhaustive list of criteria regarding the scale and effects of a cyber operation amounting to a use of force or armed attack is suggested in Michael Schmitt (ed), *Tallinn Manual 2.0 on the International Law Applicable to Cyber Operations* (CUP 2017). NATO has decided that a cyberattack can trigger Article 5 of the North Atlantic Treaty. NATO Secretary-General Jens Stoltenberg, 'Speech at the Cyber Defence Pledge Conference' (École militaire, Paris, 15 May 2018) <https://www.nato.int/cps/en/natohq/opinions_154462.htm> accessed 5 November 2019.

It should be noted that if a State gives its consent to the use of military force on its territory by another State, that does not constitute an exception to the prohibition on the use of force: force with consent does not come within the prohibition. Questions arise, however, where the government giving consent is the constitutionally elected authority but no longer in power, or is in effective control of some but not all of the territory, or is accused of being engaged in widespread and criminal attacks against its own population.[10]

2. Exceptions to the Prohibition on the Use of Force

a. *Self-Defence*

It is an 'armed attack' that triggers the right of self-defence under Article 51 of the UN Charter. As well as differences of opinion about the threshold of gravity inherent in the term,[11] there is a long-standing controversy about whether the armed attack must actually have occurred, or whether there is a right to use force in 'anticipatory' self-defence before an attack has started. Another question is whether self-defence is lawful in response to attacks on a State by non-State groups situated in another State. These questions are discussed in Section C.1.

Force used in self-defence must meet the requirements of necessity and proportionality. As mentioned in the frequently cited *Caroline* correspondence, the act must not be 'unreasonable or excessive; since the act justified by the necessity of self-defence, must be limited by that necessity, and kept clearly within it'.[12] The force used must be necessary for the purpose of defence, not to punish the attacker. As to proportionality, the State's aims in defending itself should be weighed against the harmful effects of the force taken in self-defence, and the force used should be limited to dealing with the needs of defence.

[10] See, also, Christian Henderson, Chapter 9 in this *Handbook*.

[11] See *Military and Paramilitary Activities in and against Nicaragua (Nicaragua v USA)* (Merits) [1986] ICJ Rep 14 [191], where the Court said that it was necessary 'to distinguish the most grave forms of the use of force (those constituting an armed attack) from other less grave forms'; but as noted in the ILA Report (n 7) 6, practice has shown that the gravity threshold 'is not markedly high, and would include most uses of force likely to cause casualties or significant property damage'. A gravity threshold does, however, seem to have been retained for attacks by non-State actors; see Tom Ruys, *'Armed Attack' and Article 51 of the UN Charter: Evolutions in Customary Law and Practice* (CUP 2010) 147.

[12] Letter from Mr Webster to Lord Ashburton (Department of State, Washington, 27 July 1842) <https://avalon.law.yale.edu/19th_century/br-1842d.asp#web1> accessed 5 November 2019. This correspondence followed the setting fire to, and letting loose over the Niagara Falls, of a US boat by the British Canadian militia in 1837; the boat was being used to supply arms to Canadian rebels against British rule. The subsequent correspondence between the UK and US governments has provided the *locus classicus* for the law on self-defence.

b. *Security Council Authorization*

The other exception to Article 2(4) lies in authorization by the UNSC. Under Chapter VII of the Charter, the Council may take action 'to maintain or restore international peace and security' upon finding a threat to the peace, a breach of the peace, or an act of aggression. What might be thought to be a simple exception to the prohibition on the use of force produces many problems in practice, not least because of the difficulty of drafting clear UNSC resolutions when Council Members are divided in their policies and intentions. The military intervention in Iraq in 2003, by a US-led coalition, was a notorious example of a few States claiming the authority of UNSC resolutions for their actions in the teeth of protests by much of the rest of the world.[13] The 2011 military intervention in Libya also caused controversy, in this case with regard to the extent of the force used in reliance on UNSC Resolution 1973 (2011), which had authorized States to take measures necessary to protect civilians and civilian-populated areas in the context of President Gaddafi's threats against dissidents in his own population. The outcome of the intervention was the toppling of the government and there was criticism that the intervening forces had acted beyond the mandate given by the UNSC.[14] It has to be acknowledged, however, that there may only be a thin line between repulsing government troops from civilian areas, on the one hand, and defeating those troops—leading to the fall of the government—on the other.[15]

As with self-defence, force authorized by the UNSC should be both necessary and proportionate. The Council should authorize force only if non-forcible measures 'would be inadequate or have proved to be inadequate' and if force is 'necessary to maintain or restore international peace and security' (Article 43 UN Charter). The force used by the authorized States must be necessary to comply with the Council mandate and proportionate to it.

C. Recent Developments and Contemporary Challenges

Military action taken to counter global terrorism and the proliferation of WMD has presented challenges to international law. This section discusses a few instances where

[13] The resolution in question was UNSC Res 1441 (2002), read with UNSC Res 678 (1990) and UNSC Res 687 (1991). The intervention was deemed unlawful by the UN Secretary-General and many States; and, according to Anne Marie Slaughter, then President of the American Society of International Law, 'about eighty percent of international lawyers—at least outside the United States—deemed the war on Iraq illegal'—quoted in Paulus (n 3). For one amongst many discussions of the legality of the intervention, see Marc Weller 'The Iraq War—2003' in Olivier Corten et al (eds), *The Use of Force in International Law: A Case-Based Approach* (OUP 2018).

[14] For one example, see the remarks of the Representative of South Africa in UNSC Verbatim Record (28 July 2011) UN Doc S/PV.6595, 4–5.

[15] See Ashley Deeks, 'The NATO Intervention in Libya—2011' in Corten et al (n 13) 749.

States using force to address these threats have been regarded either as distorting or ignoring the law or, alternatively, applying permissible interpretations of the law so as to enable appropriate measures to be taken.

1. International Terrorism and the Operations against the Islamic State

The main occasion for military counter-terrorism operations in the first decade of the twenty-first century was the threat posed by Al-Qaeda and its affiliates. The so-called 'war on terror' raised a number of legal questions, including on the law of self-defence.[16] Many of these questions continue to have relevance for the military operations against the next major terrorist threat, which came from the organization known as ISIL/Da'esh.

The acts of violence by ISIL/Da'esh in Iraq and Syria, as well as more widely, have been countered by military operations undertaken in those two countries by other States. The legal justification for the use of force which the intervening States put forward was, in the case of Russia in Syria, and in the case of Western States in Iraq, that the State concerned had consented to the military operations on its territory.[17]

In the case of Western States in Syria, the justification invoked was, generally, that the operations were necessary in individual or collective self-defence; they were thus the subject of notifications to the UNSC under Article 51 of the UN Charter.[18] These operations were not authorized by the UNSC,[19] nor did the Syrian government

[16] See eg Noam Lubell, *Extraterritorial Use of Force Against Non-State Actors* (OUP 2010).

[17] The Iraqi government sent letters to the UN requesting support from other States in defeating ISIL/Da'esh: UNSC 'Letter from the Permanent Representative of Iraq to the United Nations addressed to the Secretary-General' (25 June 2014) UN Doc S/2014/440 and UNSC 'Letter from the Permanent Representative of Iraq to the United Nations addressed to the President of the Security Council' (20 September 2014) UN Doc S/2014/691; subsequently, on 14 October 2015, Syria sent letters affirming its request to Russia to provide military support for its counter-terrorism efforts: UNGA/UNSC 'Identical letters from the Permanent Representative of the Syrian Arab Republic to the United Nations addressed to the Secretary-General and the President of the Security Council' (14 October 2015) UN Doc A/70/429–S/2015/789.

[18] See the letters to the UNSC from Australia (dated 9 September 2015, UN Doc S/2015/693), Belgium (dated 7 June 2016, UN Doc S/2016/523), Canada (dated 31 March 2015, UN Doc S/2015/221), Denmark (dated 11 January 2016, UN Doc S/2016/34), France (dated 8 September 2015, UN Doc S/2015/745), Germany (dated 10 December 2015, UN Doc S/2015/946), Norway (dated 3 June 2016, UN Doc S/2016/513), Turkey (dated 24 July 2015, UN Doc S/2015/563), the UK (dated 7 September 2015, UN Doc S/2015/688), and the US (dated 23 September 2014, UN Doc S/2014/695).

[19] UNSC Res 2249 (2015) affirmed that ISIL/Da'esh constituted 'a global and unprecedented threat to international peace and security' and called on States to take measures on the territory under the control of ISIL/Da'esh in Syria and Iraq to prevent and suppress its terrorist acts. The wording of the resolution was not the clearest but did not give an authorization to States to use force; the encouragement to act was subject to States' being entitled to do so under international law.

give their consent,[20] and the legality of the operations therefore depends upon whether the intervening States were entitled to rely on the right of self-defence.

The operations raise two major points of controversy with regard to the justification of self-defence. First, may armed groups lawfully be targeted in self-defence within a State which is not supporting those armed groups—namely, does the right to self-defence apply in relation to attacks by a non-State armed group which are not attributable to the host State? Secondly, may force be used in expectation of an attack by such an armed group—in anticipatory self-defence—and, if so, what are the conditions for its lawful use?

a. *Self-Defence against Non-State Actors?*

The international response to the 9/11 attacks in the US indicated support for the view that the right of self-defence encompasses force used against a non-State armed group in another State. Article 51 was in effect interpreted so that the 'armed attack' mentioned in that Article included an attack by a non-State actor.[21] There is indeed nothing in Article 51 of the Charter to restrict the right of self-defence to armed attacks by *States*.

Israel's military operations in Lebanon in 2006 give another example of force used against a non-State group. In the context of ongoing clashes between Hezbollah and the Israel Defense Forces (IDF), Hezbollah attacked an IDF border patrol and villages in northern Israel in July 2006, capturing two soldiers. In response Israel undertook extensive military operations in Lebanon. In its official statements about the armed conflict, Israel first alleged Lebanon's responsibility for Hezbollah's actions, but then changed its position and maintained that its operations were directed against Hezbollah and not against Lebanon.[22] Criticism at the UN and elsewhere directed against Israel's actions focused largely on the lack of proportionality in the exercise of Israel's operations, rather than on the claim to be acting in self-defence against Hezbollah. States' reactions to the 2006 conflict can be taken therefore as supporting the view that force may be used in self-defence against a non-State actor if it is otherwise within the criteria for self-defence.

There are commentators, however (in support of the less than clear passages in two judgments of the International Court of Justice (ICJ)), who hold the view that self-defence is permissible only against States: if the State concerned is not responsible in any

[20] After a period of silence, the Syrian government protested vigorously, stating, for example, that 'any attempt to invoke Article 51 of the Charter to justify military action on Syrian territory without coordination with the Syrian Government manipulates, distorts and misinterprets the provisions of that Article'. (UNGA/UNSC 'Identical letters from the Permanent Representative of the Syrian Arab Republic to the United Nations addressed to the Secretary-General and the President of the Security Council' (29 December 2015) UN Doc A/70/673-S/2015/1048).

[21] The UNSC specifically recognized in UNSC Res 1368 (2001) and UNSC Res 1373 (2001) the right to use force against Al-Qaeda.

[22] See Iain Scobbie, 'Southern Lebanon 2006' in Elizabeth Wilmshurst (ed), *International Law and the Classification of Conflicts* (OUP 2012) reaching the conclusion that Hezbollah's actions could not be attributed to Lebanon. Israel was primarily using its right of self-defence against Hezbollah but was also targeting Lebanese armed forces and imposing aerial and maritime blockades on Lebanon.

way for the acts of the non-State group, force is not lawful on that State's territory.[23] The negative response of Latin American States to Ecuador's incursion into Colombia in 2008 against the Revolutionary Armed Forces of Colombia (FARC) supports this view; those States regarded the incursion as a breach of Colombia's sovereignty.[24] More recently, other governments are pushing back against what they see as unjustified interpretations of the Charter in this regard.[25]

But claims by States to be entitled to defend themselves against groups located in other States are not new.[26] And to argue in such circumstances that it is not lawful to act in self-defence against non-State actors in another State may be thought to privilege the sovereignty of the 'host' State over the needs of the victims of terrorist activities. The issue is still controversial[27] but there is growing recognition that a State has a right of self-defence against non-State groups operating from other States even if those States are not responsible for the actions of the groups.[28]

As with other uses of force in self-defence, the right is available only in response to actual or imminent armed attacks. And the requirements of necessity and proportionality must be complied with. Force may lawfully be used, therefore, only if it is necessary

[23] *Legal Consequences of the Construction of a Wall in the Occupied Palestinian Territory* (Advisory Opinion) [2004] ICJ Rep 136 [139]; *Armed Activities on the Territory of the Congo* (*DRC v Uganda*) (Judgment) [2005] ICJ Rep 168 [147]. And see Olivier Corten, 'Military Operations against "Islamic State"' in Corten et al (n 13) 873 and references given by him at 897, 898.

[24] See Mónica Pinto/Marcos Kotlik, '"Operation Phoenix"—the Colombian Raid Against the FARC in Ecuador—2008' in Corten et al (n 13).

[25] See, for example, the statement by Brazil in the Security Council meeting of 17 May 2018 on upholding international law within the context of the maintenance of international peace and security (UNSC Verbatim Record (17 May 2018) UN Doc S/PV.8262).

[26] Indeed, the Caroline case itself was an act of claimed self-defence against such a group. For early practice, see Christian J Tams, 'Self-Defence against Non-State Actors: Making Sense of the "Armed Attack" Requirement' in Mary O'Connell et al (eds), *Self-Defence against Non-State Actors* (vol I, Max Planck Trialogues on the Laws of Peace and War, CUP 2019) 142–58.

[27] Indeed, Corten goes so far as to say, 'accepting the "unwilling and unable" standard, especially as broadly interpreted by the US in the Syrian crisis, would lead to a radical change in the interpretation of both the rule prohibiting the use of force and the self-defence as its main exception'. Olivier Corten, 'The "Unwilling or Unable" Test: Has it Been, and Could it be, Accepted?' (2016) 29 Leiden Journal of International Law 777, 797.

[28] This is also the conclusion of the ILA Report (n 7). See also Franklin Berman, Daniel Bethlehem, Christopher Greenwood, Vaughan Lowe, Adam Roberts, Philippe Sands, and Malcolm Shaw in Elizabeth Wilmshurst, 'Principles of International Law on the Use of Force by States in Self-Defence' (Chatham House, October 2005) ILP WP 05/01 <https://www.chathamhouse.org/publications/papers/view/108106> accessed 8 November 2019 (Chatham House Principles). In their separate opinions, Judges Kooijmans and Simma in the ICJ case *Armed Activities* (n 23) agreed that the acts of terrorist organizations without attribution to the host State could allow the victim State to take action in self-defence. Referring to an interpretation of Art 51 that would allow only self-defence against States, Judge Simma in his Separate Opinion remarked: 'Such a restrictive reading of Article 51 might well have reflected the state, or rather the prevailing interpretation, of the international law on self-defence for a long time. However, in the light of more recent developments not only in State practice but also with regard to accompanying *opinio juris*, it ought urgently to be reconsidered, also by the Court.' In support, he referred to the acceptance by the international community of that interpretation following the attacks of 9/11: *Armed Activities* (n 23) ICJ Rep 337 [11].

to do so because the host State does not itself halt and prevent the attacks by the non-State actor, whether because it is unable to do so, or unwilling to do so. This is not a new justification for resorting to force; it is part of the necessity requirement in the use of self-defence.

b. *Force Used in Anticipation of an Attack*

There is a long-standing division of opinion between those who maintain that an armed attack must have begun or taken place before defensive action is lawful (since Article 51 states 'if an armed attack occurs') and those who argue that a State may take defensive action if facing an 'imminent' attack.[29] It is difficult to see how and why States should wait for the occurrence of an actual attack before taking measures in self-defence, and this is particularly so in relation to the challenges posed by both terrorism and WMD. This 'anticipatory' self-defence in relation to specific threats has to be distinguished from so-called 'preventive' or 'pre-emptive' defence, where a threat has not yet crystallized but might arise at some time in the future.[30]

For those who accept the justifiability of anticipatory self-defence against an imminent attack, there is a need to take a view on quite what imminence means in this context. That the word does not *only* have a temporal quality is apparent from practice. It has been described as requiring that 'any further delay in countering the intended attack will result in the inability of the defending State effectively to defend itself against the attack. In this sense, necessity will determine imminence: it must be necessary to act before it is too late.'[31] Factors that may be taken into account in applying the criterion have been suggested as including the gravity of the attack, the capability of the attacker, and the nature of the threat.[32]

In the context of military counter-terrorism operations, a wider concept of imminence has been proposed. For example, it has been argued that '[t]he absence of specific evidence of where an attack will take place or of the precise nature of an attack does not preclude a conclusion that an armed attack is imminent', for purposes of self-defence.[33] But, as one writer had said,

[29] Reference is made to the Caroline incident in 1837, where it was agreed that the necessity for action must be 'instant, overwhelming, and leaving no choice of means, and no moment for deliberation'.

[30] See eg The White House, 'National Security Strategy of the United States of America' (September 2002) <https://2009-2017.state.gov/documents/organization/63562.pdf> accessed 7 November 2019. This was widely regarded as unlawful. See also UNGA 'A More Secure World: Our Shared Responsibility: Report of the High-Level Panel on Threat, Challenges and Change' (2 December 2004) UN Doc A/59/565, paras 189–90.

[31] Chatham House Principles (n 28).

[32] ibid. See also Ashley Deeks, 'Taming the Doctrine of Pre-emption' in Marc Weller (ed), *The Oxford Handbook of the Use of Force in International Law* (OUP 2015) 674–5.

[33] For example, the then Attorney General for England and Wales made a speech on 11 January 2017 describing the UK government's understanding of the law of self-defence and how it viewed an 'imminent' attack: 'Attorney General's Speech on the Modern Law of Self-Defence' (International Institute for Strategic Studies, 11 January 2017) <https://www.gov.uk/government/speeches/attorney-generals-speech-at-the-international-institute-for-strategic-studies> accessed 7 November 2019. The Attorney General of Australia delivered a speech in similar terms: Senator the Hon. George Brandis QC, Attorney-General of

> [a]ccommodating the arguments made over the threat of unpredictable terrorism could mean relinquishing the notion of imminence, and allowing for self-defence against vague unknown threats in a manner that renders the concept of self-defence open to unconscionable abuse.[34]

The discussion of imminent attacks is relevant too to the question of the use of force in relation to WMD. Israel defended its attack on the Osiraq nuclear reactor in Iraq in 1981 as necessary at that time in self-defence, but the response of the members of the UNSC was to condemn it on the ground that there was no imminent threat.[35] The question of 'imminence' will also be relevant to cyberattacks, if it is accepted that those can amount to armed attacks within the meaning of Article 51.[36]

The killing of two individuals in a UK drone strike in Syria in 2015—Reyaad Khan and Ruhul Amin, British nationals working for ISIL/Da'esh—is an example of action claimed to be in self-defence against a threat of imminent terrorist attack, which also raises other controversial points of law. The then UK Prime Minister stated that Khan was 'known to be actively engaged in planning and directing imminent armed attacks against the United Kingdom' and that the airstrike was 'a necessary and proportionate exercise of the individual right of self-defence of the United Kingdom'.[37] The government's stated position was that there was no alternative to the drone strike, since 'there is no Government we can work with; we have no military on the ground to detain those preparing plots; and there was nothing to suggest that Reyaad Khan would ever leave Syria or desist from his desire to murder us at home'.[38]

The operation illustrates the approach to the law on self-defence taken by the UK and, in varying respects, by an increasing number of Western States in counter-terrorism activities against ISIL/Da'esh. The legality of this operation depended upon the use of force being necessary, in the absence of any possibility of criminal law enforcement measures; it depended upon the threatened actions of an individual being sufficiently severe that they amounted to an 'armed attack' in terms of Article 51;[39] it required acceptance of the doctrine that self-defence is permissible against an individual in

Australia, 'The Right to Self-Defence against Imminent Armed Attack in International Law' (T C Beirne School of Law, 11 April 2017) <https://www.ejiltalk.org/the-right-of-self-defence-against-imminent-armed-attack-in-international-law/> accessed 7 November 2019. These speeches followed on from one by the US Legal Adviser in April 2016 on a similar theme: Brian Egan, 'International Law, Legal Diplomacy, and the Counter-ISIL Campaign' (ASIL, 8 April 2016) <https://www.lawfareblog.com/state-department-legal-adviser-brian-egans-speech-asil> accessed 7 November 2019.

[34] Noam Lubell, 'The Problem of Imminence in an Uncertain World' in Weller (n 32) 719.

[35] See, for example, the statement by the Permanent Representative of the UK that '[t]here was no instant or overwhelming necessity for self-defence' in UNSC Verbatim Record (15 June 1981) UN Doc S/PV/2282, para 106.

[36] See short discussion in Deeks (n 32) 673.

[37] A reference to collective self-defence in respect of Iraq was added to the UK's letter to the UNSC (S/2015/688 (n 18)).

[38] HC Deb 7 September 2015, vol 599, cols 25–6.

[39] The UK Prime Minister stated (ibid) that the 'strike was not part of coalition military action against ISIL in Syria' but was against specific threats to the UK.

another State in the absence of an armed conflict with that State, and in spite of the fact that that State, Syria, was not complicit in the threatened attacks on the UK and indeed was actively resisting ISIL/Da'esh; and, finally, the legality of the operation required the threatened attacks to be 'imminent'. In relation to all of these points, international law is not without controversy, as we have seen. And decisions on all these points have to be taken on the basis of information which, of its nature, cannot generally be disclosed to the public.

A more recent illustration of what was termed a counter-terrorism operation was the Turkish offensive into Syria, 'Operation Peace Spring', in October 2019. It had as its stated aim 'to counter the imminent terrorist threat, to ensure Turkey's border security, to neutralize terrorists starting from along the border regions adjacent to Turkish territory and to liberate Syrians from the tyranny of PKK's Syrian branch, PKK/PYD/YPG, as well as Deash' and was said to be ' in line with' the right of self-defence.[40] The same international legal questions arise as are discussed above. But while Syria complained of an act of aggression, most other international criticism was focused largely on the serious humanitarian consequences, the increase in the threat from ISIL/Da'esh, and the reports of attacks on civilians; that is, there was scarcely any allegation that the offensive was contrary to the law on the use of force. At the very least, there must be doubt as to whether it was either necessary or proportionate.[41]

2. Weapons of Mass Destruction and the Air Strikes in Syria of 2017 and 2018

The air strikes discussed here are some of the many instances of the use of force in Syria that raise questions about the efficacy of the *jus ad bellum*. They provoke discussion as to whether the use of force apparently in the common interest (in order to deter the use of chemical weapons) is becoming legally acceptable in practice, even though undertaken without UNSC authorization.

The air strikes in 2017 and 2018 have to be understood in the context of the earlier use of chemical weapons, including those in Ghouta, near Damascus, in 2013. The use of nerve agents on that occasion was confirmed by the UN mission established by the UN Secretary-General and the Organization for the Prohibition of Chemical Weapons (OPCW). Though Syria and Russia denied Syrian government responsibility, many Western States and the Arab League maintained the contrary. The US, the UK, and France all declared that they would take military action in response.

In the event, the UK Parliament refused to approve a government motion supporting military action, and it became clear that Congress would not support US action. Syria

[40] UNSC 'Letter from the Permanent Representative of Turkey to the United Nations addressed to the President of the Security Council' (9 October 2014) UN Doc S/2019/804.

[41] See UNSC Verbatim Record (24 October 2019) UN Doc S/PV/8645.

became a party to the Chemical Weapons Convention[42] and the UNSC unanimously adopted a resolution which determined that the use of chemical weapons anywhere constituted a threat to international peace and security and called for the implementation of the decision of the OPCW which contains procedures for the expeditious and verifiable destruction of Syria's chemical weapons.[43]

But there were subsequent uses of chemical weapons in Syria. On 28 February 2017, a draft resolution sponsored by forty-three States was accordingly introduced in the UNSC.[44] The resolution sought to impose economic sanctions on entities and individuals responsible for the use of chemical weapons in Syria, but it was not adopted since Russia and China used their veto.

On 4 April 2017 there was a further chemical attack at the town of Khan Shaykhun; in response, the US launched an air strike against a base of the Syrian armed forces that the US said had been used for the attack. No clear legal justification was put forward by the US.[45]

In April 2018, in response to the apparent use of chemical weapons in Douma, near Damascus, the US introduced another draft resolution in the UNSC, setting up an 'Independent Mechanism of Investigation' in Syria. It was vetoed by Russia. On 14 April 2018, the US, France, and the UK launched air strikes on three sites in Syria. Neither the US nor France put forward any clear legal justification for their actions.[46] Only the UK gave an explicit explanation of the legal justification upon which it relied: the exercise of humanitarian intervention.

The responses of other States to the threats of the three States in 2013 and to the air-strikes in 2017, by the US, and in 2018, by the US, the UK, and France, were mixed. The views expressed in the UNSC meeting following the 2018 air strikes were typical of the debate elsewhere and on other occasions: some speakers condemned the strikes as contrary to international law; others said that the strikes were understandable, without commenting on the law; others drew attention to the need to respect the Council's

[42] Convention on the Prohibition of the Development, Production, Stockpiling and Use of Chemical Weapons and on their Destruction 1974 UNTS 45.

[43] UNSC Res 2118 (2013).

[44] See UNSC Verbatim Record (28 February 2017) UN Doc S/PV.7893.

[45] In the meeting of the UNSC of 7 April 2017 the US representative said: 'when the international community consistently fails in its duty to act collectively, there are times when States are compelled to take their own action. The indiscriminate use of chemical weapons against innocent civilians is one of those times... It is in our vital national security interests to prevent the spread and use of chemical weapons... Bashar Al-Assad must never use chemical weapons again, ever.' (UNSC Verbatim Record (7 April 2017) UN Doc S/PV.7919, 17).

[46] The US representative in the UNSC meeting of 14 April 2018 stated that the three governments had acted 'to deter the future use of chemical weapons by holding the Syrian regime responsible for its crimes against humanity'. The French representative stated that the action was 'necessary in order to address the repeated violations by the Syrian regime of its obligations—obligations stemming from the law, treaties and its own commitments'. The UK stated that it was acting to 'alleviate overwhelming humanitarian suffering', that is, humanitarian intervention (UNSC Verbatim Record (14 April 2018) UN Doc S/PV.8233, 5). For further discussion on the lack of legal explanation by the US, see 'United States Bombs Syrian Government Facilities in Response to Chemical Weapons Use' (2018) 112 AJIL 522.

primary responsibility for the maintenance of peace and security.[47] The draft resolution proposed by Russia, which condemned 'the aggression against the Syrian Arab Republic by the US and its allies in violation of international law and the UN Charter' received only three votes in favour and thus was not adopted.[48]

This was a case where many governments supported, or refused to condemn, the air strikes, although most of these did not refer to any claimed legal basis for the strikes. Those opposing the strikes referred to them as unlawful. Indeed, leaving aside the claim of the UK to be acting in humanitarian intervention, it is difficult to find a legal justification for the strikes in the *jus ad bellum*. There was no authorization by the UNSC, no justification for a claim of self-defence, and Syria had not consented to the strikes. Nor does the need for the enforcement of international obligations, whether contained in UNSC resolutions or within international treaties, give individual States the legal right to use force.

This is not the place to discuss humanitarian intervention.[49] With the exception of the UK and perhaps two or three other States, international practice thus far has not supported what might once have been the development of the concept as part of the *jus ad bellum*. Human rights law, international humanitarian law and international criminal law seem to be the preferred means of protecting a State's population from their own government.[50] But even if there were a recognized humanitarian exception to the prohibition on the use of force, the UK's reliance on the concept in April 2018 raises new questions. In deciding that there was justification to intervene to meet an overwhelming

[47] 'An act of aggression against a sovereign State on the front lines in the fight against terrorism was committed without permission from the Security Council and in violation of the Charter of the United Nations and the norms and principles of international law.' See Statement by President Putin quoted by the Russian representative in UNSC Verbatim Record (14 April 2018) UN Doc S/PV.8233, 3. At that meeting representatives of Bolivia, Equatorial Guinea, Syria, and Kazakhstan spoke condemning the strikes as a violation of international law; China voted in favour of the draft resolution condemning the strikes as contrary to international law (which was not adopted); Poland and the Netherlands said that the actions of the three governments was understandable; the UN Secretary-General and others at the UNSC meeting referred to the primary responsibility for international peace and security resting with the UNSC. Elsewhere, NATO members did not refer to the law but 'expressed their full support for this action intended to degrade the Syrian regime's chemical weapons capability and deter further chemical weapon attacks against the people of Syria'; see North Atlantic Council, 'Statement on Actions Taken against the Use of Chemical Weapons in Syria' (14 April 2018) <https://www.nato.int/cps/en/natohq/news_153670.htm> accessed 8 November 2019. (The Netherlands gave an explanation of its vote, stating that it had voted in favour, on the grounds of NATO solidarity, although its position had been to express 'understanding' of the action rather than full support.) The EU supported the action: 'the Council understands that the targeted US, French and UK airstrikes on chemical weapons facilities in Syria were specific measures having been taken with the sole objective to prevent further use of chemical weapons and chemical substances as weapons by the Syrian regime to kill its own people. The Council is supportive of all efforts aimed at the prevention of the use of chemical weapons.' Council of the European Union (General Secretariat), 'Council Conclusions on Syria' (16 April 2018) Doc 7956/18, 2.

[48] UNSC 'Russian Federation draft resolution' (14 April 2018) UN Doc S/2018/355.

[49] But see Chesterman (n 5).

[50] Claus Kress, 'Major Post-Westphalian Shifts and Some Important Neo-Westphalian Hesitations in the State Practice on the International Law on the Use Of Force' (2015) 1 Journal on the Use of Force and International Law 11.

humanitarian need, the UK government took into account, amongst other things, the deaths of hundreds of thousands of civilians in the conflict in Syria as a whole. That is, the use of force by the UK was not claimed to be justified for the sole purpose of protecting the population from chemical weapons. This approach opens the door to claims that humanitarian intervention is lawful whenever there is humanitarian need because of unlawful deaths in an international or non-international armed conflict.

This is not, of course, the first occasion on which force has been used in response to possession or use of WMD. While the States intervening in Iraq in 2003 sought to justify their action by reference to supposed authorization in UNSC resolutions, their action was publicly explained by the need to ensure compliance by Iraq with its obligations to destroy and report the destruction of all its WMD. The mistaken conviction that Iraq did indeed still possess WMD was the expressed reason for the military operation.

A further instance was the 2007 airstrike by Israel against a nuclear facility in Syria, which at the time went unremarked.[51] Israel did not even attempt to put forward a legal basis for its action. Self-defence could scarcely have been available in the absence of any imminent threat.

The air strikes in Syria in 2017 and 2018—and the threats to use force in 2013—are of doubtful legality. The strike by Israel against the nuclear facility in 2007 was unlawful. At the very least, the absence of condemnation by governments which might be expected to respect international law creates the risk that a State wishing to use force to prevent the proliferation of nuclear weapons will believe itself unlikely to meet a negative international response.[52]

D. Outlook

It should perhaps go without saying that this chapter is written on the assumption that international law does indeed have an influence on governments, generally, and that most liberal democracies, most of the time, accept that it is in their national interest to act in accordance with international law.[53] A wider study of the practice of States than is here possible indicates that in most instances governments do make an effort to explain

[51] Much later, in July 2009, the Non-Aligned Movement issued a statement condemning the 2007 attack as a flagrant violation of the Charter, XV Summit of Heads of State and Government of the Non-Aligned Movement, 'Final Document' (Sharm El-Sheik, 16 July 2009) NAM2009/FD/Doc.1, para 125. The initial lack of response was in marked contrast to UNSC Res 487 (1981), adopted following Israel's attack on the Osiraq reactor in 1981, which condemned the attack as a 'clear violation of the Charter'.

[52] See, in relation to the 2007 airstrike by Israel, Christine Gray, 'The Use of Force to prevent the proliferation of Nuclear Weapons' (2009) 52 Japanese Yearbook of International Law 101, 126.

[53] The 'realist' approach to international law—that 'legal restraint is illusory' so far as military interventions by individual States are concerned—is here left to one side. See Glennon (n 3) 2. For a brief response to the realist critique, see James Crawford/Rowan Nicholson 'The Continued Relevance of Established Rules and Institutions relating to the Use of Force' in Weller (n 32).

their actions by reference to international law.[54] They frequently refer to the law in approving or condemning other governments' actions. Commentators certainly do so. Even where States' acts are of questionable legality, to put it no lower, the fact that they attempt to justify their actions by reference to the law can be seen as affirming the law's validity. As stated by the ICJ, if a State acts contrary to a rule but defends its conduct by reference to that rule, the significance of that attempted justification 'is to confirm rather than to weaken the rule'.[55] And for those who have worked inside government (or at least inside governments of liberal democracies), it is obvious that such attempts at justification are not, usually, cynical but made in the recognition that compliance with international law is in a State's interests.

Nevertheless, in some of the instances of military operations mentioned in the preceding section, the law was simply not referred to by the States concerned, and in one instance the UK put forward an extended view of humanitarian intervention shared by very few other countries. The obvious question is whether cases such as these indicate that international law is being regarded as ineffective to deal with current threats to States or populations and is therefore being distorted or ignored.

The air strikes in Syria in 2017 and 2018 show the US and France apparently unconcerned with international law, and other States approving the military actions without regard for their legal basis, in the interests of deterring the possession or use of chemical weapons. Commentators, too, have expressed the view that the *jus ad bellum* is outdated, archaic even, and fails to meet States' security interests. In the context of the threat posed by WMD, for example, it is said that the law is 'simply lagging behind the dynamics of technological and geopolitical change'.[56]

Some of the practice discussed in this chapter, on the other hand, indicates that States, in the interests of taking appropriate measures to counter security threats, have taken the law seriously while adopting pragmatic interpretations of the Charter. The growing acceptance of the permissibility of the use of force against non-State armed groups operating from other States is a good example. Reliance on self-defence as encompassing the use of force against threatened, as well as ongoing, attacks is another.

The law as thus practised is resilient. Interpretations of Charter rules can evolve; the Charter is a living instrument. While some commentators assert that it is not possible to develop interpretations of international law in this area by State practice,[57] the States concerned are indeed relying on the law as thus evolved. So are practitioners.[58] But

[54] Corten et al (n 13) examine 65 instances of the use of force and summarize the different claims of legal justification made by the States concerned.

[55] *Nicaragua* (n 11) [186].

[56] Daniel Joyner 'The Implications of the Proliferation of Weapons of Mass Destruction for the Prohibition of the Use of Force' in Weller (n 32) 1045. See, also, discussion in Matthew Waxman, 'The Use of Force Against States That *Might* Have Weapons of Mass Destruction' (2009) 31 Michigan Journal of International Law 1.

[57] For the different approaches to the interpretation of the rules on the use of force, see Olivier Corten, 'The Controversies Over the Customary Prohibition on the Use of Force: A Methodological Debate' (2006) 16 EJIL 803.

[58] See, for example, the practitioners' conclusions in Chatham House Principles (n 28).

caution is needed. Flexible approaches to the law will be used by unfriendly States, not only by allies. And those proposing, and acting upon, developing interpretations of the Charter must be prepared to take into account the judgment of others.

That sometime leaders of powerful States seem to be remarkably unconcerned about either domestic or international law need not be regarded as striking at the heart of the long-enduring law on the use of force. Whether, however, tendencies against multilateralism more generally will damage the core of international law remains to be seen.

The existence of a rules-based international order cannot be taken for granted. It is only comparatively recently that the world has had a universally agreed set of obligations to prohibit the use of force—one of the most significant powers held by a government. The legal framework is vulnerable to attack from a number of directions: from those who do not recognize the influence of international law; from those who would read the law so narrowly as to make it impossible to counter current security threats; and from those who distort the law to allow the use of force in circumstances decided unilaterally by themselves to be in the common interest. Collective action authorized by the UNSC should be the goal. A world from which any notion of collective security has disappeared will be one of global instability.

While interpretations of the law evolve, both to cover existing threats such as those from international terrorism and the proliferation of WMD, and to respond to those of the future, such as in cyberspace, the legal framework laid down by the Charter remains. It may be trite, but meaningful, to recall that the mere fact that international law does not permit the use of force in a particular instance should not of itself lead to the conclusion that the law is inadequate. And respect for a strong body of international law may be the best way to achieve global cooperation in countering security threats.

PART IV

POWER POLITICS, INTERNATIONAL LAW, AND GLOBAL SECURITY

CHAPTER 46

CHINA

CONGYAN CAI

A. Introduction

FOR most of the first four decades since its founding in 1949, the People's Republic of China (PRC) on a geopolitical level had arguably not been that relevant, neither did it pose a substantial threat, or make any significant contribution to global security. Nonetheless, global security has always been a high priority concern for China, which was highly alert to military threats from, or potential invasions by, the US and the Soviet Union during the Cold War. Since the 1980s, the landscape of global security has transformed and accordingly China has redefined its concept of security, first contending that the risk of global confrontation and, in particular, military threats to China had significantly reduced in the 1980s[1] and, secondly, by proposing the New Security Concept in the 1990s.[2] Furthermore, China was welcomed internationally for its increasing contribution to international security by, for instance, participating in the UN peacekeeping operations.

In the second decade of the twenty-first century, however, a number of events have occurred which have adversely affected global security. In February 2019, the US decided to suspend its obligations under the 1987 Intermediate-Range Nuclear Forces

[1] Literature Office of the Central Committee of the CCP (ed), *Selected Works of Deng Xiaoping* (vol 3, People's Publishing House 1993) 105 [in Chinese]; Information Office of the State Council of the People's Republic of China, 'China: Arms Control and Disarmament' (November 1995) part I <http://www.scio.gov.cn/zfbps/ndhf/1995/Document/307994/307994.htm>; in English <https://fas.org/nuke/guide/china/doctrine/wparms.htm> accessed 20 December 2019.

[2] Russian–Chinese Joint Declaration on a Multipolar World and the Establishment of a New International Order (1997) 36 International Legal Materials 986.

(INF) Treaty with Russia.[3] This had been a cornerstone treaty which not only controlled the arms race between the two parties but also significantly reduced threats to other countries, including China. Shortly after, Russia followed the US by announcing its decision to also suspend the INF Treaty.[4] The suspension, and potential termination, of the INF Treaty will allow the US and Russia to develop and deploy intermediate-range missiles, inducing a new arms race between the US, Russia, and other major powers, with resulting negative effects on both China's security environment and global security more generally.[5] It should be noted, however, that, in addition to alleged breaches of the Treaty by both parties, the failure of the INF Treaty to include China, and several other countries with the capability to develop intermediate-range missiles, was a major reason for its suspension.[6] Indeed, both the US and Russia have an interest in extending the INF Treaty to bind China and other intermediate-range missile countries.[7] More importantly, in its 2017 National Security Strategy, the US for the first time identified China as a 'revisionist power', who, by wielding its growing political, economic, and military power, aims to 'challenge American power, influence, and interests, attempting to erode American security and prosperity' and 'shape a world antithetical to U.S. values and interests'.[8] According to the 2018 US National Defense Strategy, the 'long-term, strategic competition' from China is the central challenge that the US faces.[9] For its part, China's perception of global security is somewhat the reverse. In a 2016 joint statement with Russia, China expressed its concern that there were increasing factors adversely affecting global strategic stability around the world.[10] Not explicitly naming the US, China and Russia clearly view the current negative trend as, to a large extent, being created by the US and its allies, who seek to maintain an overwhelming advantage in terms of military technology, especially anti-missile systems.[11]

[3] The White House, 'President Donald J Trump to Withdraw the United States from the Intermediate-Range Nuclear Forces (INF) Treaty' (1 February 2019) <https://www.whitehouse.gov/briefings-statements/president-donald-j-trump-withdraw-united-states-intermediate-range-nuclear-forces-inf-treaty/> accessed 30 November 2020.

[4] Mary Ilyushina et al, 'Russia Follows US in Suspending INF Nuclear Missile Treaty' (*CNN*, 2 February 2019) <https://edition.cnn.com/2019/02/02/europe/russia-inf-treaty-intl/index.html> accessed 20 December 2019.

[5] Kedi Han, 'US–Russia INF Disputes and China's Security Situation' (2018) 6 Strategic Decision Studies 46, 60–4 [in Chinese].

[6] John R Bolton/Paula A DeSutter, 'A Cold War Missile Treaty That's Doing Us Harm' (*WSJ*, 15 August 2011) <https://www.wsj.com/articles/SB10001424053111903918104576500273389091098> accessed 20 December 2019; The White House (n 3).

[7] Han (n 5) 60. In detail Jiming Jiang, 'The Globalization of the INF Treaty: Motivation, Approaches and Prospect' (2015) 4 International Forum 30.

[8] The White House, 'National Security Strategy of the United States of America' (December 2017) 25, 2 <https://www.whitehouse.gov/wp-content/uploads/2017/12/NSS-Final-12-18-2017-0905.pdf> accessed 20 December 2019 (US NSS 2017).

[9] US DoD, 'Summary of the 2018 National Defense Strategy of the United States of America: Sharpening America Military's Competitive Edge' (2018) 2, 4 <https://dod.defense.gov/Portals/1/Documents/pubs/2018-National-Defense-Strategy-Summary.pdf> accessed 20 December 2019.

[10] 'A Joint Statement by the President of the People of Republic of China and the President of Russian Federation on Strengthening Global Strategic Stability' (25 June 2016) [in Chinese] <http://www.xinhuanet.com/politics/2016-06/26/c_1119111895.htm> accessed 20 December 2019.

[11] ibid.

In short, the question of how to deal with global security concerns stemming from the rise of China is part of a far-reaching process on how a rising China treats, and is treated in, the international legal order.[12] As such, this chapter will address the following issues. First, what is the international security landscape in relation to a rising China? (Section B). Secondly, how has China transformed its traditional conception of sovereignty in order to engage with international security? (Section C). Thirdly, should any new legal regulations be considered to address security threats in relation to a rising China? (Section D). And finally, should legal means exclusively be relied on to address international security? (Section E).

B. The Changing Landscape of Global Security in Relation to a Rising China

At the beginning of the Cold War in 1948, the Chinese Communist Party (CCP), the ruling party of the PRC that had long received direction and support from the Soviet Union, took the decision to ally itself with the Soviet Union. This decision had 'a profound impact on China's foreign relations and on the entire world situation'.[13] In 1950, US concerns regarding potential communist expansion in East Asia, and Chinese fears of US invasion, led to both sides intervening in the Korean War.[14] The intervention of the US and of more than a dozen UN Member States in the Korean War was approved by the UN Security Council (UNSC).[15] China effectively found itself in a war not only with the US but also with the UN. As a result, both the US and the UN were perceived as serious threats to Chinese national security.

At the time, the Soviet Union aided China in dealing with security threats by giving substantial support, including economic assistance and transfer of nuclear technology.[16] However, such cordial relations between China and the Soviet Union did not last long. As a result of ideological differences and border disputes, the two States began to drift apart in the mid-1950s before the eventual outbreak of military conflicts at the border in the late 1960s, followed by nuclear deterrence.[17] This led to a deterioration of China's security situation. In response, China sought less hostile relations with both the US and the UN in the late 1960s. In 1972, the Shanghai Joint Communiqué between China and

[12] Congyan Cai, *The Rise of China and International Law: Taking Chinese Exceptionalism Seriously* (OUP 2019).

[13] John W Garver, *China's Quest: The History of the Foreign Relations of the People's of Republic of China* (OUP 2016) 29.

[14] Hao Yufan/Zhai Zhihai, 'China's Decision to Enter the Korean War: History Revisited' (1990) 121 The China Quarterly 94.

[15] UNSC Res 82 (1950).

[16] Zhihua Sheng, *Allies in the Cold War: Inter-State Relations in the Socialist Camp* (Jiuzhou Press 2013) 1–33, 152–88 [in Chinese].

[17] Garver (n 13) 113–45, 274–85.

the US was issued and the PRC eventually took over the Republic of China's (ROC) seat at the UN.[18]

Since the mid-1980s, as East–West tensions significantly reduced while globalization began to speed up, China updated its perception of international security. China thought it possible to postpone, if not completely avoid, a new World War and at the same time development had emerged as a new major issue on the international agenda. Consequently, it formulated a new national strategy, which prioritized economic development, persisting to this day.[19] As a result, China substantially reduced its military budget, and the number of military personnel in its armed forces decreased by over one million.[20]

Since the 1990s, a number of new trends in international relations have emerged. The process of globalization took place at breakneck speed (as can be seen at the global level in the World Trade Organization (WTO) and at the regional level in Asia-Pacific Economic Cooperation (APEC)). Many national and inter-State disputes (eg, ethnic conflicts and border disputes) have also erupted. As a result, the configuration of international security was substantially altered. In light of these trends, China proposed the New Security Concept seeking to establish military trust with several former Soviet Republics which ultimately led to the birth of the Shanghai Cooperation Organization (SCO) and the trust mechanism in Southeast Asia,[21] amongst others.

The New Security Concept formed part of the 1997 Joint Declaration with Russia on a Multipolar World and the Establishment of a New International Order.[22] The two States argued that:

> The cold war is over. The bipolar system has vanished. A positive trend towards a multipolar world is gaining momentum, and relations between major States, including former cold-war adversaries, are changing... The establishment of a peaceful, stable, just and rational new international political and economic order is becoming a pressing need of the times and an imperative of historical development.[23]

Thus, they advocated establishing 'a new and universally applicable concept of security'.[24] Additionally, perhaps in light of the fact that the US had become the sole superpower, with neither China nor Russia powerful enough to engage it, these two States favoured the UN playing a larger role in maintaining international security.[25]

China identified four core elements of the New Security Concept: mutual trust, mutual benefit, equality, and coordination. 'Mutual trust' requires that States 'discard the mentality of [the] cold war and power politics and refrain from mutual suspicion and hostility'. 'Mutual benefit' requires States to 'respect each other's security interests

[18] ibid 286–314; Samuel S Kim, *China, the United Nations, and World Order* (Princeton UP 1979) 102–4.
[19] 'China: Arms Control and Disarmament' (n 1) part I.
[20] ibid parts I and III.
[21] Dexing Song, 'Re-defining China: The ASEAN Relationship in the New Century and Its Characteristics' (1999) 4 Forum of World Economy and Politics 18 [in Chinese].
[22] 1997 Russian–Chinese Declaration (n 2).
[23] ibid para 1. [24] ibid para 3. [25] ibid para 4.

and create conditions for others' security while ensuring their own security interests with a view to achieving common security'. 'Equality' means that all States, big or small, should be treated equally and, in particular, any intervention in other countries' internal affairs should not be permitted. 'Coordination' requires that any disputes and security concerns should be addressed through negotiation and cooperation.[26]

Generally, in the 1990s China paid more attention to new means of handling security than to a new content of security. The events of 9/11 prompted China to become more sensitive to new modalities of security. In China's Position Paper on the New Security Concept submitted to the Foreign Ministers Conference of the 2002 ASEAN Regional Forum, China pointed out that

> the meaning of the security concept has evolved to be multifold with its contents extending from military and political to economic, science and technology, environment, culture and many other areas and thus States share greater common security interests and are more interdependent on one another for security.[27]

While reaffirming the diversification of the means to seek security, especially the significance of dialogue and cooperation,[28] China stressed economic cooperation as an important feature of lasting security.[29]

Given that China had rapidly expanded its economic power since the Reforming and Opening-up Policy started in the late 1970s, it was argued in the mid-1980s that China had the potential to become a great power if it could continue its economic momentum.[30] Since the mid-1990s, the existing powerful States, such as Russia,[31] France,[32] and the US,[33] have begun to recognize China as a global, or at least a regional, great power. China also reconceptualized its own identity as a State in the late 1990s. For instance, in 1999 the Research Division of China's Ministry of Foreign Affairs (MFA) used the term 'responsible power' to describe China for the first time. It wrote that 'China steadily stands out its image as a peaceful, cooperative and responsible power'.[34] In December 2003, then Premier Wen Jiabo, in a speech delivered at Harvard University, declared that China was 'a rising power dedicated to peace' and that it would follow a 'road to peaceful

[26] 'China's Position Paper on the New Security Concept' (31 July 2002) part III <https://www.fmprc.gov.cn/ce/ceun/eng/xw/t27742.htm> accessed 20 December 2019.

[27] ibid part II. [28] ibid. [29] ibid part IV.

[30] Paul Kennedy, *The Rise and Fall of the Great Powers* (Random House 1987) 447–57.

[31] China/Russia, 'Joint Statement' (September 1994) <http://www.huaxia.com/zt/2002-38/510413.html> accessed 29 December 2019 [in Chinese].

[32] China/France, 'Joint Statement' (May 1997) <http://news.xinhuanet.com/ziliao/2002-09/12/content_559463.htm> 29 January 2019 [in Chinese].

[33] China/US, 'Joint Statement' (October 1997) <http://news.xinhuanet.com/ziliao/2002-01/28/content_257084.htm> 29 January 2019 [in Chinese].

[34] Research Division of China's Ministry of Foreign Affairs (ed), *China's Diplomacy* (World Affairs Press 1999) 4 [in Chinese].

rise and development'.[35] This was the first time that China's leaders openly accepted the proposition of a 'peaceful rise' and used the phrase 'rising power'.

The change of China's identity as a State has had a number of implications in terms of security. First, China has been called on to shoulder more international responsibility since the beginning of the twenty-first century. In 2005, then US Deputy Secretary of State Robert B Zoellick, urged China to 'become a responsible stakeholder in that system' and stated that 'China has a responsibility to strengthen the international system that has enabled its success'.[36] Further, China has come under huge pressure to act in certain circumstances, such as to wield its significant influence on the Sudanese government to resolve the Darfur crisis at the beginning of the twenty-first century.[37] Secondly, as China expands its interests globally, international security is increasingly relevant to Chinese individuals and entities alike. It is widely recognized that the Belt and Road Initiative (BRI) is a grand strategy aimed at expanding Chinese economic and perhaps political influence.[38] However, the BRI involves some fragile countries that are plagued by recurring civil unrest. As a consequence, Chinese individuals and entities are exposed to numerous security threats,[39] and thus China has been more sensitive to the security situation in these countries. For instance, China seeks to strengthen international security cooperation in areas 'crucially related to China's overseas interests'.[40] Thirdly, and perhaps more profoundly, a rising China has been assumed by some countries to represent a major source of security threat in itself.

For instance, the US has stated that, in light of its behaviour as a rising power, the belief that China's 'integration into the post-war international order would liberalize China' and lead to a constructive China–US relationship,[41] has proven unfounded.[42] In contrast, the US has asserted that China has

> expanded its power at the expense of the sovereignty of others. China gathers and exploits data on an unrivaled scale and spreads features of its authoritarian system,

[35] Wen Jiabao, 'Speech: Turning Your Eyes to China' (Harvard University, 11 December 2003) <http://www.china-un.org/eng/zt/wfm/t56090.htm> accessed 1 January 2019.

[36] Robert B Zoellick, 'Whither China: From Membership to Responsibility?' (National Committee on US–China Relations, New York, 21 September 2005) <https://2001-2009.state.gov/s/d/former/zoellick/rem/53682.htm> accessed 5 January 2020.

[37] Stephanie L Kotecki, 'The Human Rights Costs of China's Arms Sales to Sudan—A Violation of International Law on Two Fronts' (2008) 17 Pacific Rim Law and Policy Journal 209; Michael J Kelly, 'Ending Corporate Impunity for Genocide: The Case against China's State-Owned Petroleum Company in Sudan' (2011) 90 Oregon Law Review 413.

[38] Zheng Yongnian/Zhang Chi, 'The Belt and Road Initiative and China's Grand Diplomacy' (2016) 56 China International Studies 52.

[39] Rosita Dellios/R James Ferguson, 'The Human Security Dimension of China's Belt and Road Initiative' (2017) 7 Journal of Management and Sustainability 48.

[40] State Council Information Office of China, 'China's Military Strategy' (May 2015) part III <http://www.scio.gov.cn/zfbps/ndhf/2015/Document/1435159/1435159.htm> accessed 6 January 2020.

[41] US NSS 2017 (n 8) 25.

[42] The White House, 'The National Security Strategy of the United States of America' (September 2002) 20, 26, 27 <https://2009-2017.state.gov/documents/organization/63562.pdf> accessed 6 January 2020.

> including corruption and the use of surveillance. It is building the most capable and well-funded military in the world, after our own. Its nuclear arsenal is growing and diversifying. Part of China's military modernization and economic expansion is due to its access to the U.S. innovation economy, including America's world-class universities.[43]

The US is of the view that China 'compete[s] across political, economic, and military arenas, and use[s] technology and information to accelerate these contests in order to shift regional balances of power in their favor'[44] and, in particular, 'seeks to displace the United States in the Indo-Pacific region, expand the reaches of its State-driven economic model, and reorder the region in its favor'.[45] The 2018 US National Defense Strategy also warned that 'long-term strategic competitions with China', together with Russia, is the 'principal priority' for the US.[46] It also views the security environment as unfavourable for it on both non-military and military fronts. On the one hand, it considers that China has 'increased efforts short of armed conflict by expanding coercion to new fronts, violating principles of sovereignty, exploiting ambiguity, and deliberately blurring the lines between civil and military goals'.[47] On the other hand, the US is aware that, '[f]or decades [it] has enjoyed uncontested or dominant superiority in every operating domain ... [but] [t]oday, every domain is contested—air, land, sea, space, and cyberspace'.[48] Similarly, in its written submission before a WTO panel in the *US-Tariff Measures on Certain Goods from China* case, the US accused China of

> a longstanding policy and practice of using governmental interventions, coercion and subterfuge to steal or otherwise improperly acquire intellectual property, trade secrets, technology and confidential business with the aim of advancing Chinese companies and advancing China's industrial policy goals.[49]

As such, China has been identified by the US as a 'revisionist power' which seeks to 'challenge American power, influence, and interests, attempting to erode American security and prosperity' and to 'shape a world antithetical to U.S. values and interests'.[50]

The new evaluation of the US of the security relationship with China, together with the growing security concerns that China faces, appears to have alarmed China, thereby apparently inducing more aggressive security policy from China's part. China recognizes that international strategic competition 'is on the rise' which, in particular, is brought about by American new security policy which 'adopted unilateral policies ... provoked and intensified competition among major countries, significantly increased its defense expenditure, [and] pushed for additional capacity in nuclear, outer space, cyber and missile defense'. Additionally, threats, like the cession pursued by the Democratic Progressive

[43] US NSS 2017 (n 8) 25. [44] ibid. [45] ibid.

[46] US National Defense Strategy 2018 (n 9) 4. [47] ibid 2. [48] ibid 3.

[49] *US-Tariff Measures on Certain Goods from China* (WT/DS543) First Written Submission of the USA (27 August 2019) para 12.

[50] US NSS 2017 (n 8) 2, 25.

Party (DPP) in Taiwan, disputes over territories and, in particular, maritime matters, and the endangering of China's growing overseas interests, outer space, and cybersecurity, are seen as intensifying.[51] Thus, China has taken more aggressive measures, for example, by deploying defensive facilities on the islands and reefs in the South China Sea, conducting patrols in the waters of Diaoyu Islands in the East China Sea,[52] conducting air reconnaissance and early warning monitoring of China's territorial air and air space and carrying out alert patrols, and conducting military training and manoeuvre 'in real combat conditions'.[53]

In addition, China is more concerned with new sources and modalities of security threats, in particular with regard to cyberspace. China recognizes that some countries are 'strengthening a cyber deterrence strategy, aggravating an arms race in cyberspace, and bringing new challenges to global peace'.[54] As a response, China views 'enhanced defense capability in cyberspace [as] an important part of China's endeavor to modernize its national defense and armed forces, which complies with the strategic guideline of active defense'.[55] To this end, China plans to

> expedite the development of a cyber force and enhance capabilities in terms of situational awareness, cyber defense, supporting state activities and participating in international cooperation, to prevent major cyber crises, safeguard cyberspace security and maintain national security and social stability.[56]

C. China's Conception of Sovereignty and its Approach to Global Security

A major concern in handling security at the international level involves State sovereignty. This has been particularly pertinent in the post-Cold War period given that many security threats do not arise from inter-State conflicts but stem from the domestic affairs of States which, in accordance with Article 2(7) UN Charter,[57] are largely within the exclusive jurisdiction of States.

[51] The State Council Information Office, 'China's National Defense in the New Era' (July 2019) part I <http://www.scio.gov.cn/zfbps/ndhf/39911/Document/1660528/1660528.htm> accessed 20 December 2019.

[52] ibid part II. [53] ibid part III.

[54] Cyberspace Administration of China, 'National Cybersecurity Strategy' (December 2016) part I.2, <http://www.cac.gov.cn/2016-12/27/c_1120195926.htm> accessed 20 December 2019 [in Chinese].

[55] Cyberspace Administration of China, 'International Strategy of Cooperation on Cyberspace' (March 2017) ch 3.1 <http://www.xinhuanet.com/english/china/2017-03/01/c_136094371.htm> accessed 20 December 2019.

[56] ibid. [57] Charter of the United Nations 1 UNTS XVI (UN Charter).

Given the humiliation to which China has been subjected by Western powers since the mid-nineteenth century,[58] and attempting to thwart the fears of some countries of a world socialist revolution, which was once assumed as being pursued by socialist China,[59] China has always been sensitive to sovereignty. China professes to being 'a most enthusiastic champion' of the principle of sovereignty.[60] The famous Five Principles of Peaceful Coexistence (Five Principles) were set out for the first time in the preamble of the Agreement between Republic of India and the People's Republic of China on the Trade and Intercourse between the Tibet Region of China and India in April 1954.[61] These Principles include (a) mutual respect for each other's territorial integrity and sovereignty; (b) mutual non-aggression; (c) mutual non-interference in each other's internal affairs; (d) equality and mutual benefit; and (e) peaceful coexistence. Taken together, the Five Principles represent the cornerstone of Chinese diplomacy.[62]

However, as Tieya Wang, a distinguished Chinese international lawyer, has stated, the Chinese approach to sovereignty has been misunderstood by many Western observers. According to Wang, China has never asserted a doctrine of absolute sovereignty.[63] Rather, sovereignty is understood by China to be a concept of intersubjectivity. In other words, China requires that other States respect its sovereignty and vice versa.[64] Furthermore, China arguably distinguishes sovereignty from the exercise of rights stemming from sovereignty.[65] This, consequently, allows China a degree of flexibility regarding issues of sovereignty whenever it deems it to be necessary.

That said, China has in the past provided policy statements, material, and personnel support to armed insurgences across Asia, Africa, Latin America, and Southeast Asia in particular. Such action was taken in the 1960s and 1970s to push back against US military containment and in the hope of achieving a global socialist revolution.[66] These activities, to some degree, contravened the principle of non-intervention that China otherwise enthusiastically has advocated.[67] This notwithstanding, China, generally speaking, is a strong supporter of the principle of sovereignty. For instance, in 1963, the spokesman of China's Ministry of Foreign Affairs denied the news appearing in Indian newspapers that China had a plan to establish a naval base in Ceylon (Sri Lanka). The spokesman stated that 'China consistently opposes the establishment of military bases by any country in other countries and consistently opposes hampering the sovereignty of other countries by any country through economic assistance'.[68] This policy has

[58] Tieya Wang, 'International Law in China: Historical and Contemporary Perspectives' (1990) 221 Recueil des Cours 199, 290, 297.

[59] Department of Unification Front of the Central Committee of the Chinese Communist Party, *Collected Work of Zhou Enlai on Unification Front* (People's Press 1984) 128 [in Chinese]; *Speech by Chairman of the Delegation of the People's Republic of China, Deng Xiaoping, at the Special Session of the U.N. General Assembly* (Foreign Language Press 1974).

[60] Wang (n 58) 288. [61] 299 UNTS 57.

[62] Constitution of the People's Republic of China (1975, as amended in 2018) preamble.

[63] Wang (n 58) 292. [64] ibid 295. [65] ibid 314, 305. [66] Garver (n 13) 196.

[67] Jerome Alan Cohen, 'China and Intervention: Theory and Practice' (1973) 121 University of Pennsylvania Law Review 471.

[68] As quoted in Wang (n 58) 294.

firmly persisted for several decades. In a 1995 White Paper on China's arms control and disarmament, China reiterated that it 'will not deploy army and establish military bases in foreign countries'.[69]

In order to address security concerns relating to the international society, a rising China has begun to soften its traditional conception of sovereignty by participating in or approving international actions, some of which are coercive or against the will of the concerned States. For instance, China's policy towards humanitarian intervention has become more pragmatic,[70] and it has often given approval to UNSC sanctions against States like Iran and North Korea.[71] More generally, China has been a major contributor to UN peacekeeping actions.[72] Amongst these developments, perhaps the most far-reaching has been China's changing policy towards humanitarian intervention or Responsibility to Protect (R2P).

There are numerous contentious issues surrounding humanitarian intervention, including its legality, legitimacy, and consequences.[73] One thing appears indisputable, however, namely that humanitarian intervention is not consistent with the principle of sovereignty (in particular, the principle of non-intervention) and, in the case of military intervention, the principle of the prohibition of the threat or use of force. These two principles are solemnly established in Article 2 of the UN Charter. Therefore, most of less powerful States are highly critical of humanitarian intervention, and China, like many other developing countries, has nearly always opposed it.[74] Likewise, Chinese commentators are always critical of humanitarian intervention. One particular commentator analysing American military actions against the Dominican Republic in April 1965 suggested that the excuses given by the US, such as 'to protect American lives', 'to save the lives of all (Dominican) people', and 'to maintain law and order', were 'ridiculous'.[75]

Gross and systematic violations of human rights committed in Rwanda, the former Yugoslavia, and other countries in the 1990s somewhat motivated new perceptions of humanitarian intervention amongst many States. Against those opponents of humanitarian intervention, especially military intervention, Secretary-General Kofi Annan contended that he agreed that the principles of sovereignty and non-interference could

[69] 'China: Arm Control and Disarmament' (n 1) part I.

[70] Jonathan E Davis, 'From Ideology to Pragmatism: China's Position on Humanitarian Intervention in the Post-Cold War Era' (2011) 44 Vanderbilt Journal of Transnational Law 217.

[71] Machiko Kanetake/Congyan Cai, 'Chinese and Japanese Perspectives on UN Sanctions' in Larissa van den Herik (ed), *Research Handbook on UN Sanctions and International Law* (Edward Elgar 2017).

[72] China currently contributes 10.25 per cent of the UN peacekeeping budget and China has also trained 8,000 People's Liberation Army troops to serve as a permanent standby militia for UN peacekeeping operations. Logan Pauley, 'China Takes the Lead in UN Peacekeeping' (*The Diplomat*, 17 April 2018) <https://thediplomat.com/2018/04/china-takes-the-lead-in-un-peacekeeping/> accessed 20 December 2019.

[73] Terry Nardin/Melissa S Williams (eds), *Humanitarian Intervention* (NY UP 2006); J L Holzgrefe/Robert O Keohane (eds), *Humanitarian Intervention: Ethnic, Legal and Political Dilemmas* (CUP 2003); UNGA 'Report of the Secretary-General: We the Peoples: The Role of the United Nations in the Twenty-First Century' (27 March 2000) UN Doc A/54/2000, para 216 ('We the Peoples').

[74] UNGA Verbatim Record (24 July 2009) UN Doc A/63/PV.98, 23.

[75] Jerome Alan Cohen/Hungdah Chiu, *People's China and International Law: A Documentary Study* (Princeton UP 1974) 1493.

'offer vital protection to small and weak States' and humanitarian intervention was 'a sensitive issue, fraught with political difficulty and not susceptible to easy answers'.[76] However, he also raised a serious question, namely: 'if humanitarian intervention is, indeed, an unacceptable assault on sovereignty, how should we respond to a Rwanda, to a Srebrenica—to gross and systematic violations of human rights that offend every precept of our common humanity?'[77]

As a response to the 'Annan Question', Canada, in September 2000, announced the establishment of an independent International Commission on Intervention and State Sovereignty (ICISS), which was given a mandate to 'build a broader understanding of the problem of reconciling intervention for human protection purpose and sovereignty'.[78] In its 2001 report entitled *Responsibility to Protect*, the ICISS decided not to use the phrase 'humanitarian intervention', but rather to refer to a 'responsibility to protect'.[79]

The concept of R2P was then included in the 2005 World Summit Outcome Document. Two important limitations were imposed, however. First, only four circumstances could trigger the application of R2P, namely genocide, war crimes, ethnic cleansing, and crimes against humanity. Most importantly, R2P action could only be authorized in accordance with the UN Charter, including Chapter VII.[80] That is, unlike in the ICISS Report, regional organizations and individual States are not allowed to take R2P actions unless authorized so by the UNSC.

China in its 2005 Position Paper on UN Reform, several months ahead of the 2005 World Summit Outcome Document, accepted the concept of R2P. The Position Paper provided that:

> [e]ach State shoulders the primary responsibility to protect its own population. However, internal unrest in a country is often caused by complex factors. Prudence is called for in judging a government's ability and will to protect its citizens. No reckless intervention should be allowed.
>
> When a massive humanitarian crisis occurs, it is the legitimate concern of the international community to ease and defuse the crisis. Any response to such a crisis should strictly conform to the UN Charter and the opinions of the country and the regional organization concerned should be respected. It falls on the Security Council to make the decision in the frame of UN in light of specific circumstances which should lead to a peaceful solution as far as possible. Wherever it involves enforcement actions, there should be more prudence in the consideration of each case.[81]

The 2005 Position Paper requires that R2P action should be authorized by the UNSC, but it does not impose the same limitation regarding the circumstances triggering R2P as the 2005 World Summit Outcome Document. Rather, it broadly refers to 'human

[76] 'We the Peoples' (n 73) paras 217, 219. [77] ibid para 217.

[78] ICISS, *Responsibility to Protect* (International Development Research Centre 2001) 2.

[79] ibid 11. [80] UNGA Res 60/1 (16 September 2005) paras 138–9.

[81] Position Paper of the People's Republic of China on the United Nations Reforms (7 June 2005) part III.1 <http://www.china-un.org/eng/hyyfy/t199101.htm> accessed 20 December 2019.

crisis'. Four reasons could explain China's hasty approval of a concept proposed by the ICISS, an international non-governmental organization. First, China, as a permanent member of the UNSC, is required to shoulder more responsibilities to prevent and stop humanitarian crises.[82] Secondly, as China rises, it seeks to protect its rapidly expanding interests around the world, especially those in fragile countries. Thirdly, R2P allows China to give the green light to UN actions based on humanitarian consideration without explicitly compromising its policy of non-intervention and without accepting humanitarian intervention. The last and perhaps most revealing explanation might be that China did not really have a proper understanding of R2P at that time.

It seems that China subsequently found that the Position Paper went too far. As such, China retreated from this position during the debates on the first UN General Assembly (UNGA) Resolution on R2P in 2009, once again emphasizing sovereignty.[83] R2P, China said, remained 'a concept' and did not constitute 'a norm of international law'.[84] China contended that 'the international society can provide assistance, but the protection of citizens [of a State] ultimately depends on the Government of that State'.[85] Unlike in the 2005 Position Paper, China stated that only the four circumstances specified in the 2005 World Summit Outcome Document could trigger R2P.[86] Furthermore, China warned that the implementation of R2P 'should not contravene the principle of State sovereignty and the principle of non-interference in the internal affairs of States', that R2P should not 'becom[e] a kind of humanitarian intervention',[87] and, in particular, that 'no States must be allowed to unilaterally implement R2P'.[88]

While still ambivalent, China's embracing of the concept of R2P is significant because, as a permanent member of the UNSC, China has the power to veto nearly all initiatives within the UNSC. Indeed, China has vetoed coercive initiatives allegedly aimed to stop humanitarian crises in Sudan,[89] Zimbabwe,[90] and Syria.[91] It should be noted, however, that, at the same time, China supported the UNSC resolutions against Sudan[92] and Libya,[93] where China has a huge economic interest. Furthermore, China reportedly used economic leverage to press Sudan to change its policy in Darfur, including by discouraging Chinese corporations from investing in Sudan and removing Sudan's

[82] David H Shinn, 'China and the Conflict in Darfur' (2009) 16 Brown Journal of World Affairs 85, 91–3.

[83] UNGA Verbatim Record (n 74) 23–4. [84] ibid 24. [85] ibid 23.

[86] ibid. [87] ibid. [88] ibid.

[89] 'UN Vote on Sudan Could Face China Veto' (*Fox News*, 18 September 2004, updated 14 January 2015) <https://www.foxnews.com/story/u-n-vote-on-sudan-could-face-china-veto> accessed 20 December 2019.

[90] Neil Macfarquhar, '2 Vetoes Quash UN Sanctions on Zimbabwe' (*The New York Times*, 12 July 2008) <http://www.nytimes.com/2008/07/12/world/africa/12zimbabwe.html?pagewanted=all> accessed 6 January 2020.

[91] 'Security Council Fails to Adopt Draft Resolution Condemning Syria's Crackdown on Anti-Government Protestors, Owing to Veto by Russian Federation, China' (UN, 4 October 2011) <https://www.un.org/press/en/2011/sc10403.doc.htm> accessed 20 December 2019.

[92] eg UNSC Res 1713 (2006); UNSC Res 1755 (2007); and UNSC Res 1769 (2007).

[93] UNSC Res 1973 (2011).

preferred trade status.[94] This indicates that China remains alert to concerns that R2P might be abused. As a matter of fact, it complained that the relevant UNSC resolutions on Libya were too broadly interpreted by some countries to justify their undue actions.[95] In light of this, China, together with Russia, blocked several coercive attempts against Syria under Chapter VII UN Charter, an act fiercely denounced by several countries including the US.[96] China has also opposed humanitarian coercive actions without the approval of the UNSC.[97]

The establishment of Chinese overseas military bases further exhibits the flexibility of China towards sovereignty when it comes to addressing security concerns. As noted above, overseas military bases had not been part of Chinese foreign policy for decades. However, in 2017 China's first overseas military base was established in Djibouti. It is reported that a major mandate of the military base is to provide logistical support for China's participation in maritime escort, peacekeeping actions, and humanitarian assistance, to facilitate military cooperation, military exercises and training, the protection and evacuation of overseas Chinese nationals, and to maintain strategic international routes.[98] It is rightly suggested that the Chinese base in Djibouti 'may be a harbinger of more to come'.[99] The establishment of this military base shows that China has significantly increased its willingness and capability to address international security issues.

D. Potential New Legal Regulations to Tackle Security Concerns in Relation to a Rising China

Arguably, the substantial transformation of security concerns in relation to a rising China, examined in Section B, requires new legal regulations. At the same time, China's

[94] Chin-Hao Huang, 'US–China Relations and Darfur' (2007) 31 Fordham International Law Journal 827, 837–8.

[95] eg Speech of Chinese Ambassador Li Baodong at the UNSC open debate on the Protection of Civilians in Armed Conflict: UNSC Verbatim Record (10 May 2011) UN Doc S/PV.6531, 20–1.

[96] Euan McKirdy, '8 Times Russia blocked a UN Security Council Resolution on Syria' (*CNN*, 13 April 2017) <https://edition.cnn.com/2017/04/13/middleeast/russia-unsc-syria-resolutions/index.html> accessed 20 December 2019.

[97] For instance, on the comment on the missile strikes launched by the US, France, and the UK against Syria in April 2018, the spokesperson said that the use of force on the ground of unilateral 'humanitarian interference' bypassing the UNSC did not conform to international law. Foreign Ministry Spokesperson Hua Chunying, 'Press Conference' (16 April 2018) <http://www.fmprc.gov.cn/mfa_eng/xwfw_665399/s2510_665401/2511_665403/t1551458.shtml> accessed 6 January 2020.

[98] Guoquan Chen/Xiaoliang Mo, 'Logics Base of the Chinese People's Liberation Army was Founded' (11 July 2017) [in Chinese] <http://www.mod.gov.cn/shouye/2017-07/11/content_4785240_2.htm> accessed 20 December 2019.

[99] Tyler Headley, 'China's Djibouti Base: A One Year Update' (*The Diplomat*, 4 December 2018) <https://thediplomat.com/2018/12/chinas-djibouti-base-a-one-year-update/> accessed 20 December 2019.

more flexible approach to sovereignty, discussed in Section C, presumably means that China may be willing to subject itself to greater legal regulations. Some of the new legal initiatives are likely to be accepted while others appear less likely, if not totally unlikely, to be put into practice.

1. From the Declaration on the Conduct to the Code of Conduct of Parties in the South China Sea

The Asia-Pacific area has been not only a major engine for international prosperity but also a major source of international confrontation. As such, in the late 2010s, the Obama Administration proposed the 'Asian Pivot' or 'Asian Rebalance' Strategy, a core component of which was to project more political and military power in the Asia-Pacific area to engage a rising China.[100] Furthermore, the US, by employing 'smart power', has sought to organize its allies and other countries in the Asia-Pacific area to contain some of the more aggressive behaviour of China.[101] For its part, it is obvious that China has recognized the Asia-Pacific area as a major source of security disputes. In January 2017, it issued a White Paper on its policy on Asia-Pacific security cooperation,[102] which was the first security document concerning this particular area.

Security issues in the Asia-Pacific region in recent years refer particularly to disputes between China and some other countries, including both regional States (like the Philippines) and non-regional States (like the US), in the South China Sea, where China has huge geopolitical, economic, and military interests. In this context, both the freedom of navigation actions carried out by the US,[103] and the arbitral proceedings initiated by the Philippines against China concerning the South China Sea[104] have posed substantial security threats to China.

In the early 1990s, ASEAN began to consider a legal regime to address such disputes with China and in July 1992 ASEAN issued a Declaration on the South China Sea (the

[100] Jonathan G Odom, 'What Does a Pivot or Rebalance Look Like: Elements of the US Strategic Turn Towards Security in the Asia-Pacific Region and Its Waters' (2012) 14 Asian-Pacific Law and Policy Journal 1.

[101] US DoS, 'Smart Power in Action' (November 2010) <https://2009-2017.state.gov/documents/organization/150505.pdf> accessed 20 December 2019.

[102] State Council Information Office of China, 'China's Policies on Asia-Pacific Security Cooperation' (January 2017) <http://www.scio.gov.cn/zfbps/ndhf/36088/Document/1539910/1539910.htm> accessed 20 December 2019.

[103] Xinjun Zhang, 'The Latest Developments of the US Freedom of Navigation Programs in the South China Sea: Deregulation or Re-Balance' (2016) 9 Journal of East Asia and International Law 167; James W Houck/Nicole M Anderson, 'The United States, China, and Freedom of Navigation in the South China Sea' (2014) 13 Washington University Global Studies Law Review 441.

[104] *Arbitration between the Republic of the Philippines and the People's Republic of China*, PCA Case No 2013-19, Award on Jurisdiction and Admissibility (29 October 2015); *Arbitration between the Republic of the Philippines and the People's Republic of China*, PCA Case No 2013-19, Award (12 July 2016). As to the South China Sea arbitration, eg Bernard H Oxman, 'The South China Sea Arbitration Award' (2017) 24 University of Miami International and Comparative Law Review 235.

Manila Declaration).[105] Although the Manila Declaration merely expressed an intention to resolve disputes through peaceful means, without referring to China at all, China perceived ASEAN as having started to view the maritime issue as a common concern. The Manila Declaration states that all parties concerned, based on the *Treaty of Amity and Cooperation* in Southeast Asia (TAC), should establish 'a code of international conduct over the South China Sea'.[106] In August 1999, the Philippines proposed a draft code of conduct on behalf of ASEAN. China rejected the draft, but ultimately had to consent to further discussions. In March 2000, China and ASEAN submitted their own drafts for discussion.[107] In 2002, ASEAN and China signed the Declaration on the Conduct of Parties in the South China Sea (DoC).[108]

The DoC is of significance because, first, ASEAN for the first time engaged 'as one side' with China on an issue of strategic importance for the rise of China. Secondly, the DoC prescribed that China and ASEAN would negotiate a Code of Conduct (CoC) in the South China Sea,[109] which is likely to impose more constraints on Chinese activities in the area. Obviously, the DoC represents a growing number of regional roadblocks and potential problems for China. Furthermore, the Declaration of ASEAN Concord II (2003) aimed to enhance cooperation amongst ASEAN countries on maritime issues. It provides that any maritime issues 'shall be addressed regionally in holistic, integrated and comprehensive manner. Maritime cooperation between and among ASEAN member countries shall contribute to the evolution of the ASEAN Security Community.' In 2012, ASEAN senior officials began to draft the CoC with the intention of attaining a common ASEAN position before submitting it to China for discussion.[110] In January 2012, the Philippines circulated an informal working draft, but ASEAN members were divided on several articles.[111] Although the final deal has not yet been reached, it is believed that the 2016 South China Sea decision, which was unfavourable to China, was instrumental in speeding up the CoC negotiations.[112] Importantly, however, neither the DoC nor the future CoC create legally binding obligations on the parties. This partly explains why the DoC failed to prevent the subsequent escalation of the South China Sea disputes.

[105] ASEAN Declaration on the South China Sea <https://cil.nus.edu.sg/wp-content/uploads/2017/07/1992-ASEAN-Declaration-on-the-South-China-Sea.pdf> accessed 20 December 2019.

[106] ibid para 4.

[107] Wu Shicun/Ren Huaifeng, 'More Than a Declaration: A Commentary on the Background and the Significance of the Declaration on the Conduct of the Parties in the South China Sea' (2003) 2 Chinese Journal of International Law 311, 313.

[108] Declaration on the Conduct of Parties in the South China Sea (ASEAN-China) <https://asean.org/?static_post=declaration-on-the-conduct-of-parties-in-the-south-china-sea-2> accessed 20 December 2019.

[109] ibid para 10.

[110] Carlyle A Thayer, 'ASEAN's Code of Conduct in the South China Sea: A Litmus Test for Community-Building?' (2012) 10 The Asia-Pacific Journal 1, 2.

[111] ibid 3.

[112] Lee YingHui, 'A South China Sea Code of Conduct: Is Real Progress Possible?' (*The Diplomat*, 18 November 2017) <https://thediplomat.com/2017/11/a-south-china-sea-code-of-conduct-is-real-progress-possible> accessed 20 December 2019.

2. China and the Future Intermediate-Range Nuclear Forces Treaty

As both the Soviet Union and the US developed and deployed intermediate-range and shorter-range missiles in the 1970s, both sides recognized that those missiles carrying nuclear warheads, namely Intermediate-Range Nuclear Forces, risked igniting nuclear war. While continuing to strengthen their INF, the Soviet Union and the US with the support of other NATO countries agreed to negotiate an arrangement concerning INF control. In December 1987, President Reagan and General Secretary Gorbachev signed the INF Treaty.[113] The INF Treaty, together with the 1972 Anti-Ballistic Missile Treaty[114] and the 1991 Strategic Arms Reduction Treaty, constituted the cornerstone of the nuclear arms control system. Given its meaningful substantive obligations of INF reduction and procedural mechanism of verification,[115] the Treaty 'has played an important role in easing the international relations, moving forward the nuclear disarmament process and safeguarding global strategic balance and stability'.[116]

In practice, the INF Treaty, both before and after its inception, caused unease amongst some States, including the US itself, which were concerned particularly with the adverse effects on their national defence arising from it.[117] This notwithstanding, a major contributing factor to the success of the INF Treaty might have been that, apart from the Soviet Union-led Warsaw Treaty Organization and the US-led NATO, other States such as China were not capable of developing and deploying advanced INF at the time. As noted above, for instance, because of its new State strategy prioritizing economic development after the beginning of the Reforming and Opening-up Policy in the late 1970s, China was neither willing to develop, nor capable of developing, INF that could constitute a meaningful threat to the US.

The situation has changed significantly in the twenty-first century. To cope with growing strategic pressure arising from the enlargement of NATO,[118] Russia allegedly began to develop INF again in violation of the Treaty (at least according to the US).[119] Additionally, more and more States including North Korea, China, India, and Pakistan, not parties to the INF Treaty, have developed more intermediate-range missiles posing threats to the US and Russia.[120]

[113] 1657 UNTS 4 (INF Treaty). [114] 944 UNTS 13.

[115] eg INF Treaty (n 113) arts 4 and 11.

[116] Foreign Ministry Spokesperson Hua Chunying, 'Press Conference' (22 October 2018) <https://www.fmprc.gov.cn/mfa_eng/xwfw_665399/s2510_665401/2511_665403/t1606198.shtml> accessed 20 December 2019.

[117] Lynn E Davis, 'Lessons of the INF Treaty' (1988) 66 Foreign Affairs 720.

[118] In 1999, Poland, Hungary, and the Czech Republic joined the NATO. Again, Bulgaria, Estonia, Latvia, Lithuania, Romania, Slovakia, and Slovenia gained the NATO membership in 2004.

[119] Amy F Woolf, 'Russian Compliance with the Intermediate Range Nuclear Forces (INF) Treaty: Background and Issues for Congress' (Congressional Research Service, 2 August 2019) 1, 2 <https://fas.org/sgp/crs/nuke/R43832.pdf> accessed 6 January 2020.

[120] ibid 24.

In light of the fact that 'an ever-greater number of countries are acquiring missile production technologies and adding such missiles to their arsenals', while the INF Treaty 'being of unlimited duration, is limiting the actions only of a few States, primarily Russia and the United States',[121] the US and Russia issued a joint statement at the UNGA in October 2007, calling on

> all interested countries to discuss the possibility of imparting a global character to this important regime through the renunciation of ground-launched ballistic and cruise missiles with ranges between 500 and 5,500 kilometers, leading to the destruction of any such missiles, and the cessation of associated programs.[122]

However, INF-producing countries, including China, did not respond positively. The US and Russia subsequently suspended the application of the INF Treaty in early 2019. Thus, the question whether China's standing outside the INF Treaty was a major factor in the suspension of the Treaty and, more importantly, whether China would be willing to join the INF regulatory regime have attracted much attention. China has firmly rebutted all accusations that the suspension of the INF Treaty should be attributed to it.[123] It has expressed its opposition to such suspension, warning that it may trigger a series of adverse consequences and has urged 'the US and Russia to properly resolve differences through constructive dialogue'.[124] At the same time, China has expressed no intention to join the INF Treaty for the time being.[125] According to China, its national defence policy justifies the opposition to the multilateralization of the INF Treaty. It has stated that its 'national defense policy is defensive in its nature' and that it has 'been adopting a highly restrained attitude when it comes to developing our military forces' with 'no intention to ... threaten any other countries'.[126] Some Chinese observers have suggested, however, that China's opposition to the multilateralization of the Treaty might be because China's strategic security faces threats from countries such as India.[127] Thus, it is safe to expect that, as the US and Russia suspended and will potentially revise or terminate the INF, China may be forced to strengthen its nuclear arsenal.

[121] 'Joint US–Russian Statement on the Treaty on the Elimination of Intermediate-Range and Shorter-Range Missiles at the 62nd Session of the UN General Assembly' (25 October 2007) <https://2001-2009.state.gov/r/pa/prs/ps/2007/oct/94141.htm> accessed 6 January 2020.

[122] ibid. [123] Chunying (n 116).

[124] Foreign Ministry Spokesperson Geng Shuang, 'Remarks on the US Suspending INF Treaty Obligations and Beginning Withdrawal Process' (2 February 2019) <https://www.fmprc.gov.cn/mfa_eng/xwfw_665399/s2510_665401/2535_665405/t1635268.shtml> accessed 20 December 2019.

[125] ibid.

[126] Foreign Ministry Spokesperson Geng Shuang, 'Press Conference' (5 December 2018) <https://www.fmprc.gov.cn/mfa_eng/xwfw_665399/s2510_665401/2511_665403/t1619268.shtml> accessed 20 December 2019.

[127] Han (n 5) 62–5.

E. Conclusion

In the past decade, whether China could rise in a peaceful manner or, more precisely, whether a rising China would bring about security threats in international society and, especially, the US as the existing hegemonic power, has invited heated debates. At one end of the spectrum is Mearsheimer, who predicted that 'the result would be an intense security competition between China and its rivals' and that China and the US 'are destined to be adversaries as China's power grows.'[128] As illustrated in this chapter, I would like to agree with Buzan who, at the other end of the spectrum, suggested that 'peaceful rise cannot be accomplished by China alone, but only by China and the rest of international society working together to create the necessary conditions.'[129] Truly, China has been continually expanding its military power, with an increasing willingness to show its muscle. This may disable the global security order, which has witnessed time and again the rise and fall of great powers in the past centuries. However, it should be stressed that not only an emerging great power but also the existing hegemonic powers should shoulder the shared responsibility to reshape the global security order.

An important issue is whether international law makes a difference in regulating security risks and potential security confrontations stemming from the rise of China. This author is of the view that China, in engaging with security issues, does take seriously into account the international obligations into which it has entered. China has supported better rule of law on the global security issue. As illustrated above, this is not just confined to rhetoric. China has started a range of efforts, including the negotiation of new rules, which are expected to reduce the security risks and confrontations arising from its rise. On the other hand, since the US, who is much more militarily powerful than China, has identified China as a strategic competitor and has taken, and continued to take, measures to impose security pressure on China, it is not reasonable to require China to make commitments which substantially prejudice China's security environment. For instance, although the reluctance of China to accede to the INF Treaty damages the viability of that Treaty, the reasons China presented are not totally unsound.

[128] John J Mearsheimer, *The Tragedy of Great Power Politics* (WW Norton and Company 2001) 4.

[129] Barry Buzan, 'China in International Society: Is "Peaceful Rise" Possible?' (2010) 3 Chinese Journal of International Policy 5, 7.

CHAPTER 47

EUROPE

ELENI METHYMAKI AND ASLI OZCELIK

A. Introduction

EXPLORING a region's role in the development of the international law of global security requires an understanding of what exactly that region entails. Yet, determining what constitutes the region of 'Europe' is not a straightforward task. According to palaeontologist Tim Flannery '[c]ontemporary Europe is not a continent in any real geographical sense'; rather, 'Europe is best defined by its rocks. So conceptualised, Europe extends from Ireland in the west to the Caucasus in the east, and from Svalbard in the north to Gibraltar and Syria in the south.'[1] He continues, '[s]o defined, Turkey is part of Europe, but Israel is not: the rocks of Turkey share a common history with the rest of Europe, while Israel's rocks originate in Africa.'[2] The geographic boundaries of regional organizations in Europe produce equally fuzzy cartographies. Membership of the North Atlantic Treaty Organization (NATO) and the European Union (EU) is open to any 'European State',[3] yet the founding treaties define neither 'Europe' nor 'European'. Although it remains contested whether Russia, Turkey, Belarus, Moldova, Ukraine, Georgia, Armenia, and Azerbaijan are geographically part of Europe, they are all members of both the Council of Europe (CoE) (except for Belarus) and the Organization for Security and Co-operation in Europe (OSCE), with Turkey being also a NATO member and an EU candidate country. Even when demarcated as such, European geography remains complex, with territorial disputes in Serbia, Moldova, Ukraine, and Georgia, amongst others, ongoing.

[1] Tim Flannery, *Europe: The First Hundred Million Years* (Penguin 2018) 2–3. [2] ibid 3.

[3] North Atlantic Treaty 34 UNTS 243 art 10 (Washington Treaty); Treaty on European Union OJ C 326 art 49 (TEU).

The complexity of delineating 'Europe' is amplified at the intersection of the 'geopolitical imaginary' of Europe with the 'European identity'[4]—a crossing that characterizes European approaches to security. In the words of political scientist William Walters:

> We cannot point to a place, state or continent called Europe which readily reveals its borders, edges or divisions to an impartial observer. On the contrary... debates about the frontiers of Europe are unavoidably political interventions which interject elements of fixture into the fluid and ambiguous space that is Europe.[5]

In the political sense, Europe has been associated with the 'European project', a political community rooted in the need to advance the security and survival of the nation-State within a framework of 'European values' and Euro-Atlantic integration. Of this project, the European Union is only the latest instalment.[6] Within this, various ideational factors are at play in determining what constitutes 'Europe' and who is to be included and excluded from the European space through state recognition, membership to the EU and NATO,[7] and entitlement to the legal protections within the European *espace juridique*.[8] In turn, what constitutes the region of 'Europe' shapes the security approaches prevalent in it: security threats are political and social constructs,[9] as much accommodating inclusion of 'us' as exclusion of the 'other'.[10]

With its global security strategy, the EU—with its Member States—has become the dominant actor in articulating a 'shared vision' and a blueprint for 'common action' for 'a stronger Europe'.[11] The fulfilment of the EU's internal and external security and 'strategic autonomy' requires 'a truly united and committed Europe' built on 'common

[4] Doris Wydra, 'Between Normative Visions and Pragmatic Possibilities: The EUropean Politics of State Recognition' (2020) 25 Geopolitics 315, 317.

[5] William Walters, 'Europe's Borders' in Chris Rumford (ed), *The SAGE Handbook of European Studies* (SAGE Publications 2009) 487.

[6] See, also, Brigid Laffan et al, *Europe's Experimental Union: Rethinking Integration* (Routledge 2000) 38–9.

[7] eg The Ministry of Defence, 'White Paper for International Security and Defence' (July 2015) <https://www.difesa.it/Primo_Piano/Documents/2015/07_Luglio/White%20book.pdf> accessed 16 May 2020 (Italy) para 40. The membership conditions of the EU, set out in the 1993 Copenhagen Criteria, include commitments to democracy, the rule of law, human rights, protection of minorities and market economy, see EC, 'Accession Criteria' <https://eur-lex.europa.eu/summary/glossary/accession_criteria_copenhague.html?locale=en> accessed 14 May 2020. The preamble of the Washington Treaty (n 3) similarly emphasizes 'the principles of democracy, individual liberty and the rule of law'.

[8] Prominent amongst such protections are those offered by the European Convention on Human Rights and Fundamental Freedoms ETS No 5 (ECHR).

[9] See, also, Audie Klotz, 'Migration' in Alexandra Gheciu/William Wohlforth (eds), *The Oxford Handbook of International Security* (OUP 2018) 446.

[10] See, also, in Antonios Tzanakopoulos, Chapter 42 in this *Handbook*, 773.

[11] EU, *Shared Vision, Common Action: A Stronger Europe—A Global Strategy for the European Union's Foreign and Security Policy* (EU Publications 2016) 3 (GSS 2016).

European interests', including 'peace, security, prosperity, democracy and a rules-based global order'.[12] As Nanopoulos notes, 'transformation of the EU's periphery, reform of the multilateral system, and strategic autonomy are all woven into a project of securing the European physical, ontological, and economic space'.[13] Within this European space the referent object for security,[14] therefore, is not just the existence of the (super)State itself, but also a mystical idea of 'European values' or the 'European way of living' that needs to be protected against existential threats. Yet, as the two case studies in this chapter demonstrate, this construction of 'Europe' as a referent object often justifies deviations from the purported values of 'European identity', including rules-based behaviour, commitment to human rights, and prosperity.[15] For example, security practices in the context of border control or extraterritorial uses of force by European States often rub up against the relevant international legal frameworks,[16] clashing with Europe's idea of itself as 'a self-styled beacon of human rights'[17] and promoter of human security.

At the intersection of these complex dynamics, we encounter European States themselves. The place of 'Europe' in the global security landscape is often analysed with a focus on the EU or NATO (or both). However, as our discussion in Section B shows, European States' security approaches are not subsumed under the policies and politics of these organizations.[18] In examining the National Security Strategies (NSSs) of nineteen European States we seek to identify the security approaches of European States' from their national perspectives, inquiring at the same time whether an embryonic 'European' security perspective emerges from them. To evaluate whether this is borne out in practice, we then turn (Section C) to two spheres of securitization which, as evident from the NSSs, are perceived as essential to the maintenance of Europe itself: security at its borders and in its wider neighbourhood. In assessing European practices in these two spheres, our objective is to examine how European States have shaped the international law of global security, appraising in the process what that tells us about Europe as an actor of both security and insecurity (Section D).

[12] ibid 4–15. [13] Eva Nanopoulos, Chapter 54 in this *Handbook*, 997.

[14] As summarized by Nigel White/Auden Davies-Bright, Chapter 1 in this *Handbook*, 21: 'the Copenhagen School [of security studies] identifies those objects that are existentially threatened as "referent objects"', citing Barry Buzan et al, *Security: A New Framework for Analysis* (Lynne Rienner 1998) 36.

[15] On those, GSS 2016 (n 11) 4–15. [16] Sections C.1 and C.2.

[17] Cathryn Costello/Itamar Mann, 'Border Justice: Migration and Accountability for Human Rights Violations' (2020) 21 German Law Journal 311, 312 (in the context of migration control).

[18] On the EU as a security actor, see Eva Nanopoulos (n 13); for NATO, see Steven Hill, Chapter 57 in this *Handbook*.

B. Current Status of the Debate: Security Governance in Europe

Security governance has been significantly 'Europeanized' and multilateralized in Europe.[19] NATO, the EU (particularly with the emergence of the Common Foreign and Security Policy[20]), and the OSCE's comprehensive approach to security dominate the institutional landscape of multilateral security governance in Europe.[21] In looser institutional settings, significant sub-regional initiatives include: the Commonwealth of Independent States (ten post-Soviet Republics in Eurasia), Weimar Triangle (Poland, Germany, France), Central European Defence Cooperation (Austria, the Czech Republic, Slovakia, Hungary, Slovenia, and Croatia), Nordic Defence Cooperation (Denmark, Finland, Iceland, Norway, and Sweden), Salzburg Forum (Central Europe: Austria, Bulgaria, Croatia, the Czech Republic, Hungary, Poland, Romania, Slovakia, and Slovenia) and the GUAM Organization for Democracy and Economic Development (Georgia, Ukraine, Azerbaijan, and Moldova).

Despite the existence of such influential actors, European States' perception of the security challenges they face and the limits of multilateralism have required unilateral and bilateral actions in addition to multilateral cooperation.[22] At the bilateral level, this includes arrangements between EU Member States, such as the Franco–German Defence and Security Council,[23] and between EU Member States and non-Member States in and beyond Europe. Within Europe, bilateral arrangements between Turkey and the EU,[24] Russia and NATO,[25] and Russia and the EU[26] seek to incorporate the periphery into the

[19] See, on 'governance', Mark Webber et al, 'The Governance of European Security' (2004) 30 Review of International Studies 3, 4. On the 'Europeanization' of security governance, Nanopoulos (n 13) Section B.3.

[20] See Nanopoulos (n 13) Section B.1 and generally.

[21] Other relevant actors are the European Atomic Energy Community, the Financial Action Task Force (FATF), and the Council of Europe.

[22] Sarah Raine, 'Europe's Strategic Future: From Crisis to Coherence?' (*International Institute for Strategic Studies*, 2019) <https://www.iiss.org/publications/adelphi/2019/europes-strategic-future-from-crisis-to-coherence> accessed 14 May 2020.

[23] 'Franco-German Defence and Security Council—Agreed Conclusions (16 October 2019)' <https://www.diplomatie.gouv.fr/en/country-files/germany/events/article/franco-german-defence-and-security-council-agreed-conclusions-16-oct-19> accessed 30 November 2020; also, Treaty of Aachen (France, Germany) <https://www.diplomatie.gouv.fr/en/country-files/germany/france-and-germany/franco-german-treaty-of-aachen/> accessed 14 May 2020.

[24] Agreement between the European Union and the Republic of Turkey on the Readmission of Persons Residing without Authorisation OJ L 134/3.

[25] 'NATO-Russia Council' <https://www.nato.int/nrc-website/en/about/index.html> accessed 14 May 2020.

[26] Agreement on Partnership and Cooperation establishing a Partnership between the European Communities and their Member States, of one part, and the Russian Federation, of the other part OJ L327/3.

core of European security governance. Post-Brexit Europe will likely see various bilateral or mixed treaties between the UK and the EU and/or its Member States.

The security approaches of individual States and unilateral or domestically led actions also remain salient. States are important—if not the dominant—actors in security governance: 80 per cent of defence investment in Europe is still spent nationally.[27] Through the politicization[28] of security across Europe, national, and even sub-national, foreign, and security perceptions have also shaped the EU's Global Security Strategy (GSS). For instance, national approaches have driven a shift in emphasis from promoting good governance to building resilience in the European neighbourhood.[29] Additionally, national security priorities have led to a securitization agenda shaped at the expense of human security, in legal and policy responses to issues such as migration.[30]

In light of this, it is necessary to examine the NSSs of European States to ask whether an embryonic European security perspective exists. Since 2000, many governments have adopted security strategy documents, laying down security threats as they perceive them and prescribing strategies and solutions.[31] Many European States have also undertaken 'horizon scanning' exercises to determine the major challenges to national and global security in the period 2030–45, and the appropriate legal and policy responses.

Such analyses provide insights into national perceptions of security challenges and appropriate responses to them. They also operate as building blocks of what can loosely be described as 'global security law', contributing to its shaping, development, and application.[32] To this end, we have reviewed the NSSs of nineteen States: Belgium, Bulgaria, Croatia, Denmark, Finland, France, Georgia, Germany, Hungary, Italy, Netherlands, Norway, Poland, Russia, Serbia, Spain, Sweden, Turkey, and the UK. Our selection reflects geographical balance, but is limited by the fact that some States, like Greece, have not adopted an NSS and some, like Ukraine's,[33] are not available in English. The aim of the review is to identify States' common and diverging approaches towards security and determine whether their strategies reflect an embryonic European perspective in relation to the *broadening, deepening* and *thickening* of security,[34] and *approaches to global security governance*.

[27] Institute of Europe Russian Academy of Sciences, 'The EU Global Strategy: A View from Russia' (January 2017) <https://wirtschaftsclubrussland.org/wp-content/uploads/2017/02/IERASReportJanuary2017.pdf> accessed 14 May 2020.

[28] Michael Zürn, 'The Politicization of World Politics and its Effects: Eight Propositions' (2014) 6 European Political Science Review 47 (Politicization: 'a subject of public discussion').

[29] See GSS 2016 (n 11) 23 and Nanopoulos (n 13). See also Ana E Juncos, 'Resilience as the New EU Foreign Policy Paradigm: A Pragmatist Turn?' (2017) 26 European Security 1, 3.

[30] Esther Barbé/Pol Morillas, 'The EU Global Strategy: The Dynamics of a More Politicized and Politically Integrated Foreign Policy' (2019) 32 Cambridge Review of International Affairs 753; and Section C.1.

[31] Alyson J K Bailes/Anna Wetter, 'Security Strategies' MPEPIL (OUP, January 2013) MN 1.

[32] ibid MN 3.

[33] See <https://zakon.rada.gov.ua/laws/show/287/2015> accessed 14 May 2020 [in Ukrainian].

[34] Ian Manners, 'European [Security] Union: Bordering and Governing a Secure Europe in a Better World?' (2013) 27 Global Society 398, 400–9.

1. A Comprehensive Approach to Security: Broadening, Deepening, and Thickening

All NSSs adopt a 'broadened' and 'deepened'[35] concept of security, extending beyond military security to dimensions of economic, societal, environmental, energy, food, health, and human security. Connectedly, the sources of insecurity have broadened.[36] The NSSs explore and address not only security 'threats'—traditionally associated with military, physical threats—but also security 'risks', 'challenges' and 'vulnerabilities'.[37] For Germany 'the range of risks to our security is becoming broader, more diverse, and increasingly unpredictable', including terrorism, cybertechnology and artificial intelligence, arms proliferation and weapons of mass destruction, climate change, migration, pandemics, resource scarcity, demographic change, inequality, populism, identity politics, nationalism, isolationism, geopolitical transitions, conflicts and fragility, transnational asymmetric threats, and espionage and disinformation. In this respect, such security strategies reflect Beck's 'global risk society':[38] 'unpredictability has become the new normal'.

The comprehensive approach to security is also evidenced in the diversification of the 'referent objects' of security, namely those objects that are threatened or challenged. Hungary's NSS exemplifies this 'deepening' of security:

> [C]hallenges, risk factors and threats appear on several levels—at individual, community, state, regional and also global level—and have an impact on a wide range of individuals, governmental and non-governmental organisations and trans-national actors.[39]

Mirroring the broader developments in international relations discourse and international law, European NSSs seemingly adopt a 'human security' approach, while also construing the environment, climate, food, or energy as 'referent objects' of security. The devil lies, of course, in the detail: most European NSSs, despite references to human rights, conceptualize human security primarily as security of *their* citizens.[40] For its

[35] On security 'broadening' and 'deepening', Ursula Schroeder, Chapter 3 in this *Handbook*, Section B.2.

[36] eg Prime Minister's Office, 'Finnish Security and Defence Policy 2012: Government Report' (2013) 14 <https://www.bbn.gov.pl/ftp/dok/07/FIN_Finnish_Security_Defence_Policy_2012_Government_Report.pdf> accessed 14 May 2020.

[37] See Hans Günter Brauch, 'Concepts of Security Threats, Challenges, Vulnerabilities and Risks' in Hans Günter Brauch et al (eds), *Coping with Global Environmental Change, Disasters and Security* (Springer 2011) 61.

[38] Ulrich Beck, 'Living in the World Risk Society' (2006) 35 Economy and Society 329, 332.

[39] Ministry of Foreign Affairs of Hungary, 'Hungary's National Security Strategy' (2012) 4 (Hungary) <https://www.eda.europa.eu/docs/default-source/documents/hungary-national-security-strategy-2012.pdf> accessed 14 May 2020.

[40] eg The National Security Council, 'National Security Strategy 2017' (2017) 8, 11 (Spain) <https://www.dsn.gob.es/eu/2017-spanish-national-security-strategy> accessed 14 May 2020; Federal Chancellery, 'Austrian Security Strategy' (July 2013) 9 (Austria) <https://www.bundesheer.at/pdf_pool/

part, the Russian conception of 'national security' seems to prioritize State security, with its emphasis on 'military security' and the 'significance of the military and security aspects of international relations'.[41] Yet, a broader notion of security, including human security and social security, seems to also underpin its NSS.[42]

In addition to the 'broadening' and 'deepening', most NSSs adopt a 'thickened' approach to security that reflects a commitment to address security issues holistically, tackling the root causes of insecurity, considering implications for peace, human rights and development, and working towards prevention. Even Denmark and Norway, which have traditionally been sceptical about the EU's comprehensive approach to security—focusing on military approaches instead,[43] today adopt a multifaceted and preventive approach towards global security. For instance, in relation to conflicts, instability, and migration in/from the European neighbourhood, their NSSs emphasize the significance of conflict prevention, sustainable development, and tackling root causes. They further commit to the use of 'aid, business development, peace and reconciliation diplomacy' in addition to military contributions.[44]

2. Globalization of Security

All NSSs reflect a common understanding of security as a *global* issue requiring *global* responses. They are based on the acknowledgement that the distinction between intra-State security, associated with 'law and order', and inter-State security, associated with deterrence and absence of war, has become blurred and has been replaced with a merged perception of internal and external security.[45] The perceived globalization of the sources and consequences of insecurity, according to the NSSs, requires multilateral legal and

publikationen/sicherheitsstrategie_engl.pdf> accessed 14 May 2020; National Security Bureau, 'National Security Strategy of the Republic of Poland' (2014) 10–11 (Poland) <https://www.bbn.gov.pl/ftp/dok/NSS_RP.pdf> accessed 14 May 2020; Norwegian Ministry of Foreign Affairs, 'Setting the Course for Norwegian Foreign and Security Policy' (21 April 2017) 27, 39 (Norway) <https://www.regjeringen.no/en/dokumenter/meld.-st.-36–20,162,017/id2549828/> accessed 14 May 2020. See, similarly, Nanopoulos (n 13) Section C.3.

[41] The Ministry of Foreign Affairs of the Russian Federation, 'National Security Concept of the Russian Federation' (10 January 2000) (Russia) <https://www.mid.ru/en/foreign_policy/official_documents/-/asset_publisher/CptICkB6BZ29/content/id/589768> accessed 14 May 2020.

[42] Decree of the President of the Russian Federation, 'National Security Strategy of the Russian Federation to 2020' (12 May 2009) para 1 <http://thailand.mid.ru/en/national-security-strategy-of-the-russian-federation> accessed 14 May 2020. cf Bakhtiyar Tuzmukhamedov, Chapter 50 in this *Handbook*.

[43] Pernille Rieker, 'The Nordic Countries and EU Security Policy: Convergent or Divergent Agendas?' in Alyson Bailes et al (eds), *The Nordic Countries and the European Security and Defence Policy* (OUP 2006) 310–11.

[44] Norway (n 40) 36–7; The Danish Government, 'Foreign and Security Policy Strategy 2019–2020' (November 2018) 15, 19 (Denmark) <https://um.dk/en/news/newsdisplaypage/?newsid=01fc577b-6bf2-4fd7-8572-5af0534cf599> accessed 14 May 2020.

[45] See Didier Bigo, 'Internal and External Aspects of Security' (2006) 15 European Security 385, 388.

institutional arrangements on global and regional levels. This is reflected in renewed commitments to international law, the UN, EU, and NATO in all NSSs.

However, there is a significant divide—and driver of insecurity, when it comes to the nature and orientation that these responses should take. For the EU and most of its Member States, the current 'rules-based international order' is constructed as a referent object.[46] Many NSSs recognize that the centres of power are moving away from Europe, especially with the retreat of the US, its long-time ally.[47] Additionally, the need to 'renew or create appropriate governance and security tools at the bilateral, regional, and global levels'[48] is acknowledged. Russia's NSS, on the other hand, takes an equally global approach, but considers the current order itself as 'an ever-increasing threat to international security', due to its 'NATO-oriented' nature and 'domination by developed Western countries in the international community'.[49]

Furthermore, beyond a perception that global responses are needed, the emphasis is put on regional and sub-regional cooperation for certain security issues. In its 2014 NSS, Poland emphasizes that 'enhanced cooperation between sub-regions of Europe in the area of security, including defence, will remain favourable from the political and economic perspective'.[50] The strategy stresses that sub-regional cooperation cannot replace allied and pan-European solutions but in the field of cybersecurity, for example, it promotes the former at the expense of the existing EU framework.[51]

All in all, despite certain divergences, the security strategies reveal an embryonic but common security perspective, characterized by a comprehensive approach to security. However, the following analysis of two case studies reveals a chasm between these policy commitments and the pursuance of European States' security objectives in practice. On the one hand, European approaches to border security and migration illustrate that in seeking to safeguard the security of the European space and States, human security of individuals and commitments under international human rights and refugee law have been sacrificed.[52] European States' practice in pursuing military operations and conflict resolution in neighbouring regions, for its part, reveals divergences between them, particularly in relation to military versus soft approaches to security, and their complex relationship with international law as it stands. All this underpins varied and at times contradictory responses to security threats, risks, and challenges deemed to emerge at the borders of Europe and in the European neighbourhood.

[46] The Federal Government, 'The 2016 White Paper: Strategic Review and Way Ahead on Security Policy and the Future of the Bundeswehr' 25 (Germany) <https://www.gmfus.org/profiles/german-ministry> accessed 14 May 2020; Norway (n 40) 6; Denmark (n 44) 18.

[47] See, also, Munich Security Conference, 'Munich Security Report 2020: Westlessness' <https://securityconference.org/en/publications/munich-security-report-2020/> accessed 30 November 2020.

[48] Delegation for Strategic Affairs, 'Strategic Horizons 2040' (2013) 19 (France) <https://www.defense.gouv.fr/english/dgris/strategic-thinking/defense-foresight/en/strategic-horizons> accessed 30 November 2020.

[49] Decree of the President of the Russian Federation (n 42). See, also, Russia (n 41).

[50] Poland (n 40) paras 7 and 42.

[51] Helena Carrapico/André Barrinha, 'The EU as a Coherent (Cyber)Security Actor?' (2017) 55 Journal of Common Market Studies 1254, 1265.

[52] See, also, White/Davies-Bright (n 14) Section B.4.

C. Contemporary Challenges

1. European Border Security

a. *Migration as a Security Threat*

Border security is inextricably linked to the idea of the State.[53] Mass migration,[54] uncontrolled and/or irregular migration,[55] refugee and migration pressures[56] and/or flows,[57] and illegal migration[58] are classified as threats and challenges in European NSSs, embodying European States' broad conception of security threats.[59] Rather than being viewed as a natural state of being, human mobility is perceived as a risk to the security of the State and its citizens, demanding strict management and regulation.[60] And this perception is not confined to migration outwith legal channels, but concerns legal migration too.[61] Even States such as Germany and France, which in their NSSs present a relatively nuanced approach, highlight migration's positive aspects only in connection to their own challenges of ageing populations and need for skilled labour.[62]

For many decades, European States have struggled with (post)colonial migration. Britain's 'Windrush Generation' scandal is one example.[63] Such struggles have translated into legal frameworks of inclusion and (mostly) exclusion from the corpus of the nation: at the most basic level, in the ability to acquire citizenship or in the possibility of being denationalized if proven an 'undeserving' citizen.[64] Securitization does not

[53] Zygmunt Bauman, *Community: Seeking Safety in an Insecure World* (Wiley 2001) 17–18.

[54] eg Croatia, 'National Security Strategy' (2017) 7 <https://www.soa.hr/files/file/National-Security-Strategy-2017.pdf> 7 accessed 14 May 2020.

[55] eg Denmark (n 44) 6; Spain (n 40) 23, 66; Ministry of Justice and Security, 'National Security Strategy' (2019) 17 (Netherlands) <https://bit.ly/2Z8Dfjy> accessed 14 May 2020.

[56] eg Denmark (n 44) 6, 7; 'National Security Strategy of the Republic of Bulgaria' (25 February 2011) 32 <https://www.me.government.bg/files/useruploads/files/national_strategy1.pdf> accessed 14 May 2020; Belgian Defence, 'Security Environment Review' (2019) 27 (Belgium) <https://www.belgianarmy.be/wp-content/uploads/2019/09/Security-environment-review-1.pdf> accessed 30 November 2020.

[57] eg Spain (n 40) 110–11; France (n 48) 113; Belgium (n 56) 23.

[58] eg Hungary (n 39) para 37; Austria (n 40) 7, 13; Croatia (n 54) 7, 9, 12.

[59] On migration as security threat in Europe, Jef Huysmans, 'The European Union and the Securitization of Migration' (2000) 38 Journal of Common Market Studies 751.

[60] Finland (n 36) 14; Austria (n 40) 11, 18. See Frédérik Mégret, 'Transnational Mobility, the International Law of Aliens, and the Origins of Global Migration Law' (2017) 111 AJIL Unbound 18 on the 'coercive management of mobility'.

[61] Hungary (n 39) para 37.

[62] Germany (n 46) 42.

[63] Huon Wardle/Laura Obermuller, '"Windrush Generation" and "Hostile Environment": Symbols and Lived Experiences in Caribbean Migration to the UK' (2019) Migration and Society 81, 82. On France, see Aida Alami, 'Three Girls from Morocco' in Zahra Hankir (ed), *Our Women on the Ground: Arab Women Reporting from the Arab World* (Harvill Secker 2019) 131.

[64] See, also, White/Davies-Bright (n 14) Section B.4; Bridget Anderson/Matthew Gibney, 'The Unworthy Citizen' in Roberto Gonzales/Nando Sigona (eds), *Within and Beyond Citizenship: Borders, Membership and Belonging* (Routledge 2017); Dimitris Papadopoulos/Vassilis Tsianos, 'After Citizenship: Autonomy of Migration, Organisational Ontology and Mobile Commons' (2013) 17 Citizenship Studies

happen only *at* the border: European citizenship is 'an even more brutally patrolled border'.[65] The plight of Shamima Begum readily illustrates this: stripped of her British nationality for leaving the UK and joining ISIL/Da'esh when she was 15 years old, she has been left stateless in a camp in northeast Syria, where living conditions would breach Article 3 ECHR,[66] and with no option of re-entering the UK. When State security and the security of the nation as a collective comes knocking on the front door, human security of the individual goes out of the window.[67] Our understanding of European States' political and legal reactions to the surge in people crossing Europe's borders in 2015–16 (and thereafter) has to be informed by this longer history. The language of 'Europe's migration/refugee crisis' cannot be taken at face value. Rather, it needs to be seen as an attempt to justify the intensification of 'Fortress Europe'[68] and the sidelining of international law in the process.

b. *State versus Human Security Spectacles at Europe's Borders: International Law at the Sidelines*

Under international law, border and migration control is considered a core aspect of State sovereignty.[69] This conception of migration as falling purely within a State's domestic jurisdiction is, however, fairly recent,[70] having materialized in the early twentieth century on racial, war-related, and economic grounds.[71] According to Chetail, much continental European discourse at the time discussed migration control as an exception to free movement on the basis of the preservation of the State.[72] Yet today States are generally considered as having a right to decide when a non-citizen may enter and stay in their territory and under what conditions, to the extent that they have not undertaken treaty obligations[73] and are not bound by rules of customary international law to the

178, 182–3. See, also, Guy Goodwin-Gill, 'Statelessness is Back (Not That It Ever Went Away…)' (*EJIL:Talk!*, 12 September 2019) <https://www.ejiltalk.org/statelessness-is-back-not-that-it-ever-went-away/> accessed 1 May 2020.

[65] Papadopoulos/Tsianos (n 64) 179.

[66] Owen Bowcott, 'Shamima Begum Loses First Stage of Appeal Against Citizenship Removal' (*The Guardian*, 7 February 2020) <https://www.theguardian.com/uk-news/2020/feb/07/shamima-begum-loses-appeal-against-removal-of-citizenship> accessed 1 May 2020.

[67] On this danger Hitoshi Nasu, 'Human Security and International Law: The Potential Scope for Legal Development within the Analytical Framework of Security' in Mary Footer et al (eds), *Security and International Law* (Hart 2016) 39–40.

[68] See Nicholas de Genova, 'Introduction' in Nicholas de Genova (ed), *The Borders of 'Europe': Autonomy of Migration, Tactics of Bordering* (Duke UP 2017)10–11, 15–16. See, also, ibid 27–9 on how the 'spectacle of terror' (another 'crisis') after the 2015 Paris attacks allowed for even harsher border controls; Evelina Gambino, 'The "Gran Ghettò": Migrant Labor and Militant Research in Southern Italy' in de Genova (n 68) 376–7.

[69] David Weissbrodt, 'Immigration' MPEPIL (OUP, March 2014) MN 3.

[70] Vincent Chetail, *International Migration Law* (OUP 2019) ch 1.

[71] ibid 48. [72] ibid 51–2.

[73] For example, the ones EU Member States have undertaken under TEU art 3(2) and TFEU art 67(2), 77, 78 and 79 to abolish internal border controls for Member State nationals and establish a common European asylum policy and a common immigration policy. From a different perspective, treaty obligations limiting the States' right of border and migration control stem from the 1951 Convention

contrary, such as the obligation of *non-refoulement* or the right of individuals to seek asylum.[74] In that respect, legally and 'in its essence', migration is a matter for both domestic and international law.[75]

In 2015–16, almost 1.5 million people[76] crossed the borders of 'Europe'; more than 1 million[77] arriving in Greece through the Eastern Mediterranean route. While lawful arrival remains open for the 'high-skilled migrant' (usually meaning from other Global North States), the increasing securitization of migration has meant that such channels have seriously diminished for those seeking international protection or fleeing regions of extreme poverty, environmental degradation, and protracted conflicts.[78] As a consequence, most people arriving at Europe's borders do so 'irregularly', faced with situations that endanger human security in multiple ways.[79]

Much of southern Europe is also the EU's external border. This is an area where national interests and policies and EU action cannot be easily disentangled:[80] individual States, including EU Member States, are in principle free to admit or not admit anyone into their territory,[81] but border security and migration control are viewed as strict duties of EU Member States and equally strict conditions for States aspiring to such membership. The increasing role played by the European Border and Coast Guard Agency (Frontex) in policing the EU's external borders,[82] the Common European Asylum System (CEAS), with its infamous Dublin Regulation,[83] and the increasing involvement of the European Asylum Support Office (EASO) in processing asylum claims[84] are manifestations of this point. The Court of Justice of the European Union

relating to the Status of Refugees (189 UNTS 137) and its 1967 Protocol (606 UNTS 267) and ECHR (n 8) art 3 (the obligation of *non-refoulement*), amongst others, concerning the international protection of individuals and human rights.

[74] Geoff Gilbert/Anna Magdalena Rusch, 'International Refugee and Migration Law' in Malcolm Evans (ed), *International Law* (5th edn, OUP 2018) 827. For a powerful, alternative argument to this mainstream understanding see E Tendayi Achiume, 'Migration as Decolonization' (2019) 71 Stanford Law Review 1509.

[75] Chetail (n 64) 5–6.

[76] UNHCR numbers <https://data2.unhcr.org/en/situations/mediterranean> accessed 14 May 2020.

[77] UNHCR numbers <https://www.unhcr.org/greece.html?query=GREECE> accessed 14 May 2020.

[78] UNGA, 'Report of the Special Rapporteur on the Human Rights of Migrants: Regional Study—Management of the External Borders of the European Union and its Impact on the Human Rights of Migrants' (24 April 2013) UN Doc A/HRC/23/46, paras 15–17.

[79] ibid paras 18–20; Cathryn Costello/Minos Mouzourakis, 'The Common European Asylum System: Where Did It All Go Wrong?' in Maria Fletcher et al (eds), *The European Union as an Area of Freedom, Security and Justice* (Taylor and Francis 2016) 278ff.

[80] This section leaves aside the actions and policies of other actors involved in this field, such as the UN High Commission for Refugees (UNHCR) or the International Organization for Migration (IOM).

[81] Under TFEU art 78 it is the Member State concerned that is responsible for examining the asylum claim and for taking the final decision. See Evangelia (Lilian) Tsourdi, 'Holding the European Asylum Support Office Accountable for its Role in Asylum Decision-Making: Mission Impossible?' (2020) 21 German Law Journal 506, 510 and 514–15.

[82] Melanie Fink, *Frontex and Human Rights: Responsibility in 'Multi-Actor Situations' under the ECHR and EU Public Liability Law* (OUP 2018) 23–9.

[83] For the architecture of the CEAS, see Costello/Mouzourakis (n 79) 266ff.

[84] Tsourdi (n 81) generally.

(CJEU), in its April 2020 judgment concerning Poland's, Hungary's, and the Czech Republic's failure to comply with relocation decisions of the Council of the EU, held that the internal and external security of individual Member States cannot be called upon unrestrictedly to evade their obligations under EU law.[85]

Lack of lawful routes to Europe and increased fortification of land borders, 'through physical obstacles and—often violent—policing',[86] has led to great numbers of people seeking to enter Europe from the Middle East and Africa to undertake deadly boat journeys across the Mediterranean.[87] Here, the clash between State and human security at Europe's borders plays out in three, interrelated, ways. First, the lack of lawful options for departure and arrival has led to an increase in human smuggling and human trafficking.[88] Secondly, those who manage to arrive at Europe's borders in such 'irregular' ways face protracted detention and long-term delays in the processing of their applications in often inhuman and degrading conditions.[89] The 'hotspot' approach to asylum processing and the 2016 EU–Turkey deal are central in this, and both highly detrimental to the human rights and security of people subjected to them.[90] Thirdly, to escape their obligations under international human rights and refugee law,[91] European States and the EU have increasingly resorted to externalization of migration control: visa restrictions and carrier sanctions,[92] alliances with (and funding for) countries such as Turkey and Libya in detaining and containing migrants beyond European territory,[93] and push-backs by Frontex and national coastguards in the Mediterranean ensure that as many people as possible will not make it to their borders and within their jurisdiction in the first place.[94] They erode, thus, international legal protection by denying ability to enter and seek asylum.[95] In its landmark 2012 judgment in *Hirsi Jamaa et al v Italy*, the

[85] CJEU Joined Cases C-715/17, 718/17, 719/17 [2020] ECLI:EU:2020:257, paras 139 et seq.

[86] Costello/Mouzourakis (n 79) 281.

[87] Another entrance point to Europe is through the Spanish enclave of Melilla in Morocco. People attempting to enter Europe there are being subjected to extensive force by border guards, illegal push-backs and collective expulsion. Shockingly, the ECtHR in *N.D. and N v Spain*, App No 86/75/15 and 8697/15, 13 February 2020, failed to condemn Spain for its conduct at Melilla.

[88] Vladislava Stoyanova, Chapter 21 in this *Handbook*; Nanopoulos (n 13) Section C.3; Costello/Mouzourakis (n 79) 279–80.

[89] Special Rapporteur (n 78) paras 20, 47–54; Costello/Mouzourakis (n 79) 291–3. For an encouraging development, see CJEU, 'Press Release No 60/20: Judgment in Joined Cases C-924/19 PPU and C-925/19 PPU' (14 May 2020) https://curia.europa.eu/jcms/upload/docs/application/pdf/2020-05/cp200060en.pdf accessed 14 May 2020.

[90] Costello/Mouzourakis (n 79); EU–Turkey Statement (18 March 2016) <https://www.consilium.europa.eu/en/press/press-releases/2016/03/18/eu-turkey-statement/> accessed 10 May 2020.

[91] On these legal obligations, see briefly Costello/Mouzourakis (n 79) 281–2.

[92] Costello/Mann (n 17) 316.

[93] Special Rapporteur (n 78) para 50. See eg the 2017 Italy–Libya Memorandum of Understanding (2017), <http://eumigrationlawblog.eu/wp-content/uploads/2017/10/MEMORANDUM_translation_finalversion.doc.pdf> accessed 10 May 2020 and renewed for another 3 years in 2020, see <https://www.aljazeera.com/news/2019/11/deal-curb-migrant-arrivals-italy-libya-renewed-191102122821537.html> accessed 10 May 2020.

[94] Special Rapporteur (n 78) para 56.

[95] See Asher Lazarus Hirsch/Nathan Bell, 'The Right to Have Rights as a Right to Enter: Addressing a Lacuna in the International Refugee Protection Regime' (2017) 18 Human Rights Review 417.

European Court of Human Rights (ECtHR) placed limitations on States Parties' migration management practices,[96] yet there has been for some time an 'apparent dilution in protection offered' by the Court with respect to detention standards and, most recently in *N.D. and N.T. v Spain*, the prohibition of collective expulsion.[97]

Although international legal developments—such as the adoption of the Global Compacts for Refugees and for Safe, Orderly and Regular Migration[98]—could signify changes to the management of human mobility,[99] at the time of writing the situation at Europe's borders is appalling. Simultaneously, the virtual collapse of the CEAS has resulted in a re-nationalization of border and migration policies,[100] including the closure of internal borders[101] and the aforementioned decision of Poland, Hungary, and the Czech Republic to defy decisions taken at EU level for relocation of third-country nationals.[102] In 2020, the situation was further exacerbated by Turkey's instrumentalization of the 2016 EU–Turkey Agreement to pressure the EU into supporting its military operations in Syria.[103] This led to another humanitarian 'crisis' at the Turkish–Greek border, where refugees were treated by Greek and FRONTEX border guards in a manner that violates international human rights and refugee law, with Greece also temporarily suspending asylum applications.[104] This latest 'crisis' needs to be again viewed within the broader geopolitical landscape of the region and the turbulent 'EU–Greece–Turkey triangle'.[105] For although European States' NSSs declare the deepening of security, shifting focus away from the State and towards human security instead, the 'macabre deathscapes'[106] of Europe's borderlands tell a different story: human security is only possible for as long as the State itself does not feel threatened.

[96] *Hirsi Jamaa and Others v Italy*, App No 27765/09, 23 February 2019.

[97] Costello/Mann (n 17) 320; *N.D. and N.T.* (n 87).

[98] UNGA Res 73/195 (11 January 2019); UNGAOR Supp 12 A/73/12 (Part II) (2018).

[99] Maria Gavouneli, 'Legislating by Compacts?—The Legal Nature of the Global Compacts' (*EJIL:Talk!*, 28 February 2019) <https://www.ejiltalk.org/legislating-by-compacts-the-legal-nature-of-the-global-compacts/> accessed 2 May 2020.

[100] Bernd Kasparek/Matthias Schmidt-Sembdner, 'Renationalisation and Spaces of Migration: the European Border Regime After 2015' in Katharyne Mitchell et al (eds), *Handbook on Critical Geographies in Migration* (Edward Elgar 2019) 214.

[101] For the EU Member States unilateral measures are taken to deal with the 'crisis' see Costello/Mouzourakis (n 79) 287–8.

[102] See n 85.

[103] 'EU–Turkey Migrant Deal Still Intact: Germany's Merkel Says' (*DW*, 17 March 2020) <https://www.dw.com/en/eu-turkey-migrant-deal-still-intact-germanys-merkel-says/a-52805142> accessed 10 May 2020.

[104] Arguably illegally. UNCHR, 'Greece: Rights Violations against Asylum Seekers at Turkey–Greece Border Must Stop—UN Special Rapporteur' (23 March 2020) <https://ohchr.org/EN/NewsEvents/Pages/DisplayNews.aspx?NewsID=25736&LangID=E> accessed 10 May 2020.

[105] Achilles Skordas, 'The Twenty-Day Greek–Turkish Border Crisis and Beyond: Geopolitics of Migration and Asylum (Part I)' (*EU Migration and Asylum Law and Policy*, 5 May 2020) <http://eumigrationlawblog.eu/the-twenty-day-greek-turkish-border-crisis-and-beyond-geopolitics-of-migration-and-asylum-law-part-i/> accessed 30 November 2020.

[106] The term from de Genova (n 68) 2.

2. Security in the European Neighbourhood

a. *Insecurity in the Neighbourhood as a Security Threat*

The entanglement of internal and external security also manifests itself in the security interests of European States (and the EU) in Europe's neighbourhood. The perceived security threats emanating from neighbouring regions range from traditional threats, such as conflicts and terrorism, to 'soft' security threats like migration as explored above. As such, securitizing and stabilizing the European neighbourhood has been an essential aspect of Europe's ontological and existential security.[107]

Underpinning the creation of the EU's European Neighbourhood Policy,[108] the conviction that security in Europe is dependent upon security near Europe also permeates the European NSSs. The Austrian NSS, for instance, states:

> All of the important challenges facing the internal security of Austria possess an international dimension. Austrian security policy, therefore, aims at making a proactive contribution to the stability and security of problematic [sic] countries of origin and transit, which are relevant to the security of Austria and the EU.[109]

According to Croatia, the 'zone of instability' surrounding Europe stretches 'from northern Africa, through the Middle East, to the Caucasus and Central Asia'.[110] Germany's NSS further provides that 'instability in Europe's neighbourhood... is thus a risk for our security'.[111]

To mitigate insecurity beyond Europe, European States undertake a variety of actions, multilaterally, through the UN, EU, NATO, and the OSCE, and individually, through transnational law enforcement operations;[112] humanitarian and rescue tasks;[113] military advice and assistance;[114] sanctions;[115] peacekeeping;[116] support for security sector reform; conflict prevention and resolution; and post-conflict assistance.[117] Additional to such traditional tools, state-building and even accession to the EU or NATO also

[107] eg Council of the European Union, 'A Secure Europe in a Better World: European Security Strategy' (12 December 2003) 15895/03 PESC 787.

[108] European Commission, 'Review of the European Neighbourhood Policy' (2015) 12 <https://ec.europa.eu/neighbourhood-enlargement/sites/near/files/neighbourhood/pdf/key-documents/151118_joint-communication_review-of-the-enp_en.pdf> accessed 30 November 2020.

[109] Austria (n 40) 14. [110] Croatia (n 54) 7. [111] Germany (n 46) 40.

[112] eg EU, 'Cocaine Route Programme: Combatting Transnational Organised Crime' <https://cocaineroute.eu> accessed 30 November 2020.

[113] See eg nn 82–4 and accompanying text; and Nanopoulos (n 13) 996.

[114] eg Ministry of Defence, 'Assistance and Support Bilateral Mission in Libya (MIASIT)' <https://www.difesa.it/EN/Operations/InternationalOperations/Libya/Pagine/default.aspx> accessed 14 May 2020.

[115] eg 'EU Sanctions Map' <https://sanctionsmap.eu/#/main> accessed 14 May 2020.

[116] eg 'EU Military and Civilian Missions and Operations' (5 March 2019) <https://eeas.europa.eu/headquarters/headquarters-homepage/430/military-and-civilian-missions-and-operations_en> accessed 14 May 2020.

[117] See Section C.2.c.

function as security practices. 'Weak States' and 'dysfunctional societies' are deemed breeding grounds for security threats such as armed conflicts, terrorism, and eventually migration. 'Governance is securitized' as ill governance is perceived as a threat to the internal security of neighbourhood States and the external security of Europe.[118] The transformation of domestic politico-legal orders, through conflict resolution, aid, or membership conditionality, is employed as a tool to promote 'good governance', or at least 'resilience', in the neighbourhood.[119]

European States' practices in responding to insecurity abroad, especially in their neighbourhood, are significant for mapping the role of 'Europe' in the (re-)making of the international law of global security. We confine our analysis to European responses to conflicts, through the use of force and diplomatic conflict resolution, as the termination of such conflicts has been at the core of European States' security interests, and actions undertaken to pursue them shape *jus ad bellum* and articulate the relevance of international law to conflict resolution, respectively.

b. *Military Operations in the Neighbourhood and jus ad bellum*

Protracted violent conflicts within Europe's geographical proximity, such as in Libya and Syria, and Russia's military actions and influence in the post-Soviet space, such as in Georgia, Moldova, and Ukraine, have led to extraterritorial uses of force by European States and a surge in military investment. Although wariness towards extensive military intervention abroad in the aftermath of Afghanistan and Iraq still dominates European responses to conflicts in neighbouring regions, the situations in Libya and Syria have prompted military responses and led to troubling consequences both for *jus ad bellum* and the humanitarian situation on the ground.

Following the failure of the Libyan government to fulfil its primary responsibility to protect its people, the UNSC authorized Member States in Resolution 1973 to use force 'to enforce compliance with the ban on flights' and 'protect civilians and civilian populated areas under threat of attack'.[120] Resolution 1970, which preceded it and had demanded immediate cessation of violence, was adopted upon the initiative of France, Germany, and the UK along with the US.[121] The ensuing NATO-led multinational military operation in pursuance of Resolution 1973, with France and the UK as the primary contributors, has raised criticism.[122] The operation went beyond the mandated use of force and undermined in the process the legitimacy of the R2P doctrine by exacerbating

[118] Laure Delcour, 'The European Union, a Security Provider in the Eastern Neighbourhood?' (2010) 19 European Security 535, 537.

[119] eg Spain (n 40) 44; Hungary (n 39) 12. See Juncos (n 29).

[120] UNSC Res 1973 (2011) paras 4–8.

[121] Ashley Deeks, 'The NATO Intervention in Libya—2011' in Olivier Corten et al (eds), *The Use of Force in International Law: A Case-Based Approach* (OUP 2018) 749.

[122] eg Olivier Corten/Vaios Koutroulis, 'The Illegality of Military Support to Rebels in the Libyan War: Aspects of *jus contra bellum* and *jus in bello*' (2013) 18 JCSL 59; Christine Gray, *International Law and the Use of Force* (OUP 2018) 380.

the conflict, contributing to the overthrow of Gaddafi, and seeking regime change in Libya.[123]

The numerous ISIL/Da'esh-connected terrorist attacks in Belgium, France, Denmark, Turkey, Germany, Sweden, Spain, Russia, and the UK from 2013 onwards have furthered perceptions about the interdependence of internal and external security, and have driven more European States to use force against ISIL/Da'esh in the territory of Syria and elsewhere. Although uses of force have been justified on different legal grounds and against varying backgrounds, a common aspect has been the expansive approach towards *jus ad bellum*, particularly in relation to the right to self-defence against non-State actors, anticipatory self-defence, humanitarian intervention, and R2P. The only exception to this is Russia's use of force against ISIL/Da'esh and other UN-designated terrorist groups justified as 'intervention by invitation' by the Syrian government.[124]

The conflict and the associated uses of force in Syria have led to increased support for the use of force against non-State armed groups in the territory of another State without its consent and, to a lesser extent, the 'unwilling and unable' test.[125] Joining the US-led coalition against ISIL/Da'esh in 2015 following a terrorist attack, Turkey adopted the 'unwilling and unable' test to justify its use of force in Syrian territory on the basis of individual and collective self-defence against imminent attacks.[126] In a 2017 speech, citing the situations in Iraq and Syria, the UK Attorney-General not only endorsed the 'unable and unwilling' test, but also espoused an interpretation of 'imminence' in relation to anticipatory self-defence that may pave the way for (unlawful) uses of force employed in the 'absence of specific evidence of where an attack will take place or of the precise nature of an attack'.[127] Other European States developed alternative, yet similarly controversial, accounts: Belgium emphasized that its use of force is 'directed against the so-called "Islamic State in Iraq and the Levant" and not against the Syrian Arab Republic',[128] while Germany associated its right to use force against ISIS in Syrian territory without

[123] cf Deeks (n 121). See also Heidarali Teimouri/Surya P Subedi, 'Responsibility to Protect and the International Military Intervention in Libya in International Law: What Went Wrong and What Lessons Could Be Learnt from It?' (2018) 23 JCSL 3, 7.

[124] See Karine Bannelier-Christakis, 'Military Interventions against ISIL in Iraq, Syria and Libya' (2016) 29 Leiden Journal of International Law 743, 760–3. For an overview of 'intervention by invitation' in civil wars, see Dapo Akande/Zachary Vermeer, 'The Airstrikes against Islamic State in Iraq and the Alleged Prohibition on Military Assistance to Governments in Civil Wars' (*EJIL: Talk!*, 2 February 2015) <https://www.ejiltalk.org/the-airstrikes-against-islamic-state-in-iraq-and-the-alleged-prohibition-on-military-assistance-to-governments-in-civil-wars/> accessed 30 November 2020.

[125] Gray (n 122) 237–48.

[126] UNSC 'Letter from the Chargé d'affaires a.i. of the Permanent Mission of Turkey to the United Nations addressed to the President of the Security Countil' (24 July 2015) UN Doc S/2015/563.

[127] See https://www.gov.uk/government/speeches/attorney-generals-speech-at-the-international-institute-for-strategic-studies citing Daniel Bethlehem's Principle 8 <https://www.un.org/law/counsel/Bethlehem%20-%20Self-Defense%20Article.pdf#page=6>. For the problems of this approach, see James Green, 'Initial Thoughts on the UK Attorney General's Self Defence Speech' (*EJIL:Talk!*, 13 January 2017) <https://www.ejiltalk.org/initial-thoughts-on-the-uk-attorney-generals-self-defence-speech/> accessed 14 May 2020.

[128] UNSC 'Letter dated 7 June 2016 from the Permanent Representative of Belgium to the United Nations addressed to the President of the Security Council' (9 June 2016) UN Doc S/2016/523.

government consent with the lack of effective control of the Syrian government over ISIL/Da'esh-occupied territory.[129]

Whether *jus ad bellum* and the current collective security architecture are fit for purpose in the face of new security threats has been contested since long before 9/11.[130] The recent violent contestations between warring parties in the European neighbourhood, as well as the surge in terrorist acts, have re-sparked the legal controversies over *jus ad bellum* and led to divergences from the established law. In that, European States have had a central role. Given the essential role of *jus ad bellum* for 'the maintenance of an international rules-based order'[131] and the uniform commitment of European States to the latter in their NSS in particular and international policies more generally, such departures reveal the contested meanings of the 'rules-based order' and international law amongst European States. On top of that, the situations in Libya and Syria readily illustrate how military responses to insecurity may drive further insecurity.[132] Beyond extraterritorial use of force, arms transfer to countries engaged in armed conflict further demonstrates how outside States can exacerbate, or become complicit in, conflict-related crimes and insecurity. The UK's arms export to Saudi Arabia, which may well have been used in the commission of serious violations of international humanitarian law in Yemen, is a case in point.[133] These shortcomings and counterproductive consequences of military approaches brings us to the significance of political solutions to (armed) conflicts—an objective which is seemingly pursued both by European States and European regional organizations.

c. *International Law and Conflict Resolution: Mediating Normative Ambition and Realpolitik*

The US-led 'War on Terror' has constricted the diplomatic space for conflict resolution and encouraged hard security approaches to armed conflicts.[134] However, with violent and non-violent conflicts in the Balkans, Ukraine, Cyprus, and the Middle East and North Africa (MENA) region, amongst others, conflict resolution, including assistance to transitional justice and peace mediation, has remained a significant field of action and objective for European security. This is especially so for the EU as part of its ambition to become a global security actor. European States self-identify as 'normative

[129] UNSC 'Letter from the Chargé d'affaires a.i. of the Permanent Mission of Germany to the United Nations addressed to the President of the Security Council' (10 December 2015) UN Doc S/2015/946.

[130] eg Thomas Franck, 'Who Killed Art 2(4)? Or: Changing Norms Governing the Use of Force by States' (1970) 64 AJIL 809.

[131] Carrie McDougall, 'The Other Enemy: Transnational Terrorists, Armed Attacks, and Armed Conflicts' in Leila Nadya Sadat (ed), *Seeking Accountability for the Unlawful Use of Force* (CUP 2018) 235.

[132] See, for similar comments, Samuel Moyn, 'The Road to Hell' (2020) 4 American Affairs 149.

[133] See *R (Campaign Against Arms Trade) v Secretary of State for International Trade* [2019] EWCA Civ 1020.

[134] See Véronique Dudouet, 'Anti-Terrorism Legislation: Impediments to Conflict Transformation' Berghof Policy Brief 02 (November 2011) <https://www.berghof-foundation.org/fileadmin/redaktion/Publications/Policy_Briefs/PolicyBrief02.pdf> accessed 14 May 2020.

powers'[135] in conflict resolution, as do the EU and the OSCE, promoting human security, compliance with international law, rule of law, transitional justice, local ownership, and inclusive conflict resolution processes and outcomes.[136] Sweden's and Norway's NSSs make particular reference to the Women, Peace and Security agenda and the inclusion of women in conflict resolution.[137] Germany's NSS emphasizes the significance of promoting respect for human rights in conflict States.[138]

This normative ambition is also evident in the laws, policies, and guidelines adopted by some European States in relation to conflict resolution, peace mediation, and peacebuilding.[139] Emphasizing the obligations of States under international law relevant to conflict resolution and transitions, these policy guidelines promote the participation of women, indigenous groups, or other historically excluded groups in official peace negotiations. Furthermore, in line with the 'thickening' of security discussed in Section B.1, there is a commitment in all NSSs to holistic and sustainable approaches to conflicts.[140] Recognizing 'the nexus between sustainable development, humanitarian action, [and] peace and security', the EU has also committed to ensuring that its security objectives are fully aligned with objectives in the fields of development policy, peacebuilding, and conflict prevention.[141]

Despite these positive developments, two problematic dynamics that characterize European States' role in (the international law of) global security are also evident in the field of conflict resolution. First, differences in their security approaches and priorities affect the coherence and complementarity of responses to armed conflicts in the neighbourhood. In Libya, different priorities and fragmented actions have undermined each

[135] On the concept of 'normative power', see Ian Manner, 'Normative Power Europe: A Contradiction in Terms?' (2002) 40 Journal of Common Market Studies 235.

[136] Council of the European Union, 'Concept on Strengthening EU Mediation and Dialogue Capacities' (10 November 2009) <http://www.eeas.europa.eu/archives/docs/cfsp/conflict_prevention/docs/concept_strengthening_eu_med_en.pdf> accessed 14 May 2020; EU, 'The EU's Policy Framework on Support to Transitional Justice' (2015) <http://eeas.europa.eu/archives/docs/top_stories/pdf/the_eus_policy_framework_on_support_to_transitional_justice.pdf> accessed 14 May 2020; OSCE, 'Guidance Note on Enhancing Gender-Responsive Mediation' (2013) <https://www.osce.org/secretariat/107533?download=true> accessed 14 May 2020; OSCE, 'Reference Guide on Mediation and Dialogue Facilitation' <https://www.osce.org/secretariat/126646?download=true> accessed 14 May 2020.

[137] Minister for Foreign Affairs, 'Statement of Government Policy' (13 February 2019) 3 (Sweden) <https://www.government.se/speeches/20192/02/the-governments-statement-of-foreign-policy-2019/> accessed 30 November 2020; Norway (n 40) 37.

[138] Germany (n 46) 48.

[139] eg Department for International Development (United Kingdom), 'Building Peaceful States and Societies: A DFID Practice Paper' (2010) (UK) <https://www.gov.uk/government/publications/building-peaceful-states-and-societies-a-dfid-practice-paper> accessed 14 May 2020; Federal Foreign Office (Germany)/Initiative Mediation Support Deutschland, 'Normativer Bezugsrahmen Und Völkerrechtliche Grundlagen Der Friedensmediation' (2017) <https://www.auswaertiges-amt.de/blob/1792316/10398297f5a3a14bdc2eb6efb56abc26/bezugsrahmen-data.pdf> accessed 14 May 2020; Bundesgesetz über Massnahmen zur zivilen Friedensförderung und Stärkung der Menschenrechte (Switzerland) (2003) <https://www.admin.ch/opc/de/classified-compilation/20021838/index.html> accessed 30 November 2020.

[140] eg Germany (n 46) 57–60.

[141] European Union 'New European Consensus on Development—"Our World, our Dignity, our Future"' (2017) <https://op.europa.eu/en/publication-detail/-/publication/5a95e892-ec76-11e8-b690-01aa75ed71a1> accessed 30 November 2020.

other. The French efforts to facilitate a peace agreement between the warring factions was not welcomed by Italy due to concerns that they might compromise its counter-migration operations.[142] Prioritizing counter-migration over conflict resolution, Italy established a bilateral Mission of Assistance and Support with the internationally recognized Libyan authorities for border and migration control.[143] The 2020 Berlin Conference on Libya had created some semblance of European unity on the conflict's resolution, whereby twelve States, including France, Germany, Italy, Russia, and Turkey, committed to ending external interference, implementing the arms embargo established by the UNSC, and promoting a Libyan-led and Libyan-owned political process.[144] This consensus, achieved ironically in the absence of the Libyan parties to the conflict,[145] seems to have collapsed within four months. Malta has withdrawn its military support to the EUNAVFOR MED Irini, an EU military operation established in the aftermath of the Conference,[146] and Turkey has reneged on its commitments by intervening in Libya in support of the Government of National Accord.[147] European responses in this case reveal how hard security priorities often clash with conflict resolution efforts that are part of the 'thickening' approach to security.

Secondly, practice tends to diverge from normative commitments at times and be, rather, driven by realpolitik. Transitional justice is an area where the clash between normative ambition and the pragmatic requirements of conflict resolution is most evident, particularly in relation to whether criminal accountability for conflict-related crimes can be negotiated away for the sake of a peace settlement. The inclusion of a blanket amnesty provision in the Minsk II Agreement, concluded under the auspices of the OSCE and the Normandy Quartet, is one example of the so-called peace versus justice dilemma.[148] In relation to the conflict in Eastern Ukraine, European States have refrained from military intervention and instead employed diplomatic efforts towards the peaceful resolution of the conflict while also adopting sanctions aiming to induce a settlement. It is within this context that the negotiations within the OSCE-led Trilateral Contact Group and the Normandy Quartet, namely Germany, France, Russia, and Ukraine, led to the adoption of the Minsk Agreement (Minsk I), followed by an

[142] Stefan Lehne, 'Is There Hope for EU Foreign Policy?' (Carnegie Endowment for International Peace, 2017) 7 <https://carnegieendowment.org/files/CP_322_Lehne_EU1.pdf> accessed 14 May 2020.

[143] See MIASIT (n 114).

[144] The Federal Government of Germany, 'The Berlin Conference on Libya: Conference Conclusions' (19 January 2020) <https://www.bundesregierung.de/breg-de/aktuelles/the-berlin-conference-on-libya-1713868> accessed 23 May 2020.

[145] Jeffrey Feltman, 'The Berlin Conference on Libya: Will Hypocrisy Undermine Results?' (*Brookings*, 21 January 2020) https://www.brookings.edu/blog/order-from-chaos/2020/01/21/the-berlin-conference-on-libya-will-hypocrisy-undermine-results/ accessed 23 May 2020.

[146] Council Decision (CFSP) 2020/472 of 31 March 2020 on a European Union military operation in the Mediterranean (EUNAVFOR MED IRINI) OJ L 101/4.

[147] Tarek Megerisi, 'It's Turkey's Libya Now' (*European Council on Foreign Relations*, 20 May 2020) <https://www.ecfr.eu/article/commentary_its_turkeys_libya_now> accessed 23 May 2020.

[148] On the 'peace versus justice' debate, see Mark Kersten, *Justice in Conflict: The Effects of the International Criminal Court's Interventions on Ending Wars and Building Peace* (OUP 2016) 2–5.

implementation agreement (Minsk II).[149] Under the latter, Ukraine undertook to '[e]nsure pardon and amnesty by enacting the law prohibiting the prosecution and punishment of persons in connection with the events that took place in certain areas of the Donetsk and Lugansk regions of Ukraine'.[150] The endorsement of the Agreement despite the promise of a seemingly blanket amnesty is at odds with the normative commitments of the OSCE and the European leads, Germany and France, to ensure criminal accountability for conflict-related crimes in transitions and with their interpretation of international law that amnesties for international crimes and serious violations of human rights are outlawed.[151] The Agreement was also endorsed by the UNSC without any caveat regarding the scope of the amnesty, although the representatives of two States expressed concern that those responsible for the MH17 attack might benefit from the amnesty.[152]

Overall, in conflict resolution, many European States, the EU, and the OSCE have led the normativization of the field through the promotion of international law and other transformative ambitions in transitions. The policy developments have been coupled with successful episodes of conflict resolution within Europe itself, the settlement of the dispute between Greece and North Macedonia regarding the latter's name being a notable example.[153] However, the tension between normative ambitions and realpolitik remains challenging for Europe's role as a crisis manager and global security provider.

D. Outlook

Europe's approach to global security is conditioned by the 'European Question', namely who and what is 'Europe'?[154] Two main consequences follow from this Euro-centric orientation. First, the securitization of migration and of Europe's relations with its neighbours has expanded the reach of European security governance and its accompanying practices in the European neighbourhood. As such, Europe has emerged as a regional (in)security provider. However, and secondly, reality falls short of Europe's

[149] Protocol on the Results of Consultations of the Trilateral Contact Group (Minsk Agreement) (5 September 2014) <https://peacemaker.un.org/UA-ceasefire-2014> accessed 14 May 2020; Package of Measures for the Implementation of the Minsk Agreements (12 February 2015) <https://peacemaker.un.org/ukraine-minsk-implementation15> accessed 14 May 2020.

[150] Package of Measures for the Implementation of the Minsk Agreements (n 149) art 5.

[151] See eg 'Normativer Bezugsrahmen Und Völkerrechtliche Grundlagen Der Friedensmediation' (n 139) 8.

[152] UNSC Res 2205 (2015) para 1. See also UNSC 'Press Release' (17 February 2015) UN Doc SC/11785 <https://www.un.org/press/en/2015/sc11785.doc.htm> accessed 14 May 2020.

[153] Final Agreement for the Settlement of the Differences as Described in the United Nations Security Council Resolution 817 (1993) and 845 (1993), the Termination of the Interim Accord of 1995, and the Establishment of a Strategic Partnership between the Parties (Greece, FYROM) art 4(d) <https://www.un.org/pga/73/wp-content/uploads/sites/53/2019/02/14-February-Letter-dated-14-February-2019.pdf> accessed 30 November 2020.

[154] For the 'European Question' see de Genova (n 68) 41–2.

ambition of becoming a *global* security actor in the geopolitical security axis, along with the US and China. Almost all NSSs identify the emergence of multipolarity, the retreat of the US in the global order, and the return of geopolitics as security challenges.[155] But, as the selection of our case studies and geographic focus of the European States' practices in these fields attest, Europe's immediate security objectives and practices have been largely confined to its neighbourhood.

Our analysis reveals that, to meet its ambitions in becoming a global security provider, Europe needs to confront two challenges that do not lend themselves to straightforward solutions. First, despite significant multilateralization and Europeanization, national perspectives remain decisive in the field of security and pose an obstacle to coherent policies and actions. As established in Section B, European NSSs stand for normative convergence on the concept of security and tend to identify security threats in a similar way. However, varying national security priorities lead to contradictory practices and stall legal and policy developments. The way forward does not necessarily rely on complete harmony, and the first required step seems to be the acknowledgement of the diversity amongst European States' security priorities.

Secondly, Europe is in need of an urgent reflection on its position vis-à-vis international law and 'global order'. As discussed in Section B.1, European NSSs increasingly refer to human rights norms, the rule of law, and development in and beyond Europe. However, as their sphere of action expands and they face the demands of realpolitik, European States depart from international law. Although in some respects the normative sphere of global security governance has expanded, in certain areas like migration and *jus ad bellum* the relevant norms of international law have been eroded instead. The practice on the ground, at least in the two case studies examined here, reveals that the security of the (European) State eventually supersedes human security, turning a blind eye to the international legal norms hindering the realization of its objectives.

This dilemma is further deepened by Europe's often unreflective defence of the 'rules-based global order'. Many of the NSSs conceptualize the increasing global contestation of the prevailing international and European order as a major security threat for the short and medium term. While upholding international law is a virtue in many respects, the contestation of existing international law and institutional architecture provides also an opportunity to establish a legal and policy framework that is truly conducive to sustainable security for all. Missing this opportunity would pave the way for further insecurity in, at the borders of, and beyond Europe.

Acknowledgements

We are grateful to Tom Western and Robin Geiß for thoughtful comments and suggestions on earlier drafts of this chapter. Many thanks are also due to Markos Karavias for insightful comments on Section C.1. All errors remain our own.

155 eg Spain (n 40) 31; Germany (n 46) 3; Belgium (n 56) 24.

CHAPTER 48

THE GLOBAL SOUTH AND THE LAW AND GOVERNANCE OF GLOBAL SECURITY

Towards a Scholarship on the Global Ecology of Insecurities

ALEJANDRO RODILES

A. Introduction

CONVENTIONAL international security has centred on inter-State conflict, especially wars and the nuclear menace. During the Cold War this story was practically circumscribed to the two superpowers which determined the bipolar security system with their respective spheres of influence: armed conflicts in the Third World were mostly viewed through the lenses of so-called 'proxy wars'. The Third World was for a long time relegated to a marginal role within 'both academic and policy debates about international security'.[1]

Today, the Global South can no longer be reduced to that peripheral role, because many States from the South have turned into both, major contributors to world security and major sources of transnational insecurity.[2] Commentators highlight the predominant

[1] Rita Abrahamsen/Adam Sandor, 'The Global South and International Security' in Alexandra Gheciu/William C Wohlforth (eds), *The Oxford Handbook of International Security* (OUP 2018). As mentioned by these authors, this was already criticized by Joseph S Nye/Sean M Lynn-Jones, 'International Security Studies: Report on a Conference on the State of the Field' (1988) 12 International Security 5, quoted in Abrahamsen/Sandor ibid 382.

[2] ibid 388–93.

role of Ethiopia and Bangladesh as troop contributing countries (TCC) to UN peacebuilding and peacekeeping operations,[3] as well as the growth in number and significance of regional and sub-regional alliances.[4] Less commented upon is that in a constantly changing global political environment, certain States from the South occupy a pivotal position when it comes to addressing specific security crises; be it due to their regional leadership or because they are otherwise regarded as indispensable brokers in highly complex political and cultural constellations.[5] In terms of insecurity, the South is no longer primarily regarded as a bloody theatre of major power confrontation, but as a source of insecurity in and of itself. Political instability, institutional weakness, and other endemic problems of some of these States have turned into primary security concerns at the global level: the ties between so-called fragile and failed States with terrorism, like in Afghanistan or Yemen, piracy off the Horn of Africa, transnational organized crime in some States of Latin America, and protracted internal conflicts, like Syria, are some of the most acute examples. Thus, the 'rise of the South' can be considered part and parcel of the changing security landscape of the post-Cold War era, which is being replaced by an interdependent and complex global ecology of insecurities where the separation between 'first', 'second', and 'third' worlds makes little to no sense.

However, the Global South should not be regarded as the avatar of the Third World in a globalized space. If the 'Global South' moniker is to make any sense, it is in that it makes clear that our diagnoses (of global security) should not be 'driven by the confident hubris of teleologies that extract the future seamlessly from the past', and that therefore our models (of law and governance) should be 'more attuned at the same time to the intricacies, ambiguities, and paradoxes of the relations between actions and their consequences, and intentions and chance contingencies that sometimes undo them'.[6] In the present context, these 'models' should be understood as the academic endeavours to explain the practices of rule that are emerging within global security, which are very different from those of classical international security law. Therefore, in Sections B and C, some of the evolving contours of the law and governance of global security will be addressed. As will be argued, there is a growing reliance on ad hoc arrangements which contribute to the decentralization and deformalization of the classical international

[3] The top-ten TCC are all from the Global South, provided China is considered part of it; United Nations Peacekeeping, 'Monthly Summary of Military and Police Contribution to United Nations Operations' (October 2019) <https://peacekeeping.un.org/sites/default/files/msr_october_2019.pdf> accessed 18 February 2020.

[4] Mark Webber, 'Security Governance' in James Sperling (ed), *Handbook of Governance and Security* (Edward Elgar 2014) 29–31, as well as the various chapters of part III of that volume on 'Regional Security Governance'; Emil J Kirchner/Roberto Domínguez (eds), *The Security Governance of Regional Organizations* (Routledge 2011).

[5] This is illustrated by the Turkish-led Group of Friends of Mediation, which consists of fifty-two UN Member States, many from the South, and promotes the use of mediation in the settlement of disputes, conflict prevention, and resolution; 'Group of Friends of Mediation' (*UN Peacemakers*) <https://peacemaker.un.org/friendsofmediation> accessed 30 November 2020.

[6] David Scott, *Conscripts of Modernity: The Tragedy of Colonial Enlightenment* (Duke UP 2004) 210, quoted in Russell West-Pavlov, 'Toward the Global South: Concept or Chimera, Paradigm or Panacea?' in Russell West-Pavlov (ed), *The Global South and Literature* (CUP 2018) 13.

security architecture centred on treaties and international institutions, most importantly the UN Charter and the UN Security Council (UNSC) (Section B). Also, the merger of security and development is undergoing profound transformations as shown by the ongoing UN peacebuilding review, and by dynamically evolving practices on counter-terrorism focused on resilience-building in communities and amongst ordinary people (Section C). Paradoxically, while these practices are, to a great extent, driven by the growing agency of the South (and of non-State actors), their consequences seem to partly curtail this agency, although in new and uncertain ways. If 'lawfare' is understood as the strategic use of law by 'the weak' in order to reduce military and other asymmetries through formal principles like sovereign equality,[7] then the deformalization and decentralization of international security law signals a retreat of lawfare which affects those who lack the resources for inserting themselves into the multiple nodes of informal networked governance. The concluding section refers to a few studies that trace the trajectories of globally informed and locally applied security practices, paying attention to the aforementioned paradox. It makes the case that this line of research is of the utmost importance for those in the South and North, West and powerful Rest (China and Russia, for example), concerned with the law and governance of today's global ecology of insecurities.

B. Global Security and the Rising South: Decentralization, Deformalization, and the Retreat of Lawfare

1. From International to Global Security

The marginalization of the Third World in post-war international security studies—a mentality which is still present in many forms today—is actually consistent with a major strand in international relations (IR) theory: systems theory. According to this theory, certain units of the system matter more than others when trying to determine the structure and functioning of the system itself. Applied to international security, the role of nuclear powers and UNSC Permanent Members (P5) is not only more important per se, but also in relation to its explanatory function in how the whole system works.[8] While

[7] This broader meaning, which does not limit itself to legal tactics in conflict, but which reflects a general disdain for reliance on international law by 'the weak', including the strategic use of 'international fora, judicial processes, and terrorism', has been articulated in the US DoD, 'National Defense Strategy of the United States of America' (March 2005) 5 <https://www.hsdl.org/?abstract&did=452255> accessed 18 February 2020. On the various usages of the term: Orde F Kittrie, *Lawfare: Law as a Weapon of War* (OUP 2016).

[8] Most clearly, Kenneth N Waltz, *Theory of International Politics* (McGraw-Hill 1979) 73; on how the agent–structure debate in IR systems theory should instead be understood as a mutually defining rela-

this approach still has some explanatory force in relation to certain instances of the international security system—for example, the composition and functioning of the UNSC which, by definition, centres around the P5[9]—it is hardly sustainable in general terms nowadays. As pointed out by Abrahamsen and Sandor, the fixation on great powers does not only denote intrinsic problems because of its 'ethnocentric biases',[10] it has also come under strain in a post-Cold War setting, where security is increasingly affected and shaped by other actors, State and non-State alike.[11] Others have noted that in a new security environment characterized by complex interdependence, systems theory is seriously questioned, both in its 'internal logics and its wider stabilizing capacity'.[12]

These shifting tendencies in IR theory are emblematic for the move from international to global security that this volume addresses. Nobody can question the existence of military powers (above all, the US), as well as of States with considerably more leverage than others. And it is also true that the latter still tend to be mainly located below the 'Brandt line'—with the great exception of China.[13] These differences notwithstanding, accelerated globalization has led to an increasing interdependence in matters ranging from the economy to climate change to pandemics. 'Complex interdependence' has only enhanced over the decades since it was articulated by Robert Keohane and Joseph S Nye in the late 1970s,[14] and the security field is one of its clearest manifestations. Today, this has become a commonplace across the UN,[15] other international organizations,[16] and within national security establishments.[17]

tion, Bear F Braumoeller, *The Great Powers and the International System—Systemic Theory in Empirical Perspective* (CUP 2013).

[9] Even here, coalitions and networks, as well as the G20, have augmented the role of the UNSC and transformed the latter into a flexible platform determined by relations that reach beyond its core.

[10] Abrahamsen/Sandor (n 1) 382. [11] ibid 386–7.

[12] Philip G Cerny, *Rethinking World Politics—A Theory of Transnational Neopluralism* (OUP 2010) 217–20.

[13] 'The line' dividing the developed North from the developing South (excluding Australia and New Zealand) goes back to the Brandt Report, called after former German Chancellor Willy Brandt, who chaired from 1977 to 1980 the Independent Commission for International Development: Independent Commission on International Development Issues, *North–South: A Programme for Survival—The Report of the Independent Commission on International Development Issues* (Pan Books 1980).

[14] Robert O Keohane/Joseph S Nye, *Power and Interdependence: World Politics in Transition* (Little, Brown and Company 1977).

[15] UNGA 'Report of the Secretary-General: Fulfilling the Promise of Globalization: Advancing Sustainable Development in an Interconnected World' (8 August 2017) UN Doc A/72/301; UNGA Res 74/228 (19 December 2019); UN Secretary-General Antonio Guterres, 'Remarks' (UNSC Open Debate on Peace and Security in Africa: Strengthening Peacekeeping Operations in Africa, 20 November 2018) <https://www.un.org/sg/en/content/sg/statement/2018-11-20/secretary-generals-remarks-security-council-open-debate-peace-and> accessed 18 February 2020.

[16] NATO's Secretary-General Lord Robertson, 'Speech: Security and Interdependence' (French Institute for International Relations, 4 November 1999) <https://www.nato.int/cps/en/natohq/opinions_27506.htm?selectedLocale=en> accessed 18 February 2020.

[17] The White House, 'National Security Strategy of the United States of America' (December 2017) 7 <https://www.whitehouse.gov/wp-content/uploads/2017/12/NSS-Final-12-18-2017-0905.pdf> accessed 18 February 2020; UK Government, 'National Security Strategy and Strategic Defence and Security Review 2015' (November 2015) Cm 9161 <https://assets.publishing.service.gov.uk/government/uploads/system/uploads/attachment_data/file/555607/2015_Strategic_Defence_and_Security_Review.pdf> accessed 18 February 2020; The State Council Information Office of the People's Republic of China,

2. Non-Polarity and Global Security *à la carte*

This tectonic shift is probably best captured by the paradigm of 'non-polarity', as explained by Richard Haass.[18] Non-polarity not only means the augment of the relative strength of several States from the South, like the BRICS, the diminishing strength of some of the former unquestionable Western powers, like the European permanent members of the UNSC,[19] and eventually the loss of dominance of the still most powerful State, the US. That would fit better with the label of 'multipolarity', which stands for a different order from the bipolar system and the unipolar moment, but which still reflects a more or less stable redistribution of power, augmented only by a few. As Haass argues, the multipolar representation does not pay sufficient attention to the significance of 'medium powers', as the growth of the 'Gs' demonstrate, which goes beyond the 20, given the different invitees to each of these summits. More importantly, non-polarity also stands for continuously shifting power constellations in international affairs. A global (dis)order without a centre of gravity, but with several nodes connecting varying actors (State and non-State alike) according to their current strength on the particular issues at hand. This strength should not be reduced to military might, which is more measurable and steadier; it crucially includes political and cultural 'relevance'.[20] Thus, contemporary global security has turned, by necessity, more context-sensitive, and accordingly many States from the South have become 'indispensable nations'[21] for solving this or that crisis, and, on a more permanent basis, for dealing efficiently with long-term security challenges, like terrorism, transnational crime, and the proliferation of weapons of mass destruction (WMD).

Continuously shifting power constellations driven not exclusively by military might but also by political and cultural relevance, translate into the necessity to address global security concerns through flexible mechanisms that 'augment' the security architecture centred on the UN and the UNSC in particular.[22] Proof of this is the mushrooming, most clearly after 9/11, of regional and sub-regional alliances, global coalitions of the

'China's National Defense in the New Era 2019' (July 2019) 2, 4 <http://www.xinhuanet.com/english/2019-07/24/c_138253389.htm> accessed 18 February 2020.

[18] Richard N Haass, *A World in Disarray—American Foreign Policy and the Crisis of the Old Order* (Penguin Press 2017) 201–5.

[19] UNSC reform is strictly related to the rising South; on non-polarity and the UN Security Council: Alejandro Rodiles, 'Non-Permanent Members of the United Nations Security Council and the Promotion of the International Rule of Law' (2013) 5 Göttingen Journal of International Law 333, 338–9.

[20] Haass (n 18) 203–5.

[21] Borrowing the expression from Madeleine Albright: Matt Lauer, Interview with United States Secretary of State Madeleine K Albright (NBC-TV 'The Today Show', New York, 19 February 1998) <https://1997-2001.state.gov/statements/1998/980219a.html> accessed 18 February 2020.

[22] In this sense, The White House, 'The National Security Strategy of the United States of America' (September 2002) preface: 'Coalitions of the willing can augment these permanent institutions' <https://2009-2017.state.gov/documents/organization/63562.pdf> accessed 18 February 2020.

willing, and networks on a variety of security concerns.[23] These coalitions are usually led by powerful States, and the US has so far been the principal nation in assembling and shaping them. At the same time, however, they are about bringing together relevant players in a selective, efficiency-driven, and purpose-oriented fashion. This '*à la carte* multilateralism'[24] or 'coalition of the willing approach'[25] certainly reproduces old hierarchies, but is also driven by non-polarity and the need to work with the 'rising South'—as well as with powerful non-State actors (just think of how meaningless efforts would be to combat terrorist propaganda online without the active involvement of Facebook, Twitter, and Google).[26] Moreover, coalition-building is not owned by the West; it has turned into a normal way of security cooperation in today's world. For instance, amongst the five main cooperation areas of the BRICS, security stands out with a strong focus on terrorism and transnational crime, and meetings of the national security advisers of the five countries (NSA) have been routinized. India, Brazil and South Africa, on their part, have created IBSAMAR, a South–South navy coalition which engages in trilateral naval, aircraft, and special forces exercises to foster military interoperability between the three nations.[27]

3. Decentralization, Deformalization, and the South

Two important and interrelated questions arise from this contemporary global security landscape where the South is more present than ever before: what are the consequences of *à la carte* security multilateralism (or 'global security by posse'[28]) for international law and for the Global South? The short answer to the first comes in the form of two

[23] Within Harvard Law School's Program on International Law and Armed Conflict (PILAC), the project 'international counter-terrorism efforts' makes a mapping exercise on the international institutions (universal, regional and sub-regional; formal and informal) involved in counter-terrorism work, identifying at least seventy 'efforts': 'International Counter-terrorism Efforts' (*HLS PILAC*) <https://pilac.law.harvard.edu/international-counterterrorism-efforts-index#international-counterterrorism-efforts-welcome> accessed 18 February 2020.

[24] Haass (n 18) 201–5.

[25] Alejandro Rodiles, *Coalitions of the Willing and International Law—The Interplay between Formality and Informality* (CUP 2018).

[26] The Global Internet Forum to Counter Terrorism (GIFCT) is a good example of how governments, in this case led by the United Kingdom (UK), coalesce with the tech industry and with networks of the former (such as *tech against terrorism*) to address the challenges posed by online terrorist propaganda and online recruitment of terrorists, most of all by ISIL/Da'esh. On the role of both initiatives in shaping global security law: Alejandro Rodiles/Gavin Sullivan, 'Global Security Assemblages: International Counter-terrorism Law in Motion' (forthcoming, on file with the author).

[27] Monica Hirst/Maria Regina Soares de Lima, 'Rethinking Global and Domestic Challenges in Brazilian Foreign Policy' in Jorge I Domínguez/Ana Covarrubias (eds), *Routledge Handbook of Latin America in the World* (Routledge 2015) 148.

[28] Rodiles (n 25) ch 4.

'Ds': decentralization and deformalization. The two Ds, for their part, show that the South can hardly win from such an approach.

The proliferation of informal global security mechanisms decentralizes the international security architecture built after the Second World War, which is mutating into a moving engineering craft. This move from a few treaty-based organs to a regime complex of formal and informal bodies gives rise to an emerging *law and governance of global security*. The emphasis is no longer on pre-established legal processes leading to valid outcomes, such as resolutions and treaties, but on continuous consultations which flow into an ongoing management of security crises. As noted by Haass, the premium is now on dexterity, not on predictability. Haass argues that consultations are likely to take place in many settings, informal and formal, bilateral and multilateral, general and ad hoc, because 'many issues are not sufficiently ripe (and may never get there) for negotiations to succeed'. He concludes that '[c]onsultations that aim to affect the actions of other governments and their leaders are likely to matter more than negotiations that aim to solve problems'.[29] Continuous consultations involve more actors, including from the Global South. 'Indispensable nations', as argued above, emerge on demand according to the issues at hand. One might think then that the law and governance of global security contributes to new forms of hybrid collective security, combining the UN Charter system with informal arrangements, thus leading to an expansion of the inner circles of power. An old dream of diplomatic elites in the South may finally come true: perhaps UNSC reform is not that important anymore, given the G20 and the growing web of coalitions on which the UNSC has to rely, and which are well-represented by States below the Brandt line.

But the elites from the Global South should be careful what they wish for. This expansion of decision-making sites is not intended to broaden participation. Quite to the contrary, it operates on a highly selective basis, and because it is spurred mainly by informal mechanisms, it is opaque as opposed to the selectivity of the UNSC, which is rules-based, in the end.[30] This apparent legalistic reasoning may sound outdated for the most powerful in the South,[31] who can bet more easily on dexterity due to their manifold resources. But for the less powerful as well as for many middle powers which rely on a thin version of the international rule of law, this game may prove to be self-defeating, a sort of self-inflected *retreat of lawfare*.

[29] Haass (n 18) 253, 288.

[30] Alejandro Rodiles, 'What Kind of Rule of Law Should Elected Members Promote?' in Nico Schrijver/Niels M Blokker (eds), *Elected Members of the Security Council: Lame Ducks or Key Players?* (Brill Nijhoff 2020) 196. Already making the case that '[f]or most states, participation in this mode [of continuous consultation; AR] is far less effective than in classical multilateralism', mainly because it pushes further the decay of state consent-based international law: Nico Krisch, 'The Decay of Consent: International Law in an Age of Global Public Goods' (2014) 108 AJIL 1, 33.

[31] Although, they too have a lot to lose from retreating from the 'culture of formalism': Rodiles (n 25) 83–8.

C. The South's Global Insecurities and the New Security–Development Paradigm

1. Protection of Global Public Goods in a Networked Order

The obsoleteness of the separation between 'different worlds', according to their economic development status, is nowhere else more pronounced as in the conception of a 'networked international order',[32] where everything is connected through multiple nodes. While there are stronger hubs and those States and other actors with the power to be linked to several nodes at the same time, in the end, the weakest link can cause major disturbances to the entire network. As observed in international security studies[33] and global public goods literature,[34] security threats, ranging from terrorism to pandemics, tend to pose the most severe weakest-link problems, where a single action by a single actor can have catastrophic consequences at the global level. Hence, such problems can only be avoided by cooperative efforts of all. This shows, again, that States from the South, including the weakest, cannot be left out of the game. But the emphasis starts shifting here to the negative side of the coin: because of the global interconnectivity of these States, endemic problems related to their structural deficiencies tend to have repercussions far beyond their borders.

This story is not new. It is the *Leitmotiv* of the well-known merger between security and development, or the securitization of development.[35] This fusion was already ingrained in post-Second World War developmental thinking, as explained by Arturo Escobar in relation to the Truman doctrine,[36] it gained ground with the shifting reference-object of security from States to individuals, namely with the consolidation of the 'human security' agenda in the course of the 1990s,[37] and it has been pushed further after 9/11.[38]

[32] Anne-Marie Slaughter, *A New World Order* (Princeton UP 2004); Anne-Marie Slaughter, *The Chessboard and the Web* (Yale UP 2017).

[33] eg Stewart Patrick, *Weak Links—Fragile States, Global Threats, and International Security* (OUP 2011).

[34] Daniel Bondansky, 'What's in a Concept? Global Public Goods, International Law, and Legitimacy' (2012) 23 EJIL 651, 660–3 (referring to nuclear security, global health, maritime security, *inter alia*).

[35] For a *locus classicus*: Mark Duffield, *Global Governance and the New Wars: The Merging of Development and Security* (Zed Books 2001); Mark Duffield, *Development, Security and Unending War—Governing the World of Peoples* (Polity Press 2007).

[36] Arturo Escobar, *Encountering Development: The Making and Unmaking of the Third World* (2nd edn, Princeton UP 2012) 3.

[37] The United Nations Development Programme (UNDP) 1994 Report is considered as the triumphant moment of the human security agenda, UNDP, *Human Development Report* (OUP 1994) 22–46.

[38] Emblematic in this respect is the US NSS 2002 (n 22) 1–2: 'The great struggle is over (…) America is now threatened less by conquering states than we are by failing ones.' And then it mentions the path

The basic idea is that through the reduction of poverty, the betterment of life conditions, and the improvement of institutional capabilities, risks of instability, violence, and State failure can be mitigated. But beyond the purpose of reducing violence in the South, the ultimate goal is to prevent the spillover of insecurities from these places of 'limited statehood'[39] to the rest of the world, through transnational organized crime, terrorist networks, and in some cases where it is regarded as a national security threat, also migration.[40] In accordance with this logic, developing the poorer South has entered the security agenda, both of major Western powers as well as of international organizations.

In the former case, it is worth recalling that during the Reagan administration, the US promoted institution-building programmes in Latin America, which focused on the administration of the justice system.[41] This development work was part and parcel of a major US security concern to fight the growing illicit narcotics business. Rule of law assistance of this kind has morphed too easily at times into pure 'law and order promotion', fuelling a failed war on drugs in several States of Latin America, most clearly in Colombia and Mexico, but also in Brazil and large parts of Central America.[42] By the 1990s, State-building had become a crucial effort of US foreign aid policy.[43] Particularly in post-conflict scenarios, it was conceived and deployed as an antidote to State weakness, so that States from the South 'can exercise a monopoly of the legitimate use of violence within their territories',[44] and take that force away from non-State actors.

Within the UN system, there are two salient conceptual and operative frames which have materialized this merger: security sector reform (SSR) and human security. While both are interrelated, especially in the goal of strengthening or building rule of law institutions which can improve the situation of ordinary people, the former is mostly present in post-conflict scenarios. Thus, it has become a standard component of multidimensional UN peacebuilding operations.[45]

ahead: 'To achieve these goals, the United States will: (…) expand the circle of development by opening societies and building the infrastructure of democracy.'

[39] On this notion: Tanja A Börzel et al, 'Governance in Areas of Limited Statehood: Conceptual Clarifications and Major Contributions of the Handbook' in Anke Draude et al (eds), *The Oxford Handbook of Governance and Limited Statehood* (OUP 2018).

[40] US NSS 2017 (n 17) 9–10; 51–2.

[41] Stephen Humphreys, *Theatre of the Rule of Law—Transnational Legal Intervention in Theory and Practice* (CUP 2012) 125.

[42] Alejandro Rodiles, 'Law and Violence in the Global South: The Legal Framing of Mexico's "Narco War"' (2018) 23 JCSL 269.

[43] Bruce Jones et al, *Power and Responsibility: Building International Order in an Era of Transnational Threats* (Brookings Institution Press 2009); for a critical appraisal: Humphreys (n 41) 149–55.

[44] David A Lake, 'Iraq: US Approaches to Statebuilding in the Twenty-First Century' in David Chandler/Timothy D Sisk (eds), *The Routledge Handbook of International Statebuilding* (Routledge 2013) 293.

[45] UNSC Res 2151 (2014).

2. Resilience as Response to Intervention Fatigue

This ambitious, security-driven, development policy has suffered a major setback in recent times, especially with the Iraq war of 2003 and the ongoing war in Afghanistan. The extreme difficulties encountered in successfully stabilizing these countries, according to liberal-democratic templates,[46] has bolstered long-standing doubts about the efficiency and legitimacy of State-building. In pragmatic terms, it has led to an intervention fatigue on behalf of Western States.[47] This fatigue is noticeable both in military and development interventions. In the first case, mention must be made to the unwillingness or inability of Western powers to intervene during the first years of the now almost decade-long Syrian civil war in order to end this humanitarian tragedy in the Middle East caused by a perverse mixture of local political insurgency, Cold War-style proxy conflict, and post-9/11 perpetual war on terror.[48] Perhaps more telling in regard to the relative retreat of Western military interventionism in the Global South, and particularly in Africa, is the growing number of ad hoc military coalitions of the willing that have emerged within the Common African Defence and Security Policy Framework.[49] Examples include the Regional Coalition Initiative against the Lord's Resistance Army (RCI-LRA), in which US troops have taken part alongside those of the Central African Republic, Democratic Republic of Congo and South Sudan, the Multinational Joint Task Force against Boko Haram (MJTF), composed of Benin, Cameroon, Chad, Niger, and Nigeria, and deployed in the Lake Chad basin, and the G5 Sahel Joint Force conformed by Burkina Faso, Chad, Mali, Mauritania, and Niger, which combats several armed groups in the Sahel region.[50]

As mentioned, intervention fatigue is also very present in relation to development work.[51] Intrusive State-building and some more invasive proposals of renewed trusteeships

[46] For Iraq: Lake (n 44) 296–301 (although making a distinction between a first (2003–2006) and a second (2006–2011) state-building period, and mentioning that the latter was at least partly successful); for Afghanistan: Péter Marton/Nik Hynek, '"Liberal" Statebuilding in Afghanistan' in Chandler/Sisk (n 44) 304–14.

[47] eg Stian Kjeksrud, 'The Future of UN Peacekeeping Operations' in Per M Norheim-Martinsen/Tore Nyhamar (eds), *International Military Operations in the 21st Century—Global Trends and the Future of Intervention* (Routledge 2015).

[48] It was not until 2014 that the US–UK coalition *Operation Inherent Resolve* started to actively confront ISIL/Da'esh in Syria, and not until 2017 that it targeted the government of Bashar Al-Assad; on the early unwillingness or incapacity of Western powers to confront the Syrian crisis: Marta Tawil Kuri, *Siria: Poder Regional, Legitimidad y Política Exterior 1996–2015* (El Colegio de México 2016) 40–2.

[49] AU, 'Solemn Declaration on a Common African Defence and Security Policy' (Sirte, 28 February 2004) <https://au.int/sites/default/files/documents/30849-doc-solemn_declaration_on_cadsp_0.pdf.> accessed 23 February 2020. This initiative complements the institutional security framework of the AU by providing a framework for ad hoc security cooperation mechanisms between AU members; Omar A Touray, 'The Common African Defence and Security Policy' (2005) 104 African Affairs 635.

[50] On these coalitions: Gustavo de Carvalho/Annette Leijenaar, 'Ad hoc Security Initiatives a Potential Force Multiplier for the AU' (*Institute for Security Studies*, 1 September 2017) <https://issafrica.org/iss-today/ad-hoc-security-initiatives-a-potential-force-multiplier-for-the-au> accessed 23 February 2020.

[51] Peter Beaumont, '"Alarming" Shortfall in Foreign Aid for World's Biggest Crises' (*The Guardian*, 16 July 2019) <https://www.theguardian.com/global-development/2019/jul/16/alarming-shortfall-foreign-aid-worlds-biggest-crises> accessed 23 February 2020.

for failing States,[52] are being replaced by the new paradigm of 'inclusive development'. This term is used because of its linkages to the 2030 Sustainable Development Agenda which establishes that '[s]ustainable development cannot be realized without peace and security; and peace and security will be at risk without sustainable development'.[53] The basic idea, namely that security presupposes the bettering of living conditions, remains, and it is arguably even reinforced by this new paradigm, since sustainability and human security are interrelated. The shifting paradigm rather consists of the underlying assumptions of what is required to achieve development. These no longer correspond to a State-centred view of improving, building, and reconstructing States and their institutions through the donor-recipient financial model and the reform of national laws and regulations. Instead, the real currency of new development work is resilience, that is, the promotion of capabilities of the underdeveloped to cope with underdevelopment.[54]

Therefore, work needs to be done directly with the affected locales. Building resilient communities, fostering resilience amongst ordinary people (youth, women, mothers, etc), and contributing to the construction of so-called 'positive resilience' between people at risk of turning into agents of (global) insecurity and their most proximate authorities (city governments, municipal authorities, local police forces, etc), are the new paths to development and, hence, to a less insecure world. Indeed, the disenchantment with the previous development model is a recurrent theme of critical resilience studies, which argue that the richer North became tired of placing resources in the hands of the (often corrupt) governmental elites of the poorer South who, most of the time, failed to deliver.[55] Resilience emerges from this donor fatigue, shifting the paradigms from donors to facilitators, from recipients to the vulnerable, from State-to-State aid and assistance to the promotion of community initiatives. Note that this implies that the new security providers are the very same agents of insecurity.

3. The New Paradigms of Security and Development (According to the 2030 Agenda)

This new approach to development and security is present both in transnational security initiatives, of which the evolution of the Mérida Initiative between Mexico and the US is a prime example,[56] as well as in documents and the day-to-day work of multilateral

[52] Stephen Krasner, 'Sharing Sovereignty: New Institutions for Collapsed and Failing States' (2004) 29 International Security 85.

[53] UNGA Res 70/1 (21 October 2015) para 35 (SDG 16).

[54] The literature on this concept is vast: David Chandler/Jon Coaffee, 'Introduction: Contested Paradigms of International Resilience' and Peter Rogers, 'The Etymology and Genealogy of a Contested Concept' in David Chandler/Jon Coaffee (eds), *The Routledge Handbook of International Resilience* (Routledge 2017).

[55] Most clearly on this, David Chandler, 'International Statebuilding and the Ideology of Resilience' (2013) 33 Politics 276.

[56] Rodiles (n 42).

organizations, especially since the adoption of the 2030 Sustainable Development Agenda in 2015. As endorsed by the heads of several international organizations, including the UN Secretary-General, during the World Humanitarian Summit of 2016:

> The 2030 Agenda places risk and vulnerability at its core. Managing crisis risks and reducing vulnerability is as much a humanitarian imperative to save lives more effectively as it is a development necessity to ensure progress towards achieving the Sustainable Development Goals (SDGs) for the more than 125 million people affected by humanitarian crises today. This is timely, given that the growing trend of repeated and protracted crises is likely to continue.[57]

New partnerships for development between the UN, the World Bank and others follow this template of risk management and resilience-building, in order to prevent, manage, and contain conflicts.[58] Most fundamentally, however, 'inclusive development and security' has been translated into 'sustaining peace':[59] the building block in the reconstruction of the UN peacebuilding architecture. This ongoing review has been endorsed by twin resolutions of the UN General Assembly (UNGA) and the UNSC,[60] and it is closely tied to the SDGs, in particular to SDG 16. Likewise, it is informed by proactive risk prevention, crisis management, and resilience, thus emphasizing the importance of engaging local stakeholders and civil society.[61]

As mentioned by the UN Secretary-General, a 'breakthrough in the twin resolutions' is the emphasis on conflict prevention.[62] Thus, sustaining peace contributes to a further blurring of the lines between the different phases (and operations) of the UN's efforts to maintain international peace and security. The enmeshment of peacemaking, peacekeeping, and peacebuilding is nothing new. Less commented upon, however, is that the contemporary collective security system is also increasingly infused by the 'inclusive development' rhetoric and practice. The UNSC not only explicitly reproduces the SDG-16 formula in the context of peacekeeping and peacebuilding,[63] it has made it part and parcel of its expansive counter-terrorism work. This goes from the call to Member States

[57] World Humanitarian Summit, 'Transcending Humanitarian-Development Divides, Changing People's Lives: From Delivering Aid to Ending Need' (Istanbul, 23 May 2016) <http://www.fao.org/fileadmin/user_upload/newsroom/docs/COMMITMENT.pdf> accessed 30 November 2020.

[58] 'UN–World Bank Joint Statement on Signing of New Framework to Build Resilience and Sustain Peace in Conflict Areas' (*The World Bank*, 22 April 2017) <https://www.worldbank.org/en/news/press-release/2017/04/22/un-world-bank-joint-statement-on-signing-of-new-framework-to-build-resilience-and-sustain-peace-in-conflict-areas> accessed 23 February 2020.

[59] The 'sustaining peace' notion goes back to the UNGA/UNSC 'Report of the Advisory Group of Experts on the Review of the Peacebuilding Architecture: Challenge of Sustaining Peace' (30 June 2015) UN Doc A/69/968-S/2015/490.

[60] UNGA Res 70/262 (27 April 2016); UNSC Res 2282 (2016); UNSC 'Statement by the President of the Security Council' (18 December 2018) UN Doc PRST/2018/20.

[61] See UNGA/UNSC 'Report of the Secretary-General: Peacebuilding and Sustaining Peace' (18 January 2018) UN Doc A/72/707-S/2018/43, 17–18.

[62] ibid 1.

[63] eg UNSC Res 2282 (2016).

to improve living conditions of those population sectors which are particularly vulnerable to be enrolled in terrorist organizations,[64] to Chapter VII resolutions on foreign terrorist fighters (FTF) and returning foreign terrorist fighters (RFTF):

> a comprehensive approach to the threat posed by foreign terrorist fighters requires addressing the conditions conducive to the spread of terrorism, including by (…) promoting (…) economic development, social cohesion and inclusiveness (…).[65]

The UNSC has endorsed the Madrid Guiding Principles on FTF of its Counter-Terrorism Committee (CTC),[66] which stress the need for inclusive development in order to address the conditions conducive to the spread of terrorism.[67] Moreover, the Madrid Principles clearly reflect the logic of proactive involvement through the building of resilience networks amongst those persons most at risk of turning into FTF and returning to their hometowns (in the North), the so-called RFTF.[68] Actually, it is in the day-to-day work of the CTC and its powerful body of experts, the Counter-Terrorism Executive Directorate (CTED), where this new face of development is most present, particularly in the mentioned realms of the fight against FTF and RFTF, as well as in the closely related field of countering violent extremism (CVE).[69] These fields reflect profound anxieties in the North about insecurities in the South, precisely because the latter circulate so easily today that the spatial categories of North and South are lifted by the global infrastructures of physical and digital communications.[70] Accordingly, the CTC has moved, from donor-recipient schemes of State-centred capacity-building and technical assistance in the national implementation of UNSC resolutions, to resilience-building strategies channelled through the direct involvement of local authorities, communities, and people, whereby the role of women and young people excels.[71] This happens through a complex amalgam of partnerships with coalitions and networks, like

[64] UNSC Res 2250 (2015) 2.

[65] UNSC Res 2396 (2017) 5.

[66] ibid 3.

[67] UNSC 'Guiding Principles on Foreign Terrorist Fighters' (23 December 2015) UN Doc S/2015/939, Annex II (Madrid Guiding Principles); UNSC '2018 Addendum to the 2015 Madrid Guiding Principles' (28 December 2018) UN Doc S/2018/1177, para 33.

[68] Madrid Guiding Principle (n 67) guiding principle 2.

[69] This should come as no surprise: the CTC, which basically endorses the work of CTED, has turned more and more into a body of Foucauldian disciplinary power: Isobel Roele, 'Disciplinary Power and the UN Security Council Counter Terrorism Committee' (2013) 19 JCSL 49.

[70] This not only implies that the 'global ecology of insecurities' (see Section D) is facilitated by infrastructures, but also that its scholarly treatment would benefit a lot from 'thinking infrastructurally', as suggested by Benedict Kingsbury, 'Infrastructure and InfraReg: On Rousing the International Law "Wizard of Is"' (2019) 8 Cambridge International Law Journal 171.

[71] Madrid Guiding Principle (n 67) guiding principles 8 and 9.

the Global Counter-terrorism Forum (GCTF) and the Abu-Dhabi based *Hedayah* Centre.[72]

4. Global Security Crises Management and the Perpetuation of Local Vulnerabilities

It is imperative to ask again how the new security and development merger affects the law on global security, in particular from the perspective of the South. And it is again not difficult to see how these evolutions accelerate the speed of the move from international security law to the law and governance of global security. The SDG-inspired concept of 'sustaining peace' is transforming the UN peacebuilding system into a multifaceted risk-management approach that could exponentially expand the scope of the security concept itself.[73] A concept of security which evolves too dynamically provides readily available grounds for UNSC elastic determinations under Article 39 UN Charter, a well-known problem which transcends legal questions of permissible interpretations via subsequent practice, posing serious legitimacy problems for the collective security system as a whole, not least due to the distinct vulnerability of the South in this regard.[74] 'Inclusive development' occupies a mounting role in the global counter-terrorism field, where the idea of building resilience amongst local authorities and ordinary people gains ground in the face of efficient terrorist propaganda and recruitment tactics. CVE has become one of the most prominent sub-fields of counter-terrorism work worldwide,[75] and it is mainly about preventing people from being turned into terrorists, especially in the form of RTFT. It is thus a preventative and proactive security practice, which operates under the authoritative umbrella of UN Charter Chapter VII, but in a continuously evolving governance mood that involves the youth, mothers, teachers, and preachers. Like in the case of the rising South, the main consequence of the globalization of the South's insecurities is less law and more governance. Moreover, it entails a tendency to perpetuate vulnerable life, here and there.[76]

[72] Rodiles/Sullivan (n 26).

[73] Ursula Schroeder, Chapter 3 in this *Handbook*.

[74] Arnulf Becker Lorca, 'Rules for the "Global War on Terror": Implying Consent and Presuming Conditions for Intervention' (2012) 45 NYU Journal of International Law and Politics 1, 35–44.

[75] This was heavily promoted by the Obama administration, Rodiles/Sullivan (n 26).

[76] Brad Evans/Julian Reid, *Resilient Life. The Art of Living Dangerously* (Polity Press 2014).

D. Conclusion: From Contagion to the Global Ecology of Insecurities (and some Notes on Further Readings)

The awareness of 'the contagion of instability'[77] internationalized the Third World's security predicament, opening the path to the merger of development and security. The securitization of development signified that the Third World as such became an object of security-driven intervention. Today, the situation is similar and dissimilar at the same time. Due to non-polarity, States from the South have become 'indispensable nations' in certain constellations, so that the very distinction between 'first', 'second', and 'third' worlds has lost its meaning: *the South has gone global*. This has led to flexible coalitions around those willing and able to secure global public goods, regardless of whether these partners are from the South or North, the West or the powerful Rest. From a legal perspective, the most important assessment is that these shifting loci of decision-making and cooperation contribute to the decentralization and deformalization of international security law. Less international law and more governance on global security can also be read as a retreat of lawfare, that is, the negative framing of reliance on international law by the less powerful.

The paradoxical global situation of the South is that while it has risen in economic, military, and populational terms, moving from the margins to the central circuits of the international security system, institutional instability and associated violence remain its security predicament. In a networked global (dis)order, complex interconnectedness has intensified to the point where the weakest node can destabilize the whole web. Therefore, the medical metaphor of 'contagion' falls short of capturing what is better described as today's *global ecology of insecurities*. Top-down intervention and State-centred donor-recipient schemes no longer work—if they ever did. Intervention fatigue is not restricted to legal and illegal uses of force in the South that cost too many lives and money to the North, it is also about the kind of development work that focused on longer-term State-building efforts.

The adaptability of the UN system and of certain national security communities to the contemporary global ecologies of insecurities has been amazing: the security and development merger continues now under the rationale of resilience (proper to ecological thinking, not surprisingly). Resilience-driven security and development has major implications for the actors and temporalities of intervention. The direct involvement of subnational and non-State actors is the new normal in trying to construct the conditions that may prevent or contain violence from spreading (mostly in the form of jihadist terrorism but increasingly so in that of transnational drug cartels). This is

[77] Mohammed Ayoob, *The Third World Security Predicament: State Making, Regional Conflict, and the International System* (Lynne Rienner Publishers 1995) 196.

sometimes praised as local ownership and the empowerment of ordinary people. But what may represent a partial triumph of those inside the Global South vis-à-vis their corrupt authorities, is also a case in point for *the securitization of everyday life*. Once education, community and family life, urban planning and public policy, are tied to global and transnational security discourses and initiatives, one can hardly speak about the end of intervention.

Perhaps, the most serious problem for the South is the temporal dimension that comes along with the new security and development paradigm. 'Sustaining peace' and 'resilience-building' have a strong managerial tone. Handling conflicts and coping with violence supersedes temporal categories of pre-conflict, conflict, and post-conflict. It is more about an ongoing administration of insecurities, and hence of blurring the lines between war and peace. The many situations of chronic violence in the Global South are the prime witness. Of course, these have many different causes, from State failure to global illegal markets to international legal regimes.[78] The new paradigm is merely a response to persistent insecurities. But in emphasizing risk management, it bears the risk of resignation to the security predicament of the Global South, which distinguishes itself from that of the Third World only (but crucially) in that it configures a global ecology of insecurities.

Ignoring this is tantamount to insisting on ethnocentric understandings (from the North) about security in an entwined landscape that makes meaningless the spatial and temporal categories construed by that very same ethnocentrism. Studies on the international law of global security, wherever situated, should refocus and take the techniques of governance within the ecology of insecurities seriously. There is no prescription for doing it, due to the rhizomorphic nature of this ecology and the evolving practices of rule. Examples that come to mind are the following.

Nathanael Tilahun Ali demonstrates the perils of proactive global security, concentrating on the perpetuating and silencing dynamics of experimentalist governance methods in counter-terrorism.[79] Gavin Sullivan explores the diachronic temporalities of UN sanctions which make legal assessments based on UN Charter law and UNSC practice insufficient.[80] He also makes the case that the global security apparatus is better understood through the lenses of assemblage thinking, an analytical tool that has the

[78] Such as the UN drug control conventions, which, through the establishment of a global prohibitionist-punitive paradigm, have favoured aggressive anti-crime strategies instead of public health approaches; on the legal regime and its clashes with human rights law: Richard Lines, *Drug Control and Human Rights in International Law* (CUP 2017); on the pernicious consequences of the international regime for the design of violence-conducive national anti-drugs and anti-crime policies in Mexico: Mónica Serrano, 'La Política Internacional de Control de Drogas: ¿Hacia una Nueva Estrategia?' in Günther Maihold/Stefan Jost (eds), *El Narcotráfico y su Combate: Sus efectos sobre las Relaciones Internacionales* (Korand Adenauer Stiftung 2014); on the political and legal difficulties to amend the conventions, María José Flores Ramírez, 'Análisis de una Reforma al Régimen Internacional de Control de Drogas y el Papel de México' (ITAM Thesis, 2019; on file with author).

[79] Nathanael Tilahun Ali, *Regulatory Counter-Terrorism: A Critical Appraisal of Proactive Global Governance* (Routledge 2018).

[80] Gavin Sullivan, *The Law of the List—UN Counter-terrorism Sanctions and the Politics of Global Security Law* (CUP 2020).

particular strength of unravelling the 'symbiotic co-functioning (...) of heterogeneous elements (...) that help to apprehend (rather than flatten) its variegated normative topology'.[81] This topology subsumes ordinary social practices into the assemblage of global security law.[82]

Writing from the theatres of postmodern violence driven by the highly lucrative narcotics business, Pablo Kalmanovitz,[83] Alejandro Roemer, and others[84] delve into the contradictory and at times even complicit relationship between the law of non-international armed conflict and the failed global war on drugs in Latin America—studies that owe much to Nathaniel Berman's emblematic piece on the legal construction of war.[85] Although not primarily concerned with security, Fleur Johns' recent work on how current developmental interventions are structured around the 'here and now' facilitated by big data, instead of making 'big plans for the future',[86] are crucial for a proper understanding of the new security and development merger. Helmut Aust's analysis of the 'secure city' shows that the placeholders of global security law have ceased to be States alone, and that models of crime prevention through 'built environments' and 'smart cities' are mimicked around the globe.[87] Zooming into the local life of the global security and development agenda, Luis Eslava and Lina Buchely illustrate the liminality of resilience and the perpetuation of insecurities in Cali,[88] a situation that not only replicates in Tijuana and Ciudad Juárez,[89] Cairo, and Marrakesh, but also in Brussels, London, and New York, and in every other place in the North, West, and powerful Rest, where a foreign terrorist fighter may eventually return.

[81] Gavin Sullivan, 'Transnational Legal Assemblages and Global Security: Topologies and Temporalities of the List' (2014) 5 Transnational Legal Theory 81, 91.

[82] Rodiles/Sullivan (n 26).

[83] Pablo Kalmanovitz, 'Entre el Deber de Proteger y la Necesidad Militar: Oscilaciones del Discurso Humanitario en Colombia, 1991–2016' (2018) 1 Latin American Law Review 33; Pablo Kalmanovitz, 'Ius Post Bellum and the Imperative to Supersede IHL' (2016) 110 AJIL Unbound 193.

[84] Alejandro Roemer, 'Entre la Guerra y la Paz: Un Estudio sobre la Instrumentalización Estratégica de la "Guerra contra el Narco"' (ITAM Thesis, 2018; on file with author); Rodiles (n 42).

[85] Nathaniel Berman, 'Privileging Combat? Contemporary Conflict and the Legal Construction of War' (2004) 43 Colombia Journal of Transnational Law 1.

[86] Fleur Johns, 'From Planning to Prototypes: New Ways of Seeing Like a State' (2019) 82 Modern Law Review 833. Connecting this approach to development in the age of the Internet of Things and big data with humanitarian work: Mark Duffield, *Post-Humanitarianism—Governing Precarity in the Digital World* (Polity Press 2019).

[87] Helmut Philipp Aust, *Das Recht der globalen Stadt* (Mohr Siebeck 2017) 325–62.

[88] Luis Eslava/Lina Buchely, 'Security and Development? A Story about Petty Crime, the Petty State and its Petty Law' (2018) 67 Revista de Estudios Sociales 40.

[89] Alejandro Rodiles, 'The Tensions Between Local Resilience-Building and Transnational Action: US–Mexican Cooperation in Crime Affected Communities in Northern Mexico, and What this Tells Us about Global Urban Governance' in Helmut Philipp Aust/Anél du Plessis (eds), *The Globalisation of Urban Governance: Legal Perspectives on Sustainable Development Goal 11* (Routledge 2019).

CHAPTER 49

INDIA

BS CHIMNI

A. Introduction

'SECURITY' is an essentially contested concept. Its meaning and scope have been debated in security studies for over five decades.[1] The terms 'national security' and 'global security' have been differently defined using statist, race, gender, and class lenses. 'National security' is also disaggregated into 'external' and 'internal' security.[2] External security involves protecting land, air, and sea borders, having an indigenous military production capacity, and possessing the means to deter enemy States and non-State actors. Internal security includes threats to nations' economic, environmental, societal, and political sectors.[3] The individuation of internal security has yielded the idea of 'human security', which is concerned not with weapons but rather 'with human life and dignity'.[4]

The concept of 'global security' has been defined by hegemonic States and powerful organs of international institutions such as the UN Security Council (UNSC). The intensified interdependence between nations in the era of accelerated globalization has also meant that national and global security can be undermined by developments in the world economy.[5] Indeed, for developing nations, enhancing national and global security today means, *inter alia*, the retrieval of critical policy space through a defence of economic sovereignty within a rules-based system in order to pursue an independent and self-reliant path of development so as to achieve for their people the goal of 'development as freedom'.

[1] For different standpoints: Columba Peoples/Nick Vaughan-Williams (eds), *Critical Security Studies: Critical Concepts in Military, Strategic and Security Studies* (Routledge 2012).

[2] Today internal security is considered as posing the foremost challenge for India: Kanti P Bajpai/Harsh V Pant, 'Introduction' in Kanti P Bajpai/Harsh V Pant (eds), *India's National Security: A Reader* (OUP 2013). On internal insurgencies: Shivaji Mukherjee, 'Insurgencies in India: Origins and Causes' in Sumit Ganguly et al (eds), *The Oxford Handbook of India's National Security* (OUP 2018).

[3] Barry Buzan et al, *Security: A New Framework for Analysis* (Lynne Rienner Publishers 1998) 3.

[4] UNDP, *Human Development Report 1994* (OUP 1994) 22.

[5] Jonathan Kirshner (ed), *Globalization and National Security* (Routledge 2006).

The approach of India, as any State, to national and global security is determined by its geography, history, nature, and stage of development.[6] A nation's approach is also shaped by notions of the self. Currently, the idea of a Hindu nation frames the worldview of the political dispensation.[7] Political Hinduism or Hindutva represents a form of hyper nationalism with implications for its minorities and oppressed classes. On the other hand, India interprets global security against the backdrop of the problems it encounters in the Asian region, which can be conceptualized as 'a single security region with several interconnected subregional clusters or complexes'.[8] The 1962 Chinese aggression and China's rapidly modernizing military have critically determined India's response to global security threats. But it is as part of the South Asian sub-region, a product of amongst other things the partition of British India, that India assigns meaning to global security threats. For example, India's commitment to the 'war against terror' focuses on State-sponsored terrorism emanating from Pakistan. Likewise, India's response to the global migration crisis is shaped by illegal migration from Bangladesh and inflows of refugees from Sri Lanka and Tibet. Beyond this, there are global security threats that are autonomous from particular national and regional interests that India grapples with, like climate change. These threats are perceived through the lens of a Third World nation.

In the backdrop of these cursory theoretical reflections on national and global security, the chapter proceeds as follows. Section B briefly reviews the general place of international law in India's conduct of international relations. It touches upon provisions of the Indian Constitution on international law and identifies the reasons why the potential of international law in realizing national security interests is yet to be tapped. Section C surveys India's response to critical areas of national and global security interests in the matrix of evolving international law. Section D draws a few salient conclusions.

B. Legal Framework: The Role of International Law

The legal framework which guides India's defence of national security interests is provided on the one hand by the UN Charter principles, as interpreted by the 1970 Friendly Relations Declaration,[9] and on the other hand by the Constitution of India.

[6] For current national and global security threats to India: Two recent books written by former foreign secretaries viz., Shivshankar Menon, *Choices: Inside the Making of India's Foreign Policy* (Allen Lane 2016); Shyam Saran, *How India Sees the World: Kautilya to the 21st Century* (Juggernaut Books 2017).

[7] Martha C Nussbaum, *The Clash Within: Democracy, Religious Violence, and India's Future* (Permanent Black 2007).

[8] Muthiah Alagappa, 'Preface' in Muthiah Alagappa (ed), *Asian Security Order: Instrumental and Normative Features* (Stanford UP 2003) xii.

[9] Charter of the United Nations 1 UNTS XVI (UN Charter); Declaration on Principles of International Law concerning Friendly Relations and Co-operation among States in accordance with the Charter of the United Nations, UNGA Res 2625(XXV) (24 October 1970).

India has, from its inception as an independent State, been firmly committed to the UN Charter principles, in particular sovereign equality of States, non-intervention, prohibition of use of force, and peaceful settlement of disputes. It is also a party to the principal UN conventions in the areas of peace, human rights, oceans, trade, and the environment.

India's Constitution embodies a progressive vision of India's role in the global order. Article 51 of the Directive Principles of State Policy (DPSP), which contains non-binding guidelines for the governance of the country, requires the State to 'promote international peace and security', 'maintain just and honorable relations between nations', 'foster respect for international law and treaty obligations in the dealings of organized peoples with one another' and 'encourage settlement of international disputes by arbitration'. The significance attached to the implementation of its international obligations is evident in Article 253 of the Constitution, titled 'Legislation for giving effect to international agreements', which empowers the Union Parliament to legislate on matters that are exclusively within the domain of individual States. It *inter alia* states:

> ... Parliament has power to make any law for the whole or any part of the territory of India for implementing any treaty, agreement or convention with any other country or countries or any decision made at any international conference, association or other body.

This provision has acquired a significance that the framers of the Constitution could not have foreseen. Since contemporary international agreements deal with many critical aspects of a nation's economic and social policies, Article 253 can significantly erode the powers of the constituent States of the Union. Thus, for instance, although agriculture is an area within the purview of constituent States, the Union can pass legislation to implement international agreements such as the WTO Agreement on Agriculture. The implication of this authorization must be determined in the context of '[a]ll legal and constitutional power to conduct foreign relations, declare war, and to sign and ratify treaties [being] with the [Union] Executive'.[10] Indian courts have also displayed a progressive vision of the role of international law. For instance, the Supreme Court has invoked international human rights law (IHRL) to constrain the actions of the State and expand the scope of fundamental rights under Part III of the Constitution.[11]

India recognizes that it 'has a stake in the norms and standards to be adopted by the global institutions'.[12] As a leader of the Third World in the first decades after independence, and today as an emerging power, India has always actively participated in the negotiations of international agreements. A US official who participated in the negotiation of the 123 Agreement with India, part of the Indo–US Civil Nuclear deal, observed that 'he had never had to explain, discuss and argue about text and language to the

[10] Menon (n 6) 194.

[11] BS Chimni, 'India' in Simon Chesterman et al (eds), *The Oxford Handbook of International Law in Asia and the Pacific* (OUP 2019).

[12] Saran (n 6) 287.

degree that he had done with the Indians'.[13] Overall, India seeks to be perceived as a good citizen in as much as it abides by foundational principles of international law, implements voluntarily undertaken obligations, and seeks changes only through peaceful means.

Yet political leaders, policymakers and international relations experts in India have rarely considered the role of international law in realizing national or global security interests. But compared to his successors, India's first Prime Minister Jawaharlal Nehru was more alert to the place of international law, in particular the role of the UN in the world order.[14] He was one of the key leaders of the Non-Aligned Movement (NAM), which routinely passed resolutions affirming the basic principles of the UN Charter. That said, even in recent times, India has proactively turned to the International Court of Justice (ICJ), such as in the *Jadhav* case, to protect its national interests.[15] Over the decades it has also attempted to further democratize the UN through, *inter alia*, expanding the membership of the UNSC.

Nonetheless, international law does not feature prominently in shaping India's foreign policy. To begin with, there is inadequate understanding of how the exponential expansion of the scope of international law in the era of accelerated globalization bears upon the framing and identification of national security interests. Thus, for instance, a lack of awareness exists regarding the constraints that IHRL imposes on State action. The government is often puzzled by the international community's critical response to India's actions when these disregard international norms; a recent example being the case of Rohingya refugees, whom India has sought to deport. The fragmented structure of decision-making on different international law issues such as trade, environment, human rights, which are dealt with by different ministries, also prevents a clear vision concerning international law's significance in the global order.[16] Furthermore, the Legal and Treaties Division of the Ministry of External Affairs, which advises the government on international law matters, is both understaffed and largely ignored on policy matters. Finally, international relations experts tend to ignore international law due to both lack of familiarity and the urge to protect their turf from cognate disciplines.[17] There is also the unexamined belief amongst policymakers that international law plays a peripheral role in international politics.

[13] Menon (n 6) 85.

[14] Generally, Jawaharlal Nehru, *India's Foreign Policy: Selected Speeches, September 1946-April 1961* (The Publications Division 1961).

[15] *Jadhav Case (India v Pakistan)* (Judgment) [2019] ICJ Rep 1. As has been noted, however, (eg, Christian Tomuschat, 'Article 36' in Andreas Zimmermann/Christian J Tams (eds), *The Statute of the International Court of Justice: A Commentary* (3rd edn, OUP 2019) MN 72) India also has one of the most complex and restrictive, in terms of reservations, optional clause declarations under Article 36(2) ICJ Statute: ICJ, 'Declarations recognizing the jurisdiction of the Court as compulsory: India' (27 September 2019) <https://www.icj-cij.org/en/declarations/in> accessed 23 March 2020.

[16] Tharoor analyses the MEA (Ministry of External Affairs) and speaks of 'administrative heterogeneity' which compounds the problems of an understaffed ministry, lack of specialization, which is also a closed shop: Shashi Tharoor, *Pax Indica: India and the World of the 21st Century* (Allen Lane 2012) 331–54.

[17] ibid.

C. Recent Developments and Contemporary Challenges

Any review of recent developments and challenges in India's engagement with international law and international organizations to realize national security goals amidst global security threats has to take into account a whole range of subjects: the bilateral relations with its South Asian neighbours; the strategic partnership with the US; India's approach to weapons of mass destruction (WMD); its maritime and water disputes; its support for the 'global war on terror'; its participation in, and defence of, the liberal economic order; its efforts to further global climate security; its position on refugee and migration issues; its contribution to UN peacekeeping; its attitude towards international Non-Governmental Organizations (NGOs); its coming-to-terms with cyberthreats; and its views on the Responsibility to Protect (R2P) doctrine.

1. India's Neighbourhood

Some of the most challenging aspects of India's national security interests relate to its neighbours, in particular to Pakistan's dogmatic and aggressive approach to Kashmir. India's legal position on Kashmir is clearly stated in a 1994 resolution of the Indian Parliament, which declared that '[t]he State of Jammu and Kashmir has been, is and shall be an integral part of India and any attempts to separate it from the rest of the country will be resisted by all necessary means.'[18] Other issues with Pakistan include the sharing of the river Indus, the conflict over Siachen and Sir Creek, Pakistan's official support of terrorists that have been persistently attacking India, and its failure to provide MFN (most favoured nation) status to Indian businesses and investors (which India granted to Pakistan in 1996).[19] It should be noted, however, that both States have taken steps to

[18] Indian Parliament, 'Parliament Resolution on Jammu and Kashmir' (22 February 1994) para (a) <http://www.satp.org/satporgtp/countries/india/document/papers/parliament_resolution_on_Jammu_and_Kashmir.htm> accessed 23 March 2020.

[19] Bajpai/Pant (n 2) 3. On the question of Pakistan's official support for terrorists, a former distinguished foreign secretary of India writes:

> Pakistan has been harboring, training, arming and otherwise assisting terrorist groups in its territory for carrying out terrorist activities not only in Jammu and Kashmir, but also in other parts of India. The links of these groups with Pakistan's military establishment, particularly its intelligence agency, have been established beyond doubt, through information revealed by visiting journalists, independent experts, people arrested while planning and executing terrorist activities and US investigating agencies.

Muchkund Dubey, *India's Foreign Policy: Coping with the Changing World* (Pearson 2013) 39; Menon (n 6) 89–120; Saran (n 6) 97; Siegfried O Wolf, 'Pakistan and State-Sponsored Terrorism in South Asia' in Paulo Casaca/Siegfried O Wolf (eds), *Terrorism Revisited: Islamism, Political Violence and State Sponsorship* (Springer 2017). On India–Pakistan bilateral relations: Ministry of External Affairs, Government of India, 'Bilateral Brief: India–Pakistan Relations' (25 September 2019) <http://www.mea.gov.in/Portal/ForeignRelation/Bilateral_Brief_pakistan.pdf> accessed 23 March 2020.

address some of these issues, for example through negotiations on Siachen and Sir Creek and the *Indus Waters Kishenganga Arbitration*.[20]

In so far as China is concerned, India has a long-standing border dispute with it. In 1993, the two countries signed the Agreement on the Maintenance of Peace and Tranquility along the Line of Actual Control in the India–China Border Areas, which 'formalized in an international treaty a bilateral commitment by India and China to maintain the status quo on the border'.[21] This was followed by the 1996 Agreement on Military Confidence-Building Measures. In 2005, the two nations signed an Agreement on the Political Parameters and Guiding Principles for the Settlement of the India–China Boundary Question.[22] Finally, in 2013 India and China signed an agreement on border defence cooperation.[23] While there have been some face-offs (as, for instance, in Doklam in 2017) the political leadership in both nations has put in place confidence-building measures as any conflict will be costly for each nation.[24]

With regard to Bangladesh, agreement has been reached on the exchange of certain enclaves. In accordance with the 1974 Land Boundary Agreement (and 2011 Protocol) 'erstwhile Bangladeshi enclaves in India and 111 erstwhile Indian enclaves in Bangladesh were physically transferred to the other country with effect from the midnight of 31 July 2015'.[25] There are, however, ongoing issues in relation to common rivers (fifty-six of them) and illegal migration.

2. Weapons of Mass Destruction

India is not a party to the 1996 Non-Proliferation Treaty (NPT) or the 1996 Comprehensive Nuclear-Test Ban Treaty (CTBT) as it considers these international agreements

[20] World Bank, 'Fact Sheet: The Indus Waters Treaty 1960 and the Role of the World Bank' (*The World Bank*, 11 June 2018) <http://www.worldbank.org/en/region/sar/brief/fact-sheet-the-indus-waters-treaty-1960-and-the-world-bank> accessed 23 March 2020.

[21] Menon (n 6) 26.

[22] Republic of India–People's Republic of China, 'Agreement on Political Parameters and Guiding Principles for the Settlement of the India–China Boundary Question' (11 April 2005) <https://www.mea.gov.in/bilateral-documents.htm?dtl/6534/Agreement+between+the+Government+of+the+Republic+of+India+and+the+Government+of+the+Peoples+Republic+of+China+on+the+Political+Parameters+and+Guiding+Principles+for+the+Settlement+of+the+IndiaChina+Bou> accessed 23 March 2020.

[23] Republic of India–People's Republic of China, 'Agreement on Border Defence Cooperation' (23 October 2013) <https://www.mea.gov.in/bilateral-documents.htm?dtl/22366/Agreement+between+the+Government+of+the+Republic+of+India+and+the+Government+of+the+Peoples+Republic+of+China+on+Border+Defence+Cooperation> accessed 23 March 2020.

[24] Manoj Joshi, 'The Wuhan Summit and the India–China Border Dispute' (June 2018) 62 ORF Special Report <https://www.orfonline.org/wp-content/uploads/2018/06/ORF_Special_Report_62_Wuhan.pdf> accessed 23 March 2020.

[25] Ministry of External Affairs, 'Exchange of Enclaves between India and Bangladesh' (20 November 2015) <https://www.mea.gov.in/press-releases.htm?dtl/26048/Exchange+of+enclaves+between+India+-and+Bangladesh> accessed 23 March 2020. For details: Ministry of External Affairs, 'India and Bangladesh Land Boundary Agreement' <https://mea.gov.in/Uploads/PublicationDocs/24529_LBA_MEA_Booklet_final.pdf> accessed 23 March 2020.

discriminatory. It has, however, been a consistent proponent of universal nuclear disarmament. This was *inter alia* evidenced in India's written submission before the ICJ in the advisory proceedings on the legality of the threat or use of nuclear weapons.[26] India argued that the 'prohibition of the use of a nuclear weapon in an armed conflict is an absolute one, compliance with which is not dependent on corresponding compliance by others but is a requisite in all circumstances'.[27] Subsequently, India carried out a nuclear test in 1998. Its position was correspondingly revised in so far as the production and manufacture of nuclear weapons is concerned. It is, however, committed to the 'no first use' principle.[28] Beyond this, India is a party to a range of conventions regulating chemical, biological, and nuclear weapons.[29] After carrying out a second peaceful nuclear explosion in 1998, India was confronted with a US sanctions regime despite the fact that 'nothing that India had done to build its own nuclear program or to test nuclear weapons flouted international law or India's commitment to others or its obligations under international law'.[30] To end its international isolation, in 2005 India entered into the 'New Framework for the US–India Defense Relationship', followed by the 2008 Indo–US Civil Nuclear Deal.[31] In 2006, the US passed domestic legislation to enable this.[32] Later, the US Congress adopted the United States–India Nuclear Cooperation Approval and Non-proliferation Enhancement Act of 2008. In September 2008, despite India not being party to the NPT, the forty-eight-nation Nuclear Suppliers Group (NSG) granted it a waiver to commence civil nuclear trade. In 2009, India signed a safeguards agreement with the International Atomic Energy Agency (IAEA) regarding 'the Application of Safeguards to Civilian Nuclear Facilities', followed by the adoption of the Civil Liability for Nuclear Damage

[26] 'Written Statement of the Government of India' (20 June 1995) HAG/POL/443/2/95 <https://www.icj-cij.org/files/case-related/95/8688.pdf> accessed 23 March 2020.

[27] ibid 2. For the ICJ opinion: *Legality of the Threat or Use of Nuclear Weapons* (Advisory Opinion) [1966] ICJ Rep 226.

[28] On reasons for adopting the policy of no first use (NFU): Menon (n 6) 157–84; Ministry of External Affairs, 'Civil Nuclear Cooperation' <http://www.mea.gov.in/in-focus-topic.htm?24/Civil+Nuclear+Cooperation> accessed 23 March 2020. In so far as the NFU doctrine is concerned, one observer notes that '[t]he caveats and internal debates notwithstanding NFU has withstood at least three internal reviews and is accepted by the military'. Gaurav Kampani, 'India's Nuclear Trajectory: New Directions Amid Enduring Myths' in Ganguly et al (n 2) 162.

[29] eg Treaty Banning Nuclear Weapons Tests in the Atmosphere, in Outer Space and Under Water 480 UNTS 43; Convention on the Prohibition of the Development, Production, Stockpiling and Use of Chemical Weapons on their Destruction 1975 UNTS 45; Convention on the Prohibition of the Development, Production and Stockpiling of Bacteriological (Biological) and Toxin Weapons and on their Destruction 1015 UNTS 163; Treaty on Principles Governing the Activities of States in the Exploration and Use of Outer Space, including the Moon and Other Celestial Bodies 610 UNTS 205 (Outer Space Treaty); Agreement Governing the Activities of States on the Moon and other Celestial Bodies 1363 UNTS 3 (Moon Treaty).

[30] Menon (n 6) 50. On the sanctions regime: Charan D Wadhwa, 'Costs of Economic Sanctions: Aftermath of Pokhran II' (1998) 33 Economic and Political Weekly 1604; Daniel Moore/Michael Carriere, 'The Economic Impacts of the 1998 Sanctions on India and Pakistan' (1999) 6 The Nonproliferation Review 1.

[31] For official statements on the 123 Agreement: 'Civil Nuclear Cooperation' (n 28).

[32] Henry J Hyde United States and India Nuclear Cooperation Promotion Act of 2006, H.R.5682, 109th Congress (2005–06); For an explanation: 'Recent Legislation' (2007) 120 Harvard Law Review 2020.

Act. The latter allows the operator to sue the supplier in case there is a technical defect in the plant. In 2016, as a follow up, India ratified the 1997 Convention on Supplementary Compensation for Nuclear Damage.[33]

The civil nuclear deal brought an end to India's isolation, which effectively prevented it from carrying out future tests, banned the stockpiling of nuclear fuel, and tied its hands (via the US Hyde Act) in pursuing an independent foreign policy with third countries like Iran. This, and the fact that they were against a strategic alliance with the US, led the Left Parties to withdraw support from the United Progressive Allowance government of the time.[34] This notwithstanding, strategic and defence ties between India and the US have grown rapidly in recent years.[35] India now has Defense Partner Status with the US.[36] This commits the US 'to facilitate technology sharing with India to a level commensurate with that of its closest allies and partners, and industry collaboration for defence co-production and co-development'.[37] This relationship has been in the making for some time. In 2002, India signed the General Security of Military Information Agreement, and in 2016 the Logistics Exchange Memorandum of Agreement, which gives the military establishment of each nation access to each other's facilities for supplies and repairs. In September 2018, the US and India signed the Communication Compatibility and Security Agreement.[38] As another example of the increasingly close relationship between the two States, the US agreed to give India

[33] IAEA, Convention on Supplementary Compensation for Nuclear Damage (22 July 1998) <https://www.iaea.org/sites/default/files/infcirc567.pdf> accessed 13 April 2020.

[34] The then General Secretary of the CPI (M) wrote : 'the left is clear that going ahead with the agreement will bind India to the United States in a manner that will seriously impair an independent foreign policy and our strategic autonomy'. Prakash Karat, 'Why the CPI (M) and the Left Oppose the Nuclear Deal' (*The Hindu*, 20 August 2007) <https://www.thehindu.com/todays-paper/tp-opinion/Why-the-CPIM-and-the-Left-oppose-the-nuclear-deal/article14819399.ece> accessed 23 March 2020; Dubey (n 19) 158, 163.

[35] For a brief summary of India–US relations: Ministry of External Affairs, 'Brief on India–US Relations' (June 2017) <https://www.mea.gov.in/Portal/ForeignRelation/India_US_brief.pdf> accessed 23 March 2020.

[36] For recognition of India as 'Defence Partner' and its implications: White House, 'Joint Statement: The United States and India: Enduring Global Partners in the 21st Century' (7 June 2016) <https://obamawhitehouse.archives.gov/the-press-office/2016/06/07/joint-statement-united-states-and-india-enduring-global-partners-21st> accessed 30 November 2020. Para 17 of the Statement reads:

> Noting that the US–India defense relationship can be an anchor of stability, and given the increasingly strengthened cooperation in defense, the United States hereby recognizes India as a Major Defense Partner. As such:
>
> The United States will continue to work toward facilitating technology sharing with India to a level commensurate with that of its closest allies and partners. The leaders reached an understanding under which India would receive license-free access to a wide range of dual-use technologies in conjunction with steps that India has committed to take to advance its export control objectives.
>
> In support of India's Make In India initiative, and to support the development of robust defense industries and their integration into the global supply chain, the United States will continue to facilitate the export of goods and technologies, consistent with U.S. law, for projects, programs and joint ventures in support of official U.S.–India defense cooperation.

Alyssa Ayres, *Our Time has Come: How India is Making its Place in the World* (OUP 2018) 222–7.

[37] 'Brief on India–US Relations' (n 35).

[38] Ministry of External Affairs, 'Joint Statement on the Inaugural India–US 2+2 Ministerial Dialogue' (6 September 2018) <https://mea.gov.in/bilateral-documents.htm?dtl/30358/Joint_Statement_on_the_Inaugural_IndiaUS_2432_Ministerial_Dialogue> accessed 23 March 2020.

licence-free exports, re-exports, and transfers under License Exception Strategic Trade Authorization.[39] The two nations are also set to negotiate an Industrial Security Annex that would allow closer collaboration between their defence industries.[40] In the future, India may sign the Basic Exchange and Cooperation Agreement for Geo-Spatial Cooperation. However, concerns have been expressed that all this may lead to India 'becoming a US acolyte in conflicts not of its choosing'.[41]

3. The War on Terror

India has contributed actively to the 'global war on terror'. It is party to all of the principal international anti-terrorism conventions, including the International Convention for the Suppression of Terrorist Bombings and the Convention for the Suppression of Financing of Terrorism.[42] In 1996, India tabled the Draft International Convention on Suppression of Terrorism in the UN General Assembly (UNGA), which is still before the Sixth Committee. In 2006, India supported the Global Counter-Terrorism Strategy adopted by the UNGA. It has also been active in the UNSC Counter-Terrorism Committee (CTC) and has enacted measures recommended by institutions like the Financial Action Task Force (FATF), the CTC, and other bodies. In 2013, the FATF concluded that '[o]verall, India has reached a satisfactory level of compliance with all of the core and key Recommendations... [c]onsequently, it is recommended that India is removed from the regular follow-up process'.[43] At the regional level, India is party to the SAARC Regional Convention on Suppression of Terrorism and the BIMSTEC Convention on Cooperation in Combating International Terrorism, Transnational Organized Crime and Illicit Drug Trafficking.[44]

At the domestic level it has, over the decades, enacted several anti-terrorism laws. In the wake of the 9/11 attacks, and the 2001 attack to the Indian Parliament, India passed the stringent Prevention of Terrorism Act 2002 (POTA). While the POTA was repealed in 2004, some of its key provisions were included as amendments to the Unlawful

[39] ibid. [40] ibid.

[41] M K Narayanan, '2+2 is Less Than the Sum of Its Parts?' (*The Hindu*, 18 September 2018) <https://www.thehindu.com/opinion/lead/22-is-less-than-the-sum-of-its-parts/article24970664.ece> accessed 23 March 2020.

[42] International Convention for the Suppression of Terrorist Bombings 2149 UNTS 256; International Convention for the Suppression of Financing of Terrorism 2178 UNTS 197.

[43] Financial Action Task Force, '8th Follow up Report: Mutual Evaluation of India' (June 2013) <http://www.fatf-gafi.org/media/fatf/documents/reports/mer/India_FUR8_2013.pdf> accessed 23 March 2020.

[44] SAARC, 'Regional Convention on Suppression of Terrorism' (4 November 1987) <https://treaties.un.org/doc/db/Terrorism/Conv18-english.pdf> accessed 24 March 2020; BIMSTEC, 'Convention on Cooperation in Combating International Terrorism, Transnational Organized Crime and Illicit Drug Trafficking' (11 December 2009) <https://mea.gov.in/bilateral-documents.htm?dtl/5070/BIMSTEC+Convention+on+Cooperation+in+Combating+International+Terrorism+Transnational+Organised+Crime+And+Illicit+Drug+Trafficking> accessed 23 March 2020.

Activities (Prevention) Act of 1967.[45] Concerns have been raised with respect to the human rights of individuals charged with offences under this and similarly contentious legislation, such as the Armed Forces Special Powers Act (AFSPA).[46] This has also found expression in judgments of the Supreme Court.[47]

Finally, India has also signed extradition treaties with several nations,[48] and has passed domestic legislation to meet its international obligations, namely, for example, the 2016 Anti-Hijacking Act.[49]

4. Maritime Security

In recent years India has striven to become a maritime power.[50] Having a coastline of 7,517 kilometres, it has to provide for security in its territorial sea and exclusive economic zone (EEZ). It is currently addressing a range of concerns, including open maritime lanes, maritime terrorism, piracy, gun running, illegal immigration, and maritime smuggling and trafficking. Apart from adopting relevant domestic legislation on these matters, India actively participated in the negotiations for the 1982 UN Convention on the Law of the Sea (UNCLOS).

India has maritime boundaries with Bangladesh, Indonesia, the Maldives, Myanmar, Thailand, Pakistan, and Sri Lanka. It has concluded maritime boundary agreements with Sri Lanka (1974 and 1976), Indonesia (1974), and the Maldives (1976), and Thailand/Indonesia (1977), Sri Lanka, the Maldives and Myanmar (1982). In the *Bay of Bengal Arbitration* under Annex VII UNCLOS, the Arbitral Tribunal was

> ... unanimous in identifying the location of the land boundary terminus between Bangladesh and India and in determining the course of the maritime boundary in the territorial sea. By a majority of four votes to one, the Tribunal determined the

[45] Anil Kalhan et al, 'Colonial Continuities: Human Rights, Terrorism and Security Laws in India' (2006) 20 Columbia Journal of Asian Law 93, 100. For an overview of anti-terror laws excluding the preventive detention legislations: Srijoni Sen et al, *Anti-Terror Law in India: A Study of Statutes and Judgments, 2001–2014* (Vidhi Centre for Legal Policy 2015).

[46] Kalhan et al (n 45); Ujjwal Kumar Singh, 'Mapping Anti-Terror Legal Regimes in India' in Victor V Ramraj et al (eds), *Global Anti-Terrorism Law and Policy* (2nd edn, CUP 2012). Anupama Roy/Ujjwal Kumar Singh, 'The Masculinist Security State and Anti-Terror Law Regimes in India' (2015) 39 Asian Studies Review 305; Surabhi Chopra, 'National Security Laws in India: The Unraveling of Constitutional Constraints' (2015) 17 Oregon Review of International Law 1.

[47] eg *Extra Judl.Exec.Victim Families... v Union Of India and Anr* (13 July 2016).

[48] For the list of countries with which India has extradition agreements/arrangements: Ministry of External Affairs, 'Countries with which India has Extradition Treaties/Arrangements' (last updated 30 August 2019) <https://www.mea.gov.in/leta.htm> accessed 23 March 2020.

[49] Ministry of Law and Justice, Anti-Hijacking Act (13 May 2016) <https://www.civilaviation.gov.in/sites/default/files/Anti-hijacking%20Act%2C%202016.pdf> accessed 23 March 2020.

[50] It has been observed that '... the fact that a rising China and emerging India are turning to the sea in ways they have not done before ... has the potential to radically alter the world's maritime environment': C Raja Mohan, *Samudra Manthan: Sino-Indian Rivalry in the Indo-Pacific* (OUP 2013).

course of the maritime boundary line between Bangladesh and India in the exclusive economic zone and the continental shelf within and beyond 200 nautical miles.[51]

The Award gave Bangladesh more of the total sea area of the Bay of Bengal. India's commitment to the international rule of law was evident in its compliance with the Award.

India's national security interests extend beyond South Asia to the Indian Ocean and Indo-Pacific regions.[52] Increasing concerns over maritime security have led India to pay attention to its economic, political, and military dimensions at both the bilateral and multilateral levels. Thus, for instance, with regard to the South China Sea, it has been reaffirming the need to keep sealanes open and safe for commerce. In the 2018 India–Vietnam Joint Statement, '[b]oth sides agreed that it is essential to strengthen cooperation in maritime domain, including... the security of sea lanes...'[53] Earlier, the 2018 Delhi Declaration of the ASEAN–India Commemorative Summit reaffirmed 'the importance of maintaining and promoting peace, stability, maritime safety and security, freedom of navigation and over flight in the region, and other lawful uses of the seas and unimpeded lawful maritime commerce and to promote peaceful resolutions of disputes...'[54]

5. International Space Law

India's space programme was launched in the early 1960s. According to Tharoor, India '... has long been an effective voice on issues like management of outer space...'[55] It is a party to, amongst others, the 1967 Outer Space Treaty, the 1968 Rescue Agreement, and the 1974 Registration Convention and has signed the 1979 Moon Treaty.[56] At first, India's space programme was 'driven by the social and developmental needs of the country'.[57] However, since the beginning of the new century its space programme has undergone change, at least in part because of 'the reality of growing missile threats in India's

[51] PCA, 'Press Release' (8 July 2014) <https://pcacases.com/web/sendAttach/410> accessed 24 March 2020; *Bay of Bengal Maritime Boundary Arbitration (People's Republic of Bangladesh v Republic of India)* PCA Case No 2010-16, Final Award (7 July 2014).

[52] Gopal Suri, *China's Expanding Military Maritime Footprint in the Indian Ocean Region* (Vivekananda International Foundation 2017). For the critical importance of maritime domain to India: Saran (n 6) 278. Menon writes vis-à-vis China that it is necessary to defend '... India's growing maritime interests when the Chinese are heading towards basing and other arrangements in Gwadar, Djibouti, and the Gulf and other portions of the Indian Ocean littoral': Menon (n 6) 36.

[53] Government of India, 'India–Vietnam Joint Statement during State visit of President of Vietnam to India' (3 March 2018) <http://pib.nic.in/newsite/PrintRelease.aspx?relid=176,933> accessed 31 May 2018.

[54] Government of India, 'Delhi Declaration of the ASEAN–India Commemorative Summit to Mark the 25th Anniversary of ASEAN–India Dialogue Relations' (25 January 2018) <http://pib.nic.in/newsite/PrintRelease.aspx?relid=175908> accessed 31 May 2018.

[55] Tharoor (n 16) 392.

[56] Outer Space Treaty (n 29); Agreement on the Rescue of Astronauts, the Return of Astronauts and the Return of Objects Launched into Outer Space 672 UNTS 119; Convention on Registration of Objects Launched into Outer Space 1023 UNTS 15; Moon Treaty (n 29).

[57] Rajeswari Pillai Rajagopalan, 'India's Space Ambitions and Capabilities' in Ganguly et al (n 2) 458, 460.

neighbourhood'.[58] On 27 March 2019 India successfully carried out an anti-satellite missile test demonstrating 'its capability to interdict and intercept a satellite in outer space based on complete indigenous technology'.[59] Yet India remains committed to the peaceful use of space technology. Its goal is to establish 'a space regime which ensures the safety of space-based assets, prohibit the deployment of space-based weapons and enable cooperation in dealing with problems such as space debris'.[60]

6. UN Peacekeeping

India has over the years made a sustained contribution to UN Peacekeeping Forces:[61]

> Out of the total 69 operations launched by the UN from 1948 till 2015, India had participated in 44 operations… As of early 2016, India was the third largest contributor to UN peacekeeping forces, participating in 11 out of the 16 missions, with total strength of 7,886 personnel, comprising 6,840 military, 995 police, and 51 other support personnel.[62]

This contribution is driven by the need to be perceived as a major power and to evidence its credentials for a permanent seat at the UNSC.[63]

7. Economic Security

India is keenly aware of both the merits and the downsides of the liberal international order in achieving economic security. However, by and large, India has supported the liberal economic order. It has been active in the Bretton Woods institutions and the WTO, even as it has called for their reform. Additionally, it has effectively used the World Trade

[58] ibid 462.

[59] Ministry of External Affairs, 'Frequently Asked Questions on Mission Shakti, India's Anti-Satellite Missile test conducted on 27 March, 2019' (27 March 2019) <https://www.mea.gov.in/press-releases.htm?dtl/31179/frequently+asked+questions+on+mission+shakti+indias+antisatellite+missile+test+conducted+on+27+march+2019> accessed 23 March 2020.

[60] ibid. Saran (n 6) 285.

[61] 'India and United Nations Peacekeeping and Peacebuilding' (*Permanent Mission of India to the UN*) <https://www.pminewyork.org/pdf/menu/49151pkeeping.pdf> accessed 24 March 2020.

[62] Geetanjali Chopra/David M Malone, 'India and United Nations Peacekeeping' in Ganguly et al (n 2) 434, 439.

[63] For the complexities of UN peacekeeping contributions: C Raja Mohan, 'India's Military Diplomacy: Legacy of International Peacekeeping' (2014) ISAS Working Paper No 190 <https://www.files.ethz.ch/isn/181075/ISAS_Working_Paper_190_-_India's_Military_Diplomacy_13062014161354.pdf> accessed 24 March 2020.

Organization (WTO) dispute settlement system.[64] India has failed to develop local capacities in the same way as Brazil and China, reflecting a lack of vision of the role of international law in the development process. In recent years, India has also favoured the creation of new development organizations such as the BRICS development and infrastructure banks.[65]

Its trading and other economic interests are increasingly subject to the global trend of competitive adoption of Free Trade Agreements. But since past agreements have not worked to its advantage, India has refused to join mega-Regional Trade Agreements, such as the Regional Comprehensive Economic Partnership Agreement, for it would mean further tariff cuts on manufactured and agricultural products without compensatory access to the services market of other States. But the fact that, in its absence, China will have a free rein in the region may eventually compel it to become a party.

8. Environmental Security

India has, since the 1972 Stockholm Conference, stressed that global environmental governance should not prevent developing countries from pursuing their development goals. It has consistently maintained that the industrialized world is primarily responsible for the ecological crisis and supported the differential treatment of developing countries. Yet despite the fact that developed nations have not delivered on their promises in the past, India promptly ratified the Paris Climate Agreement. Indeed, in the face of US withdrawal, India has been willing to play a greater role in its implementation.[66] Although there is, to date, no climate specific legislation, India has adopted a National

[64] For disputes in which India has been involved: 'Disputes by Member' (WTO) <https://www.wto.org/english/tratop_e/dispu_e/dispu_by_country_e.htm> accessed 23 March 2020; Aarshi Tirkey, 'The WTO Dispute Settlement System: An Analysis of India's Experience and Current Reform Proposals' (2019) ORF Occasional Paper No 209 <https://www.orfonline.org/wp-content/uploads/2019/09/ORF_OccasionalPaper_209_WTO.pdf> accessed 23 March 2020.

[65] Cynthia Roberts et al, *The BRICS and Collective Financial Statecraft* (OUP 2017); BRICS, 'Brasilia Declaration' (11th BRICS Summit, Brasilia, 14 November 2019) <http://www.mea.gov.in/Uploads/PublicationDocs/32042_Braslia_Declaration__1_.pdf> accessed 23 March 2020.

[66] Thus eg EU–India, 'Joint Statement on Climate Change and Clean Energy' (New Delhi, 6 October 2017) para 2:

> The EU and India are committed to lead and work together with all stakeholders to combat climate change, implement the 2030 Agenda for Sustainable Development and encourage global low greenhouse gas emissions, climate resilient and sustainable development. They underline their resolve to combat climate change and promote the global clean and low greenhouse gas emission energy transition, towards sustainable, affordable, reliable and modern energy services.

See <https://www.consilium.europa.eu/media/23517/eu-india-joint-declaration-climate-and-energy.pdf> accessed 30 May 2018.

Action Plan on Climate Change.[67] However, it has a range of domestic laws to deal with growing environmental concerns in the country.

9. Non-Governmental Organizations and Internal Security

India has always been sceptical towards international NGOs (INGOs) working in the country. In 2010 the Foreign Contribution Regulation Act (FCRA) was adopted.[68] More recently, the government has decried foreign funding of NGOs that are seen as targeting development projects. In fact, today INGOs, such as Greenpeace India or rights advocacy groups, are often seen as threats to internal security. The UN Special Rapporteur on Rights to Freedom for Peaceful Assembly and Association examined the FCRA and India's practice in the light of IHRL, and concluded that

> ... the law could be used to silence any association involved in advocating political, economic, social, environmental or cultural priorities which differ from those espoused by the government of the day. [The] restrictions as defined by the Foreign Contribution Regulation Act (2010) and Rules (2011), do not meet the obligations of the Union of India under international law, standards and principles.[69]

10. Refugees and Illegal Migration

India has a good record in hosting refugees.[70] But the government's reaction to the arrival of Rohingya refugees in India in 2017 was initially to return them to Myanmar or Bangladesh, as it was unclear on its obligations under IHRL, including international refugee law. It is true that India is not a party to the 1951 UN Convention on Refugee Status. However, it is a member of the UN High Commissioner for Refugees' Executive Committee. It is also bound by the *non-refoulement* principle which forms part of customary international law.[71] The general position of the Supreme Court on customary

[67] Government of India, Prime Minister's Council of Climate Change, 'National Action Plan on Climate Change' (2008) <http://www.nicra-icar.in/nicrarevised/images/Mission%20Documents/National-Action-Plan-on-Climate-Change.pdf> accessed 24 March 2020; Navroj K Dubash (ed), *India in a Warming World: Integrating Climate Change and Development* (OUP 2020).

[68] For information on the act and accompanying rules: 'FCRA' <http://www.fcra.co.in/> accessed 24 March 2020.

[69] OHCHR, 'Info Note: Analysis on International Law, Standards, and Principles Applicable to the Foreign Contributions Regulation Act 2010 and Foreign Contributions Regulation Rules 2011 by the UN Special Rapporteur on the Rights to Freedom of Peaceful Assembly and of Association, Maina Kiai' (20 April 2016) para 6 <http://www.ohchr.org/Documents/Issues/FAssociation/InfoNoteIndia.pdf> accessed 24 March 2020.

[70] BS Chimni, 'Status of Refugees in India: Strategic Ambiguity' in Ranabir Sammadar (ed), *Refugees and the State: Practices of Asylum and Care in India, 1947–2000* (Sage 2003).

[71] UNHCR, 'Advisory Opinion on the Extraterritorial Application of Non-Refoulement Obligations under the 1951 Convention relating to the Status of Refugees and its 1967 Protocol' (26 January 2007) <https://www.refworld.org/docid/45f17a1a4.html> accessed 24 March 2020.

international law is that it must be respected unless a contrary parliamentary statute exists. While the 1946 Foreigners Act has been interpreted by the Supreme Court in *Louis De Raedt v Union of India* to give the executive the absolute right to deport an alien, subject to the principles of natural justice, it does not distinguish between aliens in general and refugees.[72] Therefore, it has arguably no bearing upon India's obligation to respect the principle of *non-refoulement*.

A critical security issue of the recent decades are illegal migrants from Bangladesh. In *Sarbananda Sonowal vs Union of India and Anr* (2005) the Supreme Court of India noted that '[t]he large-scale influx of illegal Bangladesh immigrants has led to large tracts of sensitive international borders being occupied by foreigners. This has serious implications for internal security.'[73] It concluded from the factual record presented to it and a brief survey of the inclusive meaning of the word 'aggression' in international law that 'there can be no manner of doubt that the State of Assam is facing "external aggression and internal disturbance" on account of large scale illegal migration of Bangladeshi nationals.'[74] The problem of identifying illegal migrants entered a new phase in 2018 which saw an effort to update the National Register for Citizens (NRC), first created in 1951. The government sought to identify afresh persons who came to India after 25 March 1971, the prescribed cut-off date, and, as such, were to be declared illegal migrants.[75] The NRC process was carried out under the supervision of the Supreme Court. Nearly 1.9 million came to be excluded. One keen observer has suggested that the State should consider granting amnesty to all those who fail to make it to the NRC.[76] It is worth noting that India is not a party to the 1954 Convention on the Status of Stateless Persons and the 1961 Convention on the Reduction of Statelessness. Hannah Arendt's oft quoted phrase 'the right to have rights', used in the context of stateless peoples, succinctly captures the need to do so.

11. Water Conflicts

In recent decades, the question of transboundary water security has become a priority for India. India is not a party to the 1997 Convention on the Law of Non-Navigational Uses of International Watercourses and it abstained in the UNGA vote on the adoption of the Convention.[77] India has, however, endeavoured to reach satisfactory bilateral

[72] *Louis De Raedt v Union of India* (1991) 3 SCC 554.

[73] *Sarbananda Sonowal v Union of India and Anr* (2005) 5 SCC 665.

[74] ibid para 38.

[75] 'To be included in the NRC one has to identify an ancestor whose name appears in either the NRC of 1951 or a pre-1971 electoral roll, and provide documentary evidence of linkage with that person. Even with the substantial assistance available at the NRC Seva Kendras, this can be a challenge for many people': Sanjib Baruah, 'Non-Citizens and History' (*Frontline*, 31 August 2018) <https://www.frontline.in/the-nation/article24702054.ece> accessed 23 March 2020.

[76] Sanjib Baruah, 'The Missing 4,007,007' (*The Indian Express*, 2 August 2018) <https://indianexpress.com/article/opinion/columns/assam-nrc-draft-list-names-citizenship-5287213/> accessed 23 March 2020.

[77] For reasons of abstaining: BS Chimni, 'A Tale of Two Treaties: The Ganga and Mahakali Agreements and the Watercourses Convention' in Surya P Subedi (ed), *International Watercourses Law for the 21st Century: The Case of the River Ganges Basin* (Ashgate 2005).

solutions with its neighbours with regard to shared watercourses. In 1996, it signed the Sharing of the Ganga/Ganges Waters treaty with Bangladesh. The same year a treaty with Nepal was concluded 'Concerning the Integrated development of the Mahakali River including Sarada Barrage, Tanakpur Barrage and Pancheswar Project'. The Indus Water Treaty with Pakistan was signed in 1960.[78] It 'is the only international water treaty co-signed by a third party. This third party is the World Bank which mediated the original dispute over the Indus basin, and assisted the two parties in reaching an agreement.'[79] It is also seen as one of the most successful water treaties. As the World Bank puts it, 'it has survived frequent tensions, including conflict, and has provided a framework for irrigation and hydropower development for more than half a century'.[80] In 2005, its dispute settlement system was tested when the 'Baglihar question' was referred by the World Bank under its provisions to a Neutral Expert.[81] Both sides accepted the decision of the Neutral Expert. In 2013, following a proceeding instituted by Pakistan under the Indus Water Treaty regarding the Kishenganga Hydroelectric Project (KHEP), the Permanent Court of Arbitration issued its Award. It stated that while 'India shall release a minimum flow of 9 cumecs into the Kishenganga/Neelum River below the KHEP at all times' it 'imposes no further restrictions on the operation of the KHEP'.[82]

India has ongoing concerns regarding the activities of China on the Brahmaputra river, due to its developmental activities that may impact the flow of waters to India.[83] In that respect, there is a perceived lack of transparency and information-sharing on the part of China. However, in June 2018, the two States signed a Memorandum of understanding on the 'provision of hydrological information of the Brahmaputra river in flood season by China to India'.[84]

12. Cybersecurity

A broad definition of cybersecurity would include the phenomena of cybercrime, cyber-espionage, cyberterrorism and cyberwarfare. Cybersecurity is particularly important for India for the integrity of its electoral process, commercial transactions, unlawful surveillance, and military conflicts. An important challenge has been to put in

[78] Indus Waters Treaty 419 UNTS 125; 'Fact Sheet: The Indus Waters Treaty 1960 and the Role of the World Bank' (*World Bank*, 11 June 2018) <http://www.worldbank.org/en/region/sar/brief/fact-sheet-the-indus-waters-treaty-1960-and-the-world-bank> accessed 31 May 2018.

[79] Salman M A Salman, 'The Baglihar Difference and its Resolution Process—a Triumph for the Indus Waters Treaty?' (2008) 10 Water Policy 105, 106.

[80] Fact Sheet (n 78). [81] For summary and analysis: Salman (n 79).

[82] *Award in the Arbitration regarding the Indus Waters Kishenganga between Pakistan and India* (2013) 31 RIAA 1, 358.

[83] Brahma Chellaney, *Water, Peace, and War: Confronting the Global Water Crisis* (Rowman and Littlefield 2013); Brahma Chellaney, 'Water, Power, and Competition in Asia' (2014) 54 Asian Survey 621.

[84] Ministry of External Affairs, 'India–China Bilateral Agreements signed in Qingdao, China' (9 June 2018) <https://www.mea.gov.in/bilateral-documents.htm?dtl/29966/IndiaChina_Bilateral_Agreements_signed_in_Qingdao_China> accessed 24 March 2020.

place cyber policy, laws, infrastructure and systems to ensure cybersecurity.[85] A first attempt at regulating cybersecurity threats was the 2002 Information and Technology Act, while in 2013 India adopted a National Cyber Security Policy, later amended to define the terms 'cybersecurity' and 'cyberterrorism'.[86] Its vision is 'to build a secure and resilient cyberspace for citizens, business, and government'. But unlike the *Tallinn Manual*, in which complex legal issues were at least to an extent addressed, India has not undertaken such an exercise.[87] This is another reflection of India's absence of engagement with international law.

13. Views on the Responsibility to Protect

Finally, India has been traditionally a strong proponent of the principle of non-intervention to the internal affairs of States and has been extremely reluctant to carve out any exception to this principle. Its 1971 intervention in East Pakistan was not viewed as an instance of humanitarian intervention but as an exercise of the right to self-defence. Its sending of Indian Peacekeeping Forces (IPKF) in 1987 to Sri Lanka was pursuant to an agreement with the Sri Lankan government. But recently there has been a slight change in perspective with respect to the new doctrine of R2P. India abstained on UNSC Res 1973 (2011) which authorized 'all necessary means' and called for no-fly zones in Libya.[88] It was, however, disturbed by the fact that the mandate of the UNSC was used to bring about regime change. In fact, as a non-permanent member of the UNSC, 'India played a key role in trying to warn against the consequence of perilous interventions and attempts at regime change in Syria and Libya in the UNSC'.[89] However, Western powers had extraneous reasons for intervening in both Libya and Syria, albeit without thinking through the consequences.[90] According to Puri, in the case of armed interventions, with or without the approval of the UNSC, '[t]he action is undertaken without weighing the pros and cons, or understanding the underlying social and cultural forces and political dynamics at work, based on either an incomplete or a self-serving analysis

[85] IDSA, 'IDSA Task Force Report: India's Cyber Security Challenge' (March 2012) <http://gerdab.ir/files/fa/news/1395/4/1/32778_401.pdf> accessed 23 March 2020.

[86] Ministry of Communication and Information Technology, 'National Cyber Security Policy 2013' (2013) <https://nciipc.gov.in/documents/National_Cyber_Security_Policy-2013.pdf> accessed 24 March 2020.

[87] Michael Schmitt (ed), *Tallinn Manual 2.0 On the International Law Applicable to Cyber Operations* (CUP 2017).

[88] Manjeev Singh Puri, 'UNSC Resolution on Libya: India's Explanation of Vote' (New York, 17 March 2011) <http://mea.gov.in/press-releases.htm?dtl/639/UNSC+resolution+on+Libya++Indias+Explanation+of+Vote> accessed 24 March 2020.

[89] Hardeep Singh Puri, *Perilous Interventions: The Security Council and the Politics of Chaos* (Harper Collins 2016) 22. The book provides an 'insider's' account—the author represented India in the UNSC as a non-permanent member.

[90] ibid. The book is a good account of the factors that came into play; BS Chimni, 'R2P and Syria: Imperialism with a Human Face' (*OpenDemocracy*, 11 September 2013) <https://www.opendemocracy.net/openglobalrights/bschimni/r2p-and-syria-imperialism-with-human-face> accessed 23 March 2020.

and disregard of wise counsel'.[91] India has, therefore, long called for the expansion of the UNSC to democratize international relations and reflect the geopolitical realities of the twenty-first century.

D. Conclusion and Outlook

In responding to national and global security threats India has been firmly committed to the UN Charter principles and the international rule of law. It is wedded to the principle of peaceful settlement of disputes, including settling long-standing border disputes with its neighbours China and Pakistan. India has also made a key contribution to world peace through its extensive involvement in UN Peacekeeping. A key aspect of India's domestic and foreign policy has been the fight against terrorism. It has taken the initiative to present the draft of a comprehensive convention on terrorism. Its growing interest concerning maritime security has seen it emphasizing the freedom of navigation, especially in the context of China's expansion in the South China Sea. India has also been committed, since the early 1990s, to the liberal international economic order. Despite its concerns with the constriction of policy space, it continues to defend the multilateral trading system. It also supports the Climate Change Pact. It has sought to play a greater role in global affairs through becoming a permanent member of the UNSC.

Yet India does not seem to deeply engage with international law as a means to advance vital national security interests. A combination of deep scepticism rooted in tenets of realism, and a lack of familiarity of policymakers with the language and substance of international law, has prevented India from effectively using it to pursue national and global security interests. The fragmentation of decision-making in international law matters has made things worse as it has meant the absence of an integrated vision of the role of international law; the Legal and Treaties Division of the Ministry of External Affairs has been marginalized when it comes to policy decisions. In sum, India has yet to understand the strategy of 'lawfare'.[92] Other than on a rare occasion, such as drafting a comprehensive convention on terrorism, India has not taken the initiative to shape the world of international law doctrines, rules, and practices to advance its national and global security interests. In order to realize its national interests, a reassessment and reimagination of the role of international law is called for, along with suitable changes in relevant structures and processes of decision-making.

Acknowledgement

I would like to thank Dr P S Rao, former Additional Secretary, Legal and Treaties Division, Government of India for his comments.

[91] Puri (n 89) 5. [92] The word 'lawfare' here combines the words law and welfare.

CHAPTER 50

THE RUSSIAN FEDERATION

BAKHTIYAR TUZMUKHAMEDOV

A. Introduction

RUSSIAN, or Soviet, for that matter, doctrine of international law defines international security as constituting:

> a specific system of international relations which will only be complied with, should it express mandatory rules of conduct by a state, the latter being nothing other than principles and norms of international law. The principles and norms of international law comprising the system of international security indicate the boundaries of behavior of states, beyond which actions of one state may be detrimental to the security of others.[1]

[1] Boris Klimenko, *Mezhdunarodnoye Pravo I Mezhdunarodnaya Bezopasnost* [International Law and International Security] ('International Relations' Publishing House 1991) 13. Published simultaneously in Boris M Klimenko/Paul B Stephan (eds), *International Law and International Security* (ME Sharpe 1992); See also 'International Security and International law' in V I Kuznetsov/Bakhtiyar R Tuzmukhamedov (eds), *International Law—A Russian Introduction* (Eleven International Publishing 2009) 321–4. Or compare with the following: 'Security is a condition in which States consider that there is no danger of military attack, political pressure or economic coercion, so that they are able to pursue freely their own development and progress. International security is thus the result and the sum of the security of each and every State member of the international community accordingly' UNGA 'Report of the Secretary-General: Study on Concepts of Security' (26 August 1985) UN Doc A/40/553, para 3, and further para 223: 'It is vital for the achievement of international security that all States abide by their obligations under international law. If the corresponding provisions of the Charter were strictly observed this would lead to a drastic improvement of the international situation.'

This definition echoes Martens' vision of 'international intercourse', the objective of which should be

> the arrangement of such a structure of international legal order, which would ensure the peaceful and comprehensive development of nations, conditional on full respect for their national interests.[2]

The term 'global security' is used in Russian official statements interchangeably with 'international security', the latter being a preferred option. Sometimes, however, in international settings shades of meaning may be lost in translation, as happened, for example, in the case of the English version of remarks made by the Russian Foreign Minister at the plenary meeting of the 74th session of the UN General Assembly (UNGA). The minister, speaking in Russian, cited the UN Charter's Russian term '*vseobshchaya besopasnost'*' which corresponds to 'universal security' in the English authentic text, whereas it was translated in the Official Records as 'global security'.[3]

B. Historical Landmarks

The term 'international security' did not enter official parlance in the USSR, the State that preceded the contemporary Russian Federation and of which the latter is the continuator,[4] until the Allied Powers' conferences during the Second World War. Previously, ever since the Decree on Peace (the first executive act of the Government that came to power in post-Imperial Russia on 7 November 1917) the objective had been the attainment of 'a just or democratic peace', as a means of containing and ultimately ending the First World War.[5] Ironically, the new State, while publicly striving to break

[2] *Sovremennoye Mezhdunarodnoye Pravo Tzivilizovannykh Narodov F. Martensa* [Fyodor F Martens, *Contemporary International Law of Civilized Nations*] (vol I, 5th edn, A Benke Printers (Tipographiya A Benke) 1904) 211. Martens further outlines six foundations of the 'law of international intercourse' ibid 211–12. Excerpts from Russian sources translated by the author, unless indicated otherwise.

[3] UNGA Verbatim Record (27 September 2019) UN Doc A/74/PV.9, 51.

[4] For discussion of continuity by Russia of the legal personality of the USSR: Rein Mullerson, 'The Continuity and Succession of States, by Reference to the Former USSR and Yugoslavia' (1993) 42 International and Comparative Law Quarterly 473; and more recently: Guido Acquaviva, 'Russia as the State Continuing the Legal Personality of the USSR—An Inquiry into State Identity or Succession' (2019) Journal of the History of International Law 1.

[5] 'By a just or democratic peace, for which the overwhelming majority of the working and toiling classes of all the belligerent countries, exhausted, tormented and racked by the war, are craving—a peace that has been most definitely and insistently demanded by the Russian workers and peasants ever since the overthrow of the tsarist monarchy—by such a peace the Government means an immediate peace without annexations (i.e., without the seizure of foreign lands, without the forcible incorporation of foreign nations) and without indemnities... The Government considers it the greatest of crimes against humanity to continue this war over the issue of how to divide among the strong and rich nations the weak nationalities they have conquered, and solemnly announces its determination immediately to sign terms of peace to stop this war on the terms indicated, which are equally just for all nationalities without

away from the legacy of Imperial Russia, borrowed from the latter's peace and disarmament initiatives which had resulted in The Hague Peace Conferences of 1899 and 1907.[6]

Subsequently, disarmament and non-aggression were put into focus as means of achieving 'general peace'. Practical legislative acts included the ratification of the Protocol for the Prohibition of the Use in War of Asphyxiating, Poisonous, or Other Gases, and of Bacteriological Methods of Warfare of 1925,[7] which was a treaty additional to the conventions concluded at the Second Hague Peace Conference in 1907, and adherence to the Treaty Providing for the Renunciation of War as an Instrument of National Policy of 1928[8] (also known as the Kellogg–Briand Pact), along with several other legal instruments and multiple political initiatives on the same and related matters. Even though in 1934 the Soviet Union was admitted to the League of Nations,[9] the Covenant of which envisioned what could be perceived as component parts of international peace and security,[10] the notion of 'international security' had not been incorporated in its entirety into the foreign policy of the USSR. Whether by intention, habit, or otherwise, the official translation of the Covenant into Russian[11] seems to have been done from the French authentic text and inherited conspicuous deviations from the English, equally authentic, version. One might wish to compare the first paragraph of the preamble which stated in French as follows: 'Considérant que, pour développer la coopération entre les nations et pour leur garantir la paix et la sûreté', while in English it read: 'In order to promote international co-operation and to achieve international peace and security'. The English text appears to be more internationally oriented than the French

exception'—English translation: 'Decree on Peace' (*World Socialist Website*) <https://www.wsws.org/en/articles/2017/11/08/cen2-n08.html> accessed 23 January 2020, original Russian text published in *Documenty Vneshney Politiki SSSR* [Documents of Foreign Policy of the USSR] (vol I, Politizdat 1957) 12.

[6] Betsy Baker, 'Hague Peace Conferences (1899 and 1907)' MPEPIL (OUP, November 2009).

[7] Instruments of ratification were deposited with the Government of France on 5 April 1928 accompanied by reciprocity reservations (*Sbornik Deystvuyushchikh Dogovorov, Soglasheniy i Konventziy, Zaklyuchennikh SSSR s Inostrannymi Gosudarstvami* [Collection of Effective Treaties, Agreements and Conventions, Concluded by the USSR with Foreign States] vol V (1930) 3–5). Reservations had been withdrawn in accordance with the Federal Law No 143-FZ of 6 December 2000 (*Sobraniye Zakonodatel'stva Rossiyskoy Fetderatzii* [Collection of Legislation of the Russian Federation] (11 December 2000) No 50, Item 4866 (hereafter *SZRF*)).

[8] Text of 'Declaration of Adherence' (6 September 1928) in *Documenty Vneshney Politiki SSSR* [Documents of Foreign Policy of the USSR] vol XI (Politizdat 1966) 503–6.

[9] The League expelled the USSR in December 1939, in the aftermath of the war the latter fought on Finland.

[10] Covenant of the League of Nations 225 CTS 195 preamble:

> 'In order to promote international cooperation and to achieve international peace and security by the acceptance of obligations not to resort to war, by the prescription of open, just and honourable relations between nations by the firm establishment of the understandings of international law as the actual rule of conduct among Governments, and by the maintenance of justice and a scrupulous respect for all treaty obligations in the dealings of organised peoples with one another'.

[11] *Sbornik Deystvuyushchikh Dogovorov*, vol VIII (Izdaniye Narodnogo komossariata po inostrannym delam [Publication of the People's Commissariat of Foreign Affairs] 1935) 37.

version, with the former addressing the promotion of international security, rather than providing guarantees of security of individual nations, as does the latter.

The term 'international security' received unequivocal Soviet acceptance at the Tripartite Conference of Allied Powers, which convened from 18 October to 1 November 1943 in Moscow. The Declaration of Four Nations[12] on General Security recognized 'the necessity of... establishing and maintaining international peace and security with the least diversion of the world's human and economic resources for armaments'[13] with the 'general international organization' at its core.[14] Subsequently, however, attention concentrated on military and political dimensions of international security, ranging from disarmament (partial and, ultimately or ideally, general and complete[15]) to a variety of confidence and security-building measures, to upholding fundamental purposes and principles of the UN Charter. A doctrinal change seemed to have arrived with the advent, in 1986, of the proposal of a comprehensive system of international peace and security, attributed to, and associated with Mikhail Gorbachev, then Secretary-General of the Central Committee of the Communist Party and *ex officio* leader of the USSR. The four pillars of the system based on ideas of 'New Political Thinking',[16] included military, political, economic, and humanitarian dimensions of international security. The proposal had been entertained by the UNGA at two consecutive sessions,[17] then it morphed into a 'comprehensive approach to strengthening international peace and security'[18] before fading away.

C. Current Official Doctrine

In the immediate aftermath of the dissolution of the Soviet Union the search for the new identity of Russia as a beneficiary and benefactor of international security was reflected

[12] The Declaration was also signed by the Ambassador of China, who was specially invited for the occasion.

[13] William M Franklin/E R Perkins (eds), *Foreign Relations of the United States: Diplomatic Papers, 1943, General, Volume I* (United States Government Printing Office 1963) 755–66.

[14] A Soviet international legal authority and participant in wartime and subsequent conferences, leading to the establishment of the UN, opined that by virtue of the location of signing of the Declaration, 'Moscow became the birthplace of the United Nations Organization'—Sergey Krylov, *Istoriya Sozdaniya Organizatzii Ob'yedinennykh Natziy* [The History of Creation of the United Nations Organization] ('International Relations' Publishing House 1960) 18.

[15] For a brief discussion of early disarmament measures and proposals: Bakhtiyar Tuzmukhamedov, 'Legal Dimensions of Arms Control Agreements: An Introductory Overview' (2016) 377 Recueil des Cours 319, 340–4.

[16] For 'New Political Thinking' explained by Western analysts, and for Western audiences: David Holloway, 'Gorbachev's New Thinking' (1998) 68 Foreign Affairs 66; Alexander Dallin, 'New Thinking in Soviet Foreign Policy' in Archie Brown (ed), *New Thinking in Soviet Politics* (Palgrave Macmillan 1992).

[17] UNGA Res 41/92 (4 December 1986) and UNGA Res 42/93 (7 December 1987).

[18] UNGA Res 43/89 (7 December 1988).

in several seminal statements of contemporary Russian politicians[19] and declaratory guidelines approved by the President.[20] Russia perceived itself as 'an equal participant in international relations',[21] 'aspiring to build amicable mutually beneficial relations with all',[22] and yet a 'great power',[23] recognizing the expediency of the use of force 'in strict compliance with the UN Charter and other norms of international law to suppress acts of aggression and other threats to international peace and security'.[24] However, even though the sole continuator of the legal personality of the Soviet Union, including as permanent member of the UN Security Council (UNSC), Russia was but a fragment, though the largest, of a major world power, and no match to the latter in terms of economic and industrial capacity, population, and military power, if only except for nuclear weapons. Added to the injury of a traumatic loss of a world power was the insult of humiliating disregard of Russia's own interests and sensitivities, whether with respect to the expansion of NATO and its air campaign against Yugoslavia,[25] or the abrogation by the United States of the Treaty on the Limitation of Anti-Ballistic Missile Systems.[26] What was described by an authoritative foreign and defence policy research NGO in Russia[27] as 'voluntary dependence' on, and 'reluctant partnership' with, the United States and other Western nations, which briefly gave way to a 'moderate alternative' to Western policies,[28] has been replaced in the early 2000s by more assertive Russian approaches to world affairs, and international security in particular.

This transition is evident in several consecutive statements, primarily directed at a foreign audience, made by President Putin at the UN, with his seminal remarks at the Munich Security Conference in 2007 in between. They ranged from calls for 'peace,

[19] eg Statement of President Boris Yeltsin at the UNSC Summit Meeting on 31 January 1992. While the term 'international security' was uttered only once, and in passing, it may be assumed that Yeltsin's perception of international security comprised democracy, in its domestic and external dimensions, 'minimum defense sufficiency', and the rule of law—UNSC Verbatim Record (31 January 1992) UN Doc S/PV.3046, 43, 44, 45, 48.

[20] 'Osnovnye Polozheniya Kontzeptzii Vneshney Politiki Rossiyskoy Federatzii' [General Provisions of the Concept of the Foreign Policy of the Russian Federation] approved by the President's Directive No 284-RP (23 April 1993) cited in *Vneshyaya Politika I Bezopasnost' Sovremennoy Rossii* [Foreign Policy and National Security of Contemporary Russia] *(1991–2002): Anthology in Four Volumes* (vol IV, MGIMO (U) 2002) 19–50 (*Foreign Policy and National Security*).

[21] Yeltsin (n 19) 48. [22] *Foreign Policy and National Security* (n 20) 24. [23] ibid 19ff.

[24] ibid 22.

[25] Apparently, those were but two 'profound disillusionments' of the twentieth century to which President Putin referred in his address to the 55th session of the UNGA: UNGA Verbatim Record (6 September 2000) UN Doc A/55/PV.3, 10.

[26] George W Bush, 'President [Bush] Discusses National Missile Defense' (2001) <https://2001-2009.state.gov/t/ac/rls/rm/2001/6847.htm> accessed 30 November 2020; President Vladimir Putin, 'A Statement [by President Putin] Regarding the Decision of the Administration of the United States to Withdraw from the Antiballistic Missile Treaty of 1972' (2001) (English translation) <http://en.kremlin.ru/events/president/transcripts/21444> accessed 24 January 2020.

[27] Council on Foreign and Defense Policy <http://svop.ru/> accessed 24 January 2020.

[28] *Strategiya dlya Rossii: Povestka Dnya dlya Presidenta—2000* [Strategy for Russia—An Agenda for the President—2000] <http://www.svop.ru/files/meetings/m026013379414301.pdf> accessed 24 January 2020.

stability and prosperity by relying on the entire wealth of cultures and traditions'[29] in 2000; to concerns, in the aftermath of the invasion of Iraq, over the need 'to counter current threats to civilization only by means of collective responses whose legitimacy is not in doubt'[30] in 2003; to unite against terrorism that 'today poses the main threat to human rights and freedoms and to sustainable development of States and peoples'[31] in 2005; to warnings that 'unilateral and frequently illegitimate actions have not resolved any problems. Moreover, they have caused new human tragedies and created new centres of tension'[32] in 2007, and ultimately, in 2015, to lashing out at

> a single dominating power center [which] emerged in the world after the end of the Cold War. Those who found themselves at the top of that pyramid were tempted to think that if they were so strong and exceptional, they knew better that anyone else what should be done.[33]

However, a cross-cutting theme recurring in those and other statements has been adherence to, and supremacy of, international law—whether as a pillar of 'democracy in international relations',[34] or as the most important principle of the UN Charter-based 'equitable security and just peace'[35] that must 'have a universal character both in the conception and application of its norms',[36] or as a foundation for 'creating a space of equal and indivisible security that is not for the select few, but for everyone'.[37]

More insights into official Russian views on international security may be found in several non-normative documents under a variety of denominations: strategy (the National Security Strategy—NSS[38]), or doctrine (the Military Doctrine—MD[39]), or concept (the Foreign Policy Concept—FPC[40]). All current versions were approved under the authority of the President by a respective decree (*ukaz*), whereas of the documents that preceded them, it was the earlier version of the FPC that had been promulgated by a directive (*rasporyazheniye*), the legal and political weight of the former being superior to that of the latter. Differences in definitions might reveal shades of

[29] UNGA Verbatim Record (6 September 2000) UN Doc A/55/PV.3, 11.

[30] UNGA Verbatim Record (25 September 2003) UN Doc A/58/PV.11, 6.

[31] UNGA Verbatim Record (15 September 2005) UN Doc A/60/PV.5, 4.

[32] Vladimir Putin, 'Speech and Following Discussion' (Munich Conference on Security and Policy, 10 February 2007) <http://en.kremlin.ru/events/president/transcripts/24034> accessed 24 January 2020.

[33] UNGA Verbatim Record (28 September 2015) UN Doc A/70/PV.13, 24. President Putin further stated that 'we can no longer tolerate the current state of affairs in the world' ibid 25.

[34] UNGA Verbatim Record (n 29).

[35] UNSC Verbatim Record (7 September 2000) UN Doc S/PV.4194, 11.

[36] Putin (n 32).

[37] UNGA Verbatim Record (n 33) 26.

[38] *SZRF* (4 January 2016) No 1, Part II, Item 212 (NSS).

[39] Initially published in *SZRF* (15 February 2010) No 7, Item 724, re-drafted and amended version published in the official gazette *Rossiyskaya Gazeta* (30 December 2014) No 298 (MD).

[40] *SZRF* (5 December 2016) No 49, Item 6886. English version: 'Foreign Policy Concept of the Russian Federation—Approved by President of the Russian Federation Vladimir Putinon November 30, 2016' (*The Ministry of Foreign Affairs of the Russian Federation*, 1 December 2016) <https://www.mid.ru/en/foreign_policy/official_documents/-/asset_publisher/CptICkB6BZ29/content/id/2542248> accessed 26 January 2020 (FPC).

meaning and lead to further assumptions about the hierarchy between the three sources. The NSS is defined as

> the fundamental document of strategic planning, designating national interests and strategic national priorities of the Russian Federation, domestic and foreign policy objectives, tasks and measures, directed at strengthening of the national security of the Russian Federation and ensuring sustainable long-term development of the country.[41]

The MD 'represents a system of officially endorsed views at the preparation for armed defense, and [actual] armed defense of the Russian Federation.'[42] As for the FPC, 'it provides a systemic vision of the basic principles, priority areas, goals and objectives of the foreign policy of the Russian Federation.'[43]

The NSS defines national security as:

> a situation of protection of an individual, society and the state from internal and external threats, which ensures the realization of the constitutional rights and freedoms of citizens of the Russian Federation, dignified the quality and standard of living, sovereignty, independence, integrity of the state and territory, sustainable socio-economic development of the Russian Federation. National security includes the country's defense and all modes of security envisioned in the Constitution of the Russian Federation and the legislation of the Russian Federation, first and foremost, state, public, information, environmental, economic, transport, energy security, and personal security.[44]

While the NSS makes only two references to international security *per se*, in and of themselves they are quite noteworthy, considering that it appears to be the most senior of the three documents. In particular, paragraph 9 states that

> in the area of international security Russia maintains its adherence to, primarily, employment of political and legal tools, and mechanisms of diplomacy and peacemaking. Resort to armed force for the defense of vital national interests may only be possible, should all other non-violent means prove to be ineffective.

The MD focuses, as should be expected, on military dimensions of international security, identifying 'consolidation of international security and strategic stability at global and regional levels on the basis of supremacy of international law and, above all else, provisions of the UN Charter' as one of the principal objectives of 'military-political cooperation.'[45]

It is the FPC that suggests, if not a concise definition of international security, but certainly avenues towards enhancing it, which can be clustered as follows:

[41] NSS (n 38) para 1. [42] MD (n 39) para 1. [43] FPC (n 40) para 1.
[44] NSS (n 38) para 6. [45] MD (n 39) para 55(a).

- Arms control, non-proliferation, including military and dual-purpose technology export restrictions, confidence and security-building measures;
- Information/cybersecurity;
- Use of force within the framework of Article 51 of the UN Charter;
- Peacekeeping;
- Countering terrorism and organized crime;
- Settlement of regional conflicts by collective political and diplomatic means;
- Collective disaster management;
- Regulating of migration through international cooperation;
- Dialogue and partnership between cultures, religions, and civilizations.

The FPC proceeds from 'shared recognition that human rights, security and sustainable development are closely intertwined'.[46] As for the legal dimension, it declares, as one of the primary objectives of foreign policy,

> to further promote the efforts to strengthen international peace and ensure global security and stability with a view to establishing a fair and democratic international system that addresses international issues on the basis of collective decision-making, the rule of international law, primarily the provisions of the Charter of the United Nations, as well as equal partnership relations among States, with the central and coordinating role played by the United Nations as the key organization in charge of regulating international relations.[47]

While all three policy documents make multiple references to international law, it may be worthwhile to observe to what extent their provisions may have been informed by international legal sources or their interpretations. Two other cases may serve as illustrations: legality of the use of nuclear weapons, and the use of force under Article 51 of the UN Charter.

As for the use of nuclear weapons, in the immediate aftermath of the dissolution of the USSR, on 21 December 1991, the four former Soviet republics, namely, Belarus, Kazakhstan, Russia, and Ukraine, on whose territories most of the strategic nuclear weapons and related infrastructure had been deployed, signed the Agreement on the Joint Measures with Respect to Nuclear Weapons.[48] By virtue of Article 2 of the Agreement, States Parties reaffirmed the decade-long unilateral commitment of the predecessor State of no first-use of nuclear weapons.[49] Whether and in what terms the use of nuclear weapons had been addressed in the Basic Provisions of the Military Doctrine of the Russian Federation, approved by the Decree of the President on 2 November 1993 is unbeknownst to this author since only the Decree comprising three

[46] FPC (n 40) para 18. [47] ibid para 3(e).

[48] Diplomaticheskiy Vestnik [Diplomatic Herald], Official Bulletin of the Ministry of Foreign Affairs of the Russian Federation (1992), No 1, 9, English translation: (1992) 31 International Legal Materials 152.

[49] ibid art 2.

terse paragraphs is publicly available.[50] However, experts with first-hand knowledge of the matter opine that, although 'diluted and rather indefinite', the Basic Provisions proceeded 'from the assumption of the feasibility of the use of nuclear weapons by Russia'.[51] The 2000 MD was more explicit when it stated that

> the Russian Federation reserves the right to use nuclear weapons in response to the use against it and/or its allies of nuclear weapons or other weapons of mass destruction, as well as in response to a large-scale aggression by means of conventional weapons in situations critical for the national security of the Russian Federation.[52]

The current version of the MD has modified that provision, which now reads:

> The Russian Federation reserves the right to use nuclear weapons in response to the use against it and/or its allies of nuclear weapons or other weapons of mass destruction, as well as in response to an aggression by means of conventional weapons when the very existence of the State would be at stake.[53]

An international jurist cannot but draw a parallel with the conclusion that a divided International Court of Justice (ICJ) reached in the *Legality of the Threat or Use of Nuclear Weapons* advisory opinion, where it stated that

> in view of the current state of international law, and of the elements of fact at its disposal, the Court cannot conclude definitively whether the threat or use of nuclear weapons would be lawful or unlawful in an extreme circumstance of self-defence, in which the very survival of a State would be at stake.[54]

As to the use of force within the framework of Article 51 of the UN Charter, in 2002 and subsequently, several senior Russian officials joined a discourse, triggered by allegations that armed Chechen insurgents found refuge in neighbouring Georgia where they rested, regrouped, and re-entered Russian territory, as well as by the US President's remarks regarding readiness 'for preemptive action when necessary to defend our

[50] *Sobraniye Aktov Presidenta i Pravitelstva Rossiyskoy Federatzii* [Collected Acts of the President and the Government of the Russian Federation] (*Izdatel'stvo 'Yuridicheskaya literature'* [Publishing House 'Law Literature'] 8 November 1993) No 45, Item 4329.

[51] Vladimir Dvorkin in Nezavisimaya Gazeta [Independent Newspaper] (11 April 2019). From 1993–2001 Maj. Gen. Dvorkin (Ret.) directed Strategic Rocket Forces research, development and planning in the Ministry of Defense.

[52] *SZRF* (24 April 2000) No 17, Item 1852, para 8.

[53] MD (n 39) para 27. This provision was expounded in the Basic Principles of State Policy of the Russian Federation on Nuclear Deterrence, promulgated by the Decree of 2 June 2020—see SZRF (8 June 2020) No 23, Item 3623. English version available on the website of the Ministry of Foreign Affairs of the Russian Federation <https://www.mid.ru/en/foreign_policy/international_safety/disarmament/-/asset_publisher/rpofiUBmANaH/content/id/4152094> accessed 30 November 2020.

[54] *Legality of the Threat or Use of Nuclear Weapons* (Advisory Opinion) [1996] ICJ Rep 226, 266.

liberty and to defend our lives'.[55] Those officials had been indicating that it might be permissible to use armed force against extraterritorial sources of imminent threat to Russian security, even in the absence of an actual armed attack originating from those sources. Those statements, being made by politicians, senior military commanders, and ultimately by the President, were enthusiastically endorsed by a handful of Russian legal academics.[56] The debate eventually boiled down to a reasonable interpretation, apparently not disregarding the views expressed in the Report of the UN High-level Panel on Threats, Challenges and Change, with respect to the contemporary reading of Article 51, and Chapter VII in general, of the UN Charter.[57] The FPC indicates that

> Russia views Article 51 of the UN Charter as providing an adequate legal basis for the use of force in self-defense that is not subject to revision, including the use of force in the face of threats to peace and security such as international terrorism and the proliferation of weapons of mass destruction.[58]

However, prudence calls that this general statement be viewed in conjunction with official opinions expressed earlier, in particular that 'to exercise the right to self-defense a state, in principle, does not need to wait for the negative consequences of an armed attack to take effect. Of pivotal significance is the determination of the moment when an attack begins, hence the right to self-defense arises.'[59]

D. Domestic Legislation

The term 'international security' may be found in several federal laws of the Russian Federation, whether as a stand-alone combination, or as a component of a phrase 'international peace and security'. For example, the 1995 Federal Law 'On International Treaties of the Russian Federation' lists, amongst treaties subject to compulsory ratification,

[55] George W Bush, 'President Bush Delivers Graduation Speech at West Point. United States Miliary Academy' (West Point, New York, 1 June 2002) <https://georgewbush-whitehouse.archives.gov/news/releases/2002/06/20020601-3.html> accessed 24 January 2020.

[56] For critique of those statements: Bakhtiyar Tuzmukhamedov, 'Preemption by Armed Force of Trans-Boundary Terrorist Threats: The Russian Perspective' (2007) 83 International Law Studies 83, 83–5.

[57] UNGA 'Note by the Secretary-General' (2 December 2004) UN Doc A/59/565, 53–8.

[58] FPC (n 40) para 32.

[59] Ministry of Foreign Affairs of the Russian Federation, 'O Pozitzii Rossii na 63 Sessii General'noy Assamblei OON' [On the Position of Russia at the 63rd session of the UN General Assembly] (10 September 2008) para 14 <https://www.mid.ru/general_assembly/-/asset_publisher/lrzZMhfoyRUj/content/id/325778> accessed 10 February 2020. Compare with Martens's: 'Self-defense of a State may not be unlimited: it starts from the moment of actual attack or from the moment when clear and threatening danger arises'—Martens (n 2) 304, or with Grotius's: 'The first Cause therefore of a just War, is an Injury, which tho' not done, yet threatens our Persons or our Estates' in Hugo Grotius, *The Rights of War and Peace* (first published 1625, Liberty Fund 2005) Book II, Chapter I, para II.3, 397. And further: 'But here 'tis necessary that the Danger be present, and as it were, contained in a Point'—ibid para V.1, 398.

those dealing with 'matters related to ensuring *international peace and security*' (Article 15 (1d)).[60] The 1996 Federal Law 'On Defense' provides for the authority of the President to 'negotiate and sign international treaties...on participation of the Armed Forces of the Russian Federation in operations to maintain peace and *international security*' (Article 4 (17)).[61] A noteworthy amendment introduced in 2009 in the aftermath of a brief armed conflict between Russia and Georgia[62] envisages that

> to maintain *international peace and security* and to protect the interests of the Russian Federation and its citizens, elements of the Armed Forces of the Russian Federation may be used beyond the territory of the Russian Federation promptly, in accordance with universally recognized principles and norms of international law, international treaties of the Russian Federation, and the present Federal Law.
>
> (Article 10 (2.1))[63]

Apparently, not only does the amendment create a certain terminological discrepancy within the body of a single act, it also introduces the condition of 'promptness' which implies the bypassing of certain procedures, both domestic and international, in situations when the government, or rather the President as Supreme Commander-in-Chief, deems it necessary to resort to military force.

The 1995 Federal Law 'On the Procedure for the Provision by the Russian Federation of Military and Civilian Personnel for the Participation in the Activities for the Maintenance and Restoration of *International Peace and Security*',[64] as the name would suggest, outlines internal procedures to be followed to authorize the provision of military, police, or civilian personnel for peacekeeping or peace enforcement operations, whether formed units (battalions) or individuals (UN police officers, military observers, or

[60] *SZRF* (17 July 1995) No 29, Item 2757 (emphasis added). The current consolidated texts of this and other cited legislative acts inclusive of all amendments are available from CONSULTANT PLUS Russian electronic legal reference tool.

[61] *SZRF* (3 June 1996) No 23, Item 2750 (emphasis added).

[62] The armed conflict between Russia and Georgia started during the night of 7 to 8 August 2008 with a sustained artillery attack by Georgian forces on the South Ossetian town of Tskhinvali and other locations, including positions of the Russian component of tri-partite (Russian, Georgian, and South Ossetian) Joint Peacekeeping Forces. The Independent International Fact-Finding Mission on the Conflict in Georgia (IIFFMCG) acknowledged those attacks and made an unequivocal conclusion: 'The use of force by Georgia against Russian peacekeeping forces in Tskhinvali in the night of 7/8 August 2008 was contrary to international law'. IIFFMCG, 'Report' (September 2009) vol I, 23 <https://www.echr.coe.int/Documents/HUDOC_38263_08_Annexes_ENG.pdf> accessed 27 January 2020.

[63] Specific tasks of the Armed Forces under that amendment include: (1) to repel an armed attack on elements of the Armed Forces of the Russian Federation, other forces or organs stationed beyond the territory of the Russian Federation; (2) to repel or prevent an armed attack on another State that addressed a respective request to the Russian Federation; (3) to protect the citizens of the Russian Federation beyond the territory of the Russian Federation from an armed attack against them; (4) to repress piracy and ensure safety of maritime navigation—*SZRF* (9 November 2009) No 45, Item 5270 (emphasis added).

[64] *SZRF* (26 June 1995) No 26, Item 2401 (emphasis added).

experts on mission).[65] The 1998 Federal Law 'On Military Duty and Military Service' deals with general terms and conditions of assignment to military service with missions for the maintenance and restoration of *international peace and security* (Articles 43.1 (1), 37 (1a), 38(4), 38 (7)).[66] The 2011 Federal Law 'On Police' specifically addresses the authority of the President to decide on 'participation of police officers in activities for the maintenance and restoration of *international peace and security*' (Article 2 (2)).[67] The 1999 Federal Law 'On Export Control' establishes as one of the principles of State policy in that sphere of regulation,

> the interaction with international organizations and foreign states in the matters of export control in order to strengthen *international security* and stability and to prevent proliferation of weapons of mass destruction and means of their delivery.
> (Article 5 (2))[68]

And yet barely any Russian law in force defines international security. Moreover, there is a conspicuous void in the 2002 Federal Constitutional Law[69] 'On Martial Law'[70] where it addresses 'acts of aggression against the Russian Federation', borrowing heavily from the Definition of Aggression,[71] but never referring to international peace and security or international security per se. Neither would the term be found in the 2006 Federal Law 'On Countering Terrorism', even though it explicitly provides, in Articles 6 and 8, for the use of armed force against targets outside Russian territory, including on the high seas over the continental shelf under Russian jurisdiction.[72]

E. Concluding Remarks

The general conclusion that may be drawn from sources having a bearing on Russia's official position with respect to international security is that the term applies primarily to international security in its military and political dimensions, including the use of force in self-defence or in pursuit of an international mandate, as well as arms control and non-proliferation. Recent developments, reflective of Russia's assertive approach to its military instrument as means of maintaining security along its periphery, include reinstated military presence in Abkhazia and South Ossetia following their separation

[65] For a detailed discussion of legislative history of that Law see Bakhtiyar Tuzmukhamedov, 'Russian Federation: The Pendulum of Powers and Accountability' in Charlotte Ku/Harold K Jacobson (eds), *Democratic Accountability and the Use of Force in International Law* (CUP 2002).

[66] *SZRF* (30 March 1998) No 13, Item 1475 (emphasis added).

[67] *SZRF* (14 February 2011) No 7, Item 900 (emphasis added).

[68] *SZRF* (26 July 1999) No 30, Item 3774 (emphasis added).

[69] Federal constitutional laws, which are similar to organic laws in other jurisdictions, stand above ordinary federal laws and are adopted in pursuit of an explicit constitutional instruction.

[70] *SZRF* (4 February 2002) No 5, Item 375.

[71] UNGA Res 3314(XXIX) (14 December 1974).

[72] *SZRF* (13 March 2006) No 11, Item 1146.

from Georgia, and reinstatement of Russia's jurisdiction over Crimea. The latter was achieved by and large without violence, and with a local drive to secede from Ukraine backed by Russian military presence. Other recent developments include Russia's military support for the Government of Syria as part of international counter-terrorism efforts.[73]

It is fair to say that other facets, such as human rights, sustainable development, and environmental protection to name but a few, are also acknowledged. These, however, are more likely to be viewed as autonomous spheres of regulation, adjacent to and intertwined with, international security. Whatever the scope and embrace of international security, according to Russia's official position it hinges on the rule of international law and its supremacy, drawn from the UN Charter.

[73] For further reading on foreign deployments of Russian forces see Bakhtiyar Tuzmukhamedov, 'Russian Forces in the Former USSR and Beyond' in Dieter Fleck (ed), *The Handbook of the Law of Visiting Forces* (2nd edn, OUP 2018).

CHAPTER 51

THE UNITED STATES

MALCOLM JORGENSEN

A. Introduction

For the United States (US) the 'international law of global security' is, in a distinctive sense, synonymous with the entire project of constructing global legal order. Uniquely preponderant power enjoyed since the end of the Second World War has translated into unparalleled US influence over the design and development of international law. United States, preferences thus manifest not merely in specific rules and regimes, but in purposive development of the entire structure of global legal order to favour American security interests. The task of characterizing this complex history is itself deeply political, but advocates have increasingly settled on appeals to variants of a US-led 'liberal' or 'rules-based' international order, as the claimed foundation for global prosperity and security.[1] These accounts gravitate towards an order fixed on key post-Second World War institutions and normative principles, especially as consolidated in the immediate post-Cold War era, which were largely constructed by and designed to underpin American and global security.[2] Such formulations remain forensic constructions of an idealized and predominantly Western-led legal order that, even if never fully realized, has claimed ideals of liberal and non-discriminatory rules governing a single coherent legal system.[3] The urgency with which its main beneficiaries now seek to define the US-led order arises precisely because of unprecedented challenges created by a combination of rising geopolitical competition, most prominently from China and Russia, security threats by

[1] eg G John Ikenberry, *Liberal Leviathan: The Origins, Crisis, and Transformation of the American World Order* (Princeton UP 2011) 2; DoD, 'Summary of the 2018 National Defense Strategy of the United States of America: Sharpening America Military's Competitive Edge' (2018) 1–2 <https://dod.defense.gov/Portals/1/Documents/pubs/2018-National-Defense-Strategy-Summary.pdf> accessed 29 April 2020.

[2] G John Ikenberry, 'Why the Liberal World Order Will Survive' (2018) 32 Ethics and International Affairs 17, 23.

[3] On constructions of the 'international' according to Western interests: Anthea Roberts, *Is International Law International?* (OUP 2017) 5.

non-State and transnational actors, and by wavering ideological commitments of the US itself. As foundations of the order decline, the particularistic and often contradictory ways in which American national security interests are pursued through law have become ever more apparent behind the veil of the 'liberal international order'.

Whatever the structure of the global legal order, its function in US national security terms remains to protect 'the fundamental values and core interests necessary to the continued existence and vitality of the state'.[4] The anxiety of advocates for variations of the liberal or rules-based order is thus not that rules will disappear from key domains of global politics, but rather that fragmented and competing bodies of rules will emerge in which rights and obligations of States are incapable of reconciliation within the terms of US-led institutions. A core theme of this chapter is thus the recurrent tension, across a range of security challenges, of the US seeking to sustain universal claims in its vision for international legal order, while simultaneously pursuing competitive security advantages through law. The chapter begins by reflecting on competing US conceptions of the relationship between national security and global order as they evolved across the twentieth century. The focus then turns to three significant trends defining the contemporary field. First are US attitudes towards multilateral institutions and global security, and the ongoing contest between beliefs that they are mutually reinforcing versus beliefs that US security and global institutions sit in zero-sum opposition. Second is the impact of the generational 'War on Terror', which has yielded more permissive interpretation and development of laws governing the global use of violence. The final trend is that towards competitive geopolitical interests restructuring international law, which is evident across diverse areas ranging from global economics, to cybersecurity, to the fragmentation of global order into spheres of influence.

B. Current Status of the Debate

Contestation of American claims to the universality of its global order are nothing new, with US–Soviet confrontation throughout the Cold War effectively yielding 'two systems of international law and two systems of world public order'.[5] These divisions were especially conspicuous in the UN system and the UN Security Council (UNSC), which were originally envisioned as the formal rules-based foundations for global security. United States leadership oversaw the realization of President Franklin Roosevelt's vision of the 'Four Policemen'[6] into a UNSC structure that formalized the US role at the apex of global security as one of five permanent members (P5).[7] The almost immediate paralysis of the UNSC due to Cold War divisions did not constrain the US in exercising executive

[4] Amos A Jordan et al, *American National Security* (6th edn, Johns Hopkins UP 2009) 3–4.

[5] W Michael Reisman, 'International Law After the Cold War' (1990) 84 AJIL 859.

[6] Comprised of the USA, United Kingdom, Soviet Union, and China.

[7] Including France: Evan Luard, *A History of the United Nations: Volume 1: The Years of Western Domination, 1945–1955* (Palgrave Macmillan 1982) 18–19, 24.

type global functions, however, but merely normalized its use of military power without UNSC authorization.[8] The preference for approaching international law via unilateral interpretations was exemplified in the 'Reagan corollary' to international law, which made a virtue of the marginalized role of UN institutions in 'an attempt to pressure the international legal system into changing in a manner beneficial to United States interests'.[9] This strategy seemed close to realization in the immediate post-Cold War years, with the US promulgating the unity between its national and global security interests through law. The high-water mark was likely the 1991 Persian Gulf War in which the US reasserted a central UNSC role in forging a 'new world order—a world where the rule of law, not the law of the jungle, governs the conduct of nations'.[10] Yet appearance of consensus quickly declined, as the US met with forceful opposition to its security vision in relation to its many subsequent uses and legal justifications for force without UNSC authorization, including prominently in the 1999 NATO intervention in Kosovo, in Iraq in 2003, and throughout the ongoing Syrian Civil War.[11]

What has remained consistent across both the Cold War and post-Cold War eras is that debates over the US role in global security law have been persistently prompted by the US itself. United States claims in high-profile cases have systematically sought to achieve new developments in established understanding of the international rules and institutions governing traditional and emerging security threats. American hegemony has not meant control over every legal development but, rather, that the US has become 'the one against whose ideas regarding the system of international law all others debate'.[12] The consequence of global power preponderance is that the US is 'generally averse to limiting its scope of action via treaty; avoids being constrained by those treaties to which it has adhered; and disregards, when inconvenient, customary international law, confident that its breach will be hailed as a new rule'.[13] Under conditions of hegemony legal scholars and practitioners cannot remain silent when the US engages in such conduct, but are obliged to engage in discourse over the changes being sought in global legal order, and the legitimacy and global security implications of the US role in bringing them about.

Continuity in hegemonic incentives does not, however, equate to unity in US conceptions of security through law, which have been systematically contested according to the fortunes of domestic electoral politics, geopolitical pressures, and ideological forces.

[8] David L Bosco, *Five to Rule Them All: The UN Security Council and the Making of the Modern World* (OUP 2009) 3.

[9] Stuart S Malawer, 'Reagan's Law and Foreign Policy, 1981–1987: The "Reagan Corollary" of International Law' (1988) 29 Harvard International Law Journal 85, 85.

[10] George H W Bush, 'Address to the Nation Announcing Allied Military Action in the Persian Gulf' (White House, 16 January 1991) <www.presidency.ucsb.edu/node/265756> accessed 14 April 2020.

[11] Paul R Williams/Sophie Pearlman, 'Use of Force in Humanitarian Crises: Addressing the Limitations of UN Security Council Authorization' (2019) 51 Case Western Reserve Journal of International Law 211.

[12] Shirley V Scott, 'The Impact on International Law of US Non-Compliance' in Michael Byers/Georg Nolte (eds), *United States Hegemony and the Foundations of International Law* (CUP 2003) 450–1.

[13] Jose E Alvarez, 'Hegemonic International Law Revisited' (2003) 97 AJIL 873.

The contestation is clearly evident in the periodic National Security Strategy (NSS), in which the President fulfils a Congressional mandate to communicate a conception of national security and the strategy for its attainment.[14] Evolution of these reports over more than thirty years demonstrates that, whereas they 'are predominantly convergent on national security ends', they do in contrast display 'significant divergence' regarding the instrumental role of the law.[15] A prominent example is the marked shift between the administration of President George W Bush (Bush 43) and its 'vision of American leadership of coalitions unconstrained by formal international institutions', towards acceptance by President Barack Obama of the strategic value of adhering to 'international standards' prescribed by law.[16] Obama's preface to the NSS 2010 explicitly sets out the strongest version of the perceived positive relationship between upholding a global legal system and American national security:

> The rule of law—and our capacity to enforce it—advances our national security and strengthens our leadership ... Around the globe, it allows us to hold actors accountable, while supporting both international security and the stability of the global economy. America's commitment to the rule of law is fundamental to our efforts to build an international order that is capable of confronting the emerging challenges of the 21st century.[17]

The Trump Administration's NSS 2017, in contrast, has referred to the value of 'rules' primarily in the context of a competition for influence within multilateral forums, and avoids any such general commitment to the 'rule of law' as a security ideal at the global level.[18] Setting aside the hitherto US consensus on some variation of the liberal international order, the NSS 2017 criticizes continued assumptions that, by relying on such an order, 'American power would be unchallenged and self-sustaining'.[19] In this sense the latest NSS appears to represent a fraught transition between the security orthodoxy and a 'full-throated commitment to maintaining primacy and unbinding the US from multilateral obligations'.[20]

The dynamic interplay between alternative US national security conceptions and the development of international law has elicited an array of explanatory frameworks to explain seemingly contradictory policies. Scott interprets variability in US legal policy

[14] 50 US Code § 3043(b).

[15] Aaron Ettinger 'US National Security Strategies: Patterns of Continuity and Change 1987–2015' (2017) 36 Comparative Strategy 115, 115.

[16] ibid 119; The White House, 'National Security Strategy' (May 2010) 22 <https://www.hsdl.org/?abstract&did=24251> accessed 29 April 2020 (NSS 2010).

[17] NSS 2010 (n 16) 37, ii and 2.

[18] The White House, 'National Security Strategy of the United States of America' (December 2017) 17, 40 <https://www.whitehouse.gov/wp-content/uploads/2017/12/NSS-Final-12-18-2017-0905.pdf> accessed 29 April 2020 (NSS 2017).

[19] ibid 2.

[20] Aaron Ettinger, 'Trump's National Security Strategy: "America First" Meets the Establishment' (2018) 73 International Journal 474, 475.

as the product of a 'quest for legal security'. This has taken a 'defensive' form, in the sense of seeking 'protection of its domestic political and legal systems from external influence via law', as well as an 'offensive' strategy of influencing the 'legal and policy choices of other states via law'.[21] By identifying these strategies grounded in legal security Scott reveals a 'remarkable degree of consistency' beneath apparent contradictions.[22] Jorgensen focuses on the causal role of America's several foreign policy ideologies, which have structured competing beliefs about the relationship between security and law. 'Illiberal internationalism', for example, engages international law with a 'principal focus on national security' and seeks to develop law as a tool 'to manage rather than overcome security threats'.[23] 'Liberal internationalism', in contrast, 'addresses national security more indirectly, by externalising liberal values into an international legal environment to reinforce global security over the long term'.[24] For Meiertöns the pertinent sets of ideas are more explicit and purposive, in the form of the various 'doctrines of US security policy' that are generally named after US presidents and well known in foreign policy writings. These doctrines have, in particular, set out political principles that reframe and at times override laws on the use of force in ways seen necessary for US national security.[25] Reading the US government's own shifting accounts of national security from a range of scholarly perspectives confirms the crucial importance of understanding geopolitical and ideological context, which continue to structure responses to the full range of international legal challenges set out below.

C. Recent Developments and Contemporary Challenges

1. Multilateralism and Global Security

Its brief revival as the centrepiece of global security architecture notwithstanding, the post-Cold War fracturing of purpose between the P5 has seen the UNSC revert to a significant constraint on US security policy.[26] Frustrations have contributed to US government default on its UN dues, and to various calls for the UN to either submit to

[21] Shirley V Scott, *International Law, US Power: The United States' Quest for Legal Security* (CUP 2012) 17–18.

[22] ibid 29.

[23] Malcolm Jorgensen, *American Foreign Policy Ideology and The International Rule of Law: Contesting Power Through the International Criminal Court* (CUP 2020) 102.

[24] ibid.

[25] Heiko Meiertöns, *The Doctrines of US Security Policy: An Evaluation under International Law* (CUP 2010) 240.

[26] Sean D Murphy, 'The Security Council, Legitimacy, and the Concept of Collective Security after the Cold War' (1994) 32 Columbia Journal of Transnational Law 201, 207.

US preferences or be 'irrelevant',[27] or, for a 'supermajority' of democratic States to override the positive obligations of the UNSC where it has 'prevented free nations from keeping faith' with liberal principles.[28] Yet, despite these challenges to legitimacy in times of crisis, the US position remains complicated, with a parallel history in which the US prioritizes UNSC mechanisms in meeting a wide range of ordinary security challenges. These range from implementing State sanctions, such as those against Iran for violating its nuclear non-proliferation obligations, authorizing the deployment of peacekeeping forces, renewing missions in Afghanistan and Iraq, referring matters to the International Criminal Court (ICC), to combatting terrorist organizations.[29] Such ambivalence is in no small part a factor of the US position of global dominance, whereby advantages of multilateral cooperation are tempered by a perception that policy goals have no longer 'seemed to depend so much on reaching agreement with other states and acquiescing in the inevitable compromises that reaching such agreement often requires'.[30]

The dynamics are nowhere clearer than in the fraught US policy regarding the ICC, heralded by some as 'the most important institutional innovation since the founding of the United Nations'.[31] For ICC advocates a foundational rationale was always that: 'National security interests of the United States fundamentally concern the creation of a peaceful, liberal democratic, and economically integrated international system that allows America to flourish.' In this view the ICC promised to 'improve security for individuals and among states' by serving as 'another tool that can be used to promote the behaviours and international system that best suit the United States'.[32] Moreover, the ICC was seen as fundamentally 'linked to U.S. national security in its effect on the legitimacy of U.S. leadership'.[33]

Understanding conflicted US support and ultimate opposition to joining the ICC, as well as a range of multilateral security initiatives, necessitates an understanding of US views on the causal links between global institutions and US security. The establishment of the UN system was originally envisioned by the US in terms of a strategy for securing a global order capable of complimenting and reinforcing its internal values and institutions. Reversing this logic, US retreat from core multilateral institutions is premised on a

[27] George W Bush, 'Address to the United Nations General Assembly in New York City' (12 September 2002) <https://www.presidency.ucsb.edu/node/213436> accessed 19 April 2020.

[28] Anne-Marie Slaughter/G John Ikenberry, *Forging a World of Liberty under Law: US National Security in the 21st Century* (Woodrow Wilson School of Public and International Affairs 27 September 2006) 26.

[29] Kara C McDonald/Stewart M Patrick, 'UN Security Council Enlargement and US Interests' (2010) Council on Foreign Relations Report No 59, 16 <https://www.cfr.org/report/un-security-council-enlargement-and-us-interests> accessed 29 April 2020.

[30] William H Taft IV, 'A View from the Top: American Perspectives on International Law after the Cold War' (2006) 31 Yale Journal of International Law 503, 508.

[31] Robert C Johansen, 'A Turning Point in International Relations? Establishing a Permanent International Criminal Court' (Joan B Kroc Institute for International Peace Studies 1997) cited in William Schabas, *An Introduction to the International Criminal Court* (CUP 2011) ix.

[32] Sarah B Sewall et al, 'The United States and the International Criminal Court: An Overview' in Sarah B Sewall/Carl Kaysen (eds), *The United States and the International Criminal Court: National Security and International Law* (Rowman and Littlefield 2000) 4.

[33] ibid 4–5.

competing view that, rather than operating as guardians of US sovereignty, the diverse foreign interests embodied in global institutions pose an existential threat to particularistic US values and institutions, being the ultimate ends of national security policy. In a 2018 speech to the UN General Assembly (UNGA), President Trump defended US withdrawal from the UN Human Rights Council and opposition to the ICC in terms that the US 'will never surrender America's sovereignty to an unelected, unaccountable, global bureaucracy'. In contrast to seeking security through global law: 'America is governed by Americans. We reject the ideology of globalism, and we embrace the doctrine of patriotism.'[34] This logic now extends across a range of fields, including in US opposition to the new Global Compact on Migration, since '[m]igration should not be governed by an international body unaccountable to our own citizens', and in US intent to withdraw from both the 2015 Paris Climate Agreement[35] and from the World Health Organization (WHO) during the 2020 COVID-19 pandemic.[36] It has likewise underpinned US denouncement or withdrawal from various Cold War era agreements, including major arms-control treaties,[37] dispute resolution provisions under the 1961 Vienna Convention on Diplomatic Relations,[38] and repeated threats to withdraw from NATO.[39] Whatever the pitfalls of illiberal and nationalist perceptions, they provide a significant explanation for persistent and vigorous opposition to globalized legal frameworks as a means for achieving security at home.

2. War on Terror

It is doubtless that the US approach to global security law underwent a transformation following the 9/11 terrorist attacks, when US policy turned towards more permissive interpretations of the entire legal framework governing the 'War on Terror'.[40] One consequence of the shock and sense of vulnerability created by the attacks was a desire amongst some policymakers to restructure law in service of an illusory quest for 'absolute

[34] Donald J Trump, 'Remarks by President Trump to the 73rd Session of the United Nations General Assembly, New York, NY' (25 September 2018) <www.whitehouse.gov/briefings-statements/remarks-president-trump-73rd-session-united-nations-generalassembly-new-york-ny/> accessed 14 April 2020.

[35] Donald J Trump, 'Statement by President Trump on the Paris Climate Accord' (White House Rose Garden, 1 June 2017) <https://www.whitehouse.gov/briefings-statements/statement-president-trump-paris-climate-accord/> accessed 14 April 2020. Concluded under the United Nations Framework Convention on Climate Change 1771 UNTS 107.

[36] Donald J Trump, 'Remarks by President Trump on Actions Against China' (Remarks, 29 May 2020) <https://www.whitehouse.gov/briefings-statements/remarks-president-trump-actions-china/> accessed 25 August 2020.

[37] Jean Galbraith, 'United States Initiates Withdrawal from Intermediate-Range Nuclear Forces Treaty' (2019) 113 AJIL 631.

[38] John B Bellinger, 'The Trump Administration's Approach to International Law and Courts: Are We Seeing a Turn for the Worse?' (2019) 51 Case Western Reserve Journal of International Law 7, 19.

[39] Scott R Anderson, 'Saving NATO' (*Lawfare*, 25 July 2018) <https://www.lawfareblog.com/saving-nato> accessed 14 April 2020.

[40] Helen Duffy, *The 'War on Terror' and the Framework of International Law* (CUP 2005) 2–3.

security'.[41] Even within the discipline of international law it has been observed that national security law was subsequently elevated to a privileged position, to a degree that now distinguishes the US academy from global counterparts.[42] In most orthodox legal accounts, however, the novel dimensions of the War on Terror did not create any legal black hole or 'limbo' but, rather, invoked existing rights under 'criminal law and the law governing peaceful settlement of disputes and resort to armed force' combined with 'constraints on how those responses may be executed' as set out under international human rights and humanitarian law.[43] Yet, despite the availability of these legal frameworks, US policy has continued to diverge on the question of whether upholding universal and liberal conceptions of law are a path towards global security, or whether narrow national security imperatives should reshape the field.

a. *Use of Force Rules*

The distinctive contributions of US practice to global security remain most conspicuous and consequential in the rules governing the use of military force. States are legally entitled to use force only within the framework of the UN Charter, namely in cases of self-defence under Article 51, or when collective action is authorized by the UNSC under Chapter VII.[44] As the State with the most opportunities to exercise these powers, the US has, with mixed success, remained at the forefront of defining and developing the boundaries of relevant prohibitions. Most notoriously the US has sought expansive interpretations of the right to self-defence under Article 51, including claims to anticipatory or even pre-emptive self-defence. The so-called 'Bush Doctrine' was described by Bush 43 as a new US strategic policy to 'confront the worst threats before they emerge'.[45] The NSS 2002 argued the lawfulness of the doctrine by reference to the modern threat posed by weapons of mass destruction, which required that the US 'adapt the concept of imminent threat to the capabilities and objectives of today's adversaries'.[46] By removing limitations on self-defence embodied in the legal concept of 'imminence',[47] the administration sought to develop law into an enabling framework rather than one capable of constraining US policy. That interpretation has unsurprisingly met with almost total rejection for inviting an 'unraveling of norms on the use of force'.[48] The permissive attitude towards global security law was nevertheless evident in US justifications for

[41] David C Hendrickson, 'Toward Universal Empire: The Dangerous Quest for Absolute Security' (2002) 19 World Policy Journal 1, 9.

[42] Roberts (n 3) 104–5, 225.

[43] Duffy (n 40) 10.

[44] James Crawford, *Brownlie's Principles of Public International Law* (8th edn, OUP 2012) 746–68.

[45] George W Bush, 'Graduation Speech at West Point' (United States Military Academy, New York, 1 June 2002) <https://georgewbush-whitehouse.archives.gov/news/releases/2002/06/20020601-3.html> accessed 25 August 2020; The White House, 'The National Security Strategy of the United States of America' (September 2002) ii <https://2009-2017.state.gov/documents/organization/63562.pdf> accessed 29 April 2020 (NSS 2002).

[46] NSS 2002 (n 45) 15.

[47] Crawford (n 44) 750–2.

[48] Sean D Murphy, 'Assessing the Legality of Invading Iraq' (2004) 92 Georgetown Law Journal 173, 176–7.

the 2020 airstrikes in Iraq that killed Iranian General Qassem Soleimani.[49] The circumstances failed to meet any generally recognized threshold for the lawful use of force in self-defence—whether against an imminent threat or otherwise.[50] Yet the President and other senior officials employed the rhetoric of 'imminent' attacks in their public diplomacy, in a manner that cloaked otherwise unlawful actions with the symbols of legal authority.[51]

The US has similarly sought to extend the law to permit self-defence against non-State actors, which were recast in the context of the War on Terror as the primary threat to US security. American preferences have met with moderate success in this regard, including during the 2001 US military action in Afghanistan, which likely saw a new customary rule develop that sanctioned the use of force against States harbouring terrorists even when an attack did not emanate from the State itself.[52] In practice such a legal development benefits only States with power projection capabilities, and thereby has the effect of translating preponderant US political power into '*de facto* exceptionalism' within the doctrines of international law.[53] This precedent facilitated a further prominent example of US rule development in the so-called 'unwilling or unable' doctrine, which the US articulated in 2014 to defend the legality of its airstrikes in Syrian territory in the collective defence of Iraq against a non-State actor. In that case the US reasoned that the Assad government had shown itself to be unwilling or unable to prevent its territory being used by the Islamic State group to launch cross-border attacks.[54] Although not yet accepted as orthodoxy, the practice has been fortified by sophisticated jurisprudential articulations[55] and the explicit or tacit endorsement by a handful of States,[56] a fact that, at the very least, has unsettled any consensus against the doctrine.

[49] 'Notice on the Legal and Policy Frameworks Guiding the United States' Use of Military Force and Related National Security Operations' (14 February 2020) <https://foreignaffairs.house.gov/_cache/files/4/3/4362ca46-3a7d-43e8-a3ec-be0245705722/6E1A0F30F9204E380A7AD0C84EC572EC.doc148.pdf> accessed 29 April 2020.

[50] Ryan Goodman, 'White House "1264 Notice" and Novel Legal Claims for Military Action Against Iran' (*Just Security*, 14 February 2020) <https://www.justsecurity.org/68594/white-house-1264-notice-and-novel-legal-claims-for-military-action-against-iran/> accessed 29 April 2020.

[51] Donald J Trump, 'Remarks by President Trump on the Killing of Qasem Soleimani' (Mar-a-Lago, 3 January 2020) <https://www.whitehouse.gov/briefings-statements/remarks-president-trump-killing-qasem-soleimani/> accessed 29 April 2020.

[52] Christine Gray, *International Law and the Use of Force* (4th edn, OUP 2018) 200–2.

[53] Michael Byers, 'Preemptive Self-Defense: Hegemony, Equality and Strategies of Legal Change' (2003) 11 The Journal of Political Philosophy 171, 184–5.

[54] Statement of Samantha Power, cited in Marty Lederman, 'The War Powers Resolution and Article 51 Letters Concerning Use of Force in Syria Against ISIL and the Khorasan Group' (*Just Security*, 23 September 2014) <http://justsecurity.org/15436/war-powers-resolution-article-51-letters-force-syria-isil-khorasan-group/> accessed 14 April 2020.

[55] Ashley Deeks, '"Unwilling or Unable": Toward a Normative Framework for Extra-Territorial Self-Defense' (2012) 52 Virginia Journal of International Law 483.

[56] For a spectrum of State views ranging from explicit endorsement to objection: Elena Chachko/Ashley Deeks, 'Which States Support the "Unwilling and Unable" Test?' (*Lawfare*, 10 October 2016) <https://www.lawfareblog.com/which-states-support-unwilling-and-unable-test> accessed 14 April 2020.

The US has in parallel sought to reinterpret the scope of UNSC authorizations to use force under Chapter VII, which have been at the heart of the 'long war with Iraq', lasting (at least) from 1990 to 2011.[57] The legality of airstrikes carried out throughout the 1990s under President Clinton was based in part on implied and revived authorization of UNSC resolutions from the Persian Gulf War,[58] which became the explicit justification for the 2003 invasion.[59] Then legal adviser to the Department of State William Taft IV argued that America's use of force in 2003 'was and is lawful'.[60] Yet, the argument gained little traction outside of the US, with the 2003 invasion seen to represent 'not simply the exceptional breaking of the rules by a big power, but the beginning of a generally more liberal, or rather permissive, attitude towards the rules regarding the use of force as an instrument of state power'.[61]

Finally, beyond the War on Terror, there have been arguments for a right to use force beyond the two legally accepted grounds in the UN Charter, through various versions of a 'humanitarian' exception as encapsulated in the policy guidance of the so-called Responsibility to Protect (R2P).[62] The US resiled from fully articulating such an exception during the 1999 Kosovo intervention, which was spearheaded by the Clinton administration without UNSC authorization to prevent a 'humanitarian catastrophe'.[63] United States' lawyers presciently recognized that any articulated exception could be weaponized by US adversaries in a range of cases that bore little resemblance to the Kosovo crisis.[64] Such proved to be the case when Russia bolstered its legal case for the 2014 annexation of Crimea.[65] Nevertheless, leading US lawyers have continued to push for such an exception, with former State Department Legal Adviser Harold Koh arguing that refusal to do so is flawed for exhibiting an 'absolutist, formalist, textualist, originalist quality' that cannot be squared with beliefs that 'international law should serve human purposes'.[66] Overall, it can be concluded that, although US claims and practice rarely shift global legal consensus, they have achieved a fracturing of views on the

[57] Timothy J Lynch, 'Obama, Liberalism, and US Foreign Policy' in Inderjeet Parmar et al (eds), *Obama and the World: New Directions in US Foreign Policy* (Routledge 2014) 47.

[58] Gavin A Symes, 'Force Without Law: Seeking a Legal Justification for the September 1996 US Military Intervention in Iraq' (1998) 19 Michigan Journal of International Law 581, 602–8.

[59] Through the combined operation of UNSC Res 678 (1990), UNSC Res 687 (1991), UNSC Res 1441 (2002): William H Taft IV/Todd F Buchwald, 'Preemption, Iraq, and International Law' (2003) 97 AJIL 557, 559–60.

[60] ibid 557.

[61] Heike Krieger/Georg Nolte, 'The International Rule of Law—Rise or Decline? Approaching Current Foundational Challenges' in Heike Krieger et al (eds), *The International Rule of Law Rise or Decline?* (OUP 2019) 10.

[62] ICISS, *The Responsibility to Protect: Report of the International Commission on Intervention and State Sovereignty* (International Development Research Centre 2001).

[63] Michael P Scharf/Paul R Williams, *Shaping Foreign Policy in Times of Crisis: The Role of International Law and the State Department Legal Adviser* (CUP 2010) 166–7.

[64] Anne Peters, 'Crimea: Does "The West" Now Pay the Price for Kosovo?' (*EJIL:Talk!*, 22 April 2014) <https://www.ejiltalk.org/crimea-does-the-west-now-pay-the-price-for-kosovo/> accessed 14 April 2020.

[65] Simon Chesterman, 'Is International Law Effective: The Case of Russia and Ukraine' (2014) 108 ASIL Proc 37, 38–9.

[66] Harold H Koh, *The Trump Administration and International Law* (OUP 2018) 129–30.

legitimacy and content of international law in each case. The consequence has been to sustain an arguable case for US actions taken in the name of national and global security and in ways that few States are capable of replicating.

b. *Laws of War*

Amongst the areas of international law that the US has historically proven itself most committed to both complying with, and being seen to comply with, is in the conduct of armed conflict. Yet, as with the use of force, the security imperatives of the War on Terror have led to prominent reconsiderations of the security benefits of a liberal legal regime versus the carving out of exceptions. The Department of Defense Law of War Manual was released in 2015, which, at over 1,200 pages, 'represents the single most authoritative consolidation of US policy and legal positions regarding the lawful conduct of hostilities'.[67] In security terms, the reality of unmatched capacity to project global military power creates strong incentives for the US to increase the efficiency of military power through rules that ensure discipline in the conduct of US personnel, minimize political opposition, and ensure interoperability and reciprocity on the battlefield. Charles Dunlap noted the particular value of the Manual for building a 'counter-lawfare campaign' in cases where 'a technologically inferior opponent attempts to use allegations of violations of the law of war to undermine the public support that democracies so often need to successfully wage war'.[68]

In seeking to gain an overall understanding of US views from this sprawling document, the Manual's treatment of the role of 'specially affected states' in the development of customary international law is particularly illuminating. United States' lawyers had previously criticized a comprehensive study by the International Committee of the Red Cross on customary international law in armed conflicts for, amongst other reasons, failing 'to pay due regard to the practice of specially affected States'.[69] The Manual responds that States which have 'had significant opportunities to develop a carefully considered military doctrine, may be expected to have contributed a greater quantity and quality of State practice relevant to the law of war than States that have not'.[70] By adopting this unusually broad interpretation, the Manual 'seems to be asserting that as the leading military power, and the state perhaps most frequently resorting to the use of

[67] Michael A Newton, 'Framing Thoughts on the DoD Law of War Manual and this Commentary' in Michael A Newton (ed), *The United States Department of Defense Law of War Manual: Commentary and Critique* (CUP 2019) 4; US DoD, 'Law of War Manual' (Office of General Counsel, December 2016) <https://dod.defense.gov/Portals/1/Documents/pubs/DoD%20Law%20of%20War%20Manual%20-%20June%202015%20Updated%20Dec%202016.pdf?ver=2016-12-13-172036-190> accessed 29 April 2020.

[68] Charles J Dunlap, 'Practitioners and the Law of War Manual' in Newton (n 67) 74, 66.

[69] John B Bellinger III/William J Haynes II, cited in David Glazier et al, 'Failing Our Troops: A Critical Assessment of the Department of Defense Law of War Manual' (2017) 42 Yale Journal of International Law 215, 259; Jean-Marie Henckaerts/Louise Doswald-Beck, *Customary International Humanitarian Law: Volume I: Rules* (CUP 2005).

[70] DoD Law of War Manual (n 67) 32.

force in the modern era, the United States should have the dominant say in establishing the content of the current law of war'.[71]

Yet, despite these comprehensive aspirations, the years after 9/11 saw a determination within the US government not to apply the Geneva Conventions to detainees who themselves were not 'living up to the laws of war'.[72] Then Secretary of State Condoleezza Rice defended the 'enhanced' interrogation of detainees, including through waterboarding, as being 'consistent with our international obligations and American law'.[73] The deep divisions within US national security views were replicated in the US Supreme Court itself, which held in *Hamdan v Rumsfeld*,[74] by majority, that detainees had customary legal rights exercisable against the US government, as codified under Common Article 3 of the 1949 Geneva Conventions.[75] Rice's successor as Secretary of State Hillary Clinton declared: '[t]hat America is a nation of laws is one of our great strengths, and the Supreme Court has been clear that the fight against terrorism cannot occur in a "legal black hole" '.[76] Nevertheless, the Obama administration faced its own comparable criticisms for defending the legality of targeted killing of enemy combatants using drone technology, which was facilitated by broad rereading of the laws of combat and due process obligations.[77] By so doing, the US may have addressed immediate security objectives, but contributed to the trend towards more permissive and unaccountable uses of violence at the global level.[78]

3. The Return of Geopolitics

United States' influence extends not only to the content of specific bodies of international law, but also in restructuring the legal order as it operates across geographical domains most critical to American security. Forms of legal fragmentation along geopolitical lines pose a particular challenge to the ideal of a rules-based order and can be

[71] Glazier et al (n 69) 261–2.

[72] United States Senate, Committee on Foreign Relations, 'Nomination of Dr. Condoleezza Rice to be Secretary of State' (First Session 109th Congress, 18 January 2005) 117 <https://www.govinfo.gov/content/pkg/CHRG-109shrg22847/pdf/CHRG-109shrg22847.pdf> accessed 29 April 2020.

[73] Condoleezza Rice, *No Higher Honor: A Memoir of my Years in Washington* (Random House 2011) 117, 121, 497.

[74] (2006) 548 US 557.

[75] ibid 633 per Stevens J. cf the dissent of Thomas J ibid 718–19 referring to Protocol Additional to the Geneva Conventions of 12 August 1949, and relating to the protection of victims of international armed conflicts 1125 UNTS 3 art 75.

[76] Hillary Rodham Clinton, *Hard Choices: A Memoir* (Simon and Schuster 2014) 184.

[77] Harold H Koh, 'The Obama Administration and International Law' (ASIL Annual Meeting, 25 March 2010) <https://2009-2017.state.gov/s/l/releases/remarks/139119.htm> accessed 14 April 2020; cf Nils Melzer, *Targeted Killing in International Law* (OUP 2008) 243.

[78] Anthony Dworkin, 'Soleimani Strike Marks a Novel Shift in Targeted Killing, Dangerous to the Global Order' (*Just Security*, 7 January 2020) <https://www.justsecurity.org/67937/soleimani-strike-marks-a-novel-shift-in-targeted-killing-dangerous-to-the-global-order/> accessed 14 April 2020.

expected to increase in significance, both with the rise of regional competitors, and with the decline in US recognition of the security dividends from investing in such order.

a. *Geoeconomics*

However the 'rules-based order' is defined, the global system of economic law with the World Trade Organization (WTO) and its dispute settlement mechanism at its centre are widely recognized as amongst its greatest achievements.[79] They (and the Bretton Woods institutions) represent both the fruits of US leadership, and the divergent implications of its competing security interests. The rise in competitive security interests has led to the renewed significance of geoeconomics where, as 'territorial entities, spatially rather than functionally defined, states cannot follow a commercial logic that would ignore their own boundaries'.[80] The NSS 2017 declared that 'economic security is national security' and observed that the 'post-war order' of global institutions has been eroded by a complacency in which the US has 'stood by while countries exploited the international institutions we helped to build'.[81] Naming specifically China and Russia, the NSS continues that:

> These competitions require the United States to rethink the policies of the past two decades—policies based on the assumption that engagement with rivals and their inclusion in international institutions and global commerce would turn them into benign actors and trustworthy partners. For the most part, this premise turned out to be false.[82]

The associated policy responses have included blocking the filling of Appellate Body vacancies in the WTO to end the effective operation of the dispute settlement system. This obstruction constitutes a direct challenge to the rules-based order and is driven by broader recognition that WTO law increasingly replicates rather than impedes the decline of US dominance relative to competitors.[83]

The US now leads a global trend towards preferential trade agreements (PTAs), which ostensibly bypass the WTO system, and have been unmistakably pursued to shore up US security relationships. 'Securitization' of US foreign economic policy became especially pronounced during the Bush 43 administration, when strategic interests drove the negotiation of PTAs with a range of allies 'as a way of bolstering or rewarding good partners in the fight against terrorism'.[84] The importance of securitized interests highlights the particular strategic incoherence of US rejection of the Trans-Pacific Partnership

[79] Stewart Patrick, 'World Order: What, Exactly, Are the Rules?' (2016) 39 The Washington Quarterly 7, 14.

[80] Edward N Luttwak, 'From Geopolitics to Geo-Economics: Logic of Conflict, Grammar of Commerce' (1990) 20 The National Interest 17, 18.

[81] NSS 2017 (n 18) 2, 17. [82] ibid 3.

[83] Gregory Shaffer/Henry Gao, 'China's Rise: How It Took on the US at the WTO' (2018) 1 University of Illinois Law Review 115.

[84] Richard Higgott, 'US Foreign Policy and the "Securitization" of Economic Globalization' (2004) 41 International Politics 147, 165.

(TPP), which was touted as a 'mega-regional trade agreement' with the potential to realign global economic law in the United States' favour.[85] The TPP was always constructed upon securitized foundations, with former US Defense Secretary Ashton Carter arguing that 'passing TPP is as important to me as another aircraft carrier'.[86] For President Obama the deal was 'more than just a trade pact; it also has important strategic and geopolitical benefits. TPP is a long-term investment in our shared security and in universal human rights.'[87] US withdrawal has assisted in vacating the field for China's alternative Regional Comprehensive Economic Partnership (RCEP) trade agreement, and thereby contributed to the trend towards geographically fragmented rules-based orders.[88]

b. *Cybersecurity*

Many of the assumptions and principles guiding conduct in traditional security domains are now replicated in the new frontiers of global security, including crucially in cyberspace. In 2012 Harold Koh posed the fundamental question: 'how do we apply old laws of war to new cyber-circumstances, staying faithful to enduring principles, while accounting for changing times and technologies?'[89] Koh reaffirmed his well-established position that international law is a complete system and that existing rules and principles, including those governing the use of force, extended by analogy to cover the new terrain.[90] In this approach, the US confirmed recognition of the security benefits of being enmeshed within and bolstering a global system of laws that 'constrain the activity of all countries, including the United States'.[91] Nevertheless, the more recent National Cyber Strategy has adapted the pillars of the NSS 2017, turning to more direct recognition of geostrategic challenges and an associated desire to reassert US advantage in a domain hitherto defined by the absence of geographical borders.[92]

Cybersecurity is no hypothetical exercise in circumstances where Russian interference with the US electoral system and domestic politics has long been identified by the

[85] Arlo Poletti, 'Containment through Trade? Explaining the US Support for the Trans-Pacific Partnership' in Matteo Dian et al (eds), *US Foreign Policy in a Challenging World* (Springer 2018) 46.

[86] Ash Carter, 'Remarks on the Next Phase of the U.S. Rebalance to the Asia-Pacific' (McCain Institute, Arizona State University, 6 April 2015) <https://www.defense.gov/News/Speeches/Speech-View/Article/606660/remarks-on-the-next-phase-of-the-us-rebalance-to-the-asia-pacific-mccain-instit/> accessed 14 April 2020.

[87] Barack H Obama, 'Remarks at ASEAN Business and Investment Summit' (Kuala Lumpur, 20 November 2015) <https://obamawhitehouse.archives.gov/the-press-office/2015/11/20/remarks-president-obama-asean-business-and-investment-summit> accessed 14 April 2020.

[88] Shaffer/Gao (n 83) 181–2.

[89] Harold H Koh, 'International Law in Cyberspace' (2012) 54 Harvard International Law Journal (Online) 1, 2 (emphasis omitted).

[90] ibid 3–4.

[91] Brian J Egan, 'Cybersecurity, International Law, and the First Year of the Trump Administration' (2018) 32 Temple International and Comparative Law Journal 135, 139.

[92] The White House, 'National Cyber Strategy of the United States of America' (September 2018) 3, 20 <https://www.whitehouse.gov/wp-content/uploads/2018/09/National-Cyber-Strategy.pdf> accessed 29 April 2020.

United States' own intelligence community as a serious and ongoing threat.[93] The risk of geopolitical fragmentation became increasingly evident in 2018, however, when the UNGA adopted parallel resolutions on cybersecurity, with one sponsored by Russia and a competing one sponsored by the US and twenty-six other States.[94] The latter resolution confirmed that the 'international rules-based order' extended into cyberspace, and replicated language already familiar in the maritime domain of safeguarding a 'free' and 'open' order.[95] Russian-backed proposals for a new international cyber convention have been rejected by the US, which has preferred to develop existing norms and rules without ceding its more advanced cyber capabilities.[96] In substance, US proposals for 'defending the rule of law in cyberspace' remain deeply mindful of prevailing in competition with China, Russia, Iran, and North Korea, who 'actively work to destabilize the US-led international order, thereby promoting and advancing their own geopolitical interests'.[97]

c. *Spheres of Influence*

The structural legal ideal embedded in notions of the liberal international order is that legal rules remain unified and capable of determination within the constraints of a single coherent system. On this point, US policy has been historically contradictory, with the 'Monroe Doctrine' long subjecting legal rules to a buffer zone of exceptional rights in the Western hemisphere.[98] Although not a legal rule or regime, the claimed right to expel foreign powers from its own hemisphere provided a framework throughout the Cold War for engaging in the kinds of use of force that were ruled illegal in the 1986 *Nicaragua* case.[99] The historical reality of imperialistic US policies led the Obama administration to finally declare in 2013 that the 'era of the Monroe Doctrine is over'.[100] Yet, in recent years, the US has explicitly revived the doctrine to recalibrate the interpretation and role of international law in its foreign policy. In 2019, then National Security Advisor John Bolton defended the legitimacy of possible US intervention in Venezuela by stating: 'In this administration, we're not afraid to use the phrase "Monroe

[93] David P Fidler, 'The US Election Hacks, Cybersecurity, and International Law' (2016) 110 AJIL Unbound 337.

[94] UNGA Res 73/266 (22 December 2018).

[95] US Department of State, 'Joint Statement on Advancing Responsible State Behavior in Cyberspace' (23 September 2019) <https://www.state.gov/joint-statement-on-advancing-responsible-state-behavior-in-cyberspace/> accessed 14 April 2020.

[96] Roberts (n 3) 307.

[97] Sujit Raman, 'The Rule of Law in the Age of Great Power Competition in Cyberspace' (ABA Rule of Law Initiative Annual Issues Conference, Washington, 21 May 2019) <https://www.justice.gov/opa/speech/associate-deputy-attorney-general-sujit-raman-delivers-remarks-aba-rule-law-initiative> accessed 29 April 2020.

[98] James Monroe, '7th Annual Message to Congress' (2 December 1823) <https://avalon.law.yale.edu/19th_century/monroe.asp> accessed 14 April 2020.

[99] *Military and Paramilitary Activities in and against Nicaragua (Nicaragua v United States of America)* (Merits) [1986] ICJ Rep 14.

[100] John Kerry, 'Remarks on US Policy in the Western Hemisphere' (OAS, Washington, 18 November 2013) <https://2009-2017.state.gov/secretary/remarks/2013/11/217680.htm> accessed 14 April 2020.

Doctrine" . . . it's been the objective of presidents going back to Ronald Reagan to have a completely democratic hemisphere.'[101]

The strategy of fragmenting rules of global order into exclusionary zones of security and geopolitical power now extends beyond the United States' own backyard into other pivotal regions. These include US decisions to recognize the Golan Heights, acquired from Syria by Israeli military force in 1967, as 'part of the State of Israel',[102] and to declare that the United States will 'no longer recognize Israeli settlements [in the West Bank] as per se inconsistent with international law'.[103] Yet the security logic underpinning US policy is a double-edged sword, as China now replicates the logic of the Monroe Doctrine in its own backyard of the South China Sea,[104] and Russia in border States with Western Europe,[105] each enforcing idiosyncratic interpretations of international law to fortify regional security zones. China and Russia increasingly seek to challenge hegemonic conceptions of law, especially as they apply to these regional disputes, and in 2016 released a joint declaration on the 'Promotion of International Law' that aimed to articulate alternative political foundations for the international legal system.[106] The US has responded to China by appealing to principles of the liberal international order, including upholding 'a peaceful, prosperous and freer Asia with a free and open regional order defined by the rule of law'.[107] Pursuant to its defence of the regional security order, the US has engaged in 'Freedom of Navigation Operations' in which it sails military vessels within twelve nautical miles of constructed islands and other maritime features over which China makes excessive claims to a territorial sea.[108] Yet what these various US, Chinese and Russian cases have in common are self-judging legal claims that remain

[101] Pablo Arrocha Olabuenaga, 'The Specter of Interventionism is Haunting Latin America' (*Just Security*, 10 December 2019) <https://www.justsecurity.org/67644/the-specter-of-interventionism-is-haunting-latin-america/> accessed 14 April 2020.

[102] Michael R Pompeo/David Friedman, 'International Law Backs the Trump Golan Policy' (*Wall Street Journal*, 14 May 2019) <https://www.wsj.com/articles/international-law-backs-the-trump-golan-policy-11557875474> accessed 14 April 2020.

[103] Michael R Pompeo, 'Remarks to the Press' (Press Briefing Room, Washington, 18 November 2019) <https://www.state.gov/secretary-michael-r-pompeo-remarks-to-the-press/> accessed 14 April 2020.

[104] Steven F Jackson, 'Does China Have a Monroe Doctrine? Evidence for Regional Exclusion' (2016) 10 Strategic Studies Quarterly 64.

[105] James R Holmes, 'Goodbye Grotius, Hello Putin' (*Foreign Policy*, 29 November 2018) <https://foreignpolicy.com/2018/11/29/goodbye-grotius-hello-putin-russia-ukraine-sea-of-azov-kerch-strait-south-china-sea-unclos-law-of-sea-crimea/> accessed 14 April 2020.

[106] Ministry of Foreign Affairs of the Russian Federation, 'The Declaration of the Russian Federation and the People's Republic of China on the Promotion of International Law' (Beijing, 25 June 2016) <http://www.mid.ru/en/foreign_policy/news/-/asset_publisher/cKNonkJE02Bw/content/id/2331698> accessed 14 April 2020.

[107] James N Mattis, 'Press Gaggle by Secretary Mattis En Route to Indonesia' (22 January 2018) <https://www.defense.gov/News/Transcripts/Transcript-View/Article/1420752/press-gaggle-by-secretary-mattis-en-route-to-indonesia/> accessed 14 April 2020.

[108] Under the United Nations Convention on the Law of the Sea 1833 UNTS 3 art 57; Adam Klein/Mira Rapp-Hooper, 'Freedom of Navigation Operations in the South China Sea: What to Watch For' (*Lawfare*, 23 October 2015) <https://www.lawfareblog.com/freedom-navigation-operations-south-china-sea-what-watch> accessed 14 April 2020.

incomprehensible in terms of any recognized methods and sources of international law, yet express the effective rules operating within a sphere of geopolitical influence. Together they demonstrate the logic of security imperatives fragmenting the international legal order which, mirroring the logic of geoeconomics, is being restructured to resemble 'geolegal' orders in place of the liberal international order.[109]

D. Outlook

The return of great power competition as a primary security threat to the US, and the associated trend towards geopolitical fragmentation in the international legal order, emerges as amongst the most consequential trends reshaping the international law of global security. The COVID-19 pandemic has concentrated global attention on non-State security threats and has, for some, confirmed the indispensability of internationalized legal frameworks when addressing threats that take no heed of national boundaries.[110] Yet, even as the magnitude of the global crisis became clear, foreign ministers from the G7[111] were prevented from releasing a joint statement due to US insistence on including the terminology 'Wuhan virus' to signal the pandemic's origins in China.[112] Rather than opposing forms of fragmentation, US policy has retreated from defining security in terms of a unified rules-based order and instead reinforces the restructuring of globalized law towards differentiated orders of regional and hemispheric security.

As both global power and conceptions of law fragment, the hitherto US practice of exercising claimed rights and expecting international doctrine to follow will have decreasing power in defining the parameters of global order. Strategy under the Trump administration has expressly disconnected the US role in underwriting global security from the preservation of core national security interests. The 'trump' card for the US-led rules-based order was always assumed by its advocates to be the uniquely universal attraction of its values and interests, and their normative superiority and pull for States and citizens alike. That assumption has collapsed with the rotation of the former division between the US and its allies against the rest, to a division between advocates for a unified system of law and the rest—which now cuts through as well as between States. There is not yet confirmation that the turn from commitment to American leadership of the 'liberal international order' will crystallize as the new orthodoxy of US global

[109] Malcolm Jorgensen, 'Equilibrium and Fragmentation in the International Rule of Law: The Rising Chinese Geolegal Order' (November 2018) KFG Working Paper Series No 21<https://ssrn.com/abstract=3283626> accessed 14 April 2020.

[110] Andras Vamos-Goldman, 'When International Dysfunctionality Really Matters' (*Just Security*, 15 April 2020) <https://www.justsecurity.org/69633/when-international-dysfunctionality-really-matters/> accessed 30 April 2020.

[111] Comprised of Canada, France, Germany, Italy, Japan, the United Kingdom, and the United States.

[112] Christoph Schult, 'Streit über "Wuhan-Virus"' (*Der Spiegel*, 24 March 2020) <https://www.spiegel.de/politik/ausland/streit-um-wuhan-virus-a-6bb570bb-9f2b-4cd1-a895-fdeabf53f6b4> accessed 30 April 2020.

security policy. Polarized domestic responses to the President's unprecedented pardoning of US soldiers, convicted of war crimes, is only one salient reminder that the nexus between law and security remains deeply contested.[113] Nevertheless, the confluence of rising geopolitical competitors with divergent legal conceptions, and conflicted domestic support for the legitimacy and interests of US global leadership, are confirmed forces already recontesting the global security order.

[113] Dan Maurer, 'Should There Be a War Crime Pardon Exception?' (*Lawfare*, 3 December 2019) <https://www.lawfareblog.com/should-there-be-war-crime-pardon-exception> accessed 14 April 2020.

PART V

GLOBAL AND REGIONAL SECURITY MECHANISMS

CHAPTER 52

THE ASSOCIATION OF SOUTHEAST ASIAN NATIONS AND SOUTHEAST ASIA'S REGIONAL SECURITY

DIANE A DESIERTO

The fragmented economies of Southeast Asia (with) each country pursuing its own limited objectives and dissipating its meagre resources in the overlapping or even conflicting endeavours of sister states carry the seeds of weakness in their capacity for growth and the self-perpetuating dependence on the advanced, industrial nations. ASEAN, therefore, could marshal the still untapped potentials of this rich region through more substantial united action.[1]

Narciso Ramos, Secretary of Foreign Affairs,
Republic of the Philippines, 1997

A. Introduction

THE critical role of the Association of Southeast Asian Nations (ASEAN) in the incremental evolution of the concept of Southeast Asian regional security reflectively tracks the

[1] Cited in Andrew J Crozier, 'Festina Lente: An Introductory Sketch of the History of ASEAN' in Paul J J Welfens et al (eds), *Integration in Asia and Europe: Historical Dynamics, Political Issues, and Economic Perspectives* (Springer 2006) 19–20.

organization's gradual emergence from a loose, pluralist platform for regional cooperation, into a Charter-based intergovernmental organization with dispersed legislative and executive powers, subscribing to international law, international human rights and humanitarian law, and a rules-based multilateral economic and geopolitical system. Section B of this chapter shows how 'Southeast Asia' and ASEAN are both strategic post-Cold War constructs that evolved over decades to develop distinct regional strategies fostering peace and security in the region, and contributing to international law and the stability of the region with landmark treaties such as the 1976 Treaty of Amity and Cooperation in Southeast Asia and the construction of a nuclear weapons-free zone. Section C details the initially hesitant and incrementalist path taken by ASEAN Member States in formulating regional security cooperation strategies for siloed regional issues such as transnational crimes and maritime security, amongst others. Section D maps the significant shift from incrementalism to deliberate institutionalization of regional cooperation under the ASEAN Political-Security Community created under the 2008 ASEAN Charter and its broader implications for security governance, dispute settlement, regional security, and peace initiatives for Southeast Asia. This is particularly significant amid fraught cross-border challenges, such as in the land reclamation activities of China in the South China Sea disputes, the Rohingya refugee and migration humanitarian crisis, regional environmental disasters, and dire climate change challenges to this maritime region. Section E concludes with the centrality of consensus (musyawarah—mufakat) to ASEAN regional security decision-making, which tends to cautiously limit the region's responses against normative overreach, but at the same time generates a set of identifiably distinct Southeast Asian regional security decisions and practices that uniquely contribute to the evolving architecture of the international legal system.

B. Constructing 'Southeast Asia' and ASEAN

Geopolitical security initially drove the coinage of the phrase 'Southeast Asia', which American and European military and defence strategists after the First World War popularized to delineate a region that was distinct from the dominant Asian hegemons, namely India (in South Asia), China and Japan (in East Asia).[2] In the aftermath of decolonization, various political leaders and economic elites continued to embrace the construct of 'Southeast Asia' as a region, largely to further national interests and reinforce national identities, asserting distance from entrenched colonial pasts.[3] However,

[2] Russell H Fifield, 'Southeast Asia as a Regional Concept' (1983) 11 Southeast Asian Journal of Social Science 1; Amitav Acharya, *East of India, South of China: Sino-Indian Encounters in Southeast Asia* (OUP Press 2017) 131–78.

[3] Amitav Acharya, 'Imagined Proximities: The Making and Unmaking of Southeast Asia as a Region' (1999) 27 Southeast Asian Journal of Social Science 55.

notwithstanding its origins in narrower security discourses, it should be clear that Southeast Asia's regional security challenges are influenced by the region's complex maritime and terrestrial configuration;[4] its deep linguistic, religious, ethnic, and ideological diversity with corresponding normative and cultural pluralisms;[5] and the continuously evolving dynamics, inequalities, institutions, and ideologies of governance within and across Southeast Asian States.[6] Any conceptualization of regional security for this inherently diverse constellation of States grouped into a construct of 'Southeast Asia', would thus understandably reflect continuing tensions between fragmentation and cooperation.[7] This is not at all surprising, given that 'Southeast Asia is a region of vast pluralities'.[8]

ASEAN emerged within this history of plural ideologies, languages, religions, governance structures, and institutions.[9] After the end of three years of undeclared war (*Konfrontasi*) between Indonesia and Malaysia from 1963 to 1966,[10] both countries agreed to join the three other original ASEAN Member States (the Philippines, Singapore, and Thailand) to sign the ASEAN (Bangkok) Declaration on 8 August 1967.[11] The five foreign ministers (Indonesia's Adam Malik, Malaysia's Tun Abdul Razak, the Philippines' Narciso Ramos, Singapore's Sinnathamby Rajaratnam, and Thailand's Thamat Khoman) who signed the 1967 Bangkok Declaration expansively understood Southeast Asia's regional security to depend on some degree of political cooperation, as

[4] Brian Nichiporuk et al, 'Demographics and Security in Maritime Southeast Asia' (2006) 7 Georgetown Journal of International Affairs 83; Clive Schofield et al, 'From Disputed Waters to Seas of Opportunity: Overcoming Barriers to Maritime Cooperation in East and Southeast Asia' in John Bradford et al (eds), *Maritime Security in Southeast Asia* (National Bureau of Asian Research 2013); Joshua H Ho, 'The Security of Sea Lanes in Southeast Asia' (2006) 46 Asian Survey 558.

[5] Diane A Desierto, 'Postcolonial International Law Discourses on Regional Developments in South and Southeast Asia' (2008) 36 International Journal of Legal Information 388; Mary Margaret Steedly, 'The State of Culture Theory in the Anthropology of Southeast Asia' (1999) 28 Annual Review of Anthropology 431.

[6] Ali Farazmand, 'Governance in the Age of Globalization: Challenges and Opportunities for South and Southeast Asia' in Ishtiaq Jamil et al (eds), *Governance in South, Southeast, and East Asia: Trends, Issues, Challenges* (Springer 2015); William Case, 'Democracy's Mixed Fortunes in Southeast Asia: Torpor, Change, and Trade-Offs' in William Case (ed), *Routledge Handbook of Southeast Asian Democratization* (Routledge 2015); Mark Beeson, 'Southeast Asia and the Politics of Vulnerability' (2002) 23 Third World Quarterly 549; David Martin Jones, 'The Southeast Asian Development Model: Non-Liberal Democracy with Market Accountability' (2007) Southeast Asian Affairs 59.

[7] Michael R J Vatikiotis, 'ASEAN 10: The Political and Cultural Dimensions of Southeast Asia Unity' (1999) 27 Southeast Asia Journal of Social Science 77; Donald G McCloud, *Southeast Asia: Tradition and Modernity in the Contemporary World* (2nd edn, Routledge 2018) ch 13 (Regional Politics: Fragmentation and Cooperation).

[8] Jaclyn L Neo/Bui Ngoc Son, 'Pluralist Constitutions and the Southeast Asian Context' in Jaclyn L Neo/Bui Ngoc Son (eds), *Pluralist Constitutions in Southeast Asia* (Hart 2019) 1.

[9] Diane A Desierto, 'ASEAN's Constitutionalization of International Law: Challenges to Evolution under the ASEAN Charter' (2011) 49 Columbia Journal of Transnational Law 268.

[10] Adam Leong Kok Wey, 'The War That Gave Birth to ASEAN' (*The Diplomat*, 9 September 2016) <https://thediplomat.com/2016/09/the-war-that-gave-birth-to-asean/> accessed 10 May 2019.

[11] 'Association of Southeast Asian Nations Declaration' (1967) 6 International Legal Materials 1233 (Bangkok Declaration).

well as shared regional economic development and ensuring social stability.[12] The Bangkok Declaration stated the aims and purposes of ASEAN to include, amongst others: 'accelerat[ing] economic growth, social progress and cultural development in the region through joint endeavours in the spirit of equality and partnership in order to strengthen the foundation for a prosperous and peaceful community of South-East Asian Nations'; as well as 'promot[ing] regional peace and stability through abiding respect for justice and the rule of law in the relationship among countries of the region and adherence to the principles of the United Nations Charter'.[13] The preamble to the Bangkok Declaration stressed that

> the countries of Southeast Asia share a primary responsibility for strengthening the economic and social stability of the region and ensuring their peaceful and progressive national development, and that they are determined to ensure their stability and security from external interference in any form or manifestation in order to preserve their national identities in accordance with the ideals and aspirations of their peoples...[14]

The institutional mechanisms for achieving these strategic and expansive regional security aims were initially modest—an annual foreign ministers' meeting, with a standing committee to support the work of this annual meeting, plus ad hoc committees and national secretariats that focused on information-sharing and coordination preparatory to such foreign ministers' meetings.[15] This largely coordinative intergovernmental response (and with a very thinly staffed regional organization that was ASEAN) ran consistently with the cautious approaches taken by Southeast Asian States during the Cold War, when the original ASEAN Five (Indonesia, Malaysia, Singapore, the Philippines, and Thailand) overcame security conflicts after the creation of the Malaysian Federation, to thereafter manage post-Cold War regional uncertainties and open conflicts with Vietnam's invasion of Cambodia.[16]

However, the first ten years of ASEAN since 1967 were marked by escalating concerns over the deepening Communist threats to Southeast Asia's fragile regional security:

> ...During the first four years, nothing of substance was achieved, because much time and effort had to be directed at tearing down the 'psychological barriers', i.e. distrust among the member nations. Lee Kuan Yew (Prime Minister of Singapore)...considered the most valuable achievement of the Association to be 'the understanding and goodwill created at the frequent meetings which helped to lubricate relation-

[12] Alejandro Melchor Jr, 'Assessing ASEAN's Viability in a Changing World' (April 1978) 18 Asian Survey 422, 423; Jürgen Haacke, *ASEAN's Diplomatic and Security Culture: Origins, Development, and Prospects* (Routledge 2013) 43–4; Jamil Maidan Flores/Jun Abad, 'ASEAN at 30' (*Association of Southeast Asian Nations*, 9 July 2012) <https://asean.org/?static_post=asean-at-30> accessed 10 April 2019.

[13] Bangkok Declaration (n 11) second declaratory clause, items 1 and 2.

[14] ibid preambular para 4.

[15] ibid third declaratory clause, items (a) to (d).

[16] Evelyn Goh, 'Southeast Asia's Evolving Security Relations and Strategies' in Saadia Pekkanen et al (eds), *The Oxford Handbook of International Relations in Southeast Asia* (OUP 2014) 463.

ships which could otherwise have generated friction'... The creation of mutual trust was necessary before any serious regional efforts could be undertaken. It was not until the neutralization scheme was a common objective in 1971 that some prospects of a common policy stand could be discerned. Since then ASEAN has seemed to pay more attention to economic than to political problems, although both have been on the agenda. Political concerns were mainly triggered by the changing of great power relationships in East Asia, as well as the deteriorating situation in Indochina. ASEAN was 'shocked', and Thailand and the Philippines in particular felt 'betrayed', by President Nixon's announcement of his forthcoming visit to Peking in 1971 without consulting or informing the close allies of the U.S. beforehand. Thailand and the Philippines subsequently began to reassess and adjust their policies in line with the new development, deciding to shift from their traditional pro-U.S. policies and seek contacts and start dialogues with the Communist countries... In the 1972 Ministerial Meeting, it was decided 'to build peaceful relations with China'. There was, however, disagreement on the timing of the rapprochement. Malaysia was keen to break the ice, and established relations in 1974; the Philippines and Thailand followed suit in 1975. Indonesia, however, warned that hasty moves were dangerous, and (Indonesian Foreign Minister) Adam Malik stated bluntly that détente was no guarantee of internal security. Singapore, in view of its geopolitical position and racial considerations, preferred to be the last in the game...

... But the Communist victory in Indochina in April 1975 had a greater impact on ASEAN than Nixon's decision to withdraw U.S. troops from Vietnam. ASEAN was now more concerned about the political intentions of its new Communist neighbors than it was about a possible American lack of interest in the region. Its immediate response was a mixture of optimism, anxiety, and uncertainty. Malaysia was optimistic because an era of war was over and peace was within sight; it wanted to expand ASEAN membership to include Burma and the Indochinese states. Singapore was cautious and warned that the Vietnamese seizure of vast quantities of military supplies could be a menace to the security of the Association. Thailand was most anxious to seek détente with the Indochinese states during Kukrit's and Seni Pramoj's leadership. Indonesia... stressed the determination... to eliminate the remnants of the PKI but added that it would maintain friendship with any government on the basis of noninterference and equality. The Philippines showed restraint, but suggested economic cooperation and, if possible, economic assistance... [T]he Indochina debacle had one positive result: it gave a feeling of urgency which triggered a determination to pull together and respond collectively to the threat posed by the Communists. One could therefore argue that the Bali Summit Meeting of February 1976 and the signing of the Treaty of Amity and Cooperation, as well as the Declaration of Concord and the agreement on four ASEAN industrial projects, could not have been accomplished so soon had it not been for the changes in Indochina.[17]

The first ASEAN Summit—this time with ASEAN Heads of Government meeting in Bali, Indonesia, from 23–24 February 1976—was the first occasion for ASEAN Member

[17] Shee Poon-Kim, 'A Decade of ASEAN, 1967–1977' (August 1977) 17 Asian Survey 753, 758–9.

States to review ASEAN activities since the 1967 Bangkok Declaration.[18] This first Summit yielded two foundational regional security agreements for ASEAN Member States—the Treaty of Amity and Cooperation (TAC),[19] and the Declaration of ASEAN Concord.[20] The TAC laid down six fundamental principles central to the ASEAN Member States:

> In their relations with one another, the High Contracting Parties shall be guided by the following fundamental principles:
>
> a. Mutual respect for the independence, sovereignty, equality, territorial integrity, and national identity of all nations;
> b. The right of every State to lead its national existence free from interference, subversion, or coercion;
> c. Non-interference in the internal affairs of one another;
> d. Settlement of differences or disputes by peaceful means;
> e. Renunciation of the threat or use of force;
> f. Effective cooperation amongst themselves.[21]

ASEAN cooperation on security issues was accordingly framed from the above six principles. Amongst other commitments, the TAC broadly required 'maintain[ing] regular contacts and consultations with one another on international and regional matters with a view to coordinating their views, actions, and policies',[22] and in turn prohibited 'participat[ion] in any activity which shall constitute a threat to the political and economic stability, sovereignty, or territorial integrity of another High Contracting Party'.[23] The TAC established a High Council as a 'continuing body…comprising a Representative at ministerial level from each of the High Contracting Parties to take cognizance of the existence of disputes or situations likely to disturb regional peace and harmony'.[24] The High Council was not a supranational body that could impose decisions on ASEAN Member States, but rather was limited to recommending 'appropriate means of [dispute] settlement such as good offices, mediation, inquiry or conciliation…[as well as] appropriate measures for the prevention of a deterioration of the dispute or the situation'.[25] The design of such a mechanism in the TAC coincided with the ASEAN Member States' preferences for thin political and economic cooperation under more ad hoc and horizontal arrangements, given the delicate post-war balance of power in Southeast Asia.[26]

[18] ASEAN, 'Joint Communique' (First ASEAN Heads of Government Meeting, Bali, 23–24 February 1976) <https://asean.org/?static_post=joint-communique-the-first-asean-heads-of-government-meeting-bali-23-24-february-1976> accessed 10 April 2019.

[19] Treaty of Amity and Cooperation in Southeast Asia 1025 UNTS 316.

[20] 'The Declaration of ASEAN Concord' (Bali, 24 February 1976) <https://asean.org/?static_post=declaration-of-asean-concord-indonesia-24-february-1976> accessed 10 April 2019.

[21] TAC (n 19) art 2. [22] ibid art 9. [23] ibid art 10.

[24] ibid art 14. [25] ibid art 15.

[26] Donald E Nuechterlein, 'Prospects for Regional Security in Southeast Asia' (1968) 8 Asian Survey 806, 812–14.

Amongst ASEAN's objectives and principles in the Declaration of ASEAN Concord 'in the pursuit of political stability',[27] ASEAN Member States committed to 'take active steps for the early establishment of the Zone of Peace, Freedom, and Neutrality (ZOPFAN)'[28] as well as to 'rely exclusively on peaceful processes in the settlement of intra-regional differences'.[29] Accordingly, the programme of action adopted in the Declaration of ASEAN Concord to shape ASEAN's political cooperation entailed setting up Heads of Government meetings, signing the TAC, focusing on the peaceful settlement of intra-regional disputes, examining initial steps for a Zone of Peace, Freedom, and Neutrality (ZOPFAN), exploring the possibility of judicial cooperation amongst ASEAN Member States, and promoting 'harmonization of views, coordinating positions, and, where possible and desirable, taking common actions'.[30] With respect to security cooperation, however, the Declaration of ASEAN Concord narrowly referred to just the 'continuation of cooperation on a non-ASEAN basis between the member states in accordance with their mutual needs and interests'.[31] At the very least, at the inception and subsequent crystallization of ASEAN as an intergovernmental coordinating organization in its first ten years, the concept of regional security for Southeast Asia would still remain driven by national interests, prioritization of political stability, and a refusal to commit to any hard regional governance institution or regional process for defining regional security objectives, assessing regional security situations, or prescribing regional security actions.[32]

C. Incrementalism in Regional Security Cooperation

Subsequent ASEAN Heads of Government meetings continued the ad hoc approach to regional security. The Second ASEAN Heads of Government Meeting in Kuala Lumpur in 1977 emphasized the creation of a ZOPFAN, while explicitly welcoming the UNSC recommendation to admit Vietnam as part of the UN, since 'Vietnam would contribute

[27] Declaration of ASEAN Concord (n 20) declaratory paragraph.

[28] ibid declaratory paragraph, item 2. [29] ibid declaratory paragraph, item 6.

[30] ibid Program of Action, part A, items 1–7. [31] ibid Program of Action, part E.

[32] J L S Girling, 'Regional Security in Southeast Asia' (March 1971) 2 Journal of Southeast Asian Studies 56, 62:

> ... member states of ASEAN ... which are geographically close-knit, have very different preoccupations. Despite a common need for 'stability', a realization of the benefits of cooperation, a common awareness that internal weaknesses can be readily exploited by outside powers, a certain shared resentment of Japan's economic pre-eminence and a fear of China's domination, despite all these factors making for a sense of community, the divisive colonial past and diversity of current circumstances so far have prevented any effective combination for political purposes.

Also, Robert Fluker, 'Regionalism and the Modernization of Southeast Asia' (April 1969) 31 The Review of Politics 189; Vincent K Pollard, 'ASA and ASEAN, 1961–1967: Southeast Asian Regionalism' (March 1970) 10 Asian Survey 244.

to peace and stability necessary for the progress and prosperity of Southeast Asia.'[33] Given parallel political transitions and ongoing conflicts in Southeast Asia unfolding within the Cold War context,[34] the Third ASEAN Heads of Government Meeting would not be held until a decade later in Manila, with ASEAN declaring the hope for a 'new atmosphere of greater cooperation and accommodation between the two superpowers… [to] facilitate the speedy and just resolution of the protracted conflicts and problems in Southeast Asia….'[35] ASEAN's 1987 Manila Declaration pledged political cooperation for peace and stability in Kampuchea (Indochina), an effective solution for the plight of Indochinese refugees in Southeast Asia, the early realization of a ZOPFAN for Southeast Asia, and the establishment of a Southeast Asia Nuclear Weapon-Free Zone (SEANWFZ).[36] The 1992 Singapore Declaration,[37] issued during the Fourth ASEAN Heads of Government Meeting, opened accession of the TAC to all countries (especially Vietnam, Laos, and Cambodia),[38] declared Heads of State meetings at three-year intervals and the streamlining of ASEAN's organizational structure through the ASEAN Secretariat, and the Secretary-General of ASEAN conferred an expanded mandate as well as ministerial status.[39]

The Fifth ASEAN Heads of Government Meeting in Bangkok, Thailand, in 1995 led to the signing of the new Treaty on the Southeast Asia Nuclear Weapon-Free Zone (SEANWFZ Treaty).[40] This Treaty prohibits the development, manufacture, acquisition, possession, or control of nuclear weapons, the dumping of radioactive material or

[33] ASEAN, 'Joint Communique' (Second ASEAN Heads of Government Meeting, Kuala Lumpur, 5 August 1977) paras 7–10 <https://asean.org/?static_post=joint-communique-second-asean-heads-government-meeting-kuala-lumpur-august-51977> accessed 10 April 2019.

[34] Huynh Kim Khanh/Hans Indorf, 'Southeast Asia 1981: Two Currents Running' (1982) Southeast Asian Affairs 3, 4:

> …intra-Southeast Asian politics also drastically altered: the hopes for region-wide cooperation without external interference dwindled, yielding to the emergence of two antagonistic groups of nations drifting to acute partisanship in the global conflict between the superpowers. In the mid-1970s, there were still some optimistic hopes, if not illusions, for establishing a region free from the pervading policies of Moscow and Washington. The conditions for such a possibility were present in 1975: defeated in Indochina, the United States was on its way to withdraw to 'fortress America'; ASEAN advocated the establishment of a Zone of Peace, Freedom and Neutrality (ZOPFAN), and the Indochinese states showed every sign of a determination to maintain independence and sovereignty devoid of foreign intervention. Today, following two more military conflicts in the Indochinese peninsula, Southeast Asian nations are locked in verbal disputes, with the ZOPFAN idea laying in abeyance as the superpowers include Southeast Asia in their competitive spheres.

[35] ASEAN, 'Joint Communique' (Third ASEAN Heads of Government Meeting, Manila, 14–15 December 1987) para 8 <https://asean.org/?static_post=joint-communique-the-third-asean-heads-of-government-meeting-manila-14-15-december-1987> accessed 10 April 2019.

[36] ASEAN Manila Declaration (Manila, 15 December 1987) paras 1–6 under the section 'Political Cooperation' <https://asean.org/?static_post=manila-declaration-philippines-15-december-1987> accessed 10 April 2019.

[37] ASEAN Singapore Declaration of 1992 (Singapore, 28 January 1992) <https://asean.org/?static_post=singapore-declaration-of-1992-singapore-28-january-1992> accessed 10 April 2019.

[38] ibid para 3. [39] ibid para 8. [40] 1981 UNTS 129.

wastes in the seas or atmosphere, and permits limited uses of nuclear energy for peaceful purposes, with a control system in place to ensure verification of States Parties' compliance with all SEANWFZ Treaty obligations.[41] Significantly, Southeast Asia's Nuclear Weapons-Free Zone 'will not affect port calls, transit and overflights by nuclear-armed vessels and aircraft or innocent passage through archipelagic waters of the zone... [It] is not intended to affect the law of the sea regime of navigation'.[42] The SEANWFZ Treaty has been credited for contributing to global nuclear disarmament, improved peacebuilding and confidence-building measures in Southeast Asia, as well as relevance to ongoing counter-terrorism efforts in the region.[43]

An Informal Heads of Government Meeting in Jakarta in 1996 (held before the next scheduled ASEAN Heads of Government Meeting in 1998) publicly declared ASEAN's commitment to 'an ASEAN comprising all ten Southeast Asian countries... Cambodia, Laos, and Myanmar [should] be admitted as Members simultaneously'.[44] The ASEAN Member States also considered maritime security issues, and specifically

> reaffirmed their commitment to seek an early peaceful solution to the overlapping claims in the South China Sea in accordance with the provisions of the TAC, the ASEAN Declaration on the South China Sea of 1992, as well as international law, including the United Nations Convention on the Law of the Sea of 1982.[45]

ASEAN also published its 'ASEAN Vision 2020', where, by the year 2020, ASEAN envisioned that it shall have

> established a peaceful and stable Southeast Asia where each nation is at peace with itself and where the causes for conflict have been eliminated through abiding respect for justice and the rule of law and through the strengthening of national and regional resilience... where territorial and other disputes are resolved by peaceful means... where the ASEAN Regional Forum [is] an established means for confidence-building and preventive diplomacy and for promoting conflict-resolution.[46]

By the time ASEAN held its 6th Heads of Government Meeting in Ha Noi, Viet Nam in 1998, Cambodia was admitted as the tenth member of ASEAN,[47] joining the five original

[41] ibid arts 3, 4, and 10.

[42] ibid art 7, in relation to Surya P Subedi, 'Problems and Prospects for the Treaty on the Creation of a Nuclear Weapon-Free Zone in Southeast Asia' (January 1999) 4 International Journal of Peace Studies 63, 71.

[43] MC Abad Jr, 'A Nuclear Weapon-Free Southeast Asia and its Continuing Strategic Significance' (2005) 27 Contemporary Southeast Asia 165.

[44] ASEAN, 'Press Statement' (First Informal Heads of Government Meeting, Jakarta, 30 November 1996) para 6 <https://asean.org/?static_post=press-statement-the-first-informal-asean-heads-of-government-meeting-jakarta-30-november-1996> accessed 10 April 2019.

[45] ibid para 13.

[46] ASEAN, 'ASEAN Vision 2020' (Kuala Lumpur, 15 December 1997) <https://asean.org/?static_post=asean-vision-2020> accessed 10 April 2019.

[47] ASEAN Ha Noi Declaration of 1998 (Ha Noi, 16 December 1998) para 2 <https://asean.org/?static_post=ha-noi-declaration-of-1998-16-december-1998> accessed 10 April 2019.

ASEAN Member States, the Sultanate of Brunei Darussalam (which had joined in 1984),[48] and fellow Kampuchea/Indochinese countries Viet Nam (which had joined in 1995),[49] Laos and Myanmar (which both had joined in 1997).[50] The 7th ASEAN Summit hosted by Brunei Darussalam in 2001 yielded the 2001 ASEAN Declaration on Joint Action to Counter-Terrorism,[51] articulating an initial regional approach on counter-terrorism that has since been linked with the regularly updated ASEAN Plan of Action to Combat Transnational Crime.[52]

D. From Incrementalism to a Distinct ASEAN Political-Security Community under the ASEAN Charter

Subsequent ASEAN summits demonstrated the incrementalist approach of ASEAN Member States to reaching gradual agreement on cooperation with respect to a wider array of regional security issues. Maritime security was at the forefront of the 8th ASEAN Summit in Phnom Penh, Cambodia, which produced the 2002 Declaration on the Conduct of Parties in the South China Sea,[53] the 2002 Declaration on Terrorism,[54] as well as the 2002 Joint Declaration of ASEAN and China on Cooperation in the Field of Non-Traditional Security Issues.[55] The 9th ASEAN Summit in Indonesia produced the significant 2003 Declaration of ASEAN Concord II (Bali Concord II), where ASEAN

[48] Pushpa Thambipillai, 'Brunei Darussalam and ASEAN: Regionalism for a Small State' (1998) 6 Asian Journal of Political Science 80, 80.

[49] Anh Huyen, 'Joining ASEAN: Vietnam's Strategic International Integration' (*VOV5.VN*, 28 July 2014) <http://vovworld.vn/en-US/current-affairs/joining-asean-vietnams-strategic-international-integration-258504.vov> accessed 10 April 2019.

[50] Carolyn L Gates/Mya Than, 'ASEAN Enlargement: An Introductory Overview' in Mya Than/Carolyn L Gates (eds), *ASEAN Enlargement: Impacts and Implications* (Institute of Southeast Asian Studies 2001) 9.

[51] 2001 ASEAN Declaration on Joint Action to Counter-Terrorism (Bandar Seri Begawan, 5 November 2001) <https://asean.org/?static_post=2001-asean-declaration-on-joint-action-to-counter-terrorism> accessed 10 April 2019.

[52] ASEAN Plan of Action to Combat Transnational Crime (latest version 4 July 2012) <https://asean.org/?static_post=asean-plan-of-action-to-combat-transnational-crime> accessed 10 April 2019.

[53] ASEAN–People's Republic of China, 'Declaration on the Conduct of Parties to the South China Sea' (Phnom Penh, 4 November 2002) <https://asean.org/?static_post=declaration-on-the-conduct-of-parties-in-the-south-china-sea-2> accessed 30 November 2020.

[54] Declaration on Terrorism by the 8th ASEAN Summit (Phnom Penh, 3 November 2002) <https://asean.org/?static_post=declaration-on-terrorism-by-the-8th-asean-summit-phnom-penh-3-november-2002> accessed 30 November 2020.

[55] ASEAN–China, 'Joint Declaration on Cooperation in the Field of Non-Traditional Security Issues' (Phnom Penh, 14 May 2002) <https://asean.org/?static_post=joint-declaration-of-asean-and-china-on-cooperation-in-the-field-of-non-traditional-security-issues-6th-asean-china-summit-phnom-penh-4-november-2002-2> accessed 10 April 2019.

Member States first articulated their decision to create three distinct pillar communities: an ASEAN Security Community, ASEAN Economic Community, and ASEAN Socio-Cultural Community.[56] The ASEAN Security Community was envisaged to bring ASEAN's hitherto incrementalist political and security cooperation under a 'principle of comprehensive security…having broad political, economic, social, and cultural aspects in consonance with the ASEAN Vision 2020 rather than to a defense pact, military alliance or a joint foreign policy'.[57] The 10th ASEAN Summit in Vientiane, Laos, in 2004 produced the first ASEAN Security Community Plan of Action, focusing on political development, norm-shaping and sharing, conflict prevention, and post-conflict peacebuilding.[58] Scholars characterized ASEAN's role in regional security matters as anchored in the exercise of 'soft power, by remaining a neutral broker among its great power interlocutors and delegitimizing containment and traditional power balancing policies that would aggravate the regional security dilemma'.[59]

After nearly forty years of forging mutual trust through confidence-building cooperative activities with respect to various economic, political, security, and social issues facing Southeast Asia, the diverse constellation of ten ASEAN Member States were motivated to deepen and formalize their regional cooperative alliance into an intergovernmental organization.[60] The 13th ASEAN Summit hosted by Singapore in 2007 led to the signing of the Charter of the Association of Southeast Asian Nations (ASEAN Charter),[61] transforming ASEAN from a loose and ad hoc regional cooperation into a denser rules-based intergovernmental organization with international legal personality and specific regional institutions, with the ASEAN Summit able to take specific regional decisions deemed legally obligatory for ASEAN Member States, given the overarching Charter duty of all ASEAN Member States to 'take all necessary measures, including the enactment of appropriate domestic legislation, to effectively implement the provisions of this Charter and to comply with all obligations of membership'.[62] Two years after at the 14th ASEAN Summit in Cha-am, Thailand, ASEAN produced its landmark APSC Blueprint, outlining its three key priorities: (1) a 'rules-based community of shared values and norms'; (2) a 'cohesive, peaceful, stable, and resilient region with shared responsibility for comprehensive security'; and (3) a 'dynamic and outward-looking region in an increasingly integrated and interdependent world'.[63] Most crucially, the ASEAN Political-Security Community Blueprint echoed the ASEAN Charter in purposely aiming to

[56] ASEAN, 'Declaration of ASEAN Concord II (Bali Concord II)' (2004) 43 International Legal Materials 18.

[57] ibid part A.2, para 2.

[58] ASEAN Security Community Plan of Action (Vientiane, 29 November 2004) <https://asean.org/?static_post=asean-security-community-plan-of-action> accessed 10 April 2019.

[59] Amitav Acharya/Jillian Moo-Young, 'Constructing Security and Identity in Southeast Asia' (2006) 12 Brown Journal of World Affairs 155, 156.

[60] Desierto (n 9) 287–94.

[61] Charter of the Association of Southeast Asian Nations 2624 UNTS 223.

[62] ibid art 5(2).

[63] ASEAN Political-Security Community Blueprint (Cha-am, 1 March 2009) para 10 <https://www.asean.org/wp-content/uploads/images/archive/22337.pdf> accessed 10 April 2019.

> strengthen democracy, enhance good governance and rule of law, and to promote and protect human rights and fundamental freedoms, with due regard to the rights and responsibilities of the Member States of ASEAN, so as to ultimately create a Rules-based community of shared values and norms.[64]

ASEAN has also continually emphasized that regional security disputes must be resolved and settled peacefully in accordance with international law.[65]

The ASEAN Political-Security Community (APSC) has since been the pillar community for institutional decision-making on regional security matters,[66] ranging from traditional regional security cooperation to emerging regional security issues such as trafficking of persons in Southeast Asia,[67] regional health crises,[68] environmental threats, disaster resilience, and climate change,[69] and cybersecurity cooperation.[70] At the time of writing, the APSC includes standing bodies such as the ASEAN Foreign Ministers' Meeting, the Commission for Southeast Asia Nuclear Weapon-Free Zone (SEANWFZ Commission), the ASEAN Defence Ministers Meeting, the ASEAN Law Ministers Meeting, the ASEAN Ministerial Meeting on Transnational Crime, the ASEAN Ministerial Meeting on Drug Matters, the ASEAN Intergovernmental Commission on Human Rights (AICHR), and the ASEAN Regional Forum. The ASEAN Foreign Ministers' Meeting remains responsible for political-security cooperation and external relations in

[64] ASEAN (n 63) para 12.

[65] ASEAN, 'Bali Declaration on ASEAN Community in a Global Community of Nations—Bali Concord III Plan of Action 2013–2017' (Bali, 17 November 2011) <https://www.asean.org/wp-content/uploads/images/2013/other_documents/POA%20of%20Bali%20Concord%20III%20_final_.pdf> accessed 10 April 2019.

[66] Security Community Plan (n 58).

[67] ASEAN, 'ASEAN Leaders' Joint Statement in Enhancing Cooperation against Trafficking of Persons in Southeast Asia' (Jakarta, 8 May 2011) <https://www.asean.org/wp-content/uploads/archive/Joint_Statement_TIP.pdf> accessed 10 April 2019; ASEAN Convention Against Trafficking in Persons, Especially Women and Children (adopted 21 November 2015, entered into force 8 March 2017) <https://www.asean.org/wp-content/uploads/images/2015/November/actip/ACTIP.PDF> accessed 10 April 2019.

[68] ASEAN, 'Bandar Seri Begawan Declaration on Noncommunicable Diseases in ASEAN' (Bandar Seri Begawan, 9 October 2013) <https://www.asean.org/wp-content/uploads/images/archive/23rdASEANSummit/3.%20bsb%20declaration%20on%20ncd%20in%20asean-%20final-endorsed%2023%20september%202013.pdf> accessed 10 April 2019.

[69] ASEAN, 'Declaration on Institutionalising the Resilience of ASEAN and its Communities and Peoples to Disasters and Climate Change' (Kuala Lumpur, 27 April 2015) <https://asean.org/wp-content/uploads/2012/05/26th-DECLARATION-ON-INSTITUTIONALISING-Final.pdf> accessed 10 April 2019); ASEAN, 'ASEAN Leaders' Statement on Cooperation in Flood Prevention, Mitigation, Relief, Recovery and Rehabilitation' (Bali, 17 November 2011) <https://www.asean.org/wp-content/uploads/archive/documents/19th%20summit/Flood.pdf> accessed 10 April 2019; ASEAN Joint Statement on Climate Change (Nay Pyi Taw, 12 November 2014) <https://asean.org/wp-content/uploads/2012/05/25th-ASEAN-Joint-Statement-on-Climate-Change-2014.pdf> accessed 10 April 2019.

[70] ASEAN, 'ASEAN Leaders' Statement on Cybersecurity Cooperation' (Singapore, 28 April 2018) <https://asean.org/wp-content/uploads/2018/04/ASEAN-Leaders-Statement-on-Cybersecurity-Cooperation.pdf> accessed 10 April 2019.

ASEAN,[71] while the SEANWFZ Commission retains responsibility for the implementation of the SEANWFZ Treaty.[72] The ASEAN Defence Ministers Meeting, the Law Ministers Meeting, the Ministerial Meeting on Transnational Crime, and the Ministerial Meeting on Drug Matters implement their respective sectoral responsibilities as defined under the ASEAN Political-Security Community Blueprint, while the AICHR aspires to ensure promotion and protection of human rights in ASEAN but largely according to a strict reading of the AICHR's Terms of Reference.[73]

The ASEAN Regional Forum was formally institutionalized in 1994, to foster constructive dialogue and consultation on political and security issues of common interest and concern; and to make significant contributions to efforts towards confidence-building and preventive diplomacy in the Asia-Pacific region.[74] The Member States of ASEAN increasingly 'recognized that despite the end of the Cold War and the imminent US withdrawal from the Philippines, there were now more powers, rather than less, present, and that pressure from those powers was mounting for a forum... ASEAN States decided to claim the process in the hope that they could channel rather than resist the momentum.'[75]

The ASEAN Regional Forum is composed of all ten ASEAN Member States and ASEAN's various dialogue partners (Australia, Canada, China, the European Union, India, Japan, South Korea, Russia, New Zealand, the United States, amongst others).[76] Where before ASEAN Member States placed more emphasis on undisclosed negotiations and political-security discussions that allowed for face-saving and avoided public embarrassment or perceptions of any political divide within ASEAN, by 1997 the Regional Forum had 'agreed to move towards preventive diplomacy'. The agreement follows from the recognition of the Regional Forum, quite early on, that 'preventive diplomacy would be a natural follow-up to confidence-building measures'.[77] While the

[71] 'ASEAN Foreign Ministers Meeting (AMM)' (*Association of Southeast Asian Nations*) <https://asean.org/asean-political-security-community/asean-foreign-ministers-meeting-amm/> accessed 10 April 2019.

[72] 'Commission for the Southeast Asia Nuclear Weapon Free Zone' (*Association of Southeast Asian Nations*) <https://asean.org/asean-political-security-community/commission-for-the-southeast-asia-nuclear-weapon-free-zone-seanwfz-commission/> accessed 10 April 2019.

[73] 'ASEAN Intergovernmental Commission on Human Rights—Terms of Reference' (2009) 48 International Legal Materials 1165; John D Ciorciari, 'Institutionalizing Human Rights in Southeast Asia' (August 2012) 34 Human Rights Quarterly 695; Hsien-Li Tan, *The ASEAN Intergovernmental Commission on Human Rights: Institutionalizing Human Rights in Southeast Asia* (CUP 2011) 1–23.

[74] First ASEAN Regional Forum, 'Chairman's Statement' (Bangkok, 25 July 1994) <https://2001-2009.state.gov/t/ac/csbm/rd/4377.htm> accessed 30 November 2020.

[75] Michael Antolik, 'The ASEAN Regional Forum: The Spirit of Constructive Engagement' (September 1994) 16 Contemporary Southeast Asia 117, 119–20.

[76] Australian Government, Department of Foreign Affairs and Trade, 'ASEAN Regional Forum' <https://dfat.gov.au/international-relations/regional-architecture/Pages/asean-regional-forum-arf.aspx> accessed 10 April 2019.

[77] Simon S C Tay/Obood Talib, 'The ASEAN Regional Forum: Preparing for Preventive Diplomacy' (December 1997) 19 Contemporary Southeast Asia 252.

ASEAN Regional Forum fosters a multilateral security dialogue between ASEAN and its dialogue partners, it has been described as itself problematic for addressing regional security needs due to the different threat perceptions, security needs, lingering intraregional conflicts often primarily and preferably addressed by ASEAN Member States through national responses excluding foreign interference, ultimately reducing regional security to 'regional resilience':

> The concept of regional resilience captures ASEAN's comprehensive view of security and the different kinds of challenges faced by Southeast Asia. On the other hand, it also conceives regional security as little more than a sum of its parts... in this way, regional resilience makes the explicit link between national strength and regional strength; but it also suggests that regional resilience is achieved largely through the individual efforts of member states... ASEAN's conception of security is, in other words, a collaborative effort but not necessarily an integrated or centrally co-ordinated one.[78]

It is ultimately difficult to assess the overall effectiveness of the ASEAN Regional Forum in discharging its core function of facilitating regional security dialogue and promoting cooperation within the multilateral security architecture, given the relative opacity of its meetings, negotiations, and outcomes. The ASEAN Regional Forum stands by the core Charter-based principle of neutrality, and often for this reason treads a delicate line on complex regional disputes, especially those involving maritime security and the overlapping claims of China, Taiwan, and several ASEAN Member States (Vietnam, Philippines, Brunei Darussalam, Indonesia, Malaysia) in the South China Sea.[79] The Philippines deviated from the ASEAN collective regional security approach when it initiated and won its own landmark arbitration against China,[80] determining the unlawfulness of China's controversial 9-dash line map, the international responsibility of China for various enforcement actions taken in the South China Sea, as well as the legal characterization of various geographic features in the South China Sea according to the UN Convention on the Law of the Sea (UNCLOS). Given fraught relationships between claimants in the South China Sea, at the time of writing, the 2002 Declaration on Code of Conduct of Parties to the South China Sea has not yet led to an actual Code of Conduct, although as of August 2018 the foreign ministers of ASEAN and China were reported to have adopted a single draft negotiating text for subsequent negotiations on such a Code.[81]

[78] Alice Ba, 'The ASEAN Regional Forum: Maintaining the Regional Idea in Southeast Asia' (1997) 52 International Journal 635, 648.

[79] Ralf Emmers, 'Unpacking ASEAN Neutrality: The Quest for Autonomy and Impartiality in Southeast Asia' (2018) 40 Contemporary Southeast Asia 349, 364–5.

[80] *In the Matter of the South China Sea Arbitration (Republic of the Philippines v People's Republic of China)* PCA Case No 2013–19, Final Award (12 July 2016).

[81] Le Hong Hiep, 'Vietnam's Position on the South China Sea Code of Conduct' (2019) ISEAS Yusof Ishak Institute, Perspective No 22 <https://www.iseas.edu.sg/images/pdf/ISEAS_Perspective_2019_22.pdf> accessed 10 April 2019.

E. Conclusion: Musyawarah/Mufakat Decision-making under the ASEAN Charter and Future Regional Security

Finally, one cannot visualize regional security decision-making in ASEAN without examining the nature of consensus decision-making within the organization. Since the beginning of ASEAN in 1967, ASEAN Member States have entrenched decision-making practices by consultation and consensus (*musyawarah* and *mufakat*):

> *musyawarah* may be viewed as a pre-negotiation stage of 'intensive informal and discreet discussions that in the end bring out the general consensus of the community'. During this stage, differences can be aired and the possibility of common ground ascertained before the issues are submitted to more formal official meetings... [it] is a form of 'soft diplomacy as contrasted to saber-rattling, gunboat diplomacy of the colonial and Big Power variety'. Thus, an important aspect of the consensus-building process is the psychological setting of consultations, which must be non-hostile... Sensitive handling of intra-mural differences is a hallmark of consensus building. While parties can debate and disagree on the merit of a particular position behind closed doors, they must refrain from airing these differences in public. Even in situations where ASEAN members find it impossible to arrive at a common position, they must speak and act as though a certain level of unity has been achieved on that particular issue. This means a tendency to play down or give a positive spin to intra-mural differences. A great deal of care must be taken not to isolate or embarrass any individual ASEAN member in international fora...[82]

Several scholars attribute these particular decision-making practices as having contributed fairly significantly to building and entrenching a 'culture of peace'[83] in Southeast Asia. ASEAN concludes international agreements following this consensus decision-making rule. Its own Rules of Procedure for Conclusion of International Agreements by ASEAN requires all Member States to reach a common position first, before subsequent stages of treaty negotiation and conclusion can be undertaken.[84]

However, it should be noted that the ASEAN Charter introduced a slightly softer nuance to the consensus decision-making rule. Chapter VII of the ASEAN Charter

[82] Amitav Acharya, *Constructing a Security Community in Southeast Asia: ASEAN and the Problem of Regional Order* (Routledge 2001) 68.

[83] Kishore Mahbubani/Jeffery Sng, *The ASEAN Miracle: A Catalyst for Peace* (NUS Press 2017) 2:

> ...ASEAN has created an indispensable diplomatic platform that regularly brings all the great powers together... [it] has created conducive environments for the great powers to talk to each other. Within ASEAN, a culture of peace has evolved as a result of imbibing the Indonesian custom of *musyawarah* and *mufakat* (consultation and consensus).

[84] ASEAN, 'Rules of Procedure for Conclusion of International Agreements by ASEAN' (Bali, 17 November 2011) <https://www.asean.org/wp-content/uploads/images/archive/documents/ROP%20for%20Conclusion%20of%20International%20Agreements%20by%20ASEAN.pdf> accessed 10 April 2019.

affirms that 'as a basic principle, decision-making in ASEAN shall be based on consultation and consensus', but also stresses that 'where consensus cannot be achieved, the ASEAN Summit may decide how a specific decision can be made'.[85]

At the time of writing, these nuanced provisions in the ASEAN Charter have not yet been tested. One can anticipate, however, that the nuanced provisions on consensus decision-making may serve a purpose in case of deadlock amongst ASEAN Member States, especially for any future fraught or polarizing regional security disputes, whether these involve maritime security and overlapping claims in the South China Sea, the human rights situation and regional movement of Rohingya refugees from Myanmar, combatting extremism and transnational terrorism, as well as the resurgence of authoritarian, illiberal, and/or undemocratic governance in some ASEAN Member States and the renewed onslaught against human rights, democracy, and the rule of law in Southeast Asia.[86] The more identifiable and authoritative ASEAN Charter-based regional security decisions (premised on the distinct challenges for this maritime and topographic configuration of Southeast Asia) also exemplify and contribute a unique body of practice, usage, norms, and customs articulated jointly by ASEAN members of the 'Global South' (middle-income countries such as Malaysia, the Philippines, Indonesia, Thailand, and Vietnam; low-income emerging economies such as Myanmar, Cambodia, and Laos) and ASEAN members of the 'Global North' (Singapore and Brunei Darussalam). The proven ability to produce consensus-based regional decisions in over fifty years to date—against a shared reality of inherent ideological, political, religious, economic, social, cultural, linguistic, and geographical diversities and deep pluralisms within ASEAN's membership—sets ASEAN apart from other regional security organizations such as the European Union, the African Union, and the Organization of American States. While much can be critiqued in regard to ASEAN's distinct approach to regional security, there is also much to learn from its relative success in containing intra-regional conflicts and steadily building and deepening cooperative regional resilience in economic, social, and political dimensions as Southeast Asia's long-term strategy for international peace and security.

[85] ASEAN Charter (n 61) ch VII, art 20(1) and (2).

[86] Carolin Liss, 'New Actors and the State: Addressing Maritime Security Threats in Southeast Asia' (2013) 35 Contemporary Southeast Asia 141; Afroza Anwary, 'Atrocities Against the Rohingya Community of Myanmar' (2018) 31 Indian Journal of Asian Affairs 91; Ryamizard Ryacudu, 'Terrorism in Southeast Asia: The Need for Joint Counter-Terrorism Frameworks' (2018) 10 Counter Terrorist Trends and Analyses 1; Thitinan Pongsudhirak, 'Authoritarianism is Accelerating in Southeast Asia' (*Nikkei Asian Review*, 1 January 2018) <https://asia.nikkei.com/Editor-s-Picks/Looking-ahead-2018/Authoritarianism-is-accelerating-in-Southeast-Asia> accessed 10 April 2019; Vincent Bevins, 'It's not just Burma: Human Rights are Under Attack across Southeast Asia, Advocates Say' (*Washington Post*, 8 September 2017) <https://www.washingtonpost.com/news/worldviews/wp/2017/09/08/its-not-just-burma-human-rights-are-under-attack-across-southeast-asia-advocates-say/?utm_term=.5d52c5f8be96> accessed 10 April 2019.

CHAPTER 53

THE AFRICAN UNION

Security Governance under the African Peace and Security Architecture

JERUSHA ASIN OWINO

A. Introduction: African (In)Security and the APSA

> *...Africa needs to be protected from external enemies and from internal deviants. There is a crying need in the continent for collective military self-reliance...*
>
> —Ali Mazrui, Philosopher, December 1979[1]

> *...Nevertheless, the unfortunate truth is that Africa today is ill-prepared to adequately respond to current events, because the African Union still has to be made fit for purpose.*
>
> —President Paul Kagame, AU Chairperson, January 2017[2]

It is no lie that a mix of armed conflicts, political turbulence, and turmoil has created unrelenting and in some cases irreparably destabilizing 'crises of habitability'[3] on the

[1] Ali Mazrui, 'The African Condition: Lecture 5—Patterns of Identity' (Reith Lectures 1979, *BBC Radio 4*, 5 December 1979) 6 <http://downloads.bbc.co.uk/rmhttp/radio4/transcripts/1979_reith5.pdf> accessed 10 January 2019.

[2] Paul Kagame, 'The Imperative to Strengthen our Union: Report on the Proposed Recommendations for the Institutional Reform of the African Union' (29 January 2017) 2 <http://www.rci.uct.ac.za/sites/default/files/image_tool/images/78/News/FInal%20AU%20Reform%20Combined%20report_28012017.pdf> accessed 10 January 2020.

[3] Ali Mazrui, 'The African Condition: Lecture 1—The Garden of Eden in Decay' (Reith Lectures 1979, *BBC Radio 4*, 7 November 1979) 7 <http://downloads.bbc.co.uk/rmhttp/radio4/transcripts/1979_reith1.pdf> accessed 30 June 2018.

African continent. Granted, these are neither limited to Africa nor peculiar to the continent, but there is evidence that Africa disproportionately bears the global armed conflict burden.[4] The number of conflicts which occur in Africa is above average, seemingly unaffected by annual fluctuations, which have been discernible ever since a reported upsurge in violence in 2014.[5] From that point, in 2015, nearly one-third of all global conflicts took place in Africa,[6] dipping to a quarter of all conflicts in 2016.[7] In 2017, in addition to an increase in conflicts, the highest intensity conflicts were reported to be in sub-Saharan Africa, which surpassed the Middle East as the region most affected by wars with a total of nine full-scale wars.[8] In 2018, formidable security crises confronted the African Union's peace and security mechanisms, with differentiated manifestations in the Central African Republic (CAR), the Democratic Republic of Congo (DRC), Darfur in Sudan, Guinea Bissau, Libya, Mali and the Sahel, Somalia, South Sudan, and the Lake Chad Basin, with instability also being reported in Burundi and Madagascar.[9] Perhaps nothing quite captures the magnitude of the human cost of insecurity in the same way that the deaths of 'tens of thousands of young Africans at sea or their abandonment in the desert, in pursuit of a decent life for which they are prepared to risk everything, because they believe there is no hope at home'[10] does.

These theatres of struggle and strife compel an interrogation of the security regime of AU mechanisms mandated to promote peace and stability under the AU: the African Peace and Security Architecture (APSA), established in 2003.[11] The APSA finds legal, normative, and institutional expression through a conglomeration of declarations, treaties, protocols, and memoranda of understanding. These, however, belie the fact that alongside conventional security threats, conflict patterns and trends in Africa have not remained static from 2002 but have metastasized owing to the socio-economic and political dynamics in different African countries.[12] For instance, the maelstrom in DRC in August 2018—when the tenth outbreak of the Ebola epidemic hit in the midst of

[4] Jakkie Cilliers, 'Future (Im)perfect? Mapping Conflict, Violence and Extremism in Africa' (2015) ISS Paper 287/2015 <https://issafrica.org/research/papers/future-im-perfect-mapping-conflict-violence-and-extremism-in-africa> accessed 28 August 2018.

[5] Sophie Desmidt/Volker Hauck, 'Conflict Management under the African Peace and Security Architecture (APSA): Analysis of Conflict Prevention and Conflict Resolution Interventions by the African Union and Regional Economic Communities in Violent Conflicts in Africa for the Years 2013–2015' (2017) European Centre for Development Policy Management Discussion Paper No 211/2017, 1 <https://ecdpm.org/publications/conflict-management-under-the-apsa/> accessed 10 January 2020; Cilliers (n 4) 5.

[6] HIIK, 'Conflict Barometer 2015' (24th edn, HIIK 2016) 11.

[7] HIIK, 'Conflict Barometer 2016' (25th edn, HIIK 2017).

[8] HIIK, 'Conflict Barometer 2017' (26th edn, HIIK 2018) 14.

[9] AU Assembly, 'Report of the Peace and Security Council on its Activities and the State of Peace and Security in Africa' (1–2 July 2018) Assembly/AU/7(XXXI) (PSC Report).

[10] Kagame (n 2) 3.

[11] *African Union Handbook: A Guide for Those Working With and Within the African Union* (African Union Commission/New Zealand Crown 2014) 28.

[12] Kwesi Aning/Mustapha Abdallah, 'Confronting Hybrid Threats in Africa: Improving Multidimensional Responses' in Cedric de Coning et al (eds), *The Future of African Peace Operations: From the Janjaweed to Boko Haram* (Zed Books 2016) 20.

conflict—reveals the emergence of multifaceted security threats[13] with devastating impact. This particular outbreak is the world's first such intrusion of a lethal virus entering an active battle zone,[14] a fact which exacerbated its spread.[15] In the first instance, armed rebel militia took advantage of the outbreak to increase the frequency and intensity of their attacks in the north-eastern city of Beni, the epicentre of the pandemic.[16] The treacherous security situation compelled responders to place intervention measures on lockdown. But while they were on lockdown, Ebola was not.[17] Secondly, areas occupied by rebels, as the government does not control the entirety of its territory, and therefore designated by the World Health Organization as red zones, were out of reach to the relief agencies. The pervasive conflict situation enabled pockets of mistrust and resistance to the intervention measures based on fears of the government being involved in a conspiracy to spread the virus.[18] These multiple crises were further compounded by mass displacement and a humanitarian contingency in North Kivu involving refugees, all happening in the midst of long-delayed and eventually disputed elections.[19] On 25 June 2020, the government of the DRC announced that the tenth outbreak of Ebola,[20] which had been declared in 2018,[21] was officially over.

The situation in the DRC segues to a secondary contextual consideration, which is that the problem of security in Africa is local, regional, and global and should be approached as such, a statement as true in 2018 as it was in 1981.[22] While the APSA was crafted under the auspices of the AU, neither the AU nor its regional and international interlocutors in security governance are under any illusion that African (in)security can be addressed independently.[23] As a normative, operational, and pragmatic imperative, the APSA functions as an interlocking and hybrid system of security governance,[24] in which multiple regional, continental and global actors are integrated in order to leverage

[13] ibid 21.

[14] Kasereka Masumbuko Claude et al, 'Ebola Virus Epidemic in War-Torn Eastern DR Congo' (2018) 392 The Lancet 1399, 1400.

[15] Peter Salama, WHO Deputy Director-General for Emergency Preparedness and Response, 'Press Conference' (25 September 2018) <https://www.who.int/ebola/WHO-RUSH_Ebola_DR_Congo_update_SALAMAp_UNOG_25SEP2018-final.pdf> accessed 10 January 2020.

[16] Tedros Adhanom Ghebreyesus, WHO Director-General, 'Speech', (UNSC Meeting on the Ebola Outbreak in North Kivu, Democratic Republic of Congo, New York, 3 October 2018) <https://www.who.int/dg/speeches/2018/un-security-council-ebola-north-kivu/en/> accessed 10 January 2020.

[17] ibid. [18] Salama (n 15).

[19] AU PSC, 'Communique of the 808th Meeting on the situation on the Democratic Republic of the Congo' (19 November 2018) AU Doc PSC/PR/COMM.(DCCCVIII).

[20] WHO, 'Ebola Virus Disease: Democratic Republic of the Congo' (*Disease Outbreak News*, 10 January 2019) <https://www.who.int/csr/don/10-january-2019-ebola-drc/en/> accessed 10 January 2020.

[21] Lawrence Gostin et al, 'Ebola in the Democratic Republic of the Congo: Time to Sound a Global Alert?' (2019) 393 The Lancet 617.

[22] Francis Deng, 'Security Problems: An African Predicament' (Annual Hans Wolff Memorial Lecture, Indiana University, 23 October 1981).

[23] UNSC Verbatim Record (18 July 2018) UN Doc S/PV.8314, 2.

[24] Malte Brosig, 'Security Regime Complexity: A New Perspective in Security Studies?' in Felix Dane (ed), *Multilateral Security Governance—International Security: A European-South American Dialogue* (Konrad Adenauer Stiftung 2014).

their different capacities in managing conflicts.[25] Accordingly, the APSA is analysed within this contribution as a security regime complex.[26]

Last, the development of the APSA has been improvisational and reactive, with the AU having to respond to crises before full maturation of the APSA components.[27] To accommodate these situational exigencies, some APSA components have developed in unexpected ways. For instance, the doctrine for the African Standby Force (ASF), was formulated between 2003 to 2008 when the AU was still a neophyte in conducting peace operations[28] and was predicated on conflict trends prevailing before the year 2000. Subsequent field experience has shown that this model is vastly unsuited to confront the threat matrix posed by terrorism, violent extremism, and security environments where offensive combat is necessary to stabilize crises.[29] While the capacity of the AU and that of its regional organizations and mechanisms has expanded to mount stabilization and counter-terrorism measures either as peace support operations or as part of AU-mandated 'coalitions of the willing', none of these operations have effectuated the ASF doctrine, which is unlikely to ever be deployed as designed.[30] The ASF doctrine has been eclipsed by the specific conduct of peace support operations within the APSA.[31] This has borne significant comparative advantages within the global peace and security framework, enabling a nascent trend where either regionally led and composed forces are used to augment UN peacekeeping forces, such as was the case with the SADC (Southern African Development Community) Force Intervention Brigade in the DRC, or conversely where UN peacekeeping or dedicated support missions are used to support regional forces, as has happened in Somalia and the Sahel region with the AU Mission in Somalia and the G5 Sahel Force respectively.[32]

Keeping this analytical framework in mind, this contribution proceeds from the premise that in its designation as an instrument for the provision of regional security goods, the APSA is a conduit for global security governance. Its nesting organization, the AU, is accordingly a strategic partner in the global security architecture.[33] However, in charting the progression of the APSA, it would be disingenuous to overlook the contemporary realities belaboured at the outset, which have been known to all stakeholders at all material times. Indeed, there appears to be ongoing momentum for institutional

[25] Malte Brosig, 'Introduction: The African Security Regime Complex—Exploring Converging Actors and Policies' (2013) 6 African Security 171, 174.

[26] ibid 31.

[27] Solomon Dersso, 'Stabilization Missions and Mandates in African Peace Operations: Implications for the ASF?' in de Coning et al (n 12) 39.

[28] Cedric de Coning, 'Africa and UN Peace Operations: Implications for the Future of Regional Organisations' in Cedric de Coning/Mateja Peter (eds), *United Nations Peace Operations in a Changing Global Order* (Palgrave Macmillan 2019) 220.

[29] Yvonne Akpasom/Walter Lotze, 'The Shift to Stabilisation Operations: Considerations for African Peace Support Operations' (2014) Conflict Trends 18, 19–20.

[30] Cedric de Coning, 'Enhancing the Efficiency of the African Standby Force: The Case for a Shift to a Just-in-Time Rapid Response Model' (2014) Conflict Trends 34, 39.

[31] de Coning et al (n 12).

[32] de Coning (n 28) 218.

[33] ibid 226.

reforms at the AU, where there is acknowledgement that the AU 'is a dysfunctional organisation in which Member States see limited value, global partners find little credibility and… citizens have no trust'.[34] Moreover, the AU faces an existential crisis with regard to funding, especially given that as recently as 2016, 98 per cent of its peace and security expenditure is funded by international partners.[35] This chapter explores the relationship between the unfurling of the APSA institutions, on the one hand, and Africa's contemporary security challenges, on the other.

To that end, following this introduction, Section B outlines the historical background of the APSA. Thereafter, the chapter unpacks the dense network of partnerships that operate within the APSA (Section C), while Section D charts the institutional development of the pillars on which the APSA rests. In a similar fashion to African cultural tradition, proverbs are employed as thematic guideposts to link the narrative and support the conclusions posited in the fifth and final section of this contribution.

B. The Backstory to African Solidarity in Strife

If you know the beginning well, the end will not trouble you

—African proverb

Africa's struggles with peace and security did not begin in the recent past. All continental institutions established as a collective response reveal the security preoccupations marking distinct epochs in Pan-African life. The Organisation of African Unity (OAU) was birthed in 1963 to fight colonialism and to promote unity and solidarity amongst African States.[36] It is important to note that the OAU was established as a compromise formula between different factions of States split along two rivalling ideologies on African unity and integration.[37] The first group had a strong proclivity for a supranational institution. The second group did not wish to sacrifice individual sovereignty at the altar of African unity. Ultimately, national sovereignty won the day and the OAU was established on the basis of voluntary political and economic cooperation.[38]

[34] Kagame (n 2) 5.

[35] African Peace Fund, 'Securing Predictable and Sustainable Financing for Peace in Africa' (August 2016) 3, para 5 <https://www.peaceau.org/uploads/auhr-progress-report-final-020916-with-annexes.pdf> accessed 10 January 2019.

[36] Charter of the Organization of African Unity 479 UNTS 39 arts 2(1)(a) and (d).

[37] Monde Muyangwa/Margaret Vogt, *An Assessment of the OAU Mechanism for Conflict Prevention, Management and Resolution, 1993–2000* (International Peace Academy 2000) 4.

[38] OAU Charter (n 36) art 3(2) and (3).

Notwithstanding their views on regional integration, all OAU Member States were presumed to be committed to Pan-African solidarity.[39] Solidarity is a communal struggle for social, economic, and political equality and freedom for all persons of African descent.[40] The conception of solidarity under the OAU signalled public tolerance and support amongst African leaders that would brook no digressions once a broad continental consensus had been established.[41]

Because the underlying principles of the OAU were inter-State harmony and solidarity, there were no provisions in the Charter to monitor compliance. This was a profound mistake, which later manifested itself in the unwillingness of members to submit their own disputes to the OAU.[42] In fact, the OAU Commission, tasked with reconciliation of disputes, had to remonstrate with members to solve potential and actual conflicts.[43] OAU attempts at conflict prevention and management ended badly.[44]

In 1993, the OAU established a mechanism to anticipate and prevent conflicts, an institutional precursor of the APSA.[45] It was however ineffectual and powerless.[46] The genocide in Rwanda in 1994 marked a particularly gruesome watershed in the legacy of the OAU's non-interference policy[47] and underscored its inability to meaningfully intervene in a 'preventable genocide',[48] encumbered by outdated normative frameworks, institutional structures, and operational techniques[49] amidst the 'permissive culture of indifference'.[50]

[39] Kofi Kufuor, 'The Collapse of the Organization of African Unity: Lessons from Economics and History' (2005) 49 Journal of African Law 132, 136.

[40] Tim Murithi, 'Institutionalising Pan Africanism: Transforming African Union Values and Principles into Practice' (2007) ISS Paper 143/2007, 1 <https://www.files.ethz.ch/isn/98931/PAPER143H.pdf> accessed 10 January 2020.

[41] Thomas Tieku, 'Solidarity Intervention: Emerging Trends in AU's Interventions in African Crisis' (Workshop on Africa International: Agency and Interdependency in a changing World, Chatham House, 9 October 2009) <https://www.open.ac.uk/socialsciences/bisa-africa/confpapers/solidarity-intervention.pdf> accessed 10 January 2020.

[42] Muyangwa/Vogt (n 37) 6–7. [43] ibid.

[44] Ademola Abass, 'African Peace and Security Architecture and the Protection of Human Security' in Ademola Abass (ed), *Protecting Human Security in Africa* (OUP 2010) 252.

[45] OAU, 'Cairo Declaration of the Assembly of Heads of State and Government on the Establishment within the OAU of a Mechanism for Conflict Prevention, Management and Resolution' (adopted on 28–30 June 1993) AHG/DECL.3(XXIX).

[46] Muyangwa/Vogt (n 37) 11–15.

[47] AU, 'Rwanda: The Preventable Genocide' (International Panel of Eminent Personalities, July 2000) paras 11.32, 15.86, 15.87 <http://www.refworld.org/docid/4d1da8752.html> accessed 10 January 2020.

[48] ibid para 10.1.

[49] Solomon Dersso, 'The Role and Place of the African Standby Force within the African Peace and Security Architecture' (2010) ISS Paper 209/2010, 3 <https://www.files.ethz.ch/isn/113682/209.pdf> accessed 10 January 2020.

[50] Timothy Murithi, 'Introduction: Contextualizing the Debate on a Union Government for Africa' in Timothy Murithi (ed), 'Towards a Union Government for Africa: Challenges and Opportunities' (ISS Monograph No 140, 2008) <https://issafrica.org/chapter-1-introduction-contextualising-the-debate-on-a-union-government-for-africa-dr-tim-murithi-institute-for-security-studies-addis-ababa-eth> accessed 10 January 2020.

With the OAU in terminal decline, and a fresh set of socio-economic, political, and security challenges facing African countries close to the turn of the twentieth century, the Heads of State and Government decided to replace the OAU with the AU in 1999.[51] The transformation began in 1999 and culminated with the Durban Summit of 2002 which inaugurated the AU.

C. The Anatomy of the APSA: Partnerships

Umoja ni nguvu, utengano ni udhaifu (Unity is strength, division is weakness)

—Kiswahili Proverb

By definition, a security regime complex references a macro system[52] of at least three regimes whose activities are aligned to achieve common goals in the domain of managing security. Within the macro system, there are overlapping memberships in terms of the distinct regimes and all the substantive, normative, and operative interactions generated within the system are potentially problematic.[53] The APSA is itself the macro system in which the integrated and interdependent interactions of different actors (themselves comprising security regimes) converge and diverge in relation to their activities in managing African security.

The security regime complex enables an accurate depiction of the hybrid partnerships within the APSA and the division of work in practice. While the provisions of Chapter VIII of the UN Charter dictate a hierarchical relationship between the UN and the AU in much the same way that the PSC Protocol mandates a hierarchical relationship between the AU and the Regional Economic Communities (RECs),[54] the operational reality is different. Each actor has capacities which, depending on the circumstances, are leveraged as comparative advantages within the regime complex to respond to crises. This explains why the AU deployed military personnel to stabilize volatile crises in Somalia, the CAR, and Mali, and after a degree of stability and security was attained, the UN took over from the AU operations.[55] What the AU lacks in terms of the full multidimensional peacekeeping ability of the UN, it makes up for[56] in mobilizing

[51] OAU, 'Sirte Declaration' (Fourth Extraordinary Summit of the Assembly of Heads of State and Government, 8–9 September 1999) EAHG/Draft/Decl. (IV) Rev.1, para 6.

[52] Brosig (n 24) 30. [53] Brosig (n 25) 172.

[54] Protocol relating to the Establishment of the Peace and Security Council of the African Union AU Doc 9/7/2002, art 16(1) (PSC Protocol).

[55] Linda Darkwa, 'The Strategic Relationship between the African Union and its Partners' in de Coning et al (n 12) 69.

[56] Cedric de Coning et al, 'Towards an African Model of Peace Operations' in ibid 2.

political will and personnel, and what the UN lacks as a first responder it makes up for in terms of providing legitimacy, funding, logistical support to AU operations and, where possible, eventual takeover.[57]

There are three main APSA partnerships: that between the AU and the RECs, that between the AU and the EU (which has financially underwritten AU peace operations within the framework of the joint AU–EU partnership to support peace and security in Africa), and the third partnership between the AU and the UN.[58] Additionally, the AU has leveraged bilateral relationships with States and entities like NATO, China, Russia, Japan, Turkey, and India.[59] In certain cases, they do not directly interact with the APSA but opt to buttress the individual capacity of Member States.[60]

The regime complex does not dissolve the individual character of the actors within it. For this reason, the relationships within the APSA do not function within strict hierarchies,[61] as borne by the loosely structured agreements concluded between the AU and the EU[62] and the AU and the UN[63] on their collaborative partnerships in peace and security. While the interaction between the AU and the UN appears more structured with the 2010 establishment of the UN Office to the African Union (UNOA), the increasing joint and consultative meetings between the UN Security Council (UNSC) and the AU Peace and Security Council (PSC) have so far been informal desk to desk meetings.[64] The loose structure of the APSA allows convergence of the sub-regional, regional, and international levels as happened in the case of the SADC Force Intervention Brigade deployed to enhance the UN Stabilization Mission to the DRC (MONUSCO) in 2013. Operating as an example of positive regime convergence, the Force Intervention Brigade was deployed with the mandate to use offensive force to contain the M-23 rebel group with the support of the DRC, the African troop contributing countries from the RECs involved, and the AU, with the authority to use force being provided by the UNSC.[65] The loose structure of the APSA also allows regime actors to interact spontaneously in response to particular issues, such as the AU–EU–UN Taskforce created in November 2017 to address the migrant crisis in Libya.

The conundrum of loose structures and the absence of strict hierarchical relationships within the regime complex has predictably occasioned divergence and dissonant

[57] de Coning (n 28) 224. [58] Brosig (n 24) 30.

[59] Cedric de Coning et al, 'African Peace Operations: Trends and Future Scenarios, Conclusions and Recommendations' in de Coning et al (n 12) 136.

[60] de Coning et al (n 56) 2. [61] Brosig (n 25) 173.

[62] AU–EU, 'Memorandum of Understanding between the AU and the EU on Peace, Security and Governance' (23 May 2018) <https://eeas.europa.eu/sites/eeas/files/medghme_2018.05.23_16.31.36_5c4n7108_1.pdf> accessed 10 January 2020.

[63] UN–AU, 'Joint UN–AU Framework for enhanced partnership in Peace and Security' (19 April 2017) <https://unoau.unmissions.org/sites/default/files/jount_un-au_framework_for_an_enhanced_partnership_in_peace_and_security.pdf> accessed 10 January 2020.

[64] UNSC 'Report of the Secretary-General: Strengthening the Partnership between the United Nations and the African Union on Issues of Peace and Security in Africa, including on the Work of the United Nations Office to the African Union' (6 July 2018) UN Doc S/2018/678, para 2.

[65] de Coning (n 28) 218.

behaviour, as witnessed in the fallout between the AU PSC and the UNSC in 2011 over the management of the Libyan crisis and in 2016 between the AU and the EU over the EU's payments to troops in the AU mission in Somalia.[66]

In the same vein, the relationship between the AU and the RECs as the nucleus of the regime complex has been particularly fraught. This is because the overlapping memberships within the RECs, all of which have different historic and geographical antecedents in addressing peace and security, compounded by different interregional political dynamics,[67] complicates the operation of the operative principles of subsidiarity, complementarity, and comparative advantage in the 2008 AU–REC–RM MOU (African Union–Regional Economic Communities–Regional Mechanisms Memorandum of Understanding).[68]

While none of these concepts have been delineated in the MOU, subsidiarity would suggest that tasks should be handled at the lowest level at which results can be attained,[69] which implies that the AU relies on the RECs as first responders.[70] This is not as straightforward as it appears. In the 2015 Burundi crisis, the East African Community (EAC) (which was seized of the crisis) led a half-hearted mediation effort, with the AU in bystander mode unable to insert itself into the mediation.[71]

Where the REC is competent and marching in lock step with the AU PSC, successful outcomes have followed as, for example, with the crisis that followed the contested Gambian presidential elections in December 2016. In that case, the PSC endorsed the resolve of Economic Community of West African States (ECOWAS) to enforce the election results,[72] specifically the decision 'to use all necessary means'—parlance for 'use of force'.[73] By employing a combination of tactical, diplomatic, and military tools at the REC, AU, and UN levels, the crisis was successfully averted.[74]

[66] International Crisis Group, 'Africa Report No 255: Time to Reset African Union–European Union Relations' (17 October 2017) i <https://www.crisisgroup.org/africa/255-time-reset-african-union-european-union-relations> accessed 10 January 2020.

[67] Michelle Ndiaye, 'The Relationship between the AU and the RECs and the RMs in relation to Peace and Security in Africa: Subsidiarity and Inevitable Common Destiny' in de Coning et al (n 12) 52.

[68] AU–REC–RM, 'Memorandum of Understanding on Cooperation in the Area of Peace and Security between the African Union, the Regional Economic Communities and the Coordinating Mechanisms of the Regional Standby Brigades of Eastern Africa and Northern Africa' (June 2008) art IV(iv) <https://issafrica.s3.amazonaws.com/site/uploads/AUMOURECSJUN08.PDF> accessed 10 January 2020.

[69] Ndiaye (n 67) 53.

[70] AU–REC–RM MOU (n 68) art XX.

[71] International Crisis Group, 'Africa Briefing No 122: The African Union and the Burundi Crisis—Ambition versus Reality' (28 September 2016) 6 <https://www.crisisgroup.org/africa/central-africa/burundi/african-union-and-burundi-crisis-ambition-versus-reality> accessed 10 January 2020.

[72] ECOWAS, 'Final Communique' (50th Extraordinary Session of the ECOWAS Authority of Heads of State and Government', Abuja, 17 December 2016) para 38(g) <https://www.ecowas.int/wp-content/uploads/2016/12/Communiqu%C3%A9-Final_50th-Summit_Abuja_Dec-16_Eng.pdf> accessed 10 January 2020.

[73] AU PSC, 'Communique' (Addis Ababa, 13 January 2017) PSC/PR/COMM.(DCXLVII) para 3.

[74] Mohamed Helal, 'Crisis in The Gambia: How Africa is Rewriting Jus ad Bellum' (*Opinio Juris*, 24 January 2017) <http://opiniojuris.org/2017/01/24/crisis-in-the-gambia-how-africa-is-rewriting-jus-ad-bellum/> accessed 10 January 2020.

However, subsidiarity cannot have a monolithic application, especially in a context where, within the five AU regions, there are also eight RECs recognized by the AU.[75] This means that at any one point, there could be multiple RECs acting on the same security crises.[76] In the Malian crisis in 2012, Algeria and Mauritania, key non-ECOWAS neighbours, opposed the ECOWAS peace operation.[77] Mali's position at the crossroads of the Western, Northern, and Central AU regions and the deployment of units belonging to two different RECs presented acute coordination challenges.[78] Coupled with the fact that there were divisions within ECOWAS States, the AU stepped in to deploy a peace operation, the African-led International Support Mission in Mali (AFISMA), which was later re-hatted to become the UN-led MINUSMA (The United Nations Multidimensional Integrated Stabilization Mission in Mali).[79] In another instance, after a coup d'état in Burkina Faso in 2015, ECOWAS and the AU PSC had different views on how to manage the crisis, with ECOWAS insisting on its pre-eminence under the subsidiarity principle to manage conflict in West Africa.[80] As it emerged, four members of the AU PSC, who were also members of ECOWAS, took contradictory decisions, first as members of the PSC and thereafter as ECOWAS members, highlighting the overlapping memberships within the security regime,[81] and the potential incompatibility where some RECs consider that their activities in the field of peace and security predate both the APSA and the AU. These examples illustrate the incongruity of a singular model of subsidiarity[82] amongst the different RECs and RMs as regime actors within the APSA whose regional dynamics can and do curtail the operation of subsidiarity, and are a concrete subject for AU reform.[83]

[75] *African Union Handbook: A Guide for Those Working With and Within the African Union* (4th edn, African Union Commission/New Zealand Crown 2017) 13 (AU Handbook 2017) 128. These are: the Common Market for Eastern and Southern Africa (COMESA), the Community of Sahel–Saharan States (CEN–SAD), the East African Community (EAC), the Economic Community of Central African States (ECCAS), the Economic Community of West African States (ECOWAS), the Intergovernmental Authority on Development (IGAD), Southern African Development Community (SADC) and the Arab Maghreb Union (UMA), which has been dormant since 1989. The International Conference on the Great Lakes Region (ICGLR) and the Lake Chad Basin Commission (LCBC) are also regional organizations with a peace and security mandate.

[76] Desmidt/Hauck (n 5) 6. [77] Ndiaye (n 67) 59.

[78] AU, 'Report of the Chairperson of the Commission on the Operationalisation of the Rapid Deployment Capability of the African Standby Force and the Establishment of an African Capacity for Immediate Response to Crises' (6th Ordinary Meeting of the Specialised Technical Committee on Defence Safety and Security, 29–30 April 2013) RPT/Exp/VI/STCDSS/(i-a)2013, para 23 <https://www.peaceau.org/uploads/auc-report-cp-cdr-faa-26-04-2013-rev30.pdf> accessed 10 January 2020.

[79] ibid.

[80] ECOWAS, 'Final Communique: Extraordinary Session of the Authority of Heads of State and Government on the Political Crisis in Burkina Faso' (22 September 2015) para 23 <http://www.ecowas.int/final-communiqueextraordinary-session-of-the-authority-of-heads-of-state-and-government-on-the-political-crisis-in-burkina-faso/> accessed 10 January 2020.

[81] ISS, 'Burkina Faso a Test for the AU's Impact on Crises' (PSC Report, 2 November 2015) <https://issafrica.org/pscreport/addis-insights/burkina-faso-a-test-for-the-aus-impact-on-crises> accessed 10 January 2020.

[82] de Coning (n 28) 221. [83] Kagame (n 2) 5.

D. Institutional Interventions under the APSA

To loma oki jelo

—Bamongo Proverb

(Night comes on and we rest, thinking that we have reached land. But during the night, a storm bursts upon us and then we discover that we are on a sandbank)

The PSC is the bulwark of the APSA. Its leadership role applies at all stages of the conflict cycle and it is mandated to not only anticipate and prevent conflicts, but to also manage and resolve them.[84] In discharging this ambitious mandate, the PSC is supported by the AU Commission (AUC), a Panel of the Wise (POW), a Continental Early Warning System (CEWS), the African Standby Force (ASF), the African Peace Fund (APF),[85] the Military Staff Committee,[86] and the RECs.[87] The institutional pillars of the APSA are the CEWS, the POW, the ASF, and the APF, whose operation is designed to be sequential in terms of conflict prevention, management, and resolution.[88] As a fifteen-member-strong entity elected by the Executive Council, the PSC convenes in Addis Ababa at three levels, that of the Permanent Representatives (Ambassadors), the Ministers, and the Heads of State and Government,[89] and makes decisions either by consensus or simple majority.[90] Structures corresponding to the PSC have been established at the REC level, a robust example being the ECOWAS Mediation and Security Council and similar initiatives at COMESA and CEN-SAD.[91]

One of the most severe challenges the PSC has faced since its inception in 2003 is its abortive attempt to coercively deploy a protection force in Burundi in the midst of the political crisis in 2015. In December 2015, the PSC, meeting as permanent representatives, invoked 4(h) of the AU Constitutive Act[92] and authorized the deployment of a mission (MAPROBU) to prevent deterioration of security in Burundi.[93] The demarche demanded that Burundi consent to MAPROBU's deployment within ninety-six hours or the PSC would recommend that the AU Assembly deploy MAPROBU by force. Unsurprisingly, Bujumbura baulked, PSC resolve cracked, and it was forced to fall back with an equally unprecedented decision to rescind the deployment order in January 2016 by a PSC meeting at the level of heads of States.[94] While other dynamics contributed

[84] PSC Protocol (n 54) art 2(1). [85] ibid art 2(2).
[86] ibid art 13(8). [87] ibid art 16.
[88] Alhaji Bah et al, 'The African Peace and Security Architecture: A Handbook' (Friedrich Ebert Stiftung/AU 2014) 34–41 (APSA Handbook).
[89] PSC Protocol (n 54) art 8(2). [90] ibid art 8(13). [91] APSA Handbook (n 88) 42–5.
[92] 2158 UNTS 3.
[93] AU PSC, 'Communique' (17 December 2015) PSC/PR/COMM.(DLXV) para. 13(c)(iv).
[94] AU PSC, 'Communique' (29 January 2016) PSC/AHG/COMM.3(DLXXI).

to the derailment, this episode was disastrous for the PSC.[95] Its working processes revealed flaws and divisions within it, in addition to being understaffed and unable to develop the statecraft needed within it and the wider AU to ensure successful deployment.[96] And while the AUC worked hand in hand with the PSC, there was marginal, if any, interaction with other elements of the APSA, and the AUC is considered to have overreached itself.[97] Even though the threat of military intervention was made after violence in Bujumbura intensified, in the absence of any strategic planning or concept of operations or commitment from troop countries,[98] it amounted to a risky gamble to compel Bujumbura to negotiate.[99] It is uncertain whether this gamble paid off because in 2016, the violence between armed groups tapered off, while civilian targeting scaled up.[100] Even worse for the PSC, it was reported at the time that this debacle made it lose impetus and take a backseat in managing crises in favour of regional initiatives.[101]

This study now proceeds to assess the APSA pillars by reference to the interventions made under early warning systems, diplomacy, mediation, and peace support operations.

1. Early Warning under the Continental Early Warning System

As the early warning component of the APSA, the CEWS provides data for decision makers on crises that are likely to degenerate into full blown conflicts and corresponding policy options.[102] The CEWS operates at the AU level with equivalent early warning systems (EWSs) at IGAD, ECOWAS, COMESA, EAC and ECCAS. The SADC EWS is based on intelligence reports.[103] ECOWARN and CEWARN are the most advanced EWSs which observe a wide spectrum of conflicts.[104] The reports issued under the CEWS generate data which is aggregated and analysed and then transmitted to the AUC Commissioner for Peace and Security, who then briefs the PSC.[105]

The CEWS has however not been integrated with other pillars of the APSA to enable the anticipated early response by relevant decision makers.[106] Reportedly, CEWS staff provided early warning reports on the Mali and Guinea Bissau crises in 2012 but the PSC decided not to take any preventive action.[107] In the widely publicized case of the aborted

95 ICG, 'Africa Briefing No 122' (n 71) 7–8.

96 ibid 7–10. 97 ibid 8. 98 ibid. 99 cf ibid 7–8.

100 IPSS, 'APSA Impact Report 2016: Assessment of the Impacts of Intervention by the African Union and Regional Economic Communities in 2016 in the frame of the APSA' (October 2017) 17 <http://www.ipss-addis.org/resources/publications/apsa_impact_report_2016.php> accessed 10 January 2020.

101 ISS, 'Peace and Security Council Report No 99' (28 February 2018) 4 <https://issafrica.org/research/peace-and-security-council-report/peace-and-security-council-report-no-99> accessed 17 December 2019.

102 PSC Protocol (n 54) art 12.

103 AU, 'African Peace and Security Architecture Roadmap 2016–2020' (2015) 15 (APSA Roadmap).

104 Desmidt/Hauck (n 5) 19. 105 PSC Report (n 9) para 108.

106 APSA Roadmap (n 103) 16.

107 Adriana Lins de Albuquerque, 'The African Peace and Security Architecture: Discussing the Remaining Challenges' (October 2016) FOI-R-4301-SE, 14 <https://observatoire-boutros-ghali.org/sites/default/files/APSA.pdf> accessed 10 January 2020.

deployment of MAPROBU in Burundi, interlocutors considered that the AU lacked credible situational analysis,[108] which explains why the decision to abort the deployment was made partly on grounds of lack of sufficient data and analysis necessary to support the deployment.[109] *Prima facie*, that means that at the political level, military intervention was authorized without the hard data and situation reports that the CEWS was designed to provide.

2. Diplomatic Interventions: The Panel of the Wise

The Panel supports the PSC and the AUC Chairperson in conflict prevention through preventive diplomacy[110] but is not formally integrated into AU mediation structures. The Panel is aimed at combining the expertise of African personalities who have contributed to the continental cause of peace and development from each of the five AU regions to engage in preventive diplomacy.[111]

The Panel's thematic focus has centred on election processes.[112] While the RECS have developed corresponding structures at the regional level,[113] in 2013, the AU and the RECs established a Pan-African Network of the Wise (Panwise) to aggregate their joint activities under a single entity.[114] In March 2017, the PSC established the Network of African Women for Conflict Prevention and Mediation (Femwise-Africa) within the APSA as a subsidiary mechanism of the AU Panel of the Wise and Panwise,[115] as a means of gender mainstreaming whose operationalization is incomplete.[116]

That notwithstanding, Panwise is being operationalized at a glacial pace and there appears to be minimal interaction between the AU Panel, the PSC, and the AU Chairperson.[117] In 2018, the AU Panel decried gaps in its integration with the CEWS which would have otherwise enhanced its work[118] and allowed for the early deployment of the Panels before the escalation of conflict, highlighting gaps in integration as intended in the PSC Protocol.

[108] ICG, 'Africa Briefing No 122' (n 71) 7.

[109] Solomon Dersso, 'To Intervene or Not To Intervene? An Inside View of the AU's Decision-Making on Article 4(h) in Burundi' (2016) World Peace Foundation Occasional Paper <https://sites.tufts.edu/wpf/files/2017/05/AU-Decision-Making-on-Burundi_Dersso.pdf > accessed 10 January 2020.

[110] PSC Protocol (n 54) art 11.

[111] Ademola Jegede, 'The African Union Peace and Security Architecture: Can the Panel of the Wise make a Difference?' (2009) 9 African Human Rights Law Journal 409, 411.

[112] APSA Roadmap (n 103)16. [113] ibid. [114] AU Handbook 2017 (n 75) 63.

[115] AU, 'Strengthening African Women's Participation in Conflict Prevention, Mediation Processes and Peace Stabilisation Efforts: Operationalisation of Femwise-Africa—General Information: Implementation Period 2018–2020' <http://www.peaceau.org/uploads/final-concept-note-femwise-sept-15-short-version-clean-4-flyer.pdf> accessed 10 January 2020.

[116] PSC Report (n 9) para 122. [117] APSA Roadmap (n 103) 17.

[118] AU, 'Communique' (18th Meeting of the Panel of the Wise, Windhoek, 5–6 March 2018) 2–3 <https://www.peaceau.org/en/article/18th-meeting-of-the-panel-of-the-wise> accessed 10 January 2020.

3. Mediation at the African Union and the Regional Economic Communities

The AUC Chairperson has traditionally deployed a medley of special envoys and high-level representatives comprising political heavyweights (predominantly male) to lead AU mediation teams.[119] In a bid to structure mediation as more of a technical exercise, in 2016, the AU established the Mediation Support Unit (MSU) to provide material and logistical capacity and expertise.[120] Even though the MSU is situated in the Peace and Security Department (PSD), there is ongoing debate on how to make it accessible to the entire AU, as mediation has both pre- and post-conflict elements.[121]

The mediation capacity at the RECs appears to be stronger in certain regions than others[122] based on comparative advantage. ECOWAS, with the support of the AU, deployed robust mediation interventions following the Algiers peace deal regarding Mali and in its much-vaunted response to the crises in Gambia and Guinea Bissau.[123] Mediation interventions by other RECs have varying outcomes contingent on conflict dynamics. In that regard, the protracted mediation by IGAD and partners in the South Sudan conflict should be noted. Seized of the conflict since December 2013, IGAD was perceived to have significant comparative advantage because its frontline States had rapport with the parties and strategic interest in stability in South Sudan.[124] However, this mediation has been precarious because the warring parties lack any desire for peace[125] and have only been compelled to mediate by the double-barrelled threat of AU and UN sanctions. As a result, despite a 2015 peace agreement to resolve the conflict, its subsequent breakdown in 2016 and consequent revitalization in 2018, the peace process has neither staunched the violence, nor resolved the root causes of conflict, and has endured numerous setbacks in communication and consensus between the parties.[126] The situation has not been helped by the widespread perception that the interests of IGAD Member States have compromised IGAD's impartiality.[127] To compensate, the mediation format was expanded to include non-IGAD States, namely five AU Member States, the UN, the Troika, the EU, and China as official IGAD Plus[128] partners, in many ways

[119] GIZ, 'APSA Impact Report 2015: Impact Analysis of Interventions by the African Union and Regional Economic Communities in Conflict Prevention, Management and Resolution in Africa' (2016) 24 <http://www.ipss-addis.org/resources/publications/apsa_impact_report_2015.php> accessed 10 January 2020.

[120] Smail Chergui, Commissioner for Peace and Security, 'AU Mediation Unit' (*African Union Peace and Security*, 17 October 2016) <http://www.peaceau.org/en/page/107-au-mediation-support-unit> accessed 10 January 2020.

[121] ISS, 'Peace and Security Council Report No 107' (October 2018) 10–11 <https://issafrica.s3.amazonaws.com/site/uploads/psc107.pdf> accessed 10 January 2020.

[122] ibid. [123] APSA Impact Report 2016 (n 100) 33.

[124] Zach Vertin, 'A Poisoned Well: Lessons in Mediation from South Sudan's Troubled Peace Process' (International Peace Institute, April 2018) <https://www.ipinst.org/2018/04/mediation-lessons-south-sudan-peace-process> accessed 10 January 2020.

[125] ibid 8. [126] APSA Impact Report 2016 (n 100) 33–4. [127] ibid.

[128] Vertin (n 124) 22.

recalling the security regime complex. That there is no better alternative to resolving the South Sudanese conflict, other than mediation in an environment where mediation is deeply misaligned, speaks to the complexity of managing conflicts in Africa.[129]

4. Peace Support Operations under the African Standby Force

Ordinarily, standby denotes all systems go,[130] in the sense of pre-identified, trained, and verified military units in barracks awaiting deployment.[131] Rapid deployment capability on the other hand refers to units that are on standby readiness and can deploy within 14 days.[132]

As the peace operations and intervention instrument of the APSA, the ASF comprises multidimensional brigades of military, police, and civilian contingents from each of the AU's five regions that are on standby in their respective regions of origin and pledge availability to be called up by the AU for deployment in six pre-identified scenarios.[133] The development of these brigades was left to three RECs: ECOWAS, SADC, ECCAS,[134] and two regional mechanisms, the East African Standby Force (EASF) and the North African Regional Capability (NARC) Standby Forces because East Africa had multiple RECs and North Africa lacks an operational REC.

The ASF standby readiness model was adapted from the UN Standby High-Readiness Brigade initiative and the EU Battle Group concept. The operation of the standby readiness concept within the ASF, similar to its antecedents at the UN and the EU, has faltered.[135] This is due to three factors. First, the AU has had to respond to conflict before the ASF was fully operationalized.[136] Secondly, the AU has had to deploy stabilization and counter-terrorism measures involving offensive combat operations to match a volatile security environment.[137] And, thirdly, AU Member States have been reluctant to deploy their military capacities in high-risk combat operations as part of ASF regional standby arrangements without corresponding strategic interests.[138]

The operationalization of the ASF has been quite onerous. Following the 2012 coup in Mali, terrorist and criminal armed groups launched offensives which led to the

[129] 'Improving Prospects for Peace in South Sudan at the African Union Summit' (*International Crisis Group*, 30 June 2018) <https://www.crisisgroup.org/africa/horn-africa/south-sudan/improving-prospects-peace-south-sudan-african-union-summit> accessed 10 January 2020.

[130] Annette Leijendaar, 'African Standby Force: How the AU Can Get It Right' (*ISS*, 30 October 2015) <https://issafrica.org/iss-today/african-standby-force-how-the-au-can-get-it-right> accessed 10 January 2020; PSC Protocol (n 54) art 13.

[131] de Coning (n 30) 35.

[132] AU, 'Policy Framework for the Establishment of the African Standby Force and the Military Staff Committee' (15–16 May 2003) Exp/ASF-MSC/2 (I), 6 ('ASF Framework').

[133] Dersso (n 49) 38.

[134] ASF Framework (n 132). [135] de Coning (n 30) 38. [136] Dersso (n 49) 39.

[137] Akpasom/Lotze (n 29) 19–20. [138] de Coning (n 30) 38.

establishment of the African-led AFISMA mission, with UNSC authorization from December 2012. However, logistical and financial constraints and lack of genuine operational capacity delayed AFISMA's deployment while rebels steadily advanced on Bamako.[139] Mali called on France to intervene and restore State authority in an operation that should have been undertaken by African troops under the APSA.[140] The subsequent French intervention challenged the operationalization of the ASF, and possibly sounded the death knell for the original ASF concept. In May 2013, as a stopgap measure pending ASF operationalization, the African Capacity for Immediate Response to Crises was established to provide the AU with a Rapid deployment capability. Unlike the ASF, the African Capacity for Immediate Response to Crises is flexible, bypasses the RECs and RMs by its centralization within the AU PSC, is funded by individual Member States, is not premised on traditional peacekeeping concepts, and has a wider range of deployment scenarios.[141]

While full ASF operationalization was to have been achieved by 31 December 2015, in the Burundi crisis in 2015, the EASF which would have deployed troops as part of MAPROBU to Burundi was not ready[142] and, if actually deployed, would have relied on out-of-region troops to generate required numbers.[143] In 2017, the ASF was reported to have attained full operational capacity, which has been interpreted as a political decision,[144] rather than an objective conclusion based on the findings of the AU team validating the ASF.

Even before the ASF achieved operational capacity, the African Capacity for Immediate Response to Crises (ACIRC) was established to provide the Rapid deployment capability of the ASF with subsequent compensatory measures being ordered to streamline the ASF with the ACIRC. In terms of AU-authorized coalitions, coalitions of countries affected by a crisis with transnational implications for each of the States concerned are mandated by the AU to address the specific threats.[145] These coalitions have developed around heightened security threats like terrorism and include the Multinational Joint Task Force dealing with Boko Haram, the Mali G5 Sahel Force to

[139] AU Report (n 78) para 23.

[140] AU Assembly, 'Report of the Peace and Security Council and its Activities and the State of Peace and Security in Africa' (26–27 May 2013) Assembly/AU/5(XXI).

[141] Jason Werner, 'Complements or Competitors? The African Standby Force, the African Capacity for Immediate Response to Crises and the Future of Rapid Reaction Forces in Africa' (2015) 8 African Security 56, 61–3.

[142] ICG, 'Africa Briefing No 122' (n 71) 8.

[143] Thomas Mandrup, 'The African Peace and Security Architecture—A System for the Past or Adapting to the Future?' (2018) SIGLA Research Brief 3/2018 <https://www.sun.ac.za/english/faculty/milscience/sigla/Documents/Briefs/SIGLA%20Brief3%202018.pdf> accessed 10 January 2020.

[144] ibid.

[145] Walter Lotze, 'ZIF Policy Briefing: The Future of African Peace Operations: Time to Adjust the Operational Design' (May 2015) <http://www.zif-berlin.org/fileadmin/uploads/analyse/dokumente/veroeffentlichungen/ZIF_Policy_Briefing_Walter_Lotze_Future_African_Peace_Operations_May_2015.pdf> accessed 10 January 2020.

combat drug trafficking, and the LRA-Regional Task Force to deal with the LRA (Lord's Resistance Army).[146] While these represent flexible responses to new security threats, they subtly but deliberately undermine the APSA by lying outside it and are neither led by the AU nor an REC despite being endorsed by the AU.[147]

In addition, in all AU stabilization operations in the CAR, Mali, and Somalia, the stabilization missions have not received the requisite logistical support, which hindered their ability to effectively deliver on their stabilization mandate, with AMISOM serving as a prime example in this regard.[148] Even then, in conducting no less than eight African-led peace operations as at 2016, it is indisputable that the AU and the RECs have proven an enhanced capacity and competence to conduct peace support operations.

5. Financing the African Peace and Security Architecture under the African Union Peace Fund

The APF is a carryover instrument from the OAU and was to all extents and purposes moribund until the AU Assembly pledged in 2015 to fund 25 per cent of the AU peace and security budget by 2020.[149] Ninety-eight per cent of the peace and security expenditure of the AU is met by donors, compromising not only the AU's freedom of action but also ownership of its peace and security agenda.[150] This financial dependency has fostered powerlessness in the face of major security crises, most notably the 2011 crisis in Libya during which the AU's roadmap for a negotiated exit for Muammar Gaddafi was sidelined by international partners.[151] The shackling of the operation of the APSA to donor imperatives has led to 'strategic drift' from a holistic approach to continental security.[152] In July 2016, the AU Assembly decided to introduce a 0.2 per cent universal levy on goods imported to Africa to finance its peace and security operations, which levy was projected to generate $400 million by 2020.[153] As at December 2018, US$60 million had reportedly been collected in the Peace Fund, so it appears that the financial 'emancipation' of African security[154] is still pending.

146 APSA Impact Report 2016 (n 100) 34–40. 147 ICG, 'Africa Report No 255' (n 66) 12.

148 Akpasom/Lotze (n 29) 18. 149 AU Peace Fund (n 35) 5.

150 ICG, 'Africa Report No 255' (n 66) 3. 151 ibid.

152 AU, 'Main Successes of the AU in Peace and Security, Challenges and Mitigation Measures in Place' (Press Release, 27 January 2017) <https://au.int/en/pressreleases/20170127/main-successes-au-peace-and-security-challenges-and-mitigation-measures-place> accessed 10 January 2020.

153 AU Peace Fund (n 35) paras 39, 40.

154 Benedikte Franke/Stefan Ganzle, 'How "African" is the African Peace and Security Architecture? Conceptual and Practical Constraints of Regional Security Cooperation in Africa' (2012) 5 African Security 88, 98.

E. Conclusion

Bí a kò bá tí ì lè kọ̀lé, àgọ̀ là ǹpa (If one is yet unable to build a house, one makes a tent)

—Yoruba Proverb

The Pan-African security apparatus predicted by Ali Mazrui came to pass. It is presently embodied in the APSA as a powerful security regime complex which, as any number of APSA impact assessment reports reveal, is an indispensable and effective mechanism in addressing conflict.

However, to tap from Mazrui's philosophical vein, the APSA partly mirrors the past, present, and potential future of the large and fragmented continent it was designed for. That mirror equally reflects reality and its distortion as a paradox.[155] As a result, framing the APSA as a transformative mechanism with the AU reflects this paradox. While the APSA presupposes a strong supranational institution able to override the individual interests of Member States in the service of a regional good, it is structurally nested within an organization that is anything but supranational. The predilection for consensus as the basis for collective decision-making has consistently subordinated continental security imperatives to national interest, a flagrant example of which includes the lack of a sustainable financial framework for peace and security operations.

In addition, while APSA functions as a security regime complex whose interlocking actors at the local, regional, and international level have leveraged their respective competencies in the interests of managing conflict, in the absence of deliberate coordination, the overlapping relationships within the regime complex itself have severally complicated responses to crisis. The partnerships within the regime complex have also created a situation where donor dependency has led to the AU strategically drifting from its own peace and security agenda.

Within the APSA itself, there is ample evidence that the interaction between the respective mechanisms has not always been successful, even though the APSA relies on their interactive harmony.

Against the foregoing factors, the nature of African conflict has not remained static, with the need arising for the AU to respond to an evolving threat matrix. As a result, the development of aspects of the APSA such as the ASF has been eclipsed by events on the ground. In addition, the case of the ad hoc AU-authorized coalitions like the ACIRC, the Multinational Joint Task Force, the Mali-G5 Sahel Force, and the LRA-Regional Task Force, all of which have been established outside the APSA framework, point to non-linear expansion of the APSA. The constant push and pull within and outside APSA creates tremendous tension. It therefore does not constitute the ultimate representation of a collective security apparatus, but a steady work in progress.

[155] Mazrui (n 3) 1.

CHAPTER 54

THE EUROPEAN UNION

EVA NANOPOULOS

A. Introduction

ALTHOUGH as originally envisaged, the Community was not set up as a 'security institution', the European Union (EU) has always been a 'security policy project'.[1] That dimension of European integration is usually seen in a positive light. Security is here synonymous with peace: the EU is often understood as a 'peace project', which put an end to the violence of the European continent, a model that it has endeavoured, and should continue too, to export beyond its borders.[2] As the EU developed to encompass explicit competences in the fields traditionally associated with security, including defence, this framing of the European project has continued to play a formative role in understandings of the EU as a security actor by the EU itself[3] and third parties alike. European integration and enlargement is often presented as the EU's greatest contribution to global peace and security,[4] while the end of the Cold War and the 9/11 attacks are taken to have triggered a more explicit acknowledgement on the part of the EU of its responsibility in the management of global insecurities.[5]

But the EU as a security project has also had more negative connotations. From this perspective, the process of European integration was primarily designed to rescue the nation-State,[6] appease social conflict, manage the geopolitical antagonism between

[1] Panos Koutrakos, 'The European Union in the Global Security Architecture' in Bart Van Vooren et al (eds), *The EU's Role in Global Governance: The Legal Dimension* (OUP 2013).

[2] This is clear from the Consolidated Version of the Treaty on European Union (TEU) OJ C326/01 art 3 which states that one of the Union's objectives is to promote peace.

[3] See the opening paragraphs of the Council of the EU, 'European Security Strategy: A Secure Europe in a Better World' (12 December 2003) Doc 15895/03 PESC 787 (ESS 2003).

[4] Geert de Baere, 'The EU and the Responsibility to Protect' in Van Vooren et al (n 1).

[5] Koutrakos (n 1).

[6] Alan S Milward, *The European Rescue of the Nation State* (Routledge 1992).

major powers both within Europe (Germany and France) and in the bloc's relationship to other centres of power, as well as being a bulwark against communism. Within political science and international relations, ambivalence about the character of European integration has shaped debates about the EU's international actorness,[7] where descriptions of the EU as an imperial power[8] or empire,[9] came to stand alongside hegemonic understandings of the EU as a civilian, normative,[10] or soft power.[11] These perspectives suggest that the EU not only operates as a power bloc that is implicated in geopolitical competition and rivalries, but that the character of its project of peace diffusion and security provision requires, at the very least, further exploration.

Ambivalence regarding the EU's role as a 'security project' cannot be divorced from ambivalence for the wider global security order, which lies beyond the scope of this chapter.[12] Nonetheless, the notion of ambivalence provides a productive frame through which to approach the EU's relationship and contribution to the international law of global security,[13] for at least three reasons.

First, that relationship oscillates between symbiosis and friction. On the one hand, the EU has been gradually integrated into the global security architecture. In that context, EU law often reflects and internalizes developments at the global level, as well as shapes and develops the international legal regime. On the other hand, the EU, as a power bloc and 'autonomous' legal community, also provides a source of conflict with, disassociation from, or destabilization of, global security arrangements. This may be as a result of unilateral action but also due to normative and ideological differences and priorities. We can call this 'structural ambivalence'.

Secondly, the interaction between EU law and global security law, as well as the substantive contribution of the EU to the law of global security, produces mixed results. Both osmosis and friction have occasionally advanced the law of international security in productive directions. Yet, the EU has also played a role both in normalizing and internationalizing controversial security practices. We can call this dimension 'substantive ambivalence'.

[7] The term is generally used to refer to the EU's role in international relations. See eg Christopher Hill et al (eds), *International Relations and the European Union* (3rd edn, OUP 2017).

[8] Julian Pänke, 'The Fallout of the EU's Normative Imperialism in the Eastern Neighborhood' (2015) 62 Problems of Post-Communism 350.

[9] Jan Zielonka, *Europe as Empire: The Nature of the Enlarged European Union* (OUP 2006).

[10] Ians Manner, 'Normative Power Europe: A Contradiction in Terms?' (2002) 40 Journal of Common Market Studies 235.

[11] These are premised on an understanding of imperialism that does not equate it with colonialism (namely formal territorial and political control) but includes various formal and informal mechanisms of dependency, exploitation, and subordination.

[12] For a critical account of globalization and global international law see, for example, BS Chimni, *International Law and World Order: A Critique of Contemporary Approaches* (2nd edn, CUP 2018).

[13] The EU's role in global security governance has received increased attention. See eg Inge Govaere/Sara Poli (eds), *EU Management of Global Emergencies: Legal Framework for Combating Threats and Crises* (Brill Nijhoff 2014).

Finally, the ambivalence of the EU as a 'global security provider' has also explanatory value when it comes to contemporary developments and challenges. The ongoing crisis of the European project, as well as the broader crisis of the global liberal order, have profound implications for the law of global security. But if they tend to suggest a moment of rupture, the concept of ambivalence also brings into focus the continuities between the present conjuncture and the EU's longer-term relationship and contribution to the law of global security. In that sense, it highlights how the contemporary moment accentuates the contradictions of the EU's role, rather than fundamentally reshapes it.

Section B uses the notion of 'ambivalence' as an organizing concept to explore the legal framework that is most relevant to the EU's relationship and contribution to the law of global security. Section C then moves on to contemporary challenges and developments. Although the issues raised are by necessity selective rather than exhaustive, this section identifies two key trends that emerge from the EU's response to the increased 'questioning' of the European project and the global liberal order more generally, and that cut across several aspects of global security.

B. Legal Framework

1. EU External Security Law

Today, the core pillar of the EU's security law through which its contribution to the international law of global security is articulated and mediated is the Common Foreign and Security Policy (CFSP). The CFSP is defined in broad terms, covering 'all areas of foreign policy and all questions relating to the Union's security including the progressive framing of a common defence policy that might lead to a common defence'.[14] The latter provides the Union with 'operational capacity drawing on civilian and military assets'[15] in fulfilment of an expanded version of the so-called 'Petersberg tasks',[16] namely 'joint disarmament operations, humanitarian and rescue tasks, military advice and assistance tasks, conflict prevention and peace-keeping tasks, tasks of combat forces in crisis management, including peace-making and post-conflict stabilization'.[17] Since the entry into force of the Treaty of Lisbon, these tasks may also contribute to the fight against terrorism, which can be seen as an expression of the militarization of certain forms of criminal activity.[18]

Originally developed outside the structures of the EC Treaty under the name 'European Political Cooperation', the CFSP was gradually, although never fully,

[14] TEU (n 2) art 24. [15] ibid art 42(1).

[16] These were adopted by the now defunct Western European Union, Petersberg Declaration (June 1992) <http://www.weu.int/documents/920619peten.pdf> accessed 14 May 2020.

[17] TEU (n 2) art 43(1).

[18] See eg Council Decision 2012/392/CFSP of 16 July 2012 on EUCAP Sahel Niger OJ L187/48.

incorporated into 'mainstream' EU law. For many, this partial assimilation continues to be a major obstacle to the effectiveness and coherence of the EU as an international security actor. The CFSP remains subject to special rules and procedures, which are located in the Treaty on the European Union (TEU), as opposed to the Treaty on the Functioning of the European Union (TFEU). This includes a relatively limited role for the Court of Justice of the European Union (CJEU), an institution that has played a crucial role not only in the process of European integration, but also in the mediation between EU law and international law.[19]

Partly because of expanding notions of security at the global level and the Union's own perception of threats to its security, the EU's role in global security in reality reaches far beyond the CFSP. Legally, this is reflected and operationalized in two ways: first, in the increased blurring of internal and external security, which are seen as 'indissolubly linked'.[20] This has resulted in a growing externalization[21] of the provisions on the so-called 'area of freedom security and justice' (AFSJ).[22] Notwithstanding the EU's lack of express external competence in most fields pertaining to the AFSJ, over the years matters of internal security have been taken to require external action, as a necessary complement to internal initiatives.[23] This includes cooperation in tackling various forms of cross-border crime, from drug trafficking to corruption, in relation to which the EU has concluded multiple treaties.[24] The internal–external security nexus has also resulted in the increased mobilization of CFSP initiatives and Common Security and Defence Policy (CSDP) missions to pursue objectives traditionally attached to the construct of an area of freedom, security, and justice, such as the consolidation of the rule of law and reinforcement of the security sector in third countries.[25]

Second, there is an increased blurring between security and development and growing securitization of economic aspects of the EU's external relations. Since the Treaty of Lisbon, the EU has also had an express competence in the field of development

[19] For a recent overview of the CJEU's position as regards the relationship between international law and EU law, see Violeta Moreno-Lax/Paul Gragl, 'Introduction: Beyond Monism, Dualism, Pluralism: The Quest for a (Fully-Fledged) Theoretical Framework: Co-Implication, Embeddedness, and Interdependency between Public International Law and EU Law' (2016) 35 Yearbook of European Law 455.

[20] ESS 2003 (n 3) 2.

[21] Jörg Monar, 'The EU's Externalisation of Internal Security Objectives: Perspectives after Lisbon and Stockholm' (2010) 45 The International Spectator 23.

[22] eg Council of the EU, 'A Strategy for the External Dimension of JHA: Global Freedom, Security and Justice' (6 December 2005) Doc 15446/05 JAI 488. Recent work has begun to consider the CFSP and the AFSJ together. For an example, see Christian Kaunert/Kami Zwolski, *The EU as a Global Security Actor: A Comprehensive Analysis beyond CFSP and JHA* (Palgrave 2013).

[23] Theodore Konstadinides, 'EU Law and International Cooperation in Criminal Matters: A Tale of Legal Competence and Political Competency' in Valsamis Mitsilegas et al (eds), *Research Handbook on EU Criminal Law* (Edward Elgar 2016).

[24] eg UN Convention against Transnational Organized Crime 2225 UNTS 209.

[25] EU Police Mission for the Palestinian Territories established by Council Decision 2013/354/CFSP of 3 July 2013, OJ L 185/12.

cooperation,[26] which allows it to adopt legislative measures and conclude international agreements, with a view to eradicating poverty, in line with the wider objective of fostering sustainable development of developing countries and their integration into the world economy.[27] In 2003, the first European Security Strategy drew a direct connection between security and development,[28] a vision that was fleshed out in the EU 2005 Consensus on Development and more recently in the 2016 Renewed Consensus on Development, on the basis that security is an essential pre-condition for development. Today, development policies are considered key components of the EU's conflict prevention and peacebuilding strategy[29] and are supported by a range of financial instruments.[30] Clauses on security matters, moreover, from counter-terrorism to non-proliferation, are now routinely included in development treaties.[31] Such longer-term initiatives are typically viewed as a complement to the 'short-term' crisis management or stabilization outlook of the CFSP,[32] with a particular focus on State-building and the promotion of good governance.

The interconnections between these different aspects of the EU's security law were deepened by the Treaty of Lisbon. The Treaty for the first time provides a unified list of objectives for the EU's external relations as a whole,[33] although it should be said that this commonality of objectives did not necessarily require or imply the securitization of other aspects of the EU's external action, which is part of a longer-term trend. This contrasts with the position prior to 2009 where the objectives of the CFSP, the external dimension of internal security, and the security element of development cooperation were scattered across the three pillars that constituted the EU. Institutional links, too, have been enhanced through the creation of the High Representative for Foreign Affairs[34] and the European Union External Action Service,[35] while the Union has been expressly endowed with legal personality[36] and treaty-making powers.[37] This constellation is typically seen as both the greatest strength and weakness of the EU as a global

[26] See Consolidated version of the Treaty on the Functioning of the European Union (TFEU) OJ C326/47 arts 209–11.

[27] TEU (n 2) art 21.

[28] The Court of Justice approved the link between the two in C-91/05 *Commission of the European Communities v Council of the European Union* [2008] EU:C:2008:288, where it held that development policy could be used to combat the proliferation of small arms and light weapons.

[29] eg Commission of the European Communities, 'Communication on Conflict Prevention' (11 April 2001) COM(2001)211final.

[30] eg the Instrument for Stability: see Regulation (EC) No 1717/2006 of 15 November 2006, OJ L327/1 and Regulation (EU) No 230/2014 of 11 March 2014, OJ L77/1.

[31] See Stefaan Smis/Sevidzem Stephen Kingah, 'The Utility of Counter-Terrorism and Non-Proliferation of WMD Clauses under the EU-ACP Revised Cotonou Agreement' (2008) 57 ICLQ 149.

[32] Although the Instrument for Stability is also designed to fund short-term responses to crises situations.

[33] TEU (n 2) art 21. [34] ibid art 18.

[35] ibid art 27(3) and Council Decision 2010/427/EU of 26 July 2010 on European External Action Service OJ L201/30.

[36] TEU (n 2) art 47.

[37] See TFEU (n 26) arts 37 and 218. Within ibid art 218 a different procedure continues to apply for the conclusion of agreements falling 'exclusively or principally' within the scope of the CFSP.

security actor, creating opportunities to tackle various dimensions of security and mobilize a variety of instruments,[38] but raising issues of coordination and coherence.[39]

2. Convergence and Integration: EU Security Law as Global Security Law

International law, and particularly the UN Charter, has come to occupy a prominent position in this constellation. EU primary law displays a commitment to the substantive law of global security. Numerous provisions require compliance with international norms. External policies and actions designed to 'preserve peace, prevent conflicts and strengthen international security',[40] for example, are to be conducted in accordance with relevant principles of international law, while the new obligation of aid and assistance in the event of an armed aggression on one of the Member States is to be discharged in full compliance with Article 51 of the UN Charter on the right to self-defence.[41] The observance, development, and promotion of international law also all constitute key Union objectives, particularly in the context of its external action,[42] and form part of the Union's broader aim of advancing peace and security worldwide.[43] Economic sanctions, for example, are often adopted to enforce norms of international law, including international human rights law.[44]

EU external relations law also reflects a commitment to the structures of global security governance. The Treaties task EU institutions with building links with other international organizations and third countries, as part of the wider objective of its external action to support an 'international system based on stronger multilateral cooperation and good global governance'.[45] In that context, the EU is required to pursue multilateral solutions to 'common problems' within the framework of the UN and respect the obligations of those Member States who are part of NATO.[46]

This dual commitment mirrors the EU's vision of the international, indeed global,[47] order, first fleshed out in its 2003 Security Strategy, as (a) a multilateral and distinctively

[38] This is sometimes contrasted to the fragmentation of global security governance across different actors. Jamie Gaskarth, 'Security and Global Governance' in Sophie Harman/David Williams (eds), *Governing the World? Cases in Global Governance* (Routledge 2013).

[39] For a detailed overview, see Panos Koutrakos, *The EU Common Security and Defence Policy* (OUP 2013) ch 8.

[40] TEU (n 2) art 21(2)(c). [41] ibid art 42(7).

[42] See ibid art 21, and particularly art 21(2)(b)(c). [43] eg ibid preamble.

[44] On EU sanctions see in particular Christina Eckes, 'The Law and Practice of EU Sanctions' in Steven Blockmans/Panos Koutrakos (eds), *Research Handbook on the EU's Common Foreign and Security Policy* (Edward Elgar 2018); Charlotte Beaucillon, *Les Mesures Restrictives de l'Union Européenne* (Bruylant-Larcier 2013).

[45] TEU (n 2) art 21(2)(h). [46] ibid art 42(2).

[47] In that regard it is worth noting that references to the 'international' order in the ESS 2003 (n 3) have been replaced by references to the 'global' order in the EU's 2016 security strategy as well as most of its official discourse as reflected in particular in the various websites of the EU institutions.

rules-based order, (b) founded on shared universal rules and values, (c) at the apex of which stands the UN, which bears primary responsibility for peace and security, and (d) in which regional initiatives strengthen and complement, rather than undermine, the global regime, including by upholding and developing international law.

The vision that emerges from EU primary law and policy finds various concrete manifestations. The substantive law of global security has been furthered not only through the EU's formal participation in relevant international treaties or initiatives, such as the Kimberley process, but also through the evolution of EU law and practice to reflect developments in the international law of global security. The inter-connections between internal and external security, as well as the development–security nexus[48] are manifestations of this trend. They map onto the post-Cold War move away from negative conceptions of peace focused on military threats, as well as State-centred approaches to security focused on territorial integrity. The embrace of this 'comprehensive' approach to security was articulated most clearly in the EU's first Security Strategy, which identified five key threats to global and European security: terrorism, the proliferation of weapons of mass destruction, regional conflicts, State failure, and organized crime. Cybersecurity, climate change, and border security were added in the 2008 Implementation Report, which also includes a more elaborate discussion of energy security, a concern that has become more vivid in recent years.

Other practices, concepts, or doctrines of international law have been internalized by the EU, even if their precise meaning or content has evolved in different directions.[49] This includes the notion of 'human security' that first emerged in the development context in the early 1990s and has begun not only to appear in EU policy documents,[50] but also to shape academic debate about EU security law and practice.[51] It includes the (infamous) responsibility to protect[52] doctrine and the shift to a notion of sovereignty as responsibility. The 2008 Implementation Report, for example, emphasized the responsibility of governments for the consequences of their actions and their shared responsibility to protect populations from genocide, war crimes, ethnic cleansing, and crimes against humanity,[53] in line with the 2005 World Summit Outcome Document.[54] In many areas, EU practice has developed in line with international praxis. Most of the EU's restrictive measures are so-called 'smart' sanctions, targeting specific individuals, entities, and

[48] UNGA Res 55/2 'UN Millennium Declaration' (18 September 2000).

[49] On different conceptions of peacebuilding see Catriona Gourlay, 'EU–UN Cooperation in Peacebuilding: Natural Partners?' in Steven Blockmans et al (eds), *The European Union and Peacebuilding: Policy and Legal Aspects* (TMC Asser Press 2010).

[50] eg Council of the EU, 'Report on the implementation of the European Security Strategy: Providing Security in a Changing World' (11 December 2008) S407/08.

[51] Francesco Giumelli, 'Human Security and Sanctions, from Security to Governance: Strengthening EU Capacities and Involving the Locals' in Mary Kaldor et al (eds), *EU Global Strategy and Human Security: Rethinking Approaches to Conflict* (Routledge 2018).

[52] de Baere (n 4) 102. [53] ESS 2008 (n 50) 26.

[54] UNGA Resolution 60/1 (16 September 2005).

sectors, rather than applying to the population indiscriminately.[55] The classic 'Petersberg tasks' were expanded to cover conflict prevention and post-conflict stabilization,[56] reflecting similar developments in the system of collective security.

At the institutional level, too, there are multiple signs of the EU's gradual integration into the global security architecture. While the EU is not a member of the UN, for example, the EU's relationship with the UN has become increasingly formalized, even though the character and degree of formalization has taken different forms. That relationship can also be ad hoc. Notwithstanding ambiguities about the EU's characterization as a 'regional organization' within the meaning of Chapter VIII of the UN Charter, the UNSC has on a number of occasions either welcomed or authorized EU military and civilian missions.[57] One example is EUFOR RD Congo, which was deployed between April and November 2006 to support UN peacekeeping efforts in the region during the 2006 elections.[58] Another is Operation Artemis, the first to have been authorized under Chapter VII UN Charter.[59] A number of missions, moreover, from the EU Police Mission in Bosnia and Herzegovina[60] to the European Union Rule of Law Mission (EULEX) in Kosovo, followed in the footsteps of the UN.

But measures to enhance the UN–EU 'partnership' can also take a longer-term outlook, such as the Joint Declaration on Crisis Management concluded by both organizations in 2003,[61] the EU delegation to the UN, or the 'upgrading' of the EU to observer status at the UN General Assembly (UNGA) in 2011.[62] In some areas, finally, the EU acts as the de facto medium through which all relevant UN Resolutions are implemented and operationalized. This includes all UN sanctions regimes, as well as quasi-legislative instruments, such as UNSC Resolutions 1373 (2001) and 1540 (2004).[63] These formal or informal ties are also embedded in a wider context of material inter-relations. Today, the EU and its Member States are amongst the 'largest financial contributors to the UN system',[64] including peacekeeping missions and humanitarian activities. The European Commission is reported to have provided around €1.9 billion in support of UN external assistance programmes and projects in 2015 alone. Similar

[55] As regards counter-terrorism sanctions, see Christina Eckes, *EU Counter-Terrorist Policies and Fundamental Rights: The Case of Individual Sanctions* (OUP 2010). As regards so-called third country sanctions applying to the political leadership of third countries and their associates, see Christina Eckes, 'EU Restrictive Measures against Natural and Legal Persons: From Counterterrorist to Third Country Sanctions' (2014) 51 Common Market Law Review 869.

[56] This is now reflected in TEU (n 2) art 43.

[57] Koutrakos (n 39) 83.

[58] UNSC Res 1671 (2006).

[59] UNSC Res 1484 (2003).

[60] Council of the European Union Joint Action 2002/210/CFSP, OJ L70/1.

[61] See also Council of the EU, 'Strengthening the UN–EU Strategic Partnership on Peacekeeping and Crisis Management: Priorities 2015–2018' (27 March 2015) Doc 7632/15 COPS 95.

[62] UNGA Res 65/276 (3 May 2011).

[63] A number of EU measures have been adopted to that effect within the framework of the EU's Strategy against the Proliferation of Weapons of Mass Destruction starting with Council Joint Action 2006/419/CFSP, OJ L165/30.

[64] EEAS, 'Factsheets: How Does the EU Work at the United Nations?' (*EU External Action*, 20 September 2019) <https://eeas.europa.eu/headquarters/headquarters-homepage/9875/european-union-united-nations_en> accessed 20 November 2019.

patterns of formal, informal, and material interrelations exist with other regional security organs, particularly NATO[65] and the African Union (AU),[66] while the transnationalization of threats has resulted in greater awareness of the importance of cooperation with regional organizations on matters such as trafficking or terrorism.[67]

3. Structural Ambivalence

The EU's commitment and integration to the law of global security is, however, far from complete or harmonious. From a legal perspective, attention has often focused on the question of norm conflict, as well as the potential for competition and duplication.[68] Such concerns are often overstated. For example, the (in)famous *Kadi* decision,[69] in which the CJEU refused to grant immunity to measures intended to implement UN Security Council (UNSC) resolutions, has been portrayed as an act of 'disobedience' vis-à-vis the UN.[70] In reality, whether *Kadi* undermined rather than strengthened the global system of blacklisting is debatable. Nevertheless, the EU's self-professed legal autonomy vis-à-vis the international legal order, if it does not fully reflect the EU's actual relationship to the global security architecture, still illustrates a number of deeper tensions in the EU's role in the provision of global security.

As a bloc, the EU remains guided by its own security concerns and priorities.[71] This has had at least two implications. First, international cooperation is a means for the EU to safeguard its own 'values, fundamental interests, security, independence and integrity',[72] but it is not the only one. The 2003 ESS, for example, was implicitly premised on a model of global security based on US hegemony and remained strongly committed to the 'irreplaceable' transatlantic relationship, on which the multilateral global order was seen to hang. The EU also increasingly tends to act unilaterally. This is particularly the case in the area of sanctions, where over half of the regimes currently in force in the EU are adopted without a UN mandate, or to supplement existing UN measures. While the UNSC may not have a monopoly over economic coercion, these measures raise considerable issues from the standpoint of international law, particularly the law of

[65] See, in particular, the EU/NATO, 'Berlin-Plus Agreements' (17 March 2003) which enables the EU to draw on NATO assets.

[66] eg Africa–EU Partnership, 'Joint Africa–EU Strategy 2007' (African–EU Summit, Lisbon, 2007) and Africa–EU Partnership, 'African Peace Facility 2004' funded by the European Development Fund.

[67] Commission, 'The EU Internal Security Strategy in Action: Five Steps Towards a More Secure Europe' (Communication) COM(2010)673final.

[68] Similar concerns arise with regards to the division of labour between NATO and the EU. See Heike Krieger, 'Common European Defence: Competition or Compatibility with NATO?' in Martin Trybus/Nigel D White (eds), *EU Security Law* (OUP 2007).

[69] Joined Cases C-402/05P and C-415/05P *Kadi and Al Barakaat International Foundation v Council and Commission* [2008] ECLI:EU:C:2008:461.

[70] Antonios Tzanakopoulos, *Disobeying the Security Council: Countermeasures against Wrongful Sanctions* (OUP 2011).

[71] See TEU (n 2) art 3(5). [72] ibid art 21(2)(a).

countermeasures and the principle of non-intervention.[73] From the 1980s to the present day, the Global South has, on multiple occasions, mobilized through the UNGA to express their discontent over unilateral coercion.[74] Although they are sometimes taken to bypass inaction by the UNSC,[75] and are justified by reference to international law principles or values (in which case they could be seen as complementing rather antagonizing the system of collective security), EU sanctions also tend to fuel tension amongst the P5. Both China and Russia believe such measures undermine, rather than reinforce, multilateral efforts. This is often aggravated by the EU's tendency to enlist the support of third States for its sanctions regimes, not only encouraging solutions outside the structures of global governance, but also fuelling polarization, as neutrality is often seen as a sign of disloyalty.[76]

Secondly, this means that global security is often 'Europeanized', a phenomenon that manifests itself in at least two ways. On the one hand, alignment with EU interests and values becomes a pre-condition for the EU's engagement in the management of global insecurity. The Treaties expressly state that the EU shall 'develop relations and build partnerships with third countries, and international, regional or global organisations *which share* (emphasis added) the principles referred' to in Article 21(1) TEU, which includes respect for democracy, the rule of law, respect for human rights and the principles of the UN Charter. Assistance or aid, moreover, has often been contingent upon undertakings of reform,[77] even if, on other matters like border control or migration, the EU has been comfortable cooperating with various authoritarian regimes. The exclusionary and punitive implications of this approach were clear in the ESS 2003 Strategy, which somewhat mirrored the 'Axis of Evil' rhetoric of the Bush administration. Thus, countries that 'placed themselves outside the bounds of international society' should 'rejoin the international community' or 'understand that there is a price to be paid, including in their relationship' with the EU.

On the other hand, it also means that EU initiatives are often informed by European, rather than global or regional security concerns. The 'preservation of stability' as a medium to ensure European security has long informed the EU's relationship with its neighbours[78] and CSDP missions in Africa, for example, often tend to prioritize reforms

[73] eg Natalino Ronzitti, 'Sanctions as Instruments of Coercive Diplomacy: An International Law Perspective' in Natalino Ronzitti (ed), *Coercive Diplomacy, Sanctions and International Law* (Brill 2016).

[74] This has culminated in the creation of a Special Rapporteur on the negative impact of the unilateral coercive measures on the enjoyment of human rights.

[75] See eg Council Decision 2013/255/CFSP of 31 May 2013, OJ L147/14 and Council Regulation 36/2012 of 18 January 2012, OJ L16/1 imposing sanctions against Syria, which was adopted after a draft Resolution sponsored by France, the UK, and the US was blocked in the UNSC.

[76] Elin Hellquist, 'Either with Us or Against Us? Third-Country Alignment with EU Sanctions Against Russia/Ukraine' (2016) 29 Cambridge Review of International Affairs 997.

[77] Gourlay (n 49) 114.

[78] Roberto Roccu/Benedetta Voltolini, 'Framing and Reframing the EU's Engagement with the Mediterranean: Examining the Security–Stability Nexus before and after the Arab Uprisings' (2018) 23 Mediterranean Politics 1.

and initiatives that serve Europe's security needs.[79] In that context, the EU also tends to crystallize a particular division of labour in the provision of global and regional security: despite the EU's rhetorical commitment to an 'equal partnership' and 'joint responsibility', Europe continues primarily to serve as a financial provider, committing relatively modest missions on the ground.

4. Substantive Ambivalence

The substantive outcome of these encounters inevitably has been ambivalent. The EU has, on occasions, fostered 'improvements' to the international law of global security. In the field of smart sanctions, the *Kadi* saga, for example, is widely seen to have generated a series of reforms, most notably the creation of the UN Office of the Ombudsperson,[80] which enhanced the visibility of the individual in the State-centred structures of the UNSC and the transparency of blacklisting processes.[81] It has also helped push important questions up the global security agenda, such as the gendering of peace and security,[82] supporting steps to combat violence against women, and promote their participation in peacebuilding.

But the incorporation of the EU into global and transnational security arrangements has also helped to legitimize and normalize controversial security practices. The EU's comprehensive and integrated approach to security, reflecting changing conceptions of peace and sovereignty at the international level, also enabled increased interventionism in the internal affairs of the developing world and an asymmetrical dilution of the principle of non-intervention. The 'European security culture' of 'prevention, anticipation and early intervention,'[83] moreover, facilitated the institutionalization of pre-emption and risk, centred on the incapacitation of threats before they even arise, with significant consequences not only for human rights, but also for traditional conceptions of criminal justice and war. The security–development nexus, finally, not only securitized and transformed peacebuilding processes, but also foregrounds a gradual hierarchization of States, whereupon failed States bear the primary blame and burden for global insecurity.[84] Indeed, the EU's development policy itself was born out of its colonial encounter.[85]

[79] eg EUCAP Sahel Niger (n 18). [80] UNSC Res 1904 (2009).

[81] cf Antonios Tzanakopoulos in Cedric Ryngaert et al (eds), *Judicial Decisions on the Law of International Organizations* (OUP 2016) 229ff.

[82] See UNSC Res 1325 (2000) and UNSC 1820 (2008). See also more recently the UN–EU collaborative platform on Women, Peace, and Security.

[83] Marieke de Goede, 'European Security Culture: Preemption and Precaution in European Security' (Inaugural Lecture, University of Amsterdam, 27 May 2011) 6 <https://pure.uva.nl/ws/files/1133585/108337_361146.pdf> accessed 6 October 2018.

[84] Ben Hayes et al, 'Building Peace in Permanent War: Terrorist Listing and Conflict Transformation' (International State Crime Initiative, 2005) <https://www.tni.org/en/publication/building-peace-in-permanent-war> accessed 6 October 2018.

[85] Robert Schütze, 'EU Development Policy: Constitutional and Legislative Foundation(s)' (2013) 15 Cambridge Yearbook of European Legal Studies 699.

There are, moreover, both legal and political difficulties with authorizing the deployment of military EU missions outside its own territory, sidelining regional or local initiatives and turning Europe into a global police.[86]

The EU's own unilateral practice, moreover, not only generates geopolitical instability, but has also deepened, or directly contributed to the emergence of, controversial aspects of global security law. The former can be illustrated by the field of sanctions, where the EU has often expanded the criteria for blacklisting, loosening the link between the conduct of a particular individual and the existence of a threat to international peace and security,[87] undermining, rather than strengthening, the compatibility of blacklisting with the rule of law. The latter can be illustrated by the securitization of migration,[88] in which the Europeanization of migration policy, as a means to build and stabilize European identity as well as Europe's socio-economic and political order, played a crucial role,[89] long before the 9/11 attacks or the so-called 'migration crisis'. The securitization paradigm today has not only strained the EU's relations with the African continent, which has widely come to be seen as an extension or externalization of the European border, but risks impacting the pursuit of progressive global solutions.[90]

C. Recent Developments and Contemporary Challenges

1. An Era of 'Crises': Between Continuity and Change

Much of the recent developments and challenges are a product of, or have been shaped by, the EU's own 'multiple crises', as well as what has come increasingly to be perceived as a broader crisis of the global liberal order. The former includes the Euro-crisis, what is popularly referred to as a 'refugee' or 'migration' crisis but which could be more accurately described as a 'border crisis', as well as the rise of authoritarian regimes within Europe and Brexit. The latter includes the intensification of geopolitical antagonisms amongst the 'great powers', in which the EU is deeply implicated. Tensions with Russia in the Crimea and with the US over the US administration's decision to withdraw from

[86] See on the UNSC's authorization of operation ARTEMIS Ademola Abbas, 'Extraterritorial Collective Security: The European Union and Operation ARTEMIS' in Trybus/White (n 68).

[87] eg C-348/12 P *Council v Manufacturing Support & Procurement Kala Naft* [2013] EU:C:2013:776.

[88] See eg UNSC Res 2240 (2015) authorizing the interceptions of ships off the Libyan coast suspected of migrant smuggling.

[89] eg Jef Huysmans, 'The European Union and the Securitisation of Migration' (2000) 38 Journal of Common Market Studies 751.

[90] Eva Nanopoulos et al, 'Securitisation of Borders and the UN's Global Compact on Safe, Orderly and Regular Migration' (2018) Queen Mary School of Law Legal Studies Research Paper No 270/2018 <https://ssrn.com/abstract=3,099,996> accessed 21 November 2019.

the Iran Nuclear deal, both of which have triggered various forms of 'trade wars' or economic warfare,[91] are but two illustrations of the phenomenon.

Readings of the current conjuncture and predictions of its likely future trajectory have differed. For some, the EU's response to its changing security environment foregrounds a more assertive stance, operationalizing the legal framework introduced by the Treaty of Lisbon and translating the Union's 'overall objectives into specific policies and actions'.[92] For others, the EU's own set of crises marks a marginalization of the EU's role in global security,[93] prompted by the sidelining of security concerns in favour of economic policies and a loss of credibility vis-à-vis third countries.

In line with the broader tenor of this chapter, this section argues that the idea of a 'stronger Europe in a fragile world',[94] a frame that has been used to capture the essence of the EU's 2016 Global Security Strategy (GSS),[95] can best be seen as accentuating the contradictions and ambivalence of the EU's contribution to global and regional security governance. From a structural perspective, the EU vision of the global security architecture appears on the surface largely unchanged. The GSS 2016 conveys an urgency for reform of global governance structures, including the UNSC, to avoid the erosion of global institutions, but the message is one of deepening, and widening of, global norms and institutions and a renewed commitment to enhancing cooperation with NATO. The idea of a 'stronger Europe in a fragile order', however, denotes two shifts in the EU's approach to global security with implications both for the substantive law of global security and the EU's position in the global security architecture. One is a more general move towards 'resilience', the other is a more explicit push for greater 'strategic autonomy', characterized not necessarily by institutional disengagement, but increased militarization and polarization.

2. A 'Fragile World': From Security to Stability to Resilience

Already in 2008, the EU's emphasis had shifted from building 'security' in Europe's neighbours, to building 'stability' in Europe and beyond. This linguistic and conceptual turn was closely related to the EU's understanding of its wider security environment. The concept of 'security' that underpinned the 2003 ESS was associated with the EU's

[91] On the EU's sanctions against Russia, see Council Decision 2014/145/CFSP of 17 March 2014, OJ L78/16 and Council Regulation 269/2014 of 17 March 2014, OJ L78/6. On the EU's blocking measures against the US' sanctions against Iran, see Commission Delegated Regulation (EU) 2018/1100 of 6 June 2018, OJ L199I/1.

[92] Editorial Comments, '"We Perfectly Know What to Work For": The EU's Global Strategy for Foreign and Security Policy' (2016) 53 Common Market Law Review 1199, 1202.

[93] Koutrakos (n 39) 4.

[94] Nathalie Tocci, *Framing the EU Global Strategy: A Stronger Europe in a Fragile World* (Palgrave 2017). Dr Tocci is special adviser of the EU's High Representative.

[95] EU Global Strategy, 'Shared Vision, Common Action: A Stronger Europe: A Global Strategy for the European Union's Foreign And Security Policy' (June 2016) <https://op.europa.eu/en/publication-detail/-/publication/3eaae2cf-9ac5-11e6-868c-01aa75ed71a1> accessed 30 November 2020.

vision of a secure Europe in a 'better world', while the emphasis on 'stability' in the 2008 Implementation Report followed from the EU's recognition of the challenges of providing security in a 'changing world'. The turn to 'resilience', a concept which, like human security, was first introduced in the development context,[96] is reflective of the perceived 'fragility' and 'vulnerability' of the contemporary world order and aims to improve the ability of States and societies to reform and recover from crises.[97] Beyond Europe and its immediate borders, the responsibility for building resilient States and societies is to be shared with the UN and NATO,[98] while greater emphasis is also placed on 'cooperative regional arrangements'. As such, resilience is not only an organizing concept of the EU's internal security and its external relations,[99] but a central pillar of the EU's vision of the global security architecture.

While lawyers have tended to approach the GSS as the mere operationalization of the Treaty of Lisbon, the paradigm of 'resilience' has been seen as instantiating 'new CFSP' that redefines 'the normative framework' of the EU's security policy[100] and 'differs fundamentally from its predecessor'.[101] However, if this is usually taken to foreground a more 'protective and conservative foreign and security policy'[102] based on 'principled pragmatism', it also appears to entail a number of potentially transformative implications.

First, the shift to resilience marks a deepening, if not totalization of securitization, which is to encompass 'all individuals and the whole of society' as well as key infrastructures and public goods, from food, health, or energy, all of which constitute potential sources of vulnerability. It also signifies a deepening of the pre-emptive paradigm from pre-emptive security, which emphasized the suppression of risks and threats, to 'pre-emptive peace'[103] preparedness, and recovery, all of which entail the active building of structures and capabilities designed to enable States and societies to cope with risks and shocks, as well as adapt and transform. Both are reinforced by the EU's emphasis on the hybridity of contemporary threats, pursuant to which any act or activity—from cyberattacks to the 'disruption of critical services such as energy supplies or financial services,

[96] Commission, 'The EU Approach to Resilience: Learning from Food Security Crises' (Communication) COM(2012)586final.

[97] GSS 2016 (n 95) 23.

[98] It has already been taken up by NATO. See North Atlantic Council, 'Warsaw Summit Communiqué' (9 July 2016) <https://www.nato.int/cps/en/natohq/official_texts_133169.htm> accessed 20 May 2020.

[99] Although the GSS has a separate section on 'State and Societal Resilience to our East and South' (n 95) 23, the concept is used much more widely, both in the GSS and in other policy documents.

[100] Annegrek Bendiek, 'A Paradigm Shift in the EU's Common Foreign and Security Policy: From Transformation to Resilience' (October 2017) SWP Research Paper, Stiftung Wissenschaft und Politik German Institute for International and Security Affairs RP 11, 14 <https://www.swp-berlin.org/fileadmin/contents/products/research_papers/2017RP11_bdk.pdf> accessed 21 November 2019.

[101] ibid 5. [102] ibid 14. [103] GSS 2016 (n 95) 29.

to the undermining of public trust in government institutions or the deepening of social divisions'[104] can constitute a potential security risk.

Secondly, State and social resilience tends to further shift responsibility for security locally,[105] and, as a consequence, on the developing world. The development–security continuum and the connections between security and State failure that underpin UN and EU security law alike, already placed much of the blame and burden of global insecurity on the Global South. A similar pattern is observable in the EU's approach to piracy or smuggling, in the context of which the EU has concluded multiple transfer agreements,[106] turning third States into reception, detention or trial centres. But the paradigm of resilience has the potential to generalize that trend, embarking the global security regime upon ever more sweeping exercises of State-building. The 'State transformation-outsourcing of responsibility' continuum is particularly pronounced in Africa, but it is also becoming the dominant strategy with regards to origin and transit countries of migrants and refugees.[107]

3. A 'Stronger Europe': Autonomy, Militarization, and Polarization

At the same time as the EU's vision of global security is based on a world of resilient societies and States, the idea of a 'Stronger Europe' entails a reinforcement of the EU's own 'strategic autonomy' and, for that purpose, a turn to more traditional militarized approaches to security. The first priority listed in the GSS 2016 is now not only to promote peace, but to 'guarantee the security of its citizens and territory'. The European Defence Fund of 2017, the New European Peace Facility of 2018, the Action Plan for Military Mobility of 2018 and the Permanent Structured Cooperation between willing and able Member States, initiated in 2017, are amongst the many initiatives that have begun to put into motion the EU's vision of greater investment and cooperation in defence matters. These run in parallel to efforts to expand Europe's defence market.

In that context, the EU has continued to emphasize the importance of 'working with partners'. The more recent frictions with the Trump administration notwithstanding, Europe's vision retains a crucial role for NATO, which remains the core framework of collective defence. If anything, the NATO–EU relations appear to be deepening. The

[104] EEAS, 'Factsheet: A Europe that Protects: Countering Hybrid Threats' (EU External Action, 13 June 2018) <https://eeas.europa.eu/topics/economic-relations-connectivity-innovation/46393/europe-protects-countering-hybrid-threats_en> accessed 6 October 2018.

[105] Jonathan Joseph, 'The EU in the Horn of Africa: Building Resilience as a Distant Form of Governance' (2014) 52 Journal of Common Market Studies 285, 286.

[106] In the field of privacy see, for example, the agreement between the EU and Mauritius Council Decision 2011/640/CFSP of 12 July 2011, OJ L 254/1. In the field of migration see the infamous EU–Turkey deal: 'Press Release: EU–Turkey Statement' (18 March 2016) 144/16 <https://www.consilium.europa.eu/en/press/press-releases/2016/03/18/eu-turkey-statement/pdf> accessed 21 November 2019.

[107] See, in particular, GSS 2016 (n 95) 27–8.

Joint Declaration signed in Warsaw in 2016 agreed to enhance cooperation between the two 'partners' in seven key areas: (1) hybrid threats; (2) operational cooperation including at sea and on migration; (3) cybersecurity and defence; (4) defence capabilities; (5) defence industry and research; (6) exercises; and (7) support for Eastern and Southern partners' capacity-building efforts.

But there is now much greater emphasis on building the European arm of the transatlantic relation, enabling Europeans to 'defend themselves' building on the new clause of mutual assistance and contributing to the strengthening of the EU as a 'security community' and a 'defence union'. This vision is increasingly articulated as part of a bid for further convergence over sovereign functions, including foreign policy, defence, and the fight against terrorism.[108]

The question of militarization is not new. But while it deepens the EU's entanglement in global security governance, its implications for the international law of global security are again ambiguous. First, the EU may state that its 'higher level of ambition' in the area of defence is 'not the beginning of a militarization or an arms race with third countries'.[109] But much like the original impetus for a European defence,[110] its anxiety over defence matters is linked to a series of increased geopolitical antagonism and instability. The GSS 2016 thus explicitly mentions how the EU has had to deal with 'super-powers as well as with increasingly fractured identities'.

Secondly, the militarization of the EU takes place in the context of increased dilution of the prohibition on the use of force, expansion—indeed often abuse—of the right to self-defence, wider transformation of the military beyond traditional defence functions, as well as expansion of the notion of 'threats to the peace' under Chapter VII of the UN Charter. The creation of the CSDP mission EUNAVFROMed[111]—also known as Operation Sophia[112]—and NATO Operation Guardian, as examples of the gradual militarization of migration and border control, offer a grim picture of the likely effects of the emerging global apparatus of militarized policing. Despite the rhetoric of humanitarianism and rescue, these operations are a natural continuation of the securitization of migration. On the ground, they have not only failed to reduce the trafficking and smuggling of migrants, but have also resulted in greater loss of life, a lessening of legal protection (many are returned with little regard for the right of

[108] See eg Emmanuel Macron, 'Speech: Initiative for Europe—A Sovereign, United, Democratic Europe' (Paris, 26 September 2017) <https://uk.ambafrance.org/President-calls-for-sovereign-united-democratic-Europe#Initiative-for-Europe-A-sovereign-united-democratic-Europe-summary-of-nbsp> accessed 21 November 2019.

[109] EEAS, 'The EEAS Summer Series on EU Defense and Security: Part I: The EU Acts for Peace and Security' (1 August 2018) <https://eeas.europa.eu/headquarters/headquarters-homepage/49010/part-1-eu-acts-peace-and-security_en> accessed 8 October 2018.

[110] The Saint Malo Declaration: 'Joint Declaration on European Defence' (British–French Summit, Saint-Malo, 4 December 1998) was closely connected to the Balkan wars and particularly the situation in Kosovo.

[111] Council Decision (CFSP) 2015/778 of 18 May 2015, OJ L122/31.

[112] Council Decision (CFSP) 2015/1926 of 26 October 2015, OJ L281/13.

non-refoulement) and a co-optation, rather than vindication of human rights law and discourse.[113]

Together, these trends also signify increased polarization. The drift towards militarization and more traditional approaches to security is part and parcel of a deepening of the EU's inward-looking approach. The GSS 2016 is replete with references to protecting 'our' citizens, 'our' principles, and 'our' values. As has been remarked this is a 'foreign policy based firmly on the needs of the Union itself'.[114] In that sense, transformation of the EU's periphery, reform of the multilateral system, and strategic autonomy are all woven into a project of securing the European physical, ontological, and economic space. Such an approach can itself be a source of global insecurity, whether this is achieved by the continuous underdevelopment that policies centred on transforming Europe's periphery in accordance with European needs might produce in the Global South, or through the reinforcement of patterns of exclusion[115] and 'othering' that prevent the pursuit of genuinely global solutions.

D. Outlook

Debates about the role of the EU as security provider often centre around the EU's relevance, credibility, and effectiveness. Commentators routinely deplore the so-called 'capability–expectation' gap,[116] the EU's over-legalistic or 'process-centred'[117] approach to what are essentially political matters, the EU's utopian optimism or its lack of coherence. Proponents of the EU's contribution respond with examples where the EU has shown its might and decisively contributed to the delivery of peace and security. Viewed from that angle, the EU's relationship and contribution to the law of global security tends to emerge as a zero-sum game, where greater EU involvement is synonymous with both deeper integration into the global security architecture and better contribution to multilateral solutions and lesser EU engagement with retreat, irrelevance, or missed opportunity. This, in large part, continues to shape assessments of the current conjuncture.

The picture is, however, more complex. This chapter sought to show that there is a considerable degree of ambivalence about the EU's contribution to the law of global security, a situation that has been exacerbated by the EU's existential crisis and developments that destabilize the global liberal order, sometimes from within global security law itself. Ultimately, this chapter could but offer a sketch of some of the issues, but these

[113] On these issues see Violeta Moreno-Lax, 'The EU Humanitarian Border and the Securitization of Human Rights: The "Rescue-Through-Interdiction/Rescue-Without-Protection" Paradigm' (2018) 56 Journal of Common Market Studies 119.

[114] Editorial Comments (n 92) 1201.

[115] Gaskarth (n 38) 12.

[116] Christopher Hill, 'The Capability–Expectations Gap, Or Conceptualizing Europe's International Role' (1993) 31 Journal of Common Market Studies 305.

[117] Koutrakos (n 1) 86–9.

have to be put within the context of the character and nature of European integration. Linear approaches to the EU's contribution often rest on a vision of the EU as a peace project, where the assumption is that the EU is necessarily a 'force for good'. But European integration has always been and remains a project beset with contradictions, which only intensify when these are externalized or projected onto the global arena. In that context, the issue is not only that the EU's greater entanglement in the law of global security risks co-opting global initiatives for the pursuit of European interests, but that it will push the global security machinery in a direction that entrenches the inequality of the global security order, fuelling, rather than reducing, underdevelopment and insecurity, particularly in the Global South, as well as increasing geopolitical antagonisms.

CHAPTER 55

INTERPOL—THE INTERNATIONAL CRIMINAL POLICE ORGANIZATION

SABINE GLESS AND HELGE ELISABETH ZEITLER

A. Introduction

The International Criminal Police Organization, or Interpol, is currently the world's largest international police organization. Founded in 1923 as a private body, it has 194 Member countries as of 2020.[1] With near universal participation, it is one of the largest international organizations, second only to the UN. The turbulent history of Interpol can be seen in certain geopolitical controversies of the past, most prominently the Nazi takeover during the Second World War and its subsequent loss of significance during the Cold War. Such events presaged a gradual technical decline during the second half of last century.[2] It was only after the 9/11 attacks that Interpol's technical infrastructure and internal organization were overhauled and it was given a broader mandate to actively participate in the fight against terrorism. With an increasingly visible role in the global security architecture, Interpol is now viewed as an important stakeholder, cooperating closely with key players in the UN system as well as at a regional (eg, with the European

[1] The few non-member countries include some small island States (Micronesia, Palau, and Tuvalu) and North Korea. On the other hand, the membership also includes a few States that, while not being fully sovereign, have their own policing sovereignty: Aruba, Curacao, and Sint Maarten. See Interpol, 'Membership of INTERPOL' (Interpol, 2019) <https://www.interpol.int/Who-we-are/Legal-framework/Membership-of-INTERPOL> accessed 20 October 2019.

[2] See, also, Michael Fooner, *Interpol* (Plenum Press 1989) 7–9; Frank G Madsen, 'The Historical Evolution of the International Cooperation against Transnational Organised Crime' in Pierre Hauck/Sven Peterke (eds), *International Law and Transnational Organised Crime* (OUP 2016) 13–14.

Union (EU) and the African Union (AU)) and national levels, significantly influencing the global approach to fighting terrorism and other serious crimes.[3]

At the same time, Interpol's function as an 'apolitical and neutral' facilitator of cross-border cooperation in criminal matters has been called into question.[4] The fact that governments have tried to use 'Red Notices' (Interpol's electronic alert system which assists national law enforcement agencies in locating and arresting persons to be extradited for serious crimes) to arrest political dissidents has caused unease. Today, terror watch listings raise questions of persecutions violating human rights because they appear to be politically motivated or based on ethnicity, such as the pursuit of journalists on charges of terrorism by Turkey[5] or ethnic Uighurs in China.[6] Similarly, that Russia has pursued internationally investors and businessmen on corruption charges has raised concern.[7] Even the use of Interpol channels for solving States' internal controversies around criminal policy issues, such as prosecuting tax evasion, has triggered debates about Interpol's mission and neutrality. For example, Red Notices have been issued for bankers wanted for aiding and abetting tax fraud,[8] with such practices being particularly controversial where they are used for simple bank debts or business disputes.[9]

A growing awareness about the potential impact of the vast amounts of data stored on Interpol's databases, as well as political controversies over membership applications such as Palestine's in 2017 (approved) and Kosovo's in 2018 (rejected), have also raised concerns. Other incidents have challenged Interpol's insistence on neutrality, including the 2018 disappearance of Interpol's Chinese President (connected to corruption charges), followed by a dispute about a Russian candidate filling the Presidency (who was ultimately not elected because of concerns about Russia's controversial use of Interpol Notices in the past). Consequently, protecting Interpol's ability to operate in a neutral manner has increasingly been seen as challenging but also essential for its future success.

[3] eg UNGA Res 73/11 (26 November 2018) on UN–Interpol cooperation; Interpol Resolution No 5, GA-2019-88-RES-05 on strengthening Interpol's cooperation with the EU.

[4] cf CoE Parliamentary Assembly Resolution 2161 (26 April 2017) <http://assembly.coe.int/nw/xml/XRef/Xref-XML2HTML-EN.asp?fileid=23,714&lang=en> accessed 20 October 2019; Jessica Jaques, '"Interpol Must not be Misused to Detain Critical Writers"—EP Chair Warns Turkey' (*European Centre For Press and Media Freedom*, 30 August 2017) <https://ecpmf.eu/news/threats/hamza-yaln-ep-chair-warns-turkey-not-to-misuse-interpol> accessed 20 October 2019; and the campaign by Fair Trials <https://www.fairtrials.org/campaign/interpol> accessed 10 July 2019.

[5] Jaques (n 4).

[6] UNGA 'Report of the Special Rapporteur on the promotion and protection of the right to freedom of opinion and expression, Frank La Rue' (27 May 2011) UN Doc A/HRC/17/27/Add.1, 188.

[7] Luke Harding, 'Red Notice: How I Became Putin's No 1 Enemy by Bill Browder—Review' (*The Guardian*, 26 March 2015) <www.theguardian.com/books/2015/mar/26/red-notice-how-i-became-putin-no-1-enemy-bill-browder-review> accessed 20 October 2019.

[8] cf German Federal Constitutional Court, Bundesverfassungsgericht, Beschluss vom 24. März 2016–2 BvR 175/16.

[9] Amy Mackinnon, 'The Scourge of the Red Notice' (*Foreign Policy*, 3 December 2018) <https://foreignpolicy.com/2018/12/03/the-scourge-of-the-red-notice-interpol-uae-russia-china/> accessed 20 October 2019.

There is an increasing understanding internationally that where individual rights are affected, international organizations must either provide for the protection of such rights and for respective remedies within their internal system or do so by other means, which have to include external oversight that goes beyond a general monitoring of activities.[10] Interpol has updated its governance methods in light of technological advances and has continued to reform its internal accountability system, akin to the developments of the UN and the EU's counter-terrorism sanction regimes. Nevertheless, Interpol's more prominent and self-defined strategic goal of maximizing its role within the global security architecture between 2017 and 2020, which has been implicitly endorsed by the international community, necessitates an even more transparent and strong organizational governance.

This chapter critically examines Interpol's authority to act and the relevant legal framework. It analyses recent developments and contemporary challenges for Interpol, which has risen from an association of police authorities to an international organization, increasingly engaging in activities that influence global security and can infringe on individual liberties and human rights.

B. Legal Framework

Interpol is vital to the contemporary global security architecture. This is particularly the case because of its quasi-monopoly (at least outside the EU) on secure transnational communications between national law enforcement authorities, including the distribution of requests for national police forces to locate and arrest criminal suspects. This unique position is remarkable, particularly considering Interpol's relatively vague legal status, and attendant rights and obligations.

1. Interpol's Legal Status and Framework

Given its current position as the most significant institution for officially disseminating arrest warrants internationally, one might expect an international treaty to govern Interpol's actions. In reality, however, it is only secondary law, adopted by the Interpol General Assembly (IGA), that provides for its legal basis since its days as a Congress of police officials.[11] Even Interpol's Constitution (see Section B.2) contains, in a strict legal

[10] James Sheptycki, 'The Accountability of Transnational Policing Institutions: The Strange Case of Interpol' (2004) 19 Canadian Journal of Law and Society 107, 109–14 and 117–18; Sabine Gless, 'Police and Judicial Cooperation between the European Union Member States: Results and Prospects' in Cyrille J C F Fijnaut/Jannemieke Ouwerkerk (eds), *The Future of Police and Judicial Cooperation in the EU* (Brill 2010); Cheah Wui Ling, 'Mapping Interpol's Evolution: Functional Expansion and the Move to Legalization' (2010) 4 Policing: A Journal of Policy and Practice 30.

[11] Bettina Schöndorf-Haubold, 'The Administration of Information in International Administrative Law—The Example of Interpol (2009) 11 German Law Journal 1719.

sense, provisions for an association and not for a body of international law. But, in practice, the provisions' impact is way beyond 'club rules' as they determine the functioning of Interpol at all levels. Interpol's elusive nature by traditional legal classification seems pervasive: for instance, while a membership request has to be submitted by a country, it is the police forces that become members of the organization,[12] not the countries themselves—which is different from 'normal' international organizations.[13] And despite a 2011 Resolution of the IGA requesting its Constitution to be deposited with the UN, as is the case with many other intergovernmental treaties,[14] it has not appeared in the UN Treaty Collection so far.[15]

The prevailing view today is that Interpol is an international organization *sui generis*.[16] Proponents of such a pragmatic approach argue that Interpol ought to have such a status based on its role as a critical partner in cross-border law enforcement for nearly all governments in the world.[17] The various international agreements it has concluded, and its self-depiction as a subject of international law without States challenging it, also support this notion. The treatment it is afforded by States and international organizations suggests that Interpol has transformed into an international organization de facto,[18] at least following the adoption of the 1956 Constitution and subsequent practice. This classification draws on States' endorsements, especially regarding privileges and immunities, which are not only part of the Headquarters Agreement between Interpol and France but also appear in other agreements.[19]

As mentioned, Interpol's primary legal document is its Constitution, adopted in 1956 by the IGA consisting of representatives of all Members.[20] The Constitution lays out Interpol's mission and defines the broader legal framework, which is then operationalized by other regulations. Over time, however, conflicting goals have been

[12] Constitution of the International Criminal Police Organization I/CONS/GA/1956 (Constitution) art 4.

[13] Sheptycki (n 10) 119.

[14] Interpol Resolution AGN/80/RES/15 (2011).

[15] UNTC, 'Multilateral Treaties Deposited with the Secretary-General' <https://treaties.un.org/Pages/ParticipationStatus.aspx?clang=_en> accessed 20 October 2019.

[16] Fooner (n 2) 47–53; Bernd Hecker, *Europäisches Strafrecht* (5th edn, Springer 2015) 164–5; cf OXIO, 'Constitution of the International Criminal Police Organization-INTERPOL, 13th June 1956 (I/CONS/GA/1956 (2008))' OXIO 245 (*Oxford Public International Law*, 30 June 2017). But see also recent complaint before the US District Court of the Eastern District of New York (13 March 2019), *Oussama El Omari v Interpol*, qualifying Interpol as a non-governmental non-profit organization and objecting to Interpol's claim to immunity.

[17] For further information see Sheptycki (n 10) 119–20.

[18] Heinrich Grützner et al, *Internationaler Rechtshilfeverkehr in Strafsachen* (CF Müller 2017) III B 1, nos 10–14.

[19] See eg Executive Order by US President Ronald Reagan designating Interpol as an international organization entitled to enjoy the privileges, exemptions, and immunities conferred by the US, Ronald Reagan, 'Executive Order 12425—International Criminal Police Organizations' (*Presidential Library and Museum*, 16 June 1983) <https://www.reaganlibrary.gov/research/speeches/61683f> accessed 20 October 2019.

[20] Interpol, 'What is INTERPOL?' (*Interpol*, 2019) <https://www.interpol.int/Who-we-are/What-is-INTERPOL> accessed 20 October 2019. For further information about governance and organization see Interpol's Constitution (n 12), including on the role of the IGA (arts 6–14), the Executive Committee (arts 15–24), the General Secretariat (arts 25–33) and the Commission for the Control of Interpol's files (arts 36–7), see Rutsel Silvestre J Martha, *The Legal Foundations of INTERPOL* (Hart 2010) 66.

included in the Constitution. For instance, Article 2 promises to 'ensure and promote the widest possible mutual assistance between all criminal police authorities', but at the same time restricts such assistance to 'the limits of the laws existing in the different countries and in the spirit of the Universal Declaration of Human Rights'.[21] The Constitution emphasizes Interpol's neutral function in mutual criminal police assistance, and Article 3 expressly forbids the organization from undertaking 'any intervention or activities of a political, military, religious or racial character'.[22]

The application of the Constitution is determined by the IGA, which adopts General Regulations including the Rules of Procedure and Rules on the Processing of Data,[23] the Rules on the Control of Information and Access to Interpol's Files,[24] and the Statute of the Commission for the Control of Interpol's Files (CCF), which establishes a system of remedies for individuals affected by Interpol activity (see Section D.2.b). A large and continuously growing range of international cooperation agreements, including with the UN and its organizations and programmes, various branches of the EU, the AU, the International Criminal Court (ICC) and other international tribunals, make up Interpol's external legal framework.[25]

To fully understand Interpol's legal position, one must also take into consideration its arrangements with its host States. The Headquarters Agreement between Interpol and France regulates the organization's right to adopt its own procedures and rules while also enjoying the privileges and immunities granted by the host State. Subject to a limited number of exceptions, Interpol enjoys immunity from legal process. Furthermore, specified persons are granted privileges and immunities, including immunity from arrest and detention, immunity from legal process, and the inviolability of all official papers and documents.[26] Aside from the Headquarters in Lyon there are six Sub-Regional Bureaus plus liaison offices in Bangkok, Brussels, Addis Ababa, and at the UN, in New York. The agreements with the different host countries include immunity clauses, albeit with some variations.[27]

[21] See also Schöndorf-Haubold (n 11) 1720.

[22] See also Yaron Gottlieb, 'Article 3 of Interpol's Constitution: Balancing International Police Cooperation with the Prohibition on Engaging in Political, Military, Religious, or Racial Activities' (2011) 23 Finnish Journal of International Law 135, 146.

[23] 'Legal Framework' (*Interpol*, 2019) <https://www.interpol.int/About-INTERPOL/Legal-materials> accessed 20 October 2019.

[24] 'Commission for the Control of INTERPOL's File (CCF)' (Interpol, 2019) <https://www.interpol.int/Who-we-are/Commission-for-the-Control-of-INTERPOL-s-Files-CCF> accessed 20 October 2019.

[25] 'Cooperation Agreements' (Interpol, 2019) <https://www.interpol.int/Who-we-are/Legal-framework/Cooperation-agreements> accessed 20 October 2019.

[26] Headquarters Agreement between France and Interpol (14 April 2009), JORF No 0208 (9 September 2009) 14844, No 12 (*Legifrance*, 1 September 2009) arts 4–8 <www.legifrance.gouv.fr/eli/decret/2009/9/4/MAEJ0919137D/jo> accessed 20 October 2019.

[27] See, for example, art 3 of the host country agreement with Belgium, limiting immunity explicitly to official activities: Headquarters Agreement with Exchange of Letters between the Kingdom of Belgium and the International Criminal Police Organization-Interpol (ICPO-INTERPOL) (*Department of Foreign Affairs*, 24 October 2014) <https://www.fdfa.be/sites/default/files/atoms/files/1107_Ondertekende%20akte%20in%20het%20Engels.pdf> accessed 20 October 2019; Schöndorf-Haubold (n 11) 1732.

2. Mandate and Modus Operandi

Today, Interpol is largely considered a success due to its ability to fill a gap in cross-border cooperation amongst States who have traditionally defined criminal justice matters as domestic affairs.[28] Historically, States have had little authority in cases involving any jurisdiction other than their own, such as pursuing an alleged wrongdoer who has fled their territory. In an increasingly globalized world this traditional approach became increasingly untenable, and domestic law enforcement authorities began to rely on Interpol's assistance more often, despite its vague legal foundation.

a. *Mandate*

In line with Article 2 of its Constitution, Interpol works for the 'prevention and suppression of ordinary law crimes'. This includes all forms of crimes that are not covered by the neutrality clause in Article 3. The scope of this activity continues to be defined, as the example of terrorism demonstrates. Decisions on the interpretation of what does and does not constitute 'ordinary law crimes' take the form of IGA resolutions, adopted by simple majority.[29] This low threshold for decision-taking and the lack of a requirement for a quorum seem inversely proportional to the far-reaching consequences and the potential impact of similar decisions.[30]

Interpol currently focuses its activities around three global crime programmes: counter-terrorism, organized and emerging crime, and cybercrime (with a newly established Complex for Innovation in Singapore). It has developed separate strategies for each of them.[31]

b. *Modus Operandi*

Interpol is primarily known for fostering information exchange relating to crimes and criminals and for its Red Notices, or requests for location and provisional arrests based on arrest warrants issued by Member States. In recent years, less formal ways of sharing information and analytical work, including intelligence- and data-gathering, have become increasingly important.[32]

Since 2002, Interpol has been using the Interpol-24/7 (I-24/7) web-based communication system for secure global police communication. This system connects the General

[28] Gottlieb (n 22) 137–8.

[29] Constitution (n 12) art 14, only for special cases, such as amendments to the Constitution, requires two-thirds majority.

[30] On Interpol's decision-making process, see Schöndorf-Haubold (n 11) 1723–5.

[31] Crime overview: 'News and Events' (Interpol, 2019) A <https://www.interpol.int/News-and-Events> accessed 20 October 2019.

[32] James Sheptycki, 'Reflections on the Transnationalization of Policing; the Case of the RCMP and Serial Killers' (1998) 26 International Journal of the Sociology of Law 26, 17–31; James B Jacobs/Dimitra Blitsa, 'Sharing Criminal Records: The United States, the European Union and Interpol Compared' (2008) 30(2) Loyola LA International and Comparative Law Review 200.

Secretary in Lyon with the National Central Bureaus (NCBs) of the national police in all 194 Member countries.[33]

The I-24/7 is also used for Interpol's best-known tool, that is, the Notices. There are currently six colour-coded Notices: Red Notices, Blue,[34] Green,[35] Yellow,[36] Black,[37] and Orange Notices.[38] Red Notices are the most prominent. This is the alert published by Interpol into its databases at the request of an NCB that can be seen by police and immigration authorities globally. Its purpose is to locate a wanted person for extradition based on a valid national arrest warrant. In many States, the Red Notice alone serves as sufficient basis for a provisional arrest. Even if in other countries a domestic arrest warrant in line with national requirements is necessary for any deprivation of liberty, international courts have recognized that the circulation of the Notice alone creates legal effects for the person concerned.[39] In practical terms, any individual subject to a Red Notice will have difficultly renting a flat, obtaining a mobile phone, or opening a bank account.

Between 2001 and 2017 the number of Red Notices issued increased from approximately 1,400 to over 13,000. However, this number is exceeded by far by the number of diffusions, which reached over 50,000 in 2017.[40]

Through this lesser-known and rather informal, but equally impactful, mechanism of diffusions, law enforcement authorities directly inform other authorities about wanted persons.[41] While for Red Notices, Interpol has introduced certain ex ante control mechanisms before publishing them, for diffusions, Interpol channels serve a virtual mailbox function alone, and Interpol cannot retract those later deemed inappropriate. Any review or correction of a diffusion is done only after it has been already published online with potentially detrimental effects.[42] The CCF had to deal with a number of cases,

[33] Schöndorf-Haubold (n 11) 1736; Constitution (n 12) arts 31 and 32.

[34] To locate, identify or obtain information on a person of interest in a criminal investigation.

[35] To warn about a person's criminal activities if that person is considered to be a possible threat to public safety.

[36] To locate a missing person or to identify a person unable to identify himself/herself.

[37] To seek information on unidentified bodies.

[38] To warn of an event, a person, an object or a process representing an imminent threat and danger to persons or property.

[39] The International Court of Justice (ICJ) held in *Arrest Warrant* that an Interpol circulated arrest warrant issued by Belgium against a government member of the Democratic Republic of the Congo (DRC) who allegedly had incited genocide had a legal effect of itself and violated the DRC's sovereignty as it failed to respect the immunity from criminal jurisdiction that an incumbent minister enjoyed under international law. See*Arrest Warrant of 11 April 2000 (DRC v Belgium)* (Judgment) [2002] ICJ Rep 3 [66] and [71]; Nina Marino/Reed Grantham, 'Wanted by Interpol: Strategic Thinking about Red Notices, Diffusions, and Extradition' (2015) 30 Criminal Justice 7–9. See also *M v Bulgaria*, App No 59297/12, 25 March 2014 and *Khadzhiev v Bulgaria*, App No 44330/07, 3 June 2014.

[40] Fact Sheet Interpol, COM/FS/2018-03/GL-02.

[41] Jacobs/Blitsa (n 32) 200.

[42] Jacques Semelmann/Emily Spencer Munson, 'Interpol Red Notices and Diffusions: Powerful—And Dangerous—Tools of Global Law Enforcement' (2014) The Champion 28, 29.

where countries tried to circumvent Interpol's control mechanisms using a diffusion after a Red Notice had been rejected.[43]

With regard to Notices, Interpol gathers data that it enters into specific databases accessible by domestic police authorities and increasingly also a wide range of international partner organizations. This intense cooperation, however, is not safeguarded with closely meshed data protection.[44] Interpol's data processing compliance, for instance, is monitored by different bodies, but the options to implement decisions against the General Secretariat's will and complaint's systems remain unclear and weak.[45] Such shortcomings raise alarm when Interpol is in charge of huge databases covering suspected terrorists, other data on criminals, fingerprints, facial images, images related to child sex abuse, DNA profiles, lost or stolen travel documents, stolen artwork, and stolen motor vehicles. In 2018 alone, Interpol reported 13 million searches per day and 1.1 million database hits during that year, with 90 per cent of the records and 82 per cent of the searches coming from Europe and the Americas.[46]

c. *Operational Support*

Interpol provides also operational police support and intelligence services.[47] In 2003, a Command and Coordination Centre (CCC) was created at the General Secretariat to enable the organization to respond to support requests from any Member country faced with a particular security incident, such as a terrorist attack, or having to secure major events. Such support is provided through so-called Incident Response Teams, providing investigative support in criminal investigations but also disaster victim identification support, or teams helping with security arrangements for major international events. Interpol also participates in Joint Investigation Teams comprised of officers from the General Secretariat and Member States that can be dispatched to respond to a crisis. Interpol teams supporting national law enforcement authorities consist of officers who provide investigative and analytical support (excluding coercive techniques) at the scene of an incident in coordination with the General Secretariat.

[43] See 'Annual Report 2017' (Interpol, 2017) <https://www.google.de/url?sa=t&rct=j&q=&esrc=s&source=web&cd=1&ved=2ahUKEwibkurPvKjlAhXKzaQKHc9aDO8QFjAAegQIBBAC&url=https%3A%2F%2Fwww.interpol.int%2Fcontent%2Fdownload%2F5258%2Ffile%2FAnnual%2520Report%25202017-EN.pdf&usg=AOvVaw1tbv-H-xq2C19MHBkSkIAE> accessed 20 October 2019.

[44] Cheah Wui Ling, 'Policing Interpol: The Commission for the Control of Interpol's Files and the Right to a Remedy' (2010) 7 International Organizations Law Review 375. For a detailed analysis of the difficulties to apply data protection concepts on police intelligence, see Orla Lynskey 'Criminal Justice Profiling and EU Data Protection Law: Precarious Protection from Predictive Policing International' (2019) 15 International Journal of Law in Context 162.

[45] Ling (n 44) 402.

[46] 'Databases' (Interpol, 2019) <https://www.interpol.int/How-we-work/Databases> accessed 20 October 2019.

[47] See eg Javier Gardeazabal/Todd Sandler, 'INTERPOL's Surveillance Network in Curbing Transnational Terrorism' (2015) 34 Journal of Policy Analysis and Management 761; Ling (n 10) 32, 36.

d. *Intelligence- and Data-Gathering*

Intelligence gathering, brokering of information, and liaising between national police forces are the backbone of Interpol's work.[48] More recently, Interpol's major strategies have involved procuring intelligence through digital means: The use of machine learning to detect patterns amongst large data sets has become crucial to modern law enforcement over the last decade.[49] To achieve this, access to sufficient quantities of data is necessary and Interpol is particularly well placed in this regard as a broker of information between more than 190 States. In the area of cybercrime, Interpol cooperates with private stakeholders such as network operators or cloud service providers to jointly identify cyberthreats (while also broadening Interpol's data pool).[50] At the same time, Interpol engages in data exchange with various institutions, allowing for access to its databases in exchange for information and data being shared by the other organizations.[51] Data mining heralds a significant enhancement in global security and Interpol is a promising partner with its access to large pools of data for optimal results. But it remains unclear how Interpol's increased engagement in such data processing and intelligence work can be contained by valid accountability mechanisms.

e. *Capacity-Building and the Exchange of Expertise*

Interpol is central in the exchange of information between national law enforcement services in areas like drug trafficking, smuggling, and terrorism, but also, for example, in environmental crime.[52] This is done through the use of the aforementioned informative Notices but also through training and dedicated working groups where law enforcement officials meet and discuss.[53] Interpol also supports the capacity of domestic law enforcement agencies, and in particular, developing States, directly on the ground. Typically funded on a project basis, Interpol provides capacity-building and advises developing States on topics such as structuring their national police forces, implementing modern investigation techniques, and strategic approaches to solving crimes.[54] This

[48] Madsen (n 2) 494–6.

[49] Tim Wilson, 'Applying the Science' in Steven David Brown (ed), *Combating International Crime: The Longer Arm of the Law*' (Routledge Cavendish 2008) 229–31.

[50] cf with regard to cooperation with Europol: Maria O'Neill, 'A Europe that Protects: Moving to the Next Stage of Cross-Border Law Enforcement Cooperation' (2011) 84 The Police Journal: Theory, Practice and Principles 125, 128–9, 134–5; Francesca Bignami, 'European Versus American Liberty: A Comparative Analysis of Antiterrorism Data Mining' (2007) 48 Boston College Law Review 609.

[51] See Section C.

[52] David Higgins/Rob White, 'Collaboration at the Front Line: Interpol and NGOs in the same NEST' in Grant Pink/Rob White (eds), *Environmental Crime and Collaborative State Intervention* (Palgrave Macmillan 2016) 103.

[53] eg, on cybercrime, financial crime, different types of environmental crime.

[54] Interpol has trained 3000 law enforcement officers worldwide and has launched a global e-learning centre with currently 17,000 users. See 'Annual Report 2018' (Interpol, 2018) <https://www.google.de/url?sa=t&rct=j&q=&esrc=s&source=web&cd=1&ved=2ahUKEwjIiuHywajlAhVN46QKHVVQDUgQFjAAegQIABAC&url=https%3A%2F%2Fwww.interpol.int%2Fcontent%2Fdownload%2F13974%2Ffile%2F19COM0009%2520-%25202018%2520Annual%2520Report06_EN_LR.pdf&usg=AOvVaw32knhYkQiTII5mKPxGvLmW> accessed 20 October 2019.

capacity-building includes partnerships with other training institutions but also—more unusually—with non-governmental organizations (NGOs).[55]

C. Interpol's Place in the Global Security Architecture

Interpol's cooperation with global security actors, in particular the UN, especially in the field of counter-terrorism, demonstrates its increasingly important role in the global security architecture.[56] While not formally part of the UN system, Interpol is connected to a significant number of entities within it, including those working on counter-terrorism, the UN Office on Drugs and Crime, the UN Environment Program, the Department of Peacekeeping Operations, the Audit Office, and ten different Sanctions Committees.[57]

Interpol was granted consultative status at the UN as an NGO in 1949. In 1971, the UN granted it special treatment in certain areas due to its crucial role in cross-border law enforcement, although this did not include terrorism.[58] In 1975, Interpol was designated an Inter-Governmental Organization to allow its participation in the ECOSOC on a continual basis. Following a 1997 UN General Assembly (UNGA) Resolution, a cooperation agreement was formed, including mutual observer status at the respective General Assemblies of the UN and Interpol. In 2002, Interpol opened its databases to relevant UN bodies and, in 2004, a Special Representative Office was established in New York, followed by a Liaison Office in Vienna in 2018. Numerous UNGA and UN Security Council (UNSC) resolutions[59] refer to Interpol's role and encourage Member States to make use of all the tools provided by Interpol, not just those related to terrorism.

Since 1994, Interpol has cooperated with various international tribunals, including the ICC, in the pursuit of justice for genocide, crimes against humanity, and war crimes.

[55] See eg 'WWF Works with Interpol to Prevent Forest Crime' (WWF, 28 March 2019) <https://wwf.panda.org/knowledge_hub/where_we_work/black_sea_basin/danube_carpathian/?344,950/wwf-and-interpol—forests> accessed 20 October 2019.

[56] Schöndorf-Haubold, (n 11) 1721; Cooperation Agreement between the United Nations and the International Criminal Police Organization (INTERPOL) (Interpol, 8 July 1997) <https://www.google.de/url?sa=t&rct=j&q=&esrc=s&source=web&cd=1&cad=rja&uact=8&ved=2ahUKEwiM9taRx6jlAhXZwcQBHR-FDGAQFjAAegQIABAB&url=https%3A%2F%2Fwww.interpol.int%2FWho-we-are%2FLegal-framework%2FCooperation-agreements&usg=AOvVaw1JzsP3janep98jx3M_K6Po> accessed 20 October 2019; Karl-Heinz Kind, 'The Role of Interpol in the Fight Against the Illicit Trafficking in Cultural Property' in Stefano Manacorda/Duncan Chappell (eds), *Crime in the Art and Antiquities World* (Springer 2011) 176–80; Bernhard Kretschmer 'Transnational Organised Crime and Cultural Property' in Hauck/Peterke (n 2) 311–12.

[57] Stuart Cameron-Waller, 'Interpol, A Global Service Provider' in Steven David Brown (ed), *Combating International Crime: The Longer Arm of the Law* (Routledge-Cavendish 2008) 53–7.

[58] Gottlieb (n 22) 147–9; Grützner et al (n 18) III B 1, Nos 59–65.

[59] 'UNGA and UNSC Resolutions Highlighting INTERPOL's Role' (Interpol, 2019) <https://www.interpol.int/en/Our-partners/International-organization-partners/INTERPOL-and-the-United-Nations/UNGA-and-UNSC-resolutions-highlighting-INTERPOL-s-role> accessed 20 October 2019.

This has led to the arrest of several fugitives, but Interpol's list of Red Notices still includes twenty-one people alone wanted for crimes against humanity.[60] While this cooperation with international courts and tribunals has generally worked well, the IGA expressed in 2010 concerns about the increase in the number of requests from Member States related to genocide, war crimes, and crimes against humanity, raising doubts about possible non-compliance with Article 3 of the Constitution, which excludes political offences from the scope of Notices. It was decided that cooperation with requests submitted by Member States would continue unless these involve someone who is a national of another Member State and that State protested within 30 days.[61]

Cooperation with other actors in the global and regional security architecture is increasing.[62] Already since 2001, Interpol has, for example, a cooperation agreement with Europol, working together in many areas, particularly cybercrime, with a specific secure communication line.[63] More recently, a cooperation agreement with the African Police Cooperation Mechanism (Afripol) allows for access to Interpol's databases.[64]

D. Legal Issues

Most of the current legal issues concerning Interpol can be traced back to its origins as a private association of police officers that later transformed into a global player in international security. Notably, Interpol has never been subject to a formal system of accountability.

1. General Accountability

In strategic matters, Interpol's management bodies must answer to the IGA and the Executive Committee, but this internal governance structure is weak.[65] The quality and effectiveness of the control over Interpol's activities is therefore largely dependent upon the quality of the Member States delegations sent to the IGA and those elected to the Executive Committee.[66] No system of external accountability exists. This is quite different from the accountability mechanism that exists for other, similar entities. For example, in Europol the European Parliament, with the European Council, exercise budgetary control and the Council decides on strategic priorities around fighting organized

[60] See Red Notices database, searchable at <www.interpol.int> accessed 20 October 2019.

[61] Interpol Resolution AG-2010-RES-10 (2010). [62] See 'Cooperation Agreements' (n 25).

[63] Sabine Gless, 'Europol' in Valsamis Mitsilegas et al (eds), *Research Handbook on EU Criminal Law* (Edward Elgar 2016); see also Interpol Resolution No 5 (n 3).

[64] 'INTERPOL—African Union Agreement to Boost Fight against Terrorism and Organized Crime' (Interpol, 15 January 2019) <https://www.interpol.int/News-and-Events/News/2019/INTERPOL-African-Union-agreement-to-boost-fight-against-terrorism-and-organized-crime> accessed 20 October 2019.

[65] Schöndorf-Haubold (n 11) 1745; Sheptycki (n 10) 107–34. [66] Martha (n 20) 53.

crime, taking into account the views of Europol, but leaving the final decisions to the Ministers.[67]

2. Accountability for Infringements on Individual Rights

The alerts regarding location and provisional arrests issued by Interpol are based on national arrest warrants and information supplied by the NCBs. That said, Interpol is solely competent (and thus responsible) for issuing and maintaining Red Notices. Until 2017, Interpol's internal accountability system was limited even where Interpol activity significantly affected individual rights, such as, for example, through Red Notices or terrorist warning listings. In such situations its actions could be challenged only via a convoluted system that imposed limited obligations on the States involved, for example, alerts for the need of correction of erroneous information.[68] Since 2015, upon both political and NGO pressure,[69] a range of reforms has been adopted to enhance internal oversight.

a. *Data Protection and an Internal Review System*

Interpol has established a data protection regime for information stored in its databases as well as for the publication of Notices.[70] In addition to a data protection officer in the Secretariat General, dedicated taskforces composed of lawyers, police, and analysts have been established to review all requests for publication of Notices to avoid clerical errors and breaches of the requirements of Article 2 or 3 of the Constitution.[71] However, the exact scope of the review is not made available to the public.

Interpol's institutional data protection does not affect States' databases or diffusions that are shared directly through NCBs. On the whole, reform is necessary in order to provide the level of protection commonly found at the domestic level, particularly with regard to full disclosure of personal data and transparency in profiling. Importantly, in this regard, a review of the current data protection rules was launched at the IGA

[67] Gless (n 63) 467–8, 474–8.

[68] cf 'Promotion and Protection of the Right to Freedom of Opinion and Expression' (n 6) 188; Alex Tinsley, 'Echoes of Kadi: Reforms to Internal Remedies at INTERPOL' (*EJIL:Talk!*, 20 January 2017) <https://www.ejiltalk.org/echoes-of-kadi-reforms-to-internal-remedies-at-interpol/> accessed 20 October 2019.

[69] See eg Parliamentary Assembly, 'Report 13370: Accountability of International Organisations for Human Rights Violations' (*Council of Europe*, 17 December 2013) para 57 <https://assembly.coe.int/nw/xml/XRef/Xref-XML2HTML-en.asp?fileid=20,310&lang=en> accessed 20 October 2019; OSCE, 'Baku Declaration and Resolutions' (OSCE, 28 June–2 July 2014) para 128 <https://www.oscepa.org/documents/annual-sessions/2014-baku/declaration-2/2540-2014-baku-declaration-eng/file> accessed 20 October 2019; 'Report: Strengthening Respect for Human Rights, Strengthening INTERPOL' (Fair Trials International, November 2013) <https://www.fairtrials.org/sites/default/files/publication_pdf/Strengthening-respect-for-human-rights-strengthening-INTERPOL5.pdf> accessed 20 October 2019.

[70] 'INTERPOL's Rules on the Processing of Data' (Interpol, 2016) <https://www.interpol.int/content/download/5694/file/INTERPOL%20Rules%20on%20the%20Processing%20of%20Data-EN.pdf.> accessed 20 October 2019.

[71] Schöndorf-Haubold (n 11) 1746.

in 2018 to take into account new technical developments and new purposes such as crime prevention.[72]

b. *Remedies Under the Commission for the Control of Interpol's Files*

With the reform of the complaints mechanism and the strengthening of the CCF, today individuals can seek access to, and request correction (or deletion) of, information held about them in Interpol's systems.[73] Since the 2016 reforms, there is a two-tier remedy system where a request for revision of a decision of the CCF is allowed if new facts are discovered within six months.

The composition of the CCF, its independence, and its decision-making process and authority represent a major shift towards a more transparent remedy system able to correct errors by rendering decisions that are binding on Interpol.[74] The remedy system provides both legal protection for individuals and preserves Interpol's judicial immunity.[75] As different international courts have found, immunity is only warranted if an alternative internal justice system exists.[76]

With the introduction of the CCF internal review system, Interpol and France agreed to declare Article 24 of the Headquarters Agreement, which (although in practice was never used) provided for the possibility of arbitration for any disputes between Interpol and a private party, inapplicable to cases where the CCF could be seized.[77]

While the internal review system is now the exclusive path available to those affected by Notices, it still has certain weaknesses. First, it only works where an individual is aware that he or she is the subject of Interpol activity, which raises the question of how to strengthen other means of compliance monitoring. Even where the CCF receives an individual request, it is limited in its means of action. For instance, it must ask the NCB of the relevant State for permission to disclose whether or not there is any information on file. Only where an individual can demonstrate that there is information on him or her in Interpol's files can the CCF potentially provide access without the NCB's authorization.

[72] Interpol Resolution No 8, GA-2018-87-RES-08.

[73] See, for an overview of CCF decisions, Policy Department for External Relations, 'Misuse of Interpol's Red Notices and Impact on Human Rights—Recent Developments' (European Parliament, January 2019) Annex C <https://www.europarl.europa.eu/RegData/etudes/STUD/2019/603472/EXPO_STU(2019)603472_EN.pdf> accessed 30 November 2020.

[74] cf Interpol, Statute of the Commission for the Control of INTERPOL's Files, II.E/RCIA/GA/2016, art 3.

[75] Tinsley (n 68).

[76] *Waite and Kennedy v Germany*, App No 26083/94, 18 February 1999; *Nada v Switzerland*, App No 10593/08, 12 September 2012; Case C-584/10 P*European Commission and Others v Kadi* [2013] ECLI:EU:C:2013:518.

[77] Decree No 2016-326 (17 March 2016) promulgating the additional protocol in the form of an exchange of letters between the Government of the French Republic and the International Criminal Police Organization—INTERPOL on the interpretation and application of Article 24 of the Agreement of 14 and 24 April 2008 regarding INTERPOL's headquarters in France, signed in Paris on 9 February 2016 and in Lyon on 12 February 2016.

Such a situation would not likely be the case where someone is on a watch list and cannot determine why, for instance, he or she is rejected when applying for a lease or to open a bank account. Learning about a Blue Notice or Orange Notice is also much more difficult as these Notices primarily operate to provide internal information and intelligence gathering. Additionally, there is little to no scrutiny exercised over the diffusions that are shared directly between NCBs, which can also have a significant impact on an individual. Diffusions are not public, and the issuing country can choose to share them only with selected NCBs. In addition, in practice, CCF's ever-growing workload due to a significantly increasing volume of data being processed by Interpol and consequently a significant increase in review requests, poses challenges not yet addressed in a satisfactory manner.[78]

c. *Interim Conclusion*

The CCF reform has brought significant change but a number of problems remain, particularly around information disclosure and delisting procedures.[79] The Council of Europe has called for additional resources, including prioritizing screening mechanisms, in view of the continuously increasing number of Red Notices and NCBs submitting abusive requests.[80] In light of these weaknesses in Interpol's system, it is clear that, at least for Red Notices, additional checks by national authorities prior to acting upon the Notice are necessary to avoid further abuse.

E. Developments and Challenges

Interpol's recent reforms and regulations are a reflection of its dichotomous nature: while it seeks to efficiently facilitate cross-border cooperation and steer the global fight against crime, it must also comply with emerging legal standards, in particular with regard to a growing demand for accountability and protection of individual rights. The following section assesses Interpol's mounting role in the global security architecture and possible implications of its increasing influence on the protection of individual rights.

78 CCF, 'Activity Report of the Commission for the Control of Interpol's Files for 2017' (Interpol, 9 October 2018) paras 15–18 <https://www.google.de/url?sa=t&rct=j&q=&esrc=s&source=web&cd=2&cad=rja&uact=8&ved=2ahUKEwj3xpmW1arlAhVP6KQKHYkcCDcQFjABegQIBRAC&url=https%3A%2F%2Fwww.interpol.int%2Fcontent%2Fdownload%2F7285%2Ffile%2FCCFAnnual%2520Report%2520for%25202017%2520-%2520ENG.pdf&usg=AOvVaw3ANBv7MuTylo8GXGE5-Evf> accessed 20 October 2019.

79 See Fair Trials, 'Dismantling the Tools of Oppression—Ending the Misuse of Interpol' (*Fair Trials*, 4 October 2018) <https://www.google.de/url?sa=t&rct=j&q=&esrc=s&source=web&cd=1&cad=rja&uact=8&ved=2ahUKEwi89cKy16rlAhUG16QKHUnAC8AQFjAAegQIABAC&url=https%3A%2F%2Fwww.fairtrials.org%2Fsites%2Fdefault%2Ffiles%2Fpublication_pdf%2FDismantling%2520the%2520tools%2520of%2520oppression.pdf&usg=AOvVaw3aoEOZveVdfax_ja6P9fOK> accessed 20 October 2019.

80 Resolution 2161 (n 4).

1. Cooperation on Global Security Threats

a. *Anti-Terrorism Efforts*

The role of Interpol in the global fight against terrorism has changed dramatically since the 9/11 attacks. During the 1970s and 1980s, Interpol played a very limited role in counter-terrorism efforts, primarily due to the strict interpretation by its leadership of the neutrality requirement under Article 3 of its Constitution. Changes in this regard occurred in 1984, when the IGA allowed some engagement in cooperation on terrorism offences.[81] However, it was only after 9/11 that States started considering Interpol a necessary contributor to their activities in combating global terrorism. This triggered a willingness to agree on key reforms in the context of the IGA, including expanding the scope of terrorism-related offences excluded from Article 3 (see section E.1.a).[82]

According to the Global Strategy 2016–20,[83] Interpol is focusing its counter-terrorism activities on five areas: identification, travel documents, online activities, financing, and weapons and materials. Four regional counter-terrorism nodes have been established in addition to the Central Counter-Terrorism Node at the Interpol Headquarters.[84] Interpol keeps the details of more than 40,000 individuals deemed to be engaging in terrorist activity in a specific database and assimilates information received from a variety of sources, including UN military operations. Interpol's role has been endorsed by the UNSC,[85] and more recently at the G7 and G20 meetings. In October 2018, G7 Interior Ministers called for the implementation of a global law enforcement platform hosted by Interpol to collect and exploit terrorist content, leveraging referrals from industry and national authorities to support investigations and prosecutions.[86]

Interpol contributes to the implementation of the UN Global Counter-Terrorism Strategy, nowadays through its membership as one of two non-UN entities in the system-wide Global Counter-Terrorism Coordination Compact, to coordinate efforts across the peace and security, humanitarian, human rights, and sustainable development sectors.[87] Under a 2017 agreement with the UN Counter-Terrorism Committee Executive Directorate, a strategic action plan with joint objectives and priorities for cooperation was established.

[81] Interpol Resolution AGN/53/RES/7 (1984).

[82] Interpol Resolution AG-2004-RES-18 (2004).

[83] 'Global Counter-Terrorism Strategy' (Interpol, February 2017) <https://www.un.org/en/counterterrorism/hlc/assets/pdf/007-03_Summary_CT_Strategy_2017_01_EN%20LR.pdf> accessed 20 October 2019.

[84] 'Strategic Framework 2017–2020' (Interpol, 2019) <https://www.interpol.int/Who-we-are/Strategy/Strategic-Framework-2017-2020> accessed 20 October 2019.

[85] UNSC Res 2178 (2014).

[86] 'G7 Ministers Call for Sharing of Battlefield Data on Terrorists via INTERPOL' (Interpol, 20 October 2017) <https://www.interpol.int/News-and-Events/News/2017/G7-Ministers-call-for-sharing-of-battlefield-data-on-terrorists-via-INTERPOL> accessed 20 October 2019.

[87] 'UN Launches New Framework to Strengthen Fight Against Terrorism' (UN, 6 December 2018) <https://unicwash.org/un-launches-new-framework-to-strengthen-fight-against-terrorism/> accessed 20 October 2019.

Interpol has also maintained a decade-long cooperation with UN peacekeeping.[88] Given the increasingly close relationships between police and military worldwide, especially regarding peacekeeping operations in conflict zones, Interpol has been engaging more frequently with military actors, and for a long time has been promoting more secure and efficient exchanges of information between police, military, and the judiciary.[89] For example, in 2018, Interpol concluded an agreement with G5 Sahel, which created a joint, mixed military–police anti-terrorism task force composed of five West African States seeking to establish an institutional framework for regional security cooperation.[90] The agreement gives G5 access to Interpol databases. Similarly, through cooperation with NATO and EU military missions,[91] Interpol seeks to clarify the role of the military in evidence gathering. This increase in cooperation with military actors creates challenges in defining the limits of Article 3 of the Constitution and in ensuring appropriate rights for those affected by the transmitted intelligence.[92]

b. *Defining and Prioritizing Global Security Threats*

The wealth of data available through Interpol's databases contributes in defining international strategies for global security threats.[93] In 2017, the IGA agreed for the first time on seven Global Policing Goals to improve coherence amongst the activities of all countries: countering the threat of terrorism, promoting border integrity, protecting vulnerable communities, securing cyberspace, promoting global integrity, curbing illicit markets, and supporting environmental security and sustainability.[94] It remains to be seen whether these goals will have an impact at the national level and how they might

[88] Doreen Carvajal, 'Interpol and UN Back 'Global Policing Doctrine'' (*The New York Times*, 11 October 2009) <https://www.nytimes.com/2009/10/12/world/europe/12iht-interpol.html> accessed 20 October 2019.

[89] 'INTERPOL to Highlight Need for Military to Police Terrorism Data Flow at Global Coalition Meeting' (Interpol, 11 July 2017) <https://www.interpol.int/en/News-and-Events/News/2017/INTERPOL-to-highlight-need-for-military-to-police-terrorism-data-flow-at-Global-Coalition-meeting> accessed 20 October 2019; see for EU reflections in that regard Council of the European Union, 'Strengthening Military, Law Enforcement and Judicial Information Exchange in Counter-Terrorism' (Council of the European Union, 19 September 2017) <https://www.statewatch.org/news/2017/sep/eu-council-ctc-military-leas-battlefield-data-12,347-17-restricted.pdf> accessed 20 October 2019.

[90] Secretariat Permanent du G5 Sahel, 'Signature d'un Accord de Coopération entre le G5 Sahel et Interpol' (G5 SAHEL, 16 May 2019) <https://www.g5sahel.org/8-nos-activit%C3%A9s/1452-signature-d-un-accord-de-cooperation-entre-le-g5-sahel-et-interpol> accessed 20 October 2019.

[91] Council of the European Union, 'Council Conclusions on EU External Action on Counter-Terrorism' (Council of the European Union, 19 June 2017) <https://www.consilium.europa.eu/media/23999/st10384en17-conclusions-on-eu-external-action-on-counter-terrorism.pdf> accessed 20 October 2019; Council of the European Union, 'Strengthening Military, Law Enforcement and Judicial Information Exchange in Counter-Terrorism' (*Council of the European Union*, 11 July 2017) <https://www.eumonitor.eu/9353000/1/j9vvik7m1c3gyxp/vkfu7c4dhozk> accessed 30 November 2020; 'Strengthening Military, Law Enforcement and Judicial Information Exchange in Counter-Terrorism' (n 89).

[92] Sheptycki (n 10) 127–9. [93] ibid.

[94] 'Global Policing Goals' (Interpol, 2019) <https://www.interpol.int/en/Who-we-are/Strategy/Global-Policing-Goals> accessed 20 October 2019.

interact with other priorities such as those made every four years through the EU Policy Cycle on organized crime.[95]

Supporting environmental security is one example of Interpol's burgeoning role in the global security architecture. In light of the fact that Interpol has worked on environmental crime since 1992,[96] its IGA has acknowledged the important role of this area of crime for national, regional, and global security.[97] While discussions at the UN show increasing awareness of the link between environmental degradation, unsustainable management of natural resources, and peace and stability,[98] there is significant resistance, particularly from Russia, around a perceived 'securitization of environmental policies' and expansion of the UNSC's mandate over non-security issues.[99] However, demands are increasing on the UN Secretariat to facilitate the Council's consideration of environment-related security risks when assessing country situations.[100] Interpol's intelligence is poised to play a significant role in helping overcome resistance to the UNSC addressing such issues.

The Strategic Framework 2017–20 also includes goal 4 of 'maximizing Interpol's role in the global security architecture'.[101] This ambition is illustrated by its commitment to 'seek to federate the international community around common goals on security, and to strengthen the regional and ground-level delivery of programmes and capabilities to meet those goals [which] may also require strengthening the legal foundations of the Organization for more effective service delivery'.[102] Interpol's leadership ambitions are also reflected in the 'Dialogue on an effective multilateral policing architecture against global threats' which brings together on a yearly basis regional police organizations, and aims, amongst other things, at the alignment of strategic priorities.[103] In 2018, a new

[95] Council of the European Union, 'The EU Policy Cycle to Tackle Organized and Serious International Crime' (2014) <https://www.consilium.europa.eu/media/30232/qc0114638enn.pdf> accessed 10 July 2019.

[96] Interpol Resolution AGN/1992/RES/12; various reports, eg UNEP-INTERPOL, *The Rise of Environmental Crime* (UNEP 2016).

[97] Interpol Resolution No 3, AG-2014-RES 03.

[98] See eg UN Secretary-General, 'Secretary-General's Remarks to the Security Council on the Maintenance of International Peace and Security: The Root Causes of Conflict—The Role of Natural Resources' (UN, 16 October 2018) <https://www.un.org/sg/en/content/sg/statement/2018-10-16/secretary-generals-remarks-security-council-maintenance> accessed 30 November 2020.

[99] International Institute for Sustainable Development, 'UN Security Council Addresses Climate Change as a Security Risk' (IISD, 12 July 2018) <http://sdg.iisd.org/news/un-security-council-addresses-climate-change-as-a-security-risk/> accessed 20 October 2019; Andreas M Kravik, 'The Security Council and Climate Change—Too Hot to Handle?' (*EJIL:Talk!*, 26 April 2018) <https://www.ejiltalk.org/the-security-council-and-climate-change-too-hot-to-handle/> accessed 20 October 2019.

[100] See eg The Center for Climate and Security, 'Tag Archives: UN Security Council' (CCS, 2019) <https://climateandsecurity.org/tag/un-security-council/> accessed 20 October 2019.

[101] See Interpol (n 84) Strategic Goal 4.

[102] 'Strategy' (Interpol, 2019) <https://www.interpol.int/About-INTERPOL/Priorities> accessed 20 October 2019.

[103] 'Dialogue on an Effective Multilateral Policing Architecture Against Global Threats' (Interpol, 2019) <https://www.interpol.int/How-we-work/Dialogue-on-an-effective-multilateral-policing-architecture-against-global-threats> accessed 20 October 2019.

Working Group was established to propose means of strengthening Interpol's governance structure.[104] Unfortunately, despite an explicit request in the resolution of the IGA to make public the reflection paper on this subject,[105] neither this paper nor the recommendations under the Interpol 2020 initiative for an organizational reform process[106] are currently publicly available, which makes it difficult to ensure a transparent discussion around how to overcome current governance challenges.

2. Halting Abusive Access to Interpol Networks and Political Persecution

As Interpol seeks to integrate law enforcement cooperation worldwide, the organization has become both a tool to further international relations and a source of friction amongst its Members seeking to promote their national interests. As such, the neutrality requirement in Article 3 of the Constitution remains vital.[107] Interpol has narrowed its mission to exclude crimes of a political, military, religious, or racial character, but none of these concepts are clearly defined in international law. The ability to refuse extradition or prosecution of a foreign national based on the relevant mutual legal assistance treaties or other applicable conventions remains a powerful diplomatic tool, serving as a political statement or even refuge from an oppressive government. Member States retain this power and, therefore, a warrant transmitted by Interpol triggers only a provisional arrest, which must be followed by formal extradition procedures. These, in turn, trigger all the traditional objections to international mutual legal assistance.[108]

Remedies can only achieve results where the regulatory basis provides clear objectives. Interpol's inherently conflicting goals of pledging neutrality while simultaneously seeking to assist all governments and safeguard individuals from political persecution cannot be solved without balancing the interests involved.[109] This requires an assessment of Article 3's explicit embargo on alerts of a political, military, religious, or racial nature. Article 34(3) of the Rules on the Processing of Data provides further details about the criteria to be considered regarding potential breaches of Article 3's neutrality clause.[110]

Since Interpol's inception, the concept of a political crime has undergone two major reformulations. With the adoption of the test of predominance, Interpol took a stance of non-intervention in political cases and insisted on a case-by-case assessment. In 1984, Interpol adopted two resolutions that further developed these principles.[111] The location of a political crime, such as an act of terrorism, would be the predominant consideration in deciding whether to cooperate.[112] Acts of terrorism committed within a conflict area would be considered political crimes and international cooperation could

[104] Interpol Resolution 15, GA-2018-87-RES-15. [105] Interpol Resolution 6, AG-86-RES-6.
[106] Interpol Resolution AGN-87-RES-15; Interpol Resolution AGN-85-RES-02.
[107] Gottlieb (n 22) 153. [108] Schöndorf-Haubold (n 11) 1735. [109] Gottlieb (n 22) 162.
[110] Gottlieb (n 22) 152, 164. [111] Gottlieb (n 22) 148–9.
[112] Resolution AGN/53/RES/7 (n 81).

not be sought. If the terrorist act occurred outside the area of conflict, however, the prohibition on international cooperation could be lifted. Although the concept of national sovereignty remains strong within the Interpol framework, the 1984 resolutions indicate a willingness to recognize terrorism as a transnational concept. Later reforms broadened the definition to include membership in a terrorist organization as a non-political crime.[113] Interpol issued a 'repository of practice' for the application of Article 3 in an effort to provide guidance to practitioners with respect to the provision's interpretation but this has not been updated since 2013.[114]

The 'test of predominance'[115] has made the CCF's mandate more complex and holistic.[116] While today suspected membership in a terrorist organization can trigger a Red Notice, it must still be ascertained that the Notice does not put Interpol's political neutrality at risk, complies with standard principles of mutual legal assistance (such as the *non-refoulement* principle, the legal position of asylum seekers, and dual criminality), and does not put an individual at risk of political persecution.[117] An initial glance at the narrow interpretation of Article 3 reveals a transformation of terrorist offences from political crimes to 'alertable crimes', but also a commitment by Interpol not to assist political persecution by rogue States.[118] A more in-depth look, however, makes it apparent that these changes are the consequences of Interpol's attempt to balance its role as a stakeholder in the global fight against terrorism with its commitment to political neutrality and accountability for particular alerts.[119]

3. Protection of Individual Rights

By citing its obligation under Article 2 of the Convention to ensure and promote international police cooperation 'in the spirit of the Universal Declaration of Human Rights', Interpol stresses its commitment to human rights in the context of cross-border law enforcement.[120] One important component of this is compliance with Article 3's limits

[113] Interpol Resolution AG-2004-RES-18 (2004).

[114] Repository of Practice on Article 3, see 'INTERPOL's Constitution Forbids It from Undertaking Any Matter of a Predominantly Political, Military, Religious or Racial Nature' (Interpol, 18 September 2012) <https://www.interpol.int/News-and-Events/News/2012/INTERPOL-s-Constitution-forbids-it-from-undertaking-any-matter-of-a-predominantly-political-military-religious-or-racial-nature> accessed 20 October 2019; cf Schöndorf-Haubold (n 11) 1737.

[115] Foreseen, for example, in Interpol Resolution AGN-20-RES-11.

[116] Interpol Resolution AGN/63/RES/9 (1994); cf Schöndorf-Haubold (n 11) 1721, 1728.

[117] Gottlieb (n 22) 135, 164.

[118] cf Schöndorf-Haubold (n 11) 1721.

[119] Julia Jansson, 'Building Resilience, Demolishing Accountability? The Role of Europol in Counter-Terrorism' (2018) 28 Policing and Society 432, 434–6; Mathieu Deflem/Lindsay C Maybin, 'Interpol and the Policing of International Terrorism: Developments and Dynamics since September 11' in Lynne L Snowden/Brad C Whitsel (eds), *Terrorism: Research, Readings and Realities* (Prentice Hall 2005) 189–90.

[120] 'INTERPOL Implements New Rules on Processing of Police Information' (Interpol, 3 July 2012) <https://www.interpol.int/News-and-Events/News/2012/INTERPOL-implements-new-rules-on-processing-of-police-information> accessed 20 October 2019.

on Interpol activity, namely that the Organization is not allowed to assist in cases that pose a risk of political, ethnic, or religious persecution.[121]

In line with Interpol's 2015 refugee policy, a Red Notice will be in general withdrawn where status as a recognized asylum seeker or refugee can be confirmed by the country of refuge and the Notice comes from the prosecuting country.[122] The sensitivity of the issue is evident as the discussion about misuse of Red Notices did not start with the Turkish government asking for Turkish nationals who were seeking political asylum following the failed 2016 coup d'état or the Red Notices issued by the Chinese government for Uighurs who had received asylum in European countries.[123] The language in resolutions from both the UN and the IGA addressing concerns about the risk of abuse of asylum status by perpetrators of terrorist acts rather than the risk of Red Notices being abused against refugees demonstrates the controversial nature of the issue.[124] In the policy's application, the level of scrutiny (such as whether or not information from human rights organizations is considered) remains unclear and the public 'repertory of practice' does not clarify this either.

In principle, the importance of respecting human rights has been recognized by Interpol since 1949 when the IGA adopted a resolution condemning 'all acts of violence or inhuman treatment', including 'those contrary to human dignity committed by the police in the exercise of their judicial and criminal police duties'.[125] Article 2(a) of Interpol's Rules on the Processing of Data explicitly states that Interpol will have due respect for the basic rights of individuals when processing data.[126] The Organization works to achieve this via CCF's crucial role in providing a forum for correction or deletion of alerts. Yet, the CCF has itself conceded that compliance with Article 2 is difficult to assess, as it requires distinguishing between a possible breach of individual rights and systemic malfunctions of the human rights system in the country.[127]

Because States exchange information via Interpol on a voluntary basis, it is essential to maintain trust between Interpol and its Member States, as well as between States themselves, to foster participation in cross-border cooperation. With time, the protection of individual rights will depend on the implementation of new remedies, particularly at

[121] Gottlieb (n 22) 164.

[122] Overall Interpol's refugee policy remains vague, despite its formal endorsement through IGA Resolution, see Interpol Resolution No 9, GA-2017-86-RES-9 (2017). Excerpts can be found at 'Interpol Text on Refugee Policy—Excerpts' (*Fair Trials*, 2019) <https://www.fairtrials.org/wp-content/uploads/INTERPOL-TEXT-ON-REFUGEE-POLICY.pdf> accessed 20 October 2019.

[123] For an overview of cases, see Policy Department for External Relations (n 73) annex B. See also eg Charles R Both, 'International Police Force or Tool for Harassment of Human Rights Defenders and Political Adversaries: Interpol's Rift with the Human Rights Community' (2002) 8 ILSA Journal of International and Comparative Law 357, 359; Mario Savino, 'Global Administrative Law Meets "Soft" Powers: The Uncomfortable Case of Interpol Red Notice' (2011) 43 NYU Journal of International Law and Policy 263, 291–5; 'New Stories of INTERPOL Abuse Emphasise the Need for Reform' (*Fair Trials*, 19 December 2014) <https://www.fairtrials.org/node/717> accessed 20 October 2019.

[124] See references in Interpol Resolution AGN/86/RES/09.

[125] 'Legal documents' (Interpol, 2019) <https://www.interpol.int/Who-we-are/Legal-framework/Legal-documents> accessed 20 October 2019.

[126] 'Commission for the Control of INTERPOL's File (CCF)' (n 24).

[127] CCF (n 78) para 50.

the domestic level.[128] As long as States are unwilling to disclose all evidence underlying arrest warrants or to provide legal aid to persons who seek to challenge a Red Notice, these hurdles become a great challenge to the protection of international human rights.

F. Outlook

Interpol's growing importance in the global security architecture has gone far beyond its initial role as communication channel for national law enforcement authorities. Its key position as an information broker has made Interpol a stakeholder in UN and EU counter-terrorism operations and in many other fields. But its operations remain outside regular regimes of checks and balances. Recent reforms shed light on the need for accountability and protection of individual rights in transnational policing. The establishment of an internal remedy system may save Interpol's privileges and provide some leeway in national jurisdictions. The pledge of neutrality and independence in Interpol's actions in Article 3 of the Constitution and the promise to comply with the basic principles of mutual legal assistance and to protect individuals from abusive access to its networks add to a more reliable international legal regime. Rogue States may still be tempted to send arrest warrants to Interpol, hoping for little scrutiny and complex correction tools. That is, even if a warrant is not executed, life becomes exceedingly difficult for anyone listed in Interpol's channels and the process to be delisted is not only lengthy, but also costly.

So long as Interpol remains outside judicial supervision and detached from an institutionalized political framework, it must find a way to resolve the conflict that stems from its traditional role of facilitating cross-border law enforcement and its new commitment to individual rights, and data protection in particular. If it can achieve a sufficient standard of accountability in international law, it will have made an important contribution to modern international rules in the field of international policing.

Having to address this dichotomy between efficient law enforcement support and protection of human rights is not unique to Interpol, but, in it, it is especially difficult because of a weak accountability structure. External pressure to address this conflict in a more effective way has driven recent reforms within Interpol, but more will be required[129] if it wishes to preserve the credibility underpinning its rise in importance in the global security architecture since the attacks of 9/11.

Note

"In memoriam of James B. Jacobs, a committed advocate of police accountability".

[128] Schöndorf-Haubold (n 11) 1726.

[129] See eg recommendations in *Fair Trial* (n 69).

CHAPTER 56

NON-GOVERNMENTAL ORGANIZATIONS

Their Relevance and Impact in the International Law of Global Security

CHRISTINA BINDER

A. Introduction

SECURITY is a complex concept in today's ever-complicated world. The traditional State-centric approach to security has been complemented, albeit not replaced, by a more human-oriented aspect. With security threats stemming from both natural and man-made disasters including civil wars, poverty, climate change, and the growing terrorist threats, global security has many dimensions. Each of these endangers the security of individuals, and has given rise to more comprehensive approaches to security.

This broader understanding of global security allows for the increased involvement of non-governmental organizations (NGOs). In the traditional or classic approach, conceptualizing security as conterminous with 'high politics', where States hold tight control of information flows, mistrust of civil society is common[1] and little space left for NGO and civil society involvement.[2] The broadening of security has opened the traditionally State-centric area of 'high politics' to new actors. Today, NGOs may participate in the security discourse as increasingly relevant stakeholders, ensuring that

[1] Peter Mayer, 'Civil Society Participation in International Security Organizations: The Cases of NATO and OSCE' in Jens Steffek et al (eds), *Civil Society Participation in European and Global Governance* (Palgrave Macmillan 2008) 116.

[2] ibid.

a focus on human rights and the common interests of humankind is maintained in security debates.[3]

This chapter will explore how NGOs have engaged with international law in the field of global security and assess their contribution in developing the international legal regime. It will discuss whether NGOs have shaped relevant international standards, and if so, in what manner; whether they have influenced their implementation and enforcement; what the applicable international legal framework is and whether the ways in which NGOs engage with it have changed in view of the additional human security-related dimensions.

In addressing these questions, the chapter is organized as follows. First, the role of NGOs in global and regional security arrangements will be examined. Following that, their contribution in the field of global security in terms of standard-setting, norm application, and interpretation, as well as with regard to compliance and enforcement will be dealt with in areas where the individual is centre stage: international humanitarian law (IHL), international criminal law, and international human rights law (IHRL). Then, the applicable international legal framework regulating engagement by NGOs will be examined. Finally, the discussion will turn on whether NGO practice has been influenced by the ever-changing global security landscape. The last section concludes.

B. The Role of NGOs in Global and Regional Security Arrangements

The growing role of NGOs in the contemporary security architecture is particularly visible in relation to global and regional security arrangements. Generally, the broader the security concept adhered to by an international organization, the more room is given to NGO involvement. Unsurprisingly then, amongst security-focused organizations, by far the greatest NGO engagement has taken place in the context of the Organization for Security and Co-operation in Europe (OSCE), given its comprehensive security concept with particular emphasis on the human dimension. Non-governmental organizations' engagement with the OSCE has grown steadily since the end of the Cold War, with a turning point in the mid-1990s alongside the OSCE's increased institutionalization. Accordingly, considerable leeway is left for NGOs such as Amnesty International (AI)

[3] This contribution understands non-governmental organizations (NGOs) as '(…) [referring] to those organizations founded by private individuals, which are independent of States, oriented towards the rule of law, pursue public rather than private goals as an objective, and possess a minimum of organizational structure' (Stephan Hobe, 'Non-Governmental Organizations' MPEPIL (OUP, March 2010) MN 5; similarly ECOSOC 'Arrangements for Consultation with Non-Governmental Organizations' Res 1296 (XLIV) (23 May 1968) paras 8–14).

or Human Rights Watch (HRW), which participate in OSCE working groups on an equal footing with governmental delegations.[4] Additionally, OSCE field operations of long duration usually reach out to local NGOs in light of their knowledge about the political and social conditions on the ground.[5]

In comparison, other security-related institutions engage with NGOs far less. The UN Security Council (UNSC), the organ with primary responsibility for the maintenance of international peace and security under Article 24 UN Charter, engages only on an ad hoc and rather sporadic basis with NGOs.[6] NGOs enjoy no official status or standing before it. Rather, such organizations tend to lobby the Council membership informally.[7] Even though NGO activities in collaboration with the UNSC have intensified since the end of the Cold War, these remain minor and largely informal.[8]

Similarly, NATO is generally shut to civil society. No institutionalized NGO involvement in NATO policy planning, policymaking or implementation exists.[9] The North Atlantic Organization does not give NGOs access to deliberations or even its premises; NGOs are consequently deprived of any opportunity to lobby State representatives or NATO staff directly.[10] However, NATO officials meet with selected NGO officials (such as AI, HRW, the International Crisis Group (ICG)) from time to time for informal exchanges of views and other sporadic discussions.[11] These types of exchanges have, at least, increased over time. NGOs have also seized the opportunity to liaise when NATO engages in crisis management or post-conflict peacebuilding in situations such as in the former Yugoslavia or Afghanistan.[12] This notwithstanding, the role of NGOs in that respect remains insignificant.

Thus, NGO involvement, especially within 'high-politics' security-related arrangements such as the UNSC or NATO, is at best nascent, despite a certain trend towards their increasing involvement. This trend corresponds to the growing role of NGOs in various areas of international law in the field of global security.

[4] Mayer (n 1) 131.

[5] ibid. For details see OSCE, 'How We Work: OSCE in the Field' <www.osce.org/whatistheosce> accessed 1 May 2019.

[6] James A Paul, 'NGOs and the Security Council' (Global Policy Forum, 2004) <www.globalpolicy.org/images/pdfs/NGOs_and_the_Security_Council_2004_2.pdf> accessed 1 May 2019. See likewise the commitment to a stronger relationship with civil society in UNSC Res 2171 (2014) para 24 as well as the call for more civil society engagement by the International Service for Human Rights <www.ishr.ch/news/un-security-council-strengthen-relationship-civil-society-and-focus-human-rights-prevent> accessed 1 May 2019.

[7] See eg Martin Binder, 'The Politicization of International Security Institutions: The UN Security Council and NGOs' (Discussion Paper SP IV 2008–305, Wissenschaftszentrum Berlin für Sozialforschung 2008) 12ff.

[8] ibid. [9] Mayer (n 1) 124. [10] ibid 124.

[11] ibid 122ff. [12] ibid 124.

C. Areas of NGO Engagement with the International Law of Global Security

NGOs are diverse creatures. Scholarship traditionally differentiates between advocacy NGOs, engaging less 'on the ground', and functional or operational NGOs, such as humanitarian relief organizations.[13] Equally diverse is their role and engagement in various areas of global security. Overall, one may distinguish between their role, first, in the development of international law (standard-setting); secondly, in the judicial application and interpretation of international law (with focus on international criminal law and IHRL); and thirdly, in compliance monitoring and the enforcement of international law, including humanitarian assistance (reconstruction and relief operations) and peace mediation.[14] These three functions will be examined in turn with particular focus on the contribution of NGOs in the shaping and development of the international legal framework in the field of global security.

1. Standard-Setting

In the past twenty-five years, NGOs have actively participated in the development of international standards in the field of global security, particularly through engaging in different stages of treaty creation.[15] On the one hand, NGOs contribute to agenda-setting and raising awareness regarding the need for binding rules in particular fields through lobbying activities. Pertinent examples here are the campaigns for a ban on anti-personnel landmines, the establishment of an international criminal court, or, currently, the lobbying for the complete ban of fully autonomous weapons.[16]

[13] C de Jonge Oudraat/Virginia Haufler, *Global Governance and the Role of NGOs in International Peace and Security* (33 AICGS Policy Report, American Institute for Contemporary German Studies 2008) 14ff. Examples of advocacy NGOs are AI and HRW and of operational NGOs Oxfam and *Médecins Sans Frontières*.

[14] cf the classification by Steve Charnovitz, 'Nongovernmental Organizations and International Law' (2006) 100 AJIL 348.

[15] Generally, see Kal Raustiala, 'NGOs in International Treaty-Making' in Duncan B Hollis (ed), *The Oxford Guide to Treaties* (OUP 2012) 150ff.

[16] For details, Kenneth R Rutherford, 'The Evolving Arms Control Agenda: Implications of the Role of NGOs in Banning Antipersonnel Landmines' (200) 53 World Politics 74; Kenneth Anderson, 'The Ottawa Convention Banning Landmines, the Role of International Non-governmental Organizations and the Idea of Civil Society' (2000) 11 EJIL 91, 104; as regards the International Criminal Court (ICC), Michael J Struett, *The Politics of Constructing the International Criminal Court: NGOs, Discourse, and Agency* (Palgrave Macmillan 2008) 80, 83ff. For further information on the campaign led by HRW, see HRW <www.stopkillerrobots.org/> accessed 1 May 2019.

Beyond this, NGOs have participated in the negotiations of the respective treaties. For example, the 1998 Rome Conference for the establishment of an International Criminal Court,[17] and the drafting of the Anti-Personnel Landmine Convention (Ottawa Convention)[18] saw extensive NGO participation, with 236 NGOs being accredited in Rome,[19] and more than 1000 participating in the anti-landmine drafting process.[20] In these processes, NGOs focused on information, education, and service rather than on advocacy.[21] Since they were not entitled to officially speak or participate in the deliberations on the draft text for either the International Criminal Court (ICC) Statute or the Ottawa Convention,[22] they engaged in the process informally. They lobbied governments to stick to 'good positions' and supported especially smaller delegations with fewer resources, with information and relevant expertise.[23] In doing so, NGOs cooperated with each other. For example, the Coalition for the International Criminal Court (CICC) adopted common positions on major points, like the independent prosecutor and the de-politicization of the ICC.[24] Likewise, the International Campaign to Ban Landmines (ICBL) aimed to speak with one voice.[25] Non-governmental organizations also maintained active media relations; this way, they raised public awareness and kept the ICC and the Ottawa Convention in the news.

Due to their mostly informal participation, the NGOs' substantive influence on the treaty texts is difficult to measure. Ultimately, NGOs seem to have succeeded in making the treaties stronger from a human security-related perspective. In the case of the ICC, examples of this include the creation of an independent prosecutor; the ICC's automatic jurisdiction; victim participation; and the ICC Statute's application to internal armed conflicts.[26] With respect to the Ottawa Convention, NGOs seem to have strengthened

[17] Mahnoush H Arsanjani, 'The Rome Statute of the International Criminal Court' (1999) 93 AJIL 22, 23; also Zoe Pearson, 'Non-Governmental Organisations and the International Criminal Court: Changing Landscapes of International Law' (2006) 39 Cornell International Law Journal 243, 250ff.

[18] Nicola Short, 'The Role of NGOs in the Ottawa Process to Ban Landmines' (1999) 4 International Negotiation 481.

[19] Anna-Karin Lindblom, *Non-Governmental Organisations in International Law* (CUP 2005) 103; Struett (n 16) 106ff; William Pace/Mark Thieroff, 'Participation of Non-Governmental Organizations' in Roy S Lee (ed), *The International Criminal Court: The Making of the Rome Statute, Issues, Negotiations, Results* (Kluwer Law International 1999) 309ff.

[20] David C Atwood, 'Implementing Ottawa: Continuity and Change in the Roles of NGOs' (1999) Disarmament Forum 19, 20ff.

[21] Struett (n 16) 109ff; Pearson (n 17) 272ff; Lindblom (n 19) 472.

[22] In Rome, NGOs were allowed to participate (only) in formal meetings, to issue statements at opening and closing, and to provide written input. See UNGA Res 52/160 (15 December 1997) para 9; 'Summary records of the plenary meetings and of the meetings of the Committee of the Whole' UN Diplomatic Conference of Plenipotentiaries on the Establishment of an International Criminal Court (Rome 15 June–17 July 1998) UN Doc A/CONF.183/13 (Vol II) 60 (Rules of Procedure 63 and 64). As regards the Ottawa process see Short (n 18) 486ff.

[23] Some governments even included NGOs in their delegations, for example, during the Ottawa process. See Short (n 18) 487.

[24] Lindblom (n 19) 477; Silvia A Fernández de Gurmendi, 'The Role of the International Prosecutor' in Lee (n 19) 177.

[25] Atwood (n 20) 21; Short (n 18) 484.

[26] See eg M Cherif Bassiouni, *The Statute of the International Criminal Court: A Documentary History* (Transnational Publishers 1998) 25–6; cited after Struett (n 16) 113, 117; also Short (n 18) 488.

the text as regards its scope (particularly the definition of landmines) and the rules on international cooperation, implementation, transparency, and monitoring.[27] Non-governmental organizations also assisted in making both the Ottawa and the ICC processes more inclusive, in particular with respect to the Global South, especially African governments.[28]

Furthermore, and following the adoption of the treaties, NGOs have promoted their implementation. The CICC, for example, has launched a campaign to increase ICC Statute ratification.[29] Similar pressure is exercised by the ICBL for the Ottawa Convention.[30] Today, there are 123 States Parties to the ICC Statute and 164 parties to the Ottawa Convention.[31] The relative success of both conventions may be partly attributed to NGOs.

2. Judicial Application and Interpretation

From another footing, NGOs have contributed to the judicial application of international criminal law and IHRL and have shaped the development and interpretation of the relevant norms, especially by helping to initiate cases and by means of *amicus curiae* submissions.

Generally, NGOs have fostered norm application by advocating amongst relevant stakeholders for the acceptance of the respective institutions. For example, in the field of international criminal law, NGOs have attempted to explain the role of international criminal tribunals to local populations, engaging in relevant outreach activities.[32] They have also facilitated the work of these tribunals through the provision of relevant information and support. Operating on the ground, NGOs often witness the crimes committed and possess evidence which is important for their prosecution.[33] They may also bring major violations of IHRL and IHL to the attention of international criminal tribunals. This is sometimes done through formal procedures. For example, the Rome Statute allows NGOs to submit communications regarding the commission of international crimes to the Prosecutor.[34] In total, more than 10,000 communications have been

[27] ibid. [28] ibid 489. [29] In detail Struett (n 16) 134ff. [30] Atwood (n 20) 19ff.

[31] Rome Statute of the International Criminal Court 2187 UNTS 90 (ICC Statute); Convention on the Prohibition of the Use, Stockpiling, Production and Transfer of Anti-Personnel Mines and on Their Destruction 2056 UNTS 211(Ottawa Convention). See Section C.3 for NGOs in verification.

[32] Kjersti Lohne, 'Global Civil Society, the ICC, and Legitimacy in International Criminal Justice' in Cecilia Bailliet et al (eds), *The Legitimacy of International Criminal Tribunals* (CUP 2017) 449, 458 for references.

[33] Human Rights First, 'The Role of Human Rights NGOs in Relation to ICC Investigations' (Discussion Paper, Human Rights First, 2004) <https://www.globalpolicy.org/images/pdfs/0904hrficc.pdf> accessed 30 November 2020.

[34] ICC Statute (n 31) art 15: '(…) 2. The Prosecutor shall analyse the seriousness of the information received. For this purpose, he or she may seek additional information from (…) *non-governmental organisations* (…).' (emphasis added). William Schabas, *The International Criminal Court: A Commentary on the Rome Statute* (2nd edn, OUP 2016) 402ff.

submitted since the ICC's establishment.[35] While it is quantitatively difficult to assess how many communications came from NGOs, at least in some cases NGOs have had an obvious impact on the opening of preliminary examinations.[36]

Furthermore, NGOs have documented patterns of human rights violations and have conducted forensic examinations. For example, the Humanitarian Law Documentation Project in Kosovo, a 1999 project of the ICG, accumulated 4,700 records from victims and witnesses and handed them over to the International Criminal Tribunal for the former Yugoslavia (ICTY).[37] In the ICC, evidence submitted by NGOs seems to have played a role in the course of preliminary investigations as well as concerning decisions on the admissibility of a case.[38] Non-governmental organization support is of particular relevance when States are unwilling to cooperate with international criminal tribunals or when tribunals face other constraints, such as difficulties in accessing the territory where the crimes were committed or when a long time has passed between the commission of crimes and their prosecution. Indeed, especially in the case of the Extraordinary Criminal Chambers in the Courts of Cambodia (ECCC), NGOs substantively supported the gathering of evidence for the Khmer Rouge crimes committed in the 1970s. This proved instrumental, given the ECCC's limited financial and personnel resources.[39]

Engaging with human rights institutions, NGOs have contributed to the establishment of State responsibility and the promotion of strong human rights standards in the context of global security. Non-governmental organizations have brought several complaints for alleged human rights violations in the context of counter-terrorism. Recently, NGOs filed cases against the United Kingdom in relation to data protection under the country's surveillance laws before the European Court of Human Rights (ECtHR).[40] Broader litigation options are provided for NGOs in other regional human rights protection systems. While in the European Convention system NGOs must not act on behalf

[35] For details Kristy Brimelow et al, 'Shaping the Law: Civil Society Influence at International Criminal Courts' (International Law Programme Meeting Summary, Chatham House, 2016) 5 <www.chathamhouse.org/sites/default/files/events/160125-meeting-summary-shaping-law-civil-society-influence-international-criminal-courts.pdf> accessed 1 May 2019.

[36] For example, in June 2014 the ICC Prosecutor reopened its investigations on Iraq on the basis of ICC Statute (n 31) art 15 communications received from NGOs in relation to the responsibility of UK military officials for war crimes. See Communication submitted by the European Centre for Constitutional and Human Rights and Public Interest Lawyers, 'Preliminary Examinations: Iraq/UK' (ICC, Office of the Prosecutor) <https://www.icc-cpi.int/iraq> accessed 1 May 2019.

[37] ICG, 'Reality Demands: Documenting Violations of International Humanitarian Law in Kosovo 1999' (International Crisis Group) <www.intl-crisis-group.org/projects/showreport.cfm?reportid=57> accessed 1 May 2019; Oudraat/Haufler (n 13) 24.

[38] See eg ICC, 'Report of Preliminary Activities 2017' (Office of the Prosecutor, 4 December 2017) para 74 <www.icc-cpi.int/itemsDocuments/2017-PE-rep/2017-otp-rep-PE_ENG.pdf> accessed 1 May 2019.

[39] Chea Leang/William Smith, 'The Early Experience of the Extraordinary Chambers in the Courts of Cambodia' in Roberto Bellelli (ed), *International Criminal Justice. Law and Practice from the Rome Statute to Its Review* (Routledge 2010) 163.

[40] *Big Brother Watch and Others v UK*, App Nos 58,170/13, 62,322/14, 24,960/15, 13 September 2018. See Marko Milanovic, 'ECtHR Judgment in Big Brother Watch v UK' (*EJIL:Talk!*, 17 September 2018) <https://www.ejiltalk.org/ecthr-judgment-in-big-brother-watch-v-uk/> accessed 1 May 2019.

of victims but have to be themselves affected in their rights,[41] in the Inter-American or the African system, NGOs may also file complaints on behalf of victims in the form of *actio popularis*.[42] However, relatively little use of such mechanisms has been made so far.

The contribution of NGOs is perhaps most visible from the perspective of the individual, especially in terms of victims' rights.[43] Non-governmental organizations have fostered stronger links between victims, the Prosecutor, and the ICC.[44] They have provided victims with support, including psychological, medical, and humanitarian aid; they have organized victim participation in proceedings and reparations; and have trained lawyers to represent victims. The role of NGOs in relation to victims is formally recognized in the ICC Statute. Article 75(3)[45] presents a successful avenue for NGOs to make submissions to the ICC on reparations.[46] In proceedings before human rights tribunals, NGOs also grant extensive support to victims of human rights violations, amongst others, by providing legal advice and representing victims before the ECtHR. A prominent example of such practice was the representation by lawyers from the Kurdish Human Rights Project of victims in cases against Turkey.[47]

On top of this, NGOs have shaped the interpretation and application of norms in criminal law and IHRL through *amicus curiae* briefs. *Amicus curiae* briefs are a means to provide relevant legal (or factual) information to a tribunal without being party to a case.[48] The Rules of Procedure and Evidence (RPE) of international criminal tribunals provide avenues for the submission of such briefs.[49] While these rules are not only directed to NGOs but are phrased in more general terms, NGOs have brought *amicus curiae* on this basis. In 2015, out of the 30 NGO applications to file *amicus* submissions,

[41] See the 'victim requirement' of art 34 of the European Convention on Human Rights ETS No 5 (ECHR). More recently, the European Court of Human Rights (ECtHR) seems to move towards allowing NGOs to file complaints on behalf of individuals who are not capable of doing so themselves, see *Center for Legal Resources on Behalf of Valentin Câmpeanu v Romania*, App No 47848/08, 17 July 2014.

[42] American Convention on Human Rights, 1144 UNTS 123 (ACHR) art 44; African Charter on Human and Peoples' Rights 1520 UNTS 217 arts 55, 45; G Breton-Le Goff, 'NGOs' Perspectives on Non-State Actors' in Jean d'Aspremont (ed), *Participants in the International Legal System: Multiple Perspectives on Non-State Actors in International Law* (Routledge 2011) 253.

[43] ibid 256ff. [44] Lohne (n 32) 462. [45] For details, Schabas (n 34) 1136ff.

[46] For example, in the *Lubanga* and *Katanga* reparations hearings, NGOs were allowed to submit written representations. *Prosecutor v Thomas Lubanga Dyilo* (Judgment) ICC-01/04–01/06 (3 March 2015); see also Redress Trust observations pursuant to art 75 of the Rome Statute, *Prosecutor v Germain Katanga* (Redress Trust) ICC-01/04–01/07 (15 May 2015). See Brimelow et al (n 35) 6 for details.

[47] Breton-Le Goff (n 42) 255.

[48] Generally, Herve Ascencio, 'L'amicus curiae devant les jurisdictions internationales' (2001) 105 Revue Générale de Droit International Public 897; Sarah Williams/Hannah Woolaver, 'The Role of the Amicus Curiae Before International Criminal Tribunals' (2006) 6 International Criminal Law Review 151.

[49] Rule 103 of the ICC Rules of Procedure and Evidence, ICC-ASP/1/3 and Corr.1 (Part II-A) (as amended); Rule 74 International Criminal Tribunal for the former Yugoslavia (ICTY) Rules of Procedure and Evidence, UN Doc IT/32 and of the International Criminal Tribunal for Rwanda (ICTR) Rules of Procedure and Evidence, UN Doc ITR/3; Rule 74 of the Special Court on Sierra Leone (SCSL) Rules of Procedure and Evidence (as amended) <http://www.rscsl.org/Documents/RPE.pdf> accessed 12 February 2020; Rule 33 of the Extraordinary Chambers in the Courts of Cambodia Internal Rules (as amended) <https://www.eccc.gov.kh/en/document/legal/internal-rules> accessed 12 February 2020.

the ICC had accepted roughly one-third.[50] The ICTY, for its part, even invited *amicus briefs* in several cases (eg, in *Karadzic*[51]), displaying a proactive stance. The Special Court for Sierra Leone (SCSL) and the ECCC also sought assistance from NGOs by means of *amicus curiae*.[52]

Most notably, NGOs played a crucial role in the *Akayesu* case before the International Criminal Tribunal for Rwanda (ICTR), where the Prosecutor amended the indictment to include crimes of sexual violence after an NGO brief had requested so.[53] For their part, the SCSL and the ECCC seem to have at times explicitly adopted the conclusions reached by the *amici*.[54] More difficult is to assess the impact of *amicus curiae* briefs in relation to the ICC and the ICTY.[55] Overall, international criminal tribunals seem to have welcomed the input of NGOs especially when it has provided support to their work from a legal or a factual perspective.

Similarly, before human rights tribunals *amicus curiae* briefs have been crucial in influencing norm application and interpretation. While their acceptance lies in principle in the discretion of the ECtHR and the Inter-American Court of Human Rights, both institutions have been open to *amicus curiae* by NGOs.[56] Sometimes, their interpretation of norms in the field of global security, such as in the case of forced disappearances,[57] has been influenced by these. This exemplifies how NGOs have shaped the human rights parameters for State measures adopted in certain areas of global security.

3. Compliance Monitoring and International Law Enforcement

The engagement of NGOs with the enforcement of international law in the area of global security is diverse.[58] On the one hand, NGOs push for State compliance by engaging in

[50] Brimelow et al (n 35) 2; Schabas (n 34) 402.

[51] *Prosecutor v Karadzic* (Decision on Application for Leave to Submit an *Amicus Curiae* Brief) ICTY-IT-95-5/18-AR98bis.1, 21 September 2012.

[52] Brimelow et al (n 35) 4.

[53] *Prosecutor v AJP Akayesu* (Judgment) ICTR-96-4-T, 2 September 1998, paras 504, 594. See Breton-Le Goff (n 42) 251.

[54] As evidenced, for example, in the summarized briefs of the SCSL. See Brimelow et al (n 35) 4.

[55] Neither institution reproduces *amicus curiae* briefs at the beginning of judgments or makes any explicit reference.

[56] See Breton-Le Goff (n 42) 254; Charles Moyer, 'The Role of *Amicus Curiae* Briefs in the Inter-American Court of Human Rights' (Inter-American Court of Human Rights) <https://www.corteidh.or.cr/tablas/a11770.pdf> accessed 30 November 2020.

[57] *Kurt v Turkey*, App No 24276/94, 25 May 1998; *Timurtas v Turkey*, App No 23531/94, 13 June 2000; Breton-Le Goff (n 42) 254.

[58] On NGOs and human rights enforcement: Christian Tomuschat, *Human Rights: Between Idealism and Realism* (2nd edn, OUP 2008) 265; Olivier De Schutter, *International Human Rights Law* (2nd edn, CUP 2014) 876; on NGOs in armed conflicts: Anja Mihr, Non-State Actors in Conflict' in Ineke Boerefijn et al (eds), *Human Rights and Conflict: Essays in Honour of Bas de Gaay Fortman* (CUP 2012) 311.

their traditional advocacy role of naming and shaming, acting as 'watchdogs'. On the other, they are involved at an operational level, through the provision of humanitarian assistance (including reconstruction and relief operations). From this distinction stems the aforementioned division between advocacy and operational NGOs.[59]

Organizations such as AI, HRW, or Relief Web are well known for their action in cases of ongoing human rights violations. By publicizing major IHRL and IHL violations, they aim at gathering public support and triggering a reaction against perpetrators and non-compliant States so as to induce a change in their behaviour. Simultaneously, such advocacy raises awareness and draws the attention of the international community to (emerging) conflicts and the human rights violations committed in their context. Ideally, this in turn stimulates (re-)actions by international institutions and other States, such as diplomatic or political pressure, economic sanctions, or even military enforcement action. Examples include, amongst others, the publication by NGOs of information concerning human rights violations in Syria;[60] the campaign against 'blood diamonds';[61] or the denunciation of the humanitarian crisis in the Mediterranean in the context of the growing refugee flows and corresponding migration policies.[62]

While it is difficult to assess their actual impact on compliance monitoring, publicizing such issues and raising awareness at least ensures that they will not go unnoticed. In doing so, NGOs have a crucial role to play in early warning.[63] For example, the OSCE High Commissioner on National Minorities regularly relies on information provided by NGOs when engaging in preventive diplomacy and conflict prevention.[64] To what extent NGOs more generally induce a change in behaviour of non-compliant States or relevant (re-)actions by the international community for IHRL and IHL violations is more complex to assess; even where changes in behaviour occur or some action is taken, it would usually be difficult to causally link this back to NGO action. Still, there are certain positive examples, such as the campaign against blood diamonds, through which NGOs seem to have pushed the UNSC to act;[65] the NGO campaign in relation to the human rights violations committed by Serbian forces in Kosovo in 1999;[66] and the

[59] Oudraat/Haufler (n 13) 14ff; Anderson (n 16) 117.

[60] See eg Syrian Network for Human Rights (SNHR) <www.sn4hr.org/> accessed 1 May 2019; Violation Documentation Center in Syria (VDC) <www.vdc-sy.net/en/> accessed 1 May 2019; Syrian Observatory for Human Rights (SOHR) <www.syriahr.com/en/> accessed 1 May 2019; Syrian Justice and Accountability Center (SJAC) <https://syriaaccountability.org> accessed 30 November 2020.

[61] Binder (n 7) 15.

[62] HRW, 'The Mediterranean Migration Crisis—Why People Flee, What the EU Should Do' (*Human Rights Watch*, 19 June 2015) <https://www.hrw.org/report/2015/06/19/mediterranean-migration-crisis/why-people-flee-what-eu-should-do> accessed 30 November 2020; Médecins sans Frontières, 'Mediterranean migration' (MSF) <www.msf.org/mediterranean-migration> accessed 1 May 2019.

[63] Pamela R Aall, 'NGOs and Conflict Management' (United States Institute of Peace, 1996) 7 <www.usip.org/sites/default/files/pwks5.pdf> accessed 1 May 2019; Oudraat/Haufler (n 13) 24.

[64] As stated by Mayer (n 1) 131.

[65] Binder (n 7) 15 with further references.

[66] In this sense, Oudraat/Haufler (n 13) 24.

lobbying of the UNSC to take, at least some, action in the Rwandan genocide.[67] At the internal or domestic level, naming and shaming has proved particularly fruitful in States with leaders 'who are sensitive to their international reputation.'[68]

Of course, there are also other, including more formalized, means, apart from naming and shaming, to draw attention to human rights violations or other issues critical to global security. For example, NGOs play an active role in monitoring and verifying compliance with the Ottawa Convention. As was observed in this regard: '(…) the Ban the Landmine Campaign unofficially monitors and verifies the 1997 Landmine Treaty through "citizen verification" with 115 researchers in 85 countries. The campaign reports not only on state compliance with the treaty but even on countries that are not party to the treaty.'[69] Non-governmental organizations may also bring human rights violations to the attention of treaty monitoring bodies or the Human Rights Council through shadow reports alongside the State reporting procedure.[70] Still, since reporting cycles are long, these mechanisms mainly aim at a mid- or long-term impact, such as changes in the legal and institutional framework of a State. They are thus of only limited relevance in the context of global security where gross human rights violations usually require immediate action.

In addition to their advocacy role, NGOs contribute directly to compliance with, and the enforcement of, international (humanitarian) law through their humanitarian assistance and relief work in conflict zones. Especially operational NGOs, which are involved in programme and policy implementation, are rather active in that respect. They deliver, for example, food and services during conflicts or medical supplies. Examples include the active involvement of *Médecins Sans Frontières* in providing health care in South Sudan (with more than 1 million consultations in 2017),[71] and the distribution of food by the German NGO *Welthungerhilfe*.[72]

Further, NGOs participate in post-conflict reconstruction programmes and, increasingly, in peacebuilding activities.[73] Organizations such as CARE, Oxfam, World Vision International, Save the Children, the International Rescue Committee, *Médecins Sans*

[67] Kseniya Oksamytna, 'Civil Society and the UN Security Council: Advocacy on the Rwandan Genocide' in Raffaele Marchetti (ed), *Partnerships in International Policy-Making* (Palgrave Macmillan 2017) 131ff.

[68] David Zarnett, 'Human Rights NGOs' in Gordon DiCiacomo (ed), *Human Rights. Current Issues and Controversies* (Toronto UP 2016) 125, citing Susan D Burgerman, *Moral Victories: How Activists Provoke Multilateral Action* (Cornell UP 2001).

[69] Louise Doswald-Beck, 'Participation of Non-Governmental Entities in Treaty-Making: The Case of Conventional Weapons' in Vera Gowlland-Debbas (ed), *Multilateral Treaty Making* (Kluwer Academic Publishers 2000) 41ff; Claudia Kissling, *Civil Society and Nuclear Non-Proliferation* (Routledge 2008) 9–10.

[70] eg De Schutter (n 58) 876 on State reporting including shadow reports.

[71] Médecins Sans Frontières, 'International Activity Report 2017 South Sudan' (MFS) <www.msf.org/international-activity-report-2017/south-sudan> accessed 1 May 2019.

[72] See further Welthungerhilfe (whh) <www.welthungerhilfe.de/ueber-uns/organisation/> accessed 1 May 2019.

[73] Aall (n 63) 9; Oudraat/Haufler (n 13) 16.

Frontières, and Catholic Relief Services are crucial actors in this field. These seven NGOs together manage more than 50 per cent of the global humanitarian relief resources.[74]

The important contribution of NGOs to the reduction of human suffering through relief work in conflict zones and the amount of assistance provided by them is evidenced in concrete figures and in the billions of dollars NGOs handle when performing these tasks.[75] What is more, their relevance is illustrated by the fact that they are directly addressed by States and international organizations as partners in the delivery of humanitarian assistance and aid.[76] Major donor States like Germany or the United States rely on NGOs for the delivery of humanitarian aid and assistance.[77] Even organizations such as NATO liaise with NGOs when engaging in crisis management or post-conflict peacebuilding on the ground.[78] Furthermore, the UNSC's interaction with NGOs has intensified, especially as the Council has expanded its activities in peacekeeping and post-conflict peacebuilding.[79] Thus, operational NGOs in particular have a direct role in furthering the compliance with and the enforcement of international law in the field of global security.[80]

Occasionally, NGOs engage in peace mediation and negotiations.[81] However, while there are some examples of NGO involvement in peace negotiations, overall a formal role for NGOs has been rare. [82] Likewise, the impact of their activities in this area is generally mixed. There are some successful examples, such as the talks between the Nigerian government and Biafran rebels in the 1967–70 conflict, which were hosted and facilitated by the Quakers. Still, in other cases such direct involvement in peace negotiations is far less successful.[83] Amongst the reasons for the rare and partly unsuccessful formal involvement of NGOs in peace deals is that they 'often do not have the resources or authority to make agreements stick and are prone to be manipulated by the parties in question'.[84] In light of this, their involvement in peace negotiations is often rather indirect: they run mediation and conflict resolution workshops; engage in 'track two diplomatic efforts' where influential persons, though non-officials, from both sides are brought together; or further conflict resolution at the grassroots level.[85] These efforts notwithstanding, overall, the contribution of NGOs in this appears to be minor. This may, *inter alia*, be explained by the fact that peace negotiations tend to relate to

[74] ibid.

[75] ibid 12. Also, Daniela Irrera, 'The Humanitarian System, the EU, and NGOs: The State of the Art' in Daniela Irrera (ed), *EU Emergency Response Policies and NGOs* (Palgrave Macmillan 2018) 14.

[76] See also Section E. [77] Oudraat/Haufler (n 13) 12. [78] Mayer (n 1) 124.

[79] UNSC Res 1470 (2003) para 8; also Charnovitz (n 14) 355.

[80] Note, however, that also critical voices are heard respectively. Mihr maintains, for example, that NGOs' engagement with relief may also prolong the conflict (Mihr (n 58) 313).

[81] Tilman Pradt, *Israeli–Palestinian Negotiations in the 1990s: How NGOs Facilitated the Peace Process* (Diplomica Verlag 2012) 70; Oudraat/Haufler (n 13) 23.

[82] Oudraat/Haufler (n 13) 23; eg Pradt (n 81).

[83] Oudraat/Haufler (n 13) 24; for example, the role of Sant'Egidio in Uganda in the mid-1990s was held to undermine the negotiations with the Lord's Resistance Army (LRA).

[84] Oudraat/Haufler (n 13) 24.

[85] ibid with further references.

'high-level security' politics and thus to take place in a State-centred rather than human security-centred area, which accordingly leaves little place for NGOs.

4. Appreciation

The foregoing analysis illustrates the growing engagement of NGOs in an ever-more comprehensive security landscape, where human security has an increasingly prominent place. This is true for all the areas mentioned above, namely standard-setting, norm application and interpretation, and compliance monitoring and enforcement, especially where the rights of individuals are at stake. Notwithstanding NGOs' increasing engagement in the field of global security, it seems, however, difficult to measure their actual impact on the international legal regime for two reasons: first, due to their diversity, and, secondly, because of their frequently informal means of engagement. What may be safely stated though, is that alongside the expansion of contemporary conceptions of security to encompass human security-related issues, the contribution of NGOs becomes increasingly important. With this in mind, we now turn to the international legal framework that regulates the engagement of NGOs in the field of global security.

D. International Legal Framework

Despite the increased engagement of NGOs in the field of global security, the international legal framework that regulates their activities remains limited. It seems, however, that the so far rudimentary framework is slowly expanding, especially in human security-related fields.[86]

In many of the areas discussed above, NGO engagement remains unregulated by international law or only limited rights are conferred on NGOs. NGOs usually play an informal role and have a weak position in treaty negotiations. They may be allowed to speak but usually do not have a right to vote or participate in deliberations on the draft treaty text.[87] Also naming and shaming, the traditional role of NGOs, remains mainly in the field of international politics, not of international law. Nor does international law say much about humanitarian assistance and relief efforts effectuated by NGOs.[88] Even more informal is their role in peace negotiations.

There are more formalized avenues of participation when it comes to the interaction of NGOs with international tribunals, such as in the case of norm application and interpretation. Such avenues provide for submissions (communications, applications,

[86] Generally, one may distinguish between the very acknowledgement of NGO status and the extent of the rights granted to them.

[87] See Section C.1.

[88] Claudia Barratt, *The Status of NGOs in International Humanitarian Law* (Martinus Nijhoff 2014) 181ff. Certain NGOs have adopted codes of conduct by means of self-regulation (Mihr (n 58) 314).

amicus curiae) to international criminal[89] as well as to human rights tribunals.[90] While these procedures are often not specifically designed for NGOs, they are, as was shown, increasingly relied upon by them. As such, they contribute indirectly to an increasingly rules-based engagement of NGOs in areas of global security which are judicialized and open to litigation. Overall, however, the position of NGOs in international law remains under-regulated.

Within the UN, Article 71 UN Charter opens a formal channel for NGO participation:[91] the consultative status of NGOs at the Economic and Social Council (ECOSOC) as specified in Resolution 1996/31.[92] Tellingly, the formal status of NGOs in the UN was attached to ECOSOC, whose mandate relates to 'soft', human security-related issues, including international economic, social, cultural, educational, health, and related matters (Article 62 UN Charter).[93] Conversely, explicit rules for NGO engagement with the work of other UN organs are virtually non-existent.[94] Nonetheless, there is increasing recognition of NGOs also by the UNSC in areas where they can make a substantial contribution. At times, the UNSC has called formally on NGOs to support its work, such as in UNSC Resolution 1470 (2003) concerning the national recovery strategy in Sierra Leone.[95] In other regional security and defence organizations such as NATO, as discussed, there is usually neither a formal recognition of NGOs nor a formal framework of interaction.

OSCE, being more open to NGO participation, grants them a more established place. In the Charter of Paris, OSCE participating States recognized 'the major role that non-governmental organizations (…) have played in the achievement of the objectives of the CSCE [Conference for Security and Co-operation in Europe, which was changed on 1 January 1995 to OSCE] (…). These organizations (…) must be involved in an appropriate way in the activities and new structures of the CSCE in order to fulfil their important tasks.'[96] Also, the 1992 Helsinki summit document grants NGOs broad (though not

[89] See n 53 and Section C.2; ICC Statute (n 31) art 75 (victim reparations) and art 15(3) on communications.

[90] See generally ECHR (n 41) art 36(2); Rule 44 of ECtHR Rules of Procedure (as amended) <https://www.echr.coe.int/Documents/Rules_Court_ENG.pdf>, accessed 12 February 2020; Rule 45 of Inter-American Court of Human Rights Rules of Procedure (as amended) <https://www.cidh.oas.org/Basicos/English/Basic20.Rules%20of%20Procedure%20of%20the%20Court.htm> accessed 12 February 2020.

[91] According to Higgins et al, ECOSOC's 'Committee on Non-Governmental Organizations, (…) has been described as the "guardian of the entrance door" to the UN for NGOs (…)', Rosalyn Higgins et al, *Oppenheim's International Law: United Nations* (OUP 2017) 126.

[92] Generally, Eduard Szazi, *NGOs: Legitimate Subjects of International Law* (Leiden UP 2012) 75ff; Higgins et al (n 91) 135–7. See also the European Convention on the Recognition of the Legal Personality of International Non-Governmental Organisations ETS No 124, which was, however only ratified by twelve States <www.coe.int/en/web/conventions/full-list/-/conventions/treaty/124/signatures> accessed 1 May 2019.

[93] Jan A Scholte, 'Civil Society and NGOs' in Thomas G Weiss/Rorden Wilkinson (eds), *International Organization and Global Governance* (2nd edn, Routledge 2018) 351.

[94] Paul (n 6); Binder (n 7) 12ff. See Section B for the UNSC engagement with NGOs.

[95] UNSC Res 1470 (2003) para 8; see also Charnovitz (n 14) 355.

[96] CSCE, 'Charter of Paris for a New Europe' (Paris, 19–21 November 1990) 12; also Mayer (n 1) 129.

unlimited) access to OSCE policymaking and implementation activities.[97] The involvement of NGOs in the OSCE is even more extensive and, arguably, more formalized, when it comes to the human dimension, where NGOs are given an increasingly 'official' role in the implementation of commitments.[98] Thus, security arrangements and institutions employing a comprehensive concept of security such as the OSCE rely on NGOs; in turn this is reflected in the existence of a more detailed international legal framework.

Overall, it seems that the formal involvement of NGOs in the field of global security has been growing. Although the international legal framework still does not grant NGOs a well-established place and their engagement in the area remains largely informal, a trend towards increasing recognition is discernible, especially in fields where NGOs can play a significant role; such are the areas where the individual is centre stage.

E. Recent Developments

The ever-changing concept of security and the many more avenues open for NGO participation in the field are reflected in the working methods, structure, organization, and types of NGOs themselves. At the outset, a remarkable increase in the number of international NGOs can be witnessed. As of 2018, 5,161 NGOs had consultative status with ECOSOC.[99] The UN Human Development Report 2003 estimated that 37,000 to 50,000 NGOs were active in the field of development, human rights, and peace and security. The 2003 UN Office for the Coordination of Humanitarian Affairs roster estimated that there were approximately 2,500 NGOs in the humanitarian business while 260 major NGOs engaged in relief efforts.[100]

Indeed, especially in international humanitarian relief, NGOs play a crucial role. In view of their flexibility and their relative ability to move in and around conflict zones, NGOs have been transformed to operational partners of global and regional security arrangements, take part in UN collective enforcement efforts and collaborate with international organizations more generally.[101] Likewise, many States have started to outsource government activities to NGOs in the areas of aid delivery and humanitarian relief.[102] Non-governmental organizations (frequently State-funded) train, help, educate, mediate in conflict areas and report on what is happening on the ground. They

[97] See most importantly the CSCE, '1992 Summit Helsinki Document—The Challenges of Change' (Helsinki 9–10 July 1992) ss 14–16.

[98] For example, the High Commissioner on National Minorities is empowered to collect and receive information about national minorities from a variety of sources, including NGOs. See ibid, 'Helsinki Decisions' II. CSCE High Commissioner on National Minorities, para 23a; also Mayer (n 1) 131.

[99] UN Department of Economic and Social Affairs, 'Basic Facts about ECOSOC Status' (NGO Branch DESA) <www.csonet.org/?menu=100> accessed 1 May 2019. See also Scholte (n 93) 351.

[100] Oudraat/Haufler (n 13) 11, as regards reasons for this increase in numbers.

[101] For further details Anderson (n 16) 116ff.

[102] For details Mihr (n 58) 320–1.

channel huge amounts of money.[103] Changes in NGOs' working methods and ways of organization are thus particularly noticeable in the humanitarian field: NGOs have become professionalized and have started to act as entrepreneurs. Their (corporate) structures have been compared to small companies.[104]

But the working methods of advocacy NGOs have also changed. Their increasingly important place within international institutions and in the landscape of global security has led to new forms of cooperation between them. The rise of transnational advocacy networks (TANs) is here pertinent. Non-governmental organizations build global alliances with other international (and national) NGOs. This was noticeable, for example, with the CICC or the ICBL in the context of standard-setting.[105] Also, in the more traditional field of naming and shaming, NGOs tend to form coalitions and they engage in large lobbying campaigns as, for example, in the case of blood diamonds.[106]

As a result of these developments, the traditional distinction between operational and advocacy NGOs decreases.[107] In the modern security matrix, the ways different types of NGOs engage with international law often align. For example, humanitarian assistance-focused (namely, operational) NGOs increasingly employ a human rights lens and criticize, if necessary, governmental actions. Recently, *Médecins Sans Frontières* took an advocacy role by publicly speaking out about the humanitarian crisis suffered by refugees in the Mediterranean in the context of migration control operations.[108]

Changes are also noticeable in relation to the cooperation between international and local NGOs with new alliances being formed especially in the areas of implementation and enforcement of IHRL, IHL, or criminal law.[109] Local NGOs are increasingly recognized as important partners in many respects. First, they provide information for international campaigns, which feeds into the work of international NGOs of naming and shaming and awareness raising. For example, with respect to the conflict in Syria, international NGOs such as AI and HRW relied on information received from local NGOs to then denounce the human rights violations committed.[110] Secondly, since States with a locally organized domestic opposition are more vulnerable to

[103] Oudraat/Haufler (n 13) 11ff.

[104] Also ibid 17, see respectively, eg Gavi, 'Gavi's Business Model' (Gavi, The Vaccine Alliance), <www.gavi.org/about/gavis-business-model/> accessed 1 May 2019.

[105] Oudraat/Haufler (n 13) 15; Mihr (n 58) 321. [106] See Section C.3.

[107] In this sense Mihr (n 58) 305ff.

[108] Other examples include AI's engagement in the training of human rights defenders; Oxfam's criticism of human rights violations.

[109] Tara R Gingerich/Marc J Cohen, *Turning the Humanitarian System on its Head: Saving Lives and Livelihoods by Strengthening Local Capacity and Shifting Leadership to Local Actors* (Oxfam Research Reports, Oxfam Information 2015) <www.oxfam.org/sites/www.oxfam.org/files/file_attachments/rr-turning-humanitarian-system-local-capacity-270715-en.pdf> accessed 1 May 2019; see also the International Council of Voluntary Agencies functioning as a hub for coordination and partnerships in the field of humanitarian action (ICVA) <www.icvanetwork.org/> accessed 1 May 2019.

[110] See the reliance by AI on information provided by local NGOs in the Syrian conflict: AI, 'Syria 2017/18'(Amnesty International) <www.amnesty.org/en/countries/middle-east-and-north-africa/syria/report-syria/> accessed 1 May 2019.

transnational advocacy efforts, international NGOs partner with local actors to pressure domestic authorities from 'above' and 'below'.[111]

There is also increasing cooperation between NGOs and academia. For example, during the negotiations for the ICC Statute, NGOs were supported by LL.M students from NYU. Likewise, for litigation purposes, when acting as *amicus curiae*, NGOs increasingly join forces with academics. Law clinics and *pro bono* projects at universities are a useful resource.[112] Especially in relation to technical issues where enhanced legal (or other) knowledge is required, collaboration between NGOs and academic institutions seems to be quite fruitful.

More generally, NGO engagement in the field of global security has become increasingly powerful and effective. Working methods and information flows have been professionalized and become more stable. Sometimes, extensive resources are used. A pertinent example is the verification and monitoring in relation to the Ottawa Convention discussed above.[113] Furthermore, NGOs explore new ways to engage in interaction and monitoring. They increasingly draw on new technologies such as internet communication and satellite technology in order to detect and publicize major IHRL and IHL violations.[114]

Finally, the increased openness of international tribunals towards NGOs as regards norm application and enforcement has consequences for NGOs' working methods and their engagement with international law. Engagement has become more formalized. The traditional means of informal public denunciation (naming and shaming) is increasingly complemented (though by no means replaced) by a growing reliance on other procedures, such as litigation before human rights bodies, communications to international criminal tribunals, or the filing of *amicus curiae* briefs. Thus, NGOs take up more proceduralized avenues of denunciation.[115] At the same time, they lobby for the creation of new (judicial) institutions; as was the case with the ICC. In doing so, NGOs participate in the legalization and institutionalization of the international security landscape which, in turn, has repercussions on their working methods, which become more and more formalized. Overall, the dynamic global security environment has significantly influenced NGOs' working methods, organization, and forms of engagement with international law.

[111] Zarnett (n 68) 124. In Keck and Sikkink's view, the international advocacy efforts of local actors—which they refer to as 'boomerangs'—are crucial for the formation of a TAN. Without local NGOs which make the human rights problems known to the international community, international pressure is less likely.

[112] For example, UCLA offers a law clinic in cooperation with the Office of the Prosecutor of the ICC, see University of California Los Angeles, 'ICC Forum and Clinic' (UCLA Law) <law.ucla.edu/centers/international-law-and-human-rights/international-and-comparative-law-program/projects/icc-forum-and-clinic/> accessed 1 May 2019; see also the International Criminal and Humanitarian Law Clinic offered by the Harry Radzyner Law School, 'The International Criminal and Humanitarian Law Clinic' (IDC Herzliya) <www.idc.ac.il/en/schools/law/clinics/pages/the-international-criminal-and-humanitarian-law-clinic.aspx> accessed 1 May 2019; and the Oxford Pro Bono Publico based at the University of Oxford Faculty of Law (Oxford Human Rights Hub) <https://www.law.ox.ac.uk/research-and-subject-groups/oxford-pro-bono-publico> accessed 30 November 2020.

[113] See Section C.3.

[114] Oudraat/Haufler (n 13) 24.

[115] Breton-Le Goff (n 42) 253.

F. Conclusion and Outlook

Global security, originally limited to State security, has gradually become a more comprehensive concept. The emergence of issues associated with human rights as well as more comprehensive strategies, like post-conflict peacebuilding, opened the international arena for NGO involvement. Non-governmental organizations have plenty to offer and indeed become increasingly engaged. This goes hand in hand with a growing openness towards NGOs on behalf of intergovernmental organizations. Even traditional, 'high politics' security arrangements, such as the UNSC and NATO are gradually opening up to NGOs, especially in relation to post-conflict reconstruction. Non-governmental organizations' involvement is most extensive in the case of the OSCE in light of its inclusive conception of security. This reflects the reality that NGO involvement is directly connected to the concept of security adhered to by the international organization in question and increases in cases where human security is focal.

While NGO engagement with international law in the field of global security still remains mostly informal, a trend towards professionalization and formalization may be noticed, especially in litigation. This holds true more generally: hand in hand with the growing role of NGOs in the international arena goes the formality of their engagement and the increase of applicable international standards. This notwithstanding, development is slow and there are obvious shortcomings, including concerns on NGO accountability.[116] While not the focus of this contribution, there is greater need for stronger accountability mechanisms and transparency regarding NGO engagement in the relevant fields.

The activities of NGOs in the field of global security may be measured on the basis of their result and contribution to the field. As shown above, NGOs have advanced especially human security-related fields: they have contributed to strengthening standards and improving their judicial application and interpretation; they have enhanced compliance with international law, especially IHRL, IHL, and international criminal law; finally, they have fostered the work of international institutions in these areas, for example of international criminal and human rights tribunals, as well as of the OSCE, while they have also supported States in the delivery of humanitarian assistance.

Overall, NGOs have contributed to furthering the openness of international law towards the individual in the field of global security, traditionally reserved exclusively for States. As such, the general statement that 'NGOs make international law more responsive to the needs of the international community'[117] holds true when it comes to the field of global security.

[116] Anderson (n 16) 112; Lisa Jordan/Peter van Tuijl (eds), *NGO Accountability: Politics, Principles and Innovations* (Earthscan 2006) for further reference.

[117] Charnovitz (n 14) 360.

CHAPTER 57

THE NORTH ATLANTIC TREATY ORGANIZATION

STEVEN HILL

A. Introduction

The North Atlantic Treaty Organization (NATO) is a political–military alliance that currently includes thirty Allied Nations.[1] NATO Allies deal with a wide range of peace and security issues. NATO also cooperates with a wide range of partners in the broader Euro–Atlantic neighbourhood and across the globe. Currently there are NATO missions, operations, or activities in Afghanistan, Kosovo, the Mediterranean Sea, the Aegean Sea, and Iraq. NATO States are also in the middle of the biggest reinforcement of deterrence and defence since the end of the Cold War.[2]

NATO's foundational document is the 1949 North Atlantic Treaty,[3] which recently celebrated its seventieth anniversary. There have been commemorative events including a meeting of Ministers of Foreign Affairs in April 2019, a variety of reports and books about the Alliance's future, and even a legal conference and accompanying volume dedicated to the North Atlantic Treaty and its contribution to the international law of collective security.[4] This all culminated in a special meeting of the Heads of State and

[1] North Macedonia was invited to begin accession talks at the Brussels Summit in July 2018: 'Relations with the Republic of North Macedonia' (NATO, 30 March 2020) <https://www.nato.int/cps/en/natohq/topics_48830.htm> accessed 9 April 2020.

[2] Secretary-General Jens Stoltenberg, 'Relentless Diplomacy, Credible Defence, Strong NATO' (NATO, 13 November 2019) <https://www.nato.int/cps/en/natohq/opinions_170714.htm?selectedLocale=en> accessed 9 April 2020.

[3] North Atlantic Treaty 34 UNTS 243.

[4] 'Emory Marks NATO's 70th Anniversary with Conference' (*Emory Law News Center*) <http://law.emory.edu/news-center/releases/2019/09/emory-marks-nato-70-th-anniversary-with-conference.html#.Xb8C03k1jIU> accessed 9 April 2020.

Government in London in December 2019.[5] All of these events have in one way or another sought to assess NATO's past, present, and future role as a global security actor. International law, and the rule of law more generally, play an important part in this overall picture.

B. NATO as a Global Security Actor

This section aims to describe NATO's role as a global security actor. To that end, it reviews NATO's mission and mandate, its institutional structure, and its current priorities. In this section, a brief review of the Treaty's principal provisions will therefore help illustrate the general international legal framework in which NATO operates, the scope of its activities, and how and where it places the emphasis in its day-to-day work.

1. The North Atlantic Treaty

NATO's mission and mandate are grounded in the North Atlantic Treaty. The North Atlantic Treaty is short.[6] It has only been amended once, when Turkey joined NATO in 1952, to account for the expanded geographical scope of the Alliance's collective self-defence provision found in the famous Article 5.[7] While Article 5 is justifiably famous, it is but one part of a much more comprehensive set of tools available to the Alliance to promote security both within the Alliance and in the international system more generally.

The preamble of the North Atlantic Treaty reaffirms Allies' commitment to the purposes and principles of the UN Charter and 'their desire to live in peace with all peoples and all governments'.[8] It also describes 'the principles of democracy, individual liberty and the rule of law' on which the Alliance is founded.[9] In the same spirit as the preamble, Article 1 contains an undertaking, in accordance with the UN Charter, regarding the peaceful settlement of disputes and on the non-recourse to the threat or use of force in any manner inconsistent with the purposes of the UN.[10] This shows how NATO is anchored in the system of collective security found in the UN Charter.

Article 2 refers to the need for Allies to 'contribute toward the further development of peaceful and friendly international relations by strengthening their free institutions, by bringing about a better understanding of the principles upon which these institutions

[5] 'Secretary General Announces Dates for the Summit of NATO Heads of State and Government in London' (NATO, 22 May 2019) <https://www.nato.int/cps/en/natohq/news_166231.htm> accessed 9 April 2020.

[6] It has fourteen articles.

[7] Protocol to the North Atlantic Treaty on the Accession of Greece and Turkey <https://www.nato.int/cps/en/natohq/official_texts_17245.htm?> accessed 9 April 2020.

[8] North Atlantic Treaty (n 4) preamble. [9] ibid.

[10] ibid art 1. Charter of the United Nations 1 UNTS XVI (UN Charter) arts 2(3) and 2(4).

are founded, and by promoting conditions of stability and well-being'.[11] This reflects a broad understanding of the building blocks of security, which include strong domestic institutions, civic education, and the socio-economic foundation of peace. This Article also touches on trade and other economic policies as it refers to the need for Allies to 'seek to eliminate conflict in their international economic policies and [...] encourage economic collaboration between any or all of them'.[12] Overall, Article 2 suggests that the drafters of the North Atlantic Treaty had a broad conception of security that includes the socio-economic bases for security as well as the notion that the lack of collaboration and coordination in this area may give rise to conflict and instability. This comprehensive approach to security is reflected throughout NATO's work.

Article 3 is the 'work horse' of the North Atlantic Treaty. It describes what NATO Allies do on a day-to-day basis: '[In] order more effectively to achieve the objectives of this Treaty, the Parties, separately and jointly, by means of continuous and effective self-help and mutual aid, will maintain and develop their individual and collective capacity to resist armed attack.'[13] This system of 'continuous and effective self-help and mutual aid' has been at the foundation of the Alliance's work for the past seventy years and is key to the Allies' ability to maintain their resilience against the wide range of security threats that are present in the current international environment or that may emerge in the future.

NATO's work to this end includes the development of mutually agreed doctrine on a wide range of defence-related matters,[14] work on common standards on issues from the seemingly simple to the very complex,[15] and the design and provision of training programmes on many subjects including international humanitarian law.[16] NATO also regularly holds exercises in order to test how agreed plans and procedures work in a complicated multinational environment involving challenging conditions.

As the wording of Article 3 suggests, sometimes NATO activities are done jointly by all Allies or by groups of Allies. But the building up of capacity to resist armed attack is not only a collective enterprise. It also involves individual action in terms of building up and maintaining defence capacity and capabilities. This is where the issue of the amount spent by individual Allies on defence comes into play. In 2014, Allies pledged to spend 2 per cent of GDP on defence by 2024.[17] Allies have made considerable progress in implementing this Defence Investment Pledge, with five consecutive years of rising defence

[11] ibid art 2. [12] ibid. [13] ibid art 3.

[14] eg NATO's Declaration of Space as an Operational Domain: Heads of State and Government, 'London Declaration' (4 December 2019) para 6 <https://www.nato.int/cps/en/natohq/official_texts_171584.htm> accessed 10 April 2020.

[15] eg 'NATO Standardization Office' (NATO, 9 June 2017) <https://www.nato.int/cps/en/natohq/topics_124879.htm> accessed 9 April 2020.

[16] eg 'NATO Mission Iraq' (NATO, 17 February 2020) <https://www.nato.int/cps/en/natohq/topics_166936.htm> accessed 9 April 2020.

[17] The Defence Investment Pledge is described in: Heads of State and Government, 'Wales Summit Declaration' (5 September 2014) para 14 <https://www.nato.int/cps/ic/natohq/official_texts_112964.htm> accessed 9 April 2020.

investment.[18] By the end of 2020, Allies will have added a cumulative total of well over one hundred billion dollars to their defence spending.[19] This includes spending on research and major new equipment, ensuring that NATO will be in a good position to deal with emerging security threats in the future.

Moving from the day-to-day process of building up Allied resilience, Articles 4 and 5 deal with more specific situations of threats to the security of Allies or of the international community more generally. Article 4 contains a consultation mechanism that can be used in the case of certain threats against Allies. It reads in part: '[t]he Parties will consult together whenever, in the opinion of any of them, the territorial integrity, political independence or security of any of the Parties is threatened.'[20] It is worth noting that the Ally that is threatened does not have to be the Ally that requests consultations. Rather, consultations can be 'whenever, in the opinion of any of them' there is a threat. Nor is there a geographic limitation, as is the case with Article 5, on the threat. Article 4 has only been used in a handful of cases over the years. The most recent cases have been at the request of Turkey in response to threats from the conflict in Syria and at the request of Poland following Russia's actions against Ukraine.[21] In each case, Allies consulted with each other in a meeting of the North Atlantic Council about the threat.[22] While Article 4 remains a tool that is not used frequently, it is a useful part of NATO's response options to threats.

Article 5 is perhaps the best known of all the articles of the Treaty. It contains NATO's collective self-defence pact:

> The Parties agree that an armed attack against one or more of them in Europe or North America shall be considered an attack against them all and consequently they agree that, if such an armed attack occurs, each of them, in exercise of the right of individual or collective self-defence recognised by Article 51 of the Charter of the United Nations, will assist the Party or Parties so attacked by taking forthwith, individually and in concert with the other Parties, such action as it deems necessary, including the use of armed force, to restore and maintain the security of the North Atlantic area.[23]

The Article further provides that the armed attack and any action taken in response to it in line with Article 5 is to be immediately reported to the UN Security Council

[18] NATO Secretary-General Jens Stoltenberg, 'Press Conference ahead of the meetings of NATO Defence Ministers' (25 June 2019) <https://www.nato.int/cps/en/natohq/opinions_167065.htm?selectedLocale=en> accessed 9 April 2020.

[19] ibid. [20] North Atlantic Treaty (n 4) art 4.

[21] 'The Consultation Process and Article 4' (NATO, 28 February 2020) <https://www.nato.int/cps/en/natolive/topics_49187.htm> accessed 9 April 2020.

[22] With regards to Turkey requesting consultation in 2012 after one of its fighter jets was shot down by Syrian air defence forces and again after five Turkish civilians were killed by Syrian shells, NATO agreed to deploy Patriot missiles as a defensive measure. ibid.

[23] North Atlantic Treaty (n 4) art 5.

(UNSC).[24] Article 6 of the North Atlantic Treaty defines the geographical scope to which Article 5 applies, or in other words, where an armed attack would have to occur in order to fall within the scope of Article 5.[25] Finally, Article 11 provides that the North Atlantic Treaty shall be carried out in line with the respective constitutional processes of Allies.[26]

The first (and so far the only) time that the North Atlantic Council decided to invoke Article 5 of the North Atlantic Treaty was in response to the 9/11 attacks in the US.[27] According to the Council's statement on the day following the attacks,

> the North Atlantic Council met again in response to the appalling attacks perpetrated yesterday against the United States. The Council agreed that if it is determined that this attack was directed from abroad against the United States, it shall be regarded as an action covered by Article 5 of the Washington Treaty.[28]

Adopted by consensus in the Council, this statement formed the legal basis for a number of actions including Operation Active Endeavour, NATO's counter-terrorism operation in the Mediterranean Sea.[29] Aside from its operational impact, the Council's decision remains of lasting legal significance. It is tangible evidence of State practice in support of the proposition that non-State actors can author an armed attack that triggers the use of force resulting from the inherent right of individual or collective self-defence under international law.

Article 5 remains highly relevant to today's security environment. It is the cornerstone of NATO's policy of deterrence. It is as relevant in protecting Allies against armed attacks by traditional means as it is for defending against attacks using newer technologies. For example, in 2014 NATO Heads of State and Government decided that a cyberattack could trigger Article 5.[30] This would be decided by the North Atlantic Council on a case-by-case basis. For reasons of deterrence, NATO will not specify the threshold for an armed attack in cyberspace.[31] Along the same lines, Heads of State and Government have agreed that cases of hybrid warfare could also trigger Article 5.[32]

[24] ibid. [25] ibid art 6. [26] ibid art 11.

[27] 'Invocation of Article 5 confirmed' (NATO, 2 October 2001) <https://www.nato.int/docu/update/2001/1001/e1002a.htm> accessed 9 April 2020.

[28] North Atlantic Council, 'Statement' (12 September 2001) <https://www.nato.int/docu/pr/2001/p01-124e.htm> accessed 9 April 2020.

[29] 'Operation Active Endeavour' (NATO, 27 October 2016) <https://www.nato.int/cps/en/natohq/topics_7932.htm> accessed 9 April 2020.

[30] Wales Summit Declaration (n 17) para 72.

[31] Jens Stoltenberg, 'Why Cyber Space Matters to NATO as Much as Land, Sea and Air Defence' (*Financial Times*, 12 July 2018) ('I am often asked how significant a cyber attack would have to be to trigger an Article 5 response. My answer is: we will see.') <https://www.ft.com/content/9c3ae876-6d90-11e8-8863-a9bb262c5f53> accessed 10 April 2020.

[32] Heads of State and Government, 'Brussels Summit Declaration' (11 July 2018) <https://www.nato.int/cps/en/natohq/official_texts_156624.htm> para 21 accessed 9 April 2020.

2. Institutional Structure

The North Atlantic Organization has an institutional architecture that reflects its character as a political–military Alliance capable of addressing a wide range of issues that are relevant to global security. Article 9 of the North Atlantic Treaty establishes the North Atlantic Council.[33] In line with the principle of civilian control of the military, the Council is the supreme decision-making body in NATO. All Allies are represented on the Council, which meets at the level of Permanent Representatives on a regular basis. There are also meetings of the Council at the level of Ministers of Foreign Affairs and Ministers of Defence, usually two of each meeting each year. Finally, the Council meets at the level of Heads of State and Government approximately every two years. In recent years, these meeting have been more frequent, with meetings of leaders taking place in Brussels in 2017 and 2018, and in London in 2019.

All NATO activities are ultimately based on a decision by the Council. Allies make all decisions in NATO on the basis of consensus.[34] There is no voting within NATO bodies. All decisions represent the collective decision of all Allies. In all cases, the Secretary-General chairs the Council. NATO's International Staff is composed of civilians who support the Secretary-General in this role.

The Council is advised by a Military Committee composed of military representatives as well as an extensive committee structure that covers a wide range of topics from political, operational, and technical viewpoints.[35] These committees are staffed by representatives of Allies. NATO has a variety of agencies that cover specialized areas such as procurement and information technology.[36] There is also a military structure that includes the two NATO Supreme Allied Commanders as well as the NATO military structure.[37]

Finally, there are specialized formats that enable interactions between NATO and other States. The NATO–Ukraine Commission and the NATO–Georgia Commission are important ways to interact at the political and practical cooperation levels with those two States and contribute to regional and global security. The NATO–Russia Council remains a forum for dialogue with Russia. There are several meetings a year at the ambassadorial level to discuss a range of concerns. Practical cooperation with Russia

[33] North Atlantic Treaty (n 4) art 9 ('The Parties hereby establish a Council, on which each of them shall be represented, to consider matters concerning the implementation of this Treaty...').

[34] 'Consensus Decision-Making at NATO' (NATO, 14 March 2016) <https://www.nato.int/cps/en/natolive/topics_49178.htm> accessed 9 April 2020.

[35] 'Military Committee' (NATO, 28 May 2019) <https://www.nato.int/cps/en/natolive/topics_49633.htm> accessed 9 April 2020.

[36] 'Organisations and Agencies' (NATO, 31 March 2020) <https://www.nato.int/cps/en/natohq/topics_66470.htm> accessed 30 November 2020.

[37] 'NATO Organization' (NATO, 3 April 2020) <https://www.nato.int/cps/en/natohq/structure.htm> accessed 9 April 2020.

has been suspended in response to Russia's annexation of Crimea in 2014, which NATO considers illegal and illegitimate and will not recognize.[38]

3. Current Priorities

Just as the North Atlantic Treaty provides a broad and flexible framework for addressing the individual and collective security needs of Allies, NATO has taken a dynamic approach in defining its current priorities in order to reflect the changing global security situation. Indeed, over the course of its history, but particularly since the end of the Cold War, adaptation has been key to enabling NATO to deal with current global security challenges.

The North Atlantic Organization's conception of global security has evolved over the past decade in response to a changing security environment. At the same time, many themes have remained constant. These include the need for Allies to invest in their defence capabilities in order to meet emerging threats as well as NATO's approach to dialogue and cooperation with partners. NATO sees itself as having three core tasks: collective defence, crisis management, and cooperative security.[39] Collective defence refers broadly to the defence of Allies in line with the collective self-defence provisions of the North Atlantic Treaty. Crisis management largely refers to NATO's role in the international community's response to 'out-of-area' situations. This includes NATO's operations in the Western Balkans and Afghanistan as well as maritime operations.[40] Cooperative security encompasses NATO's considerable work with partners such as through the Euro-Atlantic Partnership Council and the Partnership for Peace.[41]

The North Atlantic Organization sees itself as part of a comprehensive approach by the international community to address global security challenges.[42] In its 2011 Comprehensive Approach Action Plan, NATO recognized that different actors contribute to a comprehensive approach based on a shared sense of responsibility, openness, and determination, taking into account their respective strengths, mandates, and roles, as well as their decision-making autonomy.[43] The Action Plan, which was last validated in December 2017, sets forth ways in which NATO can contribute to overall efforts by the

[38] 'Relations with Russia' (NATO, 5 August 2019) <https://www.nato.int/cps/en/natolive/topics_50090.htm> accessed 9 April 2020; Brussels Summit Declaration (n 32) paras 4–6.

[39] eg 'Strategic Concepts' (NATO, 12 June 2018) <https://www.nato.int/cps/en/natohq/topics_56626.htm> accessed 9 April 2020.

[40] 'Crisis Management' (NATO, 23 March 2020) <https://www.nato.int/cps/en/natolive/topics_49192.htm> accessed 9 April 2020.

[41] 'Partnerships: Projecting Stability Through Cooperation' (NATO, 24 March 2020) <https://www.nato.int/cps/en/natohq/topics_84336.htm> accessed 9 April 2020; 'Euro-Atlantic Partnership' (NATO, 23 March 2020) <https://www.nato.int/cps/en/natohq/topics_67979.htm> accessed 9 April 2020.

[42] 'A "Comprehensive Approach" to Crises' (NATO, 26 June 2018) <https://www.nato.int/cps/en/natolive/topics_51633.htm> accessed 9 April 2020.

[43] ibid.

international community.[44] These include not only the planning and conduct of operations, but also lessons learned, training, education, and exercises. Cooperation with external actors is also important. A major focus in recent years has been on cooperation between NATO and the European Union. In July 2016, the two organizations outlined areas for strengthened cooperation in light of common security challenges, including countering hybrid threats, enhancing resilience, defence capacity-building, cyber defence, maritime security, and exercises.[45] In December 2016, NATO foreign ministers endorsed a statement to which were annexed forty-two common projects to advance NATO–EU cooperation. A further thirty-two measures were agreed in December 2017.[46]

One straightforward way of understanding NATO's current priorities is to analyse the publicly available declarations and other policy documents that Heads of State and Government adopt during their periodic meetings. These documents are a good source of the latest agreed language on the overall global security environment as well as on a wide range of specific global security issues. The North Atlantic Council at the ambassadorial level also adopts statements, from time to time, that are relevant for international law issues.[47]

The 2018 Brussels Summit Declaration is the latest such high-level declaration. It gives a good snapshot of NATO's perception of the current security environment, which it characterizes as 'dangerous, unpredictable, and fluid... with enduring challenges and threats from all strategic directions; from state and non-state actors; from military forces; and from terrorist, cyber, and hybrid attacks'.[48]

The Declaration goes on to state that 'Russia's aggressive actions, including the threat and use of force to attain political goals, challenge the Alliance and are undermining Euro-Atlantic security and the rules-based international order'.[49] Reflecting the Alliance's 360 degree approach to security, the document moves beyond threats from the Alliance's east to looks to threats from the south:

> Instability and continuing crises across the Middle East and North Africa are fueling terrorism. They also contribute to irregular migration and human trafficking. The ongoing crisis in Syria has a direct effect on the stability of the region and the security of the Alliance as a whole.[50]

Referring to new technologies and techniques of conflict, leaders cite 'hybrid challenges, including disinformation campaigns and malicious cyber activities'.[51] Cyber defence

[44] ibid.
[45] 'Relations with the European Union' (NATO, 23 March 2020) <https://www.nato.int/cps/en/natohq/topics_49217.htm> accessed 9 April 2020.
[46] ibid.
[47] Good examples: North Atlantic Council, 'Statement on the Intermediate-Range Nuclear Forces (INF) Treaty' (15 December 2017) < https://www.nato.int/cps/en/natohq/news_150016.htm> accessed 10 April 2020; North Atlantic Council, 'Statement on the Intermediate-Range Nuclear Forces Treaty' (2 August 2019) <https://www.nato.int/cps/en/natohq/official_texts_168164.htm> accessed 10 April 2020.
[48] Brussels Summit Declaration (n 32) para 2. [49] ibid. [50] ibid.
[51] ibid.

has been a major area of focus for NATO over the past decade.[52] In recent years, NATO has developed a strategy to counter hybrid threats as well.[53] Finally, the document states that '[t]he proliferation of weapons of mass destruction and advanced missile technology also continues to threaten the security of our nations'.[54]

The description of the current security environment is contained in just one paragraph of the declaration, which totals seventy-nine paragraphs and contains detailed language about how NATO is addressing these challenges and others.[55] Future such documents will likely further define NATO's perspective on what security challenges lie ahead. These could include new technologies such as artificial intelligence and the strategic use of data, coupled with broader geopolitical developments such as China's role as a world power. These developments are very much on NATO's agenda at present and will continue to be in the future.

The Declaration also reaffirms NATO's commitment to its Open Door Policy under Article 10 of the North Atlantic Treaty.[56] Terming this Policy as 'one of the Alliance's greatest successes', the Declaration recognized the value that prior rounds of enlargement have had on enhancing NATO's collective security and the security of the region.[57] It once again proclaimed that

> NATO's door is open to all European democracies which share the values of our Alliance, which are willing and able to assume the responsibilities and obligations of membership, which are in a position to further the principles of the Treaty, and whose inclusion can contribute to the security of the North Atlantic area.[58]

C. NATO and the International Law of Global Security

From the perspective of NATO and its Allies, acting in accordance with international law is a core component of the Alliance's shared values and the source of its legitimacy. International law is there at the core of NATO's values and actions. This is not surprising

[52] Evidence of this focus is the Cyber Defence Pledge made by the Allies in July 2016, the pronouncement by Secretary-General Jens Stoltenberg that a serious cyberattack could trigger Article 5, and the NATO response to the GRU operation targeting the Organisation for the Prohibition of Chemical Weapons in The Hague: Allied Heads of State and Government, 'Cyber Defence Pledge' (8 July 2016) <https://www.nato.int/cps/en/natohq/official_texts_133177.htm> accessed 9 April 2020; NATO Secretary-General Jens Stoltenberg, 'NATO Will Defend Itself' (NATO, 27 August 2019) <https://www.nato.int/cps/en/natohq/news_168435.htm?selectedLocale=en> accessed 9 April 2020; NATO Secretary-General Jens Stoltenberg, 'Statement on Russian Cyber Attacks' (NATO, 4 October 2018) <https://www.nato.int/cps/en/natohq/news_158911.htm?selectedLocale=en> accessed 9 April 2020.

[53] Brussels Summit Declaration (n 32) paras 20–1. [54] ibid para 2. [55] ibid.

[56] ibid para 62. [57] ibid. [58] ibid.

given that the rule of law is listed in the preamble to the North Atlantic Treaty as one of the values that NATO was founded to defend.[59]

International law matters to NATO in a variety of ways. On the most basic level, international law provides the institutional foundation for NATO's operations. In addition to the North Atlantic Treaty, several core treaties address NATO's day-to-day functioning and status within the Allied Nations,[60] on the territory of partner States,[61] and in specific operations.[62] Part of the process of becoming a new Ally involves ensuring that there are no legal obstacles to fully implementing obligations under these treaties, which are an important part of the legal acquis for new Allies.

International law also provides the mandate for NATO's work in specific contexts. Each NATO operation, mission or activity is based on a decision of the North Atlantic Council. The international legal basis for these actions is identified on a case-by-case basis. For example, NATO's initial operation in Afghanistan was based on a UNSC resolution.[63] Additionally, the current Resolute Support Mission is based on an invitation by Afghanistan as reflected in the 2014 NATO–Afghanistan Status of Forces Agreement.[64] In some cases, there may be differing views as to the international legal basis or different interpretations of the international legal principles at stake.

The Alliance has developed a number of techniques for enabling multinational cooperation to occur despite differing legal positions. This is often referred to as 'legal interoperability'.[65] This term refers to the need for Allies to work together in a variety of contexts despite differing legal frameworks applicable to (or interpreted differently by) each Nation.[66] As one close observer of NATO operations defined it:

> '[l]egal interoperability' is understood here as the ability of the forces of two or more nations to operate effectively together in the execution of assigned missions and tasks and with full respect for their legal obligations, notwithstanding the fact that

[59] North Atlantic Treaty (n 4) preamble.

[60] Agreement on the Status of the North Atlantic Treaty Organization, National Representatives, and International Staff 200 UNTS 3 (Ottawa Agreement); Protocol on the Status of International Military Headquarters Set Up Pursuant to the North Atlantic Treaty 200 UNTS 340 (Paris Protocol).

[61] eg Agreement Among the States Party to the North Atlantic Treaty and the Other States Participating in the Partnership for Peace Regarding the Status of Their Forces <http://www.nato.int/cps/en/natohq/official_texts_24742.htm?selectedLocale=en> accessed 10 April 2020 (SOFA).

[62] eg Agreement Between the North Atlantic Treaty Organization and the Islamic Republic of Afghanistan on the Status of NATO Forces and NATO Personnel Conducting Mutually Agreed NATO-led Activities in Afghanistan <http://www.nato.int/cps/en/natohq/official_texts_116072.htm?selectedLocale=en> accessed 10 April 2020.

[63] UNSC Res 1386 (2001). [64] See n 62.

[65] Steven Hill/David Lemétayer, 'Legal Issues of Multinational Military Operations: An Alliance Perspective' (2016–17) 55 Military Law and the Law of War Review 13.

[66] ICRC, 'Report: International Humanitarian Law and the Challenges of Contemporary Armed Conflicts' (31st International Conference of the Red Cross and Red Crescent, Geneva, 28 November to 1 December 2011) 31IC/11/5.1.2, 32 (highlighting that '[a]n important practical challenge is to ensure that peace operations are conducted taking into consideration the different levels of ratification of IHL instruments and the different interprvetations of those treaties and of customary IHL by troop contributing states').

nations concerned have varying legal obligations and varying interpretations of these obligations.[67]

Another legal adviser with NATO legal experience echoed this definition and emphasized

the ability to have a generally shared single common body of law—as it allows for a critical analysis to focus, compare and identify potential areas of legal divergences and strains and, in turn, assess, for the operational commander, the impact these divergences may have on operational interoperability.[68]

International law is central to the conduct of NATO's military activities. All NATO operational documents provide that NATO operations shall be conducted in accordance with international law, including international humanitarian law.[69] Here again there is often a need for legal interoperability given differing legal obligations. Finally, NATO also pays close attention to international law compliance in its work in training, advising, and assisting partners.[70]

The North Atlantic Organization often articulates its strategic goals with respect to security threats in terms of ensuring the return to compliance with international law. For example, over the course of 2018 and 2019, the North Atlantic Council regularly called on Russia to return to compliance with the Intermediate-Range Nuclear Forces (INF) Treaty.[71] The Organization also calls on Russia to comply with its international law obligations with respect to the conflict in Ukraine.[72]

International law is also seen as an enabler of the Alliance's adaptation to new security challenges. As described above, the broad legal framework in the North Atlantic Treaty provides a flexible set of tools for reacting to threats, ranging from the day-to-day 'mutual aid and self-help' of Article 3, through the potential for consultation under Article 4, to the collective defence provisions in Article 6. At the same, a frequent

[67] Marten Zwanenburg, 'International Humanitarian Law Interoperability in Multinational Operations' (2013) 95 International Review of the Red Cross 681, 681–4.

[68] Kirby Abbott, 'A Brief Overview of Legal Interoperability Challenges for NATO Arising from the Interrelationship Between IHL and IHRL in Light of the European Convention on Human Rights' (2014) 96 International Review of the Red Cross 107.

[69] eg Steven Hill/Andreea Manea, 'Protection of Civilians: A NATO Perspective' (2018) 34 Utrecht Journal of International and European Law 146, 146–60.

[70] NATO recently reaffirmed its pledge to 'Continue a substantive dialogue with the ICRC aimed at identifying areas where training and education provided by NATO on International Humanitarian Law may be further enhanced': 'NATO Renews Pledge to Strengthen Training on International Humanitarian Law' (NATO, 16 December 2019) <https://www.nato.int/cps/en/natohq/news_172070.htm> accessed 9 April 2020.

[71] North Atlantic Council, 'Statement on Russia's failure to comply with the Intermediate-Range Nuclear Forces (INF) Treaty' (Brussels, 1 February 2019) <https://www.nato.int/cps/en/natohq/news_162996.htm?selectedLocale=en> accessed 9 April 2020; NATO Foreign Ministers, 'Statement on the Intermediate-Range Nuclear Forces (INF) Treaty' (Brussels, 4 December 2018) <https://www.nato.int/cps/en/natohq/official_texts_161122.htm?selectedLocale=en> accessed 9 April 2020.

[72] North Atlantic Council, 'Statement on Crimea' (18 March 2019) <https://www.nato.int/cps/en/natohq/news_164656.htm?selectedLocale=en> accessed 9 April 2020.

difficulty in achieving consensus decision-making in NATO has to do with different perceptions by Allies of the legal issues at stake when it comes to a particular challenge. The existence of different legal obligations amongst Allies—or different interpretations of those obligations—can make multilateral agreement more difficult. For this reason, international law considerations are included in NATO exercises—through what are frequently referred to as 'legal injects'—in order to spur, amongst Allies, discussion designed to anticipate potential legal difficulties.

Legal dialogues, or other ways of promoting exchange of legal views amongst Allies, are another common feature of NATO's work in developing new policies, especially with respect to emerging security challenges, where there might be a perception that the legal framework is in need of clarification. While the general approach in NATO tends to be that international law is well-suited to dealing with current and emerging challenges, the view is often that further clarification is needed about how the existing international legal framework applies to new security challenges. Legal discussions are often seen as part of the process of 'scoping out' new challenges and therefore shape the debate around what NATO's policy response should be.

While international law shapes the way NATO approaches security challenges, the Alliance's work also matters to the overall trajectory of international law in many of these areas. The North Atlantic Organization has clearly had a role in directly or indirectly shaping the international legal framework in the field of global security.

One important contribution relates to the North Atlantic Council's historic decision to invoke Article 5 of the North Atlantic Treaty in response to the 9/11 terrorist attacks. As mentioned above, the Council's decision remains of lasting legal significance. It is tangible evidence of State practice in support of the proposition that non-State actors can be the authors of an armed attack. Such an armed attack could trigger the use of force in inherent right of individual or collective self-defence under international law. This notion has attracted debate even in recent years where non-State actors have been at the forefront of conflict.[73] In this sense, the Council's decision can be seen as a significant contribution by NATO to the development of international law. The decision is also highly relevant to the current security environment. Non-State armed groups are part of the daily landscape of NATO's operation in Afghanistan, its work on countering piracy off the coast of Somalia, its operations in the Mediterranean, and its contribution to the international community's fight against ISIL/Da'esh, just to name a few recent NATO activities. The potential role of non-State armed groups in cyberwarfare and the challenges associated with such groups also occupies significant time in Alliance discussions of cyber doctrine and practice. Finally, non-State armed groups loom large in this area of work since Russia's 2014 annexation of Crimea, especially in adopting a strategy to address the challenges posed by hybrid warfare.

[73] eg Monica Hakimi, 'Defensive Force Against Non-State Actors: The State of Play' (2015) 91 International Law Studies 1, 3 and 4: concluding that '[t]he the law in this area has been unsettled. A broad range of legal positions might reasonably be invoked or applied in any given case' and that 'the claim that international law absolutely prohibits the use of defensive force against non-State actors is losing legal traction. That claim is increasingly difficult to sustain.'

Over the years, NATO has played a role in supporting several significant norm clarification projects, albeit often in indirect ways. Perhaps the best known of these projects has been in the field of cyber through the two *Tallinn Manuals* on the international law applicable to cyber operations.[74] These works have been influential in identifying the legal issues at stake, shaping the debate (at least to a certain extent), and contributing to the incentives for an increasing number of States to make their views known on the applicable legal framework. The two *Tallinn Manuals* were produced by independent groups of experts in processes conducted under the auspices of the NATO Cooperative Cyber Defense Center of Excellence (CCDCOE) in Tallinn, Estonia. They did not reflect official NATO positions and were not approved by Allies. Some of the positions taken by the majority of the group of experts have ended up being criticized by some NATO Allies. However, they have been influential in shaping international dialogue about the legal framework applicable to cyber operations.

The North Atlantic Organization's practice has also helped shape the development of some areas of international law related to global security. One of these is NATO's well-developed practice in the area of the status of visiting forces. As mentioned above, the status of NATO forces is governed by long-standing series of multilateral agreements focused around the NATO Status of Forces Agreement (SOFA).[75] Inasmuch as the text of the NATO SOFA has been the model for many other similar agreements, including outside the North Atlantic area, practice under the NATO SOFA can be influential in interpreting these other agreements. The Organization's practice in other areas has also been cited in reports produced under the auspices of the UN International Law Commission (ILC). For example, reports on ongoing work on the protection of the environment in relation to armed conflict have featured NATO practice as helpful in determining the scope of the obligations of States in the area of environmental protection.[76]

The North Atlantic Organization will continue to play an important role in the international law of global security in the coming years and decades. As the Heads of State and Government proclaimed in their recent 2019 London Declaration, NATO will engage in a 'forward-looking reflection process' as a means of strengthening the underpinnings of the Alliance. Work is ongoing in 2020 as to what this will shape out as, but it almost certainly looks like leveraging NATO's past experiences to tackle the novel problems of new technologies, increase resilience, and generally strengthen NATO's defence and deterrence posture. NATO will always adapt to the evolving security environment.

[74] Michael N Schmitt (ed), *Tallinn Manual on International Law Applicable to Cyber Warfare* (CUP 2013); Michael N Schmitt (ed), *Tallinn Manual 2.0 on the International Law Applicable to Cyber Operations* (CUP 2017).

[75] SOFA (n 62).

[76] 'Environment–NATO's Stake' (NATO, 9 December 2014) <https://www.nato.int/cps/en/natohq/topics_91048.htm> accessed 9 April 2020.

D. Conclusion

The commemorations of the North Atlantic Treaty's seventieth anniversary over the course of 2019 have pointed to NATO's enduring role as a key global security institution. The ability to adapt to new global security challenges has been key to the Alliance's longevity and to its effectiveness in the future. Compliance with international law is at the core of NATO's values and is part of the rule of law that the Alliance was founded to defend. While achieving consensus amongst Allies can be complicated when there are different legal obligations or interpretations at play, NATO has a good track record in fostering legal interoperability. This ability to operate in a multinational way, despite differing legal frameworks, is forged through an ongoing process of communication amongst Allies and is tested by exercises and joint operations. Promoting communication about—and ultimately more clarity on—the legal aspects of emerging security challenges is seen as important in order to lay the groundwork for NATO policies to deal with these areas. In recent years, this has been the case for cyber and hybrid threats. There will likely be demand for legal discussion within NATO on the wide-ranging military applications of artificial intelligence and the strategic use of data. The Organization's long-standing practices are both framed by international law and in turn contribute to the evolution of international law in some areas. The North Atlantic Organization, a dynamic global security actor, thus makes a contribution to defending and advancing the international law of global security.

Acknowledgement

I gratefully acknowledge the support provided by Mark Norris of the Office of Legal Affairs. The views expressed in this article are mine alone and do not necessarily represent the views of NATO or its Allies.

CHAPTER 58

THE ORGANIZATION FOR SECURITY AND CO-OPERATION IN EUROPE

THOMAS GREMINGER

A. Introduction

For several decades, the normative framework for European security has been based on the principles and commitments of the Helsinki Final Act, as agreed by consensus amongst the High Representatives of thirty-five States at the Conference on Security and Co-operation in Europe (CSCE) on 1 August 1975. The Helsinki principles and commitments, the result of more than two years of almost unbroken diplomatic negotiations, became the basis for guiding mutual relations amongst the participating States during the Cold War and helped to smooth the process of post-Communist transition. They remain relevant today as the fifty-seven participating States of the Organization for Security and Co-operation in Europe (OSCE) look to return to a rules-based system in order to enhance predictability, trust, and stability.[1]

This chapter looks at how OSCE principles and commitments have contributed to promoting security and cooperation in Europe. It explores how a political body and the norms articulated by its participating States fit into the framework of international law, and influence or are driven by it. It further looks at the impact that the unclear legal status of the OSCE has, particularly on operational activities.

[1] The 1994 CSCE Summit decided the change in name from CSCE to OSCE but stipulated that: 'The change in name from CSCE to OSCE alters neither the character of our CSCE commitments nor the status of the CSCE and its institutions.' CSCE, 'Decision I on Strengthening the CSCE' (Budapest Summit, 21 December 1994) <https://www.osce.org/mc/39554?download=true> accessed 18 February 2020.

The following sections analyse the OSCE as a political arrangement, its legal context, its structures, the status of its international legal personality and its impact, the OSCE as a regional arrangement under the UN Charter, and the various dimensions of the OSCE's work. The final section offers an outlook for the future.

B. The OSCE as a Political Arrangement

The Helsinki Final Act and some of the principal documents adopted thereafter (like the 1990 Charter of Paris for a New Europe[2] and the 1999 Charter for European Security[3]) resemble treaties in certain aspects. They were adopted at solemn diplomatic conferences at the level of Heads of State or Government and in some cases were even signed. However, some of these instruments explicitly specify that they are not eligible for registration under Article 102 of the UN Charter[4] and thus may not qualify as treaties or international agreements. In short, OSCE instruments are politically, not legally, binding. The intention of participating States to maintain the OSCE as a political forum was also expressly underscored in the 2006 OSCE Rules of Procedure which provide that its decision-making bodies have authority to take decisions and adopt documents having a politically (and not legally) binding character for all the OSCE participating States.[5] That is not necessarily a weakness. As German Chancellor Helmut Schmidt stated in 1975, '[t]his Conference created no new international law for Europe. But we have established common rules for the way in which we want to deal with each other and live together in Europe'.[6]

As discussed below, the idiosyncratic nature of the OSCE has advantages and disadvantages. The Organization's political character enables it to move quickly, flexibly, and with agility to adapt to changes and respond to crises. However, the lack of consensus to formally recognize its international legal personality can create barriers to operational efficiency.

[2] OSCE, 'Charter of Paris for a New Europe' (Paris, 21 November 1990) <https://www.osce.org/mc/39516> accessed 18 February 2020.

[3] OSCE, 'Charter for European Security' (Istanbul, 19 November 1999) <https://www.osce.org/mc/39569> accessed 18 February 2020.

[4] Charter of the United Nations 1 UNTS XVI (UN Charter).

[5] OSCE Ministerial Council, 'Rules of Procedure' (1 November 2006) MC.DOC/1/06, rules II.A.2 and II.A.3.

[6] Chancellor Helmut Schmidt quoted in English by Ulrich Fastenrath, 'The Legal Significance of CSCE/OSCE Documents: Distinction between Agreements under International Law and Non-Legal International Agreements' (1995/1996) OSCE Yearbook 411, 415.

C. Legal Context of the Organization for Security and Co-operation in Europe

1. Political Mandate and Decisions: Relationship to International Law

The Helsinki process approach has been explained by one commentator as reflecting 'the assumption that common and comprehensive security is best assured through political consensus rather than legal conditions'.[7] Such political commitments can be termed 'soft-law' and may lead to law by way of custom or eventual treaty.[8] The wide-ranging geographical participation of fifty-seven States, stretching from 'Vancouver to Vladivostok',[9] and the fact that all decisions are taken by consensus, reflecting the agreed views of participating States,[10] give the soft law OSCE decisions and documents particular importance in the emergence or crystallization of *opinio juris* and the progressive development of international law.[11]

The 'Decalogue' of principles set forth in the Helsinki Final Act can be summarized as follows: (1) sovereign equality; (2) refraining from threat or use of force; (3) inviolability of frontiers; (4) territorial integrity of States; (5) peaceful settlement of disputes; (6) non-intervention in internal affairs; (7) respect for human rights; (8) self-determination of peoples; (9) cooperation amongst States; and (10) good faith fulfilment of obligations

[7] David Galbreath/Malte Brosig, 'OSCE' in Knud Erik Jørgensen/Katie Verlin Laatikainen (eds), *Handbook on the European Union and International Institutions: Performance, Policy, Power* (Routledge 2013) 271.

[8] Dinah Shelton, 'International Law and "Relative Normativity"' in Malcolm D Evans (ed), *International Law* (2nd edn, OUP 2006); Andrew T Guzman/Timothy L Meyer, 'International Soft Law' (2010) 2 Journal of Legal Analysis 171; Dinah Shelton, 'Soft Law' in David Armstrong (ed), *Handbook of International Law* (Routledge 2009); Jean d'Aspremont, 'Softness in International Law: A Self-Serving Quest for New Legal Materials' (2008) 19 EJIL 1075; Mary Ellen O'Connell, 'The Role of Soft Law in a Global Order' in Dinah Shelton (ed), *Commitment and Compliance: The Role of Non-Binding Norms in the International Legal System* (OUP 2000); Daniel Thürer, 'Soft Law' MPEPIL (OUP, March 2009); Hartmut Hillgenberg, 'A Fresh Look at Soft Law' (1999) 10 EJIL 499.

[9] The OSCE region includes almost all the States of the northern hemisphere, with fifty-seven participating States, as well as eleven Partners for Co-operation, which do not participate in decision-making. See <https://www.osce.org/participating-states> and <https://www.osce.org/partners-for-cooperation> accessed 18 February 2020.

[10] Rules of Procedure (n 5) Rule II(A) para 2 which defines consensus as, 'the absence of any objection expressed by a participating State to the adoption of the decision [or document] in question'.

[11] For a discussion of the OSCE commitments as legal rules: Marco Odello, 'The Organization for Security and Co-operation in Europe and European Security Law' in Martin Trybus/Nigel D White (eds), *European Security Law* (OUP 2007) 302–10; Marco Odello, 'The Developing Legal Status of the Organisation for Security and Co-operation in Europe' (2006) 22 Anuario Español de Derecho Internacional 351, 371–4; Fastenrath (n 6); Eric Manton, 'The OSCE Human Dimension Process and the Process of Customary International Law Formation' (2005) OSCE Yearbook 195.

under international law. No hierarchy amongst these principles exists, nor can one pick and choose amongst them.[12]

These ten principles broadly overlap with the purposes and principles established in the UN Charter. But the fact that they were couched in a political document enabled them to be articulated more broadly than they would have been in a treaty, and, as has been argued, enabled the very creation of the CSCE.[13] Furthermore, the politically binding nature of the norms does not affect their binding nature as obligations. It simply affects the courses of action available within the OSCE realm to respond to non-compliance, namely, dispute resolution by political means, not legal proceedings.[14]

After the Helsinki Final Act was adopted, the focus shifted to implementation of the agreed principles and commitments. Work focused on three 'baskets' or 'dimensions' of security: (1) politico-military; (2) economic and environmental; and (3) the human as well as cross-dimensional aspects of security. The three dimensions are considered to be interlinked as part of the OSCE's comprehensive approach to security.

Over time, the decisions taken by the CSCE/OSCE participating States to carry out activities in and across these three dimensions resulted in the OSCE's gradual institutionalization, particularly through the establishment of decision-making bodies, institutions, and specialized units within the Secretariat. This growth was largely ad hoc. Nowhere has 'the OSCE' been formally defined. Rather, it acts under the political leadership of one of its participating States, on the basis of decisions taken by consensus by all participating States. Furthermore, it acts through its 'Executive Structures', a term explained in the OSCE Rules of Procedure as '... specific structures for the implementation of decisions taken and tasks set by the participating States. Such structures include the Secretariat, institutions, field operations, special representatives or other operational instruments of the Organization'.[15] Other structures have also been created and further instruments have been concluded within the OSCE sphere.

D. Leadership, Bodies, and Structures

Although the OSCE evolved from a conference into an organization in the early 1990s, it still very much retains its political nature, reflecting the collective views of its fifty-seven participating States. The very use of the term 'participating' rather than 'member' States

[12] OSCE, 'Helsinki Final Act' (Helsinki, 1 August 1975) <https://www.osce.org/helsinki-final-act> accessed 18 February 2020.

[13] Erika B Schlager, 'A Hard Look at Compliance with "Soft" Law: The Case of the OSCE' in Shelton, *Commitment and Compliance* (n 8) 371–2.

[14] Michael Bothe, 'The Various Dispute Settlement Procedures—General International Law and OSCE Practice' in Michael Bothe et al (eds), *The OSCE in the Maintenance of Peace and Security: Conflict Prevention, Crisis Management and Peaceful Settlement of Disputes* (Kluwer 1997) and Torsten Lohmann, 'Dispute Settlement Procedures in the OSCE—Genesis and Overview' in Bothe et al ibid.

[15] Rules of Procedure (n 5) rule II.A, para 13.

suggests the interactive and cooperative nature of the joint venture that these countries have chosen to be part of, for the sake of their national security as well as to improve their relations and contribute to peace in Europe. Decisions are taken on the basis of consensus amongst States that are sovereign equals. As first laid down in the 1973 Final Recommendations of the Helsinki Consultations (The Blue Book), 'consensus shall be understood to mean the absence of any objection expressed by a Representative and submitted by him (sic) as constituting an obstacle to the taking of the decision in question.' In other words, it is not necessary for everyone to agree as long as nobody disagrees. Still, in an organization spanning the northern hemisphere where States sometimes hold fundamentally opposing views, decision-making can be difficult. Yet once agreement is reached, the weight of the decision is considerable, since it has the unanimous support of all participating States.

The OSCE's political nature is also reflected in its leadership. Since 1991, the OSCE has had a Chair-in-Office, a function held by a participating State for one year. According to the mandate,[16] at the political level the OSCE's Secretary-General acts as the representative of the Chairperson-in-Office, with a responsibility to publicize OSCE policy and practices and is entitled to make public statements on behalf of the Organization as a whole. He or she also ensures the effective and continuous working contacts with other international organizations and institutions. Administratively, the Secretary-General is the Chief Administrative Officer of the OSCE, responsible for the efficient use of the organization's resources, and for proper implementation of the financial and staff rules and regulations.

The OSCE has several decision-making bodies. Summits are periodic meetings of Heads of State or Government. Foreign Ministers meet annually as a Ministerial Council. The Chairmanship may also convene informal meetings that do not have a decision-making capacity.[17] The Permanent Council is the principal decision-making body for regular political consultations and for governing the Organization's day-to-day work. There is a fourth decision-making body: the Forum for Security Co-operation (FSC). It is an autonomous decision-making body reviewing the implementation of OSCE commitments and negotiating measures in the fields of arms control and confidence- and security-building (CSBMs).

The OSCE has three main institutions. The Office for Democratic Institutions and Human Rights (ODIHR), established in 1990, is crucial in organizing human dimension meetings, in conducting election observations/assessments and in analysing election standards, in the provision of legislative support, in assisting in the development of democratic institutions and the protection of human rights, as well as in the promotion

[16] OSCE Ministerial Council, 'Decision No 15/04: Role of the OSCE Secretary General' (7 December 2004) MC.DEC/15/04.

[17] Such as the Informal Meeting of Foreign Ministers of OSCE Participating States in Mauerbach (11 July 2017) and in High Tatras (July 2019).

of tolerance and non-discrimination, and in issues specific to Roma and Sinti communities.[18]

The High Commissioner on National Minorities (HCNM), established in 1992, provides 'early warning' and, as appropriate, 'early action' in regard to tensions involving national minority issues which have the potential to develop into a conflict within the OSCE area, affecting peace, stability, or relations between participating States.

The third main OSCE institution is the Representative on Freedom of the Media, established in 1997 to observe relevant media developments in participating States. The Representative provides early warning on violations of freedom of expression and assists participating States by promoting full compliance with OSCE principles and commitments regarding freedom of expression and free media.[19]

The OSCE's field operations are amongst its most important assets. Indeed, the vast majority of resources are devoted to the OSCE's sixteen field operations.[20] Being the front line of its work, they give the Organization an active presence in countries that require assistance and are a cooperative vehicle through which political decisions are translated into action.

1. Other Structures and Instruments Concluded within the Organization's Sphere

In addition to the mandates and activities carried out within the OSCE executive structures, other structures and institutions have been established and instruments concluded within the OSCE sphere:

(a) The OSCE Parliamentary Assembly was established in 1991, in response to the call by Heads of State or Government in the Charter of Paris for a New Europe. It is described in the OSCE Rules of Procedure as 'an autonomous OSCE body which is composed of members of parliament from the OSCE participating States and maintains close relationships with other OSCE structures, determines its own rules of procedure and working methods'.

(b) The OSCE Court of Conciliation and Arbitration was established by the Convention on Conciliation and Arbitration within the OSCE.[21] It entered into

[18] The mandates for these thematic areas: OSCE, *Human Dimension Commitments. Vol. 1: Thematic Compilation* (3nd edn, OSCE 2011).

[19] OSCE Permanent Council, 'Decision No 193: Mandate of the OSCE Representative on Freedom of Media' (5 November 1997) PC.DEC/193.

[20] As of the autumn of 2020, the OSCE had field operations in: Albania, Bosnia and Herzegovina, Montenegro, Serbia, North Macedonia, Moldova, Ukraine (both the Project Co-ordinator and the Special Monitoring Mission), at the Russian checkpoints of Gukovo and Donetsk, in Turkmenistan, Tajikistan, Kazakhstan, Kyrgyzstan, and Uzbekistan, as well as Kosovo.

[21] CSCE Council of Ministers, 'Decision on the Peaceful Settlement of Disputes' (Stockholm, 14–15 December 1992) para 5(b).

force in 1995: thirty-four OSCE participating States had become party to the Convention. However, as yet, the Court has not been seized of a dispute.

(c) Two important treaties in the field of conventional arms control were negotiated in the 1990s. First, the 1990 Treaty on Conventional Armed Forces in Europe (CFE) focused on establishing a military balance at a lower level of armaments between NATO and the then Warsaw Treaty Organization. The dissolution of the Warsaw Pact in 1991 and the emergence of newly independent countries led to the conclusion of the Agreement on Adaptation of the CFE Treaty in 1999. The Adaptation Agreement has not, however, entered into force as it has not been ratified by all CFE States Parties and the CFE is no longer being fully implemented as intended, following the announcement by the Russian Federation in 2007 that it was suspending its implementation.[22] Secondly, the Treaty on Open Skies entered into force in 2002. It establishes a regime of unarmed aerial observation flights over the entire territory of its thirty-four States Parties, including flights quotas, notification of points of entry, and the technical details and inspection for sensors, thereby enhancing transparency and openness in military matters. Although these two treaties have membership distinct from the OSCE and are implemented outside its purview, they were intended to form a web of interlocking and mutually reinforcing arms control obligations and commitments, to enhance predictability, transparency, and military stability in Europe, thereby contributing to reducing the risk of conflict.[23]

E. Status of the Organization's International Legal Personality and its Impact

While the OSCE is called an organization and operates like one, there is a long-standing debate about whether it possesses international legal personality.[24] Although the CSCE was conceived as solely a diplomatic conference in 1975, the decisions of its decision-making bodies to create executive structures with mandates to pursue aims in the three CSCE/OSCE dimensions meant that the OSCE started to act as an organization rather than just a conference of States. One could argue that the OSCE has acquired, de facto, a legal personality.

[22] Duncan B Hollis, 'Russia Suspends CFE Treaty Participation' (2007) 11 American Society of International Law Insights <https://www.asil.org/insights/volume/11/issue/19/russia-suspends-cfe-treaty-participation> accessed 19 February 2020.

[23] OSCE, 'Arms Control' (*OSCE*) <https://www.osce.org/arms-control> accessed 18 February 2020.

[24] Mateja Steinbrück Platise et al (eds), *The Legal Framework of the OSCE* (CUP 2019).

In 1993, the CSCE Council in Rome recognized that in order to carry out the tasks that were being assigned to its various structures, the CSCE needed legal capacity, privileges, and immunities, including for its officials. Participating States were called upon to provide these through national measures.[25] In 2007, consensus was reached at expert level on the text of a Draft Convention on the International Legal Personality, Legal Capacity and Privileges and Immunities of the OSCE. However, this document remains a draft since some participating States argue that a constituent document (Charter) is a legal precondition for such a status to be granted.[26] Since 2009, the open-ended Informal Working Group on Strengthening the Legal Framework of the OSCE (IWG) has been continuously endeavouring to identify and secure consensus on a way forward.

The lack of a universally recognized legal personality seriously affects how the OSCE operates, particularly in the field.[27] A clear example is the impact on the OSCE's work in eastern Ukraine. On 21 March 2014, despite major disagreements between key stakeholders, the Permanent Council adopted Decision No 1117 establishing a new OSCE field operation—the Special Monitoring Mission to Ukraine (SMM). In that decision, the Permanent Council tasked the Secretary-General to deploy an advance team within 24 hours. It was essential to quickly negotiate and conclude an agreement to cover the mandate of the SMM which was to monitor and report on the security situation in Ukraine in teams operating 24/7.

The Memorandum of Understanding was signed on 14 April 2014 (providing for provisional application of all its provisions except privileges and immunities), ratified by the Ukrainian Parliament on 29 May 2014, and entered into force on 13 June 2014. Even so, for the first three weeks, the SMM operated with no formal legal status or capacity. For the first twelve weeks, the SMM monitors had no formal privileges or immunities covering their official activities nor the protection of security guarantees by the host country other than the courtesy that may have been extended to them as official visitors. Notwithstanding this, the SMM was still carrying out mandated activities and was exposed to an uncertain degree of liability for any damages caused or suffered by those monitors. The abduction of eight SMM monitors for one month by armed groups brought these concerns very much to the fore.[28]

[25] CSCE, 'Legal Capacity and Privileges and Immunities' (Rome, 1 December 1993) CSCE/4-C/Dec.2 in OSCE Permanent Council, 'Decision No 383: Report on OSCE Legal Capacity and on Privileges and Immunities to the Ministerial Council' (26 November 2000) PC.DEC/383, Annex 1 to Annex A (SEC.GAL/20/00).

[26] Letter from the Chair of the Informal Working Group at Expert Level to the OSCE Spanish Chairmanship (22 October 2007) CIO.GAL/159/07, annexing the Final Document of the Informal Working Group on the Draft Convention on the International Legal Personality, Legal Capacity, and Privileges and Immunities of the OSCE. cf the proposed draft 'Charter of the OSCE' tabled by the Russian Federation (18 May 2007) PC.DEL/444/07 and again by Armenia, Belarus, Kazakhstan, Kyrgyzstan, Uzbekistan, Russian Federation and Tajikistan (18 September 2007) PC.DEL/897/07.

[27] Lisa Tabassi, 'The Role of the Organisation in Asserting Legal Personality: The Position of the OSCE Secretariat on the OSCE Legal Status' in Steinbrück Platise et al (n 24).

[28] ibid Tabassi (n 27).

The case of the SMM is not unique. Although not as dramatic, similar consequences are experienced routinely in the daily operations of other OSCE executive structures, including the Secretariat, Institutions, and the other field operations. These include, most importantly:

- The need to negotiate the status of the OSCE on an ad hoc basis, with each country hosting a structure, project, event or other official activity, and the lack of leverage by the OSCE in such negotiations; and
- Ad hoc and incomplete legal capacity, privileges, and immunities provided for in the 1993 Rome Council Decision, leaving the OSCE as the object of national legislation and in a weak negotiating position.

Due to the critical need for legal status and privileges and immunities in order for the OSCE to operate effectively and carry out its mandate, the Secretariat is left with no other choice but to pragmatically assert that the OSCE enjoys them on a de facto or customary basis across the OSCE region.[29] In doing so, it relies upon the 1949 *Reparations for Injuries* Advisory Opinion. In that case, the International Court of Justice (ICJ) concluded that in order for the UN to achieve its ends, the attribution of international personality was indispensable.[30]

Absent any progress in the IWG, a short-term stopgap measure was launched in 2015: the model Standing Arrangement.[31] The model Arrangement was proposed to all participating States under the Secretary-General's executive authority and it recognizes the legal status of the OSCE and its officials in national jurisdictions in a comprehensive and harmonized manner, replacing the patchwork of arrangements across the OSCE region as envisaged by the 1993 Rome Council Decision. In 2017, two States took significant concrete steps to improve the legal status of the OSCE: Austria, by concluding a Headquarters Agreement with the OSCE[32] and Poland, by concluding an Arrangement with the OSCE, including provisions to host the OSCE ODIHR in Warsaw.[33] At least for those two States, the OSCE is a subject of international law possessing treaty-making capacity. This may represent a shift in the long-standing debate within the OSCE.

In contrast to the ongoing internal debate on the legal status of the OSCE, other international organizations recognize the OSCE's international legal personality by

[29] Michael Wood, 'Do International Organizations Enjoy Immunity Under Customary International Law?' (2013) 10 International Organizations Law Review 287; Tabassi (n 27).

[30] *Reparation for Injuries Suffered in the Service of the United Nations* (Advisory Opinion) [1949] ICJ Rep 174, 179.

[31] OSCE, 'The Secretary General's Initiative for a Bilateral Standing Arrangement with each OSCE Participating State' (8 September 2016) SEC.GAL/135/16, revised version (2017) SEC.GAL/117/17.

[32] Helmut Tichy/Catherine Quidenus, 'Consolidating the International Legal Personality of the OSCE: A Headquarters Agreement with Austria' (2017) 14 International Organizations Law Review 403.

[33] Jasna Arsic-Dapo, 'Another Brick in the Wall: Building up the OSCE as an International Organization One Agreement at a Time' (2017) 14 International Organizations Law Review 414.

routinely concluding agreements with it on an equal basis.[34] A good example is the OSCE's relationship with the UN.

F. The OSCE as a Regional Arrangement under the United Nations Charter

The OSCE is the world's largest regional organization. The organization's role as a regional arrangement of the UN was recognized in 1992 at the Helsinki Summit, when Heads of State or Government solemnly declared their

> understanding that the CSCE is a regional arrangement in the sense of Chapter VIII of the Charter of the United Nations. As such, it provides an important link between European and global security. The rights and responsibilities of the Security Council remain unaffected in their entirety. The CSCE will work together closely with the United Nations especially in preventing and settling conflicts.[35]

As a regional arrangement, the OSCE is encouraged 'to make every effort to achieve pacific settlement of local disputes' before referring them to the UN Security Council (UNSC). This suggests a degree of subsidiarity whereby the OSCE, whenever possible, would deal with issues in its region affecting international peace and security—bearing in mind of course that the UNSC has, pursuant to the UN Charter, 'primary responsibility' for establishing and maintaining international peace.

The UN General Assembly (UNGA) has welcomed the CSCE Summit declaration, '[s]tressing the need for enhanced cooperation and coordination between the CSCE and the UN'.[36] On the basis of Resolution 47/10 the 'Framework for Cooperation and Coordination between the United Nations Secretariat and the Conference on Security and Cooperation in Europe' ('1993 Framework') was agreed, in 1993.[37] That same year the UNGA granted observer status to the CSCE.[38]

[34] OSCE, 'Report to the Ministerial Council on Strengthening the Legal Framework of the OSCE' (8 December 2017) MC.GAL/7/17, para 35.

[35] CSCE, 'Helsinki Document: The Challenges of Change' (9–10 July 1992) Helsinki Declaration, para 25 <https://www.osce.org/mc/39530?download=true> accessed 19 February 2020.

[36] UNGA Res 47/10 (28 October 1992) para 1.

[37] CSCE, 'Framework for Cooperation and Coordination between the United Nations Secretariat and the Conference on Security and Cooperation in Europe' (26 May 1993) Journal No 14, Annex 2, 3 <https://www.osce.org/node/424574?download=true> accessed 12 February 2020 (1993 Framework); Exchange of Letters between UN Secretary-General Boutros-Boutros Ghali and Chairperson-in-Office of the CSCE Margaretha af Ugglas (26 May 1993) Journal No 14, Annex 2, 1–2 <https://www.osce.org/node/424574?download=true> accessed 12 February 2020.

[38] UNGA Res 48/5 (13 October 1993).

The 1993 Framework further develops the relations between the parties, specifying forms of cooperation to that end, and establishes a relationship of complementarity between the two Organizations.[39] A characteristic instance of the complementarity existing between the UN and the OSCE was the inclusion of the OSCE Mission in Kosovo (OMIK) as a component of the UN Mission in Kosovo (UNMIK), under UNSC Resolution 1244 (1999) and OSCE Permanent Council Decision No 305 (1999).

G. The Three Dimensions of the Organization's Work

1. First Dimension: Politico-Military

a. *Conventional Arms Control and Confidence- and Security-building Measures*

The Heads of State or Government who signed the 1975 Helsinki Accords, committed themselves to achieve 'general and complete disarmament under strict and effective international control',[40] undertaking specific commitments established in its 'Document on Confidence-building Measures and Certain Aspects of Security and Disarmament'. While the initial measures were voluntary in nature, the favourable political climate allowed for the gradual development of these measures, which provide for military transparency and verification measures to foster military predictability and stability.

A key OSCE document on confidence- and security-building measures (CSBMs) is the 2011 Vienna Document (and its earlier versions of 1990, 1992, 1994, and 1999). Other key documents addressing the politico-military aspects of security were consolidated in the 1996 Framework for Arms Control[41] which was adopted at the Lisbon Summit.[42] The Annex to the Framework listed the 'agreements' that constituted 'a basis for a web of interlocking and mutually reinforcing agreements, essential for building the collective and individual security of the participating States, irrespective of whether or not they are a party or signatory to these agreements'.[43] The Framework has been further developed through additional FSC decisions, including the adoption of the 2000 Document on Small Arms and Light Weapons (reissued in 2012) and the 2003 OSCE Document on Stockpiles of Conventional Ammunition (reissued in 2011). However, the failure to modernize the existing instruments as well as perceived non-compliance have resulted

[39] 1993 Framework (n 37) para 4. [40] Helsinki Final Act (n 12) s 1(b)(i).

[41] OSCE, 'Framework for Arms Control' (3 December 1996) FSC.DEC/8/96. [42] ibid para 3.

[43] These include the Treaty on Conventional Armed Forces in Europe, the Open Skies Treaty, the Concluding Act of the Negotiation on Personnel Strength of Conventional Armed Forces in Europe, Stabilizing Measures for Localized Crisis Situation, Principles Governing Conventional Arms Transfers, Global Exchange of Military Information, Vienna Document 1994, Code of Conduct on Politico-Military Aspects of Security, and Principles Governing Non-Proliferation.

in the erosion of the framework of arms control obligations and commitments in the OSCE area, a lack of trust, and ongoing debates on compliance issues.

In this context, in 2016 the Ministerial Council adopted a Declaration, in which the Foreign Ministers of OSCE participating States committed themselves to 'exploring, inter alia, how the negative developments concerning the conventional arms control and CSBM architecture in Europe can be reversed.'[44] They further underlined that 'strong commitment [. . .] to full implementation and further development of arms control agreements is essential for enhancing military and political stability within the OSCE area.'[45]

Subsequently, the 'Structured Dialogue' process was launched which has been welcomed by Ministers. In 2017 and 2018, it focused its activities on politico-military aspects, including threat perceptions, risk reduction and de-escalation, military doctrines, and military force postures. It is considered one of the few channels of communication between Russia and the West in the polarized environment, and could play an important role in rebuilding trust and cooperation.

b. *Early Warning, Conflict Prevention, and Action in the Conflict Cycle*

In the 1992 Helsinki Document, participating States agreed 'to provide for more flexible and active dialogue and better early warning and dispute settlement' with the aim of improving the CSCE's capacities for conflict prevention and resolution.[46] To that end, a number of provisions were established,[47] including the mandate of the High Commissioner on National Minorities (HCNM), who is authorized to formally draw the attention of participating States to potential crisis situations and to engage in preventive diplomacy as required.[48]

The OSCE has been described as 'a primary organization for the peaceful settlement of disputes within its region and as a key instrument for early warning, conflict prevention, crisis management and post-conflict rehabilitation.'[49] Its toolbox is best described in a landmark 2011 decision entitled 'Elements of the Conflict Cycle.'[50] That decision also added new tools, including a mandate to: develop a systematic early warning capacity; strengthen early action and crisis response capacities; and establish a systematic

[44] OSCE Ministerial Council, 'Hamburg Ministerial Declaration—From Lisbon to Hamburg: Declaration on the Twentieth Anniversary of the OSCE Framework for Arms Control' (9 December 2016) MC.DOC/4/16, para 3.

[45] ibid. [46] Helsinki Document 1992 (n 35) Decision III, para 1.

[47] OSCE, 'Mechanism and Procedures' (8 June 2004) <https://www.osce.org/cpc/39615> accessed 18 February 2020.

[48] OSCE, 'High Commission on National Minorities—Mandate' (*OSCE*) <https://www.osce.org/hcnm/107878> accessed 18 February 2020.

[49] Charter for European Security (n 3) para 7.

[50] OSCE Ministerial Council, 'Decision No 3/11 Elements of the Conflict Cycle, related to Enhancing the OSCE's Capabilities in Early Warning, Early Action, Dialogue Facilitation and Mediation Support, and Post-Conflict Rehabilitation' (7 December 2011) MC.DEC/3/11.

mediation-support capacity[51] (which resulted in the creation of a Mediation Support Team).[52] It also gave the Secretary-General a mandate to formally provide participating States with early warning on potential crisis situations. Moreover, it assigned the OSCE Conflict Prevention Centre (CPC) the function of an OSCE-wide early warning focal point.

Furthermore, in the wake of Ministerial Council Decision No. 3/11, the OSCE established a rapid deployment roster of staff as first responders in times of crisis.[53] The SMM experience highlights the critical importance of effective response capacities and the OSCE Secretariat's valuable role in providing broad support to crisis management initiatives implemented on the ground.[54]

In the early 1990s, it was envisioned that the OSCE could carry out peacekeeping operations.[55] In 1994, a High-Level Planning Group was created to plan for the deployment of a peacekeeping operation in relation to the Nagorno-Karabakh conflict. However, such a force has not yet been deployed. While the OSCE has never carried out a classic peacekeeping operation, the evolution of the UN's approach from peacekeeping to 'peace operations' covers a wider spectrum of activities.[56] As a result, many of the OSCE's field activities, principally the Ukraine SMM, could be considered peace operations.[57]

2. Second Dimension: Economic and Environmental

Within the comprehensive approach to security, the Economic and Environmental Dimension has been, since the very beginning, an integral part of OSCE activities aimed at fostering stability and cooperation amongst participating States. The founders of the Organization recognized that developing cooperation in economic and environmental matters contributes to greater stability, security, and prosperity, and also prevents conflicts and fosters reconstruction.

Over more than forty years, a number of cornerstone documents have been adopted and have set the agenda for the Organization's engagement in the economic, environmental,

[51] Claus Neukirch, 'Early Warning and Early Action—Current Developments in OSCE Conflict Prevention Activities' (2013) OSCE Yearbook 123.

[52] David Lanz et al, 'Understanding Mediation Support Structures' (*SwissPeace*, October 2017) <http://www.swisspeace.ch/fileadmin/user_upload/pdf/Mediation/swisspeace_MSS_study_new.pdf> accessed 18 February 2020.

[53] Claus Neukirch, 'The Special Monitoring Mission to Ukraine: Operational Challenges and New Horizons' (2014) OSCE Yearbook 183.

[54] Claus Neukirch, 'The Special Monitoring Mission to Ukraine in Its Second Year: Ongoing OSCE Conflict Management in Ukraine' (2015) OSCE Yearbook 220.

[55] Helsinki Document 1992 (n 35) Decision III, para 17. Gian Luca Burci, 'Division of Labour between the UN and the OSCE in Connection with Peace-Keeping' in Bothe et al, *OSCE in the Maintenance of Peace and Security* (n 14).

[56] UNGA/UNSC 'Report of the High-Level Panel on Peace Operations on Uniting our Strength for Peace: Politics, Partnership and People' (16 June 2015) UN Doc A/70/95-S/2015/446, para 56: 'the UN should embrace a dual role as one partner responding politically and operationally alongside others, as well as an enabler and facilitator of others to play their increasingly prominent roles'.

[57] Walter Kemp, *OSCE Peace Operations: Soft Security in Hard Environments* (IPI June 2016).

and energy fields. A number of Ministerial Council Decisions and other documents have been adopted since. These decisions define both commitments for the participating States and the mandates of the OSCE executive structures. Specifically, the Co-ordinator of OSCE Economic and Environmental Activities (OCEEA), established in 1997, and his Office, is tasked with monitoring both economic and environmental developments, with the aim of alerting participating States of any threat to their security and stability. Moreover, the OCEEA supports participating States to develop and implement policies and projects that promote security and cooperation in the OSCE region. In addition, the OSCE field operations play a crucial role in the implementation of economic and environmental activities in the field and in the identification of needs and requirements at the local level. Increasingly, the OSCE is helping participating States to implement the Sustainable Development Goals.

3. Third Dimension: The Human Dimension

The OSCE's third dimension is often referred to as the human dimension. The term 'human dimension' refers to the commitments made by participating States to ensure full respect for human rights and fundamental freedoms, abide by the rule of law, promote the principles of democracy and, in this regard, build, strengthen, and protect democratic institutions, as well as promote tolerance throughout the OSCE area.

Since the 1975 Helsinki Final Act, a clear link was made between security and human rights.[58] The inclusion of human rights commitments within the Helsinki Final Act inspired civil society groups to hold their leaders accountable for the promises that they had made. The commitments and guidelines outlined in the Helsinki Final Act were reviewed and refined in a series of follow-up meetings. This tradition continues in an annual Human Dimension Implementation Meeting held in Warsaw every year.

OSCE human dimension commitments apply to all participating States. The fact that all decisions are made on the basis of consensus means that no participating State can claim that certain commitments do not apply to it. Furthermore, as stated 'categorically and irrevocably' in the 1991 Moscow Document and repeated in the 2010 Astana Commemorative Declaration, 'commitments undertaken in the field of the human dimension are matters of direct and legitimate concern to all participating States and do not belong exclusively to the internal affairs of the State concerned'.[59] This suggests a degree of legitimate intrusiveness.

That said, the OSCE is a cooperative security organization. Therefore, the main emphasis is to assist States to live up to their commitments rather than to call them out or isolate them. Where this is insufficient, there are mechanisms like the Vienna or the Moscow Mechanism that oblige participating States to provide information on

[58] Helsinki Final Act (n 12) principle VII.

[59] OSCE, 'Astana Commemorative Declaration: Towards a Security Community' (3 December 2010) SUM.DOC/1/10/Corr.1, para 6.

questions relating to the human dimension or, in the case of the Moscow Mechanism, enable the deployment of missions of experts to help States resolve problems relating to the human dimension.

a. *Freedom of the Media*

The OSCE participating States consider freedom of expression a fundamental and internationally recognized human right and a basic component of a democratic society. The OSCE Representative on Freedom of the Media is mandated to observe media developments in the participating States and to advocate and promote full compliance with the Organization's principles and commitments in respect of freedom of expression and free media. Recently in the OSCE, propaganda and disinformation has been a subject of intense discussion, negotiation and policymaking. Safety of journalists has also become a higher priority.

4. Transnational Threats and Cross-Dimensional Issues

In a security environment where threats transcend borders, one of the OSCE's priorities is to help States prevent and deal with transnational threats like terrorism, organized crime, and cyberthreats. Furthermore, it addresses cross-dimensional issues like human trafficking. And it promotes gender equality.

a. *Countering International Terrorism, Enhancing Border Security, and Law Enforcement*

Following the 9/11 attacks, counter-terrorism became a central issue in the OSCE. In 2001, the 'Bucharest Plan of Action for Combating Terrorism' identified a number of core preventive actions against terrorism to be fostered in the OSCE.[60] This Action Plan has been further developed by seven more OSCE decisions, including efforts to foster implementation of UNSC Resolution 1540 (2004) which aims at preventing States from providing any form of support to non-State actors for the proliferation of weapons of mass destruction as well as the 2007 'Public–Private Partnership in Countering Terrorism', jointly sponsored by the Russian Federation and the United States. These decisions, together with fifty other relevant documents and decisions adopted by the OSCE in this field were merged in 2012 into the 'Consolidated Framework for the Fight against Terrorism'.[61]

Although the OSCE's initial steps in the fight against terrorism were perceived as tasks of the security and criminal justice sectors, recent initiatives in countering

[60] OSCE, 'The Bucharest Plan of Action for Combating Terrorism' (4 December 2001) MC(9).DEC/1, Annex, paras 9–26.

[61] OSCE Permanent Council, 'Decision No 1063: OSCE Consolidated Framework for the Fight against Terrorism' (7 December 2012) PC.DEC/1063. For a comprehensive overview: OSCE, 'Overview of OSCE Counter-Terrorism Related Commitments' (19 April 2018) SEC.GAL/69/18; OSCE, 'Consolidated Reference for OSCE Anti-Terrorism Efforts' (19 April 2018) SEC.GAL/68/18.

violent extremism and radicalization that lead to terrorism established a broader, multidimensional approach to OSCE counter-terrorism efforts. In order to prevent terrorists from travelling under false identities or aliases, OSCE's countering-terrorism and border management activities have included the strengthening of travel documents and identity management as well as the collection and use of passenger data.[62] The OSCE has been supporting countries in its region to implement UNSC Resolution 2178 (2014), which mandated all States to collect and analyse Advance Passenger Information (API)[63] in order to detect the movement of foreign terrorist fighters who may appear on watch-lists or risk profiles.

At the 2001 Bucharest Ministerial Council, police-related activities were recognized as a key element to assist in maintaining the primacy of law and to promote the development of independent judicial systems, and as an integral part of the OSCE's efforts in conflict prevention, crisis management, and post-conflict rehabilitation.[64] A police-related capacity was set up in the OSCE Secretariat immediately thereafter.[65] The focus has been on two main areas: (1) Police development and reform; (2) Addressing threats posed by criminal activity, meaning transnational organized crime, including illicit trafficking in human beings and drugs and cybercrime.[66] When implementing its police-related activities, the OSCE supports the full implementation of the UN Convention against Transnational Organized Crime (UNTOC) and the UN Convention Against Corruption.

b. *Cybersecurity*

The OSCE has been quick to adapt to cyberthreats. In particular, it has adopted sixteen practical cyber/ICT Confidence Building Measures (CBMs), aimed at making cyberspace more predictable, boosting regional cooperation, and building a stable and resilient 'cyber neighbourhood'. These CBMs contribute to international efforts to defining norms of responsible State behaviour in relation to cyberspace.[67]

[62] From the OSCE Ministerial Council, 'Decision No 7/03: Travel Documents Security' (2 December 2003) MC.DEC/7/03, the consequent OSCE Ministerial Councils have adopted four more decisions relating to strengthening travel documents, the latest being the key OSCE, 'Decision No 6/16: Enhancing the Use of Advance Passenger Information' (9 December 2016) MC.DEC/6/16.

[63] An API system is an electronic communication system that allows law enforcement officials to know in advance whether known criminal offenders are attempting to enter their countries.

[64] OSCE Ministerial Council, 'Decision No 9: Police-Related Activities' (4 December 2001) MC(9).DEC/9.

[65] OSCE Permanent Council, 'Decision No 448: Establishment of the Seconded Post of Senior Police Adviser in the OSCE Secretariat' (4 December 2001) PC.DEC/448.

[66] OSCE Permanent Council, 'Decision No 1049: OSCE Strategic Framework for Police-Related Activities' (26 July 2012) PC.DEC/1049.

[67] On international efforts: recommendations in UNGA 'Note by the Secretary-General: Group of Governmental Experts on Developments in the Field of Information and Telecommunications in the Context of International Security' (30 July 2010) UN Doc A/65/201; UNGA 'Note by the Secretary-General: Group of Governmental Experts on Developments in the Field of Information and Telecommunications in the Context of International Security' (24 June 2013) UN Doc A/68/98; UNGA 'Note by the Secretary-General: Group of Governmental Experts on Developments in the Field of Information and Telecommunications in the Context of International Security' (22 July 2015) UN Doc A/70/174.

Current efforts by participating States focus on the meaningful implementation of the CBMs, as emphasized through two consecutive Ministerial Council Decisions.[68] This means undertaking concrete activities to operationalize individual measures, building up capacities of policymakers who are in the position to integrate CBMs into their State's cyber diplomacy toolbox as well as enhancing inter-regional efforts on cyber stability.[69]

c. *Combating Trafficking in Human Beings*

Following the adoption of the UNTOC[70] together with the Protocol to Prevent, Suppress and Punish Trafficking in Persons, especially Women and Children[71], the OSCE adopted in 2003, through its MC Decision 2/03, the OSCE Action Plan to Combat Trafficking in Human Beings.[72] Complemented by its 2013 Addendum,[73] the Action Plan forms the core of the OSCE anti-trafficking commitments, a set of recommendations known as the four 'Ps': prevention, prosecution, protection of victims' rights, and partnerships. In this way, the OSCE helps, at a regional level, to promote international efforts against this modern form of slavery.

The post of Special Representative and Co-ordinator for Combating Trafficking in Human Beings (OSR/CTHB) was established in 2003 within the OSCE Secretariat to promote the implementation of the Organization's anti-trafficking commitments. In recent years, the Office of the Special Representative placed a special emphasis on addressing trafficking in human beings in crisis situations.[74] This includes a wide range of issues such as supporting States in addressing trafficking in human beings along migration routes, raising awareness of the threat facing conflict-affected populations, and exploring the nexus between terrorism and human trafficking.[75]

[68] OSCE Ministerial Council, 'Decision No 5/16: OSCE Efforts Related to Reducing the Risks of Conflict Stemming from the Use of Information and Communication Technologies' (9 December 2016) MC.DEC/5/16 and OSCE Ministerial Council, 'Decision No 5/17: Enhancing OSCE Efforts to Reduce the Risks of Conflict Stemming from the Use of Information and Communication Technologies' (8 December 2017) MC.DEC/5/17.

[69] OSCE Forum for Security Co-operation, 'Decision No 5/17: Use of the OSCE Communications Network to Support Implementation of Permanent Council Decisions No 1039, No 1106 and No 1202' (19 July 2017) FSC.DEC/5/17.

[70] 2225 UNTS 209. [71] 2237 UNTS 319.

[72] OSCE Ministerial Council, 'OSCE Action Plan to Combat Trafficking in Human Beings' (2 December 2003) MC.DEC/2/03, Annex I. The Action Plan adopts a multidimensional approach to combating trafficking in human beings.

[73] OSCE Permanent Council, 'Decision No 1107: Addendum to the OSCE Action Plan to Combat Trafficking in Human Beings: One Decade Later' (6 December 2013) PC.DEC/1107/Corr.1.

[74] OSCE, 'Report: From Reception to Recognition: Identifying and Protecting Human Trafficking Victims in Mixed Migration Flows' (2017) <https://www.osce.org/secretariat/367061?download=true> accessed 24 February 2020.

[75] On the complementarity of OSCE programmes with the global anti-trafficking agenda: UNSC 'Report of the UN Secretary-General on Trafficking in Persons in Armed Conflict Pursuant to UNSC Res 2331 (2016)' (20 November 2017) UN Doc S/2017/939.

d. *Promoting Gender Equality*

The foundations for gender equality in the OSCE were laid in the 1975 Helsinki Final Act when all participating States committed to respect human rights and fundamental freedoms 'for all without distinction as to race, sex, language or religion'.[76] A real breakthrough with respect to gender equality in the OSCE came with the 1991 Istanbul Summit and the Charter for European Security adopted at the summit, where the Heads of State or Government declared that 'the full and equal exercise by women of their human rights is essential to achieve a more peaceful, prosperous and democratic OSCE area. We are committed to making equality between men and women an integral part of our policies, both at the level of our States and within the Organization'.[77] The 2004 Gender Action Plan is, to date, the most comprehensive OSCE document on gender equality.[78] According to the Plan, OSCE executive structures assist participating States in the implementation of six priority areas of gender equality.[79] Since 2004, these commitments have been expanded upon and elaborated in more detail through a number of decisions.[80]

H. Outlook

The OSCE has been variously classified as a permanent pan-European organ,[81] or a new form of international organization consisting of a forum for trans-governmental networking, led by Heads of State, which may ripen, or not, into a more traditional organization.[82] Most recently, it has been declared a pillar of European security, which lies at the heart of the European security order.[83]

That order has been seriously shaken in recent years. Indeed, security and cooperation in the OSCE area are arguably at their lowest point since the end of the Cold War. There

[76] Helsinki Final Act (n 12) principle VII. [77] Charter for European Security (n 3) para 23.

[78] OSCE Ministerial Council, 'Decision No 14/04 2004 OSCE Action Plan for the Promotion of Gender Equality' (7 December 2004) MC.DEC/14/04, IV, paras 41–2.

[79] ibid V, para 44.

[80] These include, *inter alia*, OSCE Ministerial Council, 'Decision No 14/05: Women in Conflict Prevention, Crisis Management and Post-Conflict Rehabilitation' (6 December 2005) MC.DEC/14/05; OSCE Ministerial Council, 'Decision No 15/05: Preventing and Combating Violence against Women' (6 December 2005) MC.DEC/15/05; OSCE Ministerial Council, 'Decision No 7/09: Women's Participation in Political and Public Life' (2 December 2009) MC.DEC/07/09; OSCE Ministerial Council, 'Decision No 10/22: Promoting Equal Opportunities in the Economic Sphere' (7 December 2011) MC.DEC/10/11; OSCE Ministerial Council, 'Decision No 7/14: Preventing and Combating Violence against Women' (5 December 2014) MC.DEC/7/14/Corr.1.

[81] Marie-Claude Smouts, 'Les Suites Institutionnelles de la Conférence sur la Sécurité et la Coopération en Europe' (1974) Revue Française de Science Politique 1230, 1232.

[82] Anne-Marie Slaughter, *A New World Order* (Princeton UP 2004) 50–1.

[83] European Union, 'Shared Vision, Common Action: A Stronger Europe—Global Strategy for the European Union's Foreign and Security Policy' (June 2016) 33 <https://eeas.europa.eu/archives/docs/top_stories/pdf/eugs_review_web.pdf> accessed 25 February 2020.

is a profound lack of trust and constructive dialogue between some States. Furthermore, there is a lack of trust in the ability of governments and multilateral organizations to deal with critical and complex challenges. Many of these threats and challenges are significantly different than those faced by the founders of the CSCE. At the same time, there is an urgent need to go back to a rules-based system and work together through organizations like the OSCE to regulate spaces that require order, address common threats and challenges, reduce risks, and both build and sustain peace.

As has been described in this chapter, on the one hand the OSCE's political character enables the Organization to be agile, and to respond quickly and creatively to emerging threats and challenges. Despite being of a political character, its principles and commitments provide a normative framework for peaceful relations within and between States. On the other hand, the lack of a clear legal status of the OSCE creates operational challenges, particularly in relation to increasingly complex peace operations in hostile environments. No doubt the debate will continue about whether or not the OSCE needs a constituent legal document, like a charter, to enshrine its legal status or if it should remain as a primarily political inter-governmental organization rooted in shared principles that have been agreed to at the highest level. Until this dilemma is resolved by the participating States, the OSCE will continue its important work, despite the obstacles caused by its unclear legal status, and do its best to help States live up to their commitments.

Acknowledgement

The author would like to thank Lisa Tabassi and Walter Kemp for their support in drafting this chapter. The views expressed herein include the author's personal observations in addition to positions officially asserted in the OSCE.

CHAPTER 59

THE ROLE OF THE UNITED NATIONS IN SHAPING GLOBAL SECURITY LAW

ADAM DAY AND DAVID M MALONE

A. Introduction

THE UN Charter, negotiated at the close of the Second World War, was designed to protect sovereign powers from aggression and usher in an era of collective security. Though this placed the UN at the centre of global security, the Charter did not envisage that the Organization would legislate or enforce international law. Indeed, the Charter did not originally cast the UN as an 'international legal person' entitled to make international law.[1] Yet, over the past seventy years, the UN has played a remarkably broad, influential, and sometimes controversial role in the development and enforcement of international law, exploring, and often stretching, the limits of the Charter.

The central contention of this chapter is that the UN has contributed to the international law of global security in three related ways: (1) as a lawmaker, or something very much like it, with the UN Security Council (UNSC) empowered through the Charter to adopt decisions binding on all Member States; (2) as an interpreter of international law, with significant impact on the law of global security; and (3) as an agenda-setter, establishing norms and shaping international responses to new security challenges. In all of these, the role of the UNSC has predominated, particularly in the

[1] *Reparation for Injuries Suffered in the Service of the United Nations* (Advisory Opinion) [1949] ICJ Rep 174, finding that the UN did have a legal personality.

post-Cold War period when the pace of its engagement and its willingness to intervene in a wide range of settings increased dramatically.[2]

This does not mean that the UN is always the best or even the appropriate actor when it comes to making, shaping, and enforcing international law. Critics of the 'hegemonic international law practices'[3] of the UNSC, and those who claim that the UN has overstepped its Charter-based authority in the area of global security, are often persuasive.[4] And it is worth noting too that today's—and likely tomorrow's—security challenges often appear to outstrip the ability of the UN to respond effectively.

This chapter therefore also considers the political limitations of the UN as an actor shaping global law, and the attendant risks this contested role poses to effective management of international peace and security. But, just as it adapted in the post-Cold War period to new conflict dynamics and power constellations, the UN is likely to remain a key player in the global legal order in some respects and will need to calibrate its decisions accordingly, which it has not always done in the past. This is especially important as the future of global security will involve transnational challenges that cannot be effectively addressed outside of the multilateral system.

B. Legal Framework: The UN's Central Role in the Law of Global Security

The UN Charter is a sort of 'constitution' for the world, providing the basic rules of the international system and overriding all other treaty obligations.[5] The central intent of the Charter is quite clear: to prohibit the use of force by States other than for self-defence, and establish a system of collective security to defend States from threats to the peace and acts of aggression.[6] This notion of collective self-defence is so central to the law of global security it has been called 'the international community's right to prevent war'.[7] The Charter thus sets up a natural tension between protecting the sovereignty of States as the cornerstone of the Westphalian system, while also granting the international community the right to override sovereignty in the case of a threat to international

[2] David M Malone, 'Security Council' in Thomas G Weiss/Sam Daws (eds), *The Oxford Handbook on the United Nations* (OUP 2008).

[3] Detlev F Vagts, 'Hegemonic International Law' (2001) 95 AJIL 843. See also, José E Alvarez, 'Hegemonic International Law Revisited' (2003) 97 AJIL 873.

[4] Michael Glennon, *Limits of Law, Prerogatives of Power: Interventionism After Kosovo* (Palgrave 2001) 120.

[5] Thomas Franck, *Recourse to Force: State Action Against Threats and Armed Attacks* (CUP 2002) 5; cf Charter of the United Nations 1 UNTS XVI (UN Charter) art 103.

[6] Franck (n 5) 2.

[7] Thomas G Weiss et al, *The United Nations and Changing World Politics* (6th edn, Westview Press 2010) 5.

peace and security.[8] Navigating the murky waters between threats to collective security and the sovereignty of States has proven one of the international community's major security challenges over the past seventy years.

Importantly in this context, the UN Charter did not abolish the positivist international legal order that preceded it. States remain the entities empowered to engage in lawmaking, while the consent-based treaty system remains the major source of international rights and obligations.[9] In fact, Article 38(1) of the Statute of the International Court of Justice (ICJ)—generally considered the shorthand for the sources of international law—does not list the resolutions of the UNSC or the UN General Assembly (UNGA) as sources of international law. However, Article 25 of the UN Charter does grant the UNSC the power to make decisions that are binding on all Member States, an authority scholars call its 'lawmaking' or 'legislative' role.[10] As this chapter later discusses, the Council's capacity to formulate rules which are legally binding on States is not in question, but its legislative role can become contentious when decisions impose binding obligations on all Member States for an undefined period of time or are of an excessively sweeping nature.

Articles 39, 41, and 42 of the UN Charter, taken together, bestow an extraordinary set of powers on the UNSC. Not only is it able to determine the existence of a threat to international peace and security, but it is also given broad scope to determine the appropriate response, up to and including the use of military force. Again, it is worth noting that these rights are beyond those granted to individual Member States, even the five Permanent Members (P5). Moreover, many acts the UNSC can take to enforce its actions under these provisions, such as the imposition of sanctions regimes, some key provisions of peacekeeping operations,[11] or the creation of criminal tribunals, have the status of law, binding on all or some Member States.[12] This unprecedented award of authority was, according to the drafters of the Charter, necessary to prevent another World War and manage global security crises. However, it also set the stage for the UNSC to play a far more expansive role than mere crisis management.

The UNGA does not have as prominent a role as the UNSC in the peace and security realm, but it has a similar Charter-based right to make recommendations on 'questions relating to the maintenance of international peace and security',[13] provided the UNSC is not concurrently considering the matter. Moreover, where the UNSC fails to act as required, the UNGA has granted itself, under the famous Uniting for Peace resolution

[8] UN Charter (n 5) art 2(7).

[9] José E Alvarez, 'Legal Perspectives' in Weiss/Daws (n 2).

[10] See eg José E Alvarez, *International Organizations as Law-Makers* (OUP 2005) 184. See also, Ian Johnstone, 'The Security Council and International Law' in Sebastian von Einsiedel et al (eds), *The UN Security Council in the 21st Century* (Lynne Rienner Publishers 2016). See also, Marko Divac Öberg, 'The Legal Effects of Resolutions of the UN Security Council and General Assembly in the Jurisprudence of the ICJ' (2005) 16 EJIL 879.

[11] Simon Chesterman, *You, the People: The United Nations, Transitional Administration, and State-Building* (OUP 2004) 2.

[12] Johnstone (n 10) 773.

[13] UN Charter (n 5) art 11(2).

discussed below, the authority to consider the matter and issue recommendations.[14] Even strong opponents of this role for the UNGA acknowledge that it bestows a right, in some circumstances, to recommend deployment of military force (with the consent of the States involved) to address international security threats.[15]

Through the UNGA, the UN also acts as a forum and convenor of treaty-making conferences that contribute to the law of global security.[16] For example, treaties on aircraft hijacking,[17] terrorist bombings,[18] and nuclear terrorism,[19] all aimed to fill gaps in international law in response to worrying new security trends. Other treaties, such as the Genocide Convention[20] and the Rome Statute of the International Criminal Court,[21] were also drafted under the auspices of the UN and have helped shape the international community's response to security threats. Less clear, however, is the extent to which other UNGA resolutions and declarations may make or shape international law. The Universal Declaration of Human Rights (UDHR),[22] for example, began as a non-binding UNGA resolution, its content later codified into treaties and now overwhelmingly considered customary international law.[23] Other UNGA declarations, such as on Friendly Relations,[24] or resolutions such as the one on the definition of aggression,[25] have been subject to scholarly disagreement as to their effect on international law.[26] More generally, the role of the UNGA is most clearly obvious through the progressive development and codification of international law in dialogue with the International Law Commission (ILC), and through decades of action on long-standing issues, such as the right to self-determination.

Taken together, the principal roles of the UNSC and UNGA in making international law are: (1) binding UNSC decisions; (2) UNSC or UNGA resolutions interpreting key UN Charter provisions;[27] and (3) interpretation of other treaties (such as the 1949

[14] UNGA Res 377(V) (3 November 1950).

[15] Franck (n 5) 35. See also, *Certain Expenses of the United Nations (Article 17, paragraph 2, of the Charter)* (Advisory Opinion) [1962] Rep 151, 164; Rosalyn Higgins et al, *Oppenheim's International Law: United Nations* (vol I, OUP 2017) 20, 58–61.

[16] Rosalyn Higgins, 'The United Nations at 70 Years: The Impact Upon International Law' (2016) 65 ICLQ 1. See also, Rosalyn Higgins et al, *Oppenheim's International Law: United Nations* (vol II, OUP 2017) 973–7.

[17] Convention for the Suppression of Unlawful Seizure of Aircraft 860 UNTS 105.

[18] International Convention for the Suppression of Terrorist Bombings 2149 UNTS 256.

[19] International Convention for the Suppression of Acts of Nuclear Terrorism 2445 UNTS 89.

[20] Convention on the Prevention and Punishment of the Crime of Genocide 78 UNTS 277.

[21] Rome Statute of the International Criminal Court 2187 UNTS 3 (ICC Statute).

[22] UNGA Res 217A (III) (10 December 1948).

[23] See eg Christine Chinkin, 'Sources' in Daniel Moeckli et al (eds), *International Human Rights Law* (2nd edn, OUP 2014).

[24] Declaration on Principles of International Law concerning Friendly Relations and Co-operation among States in accordance with the Charter of the United Nations, UNGA Res 2625 (XXV) (24 October 1970).

[25] UNGA Res 3314 (XXIX) (14 December 1974).

[26] See eg Weiss et al (n 7) 186; see also, M J Peterson, 'General Assembly' in Weiss/Daws (n 2); Richard A Falk, 'On the Quasi-Legislative Competence of the General Assembly' (1966) 60 AJIL 782.

[27] UN Charter (n 5) arts 2(4), 2(7), 39, 51.

Geneva Conventions on the Laws of War).[28] This practice of both the UNGA and UNSC has contributed significantly to the development of customary international law in global security matters,[29] though the extent to which it can be said to dictate or reflect *opinio juris* remains a hotly contested issue in scholarship.[30] This chapter concerns itself less with these strictly legal questions around customary international law and focuses more on the influence of the UN in the realm of global security.

The ICJ, as the principal judicial organ of the UN, has in various ways shaped the international law relevant to global security.[31] Here, it is worth noting that the Court has touched upon several crucial security-related issues, including *inter alia* the right of self-defence,[32] armed activities on the territory of neighbouring States,[33] and the legality of the use of nuclear weapons.[34]

The UN Secretary-General, though offered no explicit lawmaking role by the Charter, has a broad scope under Articles 97–101 UN Charter to influence global security matters through what Ian Johnstone has called a 'norm entrepreneur' role.[35] This has included helping define and respond to threats to international peace,[36] suggesting limits to UNSC action,[37] calling situations to the attention of the UNSC, and generating momentum behind concepts new to international law.[38]

In sum, the above powers granted to UN organs under the Charter may not have envisaged the UN as a *de jure* legislator, but they provide wide-ranging opportunities for

[28] One of the most well-known examples of this practice was the UNSC interpretation of international humanitarian law to include the right of access to UN officials into the Federal Republic of Yugoslavia; see UNSC Res 1239 (1999). For a broader discussion of this interpretive role, see Georg Nolte, 'The Different Functions of the Security Council with Respect to Humanitarian Law' in Vaughan Lowe et al (eds), *The United Nations Security Council and War: The Evolution of Thought and Practice since 1945* (OUP 2008).

[29] *Legality of the Threat or Use of Nuclear Weapons* (Advisory Opinion) [1996] ICJ Rep 226 [70]. For an interesting non-Western analysis on this issue, see BS Chimni, 'Customary International Law: A Third World Perspective' (2018) 112 AJIL 1.

[30] In fact, the ILC has recently completed its work on the Identification of Customary International Law, during which this issue was hotly debated. See ILC, 'Conclusions on the Identification of Customary International Law' (20 December 2018) UNGA Res 73/203, Annex and in particular conclusion 12. See also, Higgins (n 16), describing the various contributions of the UN to international law, including via the ILC.

[31] For more detail, see Christian J Tams, Chapter 40 in this *Handbook*.

[32] *Military and Paramilitary Activities In and Against Nicaragua (Nicaragua v USA)* (Merits) [1986] ICJ Rep 14.

[33] *Armed Activities on the Territory of the Congo (DRC v Uganda)* (Judgment) [2005] ICJ Rep 168.

[34] *Nuclear Weapons* (n 29).

[35] Ian Johnstone, 'The Secretary-General as Norm Entrepreneur' in Simon Chesterman (ed), *Secretary or General? The UN Secretary-General in World Politics* (CUP 2007). See also, Weiss et al (n 7) 11.

[36] eg Secretary-General U Thant sent a team of observers to Yemen when civil war broke out there in 1963.

[37] eg Secretary-General Javier Pérez de Cuéllar's statement that UNSC Resolution 688 (1999) on Iraqi repression of the Kurds was 'not put in the framework of Chapter VII' and no UN force or police could therefore be deployed; Johnstone (n 35) 123.

[38] Kofi Annan's strong support for the Responsibility to Protect (R2P) agenda is perhaps the most prominent example.

the Organization to define and even create international law in the global security sphere. In the following section, we explore how the changing character of conflict and shifting geopolitical dynamics provided the UN with ever-increasing legislative, enforcement, and agenda-setting roles.

C. Changing Character of Conflict, and Response

The war-weary powers that drafted the UN Charter in 1945 centred the international legal order around the prohibition of the use of force and the requirement to respond collectively to security threats. At the time, global security risks were seen largely in inter-State terms: great power clashes and the looming threat of nuclear weapons. In the decades that followed, however, several developments prompted evolutions in the way in which the UN responded to peace and security risks. These were the advent and end of the Cold War; the growth of intra-State conflicts or civil wars as a major source of insecurity; the rapid proliferation of varying types of weapons of mass destruction; the post-colonial human rights movement; and, more recently, the rising influence of global terrorist groups.[39] Looking more closely at how the UN adapted to these changes, we identify a vital role of the Organization in shaping the law of global security.

1. The Cold War and the Veto

Following close on the heels of the UN's establishment, the Cold War nearly immediately impacted on the Organization's ability to engage with global security matters. This was most evident in the UNSC, where the veto-wielding five Permanent Members (P5) frequently prevented action during major international crises.[40] Due to this paralysis, from the 1950s through the 1980s, powerful States tended to bypass the world Organization on international security issues, although it was widely recognized after the 1956 Suez crisis as providing a valuable instrument for post-conflict stabilization through peacekeeping.[41]

While the Cold War was characterized as mostly a period of UNSC inaction, it also opened the door to other UN organs to assert a more prominent role in security matters. The most important of these initiatives was the 1950 Uniting for Peace Resolution, passed by the UNGA in the face of Soviet obstruction of UNSC debates on Korea.[42]

[39] See Franck (n 5) 2.

[40] For a summary of the Cold War veto, see Peter Wallensteen/Patrik Johansson, 'The UN Security Council: Decisions and Actions' in von Einsiedel et al (n 10).

[41] Weiss et al (n 7) xlvii.

[42] UNGA Res 377(V) (3 November 1950). See for a brief discussion, Higgins et al (n 15) 58–61.

Effectively, Uniting for Peace empowered the UNGA to consider any threat to the peace if a lack of unity within the UNSC meant it could not exercise its responsibilities under the UN Charter, and further empowered the UNGA to recommend military force in some circumstances.[43]

Uniting for Peace has been used in a range of different security settings, including the establishment of a peacekeeping mission in the context of the Suez crisis,[44] to extend and strengthen existing peacekeeping missions (eg, Korea),[45] to condemn armed interventions by States (eg, Afghanistan),[46] and to call for ceasefires (eg, Suez).[47] The resolution also raised the legal question as to whether the UNGA could itself be a source of authority for the use of force, a question that has yet to be fully answered today. Improved dynamics within the UNSC in the post-Cold War period have caused the UNGA to act less frequently on peace and security matters,[48] though as the final section of this chapter suggests, it may be useful to consider whether more inclusive decision-making might address the Council's shortcomings as a legislator.

2. Post-Cold War: The Security Council as Activist Legislator

The end of the Cold War precipitated a noticeable improvement in the relations amongst the P5 of the UNSC, allowing it to take a far more expansive approach to global security threats.[49] Iraq's 1990 invasion and annexation of Kuwait constituted a watershed moment in this regard, triggering UNSC decisions authorizing the use of force, disarmament of Iraq, protection of Iraqi minorities, and provision of humanitarian assistance.[50] This newfound unity amongst the P5 foreshadowed an era of 'new activism'[51] in which the UNSC rapidly increased its pace of work. In just over two years, the UNSC had launched fifteen new peacekeeping operations and adopted nearly 200 resolutions, dramatically redefining what constituted a 'threat to international peace' under the UN

[43] ICISS, *The Responsibility to Protect: Report of the International Commission on Intervention and State Sovereignty* (The International Development Research Centre 2001) 53; *Armed Activities* (n 33).

[44] UNGA Res 998 (ES-I) (4 November 1956). [45] UNGA Res 377(V) (3 November 1950).

[46] In its Sixth Emergency Special Session on 'The Situation in Afghanistan' UNGA Res ES-6/2 (14 January 1980) was adopted, calling for the immediate, unconditional and total withdrawal of foreign troops from Afghanistan.

[47] For a full analysis of these cases, see Dominik Zaum, 'The Security Council, the General Assembly, and War: The Uniting for Peace Resolution' in Lowe et al (n 28).

[48] In fact, Uniting for Peace has only infrequently been invoked when a US veto prevented condemnation of Israeli policies in the occupied Palestinian territories. See eg UNSC Verbatim Record (17 May 1995) UN Doc S/PV.3538 voting on UN Doc S/1995/394; and UNSC Verbatim Record (7 March 1997) UN Doc S/PV.3747 voting on UN Doc S/1997/199.

[49] See David M Malone (ed), *The UN Security Council: From the Cold War to the 21st Century* (Lynne Rienner Publishers 2004) 4.

[50] UNSC Res 678 (1990).

[51] Peter Wallensteen/Patrik Johansson, 'Security Council Decisions in Perspective' in Malone (n 49).

Charter.[52] Its decisions during this period had the effect of indirectly curtailing the use of Article 2(7) to limit intervention in domestic affairs, reshaping the normative and legal framework around the international law of humanitarian intervention, international human rights, the defensive use of force, and weapons of mass destruction, all discussed here.

3. From 'New Interventionism' to R2P: The Council's Role in Internal Wars

Perhaps the most important shift by the UNSC were its decisions on a range of predominantly internal conflicts, which helped erode traditional notions of State sovereignty and set the stage for far more intrusive international interventions. In cases of major humanitarian catastrophes (Somalia, Kosovo, Yugoslavia), systematic violations of human rights (Côte d'Ivoire), or even failed democratic processes (Haiti), the UNSC has influenced the development of international law by interpreting these circumstances as threats to international peace.[53] While the UNSC has generally been careful to articulate other factors beyond humanitarian ones or human rights as justifying intervention, such as massive refugee flows and impact beyond the State's borders, the argument that it has 'pierced the veil of sovereignty' appears borne out by the subsequent international interventions in these countries.[54]

The UNSC decision-making on internal wars contributed in important ways to the development of customary international law. In some cases, UNSC decisions reaffirmed existing norms, such as the frequent invocation of Chapter VII to demand that all conflict parties adhere to international humanitarian law (IHL) and international human rights law (IHRL).[55] In others, the UNSC waded into disputed areas where the applicability of international law was less clear, such as its decisions that non-State actors had to abide by peace agreements, or to cease hostilities.[56] And in some of its most far-reaching decisions, the Council took an expansive view of the self-defence doctrine, for example concerning the Taliban in Afghanistan.[57]

But it was the failures of the UNSC that drove the development of one of the most far-reaching recent concepts in international relations, that of responsibility to protect. The tragedies in the Balkans and Rwanda in the early 1990s featured a glaring tension between the sovereignty granted to States under the UN Charter (and the international

[52] ibid; Mats Berdal, 'The Security Council and Peacekeeping' in Lowe et al (n 28) 176.

[53] Each of these cases is considered in detail in Malone (n 49). See UNSC Res 1528 (2004); UNSC Res 1542 (2004); UNSC Res 814 (1993).

[54] Glennon (n 4) 120.

[55] Gregory H Fox et al, 'The Contributions of United Nations Security Council Resolutions to the Law of Non-International Armed Conflict: New Evidence of Customary International Law' (2018) 67 American University Law Review 649.

[56] ibid. [57] UNSC Res 1368 (2001); Fox et al (n 55) 689.

legal system in general) and the growing practice of the UN to intervene in States where large-scale humanitarian and human rights concerns were present.[58] Secretary-General Kofi Annan asked, '[i]f humanitarian intervention is, indeed, an unacceptable assault on sovereignty, how should we respond to crises such as the genocide in Rwanda, to a massacre such as that at Srebrenica—in effect to gross and systematic violations of human rights that affect every precept of our common humanity?'[59] Responding to this question, the International Commission on Intervention and State Sovereignty concluded that when States fail to protect their populations from major violations of IHL and IHRL, responsibility for such protection shifts to the international community.[60]

This so-called Responsibility to Protect (R2P) doctrine was subsequently endorsed at the 2005 World Summit Outcome Document,[61] though Member States were clear that the doctrine did not create new international law. However, R2P has been invoked in justifying UNSC enforcement action under Chapter VII. In authorizing the deployment of troops to Darfur,[62] mandating the use of force to enforce election results in Côte d'Ivoire,[63] taking a range of actions in Libya,[64] and mandating a new mission in South Sudan,[65] the Council referred to the State's responsibility to protect its own citizens. This falls short of a legislating role by the UN, as in each case the Council did not specifically identify R2P as a legal basis for enforcement, but certainly has demonstrated the strong influence of the UN on the rationales invoked for international interventions in internal conflicts.[66]

4. Human Rights and International Criminal Law

Inevitably, the UN's greater intrusion into internal conflict enhanced its role in shaping IHRL and IHL. In some cases, the UNSC itself initiated unprecedented legal developments, such as the creation of international criminal tribunals for the former Yugoslavia and Rwanda.[67] In others, the Council established specific legal liability for individual actors, including its decision providing for individual responsibility for violations of IHL in Somalia in 1992.[68] These resolutions performed both legislative and judicial

[58] Alex J Bellamy, *Responsibility to Protect: The Global Effort to End Mass Atrocities* (Polity 2009).

[59] UNGA 'Report of the Secretary-General on the Work of the Organization' (2000) UN Doc A/55/1 (Supp No 1), para 37.

[60] ICISS (n 43). [61] UNGA Res 60/1 (24 October 2005) para 138.

[62] UNSC Res 1706 (2006) para 12. [63] UNSC Res 1975 (2011).

[64] UNSC Res 1970 (2011); UNSC Res 1973 (2011). [65] UNSC Res 1996 (2011).

[66] The UN Secretary-General's annual reporting on the responsibility to protect, his 2004 creation of a Special Adviser on Genocide, and 2008 creation of a Special Adviser on Responsibility to Protect, all participate in this agenda-setting role.

[67] UNSC Res 827 (1993); UNSC Res 955 (1994).

[68] UNSC Res 794 (1992). See also, UNSC Res 687 (1991) (declaring that Iraq bore legal liability for damages caused during its invasion of Kuwait).

functions: they defined what specific acts constituted a violation of international law, and at times overtly identified those responsible for them.[69]

This notion of international criminal accountability for violations of international law represented an important precursor to the later establishment of the International Criminal Court (ICC). The ICC is not a UN entity per se, but was negotiated under the auspices of the UN and was explicitly linked to the UN by virtue of the UNSC's right to refer cases to it.[70] As such, the Council's willingness to take binding decisions establishing criminal accountability and to define breaches of international law were both legislative and agenda-setting acts, encouraging and shaping the development of international criminal law.[71]

5. Defensive Use of Force in an Era of Global Terrorism

If the 1990 Iraqi invasion of Kuwait breathed new life into the UNSC, the 2003 US-led invasion of Iraq, without Council authorization, led many experts to write obituaries for the UN's role in global security.[72] From a legal perspective, the invasion of Iraq directly challenged the UN Charter's limitation to defensive use of force, all the more so as it followed a failed attempt by several powers to convince the Council to provide authorization for it.[73] And the invasion took place at a crucial point in the development of international law, as the dual threats of weapons of mass destruction and global terrorist groups had prompted the major powers to consider stretching, or even overtly breaking with, the well-established 'just war' principles of imminent threat and proportional response.[74]

The response to the 9/11 attacks was particularly important in the context of the doctrine of self-defence. Security Council Resolution 1368 clearly stated that the terrorist attacks constituted an armed attack under Article 51, triggering the right of self-defence of the United States.[75] Whether non-State actors could be a target for Article 51 was a highly contested issue prior to UNSC Resolution 1368, and thus the decision constituted a significant expansion of the doctrine beyond purely inter-State actions. The broad set

[69] An early example of this was the resolution addressing the Iran/Iraq war, in which the Council 'deplore[d] the violation of international humanitarian law and other laws of armed conflict' via the use of chemical weapons; UNSC Res 598 (1987).

[70] ICC Statute (n 21) art 87.

[71] Steven Ratner, 'The Security Council and International Law' in Malone (n 49) 595.

[72] Even prior to 2003, the 'illegal but legitimate' intervention in Kosovo had triggered increased doubts as to the capacity of the UN Charter or its principal organs to constrain use of force between States. See eg Glennon (n 4).

[73] David M Malone/Poorvi Chitalkar, 'Iraq' in von Einsiedel et al (n 10) 559. See, also, William H Taft/Todd F Buchwald, 'Preemption, Iraq and International Law' (2003) 97 AJIL 557.

[74] For a discussion of just war principles, see Simon Chesterman, *Just War or Just Peace? Humanitarian Intervention and International Law* (OUP 2001).

[75] UNSC Res 1368 (2001).

of obligations placed on all Member States by UNSC Res 1368, and the risk that failure to snational practice far more with the US notion of 'pre-emption' at the time.[76]

While the UNSC practice points to the UN's central role in making and interpreting the laws addressing defensive use of force, this reality begs the question of whether Member States should and do feel bound by it (*opinio juris*). This is less a strictly legal question and more a normative one, without a satisfactory answer as yet. On the one hand, former President of the ICJ Rosalyn Higgins points compellingly to the 1991 UK/US action against Iraq as evidence that 'clear UN permission became a matter of deep importance' to many States wishing to use force.[77] Conversely, NATO's unauthorized intervention in Kosovo in 1999 offers a strong example of willingness to use force outside established legal parameters. Debates concerning the role of *opinio juris* (including the contentious issue whether failure to protest equals agreement that an action is lawful) are not covered here, though some implications of non-compliance with the law are discussed below.

6. The International Law of Counter-terrorism

The terrorist attacks of 9/11 not only prompted a shift in perspective on the law of self-defence, but also placed the UN in a legislative role with respect to counter-terrorism. Days after the adoption of UNSC Resolution 1368 (2001), the Council passed a second resolution calling for substantive measures to be adopted by Member States, including suppression of terrorist financing, denial of safe haven, and information exchange on terrorist activities.[78] Rather than using typical Council language, such as 'calling on' or 'requesting' Member State actions,[79] Resolution 1373 clearly created a legal requirement, deciding that States 'shall' implement the measures.

Resolution 1373 created a broad set of international legal obligations to take proactive steps to combat terrorism, making law with international and domestic effect.[80] As Paul Szasz noted, this 'broke new ground' by using Chapter VII to 'order all States to take or to refrain from specified actions in a context not limited to disciplining a particular country'.[81] This was an especially bold move by the UNSC (some would view it as brazen), as Resolution 1373 drew language directly from the UN Convention Against the Financing of Terrorist Acts, which had not yet been signed or ratified by a large number

[76] See eg The White House, 'The National Security Strategy of the United States of America' (September 2002) <https://www.state.gov/documents/organization/63562.pdf> accessed 5 March 2019 (NSS 2002); Franck (n 5) 67.

[77] Higgins (n 16). [78] UNSC Res 1373 (2001).

[79] eg UNSC Res 1269 (1999) recommending that States 'fully implement the international anti-terrorist conventions' and that they cooperate in combating international terrorism, as well as UNSC Res 1267 (1999) establishing sanctions against the Taliban both used the language 'calling on'.

[80] Jane Boulden, 'The Security Council and Terrorism' in Lowe et al (n 28) 612.

[81] Paul C Szasz, 'The Security Council Starts Legislating' (2002) 96 AJIL 901.

of Member States.[82] The UNSC claim to legislative powers beyond the treaty-based system could not have been much clearer. Resolution 1373 also established a Counter-Terrorism Committee, which subsequently has played a major (though often unpopular) role in helping States implement their 1373 obligations.[83]

Nevertheless, similar resolutions, including the Council's response to the July 2005 bombings in London, added to Member State obligations to combat terrorism, also requiring States to take measures to prohibit incitement to commit terrorism.[84] And most recently, Resolution 2396 (2017) created obligations for Member States to take affirmative steps, including adoption of criminal legislation, against the fighters returning from the Syria/Iraq conflict theatre.[85] These actions by the Council arrogate to itself a clear legislative role and dramatically broadened international legal obligations in the fight against global terrorism.[86]

Moreover, the poor drafting of sanctions resolutions and the excessively sweeping decisions of the implementing Counter-Terrorism Committee (CTC) were challenged before the Court of Justice of the European Union, which in 2008 found the Council's decisions arbitrary as applied to individuals, who were denied due process.[87] Eventually, many of the individuals earlier targeted by the Committee were 'delisted' and thus formally rehabilitated, but the Council's standing itself has suffered.

7. Containing Weapons of Mass Destruction (WMD)

The centrality of nuclear weapons to the current global order is clear: All P5 Members of the UNSC are nuclear weapons powers, and much of the UN's effort on non-proliferation over the past seventy years represents an attempt to preserve the current nuclear order. The UN has occasionally played a central role in containing WMD, though its record of success is mixed.

One of the strongest UN responses followed Iraq's 1990 invasion of Kuwait, during which the UNSC passed a series of resolutions that demanded comprehensive disarmament of Iraq's WMD, including an intrusive verification mechanism.[88] The Council's fears of Al-Qaeda's potential acquisition of WMD had previously prompted a 2004 resolution requiring all Member States to take a wide range of counter-proliferation

[82] José E Alvarez, 'The UN's War on Terrorism' (2003) 31 International Journal of Legal Information 238, 241.

[83] Jane E Stromseth, 'An Imperial Security Council? Implementing Security Council Resolutions 1373 and 1390' (2003) 97 ASIL Proc 41, 43.

[84] UNSC Res 1624 (2005).

[85] UNSC Res 2396 (2017).

[86] See Boulden (n 80) 608.

[87] Joined Cases C-402/05 P and C-415/05 P *Yassin Abdullah Kadi & Al Barakaat International Foundation v Council of the European Union and Commission of the European Communities* [2008] ECR I-6351. For a brief account of the case, see Simon Chesterman et al (eds), *The Law and Practice of the United Nations* (OUP 2016) 392–5.

[88] UNSC Res 687 (1991); UNSC Res 707 (1991); UNSC Res 1284 (1999).

measures, and to adopt national laws to prohibit the development or transport of such weapons.[89] Similarly, the 2015 UNSC Resolution on Iran's nuclear programme created additional legal obligations for Member States and put in place an international monitoring and verification mechanism run by the International Atomic Energy Authority (IAEA).[90] In these cases, the UNSC played a lawmaking role, creating new international obligations with force of law, and also an enforcement one, seeking to hold Member States accountable for their obligations under existing treaties.

The dominant legal enforcement measures of the UN with regard to WMD have been sanctions regimes intended to uphold the treaty-based obligations, limit access to weapons technology, and reaffirm the norms around non-proliferation. For instance, following a 2009 nuclear test by North Korea, the UNSC issued a resolution expanding the arms embargo and increasing inspections on vessels bound to and from the country.[91] Rather than curb activity, however, this prompted Pyongyang to conduct a series of additional tests and withdraw from the Six Party Talks.[92] The Council's wide-ranging sanctions on Iran for its nuclear programme reflect a concerted attempt to hold the country to its obligations under the Non-Proliferation Treaty (NPT).[93]

Critics have argued that the Council has been selective and inconsistent in its approach to WMD. For instance, it took no enforcement action following the chemical attacks by Iraq on Iran during the 1984–88 period, when 60,000 people were killed.[94] Such critiques also point to the mixed track record of the UN, noting that North Korea formally withdrew from the NPT in 2003, and that Israel, India, and Pakistan were never members.[95] The use of chemical weapons by, and in, Syria is another example of limited effectiveness. Nonetheless, looked at across the lifespan of the UN, respect for the widely accepted norms of non-proliferation remains remarkably high, as is the Council's willingness to move strongly against those States it deems a threat.

D. Critiques of the United Nations' Role in the Law of Global Security

We have argued above that the UN has developed and influenced the law of global security in a range of settings, and that this role has increased since the end of the Cold

[89] UNSC Res 1540 (2004).

[90] UNSC Res 2231 (2015).

[91] UNSC Res 1874 (2009).

[92] Waheguru Pal Singh Sidhu, 'Weapons of Mass Destruction: Managing Proliferation' in von Einsiedel et al (n 10).

[93] UNSC Res 1737 (2006); UNSC Res 1929 (2010).

[94] The UNSC did issue three Resolutions (582, 612 and 620) but none featured any enforcement mechanisms; see UNSC Res 582 (1986); UNSC Res 612 (1988); UNSC Res 620 (1988).

[95] Weiss et al (n 7) 5.

War. This is not to suggest, however, that the UNSC is always the best actor, or even always at all appropriately placed, to play such a lawmaking role. It is therefore worth considering briefly the major objections to the UNSC as a lawmaker, before turning to current and future challenges.

1. The Council Undermines the Treaty-based System

While the Council's lawmaking role may be implicit within the Charter, such a role can be seen as subverting the consent-based international order.[96] According to the principle of sovereignty, States are bound only by those obligations to which they have explicitly consented.[97] It is often asserted within the UN that all Member States have consented to obey the UNSC by signing the UN Charter, but well-established approaches to treaty interpretation challenge such an open-ended notion. Whenever the Council issues a resolution binding on all Member States, in one sense it works against the State-centric system upon which the UN is founded, and it also invites contestation. In the resolutions that created legal obligations on all Member States to proactively prevent terrorist activities—such as Resolution 1373 (2001)—the objection that the UNSC had taken on an 'imperial' role found many adherents and, as noted above, was highly contested by EU courts.[98]

2. The Council is Not Well Suited to Legislate

Typically, legislatures are institutions designed to deliberate meaningfully and generate thoughtful, representative laws. The UNSC's need to 'ensure prompt and effective action'[99] appears at odds with this, creating what Ian Johnstone has called a 'deliberative deficit' in the Council.[100] Indeed, by responding to immediate crises, the UNSC is by design not well equipped to balance long-term implications with short-term imperatives, as a good legislature should. Particularly in the highly charged aftermath of a terrorist attack, a high degree of risk has emerged that the UNSC will take punitive, overbroad, or otherwise myopic decisions.

3. The Council is Not Accountable or Representative

The UNSC is composed of a small group of Member States, incapable of (and typically uninterested in) representing the entire global community. The great powers within the

[96] See Szasz (n 81). [97] *SS 'Lotus' (France v Turkey)* [1927] PCIJ Ser A No 10.
[98] Stromseth (n 83). [99] UN Charter (n 5) art 24.
[100] Ian Johnstone, 'Legislation and Adjudication in the UN Security Council: Bringing Down the Deliberative Deficit' (2008) 102 AJIL 275.

Council are, in their own eyes, at times, empowered to 'rewrite international law'[101] to suit their short-term interests, distorting the international legal system in potentially harmful ways. The US pushing for Council authorization to attack or otherwise counter an undefined set of 'terrorist groups' in Resolution 1373,[102] for example, has created a global set of legal obligations that affect every Member State, but do not necessarily represent all countries' interests (nor reflect their capacities) and may well result in inconsistent targeting of groups and individuals. Unlike national legislatures, the UNSC P5, never face an electorate and have no direct accountability to any other authority for these actions.[103]

4. Major States Do Not Feel Bound by the UN Charter

A final point of critique has been articulated by Michael Glennon who asks, '[h]ow can a system indifferent to prominent and massive noncompliance rightly be called a system of law?'[104] While Kosovo offers perhaps the most concrete example of major States' disregard of the collective security system, surprisingly varied and comprehensive State practice demonstrates that States are often willing to use force, despite the clear prohibition in the UN Charter. The Charter did not manage to deter the Iraqi invasion of Kuwait (1990), the US bombing of Sudan and Afghanistan (1998), Ethiopia's attack on Eritrea (2000), the Soviet invasion of Afghanistan (1979), or well over 100 other examples of use of force in the past seventy years.[105] In a domestic setting, widespread violation of the law does not invalidate it; rather, it is considered a high crime rate. But in the international system, where States are only bound by the obligations they willingly enter into, systematic non-compliance, not least by the P5 of the UNSC, creates serious risk for the status of the law itself. And when a major power indicates that it does not feel bound by the Charter when it comes to the non-intervention principle, Glennon argues, this could render the law irrelevant.

Strong counter-arguments to this exist, including those by experts who point to the fairly consistent reduction in war and widespread violence over the past 100 years (albeit registering a recent uptick) as evidence of general compliance with international norms. But the criticism is worth considering as we turn to the future role of the UN in global security law.[106]

101 Johnstone (n 10) 777. See, also, Nico Krisch, 'The Rise and Fall of Collective Security: Terrorism, US Hegemony, and the Plight of the Security Council' in Christian Walter et al (eds), *Terrorism as a Challenge for National and International Law: Security versus Liberty?* (Springer 2004).

102 For a critique of UNSC Res 1373 (2001) along these lines, see Johanny Santana, 'In the Aftermath of Resolution 1373: Tackling the Protective Veil of Counter-Terrorism' (2015) 23 Cardozo Journal of International and Comparative Law 663.

103 Wallensteen/Johansson (n 40) 22. 104 Glennon (n 4) 145. 105 ibid.

106 Steven Pinker, 'The Decline of War and Conceptions of Human Nature' (2003) 15 International Studies Review 400. See also, Monika Hakimi, 'The Jus ad Bellum's Regulatory Form' (2018) 112 AJIL 151.

E. The Future of Global Security and the UN

The above arguments suggest that the UN may not be very well designed to legislate and enforce international law to safeguard global security. That structural weakness partly reflects the intent of the big powers in 1945, who drafted the UN Charter to protect their own interests, and partly is the result of decades of inconsistent, often highly politicized practice. Nonetheless, the UN remains a crucial player in the development and maintenance of the law of global security and will almost certainly continue to be for some time. How the Organization will need to evolve to meet current and new challenges is the question to which we now turn.

At just over seventy years of age, the UN appears to be courting a loss of authority on the world stage as it increasingly bickers in a dialogue of the deaf, while murderous conflicts in Syria and Yemen rage. Security Council paralysis, its inability to gain traction in conflict settings like Mali, South Sudan, and the Democratic Republic of the Congo, and a recent erosion of great power relations, together point to a mismatch between today's challenges and the Organization's capacities to address them. If indeed we have entered what Richard Haass has called a 'world in disarray',[107] in which well-established rules have frayed to their breaking point, the UN's role as a custodian of the international order may seem marginal at best.

The UN's ability to shape and enforce the international law of global security faces three related challenges. The first emanates from the Organization's fundamentally inter-State nature. It is poorly suited to develop effective responses to non-State actors like terrorist groups,[108] and equally badly designed to address transnational challenges like organized crime. This is in part because the sovereignty principle at the heart of the Charter limits its ability to craft more effective strategies against non-State actors unless States agree to them. As a result, though the UN has played a role in establishing a legal regime to combat key threats such as terrorism, this is principally focused on Member State obligations, rather than directed at the non-State actors involved and their members. How to develop effective legal approaches to the wide range of non-State and transnational actors in today's world is a quandary for the world body.

A second, related challenge concerns the slow pace of the UN in addressing emerging challenges. Cybersecurity, for example, poses an acute risk to global security and constitutes a top priority for many Member States.[109] To date, a universally agreed definition of cybercrime has not yet emerged, nor has a global governance system for cybersecurity

[107] Richard Haass, *A World in Disarray: American Foreign Policy and the Crisis of the Old Order* (Penguin 2017).

[108] For detail, see Helen Duffy/Larissa van den Herik, Chapter 11 in this *Handbook*.

[109] For detail, see Michael Schmitt, Chapter 36 in this *Handbook*.

yet been defined.[110] A similar example is the risk of biologically engineered pandemics, given that the basic tools and knowledge for producing a global epidemic are increasingly available to a growing number of groups and individuals.[111] Other emerging risks in the security field involve artificial intelligence, the impact of climate change, and the use of outer space, all of which appear to outstrip the current UN-based frameworks for collective action. How can the UN keep pace with, while also reflecting the will of, its diverse and often divided Member States?

The third challenge is the global order itself. The UN is founded on the notion of collective security and the principle that Member States will act together to prevent threats to the peace. If anything, however, the UN's inaction on Syria and Yemen points to a 'decollectivization' of opinion and action on security issues, where the powerful Member States are too polarized to act in unison. The deepening chill between the US and both Russia and China may well return the UN to its Cold War doldrums, not only limiting its role in the global security realm, but also encouraging the voices of ultra-nationalism and unilateralism to take matters into their own hands. If a critical element for successful lawmaking and enforcement in the past has been UNSC unity, what new approaches are needed for the UN to regain that cohesion today?

These questions point to the fact that, in many respects, the UN today is fragile. Its ability to make or promote global security through effective decision-making is at a low ebb. But in the past, failures have generated innovation and evolution. As described above, the development of international criminal accountability, the R2P doctrine, and the far-reaching legal framework on terrorism all arose from the failures of the international community to prevent major risks from materializing. They also arose out of a concerted effort by major Western powers, particularly in the immediate post-Cold War period, to project liberal democratic institutions across the world. Today, a single Western vision of world order may well be on the wane, and there are strong signs that Western capitals, singly and collectively, are incapable of addressing current trends.

Facing unprecedented challenges by the related phenomena of transnational actors, new technologies, climate change, and intractable internal conflicts, it is more crucial than ever before for the principal powers to develop widely supported multilateral responses. Indeed, these challenges point to the limits of domestic, nationally driven legislation to address global threats, and the need for more effective multilateral global governance. As we have outlined above, the UN is capable of shaping international law, practice, and norms in surprisingly impactful ways. As global security issues become increasingly complex and interrelated—often stretching beyond national boundaries—it

110 The Council of Europe Convention on Cybercrime ETS No 185, offers a partial legal framework, but this does not extend to all Member States of the UN.

111 Bill Gates, Bill and Melinda Gates Foundation, 'Bill Gates: A New Kind of Terrorism Could Wipe out 30 Million People in Less than a Year—and We Are not Prepared' (*Business Insider*, 18 February 2017) <http://www.businessinsider.com/bill-gates-op-ed-bio-terrorism-epidemic-world-threat-2017-2> accessed 10 December 2019.

is more crucial than ever that the law of global security be driven by multilateral institutions that have positioned themselves as legitimate and effective.

Acknowledgement

The authors would like to thank Simon Chesterman, Ian Johnstone, and Katarina Grenfell for their review of earlier drafts of this chapter.

Index

Note: Tables and figures are indicated by an italic "*t*" and "*f*", respectively, following the page number.
For the benefit of digital users, indexed terms that span two pages (e.g., 52–53) may, on occasion, appear on only one of those pages.